Official I

CHOOSING YOUR INDEPENDENT SCHOOL

A guide to 1,350 boarding and day schools for boys and girls aged 2–19 in the U.K. and Ireland

Editor:
D. J. WOODHEAD
National Director, ISIS

ISIS

INDEPENDENT SCHOOLS INFORMATION SERVICE

Published by
INDEPENDENT SCHOOLS INFORMATION SERVICE
56 Buckingham Gate, London SW1E 6AG
Tel. 0171-630 8793/4

© INDEPENDENT SCHOOLS INFORMATION SERVICE 1995

This book is sold subject to the condition that it shall not, by way of trade or otherwise, be lent, resold, hired out, or otherwise circulated without the publishers' prior consent in any form of binding or cover other than that in which it is published and without a similar condition being imposed on the subsequent purchaser.

Typeset by Spottiswoode Ballantyne
Colchester, Essex
Printed and bound by Benham & Co
Colchester, Essex
Data compiled by
Monkton Combe Computing Service
Designed by
Ravenscourt Design Limited, London W6

ISBN: 0-948452-14-5

CONTENTS

SECTION ONE

GENERAL INTRODUCTION	5
CHAPTER 1 Independent schools and why parents choose them	7
CHAPTER 2 Types of school and how standards are maintained	10
CHAPTER 3 Narrowing the choice	17
CHAPTER 4 Questions to ask when you visit a school	21
CHAPTER 5 How much does it cost?	30
CHAPTER 6 Scholarships and grants	35
CHAPTER 7 Where to go for further help	39
CHAPTER 8 If you live overseas	50
CHAPTER 9 How to use the directory of schools	54
SECTION TWO County directory of schools	63
SECTION THREE Maps	329
SECTION FOUR Introduction to Examination Results Sections List of English & Welsh schools' A & AS level results	347 351
SECTION FIVE List of English & Welsh schools' GCSE results List of Scottish schools' results	370 392
SECTION SIX Alphabetical index of schools	398

ACKNOWLEDGEMENTS

This book is a team effort. My warm thanks are therefore due to Julian Bewick and the Monkton Combe Computing Service for compiling the data, to Richard Davison, Carolyn Parrish, Rachel Lambert and Christopher Turrall for their help with various aspects of production and design, and to Eileen Hunter, Pat Chakravartty, Jayne Morrison and other National ISIS staff involved in many hours of laborious proofreading.

DJW

GENERAL INTRODUCTION

'Parents have a prior right to choose the kind of education that shall be given to their children.'
(Universal Declaration of Human Rights)

The best for your child

You want the best for your child. Of all the benefits you can give your son or daughter, none has more lasting value than a good education at a school where he or she will be happy and successful. There are schools to suit everyone in the independent sector, which prides itself on offering breadth of choice to parents.

The Independent Schools Information Service (ISIS) was started in 1965 by heads of schools in South Wales to meet the growing demand from parents for information about schools. There are eight regional offices throughout the UK and Ireland (see pages 39–40) and a national headquarters in London which is the official information centre for the Independent Schools Joint Council and the leading associations of independent schools in Britain. ISIS answers more than 120,000 enquiries a year, mainly from parents asking about independent schools for their children.

This book has two main purposes:

   1.   To give you details about schools which can be recommended because they belong to one of the constituent associations of ISJC/National ISIS. What this means as an assurance of quality for parents is explained in chapter 2 (pages 10–16).

   2.   To give you the best advice about choosing your independent school. Parents often ask which is the best school. The best school is the one which is best for your son or daughter.

So the choice must be yours. It is not just your right: it is also your responsibility as a parent. No other person or outside agency can do it for you. You know what would best suit your child. This book will help to narrow down the choice. It will tell you how to apply to schools, what questions to ask and what to look for when you visit them. Choosing a school is one of the most important decisions you can make. You should visit some of the schools in this book to decide which would be best for your child.

The book is in six sections. The first (pages 7–58) contains background information and helpful advice for parents thinking about independent education for their children. The second (pages 63–328) is a county directory of schools, preceded by a guide to its use. The third (pages 329–346) consists of maps to help you locate schools. The fourth section (pages 351–369) lists schools in England and Wales with their GCE A and AS level (Advanced and Advanced Supplementary) results for 1995 and average results for 1990–94. The fifth (pages 370–391) lists English and Welsh schools' 1995 General Certificate of Secondary Education (GCSE) results and average results for 1990–94. This is followed by a separate list of 1995 examination results in Scottish schools (pages 392–397; see also the note on the Scottish system on page 13). Please read carefully the introduction to the examination sections on page 347. Finally (pages 398–404) there is a complete alphabetical list of schools: those whose page number appears in bold are included in the examination results sections.

CHAPTER 1

INDEPENDENT SCHOOLS AND WHY PARENTS CHOOSE THEM

What is an independent school?

There are almost 2,500 schools in Britain which are independent of local or central government control. These schools are sometimes called fee-paying (or, more correctly, fee-charging) schools because they charge parents fees. They are also called private schools but this is not an accurate description of most of the schools in this book, because they are not run for private profit. Most of them have their own board of governors who look after the school and its finances. Any surplus income is put back at the end of the year into the running of the school. The head is responsible to the governors but is usually given a free hand to choose staff and to take day-to-day decisions.

The wide choice of independent schools throughout the country includes boarding schools and day schools; single-sex schools and coeducational ones; schools for boys and girls of every ability and age from 2 to 19.

What sort of children go to them?

Every sort. It used to be thought that only rich and privately-educated people sent their children to independent schools. This is not true. More than half of the children in independent schools have parents who were educated in the state system. The children come from every sort of background.

What advantages do independent schools have?

    1. Academic. A child's success in life will be greatly helped by academic qualifications. More than 80 per cent of pupils at independent schools (including independent special schools) gain five or more GCSEs at grades *A–C (compared with a national average of 43%). Eighty per cent of independent school A-level candidates get three or more passes, compared with a national average of 58% (and the national average is inflated by *including* independent school results!). Independent schools provide 25% of all those who achieve three or more A-levels at schools and further education colleges. Almost 90 per cent of A-level leavers go on to higher education degree courses. Seven per cent of children attend independent schools, but more than 25 per cent of university students have been educated in them.

7

SECTION ONE

The Department for Education's Statistical Bulletin of February 1995 contained evidence of pupils *at all ability levels* in independent schools achieving better examination results than candidates at other schools, including state grammar schools and sixth-form colleges. Its comparison of 1994 A and AS level grades compared with the GCSE scores gained by the same pupils two years earlier concludes:

"Candidates from independent schools tended to achieve higher GCE A/AS level scores than candidates from maintained schools. In independent schools, 33 per cent of candidates achieved a GCE A/AS level score of 25 or over compared with 14 per cent of candidates from maintained schools. In contrast, 14 per cent of candidates from independent schools compared with 35 per cent of maintained schools achieved a GCE A/AS level score of less than 10."

It goes on to say that at every level of ability "there was a clear tendency for candidates in independent schools to achieve higher GCE A/AS level scores than those in maintained schools. Of those candidates from independent schools with a GCSE score of 60 or over, 62 per cent achieved an A/AS level score of 25 or over while the equivalent figure for maintained schools was 44 per cent.

"At the lower end of GCSE achievement, of those candidates with a GCSE score of less than 40, 54 per cent of candidates from independent schools and 77 per cent of candidates from maintained schools achieved an A/AS level score of less than 10. Of those candidates with a GCSE score of less than 40, 8 per cent of candidates from independent schools achieved an A/AS level score of 25 or more compared with less than 1 per cent of candidates from maintained schools."

In other words, independent schools got more out of pupils than other schools: able and less able alike did better than might have been predicted, whereas at other schools they underperformed.

[At GCSE, a grade A scores seven points, a B six and so on down to one for a G; at A level, a grade A scores ten, a B eight and so on down to two for a E; scores for AS grades are half those for A level.]

2. A partnership with parents. In order to survive, independent schools have to satisfy parents that they are good value for money. Parents value what they pay for and are keen to encourage their children to do well.

3. Small classes and individual care. Many of the parents who contact ISIS for advice say they are looking for a school where their child can be treated as an individual. Classes in many independent schools are small, particularly for the younger age groups between 5 and 13. This is when children are especially keen to learn, the foundations of a good education can be laid and mistakes and learning difficulties recognised and put right. The average size of an independent secondary school for children aged 11 to 18 is about 450. Most independent schools are small enough for the head to know every pupil by name. The average size of ISIS schools is about 350.

4. **Traditional values.** Heads and staff at independent schools teach children to work hard and to take a pride in their work; to pay attention to detail; to have good manners; to consider other people's feelings and to grow up into responsible adults who will contribute to the community. They wish to inspire in each generation of pupils an appreciation of the richness of their European cultural heritage, in music, literature and the visual arts; to lift their eyes above the contemporary to more nourishing cultural experiences.

5. **Broad-based education.** Independent schools aim to develop the whole personality: the imaginative, practical and physical as well as the academic. Music, art and drama flourish. Team games like football, hockey and netball are encouraged, as well as individual sports such as badminton, judo, squash and sailing. There are indoor games and hobbies. Many schools, particularly those which have boarders, are open for activities in the evening and at weekends.

6. **Special needs or requirements.** Some parents choose independent schools because their children have special talents or needs which they feel cannot adequately be met by other schools. These include:

* children who are particularly gifted at academic work, music, art or sport;
* children who need a great deal of individual attention, because they suffer from dyslexia or they are slow or backward in their work or for some other reason;
* children who will benefit by being in a single-sex school. Some evidence suggests that girls at girls' schools are more likely to study science and technological subjects;
* children whose parents want them to grow up in a particular religious faith. There are schools for Roman Catholics, Methodists, Quakers and Jews, for example, as well as Anglicans. Many schools have links with the Church of England. Most schools will admit children of other beliefs, or those who have none, but they are proud of their Christian traditions and believe that religious education is important;
* children who want or need to be full or weekly boarders. Those who need boarding education may have a parent serving in the armed forces or working for a company overseas or both parents with full-time jobs in the UK. Only a few state schools have boarding places.

In ISIS surveys carried out by MORI (Market & Opinion Research International), the main reasons stated by parents for choosing independent schools included high standards of education and examination results, good discipline, small classes with individual attention, development of social responsibility and extra-curricular activities.

CHAPTER 2

TYPES OF SCHOOL AND HOW STANDARDS ARE MAINTAINED

The following chart is a summary of the ages of pupils at different kinds of independent school in England and Wales. Details for Scotland are on page 13.

England and Wales

Age	Type of School	Curriculum
2/5–16/18	ALL-THROUGH	Some schools in this book take pupils from the early ages right through to 16 or 18/19.
2–7	PRE-PREPARATORY (Pre-prep) also called nursery schools or kindergartens.	Correspond to nursery and infants stages in local authority schools. Reading, writing, numbers, learning to play. Attached to junior schools.
7–11+ or 13+	JUNIOR SCHOOLS often called preparatory schools or prep schools.	A full range of subjects leading to admission to senior schools at 11+ or through the Common Entrance Examination (described below).
11–18	SENIOR SCHOOLS	Schools which admit pupils at 11+ sometimes have a lower school for children aged 11–13. There may be a special entrance examination to the upper school at 13.
13-18	SENIOR SCHOOLS	Some boys' senior schools still have the traditional age of entry at 13. One year of general studies followed by 2 years for GCSE and 2 years for A Level.
16+	SIXTH FORM (VI Form)	Many senior schools admit students at 16+ usually for the 2-year A Level courses, or vocational courses or GCSE retakes.

1. Pre-preparatory (for children aged 2 to 7)

Many schools now have pre-preparatory departments, responding to the demand from parents who recognise the importance of early childhood education. These pre-prep departments correspond to the nursery and infants stages in the state sector, but in many parts of the country provision by local education authorities for nursery education is patchy or non-existent.

Schools with pre-prep departments hope parents will send their children on to the junior school. Many do this but there is no obligation to do so.

2. Junior Schools (for children aged 7 to 11 or 13)

Most junior independent schools are called preparatory schools (or prep schools) because they prepare children for the next stage of education. Children usually start between the ages of 7 and 9.

The heads of junior schools believe the early years are the most vital period of education. A good education at this stage will lay firm foundations in the basic skills of reading, writing and number. Staff will introduce pupils to art, music, sports and outside activities. They will seek to discover what children are good at and encourage them to do even better. The last two years are usually spent preparing children for the Common Entrance Examination (see below), for entry to independent senior schools; but some leave at 11 or later to go to a state or local authority maintained secondary school.

3. 11/12/13 (Common Entrance)

Girls: Most girls' senior schools admit pupils at any age from 11 upwards. Many will require new girls to take an examination. Sometimes the school sets its own examination, but many girls' schools use the Common Entrance Examination which can be taken for entry to the school at 11, 12 or 13. This exam is set centrally and details can be obtained from the Independent Schools' Examinations Board (see address on page 48).

The exam is marked individually by the senior school you have chosen. Each school has its own pass mark. It is not an exam in which girls are competing against each other, but a qualifying exam to see if your daughter will be able to cope with the standard of academic work the school undertakes.

* For entry at 11, your daughter will be asked to do tests in English, mathematics and science.
* For entry at 12, the subjects tested include English, mathematics, science and elementary French. There is an optional Latin paper.
* For entry at 13, she may be asked to do history, geography and religious studies as well. Latin and Greek are optional.

If your child is at a state primary school, you should apply to the Independent Schools' Examinations Board at least four months in advance. He or she may need special coaching; ISIS can advise you about tutors and tutorial colleges.

Boys: Some boys' senior schools admit boys to their lower schools at 11, usually after the same kind of tests as described for the girls at this age (see above). Others require boys to take the Common Entrance Examination for entry to the school at 13. Details of the exam can be obtained from the address on page 48.

The exam consists of papers in English, mathematics, French, science, history, geography and religious studies. Your son will not need to have learnt Latin, but there are papers in Latin (and Greek as well) if he wishes to take them. As with the girls, the exam is marked by the senior school of your choice. Each has its own pass mark. If your son does not pass, the papers can be sent on to another school. The Common Entrance examination is broadly in line with the national curriculum and the methods of the GCSE (General Certificate of Secondary Education), which will be the next landmark in your child's education.

Exam dates

The Common Entrance examinations are held in February/March, June and November, for boys and girls who wish to enter the senior school at 13. The 11+ exam is held in January, but can also be taken in November. The 12+ exam is held in February/March and in November. Heads of preparatory schools will advise you.

Please note

Some senior schools do not require pupils to take Common Entrance or any other exam. They admit pupils after interview. Some have their own entrance examination. Some use a mixture of procedures for entry at 11, 12 and 13. The entrance requirements are listed with the details about each school in this book.

4. Senior Schools (for pupils aged 11/13 to 18)

The choice is very wide: girls' schools for parents who wish their daughters to go to single-sex schools; boys' schools; boys' schools which admit girls at 16; and coeducational schools for parents who want boys and girls to be educated together. Most schools are small, while the larger ones are often divided into houses of between 40 and 60 pupils each. The traditional grammar schools usually cater for day pupils only: they select children who do best on examination for entry at 11+.

Many schools, including so-called 'public' schools, admit both boarders and day pupils of a wide range of abilities. Most stay on after 16 in the sixth form. Most students go on to higher education at colleges or universities.

Some students leave at 16 to go to further education or sixth-form colleges. Other students, who are not going on to further study, will leave at 16 or 18 having received an all-round education fitting them well for working life.

5. Scotland

Age	Type of School	Curriculum
4–13	PREPARATORY	Largely boys' schools, many of which have a number of girls, preparing for the Common Entrance Examination and entry to senior schools.
8–13 10/13–18	JUNIOR SENIOR	A variety of boys' schools, girls' schools and coeducational schools, some with junior departments. The senior schools prepare pupils for Scottish examinations and in many cases also for A Levels.
4–18	ALL-THROUGH boys, girls and co-educational	Many of the senior schools in Scotland have their own junior departments so pupils can progress through the various stages of education whilst remaining at the same school.

Scotland has its own public examination system – the Scottish Certificate of Education. In most Scottish schools, pupils study for the Scottish Certificate of Education (SCE), Standard and Higher Grade Examinations. Standard Grade is taken at the age of 15 and is approximately equivalent to GCSE. The Higher Grade is normally taken in five or six subjects a year later but can also be taken in the Scottish sixth year (upper sixth).

The Scottish Certificate of Sixth Year Studies (SCSYS) offers pupils who wish to stay on at school a further qualification after Higher Grade. Some Scottish independent schools do A Levels as well as 'Highers'. You should check which subjects are offered. The SCE and GCE are both recognised for entrance to all Scottish universities and other universities in the United Kingdom.

In Scotland all schools in membership of ISIS belong to the Scottish Council of Independent Schools, which was formed in 1978 to represent the interests of independent schools in Scotland. They are registered with the Scottish Education Department and subject to inspection by Her Majesty's Inspectorate.

For further information about Scotland, you should contact Scottish ISIS, Floor 2/1, 11 Castle Street, Edinburgh EH2 3AH.

6. How do you know if the schools ISIS recommends are good ones?

Registration

Every new independent school has to be registered with the Government and is visited by one of Her Majesty's Inspectors (HMI) for this purpose. Registration, however, simply means that the school has met the basic legal qualifications for the number of children, suitability of teachers and certain health, fire, building and other requirements.

Accreditation

Before 1978 independent schools reaching a certain standard could be 'Recognised as Efficient' by the then Department of Education & Science, which gave some guarantee about their general standards. After the Government withdrew this system, the Independent Schools Joint Council (ISJC) set up its own accreditation scheme in 1980. This is now known as the Accreditation, Review & Consultancy Service (ARCS). Accredited schools are able to use the phrase '*Accredited by the Independent Schools Joint Council*' in their literature.

On an accreditation visit a team of serving or recently retired heads, led by a team leader who is a former HMI, spends two and a half days in school after studying detailed information provided by its head. Visits are designed to assess general standards and offer advice. A discussion with the head at the end of the visit is followed by a written report which refers, in addition to general aspects of the school, to standards of achievement and the quality of teaching and learning (see below).

Accreditation is a pre-requisite for membership of the governors' and heads' associations in ISJC: Governing Bodies' Association/Governing Bodies of Girls' Schools Association (GBA/GBGSA); Girls' Schools Association (GSA); Headmasters' Conference (HMC); Incorporated Association of Preparatory Schools (IAPS); Independent Schools Association Incorporated (ISAI); Society of Headmasters & Headmistresses of Independent Schools (SHMIS).

All 1,350 schools within ISJC are members of at least one of these associations and of National ISIS. ARCS is used by all except HMC, which makes its own arrangements for accreditation.

Schools are evaluated in relation to criteria covering: aims; administration, organisation and management; curriculum; staffing; premises; resources; standards of achievement and quality of teaching and learning; assessment, recording and reporting; requirements for membership of the association.

In order to ensure consistent standards, ARCS provides written guidance for schools and teams on the purpose and conduct of visits and runs a programme of training for team leaders and members.

The benefits of the scheme are that
* **the independent sector is seen to be taking steps to maintain standards;**
* **the school receives an objective appraisal of its provision and work, and advice on further development;**
* **an association receives information on the quality of schools in membership;**
* **parents, and the general public, are given reassurance on the quality of schools using the accolade 'Accredited by ISJC.'**

Procedures for evaluating standards in independent schools are carefully monitored to ensure that regard is paid both to the needs of the school and to recent developments in education and inspection practice. ARCS works closely with the Office for Standards in Education (OFSTED), which is represented on the ARCS Committee, receives copies of all accreditation and review reports and is a major partner in the training of inspectors.

In addition, independent schools continue to be inspected by HMI and OFSTED. Boarding schools in England and Wales are also affected by the Children Act 1989, which came into force in 1991. Section 87 places a duty on their 'proprietors' (ie governing bodies and heads as well as private owners) to safeguard and promote the welfare of children in their charge. It also requires local authority social services departments to satisfy themselves that welfare arrangements are adequate by making periodic inspections of boarding schools in their areas.

Review

In 1984 some associations introduced a system of periodic review to check on whether standards were being maintained in accredited schools. Review visits are required by the school's association, usually once every ten years and/or after a change of head. Review visits are also of two and a half days and, according to the policy of the association, the purpose and procedure may be the same as for accreditation or may focus on particular aspects of the school.

In 1993, as an alternative to the review system, the Girls' Schools Association introduced a Quality & Management Audit (QMA) to evaluate and report on the management, life and work of its schools. QMA visits of two and a half days are undertaken by small teams of practising or recently retired heads led by a former HMI. Both oral and written reports are provided.

Consultancy

ISJC's consultancy service has developed since 1988 and is used by all associations. It responds to requests from schools and provides appraisal and advice tailored to their needs. Consultancy visits, using suitably qualified specialists, have included:
- large team visits akin to full HMI inspections;
- subject visits undertaken by one consultant;
- reviews of school management;
- workshops and training days;
- evaluation of, and advice on, curriculum development;
- cooperative planning of new premises with architects and teachers.

CHAPTER 3

NARROWING THE CHOICE

The first step in considering independent education is to narrow the choice. There are four basic questions which you must decide. Depending on your child's age, you may think he or she is mature enough to take part in these decisions.

1. Boarding or day?

Almost five children out of six at independent schools are day pupils. They usually come from a wider area than those at state day schools. Sometimes the children live as far as 15 or 20 miles away from their school. If day schooling would best suit your child, you should make a list of the schools within reasonable travelling distance from your home. Consider rail and bus links and if you like the look of a school, but it seems difficult to get to, check whether the school runs its own bus service. There may be other parents in your area with whom you could share the travel.

Do not dismiss the idea of a boarding education just because it is unfamiliar to you. It could be the best choice you ever made. You have a wider choice of schools and can save the trouble and expense of travelling to and from school each day. Boarding will not suit every child, but it is fun and most children enjoy living away from home during term-time. Few children would not benefit from the chance of residential education at some time during their schooldays. Don't be put off by the stereotypical images of boarding favoured by the media or the reminiscences of those who boarded many years ago. See modern boarding schools for yourself: you will understand why they are so popular with today's boarders.

The first-ever national survey of what boarders think about boarding, conducted by ISIS in 1993, was entitled *One Big Family*, because that was how boarders repeatedly described their happy school lives. A random sample of 5000 boys and girls in 335 schools found that:

* 84% of prep school boarders and 77% of senior boarders preferred to board;
* more than half of all boarders either chose their school themselves or believed their own opinion was decisive in choosing it;
* three-quarters of prep school boarders and two-thirds of seniors thought boarding was more fun;
* most thought boarding did not distance them from their parents;

* most thought boarding enabled them to get to know their teachers better and provided more opportunities for sport, music and drama.

A survey of 5000 parents in 1995 – *Boarding: A Partnership with Parents* – produced similarly positive responses from parents whose children are boarders.

Weekly or flexible boarding has become a popular option in recent years. Children go home each weekend and this often suits families where both parents have jobs. Most parents choose boarding schools within 50 miles or not more than an hour-and-a-half's journey from their homes. If they are likely to be moved abroad or to another part of the country, they may choose schools which are near relatives or close friends. Make a list of the boarding schools which might be suitable, remembering that most boarding schools admit day pupils as well. If you think your children might like to board later, you can hedge your bets by starting them off as day pupils.

2. Senior or junior or both?

Can you afford to pay for an independent education throughout your child's schooling? The financial implications are dealt with in Chapter 5.

Many parents choose a mixture of state and independent schools, making pragmatic decisions at different stages of their children's education. It may depend on the maintained schools in your area. If you have good primary schools, you may decide to use one and then send your child to an independent secondary school for the difficult years from 11 to 16 and over. More than 40% of independent senior school pupils have done this. On the other hand, many parents believe it is essential to give their children a good foundation at an independent junior school. Some children switch at 16, either moving from the state sector into the independent sector or the other way round. Independent schools have to provide flexibility as well as choice.

Most preparatory schools recommend children to stay on until the end of the course at 11 or 13 so they can be given their first taste of responsibility at school. Many secondary schools for pupils aged 11–18 feel that 16 is not a good age to change school: the best part of school is still to come when girls and boys are given responsibilities and privileges. A change during adolescence and between important examinations can be harmful.

3. Single-sex or coeducational?

Which do you want or don't you mind? At the primary stage of schooling you may think it does not matter. But you may consider that at secondary school age your son or daughter would make more progress without the distraction of the opposite sex. On the other hand, you may believe it is more natural if boys and girls spend their teens being educated together. Above all, what would best suit your child?

4. **Academic or less-academic?**

Some parents are over-ambitious for their children. Others underestimate their children's abilities and potential. It is not good for children to flounder at the bottom of the class after being over-coached and just getting through the entrance exam into a school where they find the academic pressures too great. They are too likely to be discouraged and to under-perform. On the other hand, if they can work faster than the rest it is boring and frustrating to have to pretend not to be so clever.

Will your child do better in a school where there is a good deal of academic pressure or would a school catering for a wider range of academic abilities be more suitable? If your child is bright and obviously able, and you think will do well in the type of school that used to be a grammar school, then look particularly for the schools in this book which take part in the Government's Assisted Places Scheme. This scheme is described on page 36. You may qualify for help with the fees. If your child is less academic, look for a smaller school with small classes.

Which school will choose your child?

You should now be in a position to narrow down your choice to three or four schools. If you are still undecided, you can get help from the Regional Director of ISIS who serves your area (see pages 39-40). The next part of the process is that the schools have to choose your child.

Many junior schools and a few senior schools in this book will choose their pupils on a first-come-first-served basis, so the sooner you contact the schools the better. Some very well-known schools, particularly day schools in the Greater London area and in other cities, will have waiting-lists. There are some boarding schools in this position as well, but generally it is not necessary to put children's names down at birth! Nor is it desirable to do so: the school must be right for the child and you are more likely to be sure of this two or three years before entry. You may, however, be disappointed if you leave your decision until the term before you want your child to enter the school. Two years in advance is usually the right time to book a place, but earlier in London and other big cities.

Entry to a sixth-form at 16 can be highly competitive. It is therefore advisable to plan more than a year ahead of the date of entry.

Find out about schools' entry requirements. The brief details in this guide may give you some idea, but you must know whether you are selecting the school or the school is selecting your child. If it is the latter, what is the chance of your child being successful? Should you not also consider other schools which have less demanding entrance requirements?

How to apply

Simply ring up the school and talk to the school secretary, who will be used to requests for information without obligation. Ask about vacancies. Ask for a prospectus which will tell you about the school. Please mention you have read about the school in the National ISIS guide. Read the prospectus carefully. If you approve of what the school says about itself, ring up and arrange a visit. There is no substitute for seeing the school on a normal day.

CHAPTER 4

QUESTIONS TO ASK WHEN YOU VISIT A SCHOOL

1. Read the prospectus

A school's prospectus should give you the basic facts – its fees, the numbers of children, day pupils and boarders, entry requirements, subjects and facilities (all contained in this book, too). The prospectus should also state the school's objectives. It will, of course, emphasise all those features of the school which give a good impression. It should encourage you to visit. Make a list of questions arising from the prospectus that you wish to ask and also consult the checklist which is provided at the end of this chapter. The prospectus and its supplementary information form the basis of the 'contract' between the school and parents.

Video prospectuses: A few schools have made video tapes of what they offer. These can give you a living impression of the school. This is helpful for parents overseas who cannot easily visit, but others should not judge a school entirely on its video recording. The presentation is inevitably a very selective one, put forward with professional help to present the best picture of the school.

School magazines: Many schools publish magazines about their activities. Ask for a copy of the latest issue. Use this as a further guide to life at the school.

2. What will it all cost?

The prospectus should tell you the *basic* termly or annual fees. Ask when and how often they are increased. Some schools will know what their fees will be for the next year. There are usually extras on top of the fees quoted. At some schools these are very small; at others they add substantially to the bill (perhaps another ten per cent), depending largely on activities in which your child takes part. They should be borne in mind when you consider what you can afford. Remember that a school requires parents to give a full term's notice if they intend to withdraw their child; otherwise another term's fees are payable.

Extras: Basic fees are quoted in this book. Lunches are included in these in some schools, in others they are extra: please check with individual schools. Some schools ask parents to pay for such extras as medical supplies, telephone calls and school trips. Find out if you will have to pay extra for school books and entries for public examinations. How much will you have to pay for your child to have individual lessons on a musical instrument? (See the checklist of possible extra items on page 28.)

Uniform: This can be a substantial cost throughout your child's career, if certain items have always to be bought new from the school's recommended suppliers. But if a school has its own second-hand shop selling uniforms and other clothing, you can make worthwhile savings; it makes sense when you consider how quickly children grow out of them. Find out when the school shop is open, and what essential items are not stocked there.

What about pocket money, if your child is a boarder? How much should you give, and is there a school bank where it can be put?

3. Arranging a visit

Most parents visit several schools. Your visits may be the single most influential part of the process of choosing a school. Arrange a day when you can talk to the head and meet other members of staff and their pupils; in a boarding school in particular, housemasters or housemistresses may be a key factor in your choice. The head may not be able to spend a long time with you but some will show you round personally as well as telling you about the school and discussing your concerns; others may ask a pupil or member of staff to show you round. Open days are often advertised in the local press; pupils' work is on display but you should not choose a school only on the basis of an open day. You must see the school when it is operating normally and classes are in progress. Both parents should visit the school and it is often a good idea to take your child as well.

4. First impressions

Looking at the buildings is not as important as looking at the children. A pupil prepared to stop and help you find the way to your appointment is one of the best advertisements for a school. Do the children look happy and purposeful? Speak to some of them about what they are doing and about their interests. What do they particularly like about the school? You can get some idea of the discipline of a school by watching its pupils. Are they all wearing uniform? Do they rush or walk down corridors? Do they stand aside and let you pass? In the classrooms, is the atmosphere one of orderly learning?

Try to assess whether discipline in the school is firm without being repressive. To what kind of regime will your child best respond?

5. The Head

A good head makes the school; a poor head can break it. The smaller the school, the truer this tends to be. In boarding schools, particularly, your child's housemaster or housemistress will be nearly as important as the head. You must have confidence in the person mainly responsible for looking after your child.

Do not expect heads to be super-salesmen or saleswomen. They have been trained to teach children rather than to 'sell' their school. What they must do is convince you that they will really care for your children. So do not be too impressed by the head who seems to be concerned with showing you buildings and equipment. You are not buying the school! Warm to the head who expresses an interest in your child and then explains why his or her school could be the right one. Even if heads are reserved and shy, they should be positive people, able to take decisions and prepared – and probably expecting – to answer awkward questions frankly. Take the opportunity to mention any special concerns you have or any matters which particularly interest your child. If the head is showing you round the school, you should have a good chance to assess how well your 'guide' is liked by the pupils and how well he or she knows them. Do they acknowledge him or her or look the other way? How do they and the staff react to you as visitors?

6. Staff

The staff, not the buildings, are a school's chief assets. Find out as much as you can about the teachers. How long have they taught at the school? Where have they taught before? How many are full-time? What are their qualifications? Are those teaching maths, science, English and French trained to do so? Some may not have been trained in that particular subject, but it may not matter because they are very good teachers who have been at the school for a long time. On the other hand you may find there have been frequent changes of staff and difficulties in attracting qualified teachers in certain subjects.

7. Pastoral care

In any school, and particularly in a boarding school, you will want to ask about its pastoral care system. The Children Act requires schools to provide a statement on the care of pupils. Who will have primary and immediate responsibility for your child's welfare? Is there an individual tutor? Do older pupils have responsibilities towards younger ones, especially in their first year? To whom should your child go if there is a problem? Do boarders have access to a private telephone? Is there a 'counsellor' in or outside the school to whom pupils may go? How does the school deal with bullying?

8. Discipline and contact with parents

All schools have rules. The prospectus should give you some idea of the regime. Which rules are commonsense and which seem petty? Discipline is about teaching children self-responsibility, so should it be more relaxed as children grow up?

Ask the head about the rules and the reasons for them. What are the usual punishments? What are regarded as the more serious offences and what are the punishments for these? Is corporal punishment used? If so, how often and by whom? (Very few independent schools retain it, but, unlike the state system, it is not illegal in independent schools except where children's fees are paid from public funds.) Will you be contacted if your child gets into trouble? Ask if the school has prefects or monitors and how they are appointed. If it is a single-sex school, what are the arrangements for meeting the opposite sex?

How much contact does the school have with parents? Is there a parents' association? Are there parents' evenings at which you can discuss your child's work with teachers? How often are they held? How often do teachers and other staff meet to discuss the children's work? Are there formal meetings at which this is done? How frequently do parents receive written reports on children's progress? Is there a regular newsletter to parents?

9. Curriculum

The school should have a broad and well-balanced curriculum. Most independent schools have regard to the National Curriculum, even though it does not apply by law to them, but you will expect them to provide more. How wide are subject choices for GCSE and Advanced level? Are Advanced Supplementary levels offered? Are the arts and languages well provided for? Are classics (Latin and Greek) taught? How are the sciences taught? Do pupils have the options of single sciences and dual award GCSE science (the latter enables them to continue with chemistry, physics and biology but they occupy less time and count as two GCSEs rather than three)?

Ask how children move up the school from class to class. Do some children get left behind or are some bright children held back? Are there arrangements for withdrawing slow learners or for accelerating quick ones? Are children streamed according to ability? This may not suit children who are always in the bottom class and find it so demoralising that they give up trying. Are children of all abilities mixed for some subjects and put into separate sets for subjects like maths, the sciences and French? How will this system suit your child?

10. Examinations & leavers

Examination results are not everything. A preparatory school may be sending its pupils to good state schools rather than getting top results in the Common Entrance Examination. Ask where the leavers from prep schools go. *Assess how well any type of school is doing with the kinds of children it accepts.* Ask the heads of senior schools to explain the ranges of intelligence scores they may use to admit children. If a school admits them as a result of the Common Entrance Examination, a school which has a pass mark of 60 or 65 is selecting children of high academic standard. If the pass mark is 50 or below, the school is accepting a wider range of abilities or is able to allow for differences in earlier schooling.

Your child may not be as bright as you think. A school that is prepared to take trouble over the less bright may enable your child to get more qualifications than another school with an impressive list of entrants to top universities. Nevertheless you should ask senior schools how many leavers go on to universities and how many go to colleges of further and higher education.

What subjects are offered at GCSE? The usual subjects are mentioned in the checklist on page 29. How many do pupils have to take? Do they have to do them all at the same time? (See also Curriculum above.)

Sixth form: A good school will encourage its pupils to stay on into its sixth form. Compare the size of the fifth year with the first year of the sixth form. Find out how many pupils leave the school at sixteen to go elsewhere. If there appears to be a big drop in pupils staying on, you should ask why.

Examination results: Schools may tell you that a large percentage of their pupils pass. Make sure you know whether this is the percentage of all pupils in the examination year or just a percentage of those pupils entered for the examination. Some schools enter all pupils for examinations even if they may not have a very good chance of passing. Others enter only those who have a good chance of success. Ask how many passed with 'A' & 'B' grades.

A Levels: Make sure the school offers the subjects at A Level in which your child might be interested. Ask how many students last year passed with 'A' grades. Can humanities and sciences be mixed?

Note the introduction to the examinations sections on page 000.

Careers: Whether your child goes from school into higher education or straight into a career, he or she should receive informed and up-to-date careers advice. What provision does the school make for this? What contacts does it have with the world of work, including industry? What literature on careers is available for the pupils?

11. Class size

Count the number of desks in the classes you visit. The average class in the state sector has about 30 children if the pupils are under 16. Many preparatory schools have much smaller classes with 15 to 20 pupils. Most senior independent schools have classes or teaching groups of between 20 and 25 pupils below sixth form level. Former direct grant schools and other grammar schools may have larger classes of up to 30. The size of class is different from the average pupil/teacher ratio, which includes teachers who have administrative duties and spend only part of their time teaching. Classes in boarding schools tend to be smaller than in day schools.

Ask to be taken into a few classrooms while teaching is in progress. Senior schools sometimes allow you only to look through a window or door. One sees why, and you would not like it if your child was in a class which was frequently interrupted by visitors. On the other hand, teaching is the most important activity in a school, and it is what you will be paying most for. When you go to classes in junior schools, you might ask to look at a few of the children's work books. Compare a child's books at the beginning of term with those at the end of it. You may be able to judge whether any improvement has taken place with a child's numbers, spelling or writing.

Homework: How much homework is set? Does it increase as pupils move up the school? Many boarding schools have day pupils who benefit from the longer school day and six-day week: are they able to do some of their homework at school and how satisfactorily can they study? What arrangements are made for boarders doing their 'prep'?

12. Buildings

Do not be over-impressed by splendid language laboratories, computer rooms, Olympic-size swimming pools or sports halls. Some of the schools with the most successful teaching are on fairly restricted sites.

The most important room in the school could well be the library. How well has it been stocked and to what extent are the children using the books? Is it a quiet place for private study? How well equipped are the science laboratories? Most schools have computers and teach pupils how to use them, but are pupils able to use them in their spare time? What kinds of projects are they using them for? These are important questions. But buildings and equipment are less important than people.

Other questions (mainly for boarders)

Make sure you visit the dormitories and/or study-bedrooms in a boarding school. Younger pupils may be in rooms for several children. Four or five is a popular number at that stage. Can they occupy single or double rooms in the sixth form? You will want your child to be comfortable and to have a reasonable amount of space. While you will not want him or her to live in a slum, don't be too put off by signs of normal wear and tear. Boarding accommodation has improved beyond recognition in the last ten years, but remember you are looking at schools not five-star hotels: judge them accordingly.

Parents of boarders will also want to know about sanatorium arrangements when children are ill.

Find out about chapel and provision for confirmation and first communion.

Ask when children can come home during term time ('exeats') and how often you can visit your child. Find out what is organised for pupils who stay at school during weekends. Some children become bored if their time is not fully occupied; others benefit from having time which they can organise for themselves.

At the end of the visit

Before you go, find out what are the next steps if you wish your child to come to the school. Most schools will ask you to register your child and you will have to pay a small registration fee which is often not returnable. How soon do you have to commit yourselves? Some will ask for a deposit which counts as part of one term's fees.

You should also ask for the names and telephone numbers of parents with children already at the school. Contact them and find out as much about the school as you can to help you make up your mind. Having visited it you should have plenty of questions to ask them.

ISIS CHECK-LIST OF

POINTS TO LOOK FOR AND QUESTIONS TO ASK

School roll

Parents to fill in from the details in the directory section of this book, or in the prospectus they have received, and to check with the school:

Number of Boys .... Boarders ....
Number of Girls .... Day pupils ....
Size of sixth form if appropriate .... Total ....

Fees (*Parents to check with school*):

Fees per term ....
(*These should be mentioned in details supplied with prospectus*)
Are they revised termly or yearly?
What is charged in addition (add or delete as appropriate)?

Lunches	Textbooks	Judo
School Trips	Stationery	Tennis
Music Lessons	Extra Art	Fencing
Speech (Elocution)	Technology	Phone Calls
Dancing/Ballet	Riding	Insurance
Exam entry fees		

(*These should be mentioned in the prospectus*)

Teachers

Number of full-time: .... Total equivalent of full-time teachers ....
Number of part-time: .... Staff/pupil ratio: 1 teacher to .... pupils
                              Average size of class: .... pupils

Staff qualifications

Proportion of graduates on staff: ....
Are all maths teachers qualified to teach maths? ....
Are all French teachers qualified to teach French? ....
(*Repeat for other subjects as necessary*)
How many staff are unqualified to teach? ....

Contact with parents

Are there staff meetings with parents to discuss children's work?
                                                    Yes ☐ No ☐
How often are they held? ....
Is there a parents' association? ....

Uniform

Does the school run a second hand shop?   Yes ☐ No ☐
When is it open? ....
What will you have to buy new? ....

28

Academic results

Junior Schools
How many pupils left at the end of last summer term? ....
Which schools did they go on to? (Head can usually supply a list)
Did any win scholarships? ....
How many are staying on to do scholarship exams? ....

Senior Schools
GCSE subjects usually include:

English Language	History	French
English Literature	Chemistry	Religious Education
Mathematics	Physics	Art
Geography	Biology	

Subjects at more academic schools often include:
Latin (sometimes Greek as well)
German, Spanish and other foreign languages in addition to French
Economics

How many pupils were in the year taking GCSE?
How many entered for 5 or more GCSEs?
How many passed 5 or more GCSE Grades A-C?
How many pupils stayed on for the sixth form last September?
Can the head mention any successes among pupils who came to the school with apparently low academic expectations but did well in examinations?

A Levels
Does the school offer the subjects at A Level in which my child might be interested?
How many pupils last year sat two or more A Levels?
How many passed two or more A Levels?
How many passed with top grades?

What do the school's pupils do when they leave?
Ask what last year's leavers did after they left.
How does the school help with careers advice?

'Crunch' questions
Has the head really explained what the school could do for my child?
Why should I choose this school rather than any other?

Boarding
What activities are organised at weekends?
What is the school's pastoral care system?
What arrangements are made for the child's health?

Final Questions
What are the next steps I should take if I am interested in sending my child to your school?
Can you give names and telephone numbers of a few parents of current pupils?

> Note: These are by no means all the questions you might ask. Sport, music, drama and extra-curricular activities should also be mentioned.

SECTION ONE

CHAPTER 5

HOW MUCH DOES IT COST?

Fees at the schools in this book vary widely. They depend on whether schools are educating older children or younger ones; day or boarding, and sometimes on the part of the country in which they are situated. (Schools in northern England may be less expensive).

Every January ISIS carries out a survey of its member schools and the results are published in the spring. Schools are asked to state their basic fees (which in some cases include lunches). The ranges of fees for different sorts of school are then calculated. The information has been updated for this book.

The latest figures are for 1995–6. In 1996 they will increase, possibly by about 5%.

Type of school	Approximate range of fees per term	Type of school	Approximate range of fees per term
Pre-preparatory 2–7	£400 to £1,000	Senior school 13–18	
		Girls' day	£1,200 to £2,400
		Girls' boarding	£2,500 to £4,000
Junior School 7–13			
Day pupils	£800 to £2,100	Boys' day	£1,200 to £2,900
Boarders	£2,000 to £3,000	Boys' boarding	£2,500 to £4,200

Plan early

The secret of paying school fees is to start planning early. For example, while your child is still in nappies you could pay into insurance policies to cover, or contribute towards, the cost of school fees several years later. These policies will provide a tax-free sum which can be used for other purposes if you decide after all not to choose a fee-charging school. If you have left it until later, it is still worth taking out insurance policies or other investments four or five years before the child is due to enter school. Considerable reductions on school fees can also be achieved. There are many savings vehicles available using regular contributions or payments from capital and you will need expert help. ISIS lists a number of school fees advisers at the end of this chapter who can assist you.

Grandparents can help

Many grandparents help with their grandchildren's school fees by giving occasional lump sums of money to the parents. Even small contributions on a regular basis can be useful and make it possible to afford an independent education. If grandparents are prepared to help while the child is still very young, this is one of the best ways of financing a school fees insurance policy. You should seek advice from an expert, your bank manager, accountant or any of the firms listed at the end of this section.

Lump sum payments

If you are fortunate to have a legacy or large capital sum, you can set up a trust which will pay the school fees in advance and will reduce their eventual cost quite substantially. You should consult one of the school fees experts. You could also approach the school to which you think you will send your child. Some schools have their own schemes. A lump sum put down at the time of your child's entry to cover all or part of the school fees might attract a worthwhile reduction. Bigger reductions will be achieved by putting down a lump sum four years in advance. Make sure the arrangement can be transferred if you choose another school.

If you have not been able to save in advance for school fees

The **New Perspective Range of School Fees Plans** is offered by Bowring Financial Services Ltd (regulated by the Personal Investment Authority). The plans are tailored to meet individual requirements and soften the impact of school fees by providing
* greater immediate disposable income;
* a facility for the payment of fees and
* in most cases, an increased income in later years.

Where funds are required immediately, a 'drawdown facility' can be arranged with one of the panel lenders (subject, of course, to status and, where appropriate, property valuation). This facility provides a flexible cash fund to be used to pay all or part of the fees each year. It may be secured on residential property or an appropriate insurance policy and monies can be 'drawn down' in minimum tranches of £1,000 up to four times a year.

Repayment of the capital element of any borrowing is arranged in the most cost-effective and tax-efficient manner appropriate to individual circumstances.

A brochure describing the plans and containing a short confidential questionnaire is available from National ISIS, 56 Buckingham Gate, London SW1E 6AG.

The first year's membership of FIS/Friends of Independent Schools (see page 39) is free for holders of the *New Perspective* plans.

To complement the mainly equity-based *New Perspective* plans, insurance brokers Mason & Mason and NWS Bank have launched the **School Fees Funding Plan**, which allows parents to defer the cost of school fees immediately, without the need for advance funding or initial capital outlay. A leaflet/inquiry card is available from National ISIS, or you can call the Helpline on 01625 532234.

School fees specialists

The brokers and companies listed below are specialists in school fees planning. Please note that some firms may offer only one type of fee payment scheme, which may not suit your needs. You are therefore advised to 'shop around' and approach more than one. You should also enquire whether firms are paid by commission or whether they charge a fee for their advice. If you live overseas, please see Chapter 8, page 50.

For immediate help

The New Perspective Range of School Fees Plans:

National ISIS,
56 Buckingham Gate,
London, SW1E 6AG
Telephone: 0171 630 8793/4
Fax: 0171 630 5013

or Bowring Financial
Services Ltd,
Matheson House,
141 Minories,
London EC3N 1NB
Telephone: 0171 357 3333
Fax: 0171 357 3384

School Fees Funding Plan:

National ISIS (as above)

or Mason & Mason
18/20 Manchester Road,
Wilmslow,
Cheshire SK9 1BG
Helpline 01625 532234

Private Bank

Kleinwort Benson Private Bank
PO Box 191
19 Fenchurch Street
London EC3M 3LB
Telephone: 0171 956 6600

Independent financial advisers

Hogg Robinson Financial Services Ltd
Hogg Robinson House,
42-62 Greyfriars Road,
Reading, Berks RG1 1NN
Telephone: 01734 583683
Fax: 01734 575488

Invest for School Fees
58 St James's Street,
London SW1A 1LD
Telephone: 0171 290 2510
Fax: 0171 493 4313

School Fees Insurance Agency Ltd
SFIA House,
15 Forlease Road,
Maidenhead,
Berks SL6 1JA
Telephone: 01628 502020
Fax: 01628 770447

Whitehead and Partners
Howard House,
Lloyd Street,
Altrincham, Cheshire,
WA14 2DE
Telephone: 0161 928 2209
Fax: 0161 927 7202

Insurance Companies

Ecclesiastical Insurance Group
Life Division,
Beaufort House,
Brunswick Road
Gloucester GL1 1JZ
Telephone: 01452 419221
Fax: 01452 311690

Equitable Life Assurance Society
Walton Street, Aylesbury,
Bucks HP21 7QW
Telephone: 01296 393100
Fax: 01296 386388

Standard Life Assurance Company
3 George Street,
Edinburgh EH2 2XZ
Telephone: 0131 225 2552
Fax: 0131 22 01 53 4

Financial Services Groups

Gan Financial Services Ltd
School Fees Unit,
Gan House, Harlow,
Essex CM20 2EW
Telephone: 01279 626262
Fax: 01279 451917

Sedgwick Financial Services Ltd
Norfolk House,
Wellesley Road,
Croydon CR9 3EB
Telephone: 0181 666 8108
Fax: 0181 666 8345

For immediate help

New Perspective Range of School Fees Plans & School Fees Funding Plan (see page 31).

School Fee Payment Protection Schemes

ISIS offers school fee payment protection schemes – FUTURE TERM 2000, FEESURE and EDUCARE – which provide funding for school fees when a parent is **disabled** due to illness, injury or accident, made **redundant** or becomes involuntarily **unemployed** or **bankrupt** (i.e. through the failure of his or her own business). They therefore:

* protect parents against a wide range of financial hardships, with the most competitive premiums that the market can devise, and
* protect the continuity of children's education.

Policies can be taken out individually or in group schemes.

Details of FUTURE TERM, FEESURE and EDUCARE can be obtained from: Mason & Mason, 18-20 Manchester Road, Wilmslow, Cheshire SK9 1BG (Tel. 01625 529536; Fax 01625 535447).

CHAPTER 6

SCHOLARSHIPS AND GRANTS

Many senior schools and a few junior schools offer scholarships or 'exhibitions' to attract bright pupils to the school by helping their parents with the fees. Scholarships vary in value but rarely cover the whole fees. Many schools augment scholarships with bursaries based on parental means. You must find out from the school what scholarships are offered, and what each is worth so you are not disappointed if you cannot afford the fees when your child wins one of the smaller awards. Scholarships are awarded as a result of a competitive examination, usually for academic, musical or artistic merit. Take advice from the head of your child's present school about the chances of success.

Music, art & drama

Many senior schools offer scholarships for children who are talented in music, art and drama. *Music Awards at Independent Schools*, an annual guide to music scholarships and exhibitions in senior schools published by the Music Masters' & Mistresses' Association, is available from MMA Awards Book, 29 Lillian Road, Barnes, London SW13 9JG.

Choir Schools

A child who sings well and enjoys it could win a free or heavily subsidised place at a choir school. Normal age of entry, after voice trials, is 7–9; some places are available at 10. All choristers receive a first-class musical and academic education. Further details from the Choir Schools Association (see page 46).

Bursaries

A bursary is a grant from the school to help you pay the fees. It is often awarded after a 'means test' of family income. Unlike a scholarship, it is not based on a competitive examination.

Other awards

Many schools offer grants to children of clergy, teachers, and those in the armed forces. Some give help to children of former pupils, to single parent families and orphans or concessions for brothers and sisters. About 40 schools offer Arkwright scholarships for sixth-formers intending to study engineering, technology or design-related subjects at university; further information from the Administrator, Coomery Barn, Tuckenhay, Nr Totnes, Devon TQ9 7EP (tel. 01803 732776). Some schools also make awards for all-round merit and sport.

Details

Turn to the entry details for each school under scholarships and grants.

Schol	= Academic scholarships
Art	= School offers scholarships for artistic pupils
Mus	= School offers scholarships for musical pupils
Choral	= Choral scholarships or bursaries for singing
Drama	= Scholarships for pupils talented in drama
Burs	= Bursaries and other financial assistance
Clergy	= Help is given for children of clergy
Teacher	= Help is given for children of teachers
Forces	= Help is given to members of the armed forces
AP	= School offers Government Assisted Places (see below)
VI Form	= School offers scholarships or bursaries at 16+
ARA	= All-rounder award
Sport	= Awards for sport
Siblings	= Concessions on fees for brothers/sisters

Assisted Places Scheme

The Government's Assisted Places Scheme is for day children aged 11 and over. The Government will give grants so that able children whose parents cannot afford the full cost of the fees can attend one of almost 300 academic secondary schools in England and Wales. There is also a scheme in Scotland in which 59 schools participate. National ISIS publishes a booklet listing schools participating in the scheme; the Department for Education & Employment and its Welsh and Scottish equivalents publish explanatory leaflets.

The grants are paid direct to the school in respect of individual pupils. The amount is worked out after a means test of your family income before tax with deductions of £1,165 for each of your children (except the one who may get the award). If after these deductions your family earns less than £9,572 a year, your child could win a free place; if earnings are about £15,000, you could expect to contribute about £900 a year. Above about £20,000 a year you should not expect substantial assistance.

These figures apply to the 1995–96 academic year. You should contact the school for further details. These are usually available in October or November, before schools hold examinations for assisted places in January or February. The scheme covers tuition fees only, but some schools offer boarding bursaries to pupils who win assisted places so if you do not live near an assisted place school your child could still benefit as a boarder.

See page 47 for information on the Aided Pupils Scheme for entry to specialist music schools.

Other government grants

Service families: The Ministry of Defence gives grants to children of parents in all ranks of the armed forces stationed in this country or abroad. The boarding school allowance is worth (in 1995–96) £1,883 per term for each junior school child and £2,248 per term for each senior school child. The special educational needs allowance is £2,998 per term. There are also small day allowances to enable children to be looked after by friends or guardians at day schools if you have to move home. Further information can be obtained from your local Service Education Unit or from the Service Children's Education Authority (address on page 48).

Many independent schools listed in the directory section of this book are keen to admit children of service families and to reduce their fees, particularly for boarding pupils. Look in the column headed Scholarships & Bursaries for 'Forces' to find schools offering bursaries or fee concessions for service children. The extent of this help will vary from one school to another and you should ask the schools for full details. You should check that the concessions are available to all ranks and to all children in a family. Ask also about any 'extras' for which parents have to pay which are not included in the fees.

The Foreign and Commonwealth Office gives grants to enable children of diplomats and other government servants working abroad to attend boarding schools in Britain.

Local authority grants

Some education authorities and some social service departments give grants to enable children who need to board to go to boarding schools. You should apply to the director of education or chief education officer for the area in which you live. Funds are very limited, but if you can show that boarding education is essential and if there is no room for your child at one of the few schools which admit boarders in the state system, you may be fortunate. The local authority may agree to pay part of the costs, such as tuition fees only.

Reasons commonly accepted for boarding need include:
* both parents are abroad;
* parents have to move home frequently because of their job;
* home circumstances are unhelpful to the child's development;

* child has a certain gift – e.g. music, dancing or singing – which can only be properly catered for at a boarding school;
* child suffers from a handicap which makes boarding desirable (see section on special needs, page 55);
* child lives in a remote part of the country and cannot easily travel each day to school.

Grant-giving trusts

Educational trusts help with school fees in some cases of *genuine need* and with some specific categories, such as: orphans, children of the clergy, missionaries and teachers. Genuine needs recognised by grant-making trusts include:

(a) boarding need, where the home environment is unsuitable because of the disability or illness of the parents or of siblings;
(b) unforeseen family disaster, such as the sudden death of the breadwinner when a child is already at school;
(c) need for continuity when a pupil is in the middle of a GCSE or A-level course and a change in parental circumstances threatens withdrawal from school;
(d) need for special education where there is a genuine recognised learning handicap which cannot be catered for at a local authority or grant-maintained school.

The desire for an independent education which you cannot afford to buy for your child on your own is no reason to apply to a grant-giving trust. Such applications will be rejected. Contact National ISIS for details of its Educational Grants Advisory Service, which refers genuinely deserving cases to charitable trusts.

CHAPTER 7

WHERE TO GO FOR FURTHER HELP

INDEPENDENT SCHOOLS INFORMATION SERVICE
For many parents thinking about sending their children to independent schools, ISIS is their starting point.

National ISIS was established in 1972 by the leading associations of independent schools in the UK and is now the information, public relations and political arm of the Independent Schools Joint Council (q.v.). It produces many publications for parents and schools and an annual Census. A national independent schools exhibition is held annually in October. National ISIS also runs a Press & Public Relations Office, through which it handles the independent sector's relations with the media and provides marketing and public relations services to member schools, and ISIS International and the ISIS Association (see below). It answers almost 30,000 requests for information each year from parents, schools, journalists, academics, researchers, politicians, students and others. Address: 56 Buckingham Gate, London SW1E 6AG. Tel. 0171 630 8793/4. Fax 0171 630 5013.

ISIS International helps parents living overseas to find suitable schools *in the UK* for their children. Its placement, consultancy and clearing house services are also available to UK residents and it offers a consultancy service for multi-national companies whose staff require independent schools for their children. Clients receive the personal attention of an experienced consultant with detailed knowledge of ISIS schools who tries to make sure that the school is right for the child. For further details and costs of services, please write to ISIS International, 56 Buckingham Gate, London SW1E 6AG, telephone 0171 630 8790 or fax 0171 630 5013. See also Chapter 8.

The Friends of Independent Schools is our campaigning organisation. Membership (at modest subscription rates) entitles members to regular information and discounts on various goods and services. Income is used to campaign on behalf of independent education, to lobby government and Parliament on matters affecting independent schools and to employ a political liaison officer. It has 60,000 members and donors. Full details from: 56 Buckingham Gate, London SW1E 6AG. See also the advertisement at the back of this book.

ISIS REGIONS

The United Kingdom and Ireland are divided into eight ISIS regions. Each is run by a director with detailed knowledge of independent schools in the region and publishes its own handbook. Many organise exhibitions attended by member schools. For further information, contact the appropriate Regional Director.

Central England
Woodstock, Oxon OX7 1YF
Tel. 01993 813006

London & SE England
Murray House
3 Vandon Street
London SW1H 0AN
Tel. 0171 222 7274

Northern England & N Wales

2 Overhead Cottages
Capernwray
Carnforth LA6 1AD
Tel. 01524 735 977

Eastern England
Welcome Cottage
Wiveton
Nr Holt, Norfolk NR25 7TH
Tel. 01263 741333

South and South-West England
Skippers, Shipton Lane
Burton Bradstock
Bridport
Dorset DT6 4NQ
Tel. 01308 898 045

Wales
11 High Street, St. David's
Dyfed, SA62 6SD
Tel. 01437 721 204

Scotland
Floor 2/1, 11 Castle Street
Edinburgh EH2 3AH
Tel. 0131 220 2106

Ireland
Headfort School, Kells
Co Meath
Tel. 010 353 46 40065

INDEPENDENT SCHOOLS JOINT COUNCIL

The Council, formed in 1974, is a forum in which the larger associations of independent schools exchange views and discuss policy. It is the principal organisation which negotiates with the Government on behalf of independent schools. It is responsible for an Accreditation Service, described on pages 00–00. Address: ISJC, Grosvenor Gardens House, 35–37 Grosvenor Gardens, London SW1W 0BS. Tel. 0171 630 0144. Fax. 0171 931 0036.

The constituent associations are:

GBA Governing Bodies' Association – includes the governing bodies of the boys' and coeducational schools whose heads belong to HMC and SHMIS (see below). It also includes some other boys' senior schools, which are marked as belonging to GBA in this directory. Address: The Coach House, Pickforde Lane, Ticehurst, East Sussex TN5 7BJ. Tel. 01580 200855.

GBGSA and **GSA** Governing Bodies of Girls Schools Association and the Girls' Schools Association. These are the main associations to which the girls' senior independent schools belong. Addresses: GBGSA as for GBA above; GSA, 130 Regent Road, Leicester LE1 7PA. Tel. 0116 2471797.

HMC Headmasters' Conference – boys' and coeducational senior schools whose headmasters belong to the Headmasters' Conference. Address: 130 Regent Road, Leicester LE1 7PA. Tel. 0116 2854810.

IAPS Incorporated Association of Preparatory Schools. The Association includes the heads of almost 600 boys', girls' and mixed preparatory schools for children aged usually from 7/8 to 12/13. Pupils are prepared for senior schools. Many preparatory schools have pre-prep departments for younger children. Address: 11 Waterloo Place, Leamington Spa, Warwickshire CV32 5LA. Tel. 01926 887833.

ISAI Independent Schools Association Incorporated. Members include the heads of some 300 preparatory and senior schools and schools for children of all ages. Some of these also belong to other associations. Address: Boys' British School, East Street, Saffron Walden, Essex CB10 1LS. Tel. 01799 523619.

ISBA Independent Schools Bursars' Association, to which senior school bursars belong. Address: Woodlands, Closewood Road, Denmead, Waterlooville, Hampshire PO7 6JD. Tel. 01705 264506.

SHMIS Society of Headmasters & Headmistresses of Independent Schools – comprising heads of 70 boys' and coeducational senior schools with a long tradition of boarding education. Address: The Coach House, 34a Heath Road, Upton-by-Chester, Cheshire CH2 1HX. Tel. 01244 379649.

National ISIS Independent Schools Information Service, 56 Buckingham Gate, London SW1E 6AG. Tel. 0171 630 8793/4; Fax 0171 630 5013. Described on page 39.

Reference books

Other directories which give details about independent schools include:

The Independent Schools Yearbook, published by A & C Black, 35 Bedford Row, London WC1R 1JH. Available in many public reference libraries.

Independent Schools of the United Kingdom, published by E. J. Burrows, 106 Stafford Road, Wallington, Surrey SM6 9TD.

Which School? published by John Catt Educational Ltd, Great Glemham, Saxmundham IP17 2DH.

The Equitable Schools Book, published by Bloomsbury Publishing Ltd, 2 Soho Square, London W1V 5DE.

The rest of this chapter concerns schools or organisations which can help if you or your children have particular needs.

41

SECTION ONE

1. Religious needs
Church of England (Woodard and Allied Schools & Church Schools Company)
Roman Catholic Boarding Schools
Methodist Boarding Schools
United Reformed Schools
Friends' Schools
Jewish Schools

2. Philosophical needs
'Progressive' schools
Round Square schools

3. Music and singing
Choir schools
Specialist music schools

4. Gifted children

5. Girls' Public Day School Trust

6. Other organisations

7. Careers information

1. RELIGIOUS NEEDS

Many schools in this book are Christian in ethos, tradition and observance.

Church of England

The largest group is run by the Woodard Corporation, 1 The Sanctuary, London SW1P 3JT. Telephone 0171 222 5381. The following schools belong:

BOYS & COED SENIOR SCHOOLS	GIRLS SENIOR SCHOOLS	BOYS & COED PREP SCHOOLS
Ardingly (Sussex)	Queen Mary's, York	Ardingly Jun (Sussex)
Bloxham (Oxon)	School of St Mary & St Anne (Staffs)	Hurstpierpoint Jun (Sussex)
Denstone (Staffs)		King's Jun, Taunton
Ellesmere (Salop)	St Hilary's, Cheshire	Llandaff Cathedral, Cardiff
Grenville (Devon)	St Margaret's, Exeter	Prestfelde, Cardiff
Hurstpierpoint (Sussex)	Peterborough High (Cambs)	Ranby House (Notts)
King's, Taunton		Denstone Jun (Staffs)
King's, Tynemouth		
Lancing (Sussex)		
St James' (Humberside)		
Worksop (Notts)		

42

One group is associated with The Allied Schools, 42 South Bar Street, Banbury, Oxon OX16 9XL. Tel. 01295 256441.

BOYS & COED SENIOR SCHOOLS	GIRLS SENIOR SCHOOLS	GIRLS PREP SCHOOL
Canford (Dorset)	Harrogate Ladies College	Riddlesworth Hall (Norfolk)
Stowe (Bucks)	Westonbirt (Glos)	
Wrekin (Salop)		

Another group is run by the Church Schools Company Ltd, Church Schools House, Titchmarsh, Kettering, Northants NN14 3DA. Tel. 01832 735105. They are girls' day or coeducational day/boarding schools and each has both junior and senior departments:

The Atherley School, Southampton
Guildford High School
Hull High School
Sunderland High School
Surbiton High School
York College

Roman Catholic

For information on Roman Catholic schools in both the maintained and independent sectors, you should contact the Catholic Education Council for England & Wales, 41 Cromwell Road, London SW7 2DJ. Tel. 0171 584 7491. The following boarding schools are listed according to the archdiocese/diocese in which they are situated:

Roman Catholic boarding schools
WESTMINSTER
Ware: St Edmund's College
ARUNDEL AND BRIGHTON
Crawley: Worth School
Dorking: St Teresa's Convent School
Lingfield: Notre Dame Convent School
Mayfield: Mayfield College
Mayfield: St Leonards-Mayfield
Steyning: Convent of the Blessed Sacrament
Weybridge: St George's College
Windsor: St John's Beaumont
Witley: Barrow Hills Preparatory School
Woldingham: Convent of the Sacred Heart
BIRMINGHAM
Alton: St John's Preparatory School
Birmingham: Holy Child School
Chaddesley Corbett: Winterfold House
Oxford: Rye St Anthony
Reading: Oratory Preparatory School

SECTION ONE

Reading: Douai School
Stafford: St Bede's
Woodcote: The Oratory School
BRENTWOOD
Chelmsford: New Hall
CLIFTON
Bath: Prior Park College
Cricklade: Prior Park Preparatory School
Shaftesbury: St Mary's Convent School
Shepton Mallet: All Hallows School
Stratton-on-the-Fosse: Downside School
EAST ANGLIA
Bury St Edmunds: Moreton Hall School
Cambridge: St Mary's School
Ipswich: St Joseph's College
LANCASTER
Carlisle: Austin Friars School
LIVERPOOL
Birkenhead: St Anselm's College
MIDDLESBROUGH
Ampleforth: Ampleforth Preparatory School
Ampleforth: Ampleforth College
Nawton: St Martin's Preparatory School
NOTTINGHAM
Leicester: Grace Dieu Manor Preparatory School
Leicester: Ratcliffe College
Spinkhill: Mount St Mary's College
PLYMOUTH
Sherborne: St Anthony's Convent Prep School
Sherborne: St Anthony's-Leweston
PORTSMOUTH
Andover: St Benedict's Convent High School
Andover: Farleigh School
Ascot: St Mary's Convent School
Farnborough Hill: Convent School
Romsey: La Sagesse Convent
Southsea: St John's College
Woolhampton: Douai School
SALFORD
Stonyhurst: Stonyhurst College
SHREWSBURY
Ludlow: Moor Park School
SOUTHWARK
Folkestone: St Mary's College
Kingston: Marymount International School
Tunbridge Wells: Beechwood School Sacred Heart
Westgate-on-Sea: The Ursuline College

Methodist

For information on Methodist schools and colleges you should contact the Methodist Church, Division of Education & Youth, 25 Marylebone Road, London NW1 5JP. Tel. 0171 935 3723. The following are boarding senior schools.

BOYS
Shebbear (N. Devon)

GIRLS
Edgehill (N. Devon)
Farringtons (Kent)
Kent College, Pembury
Queenswood (Herts)
Rydal Penrhos (N. Wales)

CO-EDUCATIONAL
The Leys, Cambridge
Ashville, Harrogate
Culford (Suffolk)
Kent College, Canterbury
Kingswood, Bath

Methodist College, Belfast
Queens College, Taunton
Rydal Penrhos (N. Wales)
Truro School (Cornwall)
Woodhouse Grove (W. Yorks)

United Reformed

Schools which retain their traditional links with the United Reformed Church are:

BOYS/COEDUCATIONAL
Caterham, Surrey
Eltham, London SE9
Silcoates, Wakefield

GIRLS
Walthamstow Hall, Sevenoaks
Wentworth Milton Mount, Bournemouth

Friends' Schools (Quakers)

Information can be obtained from the Friends' Schools Joint Council, Friends' House, Euston Road, London NW1 2BJ. Tel. 0171 387 3601. The Quaker schools in this book are:

BOYS
Leighton Park, Reading

GIRLS
Mount School, York
Bootham, York
Friends' School, Saffron Walden (Essex)
Sibford, Oxon
Sidcot, Avon

COEDUCATIONAL
Ackworth (Yorks)
Ayton, Middlesbrough

Jewish

There is only one Jewish school in this book: Carmel College (Oxon), a coeducational boarding school. Clifton College, Bristol, has a Jewish house. For other Jewish schools contact the Jewish Board of Deputies, Woburn House, Upper Woburn Place, London WC1. Tel. 0171 387 2681.

2. SCHOOLS WITH DIFFERENT PHILOSOPHIES
'Progressive' schools

Some independent schools have reacted against traditional education and pioneered 'progressive' teaching methods or experimented with relaxed forms of discipline based on trust and friendship between pupils and staff. Coeducational boarding schools in this book which might fall into this category include:

Bedales (Hants)   Millfield (Somerset)
Frensham Heights (Surrey)   St Christopher, Letchworth
Friends' Schools (see above)

Round Square Conference schools

An international group of schools following the principles of Kurt Hahn (founder of Salem School in Germany and Gordonstoun in Scotland) was formed in 1967. The Round Square Conference (named after Gordonstoun's circular building) now has 25 member schools in nine countries: Australia, Canada, England, Germany, India, Kenya, Scotland, Switzerland and the United States. They arrange exchange visits for pupils and undertake aid projects. All member schools uphold the five principles of outdoor adventure, community service, education for democracy, international understanding and environmental conservation.

Member schools in the United Kingdom are:

GIRLS   COEDUCATIONAL
Cobham Hall (Kent)   Abbotsholme (Derbyshire)
St. Anne's (Cumbria)   Box Hill (Surrey)
Westfield (Tyne & Wear)   Gordonstoun, Scotland
                                Rannoch, Scotland

For more information contact: Kay Holland, Secretary, Round Square Conference, Box Hill School, Dorking, Surrey RH5 6EA.

3. MUSIC AND SINGING
Choir schools

Further information is available from Caroline Legard, Administrator, Choir Schools' Association, The Minster School, Deangate, York YO1 2JA. Tel. 01904 625217. Fax. 01904 632418. The following schools in this book are members:

JUNIOR & SENIOR (AGES 7–18)
Bristol: Bristol Cathedral School   Oxford: Magdalen College
Canterbury: St Edmund's   School
Gloucester: King's School   Rochester: King's School
Grimsby: St James' School

Hereford: The Cathedral School
Liverpool: St Edward's College

Wakefield: Queen Elizabeth Grammar School
Wells: Wells Cathedral School
Worcester: King's School

JUNIOR (AGES 7–13)
Cambridge: King's College School
Cambridge: St John's College School
Chichester: The Prebendal School
Durham: The Chorister School
Ely: The Junior School, King's School
Exeter: The Cathedral School
Guildford: Lanesborough School
Lichfield: St Chad's Cathedral School
Lincoln: The Cathedral School
Llandaff: The Cathedral School
London: St Paul's Cathedral Choir School
London: Westminster Abbey Choir School
London: Westminster Cathedral Choir School
Norwich: Norwich School
Oxford: Christ Church Cathedral School
Oxford: New College School
Reigate: Reigate St Mary's Prep & Choir School
Ripon: The Cathedral Choir School
Salisbury: The Cathedral School
Tewkesbury: The Abbey School
Truro: Polwhele House School
Winchester: The Pilgrims' School
Windsor: St George's School
York: York Minster School

Specialist music schools

Many independent schools in this book have strong music departments. The following are included in the Government Aided Pupils Scheme as centres of musical excellence:

Chetham's School of Music, Manchester
The Purcell School, Harrow, Greater London
Wells Cathedral School, Somerset
The Yehudi Menuhin School, Surrey
St Mary's Music School, Manor Place, Edinburgh EH3 7EB
Royal Ballet School, Richmond, Surrey TW10 5HR

Details of the first four, which are ISIS members, can be found in the county directory section of this book.

The Aided Pupils' Scheme provides assistance with tuition and boarding fees on a scale linked to family income. Further information from the Department for Education & Employment (address on page 48).

4. GIFTED CHILDREN

For information about gifted children, please contact the National Association for Gifted Children, Park Campus, Boughton Green Road, Northampton NN2 7AL. Tel. 01604 792300.

5. GIRLS' PUBLIC DAY SCHOOL TRUST

Twenty-six girls' schools belong to the Trust, which was founded in 1872. The schools uphold high academic standards and offer a wide range of subjects, aesthetic and practical as well as academic. Further details may be obtained from: The Girls' Public Day School Trust, 26 Queen Anne's Gate, London SW1H 9AN. Tel. 0171 222 9595.

GREATER LONDON AREA	OUTSIDE GREATER LONDON
Blackheath High School	Bath High School
Bromley High School	Birkenhead High School
Croydon High School	Brighton & Hove High School
Heathfield School, Pinner	Cardiff: Howell's School, Llandaff
Kensington Prep School for Girls	Ipswich High School
Notting Hill & Ealing High School	Liverpool: The Belvedere School
Putney High School	Newcastle (Central) High School
South Hampstead High School	Norwich High School
Streatham Hill & Clapham High School	Nottingham High School
	Oxford High School
Sutton High School	Portsmouth High School
Sydenham High School	Sheffield High School
Wimbledon High School	Shrewsbury High School

6. ADDRESSES OF RELEVANT ORGANISATIONS

Boarding Schools' Association

BSA's members include 450 preparatory and senior independent boarding schools and 40 state boarding schools. Until Dec.31 1995: The Secretary, Westmorland, 43 Raglan Road, Reigate, Surrey RH2 0DU. Tel. 01737 226450. From Jan.1 1996: The Secretary, Ysgol Nant, Valley Road, Llanfairfechan, Gwynedd LL33 0ES.

Choir Schools' Association

The Minster School, Deangate, York, YO1 2JA. Tel. 01904 625217. (See pages 46–47.)

Independent Schools Examinations Board, Jordan House, Christchurch Road, New Milton, Hants BH25 6QJ. Tel. 01425 610016/621111.

Conference for Independent Further Education, Buckhall Farm, Bull Lane, Bethersden, Nr Ashford, Kent TN26 3HB. Tel. 01233 820797.

Service Children's Education Authority, HQ, DGAGC, Worthy Down, Winchester, Hants SO21 2RG. Tel. 01962 887933. See page 37.

Department for Education & Employment, Independent Schools Team, Mowden Hall, Staindrop Road, Darlington, Co. Durham DL3 9BG. Tel. 01325 392160.

7. CAREERS INFORMATION

Most independent senior schools have at least one member of staff with responsibility for careers advice and a well-stocked careers room. In addition, many schools and parents draw on the services of ISCO.

The Independent Schools Careers Organisation (ISCO) provides a complete service for boys and girls. It has over 300 schools in membership and has built up good contacts with the country's leading employers over 40 years. ISCO provides ability tests and interest questionnaires which are analysed by the schools' careers departments and show which careers might profitably be explored. It has developed a computerised careers guidance system which can be used in conjunction with the ability tests.

Further information from ISCO, 12A–18A Princess Way, Camberley, Surrey GU15 3SP. Tel. 01276 21188.

CHAPTER 8

IF YOU LIVE OVERSEAS

About one child in 21 at ISIS-member schools in Britain lives overseas. Some have British parents working abroad, but about 17,000 are boys and girls of foreign nationalities from many countries in mainland Europe, the Far East, the Middle East, Africa, Australasia and the Americas. These pupils are welcomed by independent schools throughout the United Kingdom. They come from a wide variety of cultural backgrounds and have much to offer the schools.

Increasing numbers of overseas pupils are attracted to British boarding schools by their high academic reputation; excellent examination results; high standard of English language teaching; broad curriculum; wide range of activities outside the classroom; pastoral care for every boy and girl; small classes, and good discipline.

They work, play, eat and sleep in their schools. They learn to live in a community and think of their school as one big family. They make long-lasting friendships, take advantage of sport, music, drama and clubs and benefit from a complete educational experience. Many stay on to enter British universities.

There are many schools to choose from. That is why overseas parents very often need expert help to find the right ones for their children. ISIS International provides it (see below).

How, when and where to apply

The best piece of advice is: do not leave the choice of school until the last moment. If you are moving to this country and looking for a day school in the London area, you must start looking as early as possible. A few well-known boarding schools are booked up years in advance, but generally there is less pressure on boarding than on day places. Consider the whole of Britain if you are looking for a boarding school. You will certainly not find all the best schools in the south of England within easy distance of Heathrow or Gatwick airports where, in any case, vacancies are limited.

Excellent schools with good academic traditions exist in Northern England, the South West, the Midlands and in Wales, Scotland and Ireland. There is slightly less demand for boarding places in schools over 60 miles from London and the facilities of these schools in the countryside are second to none. There are good airports too at Manchester, Birmingham, Bristol, Derby, Edinburgh, Leeds, Exeter, Newcastle upon Tyne, Glasgow, Aberdeen, Inverness, Belfast and Dublin. Communications within the United Kingdom by motorway and rail are good. Schools have long experience of arranging for pupils to be met at airports and other terminals.

Applications should be made in writing to the head of each school in which you are interested. You should ask for a prospectus and suggest dates on which you might be able to come to the UK to visit the school. You should include in your letter details of your child's name, age, date of birth, nationality, and religion, and state which term you wish your child to start. Most new children enter schools for the start of the school year in September. The school year is divided into three terms. The Autumn term begins in early September and ends in mid-December; the Spring term runs from mid-January to late March and the Summer term from late April to early July.

In your letter to the head, you should mention the schools which your child has attended, with dates, give details of any public examinations passed and enclose a report from the head of the child's present school. Remember to give the child's full name and the parents' names and occupations.

Guardians and escorts

Schools require parents who live overseas to appoint a guardian in this country to be responsible for the child over mid-term breaks and over the holidays (if the child cannot go home). Schools will want a responsible adult to turn to in case of an emergency.

Quite often guardians are relations or friends who keep an interest in your child's progress during term-time. If there is no one suitable, schools can often recommend a guardian or ISIS can put you in touch with organisations which may help. Schools will expect younger children to be accompanied by responsible adults when they are travelling between school and home. You should ask the schools for their travel arrangements and for names of escort agencies.

Age of entry

The best ages are: before the age of 9 for a junior school; at 11+ or 13+ for boys' senior schools; at 11+ or 12+ for girls' senior schools. The ages 11-13 can be particularly beneficial in a preparatory school and enable a good choice of senior school to be made. The age not recommended is about 15, when the student arrives at the school between the first two years of the GCSE course; however, arrangements can be made in these cases. Many schools will not be able to take students aged 17 for the last year of the two-year A-Level course.

Most senior schools will accept students at the age of 16 and over into their sixth forms. The main requirement will be adequate passes in the pupils' overseas certificate so that they may enter the sixth-form to study for A-levels. Schools differ in their entry requirements but as a rough guide pupils should have passed the equivalent of five GCSEs at grade C or above. Some students aged 17 and over would be best served in a college of independent further education (see page 48).

Command of English

If your child is under the age of nine, it will not matter if his or her English is weak. Many junior schools will be able to help the child catch up. Children will not normally be suitable if they are over the age of nine and cannot read English fluently as printed in text books for their age group, unless the school makes special provision for English language teaching. An ISIS booklet, *English Language for Overseas Students*, lists 400 independent schools offering varying degrees of help in English language teaching. ISIS International (see over) can arrange for children to attend additional English-language courses.

Where to go for further help

ISIS International was established in 1978 to assist parents living overseas to find places for their children in UK independent schools. It offers a comprehensive range of services to help find the most suitable school for your child and carries out this work for a number of international companies.

ISIS International's services are:

(1) **Placement Service.** This service is the one most often used by parents. After obtaining full background details of a child and personal contact with schools, ISIS International will provide a short-list of suitable schools prepared to accept your child, subject to any relevant entry tests and interviews. ISIS International will co-ordinate visit arrangements, advise on guardians and oversee all administrative arrangements until a school is finally selected.

(2) **Consultancy Service.** This service provides personal advice on suitable schools and includes follow-up action but leaves parents to apply to schools themselves.

(3) **Clearing House.** Parents wishing to obtain a short-list of schools appropriate to the child's abilities and needs can use ISISCLEAR – the ISIS International clearing house – which passes details on to schools who make their offers of a place direct to parents.

Parents pay fees for the placement and consultancy services as ISIS International takes no commission from schools for children introduced via these services. For the

ISISCLEAR service, parents pay a nominal handling charge. Full details of the above services can be obtained from ISIS International which is co-located with National ISIS in London.

A National ISIS Consultancy Service for UK parents is also available through ISIS International.

ISIS International has representatives in the following places:

Austria	Kenya	Russia
Bermuda	Korea	Singapore
Canada	Kuwait	Switzerland
Germany	Luxembourg	Taiwan
Hong Kong	Malaysia	Thailand
Indonesia	Qatar	United Arab Emirates

Overseas schools

The Heads of the following schools in mainland Europe are overseas members of the Headmasters' Conference:

Aiglon College, Switzerland; British School of Brussels; British School in the Netherlands; British School of Paris; English School, Cyprus; International School of Geneva; International School of Paris; King's College, Madrid; St Edward's College, Malta; Sir James Henderson School, Milan.

There are also overseas members of HMC in Africa (Malawi, South Africa, Zimbabwe), Australia, Canada, Hong Kong, India, Malaysia, New Zealand, Pakistan, Central and South America (Argentina, Brazil, El Salvador, Peru, Uruguay).

CHAPTER 9

HOW TO USE THIS DIRECTORY

County Directory

English schools are listed by counties. Schools in Wales are divided into North Wales and South Wales and appear after the English counties. Schools in Scotland are listed separately, as are those in Northern Ireland and the Irish Republic.

Within the English counties and the other areas mentioned above, schools are listed alphabetically. The letters **B**, **G** and **C** indicate whether they are BOYS, GIRLS or COEDUCATIONAL schools. No official definition of coeducation is used. We use **Bg** for schools which are mainly boys but also have some girls (usually entering the sixth-form at 16) and **Gb** for schools which are mainly girls but have some boys (usually in their junior departments).

The following guide will help you find your way through the school entries and should be read in conjunction with the index guide which follows this chapter. **A separate guide card is also included with this book.**

The first part of the school entry indicates the fees, numbers and age ranges of the pupils (with a breakdown of sixth-form numbers) and whether the school is for day and/or weekly/full boarding. The fees quoted represent the range of basic termly fees charged in the autumn term 1995 and reflect the fact that fees for younger children are usually lower than for older age groups. Lunches are included in the basic day fees of some schools – indicated by a knife and form symbol – but are extra in others. Fees for day pupils in boarding schools are often higher than those for day schools because pupils have longer hours at school. A dagger indicates that the school has not supplied its autumn 1995 fees. In these cases, and where fees are blank, parents should contact schools direct for details.

(N.B. Fees in Northern Ireland should be checked with the schools as there are differentials between residents and non-residents in some cases. Fees at schools in the Irish Republic are given in Irish pounds. Fees at the American schools are per semester, not per term.)

In the map reference, bold numbers indicate map numbers on pages 329–346 (between the directory and examination results sections); letters and numbers in lighter type show basic grid co-ordinates. The school's location is described as rural, urban or inner city.

A tick after 'Day' means school transport is provided for at least some day pupils.

In entry requirements, CEE is the Common Entrance Examination (see pages 11–12).

Travel times are indicated from school to the nearest major railway station and international airport.

Scholarships and bursaries are listed from the following:

Schol	Academic scholarships
Burs	Bursaries or other financial assistance
Art	Art scholarships
Mus	Music scholarships
Chor	Choral scholarships or bursaries for singing
Drama	Drama scholarships
Forces	Bursaries for children of service families
Clergy	Bursaries for children of clergy
Teachers	Bursaries for children of teachers
AP	School participates in the Government Assisted Places Scheme
VI form	School grants bursaries or scholarships for students entering the sixth-form
ARA	All-rounder award
Sport	Awards for sport
Siblings	Concessions on fees for brothers/sisters

Special needs for which the school may be able to cater are indicated from the list in the index guide. Where appropriate, schools have also categorised themselves according to their level of provision for dyslexia.

Many independent schools are able to admit a limited number of pupils with special educational needs, disabilities or illnesses. Parents should note that an entry in this list does not mean a school will definitely be able to offer a place; parents should also check precisely what provision (for dyslexia, for example) a school can actually make. Most are not 'special schools' but independent schools with their own standards of entry which in many but not all cases require evidence of academic potential or attainment. This information is therefore intended to provide general guidance for parents whose children have particular educational needs but which may be catered for in a mainstream school. In general the schools may be able to provide for limited numbers of children whose special needs are not sufficiently severe or complex to warrant a statement of special educational needs under the Education Act 1981. In all cases the schools are concerned that children should be helped to develop to the best of their ability and do not suffer academically because of their handicaps.

However, very few of these schools have been approved by the Secretary of State for Education & Employment as suitable for the placement by local authorities of 'statemented' children. This means that where a child has a statement and the parents look to a local education authority (LEA) for financial support, the authority must obtain the Secretary of State's consent before it can place the child at an independent school which has not been approved under the 1981 Act. Even where a child with a statement is placed at an independent school at the parents' own expense, the LEA maintaining the statement must be satisfied that the placement is suitable.

A full list of approved independent schools in England can be obtained free of charge from the Department for Education & Employment (DEE), Special Education Division, Sanctuary Buildings, Great Smith Street, London SW1P 3BT. Similar information about schools in Wales is available from the Welsh Office Education Department, Cathays Park, Cardiff CF1 3NQ, and about Scotland from the Scottish Education Department, New St Andrew's House, St James Centre, Edinburgh EH1 3TG.

Schools in this book which are approved by the DFE under Sections 11(3)(a) and 13 of the Education Act 1981 as being suitable for the placement of children with learning difficulties for whom LEAs maintain statements of special educational needs include: Hamilton Lodge School for Deaf Children, E Sussex; Maple Hayes Hall School, Staffs; Mark College, Somerset; More House School, Surrey.

Dietary needs for which schools can cater are explained in the index guide.

The Associations to which the governing body or head belongs are:

GBA	Governing Bodies Association
GBGSA	Governing Bodies of Girls' Schools Association
GSA	Girls' Schools Association
HMC	Headmasters' Conference
IAPS	Incorporated Association of Preparatory Schools
ISAI	Independent Schools Association Incorporated
SHMIS	Society of Headmasters & Headmistresses of Independent Schools

Some religious and philosophical affiliations (eg Methodist) are given in full; others are abbreviated, as below:

CofE	Church of England
CofI	Church of Ireland
CofS	Church of Scotland
CinW	Church in Wales

RC	Roman Catholic
UR	United Reformed Church
Inter-denom	Inter-denominational
Non-denom	Non-denominational
Chr Sci	Christian Science
7th D	Seventh Day Adventist

Sports, additional languages and subjects, extra-curricular activities, on-site facilities, retakes and National Vocational Qualifications are included in the index guide.

Examination boards are listed by their initials in the index guide. The first six are the GCSE examining groups. Scottish schools offering Scottish examinations are indicated by an asterisk; those offering English examinations are indicated by a dagger. Both symbols are used if a school offers both.

ULEAC	University of London Examinations & Assessment Council
MEG	Midland Examining Group
NEAB	Northern Examinations & Assessment Board
SEG	Southern Examining Group
WJEC	Welsh Joint Education Committee
NISEAC	Northern Ireland Schools Examination & Assessment Council
AEB	Associated Examining Board
UCLES	University of Cambridge Local Examinations Syndicate
IB	International Baccalaureate
Ox	University of Oxford Delegacy of Local Examinations
O&C	Oxford and Cambridge Schools Examination Board
SEB	Scottish Examination Board
SUJB	Southern Universities' Joint Board
Welsh	Welsh Joint Education Committee

At the end of each school's entry are shown the subjects (each represented by a letter) offered at various examination levels: Advanced level, Advanced Supplementary level, General Certificate of Secondary Education and 'Other' (which includes Common Entrance). The subjects are listed in the index guide.

An alphabetical list of schools, with their counties or countries, appears at the end of the book.

Please note that we cannot take responsibility for incorrect information. All information should be checked with individual schools. Entries for a few schools are incomplete because full details were not available at the time of publication.

DIRECTORY OF SCHOOLS

COUNTY DIRECTORY OF SCHOOLS

INDEX GUIDE TO SCHOOLS

Simply circle the category you require and then compare with your choice of school. Please also refer to Chapter 9 page 54 'How to use this directory'.

| **B** BOYS | **G** GIRLS | **Bg** BOYS including some girls | **Cb** GIRLS including some boys | **C** CO-ED | Lunches included in Day Fees |

	FEES	No. BOYS	AGE	No. GIRLS	AGE	TOTAL	SIXTH BOYS	GIRLS
DAY	£							
WEEKLY	£							
BOARDING	£							

MAP REFERENCE

See pages 329/346 for the general location of a chosen school.
Bold numbers indicates the map numbers.
Letters and numbers in the lighter type show the basic grid co-ordinates.

TRANSPORT

DAY PUPIL ✓ = yes

TRAIN
Travel time to nearest major railway station
a. Less than 15 minutes
b. 15 - 45 minutes
c. more than 45 minutes

AIR
Travel time to nearest international airport
a. Less than 60 minutes
b. 60 - 120 minutes
c. more than 120 minutes

LOCATION
Rural / Urban / Inner city

SPORT
a. Athletics
b. Basketball
c. Badminton
d. Canoeing
e. Cricket
f. Cross country
g. Fencing
h. Fitness training
i. Fives
j. Football
k. Golf
l. Gymnastics
m. Hockey
n. Lacrosse
o. Martial arts
p. Netball
q. Rounders
r. Rowing
s. Rugby
t. Sailing
u. Shooting
v. Skating
w. Squash
x. Swimming
A. Table tennis
B. Tennis
C. Volleyball
D. Curling

OTHER LANGUAGES
Subjects taught to examination level
a. EFL / ESL
b. Danish
c. Dutch
d. Flemish
e. Gaelic
f. Hebrew
g. Hindi
h. Norwegian
i. Portuguese
j. Punjabi
k. Swedish
l. Turkish
m. Urdu
n. Welsh

ACTIVITIES
a. Archery
b. Astronomy
c. Ballet / Dance
d. Bell ringing
e. CCF / ACF
f. Chess
g. Choir
h. Computing / IT
i. Debating / Public speaking
j. Drama / Theatre studies
k. Duke of Edinburgh
l. Film / Video club
m. Fishing
n. Life Saving / 1st Aid
o. Orchestra / Band
p. Orienteering
q. Outdoor pursuits
r. Philately
s. Photography
t. Pottery
u. Practical engineering
v. Printing
w. Riding
x. Scouts / Guides etc.
A. Ski-ing
B. Young Enterprise
C. Young Farmers
D. Understanding Industry

OTHER SUBJECTS
a. Current affairs
b. Health / Sex education
c. Instrumental music
d. Life skills
e. Office skills
f. Pottery
g. Secretarial skills
h. Singing

FACILITIES ON SITE
a. All-Weather pitch
b. Athletics track
c. CDT centre
d. Chapel
e. Conference facilities
f. Farm
g. Sixth Form centre
h. Sports hall
i. Swimming pool (covered)
j. Swimming pool (open air)
k. Theatre
l. Golf Course

SPECIAL NEEDS
a. Allergies
b. Asthma (severe)
c. Behavioural disorders
d. Blindness
e. Partial sight
f. Cerebral palsy
g. Coeliac disease
h. Cystic fibrosis
i. Deafness
j. Partial deafness
k. Delicate
l. Diabetics
m. Down's syndrome
n. Dyslexia
o. ESN
p. Emotional disturbance
q. Epilepsy
r. Friedrichs Ataxia
s. Haemophilia
t. Heart disease
u. Hyper-activity
v. Incontinence
w. Interrupted education
x. Kidney failure
A. Leukemia
B. Learning difficulty
C. Muscular dystrophy
D. Osteomyelitis
E. Other boarding needs
F. Paralysis
G. Physical handicap
H. Rheumatoid condition
I. Speech defect
J. Spina bifida
K. Wasting muscles
L. Wheelchair

DYSLEXIA
a. Entirely specialist
b. Mainly specialist
c. Dyslexia Unit with trained staff
d. Specifically trained staff
e. Withdrawn from class during day together with specialist help
f. Specialist help outside normal day
g. No specialist help but sympathetic staff

DIET
Dietary needs which can be catered for
a. Vegetarians
b. Vegans
c. Jews
d. Muslims

NVQ COURSES
Levels 1, 2 and 3

EXAM BOARDS
See page 57
a. LEAG
b. MEGS
c. NEA
d. SEG
e. WJEC
f. NISEC
A. AEB
B. Cam
C. IB
D. JMB
E. Lon
F. NIEB
G. Ox
H. O&C
I. SEB
J. SUJB
K. Welsh
L. etc

RETAKES
a. GCSE courses
b. A level courses

SUBJECTS TAUGHT TO EXAMINATION LEVEL
A level / AS level / GCSE / Other
a. Accounting
b. Applied science
c. Ancient hist / Classical civ
d. Art and design
e. Art
f. History of art
g. Biology
h. Business Studies
i. Chemistry
j. Commerce
k. Communication
l. Computing / IT
m. Dance
n. Drama / Theatre studies
o. Design & Technology (CDT)
p. Economics
q. Electronics
r. Engineering
s. Environmental studies
t. European studies
u. General studies
v. Geography
w. Geology
x. Government / Politics
A. Graphical / Technical
B. History
C. Home economics
D. Integrated humanities
E. Integrated science
F. Law
G. Mathematics
H. Further mathematics
I. Media studies
J. Meteorology
K. Music
L. Nautical studies
M. Philosophy
N. Photography
O. Physical education
P. Physics
Q. Psychology
R. Religious studies
S. Rural science
T. Sociology
U. Statistics
V. Surveying
W. Textiles and fashion
X. Co-ordinated science
a. *Arabic*
b. *Chinese*
c. *English literature*
d. *English language*
e. *French*
f. *German*
g. *Greek*
h. *Italian*
i. *Japanese*
j. *Latin*
k. *Russian*
l. *Spanish*

AVON

Badminton School; Westbury-on-Trym; Bristol BS9 3BA
Tel: 0117 962 3141 (Fax: 0117 962 8963) *C.J.T.Gould*

		Boys	Age	Girls	Age	TOTAL		Boys	Girls
Day	£2075			110	11-18	305	SIXTH		94
Weekly	£3750			14	11-18				
Boarding	£3750			181	11-18				

ENTRY REQUIREMENTS CEE; Exam
SCHOLARSHIPS & BURSARIES Schol; Burs; Art; Mus
SPECIAL NEEDS **DYSLEXIA** **DIET** a
ASSOCIATION GSA **FOUNDED** 1858 **RELIGIOUS AFFILIATION** Inter-denom

MAP 2 J 2
LOCATION Urban
DAY **RAIL** a **AIR** ab
SPORT acghklmopqsuvwx ABC
OTHER LANGUAGES a
ACTIVITIES cghijklnopqstuw AB
OTHER SUBJECTS abcdefgh
FACILITIES ON SITE ghik
EXAM BOARDS abcd ABDE
RETAKES a **NVQ COURSES**

A-level: efg i lmnop v x BC GH K MN P R U cdef j l
AS: f
GCSE: de g i lmnop v x N BC GH K PR U cdef j l
OTHER:

Badminton Junior School; Westbury-on-Trym; Bristol BS9 3BA
Tel: 0117 962 4733 (Fax: 0117 962 8963) *Mrs A.Lloyd*

		Boys	Age	Girls	Age	TOTAL		Boys	Girls
Day	£995-£1375			45	4-11	62	SIXTH		
Weekly	£2750			1	7-11				
Boarding	£2750			16	7-11				

ENTRY REQUIREMENTS Assessment
SCHOLARSHIPS & BURSARIES
SPECIAL NEEDS **DYSLEXIA** **DIET** a
ASSOCIATION IAPS **FOUNDED** 1858 **RELIGIOUS AFFILIATION** Non-denom

MAP 2 J 2
LOCATION Urban
DAY **RAIL** a **AIR** ab
SPORT alpqvx B
OTHER LANGUAGES
ACTIVITIES cfgjoqw A
OTHER SUBJECTS abch
FACILITIES ON SITE hik
EXAM BOARDS
RETAKES **NVQ COURSES**

A-level:
AS:
GCSE:
OTHER: e l o v B E G K O R e

Bath High School GPDST; Hope House; Lansdown; Bath BA1 5ES
Tel: 01225 422931 (Fax: 01225 484378) *Miss M.A.Winfield*

		Boys	Age	Girls	Age	TOTAL		Boys	Girls
Day	£976-£1328			631	4-18	631	SIXTH		102
Weekly									
Boarding									

ENTRY REQUIREMENTS Report & Exam & Interview
SCHOLARSHIPS & BURSARIES Schol; AP; VI Form
SPECIAL NEEDS n **DYSLEXIA** e **DIET** a
ASSOCIATION GSA **FOUNDED** 1875 **RELIGIOUS AFFILIATION** Non-denom

MAP 2 J 2
LOCATION Urban
DAY **RAIL** a **AIR** c
SPORT abfhlmopqx BC
OTHER LANGUAGES
ACTIVITIES ghijknot AB
OTHER SUBJECTS cdfh
FACILITIES ON SITE cg
EXAM BOARDS abcd ADE
RETAKES **NVQ COURSES**

A-level: c e g i p uv BC GH K M OP R U c efg j l
AS: e g l G K M efg
GCSE: de g i l o v BC G K OP R cdefgh j l
OTHER:

Bristol Cathedral School; College Square; Bristol BS1 5TS
Tel: 0117 929 1872 (Fax: 0117 930 4219) *K.J.Riley*

		Boys	Age	Girls	Age	TOTAL		Boys	Girls
Day	£1347	461	10-18	10	16-18	471	SIXTH	92	10
Weekly									
Boarding									

ENTRY REQUIREMENTS Exam; Report
SCHOLARSHIPS & BURSARIES Schol; Burs; Mus; Chor; AP; VI Form
SPECIAL NEEDS ejklnqs Bl **DYSLEXIA** efg **DIET** a
ASSOCIATION GBA **FOUNDED** 1542 **RELIGIOUS AFFILIATION** C of E

MAP 2 J 2
LOCATION Inner City
DAY **RAIL** a **AIR** a
SPORT abcefghjlmopswx AB
OTHER LANGUAGES
ACTIVITIES dfghijklnoqs AB
OTHER SUBJECTS abcdfh
FACILITIES ON SITE cdgh
EXAM BOARDS abcd ABDEH
RETAKES ab **NVQ COURSES**

A-level: c efg i p v B GH K P R cdefg j l
AS: gh G K M R ef
GCSE: c e ghi o v B G K OP R cdefg j
OTHER: l no u w K O R hi k

Bristol Grammar Lower School; Elton Road; Bristol BS8 1SR
Tel: 0117 973 6109 *Mrs Jane E.Jenkins*

		Boys	Age	Girls	Age	TOTAL		Boys	Girls
Day	£780	142	7-11	64	7-11	206	SIXTH		
Weekly									
Boarding									

ENTRY REQUIREMENTS Test
SCHOLARSHIPS & BURSARIES Schol
SPECIAL NEEDS blq H **DYSLEXIA** **DIET** a
ASSOCIATION IAPS **FOUNDED** 1532 **RELIGIOUS AFFILIATION** Inter-denom

MAP 2 J 2
LOCATION Inner City
DAY **RAIL** a **AIR** a
SPORT adefgjlmpqsx B
OTHER LANGUAGES
ACTIVITIES cfghjoqt
OTHER SUBJECTS ch
FACILITIES ON SITE abhk
EXAM BOARDS
RETAKES **NVQ COURSES**

A-level:
AS:
GCSE:
OTHER: e v B G cde

AVON continued

C | **Bristol Grammar School; University Road; Bristol BS8 1SR**
Tel: 0117 973 6006 (Fax: 0117 946 7485) *C.E.Martin*

		Boys	Age	Girls	Age	TOTAL		Boys	Girls
Day	£1296	685	7-18	334	7-18	1019	SIXTH	205	71
Weekly									
Boarding									

MAP 2 J 2
LOCATION Inner City
DAY ✓   **RAIL** b   **AIR** b
SPORT abcdefghjklmopqsuvwx AB
OTHER LANGUAGES
ACTIVITIES cfghijklnopqrs AB
OTHER SUBJECTS bcdh
FACILITIES ON SITE abcghk
EXAM BOARDS bcd ABDEHJ
RETAKES a   **NVQ COURSES**

ENTRY REQUIREMENTS Exam
SCHOLARSHIPS & BURSARIES Schol; Burs; Mus; AP
SPECIAL NEEDS bl G
DYSLEXIA   **DIET** abcd
ASSOCIATION HMC   **FOUNDED** 1532   **RELIGIOUS AFFILIATION** Non-denom

A-level: c e ghi l op v / B GH K P R / cdefg jk
AS:
GCSE: c e g i op v / B G K P R / cdefgh jk
OTHER:

C | **Clifton College Prep. School; Bristol BS8 3HE**
Tel: 0117 973 7264 (Fax: 0117 946 7565) *Dr.R.J.Acheson*

		Boys	Age	Girls	Age	TOTAL		Boys	Girls
Day	£410-£2320	X	279	3-13	93	3-13	452	SIXTH		
Weekly	£2860		12	8-13		8-13				
Boarding	£2964		44	8-13	24	8-13				

MAP 2 J 2
LOCATION Urban
DAY a   **RAIL** a   **AIR** a
SPORT abcdegijklmopqsuvwx AB
OTHER LANGUAGES afi
ACTIVITIES cfghijlmoqrstw A
OTHER SUBJECTS abcfh
FACILITIES ON SITE abcdehik
EXAM BOARDS
RETAKES   **NVQ COURSES**

ENTRY REQUIREMENTS Test; Scholarship Exam; Report & Interview
SCHOLARSHIPS & BURSARIES Schol; Mus; Forces; Clergy; AP
SPECIAL NEEDS abeghijklmnpqtuwx ABCDEFGHIJKL   **DYSLEXIA**   **DIET** acd
ASSOCIATION IAPS   **FOUNDED** 1862   **RELIGIOUS AFFILIATION** C of E

A-level:
AS:
GCSE:
OTHER: de g i lmno q v / ABC E G K NOP R / a cdefg j l

C | **Clifton College; Clifton; Bristol BS8 3JH**
Tel: 0117 973 9187 (Fax: 0117 946 6826) *A.H.Monro*

		Boys	Age	Girls	Age	TOTAL		Boys	Girls
Day	£2810	X	230	13-18	64	13-18	630	SIXTH	181	74
Weekly										
Boarding	£4050		232	13-18	104	13-18				

MAP 2 J 2
LOCATION Urban
DAY   **RAIL** a   **AIR** b
SPORT abcdefghijklmnoprstuvwx ABC
OTHER LANGUAGES acfgiln
ACTIVITIES cefghijklmnogstvw AB
OTHER SUBJECTS abcdfh
FACILITIES ON SITE abcdehik
EXAM BOARDS abcd ABDEGHJL
RETAKES   **NVQ COURSES**

ENTRY REQUIREMENTS CEE; Test & Interview
SCHOLARSHIPS & BURSARIES Schol; Burs; Art; Mus; Forces; AP; VI Form; ARA; Siblings
SPECIAL NEEDS abhjklnqtuwx BEFGIK   **DYSLEXIA** e   **DIET** abcd
ASSOCIATION HMC   **FOUNDED** 1862   **RELIGIOUS AFFILIATION**

A-level: c efg i nop uv / B GH K OP R / bcdefg ijkl
AS: f / G / ef
GCSE: de ghi nop v / B E G K PQR X / bcdefghijkl
OTHER:

G b | **Clifton High School; College Road; Clifton; Bristol BS8 3JD**
Tel: 0117 973 0201 (Fax: 0117 923 8962) *Mrs J.D.Walters*

		Boys	Age	Girls	Age	TOTAL		Boys	Girls
Day	£270-£1425		73	3-11	649	3-18	752	SIXTH		116
Weekly	£2585				6	16-18				
Boarding	£2720				24	16-18				

MAP 2 J 2
LOCATION Urban
DAY   **RAIL** a   **AIR** b
SPORT abcefghjklmpqsvwx ABC
OTHER LANGUAGES a
ACTIVITIES cfghijknogstw AB
OTHER SUBJECTS abcdfh
FACILITIES ON SITE bcgik
EXAM BOARDS abcd ABDE
RETAKES   **NVQ COURSES**

ENTRY REQUIREMENTS Exam
SCHOLARSHIPS & BURSARIES Schol; Mus; AP; VI Form
SPECIAL NEEDS   **DYSLEXIA**   **DIET** acd
ASSOCIATION GSA   **FOUNDED** 1877   **RELIGIOUS AFFILIATION** Non-denom

A-level: cd gi n p v x / BC GH K P R W / cdefg ijkl
AS: GH / def l
GCSE: cd g i l no v / BC G K P R W / cdefg j l
OTHER: l o u / NO R / h

G | **Colston's Girls' School; Cheltenham Road; Bristol BS6 5RD**
Tel: 0117 942 4328 (Fax: 0117 942 6933) *Mrs J.P.Franklin*

		Boys	Age	Girls	Age	TOTAL		Boys	Girls
Day	£1195				499	10-18	499	SIXTH		131
Weekly										
Boarding										

MAP 2 J 2
LOCATION Inner City
DAY   **RAIL** a   **AIR** a
SPORT abcfhklmpqwx ABC
OTHER LANGUAGES
ACTIVITIES cghijklnoptw AB
OTHER SUBJECTS abcdfh
FACILITIES ON SITE bch
EXAM BOARDS abcd ABDEGHJ
RETAKES   **NVQ COURSES**

ENTRY REQUIREMENTS Exam
SCHOLARSHIPS & BURSARIES Schol; Burs; AP
SPECIAL NEEDS abghjklnqtuv AI   **DYSLEXIA** g   **DIET** abcd
ASSOCIATION GSA   **FOUNDED** 1891   **RELIGIOUS AFFILIATION** Inter-denom

A-level: cd ghi nop uv / BC GH K P R W / cdef jkl
AS: GH K
GCSE: cd l o v / BC E G K O R W / cdef jkl
OTHER:

AVON *continued*

Colston's Collegiate Lower School; Stapleton; Bristol BS16 1BA
Tel: 0117 965 5297 (Fax: 0117 958 5652) *G.N.Phillips*

		Boys	Age	Girls	Age	TOTAL		Boys	Girls
Day	£840-£1270	145	3-11	60	3-11	205	SIXTH		
Weekly									
Boarding									

ENTRY REQUIREMENTS Test
SCHOLARSHIPS & BURSARIES Schol
SPECIAL NEEDS blns
DYSLEXIA ce   **DIET**
ASSOCIATION IAPS   **FOUNDED**   **RELIGIOUS AFFILIATION** C of E

MAP 2 J 2
LOCATION Urban
DAY   **RAIL** a   **AIR**
SPORT abcdefhijklmpqstuwx AB
OTHER LANGUAGES
ACTIVITIES cfghjoqt A
OTHER SUBJECTS abcdfh
FACILITIES ON SITE abcdhjk
EXAM BOARDS
RETAKES   **NVQ COURSES**

A-level
AS
GCSE
OTHER   c e g i l   o   uv
B   G I K   OP R
cde   j

Colston's Collegiate School; Stapleton; Bristol BS16 1BJ
Tel: 0117 965 5207 (Fax: 0117 958 5652) *D.G.Crawford*

		Boys	Age	Girls	Age	TOTAL		Boys	Girls
Day	£1600-£1825 ✗	309	11-18	64	11-18	427	SIXTH	93	20
Weekly	£2700-£3210	1	11-18		11-18				
Boarding	£2800-£3360	39	11-18	14	11-18				

ENTRY REQUIREMENTS CEE; Test; Scholarship Exam
SCHOLARSHIPS & BURSARIES Schol; Burs; Art; Mus; Forces; Teachers; AP; VI Form; Sport; Drama
SPECIAL NEEDS nw E   **DYSLEXIA**   **DIET** a
ASSOCIATION HMC   **FOUNDED** 1710   **RELIGIOUS AFFILIATION** C of E

MAP 2 J 2
LOCATION Urban
DAY ✓   **RAIL** a   **AIR** b
SPORT abcdefikmpqsuwx ABC
OTHER LANGUAGES
ACTIVITIES cefghijkoqst A
OTHER SUBJECTS abcfh
FACILITIES ON SITE acdghjk
EXAM BOARDS bd ABEH
RETAKES ab   **NVQ COURSES**

A-level   c e ghi   nop   v
B   GH K   OP R   W
cdef
AS   G
u
GCSE   e g i   no   v
BC   G   OP R   W
cdef   j
OTHER   l
o

Downs School,The; Charlton House; Wraxall; Bristol BS19 1PF
Tel: 01275 852008 (Fax: 01275 855840) *J.Macpherson*

		Boys	Age	Girls	Age	TOTAL		Boys	Girls
Day	£550-£1700	184	3-14	37	3-13	265	SIXTH		
Weekly	£2360		8-14		8-13				
Boarding	£2360	42	8-14	2	8-13				

ENTRY REQUIREMENTS Assessment & Interview
SCHOLARSHIPS & BURSARIES Burs; Forces; Clergy
SPECIAL NEEDS bhklnpquw AGI   **DYSLEXIA** e   **DIET** abcd
ASSOCIATION IAPS   **FOUNDED** 1894   **RELIGIOUS AFFILIATION** Inter-denom

MAP 2 I 2
LOCATION Rural
DAY   **RAIL** a   **AIR** a
SPORT abcdefklmopqrstuwx ABC
OTHER LANGUAGES
ACTIVITIES acfghijopqstx A
OTHER SUBJECTS bcfh
FACILITIES ON SITE abhjkl
EXAM BOARDS
RETAKES   **NVQ COURSES**

A-level
AS
GCSE
OTHER   b de g i   lmno   v
B   G K   OP R
cde   j

Downside School; Stratton-on-the-Fosse; Bath BA3 4RJ
Tel: 01761 232206 (Fax: 01761 233575) *Dom Antony Sutch*

		Boys	Age	Girls	Age	TOTAL		Boys	Girls
Day	£1780-£1980 ✗	4	10-18	2	16-18	326	SIXTH	133	2
Weekly		2	10-18						
Boarding	£2976-£3710	318	10-18						

ENTRY REQUIREMENTS CEE; Report & Exam & Interview
SCHOLARSHIPS & BURSARIES Schol; Burs; Art; Mus; Chor; VI Form
SPECIAL NEEDS begjlnqs BCEFGIL   **DYSLEXIA** de   **DIET** a
ASSOCIATION HMC   **FOUNDED** 1606   **RELIGIOUS AFFILIATION** R C

MAP 2 J 3
LOCATION Rural
DAY   **RAIL** b   **AIR** b
SPORT abcdefghjklmstuwx ABC
OTHER LANGUAGES a
ACTIVITIES aefghijklnopqst B
OTHER SUBJECTS abcf
FACILITIES ON SITE abcdhik
EXAM BOARDS abcd ABDEGH
RETAKES a   **NVQ COURSES**

A-level   c efghi   opq   v x
B   GH K   P R U
cdefgh jkl
AS   e
GH K   R U
c e gh j
GCSE   c e g i   opq   v
B   G K   OP R   X
cdefgh kl
OTHER   l n   u
K   O R

Fairfield PNEU School; Fairfield Way; Farleigh Road; Backwell; Avon BS19 3PD
Tel: 01275 462743 (Fax: 01275 464347) *Mrs A.Nosowska*

		Boys	Age	Girls	Age	TOTAL		Boys	Girls
Day	£325-£1080	60	3-11	67	3-11	127	SIXTH		
Weekly									
Boarding									

ENTRY REQUIREMENTS Assessment & Interview
SCHOLARSHIPS & BURSARIES Schol
SPECIAL NEEDS   **DYSLEXIA**   **DIET** a
ASSOCIATION ISAI   **FOUNDED** 1935   **RELIGIOUS AFFILIATION** C of E

MAP 2 I 2
LOCATION Rural
DAY   **RAIL** b   **AIR** a
SPORT ajpx B
OTHER LANGUAGES
ACTIVITIES cj
OTHER SUBJECTS
FACILITIES ON SITE
EXAM BOARDS
RETAKES   **NVQ COURSES**

A-level
AS
GCSE
OTHER   e   v
B   G K
cde

AVON continued

King Edward's School; North Road; Bath BA2 6HU
Tel: 01225 464313 (Fax: 01225 481363) *Peter Winter*

		Boys	Age	Girls	Age	TOTAL	SIXTH	Boys	Girls
Day	£1045-£1431	820	7-18	49	16-18	869		181	48
Weekly									
Boarding									

ENTRY REQUIREMENTS Report & Exam & Interview
SCHOLARSHIPS & BURSARIES Schol; Burs; AP; VI Form
SPECIAL NEEDS bhklq AGI
DYSLEXIA **DIET** ab
ASSOCIATION HMC **FOUNDED** 1552 **RELIGIOUS AFFILIATION** Non-denom

MAP 2 J 3
LOCATION Urban
DAY ✓ **RAIL** a **AIR** c
SPORT abcefghjkmopqrsuwx AB
OTHER LANGUAGES
ACTIVITIES befghijlnopqst AB
OTHER SUBJECTS abcdfh
FACILITIES ON SITE acghk
EXAM BOARDS bcd ABEG
RETAKES **NVQ COURSES**

A-level: d ghi l nopq v / B GH K N P R / cdef j l
AS: l q v x / G K R / ef j l
GCSE: d ghi l opq v / B G K N P R / cdef j l
OTHER:

Kingswood School; Lansdown; Bath; Avon BA1 5RG
Tel: 01225 311627 (Fax: 01225 481345) *G.M.Best*

		Boys	Age	Girls	Age	TOTAL	SIXTH	Boys	Girls
Day	£1828-£2333	116	11-18	73	11-18	437		78	54
Weekly	£2931-£3720		11-18		11-18				
Boarding	£2931-£3720	137	11-18	111	11-18				

ENTRY REQUIREMENTS CEE; Exam
SCHOLARSHIPS & BURSARIES Schol; Clergy; AP
SPECIAL NEEDS bejlnpqw EG
DYSLEXIA e **DIET** abcd
ASSOCIATION HMC **FOUNDED** 1748 **RELIGIOUS AFFILIATION** Methodist

MAP 2 J 2
LOCATION
DAY **RAIL** a **AIR** b
SPORT abcefghjkmopqstwx BC
OTHER LANGUAGES a
ACTIVITIES bcfghijlnopqstw AB
OTHER SUBJECTS bcdfh
FACILITIES ON SITE abcdeghik
EXAM BOARDS abcde ABDEGHK
RETAKES **NVQ COURSES**

A-level: efg i nop uv x / BC GH K P R U / cdefg j
AS: h l q / ef
GCSE: efg i l nop v / BC G K OP R U / cdefg j
OTHER:

Monkton Combe Junior School; Combe Down; Bath BA2 7ET
Tel: 01225 837912 (Fax: 01225 840312) *E.J.D.Clarke*

		Boys	Age	Girls	Age	TOTAL	SIXTH	Boys	Girls
Day	£620-£2040	156	3-13	44	3-13	254			
Weekly									
Boarding	£2795-£2895	52	7-13	2	7-13				

ENTRY REQUIREMENTS Test & Interview
SCHOLARSHIPS & BURSARIES Schol; Art; Mus; Clergy; Sport
SPECIAL NEEDS bjknw EGI
DYSLEXIA e **DIET** ab
ASSOCIATION IAPS **FOUNDED** 1888 **RELIGIOUS AFFILIATION** C of E

MAP 2 J 3
LOCATION Rural
DAY **RAIL** a **AIR** b
SPORT abcefjklmopqrsuwx ABC
OTHER LANGUAGES
ACTIVITIES acfghijlnoqrstx A
OTHER SUBJECTS cfh
FACILITIES ON SITE bcdhjki
EXAM BOARDS
RETAKES **NVQ COURSES**

A-level:
AS:
GCSE:
OTHER: cde g i l o v / B G K OP R / cde j

Monkton Combe School; Nr. Bath; Avon BA2 7HG
Tel: 01225 721102 (Fax: 01225 721181) *M.J.Cuthbertson*

		Boys	Age	Girls	Age	TOTAL	SIXTH	Boys	Girls
Day	£2195-£2695	34	11-18	10	11-18	311		75	49
Weekly									
Boarding	£3215-£3895	174	11-18	93	11-18				

ENTRY REQUIREMENTS CEE; Scholarship Exam; Report & Test; Assessment & Interview; Report & Exam & Interview **SCHOLARSHIPS & BURSARIES** Schol; Burs; Art; Mus; AP; VI Form; ARA; Siblings
SPECIAL NEEDS bejklnq l
DYSLEXIA e **DIET** ad
ASSOCIATION HMC **FOUNDED** 1868 **RELIGIOUS AFFILIATION** C of E (Evang)

MAP 2 J 3
LOCATION Rural
DAY ✓ **RAIL** a **AIR** b
SPORT abdefghjlmopqrstuwx ABC
OTHER LANGUAGES a
ACTIVITIES abcefghijklmnoqrsvwx AB
OTHER SUBJECTS abch
FACILITIES ON SITE acdejk
EXAM BOARDS abcd BDEH
RETAKES **NVQ COURSES**

A-level: c e g i opq v / B GH K N P R U / cdefg j
AS: c e g / B G K / U / ef
GCSE: e g i nop v / BC E G K P R / cdefg j
OTHER: l u x / o / k

Paragon School; Lyncombe House; Lyncombe Vale; Bath BA2 4LT
Tel: 01225 310837 *D.J.Martin*

		Boys	Age	Girls	Age	TOTAL	SIXTH	Boys	Girls
Day	£845-£942	118	3-11	118	3-11	236			
Weekly									
Boarding									

ENTRY REQUIREMENTS Test & Interview
SCHOLARSHIPS & BURSARIES Burs
SPECIAL NEEDS bjn B
DYSLEXIA **DIET**
ASSOCIATION IAPS **FOUNDED** 1911 **RELIGIOUS AFFILIATION** Inter-denom

MAP 2 J 3
LOCATION Urban
DAY **RAIL** a **AIR** a
SPORT aejklmpqsx B
OTHER LANGUAGES
ACTIVITIES afghjorst
OTHER SUBJECTS bcfh
FACILITIES ON SITE h
EXAM BOARDS
RETAKES **NVQ COURSES**

A-level:
AS:
GCSE:
OTHER: e l no s v / B DE G K O R / cde

AVON continued

Bg Park School; Weston Lane; Bath BA1 4AQ
Tel: 01225 421681 (Fax: 01225 428006) *The Rev.R.M.Clarke*

		Boys	Age	Girls	Age	TOTAL		Boys	Girls
Day	£865-£1295 ✗	132	3-11	18	3-4	150	SIXTH		
Weekly									
Boarding									

ENTRY REQUIREMENTS Test; Report
SCHOLARSHIPS & BURSARIES Schol; Burs
SPECIAL NEEDS befhklnqtw BGHL
DYSLEXIA e   **DIET** acd
ASSOCIATION IAPS   **FOUNDED** 1959   **RELIGIOUS AFFILIATION** Inter-denom

MAP 2 J 2
LOCATION Urban
DAY   **RAIL** a   **AIR** b
SPORT abcefgjlmoqswx BC
OTHER LANGUAGES
ACTIVITIES cfghijlopqt
OTHER SUBJECTS acdfh
FACILITIES ON SITE hk
EXAM BOARDS
RETAKES   **NVQ COURSES**

A-level: AS —   GCSE —   OTHER: e g i l no s v / B G K O R   X / cde j

---

C Prior Park College; Bath; Avon BA2 5AH
Tel: 01225 835353 (Fax: 01225 835753) *J.W.R.Goulding*

		Boys	Age	Girls	Age	TOTAL		Boys	Girls
Day	£1778-£1857 ✗	192	11-18	140	11-18	491	SIXTH	92	44
Weekly	£3358	16		10					
Boarding	£3358	94	13-18	39	13-18				

ENTRY REQUIREMENTS CEE & Interview; Report & Exam & Interview
SCHOLARSHIPS & BURSARIES Schol; Art; Mus; Chor; AP; VI Form; Siblings
SPECIAL NEEDS bgln   **DYSLEXIA** ef   **DIET** ab
ASSOCIATION HMC   **FOUNDED** 1780   **RELIGIOUS AFFILIATION** R C

MAP 2 J 3
LOCATION Urban
DAY ✓   **RAIL** a   **AIR** b
SPORT abefhkmpqsuwx AB
OTHER LANGUAGES a
ACTIVITIES acefghijklnorstuw B
OTHER SUBJECTS bcdfh
FACILITIES ON SITE acdeghik
EXAM BOARDS abcd ABDEGHJL
RETAKES   **NVQ COURSES**

A-level: c efg i op v x / B GH K M P R / c efghj l   AS —   M   GCSE: cde g i o v / B E G K   P R / cdefghj l   OTHER —

B Queen Elizabeth's Hospital; Berkeley Place; Clifton; Bristol BS8 1JX
Tel: 0117 929 1856 (Fax: 0117 929 3106) *Dr R.Gliddon*

		Boys	Age	Girls	Age	TOTAL		Boys	Girls
Day	£1305	430	10-18			504	SIXTH	117	
Weekly									
Boarding	£2319	74	10-18						

ENTRY REQUIREMENTS Exam
SCHOLARSHIPS & BURSARIES Schol; Burs; Mus; Forces; AP; VI Form
SPECIAL NEEDS ehjkl l   **DYSLEXIA**   **DIET** a
ASSOCIATION HMC   **FOUNDED** 1590   **RELIGIOUS AFFILIATION**

MAP 2 J 2
LOCATION Inner City
DAY   **RAIL** a   **AIR** b
SPORT abcefghjlorstwx ABC
OTHER LANGUAGES
ACTIVITIES aefghijklnoqrst AB
OTHER SUBJECTS bcfh
FACILITIES ON SITE cgk
EXAM BOARDS bd B
RETAKES   **NVQ COURSES**

A-level: e g i p v / B GH K P / c ef j   AS —   K   GCSE: e g i l no q v / B G K   P R / cdefghj l   OTHER: l no s u w / I K O R / g

---

G Red Maids' Junior School; Grange Court Road; Westbury-on-Trym; Bristol BS9 4DP
Tel: 0117 962 9451 (Fax: 0117 962 9451) *Mrs G.B.Rowcliffe*

		Boys	Age	Girls	Age	TOTAL		Boys	Girls
Day	£795			80	7-11	80	SIXTH		
Weekly									
Boarding									

ENTRY REQUIREMENTS Test
SCHOLARSHIPS & BURSARIES
SPECIAL NEEDS ghl   **DYSLEXIA**   **DIET** a
ASSOCIATION IAPS   **FOUNDED** 1986   **RELIGIOUS AFFILIATION**

MAP 2 J 2
LOCATION Urban
DAY   **RAIL** b   **AIR** b
SPORT almpqx B
OTHER LANGUAGES
ACTIVITIES gjoq
OTHER SUBJECTS abch
FACILITIES ON SITE
EXAM BOARDS
RETAKES   **NVQ COURSES**

A-level: —   AS —   GCSE —   OTHER: e lmno v / B G K O R / e

G Red Maids' School; Westbury-on-Trym; Bristol BS9 3AW
Tel: 0117 962 2641 (Fax: 0117 962 1687) *Miss S.Hampton*

		Boys	Age	Girls	Age	TOTAL		Boys	Girls
Day	£1240			405	11-18	501	SIXTH		125
Weekly									
Boarding	£2480			96	11-18				

ENTRY REQUIREMENTS Exam
SCHOLARSHIPS & BURSARIES Schol; Burs; Mus; AP
SPECIAL NEEDS bejqw Gl   **DYSLEXIA**   **DIET** a
ASSOCIATION GSA   **FOUNDED** 1634   **RELIGIOUS AFFILIATION**

MAP 2 J 2
LOCATION Urban
DAY   **RAIL** b   **AIR** b
SPORT abcfgjlmpqwx ABC
OTHER LANGUAGES a
ACTIVITIES dfghijkotwx B
OTHER SUBJECTS abcdfh
FACILITIES ON SITE abg
EXAM BOARDS abcd ABDEH
RETAKES   **NVQ COURSES**

A-level: c eg i p v / BC GH K P R W / c e jkl   AS: f   GCSE: e ghi o v / BC G K OP R W / cdefg jkl   OTHER: l

AVON *continued*

G — Redland High School; Redland Court; Bristol BS6 7EF
Tel: 0117 924 5796 (Fax: 0117 924 4318) Mrs Carol Lear

		Boys	Age	Girls	Age	TOTAL		Boys	Girls
Day	£650-£1322			638	4-18	638	SIXTH		119
Weekly									
Boarding									

MAP 2 J 2
LOCATION Urban
DAY   **RAIL** b   **AIR** a
SPORT acefglmpqswx AB
OTHER LANGUAGES
ACTIVITIES cghijkopqt AB

ENTRY REQUIREMENTS Test & Interview
SCHOLARSHIPS & BURSARIES Schol; Burs; Mus; AP
SPECIAL NEEDS bjlnq   **DYSLEXIA**   **DIET** abcd
ASSOCIATION GSA   **FOUNDED** 1882   **RELIGIOUS AFFILIATION** Inter-denom
OTHER SUBJECTS abcfh
FACILITIES ON SITE cg
EXAM BOARDS bd ABD
RETAKES   **NVQ COURSES**

A-level cdefghi l p s v / BC GH K P U W / cdefg j l
AS
GCSE cde g i l o v / BC G K P R U W / cdefg j l
OTHER cdef   o

Gb — Royal School, The; Lansdown Road; Bath; Avon BA1 5SZ
Tel: 01225 313877 (Fax: 01225 420338) Mrs Emma Mc Kendrick

			Boys	Age	Girls	Age	TOTAL		Boys	Girls
Day	£927-£1962	X	12	3-7	122	3-18	320	SIXTH		70
Weekly	£3086-£3667					7-18				
Boarding	£3086-£3667				186	7-18				

MAP 2 J 2
LOCATION Urban
DAY   **RAIL** a   **AIR** b
SPORT abcdefghjlmnopqtuvwx ABC
OTHER LANGUAGES ab
ACTIVITIES bcefghijklnopqstuw AB

ENTRY REQUIREMENTS CEE; Assessment & Interview
SCHOLARSHIPS & BURSARIES Schol; Burs; Art; Mus; Forces; VI Form; Sport; ARA; Drama
SPECIAL NEEDS abgjklnqstuw ABEI   **DYSLEXIA** e   **DIET** ad
ASSOCIATION GSA   **FOUNDED** 1865   **RELIGIOUS AFFILIATION** C of E
OTHER SUBJECTS abcdefgh
FACILITIES ON SITE abcdegjk
EXAM BOARDS abcd ABDEGHIJ
RETAKES ab   **NVQ COURSES** 23

A-level defgh nop e u e l no v / BC G K P W / BC FG K / TU W / BC FG K OP / WX / bcdef ef l bcdef l
AS e
GCSE
OTHER G

Gb — St. Ursula's High School; Brecon Road; Westbury-on-Trym; Bristol; Avon BS9 4DT
Tel: 0117 962 2616 (Fax: 0117 962 2616) Mrs M.A.Mac Naughton

		Boys	Age	Girls	Age	TOTAL		Boys	Girls
Day	£375-£1150	86	3-11	250	3-18	336	SIXTH		23
Weekly									
Boarding									

MAP 2 I 2
LOCATION Urban
DAY   **RAIL** b   **AIR** a
SPORT acefhjklmpqsx ABC
OTHER LANGUAGES
ACTIVITIES cfghijnoq B

ENTRY REQUIREMENTS Assessment
SCHOLARSHIPS & BURSARIES Schol; Burs; VI Form
SPECIAL NEEDS n   **DYSLEXIA**   **DIET**
ASSOCIATION GSA   **FOUNDED** 1896   **RELIGIOUS AFFILIATION** R C
OTHER SUBJECTS
FACILITIES ON SITE bcdgh
EXAM BOARDS abcd AE
RETAKES   **NVQ COURSES**

A-level e ghi n p v / B G P / c e
AS G
GCSE e o v / BC G K O R X / cde j
OTHER

C — Sidcot School; Winscombe; Avon BS25 1PD
Tel: 0193 484 3102 (Fax: 01934 844 181) C.J.Greenfield

			Boys	Age	Girls	Age	TOTAL		Boys	Girls
Day	£773-£1906	X	132	3-18	133	3-18	437	SIXTH	54	51
Weekly	£3187			9-18		9-18				
Boarding	£3187		99	9-18	73	9-18				

MAP 2 I 3
LOCATION Rural
DAY   **RAIL** b   **AIR** a
SPORT abcdefghjmpqsvwx ABC
OTHER LANGUAGES ai
ACTIVITIES abcfghijklnoqstuw ABC

ENTRY REQUIREMENTS Test
SCHOLARSHIPS & BURSARIES Schol; Burs; Mus; VI Form
SPECIAL NEEDS abegjklnqstvw B   **DYSLEXIA** ce   **DIET** acd
ASSOCIATION SHMIS   **FOUNDED** 1808   **RELIGIOUS AFFILIATION** Quaker
OTHER SUBJECTS abcdfh
FACILITIES ON SITE bcdghik
EXAM BOARDS abcde ABDEGH
RETAKES ab   **NVQ COURSES** 23

A-level e ghi n uvwx e ghi n uvwx de g i no vw / B GH K N P W / BC K P W / ABC E G K NOP R / c ef i l c ef hi abcdef ij l
AS
GCSE
OTHER h

C — Tockington Manor; Tockington; nr.Bristol; Avon BS12 4NY
Tel: 01454 613229 (Fax: 01454 615776) R.G.Tovey

			Boys	Age	Girls	Age	TOTAL		Boys	Girls
Day	£327-£1990	X	75	3-13	51	3-13	172	SIXTH		
Weekly				7-13		7-13				
Boarding	£2880		31	7-13	15	7-13				

MAP 2 J 2
LOCATION Rural
DAY ✓   **RAIL** a   **AIR** b
SPORT abcdefjklmpqstx AB
OTHER LANGUAGES a
ACTIVITIES acfghjmnopqtwx A

ENTRY REQUIREMENTS Interview
SCHOLARSHIPS & BURSARIES Forces
SPECIAL NEEDS ln   **DYSLEXIA** cdef   **DIET** a
ASSOCIATION IAPS   **FOUNDED** 1947   **RELIGIOUS AFFILIATION** C of E
OTHER SUBJECTS abcfh
FACILITIES ON SITE abchj
EXAM BOARDS
RETAKES   **NVQ COURSES**

A-level
AS
GCSE
OTHER e g i lmno q v / BC G K OP R / cdefg j l

AVON continued

Gb Westwing School; Kyneton House; Thornbury; nr.Bristol BS12 2JZ
Tel: 01454 412311 (Fax: 01454 281523) *Mrs C.A.Rispin*

	Boys	Age	Girls	Age	TOTAL		Boys	Girls
Day	£693-£1353		9	3- 6	39	3-18	98	
Weekly	£2510-£2666				50	8-18		SIXTH
Boarding	£2591-£2741					8-18		

ENTRY REQUIREMENTS Report & Interview
SCHOLARSHIPS & BURSARIES Schol; Burs; Forces
SPECIAL NEEDS abegjklnqstw ABDEGHI
ASSOCIATION ISAI **FOUNDED** 1870

DYSLEXIA cdef **DIET** a
RELIGIOUS AFFILIATION Inter-denom

MAP 2 J 1
LOCATION Rural
DAY   **RAIL** b   **AIR** b
SPORT acfhkmpqvwx ABC
OTHER LANGUAGES a
ACTIVITIES cfghijkoqtwx A
OTHER SUBJECTS abcdefgh
FACILITIES ON SITE bel
EXAM BOARDS bd ABI
RETAKES a   **NVQ COURSES**

A-level	de h mn p v	AS		GCSE	de h lmn p v	OTHER	
	BC G R U				BC G R		a hi
	bcde				bcde i l		

G Bedford High School; Bromham Road; Bedford MK40 2BS
Tel: 01234 360221 (Fax: 01234 353552) *Miss M.L.Churm*

	Boys	Age	Girls	Age	TOTAL		Boys	Girls
Day	£1158-£1583		863	7-18	918			189
Weekly	£2555-£2980		4	8-18		SIXTH		
Boarding	£2589-£3014		51	8-18				

ENTRY REQUIREMENTS Report & Exam & Interview
SCHOLARSHIPS & BURSARIES AP
SPECIAL NEEDS abeghjlnpqtvw AH
ASSOCIATION GSA **FOUNDED** 1882

DYSLEXIA e **DIET** abcd
RELIGIOUS AFFILIATION Non-denom

MAP 3 F 1
LOCATION Urban
DAY ✓   **RAIL** a   **AIR** a
SPORT abcefghlmnopqrtx ABC
OTHER LANGUAGES ao
ACTIVITIES cfghijklnopqstvwx AB
OTHER SUBJECTS abcdfh
FACILITIES ON SITE bcgi
EXAM BOARDS abcd ABDEGH
RETAKES ab   **NVQ COURSES**

A-level	cdefghi nop uvwx	AS	cdefghi op uvwx	GCSE	de g i lmno v	OTHER	j l
	BC GH K P R W		C G P R		BC G I K NOP R WX		
	c efg j l		cdefg l		cdefgh jkl		

B Bedford Modern Junior School; Manton Lane; Bedford MK41 7NT
Tel: 01234 364331 (Fax: 01234 270951) *N.R.Yelland*

	Boys	Age	Girls	Age	TOTAL		Boys	Girls
Day	£1033-£1123	205	7-11		207	SIXTH		
Weekly	£1080-£1259	1	8-11					
Boarding	£1383	1	8-11					

ENTRY REQUIREMENTS Test
SCHOLARSHIPS & BURSARIES AP
SPECIAL NEEDS blnq
ASSOCIATION IAPS **FOUNDED** 1566

DYSLEXIA e **DIET** a
RELIGIOUS AFFILIATION Inter-denom

MAP 3 F 1
LOCATION Urban
DAY   **RAIL** a   **AIR** a
SPORT acefijlswx AB
OTHER LANGUAGES
ACTIVITIES fghjnox A
OTHER SUBJECTS ch
FACILITIES ON SITE bhik
EXAM BOARDS
RETAKES   **NVQ COURSES**

A-level		AS		GCSE		OTHER	e l no v
							B E G K O R
							cdef

B Bedford Modern School; Manton Lane; Bedford MK41 7NT
Tel: 01234 364331 (Fax: 01234 270951) *P.J.Squire*

	Boys	Age	Girls	Age	TOTAL		Boys	Girls
Day	£1497	914	11-18		963	SIXTH		253
Weekly	£2577-£2756	2	11-18					
Boarding	£2880	47	11-18					

ENTRY REQUIREMENTS Test
SCHOLARSHIPS & BURSARIES Burs; Mus; AP
SPECIAL NEEDS abejlnqw ABEGI
ASSOCIATION HMC **FOUNDED** 1566

DYSLEXIA g **DIET** a
RELIGIOUS AFFILIATION Inter-denom

MAP 3 F 1
LOCATION Urban
DAY   **RAIL** a   **AIR** b
SPORT abcefghijklmrstuwx AB
OTHER LANGUAGES
ACTIVITIES defghijklorstvx AB
OTHER SUBJECTS bcfh
FACILITIES ON SITE bceghik
EXAM BOARDS abc BDE
RETAKES b   **NVQ COURSES**

A-level	c e ghi nopq uv x	AS	g u	GCSE	e g i k nopq v	OTHER	E K NO R
	AB GH K P R U		G M R		AB EFG K NOP R X		
	cdef j				cdefg j		

B Bedford Preparatory School; Burnaby Road; Bedford MK40 2TU
Tel: 01234 352740 (Fax: 01234 345048) *The Rev. Dr.B.A.Rees*

	Boys	Age	Girls	Age	TOTAL		Boys	Girls
Day	£1595-£2055	386	7-13		410	SIXTH		
Weekly	£2495-£2935	3	7-13					
Boarding	£2625-£3065	21	7-13					

ENTRY REQUIREMENTS Test
SCHOLARSHIPS & BURSARIES Schol; Teachers; AP
SPECIAL NEEDS
ASSOCIATION IAPS **FOUNDED** 1552

DYSLEXIA **DIET** abcd
RELIGIOUS AFFILIATION C of E

MAP 3 F 1
LOCATION Urban
DAY ✓   **RAIL** a   **AIR** a
SPORT abcdefghjklmorsuwx AB
OTHER LANGUAGES
ACTIVITIES fghijnot A
OTHER SUBJECTS abcfh
FACILITIES ON SITE acdhik
EXAM BOARDS
RETAKES   **NVQ COURSES**

A-level		AS	K R	GCSE		OTHER	de l no q uv
							AB E G K O R
							cde j

BEDFORDSHIRE

69

BEDFORDSHIRE continued

B | Bedford School; Burnaby Road; Bedford MK40 2TU;
Tel: 01234 340444 (Fax: 01234 340050) *Dr I.P.Evans*

		Boys	Age	Girls	Age	TOTAL	SIXTH	Boys	Girls
Day	£2335 ✗	496	13-18			713		274	
Weekly									
Boarding	£3715	217	13-18						

MAP 3 F 1
LOCATION Urban
DAY ✓ RAIL a   AIR a
SPORT abcdefghijkmorstuwx ABC
OTHER LANGUAGES a
ACTIVITIES abcefghijklmnopqrstuv AB

ENTRY REQUIREMENTS Scholarship Exam; Exam & Interview; CEE & Interview
SCHOLARSHIPS & BURSARIES Schol; Art; Mus; Teachers; AP; VI Form; ARA; Drama; Siblings
SPECIAL NEEDS blnpq H   **DYSLEXIA** f   **DIET** abcd
ASSOCIATION HMC **FOUNDED** 1552 **RELIGIOUS AFFILIATION** C of E
OTHER SUBJECTS abcdfh
FACILITIES ON SITE acdehik
EXAM BOARDS ab ABDEGHL
RETAKES a   **NVQ COURSES**

A-level: c efg i l nopq uv x   bcdefg j l
         AB GH K   P R U
AS: c   i l   q u
    G K
    efg j
GCSE: e g i   no q v
      AB G K   P R U
      bcdefg j l
OTHER: i

G | Dame Alice Harpur School; Cardington Road; Bedford MK42 0BX
Tel: 01234 340871 (Fax: 01234 344125) *Mrs R.Randle*

		Boys	Age	Girls	Age	TOTAL	SIXTH	Boys	Girls
Day	£1048-£1446			943	7-18	943			200
Weekly									
Boarding									

MAP 3 F 1
LOCATION Urban
DAY ✓ RAIL a   AIR b
SPORT abcdefghijklmopqrwx ABC
OTHER LANGUAGES
ACTIVITIES cfghjknostw ABD

ENTRY REQUIREMENTS Exam
SCHOLARSHIPS & BURSARIES AP
SPECIAL NEEDS   **DYSLEXIA**   **DIET** acd
ASSOCIATION GSA **FOUNDED** 1882 **RELIGIOUS AFFILIATION** Inter-denom
OTHER SUBJECTS abcdefgh
FACILITIES ON SITE bcghik
EXAM BOARDS abcd ABDEHL
RETAKES   **NVQ COURSES** 23

A-level: cde ghi k nop   uv   cdef j
         ABC GH K   P R U W
AS: cde   u
    ef j
GCSE: de g i kl no   v
      ABC E G K   OP R   W
      cdefg j l
OTHER: f h l n   x
       G K MN

B | Rushmoor School; 58-60 Shakespeare Road; Bedford MK40 2DL
Tel: 01234 352031 (Fax: 01234 348395) *P.J.Owen*

		Boys	Age	Girls	Age	TOTAL	SIXTH	Boys	Girls
Day	£705-£1370	218	4-16			218			
Weekly									
Boarding									

MAP 3 F 1
LOCATION Urban
DAY   RAIL a   AIR a
SPORT abcefjklmswx AC
OTHER LANGUAGES
ACTIVITIES fghjost

ENTRY REQUIREMENTS Test & Interview
SCHOLARSHIPS & BURSARIES
SPECIAL NEEDS bjlntuw ABI   **DYSLEXIA** ce   **DIET** acd
ASSOCIATION ISAI **FOUNDED** 1918 **RELIGIOUS AFFILIATION** C of E
OTHER SUBJECTS bcdf
FACILITIES ON SITE ch
EXAM BOARDS abd A
RETAKES   **NVQ COURSES**

A-level:
AS:
GCSE: de g i l o   v
      B E G   OP R
      cde
OTHER: A   G K
            h

Gb | St. Andrew's School; Kimbolton Road; Bedford MK40 2PA
Tel: 01234 267272 (Fax: 01234 355105) *Mrs Janet Mark*

		Boys	Age	Girls	Age	TOTAL	SIXTH	Boys	Girls
Day	£715-£1185	17	3-4	293	3-16	310			
Weekly									
Boarding									

MAP 3 F 1
LOCATION Urban
DAY   RAIL a   AIR b
SPORT acflmpqrwx AB
OTHER LANGUAGES
ACTIVITIES cghijkpst A

ENTRY REQUIREMENTS Exam & Interview; Assessment & Interview
SCHOLARSHIPS & BURSARIES
SPECIAL NEEDS n   **DYSLEXIA** cdf   **DIET**
ASSOCIATION GSA **FOUNDED** 1897 **RELIGIOUS AFFILIATION**
OTHER SUBJECTS bcefh
FACILITIES ON SITE
EXAM BOARDS abd
RETAKES   **NVQ COURSES**

A-level:
AS:
GCSE: de h   o   v
      ABC E G   O R   W
      cdef
OTHER: lmn
       K

BERKS

Gb | Abbey School,The; 17 Kendrick Road; Reading RG1 5DZ
Tel: 01734 872256 *Miss B.C.L.Sheldon*

		Boys	Age	Girls	Age	TOTAL	SIXTH	Boys	Girls
Day	£1100-£1380 ✗	1	4-7	990	4-18	991			173
Weekly									
Boarding									

MAP 3 D 4
LOCATION Urban
DAY ✓ RAIL a   AIR a
SPORT abcdfhlmpqrx ABC
OTHER LANGUAGES
ACTIVITIES fghjknoqw AB

ENTRY REQUIREMENTS Test & Interview
SCHOLARSHIPS & BURSARIES Schol; Burs; Mus; AP; VI Form
SPECIAL NEEDS   **DYSLEXIA**   **DIET** abcd
ASSOCIATION GSA **FOUNDED** 1887 **RELIGIOUS AFFILIATION** C of E
OTHER SUBJECTS abch
FACILITIES ON SITE dgik
EXAM BOARDS abc BEH
RETAKES   **NVQ COURSES**

A-level: d fghi l   p   v   c efg j l
         BC GH K   P R T U W
         cdef j l
AS: G
         c ef
GCSE: d ghi l n q   v
      BC G K   OP R U W
      cdefg j l
OTHER: k

BERKSHIRE *continued*

Bearwood College; Bearwood; Wokingham RG11 5BG
Tel: 01734 786915 (Fax: 01734 772687) *Dr.R.J.Belcher*

		Boys	Age	Girls	Age	TOTAL		Boys	Girls
Day	£1665-£1850	99	11-19		11-19	204	SIXTH	54	
Weekly	£3015-£3350	27	11-19		11-19				
Boarding	£3015-£3350	78	11-19		11-19				

ENTRY REQUIREMENTS CEE; Test & Interview; Report & Interview
SCHOLARSHIPS & BURSARIES Schol; Burs; Art; Mus; Chor; Forces; Clergy; Teachers; VI Form; Sport; ARA; Drama; Siblings **SPECIAL NEEDS** abegjlnqstuw ABEGIJ **DYSLEXIA** cde **DIET** acd
ASSOCIATION SHMIS **FOUNDED** 1827 **RELIGIOUS AFFILIATION** C of E

MAP 3 E 4
LOCATION Rural
DAY ✓ **RAIL** a **AIR** a
SPORT abcdefjkostuwx BC
OTHER LANGUAGES a
ACTIVITIES aefghijklmnoqsw A
OTHER SUBJECTS bcdh
FACILITIES ON SITE bcdeghikl
EXAM BOARDS abcd ABEG
RETAKES a **NVQ COURSES**

A-level e g i   l   nop   v
AB   GH K   N P R
c ef

AS G

GCSE U   e h   l no   v
AB   G I K NO R   X
cdef

OTHER l

Bradfield College; Reading; Berkshire RG7 6AR
Tel: 01734 744203 (Fax: 01734 744195) *P.B.Smith*

		Boys	Age	Girls	Age	TOTAL		Boys	Girls
Day	£3058	29	13-18	5	16-18	593	SIXTH	173	86
Weekly									
Boarding	£4075	477	13-18	82	16-18				

ENTRY REQUIREMENTS CEE
SCHOLARSHIPS & BURSARIES Schol; Burs; Art; Mus; AP; VI Form
SPECIAL NEEDS beijlnpqw EGI **DYSLEXIA** f **DIET** abcd
ASSOCIATION HMC **FOUNDED** 1850 **RELIGIOUS AFFILIATION** C of E

MAP 3 D 4
LOCATION Rural
DAY **RAIL** b **AIR** a
SPORT abcdefghijkmnopstuwx BC
OTHER LANGUAGES
ACTIVITIES befghijklmnopqrstuw AB
OTHER SUBJECTS abcfgh
FACILITIES ON SITE abcdefhik
EXAM BOARDS abd ABEGH
RETAKES **NVQ COURSES**

A-level efg i   op   v x
B   GH K   P R U
cdefg j l

AS B G R

GCSE e g i   o   v x
B   G K   P RS U
cdefg j l

OTHER hi

Brigidine School,The; King's Road; Windsor; Berks. SL4 2AX
Tel: 01753 863779 (Fax: 01753 850278) *Mrs M.B.Cairns*

		Boys	Age	Girls	Age	TOTAL		Boys	Girls
Day	£552-£1475	5	3-7	333	3-18	338	SIXTH		45
Weekly									
Boarding									

ENTRY REQUIREMENTS Report & Exam & Interview
SCHOLARSHIPS & BURSARIES Burs; VI Form; Siblings
SPECIAL NEEDS bln **DYSLEXIA** e **DIET**
ASSOCIATION GSA **FOUNDED** 1948 **RELIGIOUS AFFILIATION** R C

MAP 3 E 4
LOCATION Rural
DAY **RAIL** a **AIR** a
SPORT abchlmpqw ABC
OTHER LANGUAGES
ACTIVITIES cfghijou ABD
OTHER SUBJECTS bcdegh
FACILITIES ON SITE bdgh
EXAM BOARDS abcd AEGH
RETAKES a **NVQ COURSES**

A-level cde ghi   n p   v
BC   GH K   P R U W
c ef j l

AS G K   v
e j l

GCSE cde
BC   G K   R U WX
cdef   j l

OTHER l

Brockhurst; Marlston Hermitage; Newbury; Berks. RG16 9UL
Tel: 01635 200293 (Fax: 01635 200190) *A.J.Pudden*

		Boys	Age	Girls	Age	TOTAL		Boys	Girls
Day	£1100-£2280	104	3-11	9	3-6	148	SIXTH		
Weekly			8-13						
Boarding	£2955	35	8-13						

ENTRY REQUIREMENTS Interview
SCHOLARSHIPS & BURSARIES Schol; Forces; Siblings
SPECIAL NEEDS n **DYSLEXIA** e **DIET**
ASSOCIATION IAPS **FOUNDED** 1884 **RELIGIOUS AFFILIATION** C of E

MAP 3 C 4
LOCATION Rural
DAY ✓ **RAIL** a **AIR** a
SPORT acefgjkmsux AB
OTHER LANGUAGES
ACTIVITIES fghijloqrstw A
OTHER SUBJECTS cfh
FACILITIES ON SITE hj
EXAM BOARDS
RETAKES **NVQ COURSES**

A-level

AS

GCSE

OTHER e g i   o   v
B E G K   P R
cde g j

Cheam Hawtreys; Headley; Newbury; Berks. RG19 8LD
Tel: 01635 268242 (Fax: 01635 269345) *C.C.Evers*

		Boys	Age	Girls	Age	TOTAL		Boys	Girls
Day	£2130	32	7-13			162	SIXTH		
Weekly									
Boarding	£3015	130	8-13						

ENTRY REQUIREMENTS Report & Interview
SCHOLARSHIPS & BURSARIES Schol
SPECIAL NEEDS beijklnw BGI **DYSLEXIA** e **DIET** a
ASSOCIATION IAPS **FOUNDED** 1645 **RELIGIOUS AFFILIATION** C of E

MAP 3 C 4
LOCATION Rural
DAY ✓ **RAIL** b **AIR** a
SPORT abcdefjklmosuwx ABC
OTHER LANGUAGES a
ACTIVITIES abfghijmnoqrst
OTHER SUBJECTS abch
FACILITIES ON SITE cdhjkl
EXAM BOARDS
RETAKES **NVQ COURSES**

A-level

AS

GCSE

OTHER e g i   no q   v
B   G K   OP R
cde   j

BERKSHIRE *continued*

Claires Court School; Ray Mill Road East; Maidenhead; Berks. SL6 8TE
Tel: 01628 411470 (Fax: 01628 411466) *J.T.Wilding*

		Boys	Age	Girls	Age	TOTAL		Boys	Girls
Day	£1475-£1760	266	11-18	1	16-18	267	SIXTH	20	1
Weekly									
Boarding									

ENTRY REQUIREMENTS Report & Exam & Interview
SCHOLARSHIPS & BURSARIES Schol; Art; Mus; VI Form; ARA
SPECIAL NEEDS n   **DYSLEXIA** def   **DIET** a
ASSOCIATION ISAI   **FOUNDED** 1960   **RELIGIOUS AFFILIATION** R C

MAP 3 E 4
LOCATION Urban
DAY ✓   **RAIL** a   **AIR** a
SPORT abcefghjklmorstwx ABC
OTHER LANGUAGES
ACTIVITIES abfghijknopstw A
OTHER SUBJECTS cfh
FACILITIES ON SITE acehj
EXAM BOARDS abcd ABEH
RETAKES   **NVQ COURSES**

A-level: de ghi n p x   B GH   P T   cdef l
AS: de gh l op   G   T
GCSE: de ghi no v   B EFG K OP R   cdef hj l
OTHER: q t   f i l

Crosfields School; Shinfield; Reading RG2 9BL
Tel: 01734 871810 (Fax: 01734 310806) *F.G.Skipwith*

		Boys	Age	Girls	Age	TOTAL		Boys	Girls
Day	£950-£1730	320	4-13			320	SIXTH		
Weekly									
Boarding									

ENTRY REQUIREMENTS Report; Assessment & Interview
SCHOLARSHIPS & BURSARIES
SPECIAL NEEDS begjw G   **DYSLEXIA**   **DIET** acd
ASSOCIATION IAPS   **FOUNDED** 1946   **RELIGIOUS AFFILIATION** Inter-denom

MAP 3 D 4
LOCATION Rural
DAY b   **RAIL** b   **AIR** a
SPORT abcefjklmqsx B
OTHER LANGUAGES
ACTIVITIES fghjot A
OTHER SUBJECTS cfh
FACILITIES ON SITE chil
EXAM BOARDS
RETAKES   **NVQ COURSES**

A-level:
AS:
GCSE:
OTHER: defg i l no v   B E G K OP R   cde

Dolphin School; Hurst; Berks. RG10 0BP
Tel: 01734 341277 (Fax: 01734 344110) *Dr N.Follett*

		Boys	Age	Girls	Age	TOTAL		Boys	Girls
Day	£785-£1380	136	2-13	119	2-13	255	SIXTH		
Weekly									
Boarding									

ENTRY REQUIREMENTS Test & Interview
SCHOLARSHIPS & BURSARIES Schol; Burs; Art; Mus; Teachers; Drama
SPECIAL NEEDS abeghjlnqstuv AGH   **DYSLEXIA** f   **DIET**
ASSOCIATION IAPS   **FOUNDED** 1970   **RELIGIOUS AFFILIATION**

MAP 3 E 4
LOCATION Rural
DAY   **RAIL** a   **AIR** a
SPORT abcefhjlmnpqsx AB
OTHER LANGUAGES
ACTIVITIES bcfghijlopqtv
OTHER SUBJECTS abcdfh
FACILITIES ON SITE bchik
EXAM BOARDS
RETAKES   **NVQ COURSES**

A-level:
AS:
GCSE:
OTHER: cdefg i klmno q s vwx   BCDE G I K   OP R U W   cdefg jk

Douai School; Upper Woolhampton; Reading RG7 5TH
Tel: 01734 715200 (Fax: 01734 715241) *Father Edmund Power*

		Boys	Age	Girls	Age	TOTAL		Boys	Girls
Day	£1845-£2260 ✗	61	10-18	12	10-18	197	SIXTH	49	3
Weekly	£2715-£3415	33	10-18	1	10-18				
Boarding	£2815-£3515	88	10-18	2	10-18				

ENTRY REQUIREMENTS CEE; Scholarship Exam; Report & Interview; Report & Exam & Interview
SCHOLARSHIPS & BURSARIES Schol; Art; Mus; AP; VI Form
SPECIAL NEEDS E   **DYSLEXIA** e   **DIET** a
ASSOCIATION HMC   **FOUNDED** 1615   **RELIGIOUS AFFILIATION** R C

MAP 3 D 4
LOCATION Rural
DAY ✓   **RAIL** b   **AIR** a
SPORT abcdefghjklmopqstuwx ABC
OTHER LANGUAGES a
ACTIVITIES fghijklmnoqrst AD
OTHER SUBJECTS abcdfh
FACILITIES ON SITE abcdeghik
EXAM BOARDS abd ABDH
RETAKES a   **NVQ COURSES**

A-level: de gi l o uv   B GH K MN P R U   c efg j l
AS: e i   K N R   c e   l   v
GCSE: de gi l o q v   B E G K NOP R   cdefg j l
OTHER:

Downe House; Cold Ash; Newbury; Berks. RG16 9JJ
Tel: 01635 200286 (Fax: 01635 202026) *Miss S.R.Cameron*

		Boys	Age	Girls	Age	TOTAL		Boys	Girls
Day	£3000			32	11-18	553	SIXTH		152
Weekly									
Boarding	£4140			521	11-18				

ENTRY REQUIREMENTS CEE; Assessment
SCHOLARSHIPS & BURSARIES Schol; Mus; VI Form
SPECIAL NEEDS bjlq   **DYSLEXIA**   **DIET** a
ASSOCIATION GSA   **FOUNDED** 1907   **RELIGIOUS AFFILIATION** C of E

MAP 3 C 4
LOCATION Rural
DAY   **RAIL** a   **AIR** a
SPORT adfgklnopqrtuwx AB
OTHER LANGUAGES a
ACTIVITIES cefghijknopqstw AB
OTHER SUBJECTS abcdfh
FACILITIES ON SITE bdegik
EXAM BOARDS abd BDEGH
RETAKES   **NVQ COURSES**

A-level: c efghi l nop uv x   B GH K P R W   c efg jkl
AS: l   G K   W   ef
GCSE: egi l no v   B G K NP R W   cdefgh jkl
OTHER: m o   O   W   i

BERKSHIRE continued

Bg Elstree School; Woolhampton; Reading; Berks. RG7 5TD
Tel: 01734 713302 (Fax: 01734 714280) *S.M.Hill*

		Boys	Age	Girls	Age	TOTAL		Boys	Girls
Day	£1300-£2180 ✗	82	3-13	9	3-7	176	SIXTH		
Weekly									
Boarding	£3070	85	8-13						

ENTRY REQUIREMENTS Report; Assessment
SCHOLARSHIPS & BURSARIES Clergy
SPECIAL NEEDS bghjklpqtuw ABCDEFGHIK   **DYSLEXIA**   **DIET**
ASSOCIATION IAPS   **FOUNDED** 1848   **RELIGIOUS AFFILIATION** C of E

MAP 3 D 4
LOCATION Rural
DAY   **RAIL** b   **AIR** a
SPORT abcdefgjklmoqsuwx AB
OTHER LANGUAGES
ACTIVITIES abfghijlmnopqrstw A
OTHER SUBJECTS abcfh
FACILITIES ON SITE bcejkl
EXAM BOARDS
RETAKES   **NVQ COURSES**

A-level	AS	GCSE	OTHER
			e g i l o q v
			B G K OP R
			de j

B Eton College; Windsor SL4 6DW
Tel: 01753 671000 (Fax: 01753 671159) *J.E.Lewis*

		Boys	Age	Girls	Age	TOTAL		Boys	Girls
Day						1264	SIXTH	496	
Weekly									
Boarding	£4296	1264	12-18						

ENTRY REQUIREMENTS CEE; Scholarship Exam
SCHOLARSHIPS & BURSARIES Schol; Burs; Mus; VI Form
SPECIAL NEEDS behjklqstu ADEGI   **DYSLEXIA**   **DIET** a
ASSOCIATION HMC   **FOUNDED** 1440   **RELIGIOUS AFFILIATION** C of E

MAP 3 E 4
LOCATION Urban
DAY   **RAIL** a   **AIR** a
SPORT abcdefghijklmoprstuwx ABC
OTHER LANGUAGES i
ACTIVITIES adefghijlmnopqrstv B
OTHER SUBJECTS bcfh
FACILITIES ON SITE bcdeghijkl
EXAM BOARDS abcd HL
RETAKES   **NVQ COURSES**

A-level cdefg i nopq uv x	AS c g l p	GCSE cde g i o q v	OTHER
AB GH K P R U	G Q	AB G K P R U	ab M i
c efgh jkl	c h	cdefghijkl

Gb Eton End PNEU School; 35 Eton Road; Datchet; Slough; Berks. SL3 9AX
Tel: 01753 541075 *Mrs B.E.Ottley*

		Boys	Age	Girls	Age	TOTAL		Boys	Girls
Day	£684-£1097	77	3-7	147	3-12	224	SIXTH		
Weekly									
Boarding									

ENTRY REQUIREMENTS Interview
SCHOLARSHIPS & BURSARIES
SPECIAL NEEDS ejkn GI   **DYSLEXIA** e   **DIET** acd
ASSOCIATION IAPS   **FOUNDED** 1936   **RELIGIOUS AFFILIATION** C of E

MAP 3 E 4
LOCATION Urban
DAY   **RAIL** a   **AIR** a
SPORT aejlpqx B
OTHER LANGUAGES
ACTIVITIES cg
OTHER SUBJECTS bch
FACILITIES ON SITE bc
EXAM BOARDS
RETAKES   **NVQ COURSES**

A-level	AS	GCSE	OTHER
			e m o v
			B E G K O R
			cde

Gb Falkland St. Gabriel; Sandleford Priory; Newbury; Berks. RG15 9BD
Tel: 01635 40663 (Fax: 01635 37351) *Mrs J.H.Felton*

		Boys	Age	Girls	Age	TOTAL		Boys	Girls
Day	£592-£1369 ✗	3	3-8	187	3-11	190	SIXTH		
Weekly									
Boarding									

ENTRY REQUIREMENTS Test & Interview
SCHOLARSHIPS & BURSARIES Schol; Teachers; Siblings
SPECIAL NEEDS ejknq   **DYSLEXIA** e   **DIET** ab
ASSOCIATION IAPS   **FOUNDED** 1929   **RELIGIOUS AFFILIATION** C of E

MAP 3 C 4
LOCATION Rural
DAY ✓   **RAIL** a   **AIR** b
SPORT aflmopqx B
OTHER LANGUAGES
ACTIVITIES cfghjotw
OTHER SUBJECTS bcfh
FACILITIES ON SITE chjk
EXAM BOARDS
RETAKES   **NVQ COURSES**

A-level	AS	GCSE	OTHER
			e lm o s v
			BC E G K O R
			cde j

B Haileybury Junior School; Windsor; Berks. SL4 3RS
Tel: 01753 866330 (Fax: 01753 832819) *B.J.Hare*

		Boys	Age	Girls	Age	TOTAL		Boys	Girls
Day	£2025 ✗	121	7-13			166	SIXTH		
Weekly	£2625	14	7-13						
Boarding	£2625	31	7-13						

ENTRY REQUIREMENTS Test & Interview
SCHOLARSHIPS & BURSARIES
SPECIAL NEEDS jkn El   **DYSLEXIA** cd   **DIET** acd
ASSOCIATION IAPS   **FOUNDED** 1922   **RELIGIOUS AFFILIATION** C of E

MAP 3 E 4
LOCATION Urban
DAY   **RAIL** a   **AIR** a
SPORT abcefjkmosuwx AB
OTHER LANGUAGES
ACTIVITIES fghijloqrtv A
OTHER SUBJECTS bcfh
FACILITIES ON SITE ajkl
EXAM BOARDS
RETAKES   **NVQ COURSES**

A-level	AS	GCSE	OTHER
			de g i no v
			B G K OP R
			cde g j

BERKSHIRE *continued*

G | Heathfield School; Ascot SL5 8BQ
Tel: 01344 882955 (Fax: 01344 890689) *Mrs J.M.Benammar*

MAP 3 E 4
LOCATION Rural
DAY RAIL a AIR a

| | Boys | Age | Girls | Age | TOTAL 209 | SIXTH Boys | Girls 52 |

Day
Weekly
Boarding £4175   209 11-18

SPORT abcfglnpqvwx ABC
OTHER LANGUAGES an
ACTIVITIES ceghijnopstw B
OTHER SUBJECTS abcefgh
FACILITIES ON SITE deghj
EXAM BOARDS abd ABEH
RETAKES   NVQ COURSES

ENTRY REQUIREMENTS CEE; Assessment
SCHOLARSHIPS & BURSARIES Schol; Burs
SPECIAL NEEDS n
ASSOCIATION GSA   **FOUNDED** 1899
DYSLEXIA g   **DIET** a
RELIGIOUS AFFILIATION C of E

A-level: B FGH K N P R W   cdefghi n p v   cdef hij l
AS: d f F e l
GCSE: c e ghi n v   B G K N P R   abcdef hij l
OTHER: lmn u   C G K O

Gb | Hemdean House School; Hemdean Road; Caversham; Reading; Berks. RG4 7SD
Tel: 01734 472590 (Fax: 01734 464474) *Mrs P.Pethybridge*

MAP 3 D 4
LOCATION Urban
DAY RAIL a AIR a

| | Boys 50 | Age 3-11 | Girls 92 | Age 3-16 | TOTAL 142 | SIXTH Boys | Girls |

Day £750-£1075
Weekly
Boarding

SPORT aefhjlmpqs ABC
OTHER LANGUAGES
ACTIVITIES cghijoq
OTHER SUBJECTS abcdfgh
FACILITIES ON SITE h
EXAM BOARDS bd
RETAKES   NVQ COURSES

ENTRY REQUIREMENTS Assessment; Report & Test; Report & Exam & Interview
SCHOLARSHIPS & BURSARIES Schol; Burs; Siblings
SPECIAL NEEDS ajlnw A
ASSOCIATION ISAI   **FOUNDED** 1859
DYSLEXIA ef   **DIET**
RELIGIOUS AFFILIATION C of E

A-level:
AS:
GCSE: d g n v   BC E G K W   cdef
OTHER: lmn   K O

C | Herries School; Dean Lane; Cookham Dean; Berks. SL6 9BD
Tel: 01628 483350 *D.G Hare*

MAP 3 E 4
LOCATION Rural
DAY RAIL a AIR a

| | Boys 20 | Age 2-13 | Girls 68 | Age 2-13 | TOTAL 88 | SIXTH Boys | Girls |

Day £850-£1040
Weekly
Boarding

SPORT adjlmopqrtx B
OTHER LANGUAGES
ACTIVITIES cgjn
OTHER SUBJECTS abcfh
FACILITIES ON SITE
EXAM BOARDS
RETAKES   NVQ COURSES

ENTRY REQUIREMENTS Interview
SCHOLARSHIPS & BURSARIES Burs
SPECIAL NEEDS abgjlnw ABI
ASSOCIATION IAPS   **FOUNDED** 1947
DYSLEXIA   **DIET** a
RELIGIOUS AFFILIATION

A-level:
AS:
GCSE:
OTHER: b d e g i lmno s v x   B   G   K   OP R   W   cde   j

C | Highfield School; 2 West Road; Maidenhead; Berks. SL6 1PD
Tel: 01628 24918 (Fax: 01628 35747) *Mrs C.M.A.Lane*

MAP 3 E 4
LOCATION Urban
DAY RAIL a AIR a

| | Boys 22 | Age 3- 7 | Girls 146 | Age 3-12 | TOTAL 168 | SIXTH Boys | Girls |

Day £598-£1345 X
Weekly
Boarding

SPORT cpqx A
OTHER LANGUAGES
ACTIVITIES cgjo
OTHER SUBJECTS ch
FACILITIES ON SITE hj
EXAM BOARDS
RETAKES   NVQ COURSES

ENTRY REQUIREMENTS Interview
SCHOLARSHIPS & BURSARIES Schol; Burs; Teachers; Siblings
SPECIAL NEEDS abfghjklnpqstu AGHI
ASSOCIATION IAPS   **FOUNDED** 1918
DYSLEXIA   **DIET** abcd
RELIGIOUS AFFILIATION Inter-denom

A-level:
AS:
GCSE:
OTHER: defg i lmno s v   B E G K OP R   cde

C | Highlands School; Wardle Avenue; Tilehurst; Reading; Berks. RG3 6JR
Tel: 01734 427186 (Fax: 01734 454953) *Miss E.D.Lind-Smith*

MAP 3 D 4
LOCATION Urban
DAY RAIL a AIR a

| | Boys 54 | Age 3- 8 | Girls 127 | Age 3-11 | TOTAL 181 | SIXTH Boys | Girls |

Day £666-£1056 X
Weekly
Boarding

SPORT adpqx
OTHER LANGUAGES
ACTIVITIES go A
OTHER SUBJECTS abch
FACILITIES ON SITE
EXAM BOARDS
RETAKES   NVQ COURSES

ENTRY REQUIREMENTS Assessment
SCHOLARSHIPS & BURSARIES
SPECIAL NEEDS
ASSOCIATION ISAI   **FOUNDED** 1929
DYSLEXIA   **DIET** a
RELIGIOUS AFFILIATION Non-denom

A-level:
AS:
GCSE:
OTHER:

BERKSHIRE *continued*

C | Holme Grange; Heathlands Road; Wokingham; Berks. RG40 3AL
Tel: 01734 781566 (Fax: 01734 770810) *N.J.Brodrick*

		Boys	Age	Girls	Age	TOTAL		Boys	Girls
Day	£1196-£1536	154	4-13	105	4-13	259	SIXTH		
Weekly									
Boarding									

ENTRY REQUIREMENTS Assessment
SCHOLARSHIPS & BURSARIES Siblings
SPECIAL NEEDS jln B **DYSLEXIA** e **DIET** a
ASSOCIATION IAPS **FOUNDED** 1945 **RELIGIOUS AFFILIATION** C of E

MAP 3 E 4
LOCATION Rural
DAY **RAIL** a **AIR** a
SPORT abcefgjlmpqstx AB
OTHER LANGUAGES
ACTIVITIES cfghjot
OTHER SUBJECTS bcfh
FACILITIES ON SITE bchjk
EXAM BOARDS
RETAKES **NVQ COURSES**

A-level: e g i l no q v / B E G K OP R / cde l
AS:
GCSE:
OTHER:

B | Horris Hill; Newtown; Newbury; Berks. RG20 9DJ
Tel: 01635 40594 (Fax: 01635 35241) *M.J.Innes*

		Boys	Age	Girls	Age	TOTAL		Boys	Girls
Day	£2200	2	7-13			128	SIXTH		
Weekly									
Boarding	£3100	126	7-13						

ENTRY REQUIREMENTS None
SCHOLARSHIPS & BURSARIES Burs
SPECIAL NEEDS bjlqsw A **DYSLEXIA** **DIET** a
ASSOCIATION IAPS **FOUNDED** 1888 **RELIGIOUS AFFILIATION** C of E

MAP 3 C 4
LOCATION Rural
DAY **RAIL** a **AIR** b
SPORT abcefhijkmoqwx AB
OTHER LANGUAGES
ACTIVITIES bfghjlostv
OTHER SUBJECTS ac
FACILITIES ON SITE bcdhjkl
EXAM BOARDS
RETAKES **NVQ COURSES**

A-level: e g i l o q v / B G K R / cde g j

Gb | Hurst Lodge School; Charters Road; Sunningdale; Berks SL5 9QG
Tel: 01344 22154 (Fax: 01344 22154) *Mrs A.M.Smit*

		Boys	Age	Girls	Age	TOTAL		Boys	Girls
Day	£600-£1950	16	3- 7	131	3-19	183	SIXTH		6
Weekly	£3300			21	5-19				
Boarding	£3300			15	6-19				

ENTRY REQUIREMENTS Scholarship Exam; Report; Exam & Interview; Assessment & Interview
SCHOLARSHIPS & BURSARIES Schol; Art; Mus; Chor; Forces; VI Form; ARA; Drama; Siblings
SPECIAL NEEDS abefgjklnqtw ABEGI **DYSLEXIA** cde **DIET** ad
ASSOCIATION ISAI **FOUNDED** 1945 **RELIGIOUS AFFILIATION** Inter-denom

MAP 3 E 4
LOCATION Urban
DAY ✓ **RAIL** a **AIR** a
SPORT ckpqvwx ABC
OTHER LANGUAGES acdik
ACTIVITIES cghijlnoqstwx AB
OTHER SUBJECTS abcdfh
FACILITIES ON SITE j
EXAM BOARDS abcd ABDEGH
RETAKES ab **NVQ COURSES**

A-level: a defghi l no v / B GH K N P U / abcdef hi kl
AS: a de gh / cdef G K l
GCSE: a def h l no v / B G I K N R U WX / abcdef hijkl
OTHER: m / C O W / e

Bg | Lambrook; Winkfield Row; Bracknell; Berks. RG42 6LU
Tel: 01344 882717 (Fax: 01344 891114) *R.F.Badham-Thornhill*

		Boys	Age	Girls	Age	TOTAL		Boys	Girls
Day	£1055-£2030	45	4-13	3	4- 7	106	SIXTH		
Weekly									
Boarding	£2030-£2850	58	7-13						

ENTRY REQUIREMENTS Assessment
SCHOLARSHIPS & BURSARIES Schol; Burs; Forces; Clergy; Teachers
SPECIAL NEEDS n **DYSLEXIA** e **DIET** a
ASSOCIATION IAPS **FOUNDED** 1860 **RELIGIOUS AFFILIATION** C of E

MAP 3 E 4
LOCATION Rural
DAY **RAIL** a **AIR** a
SPORT abcefijklmsuwx AB
OTHER LANGUAGES
ACTIVITIES dfghjnopqstw
OTHER SUBJECTS cfh
FACILITIES ON SITE abcdhil
EXAM BOARDS
RETAKES **NVQ COURSES**

A-level:
AS:
GCSE:
OTHER: e l o v / B G N R / cde g j

C | Leighton Park School; Shinfield Road; Reading RG2 7DH
Tel: 01734 872065 (Fax: 01734 866959) *J.A.Chapman*

		Boys	Age	Girls	Age	TOTAL		Boys	Girls
Day	£2355-£2799	137	11-18	30	11-18	379	SIXTH	100	32
Weekly			11-18		11-18				
Boarding	£3174-£3732	164	11-18	48	11-18				

ENTRY REQUIREMENTS CEE; Report & Interview
SCHOLARSHIPS & BURSARIES Schol; Burs; Art; Mus; Teachers; AP
SPECIAL NEEDS abfgjlnqs AGL **DYSLEXIA** **DIET** abcd
ASSOCIATION HMC **FOUNDED** 1890 **RELIGIOUS AFFILIATION** Quaker

MAP 3 D 4
LOCATION Urban
DAY **RAIL** a **AIR** a
SPORT abcdefghjklmpqrstwx AB
OTHER LANGUAGES
ACTIVITIES fghijklmnopqrstv AB
OTHER SUBJECTS abcdfh
FACILITIES ON SITE abceik
EXAM BOARDS abcd ABDEGHI
RETAKES **NVQ COURSES**

A-level: cde g i op v x / B GH K N P R U / cdefg j l
AS:
GCSE: d e g i l o vwx / B G K N P R U / bcdefg jk
OTHER:

75

BERKSHIRE continued

C — Licensed Victuallers' School; London Road; Ascot; Berkshire SL5 8DR
Tel: 01344 882770 (Fax: 01344 890648) *Mrs P.M.Cowley*

		Boys	Age	Girls	Age	TOTAL	SIXTH Boys	Girls
Day	£972-£1790	312	5-18	147	5-18	655	46	24
Weekly	£2718-£3170	42	7-18	42	7-18			
Boarding	£2736-£3190	62	7-18	50	7-18			

ENTRY REQUIREMENTS Report & Interview
SCHOLARSHIPS & BURSARIES Schol; VI Form
SPECIAL NEEDS abeghjlnqsw GHL   **DYSLEXIA** def   **DIET** abcd
ASSOCIATION ISAI   **FOUNDED** 1803   **RELIGIOUS AFFILIATION** Christian

MAP 3 E 4
LOCATION Urban
DAY   **RAIL** a   **AIR** a
SPORT abcdefhjkmpqrsvwx ABC
OTHER LANGUAGES a
ACTIVITIES cefghijklmnopqrstuwx AB
OTHER SUBJECTS abcdefgh
FACILITIES ON SITE abcghik
EXAM BOARDS abcde ADEGHK
RETAKES a   **NVQ COURSES** 23

A-level: de ghi l nopq v / AB GHI K OP U / cdef l
AS: B G
GCSE: u / de ghi lmnopq v / ABC E G IJK OP U / cdef l
OTHER: hj l v / G K O / d

C — Long Close; Upton Court Road; Slough; Berks SL3 7LU
Tel: 01753 520095 (Fax: 01753 821463) *M.H.Kneath*

		Boys	Age	Girls	Age	TOTAL	SIXTH Boys	Girls
Day	£500-£1673	150	5-13	24	5-13	174		
Weekly								
Boarding								

ENTRY REQUIREMENTS Assessment & Interview
SCHOLARSHIPS & BURSARIES Schol; Burs; ARA
SPECIAL NEEDS abehklnstu BGL   **DYSLEXIA** ce   **DIET** abcd
ASSOCIATION IAPS   **FOUNDED** 1940   **RELIGIOUS AFFILIATION** C of E

MAP 3 E 4
LOCATION Urban
DAY   **RAIL** a   **AIR** a
SPORT abefhjlmpqswx ABC
OTHER LANGUAGES
ACTIVITIES fghijoqrt A
OTHER SUBJECTS cfh
FACILITIES ON SITE bchjk
EXAM BOARDS
RETAKES   **NVQ COURSES**

OTHER: e g i lmno v / B G K OP R / cdef j

G — Luckley-Oakfield School; Wokingham; Berks. RG40 3EU
Tel: 01734 784175 (Fax: 01734 770305) *R.C.Blake*

		Boys	Age	Girls	Age	TOTAL	SIXTH Boys	Girls
Day	£1643			183	11-18	274		68
Weekly	£2598			47	11-18			
Boarding	£2650			44	11-18			

ENTRY REQUIREMENTS Test & Interview
SCHOLARSHIPS & BURSARIES Schol; Mus; VI Form
SPECIAL NEEDS bjklnq EI   **DYSLEXIA** e   **DIET** a
ASSOCIATION GSA   **FOUNDED** 1918   **RELIGIOUS AFFILIATION** C of E (Evang)

MAP 3 E 4
LOCATION Rural
DAY ✓   **RAIL** a   **AIR** a
SPORT abcfglmpqtwx ABC
OTHER LANGUAGES a
ACTIVITIES acfghijknotw AB
OTHER SUBJECTS abcdegh
FACILITIES ON SITE abcghij
EXAM BOARDS abcd EGHI
RETAKES a   **NVQ COURSES**

A-level: e g ij l n p v x / BC GH K P R U / c ef
AS: C G / e
GCSE: p u x / d g ij l n v / BC E G K OP R U W / cdef l
OTHER: hj o

B — Ludgrove; Wixenford; Wokingham; Berks. RG11 3AB
Tel: 01734 789881 *G.W.P.Barber & C.N.J.Marston*

		Boys	Age	Girls	Age	TOTAL	SIXTH Boys	Girls
Day						195		
Weekly								
Boarding	£3050	195	8-13					

ENTRY REQUIREMENTS Interview
SCHOLARSHIPS & BURSARIES
SPECIAL NEEDS   **DYSLEXIA**   **DIET**
ASSOCIATION IAPS   **FOUNDED** 1892   **RELIGIOUS AFFILIATION** C of E

MAP 3 E 4
LOCATION Rural
DAY   **RAIL** b   **AIR** a
SPORT abefgijklmsuwx ABC
OTHER LANGUAGES
ACTIVITIES fghijortw
OTHER SUBJECTS acfh
FACILITIES ON SITE cdhikl
EXAM BOARDS
RETAKES   **NVQ COURSES**

OTHER: e g i v / B G K OP R / cde g j

C — Oratory Prep. School; Great Oaks; Goring Heath; Reading RG8 7SF
Tel: 01734 844511 (Fax: 01734 844806) *D.L.Sexon*

		Boys	Age	Girls	Age	TOTAL	SIXTH Boys	Girls
Day	£529-£1920	183	3-13	62	3-13	290		
Weekly								
Boarding	£2655	43	7-13	2	7-13			

ENTRY REQUIREMENTS Assessment & Interview
SCHOLARSHIPS & BURSARIES Burs
SPECIAL NEEDS bejklnqtw BEGIL   **DYSLEXIA** e   **DIET** acd
ASSOCIATION IAPS   **FOUNDED** 1859   **RELIGIOUS AFFILIATION** R C

MAP 3 D 4
LOCATION Rural
DAY   **RAIL** a   **AIR** a
SPORT abcdefgjklmopqswx ABC
OTHER LANGUAGES
ACTIVITIES abcfghijlnoqrstw A
OTHER SUBJECTS bcdfh
FACILITIES ON SITE cdhjkl
EXAM BOARDS
RETAKES   **NVQ COURSES**

OTHER: e g i l o v / B G K OP R / cde g j

76

BERKSHIRE *continued*

B Oratory School,The; Woodcote; Nr. Reading RG8 0PJ
Tel: 01491 680207 (Fax: 01491 680020) *S.W.Barrow*

		Boys	Age	Girls	Age	TOTAL		Boys	Girls
Day	£2225-£2740	132	11-18			395	SIXTH	126	
Weekly									
Boarding	£3085-£3920	263	11-18						

ENTRY REQUIREMENTS CEE; Test; Scholarship Exam
SCHOLARSHIPS & BURSARIES Schol; Art; Mus
SPECIAL NEEDS jinq Gl   **DYSLEXIA** e   **DIET**
ASSOCIATION HMC **FOUNDED** 1859 **RELIGIOUS AFFILIATION** R C

MAP 3 D 4
LOCATION Rural
DAY   **RAIL** a   **AIR** a
SPORT abcdefjkmorstuwx AB
OTHER LANGUAGES i
ACTIVITIES efghijkmoqstx A
OTHER SUBJECTS cfh
FACILITIES ON SITE cdhikl
EXAM BOARDS b HL
RETAKES   **NVQ COURSES**

A-level: cdefg i l p v x   AS: l   GCSE: e g i   OTHER:
AB GH K P   R   AB G K P
cdefgh j l   cdefgh j l
              d

Bg Pangbourne College; Pangbourne; Reading RG8 8LA
Tel: 01734 842101 (Fax: 01734 845443) *A.B.E.Hudson*

		Boys	Age	Girls	Age	TOTAL		Boys	Girls
Day	£1915-£2640 ✗	74	11-18	10	11-18	401	SIXTH	123	15
Weekly			11-18		11-18				
Boarding	£2750-£3770	312	11-18	5	11-18				

ENTRY REQUIREMENTS CEE & Interview; Report & Exam & Interview
SCHOLARSHIPS & BURSARIES Schol; Burs; Art; Mus; Forces; Clergy; ARA; Drama
SPECIAL NEEDS bfjlnqtw El   **DYSLEXIA** cef   **DIET** a
ASSOCIATION HMC **FOUNDED** 1917 **RELIGIOUS AFFILIATION** C of E

MAP 3 D 4
LOCATION Rural
DAY ✓   **RAIL** b   **AIR** a
SPORT abcefghkmnoprstuwx AB
OTHER LANGUAGES
ACTIVITIES befgijkloqst A
OTHER SUBJECTS bch
FACILITIES ON SITE ceghjk
EXAM BOARDS bd BH
RETAKES   **NVQ COURSES**

A-level: c efghi l nop v   AS   GCSE: e ghi l nopq v   OTHER:
B GH K OP   B G K OP R
cdef   cdef j l

B Papplewick; Ascot; Berks. SL5 7LH
Tel: 01344 21488 (Fax: 01344 874639) *D.R.Llewellyn*

		Boys	Age	Girls	Age	TOTAL		Boys	Girls
Day	£2392 ✗	68	7-11			191	SIXTH		
Weekly									
Boarding	£3115	123	7-13						

ENTRY REQUIREMENTS
SCHOLARSHIPS & BURSARIES Burs; Teachers
SPECIAL NEEDS aeijklnv l   **DYSLEXIA** e   **DIET** ad
ASSOCIATION IAPS **FOUNDED** 1947 **RELIGIOUS AFFILIATION** C of E

MAP 3 E 4
LOCATION Rural
DAY   **RAIL** a   **AIR** a
SPORT abefhjklmoswx ABC
OTHER LANGUAGES
ACTIVITIES afghijloqrstw A
OTHER SUBJECTS abcdfh
FACILITIES ON SITE abcdhjk
EXAM BOARDS
RETAKES   **NVQ COURSES**

A-level   AS   GCSE   OTHER: defg i l no q uv
                                   B G I K OP R
                                   a cde ghij

Bg Presentation College; 63 Bath Road; Reading RG3 2BB
Tel: 01734 572861 (Fax: 01734 572220) *Rev.S.Sullivan*

		Boys	Age	Girls	Age	TOTAL		Boys	Girls
Day	£850-£1110	386	5-18	3	16-18	389	SIXTH	60	3
Weekly									
Boarding									

ENTRY REQUIREMENTS CEE; Test & Interview; Assessment & Interview
SCHOLARSHIPS & BURSARIES
SPECIAL NEEDS ben   **DYSLEXIA** c   **DIET** ab
ASSOCIATION ISAI **FOUNDED** 1931 **RELIGIOUS AFFILIATION** R C

MAP 3 D 4
LOCATION Urban
DAY   **RAIL** a   **AIR** a
SPORT abcefhjklostwx AB
OTHER LANGUAGES
ACTIVITIES eghijklnpqr A
OTHER SUBJECTS bcdh
FACILITIES ON SITE abghk
EXAM BOARDS abcd ABDEG
RETAKES   **NVQ COURSES**

A-level: de g i l p uv   AS: G   GCSE: efg i l p v   OTHER:
B GH   P U   B G K P R U
cdef   cdef

C Prior's Court; Chieveley; Newbury; Berks. RG16 8XW
Tel: 01635 248209 (Fax: 01635 247179) *Paul High*

		Boys	Age	Girls	Age	TOTAL		Boys	Girls
Day	£1000-£1900 ✗	61	3-13	23	3-13	160	SIXTH		
Weekly			7-13		7-13				
Boarding	£2800	53	7-13	23	7-13				

ENTRY REQUIREMENTS Assessment; Report & Interview
SCHOLARSHIPS & BURSARIES Schol; AP
SPECIAL NEEDS bgjklnuw ABEI   **DYSLEXIA** cef   **DIET** ad
ASSOCIATION IAPS **FOUNDED** 1748 **RELIGIOUS AFFILIATION** Methodist

MAP 3 C 4
LOCATION Rural
DAY   **RAIL** b   **AIR** ab
SPORT abcefkmopqstx AB
OTHER LANGUAGES a
ACTIVITIES bcdfghijlnoqrstwx A
OTHER SUBJECTS bcfh
FACILITIES ON SITE bcdehjkl
EXAM BOARDS
RETAKES   **NVQ COURSES**

A-level   AS   GCSE   OTHER: de g i l no q s v
                                   BC G K OP R
                                   cde   j

BERKSHIRE continued

G — Queen Anne's School; Caversham; Reading; Berks. RG4 0DX
Tel: 01734 471582 (Fax: 01734 461498) *Mrs D.Forbes*

		Boys	Age	Girls	Age	TOTAL		Boys	Girls
Day	£2460	✗		120	11-18	322	SIXTH		83
Weekly	£3750			28					
Boarding	£3750			174	11-18				

MAP 3 D 4
LOCATION Urban
DAY **RAIL** a **AIR** a

ENTRY REQUIREMENTS CEE
SCHOLARSHIPS & BURSARIES Schol; Burs; Mus; ARA
SPECIAL NEEDS b   **DYSLEXIA**   **DIET** acd
ASSOCIATION GSA   **FOUNDED** 1894   **RELIGIOUS AFFILIATION** C of E

SPORT abcdfhklnopqrtwx ABC
OTHER LANGUAGES a
ACTIVITIES cghijknoqstw AB
OTHER SUBJECTS bcdfh
FACILITIES ON SITE bcdegik
EXAM BOARDS ab ABE
RETAKES   **NVQ COURSES**

A-level: cdefg i   n p   uv x   B GH K   P   W   c ef   j l
AS: fg i   ef   P
GCSE: cde g i   n   v   B   G   K   P R   W   cdefgh j l
OTHER:

Bg — Reading Blue Coat School; Holme Park; Sonning; Reading RG4 6SU
Tel: 01734 441005 (Fax: 01734 442690) *A.C.E.Sanders*

		Boys	Age	Girls	Age	TOTAL		Boys	Girls
Day	£1750	464	11-18	25	16-18	543	SIXTH	116	25
Weekly	£3090	35	11-18						
Boarding	£3190	19	11-18						

MAP 3 D 4
LOCATION Rural
DAY **RAIL** a **AIR** a

ENTRY REQUIREMENTS Exam & Interview; CEE & Interview
SCHOLARSHIPS & BURSARIES Schol; Burs; Mus
SPECIAL NEEDS bjl   **DYSLEXIA**   **DIET** a
ASSOCIATION HMC   **FOUNDED** 1646   **RELIGIOUS AFFILIATION** C of E

SPORT abcdefghjmprstuwx AB
OTHER LANGUAGES
ACTIVITIES abefghijkmoqstw AB
OTHER SUBJECTS bcdh
FACILITIES ON SITE bcgjk
EXAM BOARDS abd ABEG
RETAKES   **NVQ COURSES**

A-level: defg i l   op   uvwx   B   GH K   P   X   cdef
AS: G   u   l
GCSE: de g i l   o   vw   B   G   K   P R   cdef   l
OTHER: t   o

B — Ridgeway; Maidenhead Thicket; Berkshire SL6 3QE
Tel: 01628 822609 *Miss K.M.Boyd*

		Boys	Age	Girls	Age	TOTAL		Boys	Girls
Day	£1160-£1475	221	4-11			221	SIXTH		
Weekly									
Boarding									

MAP 3 E 4
LOCATION Rural
DAY ✓ **RAIL** a **AIR** a

ENTRY REQUIREMENTS None;
SCHOLARSHIPS & BURSARIES
SPECIAL NEEDS aehnsw AB   **DYSLEXIA**   **DIET** a
ASSOCIATION IAPS   **FOUNDED** 1975   **RELIGIOUS AFFILIATION** RC/Inter-denom

SPORT abcefhjklmqstx B
OTHER LANGUAGES a
ACTIVITIES afghjoqt A
OTHER SUBJECTS abcdh
FACILITIES ON SITE jl
EXAM BOARDS
RETAKES   **NVQ COURSES**

A-level:
AS:
GCSE:
OTHER: l   q   v   B   G K   O R   X   de   j

C — St. Andrew's School; Buckhold; Pangbourne; Reading RG8 8QA
Tel: 01734 744276 (Fax: 01734 745049) *J.M.Snow*

		Boys	Age	Girls	Age	TOTAL		Boys	Girls
Day	£1100-£1980	✗	130	4-13	69	4-13	242	SIXTH	
Weekly			7-13		7-13				
Boarding	£2700-£2750		28	7-13	15	7-13			

MAP 3 D 4
LOCATION Rural
DAY **RAIL** b **AIR** a

ENTRY REQUIREMENTS Report; Assessment
SCHOLARSHIPS & BURSARIES Clergy
SPECIAL NEEDS ajknw B   **DYSLEXIA** e   **DIET** ab
ASSOCIATION IAPS   **FOUNDED** 1934   **RELIGIOUS AFFILIATION** C of E

SPORT abcefhjklmopqsx ABC
OTHER LANGUAGES
ACTIVITIES cfghijlortvw A
OTHER SUBJECTS abcdfh
FACILITIES ON SITE bcdhjl
EXAM BOARDS
RETAKES   **NVQ COURSES**

A-level:
AS:
GCSE:
OTHER: e   l   o   v   B E G   K   R   cdef   j

C — St. Bernard's Prep. School; Hawtrey Close; Slough; Berks. SL1 1TB
Tel: 01753 521821 (Fax: 01753 552364) *Sister Francis Mary*

		Boys	Age	Girls	Age	TOTAL		Boys	Girls
Day	£1010-£1070	49	3-12	142	3-12	191	SIXTH		
Weekly									
Boarding									

MAP 3 E 4
LOCATION Urban
DAY **RAIL** a **AIR** a

ENTRY REQUIREMENTS Assessment & Interview
SCHOLARSHIPS & BURSARIES
SPECIAL NEEDS jknw Gl   **DYSLEXIA** g   **DIET**
ASSOCIATION IAPS   **FOUNDED** 1945   **RELIGIOUS AFFILIATION** R C

SPORT amp B
OTHER LANGUAGES
ACTIVITIES
OTHER SUBJECTS
FACILITIES ON SITE
EXAM BOARDS
RETAKES   **NVQ COURSES**

A-level:
AS:
GCSE:
OTHER: e   v   B   G   cde

BERKSHIRE continued

B — St. Edward's School; 64 Tilehurst Road; Reading RG3 2JH
Tel: 01734 574342 (Fax: 01734 454953) *J.D.T.Wall*

	Boys	Age	Girls	Age	TOTAL		Boys	Girls
Day £1030–£1070	117	7-13			117	SIXTH		
Weekly								
Boarding								

ENTRY REQUIREMENTS Test & Interview
SCHOLARSHIPS & BURSARIES
SPECIAL NEEDS kn BGI
DYSLEXIA e   **DIET**
ASSOCIATION IAPS   **FOUNDED** 1947   **RELIGIOUS AFFILIATION**

MAP 3 D 4
LOCATION Urban
DAY   **RAIL** a   **AIR** b
SPORT abdefhjlsvx A
OTHER LANGUAGES
ACTIVITIES fghjloqstw A
OTHER SUBJECTS ch
FACILITIES ON SITE ch
EXAM BOARDS
RETAKES   **NVQ COURSES**

A-level — **AS** — **GCSE** — **OTHER** cde g l o v
B E G K O RS
cdef jkl

G — S. Gabriels School; Sandleford Priory; Newbury; Berks RG15 9BD
Tel: 01635 40663 (Fax: 01635 37351) *D.J.Cobb*

	Boys	Age	Girls	Age	TOTAL		Boys	Girls
Day £1606–£1657 ✗		3-8	155	3-16	155	SIXTH		
Weekly								
Boarding								

ENTRY REQUIREMENTS Test & Interview; Exam & Interview
SCHOLARSHIPS & BURSARIES Schol; Burs; Teachers; Siblings
SPECIAL NEEDS aklnq GK
DYSLEXIA e   **DIET** abcd
ASSOCIATION GSA   **FOUNDED** 1929   **RELIGIOUS AFFILIATION** C of E

MAP 3 C 4
LOCATION Rural
DAY ✓   **RAIL** a   **AIR** b
SPORT acflmopqx B
OTHER LANGUAGES
ACTIVITIES cfghjotw A
OTHER SUBJECTS bcdefh
FACILITIES ON SITE chjk
EXAM BOARDS abd G
RETAKES   **NVQ COURSES**

A-level — **AS** — **GCSE** egiln o v
BC E G K   P R   W
cdef j
OTHER m s
o

G — St. George's School; Ascot; Berkshire SL5 7DZ
Tel: 01344 20273 (Fax: 01344 874213) *Mrs A.M.Griggs*

	Boys	Age	Girls	Age	TOTAL		Boys	Girls
Day £2275 ✗			111	11-18	278	SIXTH		65
Weekly			6					
Boarding £3875			161	11-18				

ENTRY REQUIREMENTS CEE
SCHOLARSHIPS & BURSARIES Schol; Burs; Mus; VI Form
SPECIAL NEEDS ablnpqt HI
DYSLEXIA ef   **DIET** abcd
ASSOCIATION GSA   **FOUNDED** 1877   **RELIGIOUS AFFILIATION** C of E

MAP 3 E 4
LOCATION Rural
DAY   **RAIL** b   **AIR** a
SPORT acghklnpqrvwx ABC
OTHER LANGUAGES ack
ACTIVITIES acghijknoqstw AB
OTHER SUBJECTS bcdefh
FACILITIES ON SITE bdhj
EXAM BOARDS abd ABEG
RETAKES a   **NVQ COURSES**

A-level c efg ij l n p   v
BC   G K   P R T U W
a cdef hi kl
AS G
GCSE e   j l n p   v
BC E G   K   R U W
a cdef hijkl
OTHER

B — St. George's School; Windsor Castle; Windsor; Berks. SL4 1QF
Tel: 01753 865553 (Fax: 01753 842093) *The Revd R.P.Marsh*

	Boys	Age	Girls	Age	TOTAL		Boys	Girls
Day £1930–£2130 ✗	31	7-13			69	SIXTH		
Weekly £2810	11	7-13						
Boarding £2860	27	7-13						

ENTRY REQUIREMENTS Report & Exam & Interview
SCHOLARSHIPS & BURSARIES Schol; Mus; Chor
SPECIAL NEEDS abghjklnpqstuw ABEGHIJ
DYSLEXIA e   **DIET** abcd
ASSOCIATION IAPS   **FOUNDED** 1352   **RELIGIOUS AFFILIATION** C of E

MAP 3 E 4
LOCATION Urban
DAY   **RAIL** a   **AIR** a
SPORT abefhjkmqsuvwx AB
OTHER LANGUAGES
ACTIVITIES adfghijmoqrst A
OTHER SUBJECTS abcfh
FACILITIES ON SITE bcdejkl
EXAM BOARDS
RETAKES   **NVQ COURSES**

A-level — **AS** — **GCSE** — **OTHER** cdefg i l no q   v
B   G JK   NOP R
cdefg jk

B — St. John's Beaumont; Old Windsor; Berks SL4 2JN
Tel: 01784 432428 (Fax: 01784 431307) *D.St.J.Gogarty*

	Boys	Age	Girls	Age	TOTAL		Boys	Girls
Day £1143–£2009 ✗	154	4-13			194	SIXTH		
Weekly £2777	15	8-13						
Boarding £3318	25	8-13						

ENTRY REQUIREMENTS Assessment & Interview
SCHOLARSHIPS & BURSARIES
SPECIAL NEEDS n
DYSLEXIA ce   **DIET** ab
ASSOCIATION IAPS   **FOUNDED** 1888   **RELIGIOUS AFFILIATION** R C

MAP 3 E 4
LOCATION Rural
DAY   **RAIL** a   **AIR** a
SPORT abcefgjlmsx AB
OTHER LANGUAGES
ACTIVITIES afghjloqrstx A
OTHER SUBJECTS bcfh
FACILITIES ON SITE bcdfhik
EXAM BOARDS
RETAKES   **NVQ COURSES**

A-level — **AS** — **GCSE** — **OTHER** egil o v
B   G K   OP R
cde g j

BERKSHIRE continued

G — St. Joseph's Convent School; Upper Redlands Road; Reading; Berks. RG1 5JT
Tel: 01734 661000 (Fax: 01734 269932) *Mrs V.M.Brookes*

		Boys	Age	Girls	Age	TOTAL	SIXTH	Boys	Girls
Day	£1225-£1265			372	11-18	372			78
Weekly									
Boarding									

ENTRY REQUIREMENTS Exam & Interview
SCHOLARSHIPS & BURSARIES Schol; Burs; AP; VI Form
SPECIAL NEEDS bfghjlnqtx J
ASSOCIATION GSA **FOUNDED** 1910 **RELIGIOUS AFFILIATION** R C **DYSLEXIA** **DIET** a

MAP 3 D 4
LOCATION Urban
DAY **RAIL** a **AIR** a
SPORT abchlmpqrwx ABC
OTHER LANGUAGES
ACTIVITIES cghijknos AB
OTHER SUBJECTS bcdh
FACILITIES ON SITE abdghi
EXAM BOARDS abd AG
RETAKES a **NVQ COURSES**

A-level: c e ghi i n p v
BC FGH K MN PQR U W
cdefgh j l

AS: h v
BC K M R U W
cdef h l

GCSE: e ghi p v
BC EFG K M R U W
cdef hj l

OTHER: u

G — St. Mary's School; South Ascot SL5 9JF
Tel: 01344 23721 (Fax: 01344 873281) *Sister Frances Orchard IBVM*

		Boys	Age	Girls	Age	TOTAL	SIXTH	Boys	Girls
Day	£2367			9	11-18	335			89
Weekly									
Boarding	£3945			326	11-18				

ENTRY REQUIREMENTS Exam & Interview
SCHOLARSHIPS & BURSARIES Mus
SPECIAL NEEDS jlntw G
ASSOCIATION GSA **FOUNDED** 1885 **RELIGIOUS AFFILIATION** R C **DYSLEXIA** fg **DIET** a

MAP 3 E 4
LOCATION
DAY **RAIL** ab **AIR** a
SPORT acdfghklmopqtvwx AB
OTHER LANGUAGES i
ACTIVITIES cfghijklnorst AB
OTHER SUBJECTS abcdefh
FACILITIES ON SITE bdeghik
EXAM BOARDS ab AEH
RETAKES a **NVQ COURSES**

A-level: cdefg i n p v x
B GH K MN P R
cdefgh j l

AS: G u U

GCSE: e g i n v
B G K N P R
bcdefgh jk l

OTHER:

C — St. Piran's School; Maidenhead; Berks. SL6 7LZ
Tel: 01628 27316 (Fax: 01628 32010) *A.P.Blumer*

		Boys	Age	Girls	Age	TOTAL	SIXTH	Boys	Girls
Day	£489-£1800	176	3-13	35	3-13	211			
Weekly									
Boarding									

ENTRY REQUIREMENTS Test
SCHOLARSHIPS & BURSARIES Schol
SPECIAL NEEDS ajn BG
ASSOCIATION IAPS **FOUNDED** 1872 **RELIGIOUS AFFILIATION** C of E **DYSLEXIA** de **DIET** abcd

MAP 3 E 4
LOCATION Urban
DAY **RAIL** a **AIR** a
SPORT abdefhjklmopqstuwx ABC
OTHER LANGUAGES
ACTIVITIES cdfghijlnoqst A
OTHER SUBJECTS bch
FACILITIES ON SITE adjk
EXAM BOARDS
RETAKES **NVQ COURSES**

OTHER: c e g i l o v
B G K NOP R
cdefg j

B — Sunningdale School; Sunningdale; Berks SL5 9PY
Tel: 01344 20159 (Fax: 01344 873304) *A.J.N.Dawson & T.M.E.Dawson*

		Boys	Age	Girls	Age	TOTAL	SIXTH	Boys	Girls
Day						117			
Weekly									
Boarding	£2295	117	8-13						

ENTRY REQUIREMENTS Assessment & Interview
SCHOLARSHIPS & BURSARIES
SPECIAL NEEDS bjkw l
ASSOCIATION IAPS **FOUNDED** 1874 **RELIGIOUS AFFILIATION** C of E **DYSLEXIA** **DIET**

MAP 3 E 4
LOCATION Rural
DAY **RAIL** a **AIR** a
SPORT aefijkmosuwx AB
OTHER LANGUAGES
ACTIVITIES cfghjotw
OTHER SUBJECTS acfh
FACILITIES ON SITE dhjkl
EXAM BOARDS
RETAKES **NVQ COURSES**

OTHER: e g i l m o q v
B G K P R
cde g j X

Gb — Upton House School; 115 St. Leonard's Road; Windsor SL4 3DF
Tel: 01753 862610 *Mrs Jane Woodley*

		Boys	Age	Girls	Age	TOTAL	SIXTH	Boys	Girls
Day	£548-£1251 X	63	3-7	147	3-11	210			
Weekly									
Boarding									

ENTRY REQUIREMENTS None; Assessment & Interview
SCHOLARSHIPS & BURSARIES Burs
SPECIAL NEEDS n
ASSOCIATION IAPS **FOUNDED** 1936 **RELIGIOUS AFFILIATION** C of E **DYSLEXIA** e **DIET** abcd

MAP 3 E 4
LOCATION Urban
DAY **RAIL** a **AIR** a
SPORT aejlmopqx B
OTHER LANGUAGES
ACTIVITIES cghjnt
OTHER SUBJECTS cfh
FACILITIES ON SITE ci
EXAM BOARDS
RETAKES **NVQ COURSES**

OTHER: e g i lmno v
B G K OP R
cde

BERKSHIRE *continued*

C | **Waverley School; Ravenswood Avenue; Crowthorne; Berks. RG11 6AY**
Tel: 01344 772379 (Fax: 01344 750492) *S.G.Melton*

		Boys	Age	Girls	Age	TOTAL	SIXTH	Boys	Girls
Day	£507- £975	86	3-11	75	3-11	161			
Weekly									
Boarding									

MAP 3 E 4
LOCATION Urban
DAY   **RAIL** a   **AIR** a
SPORT aejlpqx A
OTHER LANGUAGES
ACTIVITIES cfghjo

ENTRY REQUIREMENTS Interview
SCHOLARSHIPS & BURSARIES
SPECIAL NEEDS ablns B
ASSOCIATION IAPS   **FOUNDED** 1945   **RELIGIOUS AFFILIATION** Non-denom
DYSLEXIA de   **DIET** a

OTHER SUBJECTS bch
FACILITIES ON SITE
EXAM BOARDS
RETAKES   **NVQ COURSES**

A-level | **AS** | **GCSE** | **OTHER**   e   l- o   v
                                            B EG K   O R
                                              cde

B g | **Wellington College; Crowthorne; Berkshire RG11 7PU**
Tel: 01344 772261 (Fax: 01344 771725) *C.J.Driver*

		Boys	Age	Girls	Age	TOTAL	SIXTH	Boys	Girls
Day	£2985 X	146	13-18	8	16-18	810		298	54
Weekly									
Boarding	£4090	610	13-18	46	16-18				

MAP 3 E 4
LOCATION Rural
DAY   **RAIL** b   **AIR** a
SPORT abcdefghijklmnopqstuvwx ABC
OTHER LANGUAGES
ACTIVITIES abcefghijklmnopqrstuvw AB

ENTRY REQUIREMENTS CEE; Exam & Interview
SCHOLARSHIPS & BURSARIES Schol; Burs; Art; Mus; Forces; Teachers; AP; VI Form
SPECIAL NEEDS abceghjklnpqstvwx ABDGHIK   **DYSLEXIA** def   **DIET** abcd
ASSOCIATION HMC   **FOUNDED** 1853   **RELIGIOUS AFFILIATION** C of E

OTHER SUBJECTS abcdfgh
FACILITIES ON SITE abcdeghijk
EXAM BOARDS abcd ABEGH
RETAKES a   **NVQ COURSES**

A-level   c efg i l   opq   v x
              B   GH K   P R
                c efg j l
AS   G K
                ef   l
GCSE   v   cegil   o q   v
                      B G K   OP R
                      cdefg jkl
OTHER   i

C | **White House School; Finchampstead Road; Wokingham; Berks. RG11 3HD**
Tel: 01734 785151 *Mrs M.L.Blake*

		Boys	Age	Girls	Age	TOTAL	SIXTH	Boys	Girls
Day	£335-£1080	21	3- 7	92	3-11	113			
Weekly									
Boarding									

MAP 3 E 4
LOCATION Urban
DAY   **RAIL** a   **AIR** a
SPORT alpqx B
OTHER LANGUAGES
ACTIVITIES cgo

ENTRY REQUIREMENTS Interview
SCHOLARSHIPS & BURSARIES
SPECIAL NEEDS ajklnw
ASSOCIATION IAPS   **FOUNDED** 1948   **RELIGIOUS AFFILIATION** Inter-denom/Evang
DYSLEXIA g   **DIET**

OTHER SUBJECTS ch
FACILITIES ON SITE h
EXAM BOARDS
RETAKES   **NVQ COURSES**

A-level | **AS** | **GCSE** | **OTHER**   e lmno   v
                                              B EG K O R
                                                cde

C | **Winbury School; Hibbert Road; Bray; Maidenhead; Berks SL6 1UU**
Tel: 01628 27412 *Dominic Crehan*

		Boys	Age	Girls	Age	TOTAL	SIXTH	Boys	Girls
Day	£445- £895	46	3- 8	38	3- 8	84			
Weekly									
Boarding									

MAP 3 E 4
LOCATION
DAY   **RAIL** a   **AIR** a
SPORT ejpsx B
OTHER LANGUAGES
ACTIVITIES f

ENTRY REQUIREMENTS Interview
SCHOLARSHIPS & BURSARIES
SPECIAL NEEDS
ASSOCIATION ISAI   **FOUNDED**   **RELIGIOUS AFFILIATION** Non-denom
DYSLEXIA   **DIET**

OTHER SUBJECTS
FACILITIES ON SITE
EXAM BOARDS
RETAKES   **NVQ COURSES**

A-level | **AS** | **GCSE** | **OTHER**   v
                                              B   G
                                                cde

C | **Ashfold; Dorton; Aylesbury; Bucks. HP18 9NG**
Tel: 01844 238237 (Fax: 01844 238505) *D.H.M.Dalrymple*

		Boys	Age	Girls	Age	TOTAL	SIXTH	Boys	Girls
Day	£665-£2075 X	91	3-13	55	3-13	171			
Weekly	£2725	15	7-13	3	7-13				
Boarding	£2725	7	7-13		7-13				

MAP 3 E 2
LOCATION Rural
DAY   **RAIL** a   **AIR** b
SPORT abcefjklmnpqsux ABC
OTHER LANGUAGES
ACTIVITIES acfghijostw A

ENTRY REQUIREMENTS Test & Interview
SCHOLARSHIPS & BURSARIES Schol; Forces; Siblings
SPECIAL NEEDS bejknw BEGI   **DYSLEXIA** ef   **DIET** acd
ASSOCIATION IAPS   **FOUNDED** 1927   **RELIGIOUS AFFILIATION** C of E

OTHER SUBJECTS cfh
FACILITIES ON SITE cdhj
EXAM BOARDS
RETAKES   **NVQ COURSES**

A-level | **AS** | **GCSE** | **OTHER**   egil   o q   v
                                              B G K   OP R
                                              cde g j

BUCKS

BUCKINGHAMSHIRE *continued*

C — Beachborough School; Westbury; Brackley; Northants NN13 5LB
Tel: 01280 700071 (Fax: 01280 704839) *A.J.L.Boardman*

		Boys	Age	Girls	Age	TOTAL
Day	£1160-£2050	112	2-13	61	2-13	187
Weekly	£2660	8	7-13	2	7-13	
Boarding		4	7-13		7-13	

SIXTH: Boys / Girls

ENTRY REQUIREMENTS Interview
SCHOLARSHIPS & BURSARIES Siblings
SPECIAL NEEDS behijknptw ABEGI **DYSLEXIA** e **DIET** a
ASSOCIATION IAPS **FOUNDED** 1910 **RELIGIOUS AFFILIATION** C of E

MAP 3 D 1
LOCATION Rural
DAY **RAIL** b **AIR** b
SPORT abcdefhjklmopqsuwx AB
OTHER LANGUAGES
ACTIVITIES acfghijlmopqrstwx A
OTHER SUBJECTS ach
FACILITIES ON SITE ch
EXAM BOARDS
RETAKES **NVQ COURSES**

A-level / AS / GCSE
OTHER e g i l m n o q s v
BC E G K OP RS W
cde j

B — Beacon School & Winterbourn; Chesham Bois; Amersham; Bucks. HP6 5PF
Tel: 01494 433654 (Fax: 01494 727849) *J.V.Cross*

		Boys	Age	Girls	Age	TOTAL
Day	£570-£1826	305	3-13			305
Weekly						
Boarding						

ENTRY REQUIREMENTS Test & Interview
SCHOLARSHIPS & BURSARIES
SPECIAL NEEDS abjklnqtu CGH **DYSLEXIA** e **DIET** ac
ASSOCIATION IAPS **FOUNDED** 1934 **RELIGIOUS AFFILIATION** C of E

MAP 3 E 3
LOCATION Urban
DAY **RAIL** a **AIR** a
SPORT abcdejlmsx ABC
OTHER LANGUAGES
ACTIVITIES fghjoqt A
OTHER SUBJECTS bcfh
FACILITIES ON SITE abchj
EXAM BOARDS
RETAKES **NVQ COURSES**

A-level / AS / GCSE
OTHER d e g i l o v
B G K OP R
cdef j

C — Bury Lawn School; Soskin Drive; Stantonbury Fields; Milton Keynes; Bucks MK14 6DP
Tel: 01908 220345 (Fax: 01442 214346) *Mrs H.W.K.Kiff*

		Boys	Age	Girls	Age	TOTAL	SIXTH Boys	Girls
Day	£1135-£1570	172	2-18	135	2-18	307	8	5
Weekly								
Boarding								

ENTRY REQUIREMENTS Assessment & Interview
SCHOLARSHIPS & BURSARIES Burs
SPECIAL NEEDS abjln B **DYSLEXIA** e **DIET** abcd
ASSOCIATION ISAI **FOUNDED** 1970 **RELIGIOUS AFFILIATION** Inter-denom

MAP 3 E 1
LOCATION Urban
DAY ✓ **RAIL** a **AIR** a
SPORT abcefjlmpqsx ABC
OTHER LANGUAGES a
ACTIVITIES cgijko
OTHER SUBJECTS bcdh
FACILITIES ON SITE bch
EXAM BOARDS abd ABEG
RETAKES ab **NVQ COURSES**

A-level e g i no v
ABC G K P R
cdef l

AS e i
G K P R
cdef l

GCSE e g i l nop uv
ABC G K OPQR
cdef j l

OTHER

B — Caldicott; Farnham Royal; Bucks SL2 3SL
Tel: 01753 644457 (Fax: 01753 647336) *M.C.B.Spens*

		Boys	Age	Girls	Age	TOTAL
Day	£2184	118	7-13			254
Weekly						
Boarding	£2936	136	7-13			

ENTRY REQUIREMENTS Report & Exam & Interview
SCHOLARSHIPS & BURSARIES Schol
SPECIAL NEEDS **DYSLEXIA** **DIET** acd
ASSOCIATION IAPS **FOUNDED** 1904 **RELIGIOUS AFFILIATION** C of E

MAP 3 E 4
LOCATION Rural
DAY **RAIL** b **AIR** a
SPORT abcefklmsuvwx ABC
OTHER LANGUAGES
ACTIVITIES fghijoqrx
OTHER SUBJECTS ch
FACILITIES ON SITE cdhjk
EXAM BOARDS
RETAKES **NVQ COURSES**

A-level / AS / GCSE
OTHER d e g i l no v
B G K OP R
cdefg j

C — Chesham Prep. School; Orchard Leigh; Chesham; Bucks. HP5 3QF
Tel: 01494 782619 (Fax: 01494 791645) *R.J.H.Ford*

		Boys	Age	Girls	Age	TOTAL
Day	£995-£1265	175	5-13	130	5-13	305
Weekly						
Boarding						

ENTRY REQUIREMENTS None; Assessment & Interview
SCHOLARSHIPS & BURSARIES
SPECIAL NEEDS bj **DYSLEXIA** **DIET** a
ASSOCIATION IAPS **FOUNDED** 1938 **RELIGIOUS AFFILIATION** Non-denom

MAP 3 E 3
LOCATION Rural
DAY ✓ **RAIL** **AIR** a
SPORT aefjlpqstx AB
OTHER LANGUAGES
ACTIVITIES cfghjnoprtw A
OTHER SUBJECTS ch
FACILITIES ON SITE
EXAM BOARDS
RETAKES **NVQ COURSES**

A-level / AS / GCSE
OTHER de l o v
B E G K O R
cde j

BUCKINGHAMSHIRE continued

C | Crown House School; 19 London Road; High Wycombe; Bucks HP11 1BJ
Tel: 01494 529917 *L.Clark*

Day / Weekly Boarding — £1010
Boys 81 Age 4-12 | Girls 67 Age 4-12 | TOTAL 148 | SIXTH Boys — Girls —

ENTRY REQUIREMENTS Interview
SCHOLARSHIPS & BURSARIES
SPECIAL NEEDS abklnqw BGI
DYSLEXIA ce   DIET
ASSOCIATION ISAI   FOUNDED 1924   RELIGIOUS AFFILIATION Non-denom

MAP 3 E 3
LOCATION Urban
DAY   RAIL a   AIR a
SPORT ajpqx
OTHER LANGUAGES
ACTIVITIES fgj A
OTHER SUBJECTS ch
FACILITIES ON SITE bhij
EXAM BOARDS
RETAKES   NVQ COURSES

A-level | AS | GCSE | OTHER e l n v
                            B E G   K   O R
                              cde

C | Dair House School; Bishops Blake; Beaconsfield Road; Farnham Royal; Bucks SL2 3BY
Tel: 01753 643964 (Fax: 01753 642376) *Mrs T.A.Devonside*

Day / Weekly Boarding — £512-£1064
Boys 92 Age 3-8 | Girls 29 Age 3-8 | TOTAL 121 | SIXTH Boys — Girls —

ENTRY REQUIREMENTS Assessment & Interview
SCHOLARSHIPS & BURSARIES
SPECIAL NEEDS n B
DYSLEXIA e   DIET abcd
ASSOCIATION ISAI   FOUNDED 1932   RELIGIOUS AFFILIATION C of E

MAP 3 E 4
LOCATION Urban
DAY   RAIL a   AIR a
SPORT ejlpqx B
OTHER LANGUAGES
ACTIVITIES cghjr
OTHER SUBJECTS bch
FACILITIES ON SITE
EXAM BOARDS
RETAKES   NVQ COURSES

A-level | AS | GCSE | OTHER e l   v
                            B G K O
                             cd

B | Davenies School; Beaconsfield; Bucks HP9 1AA
Tel: 01494 674169 (Fax: 01494 681170) *J.R.Jones*

Day / Weekly Boarding — £1295-£1425
Boys 207 Age 4-13 | Girls — Age — | TOTAL 207 | SIXTH Boys — Girls —

ENTRY REQUIREMENTS Test; Interview
SCHOLARSHIPS & BURSARIES
SPECIAL NEEDS abjklnst
DYSLEXIA f   DIET acd
ASSOCIATION IAPS   FOUNDED 1940   RELIGIOUS AFFILIATION Inter-denom

MAP 3 E 3
LOCATION Urban
DAY   RAIL a   AIR a
SPORT abcefjlmoqsuwx ABC
OTHER LANGUAGES
ACTIVITIES cfghijopqtx AB
OTHER SUBJECTS ach
FACILITIES ON SITE achjk
EXAM BOARDS
RETAKES   NVQ COURSES

A-level | AS | GCSE | OTHER e g i lmno   vw
                            B   G K   OP RS
                            cde g j

C | Gateway School; 1 High Street; Great Missenden; Bucks. HP16 9AA;
Tel: 01494 862407 (Fax: 01494 865787) *J.L.Wade & J.H.Wade*

Day / Weekly Boarding — £384-£1275 ✗
Boys 206 Age 2-13 | Girls 150 Age 2-13 | TOTAL 356 | SIXTH Boys — Girls —

ENTRY REQUIREMENTS Interview
SCHOLARSHIPS & BURSARIES
SPECIAL NEEDS
DYSLEXIA   DIET
ASSOCIATION ISAI   FOUNDED 1940   RELIGIOUS AFFILIATION

MAP 3 E 3
LOCATION Rural
DAY   RAIL   AIR
SPORT abefjmpstx ABC
OTHER LANGUAGES
ACTIVITIES cfghjn
OTHER SUBJECTS
FACILITIES ON SITE
EXAM BOARDS
RETAKES   NVQ COURSES

A-level | AS | GCSE | OTHER e g i l no st v
                            B   G K   OP R
                            cde

B | Gayhurst School; Bull Lane; Gerrards Cross; Bucks. SL9 8RJ
Tel: 01753 882690 (Fax: 01753 887 451) *A.J.Sims*

Day / Weekly Boarding — £1140-£1570 ✗
Boys 232 Age 4-13 | Girls — Age — | TOTAL 232 | SIXTH Boys — Girls —

ENTRY REQUIREMENTS Interview
SCHOLARSHIPS & BURSARIES Burs
SPECIAL NEEDS begijklnqtuw ACGHI
DYSLEXIA ef   DIET acd
ASSOCIATION IAPS   FOUNDED 1910   RELIGIOUS AFFILIATION Christian

MAP 3 F 3
LOCATION Rural
DAY   RAIL a   AIR a
SPORT abcefgjklmqsx ABC
OTHER LANGUAGES
ACTIVITIES fghijor A
OTHER SUBJECTS bch
FACILITIES ON SITE bhjk
EXAM BOARDS
RETAKES   NVQ COURSES

A-level | AS | GCSE | OTHER cde g i l no q   v
                            B   G K   OP R
                            cde g j l

BUCKINGHAMSHIRE continued

Gb Godstowe Prep. School; High Wycombe; Bucks. HP13 6PR
Tel: 01494 529273 (Fax: 01494 452803) Mrs F.Henson

		Boys	Age	Girls	Age	TOTAL
Day	£915-£1615	25	4-8	233	4-13	370
Weekly	£2910			14	7-13	
Boarding	£2910			98	7-13	

MAP 3 E 3
LOCATION Urban
DAY   **RAIL** a   **AIR** a
SPORT acefhjklnpqsvx ABC
OTHER LANGUAGES abch
ACTIVITIES cfghjopqwx A

ENTRY REQUIREMENTS
SCHOLARSHIPS & BURSARIES
SPECIAL NEEDS ajklnw ABG
ASSOCIATION IAPS   **FOUNDED** 1900   **DYSLEXIA** e   **DIET** acd
RELIGIOUS AFFILIATION C of E
OTHER SUBJECTS abch
FACILITIES ON SITE chi
EXAM BOARDS
RETAKES   **NVQ COURSES**

A-level   AS   GCSE
OTHER   c e g i   lmno   q s   vw
     B E G   K   OP R   W
     cdefg   j

Gb Heatherton House School; Copperkins Lane; Amersham; Bucks. HP6 5QB
Tel: 01494 726433 (Fax: 01494 726433) Miss P.K.Thomson

		Boys	Age	Girls	Age	TOTAL
Day	£480-£1215	22	3-5	130	3-12	152
Weekly						
Boarding						

MAP 3 E 3
LOCATION Urban
DAY ✓   **RAIL** b   **AIR** a
SPORT lpqx AB
OTHER LANGUAGES
ACTIVITIES cfghjot

ENTRY REQUIREMENTS Assessment & Interview
SCHOLARSHIPS & BURSARIES
SPECIAL NEEDS befghjklnopqstuw ABCFGHI
ASSOCIATION IAPS   **FOUNDED** 1912   **DYSLEXIA** e   **DIET** abcd
RELIGIOUS AFFILIATION Inter-denom
OTHER SUBJECTS bcfh
FACILITIES ON SITE
EXAM BOARDS
RETAKES   **NVQ COURSES**

A-level   AS   GCSE
OTHER   e   lm o   s   v
     BC E G   K   O R
     cde

Gb High March School; Ledborough Lane; Beaconsfield; Bucks HP9 2PZ
Tel: 01494 675186 (Fax: 01494 675377) Mrs P.A.Forsyth

		Boys	Age	Girls	Age	TOTAL
Day	£450-£1390	12	3-7	292	3-13	304
Weekly						
Boarding						

MAP 3 E 3
LOCATION Urban
DAY   **RAIL** a   **AIR** a
SPORT aejlpqx B
OTHER LANGUAGES
ACTIVITIES cfghjot A

ENTRY REQUIREMENTS Interview; Assessment & Interview
SCHOLARSHIPS & BURSARIES Schol
SPECIAL NEEDS jkntw G
ASSOCIATION IAPS   **FOUNDED** 1926   **DYSLEXIA** e   **DIET** abcd
RELIGIOUS AFFILIATION Inter-denom
OTHER SUBJECTS bcfh
FACILITIES ON SITE
EXAM BOARDS
RETAKES   **NVQ COURSES**

A-level   AS   GCSE
OTHER   e g i   lmno   v
     B   G   K   OP R
     cde   j

G Maltman's Green; Gerrards Cross; Bucks. SL9 8RR
Tel: 01753 883022 (Fax: 01753 891237) Mrs M.Evans

		Boys	Age	Girls	Age	TOTAL
Day	£490-£1600			336	3-13	339
Weekly				3		
Boarding						

MAP 3 E 4
LOCATION Rural
DAY   **RAIL** a   **AIR** a
SPORT aclmnpqx AB
OTHER LANGUAGES
ACTIVITIES cghjotw A

ENTRY REQUIREMENTS Assessment
SCHOLARSHIPS & BURSARIES Schol
SPECIAL NEEDS
ASSOCIATION IAPS   **FOUNDED** 1918   **DYSLEXIA**   **DIET** abcd
RELIGIOUS AFFILIATION Non-denom
OTHER SUBJECTS abcfh
FACILITIES ON SITE chj
EXAM BOARDS
RETAKES   **NVQ COURSES**

A-level   AS   GCSE
OTHER   d g i   l m o q s   v
     B E G   K   OP R
     cdef   j l

C Milton Keynes Preparatory School; Tattenhoe Lane; Milton Keynes; Bucks MK3 7EG
Tel: 01908 642111 (Fax: 01908 366365) Mrs H.A.Pauley

		Boys	Age	Girls	Age	TOTAL
Day	£788-£1566	146	2-13	136	2-13	282
Weekly						
Boarding						

MAP 3 E 1
LOCATION Urban
DAY   **RAIL** a   **AIR** a
SPORT abcefjklmnopqsvx AB
OTHER LANGUAGES
ACTIVITIES acfghjot A

ENTRY REQUIREMENTS Exam
SCHOLARSHIPS & BURSARIES Schol; Burs
SPECIAL NEEDS bhjknq IK
ASSOCIATION IAPS   **FOUNDED** 1982   **DYSLEXIA** e   **DIET** abcd
RELIGIOUS AFFILIATION Non-denom
OTHER SUBJECTS bcdfh
FACILITIES ON SITE h
EXAM BOARDS
RETAKES   **NVQ COURSES**

A-level   AS   GCSE
OTHER   e   lm o   uv
     BC E G   K   O
     cdef   l

84

BUCKINGHAMSHIRE *continued*

G | Pipers Corner School; Great Kingshill; High Wycombe HP15 6LP
Tel: 01494 718255 (Fax: 01494 715391) *Dr M.M.Wilson*

		Boys	Age	Girls	Age	TOTAL		Boys	Girls
Day	£900-£1860			262	4-18	339	SIXTH		43
Weekly	£2545-£3070			43	7-18				
Boarding	£2585-£3110			34	7-18				

ENTRY REQUIREMENTS Exam; Interview; Report & Exam & Interview
SCHOLARSHIPS & BURSARIES Burs; Forces; VI Form
SPECIAL NEEDS abjlq   **DYSLEXIA**   **DIET** acd
ASSOCIATION GSA   **FOUNDED** 1930   **RELIGIOUS AFFILIATION** C of E

MAP 3 E 3
LOCATION Rural
DAY ✓   **RAIL** a   **AIR** a
SPORT abcfhjlmnopqx ABC
OTHER LANGUAGES a
ACTIVITIES cghijkostwx B
OTHER SUBJECTS bcdefgh
FACILITIES ON SITE bdghj
EXAM BOARDS abcd ABEG
RETAKES ab   **NVQ COURSES** 2

A-level cde g i l no uv   BC G P R T W   cdef
AS cd g i G c ef
GCSE uv P T
OTHER de g i l no v   BC G K P R W   cdef l

G | St. Mary's School; Packhorse Road; Gerrards Cross; Bucks. SL9 8JQ
Tel: 01753 883370 (Fax: 01753 890966) *Mrs J.P.G.Smith*

		Boys	Age	Girls	Age	TOTAL		Boys	Girls
Day	£505-£1695			278	3-18	278	SIXTH		28
Weekly									
Boarding									

ENTRY REQUIREMENTS CEE; Exam; Test & Interview
SCHOLARSHIPS & BURSARIES Schol; Burs; Mus; VI Form
SPECIAL NEEDS beghjklntwx ABDGHIJ   **DYSLEXIA** g   **DIET** acd
ASSOCIATION GSA   **FOUNDED** 1872   **RELIGIOUS AFFILIATION** C of E

MAP 3 E 4
LOCATION Urban
DAY   **RAIL** a   **AIR** a
SPORT abchklmnpqvwx AB
OTHER LANGUAGES
ACTIVITIES acghijkot ABD
OTHER SUBJECTS abcdefgh
FACILITIES ON SITE bcdhjk
EXAM BOARDS abd AG
RETAKES a   **NVQ COURSES**

A-level e ghi n p v   BC G K P R   cdef hj l
AS G c ef
GCSE e h l n v   BC E G K O R   cdef hj l
OTHER g i o u   de P

C | St. Teresa's School; Aylesbury Road; Princes Risborough; Bucks. HP27 0JW
Tel: 01844 345005 *Mrs C.M.Sparkes & Mrs A.M.Broom-Smith*

		Boys	Age	Girls	Age	TOTAL		Boys	Girls
Day	£284-£879	72	3-12	79	3-12	151	SIXTH		
Weekly									
Boarding									

ENTRY REQUIREMENTS Assessment; Test & Interview
SCHOLARSHIPS & BURSARIES
SPECIAL NEEDS bln JL   **DYSLEXIA** e   **DIET**
ASSOCIATION ISAI   **FOUNDED** 1970   **RELIGIOUS AFFILIATION** R C

MAP 3 E 3
LOCATION Rural
DAY   **RAIL** a   **AIR** b
SPORT aejpsx AB
OTHER LANGUAGES
ACTIVITIES cfhjo
OTHER SUBJECTS h
FACILITIES ON SITE
EXAM BOARDS
RETAKES   **NVQ COURSES**

A-level
AS
GCSE
OTHER e lmno v   B E G K O R   cde

Bg | Stowe School; Stowe; Buckingham MK18 5EH
Tel: 01280 813164 (Fax: 01280 822769) *J.G.L.Nichols*

		Boys	Age	Girls	Age	TOTAL		Boys	Girls
Day	£2985	27	13-18	6	16-18	544	SIXTH	187	88
Weekly									
Boarding	£4263	429	13-18	82	16-18				

ENTRY REQUIREMENTS CEE; Scholarship Exam; Exam & Interview
SCHOLARSHIPS & BURSARIES Schol; Burs; Art; Mus; Teachers; AP; VI Form; ARA
SPECIAL NEEDS abn Bl   **DYSLEXIA** e   **DIET** abcd
ASSOCIATION HMC   **FOUNDED** 1923   **RELIGIOUS AFFILIATION** C of E

MAP 3 E 1
LOCATION Rural
DAY   **RAIL** b   **AIR** b
SPORT abcdefghijklmnopqrstuwx ABC
OTHER LANGUAGES a
ACTIVITIES cefghijklmnopqsvw BCD
OTHER SUBJECTS abcdefgh
FACILITIES ON SITE abcdeghikl
EXAM BOARDS abcd ABEH
RETAKES a   **NVQ COURSES**

A-level cdefghi nop vwx   B GH K P R   cdefg j l
AS c h u x G R e
GCSE cde g i nop t v x   AB E G K P R   cdefgh j l
OTHER l n u   G K NO R U   de kl

C | Swanbourne House; Swanbourne; Bucks MK17 0HZ
Tel: 0129 672 0264 (Fax: 0129 672 8188) *T.V.More*

		Boys	Age	Girls	Age	TOTAL		Boys	Girls
Day	£560-£2110	140	3-13	102	3-13	287	SIXTH		
Weekly	£2745	22	7-13	8	7-13				
Boarding	£2745	7	7-13	8	7-13				

ENTRY REQUIREMENTS Assessment & Interview
SCHOLARSHIPS & BURSARIES Schol; Art; Mus; Forces; Clergy; Sport
SPECIAL NEEDS beglnqtw ABEGHI   **DYSLEXIA** e   **DIET** acd
ASSOCIATION IAPS   **FOUNDED** 1920   **RELIGIOUS AFFILIATION** C of E

MAP 3 E 2
LOCATION Rural
DAY   **RAIL** a   **AIR** a
SPORT abcdefjklmnopqstuwx ABC
OTHER LANGUAGES
ACTIVITIES cfghjmnoqrstwx AB
OTHER SUBJECTS abcfh
FACILITIES ON SITE cdhik
EXAM BOARDS
RETAKES   **NVQ COURSES**

A-level
AS
GCSE
OTHER de g i lmno q s v   AB E G K OP R   cde j

BUCKINGHAMSHIRE continued

B — Thorpe House School; Gerrards Cross; Bucks SL9 8PZ
Tel: 01753 882474 (Fax: 01753 889755) *J.Scaife*

	Boys	Age	Girls	Age	TOTAL	SIXTH	Boys	Girls
Day £1425-£1480 ×	193	7-13			193			
Weekly								
Boarding								

MAP 3 F 3
LOCATION Urban
DAY RAIL a AIR a
SPORT abefjklmsx B
OTHER LANGUAGES
ACTIVITIES fghijnow A
OTHER SUBJECTS ach
FACILITIES ON SITE abchjk
EXAM BOARDS
RETAKES NVQ COURSES

ENTRY REQUIREMENTS Test & Interview
SCHOLARSHIPS & BURSARIES
SPECIAL NEEDS   DYSLEXIA   DIET abcd
ASSOCIATION IAPS FOUNDED 1923 RELIGIOUS AFFILIATION C of E

A-level	AS	GCSE	OTHER
		e g i l no q uv B G K OP R cde g j

Gb — Thornton College; Convent of Jesus and Mary; Milton Keynes; Bucks. MK17 0HJ
Tel: 01280 812610 (Fax: 01280 824042) *Mrs E.E.Speddy*

	Boys	Age	Girls	Age	TOTAL	SIXTH	Boys	Girls
Day £1220-£1620 ×	14	3-7	187	3-16	265			
Weekly £2070-£2510			18	8-16				
Boarding £2180-£2630			46	8-16				

MAP 3 d 1
LOCATION Rural
DAY RAIL a AIR a
SPORT abcfjklmpqx ABC
OTHER LANGUAGES a
ACTIVITIES cghijknotw
OTHER SUBJECTS bcdfh
FACILITIES ON SITE bcdhj
EXAM BOARDS abd
RETAKES NVQ COURSES

ENTRY REQUIREMENTS Assessment & Interview
SCHOLARSHIPS & BURSARIES Schol
SPECIAL NEEDS aj B   DYSLEXIA   DIET ab
ASSOCIATION GBGSA FOUNDED 1917 RELIGIOUS AFFILIATION R C

A-level	AS	GCSE	OTHER
		de g i l o v BC E G K P R cde l

G — Wycombe Abbey School; High Wycombe HP11 1PE
Tel: 01494 520381 (Fax: 01494 473836) *Mrs J.M.Goodland*

	Boys	Age	Girls	Age	TOTAL	SIXTH	Boys	Girls
Day £3060 ×			9	11-18	495			146
Weekly								
Boarding £4080			486	11-18				

MAP 3 E 3
LOCATION Urban
DAY RAIL a AIR a
SPORT aglnpqwx B
OTHER LANGUAGES
ACTIVITIES cghijklnost B
OTHER SUBJECTS abcdfh
FACILITIES ON SITE bcdgik
EXAM BOARDS abcd DEH
RETAKES NVQ COURSES

ENTRY REQUIREMENTS CEE
SCHOLARSHIPS & BURSARIES Schol; Mus
SPECIAL NEEDS bgjls   DYSLEXIA   DIET abcd
ASSOCIATION GSA FOUNDED 1896 RELIGIOUS AFFILIATION C of E

A-level	AS	GCSE	OTHER
c efg i l v		e g i l o v
B GH K M R U		B G K P R
cdefgh jkl		cdefgh jkl

CAMBRIDGESHIRE

C — Horler's Pre-Preparatory School; 20 Green End; Comberton; Cambridge CB3 7DY
Tel: 01223 263189 *Mrs A.Horler*

	Boys	Age	Girls	Age	TOTAL	SIXTH	Boys	Girls
Day £1190	13	4-8	19	4-8	32			
Weekly								
Boarding								

MAP10 G 7
LOCATION Rural
DAY RAIL a AIR a
SPORT afho
OTHER LANGUAGES
ACTIVITIES jw
OTHER SUBJECTS ch
FACILITIES ON SITE
EXAM BOARDS
RETAKES NVQ COURSES

ENTRY REQUIREMENTS None; Test
SCHOLARSHIPS & BURSARIES
SPECIAL NEEDS   DYSLEXIA   DIET
ASSOCIATION ISAI FOUNDED 1983 RELIGIOUS AFFILIATION Non-denom

A-level	AS	GCSE	OTHER
		e l n s v B E G K O de

C — Kimbolton School; Kimbolton; Huntingdon; Cambs. PE18 0EA
Tel: 01480 860505 (Fax: 01480 860386) *R.V.Peel*

	Boys	Age	Girls	Age	TOTAL	SIXTH	Boys	Girls
Day £1450-£1745 ×	354	7-18	314	7-18	730		80	64
Weekly								
Boarding £2995			35	11-18	27	11-18		

MAP 9 F 7
LOCATION Rural
DAY ✓ RAIL b AIR b
SPORT abcdefghjklmopqrtuwx ABC
OTHER LANGUAGES
ACTIVITIES abdefghijklmnoqrstuvw ABD
OTHER SUBJECTS abcfh
FACILITIES ON SITE acdghjk
EXAM BOARDS abd BDEH
RETAKES NVQ COURSES

ENTRY REQUIREMENTS CEE; Report & Exam & Interview
SCHOLARSHIPS & BURSARIES Schol; Burs; Art; Mus; AP; VI Form; Sport; ARA; Siblings
SPECIAL NEEDS abegjklnqstuw DEHI   DYSLEXIA e   DIET ab
ASSOCIATION HMC FOUNDED 1600 RELIGIOUS AFFILIATION Non-denom

A-level	AS	GCSE	OTHER
defg i op uv x	f l	de g i l o v	cd l no q u w
ABC GH K P U	H	ABC G K P R U	C JK MNO R W
cde		cdef l	h l

86

CAMBRIDGESHIRE *continued*

King's College School; West Road; Cambridge CB3 9DN
Tel: 01223 365814 (Fax: 01223 461388) *A.S.R.Corbett*

		Boys	Age	Girls	Age	TOTAL		Boys	Girls
Day	£1364-£1810 ✗	142	4-13	90	4-13	277	SIXTH		
Weekly	£2804	22	7-13						
Boarding	£895	23	7-13						

ENTRY REQUIREMENTS Report; Test & Interview
SCHOLARSHIPS & BURSARIES Chor
SPECIAL NEEDS aegjlnstu BEGHI **DYSLEXIA** ce **DIET** acd
ASSOCIATION IAPS **FOUNDED** 1441 **RELIGIOUS AFFILIATION** C of E

MAP10 G 7
LOCATION Urban
DAY ✓ **RAIL** a **AIR** b
SPORT acdefgjlmpqswx ABC
OTHER LANGUAGES
ACTIVITIES cfghijlnoqstvx A
OTHER SUBJECTS bcdfh
FACILITIES ON SITE cjk
EXAM BOARDS
RETAKES **NVQ COURSES**

A-level **AS** **GCSE** **OTHER** c e g i l m n o q s v
B G K O P R
cdefg j

King's Junior School; Ely; Cambs. CB7 4DB
Tel: 01353 662491 (Fax: 01353 662187) *M.Anderson*

		Boys	Age	Girls	Age	TOTAL		Boys	Girls
Day	£620-£1798	178	4-13	137	4-13	384	SIXTH		
Weekly	£2220-£2879	16	8-13	12	8-13				
Boarding	£2300-£2959	36	8-13	5	8-13				

ENTRY REQUIREMENTS Test & Interview
SCHOLARSHIPS & BURSARIES Schol; Art; Mus; Clergy; Sport; ARA; Siblings
SPECIAL NEEDS abejklnptuw ABEGHI **DYSLEXIA** def **DIET** abcd
ASSOCIATION IAPS **FOUNDED** 970 **RELIGIOUS AFFILIATION** C of E

MAP10 H 7
LOCATION Urban
DAY ✓ **RAIL** a **AIR** a
SPORT abcefjklmpqrsux AB
OTHER LANGUAGES a
ACTIVITIES fghijortw A
OTHER SUBJECTS abcfh
FACILITIES ON SITE abcdehjkl
EXAM BOARDS
RETAKES **NVQ COURSES**

A-level **AS** **GCSE** **OTHER** c e l no v
B G K O R X
cde j

King's School; Ely; Cambs CB7 4DB
Tel: 01353 662824 (Fax: 01353 662187) *R.H.Youdale*

		Boys	Age	Girls	Age	TOTAL		Boys	Girls
Day	£2442	148	13-18	108	13-18	404	SIXTH	65	50
Weekly	£3729	41	13-18	30	13-18				
Boarding	£3829	44	13-18	33	13-18				

ENTRY REQUIREMENTS Test & Interview; Exam & Interview
SCHOLARSHIPS & BURSARIES Schol; Burs; Art; Mus; Clergy; VI Form; Siblings
SPECIAL NEEDS abejklnptuw ABEGHI **DYSLEXIA** def **DIET** abcd
ASSOCIATION HMC **FOUNDED** 970 **RELIGIOUS AFFILIATION** C of E

MAP10 H 7
LOCATION Urban
DAY ✓ **RAIL** a **AIR** a
SPORT abcdefhjkmpqrstuwx AB
OTHER LANGUAGES a
ACTIVITIES cfghijklmnoqrstuw A
OTHER SUBJECTS abcfh
FACILITIES ON SITE abdeghjkl
EXAM BOARDS abcd ABDEHI
RETAKES a **NVQ COURSES**

A-level cdefghi n pq v
B GH K OP R W
cdefg j l

AS cdefg i n q v
B GH K P R W
def hj l

GCSE de ghi n q v
B G K OP R X
cdefg j l

OTHER de lm o q uvw
ABC G K NO R U X
cdefgh j l

Leys School,The; Cambridge CB2 2AD
Tel: 01223 355327 (Fax: 01223 357053) *The Rev.Dr.J.C.A.Barrett*

		Boys	Age	Girls	Age	TOTAL		Boys	Girls
Day	£2900	139	13-18	15	13-18	416	SIXTH	128	77
Weekly									
Boarding	£3980	168	13-18	94	13-18				

ENTRY REQUIREMENTS CEE; Exam; Scholarship Exam; Report & Interview
SCHOLARSHIPS & BURSARIES Schol; Art; Mus; Forces; AP; VI Form; ARA
SPECIAL NEEDS bklnqw BEGIL **DYSLEXIA** f **DIET** ad
ASSOCIATION HMC **FOUNDED** 1875 **RELIGIOUS AFFILIATION** Methodist

MAP10 G 7
LOCATION Urban
DAY **RAIL** a **AIR** b
SPORT abcefghjkmopqrstuwx ABC
OTHER LANGUAGES a
ACTIVITIES cefghjklmnoqstuvw AB
OTHER SUBJECTS abcdfh
FACILITIES ON SITE bcdeik
EXAM BOARDS ab ABDH
RETAKES **NVQ COURSES**

A-level cd ghi nop v
B GH K P R
c efg j l

AS d

GCSE d no v
B G K O R X
cdefg j l

OTHER l no q u
K NO R

Perse Prep. School; Trumpington Road; Cambridge CB2 2EX
Tel: 01223 568270 (Fax: 01223 568273) *P.C.S.Izzett*

		Boys	Age	Girls	Age	TOTAL		Boys	Girls
Day	£1462 ✗	171	7-11			171	SIXTH		
Weekly									
Boarding									

ENTRY REQUIREMENTS Exam
SCHOLARSHIPS & BURSARIES
SPECIAL NEEDS **DYSLEXIA** **DIET** a
ASSOCIATION IAPS **FOUNDED** 1910 **RELIGIOUS AFFILIATION** Inter-denom

MAP10 G 7
LOCATION Urban
DAY **RAIL** a **AIR** b
SPORT acefjox AB
OTHER LANGUAGES
ACTIVITIES fghijort A
OTHER SUBJECTS cfh
FACILITIES ON SITE
EXAM BOARDS
RETAKES **NVQ COURSES**

A-level **AS** **GCSE** **OTHER** de l n v
B G K O R
cde

87

CAMBRIDGESHIRE continued

G — Perse School for Girls; Union Road; Cambridge CB2 1HF
Tel: 01223 359589 (Fax: 01223 467420) Miss H.S.Smith

Day £1335-£1552 ✗
Weekly
Boarding

Boys	Age	Girls	Age	TOTAL		Boys	Girls
		710	7-18	710	SIXTH		124

ENTRY REQUIREMENTS Report & Exam & Interview
SCHOLARSHIPS & BURSARIES Burs; AP; VI Form
SPECIAL NEEDS ghjl
ASSOCIATION GSA   **FOUNDED** 1881   **RELIGIOUS AFFILIATION** Non-denom
DYSLEXIA   **DIET** a

MAP 10 G 7
LOCATION Inner City
DAY   **RAIL** a   **AIR** a
SPORT acfgklmpqwx AB
OTHER LANGUAGES
ACTIVITIES acfghijkost AB
OTHER SUBJECTS abcfh
FACILITIES ON SITE bcg
EXAM BOARDS bcd ABD
RETAKES   **NVQ COURSES**

A-level: c e g i nop v
B GH K P R W
cdefgh jkl

AS: c efg opq v
B G K R
c efgh jkl

GCSE: e g i no q v
B G K P R W
cdefgh jkl

OTHER: f lm u
MNO R U
i

Bg — Perse School,The; Hills Road; Cambridge CB2 2QF
Tel: 01223 568300 (Fax: 01223 568293) N.Richardson

Day £1508
Weekly
Boarding

Boys	Age	Girls	Age	TOTAL		Boys	Girls
472	11-18		16-18	472	SIXTH		123

ENTRY REQUIREMENTS Exam; Report & Interview
SCHOLARSHIPS & BURSARIES Schol; Burs; AP
SPECIAL NEEDS agjklqs l
ASSOCIATION HMC   **FOUNDED** 1615   **RELIGIOUS AFFILIATION**
DYSLEXIA   **DIET** ac

MAP 10 G 7
LOCATION Urban
DAY   **RAIL** a   **AIR** a
SPORT abcefgikmorstuwx AB
OTHER LANGUAGES
ACTIVITIES befghijklopqrstx B
OTHER SUBJECTS acdfh
FACILITIES ON SITE agk
EXAM BOARDS abd ABEH
RETAKES   **NVQ COURSES**

A-level: cd fghi p v
B GH K P
c efg j

AS:

GCSE: d g i v
B GH K P
cdefg jk

OTHER: wx
M O R
e k

Gb — Peterborough High School; Westwood House; Thorpe Road; Peterborough PE3 6JF
Tel: 01733 343357 Mrs A.J.V.Storey

Day £681-£1371
Weekly £2583-£2753
Boarding £2583-£2753

Boys	Age	Girls	Age	TOTAL		Boys	Girls
17	4-8	200	4-18	286	SIXTH		34
		19	8-18				
		50	8-18				

ENTRY REQUIREMENTS Exam & Interview
SCHOLARSHIPS & BURSARIES Schol; Teachers
SPECIAL NEEDS abjklw G
ASSOCIATION GSA   **FOUNDED** 1895   **RELIGIOUS AFFILIATION** C of E
DYSLEXIA   **DIET** a

MAP 9 F 6
LOCATION Urban
DAY ✓   **RAIL** a   **AIR** b
SPORT acfhklmpqrtvwx ABC
OTHER LANGUAGES
ACTIVITIES gijknopqst AB
OTHER SUBJECTS abcefh
FACILITIES ON SITE bdgh
EXAM BOARDS abcd ABDEJK
RETAKES   **NVQ COURSES**

A-level: c e g i l v
BC GH K P
c ef j

AS:

GCSE: c e g i l v
BC G K OP R U
cdef j

OTHER: n u
K M O R
l

G — St Catherine's Preparatory School; 1 Brookside; Cambridge CB2 1JE
Tel: 01223 311666 Mrs S.M.Salt

Day £1278 ✗
Weekly
Boarding

Boys	Age	Girls	Age	TOTAL		Boys	Girls
		100	7-11	100	SIXTH		

ENTRY REQUIREMENTS Exam
SCHOLARSHIPS & BURSARIES
SPECIAL NEEDS abfhjnt A
ASSOCIATION IAPS   **FOUNDED** 1987   **RELIGIOUS AFFILIATION** R C
DYSLEXIA   **DIET** a

MAP 10 G 7
LOCATION Inner City
DAY   **RAIL** a   **AIR** a
SPORT alpqx B
OTHER LANGUAGES
ACTIVITIES gjo A
OTHER SUBJECTS ch
FACILITIES ON SITE bi
EXAM BOARDS
RETAKES   **NVQ COURSES**

A-level:

AS:

GCSE:

OTHER: de lmno s v
BC G K O R
ef

C — St. Colette's Preparatory School; Tenison Road; Cambridge CB1 2DP
Tel: 01223 353696 Mrs B.Y.Boyton

Day £500-£1040 ✗
Weekly
Boarding

Boys	Age	Girls	Age	TOTAL		Boys	Girls
40	2-7	130	2-7	170	SIXTH		

ENTRY REQUIREMENTS
SCHOLARSHIPS & BURSARIES
SPECIAL NEEDS abfghkiqstuwx ABCGHIJKL
ASSOCIATION ISAI   **FOUNDED** 1920   **RELIGIOUS AFFILIATION** C of E
DYSLEXIA   **DIET** abcd

MAP 10 G 7
LOCATION Inner City
DAY   **RAIL** a   **AIR** a
SPORT x B
OTHER LANGUAGES
ACTIVITIES cg
OTHER SUBJECTS ch
FACILITIES ON SITE
EXAM BOARDS
RETAKES   **NVQ COURSES**

A-level:

AS:

GCSE:

OTHER:

CAMBRIDGESHIRE *continued*

St. Faith's; Cambridge CB2 2AG
Tel: 01223 352073 (Fax: 01223 314757) *R.A.Dyson* — **C**

		Boys	Age	Girls	Age	TOTAL		Boys	Girls
Day	£1290-£1640 ✗	380	4-13	40	4-13	420	SIXTH		
Weekly									
Boarding									

ENTRY REQUIREMENTS Assessment & Interview
SCHOLARSHIPS & BURSARIES AP
SPECIAL NEEDS abehjlnqtuw GH   **DYSLEXIA** e   **DIET** abcd
ASSOCIATION IAPS   **FOUNDED** 1884   **RELIGIOUS AFFILIATION** Inter-denom

MAP10 G 7
LOCATION Urban
DAY ✓   **RAIL** a   **AIR** a
SPORT abcefjklmopqsuwx ABC
OTHER LANGUAGES
ACTIVITIES fghijoqt A
OTHER SUBJECTS abcdfh
FACILITIES ON SITE bchik
EXAM BOARDS
RETAKES   **NVQ COURSES**

A-level — **AS** — **GCSE** — **OTHER** cdefg i klmno q s uvw / ABC G K OP R / cde g j

St. John's College School; 73 Grange Road; Cambridge CB3 9AB
Tel: 01223 353532 (Fax: 01223 315535) *K.L.Jones* — **C**

		Boys	Age	Girls	Age	TOTAL		Boys	Girls
Day	£1026-£1700 ✗	218	4-13	166	4-13	428	SIXTH		
Weekly	£2686								
Boarding	£2686	44	8-13						

ENTRY REQUIREMENTS
SCHOLARSHIPS & BURSARIES Burs; Chor
SPECIAL NEEDS abefhjklnpqtuv BEHI   **DYSLEXIA** def   **DIET** abcd
ASSOCIATION IAPS   **FOUNDED** 1660   **RELIGIOUS AFFILIATION** C of E

MAP10 G 7
LOCATION Urban
DAY   **RAIL** a   **AIR** a
SPORT abcefjklmopqrsuwx ABC
OTHER LANGUAGES
ACTIVITIES fghjklmopqrst A
OTHER SUBJECTS bcfgh
FACILITIES ON SITE acdehik
EXAM BOARDS
RETAKES   **NVQ COURSES**

A-level — **AS** — **GCSE** — **OTHER** bcde l no q v / B E G K O R / cde gh jkl

St. Mary's School; Bateman Street; Cambridge CB2 1LY
Tel: 01223 353253 (Fax: 01223 357451) *Miss Michele Conway* — **G**

		Boys	Age	Girls	Age	TOTAL		Boys	Girls
Day	£1290			506	11-18	571	SIXTH		109
Weekly	£1020			65	11-18				
Boarding									

ENTRY REQUIREMENTS Report & Exam & Interview
SCHOLARSHIPS & BURSARIES AP
SPECIAL NEEDS abefhjil H   **DYSLEXIA**   **DIET** a
ASSOCIATION GSA   **FOUNDED** 1898   **RELIGIOUS AFFILIATION** R C

MAP10 G 7
LOCATION Urban
DAY   **RAIL** a   **AIR** a
SPORT acdfhklmopqrwx ABC
OTHER LANGUAGES
ACTIVITIES acghijknost B
OTHER SUBJECTS abcfh
FACILITIES ON SITE acdghk
EXAM BOARDS abd ABEJ
RETAKES   **NVQ COURSES**

A-level c efg i n pq v / BC GH K P R T W / cdefgh l — **AS** c eg / G — **GCSE** c eg i n q v x / BC G K P R W / cdefgh j l — **OTHER** F l / i

Wisbech Grammar School; North Brink; Wisbech; Cambs. PE13 1JX
Tel: 01945 583631 (Fax: 01945 476746) *R.S.Repper* — **C**

		Boys	Age	Girls	Age	TOTAL		Boys	Girls
Day	£1550	332	11-18	306	11-18	638	SIXTH	80	73
Weekly									
Boarding									

ENTRY REQUIREMENTS Exam; Exam & Interview
SCHOLARSHIPS & BURSARIES AP
SPECIAL NEEDS bjlnqst CG   **DYSLEXIA**   **DIET** acd
ASSOCIATION HMC   **FOUNDED** 1379   **RELIGIOUS AFFILIATION** C of E

MAP10 G 5
LOCATION Urban
DAY   **RAIL** b   **AIR** b
SPORT abcefhklmopstuvwx ABC
OTHER LANGUAGES
ACTIVITIES cfghijklnopqstvw AB
OTHER SUBJECTS ach
FACILITIES ON SITE bcghik
EXAM BOARDS bd AB
RETAKES ab   **NVQ COURSES**

A-level e ghi l op v / BC GH K P R W / defg j — **AS** d f / G — **GCSE** e ghi l nopq v / ABC G K P R U W / cdefg j l — **OTHER** F

Elizabeth College; Guernsey; Channel Islands GY1 2PY
Tel: 01481 726544 (Fax: 01481 714839) *J.H.F.Doulton* — **Bg**

		Boys	Age	Girls	Age	TOTAL		Boys	Girls
Day	£820	652	7-18	10	16-18	705	SIXTH	137	10
Weekly	£1870								
Boarding	£2045	43	9-18						

ENTRY REQUIREMENTS CEE; Exam
SCHOLARSHIPS & BURSARIES Schol; Burs; Mus; Chor
SPECIAL NEEDS begjlqstw AHI   **DYSLEXIA**   **DIET**
ASSOCIATION HMC   **FOUNDED** 1563   **RELIGIOUS AFFILIATION** C of E

MAP 1 A 3
LOCATION Urban
DAY   **RAIL**   **AIR** a
SPORT abcdefghjkmstuwx ABC
OTHER LANGUAGES
ACTIVITIES defghijklmnopqstx AB
OTHER SUBJECTS abcfh
FACILITIES ON SITE abchj
EXAM BOARDS bd ABEH
RETAKES ab   **NVQ COURSES**

A-level cde g i op v x / AB GH K P R U / cdef j l — **AS** — **GCSE** cde o v / AB G K O R X / cdef hj l — **OTHER** e l no s u / G O R / g

CHANNEL IS.

CHANNEL ISLANDS continued

CHANNEL ISLANDS

Gb — Ladies College; Les Gravees; St. Peter Port; Guernsey; Channel Islands GY1 1RW
Tel: 01481 721602 (Fax: 01481 724209) *Miss M.E.Macdonald*

		Boys	Age	Girls	Age	TOTAL	SIXTH	Boys	Girls
Day	£310-£760	27	3-7	509	3-18	536			76
Weekly									
Boarding									

ENTRY REQUIREMENTS Report & Exam & Interview
SCHOLARSHIPS & BURSARIES Burs; AP
SPECIAL NEEDS belt   **DYSLEXIA**   **DIET**
ASSOCIATION GSA   **FOUNDED** 1872   **RELIGIOUS AFFILIATION** Non-denom

MAP 1 A 3
LOCATION Rural
DAY   **RAIL**   **AIR** a
SPORT acfghlmpqwx AB
OTHER LANGUAGES
ACTIVITIES ghijkno B
OTHER SUBJECTS abcdeh
FACILITIES ON SITE ghjk
EXAM BOARDS ad BEH
RETAKES   **NVQ COURSES**

A-level: cd ghi l n p   v
       B   GH K   P R   W
       cdefg j

AS: c g l p x
    G K W
    d g j

GCSE: a d g i l n v
      BC E G K OP R
      cdef h j l

OTHER: l n u
       C   O R

C — St. Michael's School; Five Oaks; Jersey; JE2 7UG
Tel: 01534 856904 (Fax: 01534 856620) *R de Figueiredo*

		Boys	Age	Girls	Age	TOTAL	SIXTH	Boys	Girls
Day	£1660-£2134	149	3-13	142	3-13	291			
Weekly									
Boarding									

ENTRY REQUIREMENTS Test & Interview
SCHOLARSHIPS & BURSARIES Burs
SPECIAL NEEDS bejklnqtuw Bl   **DYSLEXIA** de   **DIET** ac
ASSOCIATION IAPS   **FOUNDED** 1965   **RELIGIOUS AFFILIATION** Non-denom

MAP 1 C 4
LOCATION Rural
DAY   **RAIL**   **AIR** a
SPORT abcdefgjlmpqstwx ABC
OTHER LANGUAGES
ACTIVITIES afghijnoqstv A
OTHER SUBJECTS abcfh
FACILITIES ON SITE bchij
EXAM BOARDS
RETAKES   **NVQ COURSES**

A-level:

AS:

GCSE:

OTHER: e g i l n o q   v
       BC G K OP R W
       cdefg j

B — Victoria College Prep.School; Jersey; Channel Islands JE2 4RR
Tel: 01534 23468 (Fax: 01534 80596) *J.H.Hibbs*

		Boys	Age	Girls	Age	TOTAL	SIXTH	Boys	Girls
Day	£525	297	8-11			297			
Weekly									
Boarding									

ENTRY REQUIREMENTS Test & Interview
SCHOLARSHIPS & BURSARIES
SPECIAL NEEDS behijklqstu DGI   **DYSLEXIA**   **DIET** a
ASSOCIATION IAPS   **FOUNDED** 1922   **RELIGIOUS AFFILIATION** Christian

MAP 1 C 4
LOCATION Urban
DAY   **RAIL**   **AIR** a
SPORT acefgjklmswx B
OTHER LANGUAGES
ACTIVITIES fghijotx A
OTHER SUBJECTS bcfh
FACILITIES ON SITE bi
EXAM BOARDS
RETAKES   **NVQ COURSES**

A-level:

AS:

GCSE:

OTHER: lm o   v
       B G K
       cde

B — Victoria College; St.Helier; Jersey; Channel Islands; JE2 4RA
Tel: 01534 37591 (Fax: 01534 27448) *J.Hydes*

		Boys	Age	Girls	Age	TOTAL	SIXTH	Boys	Girls
Day	£575	598	11-18			608			148
Weekly									
Boarding		10							

ENTRY REQUIREMENTS CEE; Exam
SCHOLARSHIPS & BURSARIES Schol
SPECIAL NEEDS bl   **DYSLEXIA**   **DIET** abcd
ASSOCIATION GBA   **FOUNDED** 1852   **RELIGIOUS AFFILIATION** Christian

MAP 1 C 4
LOCATION Urban
DAY   **RAIL**   **AIR** a
SPORT abcdefijkmstuwx AB
OTHER LANGUAGES
ACTIVITIES efghjknopqsx AB
OTHER SUBJECTS bcdh
FACILITIES ON SITE bgik
EXAM BOARDS bcd ABDH
RETAKES   **NVQ COURSES**

A-level: e ghi   nopq uvwx
         AB GH K M P R T
         c ef   l

AS:

GCSE: e g i l n o q   v
      AB E G K   P R U
      cdef   l

OTHER: O

CHESHIRE

C — Abbey Gate College; Saighton Grange; Saighton; Chester CH3 6EG
Tel: 01244 332077 (Fax: 01244 332677) *E.W.Mitchell*

		Boys	Age	Girls	Age	TOTAL	SIXTH	Boys	Girls
Day	£840-£1340	198	8-18	150	8-18	348		34	38
Weekly									
Boarding									

ENTRY REQUIREMENTS Exam
SCHOLARSHIPS & BURSARIES Schol; Burs; Mus; Chor
SPECIAL NEEDS n   **DYSLEXIA** e   **DIET**
ASSOCIATION SHMIS   **FOUNDED** 1977   **RELIGIOUS AFFILIATION**

MAP 8 H 2
LOCATION Rural
DAY   **RAIL** b   **AIR** b
SPORT aefjmpqsx AB
OTHER LANGUAGES
ACTIVITIES fghijkoq AB
OTHER SUBJECTS bcdeh
FACILITIES ON SITE abdgh
EXAM BOARDS abcd ADEGHI
RETAKES   **NVQ COURSES**

A-level: e ghi   o   uv x
         AB   GH K   PQ
         cdef j l

AS:

GCSE: e g i   o   v
      ABC G K N P
      cdef   j l

OTHER:

CHESHIRE *continued*

C — Abbey Gate School; Victoria Road; Chester CH2 2AY
Tel: 01244 380552 *Mrs S.T.Gill*

	Boys	Age	Girls	Age	TOTAL		Boys	Girls
Day £575- £605	62	3-11	74	3-11	136	SIXTH		
Weekly								
Boarding								

MAP 8 H 2
LOCATION Inner City
DAY   RAIL a   AIR a
SPORT ejpqx B
OTHER LANGUAGES
ACTIVITIES cfjo
OTHER SUBJECTS ch
FACILITIES ON SITE
EXAM BOARDS
RETAKES   NVQ COURSES

ENTRY REQUIREMENTS Interview
SCHOLARSHIPS & BURSARIES
SPECIAL NEEDS abeghjklnuw Al
DYSLEXIA g   **DIET** abcd
ASSOCIATION ISAI   **FOUNDED** 1910   **RELIGIOUS AFFILIATION** C of E

A-level   AS   GCSE   OTHER   e   o   v
                              B G   O
                              cde

B — Altrincham Prep. School; Highbury; 6 West Road; Bowdon; Altrincham; Cheshire WA14 2LE
Tel: 0161 928 3366 (Fax: 0161 929 6747) *R.J.Mc Cay*

	Boys	Age	Girls	Age	TOTAL		Boys	Girls
Day £775- £950	297	4-12			297	SIXTH		
Weekly								
Boarding								

MAP11 E 8
LOCATION Urban
DAY   RAIL b   AIR a
SPORT abefjnswx AB
OTHER LANGUAGES
ACTIVITIES fgiq
OTHER SUBJECTS
FACILITIES ON SITE
EXAM BOARDS
RETAKES   NVQ COURSES

ENTRY REQUIREMENTS Test & Interview
SCHOLARSHIPS & BURSARIES
SPECIAL NEEDS
DYSLEXIA   **DIET** c
ASSOCIATION ISAI   **FOUNDED** 1936   **RELIGIOUS AFFILIATION** Inter-denom

A-level   AS   GCSE   OTHER   de   l   v
                              B G   O
                              cde j

C — Beech Hall School; Beech Hall Drive; Macclesfield; Cheshire SK10 2EG
Tel: 01625 422192 (Fax: 01625 502424) *J.S.Fitz-Gerald*

	Boys	Age	Girls	Age	TOTAL		Boys	Girls
Day £950-£1495 X	127	2-13	77	2-13	204	SIXTH		
Weekly								
Boarding								

MAP 8 J 2
LOCATION Urban
DAY   RAIL a   AIR a
SPORT abcdejlmpqsuwx AB
OTHER LANGUAGES
ACTIVITIES acghjpt A
OTHER SUBJECTS c
FACILITIES ON SITE bchjk
EXAM BOARDS
RETAKES   NVQ COURSES

ENTRY REQUIREMENTS Interview
SCHOLARSHIPS & BURSARIES Burs
SPECIAL NEEDS nw l
DYSLEXIA e   **DIET** a
ASSOCIATION IAPS   **FOUNDED** 1926   **RELIGIOUS AFFILIATION** C of E

A-level   AS   GCSE   OTHER   e   o   v
                              B G K O R
                              cde g j

C — Brabyns School; 34/36 Arkwright Road; Marple; Cheshire SK6 7DB
Tel: 0161 427 2395 *Mrs A.D.Briggs*

	Boys	Age	Girls	Age	TOTAL		Boys	Girls
Day £510- £782	90	2-11	95	2-11	185	SIXTH		
Weekly								
Boarding								

MAP 8 J 1
LOCATION Rural
DAY   RAIL b   AIR a
SPORT aefjlmpqx B
OTHER LANGUAGES
ACTIVITIES cfgjo
OTHER SUBJECTS ch
FACILITIES ON SITE
EXAM BOARDS
RETAKES   NVQ COURSES

ENTRY REQUIREMENTS Assessment & Interview
SCHOLARSHIPS & BURSARIES
SPECIAL NEEDS
DYSLEXIA   **DIET** a
ASSOCIATION ISAI   **FOUNDED** 1899   **RELIGIOUS AFFILIATION** Non-denom

A-level   AS   GCSE   OTHER   e   Imno st v
                              B G K O R
                              cd

C — Cheadle Hulme School; Claremont Road; Cheadle Hulme; Cheadle; Cheshire SK8 6EF
Tel: 0161 485 4142 (Fax: 0161 488 4540) *D.J.Wilkinson*

	Boys	Age	Girls	Age	TOTAL		Boys	Girls
Day £1091-£1362	558	7-18	571	7-18	1129	SIXTH	114	121
Weekly								
Boarding								

MAP 8 J 1
LOCATION Urban
DAY   RAIL a   AIR a
SPORT acekmnopswx B
OTHER LANGUAGES
ACTIVITIES acfghijloqrt A
OTHER SUBJECTS bcdfh
FACILITIES ON SITE bci
EXAM BOARDS bcd ABD
RETAKES   NVQ COURSES

ENTRY REQUIREMENTS Exam & Interview
SCHOLARSHIPS & BURSARIES Art; Mus; AP
SPECIAL NEEDS bklqst
DYSLEXIA   **DIET** abcd
ASSOCIATION HMC   **FOUNDED** 1855   **RELIGIOUS AFFILIATION** Non-denom

A-level   e ghi   n p   uvwx   AS   GCSE e ghi   no   v   OTHER
        ABC GH K   P R U   ABC   G JK   P U
        cdefgh j l   cdefgh j l

CHESHIRE continued

Cransley School; Belmont Hall; Great Budworth; Northwich; Cheshire CW9 6NQ
Tel: 01606 891747 (Fax: 01606 892122) M.A.Eagar

		Boys	Age	Girls	Age	TOTAL	SIXTH Boys	Girls
Day	£770-£1385	15	3-11	177	3-16	192		
Weekly								
Boarding								

MAP 8 | 2
LOCATION Rural
DAY ✓ **RAIL** b **AIR** a
SPORT abcfhjlmpqx ABC
OTHER LANGUAGES
ACTIVITIES cghijknotw AB

ENTRY REQUIREMENTS Assessment; Exam & Interview
SCHOLARSHIPS & BURSARIES Schol; Burs; Mus; Teachers
SPECIAL NEEDS aefijnq B   **DYSLEXIA** e   **DIET** abd
ASSOCIATION ISAI   **FOUNDED** 1953   **RELIGIOUS AFFILIATION**

OTHER SUBJECTS bcdfgh
FACILITIES ON SITE bfh
EXAM BOARDS bc H
RETAKES a   **NVQ COURSES**

A-level
AS
GCSE de g i n v
BC G K P
cde l
OTHER l
H
jk

Culcheth Hall; Ashley Road; Altrincham; Cheshire WA14 2LT
Tel: 0161 928 1862 (Fax: 0161 929 6893)

		Boys	Age	Girls	Age	TOTAL	SIXTH Boys	Girls
Day	£620-£1230	11	2-4	218	2-18	229		13
Weekly								
Boarding								

MAP 8 | 1
LOCATION Urban
DAY ✓ **RAIL** a **AIR** a
SPORT abcfhlmpqwx BC
OTHER LANGUAGES
ACTIVITIES cfghijkot A

ENTRY REQUIREMENTS Test & Interview; Report & Exam & Interview
SCHOLARSHIPS & BURSARIES Schol; Burs; VI Form
SPECIAL NEEDS bjln A   **DYSLEXIA** f   **DIET**
ASSOCIATION ISAI   **FOUNDED** 1891   **RELIGIOUS AFFILIATION** Non-denom

OTHER SUBJECTS abcfgh
FACILITIES ON SITE bcgh
EXAM BOARDS c DL
RETAKES a   **NVQ COURSES**

A-level d g i uv
BC GH K P R X
c ef l
AS d g i l u
ef l
GCSE B G l v
BC G K R X
cdef l
OTHER l

Forest Park School; Lauriston House; 27 Oakfield; Sale M33 6NB
Tel: 0161 973 4835 (Fax: 0161 282 9021) Mrs R.Smart

		Boys	Age	Girls	Age	TOTAL	SIXTH Boys	Girls
Day	£785-£890 X	72	3-11	40	3-11	112		
Weekly								
Boarding								

MAP 11 E 8
LOCATION Urban
DAY **RAIL** a **AIR** a
SPORT ejpqx B
OTHER LANGUAGES
ACTIVITIES g

ENTRY REQUIREMENTS Interview
SCHOLARSHIPS & BURSARIES
SPECIAL NEEDS abl   **DYSLEXIA**   **DIET** ad
ASSOCIATION ISAI   **FOUNDED** 1989   **RELIGIOUS AFFILIATION** Non-denom

OTHER SUBJECTS
FACILITIES ON SITE
EXAM BOARDS
RETAKES   **NVQ COURSES**

A-level
AS
GCSE
OTHER

Forest School; Moss Lane; Timperley; Altrincham; Cheshire WA15 6LJ
Tel: 0161 980 4075 (Fax: 0161 903 9275) Mrs J.Quest

		Boys	Age	Girls	Age	TOTAL	SIXTH Boys	Girls
Day	£785-£890 X	101	3-11	62	3-11	163		
Weekly								
Boarding								

MAP 11 E 8
LOCATION Urban
DAY **RAIL** a **AIR** a
SPORT acjlpqx B
OTHER LANGUAGES
ACTIVITIES cfg

ENTRY REQUIREMENTS Assessment & Interview
SCHOLARSHIPS & BURSARIES
SPECIAL NEEDS l   **DYSLEXIA**   **DIET** acd
ASSOCIATION ISAI   **FOUNDED** 1924   **RELIGIOUS AFFILIATION** Inter-denom

OTHER SUBJECTS ch
FACILITIES ON SITE
EXAM BOARDS
RETAKES   **NVQ COURSES**

A-level
AS
GCSE
OTHER e l n v
B G K O
cde

Grange School, The; Bradburns Lane; Hartford; Northwich; Cheshire CW8 1LU
Tel: 01606 74007 (Fax: 01606 784581) E.S.Marshall

		Boys	Age	Girls	Age	TOTAL	SIXTH Boys	Girls
Day	£825-£1155	536	4-18	554	4-18	1090	60	69
Weekly								
Boarding								

MAP 8 | 2
LOCATION Urban
DAY **RAIL** a **AIR** a
SPORT abcefhjklmpqrswx AB
OTHER LANGUAGES
ACTIVITIES cfghijkorst AB

ENTRY REQUIREMENTS Exam & Interview
SCHOLARSHIPS & BURSARIES Schol; Burs; Mus; VI Form; Sport; Drama
SPECIAL NEEDS   **DYSLEXIA**   **DIET** a
ASSOCIATION ISAI   **FOUNDED** 1933   **RELIGIOUS AFFILIATION** Christian

OTHER SUBJECTS ch
FACILITIES ON SITE bchk
EXAM BOARDS bcde ABDEH
RETAKES   **NVQ COURSES**

A-level defghi l nop s uv x
BC GH K M P R
c ef jl
AS et l
GCSE cde g i l no v
BC G K P R W
cdef jl
OTHER

CHESHIRE *continued*

C — Greenbank School; Heathbank Road; Cheadle Hulme; Cheadle; Cheshire SK8 6HU
Tel: 0161 485 3724 (Fax: 0161 485 5519) *N Brown*

	Boys	Age	Girls	Age	TOTAL	Boys	Girls
Day £557- £962	111	2-11	73	2-11	184		
Weekly							
Boarding							

MAP 8 J 1
LOCATION Urban
DAY ✓ RAIL a AIR a
SPORT aejmpqsx B
OTHER LANGUAGES
ACTIVITIES fghjo
OTHER SUBJECTS ch
FACILITIES ON SITE h
EXAM BOARDS
RETAKES   NVQ COURSES

ENTRY REQUIREMENTS Assessment & Interview
SCHOLARSHIPS & BURSARIES Siblings
SPECIAL NEEDS bhlns   DYSLEXIA e   DIET
ASSOCIATION ISAI   FOUNDED 1951   RELIGIOUS AFFILIATION Non-denom

A-level | AS | GCSE cde: e n v / B G K O | OTHER

C — Hale Prep. School; Broomfield Lane; Hale; Altrincham; Cheshire WA15 9AS
Tel: 0161 928 2386 *J.F.Connor*

	Boys	Age	Girls	Age	TOTAL	Boys	Girls
Day £815	110	4-10	72	4-10	182		
Weekly							
Boarding							

MAP 11 E 8
LOCATION Urban
DAY ✓ RAIL a AIR a
SPORT acefjpqx B
OTHER LANGUAGES
ACTIVITIES cgj A
OTHER SUBJECTS ch
FACILITIES ON SITE
EXAM BOARDS
RETAKES   NVQ COURSES

ENTRY REQUIREMENTS Assessment & Interview
SCHOLARSHIPS & BURSARIES
SPECIAL NEEDS   DYSLEXIA   DIET ac
ASSOCIATION ISAI   FOUNDED 1980   RELIGIOUS AFFILIATION

A-level | AS | GCSE cde: e l v / B G | OTHER

Gb — Hammond School; Hoole Bank House; Mannings Lane; Hoole; Chester CH2 2PB
Tel: 01244 328542 (Fax: 01244 315845) *Mrs M.P.Dangerfield*

	Boys	Age	Girls	Age	TOTAL	Boys	Girls
Day £1280			85	11-15	120		
Weekly £1110							
Boarding £1550	7	11-15	28	11-15			

MAP 8 H 2
LOCATION
DAY ✓ RAIL a AIR a
SPORT almpqx B
OTHER LANGUAGES
ACTIVITIES cgjoqs
OTHER SUBJECTS abcdh
FACILITIES ON SITE b
EXAM BOARDS ac
RETAKES   NVQ COURSES

ENTRY REQUIREMENTS Exam
SCHOLARSHIPS & BURSARIES Burs
SPECIAL NEEDS abn G   DYSLEXIA g   DIET abcd
ASSOCIATION ISAI   FOUNDED 1962   RELIGIOUS AFFILIATION C of E

A-level | AS | GCSE: de g i v / BC E G K P X / cde | OTHER: h lmn s / f NO R

C — Hillcrest Grammar School; Beech Avenue; Stockport; Cheshire SK3 8HB
Tel: 0161 480 0329 (Fax: 0161 476 2814) *D.K.Blackburn*

	Boys	Age	Girls	Age	TOTAL	Boys	Girls
Day £755-£1040	212	3-16	103	3-16	315		
Weekly							
Boarding							

MAP 8 J 1
LOCATION Urban
DAY ✓ RAIL a AIR a
SPORT abcefjlmpqx AB
OTHER LANGUAGES
ACTIVITIES cfghijoqt A
OTHER SUBJECTS bcfgh
FACILITIES ON SITE h
EXAM BOARDS bcde
RETAKES   NVQ COURSES

ENTRY REQUIREMENTS Assessment & Interview
SCHOLARSHIPS & BURSARIES Burs; Teachers
SPECIAL NEEDS n GL   DYSLEXIA e   DIET
ASSOCIATION ISAI   FOUNDED 1940   RELIGIOUS AFFILIATION Non-denom

A-level | AS | GCSE: de g i l uv / BC E G K OP / cde l | OTHER

C — Hulme Hall Schools; 75 Hulme Hall Road; Cheadle Hulme SK8 6LA
Tel: 0161 485 3524 (Fax: 0161 485 5966) *G.Kellock*

	Boys	Age	Girls	Age	TOTAL	Boys	Girls
Day £630-£1190	291	2-16	169	2-16	460		
Weekly							
Boarding							

MAP 8 J 1
LOCATION Urban
DAY ✓ RAIL b AIR a
SPORT abcefhjlmopqwx ABC
OTHER LANGUAGES a
ACTIVITIES fghjoqs A
OTHER SUBJECTS bcdefgh
FACILITIES ON SITE abchk
EXAM BOARDS acde AL
RETAKES a   NVQ COURSES

ENTRY REQUIREMENTS Test & Interview
SCHOLARSHIPS & BURSARIES
SPECIAL NEEDS abfijklnpqtuw ABCDHIJ   DYSLEXIA e   DIET acd
ASSOCIATION ISAI   FOUNDED 1929   RELIGIOUS AFFILIATION

A-level | AS | GCSE: d g i l no v / ABC E G K OP / cdef l | OTHER: mn v / d O

CHESHIRE continued

B | King's School; Chester CH4 7QL
Tel: 01244 680026 (Fax: 01244 678008) *A.R.D.Wickson*

Day	£880-£1344	Boys 671	Age 7-18	Girls	Age	TOTAL 671	SIXTH	Boys 142	Girls
Weekly									
Boarding									

ENTRY REQUIREMENTS Exam
SCHOLARSHIPS & BURSARIES Schol; Burs; AP
SPECIAL NEEDS abeghjlqst ADGHIKL
ASSOCIATION HMC **FOUNDED** 1541 **RELIGIOUS AFFILIATION** C of E **DYSLEXIA** **DIET** abcd

MAP 8 H 2
LOCATION Urban
DAY **RAIL** a **AIR** a
SPORT abcdefghjklmrswx ABC
OTHER LANGUAGES a
ACTIVITIES efghijknoq AB
OTHER SUBJECTS bc
FACILITIES ON SITE bcghi
EXAM BOARDS abcd D
RETAKES **NVQ COURSES**

A-level	c e g i p u v B GH K P R cdef j l	AS	e R	GCSE	e o v B G K R X cdef j l	OTHER	f l q A O U

C | King's School,The; Macclesfield; Cheshire SK10 1DA
Tel: 01625 618586 (Fax: 01625 614784) *A.G.Silcock*

Day	£1110-£1415	Boys 933	Age 7-18	Girls 322	Age 7-18	TOTAL 1255	SIXTH	Boys 221	Girls 58
Weekly									
Boarding									

ENTRY REQUIREMENTS CEE; Report & Interview; Report & Exam & Interview
SCHOLARSHIPS & BURSARIES Schol; Burs; Mus; AP
SPECIAL NEEDS ajlq G
ASSOCIATION HMC **FOUNDED** 1502 **RELIGIOUS AFFILIATION** C of E **DYSLEXIA** **DIET** acd

MAP 8 J 2
LOCATION Urban
DAY **RAIL** a **AIR** a
SPORT abcefhjklmpqstwx AB
OTHER LANGUAGES
ACTIVITIES fghijkmnopqrstu ABD
OTHER SUBJECTS abcdfh
FACILITIES ON SITE abcghik
EXAM BOARDS bc BDH
RETAKES **NVQ COURSES**

A-level	d e ghi l nop uvw AB GH K P R U c ef j	AS	g l s d	GCSE	d e g i l no v AB G K P R U cdef j l	OTHER	d g i l n u K NOP R f

C | Lady Barn House School; Schools Hill; Cheadle; Cheshire SK8 1JE
Tel: 0161 428 2912 (Fax: 0161 428 5798) *E.J.Bonner*

Day	£530-£915	Boys 250	Age 3-10	Girls 186	Age 3-10	TOTAL 436	SIXTH	Boys	Girls
Weekly									
Boarding									

ENTRY REQUIREMENTS Interview; Assessment
SCHOLARSHIPS & BURSARIES
SPECIAL NEEDS
ASSOCIATION ISAI **FOUNDED** 1873 **RELIGIOUS AFFILIATION** Inter-denom **DYSLEXIA** **DIET** ab

MAP 8 J 1
LOCATION Urban
DAY **RAIL** b **AIR** a
SPORT abdefjlnpqstux
OTHER LANGUAGES
ACTIVITIES cgjoq
OTHER SUBJECTS ch
FACILITIES ON SITE h
EXAM BOARDS
RETAKES **NVQ COURSES**

A-level		AS		GCSE		OTHER	e lmno v B E G K O R cde

Gb | Loreto Convent Preparatory School; Dunham Road; Altrincham; Cheshire WA14 4AH
Tel: 0161 928 8310 *Sister Catherine A.Fay*

Day	£610	Boys 11	Age 4-7	Girls 185	Age 4-11	TOTAL 196	SIXTH	Boys	Girls
Weekly									
Boarding									

ENTRY REQUIREMENTS Test & Interview
SCHOLARSHIPS & BURSARIES
SPECIAL NEEDS n
ASSOCIATION ISAI **FOUNDED** 1909 **RELIGIOUS AFFILIATION** R C **DYSLEXIA** g **DIET**

MAP 11 E 8
LOCATION Urban
DAY ✓ **RAIL** b **AIR** a
SPORT aflpqx B
OTHER LANGUAGES
ACTIVITIES go
OTHER SUBJECTS ch
FACILITIES ON SITE
EXAM BOARDS
RETAKES **NVQ COURSES**

A-level		AS		GCSE		OTHER	e lmno s v B G K O R cd

C | Mostyn House School; Parkgate; South Wirral; Cheshire L64 6SG
Tel: 0151 336 1010 (Fax: 0151 353 1040) *A.D.J.Grenfell*

Day	£440-£1495	Boys 182	Age 4-18	Girls 136	Age 4-18	TOTAL 318	SIXTH	Boys 25	Girls 20
Weekly									
Boarding									

ENTRY REQUIREMENTS Exam; Interview
SCHOLARSHIPS & BURSARIES Schol
SPECIAL NEEDS bejklnpqw BGI
ASSOCIATION ISAI **FOUNDED** 1854 **RELIGIOUS AFFILIATION** Inter-denom **DYSLEXIA** de **DIET** a

MAP 8 G 2
LOCATION Urban
DAY ✓ **RAIL** b **AIR** a
SPORT abcefjlmpquwx BC
OTHER LANGUAGES a
ACTIVITIES cdfghijknos B
OTHER SUBJECTS abcdh
FACILITIES ON SITE bcdgik
EXAM BOARDS ce ABDEGHK
RETAKES ab **NVQ COURSES**

A-level	e ghi l nop uv BC G K OP cde j l	AS		GCSE	d lm o v BC E G K O U cde j l	OTHER	

CHESHIRE continued

Mount Carmel Junior School; Wilmslow Road; Alderley Edge SK9 7QE
Tel: 01625 583028 (Fax: 01625 590271) *Mrs.M.Y.Debio*

		Boys	Age	Girls	Age	TOTAL		Boys	Girls
Day	£750- £936	11	4- 7	160	4-11	171	SIXTH		
Weekly									
Boarding									

ENTRY REQUIREMENTS Interview; Report; Assessment
SCHOLARSHIPS & BURSARIES
SPECIAL NEEDS   **DYSLEXIA**   **DIET** a
ASSOCIATION ISAI   **FOUNDED** 1945   **RELIGIOUS AFFILIATION** R C

MAP 8 | 2
LOCATION Rural
DAY   **RAIL** a   **AIR** a
SPORT aflmpqx B
OTHER LANGUAGES
ACTIVITIES cfgh
OTHER SUBJECTS ch
FACILITIES ON SITE b
EXAM BOARDS
RETAKES   **NVQ COURSES**

A-level	AS	GCSE	OTHER
			e l o v B G K O R de

Mount Carmel School; Wilmslow Road; Alderley Edge SK9 7QE
Tel: 01625 583028 (Fax: 01625 590271) *Mrs K.Mills*

		Boys	Age	Girls	Age	TOTAL		Boys	Girls
Day	£1196			373	11-18	373	SIXTH		83
Weekly									
Boarding									

ENTRY REQUIREMENTS Exam
SCHOLARSHIPS & BURSARIES Schol; AP; VI Form
SPECIAL NEEDS   **DYSLEXIA**   **DIET**
ASSOCIATION GBGSA   **FOUNDED** 1945   **RELIGIOUS AFFILIATION** R C

MAP 8 | 2
LOCATION Rural
DAY   **RAIL** a   **AIR** a
SPORT acmpwx AB
OTHER LANGUAGES
ACTIVITIES cghijko A
OTHER SUBJECTS bcdh
FACILITIES ON SITE
EXAM BOARDS acd AD
RETAKES   **NVQ COURSES**

A-level	AS	GCSE	OTHER
e ghi p uv x BC GH K P R U cdef j	e g B G K ef	u	e g i p v x BC G K P R U cdef j	l h l

North Cestrian Grammar School; Dunham Road; Altrincham; Cheshire WA14 4AJ
Tel: 0161 928 1856 *P.F.Morton*

		Boys	Age	Girls	Age	TOTAL		Boys	Girls
Day	£1150	364	11-18			364	SIXTH	60	
Weekly									
Boarding									

ENTRY REQUIREMENTS Exam
SCHOLARSHIPS & BURSARIES Schol; Siblings
SPECIAL NEEDS bfn   **DYSLEXIA** f   **DIET** abcd
ASSOCIATION ISAI   **FOUNDED** 1951   **RELIGIOUS AFFILIATION**

MAP11 E 8
LOCATION Urban
DAY √   **RAIL** a   **AIR** a
SPORT abcefjklmx ABC
OTHER LANGUAGES
ACTIVITIES fghijknoqrst A
OTHER SUBJECTS cf
FACILITIES ON SITE bgh
EXAM BOARDS c ADH
RETAKES   **NVQ COURSES**

A-level	AS	GCSE	OTHER
e g i p uv B G K P cde		e g i p v B G K N P cdef j l	

Oriel Bank High School; Devonshire Park Road; Davenport; Stockport SK2 6JP
Tel: 0161 483 2935 *Mrs A.P.Perrett*

		Boys	Age	Girls	Age	TOTAL		Boys	Girls
Day	£485-£1180			193	3-16	193	SIXTH		
Weekly									
Boarding									

ENTRY REQUIREMENTS
SCHOLARSHIPS & BURSARIES Siblings
SPECIAL NEEDS abcjklnpqtw BGHI   **DYSLEXIA** g   **DIET** abcd
ASSOCIATION ISAI   **FOUNDED** 1887   **RELIGIOUS AFFILIATION** C of E

MAP 8 J 1
LOCATION Urban
DAY √   **RAIL** a   **AIR** a
SPORT abcfhklmpqwx ABC
OTHER LANGUAGES
ACTIVITIES cghijknoqt A
OTHER SUBJECTS abcdefh
FACILITIES ON SITE abch
EXAM BOARDS c
RETAKES   **NVQ COURSES**

A-level	AS	GCSE	OTHER
		de g i l o v BC E G K P R W cdef	n o

Pownall Hall School; Carrwood Road; Wilmslow; Cheshire SK9 5DW
Tel: 01625 523141 (Fax: 01625 525209) *J.J.Meadmore*

		Boys	Age	Girls	Age	TOTAL		Boys	Girls
Day	£400-£1425 ✕	192	3-13			192	SIXTH		
Weekly									
Boarding									

ENTRY REQUIREMENTS Interview; Assessment & Interview
SCHOLARSHIPS & BURSARIES Clergy; Teachers
SPECIAL NEEDS bglnuw B   **DYSLEXIA** ce   **DIET** abcd
ASSOCIATION IAPS   **FOUNDED** 1895   **RELIGIOUS AFFILIATION** Inter-denom

MAP 8 | 2
LOCATION
DAY   **RAIL** a   **AIR** a
SPORT abcdefjklmnqwx ABC
OTHER LANGUAGES
ACTIVITIES fghijmopqrtw A
OTHER SUBJECTS abcfh
FACILITIES ON SITE bchjk
EXAM BOARDS
RETAKES   **NVQ COURSES**

A-level	AS	GCSE	OTHER
			e g i l no v B G K P R cde g j

CHESHIRE continued

Gb Queen's School,The; City Walls Road; Chester CH1 2NN
Tel: 01244 312078 (Fax: 01244 321507) *Miss D.M.Skilbeck*

		Boys	Age	Girls	Age	TOTAL	SIXTH Boys	Girls
Day	£795-£1440	26	5- 8	608	4-18	634		115
Weekly								
Boarding								

ENTRY REQUIREMENTS Exam
SCHOLARSHIPS & BURSARIES Burs; AP
SPECIAL NEEDS **DYSLEXIA** **DIET** acd
ASSOCIATION GSA **FOUNDED** 1878 **RELIGIOUS AFFILIATION** C of E

MAP 8 H 2
LOCATION
DAY **RAIL** a **AIR**
SPORT acefhjlmnopqwx ABC
OTHER LANGUAGES
ACTIVITIES fghijko AB
OTHER SUBJECTS bch
FACILITIES ON SITE bi
EXAM BOARDS acd D
RETAKES **NVQ COURSES**

A-level	cde ghi p uv	AS	GCSE cde g i v	OTHER l o
	BC GH K P R U		BC G K P R X	
	c efg j e		cdefgh j l	

C Ramillies Hall; Cheadle Hulme; Cheshire SK8 7AJ
Tel: 0161 485 3804 (Fax: 0161 485 3804) *Mrs A.L.Poole & M.F.Brown*

		Boys	Age	Girls	Age	TOTAL	SIXTH Boys	Girls
Day	£985-£1285 X	60	2-13	41	2-13	121		
Weekly	£2050-£2300	5	6-13		6-13			
Boarding	£2200-£2500	9	6-13	6	6-13			

ENTRY REQUIREMENTS Assessment; Report & Interview
SCHOLARSHIPS & BURSARIES Forces
SPECIAL NEEDS bjklnw BEGI **DYSLEXIA** cdef **DIET** acd
ASSOCIATION IAPS **FOUNDED** 1884 **RELIGIOUS AFFILIATION** Inter-denom

MAP 8 J 1
LOCATION Rural
DAY **RAIL** a **AIR** a
SPORT adefjmpqsx AB
OTHER LANGUAGES a
ACTIVITIES cghijnpqw
OTHER SUBJECTS abch
FACILITIES ON SITE bcj
EXAM BOARDS
RETAKES **NVQ COURSES**

A-level	AS	GCSE	OTHER e g i lmno v
			BCDE G K OP R
			cde

B Ryleys,The; Alderley Edge; Cheshire SK9 7UY
Tel: 01625 583241 (Fax: 01625 583241) *J.C.Mackay*

		Boys	Age	Girls	Age	TOTAL	SIXTH Boys	Girls
Day	£720-£1350 X	272	3-13			272		
Weekly			8-13					
Boarding								

ENTRY REQUIREMENTS
SCHOLARSHIPS & BURSARIES
SPECIAL NEEDS jkln l **DYSLEXIA** e **DIET** abcd
ASSOCIATION IAPS **FOUNDED** 1877 **RELIGIOUS AFFILIATION** Non-denom

MAP 8 I 2
LOCATION Rural
DAY **RAIL** a **AIR** a
SPORT abcdefjkmsx ABC
OTHER LANGUAGES
ACTIVITIES afghijnopq A
OTHER SUBJECTS abch
FACILITIES ON SITE bchjk
EXAM BOARDS
RETAKES **NVQ COURSES**

A-level	AS	GCSE	OTHER e g i no q v
			B E G K OP RS
			cde g j

B St Ambrose College; Wicker Lane; Hale Barns; Altrincham; Cheshire WA15 0HE
Tel: 0161 980 2711 (Fax: 0161 980 2323) *G.E.Hester*

		Boys	Age	Girls	Age	TOTAL	SIXTH Boys	Girls
Day	£820-£1150	908	4-18			908		152
Weekly								
Boarding								

ENTRY REQUIREMENTS Exam
SCHOLARSHIPS & BURSARIES
SPECIAL NEEDS bjl l **DYSLEXIA** **DIET** abcd
ASSOCIATION HMC **FOUNDED** 1946 **RELIGIOUS AFFILIATION** R C

MAP 11 E 8
LOCATION Urban
DAY ✓ **RAIL** b **AIR** a
SPORT abcefhkloswx AB
OTHER LANGUAGES
ACTIVITIES fghijlnogrs A
OTHER SUBJECTS bch
FACILITIES ON SITE cgi
EXAM BOARDS bc D
RETAKES b **NVQ COURSES**

A-level	de ghi l p uv x	AS g l	GCSE cde g i l o v	OTHER
	B GH K OP R U		B G K OP R U	
	c ef j	h l	cdef hj l	

C St. Catherine's Preparatory School; Hollins Lane; Marple Bridge; Stockport; Cheshire SK6 5BB
Tel: 0161 449 8800 (Fax: 0161 449 8800) *Mrs M.A.Sidwell*

		Boys	Age	Girls	Age	TOTAL	SIXTH Boys	Girls
Day	£705- £740	80	3-11	81	3-11	161		
Weekly								
Boarding								

ENTRY REQUIREMENTS Assessment & Interview
SCHOLARSHIPS & BURSARIES
SPECIAL NEEDS **DYSLEXIA** **DIET**
ASSOCIATION ISAI **FOUNDED** 1977 **RELIGIOUS AFFILIATION** RC/Christian

MAP 8 J 1
LOCATION Urban
DAY **RAIL** a **AIR** a
SPORT efjlpqx
OTHER LANGUAGES
ACTIVITIES cfgh
OTHER SUBJECTS ach
FACILITIES ON SITE
EXAM BOARDS
RETAKES **NVQ COURSES**

A-level	AS	GCSE	OTHER

CHESHIRE continued

St. Hilary's School; Alderley Edge; Cheshire SK9 7AG
Tel: 01625 583532 (Fax: 01625 586110) *Mrs G.M.Case*

		Boys	Age	Girls 254	Age 3-18	TOTAL 254	SIXTH	Boys	Girls 26
Day Weekly Boarding	£725-£1347								

MAP 8 I 2
LOCATION Rural
DAY **RAIL** a **AIR** a
SPORT abclmpqx ABC
OTHER LANGUAGES
ACTIVITIES cghijostx A

ENTRY REQUIREMENTS Report & Exam & Interview
SCHOLARSHIPS & BURSARIES Schol; Burs
SPECIAL NEEDS
DYSLEXIA **DIET** ad
ASSOCIATION GSA **FOUNDED** 1880 **RELIGIOUS AFFILIATION** C of E
OTHER SUBJECTS abcdh
FACILITIES ON SITE bdh
EXAM BOARDS cd DG
RETAKES **NVQ COURSES**

A-level: efghi uv / BC GH K P R U / cdef
AS:
GCSE: de g i v / BC G K P R / cdef j
OTHER: lmn / o

Stockport Grammar Junior School; Buxton Road; Stockport SK2 7AF
Tel: 0161 456 4250 (Fax: 0161 483 1797) *A.J.Carter*

		Boys 139	Age 4-11	Girls 135	Age 4-11	TOTAL 274	SIXTH	Boys	Girls
Day Weekly Boarding	£999								

MAP 8 J 1
LOCATION Urban
DAY **RAIL** a **AIR** a
SPORT aefjmpqx AB
OTHER LANGUAGES
ACTIVITIES fghijo

ENTRY REQUIREMENTS Test
SCHOLARSHIPS & BURSARIES
SPECIAL NEEDS
DYSLEXIA **DIET** a
ASSOCIATION ISAI **FOUNDED** **RELIGIOUS AFFILIATION** Inter-denom
OTHER SUBJECTS bc
FACILITIES ON SITE ai
EXAM BOARDS
RETAKES **NVQ COURSES**

A-level:
AS:
GCSE:
OTHER: e lm o v / B G / cde

Stockport Grammar School; Buxton Road; Stockport; Cheshire SK2 7AF
Tel: 0161 456 9000 (Fax: 0161 483 1797) *D.R.J.Bird*

		Boys 498	Age 11-18	Girls 513	Age 11-18	TOTAL 1011	SIXTH	Boys 124	Girls 138
Day Weekly Boarding	£1299								

MAP 8 J 1
LOCATION Urban
DAY **RAIL** a **AIR** a
SPORT abcemnpqstwx AB
OTHER LANGUAGES
ACTIVITIES bcfghijknoqst ABD

ENTRY REQUIREMENTS Report & Exam & Interview
SCHOLARSHIPS & BURSARIES AP
SPECIAL NEEDS bej Gl
DYSLEXIA **DIET** a
ASSOCIATION HMC **FOUNDED** 1487 **RELIGIOUS AFFILIATION** Non-denom
OTHER SUBJECTS abcdfh
FACILITIES ON SITE acdik
EXAM BOARDS bcd BD
RETAKES **NVQ COURSES**

A-level: c e ghi p uv / B GH K P / c ef j
AS:
GCSE: c e g i o v / BC G K P / cdef
OTHER:

Syddal Park School; 33 Syddal Road; Bramhall; Cheshire SK7 1AB
Tel: 0161 439 1751 *Mrs P.Hamel*

		Boys 39	Age 3-7	Girls 34	Age 3-7	TOTAL 73	SIXTH	Boys	Girls
Day Weekly Boarding	£490- £790								

MAP 8 J 1
LOCATION
DAY **RAIL** **AIR**
SPORT x
OTHER LANGUAGES
ACTIVITIES

ENTRY REQUIREMENTS
SCHOLARSHIPS & BURSARIES
SPECIAL NEEDS
DYSLEXIA **DIET**
ASSOCIATION ISAI **FOUNDED** 1919 **RELIGIOUS AFFILIATION**
OTHER SUBJECTS
FACILITIES ON SITE
EXAM BOARDS
RETAKES **NVQ COURSES**

A-level:
AS:
GCSE:
OTHER: e v / B G K / cd

Terra Nova; Jodrell Bank; Holmes Chapel; Cheshire CW4 8BT
Tel: 01477 571251 (Fax: 01477 571646) *T.R.Lewis*

		Boys 88 / 27 / 13	Age 3-13 / 8-13 / 8-13	Girls 56 / 10 /	Age 3-13 / 8-13 / 8-13	TOTAL 194	SIXTH	Boys	Girls
Day Weekly Boarding	£520-£2005 £2500 £2500								

MAP 8 I 2
LOCATION Rural
DAY **RAIL** b **AIR** a
SPORT abcefghjlmpqsux ABC
OTHER LANGUAGES a
ACTIVITIES cfghijoqstwx A

ENTRY REQUIREMENTS Interview
SCHOLARSHIPS & BURSARIES Schol; Forces; Clergy
SPECIAL NEEDS abegjlntuvw BEHI
DYSLEXIA e **DIET** ac
ASSOCIATION IAPS **FOUNDED** 1897 **RELIGIOUS AFFILIATION** C of E
OTHER SUBJECTS abcfh
FACILITIES ON SITE bcdhj
EXAM BOARDS
RETAKES **NVQ COURSES**

A-level:
AS:
GCSE:
OTHER: c e l o s v / B E G K O R / cdefg j

CHESHIRE continued

G — Wilmslow Prep. School; Grove Avenue; Wilmslow; Cheshire SK9 5EG
Tel: 01625 524246 (Fax: 01625 536660) Mrs M.Grant

	Boys	Age	Girls	Age	TOTAL	Boys	Girls
Day £300–£1200 Weekly Boarding			171	3–11	171	SIXTH	

- **ENTRY REQUIREMENTS** Assessment & Interview
- **SCHOLARSHIPS & BURSARIES**
- **SPECIAL NEEDS** k l   **DYSLEXIA**   **DIET** ac
- **ASSOCIATION** IAPS   **FOUNDED** 1909   **RELIGIOUS AFFILIATION** Non-denom

- **MAP** 8 I 2
- **LOCATION** Urban
- **DAY**   **RAIL** a   **AIR** a
- **SPORT** almpqx B
- **OTHER LANGUAGES**
- **ACTIVITIES** ghij
- **OTHER SUBJECTS** cfh
- **FACILITIES ON SITE**
- **EXAM BOARDS**
- **RETAKES**   **NVQ COURSES**

A-level | AS | GCSE e o v / B E G K O R / cde | OTHER

CLEVELAND

C — Red House School Ltd; 36 The Green; Norton; Stockton-on-Tees; Cleveland TS20 1DX
Tel: 01642 553370 (Fax: 01642 361031) M.England

	Boys	Age	Girls	Age	TOTAL	Boys	Girls
Day £875–£1010 Weekly Boarding	232	4–16	179	4–16	411	SIXTH	

- **ENTRY REQUIREMENTS** CEE; Exam; Test & Interview
- **SCHOLARSHIPS & BURSARIES** Schol
- **SPECIAL NEEDS** abfjlnopqst ABGHI   **DYSLEXIA**   **DIET** abcd
- **ASSOCIATION** ISAI   **FOUNDED** 1929   **RELIGIOUS AFFILIATION** Non-denom

- **MAP** 12 H 3
- **LOCATION** Urban
- **DAY**   **RAIL** b   **AIR**
- **SPORT** abcdefjlmopswx B
- **OTHER LANGUAGES**
- **ACTIVITIES** fghkmo
- **OTHER SUBJECTS** bc
- **FACILITIES ON SITE** bh
- **EXAM BOARDS** c
- **RETAKES**   **NVQ COURSES**

A-level | AS | GCSE d g i l vw / ABC G K P R / cdefg j | OTHER

G — Teesside High School for Girls; The Avenue; Eaglescliffe; Stockton-on-Tees TS16 9AT
Tel: 01642 782095 (Fax: 01642 791207) Miss J.F.Hamilton

	Boys	Age	Girls	Age	TOTAL	Boys	Girls
Day £875–£1235 ✗ Weekly Boarding			553	3–18	553	SIXTH	60

- **ENTRY REQUIREMENTS** Report & Exam & Interview
- **SCHOLARSHIPS & BURSARIES** AP; VI Form
- **SPECIAL NEEDS** bejklnqw GI   **DYSLEXIA** e   **DIET** a
- **ASSOCIATION** GSA   **FOUNDED** 1970   **RELIGIOUS AFFILIATION** Non-denom

- **MAP** 12 G 3
- **LOCATION** Rural
- **DAY** ✓   **RAIL** a   **AIR** a
- **SPORT** acefklmpqwx ABC
- **OTHER LANGUAGES** a
- **ACTIVITIES** cgijkopt A
- **OTHER SUBJECTS** bcfh
- **FACILITIES ON SITE** bghk
- **EXAM BOARDS** abcd ABDE
- **RETAKES** ab   **NVQ COURSES**

A-level cde g i l uv / BC GH K P R / c efg j l | AS l u / ef j | GCSE cde g i n vw / BC G K P R / cdefg j l | OTHER

Bg — Yarm School; The Friarage; Yarm; Cleveland TS15 9EJ
Tel: 01642 786023 (Fax: 01642 789216) R.Neville Tate

	Boys	Age	Girls	Age	TOTAL	Boys	Girls
Day £930–£1680 ✗ Weekly Boarding	700	5–18	10	16–18	710	SIXTH 130	10

- **ENTRY REQUIREMENTS** Exam & Interview; CEE & Interview
- **SCHOLARSHIPS & BURSARIES** Schol; Burs; Mus; AP; VI Form
- **SPECIAL NEEDS** jlnqt   **DYSLEXIA** g   **DIET** acd
- **ASSOCIATION** HMC   **FOUNDED** 1978   **RELIGIOUS AFFILIATION** Christian

- **MAP** 12 G 3
- **LOCATION** Urban
- **DAY**   **RAIL** a   **AIR** a
- **SPORT** abcdefghjklmoprswx ABC
- **OTHER LANGUAGES**
- **ACTIVITIES** efghijklmnopqsu AB
- **OTHER SUBJECTS** ac
- **FACILITIES ON SITE** acghk
- **EXAM BOARDS** abcd ABDEHI
- **RETAKES**   **NVQ COURSES**

A-level cde ghi l nop uvwx / B GH K PQ U / cdef hj l | AS cde g i l / GH K / cdef j | GCSE cde ghi l o q vwx / AB E G K OP R U / cdefgh j l | OTHER n q / K N R

CORNWALL

Gb — Bolitho School,The; (formerly The School of St. Clare); Polwithen; Penzance; Cornwall TR18 4JR
Tel: 01736 63271 (Fax: 01736 330960) I.Halford

	Boys	Age	Girls	Age	TOTAL	Boys	Girls
Day £355–£1472 ✗ Weekly £2548–£2625 Boarding £2661–£2787	28	3–11 7–11 7–11	93 12 24	3–18 7–18 7–18	157	SIXTH	14

- **ENTRY REQUIREMENTS** Scholarship Exam; Assessment & Interview; Report & Exam & Interview
- **SCHOLARSHIPS & BURSARIES** Schol; Burs; Mus; Forces; Clergy; VI Form; Siblings
- **SPECIAL NEEDS** abceghjklnpqw BEGI   **DYSLEXIA** d   **DIET** a   **ASSOCIATION** GSA   **FOUNDED** 1889   **RELIGIOUS AFFILIATION** C of E

- **MAP** 1 A 8
- **LOCATION** Rural
- **DAY**   **RAIL** a   **AIR** b
- **SPORT** abcdefhjlmopqstx ABC
- **OTHER LANGUAGES** a
- **ACTIVITIES** abcdefghijknopqstwx AB
- **OTHER SUBJECTS** abcdefgh
- **FACILITIES ON SITE** cdegjk
- **EXAM BOARDS** abd ABEGHL
- **RETAKES** a   **NVQ COURSES**

A-level e g i v / BC G K P R / cdef j | AS | GCSE e g i no v / BC G K P R W / cdef j l | OTHER c e g i mno v / BC G K NOP R W / cdefg j l

CORNWALL *continued*

Duchy Grammar School,The; Carnon Downs; Tregye; Truro; Cornwall TR3 6JH
Tel: 01872 862289 *M.L.Fuller*

		Boys	Age	Girls	Age	TOTAL		Boys	Girls
Day	£710-£1615	54	3-18	23	3-18	102	SIXTH	4	5
Weekly	£2404-£2694	12	7-18		7-18				
Boarding	£2498-£2788	7	7-18	6	7-18				

ENTRY REQUIREMENTS Assessment & Interview
SCHOLARSHIPS & BURSARIES Schol; VI Form
SPECIAL NEEDS nw B   **DYSLEXIA**   **DIET** a
ASSOCIATION ISAI   **FOUNDED** 1982   **RELIGIOUS AFFILIATION** Non-denom

MAP 1 C 8
LOCATION Rural
DAY √   **RAIL** a   **AIR** c
SPORT abcdefghjmpqstwx ABC
OTHER LANGUAGES a
ACTIVITIES cfghjknpqstuw A
OTHER SUBJECTS abcdefgh
FACILITIES ON SITE bc
EXAM BOARDS bcd BG
RETAKES a   **NVQ COURSES**

A-level	e ghi l o v	AS	g i	GCSE	de ghi l no v	OTHER	
	ABC G K P		B G		ABC E G KL OP R X		X
	cdef				cdef j		

Polwhele House School; Truro; Cornwall TR4 9AE
Tel: 01872 73011 (Fax: 01872 73011) *Mr & Mrs R.I.White*

		Boys	Age	Girls	Age	TOTAL		Boys	Girls
Day	£160-£1525	79	3-13	71	3-13	158	SIXTH		
Weekly	£2490-£2700	6	8-13	2	8-13				
Boarding									

ENTRY REQUIREMENTS Assessment & Interview
SCHOLARSHIPS & BURSARIES Chor; Clergy; Teachers
SPECIAL NEEDS abeghjklnqtuw AGI   **DYSLEXIA** ef   **DIET** acd
ASSOCIATION ISAI   **FOUNDED** 1976   **RELIGIOUS AFFILIATION** Inter-denom

MAP 1 C 7
LOCATION Rural
DAY   **RAIL** a   **AIR** c
SPORT acdefhjklmpqstx ABC
OTHER LANGUAGES
ACTIVITIES cfghjnopqtw A
OTHER SUBJECTS abcdfh
FACILITIES ON SITE bcfhk
EXAM BOARDS
RETAKES   **NVQ COURSES**

A-level		AS		GCSE		OTHER	de g i klmno s v
							BC E G K OP RS
							cdef j

Roselyon School; Par; Cornwall PL24 2HZ
Tel: 01726 812110 *A.J.H.Stone*

		Boys	Age	Girls	Age	TOTAL		Boys	Girls
Day	£285-£890	39	3-11	39	3-11	78	SIXTH		
Weekly									
Boarding									

ENTRY REQUIREMENTS Test & Interview
SCHOLARSHIPS & BURSARIES Schol; Burs; Siblings
SPECIAL NEEDS   **DYSLEXIA**   **DIET**
ASSOCIATION ISAI   **FOUNDED** 1953   **RELIGIOUS AFFILIATION** C of E

MAP 1 D 7
LOCATION Rural
DAY √   **RAIL** a   **AIR**
SPORT acefjkpx AB
OTHER LANGUAGES
ACTIVITIES cfghjqt
OTHER SUBJECTS cfh
FACILITIES ON SITE
EXAM BOARDS
RETAKES   **NVQ COURSES**

A-level		AS		GCSE		OTHER	de l v
							B E G
							cde

St. Joseph's School; 15 St. Stephen's Hill; Launceston PL15 8HN
Tel: 01566 772988 (Fax: 01566 775902) *P.S.Larkman*   **Gb**

		Boys	Age	Girls	Age	TOTAL		Boys	Girls
Day	£835-£1198	34	4-11	146	4-16	203	SIXTH		
Weekly	£1920-£2190	3	7-11	19	8-16				
Boarding	£2320-£2590			1	8-16				

ENTRY REQUIREMENTS Exam & Interview
SCHOLARSHIPS & BURSARIES Schol
SPECIAL NEEDS abln   **DYSLEXIA** e   **DIET** a
ASSOCIATION ISAI   **FOUNDED** 1915   **RELIGIOUS AFFILIATION** R C

MAP 1 E 6
LOCATION Rural
DAY √   **RAIL** b   **AIR** c
SPORT afjlmpqwx B
OTHER LANGUAGES
ACTIVITIES cghijknox A
OTHER SUBJECTS bcdeh
FACILITIES ON SITE bdeh
EXAM BOARDS abcd
RETAKES   **NVQ COURSES**

A-level		AS		GCSE	e gi l o v	OTHER	
			e		BC G K P R W		
					cdef l		

St. Petroc's School; Bude; Cornwall EX23 8NJ
Tel: 01288 352876 (Fax: 01288 352876) *M.J.Glen*

		Boys	Age	Girls	Age	TOTAL		Boys	Girls
Day	£1315	50	3-14	37	3-14	105	SIXTH		
Weekly	£1980	7	7-14	4	7-14				
Boarding	£2110-£2400	6	7-14	1	7-14				

ENTRY REQUIREMENTS Interview
SCHOLARSHIPS & BURSARIES Schol; Burs; Art; Mus; Forces; Clergy; Teachers; Sport; Siblings
SPECIAL NEEDS abn   **DYSLEXIA** e   **DIET** abcd
ASSOCIATION IAPS   **FOUNDED** 1912   **RELIGIOUS AFFILIATION** C of E

MAP 1 D 5
LOCATION Urban
DAY √   **RAIL** c   **AIR** c
SPORT abcefjklmopqsuwx AB
OTHER LANGUAGES
ACTIVITIES bcfgijoqrstwx A
OTHER SUBJECTS acfh
FACILITIES ON SITE c
EXAM BOARDS
RETAKES   **NVQ COURSES**

A-level		AS		GCSE		OTHER	de g i lmno s uv
							BC G K OP R
							cde j

CORNWALL

99

CORNWALL continued

C — Treliske Preparatory School; Truro; Cornwall TR1 3QN
Tel: 01872 72616 (Fax: 01872 223431) *R.L.Hollins*

		Boys	Age	Girls	Age	TOTAL		Boys	Girls
Day	£917-£1398	129	3-11	51	3-11	198	SIXTH		
Weekly	£2493								
Boarding	£2493	14	7-11	4	7-11				

ENTRY REQUIREMENTS Scholarship Exam; Report & Exam & Interview
SCHOLARSHIPS & BURSARIES Schol; Burs
SPECIAL NEEDS abeghjlqs B   **DYSLEXIA**   **DIET** a
ASSOCIATION IAPS   **FOUNDED** 1934   **RELIGIOUS AFFILIATION** Methodist

MAP 1 C 7
LOCATION Rural
DAY   **RAIL** a   **AIR** c
SPORT abcdefjklmpqstwx AB
OTHER LANGUAGES
ACTIVITIES acfghijmnoptx A
OTHER SUBJECTS cfh
FACILITIES ON SITE bchi
EXAM BOARDS
RETAKES   **NVQ COURSES**

A-level: **AS**:   **GCSE**:   **OTHER**: de lmno s v / B E G K O R / cde

---

Gb — Truro High School for Girls; Falmouth Road; Truro; Cornwall TR1 2HU
Tel: 01872 72830 *J.M.H.Graham-Brown*

		Boys	Age	Girls	Age	TOTAL		Boys	Girls
Day	£447-£1460	✗ 9	3-5	319	3-18	392	SIXTH		81
Weekly	£2526-£2630			21	8-18				
Boarding	£2561-£2665			43	8-18				

ENTRY REQUIREMENTS Exam & Interview
SCHOLARSHIPS & BURSARIES Schol; Mus; Clergy; AP; VI Form
SPECIAL NEEDS begjlnqstw AEGHIK   **DYSLEXIA** g   **DIET** abcd
ASSOCIATION GSA   **FOUNDED** 1880   **RELIGIOUS AFFILIATION** C of E

MAP 1 C 7
LOCATION Urban
DAY ✓   **RAIL** a   **AIR** c
SPORT abcdefhjklmopqtx AB
OTHER LANGUAGES
ACTIVITIES cdfghijklnopqrstwx A
OTHER SUBJECTS abcfh
FACILITIES ON SITE abcghi
EXAM BOARDS abcd ABDL
RETAKES   **NVQ COURSES**

A-level: de ghi n v / BC GH K P R W / cdefgh j l
AS: de g i / BC K G K P U / c ef h l
GCSE: de g i n vw / BC E G K P R W / cdefgh j l
OTHER: de no q s v / C I K NOP / ef h l

C — Truro School; Trennick Lane; Truro; Cornwall TR1 1TH
Tel: 01872 72763 (Fax: 01872 223431) *G.A.G.Dodd*

		Boys	Age	Girls	Age	TOTAL		Boys	Girls
Day	£1536	451	11-18	204	11-18	793	SIXTH	139	76
Weekly			11-18		11-18				
Boarding	£2860	94	11-18	44	11-18				

ENTRY REQUIREMENTS CEE; Exam; Report & Interview
SCHOLARSHIPS & BURSARIES Schol; Art; Mus; AP; Siblings
SPECIAL NEEDS bjklnqs BGI   **DYSLEXIA** e   **DIET** abcd
ASSOCIATION HMC   **FOUNDED** 1880   **RELIGIOUS AFFILIATION** Methodist

MAP 1 C 7
LOCATION Urban
DAY   **RAIL** a   **AIR** c
SPORT abcdefghjklmpqstuwx ABC
OTHER LANGUAGES a
ACTIVITIES abfghijklmnopqrstuw ABD
OTHER SUBJECTS bcdfh
FACILITIES ON SITE abcdeghj
EXAM BOARDS abcd BDEGH
RETAKES ab   **NVQ COURSES**

A-level: cdefghi op vwx / B GH K P R U / cdefg j l
AS: g i / ef l / P U
GCSE: de ghi op vw / B G K OP R U X / cdefga j l
OTHER: d l n qr u / A K NO

CUMBRIA

C — Austin Friars School; St. Ann's Hill; Carlisle CA3 9PB
Tel: 01228 28042 (Fax: 01228 810327) *Michael G.Taylor*

		Boys	Age	Girls	Age	TOTAL		Boys	Girls
Day	£1446	154	11-18	113	11-18	298	SIXTH	46	31
Weekly	£2457	3	11-18						
Boarding	£2526	28	11-18						

ENTRY REQUIREMENTS CEE; Exam; Report & Interview
SCHOLARSHIPS & BURSARIES Schol; Burs; Forces; AP; VI Form
SPECIAL NEEDS bijnqs GI   **DYSLEXIA** e   **DIET** a
ASSOCIATION SHMIS   **FOUNDED** 1951   **RELIGIOUS AFFILIATION** R C

MAP 11 C 1
LOCATION Rural
DAY ✓   **RAIL** a   **AIR** b
SPORT abcdefhjklmopqstx ABC
OTHER LANGUAGES a
ACTIVITIES cfghijklnoqs AB
OTHER SUBJECTS bch
FACILITIES ON SITE bcdhk
EXAM BOARDS bcd DEH
RETAKES b   **NVQ COURSES**

A-level: c efg i p uv / B GH K P R / c ef l
AS: c / G / P / j
GCSE: c egi op v / AB GH K N P R / cdef j
OTHER: lmno q x / E K MNO R / g l

Gb — Casterton School; Kirkby Lonsdale; Cumbria LA6 2SG
Tel: 015242 71202 (Fax: 015242 71146) *A.F.Thomas*

		Boys	Age	Girls	Age	TOTAL		Boys	Girls
Day	£1640-£1888	✗ 3	4-7	90	4-18	359	SIXTH		81
Weekly	£2350-£2518			8	8-11				
Boarding	£2410-£3010			258	8-18				

ENTRY REQUIREMENTS Exam
SCHOLARSHIPS & BURSARIES Schol; Mus; Clergy; AP
SPECIAL NEEDS bjlnt GHK   **DYSLEXIA** d   **DIET** a
ASSOCIATION GSA   **FOUNDED** 1823   **RELIGIOUS AFFILIATION** C of E

MAP 11 D 4
LOCATION Rural
DAY   **RAIL** b   **AIR** b
SPORT acdefklmnpqtwx AB
OTHER LANGUAGES a
ACTIVITIES acfghijknopqrstvwx AB
OTHER SUBJECTS abcdefgh
FACILITIES ON SITE bcdghik
EXAM BOARDS bc ABDEH
RETAKES ab   **NVQ COURSES**

A-level: efghi p uv / BC GH K P R W / cdef j l
AS: h l / T
GCSE: e g ij l v x / BC G K P R T W / cdef j l
OTHER: j mn o / h

100

CUMBRIA *continued*

C — Harecroft School; Gosforth; Seascale; Cumbria CA20 1HS
Tel: 019467 25220 (Fax: 019467 25885) *D.G.Hoddy*

		Boys	Age	Girls	Age	TOTAL		Boys	Girls
Day	£1134-£1585	40	4-13	32	4-13	84	SIXTH		
Weekly	£2175	4	6-13	1	6-13				
Boarding	£2280	2	7-13	5	7-13				

ENTRY REQUIREMENTS
SCHOLARSHIPS & BURSARIES Schol; Forces
SPECIAL NEEDS bjklntuw CDEI **DYSLEXIA** e **DIET** abcd
ASSOCIATION ISAI **FOUNDED** 1925 **RELIGIOUS AFFILIATION** C of E

MAP11 B 4
LOCATION Rural
DAY ✓ **RAIL** b **AIR** b
SPORT abcdfjklmpqstux AB
OTHER LANGUAGES
ACTIVITIES acfghijopqrtw A
OTHER SUBJECTS abcfh
FACILITIES ON SITE ab
EXAM BOARDS
RETAKES e **NVQ COURSES**

A-level: c e g i lmno s uv
BC G K OP RS
cdef j l

AS:

GCSE:

OTHER:

C — Lime House School; Holm Hill; Dalston; Carlisle; Cumbria CA5 7BX
Tel: 01228 710225 (Fax: 01228 710508) *Nigel A.Rice*

		Boys	Age	Girls	Age	TOTAL		Boys	Girls
Day	£500-£1150 X	46	4-18	32	4-18	242	SIXTH	30	16
Weekly	£1400-£2250	2	4-18		4-18				
Boarding	£1600-£2700	100	4-18	62	4-18				

ENTRY REQUIREMENTS CEE; Exam
SCHOLARSHIPS & BURSARIES Forces; Sport
SPECIAL NEEDS beijklnquwx ABEHI **DYSLEXIA** cdef **DIET** abc
ASSOCIATION ISAI **FOUNDED** 1899 **RELIGIOUS AFFILIATION** Inter-denom

MAP14 I 8
LOCATION Rural
DAY ✓ **RAIL** a **AIR** a
SPORT abcdefghjklmopqstuvwx ABC
OTHER LANGUAGES a
ACTIVITIES acefghijklmnoqrstvw AC
OTHER SUBJECTS bcdefh
FACILITIES ON SITE abcefghil
EXAM BOARDS abcd ABDEGIKL
RETAKES ab **NVQ COURSES** 12

A-level: abcdefghijklmnopqrs v x
ABC G OPQ U
abcdefghijkl

AS: de
G
b

GCSE: de ghij lm op s uvwx
ABC E G K NOP U X
bcdef j l

OTHER: d
K N
b

Gb — St. Anne's School; Windermere; Cumbria LA23 1NW
Tel: 015394 46164 (Fax: 015394 88414) *C.M.G.R.Jenkins*

		Boys	Age	Girls	Age	TOTAL		Boys	Girls
Day	£788-£2017 X	17	3-11	122	3-19	342	SIXTH		66
Weekly	£2140-£3042			29	7-19				
Boarding	£2450-£3042			174	7-19				

ENTRY REQUIREMENTS Report & Exam & Interview
SCHOLARSHIPS & BURSARIES Schol; Burs; Art; Mus; Forces; Teachers; VI Form; Sport; Drama
SPECIAL NEEDS ajlnq B **DYSLEXIA** ef **DIET** acd
ASSOCIATION GSA **FOUNDED** 1863 **RELIGIOUS AFFILIATION** Non-denom

MAP11 C 4
LOCATION Rural
DAY **RAIL** b **AIR** b
SPORT abcdfghlmpqtux AB
OTHER LANGUAGES abi
ACTIVITIES abcfghjknopqstuwx AB
OTHER SUBJECTS abcdefgh
FACILITIES ON SITE abceghk
EXAM BOARDS abc ABDEL
RETAKES ab **NVQ COURSES**

A-level: defg i n uv x
BC GH K P R
c ef h l

AS: g m v
G M R

GCSE: de g i lmn v
BC G K P R W
cdef hj l

OTHER: l
j

C — St. Bees School; St. Bees; Cumbria CA27 0DU
Tel: 01946 822 263 (Fax: 01946 823657) *P.A.Chamberlain*

		Boys	Age	Girls	Age	TOTAL		Boys	Girls
Day	£1951-£2406 X	88	11-18	87	11-18	287	SIXTH	42	39
Weekly	£2356-£3331	31	11-18	32	11-18				
Boarding	£2558-£3497	28	11-18	21	11-18				

ENTRY REQUIREMENTS CEE; Exam
SCHOLARSHIPS & BURSARIES Schol; Burs; Art; Mus; Forces; Clergy; AP; Sport
SPECIAL NEEDS ejklnqw EGI **DYSLEXIA** ce **DIET** abcd
ASSOCIATION HMC **FOUNDED** 1583 **RELIGIOUS AFFILIATION** C of E

MAP11 B 3
LOCATION Rural
DAY ✓ **RAIL** c **AIR** c
SPORT abcdefghjklmpqsuwx ABC
OTHER LANGUAGES a
ACTIVITIES abcdefghijklmnopqstwx ABC
OTHER SUBJECTS abcdfh
FACILITIES ON SITE adehikl
EXAM BOARDS bcd ABDEGH
RETAKES b **NVQ COURSES**

A-level: defghi p uv
AB GH K NOP R U W
cdef

AS:

GCSE: de g i l v
ABC G K N P R U W
cdef j

OTHER: mno q
g i

B — Sedbergh School; Sedbergh; Cumbria LA10 5HG
Tel: 015396 20535 (Fax: 015396 21301) *C.H.Hirst*

		Boys	Age	Girls	Age	TOTAL		Boys	Girls
Day	£1930-£2715	11	11-18			376	SIXTH	143	
Weekly									
Boarding	£2760-£3880	365	11-18						

ENTRY REQUIREMENTS CEE; Exam; Scholarship Exam
SCHOLARSHIPS & BURSARIES Schol; Burs; Art; Mus; Clergy; Teachers; AP; VI Form
SPECIAL NEEDS blqu **DYSLEXIA** **DIET** abcd
ASSOCIATION HMC **FOUNDED** 1525 **RELIGIOUS AFFILIATION** C of E

MAP11 D 4
LOCATION Rural
DAY **RAIL** b **AIR** b
SPORT abcdefhijklmstuwx ABC
OTHER LANGUAGES a
ACTIVITIES abdefghijklmnopqrst A
OTHER SUBJECTS abcdfh
FACILITIES ON SITE bcdeghik
EXAM BOARDS bcd BDHL
RETAKES **NVQ COURSES**

A-level: cd ghi op uv
B GH K OP R
c efg j

AS: ghi
G
ef

GCSE: e g i o vw
B G K NOP R X
cdefg jk

OTHER: e l no q s u
K O R

DERBYSHIRE

Ashbourne PNEU School; St Monica's House; Windmill Lane; Ashbourne; Derbyshire DE6 1EY Tel: 01335 343294 (Fax: 01335 343294) *M.Broadbent*

Grade: C

		Boys	Age	Girls	Age	TOTAL		Boys	Girls
Day	£330-£1100	50	3-12	54	3-12	104	SIXTH		
Weekly									
Boarding									

ENTRY REQUIREMENTS
SCHOLARSHIPS & BURSARIES
SPECIAL NEEDS aijnuw **DYSLEXIA** **DIET** a
ASSOCIATION ISAI **FOUNDED** 1942 **RELIGIOUS AFFILIATION** C of E

MAP 9 B 4
LOCATION Urban
DAY **RAIL** b **AIR** a
SPORT aefhjlmpqsx B
OTHER LANGUAGES
ACTIVITIES cfgjors
OTHER SUBJECTS ch
FACILITIES ON SITE
EXAM BOARDS
RETAKES **NVQ COURSES**

A-level: **AS:** **GCSE:** **OTHER:** e g i lm o v / B G K OP R / ef

---

Derby High School; Hillsway; Littleover; Derby DE23 7DT
Tel: 01332 514267 (Fax: 01332 516085) *Dr G.H.Goddard*

Grade: Gb

		Boys	Age	Girls	Age	TOTAL		Boys	Girls
Day	£1070-£1450	66	3-11	485	3-18	551	SIXTH		58
Weekly									
Boarding									

ENTRY REQUIREMENTS Exam & Interview
SCHOLARSHIPS & BURSARIES Schol; Burs; Mus; Clergy; AP
SPECIAL NEEDS Inq **DYSLEXIA** e **DIET** acd
ASSOCIATION GSA **FOUNDED** 1892 **RELIGIOUS AFFILIATION** C of E

MAP 9 C 4
LOCATION Urban
DAY a **RAIL** a **AIR** a
SPORT acefghjklmopqtx AB
OTHER LANGUAGES a
ACTIVITIES fghijknoqs A
OTHER SUBJECTS abcdeh
FACILITIES ON SITE bcghk
EXAM BOARDS abcde ABDEHKL
RETAKES **NVQ COURSES**

A-level: d e g i l op uv / BC GH K P R / cdef
AS: d e g i q / BC G
GCSE: d e g i l no v / BC G K P R / cdef
OTHER: l / K

Mount St. Mary's College; Spinkhill; Via Sheffield S31 9YL
Tel: 01246 433388 (Fax: 01246 435511) *P.B.Fisher*

Grade: C

		Boys	Age	Girls	Age	TOTAL		Boys	Girls
Day	£1876	76	13-18	21	13-18	296	SIXTH	66	31
Weekly	£2767	21	13-18	17	13-18				
Boarding	£2990	105	13-18	56	13-18				

ENTRY REQUIREMENTS CEE; Report & Interview
SCHOLARSHIPS & BURSARIES Burs; AP
SPECIAL NEEDS n GL **DYSLEXIA** e **DIET** a
ASSOCIATION HMC **FOUNDED** 1842 **RELIGIOUS AFFILIATION** R C

MAP 9 C 3
LOCATION Rural
DAY ✓ **RAIL** b **AIR** b
SPORT abcdefghjklmpqstuwx ABC
OTHER LANGUAGES a
ACTIVITIES abefghijklnopqsw A
OTHER SUBJECTS bcdh
FACILITIES ON SITE bdehik
EXAM BOARDS bc ABDEHL
RETAKES a **NVQ COURSES**

A-level: c efg i l op vwx / AB GH K OP R / cdefg j l
AS: g i l / B G / e
GCSE: e g i l o v / AB G K OP R / cdefg j l
OTHER: N

Ockbrook School; The Settlement; Ockbrook; Nr. Derby DE72 3RJ
Tel: 01332 673532 (Fax: 01332 665184) *Mrs D.Bolland*

Grade: Gb

		Boys	Age	Girls	Age	TOTAL		Boys	Girls
Day	£891-£1241	49	3-11	328	3-18	396	SIXTH		18
Weekly	£2019-£2302			4	8-18				
Boarding	£2019-£2302			15	8-18				

ENTRY REQUIREMENTS Exam; Interview; Report
SCHOLARSHIPS & BURSARIES VI Form
SPECIAL NEEDS n **DYSLEXIA** e **DIET** ab
ASSOCIATION GSA **FOUNDED** 1799 **RELIGIOUS AFFILIATION** Inter-denom

MAP 9 C 4
LOCATION Rural
DAY ✓ **RAIL** b **AIR** a
SPORT abcdefghjklmpqwx ABC
OTHER LANGUAGES a
ACTIVITIES acfghijknoqstx A
OTHER SUBJECTS bcdfh
FACILITIES ON SITE bcdi
EXAM BOARDS abcd ABDEGI
RETAKES **NVQ COURSES**

A-level: d e ghi p v / BC G K P R / cdef
AS: B
GCSE: d e g i o v / BC E G K NOP R / cdef
OTHER: l n u

Repton Prep. School; Foremarke Hall; Milton; Derby DE65 6EJ
Tel: 01283 703269 (Fax: 01283 702957) *R.C.Theobald*

Grade: C

		Boys	Age	Girls	Age	TOTAL		Boys	Girls
Day	£1929	173	7-13	81	7-13	353	SIXTH		
Weekly	£2563	34	7-13	22	7-13				
Boarding	£2563	31	7-13	12	7-13				

ENTRY REQUIREMENTS Test & Interview
SCHOLARSHIPS & BURSARIES Mus; Clergy; AP
SPECIAL NEEDS bjlnsw ADHIK **DYSLEXIA** de **DIET** abcd
ASSOCIATION IAPS **FOUNDED** 1940 **RELIGIOUS AFFILIATION** C of E

MAP 9 C 5
LOCATION Rural
DAY **RAIL** b **AIR** a
SPORT abcdefgjklmopqtux AB
OTHER LANGUAGES
ACTIVITIES cfghijmoqrstw A
OTHER SUBJECTS bcfh
FACILITIES ON SITE bchik
EXAM BOARDS
RETAKES **NVQ COURSES**

A-level: **AS:** **GCSE:** **OTHER:** e g i l no v / B G K OP R / cde jk

DERBYSHIRE *continued*

C — Repton School; Repton; Derby DE65 6FH
Tel: 01283 702375 (Fax: 01283 701468) *G.E.Jones*

		Boys	Age	Girls	Age	TOTAL		Boys	Girls
Day	£2910	123	13-18	47	13-18	988	SIXTH	194	61
Weekly									
Boarding	£3868	317	13-18	61	13-18				

ENTRY REQUIREMENTS CEE
SCHOLARSHIPS & BURSARIES Schol; Burs; Art; Mus; Clergy; AP
SPECIAL NEEDS bejknq EGI **DYSLEXIA** def **DIET** a
ASSOCIATION HMC **FOUNDED** 1557 **RELIGIOUS AFFILIATION** C of E

MAP 9 C 5
LOCATION Rural
DAY **RAIL** b **AIR** a
SPORT abcdefgijkmnopqrstuwx BC
OTHER LANGUAGES
ACTIVITIES bcefghijkloqst AB
OTHER SUBJECTS cfh
FACILITIES ON SITE abcdehik
EXAM BOARDS abcd ABDEH
RETAKES a **NVQ COURSES**

- **A-level**: c e g i op uv x / B GH K P U / cdefg j
- **AS**: G / de
- **q**: R
- **GCSE**: c e g i l no v / B G K OP R U / cdef h j
- **OTHER**: b

C — S. Anselm's School; Bakewell; Derbyshire DE45 1DP
Tel: 01629 812 734 (Fax: 01629 814742) *R.J.Foster*

		Boys	Age	Girls	Age	TOTAL		Boys	Girls
Day	£1040-£2262	44	3-13	36	3-13	165	SIXTH		
Weekly									
Boarding	£2964	60	7-13	25	7-13				

ENTRY REQUIREMENTS Report
SCHOLARSHIPS & BURSARIES Forces; Clergy; Teachers; Siblings
SPECIAL NEEDS abefijklnpqtuvw ABDEGHIJ **DYSLEXIA** e **DIET** ac
ASSOCIATION IAPS **FOUNDED** 1888 **RELIGIOUS AFFILIATION** C of E

MAP 9 B 3
LOCATION Rural
DAY **RAIL** b **AIR** a
SPORT abcefjlmnpqstux ABC
OTHER LANGUAGES
ACTIVITIES cfghijmnoqstw A
OTHER SUBJECTS bch
FACILITIES ON SITE abcejk
EXAM BOARDS
RETAKES **NVQ COURSES**

- **A-level**:
- **AS**:
- **GCSE**:
- **OTHER**: e g i lmno q   v / B   G K   NOP R / cde g j l

Gb — St. Elphin's School; Darley Dale; Matlock DE4 2HA
Tel: 01629 732687 (Fax: 01629 733956) *Mrs V.E.Fisher*

		Boys	Age	Girls	Age	TOTAL		Boys	Girls
Day	£753-£1886	1	3-7	155	3-18	226	SIXTH		32
Weekly	£2774-£3075			21	7-18				
Boarding	£2920-£3237			49	7-18				

ENTRY REQUIREMENTS Exam
SCHOLARSHIPS & BURSARIES Schol; Burs; Mus; Forces; Clergy
SPECIAL NEEDS bejknqw GH **DYSLEXIA** c **DIET** acd
ASSOCIATION GSA **FOUNDED** 1844 **RELIGIOUS AFFILIATION** C of E

MAP 9 B 3
LOCATION Rural
DAY ✓ **RAIL** b **AIR** a
SPORT abcfghlmopqvwx AB
OTHER LANGUAGES a
ACTIVITIES cdghijknoqtw AB
OTHER SUBJECTS abcfh
FACILITIES ON SITE abdehk
EXAM BOARDS abc BDE
RETAKES ab **NVQ COURSES** 12

- **A-level**: cde ghi l n p   uv / BC GH K   P R   W / c efg j
- **AS**: cd gh l   p   u / C GH K   R / j
- **GCSE**: cde g i l   v / BC G K   OP R W / cdefgh jkl
- **OTHER**: o

C — St. Wystan's School; 11a High Street; Repton; Derbyshire DE65 6GE
Tel: 01283 703258 *Mrs J.Roberts*

		Boys	Age	Girls	Age	TOTAL		Boys	Girls
Day	£440- £910	55	2-11	59	2-11	114	SIXTH		
Weekly									
Boarding									

ENTRY REQUIREMENTS Assessment & Interview
SCHOLARSHIPS & BURSARIES
SPECIAL NEEDS n **DYSLEXIA** e **DIET**
ASSOCIATION ISAI **FOUNDED** 1926 **RELIGIOUS AFFILIATION** C of E

MAP 9 C 5
LOCATION Rural
DAY **RAIL** **AIR**
SPORT acejlpqx B
OTHER LANGUAGES
ACTIVITIES ghjor
OTHER SUBJECTS ac
FACILITIES ON SITE
EXAM BOARDS
RETAKES **NVQ COURSES**

- **A-level**:
- **AS**:
- **GCSE**:
- **OTHER**: e   no v / B G K O R / cde

C — Stancliffe Hall; Darley Dale; Matlock; Derbyshire DE4 2HJ
Tel: 01629 732310 *A.R.R.Wareham*

		Boys	Age	Girls	Age	TOTAL		Boys	Girls
Day	£910-£2030	109	3-13	47	3-13	179	SIXTH		
Weekly	£2520	10	7-13	2	7-13				
Boarding	£2520	10	7-13	1	7-13				

ENTRY REQUIREMENTS
SCHOLARSHIPS & BURSARIES Forces; Clergy; Teachers
SPECIAL NEEDS bnq **DYSLEXIA** e **DIET** a
ASSOCIATION IAPS **FOUNDED** 1898 **RELIGIOUS AFFILIATION** Inter-denom

MAP 9 B 3
LOCATION Rural
DAY **RAIL** **AIR** a
SPORT acdefjklmpqswx AB
OTHER LANGUAGES
ACTIVITIES cfghijopqstw A
OTHER SUBJECTS cfh
FACILITIES ON SITE cdhjkl
EXAM BOARDS
RETAKES **NVQ COURSES**

- **A-level**:
- **AS**:
- **GCSE**:
- **OTHER**: e g i l no q   v / B G K   OP R / cdef j

DERBYSHIRE continued

C Trent College; Long Eaton; Nottingham NG10 4AD
Tel: 0115 973 2737 (Fax: 0115 946 3284) *J.S.Lee*

	Fees		Boys	Age	Girls	Age	TOTAL	SIXTH	Boys	Girls
Day	£1973-£2125	X	315	11-18	117	11-18	688		150	53
Weekly				11-18		11-18				
Boarding	£2982-£3475		206	11-18		11-18				

MAP 9 C 5
LOCATION Urban
DAY **RAIL** a **AIR** a
SPORT abcdefghkmopqrstuvwx AB
OTHER LANGUAGES
ACTIVITIES abefghijklnopqrsuvwx AB
OTHER SUBJECTS abcdh
FACILITIES ON SITE abcdeghik
EXAM BOARDS b ADEGH
RETAKES a **NVQ COURSES**

ENTRY REQUIREMENTS CEE; Scholarship Exam; Exam & Interview
SCHOLARSHIPS & BURSARIES Schol; Burs; Art; Mus; Forces; Clergy; AP; VI Form; Drama
SPECIAL NEEDS abegjkInqtuw EGHI   **DYSLEXIA** e   **DIET** acd
ASSOCIATION HMC   **FOUNDED** 1866   **RELIGIOUS AFFILIATION** C of E

- **A-level**: cde ghi l opq uv / B GH K P R U / cdefg j l
- **AS**: l q u / G K / ef j
- **GCSE**: de g i l o v / B G K P R / cdefg jkl
- **OTHER**:

C Blundell's School; Tiverton; Devon EX16 4DN
Tel: 01884 252543 (Fax: 01884 243232) *J.Leigh*

	Fees		Boys	Age	Girls	Age	TOTAL	SIXTH	Boys	Girls
Day	£1880-£2350	X	111	11-18	28	11-18	372		131	45
Weekly				11-18		11-18				
Boarding	£3380-£3850		190	11-18	43	11-18				

MAP 2 G 5
LOCATION Rural
DAY ✓ **RAIL** a **AIR** b
SPORT abcdefghijkmopqstuwx AB
OTHER LANGUAGES a
ACTIVITIES abefghijklmnoqstuw AC
OTHER SUBJECTS abcdfh
FACILITIES ON SITE bcdeghjk
EXAM BOARDS abcd ABDEGH
RETAKES ab **NVQ COURSES**

ENTRY REQUIREMENTS Scholarship Exam; Report & Interview; CEE & Interview; Report & Exam & Interview
SCHOLARSHIPS & BURSARIES Schol; Burs; Art; Mus; Forces; Teachers; VI Form; ARA; Drama
SPECIAL NEEDS begjlnqtuvw ABEGHI   **DYSLEXIA** def   **DIET** ad
ASSOCIATION HMC   **FOUNDED** 1604   **RELIGIOUS AFFILIATION** C of E

- **A-level**: cdefg i nop v / B GH K NOP R / cdefg j l
- **AS**: G / ef
- **GCSE**: de g i no vw / B G K NOP R / cdefg j l
- **OTHER**: l u / A Q

C Edgehill College; Bideford; Devon EX39 3LY
Tel: 01237 426200 (Fax: 01237 425981) *Mrs E.M.Burton*

	Fees	Boys	Age	Girls	Age	TOTAL	SIXTH	Boys	Girls
Day	£845-£1725	73	3-18	302	3-18	507		8	76
Weekly	£2070-£2850	1	5-18	27	5-18				
Boarding	£2290-£3160	24	5-18	80	5-18				

MAP 1 E 4
LOCATION Rural
DAY ✓ **RAIL** b **AIR** c
SPORT acefhjlmpqstwx ABC
OTHER LANGUAGES a
ACTIVITIES abcfghijknopqrstwx ABC
OTHER SUBJECTS bcdefh
FACILITIES ON SITE abceghj
EXAM BOARDS abd AB
RETAKES a **NVQ COURSES**

ENTRY REQUIREMENTS Exam & Interview; CEE & Interview
SCHOLARSHIPS & BURSARIES Schol; Burs; Art; Mus; Forces; Clergy; AP; VI Form
SPECIAL NEEDS bejlnpqw AGHI   **DYSLEXIA** f   **DIET** ab
ASSOCIATION GSA   **FOUNDED** 1884   **RELIGIOUS AFFILIATION** Methodist

- **A-level**: e ghi l n s v x / BC GH K P R W / c ef j
- **AS**: f i / G K / ef
- **GCSE**: e ghi l n v / BC G K OPQR T W / cdef hj l
- **OTHER**: m o t / A K O

C Exeter Cathedral School; The Chantry; Palace Gate; Exeter EX1 1HX
Tel: 01392 55298 (Fax: 01392 498769) *R.A.C.Hay*

	Fees	Boys	Age	Girls	Age	TOTAL	SIXTH	Boys	Girls
Day	£775-£1410	92	4-13	13	4-13	143			
Weekly	£2180-£2230	6	8-13	5	8-13				
Boarding	£2250-£2300	21	8-13	6	8-13				

MAP 2 G 6
LOCATION Inner City
DAY **RAIL** a **AIR** a
SPORT abcdefgjmopqstwx A
OTHER LANGUAGES
ACTIVITIES fghijopqstw
OTHER SUBJECTS cfh
FACILITIES ON SITE bcdeik
EXAM BOARDS
RETAKES **NVQ COURSES**

ENTRY REQUIREMENTS Report & Test
SCHOLARSHIPS & BURSARIES Schol; Burs; Mus; Chor; Clergy; Siblings
SPECIAL NEEDS ejknpqtvw EGHI   **DYSLEXIA**   **DIET** ab
ASSOCIATION IAPS   **FOUNDED**   **RELIGIOUS AFFILIATION** C of E

- **A-level**:
- **AS**:
- **GCSE**:
- **OTHER**: de g i l no v / B G K OP R / cde g j

B Exeter Preparatory School; Victoria Park Road; Exeter; Devon; EX2 4NS
Tel: 01392 58712 (Fax: 01392 498144) *J.B.D.Lawford*

	Fees	Boys	Age	Girls	Age	TOTAL	SIXTH	Boys	Girls
Day	£1205	98	7-11			98			
Weekly									
Boarding									

MAP 2 G 5
LOCATION Urban
DAY ✓ **RAIL** a **AIR** a
SPORT abcfgjlmswx AB
OTHER LANGUAGES a
ACTIVITIES fghjopqt A
OTHER SUBJECTS ch
FACILITIES ON SITE abdhjk
EXAM BOARDS
RETAKES **NVQ COURSES**

ENTRY REQUIREMENTS Report & Exam & Interview
SCHOLARSHIPS & BURSARIES Burs; Siblings
SPECIAL NEEDS bejklpqtw GIJ   **DYSLEXIA**   **DIET** abcd
ASSOCIATION IAPS   **FOUNDED** 1884   **RELIGIOUS AFFILIATION** C of E

- **A-level**:
- **AS**:
- **GCSE**:
- **OTHER**: d l no v / B E G K O R / cde

DEVON

104

DEVON *continued*

Bg Exeter School; Exeter EX2 4NS
Tel: 01392 73679 (Fax: 01392 498144) *N.W.Gamble*

		Boys	Age	Girls	Age	TOTAL		Boys	Girls
Day	£1400	645	10-18	38	16-18	730	SIXTH	208	38
Weekly			10-18						
Boarding	£1250	47	10-18						

ENTRY REQUIREMENTS CEE; Exam; Scholarship Exam; Test & Interview; Assessment & Interview
SCHOLARSHIPS & BURSARIES Schol; Art; Mus; AP
SPECIAL NEEDS bejklqtu GH **DYSLEXIA** **DIET** a
ASSOCIATION HMC **FOUNDED** 1633 **RELIGIOUS AFFILIATION** C of E

MAP 2 G 5
LOCATION Urban
DAY **RAIL** a **AIR** a
SPORT abcdefhjkmpqstuwx BC
OTHER LANGUAGES
ACTIVITIES efghijknopqstu AB
OTHER SUBJECTS abcfh
FACILITIES ON SITE acdeghjk
EXAM BOARDS bd ABEGH
RETAKES ab **NVQ COURSES**

| A-level | cdefg i l nopq uv x
ABC GH K   P R TU W
cdefg jkl | AS | cdefg i l   uv
G K   P R
cdef   j | GCSE | de g i l nopq   vwx
AB G K   P R U
cdefgh jkl | OTHER |

C Grenville College; Bideford; Devon EX39 3JR
Tel: 01237 472212 (Fax: 01237 477020) *M.C.V.Cane*

		Boys	Age	Girls	Age	TOTAL		Boys	Girls
Day	£1627	×	95	11-18	122	11-18	390	SIXTH	55	30
Weekly									
Boarding	£3272-£3318	117	11-18	56	11-18				

ENTRY REQUIREMENTS CEE; ; Test & Interview
SCHOLARSHIPS & BURSARIES Schol; Burs; Art; Mus; Forces; Clergy; Sport; Siblings
SPECIAL NEEDS ln **DYSLEXIA** c **DIET** abc
ASSOCIATION SHMIS **FOUNDED** 1954 **RELIGIOUS AFFILIATION** C of E

MAP 1 E 4
LOCATION Rural
DAY ✓ **RAIL** c **AIR** c
SPORT abcdefghjkImopqrstuwx ABC
OTHER LANGUAGES a
ACTIVITIES acefghijkImnopqstwx A
OTHER SUBJECTS abcdfh
FACILITIES ON SITE abcdehijk
EXAM BOARDS abcd ABDEGHKL
RETAKES ab **NVQ COURSES** 23

| A-level | de ghi   op uv
B   GH K   P R
c ef | AS | B   G K
ef | GCSE | de g ij l nopq uv
BC FG   K   OP R   WX
cdef | OTHER |

C Kelly College; Tavistock; Devonshire PL19 0HZ
Tel: 01822 613005 (Fax: 01822 616628) *M.Turner*

		Boys	Age	Girls	Age	TOTAL		Boys	Girls
Day	£1695-£2385	100	11-18	53	11-18	326	SIXTH	72	39
Weekly	£3635	33	11-18	15	11-18				
Boarding	£3795	79	11-18	46	11-18				

ENTRY REQUIREMENTS CEE; Scholarship Exam; Exam & Interview; Report & Interview
SCHOLARSHIPS & BURSARIES Schol; Burs; Art; Mus; Forces; Teachers; VI Form; ARA
SPECIAL NEEDS blntw GL **DYSLEXIA** e **DIET** a
ASSOCIATION HMC **FOUNDED** 1877 **RELIGIOUS AFFILIATION** C of E

MAP 1 E 6
LOCATION Rural
DAY   **RAIL** b **AIR** c
SPORT abcdefghijkImopqrstuwx ABC
OTHER LANGUAGES
ACTIVITIES abcefghijkImnopqstuvw A
OTHER SUBJECTS abcfh
FACILITIES ON SITE abcdegik
EXAM BOARDS bc ABDEGH
RETAKES ab **NVQ COURSES**

| A-level | c efg i l   opq uv
B   GH K   NOP
c ef   j l | AS | c
GH
ef   l | p u
P R | GCSE | e g i l   o   v
B   GH K   P R
cdef   j l | OTHER |

C Kelly College Junior School - St. Michael's; Hazeldon; Parkwood Road; Tavistock; Devon PL19 0JS Tel: 01822 612919 (Fax: 01822 616628) *M.J.Nicholls*

		Boys	Age	Girls	Age	TOTAL		Boys	Girls
Day	£420-£1075	49	4-11	51	4-11	100	SIXTH		
Weekly									
Boarding									

ENTRY REQUIREMENTS Assessment & Interview
SCHOLARSHIPS & BURSARIES
SPECIAL NEEDS n **DYSLEXIA** **DIET** a
ASSOCIATION ISAI **FOUNDED** 1910 **RELIGIOUS AFFILIATION** C of E

MAP 1 E 6
LOCATION Rural
DAY ✓ **RAIL** b **AIR** c
SPORT aefjlpqsx B
OTHER LANGUAGES
ACTIVITIES chjo
OTHER SUBJECTS
FACILITIES ON SITE i
EXAM BOARDS
RETAKES **NVQ COURSES**

| A-level | | AS | | GCSE | | OTHER | e   lmn   v
B   G K   O R
cde |

C Manor House School; Honiton; Devon EX14 8TL
Tel: 01404 42026 (Fax: 01404 41153) *P.A.J.Eyles*

		Boys	Age	Girls	Age	TOTAL		Boys	Girls
Day	£725- £930	86	3-13	74	3-13	171	SIXTH		
Weekly	£1610	6	7-13	5	7-13				
Boarding									

ENTRY REQUIREMENTS Interview
SCHOLARSHIPS & BURSARIES Burs
SPECIAL NEEDS n L **DYSLEXIA** **DIET** a
ASSOCIATION ISAI **FOUNDED** 1958 **RELIGIOUS AFFILIATION** C of E

MAP 2 H 5
LOCATION Rural
DAY ✓ **RAIL** b **AIR** c
SPORT acejmopqsx B
OTHER LANGUAGES
ACTIVITIES cghjot A
OTHER SUBJECTS bch
FACILITIES ON SITE bh
EXAM BOARDS
RETAKES **NVQ COURSES**

| A-level | | AS | | GCSE | | OTHER | e   v
B   G
cde |

DEVON continued

G — Maynard School; Exeter; Devon EX1 1SJ
Tel: 01392 73417 (Fax: 01392 496199) *Miss F.Murdin*

		Boys	Age	Girls	Age	TOTAL	SIXTH	Boys	Girls
Day	£1118-£1391			540	7-18	540			103
Weekly									
Boarding									

ENTRY REQUIREMENTS Exam; Test
SCHOLARSHIPS & BURSARIES Schol; Mus; AP
SPECIAL NEEDS ejknqw Gl   **DYSLEXIA** g   **DIET** a
ASSOCIATION GSA   **FOUNDED** 1658   **RELIGIOUS AFFILIATION** Non-denom

MAP 2 G 6
LOCATION Urban
DAY ✓   **RAIL** a   **AIR** a
SPORT abcdfghlmpqwx ABC
OTHER LANGUAGES
ACTIVITIES acfghijknoqrt AB
OTHER SUBJECTS bcdfh
FACILITIES ON SITE acghj
EXAM BOARDS acd EL
RETAKES   **NVQ COURSES**

A-level: c efg i n p v / BC G K P R U / c efg jkl
AS: B G n / e R
GCSE: e g i l n v / BC G K P R / cdefg jkl
OTHER: h l o u / K O R U

B — Mount House School; Tavistock; Devon PL19 9JL
Tel: 01822 612244 (Fax: 01822 610042) *C.D.Price*

		Boys	Age	Girls	Age	TOTAL	SIXTH	Boys	Girls
Day	£1974 ✗	34	7-13			151			
Weekly	£2723	117	7-13						
Boarding									

ENTRY REQUIREMENTS Test & Interview
SCHOLARSHIPS & BURSARIES
SPECIAL NEEDS ij l   **DYSLEXIA**   **DIET** a
ASSOCIATION IAPS   **FOUNDED** 1881   **RELIGIOUS AFFILIATION** C of E

MAP 1 E 6
LOCATION Rural
DAY   **RAIL** b   **AIR** a
SPORT abcdefhjklmostuwx ABC
OTHER LANGUAGES
ACTIVITIES afghijlmnopqrst A
OTHER SUBJECTS abcfh
FACILITIES ON SITE bchjkl
EXAM BOARDS
RETAKES   **NVQ COURSES**

A-level:
AS:
GCSE: cde g i l o q v / B G K OP R / cde g j
OTHER:

Gb — Mount St. Mary's Convent School; Wonford Road; Exeter; Devon EX2 4PF
Tel: 01392 436770 (Fax: 01392 423572) *Sister E Delaney*

		Boys	Age	Girls	Age	TOTAL	SIXTH	Boys	Girls
Day	£595-£1150	17	3-7	297	3-18	314			22
Weekly									
Boarding									

ENTRY REQUIREMENTS Exam
SCHOLARSHIPS & BURSARIES
SPECIAL NEEDS abghklnqstw GIK   **DYSLEXIA** e   **DIET**
ASSOCIATION GSA   **FOUNDED** 1896   **RELIGIOUS AFFILIATION** R C

MAP 2 G 5
LOCATION Urban
DAY   **RAIL** a   **AIR** c
SPORT abcefghlmpqwx ABC
OTHER LANGUAGES
ACTIVITIES cdeghijkopqst ABD
OTHER SUBJECTS abcdefgh
FACILITIES ON SITE dgh
EXAM BOARDS abcd ABDEHI
RETAKES ab   **NVQ COURSES** 3

A-level: cdefghi mn uv / BC G K O R T W / c ef j l
AS: g / BC K / e
GCSE: de ghi mno v / BC E G K OP R WX / cdef j l
OTHER: ij l / N R

C — Plymouth College Prep. School; Hartley Road; Plymouth PL3 5LW
Tel: 01752 772283 (Fax: 01752 769963) *Guy Pessell*

		Boys	Age	Girls	Age	TOTAL	SIXTH	Boys	Girls
Day	£750-£1060	228	4-11	129	4-11	357			
Weekly									
Boarding									

ENTRY REQUIREMENTS Test & Interview
SCHOLARSHIPS & BURSARIES
SPECIAL NEEDS n   **DYSLEXIA** e   **DIET** a
ASSOCIATION IAPS   **FOUNDED** 1879   **RELIGIOUS AFFILIATION** C of E

MAP 1 E 7
LOCATION Urban
DAY ✓   **RAIL** a   **AIR** a
SPORT abcefgjlmpqswx AB
OTHER LANGUAGES
ACTIVITIES acfghjort A
OTHER SUBJECTS bch
FACILITIES ON SITE bchi
EXAM BOARDS
RETAKES   **NVQ COURSES**

A-level:
AS:
GCSE:
OTHER: e lmn v / B E G K O R / cde

C — Plymouth College; Ford Park; Plymouth; Devon PL4 6RN
Tel: 01752 228596 (Fax: 01752 221267) *A.J.Morsley*

		Boys	Age	Girls	Age	TOTAL	SIXTH	Boys	Girls
Day	£1550	481	11-18	40	16-18	602		186	42
Weekly	£2950	30	11-18	1	11-18				
Boarding	£2970	48	11-18	2	16-18				

ENTRY REQUIREMENTS Exam; Report
SCHOLARSHIPS & BURSARIES Schol; Burs; Art; Mus; AP; VI Form
SPECIAL NEEDS n   **DYSLEXIA** e   **DIET** a
ASSOCIATION HMC   **FOUNDED** 1877   **RELIGIOUS AFFILIATION** Christian

MAP 1 D 7
LOCATION Urban
DAY ✓   **RAIL** a   **AIR** c
SPORT abcdefghklmopstuwx AB
OTHER LANGUAGES a
ACTIVITIES efghijkmnoqrstw AB
OTHER SUBJECTS bcfh
FACILITIES ON SITE cdhj
EXAM BOARDS abcd ABDEGH
RETAKES b   **NVQ COURSES**

A-level: cde g i opq uv / B GH K N P R / cdefg j
AS: h l q / GH
GCSE: cde ghi l o q v / B G NOP R / cdefg j
OTHER: K   R

DEVON *continued*

C St. Aubyn's School; Tiverton; Devon EX16 5PB
Tel: 01884 252393 (Fax: 01884 243122) *A.C.C.Herniman*

		Boys	Age	Girls	Age	TOTAL		Boys	Girls
Day	£176-£1353	147	3-13	81	3-13	260	SIXTH		
Weekly	£1980-£2298	7	6-13	8	6-13				
Boarding	£1980-£2298	8	6-13	9	6-13				

ENTRY REQUIREMENTS Report; Assessment & Interview
SCHOLARSHIPS & BURSARIES Schol; Forces; Clergy; Teachers
SPECIAL NEEDS begjlmnqw BEI **DYSLEXIA** e **DIET** a
ASSOCIATION IAPS **FOUNDED** 1929 **RELIGIOUS AFFILIATION** Christian

MAP 2 G 5
LOCATION Rural
DAY   **RAIL** a   **AIR** a
SPORT acdefghjlmopqsux AB
OTHER LANGUAGES a
ACTIVITIES cfghjoqstuvwx
OTHER SUBJECTS abcfh
FACILITIES ON SITE achj
EXAM BOARDS
RETAKES   **NVQ COURSES**

A-level: AS: GCSE: OTHER: d e g i l no q   v
B G K NOP R
cde j

Gb St. Dunstan's Abbey School; Plymouth PL1 5DH
Tel: 01752 663998 (Fax: 01752 260106) *R.A.Bye*

		Boys	Age	Girls	Age	TOTAL		Boys	Girls
Day	£760-£1500	2	4-7	256	4-18	299	SIXTH		55
Weekly	£1710-£2370			31	9-18				
Boarding	£2010-£2670			10					

ENTRY REQUIREMENTS Exam
SCHOLARSHIPS & BURSARIES Schol; VI Form
SPECIAL NEEDS bhjlnqw E **DYSLEXIA** fg **DIET** ab
ASSOCIATION GSA **FOUNDED** 1850 **RELIGIOUS AFFILIATION** C of E

MAP 1 E 7
LOCATION Inner City
DAY   **RAIL** a   **AIR** c
SPORT acglmopqtvwx ABC
OTHER LANGUAGES a
ACTIVITIES acfghijknoqwx AB
OTHER SUBJECTS abcdfh
FACILITIES ON SITE degk
EXAM BOARDS abcd ADEGJL
RETAKES b   **NVQ COURSES**

A-level: efghi n   uv   AS: fghi n uv   GCSE: e ghi n   v   OTHER: c   l no
BC GH K   P R U W   B   GH   R   W   BC G K   P R U W
bcdef   j l   ef j l   cdef j

C St. John's School; Sidmouth; Devon EX10 8RG
Tel: 01395 513984 (Fax: 01395 514539) *N.Pockett*

		Boys	Age	Girls	Age	TOTAL		Boys	Girls
Day	£345-£1225	105	3-13	62	3-13	250	SIXTH		
Weekly	£2065	15	5-13	9	5-13				
Boarding	£2065	41	5-13	18	5-13				

ENTRY REQUIREMENTS Assessment; Test & Interview
SCHOLARSHIPS & BURSARIES Schol; Burs; Teachers; Siblings
SPECIAL NEEDS lnw BE **DYSLEXIA** **DIET** acd
ASSOCIATION IAPS **FOUNDED** 1976 **RELIGIOUS AFFILIATION** RC/C of E

MAP 2 H 6
LOCATION Rural
DAY ✓   **RAIL** b   **AIR** c
SPORT abcdefghjlmopqstuwx ABC
OTHER LANGUAGES a
ACTIVITIES cfghijopqtwx A
OTHER SUBJECTS abcfh
FACILITIES ON SITE dhj
EXAM BOARDS
RETAKES   **NVQ COURSES**

A-level: AS: GCSE: OTHER: d e g i l   o q   v
B G K   OP R
cde j

G St. Margaret's School for Girls; Magdalen Road; Exeter EX2 4TS
Tel: 01392 73197 (Fax: 01392 51402) *Maureen D'Albertanson*

		Boys	Age	Girls	Age	TOTAL		Boys	Girls
Day	£875-£1360			416	5-18	429	SIXTH		72
Weekly	£2235			13	11-18				
Boarding									

ENTRY REQUIREMENTS Report & Test
SCHOLARSHIPS & BURSARIES Mus; Clergy; AP
SPECIAL NEEDS abgjl **DYSLEXIA** **DIET** a
ASSOCIATION GSA **FOUNDED** 1904 **RELIGIOUS AFFILIATION** C of E

MAP 2 G 5
LOCATION Urban
DAY   **RAIL** a   **AIR** b
SPORT acfghlmpqrx ABCDE
OTHER LANGUAGES
ACTIVITIES efghijknoqs AB
OTHER SUBJECTS abceh
FACILITIES ON SITE
EXAM BOARDS cd AEG
RETAKES   **NVQ COURSES**

A-level: c efg i   nopq uv x   AS: GCSE: d e g i n   v x   OTHER: l   u
BC GH K   P R TU   BC E G K   P R T W   o
cdef   j l   e   cdef hj l

C St. Michael's; Tawstock Court; Barnstaple; Devon EX31 3HY
Tel: 01271 43242 (Fax: 01271 46771) *R.K.Yetzes*

		Boys	Age	Girls	Age	TOTAL		Boys	Girls
Day	£810-£1625	106	3-13	67	3-13	201	SIXTH		
Weekly	£1950-£2640	6	6-13	2	6-13				
Boarding	£1950-£2640	13	6-13	7	6-13				

ENTRY REQUIREMENTS Exam & Interview
SCHOLARSHIPS & BURSARIES Schol; Art; Mus; Clergy; Sport
SPECIAL NEEDS blnw E **DYSLEXIA** **DIET** a
ASSOCIATION IAPS **FOUNDED** 1832 **RELIGIOUS AFFILIATION** C of E

MAP 1 F 4
LOCATION Rural
DAY ✓   **RAIL** c   **AIR** c
SPORT abcefghijklmopqsuwx ABC
OTHER LANGUAGES a
ACTIVITIES acfghijnoqrstwx A
OTHER SUBJECTS cdfh
FACILITIES ON SITE abdhjkl
EXAM BOARDS
RETAKES   **NVQ COURSES**

A-level: AS: GCSE: OTHER: e   lm o   v
ABC E G   K   NO R
cdef   l

DEVON continued

St. Peter's School; Lympstone; nr.Exmouth; Devon EX8 5AU
Tel: 01395 272148 (Fax: 01395 222410) *C.N.C.Abram* — **C**

		Boys	Age	Girls	Age	TOTAL	Boys	Girls
Day	£1025-£1460	123	5-13	49	5-13	213		
Weekly	£2095	24	7-13	17	7-13			
Boarding								

SIXTH

MAP 2 G 6
LOCATION Rural
DAY · **RAIL** b **AIR** c
SPORT abcefjmpqstwx AB
OTHER LANGUAGES
ACTIVITIES acfghjorst A

ENTRY REQUIREMENTS Test & Interview; Report & Interview
SCHOLARSHIPS & BURSARIES Schol; Burs
SPECIAL NEEDS jw l   **DYSLEXIA**   **DIET**
ASSOCIATION IAPS   **FOUNDED** 1882   **RELIGIOUS AFFILIATION**

OTHER SUBJECTS
FACILITIES ON SITE chj
EXAM BOARDS
RETAKES   **NVQ COURSES**

A-level: AS: GCSE: e / cde j   OTHER: B G v

Shebbear College; Beaworthy; Devon EX21 5HJ
Tel: 01409 281228 (Fax: 01409 281784) *R.J.Buley* — **C**

		Boys	Age	Girls	Age	TOTAL	Boys	Girls
Day	£680-£1670	137	3-18	48	3-18	284	46	13
Weekly	£1775-£2960	6	7-18	3	7-18			
Boarding	£1925-£3110	86	7-18	4	7-18			

SIXTH

MAP 2 G 5
LOCATION Rural
DAY · **RAIL** c **AIR** c
SPORT abcdefghjklmopqstuwx ABC
OTHER LANGUAGES a
ACTIVITIES acdefghijklmnopqrstux AB

ENTRY REQUIREMENTS CEE; Exam
SCHOLARSHIPS & BURSARIES Schol; Burs; Art; Forces; Clergy; VI Form; Sport
SPECIAL NEEDS beglnstv BEG   **DYSLEXIA** def   **DIET** abcd
ASSOCIATION SHMIS   **FOUNDED** 1841   **RELIGIOUS AFFILIATION** Methodist

OTHER SUBJECTS bcdefh
FACILITIES ON SITE bcdeghjl
EXAM BOARDS abd AEGH
RETAKES a   **NVQ COURSES**

A-level: de ghi l o v / B G K OP R / cdef l
AS: de ghi l o u / GH K R / c
GCSE: de ghi l o v / B E G K OP R X / cdef l
OTHER: kl

Stella Maris (Grenville Coll Jnr Sch); The Strand; Bideford; North Devon EX39 2PW
Tel: 01237 472208 (Fax: 01237 477020) *Mrs L.Maggs-Wellings* — **C**

		Boys	Age	Girls	Age	TOTAL	Boys	Girls
Day	£625-£1260	64	2-11	91	2-11	156		
Weekly					7-11			
Boarding	£2575			1	7-11			

SIXTH

MAP 1 E 4
LOCATION Urban
DAY · **RAIL** b **AIR** c
SPORT aefjlmopqsx B
OTHER LANGUAGES
ACTIVITIES cgjnort

ENTRY REQUIREMENTS Interview
SCHOLARSHIPS & BURSARIES Schol
SPECIAL NEEDS n   **DYSLEXIA** e   **DIET** abcd
ASSOCIATION ISAI   **FOUNDED** 1929   **RELIGIOUS AFFILIATION** C of E

OTHER SUBJECTS bcfh
FACILITIES ON SITE abcdehi
EXAM BOARDS
RETAKES   **NVQ COURSES**

A-level: AS: GCSE: OTHER: e mno v / B E G K O R / e

Stover School; Newton Abbot TQ12 6QG
Tel: 01626 54505 (Fax: 01626 335240) *P.Bujak* — **G**

		Boys	Age	Girls	Age	TOTAL	Boys	Girls
Day	£1475			76	10-18	155		23
Weekly	£2750			21	10-18			
Boarding	£2825			58	10-18			

SIXTH

MAP 2 G 6
LOCATION Rural
DAY · **RAIL** a **AIR** c
SPORT acfklmnnpqsux AB
OTHER LANGUAGES a
ACTIVITIES cghijknopqtw AB

ENTRY REQUIREMENTS Report & Exam & Interview
SCHOLARSHIPS & BURSARIES Schol; Burs; Mus
SPECIAL NEEDS jln B   **DYSLEXIA**   **DIET** ad
ASSOCIATION GSA   **FOUNDED** 1932   **RELIGIOUS AFFILIATION** C of E

OTHER SUBJECTS abcdgh
FACILITIES ON SITE bdghj
EXAM BOARDS bcd ABD
RETAKES a   **NVQ COURSES**

A-level: efghi l n p s v / BC GH K P R U / cdef j
AS: ghi l / G K P U
GCSE: e g i lmn p v / BC B E G K OP R W / cdef j
OTHER:

Trinity School; Buckeridge Road; Teignmouth TQ14 8LY
Tel: 01626 774138 (Fax: 01626 775491) *C.J.Ashby* — **C**

		Boys	Age	Girls	Age	TOTAL	Boys	Girls
Day	£860-£1370	103	3-18	111	3-18	291	6	1
Weekly	£2500-£2780		6-18	2	6-18			
Boarding	£2500-£2780	51	6-18	24	6-18			

SIXTH

MAP 2 G 6
LOCATION Rural
DAY · **RAIL** a **AIR** ac
SPORT abcdefhjklmopqstwx ABC
OTHER LANGUAGES a
ACTIVITIES abcfghijkloqw A

ENTRY REQUIREMENTS Exam; Scholarship Exam; Report & Test; Report & Exam & Interview
SCHOLARSHIPS & BURSARIES Schol; Burs; Art; Mus; Chor; Forces; Clergy; Teachers; VI Form; Sport; Drama; Siblings   **SPECIAL NEEDS** bjklnt E   **DYSLEXIA** def   **DIET** abcd
ASSOCIATION ISAI   **FOUNDED** 1979   **RELIGIOUS AFFILIATION** RC/C of E

OTHER SUBJECTS bcdegh
FACILITIES ON SITE bcdeghjk
EXAM BOARDS abcd ADEG
RETAKES ab   **NVQ COURSES** 23

A-level: e g i n p uv / G OP / bc ef kl
AS: l
GCSE: e g i j l o v / ABC B E G K OP R X / bcdef
OTHER: h / l O R / l

DEVON continued

C **West Buckland School; Barnstaple; Devon EX32 0SX**
Tel: 01598 760281 (Fax: 01598 760546) *M.Downward*

		Boys	Age	Girls	Age	TOTAL		Boys	Girls
Day	£820-£1622	185	5-18	133	5-18	451	SIXTH	68	42
Weekly	£2055-£2990	24	8-18	10	8-18				
Boarding	£2055-£2990	71	8-18	28	8-18				

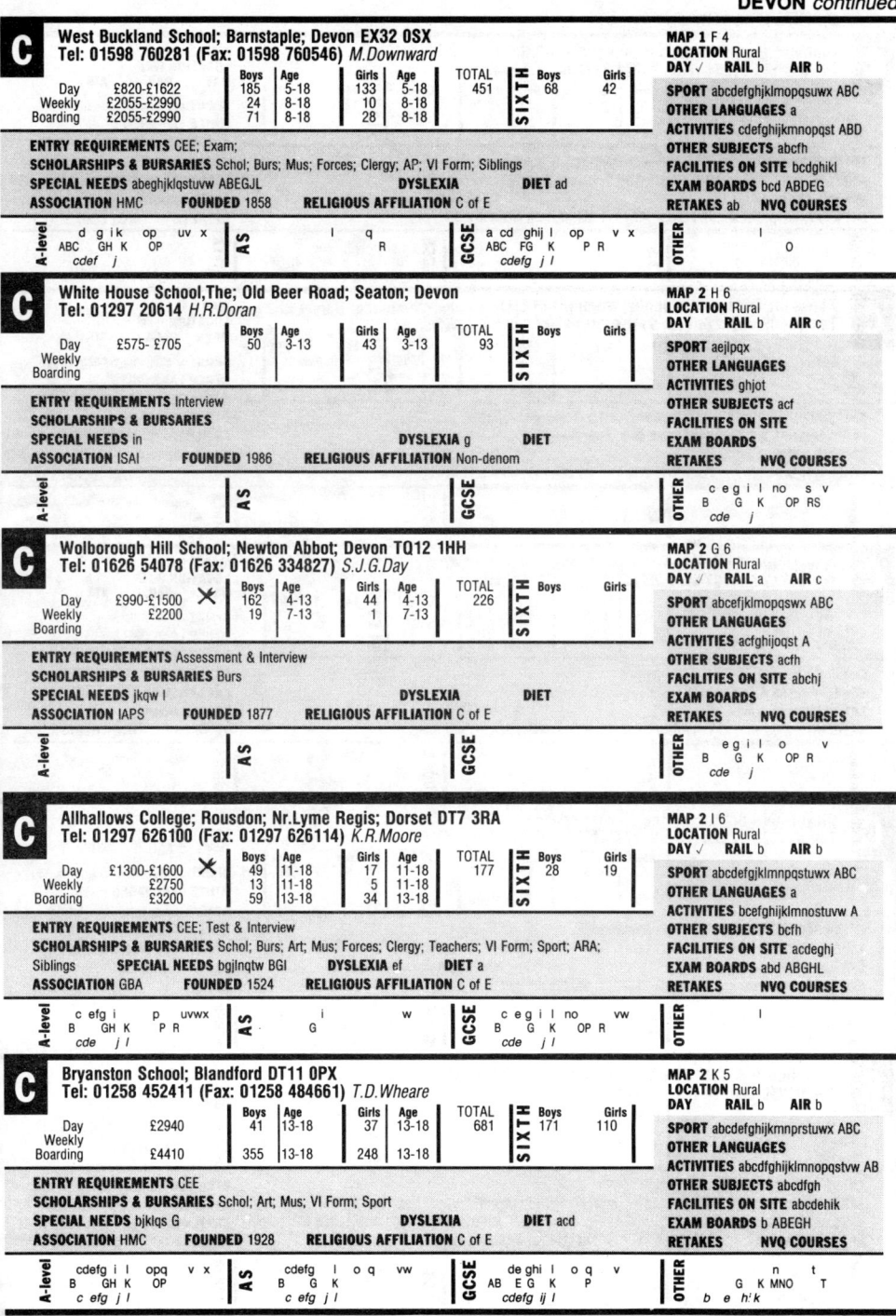

MAP 1 F 4
LOCATION Rural
DAY ✓ **RAIL** b **AIR** b
SPORT abcdefghjklmopqsuwx ABC
OTHER LANGUAGES a
ACTIVITIES cdefghijkmnopqst ABD

ENTRY REQUIREMENTS CEE; Exam;
SCHOLARSHIPS & BURSARIES Schol; Burs; Mus; Forces; Clergy; AP; VI Form; Siblings
SPECIAL NEEDS abeghjklqstuvw ABEGJL   **DYSLEXIA**   **DIET** ad
ASSOCIATION HMC   **FOUNDED** 1858   **RELIGIOUS AFFILIATION** C of E
OTHER SUBJECTS abcfh
FACILITIES ON SITE bcdghikl
EXAM BOARDS bcd ABDEG
RETAKES ab   **NVQ COURSES**

A-level: d g i k   op   uv x / ABC   GH K   OP / cdef   j
AS: l   q / R
GCSE: a cd ghij l   op   v x / ABC   FG   K   P R / cdefg   j l
OTHER: l / o

C **White House School,The; Old Beer Road; Seaton; Devon**
Tel: 01297 20614 *H.R.Doran*

		Boys	Age	Girls	Age	TOTAL		Boys	Girls
Day	£575- £705	50	3-13	43	3-13	93	SIXTH		
Weekly									
Boarding									

MAP 2 H 6
LOCATION Rural
DAY **RAIL** b **AIR** c
SPORT aejlpqx
OTHER LANGUAGES
ACTIVITIES ghjot

ENTRY REQUIREMENTS Interview
SCHOLARSHIPS & BURSARIES
SPECIAL NEEDS in   **DYSLEXIA** g   **DIET**
ASSOCIATION ISAI   **FOUNDED** 1986   **RELIGIOUS AFFILIATION** Non-denom
OTHER SUBJECTS acf
FACILITIES ON SITE
EXAM BOARDS
RETAKES   **NVQ COURSES**

A-level: ABC   GH K   OP
AS:
GCSE:
OTHER: c e g i l   no   s v / B   G K   OP RS / cde   j

C **Wolborough Hill School; Newton Abbot; Devon TQ12 1HH**
Tel: 01626 54078 (Fax: 01626 334827) *S.J.G.Day*

		Boys	Age	Girls	Age	TOTAL		Boys	Girls
Day	£990-£1500 ✗	162	4-13	44	4-13	226	SIXTH		
Weekly	£2200	19	7-13	1	7-13				
Boarding									

MAP 2 G 6
LOCATION Rural
DAY ✓ **RAIL** a **AIR** c
SPORT abcefjklmopqswx ABC
OTHER LANGUAGES
ACTIVITIES acfghijoqst A

ENTRY REQUIREMENTS Assessment & Interview
SCHOLARSHIPS & BURSARIES Burs
SPECIAL NEEDS jkqw l   **DYSLEXIA**   **DIET**
ASSOCIATION IAPS   **FOUNDED** 1877   **RELIGIOUS AFFILIATION** C of E
OTHER SUBJECTS acfh
FACILITIES ON SITE abchj
EXAM BOARDS
RETAKES   **NVQ COURSES**

A-level:
AS:
GCSE:
OTHER: e g i l   v / B   G K   OP R / cde   j

C **Allhallows College; Rousdon; Nr.Lyme Regis; Dorset DT7 3RA**
Tel: 01297 626100 (Fax: 01297 626114) *K.R.Moore*

		Boys	Age	Girls	Age	TOTAL		Boys	Girls
Day	£1300-£1600 ✗	49	11-18	17	11-18	177	SIXTH	28	19
Weekly	£2750	13	11-18	5	11-18				
Boarding	£3200	59	13-18	34	13-18				

MAP 2 I 6
LOCATION Rural
DAY ✓ **RAIL** b **AIR** b
SPORT abcdefgjklmnpqstuwx ABC
OTHER LANGUAGES a
ACTIVITIES bcefghijklmnostuvw A

ENTRY REQUIREMENTS CEE; Test & Interview
SCHOLARSHIPS & BURSARIES Schol; Burs; Art; Mus; Forces; Clergy; Teachers; VI Form; Sport; ARA; Siblings   **SPECIAL NEEDS** bgjlnqtw BGI   **DYSLEXIA** ef   **DIET** a
ASSOCIATION GBA   **FOUNDED** 1524   **RELIGIOUS AFFILIATION** C of E
OTHER SUBJECTS bcfh
FACILITIES ON SITE acdeghj
EXAM BOARDS abd ABGHL
RETAKES   **NVQ COURSES**

A-level: c efg i   p   uvwx / B   GH K   P R / cde   j l
AS: i / G
GCSE: w / c e g i l   no   vw / B   G K   OP R / cde   j l
OTHER: l

C **Bryanston School; Blandford DT11 0PX**
Tel: 01258 452411 (Fax: 01258 484661) *T.D.Wheare*

		Boys	Age	Girls	Age	TOTAL		Boys	Girls
Day	£2940	41	13-18	37	13-18	681	SIXTH	171	110
Weekly									
Boarding	£4410	355	13-18	248	13-18				

MAP 2 K 5
LOCATION Rural
DAY ✓ **RAIL** b **AIR** b
SPORT abcdefghijkmnprstuwx ABC
OTHER LANGUAGES
ACTIVITIES abcdfghijklmnopqstvw AB

ENTRY REQUIREMENTS CEE
SCHOLARSHIPS & BURSARIES Schol; Art; Mus; VI Form; Sport
SPECIAL NEEDS bjklqs G   **DYSLEXIA**   **DIET** acd
ASSOCIATION HMC   **FOUNDED** 1928   **RELIGIOUS AFFILIATION** C of E
OTHER SUBJECTS abcdfgh
FACILITIES ON SITE abcdehik
EXAM BOARDS b ABEGH
RETAKES   **NVQ COURSES**

A-level: cdefg i l   opq   v x / B   GH K   OP / c efg   j l
AS: cdefg   l   o q   vw / B   G K / c efg   j l
GCSE: de ghi   l   o q   v / AB   E G K   P / cdefg   ij l
OTHER: n   t / G   K MNO   T / b e h'k

DORSET

109

DORSET continued

Canford School; Wimborne; Dorset BH21 3AD
Tel: 01202 841254 (Fax: 01202 881009) *J.D.Lever*

		Boys	Age	Girls	Age	TOTAL		Boys	Girls
Day	£3050	110	13-18	13	13-18	467	SIXTH	170	48
Weekly									
Boarding	£4070	309	13-18	35	13-18				

MAP 2 K 5
LOCATION Rural
DAY ✓ RAIL a AIR a
SPORT abcdefghjklmnprstuwx ABC
OTHER LANGUAGES defghijklmnoqstv ABD
ACTIVITIES
OTHER SUBJECTS bcdfh
FACILITIES ON SITE abcdeghijkl
EXAM BOARDS abcd AEGH
RETAKES   NVQ COURSES

ENTRY REQUIREMENTS CEE; Scholarship Exam; Test & Interview
SCHOLARSHIPS & BURSARIES Schol; Burs; Art; Mus; Clergy; AP; VI Form; ARA
SPECIAL NEEDS ejlnqw EGI   DYSLEXIA df   DIET ad
ASSOCIATION HMC   FOUNDED 1923   RELIGIOUS AFFILIATION C of E

A-level: d ghi op v x / B GH K OP / c ef j
AS:
GCSE: cd g i nop v / B G K P R U / cdef hj l
OTHER: l n u

Castle Court; The Knoll House; Knoll Lane; Corfe Mullen; Wimborne; Dorset BH21 3RF
Tel: 01202 694 438 (Fax: 01202 659 063) *R.E.T.Nicholl*

		Boys	Age	Girls	Age	TOTAL		Boys	Girls
Day	£1125-£2190	171	3-13	104	3-13	275	SIXTH		
Weekly									
Boarding									

MAP 2 K 5
LOCATION Rural
DAY ✓ RAIL b AIR c
SPORT abefhjlmnpqstuwx ABC
OTHER LANGUAGES
ACTIVITIES cfghijnoqstw A
OTHER SUBJECTS bcfh
FACILITIES ON SITE bcgjk
EXAM BOARDS
RETAKES   NVQ COURSES

ENTRY REQUIREMENTS Test & Interview
SCHOLARSHIPS & BURSARIES Schol; Burs; Mus; Clergy
SPECIAL NEEDS abgjknw l   DYSLEXIA e   DIET acd
ASSOCIATION IAPS   FOUNDED 1948   RELIGIOUS AFFILIATION Inter-denom

A-level:
AS:
GCSE:
OTHER: cde g i lm o q s uv / AB G K NOP R / cdefg j

Clayesmore Prep. School; Iwerne Minster; Blandford; Dorset DT11 8PH
Tel: 01747 811707 (Fax: 01747 811692) *M.G.Cooke*

		Boys	Age	Girls	Age	TOTAL		Boys	Girls
Day	£950-£2000	105	3-13	56	3-13	230	SIXTH		
Weekly	£2810	3	8-13	3	8-13				
Boarding	£2810	36	8-13	27	8-13				

MAP 2 K 5
LOCATION Rural
DAY ✓ RAIL b AIR b
SPORT abcdeglmopqsuwx AB
OTHER LANGUAGES a
ACTIVITIES acfghjlopqrstw AB
OTHER SUBJECTS abcdefh
FACILITIES ON SITE abcdhik
EXAM BOARDS
RETAKES   NVQ COURSES

ENTRY REQUIREMENTS Report & Interview
SCHOLARSHIPS & BURSARIES Schol; Art; Mus; Forces
SPECIAL NEEDS bjlnqw BEI   DYSLEXIA ce   DIET abd
ASSOCIATION IAPS   FOUNDED 1929   RELIGIOUS AFFILIATION C of E

A-level:
AS:
GCSE:
OTHER: ef i lmno s v / BC G K NOP R / cde j

Clayesmore School; Iwerne Minster; Blandford; Dorset DT11 8LL
Tel: 01747 812122 (Fax: 01747 811343) *D.J.Beeby*

		Boys	Age	Girls	Age	TOTAL		Boys	Girls
Day	£2619	46	13-18	25	13-18	286	SIXTH	49	34
Weekly									
Boarding	£3730	138	13-18	77	13-18				

MAP 2 K 5
LOCATION Rural
DAY ✓ RAIL b AIR b
SPORT abcdefghjklmnopqstuwx AB
OTHER LANGUAGES a
ACTIVITIES aceghijkmnopqstw A
OTHER SUBJECTS abcfh
FACILITIES ON SITE abcdghik
EXAM BOARDS abde AEGHK
RETAKES ab   NVQ COURSES

ENTRY REQUIREMENTS CEE; Report & Interview
SCHOLARSHIPS & BURSARIES Schol; Burs; Art; Mus; Chor; Forces; Clergy; VI Form; ARA
SPECIAL NEEDS bejlnqsw BEI   DYSLEXIA cde   DIET abd
ASSOCIATION SHMIS   FOUNDED 1896   RELIGIOUS AFFILIATION C of E

A-level: c efghi l uv / ABC GHI K P / cdef j
AS: e i / G P
GCSE: e g ij l o v / ABC E G K P R W / cdef j
OTHER: n o

Croft House School; Shillingstone; Blandford; Dorset DT11 0QS
Tel: 01258 860295 (Fax: 01258 860552) *Michael Hawkins*

		Boys	Age	Girls	Age	TOTAL		Boys	Girls
Day	£2295			20	11-18	102	SIXTH		33
Weekly	£3250			23	11-18				
Boarding	£3250			59	11-18				

MAP 2 K 5
LOCATION Rural
DAY ✓ RAIL b AIR b
SPORT abcdflmopqx ABC
OTHER LANGUAGES a
ACTIVITIES cghijknoqstw
OTHER SUBJECTS abcefgh
FACILITIES ON SITE bdehjk
EXAM BOARDS abd ABDEGL
RETAKES ab   NVQ COURSES 2

ENTRY REQUIREMENTS Report & Exam & Interview
SCHOLARSHIPS & BURSARIES Schol; Art; Mus; Forces; Teachers; VI Form; Drama
SPECIAL NEEDS abefjklnqtw AGHIK   DYSLEXIA e   DIET abcd
ASSOCIATION GSA   FOUNDED 1941   RELIGIOUS AFFILIATION C of E

A-level: efg i n v / BC G K P R U W / cde
AS: f
GCSE: de ghi n v / BC E G K P R WX / cdef l
OTHER: l NO l

DORSET *continued*

C **Dorchester Preparatory School; 25-26 Icen Way; Dorchester; Dorset DT1 1EP**
Tel: 01305 264925 *J.M.Rose*

		Boys	Age	Girls	Age	TOTAL		Boys	Girls
Day	£370- £940	102	3-13	68	3-13	170	SIXTH		
Weekly									
Boarding									

ENTRY REQUIREMENTS Test & Interview
SCHOLARSHIPS & BURSARIES
SPECIAL NEEDS n   **DYSLEXIA** e   **DIET** a
ASSOCIATION ISAI   **FOUNDED** 1947   **RELIGIOUS AFFILIATION** Non-denom

MAP 2 J 6
LOCATION Rural
DAY **RAIL** a   **AIR** a
SPORT aejklmpqsux AB
OTHER LANGUAGES
ACTIVITIES cfghijlrt
OTHER SUBJECTS cfh
FACILITIES ON SITE
EXAM BOARDS
RETAKES   **NVQ COURSES**

A-level   AS   GCSE   OTHER d e g i lm o s v
B G K OP R
cde j

C **Dumpton School; Wimborne; Dorset BH21 7AF**
Tel: 01202 883818 (Fax: 01202 848760) *A.G.M.Watson*

		Boys	Age	Girls	Age	TOTAL		Boys	Girls
Day	£960-£1990 ✗	166	3-13	16	3-13	213	SIXTH		
Weekly	£2575	27	7-13		7-13				
Boarding	£2575	4	7-13		7-13				

ENTRY REQUIREMENTS Assessment & Interview
SCHOLARSHIPS & BURSARIES Schol; Burs
SPECIAL NEEDS jklnqw EGl   **DYSLEXIA** e   **DIET** a
ASSOCIATION IAPS   **FOUNDED** 1903   **RELIGIOUS AFFILIATION** C of E

MAP 2 K 5
LOCATION Rural
DAY ✓   **RAIL** b   **AIR** b
SPORT abcefgjkmopqstuwx AB
OTHER LANGUAGES
ACTIVITIES acfghijnoqrtw A
OTHER SUBJECTS abcfh
FACILITIES ON SITE ahjk
EXAM BOARDS
RETAKES   **NVQ COURSES**

A-level   AS   GCSE   OTHER e g i l o s v
B G K OP R
cde g j

G **Hanford School; Childe Okeford; Blandford; Dorset DT11 8HL** Tel: 01258 860219
(Fax: 01258 861255) *Miss S.Canning & Mr & Mrs R.A.Mc Kenzie Johnston*

		Boys	Age	Girls	Age	TOTAL		Boys	Girls
Day						123	SIXTH		
Weekly									
Boarding	£2700			123	7-13				

ENTRY REQUIREMENTS None
SCHOLARSHIPS & BURSARIES
SPECIAL NEEDS jklnpqw Gl   **DYSLEXIA** de   **DIET** a
ASSOCIATION IAPS   **FOUNDED** 1947   **RELIGIOUS AFFILIATION** C of E

MAP 2 K 5
LOCATION Rural
DAY   **RAIL** b   **AIR** c
SPORT almnpqx AB
OTHER LANGUAGES
ACTIVITIES cghjotw
OTHER SUBJECTS acfh
FACILITIES ON SITE dj
EXAM BOARDS
RETAKES   **NVQ COURSES**

A-level   AS   GCSE   OTHER c efg i lm o v
B G K OP R
cde j

C **Homefield School; Salisbury Road; Winkton; Christchurch; Dorset BH23 7AR**
Tel: 01202 476644 (Fax: 01202 477923) *A.C.Partridge*

		Boys	Age	Girls	Age	TOTAL		Boys	Girls
Day	£860-£1340	194	2-16	99	2-16	345	SIXTH		
Weekly	£3225	3	4-16		4-16				
Boarding	£3225	36	4-16	13	4-16				

ENTRY REQUIREMENTS Interview
SCHOLARSHIPS & BURSARIES Schol; Mus; Forces; Sport
SPECIAL NEEDS bejln BL   **DYSLEXIA** cdef   **DIET** a
ASSOCIATION ISAI   **FOUNDED** 1924   **RELIGIOUS AFFILIATION** Inter-denom

MAP 2 L 5
LOCATION Rural
DAY ✓   **RAIL** a   **AIR** b
SPORT abcefjklmpqstux AB
OTHER LANGUAGES a
ACTIVITIES eghjkotu A
OTHER SUBJECTS bcdfh
FACILITIES ON SITE ah
EXAM BOARDS abd AB
RETAKES a   **NVQ COURSES**

A-level l   AS   GCSE de g i l r v
ABC G K OP R
cdef l
OTHER

Gb **Knighton House; Durweston; Blandford; Dorset DT11 0PY**
Tel: 01258 452065 (Fax: 01258 450744) *R.P.Weatherly*

		Boys	Age	Girls	Age	TOTAL		Boys	Girls
Day	£795-£2145 ✗	26	4- 7	57	4-13	161	SIXTH		
Weekly	£2920			38	7-13				
Boarding	£2920			40	7-13				

ENTRY REQUIREMENTS Assessment & Interview
SCHOLARSHIPS & BURSARIES Clergy; Teachers
SPECIAL NEEDS aknw   **DYSLEXIA** ef   **DIET** a
ASSOCIATION IAPS   **FOUNDED** 1950   **RELIGIOUS AFFILIATION** C of E

MAP 2 K 5
LOCATION Rural
DAY   **RAIL** b   **AIR** b
SPORT acjlmpqx AB
OTHER LANGUAGES
ACTIVITIES cfghjnoqrtw A
OTHER SUBJECTS abcfh
FACILITIES ON SITE abcdehj
EXAM BOARDS
RETAKES   **NVQ COURSES**

A-level   AS   GCSE   OTHER e g i l o v
B G K OP R
cde j

111

DORSET *continued*

B | **Milton Abbey School; Blandford; Dorset DT11 0BZ**
Tel: 01258 880 484 (Fax: 01258 881194) *W.J.Hughes-D'Aeth*

		Boys	Age	Girls	Age	TOTAL		Boys	Girls
Day	£2582	9	13-18			209	SIXTH	95	
Weekly									
Boarding	£3868	200	13-18						

MAP 2 K 5
LOCATION Rural
DAY ✓ **RAIL** b **AIR** c
SPORT abcdefgjklmostuwx AB
OTHER LANGUAGES a
ACTIVITIES abdefghijklmnoqrstvw A

ENTRY REQUIREMENTS CEE & Interview
SCHOLARSHIPS & BURSARIES Schol; Burs; Art; Mus; VI Form; ARA
SPECIAL NEEDS behjklnw G   **DYSLEXIA** cf   **DIET** ad
ASSOCIATION SHMIS   **FOUNDED** 1954   **RELIGIOUS AFFILIATION** C of E
OTHER SUBJECTS abcf
FACILITIES ON SITE abcdghikl
EXAM BOARDS abcd ADEHI
RETAKES a   **NVQ COURSES**

A-level: AB de ghi k nop v GH K P R cde l
AS: h G K P uv e
GCSE: B de g i l no v G K N P R X cde j l
OTHER: e l o K O R

C | **Newell House School; Cornhill; Sherborne; Dorset DT9 3PL**
Tel: 01935 812584 *P.J.R.Dale*

		Boys	Age	Girls	Age	TOTAL		Boys	Girls
Day	£625-£725	13	2-11	20	2-11	33	SIXTH		
Weekly									
Boarding									

MAP 2 J 9
LOCATION Urban
DAY **RAIL** a **AIR** c
SPORT aejlmpqsx B
OTHER LANGUAGES
ACTIVITIES cjs

ENTRY REQUIREMENTS Assessment & Interview
SCHOLARSHIPS & BURSARIES
SPECIAL NEEDS j   **DYSLEXIA**   **DIET**
ASSOCIATION ISAI   **FOUNDED** 1947   **RELIGIOUS AFFILIATION** Inter-denom
OTHER SUBJECTS ch
FACILITIES ON SITE
EXAM BOARDS
RETAKES   **NVQ COURSES**

A-level:
AS:
GCSE:
OTHER: e l o v B G NO S cde j

Bg | **Old Malthouse,The; Langton Matravers; Swanage; Dorset BH19 3HB**
Tel: 01929 422302 (Fax: 01929 422154) *J.H.L.Phillips*

		Boys	Age	Girls	Age	TOTAL		Boys	Girls
Day	£825-£2175	41	4-13	10	4-7	120	SIXTH		
Weekly	£2870	10	8-10						
Boarding	£2870	59	8-13						

MAP 2 K 6
LOCATION Rural
DAY **RAIL** b **AIR** c
SPORT abcefjlmoqstuwx ABC
OTHER LANGUAGES a
ACTIVITIES fghijloqrst A

ENTRY REQUIREMENTS Test & Interview
SCHOLARSHIPS & BURSARIES Schol
SPECIAL NEEDS bhjnw G   **DYSLEXIA** e   **DIET** acd
ASSOCIATION IAPS   **FOUNDED** 1906   **RELIGIOUS AFFILIATION** C of E
OTHER SUBJECTS abcfh
FACILITIES ON SITE abcefhjk
EXAM BOARDS
RETAKES   **NVQ COURSES**

A-level:
AS:
GCSE:
OTHER: cde g i l no q stuvw AB E G K NOP RS UV cde g j

C | **Park School,The; 45 Queen's Park South Drive; Bournemouth BH8 9BJ**
Tel: 01202 396640 (Fax: 01202 392705) *M.M.Smyth*

		Boys	Age	Girls	Age	TOTAL		Boys	Girls
Day	£705-£955	128	4-12	121	4-12	249	SIXTH		
Weekly									
Boarding									

MAP 3 B 7
LOCATION Urban
DAY **RAIL** a **AIR** a
SPORT abcefhjlmopqswx ABC
OTHER LANGUAGES
ACTIVITIES cfghjoq A

ENTRY REQUIREMENTS Assessment & Interview
SCHOLARSHIPS & BURSARIES Schol; Burs; Mus
SPECIAL NEEDS ejlnw l   **DYSLEXIA** e   **DIET** acd
ASSOCIATION ISAI   **FOUNDED** 1928   **RELIGIOUS AFFILIATION** Inter-denom
OTHER SUBJECTS acdh
FACILITIES ON SITE ch
EXAM BOARDS
RETAKES   **NVQ COURSES**

A-level:
AS:
GCSE:
OTHER: de g lmno stuv BC E G K O RS X cde

C | **Port Regis; Motcombe Park; Shaftesbury; Dorset SP7 9QA**
Tel: 01747 852566 (Fax: 01747 854684) *P.A.E.Dix*

		Boys	Age	Girls	Age	TOTAL		Boys	Girls
Day	£845-£2585	42	4-14	44	4-14	323	SIXTH		
Weekly	£3510	37	7-14	13	7-14				
Boarding	£3510	122	7-14	65	7-14				

MAP 2 K 4
LOCATION Rural
DAY **RAIL** a **AIR** b
SPORT abcdefghjklmopqrstuwx ABC
OTHER LANGUAGES
ACTIVITIES acfghijlmnopqrstvw A

ENTRY REQUIREMENTS Interview; Report; Report & Interview
SCHOLARSHIPS & BURSARIES Schol; Mus; Siblings
SPECIAL NEEDS ajklntuw BEGI   **DYSLEXIA** e   **DIET** acd
ASSOCIATION IAPS   **FOUNDED** 1881   **RELIGIOUS AFFILIATION** Inter-denom
OTHER SUBJECTS cdfh
FACILITIES ON SITE cehikl
EXAM BOARDS
RETAKES   **NVQ COURSES**

A-level:
AS:
GCSE:
OTHER: de g i lmno qr v BC G K NOP R cdefg j l

DORSET *continued*

Gb St. Antony's-Leweston School; Sherborne; Dorset DT9 6EN
Tel: 01963 210691 (Fax: 01963 210786) *Miss C.Denley-Lloyd*

		Boys	Age	Girls	Age	TOTAL		Boys	Girls
Day	£430-£2287	9	2-8	175	2-18	339	SIXTH		68
Weekly Boarding	£2265-£3505			155	8-18				

MAP 2 J 9
LOCATION Rural
DAY   **RAIL** b   **AIR** b
SPORT abcfghjklmopqstuvwx ABC
OTHER LANGUAGES a
ACTIVITIES cdghijklnopqstvw AB
OTHER SUBJECTS abcdefgh
FACILITIES ON SITE bcdehj
EXAM BOARDS abd ABEG
RETAKES a   **NVQ COURSES**

ENTRY REQUIREMENTS CEE
SCHOLARSHIPS & BURSARIES Schol; Mus; VI Form
SPECIAL NEEDS bgln Bl   **DYSLEXIA** e   **DIET** a
ASSOCIATION GSA   **FOUNDED** 1891   **RELIGIOUS AFFILIATION** R C

A-level: efg i op v   BC GH K   P R   *cdef h j l*
AS:
GCSE: d ghi k o v   B G K   OP R   *cdefgh jkl*
OTHER: f j mn   u   K

G St. Mary's School; Shaftesbury; Dorset SP7 9LP
Tel: 01747 854005 (Fax: 01747 851557) *Sister Campion Livesey*

		Boys	Age	Girls	Age	TOTAL		Boys	Girls
Day	£1950-£2050			81	9-18	299	SIXTH		67
Weekly Boarding	£3050-£3200			218	9-18				

MAP 2 K 4
LOCATION Rural
DAY   **RAIL** b   **AIR** b
SPORT abcfghlmpqx ABC
OTHER LANGUAGES
ACTIVITIES gijklnostw AB
OTHER SUBJECTS abcdfh
FACILITIES ON SITE bdghj
EXAM BOARDS abd BEGH
RETAKES   **NVQ COURSES**

ENTRY REQUIREMENTS CEE & Interview; Report & Exam & Interview
SCHOLARSHIPS & BURSARIES Art; Mus; VI Form; ARA
SPECIAL NEEDS bejkln l   **DYSLEXIA**   **DIET** a
ASSOCIATION GSA   **FOUNDED** 1945   **RELIGIOUS AFFILIATION** R C

A-level: cefg i n p v   B G K   P R   *c ef j l*
AS: c f   G K   u R
GCSE: c e l n   v x   B G K   R X   *cdefgh j l*
OTHER: c   NO   W

C St. Monica's; The Yarrells; Upton; Poole; Dorset BH16 5EU
Tel: 01202 622229 *Mrs N.A.Covell*

		Boys	Age	Girls	Age	TOTAL		Boys	Girls
Day	£452-£1471	39	3-12	144	3-12	183	SIXTH		
Weekly Boarding									

MAP 2 K 6
LOCATION Urban
DAY   **RAIL** a   **AIR**
SPORT acfjlmpqx AB
OTHER LANGUAGES
ACTIVITIES cghijoptw
OTHER SUBJECTS abch
FACILITIES ON SITE bi
EXAM BOARDS
RETAKES   **NVQ COURSES**

ENTRY REQUIREMENTS Scholarship Exam; Test & Interview; Assessment & Interview
SCHOLARSHIPS & BURSARIES Schol; Mus; Forces; Clergy; Teachers; Sport
SPECIAL NEEDS abjknw Bl   **DYSLEXIA** de   **DIET** ac
ASSOCIATION IAPS   **FOUNDED** 1927   **RELIGIOUS AFFILIATION** C of E

A-level:
AS:
GCSE:
OTHER: e g i lmno   s v   B G K   OP R   *cde*

C Sherborne Preparatory School; Sherborne; Dorset DT9 3NY
Tel: 01935 812097 (Fax: 01935 813948) *R.T.M.Lindsay*

		Boys	Age	Girls	Age	TOTAL		Boys	Girls
Day	£405-£1662	92	3-13	54	3-13	193	SIXTH		
Weekly	£2493	10	7-13	4	7-13				
Boarding	£2493	29	7-13	4	7-13				

MAP 2 J 4
LOCATION
DAY   **RAIL** a   **AIR** b
SPORT abcefhlmpqsux AB
OTHER LANGUAGES
ACTIVITIES cfghjoptw A
OTHER SUBJECTS bch
FACILITIES ON SITE adhi
EXAM BOARDS
RETAKES   **NVQ COURSES**

ENTRY REQUIREMENTS Report & Interview
SCHOLARSHIPS & BURSARIES Burs; Forces
SPECIAL NEEDS anv   **DYSLEXIA** e   **DIET** acd
ASSOCIATION IAPS   **FOUNDED** 1885   **RELIGIOUS AFFILIATION** C of E

A-level:
AS:
GCSE:
OTHER: e g i l o q v   B G K   P R   *cde   j*

G Sherborne School For Girls; Sherborne; Dorset DT9 3QN
Tel: 01935 812245 (Fax: 01935 814973) *Miss J.M.Taylor*

		Boys	Age	Girls	Age	TOTAL		Boys	Girls
Day	£2650			11	12-18	453	SIXTH		163
Weekly Boarding	£3850			442	12-18				

MAP 2 J 4
LOCATION Rural
DAY   **RAIL** a   **AIR** c
SPORT abcdefglmntwx BC
OTHER LANGUAGES
ACTIVITIES aghijkoqstw B
OTHER SUBJECTS cfh
FACILITIES ON SITE achj
EXAM BOARDS abcd BEGH
RETAKES   **NVQ COURSES**

ENTRY REQUIREMENTS CEE
SCHOLARSHIPS & BURSARIES Schol; Mus
SPECIAL NEEDS ahln A   **DYSLEXIA**   **DIET** ad
ASSOCIATION GSA   **FOUNDED** 1899   **RELIGIOUS AFFILIATION** C of E

A-level: cd fg i op v   BC GH K   P R   *c efgh jkl*
AS: d   K   ef l
GCSE: cd g i   o v   BC G K   P R   *cdefg j l*
OTHER:

DORSET continued

B — Sherborne School; Sherborne; Dorset DT9 3AP
Tel: 01935 812249 (Fax: 01935 816628) *P.H.Lapping*

		Boys	Age	Girls	Age	TOTAL		Boys	Girls
Day	£3190	33	13-18	X		634	SIXTH	246	
Weekly									
Boarding	£4185	601	13-18						

ENTRY REQUIREMENTS CEE
SCHOLARSHIPS & BURSARIES Schol; Art; Mus; VI Form
SPECIAL NEEDS ew G   **DYSLEXIA**   **DIET** ad
ASSOCIATION HMC   **FOUNDED** 1550   **RELIGIOUS AFFILIATION** C of E

MAP 2 J 4
LOCATION Rural
DAY   **RAIL** a   **AIR** b
SPORT abcdefghijkmostuwx AB
OTHER LANGUAGES
ACTIVITIES befghijklmnopqsvw AB
OTHER SUBJECTS abcdh
FACILITIES ON SITE abcdeghik
EXAM BOARDS abcd BDEGH
RETAKES   **NVQ COURSES**

A-level: c e g i   opq   v / B GH K   OP R / c efg j l
AS: q / G   M
GCSE: c e g i   no q   v / B G K   P R / cdefg j l
OTHER: l no / K O R / a   ef h kl

C — Sunninghill Prep. School; 6 Herringston Road; Dorchester DT1 2BS
Tel: 01305 262306 *C.S.Pring*

		Boys	Age	Girls	Age	TOTAL		Boys	Girls
Day	£425-£935	74	3-13	97	3-13	171	SIXTH		
Weekly									
Boarding									

ENTRY REQUIREMENTS Test & Interview
SCHOLARSHIPS & BURSARIES
SPECIAL NEEDS knw l   **DYSLEXIA** e   **DIET**
ASSOCIATION IAPS   **FOUNDED** 1939   **RELIGIOUS AFFILIATION** Non-denom

MAP 2 J 6
LOCATION Urban
DAY   **RAIL** a   **AIR** c
SPORT aejmopqsx B
OTHER LANGUAGES
ACTIVITIES cfghjoq
OTHER SUBJECTS bch
FACILITIES ON SITE
EXAM BOARDS
RETAKES   **NVQ COURSES**

GCSE: e g i l   o   v / B   G   OP R / cde

Gb — Talbot Heath School; Rothesay Road; Bournemouth BH4 9NJ
Tel: 01202 761881 (Fax: 01202 768155) *Mrs C.Dipple*

		Boys	Age	Girls	Age	TOTAL		Boys	Girls
Day	£520-£1650	1	3-7	515	3-18	545	SIXTH		76
Weekly	£2405-£2900			4	10-18				
Boarding	£2480-£2930			25	10-18				

ENTRY REQUIREMENTS Report & Exam & Interview
SCHOLARSHIPS & BURSARIES Schol; Burs; Mus; Forces; AP; VI Form
SPECIAL NEEDS abln   **DYSLEXIA**   **DIET** acd
ASSOCIATION GSA   **FOUNDED** 1886   **RELIGIOUS AFFILIATION** C of E

MAP 3 B 7
LOCATION Urban
DAY ✓   **RAIL** a   **AIR** a
SPORT acefghjklmopqstwx ABC
OTHER LANGUAGES a
ACTIVITIES acdfghijklnopstw ABD
OTHER SUBJECTS bcdefgh
FACILITIES ON SITE bcdehj
EXAM BOARDS abc ABE
RETAKES a   **NVQ COURSES**

A-level: c e g i   np   v / B GH K   P R U / cdefgh jkl
AS: ef h kl
GCSE: c e g i l   v / BC E G K   P R   W / cdefgh jkl
OTHER: h l m o q   u   x / E l   MNO

C — Thornlow School; Sandesfort House; Buxton Road; Weymouth DT4 9PR
Tel: 01305 782977 (Fax: 01305 778403) *D.H.Crocker*

		Boys	Age	Girls	Age	TOTAL		Boys	Girls
Day	£745-£1220	74	5-16	29	5-16	161	SIXTH		
Weekly	£2335-£2620	19	7-16	7	7-16				
Boarding	£2535-£2725	25	7-16	7	7-16				

ENTRY REQUIREMENTS Test & Interview
SCHOLARSHIPS & BURSARIES Burs; Forces
SPECIAL NEEDS bejklnqw ABEGI   **DYSLEXIA** df   **DIET** ad
ASSOCIATION ISAI   **FOUNDED** 1872   **RELIGIOUS AFFILIATION** Free Church

MAP 2 J 6
LOCATION Urban
DAY ✓   **RAIL** a   **AIR** c
SPORT adefjkmoptuwx AB
OTHER LANGUAGES a
ACTIVITIES cehjkmnotx AB
OTHER SUBJECTS bfh
FACILITIES ON SITE ci
EXAM BOARDS bd IL
RETAKES a   **NVQ COURSES**

GCSE: d g i l   o   v / BC   G   P R

C — Uplands School; St.Osmund's Road; Parkstone; Poole; Dorset BH14 9JY
Tel: 01202 742626 (Fax: 01202 731037) *Mrs L.Dummett*

		Boys	Age	Girls	Age	TOTAL		Boys	Girls
Day	£505-£1225	183	3-16	159	3-16	342	SIXTH		
Weekly									
Boarding									

ENTRY REQUIREMENTS Exam
SCHOLARSHIPS & BURSARIES Schol
SPECIAL NEEDS bejlns   **DYSLEXIA**   **DIET** acd
ASSOCIATION ISAI   **FOUNDED** 1895   **RELIGIOUS AFFILIATION** Non-denom

MAP 2 K 6
LOCATION Urban
DAY   **RAIL** b   **AIR** b
SPORT abcejklmpqswx ABC
OTHER LANGUAGES
ACTIVITIES cfghjot A
OTHER SUBJECTS bch
FACILITIES ON SITE i
EXAM BOARDS abcd
RETAKES   **NVQ COURSES**

GCSE: e g i l   no   v / B D G K   P R U / cdef

DORSET *continued*

Wentworth Milton Mount School; College Road; Boscombe; Bournemouth BH5 2DY
Tel: 01202 423266 (Fax: 01202 418030) *Miss S.Coe*

	Boys	Age	Girls	Age	TOTAL		Boys	Girls
Day	£1847		153	11-18	239	SIXTH		55
Weekly	£2945		30	11-18				
Boarding	£2945		56	11-18				

ENTRY REQUIREMENTS CEE & Interview; Report & Exam & Interview
SCHOLARSHIPS & BURSARIES Schol; Burs; VI Form
SPECIAL NEEDS bejlnpquw DEHI   **DYSLEXIA** ef   **DIET** abcd
ASSOCIATION GSA   **FOUNDED** 1871   **RELIGIOUS AFFILIATION** Inter-denom

MAP 3 B 7
LOCATION Urban
DAY ✓   **RAIL** a   **AIR** b
SPORT abcdfhlnopqtwx ABC
OTHER LANGUAGES a
ACTIVITIES cghijklnoqstwx AB
OTHER SUBJECTS abcdefgh
FACILITIES ON SITE bceghi
EXAM BOARDS abd ABDEH
RETAKES a   **NVQ COURSES**

A-level: BC GH K de ghi l p P R v W x
bcdef j l
AS: g G u P R
GCSE: BC E G K de gil l o P R v WX
bcdef j l
OTHER: BC c efg I K lm OP R p st v x W
cde

Barnard Castle School; Barnard Castle; Co.Durham DL12 8UN
Tel: 01833 690222 (Fax: 01833 38985) *F.S.Mc Namara*

	Boys	Age	Girls	Age	TOTAL		Boys	Girls
Day	£1147-£1649	346	7-18	71	7-18	624	SIXTH	109	38
Weekly								
Boarding	£2135-£2786	182	7-18	25	7-18			

ENTRY REQUIREMENTS CEE; Exam
SCHOLARSHIPS & BURSARIES Schol; Mus; AP; VI Form
SPECIAL NEEDS jlnqw EG   **DYSLEXIA** cde   **DIET** acd
ASSOCIATION HMC   **FOUNDED** 1883   **RELIGIOUS AFFILIATION** Inter-denom

MAP 11 F 3
LOCATION Rural
DAY ✓   **RAIL** b   **AIR** a
SPORT abcdefghjklmnopstuwx AB
OTHER LANGUAGES
ACTIVITIES aefghijklmnopqstuvw A
OTHER SUBJECTS abcfh
FACILITIES ON SITE bcdghik
EXAM BOARDS bcd BDEH
RETAKES   **NVQ COURSES**

A-level: AB c efg i GH op K uv P R U x
cdef j
AS: c cdef l o K R
GCSE: AB c egi l GH op K uv P R U x
cdef j l
OTHER:

Bow School; South Road; Durham DH1 3LS
Tel: 0191 384 8233 (Fax: 0191 384 1371) *J.P.Wansey*

	Boys	Age	Girls	Age	TOTAL		Boys	Girls
Day	£1000-£1596	107	4-13	1		113	SIXTH		
Weekly								
Boarding	£2244	5	7-13					

ENTRY REQUIREMENTS Test; Interview
SCHOLARSHIPS & BURSARIES
SPECIAL NEEDS jnw l   **DYSLEXIA** e   **DIET** abcd
ASSOCIATION IAPS   **FOUNDED** 1885   **RELIGIOUS AFFILIATION** C of E

MAP 12 G 2
LOCATION Urban
DAY ✓   **RAIL** a   **AIR** a
SPORT aefijswx
OTHER LANGUAGES
ACTIVITIES fghjloqstw A
OTHER SUBJECTS cfh
FACILITIES ON SITE cdhik
EXAM BOARDS
RETAKES   **NVQ COURSES**

A-level:
AS:
GCSE:
OTHER: B e gi l G K o q OP R v
cde j

Chorister School,The; Durham DH1 3EL
Tel: 0191 3842935 *C.S.S.Drew*

	Boys	Age	Girls	Age	TOTAL		Boys	Girls
Day	£922-£1320	132	4-13	6	4-4	176	SIXTH		
Weekly	£1920	4	7-13					
Boarding	£1920	34	7-13					

ENTRY REQUIREMENTS Test; Interview
SCHOLARSHIPS & BURSARIES Burs; Chor; Clergy
SPECIAL NEEDS abeijklntuw EGI   **DYSLEXIA** e   **DIET** ad
ASSOCIATION IAPS   **FOUNDED** 1416   **RELIGIOUS AFFILIATION** C of E

MAP 12 G 2
LOCATION Urban
DAY   **RAIL** a   **AIR** a
SPORT abcefghjlsux ABC
OTHER LANGUAGES
ACTIVITIES fghijox
OTHER SUBJECTS abch
FACILITIES ON SITE h
EXAM BOARDS
RETAKES   **NVQ COURSES**

A-level:
AS:
GCSE:
OTHER: B e gi lm o G K OP R v
cdef j

Durham High School for Girls; Farewell Hall; Durham DH1 3TB
Tel: 0191 384 3226 (Fax: 0191 386 7381) *Miss M.L.Walters*

	Boys	Age	Girls	Age	TOTAL		Boys	Girls
Day	£864-£1459		4- 7	427	4-18	427	SIXTH		53
Weekly								
Boarding								

ENTRY REQUIREMENTS Test & Interview
SCHOLARSHIPS & BURSARIES Schol; Burs; VI Form
SPECIAL NEEDS abjklnqtuw H   **DYSLEXIA** g   **DIET** ad
ASSOCIATION GSA   **FOUNDED** 1884   **RELIGIOUS AFFILIATION** C of E

MAP 12 G 2
LOCATION Rural
DAY   **RAIL** a   **AIR** a
SPORT achjlmopqrwx ABC
OTHER LANGUAGES
ACTIVITIES cghijkopqs A
OTHER SUBJECTS bcfh
FACILITIES ON SITE cgh
EXAM BOARDS bc ABDL
RETAKES   **NVQ COURSES**

A-level: BC cde ghi l GH p P R v W
c efg j
AS: BC cde ghi l G K p R ef
GCSE: BC E G K de g i l P R v W
cdefgh j
OTHER: o O u l

DURHAM

DURHAM continued

C — Durham School; Durham DH1 4SZ
Tel: 0191 384 7977 (Fax: 0191 383 1025) *M.A.Lang*

	Fees		Boys	Age	Girls	Age	TOTAL		Boys	Girls
Day	£1695-£2473	✗	166	11-18	13	16-18	315	SIXTH	96	39
Weekly				11-18		16-18				
Boarding	£3231-£3802		110	11-18	26	16-18				

ENTRY REQUIREMENTS CEE; Scholarship Exam; Exam & Interview
SCHOLARSHIPS & BURSARIES Schol; Burs; Art; Mus; Forces; Clergy; Teachers; AP; VI Form; Sport; ARA; Siblings   **SPECIAL NEEDS** begjklnq EGI   **DYSLEXIA** ef   **DIET** abcd
ASSOCIATION HMC   **FOUNDED** 1414   **RELIGIOUS AFFILIATION** C of E

MAP 12 G 2
LOCATION Urban
DAY ✓   **RAIL** a   **AIR** a
SPORT abcdefghikmprstuvwx B
OTHER LANGUAGES ah
ACTIVITIES befghijklnopqsvw A
OTHER SUBJECTS bch
FACILITIES ON SITE bcdehik
EXAM BOARDS abcd BDEGHL
RETAKES   **NVQ COURSES**

A-level cde ghi l op uv
B GH K OP R
cdefg j

AS cde l op v x
G K R
efg j

GCSE de g i l op v
B G K NOP R T
cdefg j l

OTHER 0
d

G — Polam Hall Junior School; Grange Road; Darlington; Durham DL1 5PA
Tel: 01325 350697 (Fax: 01325 383539) *Mrs D.M.Blackburn*

	Fees	Boys	Age	Girls	Age	TOTAL		Boys	Girls
Day	£656-£1010			125	4-11	129	SIXTH		
Weekly	£2325			1	8-11				
Boarding	£2350			3	8-11				

ENTRY REQUIREMENTS Test & Interview
SCHOLARSHIPS & BURSARIES Schol; Forces
SPECIAL NEEDS ejklnqw GI   **DYSLEXIA** e   **DIET** abcd
ASSOCIATION IAPS   **FOUNDED** 1848   **RELIGIOUS AFFILIATION** Inter-denom

MAP 12 G 3
LOCATION Urban
DAY ✓   **RAIL** a   **AIR** a
SPORT aglpqx B
OTHER LANGUAGES
ACTIVITIES cgowx
OTHER SUBJECTS c
FACILITIES ON SITE hk
EXAM BOARDS
RETAKES   **NVQ COURSES**

A-level   **AS**   **GCSE**   **OTHER**

G — Polam Hall School; Grange Road; Darlington DL1 5PA
Tel: 01325 463383 (Fax: 01325 383539) *Mrs H.C.Hamilton*

	Fees	Boys	Age	Girls	Age	TOTAL		Boys	Girls
Day	£656-£1422			237	11-18	288	SIXTH		48
Weekly	£2325-£2883			6	11-18				
Boarding	£2350-£2908			45	11-18				

ENTRY REQUIREMENTS Exam
SCHOLARSHIPS & BURSARIES Schol; Burs; Forces; VI Form
SPECIAL NEEDS abejklnqtw EGH   **DYSLEXIA** de   **DIET** abcd
ASSOCIATION GSA   **FOUNDED** 1848   **RELIGIOUS AFFILIATION** Inter-denom

MAP 12 G 3
LOCATION Urban
DAY ✓   **RAIL** a   **AIR** a
SPORT abcdfghklmnopqtwx ABC
OTHER LANGUAGES a
ACTIVITIES cdfgijklnoqstwx A
OTHER SUBJECTS abcefgh
FACILITIES ON SITE bceghk
EXAM BOARDS abcd ABDEG
RETAKES ab   **NVQ COURSES**

A-level defghi n p uv
BC GH K P U W
bcdef i l

AS fg i x
K R

GCSE de ghij lmn v
BC G K OP R
bcdef ij l

OTHER m o x
A E O

C — St Anne's High School; Angate Square; Wolsingham; Bishop Auckland; County Durham DL13 3AL Tel: 01388 527298 *Sister Mary Michael*

	Fees		Boys	Age	Girls	Age	TOTAL		Boys	Girls
Day	£810-£870	✗	17	4-11	168	4-16	185	SIXTH		
Weekly										
Boarding										

ENTRY REQUIREMENTS
SCHOLARSHIPS & BURSARIES
SPECIAL NEEDS fhjnrw A   **DYSLEXIA**   **DIET** a
ASSOCIATION ISAI   **FOUNDED** 1890   **RELIGIOUS AFFILIATION** RC/Christian

MAP 11 F 3
LOCATION Rural
DAY ✓   **RAIL** b   **AIR** b
SPORT cfmopq B
OTHER LANGUAGES
ACTIVITIES cghjk
OTHER SUBJECTS bcdegh
FACILITIES ON SITE dh
EXAM BOARDS acd AE
RETAKES a   **NVQ COURSES**

A-level   **AS**   **GCSE** d ghi l v
BC G P R
cde

OTHER

ESSEX

C — Alleyn Court and Eton House; Southend-on-Sea; Essex SS3 0PW
Tel: 01702 582553 (Fax: 01702 584574) *P.Green & S Bishop*

	Fees	Boys	Age	Girls	Age	TOTAL		Boys	Girls
Day	£871-£1520	274	3-16	69	3-16	343	SIXTH	1	
Weekly									
Boarding									

ENTRY REQUIREMENTS
SCHOLARSHIPS & BURSARIES Schol; Burs; Art; Mus; Clergy; Teachers
SPECIAL NEEDS bklnpsuw B   **DYSLEXIA**   **DIET** abcd
ASSOCIATION IAPS   **FOUNDED** 1904   **RELIGIOUS AFFILIATION** C of E

MAP 4 I 4
LOCATION Rural
DAY ✓   **RAIL** a   **AIR** b
SPORT abcefhjmpswx AB
OTHER LANGUAGES
ACTIVITIES cfghjnos A
OTHER SUBJECTS abcdh
FACILITIES ON SITE c
EXAM BOARDS abd AB
RETAKES a   **NVQ COURSES**

A-level   **AS** G   **GCSE** c e ghi l no v
B G K NOP
cde j l

OTHER R

ESSEX continued

C — Bancroft's School; Woodford Green; Essex IG8 0RF;
Tel: 0181 505 4821 (Fax: 0181 559 0032) *Dr P.C.D.Southern*

		Boys	Age	Girls	Age	TOTAL		Boys	Girls
Day	£1436-£1898 ✗	441	7-18	502	7-18	943	SIXTH	114	106
Weekly									
Boarding									

ENTRY REQUIREMENTS Exam; Test & Interview
SCHOLARSHIPS & BURSARIES Schol; Burs; Mus; AP
SPECIAL NEEDS abglnqstux H **DYSLEXIA** **DIET** abcd
ASSOCIATION HMC **FOUNDED** 1737 **RELIGIOUS AFFILIATION** C of E

MAP 6 G 2
LOCATION Urban
DAY **RAIL** a **AIR** a
SPORT abcefhjklmpqsuwx AB
OTHER LANGUAGES
ACTIVITIES abcefghijknopqstx A
OTHER SUBJECTS abcdfh
FACILITIES ON SITE abcdhik
EXAM BOARDS abcd BEH
RETAKES **NVQ COURSES**

A-level: cdefghi pq v / B GH K P R / c efg j l
AS: d / G K
o q v / P / e g j
GCSE: cde o q v / B G K R X / cdefgh j l
OTHER:

G — Braeside School For Girls; 130 High Road; Buckhurst Hill; Essex IG9 5SD
Tel: 0181 504 1133 *Mrs.C.Naismith*

		Boys	Age	Girls	Age	TOTAL		Boys	Girls
Day	£985-£1300			198	4-16	198	SIXTH		
Weekly									
Boarding									

ENTRY REQUIREMENTS Test & Interview
SCHOLARSHIPS & BURSARIES
SPECIAL NEEDS bil **DYSLEXIA** **DIET** acd
ASSOCIATION ISAI **FOUNDED** 1943 **RELIGIOUS AFFILIATION** Inter-denom

MAP 6 G 2
LOCATION Urban
DAY **RAIL** **AIR** b
SPORT aflmpqx AB
OTHER LANGUAGES
ACTIVITIES gjkn
OTHER SUBJECTS ch
FACILITIES ON SITE
EXAM BOARDS ad
RETAKES **NVQ COURSES**

A-level:
AS:
GCSE: d g i l v / B G K P R / cde
OTHER: o / o

B — Brentwood Preparatory School; Middleton Hall; Brentwood; Essex CM15 8EQ
Tel: 01277 220045 (Fax: 01277 260218) *T.J.G.Marchant*

		Boys	Age	Girls	Age	TOTAL		Boys	Girls
Day	£1475 ✗	217	3-11		3-11	217	SIXTH		
Weekly									
Boarding									

ENTRY REQUIREMENTS Test
SCHOLARSHIPS & BURSARIES
SPECIAL NEEDS ehjknq GI **DYSLEXIA** ef **DIET** acd
ASSOCIATION IAPS **FOUNDED** 1892 **RELIGIOUS AFFILIATION** C of E

MAP 4 H 3
LOCATION Urban
DAY ✓ **RAIL** a **AIR** b
SPORT acefgjlqwx B
OTHER LANGUAGES
ACTIVITIES fghjot
OTHER SUBJECTS cfh
FACILITIES ON SITE bdhjk
EXAM BOARDS
RETAKES **NVQ COURSES**

A-level:
AS:
GCSE:
OTHER: e o v / B G K O R / cde j

C — Brentwood School; Brentwood; Essex CM15 8AS
Tel: 01277 212271 (Fax: 01277 260218) *J.A.B.Kelsall*

		Boys	Age	Girls	Age	TOTAL		Boys	Girls
Day	£1924 ✗	874	11-18	333	11-18	1259	SIXTH	193	71
Weekly	£3365		11-18		11-18				
Boarding	£3365	44	11-18	8	11-18				

ENTRY REQUIREMENTS CEE; Exam; Assessment
SCHOLARSHIPS & BURSARIES Schol; Burs; Art; Mus; AP
SPECIAL NEEDS abghlntuw EGH **DYSLEXIA** g **DIET** abcd
ASSOCIATION HMC **FOUNDED** 1557 **RELIGIOUS AFFILIATION** C of E

MAP 4 H 3
LOCATION Urban
DAY **RAIL** a **AIR** a
SPORT abcefghjklmpqstuwx ABC
OTHER LANGUAGES
ACTIVITIES abcefghijklnopqrstuv A
OTHER SUBJECTS abcdfh
FACILITIES ON SITE bcdghjk
EXAM BOARDS abcd ABEGH
RETAKES b **NVQ COURSES**

A-level: cdefghi l pq v x / B GH K OP R U / cdefg j
AS: e h l pq / G R / ef
GCSE: cde g i l no v / B G K NOP R U W / cdefgh jkl
OTHER: N

B — Chigwell Junior School; Chigwell; Essex IG7 6QF
Tel: 0181 500 1396 (Fax: 0181 500 6232) *P.R.Bowden*

		Boys	Age	Girls	Age	TOTAL		Boys	Girls
Day	£1299-£1997	276	7-13			289	SIXTH		
Weekly	£1927-£2874	5	7-13						
Boarding	£2038-£3036	8	7-13						

ENTRY REQUIREMENTS Scholarship Exam; Report & Exam & Interview
SCHOLARSHIPS & BURSARIES Schol; Mus; Forces; AP
SPECIAL NEEDS bglnt **DYSLEXIA** f **DIET** ab
ASSOCIATION IAPS **FOUNDED** 1629 **RELIGIOUS AFFILIATION** C of E

MAP 6 H 2
LOCATION Rural
DAY ✓ **RAIL** b **AIR** a
SPORT abcefhjklmosuwx AB
OTHER LANGUAGES
ACTIVITIES abfghijoqstvx
OTHER SUBJECTS abcdfh
FACILITIES ON SITE abcdhjl
EXAM BOARDS
RETAKES **NVQ COURSES**

A-level:
AS:
GCSE:
OTHER: ef l no v / B E G K O R / cdef j

ESSEX *continued*

Bg Chigwell School; Chigwell; Essex IG7 6QF
Tel: 0181 500 1396 (Fax: 0181 500 6232) *A.R.M.Little*

		Boys	Age	Girls	Age	TOTAL	SIXTH	Boys	Girls
Day	£1351-£2077	318	13-18	17	16-18	379		117	23
Weekly	£2004-£2989	19	13-18	2	16-18				
Boarding	£2120-£3157	19	13-18	4	16-18				

ENTRY REQUIREMENTS CEE; Report & Exam & Interview
SCHOLARSHIPS & BURSARIES Schol; Burs; Art; Mus; Forces; AP; VI Form
SPECIAL NEEDS bgjlnqw   **DYSLEXIA** f   **DIET** ab
ASSOCIATION HMC   **FOUNDED** 1629   **RELIGIOUS AFFILIATION** C of E

MAP 6 H 2
LOCATION Rural
DAY ✓ **RAIL** b **AIR** a
SPORT abcefghjklmopsuwx ABC
OTHER LANGUAGES ac
ACTIVITIES abfghijklnopqstvwx AB
OTHER SUBJECTS abcdfh
FACILITIES ON SITE abcdhjl
EXAM BOARDS abc ABDEH
RETAKES   **NVQ COURSES**

A-level: cde g i   nopq   v
B   GH K   N P R
c efg j

AS

GCSE: de g i   nopq   uv
B   GH K   N P R   X
cdefg j

OTHER: d f   l
F   M O
b   i l

Bg Colchester Boys High School; Wellesley Road; Colchester; Essex CO3 3HD
Tel: 01206 573389 (Fax: 01206 573114) *A.T.Moore*

		Boys	Age	Girls	Age	TOTAL	SIXTH	Boys	Girls
Day	£395-£1200	359	3-16	10	3- 7	369			
Weekly									
Boarding									

ENTRY REQUIREMENTS Exam & Interview
SCHOLARSHIPS & BURSARIES Schol; Burs
SPECIAL NEEDS ajklnq B   **DYSLEXIA** cde   **DIET** acd
ASSOCIATION ISAI   **FOUNDED** 1882   **RELIGIOUS AFFILIATION** C of E

MAP 4 J 2
LOCATION Urban
DAY   **RAIL** a **AIR** a
SPORT abcdefhjlmqsx ABC
OTHER LANGUAGES
ACTIVITIES cfghijnopqrt
OTHER SUBJECTS abcdfh
FACILITIES ON SITE bchi
EXAM BOARDS abd A
RETAKES   **NVQ COURSES**

A-level

AS

GCSE: defghi   l   o   uv
AB   E G   K   P R
cdef

OTHER: mn   s
JK   O

C Crowstone Prep. School; 121-123 Crowstone Road; Westcliff-on-Sea; Essex SS0 8LH
Tel: 01702 346758 (Fax: 01702 390632) *J.P.Thayer*

		Boys	Age	Girls	Age	TOTAL	SIXTH	Boys	Girls
Day	£575- £945	126	3-11	119	3-11	245			
Weekly									
Boarding									

ENTRY REQUIREMENTS
SCHOLARSHIPS & BURSARIES
SPECIAL NEEDS bnw B   **DYSLEXIA** e   **DIET**
ASSOCIATION ISAI   **FOUNDED** 1943   **RELIGIOUS AFFILIATION**

MAP 4 I 4
LOCATION
DAY   **RAIL** a **AIR** a
SPORT aefhjlmpq B
OTHER LANGUAGES
ACTIVITIES cdghjn
OTHER SUBJECTS bcdh
FACILITIES ON SITE bh
EXAM BOARDS
RETAKES   **NVQ COURSES**

A-level   **AS**   **GCSE**   **OTHER**

B Daiglen School,The; 68 Palmerston Road; Buckhurst Hill; Essex IG9 5LG
Tel: 0181 504 7108 *D.E.Wood*

		Boys	Age	Girls	Age	TOTAL	SIXTH	Boys	Girls
Day	£835	152	4-11			152			
Weekly									
Boarding									

ENTRY REQUIREMENTS Interview; Test & Interview
SCHOLARSHIPS & BURSARIES
SPECIAL NEEDS abn Bl   **DYSLEXIA**   **DIET** abcd
ASSOCIATION ISAI   **FOUNDED** 1916   **RELIGIOUS AFFILIATION**

MAP 6 G 2
LOCATION Urban
DAY   **RAIL** a **AIR** a
SPORT abefhjlqx AB
OTHER LANGUAGES
ACTIVITIES fghij
OTHER SUBJECTS abcfh
FACILITIES ON SITE ch
EXAM BOARDS
RETAKES   **NVQ COURSES**

A-level   **AS**   **GCSE**

OTHER: e g   l   no   stuv
BCDE G   K   OP RS
cde   j

C Dame Johane Bradbury's School; Ashdon Road; Saffron Walden; Essex CB10 2AL
Tel: 01799 522348 *Mrs R.M.Rainey*

		Boys	Age	Girls	Age	TOTAL	SIXTH	Boys	Girls
Day	£785-£1040	108	4-11	156	4-11	264			
Weekly									
Boarding									

ENTRY REQUIREMENTS Interview
SCHOLARSHIPS & BURSARIES Burs; Teachers; Siblings
SPECIAL NEEDS bgjklnqw Bl   **DYSLEXIA** de   **DIET** a
ASSOCIATION IAPS   **FOUNDED** 1517   **RELIGIOUS AFFILIATION** Non-denom

MAP 4 H 1
LOCATION Rural
DAY   **RAIL** a **AIR** a
SPORT aejlpqx AB
OTHER LANGUAGES
ACTIVITIES cfghjot
OTHER SUBJECTS bcfh
FACILITIES ON SITE h
EXAM BOARDS
RETAKES   **NVQ COURSES**

A-level   **AS**   **GCSE**

OTHER: e g   l   o   s   v
B   G K   O R
cde

ESSEX *continued*

Elm Green Prep.School; Parsonage Lane; Lt.Baddow; Chelmsford; Essex CM3 4SU
Tel: 01245 225230 (Fax: 01245 226008) *Mrs E.L.Mimpriss*

		Boys	Age	Girls	Age	TOTAL		Boys	Girls
Day	£1030	117	4-11	93	4-11	210	SIXTH		
Weekly									
Boarding									

ENTRY REQUIREMENTS Interview
SCHOLARSHIPS & BURSARIES
SPECIAL NEEDS abnqw Gl   **DYSLEXIA** e   **DIET** abd
ASSOCIATION IAPS   **FOUNDED** 1944   **RELIGIOUS AFFILIATION** Non-denom

MAP 4 I 3
LOCATION Rural
DAY   **RAIL** b   **AIR** a
SPORT acefjlmpqx AB
OTHER LANGUAGES
ACTIVITIES cfghijnort
OTHER SUBJECTS abcfh
FACILITIES ON SITE cj
EXAM BOARDS
RETAKES   **NVQ COURSES**

A-level   **AS**   **GCSE**   **OTHER** c e lmno q s v B E G K O R cde j

---

Felsted Preparatory School; Felsted; Dunmow; Essex CM6 3JL
Tel: 01371 820252 (Fax: 01371 821179) *M.P.Pomphrey*

		Boys	Age	Girls	Age	TOTAL		Boys	Girls
Day	£920-£2500	X	119	4-13	78	4-13	232	SIXTH	
Weekly					1				
Boarding	£3075		23	8-13	11	8-13			

ENTRY REQUIREMENTS Assessment
SCHOLARSHIPS & BURSARIES Schol; Forces; AP
SPECIAL NEEDS ablnqs BG   **DYSLEXIA** e   **DIET** a
ASSOCIATION IAPS   **FOUNDED** 1895   **RELIGIOUS AFFILIATION** C of E

MAP 4 H 2
LOCATION Rural
DAY   **RAIL** b   **AIR** a
SPORT abeflmpqsuwx AB
OTHER LANGUAGES
ACTIVITIES cfghijnorstw A
OTHER SUBJECTS abcfh
FACILITIES ON SITE abcdhijk
EXAM BOARDS
RETAKES   **NVQ COURSES**

A-level   **AS**   **GCSE**   **OTHER** egilo v B EGIK OP R cde g j l

---

Felsted School; Dunmow; Essex CM6 3LL
Tel: 01371 820258 (Fax: 01371 821232) *S.C.Roberts*

		Boys	Age	Girls	Age	TOTAL		Boys	Girls
Day	£3010-£3250	X	51	13-18	9	13-18	363	SIXTH	142	37
Weekly									
Boarding	£4120		244	13-18	59	13-18			

ENTRY REQUIREMENTS CEE; Scholarship Exam; Report & Exam & Interview
SCHOLARSHIPS & BURSARIES Schol; Burs; Art; Mus; Forces; Teachers; AP; VI Form
SPECIAL NEEDS bejlst EG   **DYSLEXIA** f   **DIET** ad
ASSOCIATION HMC   **FOUNDED** 1564   **RELIGIOUS AFFILIATION** C of E

MAP 4 H 2
LOCATION Rural
DAY ✓   **RAIL** b   **AIR** ab
SPORT abcefhijklmpqstuwx ABC
OTHER LANGUAGES a
ACTIVITIES cefghijklnoqstuw ABC
OTHER SUBJECTS abcdfh
FACILITIES ON SITE abcdeghik
EXAM BOARDS abcd ABEH
RETAKES   **NVQ COURSES**

A-level defghi l nop v B GH K P R cdefg j l   **AS**   **GCSE** de g i l o v B G K OP R cdefg j l   **OTHER** c M O Q X e kl q u

---

Friends School; Saffron Walden; Essex CB11 3EB
Tel: 01799 525351 (Fax: 01799 523808) *Sarah H.Evans*

		Boys	Age	Girls	Age	TOTAL		Boys	Girls
Day	£1119-£2022	X	116	4-18	131	4-18	347	SIXTH	21	25
Weekly			11-18		11-18				
Boarding	£2008-£3338		52	11-18	48	11-18			

ENTRY REQUIREMENTS Report & Exam & Interview
SCHOLARSHIPS & BURSARIES AP; VI Form
SPECIAL NEEDS abegln BE   **DYSLEXIA** ce   **DIET** acd
ASSOCIATION SHMIS   **FOUNDED** 1702   **RELIGIOUS AFFILIATION** Quaker

MAP 4 H 1
LOCATION Urban
DAY   **RAIL** a   **AIR** a
SPORT abcefhjmpsx ABC
OTHER LANGUAGES a
ACTIVITIES fghijnostvx AB
OTHER SUBJECTS bcdfh
FACILITIES ON SITE bcehik
EXAM BOARDS abc BE
RETAKES a   **NVQ COURSES**

A-level defghi no uv AB GH K P cdef   **AS** ef o w G K c ef   **GCSE** e g i o v ABC G K P R T W cdef   **OTHER** l O

Gosfield School; Halstead Road; Gosfield; Halstead; Essex CO9 1PF
Tel: 01787 474040 (Fax: 01787 478228) *John Shaw*

		Boys	Age	Girls	Age	TOTAL		Boys	Girls
Day	£1035-£1615	X	39	4-18	14	4-18	102	SIXTH	4	
Weekly	£1975-£2575		17		1				
Boarding	£2195-£2885		26	4-18	5	4-18			

ENTRY REQUIREMENTS Exam & Interview
SCHOLARSHIPS & BURSARIES
SPECIAL NEEDS n   **DYSLEXIA** g   **DIET** a
ASSOCIATION ISAI   **FOUNDED** 1930   **RELIGIOUS AFFILIATION** C of E

MAP 4 I 2
LOCATION Rural
DAY ✓   **RAIL** a   **AIR**
SPORT abcdefhjkmpqstwx ABC
OTHER LANGUAGES a
ACTIVITIES acdefghijklmnpqrtuwx A
OTHER SUBJECTS abcdfgh
FACILITIES ON SITE abce
EXAM BOARDS abd BE
RETAKES   **NVQ COURSES**

A-level e h o v B G P cde   **AS** G   **GCSE** egilo s v B G OP cdef   **OTHER**

ESSEX *continued*

C — Heathcote School; Eves Corner; Danbury; Chelmsford; Essex CM3 4QB
Tel: 01245 223131 *Mr. & Mrs.R.H.Greenland*

		Boys	Age	Girls	Age	TOTAL		Boys	Girls
Day	£382-£955 ✗	102	3-11	70	3-11	172	SIXTH		
Weekly									
Boarding									

MAP 4 I 3
LOCATION Rural
DAY **RAIL** a **AIR** b
SPORT abefjlopqx B
OTHER LANGUAGES
ACTIVITIES cfghjnot A

ENTRY REQUIREMENTS
SCHOLARSHIPS & BURSARIES
SPECIAL NEEDS abeghjnqsuw BCGIL
DYSLEXIA e **DIET** a
ASSOCIATION ISAI **FOUNDED** 1935 **RELIGIOUS AFFILIATION** Non-denom

OTHER SUBJECTS cfh
FACILITIES ON SITE chijk
EXAM BOARDS
RETAKES **NVQ COURSES**

A-level | AS | GCSE | OTHER: e lmno v / B E G K O / cde

Gb — Herington House School; Mount Avenue; Hutton; Brentwood; Essex CM13 2NS
Tel: 01277 211595 (Fax: 01462 420416) *R.Dudley-Cooke*

		Boys	Age	Girls	Age	TOTAL		Boys	Girls
Day	£535-£1135	39	3-7	103	3-11	142	SIXTH		
Weekly									
Boarding									

MAP 4 H 3
LOCATION Urban
DAY **RAIL** a **AIR** b
SPORT aejmpqwx
OTHER LANGUAGES
ACTIVITIES cfgjq

ENTRY REQUIREMENTS Interview
SCHOLARSHIPS & BURSARIES
SPECIAL NEEDS
DYSLEXIA **DIET** a
ASSOCIATION ISAI **FOUNDED** 1936 **RELIGIOUS AFFILIATION** Inter-denom

OTHER SUBJECTS ch
FACILITIES ON SITE
EXAM BOARDS
RETAKES **NVQ COURSES**

A-level | AS | GCSE | OTHER: e lm s v / B G K O R / cde j

C — Holmwood House; Lexden; Colchester CO3 5ST
Tel: 01206 574305 (Fax: 01206 768269) *H.S.Thackrah*

		Boys	Age	Girls	Age	TOTAL		Boys	Girls
Day	£1295-£2305 ✗	199	4-13	93	4-13	330	SIXTH		
Weekly	£2655-£2975		8-13		8-13				
Boarding	£2655-£2975	24	8-13	14	8-13				

MAP 4 J 2
LOCATION Rural
DAY **RAIL** a **AIR** a
SPORT acefjklmnpqswx AB
OTHER LANGUAGES
ACTIVITIES cdfghijlnopqrstv A

ENTRY REQUIREMENTS
SCHOLARSHIPS & BURSARIES Schol; Burs; Mus
SPECIAL NEEDS bgjklntu BEH
DYSLEXIA c **DIET** a
ASSOCIATION IAPS **FOUNDED** 1922 **RELIGIOUS AFFILIATION** Inter-denom

OTHER SUBJECTS bcfh
FACILITIES ON SITE behik
EXAM BOARDS
RETAKES **NVQ COURSES**

A-level | AS | GCSE | OTHER: cde g i lmno v / B E G K OP R / cdefg j

C — Littlegarth School; Horkesley Park; Nayland; Colchester; Essex CO6 4JR
Tel: 01206 262332 *Mrs M-L.Harvey*

		Boys	Age	Girls	Age	TOTAL		Boys	Girls
Day	£320-£960	89	2-13	120	2-13	209	SIXTH		
Weekly									
Boarding									

MAP 4 J 2
LOCATION Rural
DAY **RAIL** b **AIR** b
SPORT acefjlmpqsx AB
OTHER LANGUAGES
ACTIVITIES cfghijnoq

ENTRY REQUIREMENTS Assessment; Test & Interview
SCHOLARSHIPS & BURSARIES
SPECIAL NEEDS abefgjklnquw BGIL
DYSLEXIA de **DIET** abcd
ASSOCIATION ISAI **FOUNDED** 1940 **RELIGIOUS AFFILIATION** Non-denom

OTHER SUBJECTS ach
FACILITIES ON SITE bch
EXAM BOARDS
RETAKES **NVQ COURSES**

A-level | AS | GCSE | OTHER: cde g i klmno s v / B E G K OP R W / cdef j

B — Loyola Prep. School; 103 Palmerston Road; Buckhurst Hill; Essex IG9 5NH
Tel: 0181 504 7372 *P.G.M.Nicholson*

		Boys	Age	Girls	Age	TOTAL		Boys	Girls
Day	£1040 ✗	185	4-11			185	SIXTH		
Weekly									
Boarding									

MAP 6 G 2
LOCATION Urban
DAY **RAIL** b **AIR** b
SPORT aefjqsvx B
OTHER LANGUAGES
ACTIVITIES fghjoq A

ENTRY REQUIREMENTS Test & Interview
SCHOLARSHIPS & BURSARIES Siblings
SPECIAL NEEDS l
DYSLEXIA **DIET** a
ASSOCIATION IAPS **FOUNDED** 1894 **RELIGIOUS AFFILIATION** R C

OTHER SUBJECTS ach
FACILITIES ON SITE
EXAM BOARDS
RETAKES **NVQ COURSES**

A-level | AS | GCSE | OTHER: ce l o v / B E G K O R / cde j

ESSEX *continued*

Maldon Court Preparatory School; Silver Street; Maldon; Essex CM9 7QE
Tel: 01621 853529 *A.G.Sutton*

		Boys	Age	Girls	Age	TOTAL		Boys	Girls
Day	£885- £925	70	4-11	51	4-11	121	SIXTH		
Weekly									
Boarding									

ENTRY REQUIREMENTS Interview
SCHOLARSHIPS & BURSARIES
SPECIAL NEEDS bejklnquw GIJ
ASSOCIATION IAPS **FOUNDED** 1956 **RELIGIOUS AFFILIATION** Inter-denom
DYSLEXIA e **DIET** ad

MAP 4 I 3
LOCATION Urban
DAY **RAIL** b **AIR** b
SPORT ajlmpwx
OTHER LANGUAGES
ACTIVITIES jt
OTHER SUBJECTS abcfh
FACILITIES ON SITE
EXAM BOARDS
RETAKES **NVQ COURSES**

A-level / AS / GCSE / OTHER:
e l no s v
B G K O R
cde

New Hall School; Boreham; Chelmsford CM3 3HT
Tel: 01245 467588 (Fax: 01245 467188) *Sister Margaret Mary Horton*

		Boys	Age	Girls	Age	TOTAL		Boys	Girls
Day	£1020-£2201	X 12	4-11	270	4-18	493	SIXTH		111
Weekly	£2388-£3370			83	9-18				
Boarding	£2388-£3438			128	9-18				

ENTRY REQUIREMENTS Report & Exam & Interview
SCHOLARSHIPS & BURSARIES Schol; Burs; Mus; Forces; VI Form; Drama
SPECIAL NEEDS abeghjklnpqtw ABCEFGHIJKL **DYSLEXIA** e **DIET** abcd
ASSOCIATION GSA **FOUNDED** 1642 **RELIGIOUS AFFILIATION** R C

MAP 4 I 3
LOCATION Rural
DAY ✓ **RAIL** a **AIR** a
SPORT abcdefghjklmnopqtvwx ABC
OTHER LANGUAGES a
ACTIVITIES acfghijklnopqstvwx ABD
OTHER SUBJECTS abcdefh
FACILITIES ON SITE abcdefghjk
EXAM BOARDS abcd ABDEGHJ
RETAKES a **NVQ COURSES**

A-level: cdefghi n p v
BC GH K N P R W
c ef j l

AS: de gh v
G K
c ef l

GCSE: de ghi l no v
BC E G K N PQR U W
cdef hj l

OTHER: j lm u
C FG K O R
e

Oxford House; 2 & 4 Lexden Road; Colchester CO3 3NE
Tel: 01206 576686 *R.P.Spendlove*

		Boys	Age	Girls	Age	TOTAL		Boys	Girls
Day	£515-£1025	X 62	2-11	65	2-11	127	SIXTH		
Weekly									
Boarding									

ENTRY REQUIREMENTS Interview
SCHOLARSHIPS & BURSARIES
SPECIAL NEEDS **DYSLEXIA** **DIET** a
ASSOCIATION ISAI **FOUNDED** 1959 **RELIGIOUS AFFILIATION** Inter-denom

MAP 4 J 2
LOCATION Urban
DAY **RAIL** a **AIR** b
SPORT efjmqx
OTHER LANGUAGES
ACTIVITIES cfgjnt
OTHER SUBJECTS abcfh
FACILITIES ON SITE
EXAM BOARDS
RETAKES **NVQ COURSES**

OTHER:
e g lmno s v
B G K R
cde

Park School for Girls; 20-22 Park Avenue; Ilford; Essex IG1 4RS
Tel: 0181 554 2466 *Mrs N.E.O'Brien*

		Boys	Age	Girls	Age	TOTAL		Boys	Girls
Day	£910-£1210			204	7-18	204	SIXTH		19
Weekly									
Boarding									

ENTRY REQUIREMENTS Exam
SCHOLARSHIPS & BURSARIES
SPECIAL NEEDS bkq **DYSLEXIA** **DIET**
ASSOCIATION ISAI **FOUNDED** 1974 **RELIGIOUS AFFILIATION** Inter-denom

MAP 6 H 3
LOCATION Urban
DAY **RAIL** a **AIR**
SPORT acmpqtx AB
OTHER LANGUAGES
ACTIVITIES ghijk
OTHER SUBJECTS cdh
FACILITIES ON SITE
EXAM BOARDS ab BE
RETAKES **NVQ COURSES**

A-level: c e g i p v
B G P R
c e j l

GCSE: c e g i p v
B G P R W
cde j l

St. Anne's Preparatory School; 154 New London Road; Chelmsford; Essex CM2 0AW
Tel: 01245 353488 *Mrs.K.Darby*

		Boys	Age	Girls	Age	TOTAL		Boys	Girls
Day	£770- £905	48	3-11	92	3-11	140	SIXTH		
Weekly									
Boarding									

ENTRY REQUIREMENTS Interview
SCHOLARSHIPS & BURSARIES
SPECIAL NEEDS kln l **DYSLEXIA** e **DIET**
ASSOCIATION ISAI **FOUNDED** 1925 **RELIGIOUS AFFILIATION** Non-denom

MAP 4 I 3
LOCATION Urban
DAY **RAIL** a **AIR** a
SPORT acejmpqx
OTHER LANGUAGES
ACTIVITIES cgijt
OTHER SUBJECTS bcfh
FACILITIES ON SITE
EXAM BOARDS
RETAKES **NVQ COURSES**

OTHER:
e g lmo s v
B G K O R
cde

ESSEX continued

Bg St. Aubyn's School; Bunces Lane; Woodford Green; Essex; IG8 9DU
Tel: 0181 504 1577 (Fax: 0181 504 2053) *Gordon James*

		Boys	Age	Girls	Age	TOTAL		Boys	Girls
Day Weekly Boarding	£915–£1254 ✗	261	3-13	20	3- 4	281	SIXTH		

MAP 6 G 2
LOCATION Urban
DAY RAIL a AIR

SPORT abefjklsx A
OTHER LANGUAGES
ACTIVITIES dfghj

ENTRY REQUIREMENTS Interview; Test & Interview
SCHOLARSHIPS & BURSARIES
SPECIAL NEEDS   DYSLEXIA   DIET acd
ASSOCIATION IAPS   FOUNDED 1884   RELIGIOUS AFFILIATION Non-denom

OTHER SUBJECTS c
FACILITIES ON SITE aj
EXAM BOARDS
RETAKES   NVQ COURSES

A-level	AS	GCSE	OTHER
	de i l o v / B E G K O R / cde j

C St. Cedd's School; Maltese Road; Chelmsford; Essex CM1 2PB
Tel: 01245 354380 (Fax: 01245 348635) *Dr S.A.Foster*

		Boys	Age	Girls	Age	TOTAL		Boys	Girls
Day Weekly Boarding	£900–£1033 ✗	167	4-11	164	4-11	331	SIXTH		

MAP 4 I 3
LOCATION Urban
DAY RAIL a AIR a

SPORT aefjlmpqsx B
OTHER LANGUAGES
ACTIVITIES fghjot

ENTRY REQUIREMENTS Assessment & Interview
SCHOLARSHIPS & BURSARIES Chor
SPECIAL NEEDS   DYSLEXIA   DIET acd
ASSOCIATION IAPS   FOUNDED 1931   RELIGIOUS AFFILIATION Inter-denom

OTHER SUBJECTS cfh
FACILITIES ON SITE
EXAM BOARDS
RETAKES   NVQ COURSES

A-level	AS	GCSE	OTHER
		e lm o s v / B G K O R / cde j

G St. Hilda's School; 15 Imperial Avenue; Westcliff-on-Sea; Essex SS0 8NE
Tel: 01702 344542 (Fax: 01702 435945) *Mrs V.M.Tunnicliffe*

		Boys	Age	Girls	Age	TOTAL		Boys	Girls
Day Weekly Boarding	£852–£1050		3- 7	189	3-16	189	SIXTH		

MAP 4 I 4
LOCATION Urban
DAY RAIL a AIR b

SPORT aflpqx BC
OTHER LANGUAGES
ACTIVITIES cgjo A

ENTRY REQUIREMENTS Exam; Interview
SCHOLARSHIPS & BURSARIES
SPECIAL NEEDS abjnq H   DYSLEXIA e   DIET
ASSOCIATION ISAI   FOUNDED 1947   RELIGIOUS AFFILIATION Inter-denom

OTHER SUBJECTS bcdh
FACILITIES ON SITE h
EXAM BOARDS ab B
RETAKES   NVQ COURSES

A-level	AS	GCSE	OTHER
		e g v / B E G R / cdef	l / K O

C St. John's School; Stock Road; Billericay; Essex CM12 0AR
Tel: 01277 623070 *Mrs S.E.Hillier & Mrs F.Armour*

		Boys	Age	Girls	Age	TOTAL		Boys	Girls
Day Weekly Boarding	£520–£1298	174	3-16	126	3-16	300	SIXTH		

MAP 6 K 2
LOCATION Urban
DAY RAIL a AIR a

SPORT acefgjmopqsx B
OTHER LANGUAGES
ACTIVITIES acghijkoq A

ENTRY REQUIREMENTS Scholarship Exam; Report; Exam & Interview
SCHOLARSHIPS & BURSARIES Schol; Burs
SPECIAL NEEDS In B   DYSLEXIA cde   DIET abcd
ASSOCIATION ISAI   FOUNDED 1928   RELIGIOUS AFFILIATION C of E

OTHER SUBJECTS bch
FACILITIES ON SITE c
EXAM BOARDS abcd
RETAKES a   NVQ COURSES

A-level	AS	GCSE	OTHER
		e ghi l v / B E G I K OP R T WX / cde l	lmnop / A C

C St. Margaret's Preparatory School; Gosfield Hall Park; Gosfield; Halstead; Essex
CO9 1SE Tel: 01787 472134 (Fax: 01787 478207) *John Dann*

		Boys	Age	Girls	Age	TOTAL		Boys	Girls
Day Weekly Boarding	£882–£1055 ✗	58	3-13	66	3-13	124	SIXTH		

MAP 4 I 2
LOCATION Rural
DAY RAIL b AIR a

SPORT acefjlmpqsx B
OTHER LANGUAGES
ACTIVITIES cfghijrt

ENTRY REQUIREMENTS Interview; Test & Interview
SCHOLARSHIPS & BURSARIES Burs
SPECIAL NEEDS ajlnqstu A   DYSLEXIA g   DIET abcd
ASSOCIATION ISAI   FOUNDED 1947   • RELIGIOUS AFFILIATION Non-denom

OTHER SUBJECTS ach
FACILITIES ON SITE h
EXAM BOARDS
RETAKES   NVQ COURSES

A-level	AS	GCSE	OTHER
			e gi l n s v / B G K OP R / e j

ESSEX continued

St. Mary's School; Lexden Road; Colchester; Essex CO3 3RB
Tel: 01206 572544 *Mrs G.M.G.Mouser*

Day / Weekly Boarding £880-£1230 ✗

Boys	Age	Girls	Age	TOTAL
		514	4-17	514

SIXTH: Boys / Girls

ENTRY REQUIREMENTS Exam & Interview; Assessment & Interview
SCHOLARSHIPS & BURSARIES ARA; Siblings
SPECIAL NEEDS bhjlnqt G   **DYSLEXIA** ef   **DIET** a
ASSOCIATION GSA   **FOUNDED** 1908   **RELIGIOUS AFFILIATION** C of E

MAP 4 J 2
LOCATION
DAY   **RAIL** a   **AIR** b
SPORT abcfghklmopqwx BC
OTHER LANGUAGES
ACTIVITIES fghijknoq A
OTHER SUBJECTS bcdfh
FACILITIES ON SITE j
EXAM BOARDS abcd BEL
RETAKES   **NVQ COURSES**

A-level: AS
GCSE: cde g i l n p v / BCDE G K P R W / cdef h j l
OTHER: l / C   O R

St. Michael's School; 198 Hadleigh Road; Leigh-on-Sea; Essex SS9 2LP
Tel: 01702 78719 (Fax: 01702 710183) *Mrs S.Stokes*

Day / Weekly Boarding £900

Boys	Age	Girls	Age	TOTAL
141	3-11	151	3-11	292

SIXTH: Boys / Girls

ENTRY REQUIREMENTS Interview; Test & Interview
SCHOLARSHIPS & BURSARIES Clergy
SPECIAL NEEDS ns   **DYSLEXIA**   **DIET**
ASSOCIATION IAPS   **FOUNDED** 1922   **RELIGIOUS AFFILIATION** C of E

MAP 4 I 4
LOCATION Urban
DAY   **RAIL** b   **AIR** b
SPORT adefhjlmpqtx ABC
OTHER LANGUAGES
ACTIVITIES cfghjnopq A
OTHER SUBJECTS bch
FACILITIES ON SITE di
EXAM BOARDS
RETAKES   **NVQ COURSES**

A-level: AS
GCSE
OTHER: defg lmno st v / BC E G K O R / cdef l

St. Nicholas School; Hillingdon House; Hobbs Cross Road; Old Harlow; Essex CM17 0NJ
Tel: 01279 429910 (Fax: 01279 450224) *G.W.Brant*

Day / Weekly Boarding £1010-£1360

Boys	Age	Girls	Age	TOTAL
142	4-16	142	4-16	284

SIXTH: Boys / Girls

ENTRY REQUIREMENTS Test & Interview
SCHOLARSHIPS & BURSARIES
SPECIAL NEEDS   **DYSLEXIA**   **DIET**
ASSOCIATION ISAI   **FOUNDED** 1939   **RELIGIOUS AFFILIATION** Inter-denom

MAP 4 G 3
LOCATION Rural
DAY   **RAIL** a   **AIR** a
SPORT abcefhjlmpqsx ABC
OTHER LANGUAGES
ACTIVITIES cfghijoqt A
OTHER SUBJECTS ch
FACILITIES ON SITE bcj
EXAM BOARDS abc B
RETAKES   **NVQ COURSES**

A-level: AS
GCSE: de g i l o v / BC G K P / cdef j
OTHER

Thorpe Hall School; Wakering Road; Thorpe Bay; Southend-on-Sea; Essex SS1 3RD
Tel: 01702 582340 (Fax: 01702 587070) *T.Fawell*

Day / Weekly Boarding £780-£1120

Boys	Age	Girls	Age	TOTAL
234	3-16	134	3-16	368

SIXTH: Boys / Girls

ENTRY REQUIREMENTS Test & Interview
SCHOLARSHIPS & BURSARIES
SPECIAL NEEDS n Bl   **DYSLEXIA** ce   **DIET** acd
ASSOCIATION ISAI   **FOUNDED** 1925   **RELIGIOUS AFFILIATION** C of E

MAP 4 I 4
LOCATION Rural
DAY ✓   **RAIL** a   **AIR** a
SPORT abcdefghjklmopqsuwx ABC
OTHER LANGUAGES a
ACTIVITIES fghjoq A
OTHER SUBJECTS abcdeh
FACILITIES ON SITE bchk
EXAM BOARDS abcd AE
RETAKES a   **NVQ COURSES**

A-level: AS
GCSE: e ghij l nop v x / ABC GH K OP W / cdef h
OTHER: o

Widford Lodge; Chelmsford; Essex CM2 9AN
Tel: 01245 352581 (Fax: 01245 281329) *H.C.Witham*

Day / Weekly Boarding £870-£1240

Boys	Age	Girls	Age	TOTAL
150	2-13	2	2-4	152

SIXTH: Boys / Girls

ENTRY REQUIREMENTS Test
SCHOLARSHIPS & BURSARIES
SPECIAL NEEDS ejnw   **DYSLEXIA**   **DIET** abcd
ASSOCIATION IAPS   **FOUNDED** 1935   **RELIGIOUS AFFILIATION** C of E

MAP 4 I 3
LOCATION Urban
DAY   **RAIL** a   **AIR** a
SPORT acefjksx AB
OTHER LANGUAGES
ACTIVITIES fghjmot A
OTHER SUBJECTS ch
FACILITIES ON SITE cj
EXAM BOARDS
RETAKES   **NVQ COURSES**

A-level: AS
GCSE
OTHER: e l o v / B G / cde l

ESSEX continued

Woodford Green Prep. School; Glengall Road; Snakes Lane; Woodford Green; Essex IG8 0BZ Tel: 0181 504 5045 (Fax: 0181 505 0639) *I.P.Stroud*

		Boys	Age	Girls	Age	TOTAL		Boys	Girls
Day	£450-£960 ×	160	3-11	215	3-11	375	SIXTH		
Weekly									
Boarding									

ENTRY REQUIREMENTS None
SCHOLARSHIPS & BURSARIES Burs
SPECIAL NEEDS   **DYSLEXIA**   **DIET** abcd
ASSOCIATION IAPS   **FOUNDED** 1932   **RELIGIOUS AFFILIATION** Inter-denom

MAP 6 G 2
LOCATION Urban
DAY   **RAIL**   **AIR**
SPORT aefjmpqsx B
OTHER LANGUAGES
ACTIVITIES cgjo A
OTHER SUBJECTS ch
FACILITIES ON SITE ack
EXAM BOARDS
RETAKES   **NVQ COURSES**

A-level   AS   GCSE   OTHER: e l o v / B G K O R / cde

GLOUCESTERSHIRE

Abbey School; Church Street; Tewkesbury; Glos. GL20 5PD
Tel: 01684 294460 *J.H.Milton*

		Boys	Age	Girls	Age	TOTAL		Boys	Girls
Day	£330-£1765 ×	63	3-13	37	3-13	108	SIXTH		
Weekly	£2140-£2455	8	8-13		8-13				
Boarding									

ENTRY REQUIREMENTS Test; Interview
SCHOLARSHIPS & BURSARIES Burs; Chor
SPECIAL NEEDS   **DYSLEXIA**   **DIET** a
ASSOCIATION IAPS   **FOUNDED** 1973   **RELIGIOUS AFFILIATION** C of E

MAP 8 J 8
LOCATION Urban
DAY   **RAIL** b   **AIR** b
SPORT acefjlmpqstx AB
OTHER LANGUAGES
ACTIVITIES cfghjorst
OTHER SUBJECTS ch
FACILITIES ON SITE h
EXAM BOARDS
RETAKES   **NVQ COURSES**

A-level   AS   GCSE   OTHER: d e g i l n v / B G K OP R / cde j

---

Beaudesert Park; Minchinhampton; Stroud; Glos. GL6 9AF
Tel: 01453 832072 (Fax: 01453 836040) *J.R.W.Beasley*

		Boys	Age	Girls	Age	TOTAL		Boys	Girls
Day	£1050-£2100 ×	98	4-13	96	4-13	267	SIXTH		
Weekly	£2853	31	8-13	14	8-13				
Boarding	£2853	19	8-13	9	8-13				

ENTRY REQUIREMENTS Test & Interview
SCHOLARSHIPS & BURSARIES Forces
SPECIAL NEEDS abgjklnq G   **DYSLEXIA** e   **DIET** acd
ASSOCIATION IAPS   **FOUNDED** 1908   **RELIGIOUS AFFILIATION** C of E

MAP 2 K 1
LOCATION Rural
DAY ✓   **RAIL** a   **AIR** b
SPORT abcefgjklmopqstuwx ABC
OTHER LANGUAGES
ACTIVITIES abcfghijlnoqrstw A
OTHER SUBJECTS abcfh
FACILITIES ON SITE chijk
EXAM BOARDS
RETAKES   **NVQ COURSES**

A-level   AS   GCSE   OTHER: e g i lmno q v / B G K OP R / cdef j

---

Bredon School; Pull Court; Bushley; Tewkesbury; Glos. GL20 6AH
Tel: 01684 293156 (Fax: 01684 298008) *Colin E.Wheeler*

		Boys	Age	Girls	Age	TOTAL		Boys	Girls
Day	£800-£2320	89	3-18	34	3-18	301	SIXTH	58	7
Weekly	£2650-£3990	38	7-18	5	7-18				
Boarding	£2710-£4050	121	7-18	14	7-18				

ENTRY REQUIREMENTS Report & Interview
SCHOLARSHIPS & BURSARIES Schol; Burs
SPECIAL NEEDS abejlnqvw BGI   **DYSLEXIA** cde   **DIET** ad
ASSOCIATION ISAI   **FOUNDED** 1962   **RELIGIOUS AFFILIATION** C of E

MAP 8 J 8
LOCATION Rural
DAY ✓   **RAIL** b   **AIR** a
SPORT abcdefghjklmpqrstuwx ABC
OTHER LANGUAGES a
ACTIVITIES abfghijklmnopqstuw AC
OTHER SUBJECTS bcdfh
FACILITIES ON SITE abcfghj
EXAM BOARDS abcde ABDEGHKL
RETAKES a   **NVQ COURSES** 123

A-level: de hj p v / B G N / cde
AS: e / G / cd
GCSE: p v / U
OTHER e ghij l op v / AB E G I NOP S / cde
OTHER: d h r / S

Cheltenham College Junior School; Thirlestaine Road; Cheltenham GL53 7AB
Tel: 01242 522697 (Fax: 01242 256553) *N.I.Archdale*

		Boys	Age	Girls	Age	TOTAL		Boys	Girls
Day	£565-£2220 ×	194	3-13	32	3-11	294	SIXTH		
Weekly		68	7-13		7-11				
Boarding	£2310-£2870								

ENTRY REQUIREMENTS Test & Interview
SCHOLARSHIPS & BURSARIES Schol; Art; Mus; Sport; Drama
SPECIAL NEEDS abjklnqstuw ABDEGH   **DYSLEXIA**   **DIET** abcd
ASSOCIATION IAPS   **FOUNDED** 1841   **RELIGIOUS AFFILIATION** C of E

MAP 8 J 8
LOCATION Urban
DAY ✓   **RAIL** a   **AIR** b
SPORT abcdefghjl mopqrstuwx AB
OTHER LANGUAGES a
ACTIVITIES acfghijlmnopqrstwx A
OTHER SUBJECTS abcdfh
FACILITIES ON SITE abcdik
EXAM BOARDS
RETAKES   **NVQ COURSES**

A-level   AS   GCSE   OTHER: c e g i lmno q v / AB G K OP R / cdefg ij l

GLOUCESTERSHIRE continued

Cheltenham College; Bath Road; Cheltenham GL53 7LD
Tel: 01242 513540 (Fax: 01242 577746) *P.D.V Wilkes*

		Boys	Age	Girls	Age	TOTAL		Boys	Girls
Day	£3075	164	13-18	15	16-18	577	SIXTH	192	103
Weekly									
Boarding	£4070	316	13-18	82	16-18				

ENTRY REQUIREMENTS CEE
SCHOLARSHIPS & BURSARIES Schol; Art; Mus; VI Form; ARA
SPECIAL NEEDS eij   **DYSLEXIA**   **DIET** a
ASSOCIATION HMC   **FOUNDED** 1841   **RELIGIOUS AFFILIATION** C of E

MAP 8 J 8
LOCATION Urban
DAY   **RAIL** a   **AIR** a
SPORT acefikmprstuwx B
OTHER LANGUAGES
ACTIVITIES abefghijkmopqst AB
OTHER SUBJECTS bcdfh
FACILITIES ON SITE abcdehik
EXAM BOARDS bd ADEH
RETAKES   **NVQ COURSES**

A-level: c efg i opq uv x / B GH K P R / cdefgh jkl
AS: q
GCSE: G / j
GCSE: e g i o q vw / B GH K N P R / cdefg j l
OTHER:

Cheltenham Ladies' College,The; Cheltenham GL50 3EP
Tel: 01242 520691 (Fax: 01242 227882) *Miss E.Castle*

		Boys	Age	Girls	Age	TOTAL		Boys	Girls
Day	£2600			201	11-18	853	SIXTH		277
Weekly									
Boarding	£4095			652	11-18				

ENTRY REQUIREMENTS CEE; Scholarship Exam
SCHOLARSHIPS & BURSARIES Schol; Burs; Art; Mus; AP; VI Form
SPECIAL NEEDS abglnqw   **DYSLEXIA** e   **DIET** abcd
ASSOCIATION GSA   **FOUNDED** 1853   **RELIGIOUS AFFILIATION** Christian

MAP 8 J 8
LOCATION Urban
DAY   **RAIL** a   **AIR** b
SPORT abceghklmnpqrtuwx ABC
OTHER LANGUAGES
ACTIVITIES acfghijklnoqrstw AB
OTHER SUBJECTS abcfh
FACILITIES ON SITE abceghik
EXAM BOARDS abcd ABDEH
RETAKES a   **NVQ COURSES**

A-level: cdefg i l n p v x / BC GH K P R W / cdefgh jkl
AS:
GCSE: c e g i no q v / BC G K P R / bcdefg ijkl
OTHER:

Dean Close Junior School; Cheltenham; Glos. GL51 6QS
Tel: 01242 512217 (Fax: 01242 221195) *I.F.M.Ferguson*

		Boys	Age	Girls	Age	TOTAL		Boys	Girls
Day	£910-£2025 X	89	3-13	82	3-13	249	SIXTH		
Weekly	£2500		7- 9						
Boarding	£2960	49	7-13	29	7-13				

ENTRY REQUIREMENTS Test; Assessment
SCHOLARSHIPS & BURSARIES Schol; Burs; Mus; Forces; Clergy; Teachers
SPECIAL NEEDS jknw l   **DYSLEXIA** de   **DIET** a
ASSOCIATION IAPS   **FOUNDED** 1926   **RELIGIOUS AFFILIATION** C of E

MAP 8 J 8
LOCATION Urban
DAY   **RAIL** a   **AIR** b
SPORT abcdefgjklmopqsuwx ABC
OTHER LANGUAGES a
ACTIVITIES cfghijlopqrstuw A
OTHER SUBJECTS abcfh
FACILITIES ON SITE acdhik
EXAM BOARDS
RETAKES   **NVQ COURSES**

A-level:
AS:
GCSE:
OTHER: e lmno v / B K NOP R / cde g j

Dean Close School; Cheltenham; Glos. GL51 6HE
Tel: 01242 522640 (Fax: 01242 244758) *C.J.Bacon*

		Boys	Age	Girls	Age	TOTAL		Boys	Girls
Day	£2845	96	13-18	79	13-18	448	SIXTH	96	77
Weekly									
Boarding	£4075	160	13-18	113	13-18				

ENTRY REQUIREMENTS CEE; Scholarship Exam; Report & Exam & Interview
SCHOLARSHIPS & BURSARIES Schol; Burs; Art; Mus; Forces; Teachers; VI Form
SPECIAL NEEDS abegjklnqstuw ABEGI   **DYSLEXIA** c   **DIET** abcd
ASSOCIATION HMC   **FOUNDED** 1886   **RELIGIOUS AFFILIATION** C of E

MAP 8 J 8
LOCATION Urban
DAY   **RAIL** a   **AIR** b
SPORT abcdefghijklmopqstuwx ABC
OTHER LANGUAGES a
ACTIVITIES abcefghijklnopqrstuw A
OTHER SUBJECTS bcfh
FACILITIES ON SITE abcdhik
EXAM BOARDS abcd ABDEGH
RETAKES   **NVQ COURSES**

A-level: cd fg i l op v x / B GH K M OP / c efg j l
AS: h / ef l
GCSE: cd g i no q v / BC G K N P R / cdefg j l
OTHER:

Hatherop Castle Preparatory School; Cirencester; Glos. GL7 3NB
Tel: 01285 750206 (Fax: 01285 750430) *P.Easterbrook*

		Boys	Age	Girls	Age	TOTAL		Boys	Girls
Day	£1000-£1600 X	99	2-13	130	2-13	248	SIXTH		
Weekly	£2500	7	7-13	8	7-13				
Boarding	£2500	3	7-13	1	7-13				

ENTRY REQUIREMENTS Exam; Test; Scholarship Exam; Interview; Report; Assessment & Interview
SCHOLARSHIPS & BURSARIES Schol; Burs; Art; Mus; Forces
SPECIAL NEEDS ablnw ABEI   **DYSLEXIA** de   **DIET** a
ASSOCIATION ISAI   **FOUNDED** 1926   **RELIGIOUS AFFILIATION** C of E

MAP 2 K 1
LOCATION Rural
DAY ✓   **RAIL** b   **AIR** b
SPORT abcefhijlmnpqswx ABC
OTHER LANGUAGES
ACTIVITIES abcfghjloqrstvw
OTHER SUBJECTS abcfh
FACILITIES ON SITE cdehj
EXAM BOARDS
RETAKES   **NVQ COURSES**

A-level:
AS:
GCSE:
OTHER: de g i lmno q s v / BCDE G K   OP RS   W / cdef

GLOUCESTERSHIRE continued

King's School; Pitt Street; Gloucester GL1 2BG
Tel: 01452 521251 (Fax: 01452 385275) *P.R.Lacey*

		Boys	Age	Girls	Age	TOTAL	Boys	Girls
Day	£595-£1890	305	3-19	142	3-19	500	61	22
Weekly	£2450-£3075	2	11-19	2	11-19			
Boarding	£2515-£3140	39	11-19	10	11-19			

MAP 8 J 8
LOCATION Urban
DAY ✓ **RAIL** a **AIR** b
SPORT abcefhklmpqrstwx BC
OTHER LANGUAGES
ACTIVITIES abcdefghijkloqt AB

ENTRY REQUIREMENTS CEE; Test & Interview
SCHOLARSHIPS & BURSARIES Schol; Mus; Chor; Forces
SPECIAL NEEDS glnq AB
ASSOCIATION SHMIS **FOUNDED** 1541 **RELIGIOUS AFFILIATION** C of E
DYSLEXIA **DIET** ad
OTHER SUBJECTS cdfh
FACILITIES ON SITE acdegj
EXAM BOARDS abd ABDEHL
RETAKES a **NVQ COURSES**

A-level: de ghi no vw B GH K P R U W cdefg j
AS: B G K
GCSE: i l q u P R e ghi B G K cdefg j o v OP R U W
OTHER: h mn F I K k

Kitebrook House; Moreton-in-Marsh; Glos. GL56 0RP
Tel: 01608 674 350 *Mrs A.Mc Dermott*

		Boys	Age	Girls	Age	TOTAL	Boys	Girls
Day	£580-£1580	40	4-8	93	4-13	168		
Weekly	£1900-£2400			35	7-13			
Boarding								

MAP 8 K 8
LOCATION Rural
DAY **RAIL** a **AIR** b
SPORT afjlpqx AB
OTHER LANGUAGES a
ACTIVITIES aghijot

ENTRY REQUIREMENTS Interview
SCHOLARSHIPS & BURSARIES
SPECIAL NEEDS eijlnw BC
ASSOCIATION IAPS **FOUNDED** 1955 **RELIGIOUS AFFILIATION** C of E
DYSLEXIA d **DIET**
OTHER SUBJECTS abcfhk
FACILITIES ON SITE i
EXAM BOARDS
RETAKES **NVQ COURSES**

A-level:
AS:
GCSE:
OTHER: de gil o qs v B E G K OP R cdef j

Rendcomb College; Nr. Cirencester; Glos. GL7 7HA
Tel: 01285 831213 (Fax: 01285 831331) *J.N.Tolputt*

		Boys	Age	Girls	Age	TOTAL	Boys	Girls
Day	£2144-£2814	23	11-18	23	11-18	247	53	17
Weekly								
Boarding	£2769-£3558	158	11-18	43	11-18			

MAP 2 K 1
LOCATION Rural
DAY **RAIL** b **AIR** b
SPORT abcdefhjkmopstuwx AB
OTHER LANGUAGES a
ACTIVITIES acdfghijklmnoqrstw A

ENTRY REQUIREMENTS CEE; Exam
SCHOLARSHIPS & BURSARIES Schol; Burs; Art; Mus; Forces; VI Form; Sport; Drama
SPECIAL NEEDS bjlns EH
ASSOCIATION HMC **FOUNDED** 1920 **RELIGIOUS AFFILIATION** C of E
DYSLEXIA **DIET** a
OTHER SUBJECTS bcdfh
FACILITIES ON SITE bcdehjkl
EXAM BOARDS bd ABEG
RETAKES a **NVQ COURSES**

A-level: e h l o v x BC G K cdef j
AS: h
GCSE: e h l o v x BC G K cdef j
OTHER:

Richard Pate School,The; Southern Road; Leckhampton; Cheltenham; Glos. GL53 9RP
Tel: 01242 522086 (Fax: 01242 522086) *E.L.Rowland*

		Boys	Age	Girls	Age	TOTAL	Boys	Girls
Day	£437-£1014	164	3-11	120	3-11	284		
Weekly								
Boarding								

MAP 8 J 8
LOCATION Rural
DAY **RAIL** a **AIR** b
SPORT abcefjlmpqsx A
OTHER LANGUAGES
ACTIVITIES cfghjot

ENTRY REQUIREMENTS Test & Interview
SCHOLARSHIPS & BURSARIES
SPECIAL NEEDS ejkw
ASSOCIATION IAPS **FOUNDED** 1946 **RELIGIOUS AFFILIATION** Inter-denom
DYSLEXIA **DIET** a
OTHER SUBJECTS abcfh
FACILITIES ON SITE h
EXAM BOARDS
RETAKES **NVQ COURSES**

A-level:
AS:
GCSE:
OTHER: e lmno s v B E G K O R cde j

Rose Hill School; Alderley; Wotton-under-Edge; Glos. GL12 7QT
Tel: 01453 843196 (Fax: 01453 842765) *R.C.G.Lyne-Pirkis*

		Boys	Age	Girls	Age	TOTAL	Boys	Girls
Day	£960-£2100	64	2-13	52	2-13	154		
Weekly	£2100-£2780	13	6-13	6	6-13			
Boarding	£2100-£2780	11	6-13	8	6-13			

MAP 2 J 1
LOCATION Rural
DAY **RAIL** b **AIR** b
SPORT abcdefjklmopqstuwx ABC
OTHER LANGUAGES
ACTIVITIES cfghjnopqw A

ENTRY REQUIREMENTS Report & Interview
SCHOLARSHIPS & BURSARIES Schol; Burs; Mus; Forces; Clergy; Siblings
SPECIAL NEEDS bn Bl
ASSOCIATION IAPS **FOUNDED** 1832 · **RELIGIOUS AFFILIATION** C of E
DYSLEXIA ce **DIET** a
OTHER SUBJECTS abch
FACILITIES ON SITE dehj
EXAM BOARDS
RETAKES **NVQ COURSES**

A-level:
AS:
GCSE:
OTHER: c e g i lmno q v B G K OP R cde j

GLOUCESTERSHIRE continued

St Clotilde's School; Lechlade Manor; Lechlade; Glos. GL7 3BB
Tel: 01367 252259 (Fax: 01367 253668) *Miss A.G.Wood*

		Boys	Age	Girls	Age	TOTAL		Boys	Girls
Day	£460-£1690	~20	3-9	100	3-18	160	SIXTH		9
Weekly	£2620-£2830			40	9-18				
Boarding									

ENTRY REQUIREMENTS Report & Exam & Interview
SCHOLARSHIPS & BURSARIES Burs
SPECIAL NEEDS n B   **DYSLEXIA** e   **DIET** a
ASSOCIATION GBGSA **FOUNDED** 1903   **RELIGIOUS AFFILIATION** RC/Inter-denom

LOCATION Rural   MAP 2 L 1
DAY **RAIL** b **AIR** b
SPORT chlmpqx AB
OTHER LANGUAGES a
ACTIVITIES dfghijknostwx
OTHER SUBJECTS bcfgh
FACILITIES ON SITE dghj
EXAM BOARDS bd ABDEG
RETAKES   **NVQ COURSES**

A-level: efg i   p   v   BC G K   R   c ef
AS: g   p   K   c
GCSE: de g i   n   v   BC G K   R W   cdef
OTHER: l   K

St. Edward's School; Ashley Road; Charlton Kings; Cheltenham; Glos. GL52 6NT
Tel: 01242 526697 (Fax: 01242 260986) *Anthony J Martin*

		Boys	Age	Girls	Age	TOTAL		Boys	Girls
Day	£770-£1795	358	2-18	361	2-18	719	SIXTH	46	44
Weekly									
Boarding									

ENTRY REQUIREMENTS Exam
SCHOLARSHIPS & BURSARIES Schol; Burs; VI Form
SPECIAL NEEDS begjlnw B   **DYSLEXIA** def   **DIET** ab
ASSOCIATION ISAI   **FOUNDED** 1987   **RELIGIOUS AFFILIATION** R C

LOCATION Rural   MAP 8 J 8
DAY **RAIL** b **AIR** b
SPORT abcefghjklmopqswx ABC
OTHER LANGUAGES a
ACTIVITIES bcfghijklnost AB
OTHER SUBJECTS bcefgh
FACILITIES ON SITE abcdghi
EXAM BOARDS bd ABEG
RETAKES a **NVQ COURSES**

A-level: e ghi l n p   uv   BC   GH K   OP R U   cdef j l
AS: C   K   P R   u
GCSE: e ghi l n   v   BC G K   OP R   cdefgh j l
OTHER: i

Selwyn School; Matson House; Matson Lane; Gloucester GL4 9DY
Tel: 01452 305663 (Fax: 01452 385907) *Miss L.M.Brown*

		Boys	Age	Girls	Age	TOTAL		Boys	Girls
Day	£685-£1600	44	3-11	219	3-18	311	SIXTH		21
Weekly	£2020-£2650			9	9-18				
Boarding	£2180-£2810			39	9-18				

ENTRY REQUIREMENTS Test & Interview
SCHOLARSHIPS & BURSARIES Schol; Mus; VI Form; Sport; Drama; Siblings
SPECIAL NEEDS aeghjlnqwx ABEI   **DYSLEXIA** ef   **DIET** acd
ASSOCIATION GSA   **FOUNDED** 1958   **RELIGIOUS AFFILIATION** C of E

LOCATION Rural   MAP 8 J 8
DAY ✓ **RAIL** a **AIR** b
SPORT acfghjklmpqswx ABC
OTHER LANGUAGES a
ACTIVITIES cfghijknoqtw AB
OTHER SUBJECTS abcdefh
FACILITIES ON SITE bg
EXAM BOARDS abcd ABDEGIJ
RETAKES ab **NVQ COURSES**

A-level: de ghi   n   uv   BC G K   P R TU W   bcdef l
AS: d ghi   G K   P R   v   W   c e
GCSE: de ghi   no   v   BC G K   P R W   bcdef j l
OTHER: h

Westonbirt School; Tetbury; Glos. GL8 8QG
Tel: 01666 880333 (Fax: 01666 880364) *Mrs G.Hylson-Smith*

		Boys	Age	Girls	Age	TOTAL		Boys	Girls
Day	£2312			30	11-18	241	SIXTH		65
Weekly	£3595			2	11-18				
Boarding	£3595			209	11-18				

ENTRY REQUIREMENTS CEE; Test & Interview
SCHOLARSHIPS & BURSARIES Schol; Mus; Forces; Clergy; VI Form
SPECIAL NEEDS begjklnqstw DEGHI   **DYSLEXIA** def **DIET** ab
ASSOCIATION GSA   **FOUNDED** 1928   **RELIGIOUS AFFILIATION** C of E

LOCATION Rural   MAP 2 K 1
DAY ✓ **RAIL** b **AIR** b
SPORT abcdfklmnpqtuwx AB
OTHER LANGUAGES a
ACTIVITIES cghijklnostuwx AB
OTHER SUBJECTS bcdefgh
FACILITIES ON SITE bcdeikl
EXAM BOARDS abcd ADEGHI
RETAKES   **NVQ COURSES**

A-level: cdefghi   nop   v   BC GH K   P   cde j l
AS: c   p
GCSE: e   i   no   v x   BC G K N P R   W   cde g j l
OTHER: c   l

Wycliffe College Jnr School; Ryeford Hall; Stonehouse; Glos. GL10 2LD
Tel: 01453 823233 (Fax: 01453 825604) *R.Outwin-Flinders*

		Boys	Age	Girls	Age	TOTAL		Boys	Girls
Day	£810-£1925	137	4-13	96	4-13	285	SIXTH		
Weekly	£2040-£2595	11	8-13	6	8-13				
Boarding	£2105-£2690	24	8-13	11	8-13				

ENTRY REQUIREMENTS Interview; Report & Test
SCHOLARSHIPS & BURSARIES Schol; AP
SPECIAL NEEDS ejknqw GI   **DYSLEXIA** e   **DIET** a
ASSOCIATION IAPS   **FOUNDED** 1928   **RELIGIOUS AFFILIATION** Inter-denom

LOCATION Rural   MAP 2 J 1
DAY **RAIL** a **AIR** a
SPORT abdefgjlmpqrswx AB
OTHER LANGUAGES
ACTIVITIES cfghjmnoqrtvwx A
OTHER SUBJECTS fh
FACILITIES ON SITE bdik
EXAM BOARDS
RETAKES   **NVQ COURSES**

A-level:
AS:
GCSE:
OTHER: de g i l   no   v   B G K   OP R   W   cde j

GLOUCESTERSHIRE continued

C — Wycliffe College; Stonehouse GL10 2JQ
Tel: 01453 822432 (Fax: 01453 827634) *D.C.M.Prichard*

		Boys	Age	Girls	Age	TOTAL		Boys	Girls
Day	£2730	94	13-18	43	13-18	324	SIXTH	88	55
Weekly			13-18		13-18				
Boarding	£3995	123	13-18	64	13-18				

ENTRY REQUIREMENTS CEE; Scholarship Exam; Report & Interview
SCHOLARSHIPS & BURSARIES Schol; Burs; Art; Mus; Forces; Teachers; AP; VI Form; Sport; Drama
SPECIAL NEEDS bejlntuw BEGI   **DYSLEXIA** ef   **DIET** ad
ASSOCIATION HMC   **FOUNDED** 1882   **RELIGIOUS AFFILIATION** Inter-denom

MAP 2 J 1
LOCATION Rural
DAY ✓   **RAIL** a   **AIR** b
SPORT abcefghjklmopqrsuwx B
OTHER LANGUAGES a
ACTIVITIES acefghijklnoqstvwx ABC
OTHER SUBJECTS abcdfh
FACILITIES ON SITE abcdeghjk
EXAM BOARDS abcd ABDEGHI
RETAKES a   **NVQ COURSES**

A-level: defghi lmnop v x   AB GH K OP   cdef j l
AS: de l   GH K   ef l
GCSE: de g i lmno v   AB G I K OP R   cdef j l
OTHER: h l u   G

HAMPSHIRE

Gb — Atherley School,The; Hill Lane; Southampton SO15 5RG
Tel: 01703 772 898 (Fax: 01703 779971) *Mrs C.Madina*

		Boys	Age	Girls	Age	TOTAL		Boys	Girls
Day	£472-£1424	46	3-11	391	3-18	437	SIXTH		23
Weekly									
Boarding									

ENTRY REQUIREMENTS Report & Interview
SCHOLARSHIPS & BURSARIES Schol; Clergy; Teachers; VI Form; Siblings
SPECIAL NEEDS bejklntw C   **DYSLEXIA** g   **DIET** acd
ASSOCIATION GSA   **FOUNDED** 1926   **RELIGIOUS AFFILIATION** C of E

MAP 3 C 7
LOCATION Urban
DAY   **RAIL** a   **AIR** a
SPORT abcfhlnpqwx ABC
OTHER LANGUAGES
ACTIVITIES cghijkost A
OTHER SUBJECTS bcdefgh
FACILITIES ON SITE bghk
EXAM BOARDS abd ABG
RETAKES ab   **NVQ COURSES** 12

A-level: cdefghi p v   BC GH K P R   cdef j l
AS: ef
GCSE: cde g i p v   BC G K P R   cdefg j l
OTHER: lm q uv   BC E G K NOP R U W   c ef kl

G — Ballard College; New Milton; Hampshire BH25 5JL
Tel: 01425 611090 (Fax: 01425 638847) *The Rev A.Folks*

		Boys	Age	Girls	Age	TOTAL		Boys	Girls
Day	£1770	X		69	11-18	115	SIXTH		17
Weekly	£2630			8	11-18				
Boarding	£2795			38	11-18				

ENTRY REQUIREMENTS CEE; Test & Interview
SCHOLARSHIPS & BURSARIES Schol; Mus; VI Form
SPECIAL NEEDS bejlp BG   **DYSLEXIA**   **DIET** abd
ASSOCIATION GSA   **FOUNDED** 1906   **RELIGIOUS AFFILIATION** C of E

MAP 3 B 7
LOCATION Rural
DAY   **RAIL** a   **AIR** b
SPORT abcfghlmpvwx AB
OTHER LANGUAGES a
ACTIVITIES agijknopstwx AB
OTHER SUBJECTS acfh
FACILITIES ON SITE bcdeghjk
EXAM BOARDS abcd ABDEH
RETAKES a   **NVQ COURSES**

A-level: egil op v   BC GH K P R   cdef j
AS: c
GCSE: egil op v   BC G K P R   cdef j
OTHER:

G — Ballard Lake Prep School; New Milton; Hampshire BH25 5JL
Tel: 01425 611153 (Fax: 01425 622099) *Miss G.R.Morris*

		Boys	Age	Girls	Age	TOTAL		Boys	Girls
Day	£270-£1770	X		93	3-11	97	SIXTH		
Weekly	£2445			4	7-11				
Boarding	£2615				7-11				

ENTRY REQUIREMENTS Interview
SCHOLARSHIPS & BURSARIES
SPECIAL NEEDS abejlnp BG   **DYSLEXIA** cef   **DIET** abd
ASSOCIATION IAPS   **FOUNDED** 1906   **RELIGIOUS AFFILIATION** C of E

MAP 3 B 7
LOCATION Rural
DAY   **RAIL** a   **AIR** b
SPORT ahlpqx AB
OTHER LANGUAGES
ACTIVITIES cdghijlnotx
OTHER SUBJECTS abcfh
FACILITIES ON SITE bcdehjk
EXAM BOARDS
RETAKES   **NVQ COURSES**

A-level:
AS:
GCSE:
OTHER: e lmno v   BC G K O R   cde

C — Bedales School; Petersfield; Hants. GU32 2DG
Tel: 01730 263286 (Fax: 01730 267411) *Mrs A.A.Willcocks*

		Boys	Age	Girls	Age	TOTAL		Boys	Girls
Day	£3189	X	44	13-18	43	13-18	405	SIXTH	62	89
Weekly									
Boarding	£4332	145	13-18	173	13-18				

ENTRY REQUIREMENTS Report & Exam & Interview
SCHOLARSHIPS & BURSARIES Schol; Burs; Mus; AP
SPECIAL NEEDS abegijlnqstvw ADEFGHIK •   **DYSLEXIA** f   **DIET** ac
ASSOCIATION HMC   **FOUNDED** 1893   **RELIGIOUS AFFILIATION** Non-denom

MAP 3 D 6
LOCATION Rural
DAY   **RAIL** a   **AIR** b
SPORT abcdefhjlmopqtwx AB
OTHER LANGUAGES
ACTIVITIES bcdfghijklnoqstw
OTHER SUBJECTS abcfh
FACILITIES ON SITE abcfghik
EXAM BOARDS abcd ABDEGHL
RETAKES   **NVQ COURSES**

A-level: egi nop v   B GH K P   c ef j l
AS: l   ef l
GCSE: egil no v   B G K P   cdefg j l
OTHER: c f lmn q s u x   I K MNO QR   h

HAMPSHIRE *continued*

C **Boundary Oak School; Roche Court; Fareham; Hants. PO17 5BL**
Tel: 01329 280955 (Fax: 01329 827 656) *R.B.Bliss*

			Boys	Age	Girls	Age	TOTAL		Boys	Girls
Day	£495-£1752	✗	138	3-13	28	3-9	200	SIXTH		
Weekly	£1905-£2580		33	7-13						
Boarding	£1905-£2580		1	8-13						

ENTRY REQUIREMENTS Assessment & Interview
SCHOLARSHIPS & BURSARIES Schol; Mus
SPECIAL NEEDS egjknq IL **DYSLEXIA** e **DIET** acd
ASSOCIATION IAPS **FOUNDED** 1908 **RELIGIOUS AFFILIATION** Inter-denom

MAP 3 D 7
LOCATION Rural
DAY ✓ **RAIL** a **AIR** b
SPORT abcefhjklmostuwx AB
OTHER LANGUAGES
ACTIVITIES bfghjlrst A
OTHER SUBJECTS bch
FACILITIES ON SITE bcjk
EXAM BOARDS
RETAKES **NVQ COURSES**

A-level: efg i lm o q v B G K OP R cde j
AS:
GCSE:
OTHER:

C **Churcher's College; London Road; Petersfield GU31 4AS**
Tel: 01730 263033 (Fax: 01730 231437) *G.W.Buttle*

		Boys	Age	Girls	Age	TOTAL		Boys	Girls
Day	£870-£1665	435	4-18	222	4-18	698	SIXTH	91	33
Weekly	£3065	14	11-18	3	11-18				
Boarding	£3115	19	11-18	5	11-18				

ENTRY REQUIREMENTS CEE & Interview; Report & Exam & Interview
SCHOLARSHIPS & BURSARIES Schol; Burs; AP
SPECIAL NEEDS ilnq BFGIL **DYSLEXIA**   **DIET** a
ASSOCIATION HMC **FOUNDED** 1722 **RELIGIOUS AFFILIATION** Non-denom

MAP 3 D 6
LOCATION Rural
DAY   **RAIL** a **AIR** a
SPORT abcdefhjkmopqstuwx ABC
OTHER LANGUAGES
ACTIVITIES acefghijklnoqstv AB
OTHER SUBJECTS abcdfh
FACILITIES ON SITE cdghj
EXAM BOARDS abcd ABDEGHKL
RETAKES ab **NVQ COURSES**

A-level: e ghi opq v AB GH K OP R U c ef l
AS: e ghi pq G R ef l
GCSE: e g i l opq v AB E G K P R cdef j l
OTHER:

C **Daneshill School; Stratfield Turgis; Basingstoke RG27 0AR**
Tel: 01256 882707 (Fax: 01256 882007) *S.V.Spencer*

			Boys	Age	Girls	Age	TOTAL		Boys	Girls
Day	£1030-£1360	✗	126	4-11	206	4-12	332	SIXTH		
Weekly										
Boarding										

ENTRY REQUIREMENTS
SCHOLARSHIPS & BURSARIES Teachers
SPECIAL NEEDS ehjkn BGI **DYSLEXIA** e **DIET** a
ASSOCIATION IAPS **FOUNDED** 1950 **RELIGIOUS AFFILIATION** C of E

MAP 3 D 5
LOCATION Rural
DAY   **RAIL** b **AIR** b
SPORT aefjlmnpqsx B
OTHER LANGUAGES
ACTIVITIES cghjo
OTHER SUBJECTS acfh
FACILITIES ON SITE bhi
EXAM BOARDS
RETAKES **NVQ COURSES**

A-level:
AS:
GCSE:
OTHER: e lm o v B G K O R cde j

C **Ditcham Park School; Ditcham Park; Petersfield; Hants. GU31 5RN**
Tel: 01730 825659 (Fax: 01730 825070) *Mrs P.M.Holmes*

		Boys	Age	Girls	Age	TOTAL		Boys	Girls
Day	£1020-£1710	172	4-16	134	4-16	306	SIXTH		
Weekly									
Boarding									

ENTRY REQUIREMENTS Test; Report & Interview
SCHOLARSHIPS & BURSARIES Schol
SPECIAL NEEDS aegjlqtx AB **DYSLEXIA**   **DIET** a
ASSOCIATION ISAI **FOUNDED** 1976 **RELIGIOUS AFFILIATION** Inter-denom

MAP 3 D 6
LOCATION Rural
DAY   **RAIL** b **AIR** b
SPORT abcefjklmpqsx AB
OTHER LANGUAGES
ACTIVITIES cfghijot A
OTHER SUBJECTS bcdfh
FACILITIES ON SITE bck
EXAM BOARDS bd
RETAKES **NVQ COURSES**

A-level:
AS:
GCSE: e g i no v B E G K P cdef j
OTHER: lm q O RS

C **Dunhurst (Bedales Junior School); Alton Road; Steep; Petersfield; Hants. GU32 2DP**
Tel: 01730 262984 (Fax: 01730 267411) *Mr & Mrs M.L.Heslop*

		Boys	Age	Girls	Age	TOTAL		Boys	Girls
Day	£1981-£2132	96	3-13	84	3-13	248	SIXTH		
Weekly									
Boarding	£2937-£3123	29	8-13	39	8-13				

ENTRY REQUIREMENTS Test & Interview
SCHOLARSHIPS & BURSARIES Burs; Mus
SPECIAL NEEDS ijlnw **DYSLEXIA** c **DIET** abcd
ASSOCIATION IAPS **FOUNDED** 1893 **RELIGIOUS AFFILIATION** Non-denom

MAP 3 D 6
LOCATION Rural
DAY   **RAIL** a **AIR** b
SPORT abcdefhjklmopqvwx ABC
OTHER LANGUAGES
ACTIVITIES cfghijnopqstw A
OTHER SUBJECTS abcdfgh
FACILITIES ON SITE abcfhik
EXAM BOARDS
RETAKES **NVQ COURSES**

A-level:
AS:
GCSE:
OTHER: e lmno v BC G I cde j

HAMPSHIRE continued

C — Durlston Court; Barton-on-Sea; New Milton; Hants. BH25 7AQ
Tel: 01425 610010 (Fax: 01425 622731) *J.T.Seddon*

MAP 3 B 7
LOCATION Rural
DAY ✓   RAIL a   AIR b

		Boys	Age	Girls	Age	TOTAL		Boys	Girls
Day	£550-£1870	122	3-13	90	3-13	260	SIXTH		
Weekly			8-13		8-13				
Boarding	£2640	28	8-13	20	8-13				

SPORT abcefhjklmpqstwx AB
OTHER LANGUAGES a
ACTIVITIES cdfghijopqrtw A
OTHER SUBJECTS bcfh
FACILITIES ON SITE bdhj
EXAM BOARDS
RETAKES   NVQ COURSES

ENTRY REQUIREMENTS Report & Interview
SCHOLARSHIPS & BURSARIES Schol; Art; Mus; Forces; Sport
SPECIAL NEEDS abeijklnqw BEGI   DYSLEXIA cdef   DIET abcd
ASSOCIATION IAPS   FOUNDED 1903   RELIGIOUS AFFILIATION C of E

A-level   AS   GCSE
OTHER   e g i l   q   v
         BC E G   K   OP R
         cdefg j

C — Embley Park School; Romsey; Hants SO51 6ZE
Tel: 01794 512206 (Fax: 01794 518737) *David Chapman*

MAP 3 C 6
LOCATION Rural
DAY   RAIL a   AIR b

		Boys	Age	Girls	Age	TOTAL		Boys	Girls
Day	£1845-£1945	126	11-18	6	11-18	224	SIXTH	42	6
Weekly	£3090-£3190	47	11-18	5	11-18				
Boarding	£3090-£3190	34	11-18	6	11-18				

SPORT abcdefhjklmopqstuwx ABC
OTHER LANGUAGES a
ACTIVITIES fghijklmnopqstuw AB
OTHER SUBJECTS bcfh
FACILITIES ON SITE bcdghjkl
EXAM BOARDS abcd ABDEGI
RETAKES ab   NVQ COURSES

ENTRY REQUIREMENTS CEE; Exam; Exam & Interview; Report & Interview; CEE & Interview; Report & Exam & Interview   SCHOLARSHIPS & BURSARIES Schol; Burs; Forces; Clergy; Teachers; VI Form; ARA
SPECIAL NEEDS ablnqtuw ABEGI   DYSLEXIA f   DIET abcd
ASSOCIATION SHMIS   FOUNDED 1946   RELIGIOUS AFFILIATION C of E

A-level   e ghi l   op s uv x
AB   GH K   OP
cdef

AS   gh l   p   u x
      G O
      e

GCSE   e g i   op   v
AB E G K   OP R
cdef j

OTHER   h l
         NO

C — Farleigh School; Red Rice; Andover; Hants SP11 7PW
Tel: 01264 710766 *J.E.Murphy*

MAP 3 C 5
LOCATION Rural
DAY ✓   RAIL a   AIR a

		Boys	Age	Girls	Age	TOTAL		Boys	Girls
Day	£452-£1980	155	3-13	75	3-13	304	SIXTH		
Weekly	£2789	16	7-13						
Boarding	£2789	56	7-13	2					

SPORT abcefjklmopqsuvwx AB
OTHER LANGUAGES
ACTIVITIES acfghjoqrstvw
OTHER SUBJECTS acfh
FACILITIES ON SITE bcdhjkl
EXAM BOARDS
RETAKES   NVQ COURSES

ENTRY REQUIREMENTS Report & Interview
SCHOLARSHIPS & BURSARIES
SPECIAL NEEDS biln G   DYSLEXIA ef   DIET a
ASSOCIATION IAPS   FOUNDED 1953   RELIGIOUS AFFILIATION R C

A-level   AS   GCSE
OTHER   e g i l m o q   v
         B G K   OP R
         cde   j

G — Farnborough Hill; Farnborough; Hants. GU14 8AT
Tel: 01252 545197 (Fax: 01252 375962) *Sister Elizabeth Mc Cormack*

MAP 3 E 5
LOCATION Urban
DAY ✓   RAIL a   AIR a

		Boys	Age	Girls	Age	TOTAL		Boys	Girls
Day	£1476			536	11-18	536	SIXTH		110
Weekly									
Boarding									

SPORT abcfhjklmnpqx ABC
OTHER LANGUAGES
ACTIVITIES acghijlnostw AB
OTHER SUBJECTS abcdefgh
FACILITIES ON SITE abcdghi
EXAM BOARDS abcd ABEG
RETAKES   NVQ COURSES

ENTRY REQUIREMENTS Exam; Interview; Report
SCHOLARSHIPS & BURSARIES Burs; AP; VI Form
SPECIAL NEEDS bhjlnqt A   DYSLEXIA efg   DIET a
ASSOCIATION GSA   FOUNDED 1889   RELIGIOUS AFFILIATION R C

A-level   cd ghi   n p   v
BC   GH K   P R U W
c efg j l

AS   d g
      G K   U

GCSE   cd g i   n   v
BC   G K   P R T WX
cdefg j l

OTHER   e   klmno   u x
              MNO Q

C — Forres Sandle Manor; Fordingbridge; Hants. SP6 1NS
Tel: 01425 653181 (Fax: 01425 655676) *R.P.J.Moore*

MAP 3 B 7
LOCATION Rural
DAY   RAIL b   AIR b

		Boys	Age	Girls	Age	TOTAL		Boys	Girls
Day	£596-£1525	82	3-13	70	3-13	235	SIXTH		
Weekly	£1995	20	7-13	11	7-13				
Boarding	£2795	36	7-13	16	7-13				

SPORT acdejklmopqstux AB
OTHER LANGUAGES
ACTIVITIES cfghjoqrstvwx A
OTHER SUBJECTS abcdfh
FACILITIES ON SITE bchj
EXAM BOARDS
RETAKES   NVQ COURSES

ENTRY REQUIREMENTS Interview
SCHOLARSHIPS & BURSARIES Forces; Siblings
SPECIAL NEEDS knqw GI   DYSLEXIA   DIET acd
ASSOCIATION IAPS   FOUNDED 1880   RELIGIOUS AFFILIATION C of E

A-level   AS   GCSE
OTHER   cde g i   lmno   s v
         BC E G   K   OP R
         cde   j

HAMPSHIRE *continued*

Gregg School, The; Townhill Park House; Cutbush Lane; Southampton SO18 2GF
Tel: 01703 472133 (Fax: 01703 471080) *R.D.Hart*

		Boys	Age	Girls	Age	TOTAL
Day	£1400	116	10-17	77	10-17	193
Weekly						
Boarding						

SIXTH: Boys — Girls —

ENTRY REQUIREMENTS Exam; Scholarship Exam; Interview
SCHOLARSHIPS & BURSARIES Schol; Burs; Art; Mus; Teachers
SPECIAL NEEDS ejln B **DYSLEXIA** de **DIET** ab
ASSOCIATION ISAI **FOUNDED** 1901 **RELIGIOUS AFFILIATION** Non-denom

MAP 3 C 7
LOCATION Rural
DAY ✓ **RAIL** a **AIR** a
SPORT abcdefhjklmpqswx ABC
OTHER LANGUAGES
ACTIVITIES cfgjkoqw
OTHER SUBJECTS bcdegh
FACILITIES ON SITE c
EXAM BOARDS abcd K
RETAKES a **NVQ COURSES**

A-level —
AS G
GCSE: d e g i l no v / AB E G K P R W / cdef
OTHER: h / C G O / cd

Hawley Place School; Fernhill Road; Blackwater; Camberley; Surrey GU17 9HU
Tel: 01276 32028 *T.G.Pipe & Mrs M.L.Pipe*

		Boys	Age	Girls	Age	TOTAL
Day	£980-£1250	42	2-11	124	2-16	166
Weekly						
Boarding						

SIXTH: Boys — Girls —

ENTRY REQUIREMENTS Scholarship Exam; Exam & Interview
SCHOLARSHIPS & BURSARIES Schol; Burs; Mus; Sport; Siblings
SPECIAL NEEDS n B **DYSLEXIA** ef **DIET**
ASSOCIATION ISAI **FOUNDED** 1952 **RELIGIOUS AFFILIATION** Inter-denom

MAP 3 E 5
LOCATION Rural
DAY **RAIL** a **AIR** a
SPORT acflmpqwx BC
OTHER LANGUAGES
ACTIVITIES aghijn
OTHER SUBJECTS ch
FACILITIES ON SITE abck
EXAM BOARDS abd A
RETAKES **NVQ COURSES**

A-level —
AS —
GCSE: d l n v / BC E G K / cdef j
OTHER: l o / O R

Highfield School; Liphook; Hants. GU30 7LQ
Tel: 01428 722228 (Fax: 01428 727164) *N.O.Ramage*

		Boys	Age	Girls	Age	TOTAL
Day	£2000-£2320	27	7- 9	21	7- 9	169
Weekly						
Boarding	£2650-£2990	73	7-13	48	7-13	

SIXTH: Boys — Girls —

ENTRY REQUIREMENTS Report & Interview
SCHOLARSHIPS & BURSARIES Clergy
SPECIAL NEEDS abegjklnpqtuvw Gl **DYSLEXIA** de **DIET** a
ASSOCIATION IAPS **FOUNDED** 1907 **RELIGIOUS AFFILIATION** C of E

MAP 3 E 6
LOCATION Rural
DAY **RAIL** a **AIR** b
SPORT abcefjlmnopqsuwx ABC
OTHER LANGUAGES
ACTIVITIES bcfghijlnopqstw
OTHER SUBJECTS bcdfh
FACILITIES ON SITE bcdhjk
EXAM BOARDS
RETAKES **NVQ COURSES**

A-level —
AS —
GCSE —
OTHER: e g i lm o v / B G K OP R / cde j

Hordle House Preparatory School; Cliff Road; Milford-on-Sea; Lymington; Hants. SO41 0NW
Tel: 01590 642104 (Fax: 01590 645935) *R.H.C.Phillips*

		Boys	Age	Girls	Age	TOTAL
Day	£495-£1990	73	3-14	63	3-14	183
Weekly	£2250-£2650	7		1		
Boarding	£2250-£2650	22	7-13	17	7-13	

SIXTH: Boys — Girls —

ENTRY REQUIREMENTS Report
SCHOLARSHIPS & BURSARIES Schol; Burs; Mus; Chor
SPECIAL NEEDS bjn BG **DYSLEXIA** ce **DIET** abcd
ASSOCIATION IAPS **FOUNDED** 1926 **RELIGIOUS AFFILIATION** C of E

MAP 3 C 7
LOCATION Rural
DAY ✓ **RAIL** a **AIR** b
SPORT aefjklmpqstuwx AB
OTHER LANGUAGES
ACTIVITIES cfghijortwx A
OTHER SUBJECTS acfh
FACILITIES ON SITE bcdjk
EXAM BOARDS
RETAKES **NVQ COURSES**

A-level —
AS —
GCSE —
OTHER: e g i lmno s v / B G K OP R / cdef j

King Edward VI School; Kellett Road; Southampton SO15 7UQ
Tel: 01703 704561 (Fax: 01703 705937) *T.R.Cookson*

		Boys	Age	Girls	Age	TOTAL
Day	£1570	836	11-18	103	11-18	939
Weekly						
Boarding						

SIXTH: Boys 210 Girls 59

ENTRY REQUIREMENTS Report & Exam & Interview
SCHOLARSHIPS & BURSARIES Schol; Burs; Mus; AP
SPECIAL NEEDS abeijlnquvw H **DYSLEXIA** g **DIET** abcd
ASSOCIATION HMC **FOUNDED** 1553 **RELIGIOUS AFFILIATION** Inter-denom

MAP 3 C 7
LOCATION Urban
DAY **RAIL** a **AIR** b
SPORT abcdefhjklmpqstwx ABC
OTHER LANGUAGES
ACTIVITIES bcfghijkopqrstvw ABD
OTHER SUBJECTS cf
FACILITIES ON SITE chk
EXAM BOARDS abcd BDEGH
RETAKES **NVQ COURSES**

A-level: c e g i op v / AB GH P R / c efg j l
AS —
GCSE: e g i nop v / AB G K P R / cdefg j l
OTHER: l n u / O / h k

HAMPSHIRE *continued*

C | Lord Mayor Treloar College; Holybourne; Alton; Hants GU34 4EN;
Tel: 01420 547425 (Fax: 01420 542708) *Hartley Heard*

MAP 3 D 5
LOCATION Rural
DAY RAIL a   AIR a

	Fees	Boys	Age	Girls	Age	TOTAL	Boys	Girls
Day	£4763-£9867	17	8-19	11	8-19	260	78	54
Weekly	£6160-12760	7	8-19	4	8-19	SIXTH		
Boarding	£6351-13155	130	8-19	91	8-19			

SPORT abcdefhjmqtuwx A
OTHER LANGUAGES a
ACTIVITIES afghijkmnopsvwx A

ENTRY REQUIREMENTS Assessment & Interview
SCHOLARSHIPS & BURSARIES
SPECIAL NEEDS abefhijklnpqrstuvwx ABCDEFGHIJKL
ASSOCIATION SHMIS **FOUNDED** 1908 **RELIGIOUS AFFILIATION** Non-denom
DYSLEXIA ef **DIET** abcd

OTHER SUBJECTS abcdefgh
FACILITIES ON SITE bcehik
EXAM BOARDS abcd ABDEGI
RETAKES ab   NVQ COURSES 123

A-level: defghi kl nopq uv B GH K PQ T c ef l
AS:
GCSE: de l no v ABC E G K N R W cde l
OTHER: hj l o q s A G I K N S W j

C | Lord Wandsworth College; Long Sutton; Hook; Hants. RG29 1TB
Tel: 01256 862482 (Fax: 01256 862563) *G. de W.Waller*

MAP 3 D 5
LOCATION Rural
DAY RAIL a   AIR a

	Fees	Boys	Age	Girls	Age	TOTAL	Boys	Girls
Day	£2364-£2460	132	11-18	—	16-18	455	105	33
Weekly	£3028-£3164	228	11-18	26	16-18	SIXTH		
Boarding	£3028-£3164	62	11-18	7	16-18			

SPORT abcdefhjklmpstuwx BC
OTHER LANGUAGES
ACTIVITIES efghijklmnoqstv ABCD

ENTRY REQUIREMENTS CEE; Test & Interview
SCHOLARSHIPS & BURSARIES Schol; Burs; Mus; AP
SPECIAL NEEDS I EG
ASSOCIATION HMC **FOUNDED** 1912 **RELIGIOUS AFFILIATION** Inter-denom
DYSLEXIA **DIET** ab

OTHER SUBJECTS abcdfh
FACILITIES ON SITE acdefghijl
EXAM BOARDS abcd ABDEGHL
RETAKES a   NVQ COURSES

A-level: cde ghi nop v B GH K P U cdef j l
AS:
GCSE: c e g i o v B G K P X cdef j l
OTHER: l no q u G JK MNO R ef j l

C | Mayfield Preparatory School; 103 Anstey Road; Alton GU34 2RN
Tel: 01420 83105 *T.T.Incles*

MAP 3 D 5
LOCATION Urban
DAY RAIL a   AIR a

	Fees	Boys	Age	Girls	Age	TOTAL	Boys	Girls
Day	£796-£816	63	3-11	45	3-11	108		
Weekly						SIXTH		
Boarding								

SPORT aefjmpqs B
OTHER LANGUAGES
ACTIVITIES fghjo

ENTRY REQUIREMENTS Test & Interview
SCHOLARSHIPS & BURSARIES Schol; Burs; Siblings
SPECIAL NEEDS n
ASSOCIATION ISAI **FOUNDED** 1944 **RELIGIOUS AFFILIATION** Non-denom
DYSLEXIA e **DIET**

OTHER SUBJECTS ach
FACILITIES ON SITE
EXAM BOARDS
RETAKES   NVQ COURSES

A-level:
AS:
GCSE:
OTHER: e l o s v B E G K O R cde

Gb | Mayville High School; 35 St Simons Road; Southsea; Hants PO5 2PE
Tel: 01705 734847 (Fax: 01705 863510) *Mrs L.A.Owens*

MAP 3 D 7
LOCATION Inner City
DAY RAIL a   AIR b

	Fees	Boys	Age	Girls	Age	TOTAL	Boys	Girls
Day	£800-£1150	43	2-8	205	2-16	248		
Weekly						SIXTH		
Boarding								

SPORT acjlfmpqx BC
OTHER LANGUAGES
ACTIVITIES cfghijnr A

ENTRY REQUIREMENTS Interview; Test & Interview; Exam & Interview
SCHOLARSHIPS & BURSARIES Burs
SPECIAL NEEDS n
ASSOCIATION ISAI **FOUNDED** 1911 **RELIGIOUS AFFILIATION** Non-denom
DYSLEXIA ce **DIET**

OTHER SUBJECTS bch
FACILITIES ON SITE
EXAM BOARDS acd
RETAKES   NVQ COURSES

A-level:
AS:
GCSE: e g i n v B E G OP R cdef l
OTHER: l

C | Moyles Court School; Moyles Court; Ringwood; Hants BH24 3NF
Tel: 01425 472856 (Fax: 01425 474715) *R.A.Dean*

MAP 3 B 7
LOCATION Rural
DAY ✓ RAIL b   AIR ab

	Fees	Boys	Age	Girls	Age	TOTAL	Boys	Girls
Day	£720-£1695	54	3-16	33	3-16	156		
Weekly		3	8-16	7	8-16	SIXTH		
Boarding	£2360-£2680	31	8-16	28	8-16			

SPORT abcefhjklmopqstuwx ABC
OTHER LANGUAGES
ACTIVITIES cfghijknpqtwx A

ENTRY REQUIREMENTS Exam; Interview; Report
SCHOLARSHIPS & BURSARIES Schol; Burs
SPECIAL NEEDS bjklnqtw BE
ASSOCIATION ISAI **FOUNDED** 1940 **RELIGIOUS AFFILIATION** C of E
DYSLEXIA e **DIET** abcd

OTHER SUBJECTS abcdfh
FACILITIES ON SITE abce
EXAM BOARDS abc BDE
RETAKES   NVQ COURSES

A-level:
AS:
GCSE: de o v B G WX cdef
OTHER:

HAMPSHIRE *continued*

C | **Nethercliffe School; Hatherley Road; Winchester; Hants. SO22 6RS**
Tel: 01962 854570 *R.F.G.Whitfield*

		Boys	Age	Girls	Age	TOTAL		Boys	Girls
Day	£519-£1177 ✗	86	3-11	28	3-11	114	SIXTH		
Weekly									
Boarding									

MAP 3 C 6
LOCATION Urban
DAY   **RAIL** a   **AIR** b
SPORT aejlmopqsx B
OTHER LANGUAGES
ACTIVITIES cgjno

ENTRY REQUIREMENTS Interview
SCHOLARSHIPS & BURSARIES
SPECIAL NEEDS   **DYSLEXIA**   **DIET**
ASSOCIATION ISAI   **FOUNDED** 1931   **RELIGIOUS AFFILIATION** C of E

OTHER SUBJECTS ch
FACILITIES ON SITE h
EXAM BOARDS
RETAKES   **NVQ COURSES**

A-level | AS | GCSE | OTHER: e l n uv / B E G K O R / cde

C | **Norman Court; West Tytherley; Nr. Salisbury SP5 1NH**
Tel: 01980 862345 (Fax: 01980 862082) *K.N.Foyle*

		Boys	Age	Girls	Age	TOTAL		Boys	Girls
Day	£920-£1940 ✗	44	3-13	33	4-13	145	SIXTH		
Weekly	£2610	22		7					
Boarding	£2610	26	7-13	13	7-13				

MAP 3 B 6
LOCATION Rural
DAY   **RAIL** a   **AIR** b
SPORT abcefjklmopqsuwx AB
OTHER LANGUAGES a
ACTIVITIES cfghijloqrstw

ENTRY REQUIREMENTS Report & Interview
SCHOLARSHIPS & BURSARIES
SPECIAL NEEDS   **DYSLEXIA**   **DIET** a
ASSOCIATION IAPS   **FOUNDED** 1881   **RELIGIOUS AFFILIATION** C of E

OTHER SUBJECTS acfh
FACILITIES ON SITE dhjk
EXAM BOARDS
RETAKES   **NVQ COURSES**

A-level | AS | GCSE | OTHER: e l o v / B G O R / cde g j

G | **North Foreland Lodge; Sherfield-on-Loddon; Basingstoke; Hants RG27 0HT**
Tel: 01256 882431 (Fax: 01256 883305) *Miss D.L.Matthews*

		Boys	Age	Girls	Age	TOTAL		Boys	Girls
Day	£2200					171	SIXTH		41
Weekly									
Boarding	£3600			171	11-18				

MAP 3 D 5
LOCATION Rural
DAY   **RAIL** a   **AIR** a
SPORT abglnpqx ABC
OTHER LANGUAGES
ACTIVITIES cghijklnost B

ENTRY REQUIREMENTS CEE & Interview
SCHOLARSHIPS & BURSARIES VI Form
SPECIAL NEEDS bghj   **DYSLEXIA**   **DIET** a
ASSOCIATION GSA   **FOUNDED** 1909   **RELIGIOUS AFFILIATION** C of E

OTHER SUBJECTS abcefh
FACILITIES ON SITE cdhj
EXAM BOARDS abd AEG
RETAKES   **NVQ COURSES**

A-level: cdefghi p v x / BC GH K P T W / cde j l
AS
GCSE: e g i l no v / BC E G K P W / cdef j l
OTHER

B | **Pilgrims' School; Winchester; Hants. SO23 9LT**
Tel: 01962 854189 (Fax: 01962 843610) *M.E.K.Kefford*

		Boys	Age	Girls	Age	TOTAL		Boys	Girls
Day	£1975 ✗	112	8-13			187	SIXTH		
Weekly	£2705		8-13						
Boarding	£2705	75	8-13						

MAP 3 C 6
LOCATION Urban
DAY   **RAIL** a   **AIR** a
SPORT abcefhijlmrstuwx AB
OTHER LANGUAGES
ACTIVITIES fghjmort A

ENTRY REQUIREMENTS Test & Interview
SCHOLARSHIPS & BURSARIES Chor
SPECIAL NEEDS   **DYSLEXIA**   **DIET** a
ASSOCIATION IAPS   **FOUNDED** 1931   **RELIGIOUS AFFILIATION** C of E

OTHER SUBJECTS acdfh
FACILITIES ON SITE chijk
EXAM BOARDS
RETAKES   **NVQ COURSES**

A-level | AS | GCSE | OTHER: e g i l no v / B G K OP R / cdefg j

---

C | **Portsmouth Grammar Lower School,The; High Street; Portsmouth PO1 2LN**
Tel: 01705 819125 (Fax: 01705 870184) *R.J.Mathrick*

		Boys	Age	Girls	Age	TOTAL		Boys	Girls
Day	£1062	143	8-11	67	8-11	210	SIXTH		
Weekly									
Boarding									

MAP 3 D 7
LOCATION Urban
DAY   **RAIL** a   **AIR** b
SPORT abefjlmpqsx AB
OTHER LANGUAGES
ACTIVITIES cfghjnot A

ENTRY REQUIREMENTS Report & Exam & Interview
SCHOLARSHIPS & BURSARIES Schol
SPECIAL NEEDS abejklntu GHI   **DYSLEXIA**   **DIET** acd
ASSOCIATION IAPS   **FOUNDED** 1928   **RELIGIOUS AFFILIATION** Non-denom

OTHER SUBJECTS bcfh
FACILITIES ON SITE hik
EXAM BOARDS
RETAKES   **NVQ COURSES**

A-level | AS | GCSE | OTHER: de lmno   v / B E G K O R / cdef

HAMPSHIRE continued

C — Portsmouth Grammar School,The; High Street; Portsmouth PO1 2LN
Tel: 01705 819125 (Fax: 01705 870184) *A.C.V.Evans*

		Boys	Age	Girls	Age	TOTAL		Boys	Girls
Day	£1495	639	11-18	168	11-18	807	SIXTH	172	30
Weekly									
Boarding									

ENTRY REQUIREMENTS CEE; Exam
SCHOLARSHIPS & BURSARIES AP; VI Form
SPECIAL NEEDS jnw G
DYSLEXIA f   **DIET** a
ASSOCIATION HMC   **FOUNDED** 1732   **RELIGIOUS AFFILIATION** Non-denom

MAP 3 D 7
LOCATION
DAY   **RAIL** a   **AIR** a
SPORT abcefghkmopqrstwx ABC
OTHER LANGUAGES
ACTIVITIES efghijknoqstv AB
OTHER SUBJECTS abcdf
FACILITIES ON SITE cghik
EXAM BOARDS abcd ABEGH
RETAKES   **NVQ COURSES**

A-level: cd g i opq v x / B GH K P R / c ef j l
AS: e K / ef l
GCSE: cd ghi no t v / B G K OP R / cdef ij l
OTHER: d l u / FG K R

G — Portsmouth High School GPDST; Kent Road; Southsea; Hants. PO5 3EQ
Tel: 01705 826714 (Fax: 01705 814814) *Mrs J.M.Dawtrey*

		Boys	Age	Girls	Age	TOTAL		Boys	Girls
Day	£976-£1328			743	4-18	743	SIXTH		127
Weekly									
Boarding									

ENTRY REQUIREMENTS Report & Test
SCHOLARSHIPS & BURSARIES Schol; AP; VI Form
SPECIAL NEEDS
DYSLEXIA   **DIET** a
ASSOCIATION GSA   **FOUNDED** 1882   **RELIGIOUS AFFILIATION** Non-denom

MAP 3 D 7
LOCATION Urban
DAY   **RAIL** a   **AIR** a
SPORT acejlmnpqtwx ABC
OTHER LANGUAGES
ACTIVITIES fghijknost ABD
OTHER SUBJECTS bcdfh
FACILITIES ON SITE cgh
EXAM BOARDS abd BE
RETAKES   **NVQ COURSES**

A-level: de g i p v x / B GH K P R / c efg j l
AS: de / ef l
GCSE: de g i no v / B G K P R X / cdefgh j l
OTHER: f lm o q u / K NO

C — Prince's Mead School; 43 Edgar Road; Winchester; Hants SO23 9TN
Tel: 01962 853416 (Fax: 01962 842217) *Mrs D.Moore*

		Boys	Age	Girls	Age	TOTAL		Boys	Girls
Day	£1015-£1215 X	120	3-11	131	3-11	251	SIXTH		
Weekly									
Boarding									

ENTRY REQUIREMENTS Assessment & Interview
SCHOLARSHIPS & BURSARIES Schol; Mus
SPECIAL NEEDS
DYSLEXIA   **DIET** a
ASSOCIATION IAPS   **FOUNDED** 1949   **RELIGIOUS AFFILIATION** C of E

MAP 3 C 6
LOCATION Urban
DAY   **RAIL** a   **AIR** b
SPORT aejmpqsx B
OTHER LANGUAGES
ACTIVITIES cfgijo
OTHER SUBJECTS ch
FACILITIES ON SITE
EXAM BOARDS
RETAKES   **NVQ COURSES**

A-level:
AS:
GCSE:
OTHER: e m o v / B G O R / cde

G — Rookesbury Park School; Wickham; Hants. PO17 6HT
Tel: 01329 833108 (Fax: 01329 835090) *Miss L.Appleyard*

		Boys	Age	Girls	Age	TOTAL		Boys	Girls
Day	£515-£1790 X			83	3-13	126	SIXTH		
Weekly	£2215				7-13				
Boarding	£2215-£2605			43	7-13				

ENTRY REQUIREMENTS Report & Interview
SCHOLARSHIPS & BURSARIES Schol; Burs; Siblings
SPECIAL NEEDS bcklnw Gl
DYSLEXIA ef   **DIET** acd
ASSOCIATION IAPS   **FOUNDED** 1929   **RELIGIOUS AFFILIATION** C of E

MAP 3 D 7
LOCATION Rural
DAY ✓   **RAIL** a   **AIR** b
SPORT adfglnpqtx AB
OTHER LANGUAGES
ACTIVITIES acfghjlnoqtwx A
OTHER SUBJECTS bcfh
FACILITIES ON SITE bdejk
EXAM BOARDS
RETAKES   **NVQ COURSES**

A-level:
AS:
GCSE:
OTHER: cde g i lmno q s v / BC E G K OP R / cdef j

C — Rookwood School; Weyhill Road; Andover; Hants; SP10 3AL
Tel: 01264 352855 *Mrs S.Hindle*

		Boys	Age	Girls	Age	TOTAL		Boys	Girls
Day	£700-£1512 X	82	3-11	168	3-16	273	SIXTH		
Weekly	£2025-£2702			21	7-16				
Boarding	£2200-£2877			2	7-16				

ENTRY REQUIREMENTS Test & Interview; Report & Interview
SCHOLARSHIPS & BURSARIES Schol
SPECIAL NEEDS abjklntw BEHI
DYSLEXIA ef   **DIET** abcd
ASSOCIATION ISAI   **FOUNDED** 1934   **RELIGIOUS AFFILIATION** Non-denom

MAP 3 C 5
LOCATION Urban
DAY   **RAIL** a   **AIR** b
SPORT acejlmpqx ABC
OTHER LANGUAGES
ACTIVITIES cghijknoqwx
OTHER SUBJECTS bch
FACILITIES ON SITE hj
EXAM BOARDS acd L
RETAKES   **NVQ COURSES**

A-level:
AS:
GCSE: d v / BC E G K R / cdef
OTHER: C l

HAMPSHIRE continued

Rushmoor Independent School; 40 Reading Road; Farnborough; Hants. GU14 6NB
Tel: 01252 544738 *Mrs Julie Morrish*

		Boys	Age	Girls	Age	TOTAL		Boys	Girls
Day	£898	18	3-16	7	3-16	25	SIXTH		
Weekly									
Boarding									

MAP 3 E 5
LOCATION Urban
DAY **RAIL** a **AIR** b
SPORT
OTHER LANGUAGES
ACTIVITIES

ENTRY REQUIREMENTS Exam & Interview; Assessment & Interview
SCHOLARSHIPS & BURSARIES
SPECIAL NEEDS **DYSLEXIA** **DIET**
ASSOCIATION ISAI **FOUNDED** **RELIGIOUS AFFILIATION** Non-denom

OTHER SUBJECTS
FACILITIES ON SITE
EXAM BOARDS d
RETAKES **NVQ COURSES**

A-level | AS | GCSE d e g i v / B G OP R / e | OTHER l

St. Benedict's Convent School; Penton Lodge; Andover; Hants SP11 0RD
Tel: 01264 772291 *Mrs R.M.Wheelwright*

		Boys	Age	Girls	Age	TOTAL		Boys	Girls
Day	£550-£995	31	3-9	51	3-16	103	SIXTH		
Weekly									
Boarding	£1965-£2395			21	6-16				

MAP 3 C 5
LOCATION Rural
DAY **RAIL** a **AIR** a
SPORT cflmpqx AB
OTHER LANGUAGES
ACTIVITIES cghjnqwx A

ENTRY REQUIREMENTS Test & Interview
SCHOLARSHIPS & BURSARIES Burs
SPECIAL NEEDS abejkqw EI **DYSLEXIA** **DIET**
ASSOCIATION ISAI **FOUNDED** 1930 **RELIGIOUS AFFILIATION** R C

OTHER SUBJECTS bch
FACILITIES ON SITE d
EXAM BOARDS abcd ADE
RETAKES **NVQ COURSES**

A-level | AS | GCSE d g i v / B G K P R / cdef | OTHER m K O

St. John's College; Southsea PO5 3QW
Tel: 01705 815118 (Fax: 01705 873603) *J.R.Davies*

		Boys	Age	Girls	Age	TOTAL		Boys	Girls
Day	£900-£1295	678	5-18	9	16-18	777	SIXTH	106	9
Weekly	£2215-£2670	90	8-18						
Boarding	£2215-£2670								

MAP 3 D 7
LOCATION Urban
DAY **RAIL** a **AIR** b
SPORT abcefghjklmprstwx ABC
OTHER LANGUAGES
ACTIVITIES bfghijklmnoqrstx AB

ENTRY REQUIREMENTS Report & Test
SCHOLARSHIPS & BURSARIES AP
SPECIAL NEEDS **DYSLEXIA** **DIET** a
ASSOCIATION GBA **FOUNDED** 1908 **RELIGIOUS AFFILIATION** R C

OTHER SUBJECTS cfh
FACILITIES ON SITE bcdhk
EXAM BOARDS abcde ADEG
RETAKES **NVQ COURSES**

A-level e g i l op v x / B GH K OP R / cdef | AS | GCSE e g i l op v / B G K OP R / cdef | OTHER h

St. Neots; Eversley; Basingstoke; Hants. RG27 0PN
Tel: 01734 732118 *R.J.Thorp*

		Boys	Age	Girls	Age	TOTAL		Boys	Girls
Day	£450-£1962 X	101	3-13	44	3-11	160	SIXTH		
Weekly	£2570	15	8-13						
Boarding									

MAP 3 D 5
LOCATION Rural
DAY **RAIL** b **AIR** a
SPORT abcefjklmopqux AB
OTHER LANGUAGES
ACTIVITIES cfghijopqt A

ENTRY REQUIREMENTS Report & Interview
SCHOLARSHIPS & BURSARIES Forces; Siblings
SPECIAL NEEDS j BI **DYSLEXIA** **DIET**
ASSOCIATION IAPS **FOUNDED** 1888 **RELIGIOUS AFFILIATION** C of E

OTHER SUBJECTS ach
FACILITIES ON SITE hi
EXAM BOARDS
RETAKES **NVQ COURSES**

A-level | AS | GCSE e g i l v / B G K OP R / cde j | OTHER

St. Nicholas' School; Falklands; Branksomewood Road; Fleet; Hampshire GU13 8JT
Tel: 01252 614864 *Mrs L.G.Smith*

		Boys	Age	Girls	Age	TOTAL		Boys	Girls
Day	£606-£1250	13	3-7	334	3-18	347	SIXTH		11
Weekly									
Boarding									

MAP 3 E 5
LOCATION Urban
DAY **RAIL** a **AIR** b
SPORT abcfhlnpqx ABC
OTHER LANGUAGES
ACTIVITIES cghijoqtwx A

ENTRY REQUIREMENTS Test & Interview; Report & Interview
SCHOLARSHIPS & BURSARIES Burs
SPECIAL NEEDS ajlnt B **DYSLEXIA** eg **DIET**
ASSOCIATION GBGSA **FOUNDED** 1935 **RELIGIOUS AFFILIATION** C of E

OTHER SUBJECTS cfgh
FACILITIES ON SITE dhk
EXAM BOARDS abd ABEG
RETAKES ab **NVQ COURSES**

A-level efghi l p v / BC GH K P R / cdef j l | AS | GCSE G | GCSE e g i l v / BC G K OP R / cdef j l | OTHER cde l n / d

HAMPSHIRE continued

C — St. Swithun's Junior School; Winchester; Hants; SO21 1HA
Tel: 01962 852634 (Fax: 01962 841874) Mrs V.A.M.Lewis

		Boys	Age	Girls	Age	TOTAL		Boys	Girls
Day	£565-£1435	35	3-8	156	3-11	191	SIXTH		
Weekly									
Boarding									

ENTRY REQUIREMENTS Assessment
SCHOLARSHIPS & BURSARIES
SPECIAL NEEDS abejklnqt ABGI **DYSLEXIA** e **DIET** ab
ASSOCIATION IAPS **FOUNDED** 1884 **RELIGIOUS AFFILIATION** C of E

MAP 3 C 6
LOCATION Rural
DAY **RAIL** a **AIR** b
SPORT cejlopqx B
OTHER LANGUAGES
ACTIVITIES cfghjno
OTHER SUBJECTS bch
FACILITIES ON SITE hi
EXAM BOARDS
RETAKES **NVQ COURSES**

A-level:
AS:
GCSE:
OTHER: e lmno s v B DE G K O R cde

G — St. Swithun's School; Winchester SO21 1HA
Tel: 01962 861316 (Fax: 01962 841874) Dr H.L.Harvey

		Boys	Age	Girls	Age	TOTAL		Boys	Girls
Day	£2240			234	11-18	457	SIXTH		104
Weekly	£3710			155	11-18				
Boarding	£3710			68	11-18				

ENTRY REQUIREMENTS CEE; Test
SCHOLARSHIPS & BURSARIES Schol; Burs; Mus; AP; VI Form
SPECIAL NEEDS bglnquw EGI **DYSLEXIA** e **DIET** a
ASSOCIATION GSA **FOUNDED** 1884 **RELIGIOUS AFFILIATION** C of E

MAP 3 C 6
LOCATION Rural
DAY **RAIL** a **AIR** a
SPORT cgklnopx ABC
OTHER LANGUAGES
ACTIVITIES acfghijklow A
OTHER SUBJECTS abceh
FACILITIES ON SITE ceghi
EXAM BOARDS abcd ABDE
RETAKES **NVQ COURSES**

A-level: cd fg i nop uv x B GH K P R cdefg j l
AS: K
GCSE: cd g i o v BC E G K P R cdefg jkl
OTHER: lmn O

C — Sherborne House School; Lakewood Road; Chandlers Ford; Hants. SO53 1EU;
Tel: 01703 252440 (Fax: 01703 252553) Mrs S.M.Warner

		Boys	Age	Girls	Age	TOTAL		Boys	Girls
Day	£365-£990	21	3-8	164	3-11	185	SIXTH		
Weekly									
Boarding									

ENTRY REQUIREMENTS Report & Interview
SCHOLARSHIPS & BURSARIES
SPECIAL NEEDS ejknpqw GI **DYSLEXIA** e **DIET** a
ASSOCIATION IAPS **FOUNDED** 1933 **RELIGIOUS AFFILIATION** Inter-denom

MAP 3 C 6
LOCATION Rural
DAY **RAIL** a **AIR** b
SPORT pq
OTHER LANGUAGES
ACTIVITIES cghjo
OTHER SUBJECTS bch
FACILITIES ON SITE ac
EXAM BOARDS
RETAKES **NVQ COURSES**

A-level:
AS:
GCSE:
OTHER: lmno v B G K O R cde

C — Stanbridge Earls School; Romsey; Hants. SO51 0ZS
Tel: 01794 516777 (Fax: 01794 511201) H.Moxon

		Boys	Age	Girls	Age	TOTAL		Boys	Girls
Day	£2665-£2915	13	11-18	7	11-18	183	SIXTH	26	7
Weekly			11-18		11-18				
Boarding	£3555-£3885	131	11-18	32	11-18				

ENTRY REQUIREMENTS Report & Interview
SCHOLARSHIPS & BURSARIES Schol; Burs; Art
SPECIAL NEEDS begijklnqtuwx ABCDEGIJKL **DYSLEXIA** bcd **DIET** a
ASSOCIATION SHMIS **FOUNDED** 1952 **RELIGIOUS AFFILIATION** Inter-denom

MAP 3 C 6
LOCATION Rural
DAY **RAIL** b **AIR** b
SPORT abcefhjkmopqstuwx ABC
OTHER LANGUAGES a
ACTIVITIES afghijklmnqsuw AB
OTHER SUBJECTS bcdh
FACILITIES ON SITE abcdhik
EXAM BOARDS abcde ABDEG
RETAKES ab **NVQ COURSES**

A-level: defg i l nop v B G I K NOP c e l
AS: f h n p u
GCSE: de ghij nop v BC E G I K NOP T W cdef h l
OTHER: N

C — Stroud School; Highwood House; Romsey; Hants. SO51 9ZH
Tel: 01794 513231 (Fax: 01794 513231) A.J.L.Dodds

		Boys	Age	Girls	Age	TOTAL		Boys	Girls
Day	£543-£1926	185	3-13	63	3-13	248	SIXTH		
Weekly									
Boarding									

ENTRY REQUIREMENTS Test & Interview
SCHOLARSHIPS & BURSARIES Schol; Art; Mus; Clergy; Sport; ARA; Siblings
SPECIAL NEEDS abn **DYSLEXIA** de **DIET** abcd
ASSOCIATION IAPS **FOUNDED** 1926 **RELIGIOUS AFFILIATION** Inter-denom

MAP 3 C 6
LOCATION Rural
DAY **RAIL** b **AIR** b
SPORT abcdefjlmpqstuwx ABC
OTHER LANGUAGES
ACTIVITIES cfghijnopqtw A
OTHER SUBJECTS abcfh
FACILITIES ON SITE bcj
EXAM BOARDS
RETAKES **NVQ COURSES**

A-level:
AS:
GCSE:
OTHER: c e g i lmno t v BC G K OP R cde j l

HAMPSHIRE *continued*

C | **Twyford School; Winchester; Hants. SO21 1NW**
Tel: 01962 712269 (Fax: 01962 712100) *P.R.D.Gould*

		Boys	Age	Girls	Age	TOTAL		Boys	Girls
Day	£590-£2120 ✗	154	3-13	56	3-13	267	SIXTH		
Weekly		53	7-13	4	7-13				
Boarding	£2900								

ENTRY REQUIREMENTS Assessment & Interview
SCHOLARSHIPS & BURSARIES
SPECIAL NEEDS jw **DYSLEXIA** **DIET**
ASSOCIATION IAPS **FOUNDED** 1809 **RELIGIOUS AFFILIATION** C of E

MAP 3 C 6
LOCATION Rural
DAY   **RAIL** a   **AIR** b
SPORT abcefjklmopqsuwx ABC
OTHER LANGUAGES
ACTIVITIES acdfghijmnopqrtvw A
OTHER SUBJECTS abcfh
FACILITIES ON SITE cdhik
EXAM BOARDS
RETAKES   **NVQ COURSES**

A-level   **AS**   **GCSE**   **OTHER** cdefg i lmno q s v
AB E G K OP R W
cdefg j

C | **Walhampton School; Lymington; Hants. SO41 5ZG**
Tel: 01590 672013 (Fax: 01590 678498) *A.W.S.Robinson*

		Boys	Age	Girls	Age	TOTAL		Boys	Girls
Day	£1100-£2340 ✗	76	4-13	51	4-13	221	SIXTH		
Weekly		57	7-13	37	8-13				
Boarding	£3060								

ENTRY REQUIREMENTS Test; Assessment
SCHOLARSHIPS & BURSARIES Schol; Burs
SPECIAL NEEDS ajln **DYSLEXIA** e **DIET** a
ASSOCIATION IAPS **FOUNDED** 1948 **RELIGIOUS AFFILIATION** C of E

MAP 3 C 7
LOCATION Rural
DAY   **RAIL** a   **AIR** b
SPORT abcefgjklmopqstux AB
OTHER LANGUAGES
ACTIVITIES acfghijmnortw
OTHER SUBJECTS abcdfh
FACILITIES ON SITE bcdj
EXAM BOARDS
RETAKES   **NVQ COURSES**

A-level   **AS**   **GCSE**   **OTHER** egi l no q   v
B   G K   OP R
cde   j

C | **West Hill Park; Titchfield; Fareham; Hants. PO14 4BS**
Tel: 01329 842356 (Fax: 01329 842911) *E.P.K.Hudson*

		Boys	Age	Girls	Age	TOTAL		Boys	Girls
Day	£485-£1890	118	3-13	78	3-13	253	SIXTH		
Weekly		40	7-13	17	7-13				
Boarding	£2555								

ENTRY REQUIREMENTS Test
SCHOLARSHIPS & BURSARIES
SPECIAL NEEDS ejkl Gl **DYSLEXIA** **DIET**
ASSOCIATION IAPS **FOUNDED** 1920 **RELIGIOUS AFFILIATION** C of E

MAP 3 D 7
LOCATION Rural
DAY   **RAIL** a   **AIR** b
SPORT abcdefjklmopqsuwx ABC
OTHER LANGUAGES
ACTIVITIES acfghjnoqrstw A
OTHER SUBJECTS cfh
FACILITIES ON SITE bcdhik
EXAM BOARDS
RETAKES   **NVQ COURSES**

A-level   **AS**   **GCSE**   **OTHER**   e lm o   v
AB G
cde g j

B | **Winchester College; College Street; Winchester; Hants. SO23 9NA**
Tel: 01962 854328 (Fax: 01962 842972) *J.P.Sabben-Clare*

		Boys	Age	Girls	Age	TOTAL		Boys	Girls
Day	£3322 ✗	26	13-18			667	SIXTH	264	
Weekly		641	13-18						
Boarding	£4430								

ENTRY REQUIREMENTS Report & Exam & Interview
SCHOLARSHIPS & BURSARIES Schol; Mus; AP; VI Form
SPECIAL NEEDS abglq **DYSLEXIA** **DIET** a
ASSOCIATION HMC **FOUNDED** 1382 **RELIGIOUS AFFILIATION** C of E

MAP 3 C 6
LOCATION Urban
DAY   **RAIL** a   **AIR** b
SPORT abcdefhijklmortuwx ABC
OTHER LANGUAGES
ACTIVITIES bdefghijlmnopqrstv D
OTHER SUBJECTS abcdfh
FACILITIES ON SITE cdhikl
EXAM BOARDS abcd ABDEGHL
RETAKES   **NVQ COURSES**

A-level defg i   opq v   **AS** c fg i   **GCSE** egi o v   **OTHER** B F L q
B GH K   P R   G   P   G K   P   bc hi O R
cdefg jkl   b defg jkl

G | **Wykeham House School; East Street; Fareham; Hants PO16 0BW;**
Tel: 01329 280178 (Fax: 01329 823964) *Mrs E.M.Moore*

		Boys	Age	Girls	Age	TOTAL		Boys	Girls
Day	£963-£1290			316	4-16	316	SIXTH		
Weekly									
Boarding									

ENTRY REQUIREMENTS CEE; Exam; Assessment & Interview
SCHOLARSHIPS & BURSARIES Schol; Burs
SPECIAL NEEDS **DYSLEXIA** **DIET**
ASSOCIATION GSA **FOUNDED** 1913 **RELIGIOUS AFFILIATION** C of E

MAP 3 D 7
LOCATION Urban
DAY   **RAIL** a   **AIR** b
SPORT achmnpqx B
OTHER LANGUAGES
ACTIVITIES fghijko
OTHER SUBJECTS bc
FACILITIES ON SITE
EXAM BOARDS bd B
RETAKES   **NVQ COURSES**

A-level   **AS**   **GCSE** egi l q v   **OTHER** G
B E G K P R W
cdef l

HEREFORD & WORCESTER

Bg Abberley Hall; Worcester WR6 6DD
Tel: 01299 896275 (Fax: 01299 896875) *M.V.D.Haggard*

		Boys	Age	Girls	Age	TOTAL		Boys	Girls
Day	£690-£2100	75	2-13	23	2-8	223			
Weekly	£2800		7-13				SIXTH		
Boarding	£2800	125	7-13						

ENTRY REQUIREMENTS None
SCHOLARSHIPS & BURSARIES Schol; Burs; Mus; Teachers
SPECIAL NEEDS bejklnuw GHI   **DYSLEXIA** ce   **DIET** acd
ASSOCIATION IAPS   **FOUNDED** 1880   **RELIGIOUS AFFILIATION** C of E

MAP 8 J 7
LOCATION Rural
DAY   **RAIL** b   **AIR** a
SPORT abcdefgjklmosux ABC
OTHER LANGUAGES
ACTIVITIES afghijmopqrst A
OTHER SUBJECTS abcfh
FACILITIES ON SITE abcdhjkl
EXAM BOARDS
RETAKES   **NVQ COURSES**

A-level
AS
GCSE
OTHER e g i l n o q v / B G K O P R / c d e f g j

G Alice Ottley School,The; Upper Tything; Worcester WR1 1HW
Tel: 01905 27061 (Fax: 01905 724626) *Miss C.Sibbit*

		Boys	Age	Girls	Age	TOTAL		Boys	Girls
Day	£742-£1595			704	3-18	704	SIXTH		136
Weekly									
Boarding									

ENTRY REQUIREMENTS Scholarship Exam; Report & Interview; Report & Test
SCHOLARSHIPS & BURSARIES Schol; Burs; Mus; Clergy; AP; VI Form; Siblings
SPECIAL NEEDS bejlw   **DYSLEXIA**   **DIET** abcd
ASSOCIATION GSA   **FOUNDED** 1883   **RELIGIOUS AFFILIATION** C of E

MAP 8 J 7
LOCATION Urban
DAY   **RAIL** a   **AIR** a
SPORT acfhlmnopqx ABC
OTHER LANGUAGES
ACTIVITIES acghijklnostwx AB
OTHER SUBJECTS bcdfh
FACILITIES ON SITE bcgh
EXAM BOARDS abcde ABDEG
RETAKES a   **NVQ COURSES**

A-level cd g i op uv / BC GH K P R W / c efg j l
AS cd g / C G K P / e g j l
GCSE e g i op v / BC E G K P R W / c d e f g j k l
OTHER l

B Aymestrey School; Crown East; Worcester WR2 5TR
Tel: 01905 42 5619 *D.H.Griffith*

		Boys	Age	Girls	Age	TOTAL		Boys	Girls
Day	£1300	17	7-13			31	SIXTH		
Weekly									
Boarding	£1750	14	7-13						

ENTRY REQUIREMENTS Interview
SCHOLARSHIPS & BURSARIES Clergy; Teachers
SPECIAL NEEDS abejklnpquw BEGI   **DYSLEXIA** e   **DIET** a
ASSOCIATION IAPS   **FOUNDED** 1909   **RELIGIOUS AFFILIATION** C of E

MAP 8 J 7
LOCATION Rural
DAY   **RAIL** b   **AIR** a
SPORT abefhjloqsx AB
OTHER LANGUAGES a
ACTIVITIES fghjmnoqvw
OTHER SUBJECTS abcfh
FACILITIES ON SITE aj
EXAM BOARDS
RETAKES   **NVQ COURSES**

A-level
AS
GCSE
OTHER c e g i l n q v / B G K O P R / c d e j

C Bowbrook House School; Peopleton; Pershore; Worcs. WR10 2EE
Tel: 01905 841242 (Fax: 01905 840716) *S.W.Jackson*

		Boys	Age	Girls	Age	TOTAL		Boys	Girls
Day	£530-£1200	52	3-16	49	3-16	101	SIXTH		
Weekly									
Boarding									

ENTRY REQUIREMENTS Report & Test
SCHOLARSHIPS & BURSARIES Burs; Art; Mus; Sport
SPECIAL NEEDS bnw B   **DYSLEXIA** e   **DIET**
ASSOCIATION ISAI   **FOUNDED** 1954   **RELIGIOUS AFFILIATION** Non-denom

MAP 8 J 7
LOCATION Rural
DAY   **RAIL** b   **AIR** b
SPORT aefjmpqsx AB
OTHER LANGUAGES
ACTIVITIES fghjo
OTHER SUBJECTS ch
FACILITIES ON SITE j
EXAM BOARDS b H
RETAKES   **NVQ COURSES**

A-level
AS
GCSE e g i v / B G K O P R / c d e
OTHER

C Bowbrook School; The Village; Hartlebury; Worcestershire DY11 7TE
Tel: 01299 250258 (Fax: 01299 250379) *David Bolam*

		Boys	Age	Girls	Age	TOTAL		Boys	Girls
Day	£665-£1565	54	2-16	50	2-16	104	SIXTH		
Weekly									
Boarding									

ENTRY REQUIREMENTS Assessment & Interview
SCHOLARSHIPS & BURSARIES
SPECIAL NEEDS n BL   **DYSLEXIA**   **DIET** acd
ASSOCIATION ISAI   **FOUNDED** 1977   **RELIGIOUS AFFILIATION**

MAP 8 I 6
LOCATION Rural
DAY ✓   **RAIL** b   **AIR** a
SPORT acefhjmpqx BC
OTHER LANGUAGES
ACTIVITIES fgh
OTHER SUBJECTS cd
FACILITIES ON SITE j
EXAM BOARDS b
RETAKES a   **NVQ COURSES** 12

A-level
AS
GCSE d e g i l v / B G K P / c d e l
OTHER e m o v / B G O / c d

HEREFORD & WORCESTER *continued*

C — Bromsgrove Lower School; Cobham House; Conway Road; Bromsgrove; Worcs. B60 2AD Tel: 01527 579600 (Fax: 01527 579571) *E.J.Ormerod*

		Boys	Age	Girls	Age	TOTAL		Boys	Girls
Day	£1530-£1975	255	7-13	187	7-13	538	SIXTH		
Weekly									
Boarding	£2615-£2995	57	7-13	39	7-13				

ENTRY REQUIREMENTS Test
SCHOLARSHIPS & BURSARIES Schol; Burs; Forces; AP
SPECIAL NEEDS B **DYSLEXIA** **DIET** abcd
ASSOCIATION IAPS **FOUNDED** 1940 **RELIGIOUS AFFILIATION** C of E

MAP 8 J 6
LOCATION Urban
DAY **RAIL** b **AIR** a
SPORT abcdefgjklmnopqrsuwx AB
OTHER LANGUAGES
ACTIVITIES acfghjopstwx A
OTHER SUBJECTS bcfh
FACILITIES ON SITE acdhij
EXAM BOARDS
RETAKES **NVQ COURSES**

A-level / AS / GCSE / OTHER:
OTHER: de lmno s v AB E G K NO R cdef j l

C — Bromsgrove School; Bromsgrove B61 7DU Tel: 01527 579679 (Fax: 01527 576177) *T.M.Taylor*

		Boys	Age	Girls	Age	TOTAL		Boys	Girls
Day	£2050	232	13-18	151	13-18	637	SIXTH	142	87
Weekly									
Boarding	£3275	157	13-18	97	13-18				

ENTRY REQUIREMENTS Scholarship Exam; CEE & Interview; Report & Exam & Interview
SCHOLARSHIPS & BURSARIES Schol; Burs; Art; Mus; Chor; Forces; Teachers; AP; VI Form; Sport
SPECIAL NEEDS n **DYSLEXIA** e **DIET** acd
ASSOCIATION HMC **FOUNDED** 1548 **RELIGIOUS AFFILIATION** C of E

MAP 8 J 6
LOCATION Urban
DAY ✓ **RAIL** b **AIR** a
SPORT abcdefghjklmopqstuwx AB
OTHER LANGUAGES a
ACTIVITIES abcefghijklnoqstw AB
OTHER SUBJECTS bcefh
FACILITIES ON SITE abcdehik
EXAM BOARDS bc ABDEH
RETAKES **NVQ COURSES** 3

A-level: c e ghi op uv x B GH K P U cdef j l
AS: c ghi n p v x B GH K P U c ef l
GCSE: cde ghi l no q v B GH K OP R X cdef hj l
OTHER: l O R

G — Dodderhill School; Droitwich; Worcs. WR9 0BE Tel: 01905 778290 *Mrs M.A.Maybee*

		Boys	Age	Girls	Age	TOTAL		Boys	Girls
Day	£1285-£1445			106	9-16	106	SIXTH		
Weekly									
Boarding									

ENTRY REQUIREMENTS Report & Exam & Interview
SCHOLARSHIPS & BURSARIES Schol; Mus; Siblings
SPECIAL NEEDS bejklnqw **DYSLEXIA** e **DIET** ac
ASSOCIATION ISAI **FOUNDED** 1973 **RELIGIOUS AFFILIATION** C of E

MAP 8 J 6
LOCATION Urban
DAY ✓ **RAIL** b **AIR** b
SPORT acflmpqx ABC
OTHER LANGUAGES
ACTIVITIES ghijkn A
OTHER SUBJECTS abch
FACILITIES ON SITE bh
EXAM BOARDS bd A
RETAKES **NVQ COURSES**

A-level / AS: G / GCSE: d v BC G K R WX cdef
OTHER: l no u E O

C — Downs School,The; Colwall; Malvern; Worcs. WR13 6EY Tel: 01684 540277 (Fax: 01684 540094) *J.M.Griggs*

		Boys	Age	Girls	Age	TOTAL		Boys	Girls
Day	£442-£1945	64	3-13	37	3-13	151	SIXTH		
Weekly	£2645	10	7-13	8	7-13				
Boarding	£2645	13	7-13	19	7-13				

ENTRY REQUIREMENTS Report & Interview
SCHOLARSHIPS & BURSARIES Schol; Burs; Mus; Forces; Teachers; AP
SPECIAL NEEDS bejmnuvw ABEG **DYSLEXIA** ef **DIET** abcd
ASSOCIATION IAPS **FOUNDED** 1900 **RELIGIOUS AFFILIATION** Inter-denom

MAP 8 I 7
LOCATION Rural
DAY **RAIL** b **AIR** a
SPORT abcefghjklmpqswx ABC
OTHER LANGUAGES
ACTIVITIES acdfghijnopqrstuwx A
OTHER SUBJECTS abcfh
FACILITIES ON SITE abcefjkl
EXAM BOARDS
RETAKES **NVQ COURSES**

OTHER: de g i klmno rs v ABCDE G JK NOP RS W cdefg jkl

B g — Elms,The; Colwall; nr.Malvern; Worcs WR13 6EF Tel: 01684 540344 (Fax: 01684 541174) *L.A.C.Ashby*

		Boys	Age	Girls	Age	TOTAL		Boys	Girls
Day	£520-£2400	42	3-13	42	3-12	149	SIXTH		
Weekly									
Boarding	£2800	45	8-13	20	8-12				

ENTRY REQUIREMENTS Interview
SCHOLARSHIPS & BURSARIES Schol; Forces; Clergy; Teachers
SPECIAL NEEDS bkqw G **DYSLEXIA** **DIET** a
ASSOCIATION IAPS **FOUNDED** 1620 **RELIGIOUS AFFILIATION** C of E

MAP 8 I 7
LOCATION Rural
DAY ✓ **RAIL** b **AIR** a
SPORT acefijklmpqsux AB
OTHER LANGUAGES
ACTIVITIES cfghijmnortw ABC
OTHER SUBJECTS acfh
FACILITIES ON SITE bcdfhik
EXAM BOARDS
RETAKES **NVQ COURSES**

OTHER: e g i lmn v B E G K OP RS cde g j l

HEREFORD & WORCESTER *continued*

Hawford Lodge; Worcester WR3 7SE
Tel: 01905 451292 (Fax: 01905 756502) *A.Race*

		Boys	Age	Girls	Age	TOTAL
Day	£905-£1596 ✗	120	3-13	39	3-13	159
Weekly						
Boarding						

SIXTH: Boys — Girls —

MAP 8 J 7
LOCATION Rural
DAY — **RAIL** a **AIR** a
SPORT abdefjmpqstuwx AB
OTHER LANGUAGES
ACTIVITIES cfghjmopqt
OTHER SUBJECTS bch
FACILITIES ON SITE jk
EXAM BOARDS
RETAKES **NVQ COURSES**

ENTRY REQUIREMENTS Assessment & Interview
SCHOLARSHIPS & BURSARIES Schol; Clergy
SPECIAL NEEDS begijklnqtw GHI
DYSLEXIA **DIET** abcd
ASSOCIATION IAPS **FOUNDED** 1955 **RELIGIOUS AFFILIATION** C of E

A-level —
AS —
GCSE — e g i l — no q — v
BC — G — K — OP R
cde g j
OTHER —

Heathfield School; Wolverley; nr.Kidderminster DY10 3QE
Tel: 01562 850204 *G.L.Sinton*

		Boys	Age	Girls	Age	TOTAL
Day	£285-£1355	167	3-16	88	3-16	255
Weekly						
Boarding						

SIXTH: Boys — Girls —

MAP 8 I 6
LOCATION Rural
DAY — **RAIL** a **AIR** a
SPORT abcefjlmopqsx AB
OTHER LANGUAGES
ACTIVITIES cfghjlmnqstx A
OTHER SUBJECTS bcfh
FACILITIES ON SITE bchk
EXAM BOARDS b
RETAKES **NVQ COURSES**

ENTRY REQUIREMENTS Test & Interview
SCHOLARSHIPS & BURSARIES Schol; Burs
SPECIAL NEEDS abjklnqtu BI **DYSLEXIA** e **DIET** abcd
ASSOCIATION ISAI **FOUNDED** 1970 **RELIGIOUS AFFILIATION** Non-denom

A-level —
AS —
GCSE — e g i l — v
B — G — OP
cdef
OTHER —

Hereford Cathedral Junior School; Hereford HR1 2NW
Tel: 01432 353726 (Fax: 01432 272362)

		Boys	Age	Girls	Age	TOTAL
Day	£770-£1130	175	3-11	64	3-11	248
Weekly	£1915-£2140	6	7-11	1		
Boarding	£1915-£2140	2	8-11			

SIXTH: Boys — Girls —

MAP 8 H 7
LOCATION Urban
DAY — **RAIL** b **AIR** b
SPORT abefjlmpqsx B
OTHER LANGUAGES
ACTIVITIES cfghijloqrtx
OTHER SUBJECTS ch
FACILITIES ON SITE ck
EXAM BOARDS
RETAKES **NVQ COURSES**

ENTRY REQUIREMENTS Interview; Test & Interview
SCHOLARSHIPS & BURSARIES Chor; Clergy; Siblings
SPECIAL NEEDS n B **DYSLEXIA** e **DIET** a
ASSOCIATION IAPS **FOUNDED** 1897 **RELIGIOUS AFFILIATION** C of E

A-level —
AS —
GCSE — e — l no s v
B E G K O R W
cde j
OTHER —

Hereford Cathedral School; Old Deanery; The Cathedral Close; Hereford HR1 2NG
Tel: 01432 363522 (Fax: 01432 363525) *Dr H.C.Tomlinson*

		Boys	Age	Girls	Age	TOTAL
Day	£1510	307	11-18	279	11-18	634
Weekly						
Boarding	£2660	33	11-18	15	11-18	

SIXTH: Boys 97 Girls 83

MAP 8 H 7
LOCATION Inner City
DAY — **RAIL** a **AIR** b
SPORT abcdefghkmpqrstuwx BC
OTHER LANGUAGES
ACTIVITIES cefghijklnostwx AB
OTHER SUBJECTS abcdf
FACILITIES ON SITE cek
EXAM BOARDS abcde DEGH
RETAKES **NVQ COURSES**

ENTRY REQUIREMENTS CEE; Report & Exam & Interview
SCHOLARSHIPS & BURSARIES Schol; Mus; Chor; Forces; Clergy; Teachers; AP
SPECIAL NEEDS **DYSLEXIA** **DIET** a
ASSOCIATION HMC **FOUNDED** **RELIGIOUS AFFILIATION** C of E

A-level: c efg i — op — uv
B — GH K — P R
c efg j

AS: c — l o q
B — GH K — R
ef j

GCSE: c e g i l nopq vw
B — G K — P R
cdefg j l

OTHER: i k

Hillstone School; Malvern College; Abbey Road; Malvern WR14 3HF
Tel: 01684 573057 (Fax: 01684 572398) *R.G.Gillard*

		Boys	Age	Girls	Age	TOTAL
Day	£460-£2025 ✗	115	3-13	56	3-13	223
Weekly	£1340-£2680	6	7-13	2	7-13	
Boarding	£1340-£2680	30	7-13	14	7-13	

SIXTH: Boys — Girls —

MAP 8 I 7
LOCATION Urban
DAY — **RAIL** a **AIR** b
SPORT abcefhjklmnopqsx ABC
OTHER LANGUAGES a
ACTIVITIES bcfghijnoqrstw A
OTHER SUBJECTS abcfh
FACILITIES ON SITE bcdhikl
EXAM BOARDS
RETAKES **NVQ COURSES**

ENTRY REQUIREMENTS ; Exam & Interview; Report & Interview
SCHOLARSHIPS & BURSARIES Schol; Art; Mus; Chor; Forces; AP
SPECIAL NEEDS abjknquvw BGI **DYSLEXIA** cde **DIET** abcd
ASSOCIATION IAPS **FOUNDED** 1883 **RELIGIOUS AFFILIATION** C of E

A-level —
AS —
GCSE —
OTHER: defg i — lmno q s v
BC — G — K — OP R
cdef j

140

HEREFORD & WORCESTER *continued*

Gb Holy Trinity School; Birmingham Road; Kidderminster DY10 2BY
Tel: 01562 822929 (Fax: 01562 865137) *Mrs S.M.Bell*

		Boys	Age	Girls	Age	TOTAL		Boys	Girls
Day	£625-£1183	6	3- 8	300	3-18	306	SIXTH		26
Weekly									
Boarding									

ENTRY REQUIREMENTS Report & Exam & Interview
SCHOLARSHIPS & BURSARIES Schol; Burs
SPECIAL NEEDS jlntux l   **DYSLEXIA**   **DIET**
ASSOCIATION GSA   **FOUNDED** 1903   **RELIGIOUS AFFILIATION** R C

MAP 8 | 6
LOCATION Urban
DAY ✓ **RAIL** a **AIR** a
SPORT acdfhlmopqtvwx AB
OTHER LANGUAGES
ACTIVITIES cfghijknopqt AB
OTHER SUBJECTS bcdfh
FACILITIES ON SITE cdghik
EXAM BOARDS bcd ABDEGH
RETAKES ab   **NVQ COURSES**

A-level: d fg i n uv BC GH K P R W cde
AS: d g B GH K uv R W cdef
GCSE: d fg i lmn uv BCD G K OP R W cdef
OTHER: h m k

C King's Junior School; Mill Street; Worcester WR1 2NJ
Tel: 01905 354906 (Fax: 01905 763075) *John A.Allcott*

		Boys	Age	Girls	Age	TOTAL		Boys	Girls
Day	£1190-£1574	97	7-11	64	7-11	163	SIXTH		
Weekly			7-11		11				
Boarding	£2334-£2718	2	7-11		7-11				

ENTRY REQUIREMENTS Exam
SCHOLARSHIPS & BURSARIES Schol; Burs; Mus; Chor
SPECIAL NEEDS bjq Gl   **DYSLEXIA**   **DIET** abd
ASSOCIATION IAPS   **FOUNDED** 1541   **RELIGIOUS AFFILIATION** C of E

MAP 8 J 7
LOCATION
DAY   **RAIL** a   **AIR** a
SPORT abcefgjlmopqsx AB
OTHER LANGUAGES
ACTIVITIES acfghjopqrtv A
OTHER SUBJECTS bch
FACILITIES ON SITE bdhik
EXAM BOARDS
RETAKES   **NVQ COURSES**

A-level:
AS:
GCSE:
OTHER: e I no s v B E G K O R cde

C King's School,The; Worcester WR1 2LH
Tel: 01905 23016 (Fax: 01905 25511) *Dr J.M.Moore*

		Boys	Age	Girls	Age	TOTAL		Boys	Girls
Day	£1100-£1697	509	11-18	184	11-18	758	SIXTH	167	67
Weekly			11-18		11-18				
Boarding	£2334-£2931	47	11-18	18	11-18				

ENTRY REQUIREMENTS CEE; Exam
SCHOLARSHIPS & BURSARIES Schol; Burs; Mus; Chor; Forces; Clergy; AP; VI Form
SPECIAL NEEDS befjklqst EGH   **DYSLEXIA**   **DIET** acd
ASSOCIATION HMC   **FOUNDED** 1541   **RELIGIOUS AFFILIATION** C of E

MAP 8 J 7
LOCATION Urban
DAY   **RAIL** a   **AIR** b
SPORT abcdefghijkmpqrstux AB
OTHER LANGUAGES a
ACTIVITIES bcefghijklopqrst AB
OTHER SUBJECTS bcdh
FACILITIES ON SITE bcdhik
EXAM BOARDS abc ABDEH
RETAKES b   **NVQ COURSES**

A-level: c efg i op v B GH K NPR U c ef j l
AS: e K e
GCSE: cde g i no v B GH K N P R U X cdefgh j l
OTHER: e lm o q u G K O R d hj l

C Knoll School,The; Manor Avenue; Kidderminster DY11 6EA
Tel: 01562 822622 (Fax: 01562 822622) *N.J.Humphreys*

		Boys	Age	Girls	Age	TOTAL		Boys	Girls
Day	£210- £800	78	3-11	55	3-11	133	SIXTH		
Weekly									
Boarding									

ENTRY REQUIREMENTS Interview
SCHOLARSHIPS & BURSARIES Schol
SPECIAL NEEDS n   **DYSLEXIA** e   **DIET** acd
ASSOCIATION ISAI   **FOUNDED** 1917   **RELIGIOUS AFFILIATION** C of E

MAP 8 | 6
LOCATION Urban
DAY   **RAIL** a   **AIR** b
SPORT aejlmpqx AB
OTHER LANGUAGES
ACTIVITIES cghjt
OTHER SUBJECTS bch
FACILITIES ON SITE ac
EXAM BOARDS
RETAKES   **NVQ COURSES**

A-level:
AS:
GCSE:
OTHER: de I mno s v B DE G K O R cde

C Lea House School; The Lea; Bewdley Hill; Kidderminster; Worcs. DY11 6JR
Tel: 01562 822376 *Mrs.B.A.Bartter*

		Boys	Age	Girls	Age	TOTAL		Boys	Girls
Day	£685- £950 ✗	48	2-11	44	2-11	92	SIXTH		
Weekly									
Boarding									

ENTRY REQUIREMENTS Interview
SCHOLARSHIPS & BURSARIES
SPECIAL NEEDS n   **DYSLEXIA** e   **DIET** abcd
ASSOCIATION ISAI   **FOUNDED** 1926   **RELIGIOUS AFFILIATION** Non-denom

MAP 8 | 6
LOCATION Rural
DAY   **RAIL** b   **AIR** a
SPORT aefjlmpqsx AB
OTHER LANGUAGES
ACTIVITIES cfghj
OTHER SUBJECTS ch
FACILITIES ON SITE abch
EXAM BOARDS
RETAKES   **NVQ COURSES**

A-level:
AS:
GCSE:
OTHER: e lmno s v B G K O R cde

141

HEREFORD & WORCESTER *continued*

C — Malvern College; Malvern; Worcs. WR14 3DF
Tel: 01684 892333 (Fax: 01684 572398) *R.de C.Chapman*

		Boys	Age	Girls	Age	TOTAL		Boys	Girls
Day	£2960	X	61	13-18	47	13-18	663	SIXTH	229	94
Weekly Boarding	£4070		412	13-18	143	13-18				

ENTRY REQUIREMENTS CEE; Report & Exam & Interview
SCHOLARSHIPS & BURSARIES Schol; Art; Mus; AP
SPECIAL NEEDS bjln B **DYSLEXIA** ef **DIET** abcd
ASSOCIATION HMC **FOUNDED** 1865 **RELIGIOUS AFFILIATION** C of E

MAP 8 I 7
LOCATION Rural
DAY **RAIL** a **AIR** a
SPORT abcdefghijklmnopqrstuwx ABC
OTHER LANGUAGES a
ACTIVITIES cefghijklnoqstvw AB
OTHER SUBJECTS bcdfh
FACILITIES ON SITE bcdhik
EXAM BOARDS abcde ABCDEHJ
RETAKES **NVQ COURSES**

A-level: c efg i   op   uv x
AB   GH K   OP R
c efg j l

AS: c

GCSE: B   G   v
ef   j l
R

OTHER: d g i   no   v
BC   G   K   OP R   WX
cdefg j l

G — Malvern Girls' College; Malvern; Worcs. WR14 3BA
Tel: 01684 892288 (Fax: 01684 566204) *Dr Anne Lee*

		Boys	Age	Girls	Age	TOTAL		Boys	Girls
Day	£2600	X			55	11-18	462	SIXTH		173
Weekly Boarding	£3900				407	11-18				

ENTRY REQUIREMENTS CEE; Report & Exam & Interview
SCHOLARSHIPS & BURSARIES Schol; Burs; Art; Mus; VI Form
SPECIAL NEEDS jn G **DYSLEXIA** d **DIET** ad
ASSOCIATION GSA **FOUNDED** 1893 **RELIGIOUS AFFILIATION** C of E

MAP 8 I 7
LOCATION Rural
DAY **RAIL** a **AIR** b
SPORT abcdfghklmnopqtwx ABC
OTHER LANGUAGES a
ACTIVITIES cfghijklnopqstuw AB
OTHER SUBJECTS abcdfh
FACILITIES ON SITE abcdehik
EXAM BOARDS abcd ADEGH
RETAKES **NVQ COURSES**

A-level: cdefg i   p   uv
BC   GH K   P R
cdefg j l

AS: cdefg i
BC   GH K   P R
c efg j l

GCSE: cdefg i   nop   v
BC   G   K   N P R
cdefghj l

OTHER: l

G — Margaret Allen Preparatory School; 32 Broomy Hill; Hereford HR4 0LH
Tel: 01432 273594 (Fax: 01432 273594) *Lady Mynors*

		Boys	Age	Girls	Age	TOTAL		Boys	Girls
Day	£770-£1010				104	3-11	104	SIXTH		
Weekly Boarding										

ENTRY REQUIREMENTS Interview
SCHOLARSHIPS & BURSARIES
SPECIAL NEEDS ejknqvw Gl **DYSLEXIA** e **DIET** ad
ASSOCIATION IAPS **FOUNDED** 1923 **RELIGIOUS AFFILIATION** Non-denom

MAP 8 H 7
LOCATION Urban
DAY ✓ **RAIL** a **AIR**
SPORT almnpqx
OTHER LANGUAGES
ACTIVITIES cfgjoq
OTHER SUBJECTS abch
FACILITIES ON SITE
EXAM BOARDS
RETAKES **NVQ COURSES**

A-level:

AS:

GCSE:

OTHER: de   lmno   s v
B EG   K   O R
cde

C — Moffats School; Kinlet Hall; nr.Bewdley; Worcs. DY12 3AY
Tel: 01299 841230 (Fax: 01299 841444) *M. & A.Daborn*

		Boys	Age	Girls	Age	TOTAL		Boys	Girls
Day	£1260		2	6-13	1	6-13	78	SIXTH		
Weekly Boarding	£2075		48	7-13	27	7-13				

ENTRY REQUIREMENTS Assessment & Interview
SCHOLARSHIPS & BURSARIES Schol; Mus; Forces; Clergy; Teachers
SPECIAL NEEDS abefjknuwx DEGH **DYSLEXIA** e **DIET** a
ASSOCIATION ISAI **FOUNDED** 1934 **RELIGIOUS AFFILIATION**

MAP 8 I 6
LOCATION Rural
DAY **RAIL** b **AIR** a
SPORT acefjmpqtx AB
OTHER LANGUAGES
ACTIVITIES cfghjqw
OTHER SUBJECTS ach
FACILITIES ON SITE bfjk
EXAM BOARDS
RETAKES **NVQ COURSES**

A-level:

AS:

GCSE:

OTHER: egilm   v
B   G K   P R
cdefg j

C — Mount School; 277 Birmingham Road; Bromsgrove; Worcs. B61 0EP
Tel: 01527 877772 (Fax: 01527 877772) *B.J.Maybee*

		Boys	Age	Girls	Age	TOTAL		Boys	Girls
Day	£679-£1096		78	3-12	59	3-12	137	SIXTH		
Weekly Boarding										

ENTRY REQUIREMENTS Interview
SCHOLARSHIPS & BURSARIES
SPECIAL NEEDS bejmntuw ABI **DYSLEXIA** def **DIET**
ASSOCIATION ISAI **FOUNDED** 1927 **RELIGIOUS AFFILIATION**

MAP 8 J 6
LOCATION Rural
DAY **RAIL** c **AIR**
SPORT acfjlmpqx
OTHER LANGUAGES
ACTIVITIES cfgjor
OTHER SUBJECTS bch
FACILITIES ON SITE
EXAM BOARDS
RETAKES **NVQ COURSES**

A-level:

AS:

GCSE:

OTHER: e   lm o   v
B EG   K   O R
cde

HEREFORD & WORCESTER *continued*

C — R.N.I.B. New College Worcester; Whittington Road; Worcester WR5 2JX
Tel: 01905 763933 (Fax: 01905 763277) *Mrs Helen Williams*

	Boys	Age	Girls	Age	TOTAL		Boys	Girls
Day	2		1		120	**SIXTH**	20	17
Weekly	4		4					
Boarding	55	11-19	54	11-19				

ENTRY REQUIREMENTS Assessment
SCHOLARSHIPS & BURSARIES
SPECIAL NEEDS bdefgijklnpqstuvwx BCDEFGHIKL   **DYSLEXIA**   **DIET** abcd
ASSOCIATION HMC   **FOUNDED** 1866   **RELIGIOUS AFFILIATION** C of E

MAP 8 J 7
LOCATION
DAY   **RAIL** a   **AIR** a
SPORT adehjklortx A
OTHER LANGUAGES
ACTIVITIES afghijknoqtwx AB
OTHER SUBJECTS bcdefh
FACILITIES ON SITE bdghi
EXAM BOARDS abd GH
RETAKES ab   **NVQ COURSES**

A-level: d e g i l n p   v x   BC   GH K   P R TU   c ef   j l
AS: g i   GH   e   P
GCSE: cd   l   p   v   BC   G K   U X   cdef   ij l
OTHER:

B — Royal Grammar School; Upper Tything; Worcester WR1 1HP
Tel: 01905 613391 (Fax: 01905 726892) *Walter Jones*

		Boys	Age	Girls	Age	TOTAL		Boys	Girls
Day	£1158-£1446	924	7-18			924	**SIXTH**	200	
Weekly									
Boarding									

ENTRY REQUIREMENTS Exam
SCHOLARSHIPS & BURSARIES Schol; Burs; AP
SPECIAL NEEDS n   **DYSLEXIA** g   **DIET** a
ASSOCIATION HMC   **FOUNDED**   **RELIGIOUS AFFILIATION** Non-denom

MAP 8 J 7
LOCATION Urban
DAY   **RAIL** a   **AIR** a
SPORT abcdefghjklmrstuwx ABC
OTHER LANGUAGES
ACTIVITIES befghijklmnopqsu AB
OTHER SUBJECTS bch
FACILITIES ON SITE bcghk
EXAM BOARDS bcd ABDEGH
RETAKES b   **NVQ COURSES**

A-level: cde ghi l   opq   uv x   B   GH K   NOP   c ef   jk
AS: cde hi l   nopq   u wx   GH K   N   c ef   jk
GCSE: cde g i l   o q   v   AB   G K   N P R   cdef   jk
OTHER:

G — St. James's and The Abbey; West Malvern WR14 4DF
Tel: 01684 560851 (Fax: 01684 569252) *Miss E.M.Mullenger*

		Boys	Age	Girls	Age	TOTAL		Boys	Girls
Day	£2436			30		184	**SIXTH**		51
Weekly	£3654			36					
Boarding	£3654			118	11-18				

ENTRY REQUIREMENTS CEE & Interview; Report & Exam & Interview
SCHOLARSHIPS & BURSARIES Schol; Art; Mus; Forces; VI Form; ARA
SPECIAL NEEDS bgln   **DYSLEXIA** e   **DIET** a
ASSOCIATION GSA   **FOUNDED** 1896   **RELIGIOUS AFFILIATION** C of E

MAP 8 I 7
LOCATION Rural
DAY ✓   **RAIL** a   **AIR** b
SPORT acefgmpwx ABC
OTHER LANGUAGES a
ACTIVITIES acghijklnoqstw B
OTHER SUBJECTS bcdfh
FACILITIES ON SITE bcdejk
EXAM BOARDS bcd ABDEGL
RETAKES a   **NVQ COURSES**

A-level: efghi   n p   v   BC   GHI K   OP R T W   c def   hi l
AS: i   o   G   e
GCSE: e g i   no   v   BC   G K   OP R   W   c def   hj l
OTHER: h l   o   E   K   ef

Gb — St. Mary's Convent School; Mount Battenhall; Worcester WR5 2HP
Tel: 01905 357786 (Fax: 01905 351718) *Miss Gertrude Morrissey*

		Boys	Age	Girls	Age	TOTAL		Boys	Girls
Day	£715-£1200	17	3-8	349	3-18	366	**SIXTH**		
Weekly									
Boarding									

ENTRY REQUIREMENTS Test & Interview
SCHOLARSHIPS & BURSARIES Schol; Burs; VI Form
SPECIAL NEEDS ejkln   **DYSLEXIA**   **DIET** a
ASSOCIATION GSA   **FOUNDED** 1934   **RELIGIOUS AFFILIATION** R C

MAP 8 J 7
LOCATION Urban
DAY   **RAIL** ab   **AIR** b
SPORT acflmprsx BC
OTHER LANGUAGES
ACTIVITIES ghijkopq AB
OTHER SUBJECTS g
FACILITIES ON SITE abdgh
EXAM BOARDS abcd DEG
RETAKES   **NVQ COURSES**

A-level: defg i   v x   BC   PR   W   c ef   j
AS: ef
GCSE: e g i l   v   BC   G K   OP R   W   cdef   j l
OTHER: B   e   G   v   cd

C — St. Richard's; Bredenbury Court; Bromyard; Herefordshire; HR7 4TD
Tel: 01885 482491 (Fax: 01885 488982) *R.E.H.Coghlan*

		Boys	Age	Girls	Age	TOTAL		Boys	Girls
Day	£274-£1614 X	31	4-13	23	4-13	121	**SIXTH**		
Weekly	£2225	6	7-13	4	7-13				
Boarding	£2380	32	7-13	25	7-13				

ENTRY REQUIREMENTS Interview
SCHOLARSHIPS & BURSARIES Forces; Teachers
SPECIAL NEEDS abgkn BG   **DYSLEXIA**   **DIET** a
ASSOCIATION IAPS   **FOUNDED** 1921   **RELIGIOUS AFFILIATION** R C

MAP 8 H 7
LOCATION Rural
DAY ✓   **RAIL** b   **AIR** b
SPORT acdefjlmpqstux ABC
OTHER LANGUAGES
ACTIVITIES acfghijmopqrstw
OTHER SUBJECTS acfh
FACILITIES ON SITE cdhj
EXAM BOARDS
RETAKES   **NVQ COURSES**

A-level:
AS:
GCSE:
OTHER: e g i   lmno   v   B   G K   OP R   cde g   j

143

HEREFORD & WORCESTER *continued*

C | Whitford Hall School; Bromsgrove; Worcs. B61 7LB
Tel: 01527 831631 *Mrs S.Brooks*

		Boys	Age	Girls	Age	TOTAL		Boys	Girls
Day	£460-£1310	44	3-11	110	3-11	154	SIXTH		
Weekly									
Boarding									

MAP 8 J 6
LOCATION Urban
DAY   **RAIL** b   **AIR** a

ENTRY REQUIREMENTS Report; Assessment & Interview
SCHOLARSHIPS & BURSARIES Schol; Siblings
SPECIAL NEEDS abegjklnpqtuw ABCDGHIJK   **DYSLEXIA** ef   **DIET** acd
ASSOCIATION ISAI   **FOUNDED** 1945   **RELIGIOUS AFFILIATION** Inter-denom

SPORT afjlmpqx B
OTHER LANGUAGES
ACTIVITIES cgjot
OTHER SUBJECTS abcfh
FACILITIES ON SITE acjk
EXAM BOARDS
RETAKES   **NVQ COURSES**

A-level   AS   GCSE   e g i lmno   v
                         B G K   OP R
                         cde   j

C | Winterfold House; Chaddesley Corbett; Worcs. DY10 4PL
Tel: 01562 777234 (Fax: 01562 777234) *S.D.Arbuthnott*

		Boys	Age	Girls	Age	TOTAL		Boys	Girls
Day	£630-£1550	109	2-13	20	2-13	129	SIXTH		
Weekly	£1950		7-13						
Boarding									

MAP 8 I 6
LOCATION Rural
DAY   **RAIL** b   **AIR** a

ENTRY REQUIREMENTS Test
SCHOLARSHIPS & BURSARIES Schol; Burs; Art; Mus
SPECIAL NEEDS abknw BEG   **DYSLEXIA** cde   **DIET** a
ASSOCIATION IAPS   **FOUNDED** 1923   **RELIGIOUS AFFILIATION** R C

SPORT abefgjklmopqsux AB
OTHER LANGUAGES
ACTIVITIES acfghijmostw A
OTHER SUBJECTS cfh
FACILITIES ON SITE abcdhjkl
EXAM BOARDS
RETAKES   **NVQ COURSES**

A-level   AS   GCSE   cde g i lmno   v
                         B E G K NOP R   X
                         cde   j l

HERTFORDSHIRE

G | Abbot's Hill; Bunkers Lane; Hemel Hempstead HP3 8RP
Tel: 01442 240333 (Fax: 01442 69981) *Mrs J.S.Kingsley*

		Boys	Age	Girls	Age	TOTAL		Boys	Girls
Day	£2020			88	11-16	166	SIXTH		
Weekly	£3400			51	11-16				
Boarding	£3425			27	11-16				

MAP 3 F 3
LOCATION Rural
DAY   **RAIL** a   **AIR** a

ENTRY REQUIREMENTS Exam & Interview
SCHOLARSHIPS & BURSARIES Schol; Burs; Art; Mus; Chor; Forces; Clergy; Teachers; Sport
SPECIAL NEEDS bgknpqw EI   **DYSLEXIA** ef   **DIET** acd
ASSOCIATION GSA   **FOUNDED** 1912   **RELIGIOUS AFFILIATION** C of E

SPORT abcfhlnpqwx ABC
OTHER LANGUAGES a
ACTIVITIES cghijklnpqstw A
OTHER SUBJECTS abcefgh
FACILITIES ON SITE bdejk
EXAM BOARDS abcd GL
RETAKES   **NVQ COURSES**

A-level   AS   GCSE   d l n   v   OTHER m
                         BC E G K O R   W
                         bcdef   l

B g | Aldenham School; Elstree; Herts. WD6 3AJ
Tel: 01923 858122 (Fax: 01923 854410) *Stephen Borthwick*

		Boys	Age	Girls	Age	TOTAL		Boys	Girls
Day	£1665-£3110	249	11-18	7	16-18	352	SIXTH	94	12
Weekly			13-18		16-18				
Boarding	£3820	91	13-18	5	16-18				

MAP 5 D 2
LOCATION Rural
DAY ✓   **RAIL** a   **AIR** a

ENTRY REQUIREMENTS CEE; Test & Interview
SCHOLARSHIPS & BURSARIES Schol; Burs; Art; Mus; Forces; AP; VI Form; Sport; ARA
SPECIAL NEEDS abejklnpqstw AEGH   **DYSLEXIA** de   **DIET** acd
ASSOCIATION HMC   **FOUNDED** 1597   **RELIGIOUS AFFILIATION** C of E

SPORT abcdefghijkmnopqstuwx ABC
OTHER LANGUAGES
ACTIVITIES fghijknopqrstuvw AB
OTHER SUBJECTS abcdefh
FACILITIES ON SITE abcdeghk
EXAM BOARDS abd ABEHL
RETAKES a   **NVQ COURSES** 3

A-level c eghi   op   v x   AS   GCSE egi l o v   OTHER c f kl no q tu wx
         B GH K   OP R U   B G K   PR   JK M O R
         cdef   l   cdef j l   ef

B g | Aldwickbury School; Wheathampstead Road; Harpenden; Herts. AL5 1AE
Tel: 01582 713022 *P.H.Jeffery*

		Boys	Age	Girls	Age	TOTAL		Boys	Girls
Day	£1060-£1500	232	4-13	15	4- 6	279	SIXTH		
Weekly	£1825-£2025	32	10-13						
Boarding									

MAP 3 F 2
LOCATION Rural
DAY   **RAIL** a   **AIR** a

ENTRY REQUIREMENTS Test
SCHOLARSHIPS & BURSARIES Schol
SPECIAL NEEDS bj G   **DYSLEXIA**   **DIET**
ASSOCIATION IAPS   **FOUNDED** 1937   **RELIGIOUS AFFILIATION** C of E

SPORT abefjlmsx AB
OTHER LANGUAGES
ACTIVITIES fghijor A
OTHER SUBJECTS abch
FACILITIES ON SITE i
EXAM BOARDS
RETAKES   **NVQ COURSES**

A-level   AS   GCSE   egi l o   v
                         B E G K   OP R
                         cde   j

HERTFORDSHIRE *continued*

C — Arts Educational School; Tring Park; Tring; Herts. HP23 5LX
Tel: 01442 824255 (Fax: 01442 891069) Mrs J.D.Billing

		Boys	Age	Girls	Age	TOTAL	SIXTH	Boys	Girls
Day	£1505-£2226	1	8-18	62	8-18	209			51
Weekly									
Boarding	£2512-£3604	11	8-18	135	8-18				

ENTRY REQUIREMENTS Test
SCHOLARSHIPS & BURSARIES Siblings
SPECIAL NEEDS n **DYSLEXIA** **DIET** a
ASSOCIATION ISAI **FOUNDED** 1919 **RELIGIOUS AFFILIATION** Inter-denom

MAP 3 E 3
LOCATION Rural
DAY **RAIL** a **AIR** a
SPORT x AB
OTHER LANGUAGES
ACTIVITIES cgijotw
OTHER SUBJECTS abcfgh
FACILITIES ON SITE gik
EXAM BOARDS bcd A
RETAKES **NVQ COURSES**

A-level: d fg mn / B G K / c e
AS:
GCSE: d n uv / B E G K / cde
OTHER: h F

C — Beechwood Park; Markyate; St.Albans; Herts. AL3 8AW
Tel: 01582 840333 (Fax: 01582 842372) D.S.Macpherson

		Boys	Age	Girls	Age	TOTAL	SIXTH	Boys	Girls
Day	£1305-£1785	241	4-13	30	4-13	303			
Weekly	£2435	2	7-9		7-9				
Boarding	£2575	30	8-13		8-13				

ENTRY REQUIREMENTS Test
SCHOLARSHIPS & BURSARIES Schol; Mus; Forces; Clergy; Siblings
SPECIAL NEEDS n **DYSLEXIA** **DIET** abcd
ASSOCIATION IAPS **FOUNDED** 1964 **RELIGIOUS AFFILIATION** C of E

MAP 3 F 3
LOCATION Rural
DAY **RAIL** b **AIR** a
SPORT abcefgjkmpqswx AB
OTHER LANGUAGES a
ACTIVITIES fghijoqtvw A
OTHER SUBJECTS bcfh
FACILITIES ON SITE bcdhjl
EXAM BOARDS
RETAKES **NVQ COURSES**

A-level:
AS:
GCSE:
OTHER: e l o v / B E G K O R / cde g j

B — Berkhamsted Junior School; Castle Street; Berkhamsted; Herts. HP4 2BB
Tel: 01442 863236 (Fax: 01442 877657) E.T.Sneddon

		Boys	Age	Girls	Age	TOTAL	SIXTH	Boys	Girls
Day	£1465-£1897	239	7-13			246			
Weekly	£3077		10-13						
Boarding	£3077	7	10-13						

ENTRY REQUIREMENTS Report & Exam & Interview
SCHOLARSHIPS & BURSARIES Schol; Burs; AP
SPECIAL NEEDS aejklnqw DEG **DYSLEXIA** de **DIET** abcd
ASSOCIATION IAPS **FOUNDED** 1888 **RELIGIOUS AFFILIATION** C of E

MAP 3 E 3
LOCATION Urban
DAY ✓ **RAIL** a **AIR** a
SPORT abcefgijkmosuwx ABC
OTHER LANGUAGES
ACTIVITIES fghijmot A
OTHER SUBJECTS bcfh
FACILITIES ON SITE abcdeik
EXAM BOARDS
RETAKES **NVQ COURSES**

A-level:
AS:
GCSE:
OTHER: c e l no v / B E G K O R / cdef ij

Gb — Berkhamsted School for Girls; King's Road; Berkhamsted HP4 3BG
Tel: 01442 862168 (Fax: 01442 876732) Miss V.E.M.Shepherd

		Boys	Age	Girls	Age	TOTAL	SIXTH	Boys	Girls
Day	£1158-£1829	28	3-7	468	3-18	550			109
Weekly	£3109			30	10-18				
Boarding	£3109			24	10-18				

ENTRY REQUIREMENTS Report & Exam & Interview
SCHOLARSHIPS & BURSARIES Schol; Burs; Mus; AP
SPECIAL NEEDS abgjlnq E **DYSLEXIA** e **DIET** abcd
ASSOCIATION GSA **FOUNDED** 1888 **RELIGIOUS AFFILIATION** Non-denom

MAP 3 E 3
LOCATION Rural
DAY **RAIL** a **AIR** a
SPORT abcginpqwx ABC
OTHER LANGUAGES
ACTIVITIES ceghijknos AB
OTHER SUBJECTS abch
FACILITIES ON SITE bcegjk
EXAM BOARDS abd ABDEG
RETAKES **NVQ COURSES**

A-level: c e g i p v / BC GH K P R W / cdefg j l
AS: cdef
GCSE: T / c e o v / BC G K R WX / cdefg j l
OTHER: l

Bg — Berkhamsted School; Castle Street; Berkhamsted; Herts. HP4 2BB
Tel: 01442 863236 (Fax: 01442 877657) The Revd.K.H.Wilkinson

		Boys	Age	Girls	Age	TOTAL	SIXTH	Boys	Girls
Day	£2258	369	13-18	3	16-18	436		147	3
Weekly	£3678		13-18						
Boarding	£3678	64	13-18						

ENTRY REQUIREMENTS CEE; Test & Interview
SCHOLARSHIPS & BURSARIES Schol; Burs; Art; Mus; Forces; AP; VI Form
SPECIAL NEEDS aejklnq DEG **DYSLEXIA** d **DIET** abcd
ASSOCIATION HMC **FOUNDED** 1541 **RELIGIOUS AFFILIATION** C of E

MAP 3 E 3
LOCATION Urban
DAY ✓ **RAIL** a **AIR** a
SPORT abcdefghijkmorstuwx B
OTHER LANGUAGES a
ACTIVITIES efghijkmnoqstv AB
OTHER SUBJECTS abcfh
FACILITIES ON SITE abcdegik
EXAM BOARDS abde AEHL
RETAKES a **NVQ COURSES**

A-level: cde g i nop uv x / B GH K N P R / c ef j
AS: c o q / GH K U / c e
GCSE: cde ghi l o q vw / B E G H K N P R U / cdefg jkl
OTHER: M O / i

HERTFORDSHIRE continued

C — Bishop's Stortford College; Maze Green Road; Bishop's Stortford; Herts. CM23 2QZ
Tel: 01279 758575 (Fax: 01279 755865) *S.G.G.Benson*

MAP 4 H 2
LOCATION Urban
DAY   RAIL a   AIR a

		Boys	Age	Girls	Age	TOTAL	SIXTH	Boys	Girls
Day	£2480	169	13-18	25	13-18	337		106	33
Weekly									
Boarding	£3440	130	13-18	13	13-18				

SPORT abcdefhjkmpqstwx ABC
OTHER LANGUAGES
ACTIVITIES afghijklnopqstuw AB

ENTRY REQUIREMENTS CEE; Test & Interview
SCHOLARSHIPS & BURSARIES Schol; Burs; Art; Mus; Chor; Forces; AP; VI Form
SPECIAL NEEDS abjklqtw BE   DYSLEXIA de   DIET ad
ASSOCIATION HMC   FOUNDED 1868   RELIGIOUS AFFILIATION Inter-denom

OTHER SUBJECTS abcdfgh
FACILITIES ON SITE abcdghijkl
EXAM BOARDS abd AH
RETAKES   NVQ COURSES

A-level: efghi nop v / B GH K P / c ef
AS: h / G / c
GCSE: e g i l o v / B G K P / cdef j l
OTHER: i

C — Bishop's Stortford College Junior School; Maze Green Road; Bishop's Stortford; Herts CM23 2PH Tel: 01279 653616 (Fax: 01279 755865) *D.J.Defoe*

MAP 4 H 2
LOCATION Rural
DAY   RAIL b   AIR a

		Boys	Age	Girls	Age	TOTAL	SIXTH	Boys	Girls
Day	£1770-£1990	187	4-13	22	4-13	261			
Weekly	£2400-£2620	10	7-13		7-13				
Boarding	£2400-£2620	37	7-13	5	7-13				

SPORT abcdefklmopswx ABC
OTHER LANGUAGES
ACTIVITIES acfghijopqrstwx A

ENTRY REQUIREMENTS Test & Interview
SCHOLARSHIPS & BURSARIES Schol; Burs; Art; Mus; AP
SPECIAL NEEDS bejklqtw EGI   DYSLEXIA   DIET abcd
ASSOCIATION IAPS   FOUNDED 1902   RELIGIOUS AFFILIATION Inter-denom

OTHER SUBJECTS bcfh
FACILITIES ON SITE abcdhijkl
EXAM BOARDS
RETAKES   NVQ COURSES

A-level:
AS:
GCSE:
OTHER: c e g i l n o q t v / B G K OP R / cde j

C — Duncombe School; 4 Warren Park Road; Bengeo; Hertford; Herts SG14 3JA
Tel: 01992 582653 *Miss R.M.Martin*

MAP 4 G 2
LOCATION Urban
DAY   RAIL c   AIR b

		Boys	Age	Girls	Age	TOTAL	SIXTH	Boys	Girls
Day	£486-£1367	103	4-11	110	4-11	213			
Weekly									
Boarding									

SPORT aejpqx B
OTHER LANGUAGES
ACTIVITIES cfgh

ENTRY REQUIREMENTS Test; Interview
SCHOLARSHIPS & BURSARIES
SPECIAL NEEDS   DYSLEXIA   DIET a
ASSOCIATION ISAI   FOUNDED 1939   RELIGIOUS AFFILIATION C of E

OTHER SUBJECTS c
FACILITIES ON SITE a
EXAM BOARDS
RETAKES   NVQ COURSES

A-level:
AS:
GCSE:
OTHER: e l o v / B G K OR R / cde

B — Edge Grove; Aldenham; Herts. WD2 8BL
Tel: 01923 855724 (Fax: 01923 859920) *K.J.Waterfield*

MAP 5 D 1
LOCATION Rural
DAY ✓   RAIL a   AIR a

		Boys	Age	Girls	Age	TOTAL	SIXTH	Boys	Girls
Day	£1500-£1950	61	2-13		2-7	132			
Weekly	£2625		7-13						
Boarding	£2725	71	7-13						

SPORT abcefjlmsx AB
OTHER LANGUAGES
ACTIVITIES afghjopqtwx A

ENTRY REQUIREMENTS Test
SCHOLARSHIPS & BURSARIES
SPECIAL NEEDS   DYSLEXIA   DIET
ASSOCIATION IAPS   FOUNDED 1935   RELIGIOUS AFFILIATION C of E

OTHER SUBJECTS acfh
FACILITIES ON SITE djk
EXAM BOARDS
RETAKES   NVQ COURSES

A-level:
AS:
GCSE:
OTHER: e l q v / B G K OP R / cdefg j

C — Egerton-Rothesay School Limited; Durrants Lane; Berkhamsted; Herts. HP4 3UJ
Tel: 01442 865275 (Fax: 01442 864977) *J.R.Adkins*

MAP 3 E 3
LOCATION
DAY ✓   RAIL a   AIR a

		Boys	Age	Girls	Age	TOTAL	SIXTH	Boys	Girls
Day	£175-£1760	281	2-18	229	2-18	510		2	3
Weekly	£1740-£2760								
Boarding	£1990-£3260								

SPORT abcefhjlmnpqswx ABC
OTHER LANGUAGES l
ACTIVITIES cfghijknot B

ENTRY REQUIREMENTS Test & Interview
SCHOLARSHIPS & BURSARIES Schol; Burs
SPECIAL NEEDS abcejlnpqtuw ABGHIL   DYSLEXIA cde   DIET abcd
ASSOCIATION ISAI   FOUNDED 1922   RELIGIOUS AFFILIATION Inter-denom

OTHER SUBJECTS bcdfh
FACILITIES ON SITE bc
EXAM BOARDS abd BEG
RETAKES a   NVQ COURSES

A-level: de gh p v / BC FGHI K PQR TU / cdef jkl
AS:
GCSE: de ghi no t v / BC G K OPQR T / cdefg jkl
OTHER: f klm x W

HERTFORDSHIRE continued

B | Haberdashers' Aske's Prep Sch,The; Butterfly Lane; Elstree; Borehamwood; Herts WD6 3AF Tel: 0181 207 4323 (Fax: 0181 207 4439) Mrs P.A.Bryant

		Boys	Age	Girls	Age	TOTAL	SIXTH	Boys	Girls
Day	£1712	205	7-11			205			
Weekly									
Boarding									

ENTRY REQUIREMENTS Report & Exam & Interview
SCHOLARSHIPS & BURSARIES
SPECIAL NEEDS behjlq Gl   **DYSLEXIA**   **DIET** a
ASSOCIATION IAPS   **FOUNDED** 1690   **RELIGIOUS AFFILIATION** C of E

MAP 5 D 2
LOCATION Rural
DAY   **RAIL** b   **AIR** a
SPORT aefhjlmqsx B
OTHER LANGUAGES
ACTIVITIES fghjoq A
OTHER SUBJECTS abch
FACILITIES ON SITE abcdhik
EXAM BOARDS
RETAKES   **NVQ COURSES**

A-level | AS | GCSE | OTHER
e   l no   s v
B E G   K   O   R
cde

G | Haberdashers' Aske's Sch. for Girls; Aldenham Road; Elstree; Herts WD6 3BT Tel: 0181 953 4261 Mrs P.Penney

		Boys	Age	Girls	Age	TOTAL	SIXTH	Boys	Girls
Day	£1155-£1380			1138	4-18	1138			233
Weekly									
Boarding									

ENTRY REQUIREMENTS Exam & Interview
SCHOLARSHIPS & BURSARIES Schol; Burs; Mus; Clergy; AP
SPECIAL NEEDS ablq   **DYSLEXIA**   **DIET** abcd
ASSOCIATION GSA   **FOUNDED** 1690   **RELIGIOUS AFFILIATION** C of E

MAP 5 D 2
LOCATION Rural
DAY ✓   **RAIL** b   **AIR** a
SPORT abcfghjklnopquwx ABC
OTHER LANGUAGES f
ACTIVITIES fghijknoqstw AB
OTHER SUBJECTS abcdfh
FACILITIES ON SITE chi
EXAM BOARDS abcd AEGH
RETAKES   **NVQ COURSES**

A-level c e g i   o p   v
B   GH K   P R
c ef   j l

AS   e   x
G   R
ef   j l

GCSE c e g i   no   v
B   G K   P R   X
cdefgh j l

OTHER   u
i

B | Haberdashers' Aske's School,The; Butterfly Lane; Elstree; Borehamwood; Herts. WD6 3AF Tel: 0181 207 4323 (Fax: 0181 207 4439) Keith Dawson

		Boys	Age	Girls	Age	TOTAL	SIXTH	Boys	Girls
Day	£1867	1096	11-18			1096		309	
Weekly									
Boarding									

ENTRY REQUIREMENTS Exam & Interview; Report & Exam & Interview
SCHOLARSHIPS & BURSARIES Schol; Burs; AP
SPECIAL NEEDS behjklnqstw AGHI   **DYSLEXIA**   **DIET** a
ASSOCIATION HMC   **FOUNDED** 1690   **RELIGIOUS AFFILIATION** C of E

MAP 5 D 2
LOCATION Rural
DAY ✓   **RAIL** b   **AIR** a
SPORT abcdefghjklmostuwx AB
OTHER LANGUAGES
ACTIVITIES abefghijklmnoqrstuv ABD
OTHER SUBJECTS abcdfh
FACILITIES ON SITE abcdghik
EXAM BOARDS abcd ABEH
RETAKES   **NVQ COURSES**

A-level e g i   o p   v x
AB   GH K M   P R U
cdefg   j l

AS   A   l o   vw
G K M
def   l

GCSE e g i l   no q t v
AB   G K   P R U
cdefgh j l

OTHER   u
I L NO Q
a   h

Bg | Haileybury; Hertford SG13 7NU Tel: 01992 462352 (Fax: 01992 467603) D.J.Jewell

		Boys	Age	Girls	Age	TOTAL	SIXTH	Boys	Girls
Day	£3075	175	11-18	10	16-18	586		179	58
Weekly									
Boarding	£4240	354	13-18	47	16-18				

ENTRY REQUIREMENTS CEE; Scholarship Exam; Report & Test
SCHOLARSHIPS & BURSARIES Schol; Burs; Art; Mus; Clergy; Teachers; AP; VI Form; ARA
SPECIAL NEEDS abgijlqtv GHL   **DYSLEXIA**   **DIET** abcd
ASSOCIATION HMC   **FOUNDED** 1862   **RELIGIOUS AFFILIATION** C of E

MAP 4 G 2
LOCATION Rural
DAY   **RAIL** a   **AIR** a
SPORT abcdefghijklmnopqstuwx ABC
OTHER LANGUAGES
ACTIVITIES abcefghijklmnopqrst A
OTHER SUBJECTS abcdfh
FACILITIES ON SITE abcdeghjk
EXAM BOARDS abd ABDEGHI
RETAKES   **NVQ COURSES**

A-level cd fg i   nop   uv v x
B   GH K   OP R
cdefg   j l

AS   cd f   op   v
B   G K   R
efg   j l

GCSE   cd   o   v
B   G K   O R   X
cdefg   j l

OTHER
k

C | Haresfoot Senior School; Amersfort; The Common; Berkhamsted; Herts. HP4 2QF Tel: 01442 877215 (Fax: 01442 872742) D.L.Davies

		Boys	Age	Girls	Age	TOTAL	SIXTH	Boys	Girls
Day	£1535-£1865	✗	41	11-18	17	11-18	58		7	2
Weekly									
Boarding									

ENTRY REQUIREMENTS Assessment & Interview
SCHOLARSHIPS & BURSARIES Burs; Siblings
SPECIAL NEEDS aejklnw BGHI   **DYSLEXIA** de   **DIET** ab
ASSOCIATION ISAI   **FOUNDED** 1989   **RELIGIOUS AFFILIATION** Non-denom

MAP 3 E 3
LOCATION Rural
DAY   **RAIL** a   **AIR** a
SPORT abcefhjkmopqswx ABC
OTHER LANGUAGES a
ACTIVITIES acfghjknopqst B
OTHER SUBJECTS bcdefgh
FACILITIES ON SITE cg
EXAM BOARDS abd ABEK
RETAKES ab   **NVQ COURSES**

A-level de g i l   nop   uvwx
BC   G K   PQR T   W
cdef   l

AS   d g i
G   K   P
cdef

GCSE de g i l   no   vw
BC E G   K   OP R
cdef   l

OTHER   d ghi   l n p   tu x
l   PQ T
ef

147

HERTFORDSHIRE *continued*

Haresfoot Preparatory School; Chesham Road; Berkhamsted; Herts HP4 2SZ
Tel: 01442 872742 (Fax: 01442 872742) *Mrs G.R.Waterhouse*

MAP 3 E 3
LOCATION Rural
DAY RAIL a AIR a

		Boys	Age	Girls	Age	TOTAL
Day	£75-£1140	105	2-12	125	2-12	230
Weekly						
Boarding						

SIXTH: Boys Girls

SPORT abcefjlmopqsx BC
OTHER LANGUAGES
ACTIVITIES cfghjoqt

ENTRY REQUIREMENTS Test & Interview; Assessment & Interview
SCHOLARSHIPS & BURSARIES Burs; Siblings
SPECIAL NEEDS bjlnqtw Bl   **DYSLEXIA** de   **DIET** a
ASSOCIATION ISAI   **FOUNDED** 1985   **RELIGIOUS AFFILIATION** Non-denom

OTHER SUBJECTS abcfh
FACILITIES ON SITE h
EXAM BOARDS
RETAKES   NVQ COURSES

A-level   AS   GCSE
OTHER: e lmno q s v
B E G K O
cde l

Heath Mount School; Woodhall Park; Watton-at-Stone; Hertford SG14 3NG
Tel: 01920 830 230 (Fax: 01920 830 357) *The Rev.H.J.Matthews*

MAP 4 G 2
LOCATION Rural
DAY RAIL a AIR a

		Boys	Age	Girls	Age	TOTAL
Day	£525-£1936	164	3-13	79	3-13	285
Weekly	£2268-£2429	14	7-13	14	7-13	
Boarding		12		2		

SPORT abcefghjklmnpqsx ABL
OTHER LANGUAGES
ACTIVITIES fghijlmorstw A

ENTRY REQUIREMENTS Test & Interview; Assessment & Interview
SCHOLARSHIPS & BURSARIES Schol; Burs; Art; Mus; Forces; Sport; ARA; Siblings
SPECIAL NEEDS abegjklnqstw ABEGI   **DYSLEXIA** de   **DIET** acd
ASSOCIATION IAPS   **FOUNDED** 1817   **RELIGIOUS AFFILIATION** C of E

OTHER SUBJECTS abcfh
FACILITIES ON SITE acdhjkl
EXAM BOARDS
RETAKES   NVQ COURSES

A-level AS GCSE
OTHER: e g i l no   v
B E G K OP R
cdefg j

Homewood Independent School; Hazel Road; Park Street; St Albans; Herts AL2 2AH
Tel: 01727 873542 *Mrs C.Erwin*

MAP 3 F 3
LOCATION Rural
DAY RAIL a AIR a

		Boys	Age	Girls	Age	TOTAL
Day	£580-£975	39	3-8	27	3-8	66
Weekly						
Boarding						

SPORT
OTHER LANGUAGES
ACTIVITIES

ENTRY REQUIREMENTS None
SCHOLARSHIPS & BURSARIES
SPECIAL NEEDS abjln BGIL   **DYSLEXIA** g   **DIET**
ASSOCIATION ISAI   **FOUNDED** 1949   **RELIGIOUS AFFILIATION** Non-denom

OTHER SUBJECTS bc
FACILITIES ON SITE
EXAM BOARDS
RETAKES   NVQ COURSES

A-level AS GCSE OTHER

Howe Green House School; Great Hallingbury; Bishop's Stortford; Herts. CM22 7UF
Tel: 01279 657706 (Fax: 01279 501333) *Mrs N.R.J.Garrod*

MAP 4 H 2
LOCATION Rural
DAY RAIL a AIR a

		Boys	Age	Girls	Age	TOTAL
Day	£920-£1485	59	3-11	77	3-11	136
Weekly						
Boarding						

SPORT aijlmpqx
OTHER LANGUAGES
ACTIVITIES cghot

ENTRY REQUIREMENTS Assessment & Interview
SCHOLARSHIPS & BURSARIES
SPECIAL NEEDS   **DYSLEXIA**   **DIET**
ASSOCIATION ISAI   **FOUNDED** 1987   **RELIGIOUS AFFILIATION** Non-denom

OTHER SUBJECTS bc
FACILITIES ON SITE c
EXAM BOARDS
RETAKES   NVQ COURSES

A-level AS GCSE
OTHER: de l o   v
B   G K O R
de

Kingshott School; St. Ippolyts; Hitchin; Herts. SG4 7JX
Tel: 01462 432009 (Fax: 01462 421652) *The Rev'd.D.Highton*

MAP 3 F 2
LOCATION Rural
DAY RAIL a AIR a

		Boys	Age	Girls	Age	TOTAL
Day	£1005-£1350 ✗	221	4-13	107	4-13	328
Weekly						
Boarding						

SPORT abcefjklmnopqsux AB
OTHER LANGUAGES
ACTIVITIES cfghijnost A

ENTRY REQUIREMENTS Test
SCHOLARSHIPS & BURSARIES Schol
SPECIAL NEEDS blnw l   **DYSLEXIA** e   **DIET** abcd
ASSOCIATION IAPS   **FOUNDED** 1930   **RELIGIOUS AFFILIATION** C of E

OTHER SUBJECTS abcfh
FACILITIES ON SITE cik
EXAM BOARDS
RETAKES   NVQ COURSES

A-level AS GCSE
OTHER: e lm o   v
B E G K O R
cdefg j

HERTFORDSHIRE continued

B — Lochinver House School; Heath Road; Little Heath; Potters Bar; Herts. EN6 1LW
Tel: 01707 653064 (Fax: 01707 653064) *P.C.E.Atkinson*

		Boys	Age	Girls	Age	TOTAL		Boys	Girls
Day	£1260-£1680	325	4-13			325	SIXTH		
Weekly									
Boarding									

MAP 5 E 1
LOCATION Urban
DAY ✓   **RAIL** b   **AIR** b
SPORT abcdefjklstwx AB
OTHER LANGUAGES
ACTIVITIES fghijlopqrt A
OTHER SUBJECTS bcfh
FACILITIES ON SITE ch
EXAM BOARDS
RETAKES   **NVQ COURSES**

ENTRY REQUIREMENTS Interview
SCHOLARSHIPS & BURSARIES
SPECIAL NEEDS ejkn Gl
ASSOCIATION IAPS   **FOUNDED** 1947   **DYSLEXIA** cde   **DIET** a   **RELIGIOUS AFFILIATION** Christian

A-level   **AS**   **GCSE**   **OTHER** e g i l   o   v
BC   G   K   OP R
cdef   j

B — Lockers Park School; Hemel Hempstead; Herts. HP1 1TL
Tel: 01442 251712 (Fax: 01442 234150) *N.J.Chapman*

		Boys	Age	Girls	Age	TOTAL		Boys	Girls
Day	£1695-£1995	28	7-10			103	SIXTH		
Weekly									
Boarding	£2745	75	7-13						

MAP 3 F 3
LOCATION Urban
DAY   **RAIL** a   **AIR** a
SPORT abcefjklmsuwx AB
OTHER LANGUAGES
ACTIVITIES fghjlmopst A
OTHER SUBJECTS afh
FACILITIES ON SITE bcdhjkl
EXAM BOARDS
RETAKES   **NVQ COURSES**

ENTRY REQUIREMENTS Test & Interview
SCHOLARSHIPS & BURSARIES Burs; Art; Mus; Forces; Sport; ARA
SPECIAL NEEDS blnqs Gl   **DYSLEXIA** e   **DIET** abcd
ASSOCIATION IAPS   **FOUNDED** 1874   **RELIGIOUS AFFILIATION** C of E

A-level   **AS**   **GCSE**   **OTHER** e g i l   o q   v
B   G   K   OP R
cde g   j

Gb — Northfield School; Church Road; Watford; Herts. WD1 3QB
Tel: 01923 229758 *Mrs P.Hargreaves*

		Boys	Age	Girls	Age	TOTAL		Boys	Girls
Day	£449-£1400	12	3-7	117	3-18	129	SIXTH		8
Weekly									
Boarding									

MAP 5 C 2
LOCATION Urban
DAY   **RAIL** a   **AIR** a
SPORT abcflmpqx ABC
OTHER LANGUAGES
ACTIVITIES ghijkot B
OTHER SUBJECTS abcdegh
FACILITIES ON SITE
EXAM BOARDS ab ABL
RETAKES a   **NVQ COURSES**

ENTRY REQUIREMENTS Exam; Interview
SCHOLARSHIPS & BURSARIES Burs; VI Form
SPECIAL NEEDS jnw I
ASSOCIATION ISAI   **FOUNDED** 1870   **DYSLEXIA** fg   **DIET**   **RELIGIOUS AFFILIATION** Inter-denom

A-level cdefghi kl   no   uv
BC   GH K   P R T
cdef
AS d fghi k   uv
BC   GH K   P R T
cdef
GCSE de h   l   no   uv
BC E G   K   R T
cdef
OTHER

B — Northwood Preparatory School; Moor Farm; Sandy Lodge Road; Rickmansworth WD3 1LW
Tel: 01923 825648 (Fax: 01923 835802) *N.D.Flynn*

		Boys	Age	Girls	Age	TOTAL		Boys	Girls
Day	£1200-£1450	249	4-13			249	SIXTH		
Weekly									
Boarding									

MAP 5 B 2
LOCATION Rural
DAY   **RAIL** b   **AIR** a
SPORT abefghjklmqsuwx AB
OTHER LANGUAGES
ACTIVITIES fghjoqr A
OTHER SUBJECTS ch
FACILITIES ON SITE
EXAM BOARDS
RETAKES   **NVQ COURSES**

ENTRY REQUIREMENTS Test; Interview
SCHOLARSHIPS & BURSARIES
SPECIAL NEEDS f GL
ASSOCIATION IAPS   **FOUNDED** 1910   **DYSLEXIA**   **DIET** a   **RELIGIOUS AFFILIATION** C of E

A-level   **AS**   **GCSE**   **OTHER** c e g i l   o q   v
B   G   K   OP R
cdef   j l

G — Princess Helena College, The; Preston; Hitchin; Herts. SG4 7RT
Tel: 01462 432100 (Fax: 01462 431497) *John Jarvis*

		Boys	Age	Girls	Age	TOTAL		Boys	Girls
Day	£2320			43	11-18	143	SIXTH		37
Weekly	£3330			47	11-18				
Boarding	£3330			53	11-18				

MAP 3 F 2
LOCATION Rural
DAY ✓   **RAIL** a   **AIR** a
SPORT acdfhlmnpqtvwx ABC
OTHER LANGUAGES a
ACTIVITIES cdghijklnoqstw AB
OTHER SUBJECTS bcdfh
FACILITIES ON SITE bceghj
EXAM BOARDS abd ABDEH
RETAKES ab   **NVQ COURSES**

ENTRY REQUIREMENTS CEE; Report & Exam & Interview
SCHOLARSHIPS & BURSARIES Schol; Burs; Mus; Forces; Clergy
SPECIAL NEEDS abfjln ADGHI   **DYSLEXIA** de   **DIET** abcd
ASSOCIATION GSA   **FOUNDED** 1820   **RELIGIOUS AFFILIATION** C of E

A-level defghi   v
B   GH K   P
cdef   hj l
AS d fghi
GH K   P
c ef hj l
GCSE e g i   no   v
B   G   K   OP
cdef hj l
OTHER c e ghi lmno   uv
B E G   K   O P R   W
cdef hj l

HERTFORDSHIRE *continued*

Queenswood School; Shepherds Way; Brookmans Park; Hatfield AL9 6NS
Tel: 01707 652262 (Fax: 01707 649267) *A.M.B.Butler*

MAP 4 G 3
LOCATION Rural
DAY   RAIL a   AIR a

	Boys	Age	Girls	Age	TOTAL		Boys	Girls
Day £2256			49	11-15	388	SIXTH		101
Weekly £3658-£3814			339	11-18				
Boarding								

ENTRY REQUIREMENTS CEE & Interview; Report & Exam & Interview
SCHOLARSHIPS & BURSARIES Schol; Burs; Mus; Sport
SPECIAL NEEDS bnw   DYSLEXIA ef   DIET a
ASSOCIATION GSA   FOUNDED 1894   RELIGIOUS AFFILIATION Inter-denom

SPORT acdghklmopqtuwx ABC
OTHER LANGUAGES a
ACTIVITIES cfghijklnopqstuw AB
OTHER SUBJECTS abcdfh
FACILITIES ON SITE abdeghil
EXAM BOARDS abc ABEL
RETAKES   NVQ COURSES

A-level: defghi n p   v
B   GH K   P R
c ef j l

AS: B   K   R
         e   v

GCSE: de   n   v
B E G K   O R
a cdef hj l

OTHER: m o   tu
         O

Rickmansworth Masonic School; Rickmansworth Park; Rickmansworth; Herts. WD3 4HF
Tel: 01923 773168 (Fax: 01923 896729) *Mrs I.M.Andrews*

MAP 5 B 2
LOCATION Rural
DAY   RAIL a   AIR a

	Boys	Age	Girls	Age	TOTAL		Boys	Girls
Day £876-£1702 ✗			399	4-18	687	SIXTH		122
Weekly £1660-£2797			108	7-18				
Boarding £1660-£2797			180	7-18				

ENTRY REQUIREMENTS Exam & Interview; Assessment & Interview
SCHOLARSHIPS & BURSARIES Schol; Art; Mus; VI Form
SPECIAL NEEDS ln   DYSLEXIA ce   DIET abcd
ASSOCIATION GSA   FOUNDED 1788   RELIGIOUS AFFILIATION C of E

SPORT acfghkmpqtwx ABC
OTHER LANGUAGES
ACTIVITIES bcfghijklnorstwx ABD
OTHER SUBJECTS abcdefgh
FACILITIES ON SITE bcdegi
EXAM BOARDS abcde ABEFGK
RETAKES ab   NVQ COURSES 3

A-level: cde g i   n p   vwx
BC GH K   PQR   W
c ef j l

AS: cde g i   vwx
C   K   R T W
cd

GCSE: b de ghi l no   t vw
BC E G   K   N PQR   W
cdef j l

OTHER: h j lm   u
         G   K   NO
         i

Rickmansworth P.N.E.U. School; 88 The Drive; Rickmansworth; Herts. WD3 4DU
Tel: 01923 772101 *Mrs S.K.Marshall-Taylor*

MAP 5 B 2
LOCATION Urban
DAY   RAIL b   AIR a

	Boys	Age	Girls	Age	TOTAL		Boys	Girls
Day £356-£1023	3	3-7	134	3-11	137	SIXTH		
Weekly								
Boarding								

ENTRY REQUIREMENTS Assessment & Interview
SCHOLARSHIPS & BURSARIES
SPECIAL NEEDS   DYSLEXIA   DIET
ASSOCIATION IAPS FOUNDED 1931   RELIGIOUS AFFILIATION

SPORT apx B
OTHER LANGUAGES
ACTIVITIES cj
OTHER SUBJECTS
FACILITIES ON SITE
EXAM BOARDS
RETAKES   NVQ COURSES

A-level:
AS:
GCSE:
OTHER: e   l o   v
B E G
cde

St. Albans High School for Girls; Townsend Avenue; St. Albans AL1 3SJ
Tel: 01727 853800 (Fax: 01727 845011) *Mrs C.Y.Daly*

MAP 3 F 3
LOCATION Urban
DAY ✓ RAIL a   AIR a

	Boys	Age	Girls	Age	TOTAL		Boys	Girls
Day £1300-£1570			697	7-18	697	SIXTH		127
Weekly								
Boarding								

ENTRY REQUIREMENTS Report & Exam & Interview
SCHOLARSHIPS & BURSARIES Schol; Burs; Mus; Clergy; AP; VI Form
SPECIAL NEEDS e   DYSLEXIA   DIET a
ASSOCIATION GSA FOUNDED 1889   RELIGIOUS AFFILIATION C of E

SPORT acghklnopqwx ABC
OTHER LANGUAGES
ACTIVITIES cghijknost AB
OTHER SUBJECTS abcfh
FACILITIES ON SITE bcghj
EXAM BOARDS abd BEHL
RETAKES   NVQ COURSES

A-level: c e g i   n p   uv
BC GH K   P R U W
c ef j l

AS: c   g i   p   v x
BC GH K   P R U W
c ef j l

GCSE: c e   no   v x
BC E G   K   R U W
cdef j l

OTHER: lmno q   u
I   NO
h

St. Albans School; Abbey Gateway; St. Albans AL3 4HB
Tel: 01727 855521 (Fax: 01727 843447) *A.R.Grant*

MAP 3 F 3
LOCATION Urban
DAY ✓ RAIL a   AIR a

	Boys	Age	Girls	Age	TOTAL		Boys	Girls
Day £1820	610	11-18	25	16-18	635	SIXTH	165	25
Weekly								
Boarding								

ENTRY REQUIREMENTS CEE & Interview; Report & Exam & Interview
SCHOLARSHIPS & BURSARIES Schol; Art; Mus; AP
SPECIAL NEEDS bjlq G   DYSLEXIA   DIET a
ASSOCIATION HMC FOUNDED 948   RELIGIOUS AFFILIATION Inter-denom

SPORT abcefhjklmostuwx ABC
OTHER LANGUAGES k
ACTIVITIES cefghijkmopqstv AB
OTHER SUBJECTS bcdfh
FACILITIES ON SITE cgk
EXAM BOARDS abd ABEHL
RETAKES   NVQ COURSES

A-level: cd fghi l nop   v x
B   GH K   P R U
c efg j l

AS: a   g   u x
     G K
     e

GCSE: d   nop   v
B   G K   R U X
cdefg jkl

OTHER: lmn   u
E   I   MNO   R
h

150

HERTFORDSHIRE continued

C — St. Christopher School; Letchworth; Herts. SG6 3JZ
Tel: 01462 679301 (Fax: 01462 481578) *Colin Reid*

		Boys	Age	Girls	Age	TOTAL		Boys	Girls
Day	£703–£2062	188	2-19	115	3-19	475	SIXTH	42	42
Weekly	£2914–£3640								
Boarding	£2914–£3640	103	8-18	69	8-18				

ENTRY REQUIREMENTS
SCHOLARSHIPS & BURSARIES Mus
SPECIAL NEEDS bghijklnqtvw EL   **DYSLEXIA** e   **DIET** ab
ASSOCIATION SHMIS   **FOUNDED** 1915   **RELIGIOUS AFFILIATION** Non-denom

MAP 3 F 2
LOCATION Urban
DAY   **RAIL** a   **AIR** a
SPORT abcdefjkmnpstwx ABC
OTHER LANGUAGES ago
ACTIVITIES acfghijklnopqstvw AB
OTHER SUBJECTS abcdfh
FACILITIES ON SITE cehjk
EXAM BOARDS abcd ADHL
RETAKES ab   **NVQ COURSES**

A-level: c efghi nop v x   ABC GH K P   c ef ij l
AS: g   B G   ef
GCSE: e g i l nopq v   ABC G K N P   cdefghijkl   X
OTHER:

C — St. Edmund's College; Old Hall Green; Ware; Herts SG11 1DS;
Tel: 01920 821504 (Fax: 01920 823011) *D.J.J.Mc Ewen*

		Boys	Age	Girls	Age	TOTAL		Boys	Girls
Day	£1695–£2040 ✗	220	7-18	139	7-18	535	SIXTH	71	35
Weekly	£2420–£2955	31	7-18	15	7-18				
Boarding	£2575–£3185	82	7-18	48	7-18				

ENTRY REQUIREMENTS CEE; Test & Interview
SCHOLARSHIPS & BURSARIES Schol; Mus; Forces; AP
SPECIAL NEEDS bjn   **DYSLEXIA** e   **DIET** a
ASSOCIATION HMC   **FOUNDED** 1568   **RELIGIOUS AFFILIATION** R C

MAP 4 G 2
LOCATION Rural
DAY ✓   **RAIL** b   **AIR** a
SPORT abcefjklmpqsuwx AB
OTHER LANGUAGES
ACTIVITIES efghijklmnoqtw A
OTHER SUBJECTS bcfh
FACILITIES ON SITE bcdghik
EXAM BOARDS abd ABEHJ
RETAKES ab   **NVQ COURSES**

A-level: de g i op uv   B GH K P R   c ef l
AS: d   FGH   c e j   R
GCSE: de g i op v   ABC G K OP R   cdef j l
OTHER: d   K

Gb — St. Francis' College; Broadway; Letchworth; Herts SG6 3PJ
Tel: 01462 670511 (Fax: 01462 682361) *Miss M.Hegarty*

		Boys	Age	Girls	Age	TOTAL		Boys	Girls
Day	£315–£1675	16	3-5	268	3-18	335	SIXTH		54
Weekly	£2845–£3270			11	7-18				
Boarding	£2845–£3270			40	7-19				

ENTRY REQUIREMENTS Test & Interview; Exam & Interview
SCHOLARSHIPS & BURSARIES Schol; Burs; Mus
SPECIAL NEEDS   **DYSLEXIA**   **DIET** a
ASSOCIATION GSA   **FOUNDED** 1933   **RELIGIOUS AFFILIATION** Christian

MAP 3 F 2
LOCATION Rural
DAY ✓   **RAIL** a   **AIR** a
SPORT acdfhklmopqstvwx ABC
OTHER LANGUAGES acgj
ACTIVITIES cfghijknopqtw AB
OTHER SUBJECTS bcdfh
FACILITIES ON SITE bcdegik
EXAM BOARDS abcd ABDEG
RETAKES a   **NVQ COURSES**

A-level: e ghi n p v   BC GH K P R U   c ef j
AS: e g i p v   c ef   R
GCSE: e l n v   BC E G K   cdef j   R
OTHER:

G — St. Hilda's School; 28 Douglas Road; Harpenden; Herts. AL5 2ES
Tel: 01582 712307 (Fax: 01582 763892) *Mrs M.Piachaud*

		Boys	Age	Girls	Age	TOTAL		Boys	Girls
Day	£195–£1045 ✗			167	2-11	167	SIXTH		
Weekly									
Boarding									

ENTRY REQUIREMENTS Interview
SCHOLARSHIPS & BURSARIES Clergy; Siblings
SPECIAL NEEDS bnt BG   **DYSLEXIA** df   **DIET** a
ASSOCIATION ISAI   **FOUNDED** 1890   **RELIGIOUS AFFILIATION** C of E

MAP 3 F 2
LOCATION Urban
DAY   **RAIL** ab   **AIR** a
SPORT alpqx B
OTHER LANGUAGES
ACTIVITIES gjo
OTHER SUBJECTS bcfh
FACILITIES ON SITE bhj
EXAM BOARDS
RETAKES   **NVQ COURSES**

A-level:
AS:
GCSE:
OTHER: e l no s v   B EG K O R   cde j

Gb — St. Hilda's School; High Street; Bushey; Herts. WD2 3DA
Tel: 0181 950 1751 (Fax: 0181 420 4523) *Mrs L.E.G.Cavanagh*

		Boys	Age	Girls	Age	TOTAL		Boys	Girls
Day	£895–£1315	4		122	3-11	126	SIXTH		
Weekly									
Boarding									

ENTRY REQUIREMENTS Test & Interview; Assessment & Interview
SCHOLARSHIPS & BURSARIES Burs
SPECIAL NEEDS bklntw Bl   **DYSLEXIA** e   **DIET** abcd
ASSOCIATION IAPS   **FOUNDED** 1918   **RELIGIOUS AFFILIATION** Non-denom

MAP 5 C 2
LOCATION Urban
DAY   **RAIL** a   **AIR** a
SPORT lmopqx B
OTHER LANGUAGES
ACTIVITIES cghj
OTHER SUBJECTS abcdfh
FACILITIES ON SITE hi
EXAM BOARDS
RETAKES   **NVQ COURSES**

A-level:
AS:
GCSE:
OTHER:

HERTFORDSHIRE *continued*

G — St. Margaret's School; Bushey; Herts. WD2 1DT
Tel: 0181 950 1548 (Fax: 0181 950 1677) *Miss M.de Villiers*

		Boys	Age	Girls	Age	TOTAL		Boys	Girls
Day	£1025-£1825			286	4-18	420	SIXTH		84
Weekly	£2530-£2920			51	8-18				
Boarding	£2530-£2920			83	8-18				

ENTRY REQUIREMENTS Report & Exam & Interview
SCHOLARSHIPS & BURSARIES Schol; Burs; Art; Mus; AP; VI Form
SPECIAL NEEDS jn **DYSLEXIA** g **DIET** abcd
ASSOCIATION GSA **FOUNDED** 1749 **RELIGIOUS AFFILIATION** C of E

MAP 5 C 2
LOCATION Urban
DAY ✓ **RAIL** a **AIR** a
SPORT acflnpqx B
OTHER LANGUAGES a
ACTIVITIES gijknoqstw B
OTHER SUBJECTS bcdefgh
FACILITIES ON SITE bdj
EXAM BOARDS ab BE
RETAKES a **NVQ COURSES**

A-level: cdefg i n p v / B GH K P R / bc efg j l
AS: d / G K R / c efg l
GCSE: cde h l n v / BC E G K NO R W / bcdefg j l
OTHER:

C — St. Nicholas House Preparatory School; Bunkers Lane; Hemel Hempstead HP3 8RP
Tel: 01442 211156 (Fax: 01442 69981) *Mrs D.Harrison*

		Boys	Age	Girls	Age	TOTAL		Boys	Girls
Day	£1075-£1325	17	3-7	116	3-11	133	SIXTH		
Weekly	£3240								
Boarding									

ENTRY REQUIREMENTS Assessment & Interview
SCHOLARSHIPS & BURSARIES
SPECIAL NEEDS bjknw l **DYSLEXIA** ef **DIET** abcd
ASSOCIATION IAPS **FOUNDED** 1923 **RELIGIOUS AFFILIATION** C of E

MAP 3 E 3
LOCATION Rural
DAY **RAIL** a **AIR** a
SPORT ajlnpqx B
OTHER LANGUAGES
ACTIVITIES cfghjnot A
OTHER SUBJECTS acfh
FACILITIES ON SITE bhj
EXAM BOARDS
RETAKES **NVQ COURSES**

A-level:
AS:
GCSE:
OTHER: e m o v / B G O R / cd

C — Sherrardswood School; Welwyn Garden City AL8 7JN
Tel: 01707 322281 (Fax: 01438 840616) *M.C.Lloyd*

		Boys	Age	Girls	Age	TOTAL		Boys	Girls
Day	£902-£1479	145	4-19	116	4-19	299	SIXTH	6	5
Weekly	£2268-£2795		8-19		8-19				
Boarding	£2268-£2795	18	8-19	20	8-19				

ENTRY REQUIREMENTS Report & Exam & Interview
SCHOLARSHIPS & BURSARIES Schol; Burs; Forces; VI Form
SPECIAL NEEDS abejklnuw Gl **DYSLEXIA** **DIET** a
ASSOCIATION ISAI **FOUNDED** 1928 **RELIGIOUS AFFILIATION** C of E

MAP 4 G 2
LOCATION
DAY **RAIL** a **AIR** a
SPORT abcefjmpx AB
OTHER LANGUAGES a
ACTIVITIES fghijklos A
OTHER SUBJECTS bcdegh
FACILITIES ON SITE bcej
EXAM BOARDS abcd ABD
RETAKES **NVQ COURSES**

A-level: e g i op uv / B GH K P / cdef
AS: g / K
GCSE: e g i op v / B E G K OP X / cdef
OTHER: h l u / C NO R

C — Stanborough School; Stanborough Park; Garston; Watford; Herts. WD2 6JT
Tel: 01923 673268 (Fax: 01923 893943) *Dr Andrea Luxton*

		Boys	Age	Girls	Age	TOTAL		Boys	Girls
Day	£610-£970	92	3-18	78	3-18	215	SIXTH	3	3
Weekly	£1710-£2055	15	11-18	10	11-18				
Boarding	£1990-£2335	14	11-18	6	11-18				

ENTRY REQUIREMENTS Assessment & Interview
SCHOLARSHIPS & BURSARIES
SPECIAL NEEDS ajknuw B **DYSLEXIA** **DIET** abcd
ASSOCIATION ISAI **FOUNDED** 1941 **RELIGIOUS AFFILIATION**

MAP 5 C 2
LOCATION Urban
DAY **RAIL** b **AIR** a
SPORT bcefjmpqx ABC
OTHER LANGUAGES a
ACTIVITIES ghjno
OTHER SUBJECTS abcdfg
FACILITIES ON SITE cdeh
EXAM BOARDS abd EG
RETAKES ab **NVQ COURSES**

A-level: e g i / B G P / c e
AS:
GCSE: e ghi l o v / BC E G P R / cde
OTHER: st / K O

G — Stormont; The Causeway; Potters Bar; Herts. EN6 5HA
Tel: 01707 654037 (Fax: 01707 663295) *Mrs M.E.Johnston*

		Boys	Age	Girls	Age	TOTAL		Boys	Girls
Day	£1120-£1350			169	4-11	169	SIXTH		
Weekly									
Boarding									

ENTRY REQUIREMENTS
SCHOLARSHIPS & BURSARIES Schol; Burs
SPECIAL NEEDS ghkntw Al **DYSLEXIA** **DIET** a
ASSOCIATION IAPS **FOUNDED** 1944 **RELIGIOUS AFFILIATION** Inter-denom

MAP 5 E 1
LOCATION Urban
DAY **RAIL** b **AIR** b
SPORT ajlnpqx B
OTHER LANGUAGES
ACTIVITIES cfghjot A
OTHER SUBJECTS bcfh
FACILITIES ON SITE c
EXAM BOARDS
RETAKES **NVQ COURSES**

A-level:
AS:
GCSE:
OTHER: de lmno v / B E G K O R / cde

HERTFORDSHIRE continued

C — Westbrook Hay Educational Trust Ltd; London Road; Hemel Hempstead; Herts HP1 2RF Tel: 01442 256143 (Fax: 01442 232076) *J.A.Allen*

		Boys	Age	Girls	Age	TOTAL		Boys	Girls
Day	£70-£1970	104	2-13	36	2-13	170			
Weekly			8-13		8-13		SIXTH		
Boarding	£2735	27	8-13	3	8-13				

ENTRY REQUIREMENTS Assessment & Interview
SCHOLARSHIPS & BURSARIES Schol; Burs; Art; Mus; Forces; Sport
SPECIAL NEEDS aejknqw E   **DYSLEXIA**   **DIET** acd
ASSOCIATION IAPS   **FOUNDED** 1892   **RELIGIOUS AFFILIATION** C of E

MAP 3 F 3
LOCATION Rural
DAY   **RAIL** a   **AIR** a
SPORT abcdefjklmopqsux ABC
OTHER LANGUAGES
ACTIVITIES cfghjlmnqrwx A
OTHER SUBJECTS bch
FACILITIES ON SITE bcdhjl
EXAM BOARDS
RETAKES   **NVQ COURSES**

A-level: AS: GCSE: OTHER: e g i l m n o q s v / B G K OP R / cde

---

B — York House School; Redheath; Croxley Green; Rickmansworth; Herts WD3 4LW Tel: 01923 772395 (Fax: 01923 772395) *P.B.Moore*

		Boys	Age	Girls	Age	TOTAL		Boys	Girls
Day	£918-£1448	211	4-13			211	SIXTH		
Weekly									
Boarding									

ENTRY REQUIREMENTS Assessment & Interview
SCHOLARSHIPS & BURSARIES Schol; Burs; Teachers
SPECIAL NEEDS begjkln l   **DYSLEXIA** e   **DIET** acd
ASSOCIATION IAPS   **FOUNDED** 1910   **RELIGIOUS AFFILIATION** C of E

MAP 5 B 2
LOCATION Rural
DAY ✓   **RAIL** a   **AIR** a
SPORT abcdefgjilosx AB
OTHER LANGUAGES
ACTIVITIES afghijnopqr A
OTHER SUBJECTS ch
FACILITIES ON SITE i
EXAM BOARDS
RETAKES   **NVQ COURSES**

A-level: AS: GCSE: OTHER: c e g i l   o q   v / B G K OP R / cde g j

---

C — Brigg Preparatory School; Bigby Street; Brigg; Sth.Humberside DN20 8EF Tel: 01652 653237 *L.J.Shephard*

		Boys	Age	Girls	Age	TOTAL		Boys	Girls
Day	£680-£725	98	3-11	77	3-11	175	SIXTH		
Weekly									
Boarding									

ENTRY REQUIREMENTS Interview
SCHOLARSHIPS & BURSARIES
SPECIAL NEEDS jklnw Gl   **DYSLEXIA** e   **DIET** a
ASSOCIATION IAPS   **FOUNDED** 1926   **RELIGIOUS AFFILIATION** C of E

MAP 12 J 7
LOCATION Urban
DAY   **RAIL** b   **AIR** a
SPORT acefjlmpqswx AB
OTHER LANGUAGES
ACTIVITIES cgjo A
OTHER SUBJECTS ch
FACILITIES ON SITE h
EXAM BOARDS
RETAKES   **NVQ COURSES**

A-level: AS: GCSE: OTHER: e   o   v / B   G / cde

C — Hull Grammar School; Cottingham Road; Kingston upon Hull; North Humberside HU5 2DL Tel: 01482 440144 (Fax: 01482 441312) *R.Haworth*

		Boys	Age	Girls	Age	TOTAL		Boys	Girls
Day	£750-£1275	237	4-19	182	4-19	419	SIXTH	38	28
Weekly									
Boarding									

ENTRY REQUIREMENTS Interview; Assessment; Exam & Interview
SCHOLARSHIPS & BURSARIES Schol; VI Form; Siblings
SPECIAL NEEDS abegjklnpqstuvwx AGHIL   **DYSLEXIA** g   **DIET** acd
ASSOCIATION ISAI   **FOUNDED**   **RELIGIOUS AFFILIATION** C of E

MAP 12 J 7
LOCATION Urban
DAY ✓   **RAIL** a   **AIR** b
SPORT abcefhjlmopqsx AC
OTHER LANGUAGES a
ACTIVITIES cdfghjkoqs A
OTHER SUBJECTS abcdgh
FACILITIES ON SITE cgh
EXAM BOARDS bcd BDE
RETAKES   **NVQ COURSES**

A-level: e ghi   p   uv / BC GH K   P / c ef j
AS: l / G / e j
GCSE: e g i l   o   v / BC E G K   OP R / cdef j
OTHER: l / K

Gb — Hull High School; Tranby Croft; Anlaby; North Humberside HU10 7EH Tel: 01482 657016 (Fax: 01482 655389) *Mrs A.Benson*

		Boys	Age	Girls	Age	TOTAL		Boys	Girls
Day	£842-£1319	57	3-11	297	3-18	361	SIXTH		32
Weekly				7	11-18				
Boarding									

ENTRY REQUIREMENTS Exam; Test & Interview
SCHOLARSHIPS & BURSARIES Schol; VI Form
SPECIAL NEEDS abjq   **DYSLEXIA**   **DIET** ac
ASSOCIATION GSA   **FOUNDED** 1890   **RELIGIOUS AFFILIATION** C of E

MAP 12 J 7
LOCATION Rural
DAY ✓   **RAIL** b   **AIR** b
SPORT abcfhjklmpqwx ABC
OTHER LANGUAGES
ACTIVITIES cfghijkorst A
OTHER SUBJECTS bcefgh
FACILITIES ON SITE g
EXAM BOARDS acd ADEL
RETAKES a   **NVQ COURSES**

A-level: d fg i   n   uv x / BC GH K   P R / c ef j
AS: d   g / B   H / ef
GCSE: e g i   o   v / BC E G K   OP R W / cdef j l
OTHER: l

HUMBERSIDE

HUMBERSIDE continued

Hymers College; Hymers Avenue; Hull; N.Humberside HU3 1LW
Tel: 01482 343555 (Fax: 01482 472854) *J.C.Morris*

MAP12 J 7
LOCATION Urban
DAY RAIL a AIR a

		Boys	Age	Girls	Age	TOTAL		Boys	Girls
Day	£1041-£1185	595	8-18	325	8-18	920	SIXTH	147	50
Weekly									
Boarding									

SPORT abcefghjkmpqswx ABC
OTHER LANGUAGES
ACTIVITIES efghijkopqst AB

ENTRY REQUIREMENTS Exam & Interview
SCHOLARSHIPS & BURSARIES Burs; AP
SPECIAL NEEDS abeijklqstwx ACDGHIKL
ASSOCIATION HMC **FOUNDED** 1889

DYSLEXIA DIET abcd
RELIGIOUS AFFILIATION

OTHER SUBJECTS abcdfh
FACILITIES ON SITE cghk
EXAM BOARDS abc ABDEGHL
RETAKES NVQ COURSES

A-level: d ghi op uv / B GH K P / c ef j l
AS: l q / M
GCSE: a d ghi no v x / AB G K P / cdef j l
OTHER: l / F NO R

Pocklington School; West Green; Pocklington; York YO4 2NJ
Tel: 01759 303125 (Fax: 01759 306366) *J N D Gray*

MAP12 I 6
LOCATION Rural
DAY RAIL b AIR b

		Boys	Age	Girls	Age	TOTAL		Boys	Girls
Day	£956-£1614	393	7-18	225	7-18	735	SIXTH	119	47
Weekly			11-18		11-18				
Boarding	£2399-£2896	89	11-18	28	11-18				

SPORT abcdefhjklmopqsuwx ABC
OTHER LANGUAGES a
ACTIVITIES abcdefghijklnopqrstuwx ABD

ENTRY REQUIREMENTS CEE; Exam; Test; Report & Interview
SCHOLARSHIPS & BURSARIES Schol; Burs; Art; Mus; Chor; Forces; AP; VI Form
SPECIAL NEEDS befjlnqw GL
ASSOCIATION HMC **FOUNDED** 1514

DYSLEXIA df DIET acd
RELIGIOUS AFFILIATION C of E

OTHER SUBJECTS abcdfh
FACILITIES ON SITE abcdeghik
EXAM BOARDS abcd ABDEGHI
RETAKES NVQ COURSES

A-level: cdefg i l nopq uv x / AB GH K P R U / c efg j l
AS: e l pq v x / G M / c ef
GCSE: cde g i l opq v x / AB GH K P R U / cdefg j l
OTHER: d h lm / NO

St. James School; 22 Bargate; Grimsby DN34 4SY
Tel: 01472 362093 (Fax: 01472 351437) *D.J.Berisford*

MAP12 K 7
LOCATION Urban
DAY RAIL a AIR a

		Boys	Age	Girls	Age	TOTAL		Boys	Girls
Day	£723-£1526	115	3-19	71	3-19	246	SIXTH	19	17
Weekly	£1816-£2484	12	6-19	8	6-19				
Boarding	£1949-£2617	23	6-19	17	6-19				

SPORT abcefghjmopqswx AB
OTHER LANGUAGES a
ACTIVITIES cdfghijkmnopqrswx AB

ENTRY REQUIREMENTS Report & Exam & Interview
SCHOLARSHIPS & BURSARIES Burs; Chor; Forces; Clergy; Teachers
SPECIAL NEEDS abejlnqw BGI
ASSOCIATION ISAI **FOUNDED** 1880

DYSLEXIA def DIET ad
RELIGIOUS AFFILIATION C of E

OTHER SUBJECTS abcdh
FACILITIES ON SITE bceg
EXAM BOARDS abcd ABCDE
RETAKES ab NVQ COURSES

A-level: de ghi o uv / ABC G K / cde j
AS: de gi / G K P
GCSE: cde g i l v / ABC G K N P R WX / bcdef j
OTHER: l no / o

St. Martin's Preparatory School; Bargate; Grimsby; South Humberside DN34 5AA
Tel: 01472 878907 *Mrs M.Preston*

MAP12 K 7
LOCATION
DAY RAIL AIR

		Boys	Age	Girls	Age	TOTAL		Boys	Girls
Day	£405-£775	104	3-11	137	3-11	241	SIXTH		
Weekly									
Boarding									

SPORT cejlpqx AB
OTHER LANGUAGES
ACTIVITIES cfghjo

ENTRY REQUIREMENTS Interview
SCHOLARSHIPS & BURSARIES
SPECIAL NEEDS
ASSOCIATION ISAI **FOUNDED** 1930

DYSLEXIA DIET
RELIGIOUS AFFILIATION Inter-denom

OTHER SUBJECTS
FACILITIES ON SITE
EXAM BOARDS
RETAKES NVQ COURSES

A-level:
AS:
GCSE:
OTHER: b e l o v / B G K O R / cde

ISLE OF MAN

Buchan School,The; Prep Sch to King William's College; Westhill; Castletown; Isle of Man IM9 1RD Tel: 01624 822526 (Fax: 01624 823220) *P.H.Moody*

MAP11 A 8
LOCATION Rural
DAY ✓ RAIL AIR a

		Boys	Age	Girls	Age	TOTAL		Boys	Girls
Day	£1135-£1760 ×	99	3-11	99	3-11	208	SIXTH		
Weekly			7-11		7-11				
Boarding	£2830	5	7-11	5	7-11				

SPORT abefjklmpqstx AB
OTHER LANGUAGES
ACTIVITIES

ENTRY REQUIREMENTS Interview; Report
SCHOLARSHIPS & BURSARIES Schol; Siblings
SPECIAL NEEDS
ASSOCIATION IAPS **FOUNDED** 1875

DYSLEXIA DIET a
RELIGIOUS AFFILIATION Non-denom

OTHER SUBJECTS bch
FACILITIES ON SITE c
EXAM BOARDS
RETAKES NVQ COURSES

A-level:
AS:
GCSE:
OTHER: de g i lmno v / BC G K OP R / cdef l

ISLE OF MAN continued

C — King William's College; Castletown; Isle of Man IM9 1TP
Tel: 01624 822551 (Fax: 01624 824287) *S.A.Westley*

	Fees	Boys	Age	Girls	Age	TOTAL	Sixth Boys	Girls
Day	£1915-£2650	112	11-18	96	11-18	313	60	28
Weekly	£2985-£3720	79	11-18	26	11-18			
Boarding								

ENTRY REQUIREMENTS CEE; Exam; Test; Report
SCHOLARSHIPS & BURSARIES Schol; Burs; Mus; Forces; Clergy; VI Form
SPECIAL NEEDS abejklnpqstw BEGI **DYSLEXIA** cde **DIET** ad
ASSOCIATION HMC **FOUNDED** 1833 **RELIGIOUS AFFILIATION** C of E

MAP 10 A 8
LOCATION Rural
DAY ✓ **RAIL**   **AIR** a
SPORT abcdefghjklmpqstuwx ABC
OTHER LANGUAGES a
ACTIVITIES efghijklmnopqrstuvw AB
OTHER SUBJECTS abcfgh
FACILITIES ON SITE bcdeghikl
EXAM BOARDS abc ABEH
RETAKES a **NVQ COURSES**

A-level: c efghi o uv x / B GH K P R / c ef l
AS: g o u / G U
GCSE: c e g i o v / B G K P R / cdef j l
OTHER: c l / e MNO R

C — Bembridge School; Bembridge; Isle of Wight PO35 5PH
Tel: 0198 387 2101 (Fax: 0198 387 2576) *J.High*

	Fees	Boys	Age	Girls	Age	TOTAL	Sixth Boys	Girls
Day	£495-£1480	83	3-18	49	3-18	256	37	20
Weekly	£2365-£2845	10	7-18	3	7-18			
Boarding	£2490-£2970	80	7-18	31	7-18			

ENTRY REQUIREMENTS CEE; Test & Interview
SCHOLARSHIPS & BURSARIES Schol; Art; Mus; Forces
SPECIAL NEEDS bjklnqtw DEGI **DYSLEXIA** ce **DIET** acd
ASSOCIATION SHMIS **FOUNDED** 1919 **RELIGIOUS AFFILIATION** Non-denom

MAP 3 D 8
LOCATION Rural
DAY ✓ **RAIL** b **AIR** b
SPORT abcdefhjklmopqstuvwx ABC
OTHER LANGUAGES a
ACTIVITIES abcfghijkmnoqrstuvw AB
OTHER SUBJECTS bcfh
FACILITIES ON SITE bcdeghkl
EXAM BOARDS abcd ABDEH
RETAKES ab **NVQ COURSES** 2

A-level: defghij l op v / AB G K OP / cdef
AS: h u / B G
GCSE: e ghij nop v / BC G K P / cdef
OTHER: C

C — Ryde School (Junior School); Queen's Road; Ryde; Isle of Wight PO33 3BE
Tel: 01983 562229 (Fax: 01983 614973) *J.T.Coakley*

	Fees	Boys	Age	Girls	Age	TOTAL	Sixth Boys	Girls
Day	£575-£1259	115	3-11	83	3-11	201		
Weekly	£1105	1						
Boarding	£1254	2						

ENTRY REQUIREMENTS Test & Interview
SCHOLARSHIPS & BURSARIES Siblings
SPECIAL NEEDS bejlnw **DYSLEXIA** e **DIET** ad
ASSOCIATION IAPS **FOUNDED** 1921 **RELIGIOUS AFFILIATION** C of E

MAP 3 D 7
LOCATION Urban
DAY ✓ **RAIL** a **AIR** b
SPORT abefgjlmopqsx B
OTHER LANGUAGES
ACTIVITIES cfghjnotx
OTHER SUBJECTS cdh
FACILITIES ON SITE chjk
EXAM BOARDS
RETAKES **NVQ COURSES**

OTHER: e l no v / B G K O R / cde

C — Ryde School with Upper Chine; Queen's Road; Ryde; Isle of Wight PO33 3BE
Tel: 01983 562229 (Fax: 01983 564714) *M.D.Featherstone*

	Fees	Boys	Age	Girls	Age	TOTAL	Sixth Boys	Girls
Day	£1394	228	11-18	205	11-18	488	60	58
Weekly	£2673	1	11-18	7	11-18			
Boarding	£2845	19	11-18	28	11-18			

ENTRY REQUIREMENTS Report & Interview
SCHOLARSHIPS & BURSARIES Schol; Burs; AP
SPECIAL NEEDS bejklnqsuw EGI **DYSLEXIA** e **DIET** a
ASSOCIATION HMC **FOUNDED** 1921 **RELIGIOUS AFFILIATION** C of E

MAP 3 D 7
LOCATION
DAY ✓ **RAIL** b **AIR** b
SPORT abcdefghjlmopqstuvwx ABC
OTHER LANGUAGES a
ACTIVITIES cefghijklmnopqstw AB
OTHER SUBJECTS bcdfh
FACILITIES ON SITE bcdeghjk
EXAM BOARDS abcd ABDEH
RETAKES ab **NVQ COURSES**

A-level: d fghi nop v x / B GH K OP / c ef j l
AS: G K l / cdef
GCSE: s uv x / e ghi mno v / B E G K OP R / cdef j l
OTHER: l u / R

G — Ashford Junior School; East Hill; Ashford; Kent TN24 8PB
Tel: 01233 625171 (Fax: 01233 647185) *P.H.Power*

	Fees	Boys	Age	Girls	Age	TOTAL	Sixth Boys	Girls
Day	£318-£1462		3-7	181	3-11	181		
Weekly	£2972				9-11			
Boarding	£3007				9-11			

ENTRY REQUIREMENTS Report & Test
SCHOLARSHIPS & BURSARIES Schol
SPECIAL NEEDS bjklqt GHI **DYSLEXIA**   **DIET** abcd
ASSOCIATION IAPS **FOUNDED** 1910 **RELIGIOUS AFFILIATION** Inter-denom

MAP 4 J 5
LOCATION Urban
DAY ✓ **RAIL** a **AIR** b
SPORT aclmpqx AB
OTHER LANGUAGES
ACTIVITIES cfghijo
OTHER SUBJECTS ch
FACILITIES ON SITE behi
EXAM BOARDS
RETAKES **NVQ COURSES**

OTHER: de mno v / B E G K O RS / cde

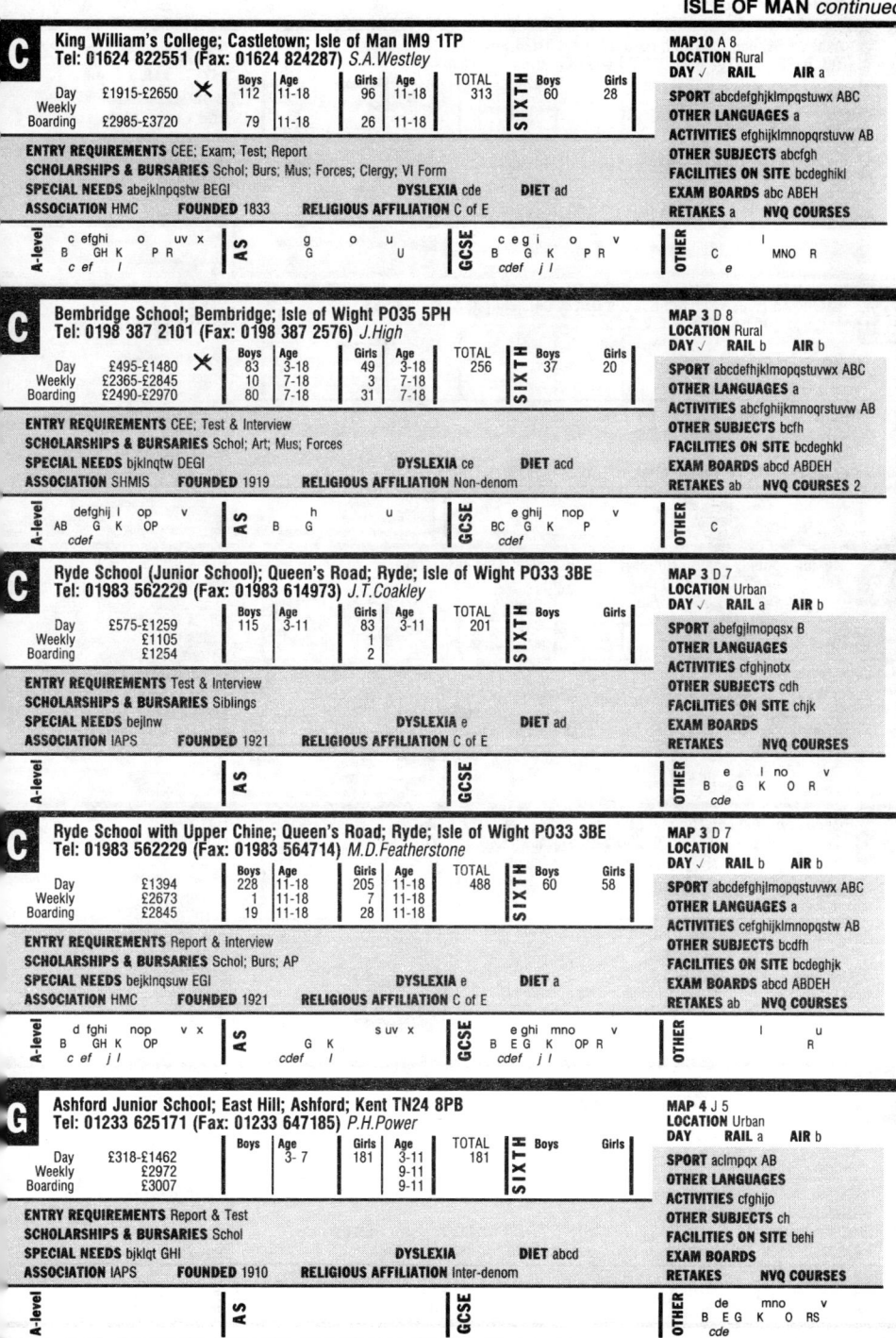

ISLE OF WIGHT — **KENT**

KENT *continued*

G — Ashford School; East Hill; Ashford; Kent TN24 8PB
Tel: 01233 625171 (Fax: 01233 647185) *Mrs P.Metham*

	Boys	Age	Girls	Age	TOTAL	SIXTH	Boys	Girls
Day £1950			288	11-18	377			116
Weekly £3448			19	11-18				
Boarding £3493			70	11-18				

MAP 4 J 5
LOCATION Urban
DAY **RAIL** a **AIR** a
SPORT abcghklmopwx BC
OTHER LANGUAGES
ACTIVITIES cfghijklnoqsw ABD

ENTRY REQUIREMENTS Test & Interview
SCHOLARSHIPS & BURSARIES Schol; Mus; AP
SPECIAL NEEDS abejklqt GHI
ASSOCIATION GSA **FOUNDED** 1898
DYSLEXIA **DIET** acd
RELIGIOUS AFFILIATION Inter-denom
OTHER SUBJECTS bcdh
FACILITIES ON SITE bceghi
EXAM BOARDS abcd AE
RETAKES **NVQ COURSES**

A-level: c efghi n p v / B GH K P R U W / c efg j l
AS: e o / G
GCSE: c e g i no v / BC E G K P R W / cdefghij l
OTHER: e lmno q u / C K O R / l

Gb — Babington House School; Grange Drive; Chislehurst; Kent BR7 5ES
Tel: 0181 467 5537 *Mrs E.V.Walter*

	Boys	Age	Girls	Age	TOTAL	SIXTH	Boys	Girls
Day £725-£1450	59	3-7	169	3-16	228			
Weekly								
Boarding								

MAP 6 H 6
LOCATION Urban
DAY **RAIL** a **AIR** a
SPORT achlptvx ABC
OTHER LANGUAGES
ACTIVITIES cgjopqt A

ENTRY REQUIREMENTS Assessment & Interview
SCHOLARSHIPS & BURSARIES Schol; Siblings
SPECIAL NEEDS bknw
ASSOCIATION ISAI **FOUNDED** 1887
DYSLEXIA **DIET** abcd
RELIGIOUS AFFILIATION C of E
OTHER SUBJECTS abcdegh
FACILITIES ON SITE h
EXAM BOARDS abcd E
RETAKES **NVQ COURSES**

A-level:
AS:
GCSE: e ghijkl v / B G K P R W / cdef
OTHER: h j lm / G K O / d

G — Baston School; Baston Road; Hayes; Bromley; Kent BR2 7AB
Tel: 0181 462 1010 (Fax: 0181 462 0438) *C.R.C.Wimble*

	Boys	Age	Girls	Age	TOTAL	SIXTH	Boys	Girls
Day £330-£1485			210	3-18	238			27
Weekly £2850			3	9-18				
Boarding £2900			25	9-18				

MAP 6 G 6
LOCATION Rural
DAY **RAIL** a **AIR** a
SPORT abfhjlnpqwx AB
OTHER LANGUAGES a
ACTIVITIES ghjknoqt AD

ENTRY REQUIREMENTS Report & Exam & Interview
SCHOLARSHIPS & BURSARIES Schol; Burs; Mus; Siblings
SPECIAL NEEDS bhjln
ASSOCIATION ISAI **FOUNDED** 1933
DYSLEXIA ef **DIET** abcd
RELIGIOUS AFFILIATION C of E
OTHER SUBJECTS bcdfgh
FACILITIES ON SITE bgj
EXAM BOARDS abd AEG
RETAKES b **NVQ COURSES**

A-level: a e ghi l v / BC GH K P U W / cdef l
AS: G
GCSE: e ghi l o v / BC G K OP R T W / cdef l
OTHER: mn u / O R

Gb — Bedgebury School; Goudhurst; Cranbrook; Kent TN17 2SH
Tel: 01580 211221 (Fax: 01580 212252) *Mrs L.J.Griffin*

	Boys	Age	Girls	Age	TOTAL	SIXTH	Boys	Girls
Day £1079-£2226	14	3-8	145	3-18	366			81
Weekly £2363-£3596			103	8-18				
Boarding £2363-£3596			104	8-18				

MAP 4 I 6
LOCATION Rural
DAY ✓ **RAIL** b **AIR** b
SPORT abcdfghjklmnopqrstuwx ABC
OTHER LANGUAGES a
ACTIVITIES acdghijklnopqstwx AB

ENTRY REQUIREMENTS Report & Exam & Interview
SCHOLARSHIPS & BURSARIES Schol; Art; Mus; Forces; Clergy; VI Form; Drama
SPECIAL NEEDS aejklnw BEGI
ASSOCIATION GSA **FOUNDED** 1860
DYSLEXIA c **DIET** acd
RELIGIOUS AFFILIATION C of E
OTHER SUBJECTS bcdefgh
FACILITIES ON SITE bcdeghjl
EXAM BOARDS abcd ABDEGHKL
RETAKES ab **NVQ COURSES** 2

A-level: de ghi kl nop uv / AB GHI K P R U W / cdefghij l
AS: de ghi l op uv / G K P R / cde l
GCSE: de ghi l no v / B EGI K NOP R WX / cdefghij l
OTHER: de ghi klmnop uv / B C GHI K OP W / cdefgh j l

Gb — Beechwood School Sacred Heart; Beechwood; Pembury Road; Tunbridge Wells TN2 3QD
Tel: 01892 532747 (Fax: 01892 536164) *T.S.Hodkinson*

	Boys	Age	Girls	Age	TOTAL	SIXTH	Boys	Girls
Day £850-£2110	7	3-7	129	3-18	216			56
Weekly £1995-£2810			2	9-18				
Boarding £2720-£3535			78	9-18				

MAP 4 H 5
LOCATION Rural
DAY **RAIL** a **AIR** a
SPORT abcefmpqwx ABC
OTHER LANGUAGES a
ACTIVITIES cfghijkopstw A

ENTRY REQUIREMENTS CEE & Interview
SCHOLARSHIPS & BURSARIES Schol; Art; Mus; VI Form
SPECIAL NEEDS jntv E
ASSOCIATION GSA **FOUNDED** 1915
DYSLEXIA e **DIET** a
RELIGIOUS AFFILIATION R C
OTHER SUBJECTS acefgh
FACILITIES ON SITE dhjk
EXAM BOARDS abcd ABDEG
RETAKES **NVQ COURSES**

A-level: a de ghi l n v / BC FGH K P / cdef h
AS: a de h l / GH K U / cde l
GCSE: a de ghi l no v / BC FG K P R W / cde hj l
OTHER: u / NO R

156

KENT continued

G Benenden School; Cranbrook; Kent TN17 4AA
Tel: 01580 240592 (Fax: 01580 240280) *Mrs G.du Charme*

		Boys	Age	Girls	Age	TOTAL		Boys	Girls
Day						444	SIXTH		136
Weekly									
Boarding	£4210			444	11-18				

ENTRY REQUIREMENTS CEE; Test & Interview
SCHOLARSHIPS & BURSARIES Schol; Art; Mus; VI Form; Siblings
SPECIAL NEEDS n E   **DYSLEXIA** f   **DIET** abcd
ASSOCIATION GSA   **FOUNDED** 1923   **RELIGIOUS AFFILIATION** C of E

MAP 4 I 5
LOCATION Rural
DAY   **RAIL** a   **AIR** b
SPORT abcefghlnopquwx ABC
OTHER LANGUAGES a
ACTIVITIES cghijklnoqstw AB
OTHER SUBJECTS abch
FACILITIES ON SITE cdeghi
EXAM BOARDS abd ABE
RETAKES   **NVQ COURSES**

A-level: cd fg i   n p   v   B GH K   P R U   cdefg j l
AS: d   G K   defg
GCSE: o   u   U
OTHER: d g i   no   v   B G K   P R W   cdefg j l
: C   lm   o   hi k

C Bethany School; Goudhurst; Cranbrook; Kent TN17 1LB
Tel: 01580 211273 (Fax: 01580 211151) *W.M.Harvey*

		Boys	Age	Girls	Age	TOTAL		Boys	Girls
Day	£2013	X	105	11-18	17	11-18	265	SIXTH		52
Weekly	£3147			11-18		11-18				
Boarding	£3147		134	11-18	9	11-18				

ENTRY REQUIREMENTS CEE; Test
SCHOLARSHIPS & BURSARIES Schol; Art; Mus; Forces; Clergy; VI Form; Sport
SPECIAL NEEDS bejlntw D   **DYSLEXIA** cd   **DIET** ad
ASSOCIATION SHMIS   **FOUNDED** 1866   **RELIGIOUS AFFILIATION** C of E

MAP 4 I 5
LOCATION Rural
DAY ✓   **RAIL** a   **AIR** a
SPORT abcefghjklmopqrstuwx ABC
OTHER LANGUAGES
ACTIVITIES acfghijknopqrstuw AC
OTHER SUBJECTS bcfh
FACILITIES ON SITE bcdeghj
EXAM BOARDS abcde ABDEK
RETAKES ab   **NVQ COURSES** 3

A-level: e ghi   l   o   vw   AB   G   OPQR   cdef
AS: g i   G
GCSE: e ghi   l   no   vw   AB   G   K NOP R   X   cdef   l
OTHER:

G Bromley High School GPDST; Blackbrook Lane; Bickley; Bromley; Kent BR1 2TW
Tel: 0181 468 7981 (Fax: 0181 295 1062) *Mrs E.J.Hancock*

		Boys	Age	Girls	Age	TOTAL		Boys	Girls
Day	£1192-£1548				792	4-18	792	SIXTH		128
Weekly										
Boarding										

ENTRY REQUIREMENTS Report & Exam & Interview
SCHOLARSHIPS & BURSARIES Schol; Burs; Mus; AP; VI Form
SPECIAL NEEDS bfjn   **DYSLEXIA**   **DIET** abcd
ASSOCIATION GSA   **FOUNDED** 1883   **RELIGIOUS AFFILIATION** Inter-denom

MAP 6 G 6
LOCATION Urban
DAY   **RAIL** a   **AIR** a
SPORT acfgjklmpqrwx ABC
OTHER LANGUAGES
ACTIVITIES acfghijklnoqst ABD
OTHER SUBJECTS abcdefgh
FACILITIES ON SITE abcghi
EXAM BOARDS abd ABEG
RETAKES   **NVQ COURSES**

A-level: de ghi   l   pq   v x   B GH K   P R U   cdef j l
AS: e   l
GCSE: de   l no q   v   B G K   O R U WX   cdef j l
OTHER: C   u   i k

C Bronte School; 5 & 7 Parrock Road; Gravesend; Kent DA12 1PY
Tel: 01474 533805 (Fax: 01474 352003) *Mrs R.M.Roberts*

		Boys	Age	Girls	Age	TOTAL		Boys	Girls
Day	£890		44	3-11	35	3-11	79	SIXTH		
Weekly										
Boarding										

ENTRY REQUIREMENTS Assessment & Interview
SCHOLARSHIPS & BURSARIES
SPECIAL NEEDS   **DYSLEXIA**   **DIET**
ASSOCIATION ISAI   **FOUNDED** 1905   **RELIGIOUS AFFILIATION** C of E

MAP 6 K 5
LOCATION Urban
DAY   **RAIL** a   **AIR** a
SPORT aejlmpqx B
OTHER LANGUAGES
ACTIVITIES fghjr
OTHER SUBJECTS ch
FACILITIES ON SITE
EXAM BOARDS
RETAKES   **NVQ COURSES**

A-level:
AS:
GCSE:
OTHER: e   lm o   v   B G K O R   cde

G Cobham Hall School; Cobham; Nr. Gravesend; Kent DA12 3BL
Tel: 01474 823371 (Fax: 01474 822995) *Mrs R.J.Mc Carthy*

		Boys	Age	Girls	Age	TOTAL		Boys	Girls
Day	£2200-£2750	X			22	11-18	160	SIXTH		73
Weekly	£4285					11-18				
Boarding	£4285				138	11-18				

ENTRY REQUIREMENTS Report & Exam & Interview
SCHOLARSHIPS & BURSARIES Schol; Burs; VI Form; Siblings
SPECIAL NEEDS abehijklnqstuw ABEGHI   **DYSLEXIA** cd   **DIET** abcd
ASSOCIATION GSA   **FOUNDED** 1962   **RELIGIOUS AFFILIATION** Inter-denom

MAP 6 K 5
LOCATION Rural
DAY   **RAIL** a   **AIR** a
SPORT acdfhklmopqtuvwx ABC
OTHER LANGUAGES ai
ACTIVITIES cfghijklnopqstw AB
OTHER SUBJECTS abcdfh
FACILITIES ON SITE bceghi
EXAM BOARDS abcd ABDEH
RETAKES ab   **NVQ COURSES**

A-level: b defgh   l nop   uv   B GH K N P   cdef   jkl
AS:
GCSE: de ghi   l   no   v   B E G K N P   cdef jkl
OTHER: s u   M O R   g

KENT continued

Gb — Combe Bank School; Sundridge; Nr. Sevenoaks; Kent TN14 6AE
Tel: 01959 563720 (Fax: 01959 561997) *Miss N.Spurr*

		Boys	Age	Girls	Age	TOTAL		Boys	Girls
Day	£595-£1820	16	3-5	402	3-18	418	SIXTH		50
Weekly									
Boarding									

MAP 4 H 5
LOCATION Rural
DAY ✓ RAIL a AIR a
SPORT abcfhklmopqx ABC
OTHER LANGUAGES a
ACTIVITIES cghijknoqst AB
OTHER SUBJECTS bcdefgh
FACILITIES ON SITE bcdgi
EXAM BOARDS abd ABEG
RETAKES ab NVQ COURSES 23

ENTRY REQUIREMENTS Exam; Interview
SCHOLARSHIPS & BURSARIES Schol; Mus; VI Form
SPECIAL NEEDS abhklnqw   DYSLEXIA ef   DIET a
ASSOCIATION GSA   FOUNDED 1972   RELIGIOUS AFFILIATION R C

A-level: d ghi v / BC G K P R T / c ef l
AS: d / G K / ef l
GCSE: de ghi l n v / ABC G K OP R / cdef l
OTHER:

G — Derwent Lodge Preparatory School for Girls; Somerhill; Tonbridge; Kent TN11 0NJ
Tel: 01732 352124 (Fax: 01732 363381) *Mrs C.M.York*

		Boys	Age	Girls	Age	TOTAL		Boys	Girls
Day	£1475	✗		76	7-11	76	SIXTH		
Weekly									
Boarding									

MAP 4 H 5
LOCATION Rural
DAY ✓ RAIL a AIR a
SPORT alpqx B
OTHER LANGUAGES
ACTIVITIES cgjt
OTHER SUBJECTS cfh
FACILITIES ON SITE bj
EXAM BOARDS
RETAKES NVQ COURSES

ENTRY REQUIREMENTS Report & Interview; Assessment & Interview
SCHOLARSHIPS & BURSARIES Schol; Burs; Mus; Siblings
SPECIAL NEEDS alnw   DYSLEXIA e   DIET abcd
ASSOCIATION ISAI   FOUNDED 1952   RELIGIOUS AFFILIATION Christian

A-level:
AS:
GCSE:
OTHER: e lmno v / B E G K O R / cde

C — Dover College; Dover; Kent CT17 9RH
Tel: 01304 205969 (Fax: 01304 242208) *M.P.G.Wright*

		Boys	Age	Girls	Age	TOTAL		Boys	Girls
Day	£1200-£1500	✗ 62	11-18	38	11-18	221	SIXTH	47	22
Weekly	£3520	13	13-18	2	13-18				
Boarding	£3725	72	13-18	34	13-18				

MAP 4 K 5
LOCATION Urban
DAY a RAIL a AIR b
SPORT abcfhjkmopstwx ABC
OTHER LANGUAGES ac
ACTIVITIES bcfghijknoqstw AB
OTHER SUBJECTS abcdfh
FACILITIES ON SITE acdegh
EXAM BOARDS abcd ABDEGHIJ
RETAKES ab NVQ COURSES

ENTRY REQUIREMENTS CEE; Exam; Assessment; Test & Interview; Report & Test
SCHOLARSHIPS & BURSARIES Schol; Burs; Art; Mus; Chor; Forces; Clergy; Teachers; AP; VI Form; Sport; ARA; Siblings   SPECIAL NEEDS bjln C   DYSLEXIA def   DIET abcd
ASSOCIATION HMC   FOUNDED 1871   RELIGIOUS AFFILIATION C of E

A-level: c e ghi l p v x / B GH K P / cdefgh j l
AS: c g i o / G / ef
GCSE: e g i l no q v x / B E G K NOP R / cdefgh j l
OTHER: N

C — Duke of York's Royal Military School; Dover; Kent CT15 5EQ
Tel: 01304 245024 (Fax: 01304 245019) *Colonel G.H.Wilson*

		Boys	Age	Girls	Age	TOTAL		Boys	Girls
Day						464	SIXTH	99	7
Weekly									
Boarding	£250	414	11-18	50	11-18				

MAP 4 K 5
LOCATION Rural
DAY RAIL a AIR c
SPORT abcdefgjklmopqstuwx ABC
OTHER LANGUAGES
ACTIVITIES cefghijklmnopqstuw A
OTHER SUBJECTS abcdh
FACILITIES ON SITE abdeikl
EXAM BOARDS abcdef AEGH
RETAKES NVQ COURSES 3

ENTRY REQUIREMENTS Exam; Report
SCHOLARSHIPS & BURSARIES
SPECIAL NEEDS   DYSLEXIA   DIET a
ASSOCIATION SHMIS   FOUNDED 1803   RELIGIOUS AFFILIATION C of E

A-level: de ghi l no uv / B GH K P R / cdef
AS: u
GCSE: d g i l no q v / BC G K OP R / cdef
OTHER: h l n p r u x / K O R / cdef

C — Dulwich College Prep. School; Coursehorn; Cranbrook; Kent TN17 3NP
Tel: 01580 712179 (Fax: 01580 715322) *M.C.Wagstaffe*

		Boys	Age	Girls	Age	TOTAL		Boys	Girls
Day	£645-£1865	✗ 228	3-13	236	3-13	534	SIXTH		
Weekly	£2785	31	8-13	16	8-13				
Boarding	£2865	11	8-13	12	8-13				

MAP 4 I 5
LOCATION Rural
DAY RAIL a AIR b
SPORT abcefhjlmnpqsux ABC
OTHER LANGUAGES
ACTIVITIES cfghijoqstw A
OTHER SUBJECTS bch
FACILITIES ON SITE abchjk
EXAM BOARDS
RETAKES NVQ COURSES

ENTRY REQUIREMENTS Test
SCHOLARSHIPS & BURSARIES
SPECIAL NEEDS abegjklnqstux ABHI   DYSLEXIA ce   DIET abcd
ASSOCIATION IAPS   FOUNDED 1946   RELIGIOUS AFFILIATION Christian

A-level:
AS:
GCSE:
OTHER: e g i lmno v / B G K NOP R X / cde j l

KENT *continued*

Farringtons and Stratford House; Chislehurst BR7 6LR
Tel: 0181 467 0256 (Fax: 0181 295 1575) *Mrs B.J.Stock*

	Boys	Age	Girls	Age	TOTAL		Boys	Girls
Day £1159-£1654 ✗			384	4-18	509	SIXTH		64
Weekly £2765-£3071			20	7-18				
Boarding £2887-£3187			105	7-18				

ENTRY REQUIREMENTS Exam & Interview
SCHOLARSHIPS & BURSARIES Forces
SPECIAL NEEDS abjlnq EGH **DYSLEXIA** g **DIET** acd
ASSOCIATION GSA **FOUNDED** 1911 **RELIGIOUS AFFILIATION** Methodist

MAP 6 H 6
LOCATION Urban
DAY ✓ **RAIL** b **AIR** a
SPORT abcghlmnpqwx ABC
OTHER LANGUAGES a
ACTIVITIES cfghijknoqrst AB
OTHER SUBJECTS bcefgh
FACILITIES ON SITE cdeghj
EXAM BOARDS abcd ABEGL
RETAKES a **NVQ COURSES**

A-level: defgh l n v BC GH K P R U W cdef l
AS: d g i l BC G K P R cdef l
GCSE: de g i l no v BC G K OP R W cdef l
OTHER: cde ghij BC G K OP R W uv cdef l

Friars School; Great Chart; Ashford; Kent TN23 3DJ
Tel: 01233 620493 *P.M.Ashley*

	Boys	Age	Girls	Age	TOTAL		Boys	Girls
Day £400-£1775 ✗	89	3-13	9	3-13	105	SIXTH		
Weekly £2475	7	7-13						
Boarding								

ENTRY REQUIREMENTS Test; Test & Interview
SCHOLARSHIPS & BURSARIES Schol; Forces; Clergy
SPECIAL NEEDS bejklnpqstuwx ABCDGHK **DYSLEXIA** ef **DIET** acd
ASSOCIATION IAPS **FOUNDED** 1949 **RELIGIOUS AFFILIATION** Non-denom

MAP 4 J 5
LOCATION Rural
DAY ✓ **RAIL** a **AIR** b
SPORT abcefhjklmpqsuwx ABC
OTHER LANGUAGES
ACTIVITIES cfghijmoqtwx A
OTHER SUBJECTS abcfh
FACILITIES ON SITE aehjk
EXAM BOARDS
RETAKES **NVQ COURSES**

OTHER: d g i lmno q s v B G K OP R cde j

Granville School,The; Sevenoaks; Kent TN13 3LJ
Tel: 01732 453039 (Fax: 01732 743634) *Mrs J.Evans*

	Boys	Age	Girls	Age	TOTAL		Boys	Girls
Day £525-£1320	11	3-5	176	3-11	187	SIXTH		
Weekly								
Boarding								

ENTRY REQUIREMENTS Interview
SCHOLARSHIPS & BURSARIES Burs
SPECIAL NEEDS bjknuw GHIJ **DYSLEXIA** e **DIET** ad
ASSOCIATION IAPS **FOUNDED** 1945 **RELIGIOUS AFFILIATION** Inter-denom

MAP 4 H 5
LOCATION Urban
DAY **RAIL** a **AIR** a
SPORT acdhlmnpqx AB
OTHER LANGUAGES
ACTIVITIES cghijopqt A
OTHER SUBJECTS abcfh
FACILITIES ON SITE ci
EXAM BOARDS
RETAKES **NVQ COURSES**

OTHER: e Imno s v B E G K O R cde

Greenhayes School for Boys; Corkscrew Hill; West Wickham; Kent BR4 9BA
Tel: 0181 777 2093 (Fax: 0181 777 2093) *D.J.Cozens*

	Boys	Age	Girls	Age	TOTAL		Boys	Girls
Day £750-£830	95	4-11			95	SIXTH		
Weekly								
Boarding								

ENTRY REQUIREMENTS None; Interview; Test & Interview
SCHOLARSHIPS & BURSARIES
SPECIAL NEEDS n **DYSLEXIA** e **DIET**
ASSOCIATION ISAI **FOUNDED** 1931 **RELIGIOUS AFFILIATION** Non-denom

MAP 6 G 6
LOCATION Urban
DAY **RAIL** a **AIR** a
SPORT aefjlqx A
OTHER LANGUAGES
ACTIVITIES fg
OTHER SUBJECTS abch
FACILITIES ON SITE
EXAM BOARDS
RETAKES **NVQ COURSES**

OTHER: e l v B E G K O R e

Harenc School; 167 Rectory Lane; Footscray; Sidcup; Kent DA14 5BU
Tel: 0181 309 0619 (Fax: 0181 309 5051) *S.H.D.Cassidy*

	Boys	Age	Girls	Age	TOTAL		Boys	Girls
Day £465-£1045	138	3-11			138	SIXTH		
Weekly								
Boarding								

ENTRY REQUIREMENTS Assessment & Interview
SCHOLARSHIPS & BURSARIES
SPECIAL NEEDS blt A **DYSLEXIA** **DIET**
ASSOCIATION ISAI **FOUNDED** 1983 **RELIGIOUS AFFILIATION** Inter-denom

MAP 6 H 5
LOCATION Urban
DAY **RAIL** a **AIR** a
SPORT aefjqx
OTHER LANGUAGES
ACTIVITIES fghjm A
OTHER SUBJECTS bh
FACILITIES ON SITE
EXAM BOARDS
RETAKES **NVQ COURSES**

OTHER: e l n s v B G K O R cde

KENT continued

C — Hilden Grange School; Tonbridge; Kent TN10 3BX
Tel: 01732 352706 *J.A.Stewart & J.Withers*

		Boys	Age	Girls	Age	TOTAL		Boys	Girls
Day	£1000-£1600	210	3-13	81	3-13	291	SIXTH		
Weekly									
Boarding									

ENTRY REQUIREMENTS Assessment & Interview
SCHOLARSHIPS & BURSARIES Schol; Art; Mus; Teachers
SPECIAL NEEDS bej   **DYSLEXIA**   **DIET**
ASSOCIATION IAPS   **FOUNDED** 1946   **RELIGIOUS AFFILIATION** C of E

MAP 4 H 5
LOCATION Urban
DAY   RAIL b   AIR a
SPORT abcefjlmnopqsx BC
OTHER LANGUAGES
ACTIVITIES cfghjnot A
OTHER SUBJECTS abcfh
FACILITIES ON SITE hj
EXAM BOARDS
RETAKES   NVQ COURSES

A-level / AS / GCSE
OTHER: c e g i lmno v / B G K OP R / cde j l

Gb — Hilden Oaks; 38 Dry Hill Park Road; Tonbridge; Kent TN10 3BW
Tel: 01732 353941 (Fax: 01732 353941) *Mrs.H.J.Bacon*

		Boys	Age	Girls	Age	TOTAL		Boys	Girls
Day	£495-£1075 ✗	35	3-7	136	3-11	171	SIXTH		
Weekly									
Boarding									

ENTRY REQUIREMENTS Interview
SCHOLARSHIPS & BURSARIES
SPECIAL NEEDS   **DYSLEXIA**   **DIET** a
ASSOCIATION IAPS   **FOUNDED** 1920   **RELIGIOUS AFFILIATION** C of E

MAP 4 H 5
LOCATION
DAY   RAIL a   AIR a
SPORT jpq
OTHER LANGUAGES
ACTIVITIES hj
OTHER SUBJECTS ah
FACILITIES ON SITE
EXAM BOARDS
RETAKES   NVQ COURSES

C — Hill School; Westerham; Kent TN16 2DU
Tel: 01959 563381 *R.G.A Balchin & N.J.R.Sanceau*

		Boys	Age	Girls	Age	TOTAL		Boys	Girls
Day	£1195	66	7-13	5	7-13	71	SIXTH		
Weekly									
Boarding									

ENTRY REQUIREMENTS Assessment & Interview
SCHOLARSHIPS & BURSARIES Forces; Clergy; Teachers
SPECIAL NEEDS lnw B   **DYSLEXIA** e   **DIET** acd
ASSOCIATION IAPS   **FOUNDED** 1950   **RELIGIOUS AFFILIATION**

MAP 4 H 5
LOCATION Rural
DAY ✓   RAIL b   AIR a
SPORT abefjmopqsx AB
OTHER LANGUAGES
ACTIVITIES cfghijno A
OTHER SUBJECTS ch
FACILITIES ON SITE j
EXAM BOARDS
RETAKES   NVQ COURSES

OTHER: e g i l o q v / AB G K OP R / cde j

C — Holmewood House; Langton Green; Tunbridge Wells; Kent TN3 0EB
Tel: 01892 86 2088 (Fax: 01892 863970) *D.G.Ives*

		Boys	Age	Girls	Age	TOTAL		Boys	Girls
Day	£635-£2340 ✗	259	3-13	135	3-13	457	SIXTH		
Weekly	£3485	27	7-13	7	7-13				
Boarding	£3485	18	7-13	11	7-13				

ENTRY REQUIREMENTS Interview
SCHOLARSHIPS & BURSARIES Schol; Art; Mus; Forces
SPECIAL NEEDS beghijklqrstvwx ADGHIK   **DYSLEXIA**   **DIET** acd
ASSOCIATION IAPS   **FOUNDED** 1945   **RELIGIOUS AFFILIATION** Inter-denom

MAP 4 H 5
LOCATION Rural
DAY   RAIL a   AIR a
SPORT abcefgjklmopqsuwx AB
OTHER LANGUAGES a
ACTIVITIES acfghjmnopqtw
OTHER SUBJECTS bcfh
FACILITIES ON SITE abchjk
EXAM BOARDS
RETAKES   NVQ COURSES

OTHER: e g i lmno uv / B G K OP R / cdefg ij

Gb — Holy Trinity College; 81 Plaistow Lane; Bromley; Kent BR1 3LL
Tel: 0181 313 0399 (Fax: 0181 466 0151) *Mrs Doreen Bradshaw*

		Boys	Age	Girls	Age	TOTAL		Boys	Girls
Day	£1010-£1380	15	3-4	583	3-18	598	SIXTH		57
Weekly									
Boarding									

ENTRY REQUIREMENTS Report & Exam & Interview
SCHOLARSHIPS & BURSARIES Schol; Mus; VI Form
SPECIAL NEEDS alnqw   **DYSLEXIA** g   **DIET**
ASSOCIATION GSA   **FOUNDED** 1886   **RELIGIOUS AFFILIATION** R C

MAP 6 G 6
LOCATION Urban
DAY   RAIL a   AIR b
SPORT abcfhklmnpqwx ABC
OTHER LANGUAGES
ACTIVITIES cfghijknostw AB
OTHER SUBJECTS abcdfh
FACILITIES ON SITE adj
EXAM BOARDS abcd ABEHL
RETAKES   NVQ COURSES

A-level: cde g i l n p uv / B G K OP R U / c ef
AS: c / G / c ef
GCSE: de g i l n v / B G K OP R / cdef j
OTHER: l o / C E K O

160

KENT *continued*

Junior King's School; Milner Court; Sturry; Canterbury CT2 0AY
Tel: 01227 710245 (Fax: 01227 713171) *R.G.Barton*

		Boys	Age	Girls	Age	TOTAL		Boys	Girls
Day	£1100-£1970	130	4-13	71	4-13	263	SIXTH		
Weekly	£2820	10	8-13	8	8-13				
Boarding	£2820	32	8-13	12	8-13				

ENTRY REQUIREMENTS Report & Test
SCHOLARSHIPS & BURSARIES Burs
SPECIAL NEEDS abegjklnqtw Gl   **DYSLEXIA** e   **DIET** a
ASSOCIATION IAPS   **FOUNDED** 1879   **RELIGIOUS AFFILIATION** C of E

MAP 4 J 5
LOCATION Rural
DAY ✓   **RAIL** a   **AIR** b
SPORT adegjlmpqstuwx AB
OTHER LANGUAGES
ACTIVITIES acfghijmot A
OTHER SUBJECTS ch
FACILITIES ON SITE acj
EXAM BOARDS
RETAKES   **NVQ COURSES**

A-level
AS
GCSE
OTHER: d e g i l o v / B G K OP R / cde g j

Kent College Infant & Junior School; Vernon Holme; Harbledown; Canterbury CT2 9AQ
Tel: 01227 762436 *T.J.Smith*

		Boys	Age	Girls	Age	TOTAL		Boys	Girls
Day	£921-£1843	95	3-11	90	3-11	193	SIXTH		
Weekly	£2666		7-11		7-11				
Boarding	£2666	6	7-11	2	7-11				

ENTRY REQUIREMENTS Report; Assessment
SCHOLARSHIPS & BURSARIES Forces
SPECIAL NEEDS lnqw El   **DYSLEXIA** ce   **DIET** abcd
ASSOCIATION IAPS   **FOUNDED** 1947   **RELIGIOUS AFFILIATION** Methodist

MAP 4 J 5
LOCATION Rural
DAY ✓   **RAIL** a   **AIR** b
SPORT aefjmpqx AB
OTHER LANGUAGES a
ACTIVITIES acfghijoqtw A
OTHER SUBJECTS abcfh
FACILITIES ON SITE abcfhjk
EXAM BOARDS
RETAKES   **NVQ COURSES**

A-level
AS
GCSE
OTHER: e lm o v / B G / cde

Kent College Junior School; Aultmore House; Old Church Road; Pembury; Tunbridge Wells; Kent TN2 4AX
Tel: 01892 820204 (Fax: 01892 820221) *Mrs D.C.Dunham*

		Boys	Age	Girls	Age	TOTAL		Boys	Girls
Day	£945-£1455	132	3-11			138	SIXTH		
Weekly	£2425			3	7-11				
Boarding	£2756			3	7-11				

ENTRY REQUIREMENTS Test; Report & Interview
SCHOLARSHIPS & BURSARIES Clergy
SPECIAL NEEDS jnw BEl   **DYSLEXIA** ef   **DIET** acd
ASSOCIATION IAPS   **FOUNDED** 1886   **RELIGIOUS AFFILIATION** Methodist

MAP 4 H 5
LOCATION Rural
DAY ✓   **RAIL** a   **AIR** a
SPORT lmpqx AB
OTHER LANGUAGES
ACTIVITIES gjotx
OTHER SUBJECTS cfh
FACILITIES ON SITE bhi
EXAM BOARDS
RETAKES   **NVQ COURSES**

A-level
AS
GCSE
OTHER: e ln v / B G K O R / cde

Kent College; Canterbury; Kent CT2 9DT
Tel: 01227 763231 (Fax: 01227 764777) *E.B.Halse*

		Boys	Age	Girls	Age	TOTAL		Boys	Girls
Day	£1888	168	11-18	135	11-18	512	SIXTH	85	70
Weekly									
Boarding	£3366	132	11-18	77	11-18				

ENTRY REQUIREMENTS Report & Test
SCHOLARSHIPS & BURSARIES Schol; Burs; Mus; Forces; AP
SPECIAL NEEDS abefjklnpqtuw EGHI   **DYSLEXIA** cde   **DIET** abcd
ASSOCIATION HMC   **FOUNDED** 1885   **RELIGIOUS AFFILIATION** Methodist

MAP 4 K 5
LOCATION
DAY ✓   **RAIL** a   **AIR** b
SPORT abcefghjlmpqstwx ABC
OTHER LANGUAGES ac
ACTIVITIES cfghijknoprstvw AC
OTHER SUBJECTS bcfh
FACILITIES ON SITE cdefhjk
EXAM BOARDS abd BDH
RETAKES   **NVQ COURSES**

A-level: de ghi l opq v x / AB GH K P R U / cdefg j l
AS: de g opq tuvw / B G K PQ U / cdef j l
GCSE: de g i l opq v x / AB G K P RS U / cdefg j l
OTHER: mn s u / K NO

Kent College Pembury; Pembury; Tunbridge Wells; Kent TN2 4AX
Tel: 01892 822006 (Fax: 01892 820221) *Miss B.J.Crompton*

		Boys	Age	Girls	Age	TOTAL		Boys	Girls
Day	£2110-£2185			137	11-18	240	SIXTH		62
Weekly	£3276-£3426			30	11-18				
Boarding	£3528-£3678			73	11-18				

ENTRY REQUIREMENTS Report & Exam & Interview
SCHOLARSHIPS & BURSARIES Schol; Burs; Mus; Forces; Clergy; Teachers; VI Form; Drama
SPECIAL NEEDS behijklnpqstuvwx ABCDEGHIJK   **DYSLEXIA** ef   **DIET** abd
ASSOCIATION GSA   **FOUNDED** 1886   **RELIGIOUS AFFILIATION** Methodist

MAP 4 H 5
LOCATION Rural
DAY ✓   **RAIL** a   **AIR** a
SPORT abcdfhjlmpqtwx ABC
OTHER LANGUAGES a
ACTIVITIES acfghijklnoqstwx AB
OTHER SUBJECTS abcdefh
FACILITIES ON SITE bcdeghi
EXAM BOARDS abd ABDE
RETAKES a   **NVQ COURSES**

A-level: c eghi n p uv / BC GH K P R / c e
AS: efgh / G R T / e
GCSE: cde ghi no v / BC E G K P RT W / cdef j l
OTHER: l

KENT *continued*

King's Preparatory School; Rochester; King Edward Road; Rochester; Kent ME1 1UB
Tel: 01634 843657 (Fax: 01634 840569) *C.J.Nickless*

		Boys	Age	Girls	Age	TOTAL		Boys	Girls
Day	£1817-£2009	185	8-13	25	8-13	225			
Weekly	£3182-£3374				8-13				
Boarding	£3182-£3374	15	8-13		8-13		SIXTH		

MAP 4 I 4
LOCATION Urban
DAY **RAIL** a **AIR** b
SPORT abefgjkmpqsuwx B
OTHER LANGUAGES
ACTIVITIES cdfghijort A

ENTRY REQUIREMENTS Report & Exam & Interview
SCHOLARSHIPS & BURSARIES Schol; Chor; Clergy; AP
SPECIAL NEEDS w   **DYSLEXIA**   **DIET** ad
ASSOCIATION IAPS   **FOUNDED** 604   **RELIGIOUS AFFILIATION** C of E
OTHER SUBJECTS cfh
FACILITIES ON SITE bchjk
EXAM BOARDS
RETAKES   **NVQ COURSES**

A-level   **AS**   **GCSE**   **OTHER** e g i l   o   v
B E G K   OP R
cdef   j

King's School; Canterbury; Kent CT1 2ES
Tel: 01227 595501 (Fax: 01227 595595) *The Revd.Canon A.C.J.Phillips*

		Boys	Age	Girls	Age	TOTAL		Boys	Girls
Day	£2945	79	12-18	56	12-18	705	SIXTH	170	91
Weekly									
Boarding	£4265	356	12-18	214	12-18				

MAP 4 J 5
LOCATION Urban
DAY **RAIL** a **AIR** b
SPORT abcdefghjklmnoprstuwx AB
OTHER LANGUAGES i
ACTIVITIES bcefghijklorstvw

ENTRY REQUIREMENTS CEE
SCHOLARSHIPS & BURSARIES Schol; Burs; Art; Mus; Clergy
SPECIAL NEEDS jq   **DYSLEXIA**   **DIET** a
ASSOCIATION HMC   **FOUNDED** 1541   **RELIGIOUS AFFILIATION** C of E
OTHER SUBJECTS bcfh
FACILITIES ON SITE abcdhi
EXAM BOARDS abcd ABDEH
RETAKES   **NVQ COURSES**

A-level efg i   nop   uvwx
B   GH K   P R
c efgh jkl
AS c efg   l   o   vw
B   G K M   R
cdef   kl
GCSE e g i l   no   v
AB   G K   P R   WX
cdefgh jkl
OTHER

King's School Rochester; Satis House; Boley Hill; Rochester; Kent ME1 1TE
Tel: 01634 843913 (Fax: 01634 832493) *Dr I.R.Walker*

		Boys	Age	Girls	Age	TOTAL		Boys	Girls
Day	£2234	233	13-18	45	13-18	324	SIXTH	111	24
Weekly	£3894		13-18		13-18				
Boarding	£3894	45	13-18	1	13-18				

MAP 4 I 4
LOCATION Urban
DAY ✓ **RAIL** a **AIR** a
SPORT abcefghikmpqrstuwx ABC
OTHER LANGUAGES
ACTIVITIES defghijkoqst AB

ENTRY REQUIREMENTS CEE; Exam
SCHOLARSHIPS & BURSARIES Schol; Art; Mus; Chor; Clergy; AP
SPECIAL NEEDS aq   **DYSLEXIA**   **DIET** a
ASSOCIATION HMC   **FOUNDED** 604   **RELIGIOUS AFFILIATION** C of E
OTHER SUBJECTS bcdfh
FACILITIES ON SITE cdghjk
EXAM BOARDS abcde BDEH
RETAKES   **NVQ COURSES**

A-level e g i   op   uv
B   GH K   P R
cdef   j
AS   **GCSE** v
R
OTHER e g i l   o   vw
B   G K   P R
cdefgh jk
l

Marlborough House School; Hawkhurst; Kent TN18 4PY
Tel: 01580 753555 (Fax: 01580 754281) *D.N.Hopkins*

		Boys	Age	Girls	Age	TOTAL		Boys	Girls
Day	£595-£2235	89	3-13	69	3-13	193	SIXTH		
Weekly	£2915	20	6-13	5	6-13				
Boarding	£2935	9	6-13	1	6-13				

MAP 4 I 5
LOCATION Rural
DAY ✓ **RAIL** a **AIR** a
SPORT abcefjklmnopqstuwx AB
OTHER LANGUAGES a
ACTIVITIES abcfghijlmopqtw A

ENTRY REQUIREMENTS Interview
SCHOLARSHIPS & BURSARIES Forces; Clergy
SPECIAL NEEDS aegjkn AGI   **DYSLEXIA** e   **DIET** acd
ASSOCIATION IAPS   **FOUNDED** 1874   **RELIGIOUS AFFILIATION** C of E
OTHER SUBJECTS abcdfgh
FACILITIES ON SITE abcdhjkl
EXAM BOARDS
RETAKES   **NVQ COURSES**

A-level   **AS**   **GCSE**   **OTHER** d e g i lmno   s   v
ABC   G K   OP R
cde g j l

Mead School; 16 Frant Road; Tunbridge Wells; Kent TN2 5SN
Tel: 01892 525837 *Mrs A.Culley*

		Boys	Age	Girls	Age	TOTAL		Boys	Girls
Day	£480-£1160	67	3-11	79	3-11	146	SIXTH		
Weekly									
Boarding									

MAP 4 H 5
LOCATION Urban
DAY **RAIL** a **AIR** a
SPORT aefjlmpqx B
OTHER LANGUAGES
ACTIVITIES cgjo

ENTRY REQUIREMENTS
SCHOLARSHIPS & BURSARIES
SPECIAL NEEDS ln   **DYSLEXIA** g   **DIET** ab
ASSOCIATION ISAI   **FOUNDED** 1987   **RELIGIOUS AFFILIATION** Inter-denom
OTHER SUBJECTS acdh
FACILITIES ON SITE
EXAM BOARDS
RETAKES   **NVQ COURSES**

A-level   **AS**   **GCSE**   **OTHER**

162

KENT *continued*

B | New Beacon, The; Sevenoaks; Kent TN13 2PB
Tel: 01732 452131 (Fax: 01732 459509) *R.Constantine*

		Boys	Age	Girls	Age	TOTAL		Boys	Girls
Day	£845-£1490	355	4-13			372	SIXTH		
Weekly	£2360	17	9-13						
Boarding									

ENTRY REQUIREMENTS Interview
SCHOLARSHIPS & BURSARIES
SPECIAL NEEDS efjknqw Gl **DYSLEXIA** cef **DIET**
ASSOCIATION IAPS **FOUNDED** 1882 **RELIGIOUS AFFILIATION** C of E

MAP 4 H 5
LOCATION Rural
DAY   **RAIL** a   **AIR** a
SPORT abcejkosux AB
OTHER LANGUAGES
ACTIVITIES fghijow A
OTHER SUBJECTS
FACILITIES ON SITE bhik
EXAM BOARDS
RETAKES   **NVQ COURSES**

A-level | AS | GCSE | OTHER: B e G v cde j

C | Northbourne Park; Betteshanger; Deal; Kent CT14 0NW
Tel: 01304 611215 (Fax: 01304 619020) *F.W.Roche*

		Boys	Age	Girls	Age	TOTAL		Boys	Girls
Day	£1070-£1915	87	3-13	71	3-13	202	SIXTH		
Weekly	£2680		7-13		7-13				
Boarding	£2680	29	7-13	15	7-13				

ENTRY REQUIREMENTS Report & Interview
SCHOLARSHIPS & BURSARIES Schol; Burs; Art; Mus; Chor; Forces; Clergy; Sport
SPECIAL NEEDS abefjknqw Gl **DYSLEXIA**   **DIET** ad
ASSOCIATION IAPS **FOUNDED** 1980 **RELIGIOUS AFFILIATION** C of E

MAP 4 K 5
LOCATION Rural
DAY   **RAIL** b   **AIR** b
SPORT abcefgjkmpqstx AB
OTHER LANGUAGES
ACTIVITIES acfghjoqtw A
OTHER SUBJECTS abcdfh
FACILITIES ON SITE bcdhj
EXAM BOARDS
RETAKES   **NVQ COURSES**

A-level | AS | GCSE | OTHER: B e g i lm o v G K OP R cde j

C | Rose Hill School; Culverden Down; Tunbridge Wells; Kent TN4 9SY
Tel: 01892 525591 (Fax: 01892 533312) *J.G.L.Parker*

		Boys	Age	Girls	Age	TOTAL		Boys	Girls
Day	£580-£1880	133	3-14	61	3-14	194	SIXTH		
Weekly									
Boarding									

ENTRY REQUIREMENTS Report & Interview
SCHOLARSHIPS & BURSARIES Schol; Burs; Art; Mus; Chor; Teachers; Sport; ARA
SPECIAL NEEDS abdegijklnpqstuw ABGHIJKL **DYSLEXIA** e **DIET** abcd
ASSOCIATION IAPS **FOUNDED** 1832 **RELIGIOUS AFFILIATION** Inter-denom

MAP 4 H 5
LOCATION
DAY ✓   **RAIL** a   **AIR** a
SPORT abcefhjklmpqswx ABC
OTHER LANGUAGES
ACTIVITIES cfghijlnopqrstx A
OTHER SUBJECTS abcdfh
FACILITIES ON SITE abchjkl
EXAM BOARDS
RETAKES   **NVQ COURSES**

A-level | AS | GCSE | OTHER: de g i lmno q uv BC E G K OP RS cdefg j

C | Russell House School; Station Road; Otford; Sevenoaks; Kent TN14 5QU
Tel: 01959 522352 (Fax: 01959 524913) *Mrs E.N.Lindsay & A.Duffy*

		Boys	Age	Girls	Age	TOTAL		Boys	Girls
Day	£675-£1320	97	3-11	103	3-11	200	SIXTH		
Weekly									
Boarding									

ENTRY REQUIREMENTS Interview
SCHOLARSHIPS & BURSARIES
SPECIAL NEEDS   **DYSLEXIA**   **DIET** acd
ASSOCIATION IAPS **FOUNDED** 1938 **RELIGIOUS AFFILIATION** C of E

MAP 4 H 5
LOCATION Rural
DAY   **RAIL** b   **AIR** a
SPORT aejlopqx B
OTHER LANGUAGES
ACTIVITIES cfghjo
OTHER SUBJECTS bch
FACILITIES ON SITE ah
EXAM BOARDS
RETAKES   **NVQ COURSES**

A-level | AS | GCSE | OTHER: e lmo s v BC E G K O cde

C | Sackville School; Tonbridge Road; Hildenborough; Kent TN11 9HN
Tel: 01732 838888 (Fax: 01732 838688) *J.G.Langdale*

		Boys	Age	Girls	Age	TOTAL		Boys	Girls
Day	£1540-£1931	109	11-16	6	11-16	115	SIXTH		
Weekly									
Boarding									

ENTRY REQUIREMENTS CEE; Scholarship Exam; Test & Interview; Report & Test; Assessment & Interview; Report & Exam & Interview **SCHOLARSHIPS & BURSARIES** Schol; Burs; Art; Mus; Sport; ARA; Drama; Siblings **SPECIAL NEEDS** aenw BG **DYSLEXIA** e **DIET** a
ASSOCIATION ISAI **FOUNDED** 1987 **RELIGIOUS AFFILIATION** C of E

MAP 4 H 5
LOCATION Rural
DAY ✓   **RAIL** a   **AIR** a
SPORT abcefhjklmnpqsux ABC
OTHER LANGUAGES
ACTIVITIES afghijklmnoqt B
OTHER SUBJECTS abcfh
FACILITIES ON SITE ch
EXAM BOARDS abd
RETAKES a   **NVQ COURSES**

A-level | AS | GCSE: de ghij l o t v B G K OP R X cde | OTHER: X

163

KENT continued

St. Edmund's Junior School; Canterbury; Kent CT2 8HU
Tel: 01227 454575 (Fax: 01227 471083) *D.C.Gahan*

			Boys	Age	Girls	Age	TOTAL		Boys	Girls
Day	£1030-£1960	✗	95	4-13	62	4-13	220	SIXTH		
Weekly	£2805			7-13		10-13				
Boarding	£2770-£2805		56	7-13	7	10-13				

ENTRY REQUIREMENTS Test & Interview
SCHOLARSHIPS & BURSARIES Chor; Forces; Clergy; Siblings
SPECIAL NEEDS abegjklnqtw EG **DYSLEXIA** e **DIET** ad
ASSOCIATION IAPS **FOUNDED** 1749 **RELIGIOUS AFFILIATION** C of E

MAP 4 J 5
LOCATION Urban
DAY ✓ **RAIL** a **AIR** b
SPORT abcdefgjklmopqstuwx ABC
OTHER LANGUAGES
ACTIVITIES cfghijoqstv A
OTHER SUBJECTS bcdfh
FACILITIES ON SITE bcdhjkl
EXAM BOARDS
RETAKES **NVQ COURSES**

A-level	**AS**	**GCSE**	**OTHER**
		e g i l o uv
		ABC G K OP R
		cde j

St. Edmund's School; Canterbury CT2 8HU; Kent
Tel: 01227 454575 (Fax: 01227 471083) *A.N.Ridley*

			Boys	Age	Girls	Age	TOTAL		Boys	Girls
Day	£2620	✗	105	13-18	57	13-18	278	SIXTH	73	32
Weekly	£4010-£4120			13-18		13-18				
Boarding	£4010-£4120		85	13-18	31	13-18				

ENTRY REQUIREMENTS CEE; Test; Scholarship Exam; Report
SCHOLARSHIPS & BURSARIES Schol; Art; Mus; Forces; Clergy; VI Form; Sport; Siblings
SPECIAL NEEDS abegjlnqtw EG **DYSLEXIA** e **DIET** ad
ASSOCIATION HMC **FOUNDED** 1749 **RELIGIOUS AFFILIATION** C of E

MAP 4 J 5
LOCATION Urban
DAY **RAIL** a **AIR** b
SPORT abcdefghjkmopqtuvwx ABC
OTHER LANGUAGES ac
ACTIVITIES bdefgijkmopqstuv AB
OTHER SUBJECTS abcdfh
FACILITIES ON SITE bcdehjkl
EXAM BOARDS abcde ADEHL
RETAKES **NVQ COURSES**

A-level	**AS**	**GCSE**	**OTHER**
de ghi nop v x	GH	de l o t v	l n u
B GH K OP R		BC G K NO R X
cdef		cdef j l

St. Lawrence College Junior School; Ramsgate CT11 7AF
Tel: 01843 591788 (Fax: 01843 853271) *D.A.Heaton*

			Boys	Age	Girls	Age	TOTAL		Boys	Girls
Day	£800-£1830	✗	65	4-13	48	4-13	167	SIXTH		
Weekly	£2790			5-13		5-13				
Boarding	£2790		36	5-13	18	5-13				

ENTRY REQUIREMENTS Test; Report; Assessment; Test & Interview
SCHOLARSHIPS & BURSARIES Schol; Forces; Clergy
SPECIAL NEEDS jkn **DYSLEXIA** e **DIET** acd
ASSOCIATION IAPS **FOUNDED** 1884 **RELIGIOUS AFFILIATION** C of E

MAP 4 K 5
LOCATION
DAY **RAIL** a **AIR** b
SPORT abcefjlmopqsuwx AB
OTHER LANGUAGES a
ACTIVITIES cfghjorsw A
OTHER SUBJECTS ch
FACILITIES ON SITE bcdik
EXAM BOARDS
RETAKES **NVQ COURSES**

A-level	**AS**	**GCSE**	**OTHER**
		e g i l m o s v
		BC G K OP R
		cde g j

St. Lawrence College; Ramsgate CT11 7AE
Tel: 01843 592680 (Fax: 01843 851123) *J.H.Binfield*

			Boys	Age	Girls	Age	TOTAL		Boys	Girls
Day	£1830-£2485	✗	114	11-18	69	11-18	357	SIXTH	82	43
Weekly	£2790-£3720			11-18		11-18				
Boarding	£2790-£3720		114	11-18	60	11-18				

ENTRY REQUIREMENTS CEE; Test; Scholarship Exam; Test & Interview
SCHOLARSHIPS & BURSARIES Schol; Mus; Forces; Clergy; AP
SPECIAL NEEDS bejlnqsw AEGI **DYSLEXIA** f **DIET** a
ASSOCIATION HMC **FOUNDED** 1879 **RELIGIOUS AFFILIATION** C of E

MAP 4 K 5
LOCATION Urban
DAY **RAIL** a **AIR** b
SPORT acefjklmpqsuwx AB
OTHER LANGUAGES a
ACTIVITIES efghijklnorstuw
OTHER SUBJECTS bcefh
FACILITIES ON SITE abcdeghik
EXAM BOARDS abcd BEHL
RETAKES a **NVQ COURSES**

A-level	**AS**	**GCSE**	**OTHER**
cde g i op v	cde g i v	cde g i l o v	l q u x
B GH K P R U	GH K P R U	BC G K P R	o
c efg j l	c efg j l	cdefg j l	f h l

St. Mary's College; Ravenlea Road; Folkestone; Kent CT20 2JU
Tel: 01303 851363 *Sister B.Milligan*

			Boys	Age	Girls	Age	TOTAL		Boys	Girls
Day	£940-£1780		57	4-16	92	4-16	149	SIXTH		
Weekly										
Boarding										

ENTRY REQUIREMENTS Interview; Report & Interview
SCHOLARSHIPS & BURSARIES Schol; Mus
SPECIAL NEEDS nw B **DYSLEXIA** cef **DIET** ad
ASSOCIATION ISAI **FOUNDED** 1904 **RELIGIOUS AFFILIATION** R C

MAP 4 K 6
LOCATION Urban
DAY **RAIL** a **AIR** b
SPORT cehjlpqwx ABC
OTHER LANGUAGES a
ACTIVITIES fghjknt A
OTHER SUBJECTS cfh
FACILITIES ON SITE cd
EXAM BOARDS abde BEGKL
RETAKES a **NVQ COURSES**

A-level	**AS**	**GCSE**	**OTHER**
	d l no v
	BC E G K R
	cdef

KENT continued

C | St. Michael's; Otford Court; nr.Sevenoaks; Kent TN14 5SA
Tel: 01959 522137 (Fax: 01959 522137) *Simon Cummins*

	Fees		Boys	Age	Girls	Age	TOTAL		Boys	Girls
Day	£1085-£1502	✗	220	2-13	110	2-13	330	SIXTH		
Weekly										
Boarding										

ENTRY REQUIREMENTS Test & Interview
SCHOLARSHIPS & BURSARIES Schol; Art; Mus; Chor; Teachers; Sport
SPECIAL NEEDS abefjklnpquvw BEGI **DYSLEXIA** cde **DIET** abcd
ASSOCIATION IAPS **FOUNDED** 1872 **RELIGIOUS AFFILIATION** C of E

MAP 4 H 5
LOCATION Rural
DAY   **RAIL** a   **AIR** a
SPORT abcdefhjklmnopqstuwx ABC
OTHER LANGUAGES
ACTIVITIES acfghijlnopqstw A
OTHER SUBJECTS abcdfh
FACILITIES ON SITE bcdhi
EXAM BOARDS
RETAKES   **NVQ COURSES**

A-level   **AS**   **GCSE**   **OTHER** e g i lmno q uv
                                            B   G   K   OP R
                                            cde   j

B | St. Ronan's; Hawkhurst; Kent TN18 5DJ
Tel: 0158075 2271 *J.R.Vassar-Smith*

	Fees		Boys	Age	Girls	Age	TOTAL		Boys	Girls
Day	£555-£1985	✗	38	3-13	4	3-8	82	SIXTH		
Weekly	£2560		19	7-13						
Boarding	£2560		21	7-13						

ENTRY REQUIREMENTS Interview
SCHOLARSHIPS & BURSARIES
SPECIAL NEEDS n **DYSLEXIA** g **DIET**
ASSOCIATION IAPS **FOUNDED** 1883 **RELIGIOUS AFFILIATION** C of E

MAP 4 I 5
LOCATION Rural
DAY   **RAIL** b   **AIR** b
SPORT aefhjkmux AB
OTHER LANGUAGES
ACTIVITIES fghj
OTHER SUBJECTS c
FACILITIES ON SITE dhi
EXAM BOARDS
RETAKES   **NVQ COURSES**

A-level   **AS**   **GCSE**   **OTHER** e g i l   v
                                            B   G   P R
                                            cde g j

C | Sevenoaks Prep. School; Godden Green; Sevenoaks; Kent TN15 0JU
Tel: 01732 762336 (Fax: 01732 762336) *E.H.Oatley*

	Fees		Boys	Age	Girls	Age	TOTAL		Boys	Girls
Day	£500-£1400	✗	210	3-13	36	3-13	246	SIXTH		
Weekly										
Boarding										

ENTRY REQUIREMENTS
SCHOLARSHIPS & BURSARIES Teachers; Siblings
SPECIAL NEEDS bejnqtw GI **DYSLEXIA** cef **DIET** abcd
ASSOCIATION IAPS **FOUNDED** 1918 **RELIGIOUS AFFILIATION**

MAP 4 H 5
LOCATION Rural
DAY   **RAIL** a   **AIR** a
SPORT abcefjlmopqswx AB
OTHER LANGUAGES
ACTIVITIES cfghijloqrst A
OTHER SUBJECTS bcdefh
FACILITIES ON SITE bck
EXAM BOARDS
RETAKES   **NVQ COURSES**

A-level   **AS**   **GCSE**   **OTHER** e ghij lmnop   v
                                            B   G   K   OP R
                                            cde   j l

C | Sevenoaks School; Sevenoaks TN13 1HU
Tel: 01732 455133 (Fax: 01732 456143) *R.P.Barker*

	Fees		Boys	Age	Girls	Age	TOTAL		Boys	Girls
Day	£2358-£2628	✗	362	11-18	242	11-18	931	SIXTH	210	182
Weekly										
Boarding	£3873-£4143		161	11-18	166	11-18				

ENTRY REQUIREMENTS CEE; Scholarship Exam; Exam & Interview; Report & Interview
SCHOLARSHIPS & BURSARIES Schol; Mus; AP; VI Form; Sport; ARA
SPECIAL NEEDS bdeijkqsw GI **DYSLEXIA**   **DIET** acd
ASSOCIATION HMC **FOUNDED** 1432 **RELIGIOUS AFFILIATION** Inter-denom

MAP 4 H 5
LOCATION Rural
DAY ✓ **RAIL** a   **AIR** a
SPORT abcdefghjklmopqrstuwx ABC
OTHER LANGUAGES achk
ACTIVITIES bcefghijklnoqrstuw A
OTHER SUBJECTS bcdfh
FACILITIES ON SITE abcehjk
EXAM BOARDS abd BCEGH
RETAKES   **NVQ COURSES**

A-level cde ghi l nop   v
             AB   GH K M P   U
             cdefgh jkl
AS
GCSE cde g i l nop   v
          AB   GHI K M   P R U
          cdefghijkl
OTHER   m   q
                         o
                      i

Gb | Sibton Park Girls' Preparatory School; Sibton Park; Lyminge; nr.Folkestone; Kent CT18 8HB **Tel: 01303 862284 (Fax: 01303 863429)** *Mr & Mrs C.E.R.Blackwell*

	Fees		Boys	Age	Girls	Age	TOTAL		Boys	Girls
Day	£645-£1957	✗	16	1-8	44	1-13	101	SIXTH		
Weekly					4	7-13				
Boarding	£2288-£2995				37	7-13				

ENTRY REQUIREMENTS Test & Interview
SCHOLARSHIPS & BURSARIES Schol; Burs; Mus; Forces; Clergy; Teachers; Siblings
SPECIAL NEEDS abejklnoqtuw BE **DYSLEXIA** e **DIET** acd
ASSOCIATION IAPS **FOUNDED** 1948 **RELIGIOUS AFFILIATION** C of E

MAP 4 K 5
LOCATION Rural
DAY ✓ **RAIL** b   **AIR** b
SPORT acefhlmnopqux AB
OTHER LANGUAGES a
ACTIVITIES cfghijnoqwx A
OTHER SUBJECTS abcfh
FACILITIES ON SITE abchj
EXAM BOARDS
RETAKES   **NVQ COURSES**

A-level   **AS**   **GCSE**   **OTHER** cdefg i lmno q   v
                                            BC   G   K   OP R   W
                                            cdef   j

KENT continued

B | Solefield School; Sevenoaks; Kent TN13 1PH
Tel: 01732 452142 (Fax: 01732 740388) *J Baugh*

		Boys	Age	Girls	Age	TOTAL	SIXTH	Boys	Girls
Day	£820-£1395	200	4-13			200			
Weekly									
Boarding									

ENTRY REQUIREMENTS
SCHOLARSHIPS & BURSARIES Burs
SPECIAL NEEDS ejklnqw GI   **DYSLEXIA** e   **DIET** a
ASSOCIATION IAPS   **FOUNDED** 1948   **RELIGIOUS AFFILIATION** C of E

MAP 4 H 5
LOCATION Rural
DAY   **RAIL** a   **AIR** a
SPORT abcefjmoswx B
OTHER LANGUAGES
ACTIVITIES fghijlost A
OTHER SUBJECTS ch
FACILITIES ON SITE h
EXAM BOARDS
RETAKES   **NVQ COURSES**

A-level: efg i l q v B G K N P R cdefg j l
AS:
GCSE:
OTHER:

C | Sutton Valence School; Sutton Valence; Maidstone; Kent ME17 3HN;
Tel: 01622 842281 (Fax: 01622 844093) *N.Sampson*

		Boys	Age	Girls	Age	TOTAL	SIXTH	Boys	Girls
Day	£1750-£2365	281	3-18	241	3-18	636		74	49
Weekly			11-18		11-18				
Boarding	£3415-£3695	78	11-18	36	11-18				

ENTRY REQUIREMENTS CEE; Exam & Interview
SCHOLARSHIPS & BURSARIES Schol; Burs; Art; Mus; Forces; AP; VI Form; Sport; Siblings
SPECIAL NEEDS beinstuv EJ   **DYSLEXIA** ef   **DIET** a
ASSOCIATION HMC   **FOUNDED** 1576   **RELIGIOUS AFFILIATION** C of E

MAP 4 I 5
LOCATION Rural
DAY ✓   **RAIL** a   **AIR** a
SPORT abcefghijkmnopqstuwx ABC
OTHER LANGUAGES a
ACTIVITIES bcdefghijklnoqstw AB
OTHER SUBJECTS bcefgh
FACILITIES ON SITE abcdegjl
EXAM BOARDS abd ABDEH
RETAKES a   **NVQ COURSES**

A-level: cdefg i nop uv   BC GH K   P R   c ef j
AS: cde g i l   C GH K   ef
GCSE: uv   de g i l   op   v   BC   GH K   NOP R   X   cdef j l
OTHER: cdefg i l   o   v   BC G K   OP R   cdef j l

B | Tonbridge School; Tonbridge; Kent TN9 1JP
Tel: 01732 365555 (Fax: 01732 363424) *J.M.Hammond*

		Boys	Age	Girls	Age	TOTAL	SIXTH	Boys	Girls
Day	£3051 ✗	232	13-18			660		263	
Weekly									
Boarding	£4323	428	13-18						

ENTRY REQUIREMENTS CEE; Scholarship Exam
SCHOLARSHIPS & BURSARIES Schol; Art; Mus; Chor
SPECIAL NEEDS begjklnqstuw ADGHIK   **DYSLEXIA** g   **DIET** acd
ASSOCIATION HMC   **FOUNDED** 1553   **RELIGIOUS AFFILIATION** C of E

MAP 4 H 5
LOCATION
DAY   **RAIL** a   **AIR** a
SPORT abcdefghijkmorstuwx ABC
OTHER LANGUAGES
ACTIVITIES abdefghijklmnopqstuw ABC
OTHER SUBJECTS abcfh
FACILITIES ON SITE abcdegik
EXAM BOARDS abd ABEGH
RETAKES   **NVQ COURSES**

A-level: c e ghi l   p   v x   B   GH K   P R   c efg jkl
AS: c   l o q   G
GCSE: c e g i l no q   vw   BC G K   P R   cdefg ijkl
OTHER: ef   n   u   F K M O QR   a   f i

G | Ursuline College; 225 Canterbury Road; Westgate-on-Sea; Kent CT8 8LX
Tel: 01843 834431 (Fax: 01843 835365) *Sister Alice Montgomery*

		Boys	Age	Girls	Age	TOTAL	SIXTH	Boys	Girls
Day	£1785			116	11-18	216			47
Weekly	£2513			7					
Boarding	£3060-£3521			93	11-18				

ENTRY REQUIREMENTS Report & Exam & Interview
SCHOLARSHIPS & BURSARIES Forces; AP
SPECIAL NEEDS hjlnpqw Bl   **DYSLEXIA** de   **DIET** ab
ASSOCIATION GSA   **FOUNDED** 1904   **RELIGIOUS AFFILIATION** R C

MAP 4 K 4
LOCATION Rural
DAY ✓   **RAIL** a   **AIR** b
SPORT abclmopqwx ABC
OTHER LANGUAGES a
ACTIVITIES cfghijkortwx A
OTHER SUBJECTS bcefgh
FACILITIES ON SITE cdeg
EXAM BOARDS abcd ADEG
RETAKES   **NVQ COURSES**

A-level: c e ghi l   p   v   BC GH K   P   U W   cdef hj l
AS: e h G   e hj
GCSE: c e g i l   o   v   BC G K   OP R U WX   cdef h jkl
OTHER: l n   K

G | Walthamstow Hall; Hollybush Lane; Sevenoaks TN13 3UL
Tel: 01732 451334 (Fax: 01732 456156) *Mrs J.S.Lang*

		Boys	Age	Girls	Age	TOTAL	SIXTH	Boys	Girls
Day	£90-£2115			478	3-18	528			104
Weekly	£3185-£3925			13	8-18				
Boarding	£3185-£3925			37	8-18				

ENTRY REQUIREMENTS Report & Exam & Interview
SCHOLARSHIPS & BURSARIES Schol; Burs; Mus; Clergy; AP; VI Form
SPECIAL NEEDS bejlqt AGJL   **DYSLEXIA**   **DIET** ad
ASSOCIATION GSA   **FOUNDED** 1838   **RELIGIOUS AFFILIATION** Inter-denom

MAP 4 H 5
LOCATION Urban
DAY ✓   **RAIL** a   **AIR** a
SPORT abcfgklnopqwx ABC
OTHER LANGUAGES a
ACTIVITIES cfghijklnoqstw AB
OTHER SUBJECTS bcdfh
FACILITIES ON SITE gijk
EXAM BOARDS abd ABEGHJL
RETAKES   **NVQ COURSES**

A-level: cde g   i l n p s v x   BC   GH K   P R T   c efg jl
AS: cde g   c e
GCSE: s v   R   de ghi l n   v   BCD G K   OP R   X   cdefg j
OTHER: def   lmn q u   C   K MNO R   e h

KENT *continued*

C | **Wellesley House; Broadstairs; Kent CT10 2DG**
Tel: 01843 862991 (Fax: 01843 602068) *R.R.Steel*

		Boys	Age	Girls	Age	TOTAL		Boys	Girls
Day	£2150	4	7-13	6	7-13	162	SIXTH		
Weekly	£2850	12	7-13	7	7-13				
Boarding	£2950	95	7-13	38	7-13				

ENTRY REQUIREMENTS Assessment & Interview
SCHOLARSHIPS & BURSARIES Burs; Clergy; Teachers
SPECIAL NEEDS abegjklnpqtuvw BEGI
ASSOCIATION IAPS **FOUNDED** 1900 **RELIGIOUS AFFILIATION** C of E
DYSLEXIA e **DIET** acd

MAP 4 K 4
LOCATION Urban
DAY **RAIL** a **AIR** b
SPORT abcefgjklmpqsuwx AB
OTHER LANGUAGES f
ACTIVITIES bcfghijloqrtw A
OTHER SUBJECTS abcdfh
FACILITIES ON SITE bcdhik
EXAM BOARDS
RETAKES **NVQ COURSES**

A-level | AS | GCSE | OTHER: e g i lm o v / BC G K OP R / cdefg j

---

C | **Westbrook House; Shorncliffe Road; Folkestone CT20 2NQ**
Tel: 01303 851222 (Fax: 01303 249901) *S.M.Abbott*

		Boys	Age	Girls	Age	TOTAL		Boys	Girls
Day	£450-£1700	77	3-13	60	3-13	183	SIXTH		
Weekly	£2270		7-13		7-13				
Boarding	£2575	33	7-13	13	7-13				

ENTRY REQUIREMENTS Scholarship Exam; Assessment; Report & Test
SCHOLARSHIPS & BURSARIES Schol; Burs; Mus; Forces; Sport
SPECIAL NEEDS nw BI
ASSOCIATION IAPS **FOUNDED** 1893 **RELIGIOUS AFFILIATION** C of E
DYSLEXIA e **DIET** ad

MAP 4 K 6
LOCATION Urban
DAY **RAIL** a **AIR** b
SPORT abcefhjlmopqstx AB
OTHER LANGUAGES a
ACTIVITIES cghijost A
OTHER SUBJECTS bcfh
FACILITIES ON SITE bchjk
EXAM BOARDS
RETAKES **NVQ COURSES**

A-level | AS | GCSE | OTHER: de g i lm o s v / ABC G K OP R / cde j

---

G | **West Heath School; Sevenoaks TN13 1SR**
Tel: 01732 452541 (Fax: 01732 459359) *Mrs A.Williamson*

		Boys	Age	Girls	Age	TOTAL		Boys	Girls
Day	£2585			18	11-18	93	SIXTH		18
Weekly									
Boarding	£3680			75	11-18				

ENTRY REQUIREMENTS CEE; Assessment & Interview
SCHOLARSHIPS & BURSARIES Schol; VI Form
SPECIAL NEEDS abklnw I
ASSOCIATION GSA **FOUNDED** 1865 **RELIGIOUS AFFILIATION** C of E
DYSLEXIA **DIET** ab

MAP 4 H 5
LOCATION Rural
DAY **RAIL** a **AIR** a
SPORT acgklmnpqtwx ABC
OTHER LANGUAGES
ACTIVITIES cghijknoqstw AB
OTHER SUBJECTS abcefgh
FACILITIES ON SITE chi
EXAM BOARDS abcd ADGHI
RETAKES a **NVQ COURSES**

A-level: cdefghi l n p uv x / B GH K N P R T / cdefgh j l
AS: uv / G
GCSE: cde g i l n v / B E G K NOP R W / cdefgh j l
OTHER: m u / C NO

Bg | **Yardley Court Prep. School; Somerhill; Tonbridge; Kent TN11 0NJ**
Tel: 01732 35 2124 (Fax: 01732 363381) *A.M.Brooke*

		Boys	Age	Girls	Age	TOTAL		Boys	Girls
Day	£495-£1935	202	3-13	33	3-7	235	SIXTH		
Weekly									
Boarding									

ENTRY REQUIREMENTS Interview
SCHOLARSHIPS & BURSARIES Schol; Mus; Siblings
SPECIAL NEEDS n BI
ASSOCIATION IAPS **FOUNDED** 1898 **RELIGIOUS AFFILIATION** Christian
DYSLEXIA e **DIET** a

MAP 4 H 5
LOCATION Rural
DAY √ **RAIL** a **AIR** a
SPORT abcefjlmpqsx ABC
OTHER LANGUAGES
ACTIVITIES abfghijmnoprstw A
OTHER SUBJECTS cfh
FACILITIES ON SITE bj
EXAM BOARDS
RETAKES **NVQ COURSES**

A-level | AS | GCSE | OTHER: c e g i l no v / B G K OP R / cdef j l

---

C | **Arnold Junior School; Lytham Road; Blackpool FY4 1JG**
Tel: 01253 348314 (Fax: 01253 407245) *Miss J.E.Hilton*

		Boys	Age	Girls	Age	TOTAL		Boys	Girls
Day	£840-£961	169	4-11	145	4-11	315	SIXTH		
Weekly		1							
Boarding									

ENTRY REQUIREMENTS Exam & Interview
SCHOLARSHIPS & BURSARIES Schol
SPECIAL NEEDS
ASSOCIATION IAPS **FOUNDED** 1896 **RELIGIOUS AFFILIATION** Inter-denom
DYSLEXIA **DIET** acd

MAP 11 C 6
LOCATION Urban
DAY **RAIL** a **AIR** b
SPORT acejlpqsx
OTHER LANGUAGES
ACTIVITIES cfghjqrw
OTHER SUBJECTS ch
FACILITIES ON SITE a
EXAM BOARDS
RETAKES **NVQ COURSES**

A-level | AS | GCSE | OTHER: e lm v / BC G O R / cde

LANCS

LANCASHIRE continued

C — Arnold School; Lytham Road; Blackpool FY4 1JG
Tel: 01253 346391 (Fax: 01253 407245) *W.T.Gillen*

		Boys	Age	Girls	Age	TOTAL		Boys	Girls
Day	£1245	425	11-18	366	11-18	834	SIXTH	129	84
Weekly	£2341	4	11-18	1	11-18				
Boarding	£2510	26	11-18	12	11-18				

MAP11 C 6
LOCATION Urban
DAY ✓ **AIR** b

SPORT acefklmopqstuwx AB
OTHER LANGUAGES
ACTIVITIES cefghijknopqrstw AB

ENTRY REQUIREMENTS CEE; Exam
SCHOLARSHIPS & BURSARIES Schol; Mus; AP; VI Form
SPECIAL NEEDS bjlnw
ASSOCIATION HMC **FOUNDED** 1896 **RELIGIOUS AFFILIATION** C of E
DYSLEXIA   **DIET** acd
OTHER SUBJECTS bcdefgh
FACILITIES ON SITE acdg
EXAM BOARDS cd ADGI
RETAKES a **NVQ COURSES** 1

A-level: cde ghi l op uvw / ABC FGH K N P W / cdef j
AS: G / ef
GCSE: u / de ghi lmnopq v / ABC G K N PQ W / cdefg j l
OTHER:

B — Bolton School (Boys Div.); Chorley New Road; Bolton BL1 4PA
Tel: 01204 840201 (Fax: 01204 849477) *A.W.Wright*

		Boys	Age	Girls	Age	TOTAL		Boys	Girls
Day	£1075-£1492 ✗	1008	8-18			1008	SIXTH	219	
Weekly									
Boarding									

MAP11 E 7
LOCATION Urban
DAY **RAIL** a **AIR** a

SPORT abcdefhjklmstx ABC
OTHER LANGUAGES
ACTIVITIES afghijknoqstux AB

ENTRY REQUIREMENTS Report & Exam & Interview
SCHOLARSHIPS & BURSARIES Burs; Mus; AP; VI Form
SPECIAL NEEDS bejklnq GIL
ASSOCIATION HMC **FOUNDED** 1524 **RELIGIOUS AFFILIATION** Non-denom
DYSLEXIA g **DIET** abcd
OTHER SUBJECTS abcfh
FACILITIES ON SITE bcghik
EXAM BOARDS bcd ABDE
RETAKES **NVQ COURSES**

A-level: c e ghi op uv / B GH K P R U / cdefg jk
AS: l q / K / ef
GCSE: e gi n p v / B G K P / cdefg jk
OTHER: c e f h l n o q s x / A K MNO R / hi l

Gb — Bolton School (Girls Div.); Chorley New Road; Bolton BL1 4PB
Tel: 01204 840201 (Fax: 01204 849477) *Miss E.J.Panton*

		Boys	Age	Girls	Age	TOTAL		Boys	Girls
Day	£1075-£1492 ✗	101	4-7	1061	4-18	1162	SIXTH		209
Weekly									
Boarding									

MAP11 E 7
LOCATION Urban
DAY ✓ **RAIL** b **AIR** a

SPORT abcdfhjklnopqtwx BC
OTHER LANGUAGES
ACTIVITIES cghijknopqt B

ENTRY REQUIREMENTS Exam & Interview
SCHOLARSHIPS & BURSARIES Schol; Burs; Mus; Teachers; AP; VI Form
SPECIAL NEEDS
ASSOCIATION GSA **FOUNDED** 1877 **RELIGIOUS AFFILIATION** Inter-denom
DYSLEXIA   **DIET** a
OTHER SUBJECTS bcdfh
FACILITIES ON SITE bchik
EXAM BOARDS bcd ABDEHL
RETAKES **NVQ COURSES**

A-level: cd ghi l op uv / BC GH K P R W / cdefg j l
AS: h / ef l
GCSE: d l no v / BC G K O R WX / cdefg j l
OTHER: m / o

B — Bury Grammar School; Tenterden Street; Bury BL9 0HN
Tel: 0161 797 2700 (Fax: 0161 763 4655) *K.Richards*

		Boys	Age	Girls	Age	TOTAL		Boys	Girls
Day	£879-£1234	850	7-18			850	SIXTH	160	
Weekly									
Boarding									

MAP11 E 7
LOCATION Urban
DAY **RAIL** b **AIR** a

SPORT abcefjmsux AB
OTHER LANGUAGES
ACTIVITIES efghijloqtu BD

ENTRY REQUIREMENTS Exam & Interview
SCHOLARSHIPS & BURSARIES Schol; Burs; AP
SPECIAL NEEDS abghjklpqstu DHI
ASSOCIATION HMC **FOUNDED** 1634 **RELIGIOUS AFFILIATION** Non-denom
DYSLEXIA   **DIET**
OTHER SUBJECTS bcfh
FACILITIES ON SITE abcghi
EXAM BOARDS bcd BDH
RETAKES **NVQ COURSES**

A-level: cd ghi l p uvwx / B GH K P R / c efg j
AS: G
GCSE: cd ghi l v / B G K P R / cdefg j l
OTHER: o / o / d

Gb — Bury Grammar School (Girls); Bridge Road; Bury BL9 0HH
Tel: 0161 797 2808 (Fax: 0161 763 4658) *Miss J.M.Lawley*

		Boys	Age	Girls	Age	TOTAL		Boys	Girls
Day	£840-£1234	70	4-7	1042	4-18	1112	SIXTH		206
Weekly									
Boarding									

MAP11 E 7
LOCATION Urban
DAY **RAIL** a **AIR** a

SPORT abcdhklmopqrwx ABC
OTHER LANGUAGES
ACTIVITIES cfghijnos ABD

ENTRY REQUIREMENTS Exam & Interview
SCHOLARSHIPS & BURSARIES AP; VI Form
SPECIAL NEEDS bgjlnq
ASSOCIATION GSA **FOUNDED** 1884 **RELIGIOUS AFFILIATION**
DYSLEXIA   **DIET**
OTHER SUBJECTS abcdfo
FACILITIES ON SITE bcghi
EXAM BOARDS abce BDHK
RETAKES **NVQ COURSES**

A-level: cd g il op uv x / BC GH KM P R U / cdef j
AS: l p / C G KM R U / def
GCSE: d g il o v / BC E G K P R W / cdef hj l
OTHER: e m q / o / kl

LANCASHIRE *continued*

G — Elmslie Girls School; 194 Whitegate Drive; Blackpool; Lancs FY3 9HL
Tel: 01253 763775 *Miss E.M.Smithies*

		Boys	Age	Girls	Age	TOTAL	SIXTH	Boys	Girls
Day	£815-£1295	4	3-7	251	3-18	255			19
Weekly									
Boarding									

MAP11 C 6
LOCATION Urban
DAY ✓ **RAIL** b **AIR** c
SPORT aceflmpqvwx B
OTHER LANGUAGES
ACTIVITIES cghijkoqt ABD
OTHER SUBJECTS acefgh
FACILITIES ON SITE dg
EXAM BOARDS ce ABDE
RETAKES   **NVQ COURSES**

ENTRY REQUIREMENTS Exam; Scholarship Exam
SCHOLARSHIPS & BURSARIES Schol; Burs; Mus; Teachers
SPECIAL NEEDS   **DYSLEXIA**   **DIET**
ASSOCIATION GSA   **FOUNDED** 1918   **RELIGIOUS AFFILIATION** C of E

A-level: efg i   o   uv
BC GH K   P R U W
c ef   j
AS: u
e
GCSE: efg i   o   v
BC   G K   OP R   W
cdef   j
OTHER: h l

C — Highfield Priory School; Fulwood Row; Preston; Lancs. PR2 6SL
Tel: 01772 709624 (Fax: 01772 709624) *B.C.Duckett*

		Boys	Age	Girls	Age	TOTAL	SIXTH	Boys	Girls
Day	£887 ✗	156	3-11	157	3-11	313			
Weekly									
Boarding									

MAP11 D 6
LOCATION Rural
DAY ✓ **RAIL** a **AIR** a
SPORT acefjlmpqsx AB
OTHER LANGUAGES
ACTIVITIES acfghjoqst A
OTHER SUBJECTS cfh
FACILITIES ON SITE ah
EXAM BOARDS
RETAKES   **NVQ COURSES**

ENTRY REQUIREMENTS Test & Interview
SCHOLARSHIPS & BURSARIES
SPECIAL NEEDS bjt   **DYSLEXIA**   **DIET** ad
ASSOCIATION ISAI   **FOUNDED** 1940   **RELIGIOUS AFFILIATION** Inter-denom

A-level:
AS:
GCSE:
OTHER: e   lmn   v
B   G K   O R
cde

G — Hulme Grammar School for Girls; Chamber Road; Oldham OL8 4BX
Tel: 0161 624 2523 (Fax: 0161 620 0234) *Miss M.S.Smolenski*

		Boys	Age	Girls	Age	TOTAL	SIXTH	Boys	Girls
Day	£845-£1183			620	7-18	620			114
Weekly									
Boarding									

MAP11 F 8
LOCATION Urban
DAY   **RAIL** a **AIR** a
SPORT abcdflmpqx ABC
OTHER LANGUAGES
ACTIVITIES fghijklnopqt AB
OTHER SUBJECTS abcdfh
FACILITIES ON SITE aghi
EXAM BOARDS ac DEL
RETAKES   **NVQ COURSES**

ENTRY REQUIREMENTS Exam & Interview
SCHOLARSHIPS & BURSARIES Burs; AP
SPECIAL NEEDS bl A   **DYSLEXIA**   **DIET** a
ASSOCIATION GSA   **FOUNDED** 1895   **RELIGIOUS AFFILIATION** Non-denom

A-level: c e ghi   op   uv x
BC   GH K   P R
cdefg   j
AS: g   p
BC   G K   R
def
GCSE: c e g i   o   vw
BC   G K   P R
cdefg   j
OTHER: l

B — Hulme Grammar School; Chamber Road; Oldham; Lancs. OL8 4BX
Tel: 0161 624 4497 (Fax: 0161 652 4107) *G.F.Dunkin*

		Boys	Age	Girls	Age	TOTAL	SIXTH	Boys	Girls
Day	£834-£1170	808	7-18			808		171	
Weekly									
Boarding									

MAP11 F 8
LOCATION Urban
DAY   **RAIL** a **AIR** a
SPORT abcdefjklmuwx AB
OTHER LANGUAGES
ACTIVITIES efghijklqrst
OTHER SUBJECTS bcfh
FACILITIES ON SITE acghi
EXAM BOARDS abc DHL
RETAKES   **NVQ COURSES**

ENTRY REQUIREMENTS Exam & Interview; Report & Interview
SCHOLARSHIPS & BURSARIES Schol; Burs; AP
SPECIAL NEEDS   **DYSLEXIA**   **DIET** abcd
ASSOCIATION HMC   **FOUNDED** 1611   **RELIGIOUS AFFILIATION** Non-denom

A-level: c e ghi   op   uv x
AB   GH K MN P R U
c ef   j
AS: AB   G
GCSE: c e ghi   o   v x
AB   G K   P R U
cdef   j l
OTHER: f   l   x
B   G K M O
g

B — King Edward VII School; Lytham; Lancs. FY8 1DT
Tel: 01253 736459 (Fax: 01253 731623) *P.J.Wilde*

		Boys	Age	Girls	Age	TOTAL	SIXTH	Boys	Girls
Day	£820-£1230	530	3-18	70	3-11	600		100	
Weekly									
Boarding									

MAP11 C 7
LOCATION Urban
DAY ✓ **RAIL** a **AIR** b
SPORT abcdefhjklmstuvwx AB
OTHER LANGUAGES
ACTIVITIES afghijkmopqstw AB
OTHER SUBJECTS abcfh
FACILITIES ON SITE bcgh
EXAM BOARDS c ABDEG
RETAKES ab   **NVQ COURSES**

ENTRY REQUIREMENTS Exam & Interview
SCHOLARSHIPS & BURSARIES Schol; Burs; Mus; AP
SPECIAL NEEDS bjn   **DYSLEXIA**   **DIET**
ASSOCIATION HMC   **FOUNDED** 1908   **RELIGIOUS AFFILIATION** Inter-denom

A-level: d ghi   nop   uv x
B   GH K   P R U
c ef
AS: g   l o
B
ef
GCSE: d g i l   o   v
B   G K   P R
cdef   j
OTHER: l
k

LANCASHIRE *continued*

C — **Kirkham Grammar School; Ribby Road; Kirkham; Preston; Lancs PR4 2BH**
Tel: 01772 671079 (Fax: 01772 672747) *B.Stacey*

		Boys	Age	Girls	Age	TOTAL		Boys	Girls
Day	£925-£1225	359	4-18	312	4-18	742	SIXTH	60	64
Weekly	£2270	9	11-18	6	11-18				
Boarding	£2325	28	11-18	28	11-18				

ENTRY REQUIREMENTS Exam; Scholarship Exam
SCHOLARSHIPS & BURSARIES Schol; Burs; Mus; AP; VI Form; Siblings
SPECIAL NEEDS bl EG   **DYSLEXIA**   **DIET** a
ASSOCIATION SHMIS   **FOUNDED** 1549   **RELIGIOUS AFFILIATION** Non-denom

MAP 1 D 6
LOCATION Rural
DAY ✓   **RAIL** b   **AIR** b
SPORT abcefhklmpqsuwx BC
OTHER LANGUAGES
ACTIVITIES efghijoqs AB
OTHER SUBJECTS bcdh
FACILITIES ON SITE abcgh
EXAM BOARDS acd ADEH
RETAKES ab   **NVQ COURSES**

A-level: d ghi no uv x / AB GH K P R U / c ef
AS: B g / ef
GCSE: d ghi l no v / AB E G K P R / cdef
OTHER:

C — **Moorland School; Ribblesdale Avenue; Clitheroe; Lancs. BB7 2JA**
Tel: 01200 23833 (Fax: 01200 29339) *Mrs J.E.Harrison*

		Boys	Age	Girls	Age	TOTAL		Boys	Girls
Day	£660-£1116	61	2-16	68	2-16	164	SIXTH		
Weekly	£2323-£2441	1	7-16		7-16				
Boarding	£2353-£2471	19	7-16	15	7-16				

ENTRY REQUIREMENTS Report & Test
SCHOLARSHIPS & BURSARIES Forces
SPECIAL NEEDS   **DYSLEXIA**   **DIET** abd
ASSOCIATION ISAI   **FOUNDED** 1912   **RELIGIOUS AFFILIATION** Inter-denom

MAP11 E 6
LOCATION Rural
DAY ✓   **RAIL** b   **AIR** b
SPORT acdefhjlmopqwx ABC
OTHER LANGUAGES a
ACTIVITIES acfghijlmqwx A
OTHER SUBJECTS bch
FACILITIES ON SITE bch
EXAM BOARDS abcd ABE
RETAKES a   **NVQ COURSES**

A-level:
AS:
GCSE: e g i l o q v / BC G P / bcdef
OTHER:

Bg — **Queen Elizabeth's Grammar School; Blackburn BB2 6DF;**
Tel: 01254 59911 (Fax: 01254 692314) *D.S.Hempsall*

		Boys	Age	Girls	Age	TOTAL		Boys	Girls
Day	£1040-£1314	1084	8-18	48	16-18	1132	SIXTH	247	48
Weekly									
Boarding									

ENTRY REQUIREMENTS Exam
SCHOLARSHIPS & BURSARIES Burs; AP
SPECIAL NEEDS bijstu G   **DYSLEXIA**   **DIET** abcd
ASSOCIATION HMC   **FOUNDED** 1509   **RELIGIOUS AFFILIATION** C of E

MAP11 E 7
LOCATION Urban
DAY ✓   **RAIL** a   **AIR** a
SPORT abcefhjkmpstwx B
OTHER LANGUAGES
ACTIVITIES fghijklnopqstx AB
OTHER SUBJECTS bcf
FACILITIES ON SITE aghik
EXAM BOARDS abcde ABDHIL
RETAKES   **NVQ COURSES**

A-level: c eghij l op uv x / AB GH K P R / cdefg j
AS:
GCSE: c eghij l nop vwx / AB G K OP R / cdefgh j l
OTHER: kl

Gb — **Queen Mary School; Lytham; Lancs FY8 1DS**
Tel: 01253 723246 (Fax: 01253 781766) *Miss M.C.Ritchie*

		Boys	Age	Girls	Age	TOTAL		Boys	Girls
Day	£820-£1230	100	3-10	592	3-18	692	SIXTH		101
Weekly									
Boarding									

ENTRY REQUIREMENTS Exam
SCHOLARSHIPS & BURSARIES Schol; Burs; Mus; AP
SPECIAL NEEDS   **DYSLEXIA**   **DIET**
ASSOCIATION GSA   **FOUNDED** 1930   **RELIGIOUS AFFILIATION**

MAP11 C 7
LOCATION Urban
DAY   **RAIL** a   **AIR** b
SPORT aceflmpx B
OTHER LANGUAGES
ACTIVITIES cfghijknot AB
OTHER SUBJECTS c
FACILITIES ON SITE bcgh
EXAM BOARDS cd ABD
RETAKES   **NVQ COURSES**

A-level: egil no uv x / B GH K P R / cdef j l
AS: l / C G
GCSE: egil no vw / BC G K OP R / cdef j l
OTHER:

C — **Rossall Preparatory School; Fleetwood; Lancs. FY7 8JW**
Tel: 01253 774222 (Fax: 01253 774248) *A.N.Rostron*

		Boys	Age	Girls	Age	TOTAL		Boys	Girls
Day	£880-£900	122	2-11	104	2-11	267	SIXTH		
Weekly	£2570	7	7-11	1	7-11				
Boarding	£2570	18	7-11	15	7-11				

ENTRY REQUIREMENTS Test & Interview
SCHOLARSHIPS & BURSARIES
SPECIAL NEEDS ejklnpqtuw BGI   **DYSLEXIA** e   **DIET** abcd
ASSOCIATION IAPS   **FOUNDED** 1861   **RELIGIOUS AFFILIATION** C of E

MAP11 C 6
LOCATION Urban
DAY   **RAIL** a   **AIR** b
SPORT abcefjklmpqstuwx AB
OTHER LANGUAGES
ACTIVITIES acfghijoqtw A
OTHER SUBJECTS abcfh
FACILITIES ON SITE abcdehik
EXAM BOARDS
RETAKES   **NVQ COURSES**

A-level:
AS:
GCSE:
OTHER: c egi lmno uv / B G K OP R / cde j

LANCASHIRE continued

C | Rossall School; Fleetwood; Lancs FY7 8JW
Tel: 01253 774201 (Fax: 01253 772052) *R.D.W.Rhodes*

		Boys	Age	Girls	Age	TOTAL		Boys	Girls
Day	£1400	64	11-19	54	11-19	411	SIXTH	92	50
Weekly			11-19		11-19				
Boarding	£2570-£3800	198	11-19	95	11-19				

ENTRY REQUIREMENTS CEE; Exam; Scholarship Exam; Report & Exam & Interview
SCHOLARSHIPS & BURSARIES Schol; Burs; Art; Mus; Forces; Clergy; AP; VI Form
SPECIAL NEEDS bjklnqw BGI **DYSLEXIA** cef **DIET** abcd
ASSOCIATION HMC **FOUNDED** 1844 **RELIGIOUS AFFILIATION** C of E

MAP11 C 6
LOCATION Rural
DAY ✓ **RAIL** a **AIR** a
SPORT abcdefghijkmopstuvwx BC
OTHER LANGUAGES a
ACTIVITIES abcefghijklmnoqrtw A
OTHER SUBJECTS abcdefh
FACILITIES ON SITE abcdeghik
EXAM BOARDS b HL
RETAKES ab **NVQ COURSES**

A-level: c e ghi op uv / BC GH K OP R / c ef j
AS: h l
GCSE: P / e ghi l nop v / BC G K OP R / cdef j
OTHER:

B | St. Mary's Hall; Stonyhurst; Lancs BB7 9PU
Tel: 01254 826 242 (Fax: 01254 826 382) *R.F.O'Brien*

		Boys	Age	Girls	Age	TOTAL		Boys	Girls
Day	£1269-£1830	99	7-13			173	SIXTH		
Weekly									
Boarding	£2581	74	7-13						

ENTRY REQUIREMENTS Test & Interview
SCHOLARSHIPS & BURSARIES Burs; Forces; AP
SPECIAL NEEDS abjklnpqtvw BGHI **DYSLEXIA** e **DIET** a
ASSOCIATION IAPS **FOUNDED** 1946 **RELIGIOUS AFFILIATION** R C

MAP11 E 6
LOCATION Rural
DAY **RAIL** b **AIR** b
SPORT abcefhjklsuwx ABC
OTHER LANGUAGES
ACTIVITIES afghijlmoqrstvw A
OTHER SUBJECTS acfh
FACILITIES ON SITE cdefhik
EXAM BOARDS
RETAKES **NVQ COURSES**

A-level:
AS:
GCSE:
OTHER: e g i l no s v / B G I K OP R / cde g j

C | St. Pius X Preparatory School; 200 Garstang Road; Fulwood; Preston PR2 8RD
Tel: 01772 719937 (Fax: 01772 787535) *Miss B.Banks*

		Boys	Age	Girls	Age	TOTAL		Boys	Girls
Day	£790-£893	159	3-11	167	3-11	326	SIXTH		
Weekly									
Boarding									

ENTRY REQUIREMENTS Exam; Assessment
SCHOLARSHIPS & BURSARIES
SPECIAL NEEDS abjklnqsuw ABGI **DYSLEXIA** g **DIET** abcd
ASSOCIATION IAPS **FOUNDED** 1955 **RELIGIOUS AFFILIATION** R C

MAP11 D 6
LOCATION
DAY **RAIL** b **AIR** a
SPORT aefjlmpqsx AB
OTHER LANGUAGES
ACTIVITIES cfghj
OTHER SUBJECTS ch
FACILITIES ON SITE bch
EXAM BOARDS
RETAKES **NVQ COURSES**

A-level:
AS:
GCSE:
OTHER: e lmno s v / AB G K O R / cde

C | Scarisbrick Hall School; Ormskirk; Lancs. L40 9RQ
Tel: 01704 880200 (Fax: 01704 880032) *D.M.Raynor*

		Boys	Age	Girls	Age	TOTAL		Boys	Girls
Day	£593-£894	260	3-18	266	3-18	526	SIXTH	15	13
Weekly									
Boarding									

ENTRY REQUIREMENTS Exam
SCHOLARSHIPS & BURSARIES Schol; VI Form; Siblings
SPECIAL NEEDS abln GL **DYSLEXIA** g **DIET** abcd
ASSOCIATION ISAI **FOUNDED** 1964 **RELIGIOUS AFFILIATION** Inter-denom/Evang

MAP11 D 7
LOCATION Rural
DAY ✓ **RAIL** b **AIR** a
SPORT abcefghjlmpqswx ABC
OTHER LANGUAGES
ACTIVITIES fghijos A
OTHER SUBJECTS c
FACILITIES ON SITE abdj
EXAM BOARDS abc DEI
RETAKES b **NVQ COURSES**

A-level: e g i uv / B GH K P R U / c ef
AS: G / e
GCSE: de g / B E G K P R / cdef j
OTHER: l / o

Bg | Stonyhurst College; Stonyhurst; Clitheroe; Lancs BB7 9PZ
Tel: 01254 826345 (Fax: 01254 826732) *Dr R.G.G.Mercer*

		Boys	Age	Girls	Age	TOTAL		Boys	Girls
Day	£2375	56	13-18	3	17-18	391	SIXTH	151	5
Weekly									
Boarding	£3824	330	13-18	2					

ENTRY REQUIREMENTS CEE
SCHOLARSHIPS & BURSARIES Schol; Burs; Mus; AP
SPECIAL NEEDS befgklnqtvwx ACGI **DYSLEXIA** ef **DIET** a
ASSOCIATION HMC **FOUNDED** 1593 **RELIGIOUS AFFILIATION** R C

MAP11 E 6
LOCATION Rural
DAY **RAIL** b **AIR** b
SPORT abcdefgijkmostuwx AB
OTHER LANGUAGES a
ACTIVITIES abefghijklmopqt
OTHER SUBJECTS cfh
FACILITIES ON SITE bcehikl
EXAM BOARDS abcde ABDEGH
RETAKES **NVQ COURSES**

A-level: cde g i op vwx / B GH K P R / cdefghij l
AS:
GCSE: R / cd g i o v / B G K PQR / cdefg j l
OTHER: l

LANCASHIRE continued

Gb Westholme School; Meins Road; Blackburn BB2 6QU
Tel: 01254 53447 (Fax: 01254 681459) *Mrs L.Croston*

	Boys	Age	Girls	Age	TOTAL		Boys	Girls
Day £835-£1175	84	4-8	925	4-18	1009	SIXTH		117
Weekly								
Boarding								

MAP 11 E 7
LOCATION Rural
DAY   **RAIL** b   **AIR** a
SPORT abcfhjklmopqvwx ABC
OTHER LANGUAGES
ACTIVITIES cdfghijklnopqsvw ABD
OTHER SUBJECTS abcdh
FACILITIES ON SITE abcghi
EXAM BOARDS c ADEG
RETAKES ab   **NVQ COURSES** 1

ENTRY REQUIREMENTS Exam; Interview; Report
SCHOLARSHIPS & BURSARIES Burs; Teachers; AP
SPECIAL NEEDS bfjklnw GL
ASSOCIATION GSA   **FOUNDED** 1923   **RELIGIOUS AFFILIATION** Inter-denom
DYSLEXIA g   **DIET** ad

A-level   c efg i l   op   uv
     BC   GH   K   PQR TU W
     cdef   j l

AS   G   K
     ef

GCSE   c e g i   lmnop   v
     BC EFG   K   PQR   U W
     cdef   j l

OTHER   de g i   lmno q   v
     BC   G   JK   NOP R   W
     cdefg   j l

LEICESTERSHIRE

C Dixie Grammar & Wolstan Prep Schools; Market Bosworth; Nuneaton; Warks. CV13 0LE
Tel: 01455 292244 (Fax: 01455 292151) *R.S.Willmott*

	Boys	Age	Girls	Age	TOTAL		Boys	Girls
Day £860-£1150	230	4-18	199	4-18	429	SIXTH	12	11
Weekly								
Boarding								

MAP 9 C 6
LOCATION Rural
DAY ✓   **RAIL** b   **AIR** a
SPORT acefjlmpqswx BC
OTHER LANGUAGES
ACTIVITIES cfghijklnops AB
OTHER SUBJECTS abcdfh
FACILITIES ON SITE bc
EXAM BOARDS abc ABDE
RETAKES a   **NVQ COURSES**

ENTRY REQUIREMENTS Exam; Test & Interview
SCHOLARSHIPS & BURSARIES Schol; Burs; Mus; VI Form; Siblings
SPECIAL NEEDS
ASSOCIATION ISAI   **FOUNDED** 1987   **RELIGIOUS AFFILIATION** Non-denom
DYSLEXIA   **DIET** a

A-level   d ghi l   o   uv
     BC   GH K   P
     c ef   j

AS   d ghi l   o   v
     BC   G   K   P
     c ef j

GCSE   d g i l   o   v
     BC E G   K   P
     cdef j

OTHER   c   lmn   q
     C   G   K   O   R

C Fairfield School; Leicester Road; Loughborough; Leics. LE11 2AE
Tel: 01509 215172 (Fax: 01509 210486) *T.A.Eadon*

	Boys	Age	Girls	Age	TOTAL		Boys	Girls
Day £1032	266	4-11	210	4-11	476	SIXTH		
Weekly								
Boarding								

MAP 9 C 5
LOCATION Urban
DAY ✓   **RAIL** a   **AIR** a
SPORT acefjlmpqx BC
OTHER LANGUAGES
ACTIVITIES fghjostx
OTHER SUBJECTS cfh
FACILITIES ON SITE bi
EXAM BOARDS
RETAKES   **NVQ COURSES**

ENTRY REQUIREMENTS Report & Exam & Interview
SCHOLARSHIPS & BURSARIES
SPECIAL NEEDS abjlnq
ASSOCIATION IAPS   **FOUNDED** 1969   **RELIGIOUS AFFILIATION** Non-denom
DYSLEXIA e   **DIET** abcd

A-level
AS
GCSE
OTHER   e   l   o   v
     B   G   K   O   R
     cde

C Grace Dieu Manor Preparatory School; Grace Dieu; Coalville; Leic. LE67 5UG
Tel: 01530 222276 (Fax: 01530 223184) *Rev.Fr.G.J.Duffy*

	Boys	Age	Girls	Age	TOTAL		Boys	Girls
Day £884-£1531 ✗	232	3-13	65	3-13	327	SIXTH		
Weekly £2268	1	7-13	4	7-13				
Boarding £2296	18	7-13	7	7-13				

MAP 9 C 5
LOCATION Rural
DAY   **RAIL** b   **AIR** a
SPORT aefjlmopqsx B
OTHER LANGUAGES a
ACTIVITIES cdfgjoprstw
OTHER SUBJECTS ch
FACILITIES ON SITE di
EXAM BOARDS
RETAKES   **NVQ COURSES**

ENTRY REQUIREMENTS Interview; Report
SCHOLARSHIPS & BURSARIES Schol; Forces; AP; Siblings
SPECIAL NEEDS afgjklnuw ABGI
ASSOCIATION IAPS   **FOUNDED** 1933   **RELIGIOUS AFFILIATION** R C
DYSLEXIA e   **DIET** acd

A-level
AS
GCSE
OTHER   e   lmno   v
     B E G   K   O   R
     cde

C Leicester Grammar School; 8 Peacock Lane; Leicester LE1 5PX
Tel: 0116 262 1221 (Fax: 0116 253 6482) *J.B.Sugden*

	Boys	Age	Girls	Age	TOTAL		Boys	Girls
Day £1360	286	10-18	298	10-18	584	SIXTH	65	72
Weekly								
Boarding								

MAP 9 D 6
LOCATION Inner City
DAY ✓   **RAIL** a   **AIR** a
SPORT abcefghkImpqswx AB
OTHER LANGUAGES
ACTIVITIES fghijknoq AB
OTHER SUBJECTS c
FACILITIES ON SITE cg
EXAM BOARDS abcd ADEHI
RETAKES   **NVQ COURSES**

ENTRY REQUIREMENTS Exam; Report
SCHOLARSHIPS & BURSARIES Schol; Burs; Mus; AP; VI Form; Siblings
SPECIAL NEEDS abghijklnpqstuvwx ACDGHI
ASSOCIATION HMC   **FOUNDED** 1981   **RELIGIOUS AFFILIATION** C of E
DYSLEXIA   **DIET** abcd

A-level   cde g i   nop   uv
     B   GH K   P R U
     c efg jk

AS   c
     G   K   R U
     efg j

GCSE   cde g i l   no   v
     B   G   K   OP R   W
     cdefg jkl

OTHER   l   u   x
     C E G   KM O R   W

LEICESTERSHIRE continued

G | Leicester High School for Girls; 454 London Road; Leicester LE2 2PP
Tel: 0116 270 5338 *Mrs P.A.Watson*

MAP 9 D 6
LOCATION Urban
DAY ✓ **RAIL** a **AIR** b

		Boys	Age	Girls	Age	TOTAL	SIXTH	Boys	Girls
Day	£895-£1425			406	3-18	406			43
Weekly									
Boarding									

SPORT acghlmopqx ABC
OTHER LANGUAGES
ACTIVITIES cfghijnotv A

ENTRY REQUIREMENTS Exam
SCHOLARSHIPS & BURSARIES Schol; Burs; Mus; Teachers; VI Form; Siblings
SPECIAL NEEDS n   **DYSLEXIA** g   **DIET** a
ASSOCIATION GSA **FOUNDED** 1906 **RELIGIOUS AFFILIATION** C of E

OTHER SUBJECTS abcfh
FACILITIES ON SITE h
EXAM BOARDS abcd ABDEG
RETAKES   **NVQ COURSES**

A-level: cd fg i l n p uv / BC GH K PQR TU W / c ef
AS: G
GCSE: cd g i l n v / BC E G K OP R WX / cdef j
OTHER: m

B | Loughborough Grammar School; Burton Walks; Loughborough LE11 2DU
Tel: 01509 233233 (Fax: 01509 210486) *D.N.Ireland*

MAP 9 C 5
LOCATION Urban
DAY **RAIL** a **AIR** a

		Boys	Age	Girls	Age	TOTAL	SIXTH	Boys	Girls
Day	£1455	899	10-18			940		264	
Weekly	£2373	8	10-18						
Boarding	£2700	33	10-18						

SPORT abcdefghkmostuwx ABC
OTHER LANGUAGES
ACTIVITIES efghijklnoqrstux ABD

ENTRY REQUIREMENTS CEE; Exam
SCHOLARSHIPS & BURSARIES Schol; Burs; Mus; Chor; Forces; Clergy; AP;.
SPECIAL NEEDS bejklnqt AGI   **DYSLEXIA**   **DIET** acd
ASSOCIATION HMC **FOUNDED** 1495 **RELIGIOUS AFFILIATION** Non-denom

OTHER SUBJECTS acfh
FACILITIES ON SITE cdghi
EXAM BOARDS abce ADEHK
RETAKES   **NVQ COURSES**

A-level: cde ghi l op uv x / B GH K N P R / c ef j
AS: o / g j
GCSE: cde g i l o v / B G K N P R / cdefgh jk
OTHER:

G | Loughborough High School; Burton Walks; Loughborough; Leicestershire LE11 2DU
Tel: 01509 212 348 (Fax: 01509 210 486) *Miss J.E.L.Harvatt*

MAP 9 C 5
LOCATION Urban
DAY **RAIL** b **AIR** b

		Boys	Age	Girls	Age	TOTAL	SIXTH	Boys	Girls
Day	£1308			522	11-18	534			147
Weekly				12					
Boarding									

SPORT acgklmnpqwx ABC
OTHER LANGUAGES
ACTIVITIES cdfghijklnortx AB

ENTRY REQUIREMENTS Exam
SCHOLARSHIPS & BURSARIES Schol; Burs; Mus; AP; VI Form
SPECIAL NEEDS abghln   **DYSLEXIA**   **DIET** abcd
ASSOCIATION GSA **FOUNDED** 1850 **RELIGIOUS AFFILIATION** Non-denom

OTHER SUBJECTS abcdfh
FACILITIES ON SITE bchi
EXAM BOARDS abcd DEGH
RETAKES   **NVQ COURSES**

A-level: d fg i p uv / BC GH K P R U W / c efg j
AS:
GCSE: d g i l m o v / BC E G K P R W / cdefg j l
OTHER:

C | Manor House Prep. School; Ashby-de-la-Zouch; Leicestershire LE65 1BR
Tel: 01530 412932 *R.J.Sill*

MAP 9 C 5
LOCATION Rural
DAY **RAIL** b **AIR** a

		Boys	Age	Girls	Age	TOTAL	SIXTH	Boys	Girls
Day	£848-£1340 ✗	127	3-14	87	3-14	214			
Weekly									
Boarding									

SPORT acefjlopqsx AB
OTHER LANGUAGES
ACTIVITIES cfghjot

ENTRY REQUIREMENTS Test & Interview
SCHOLARSHIPS & BURSARIES Burs
SPECIAL NEEDS abejklnstuvw BGHI **DYSLEXIA** **DIET** abcd
ASSOCIATION ISAI **FOUNDED** 1951 **RELIGIOUS AFFILIATION** Non-denom

OTHER SUBJECTS bcfh
FACILITIES ON SITE achi
EXAM BOARDS
RETAKES   **NVQ COURSES**

A-level:
AS:
GCSE:
OTHER: e g i l no v / B G K OP R / cdef j

C | Nevill Holt; nr.Market Harborough; Leics. LE16 8EG
Tel: 01858 565234 (Fax: 01858 565303) *I.D.Mackenzie*

MAP 9 E 6
LOCATION Rural
DAY **RAIL** b **AIR** b

		Boys	Age	Girls	Age	TOTAL	SIXTH	Boys	Girls
Day	£860-£1870 ✗	59	4-13	37	4-13	126			
Weekly	£2480	8	7-13	10	7-13				
Boarding	£2585	10	7-13	2	7-13				

SPORT abefhjklmpqstux ABC
OTHER LANGUAGES
ACTIVITIES abcfghijmopqtw

ENTRY REQUIREMENTS Interview
SCHOLARSHIPS & BURSARIES Schol; Burs; Forces; Clergy; Teachers
SPECIAL NEEDS bn   **DYSLEXIA** e   **DIET** a
ASSOCIATION IAPS **FOUNDED** 1868 **RELIGIOUS AFFILIATION** C of E

OTHER SUBJECTS cfh
FACILITIES ON SITE bdikl
EXAM BOARDS
RETAKES   **NVQ COURSES**

A-level:
AS:
GCSE:
OTHER: de g i l mno v / B G K OP R / cde g j

LEICESTERSHIRE continued

C — Oakham School; Chapel Close; Oakham; Rutland LE15 6DT
Tel: 01572 722487 (Fax: 01572 755786) *G.Smallbone*

		Boys	Age	Girls	Age	TOTAL	Boys	Girls
Day	£2150	243	10-18	218	10-18	1005	151	145
Weekly								
Boarding	£3890	269	10-18	275	10-18			

(SIXTH)

ENTRY REQUIREMENTS CEE; Scholarship Exam; Report & Exam & Interview
SCHOLARSHIPS & BURSARIES Schol; Burs; Art; Mus; AP; Drama
SPECIAL NEEDS abeghjklnqstwx ABDEGHIK **DYSLEXIA** ef **DIET** abcd
ASSOCIATION HMC **FOUNDED** 1584 **RELIGIOUS AFFILIATION** C of E

MAP 9 E 6
LOCATION Rural
DAY **RAIL** a **AIR** b
SPORT abcdefghijklmnpqstuwx ABC
OTHER LANGUAGES a
ACTIVITIES acefghijklmnopqstw A
OTHER SUBJECTS abcdefgh
FACILITIES ON SITE abcdeghik
EXAM BOARDS abcd ABDEGH
RETAKES **NVQ COURSES**

- **A-level**: B efghi GH K M P nop W v x / cdefg jkl
- **AS**: C G l M q
- **GCSE**: BC G e K h nop v x WX / cdefgh jkl
- **OTHER**: c e K I no O R q U u W / f h j l

C — Ratcliffe College; Fosse Way; Ratcliffe on the Wreake; Leicester LE7 4SG
Tel: 01509 817000 (Fax: 01509 817004) *The Rev.K.A.Tomlinson*

		Boys	Age	Girls	Age	TOTAL	Boys	Girls
Day	£1608-£2022	222	11-18	102	11-18	480	80	47
Weekly	£2411-£3032	25	11-18	6	11-18			
Boarding	£3032	79	11-18	46	11-18			

ENTRY REQUIREMENTS CEE; Scholarship Exam; Report & Exam & Interview
SCHOLARSHIPS & BURSARIES Schol; Art; Mus; Forces; Teachers; AP; VI Form
SPECIAL NEEDS bjklnpqtuvw EGIL **DYSLEXIA** e **DIET** abd
ASSOCIATION HMC **FOUNDED** 1844 **RELIGIOUS AFFILIATION** R C

MAP 9 D 5
LOCATION Rural
DAY ✓ **RAIL** b **AIR** a
SPORT abcefghjklmpqrstuwx ABC
OTHER LANGUAGES a
ACTIVITIES efghijknopstvwx A
OTHER SUBJECTS cfh
FACILITIES ON SITE bcdeghjkl
EXAM BOARDS bd BDEH
RETAKES ab **NVQ COURSES**

- **A-level**: B efg GH K i l nopq P R s uv x
- **AS**: cdef
- **GCSE**: BC G e g i l I bcdef j l NOP nopq R v x
- **OTHER**: E I K u O R W

B — St. Crispin's School; St. Mary's Road; Leicester LE2 1XA
Tel: 0116 270 7648 (Fax: 0116 270 7648) *B.Harrild*

		Boys	Age	Girls	Age	TOTAL	Boys	Girls
Day	£1025-£1140	103	7-13	14	7-13	117		
Weekly								
Boarding								

ENTRY REQUIREMENTS Interview
SCHOLARSHIPS & BURSARIES
SPECIAL NEEDS n B **DYSLEXIA** ce **DIET** abcd
ASSOCIATION IAPS **FOUNDED** 1945 **RELIGIOUS AFFILIATION** Inter-denom

MAP 9 D 6
LOCATION Urban
DAY **RAIL** a **AIR** a
SPORT abcefjlmpqsx ABC
OTHER LANGUAGES
ACTIVITIES fgjqt A
OTHER SUBJECTS bch
FACILITIES ON SITE ch
EXAM BOARDS
RETAKES **NVQ COURSES**

- **A-level**:
- **AS**:
- **GCSE**:
- **OTHER**: B de G g i l K no OP R v / cde j

C — Stoneygate College; 2 Albert Road; Stoneygate; Leicester LE2 2AA
Tel: 0116 270 7414 (Fax: 0116 270 7414) *J.Bourlet*

		Boys	Age	Girls	Age	TOTAL	Boys	Girls
Day	£420-£995	61	3-11	83	3-11	144		
Weekly								
Boarding								

ENTRY REQUIREMENTS Assessment & Interview
SCHOLARSHIPS & BURSARIES Siblings
SPECIAL NEEDS b **DYSLEXIA** **DIET** acd
ASSOCIATION ISAI **FOUNDED** 1886 **RELIGIOUS AFFILIATION** Christian

MAP 9 D 6
LOCATION Urban
DAY **RAIL** a **AIR** a
SPORT aejlpqx B
OTHER LANGUAGES
ACTIVITIES gjnq
OTHER SUBJECTS ch
FACILITIES ON SITE
EXAM BOARDS
RETAKES **NVQ COURSES**

- **A-level**:
- **AS**:
- **GCSE**:
- **OTHER**: B e G k K o O R v / cde

C — Stoneygate Prep. School; 254 London Road; Leicester LE2 1RP
Tel: 0116 270 7536 (Fax: 0116 244 8592) *J.B.Josephs*

		Boys	Age	Girls	Age	TOTAL	Boys	Girls
Day	£1030-£1425	261	3-13	146	3-13	407		
Weekly								
Boarding								

ENTRY REQUIREMENTS Assessment & Interview
SCHOLARSHIPS & BURSARIES Burs
SPECIAL NEEDS bjlnw **DYSLEXIA** e **DIET** a
ASSOCIATION IAPS **FOUNDED** 1850 **RELIGIOUS AFFILIATION** C of E

MAP 9 D 6
LOCATION Urban
DAY **RAIL** a **AIR** a
SPORT abefjlmopqswx B
OTHER LANGUAGES
ACTIVITIES cfghjo A
OTHER SUBJECTS bch
FACILITIES ON SITE cjk
EXAM BOARDS
RETAKES **NVQ COURSES**

- **A-level**:
- **AS**:
- **GCSE**:
- **OTHER**: BC cde g j G i l K o OP q s v

LEICESTERSHIRE *continued*

Bg Uppingham School; Uppingham LE15 9QE;
Tel: 0157 282 2216 (Fax: 0157 282 2332) *Dr S.C.Winkley*

		Boys	Age	Girls	Age	TOTAL		Boys	Girls
Day	£1990-£2550	✗	13	11-18	4	16-18	604	205	126
Weekly									
Boarding	£4250		465	13-18	122	16-18	SIXTH		

MAP 9 E 6
LOCATION Rural
DAY ✓ **RAIL** b **AIR** b
SPORT abcdefghijklmnpqstuwx ABC
OTHER LANGUAGES
ACTIVITIES cefghijklmnoqstuv ABC
OTHER SUBJECTS abcdfh
FACILITIES ON SITE abcdeghik
EXAM BOARDS abcd ABDEGH
RETAKES a   **NVQ COURSES**

ENTRY REQUIREMENTS CEE; Report & Interview
SCHOLARSHIPS & BURSARIES Schol; Burs; Art; Mus; Chor; Clergy; VI Form; ARA
SPECIAL NEEDS jn   **DYSLEXIA** ef   **DIET** acd
ASSOCIATION HMC   **FOUNDED** 1584   **RELIGIOUS AFFILIATION** C of E

A-level	cdefg i l nopq vwx	AS	c gh l p w	GCSE	cde g i o q v	OTHER	de l n u
	B GH K P		G K		B G K P R		K O
	c efg j l		c ef j l		cdefg j l		

C Kirkstone House School; Main Street; Baston; Peterborough PE6 9NU
Tel: 01778 560 547 (Fax: 01778 560 350) *Mrs P.M.G.Little*

		Boys	Age	Girls	Age	TOTAL		Boys	Girls
Day	£792-£1394		105	3-16	58	3-16	163		
Weekly							SIXTH		
Boarding									

MAP 9 F 5
LOCATION Rural
DAY ✓ **RAIL** b **AIR** c
SPORT abcdefhjklmpqsx ABC
OTHER LANGUAGES a
ACTIVITIES cfghijklmnoqt A
OTHER SUBJECTS cefh
FACILITIES ON SITE h
EXAM BOARDS bd AL
RETAKES   **NVQ COURSES**

ENTRY REQUIREMENTS Test & Interview
SCHOLARSHIPS & BURSARIES Schol; Art; Mus; Teachers; ARA; Siblings
SPECIAL NEEDS ajln   **DYSLEXIA** e   **DIET** acd
ASSOCIATION ISAI   **FOUNDED** 1967   **RELIGIOUS AFFILIATION** C of E

A-level		AS		GCSE	de ghi l no v	OTHER	
					BC E GH K OP		d h
					cde h		

C Lincoln Cathedral School; Eastgate; Lincoln LN2 1QE
Tel: 01522 523769 (Fax: 01522 514778) *The Rev.Canon R.G.Western*

		Boys	Age	Girls	Age	TOTAL		Boys	Girls
Day	£915-£1030		61	2-13	22	2-13	101		
Weekly	£1245-£2300		2	7-13				SIXTH	
Boarding	£2300		16	7-13					

MAP 9 E 3
LOCATION Urban
DAY ✓ **RAIL** b **AIR** a
SPORT abefgjmostx AB
OTHER LANGUAGES
ACTIVITIES bcfghjlor
OTHER SUBJECTS abch
FACILITIES ON SITE ad
EXAM BOARDS
RETAKES   **NVQ COURSES**

ENTRY REQUIREMENTS Assessment & Interview
SCHOLARSHIPS & BURSARIES Mus; Chor
SPECIAL NEEDS n   **DYSLEXIA** ef   **DIET** ad
ASSOCIATION IAPS   **FOUNDED** 1961   **RELIGIOUS AFFILIATION** C of E

A-level		AS		GCSE		OTHER	de g i l o q v
							B G K OP R
							cde j

C St. Hugh's; Woodhall Spa; Lincs. LN10 6TQ
Tel: 01526 352169 *P.M.Wells*

		Boys	Age	Girls	Age	TOTAL		Boys	Girls
Day	£992-£1836	✗	33	4-13	17	4-13	134		
Weekly	£2425-£2482		19	7-10	7	7-10		SIXTH	
Boarding	£2425-£2482		38	7-13	20	7-13			

MAP 9 F 3
LOCATION Rural
DAY ✓ **RAIL** b **AIR** b
SPORT abcefjklmpqsux ABC
OTHER LANGUAGES
ACTIVITIES cfghijlmnopqrstw A
OTHER SUBJECTS bcdfh
FACILITIES ON SITE bcehik
EXAM BOARDS
RETAKES   **NVQ COURSES**

ENTRY REQUIREMENTS Assessment & Interview
SCHOLARSHIPS & BURSARIES Schol; Burs; Art; Mus; Forces; Clergy; Teachers; Sport
SPECIAL NEEDS bjklntuv BDEG   **DYSLEXIA** c   **DIET** abcd
ASSOCIATION IAPS   **FOUNDED** 1925   **RELIGIOUS AFFILIATION** C of E (Evang)

A-level		AS		GCSE		OTHER	cdefg i klmno v
							AB G JK NOP R W
							cdef j

Gb St. Joseph's School; Upper Lindum Street; Lincoln LN2 5RW
Tel: 01522 543764 (Fax: 01522 537938) *Mrs Maureen Bradley*

		Boys	Age	Girls	Age	TOTAL		Boys	Girls
Day	£835-£1415			4-11	172	4-18	203		28
Weekly	£2605-£2665				15	9-18		SIXTH	
Boarding	£2725-£2890				16	9-18			

MAP 9 E 3
LOCATION Urban
DAY ✓ **RAIL** a **AIR** b
SPORT abcfghjklmopqtw BC
OTHER LANGUAGES a
ACTIVITIES acfghijkoqt AB
OTHER SUBJECTS abcdefgh
FACILITIES ON SITE cdg
EXAM BOARDS abcd BDEI
RETAKES ab   **NVQ COURSES**

ENTRY REQUIREMENTS Report & Interview
SCHOLARSHIPS & BURSARIES Schol; Burs; Teachers
SPECIAL NEEDS bjkln H   **DYSLEXIA** f   **DIET** abcd
ASSOCIATION GSA   **FOUNDED** 1905   **RELIGIOUS AFFILIATION** Inter-denom

A-level	de g i p uv	AS	d g i v	GCSE	de g i p v	OTHER	h lmno s
	BC GH K P W		G W		BC E G K OP R WX		K O R U
	cdef l		ef		cdef		cd

LINCOLNSHIRE

LINCOLNSHIRE continued

C — St. Mary's School; 5 Pottergate; Lincoln; Lincolnshire LN2 1PH
Tel: 01522 524622 (Fax: 01522 524622) *P.H.Brewster*

	Boys	Age	Girls	Age	TOTAL
Day £1100-£1150	91	3-11	83	3-11	174
Weekly					
Boarding					

SIXTH: Boys / Girls

MAP 9 E 3
LOCATION Urban
DAY   RAIL a   AIR a
SPORT abcejlpqsx AB
OTHER LANGUAGES
ACTIVITIES cfghjot

ENTRY REQUIREMENTS Test; Interview; Test & Interview
SCHOLARSHIPS & BURSARIES
SPECIAL NEEDS   **DYSLEXIA**   **DIET**
ASSOCIATION IAPS   **FOUNDED** 1949   **RELIGIOUS AFFILIATION** Non-denom

OTHER SUBJECTS cfh
FACILITIES ON SITE ch
EXAM BOARDS
RETAKES   NVQ COURSES

A-level:
AS:
GCSE: e lm o v
OTHER: B G O X
       cde j

Gb — Stamford High Junior School; Kettering Road; Stamford; Lincs. PE9 2LR
Tel: 01780 63367 (Fax: 01780 481100) *Mrs J.M.Lea*

	Boys	Age	Girls	Age	TOTAL
Day £1091	68	4-7	170	4-11	245
Weekly £2428				8-11	
Boarding £2454			7	8-11	

MAP 9 F 6
LOCATION Rural
DAY   RAIL b   AIR b
SPORT aejlpqsx B
OTHER LANGUAGES
ACTIVITIES cfghjnoq

ENTRY REQUIREMENTS Interview; Report & Test
SCHOLARSHIPS & BURSARIES
SPECIAL NEEDS bjklnqt ACGIJL   **DYSLEXIA** e   **DIET** abcd
ASSOCIATION IAPS   **FOUNDED** 1877   **RELIGIOUS AFFILIATION** Non-denom

OTHER SUBJECTS bch
FACILITIES ON SITE bhi
EXAM BOARDS
RETAKES   NVQ COURSES

A-level:
AS:
GCSE:
OTHER: bcde lmno s v
       BC E G I K O R
       cd

G — Stamford High School for Girls; St. Martins; Stamford PE9 2LJ
Tel: 01780 62330 (Fax: 01780 481100) *Miss G.K.Bland*

	Boys	Age	Girls	Age	TOTAL	SIXTH Boys	Girls
Day £1363			599	10-18	711		167
Weekly £2700			19	10-18			
Boarding £2726			93	10-18			

MAP 9 F 6
LOCATION Rural
DAY ✓ RAIL b AIR b
SPORT abcdfghklmopqtuwx ABC
OTHER LANGUAGES
ACTIVITIES cdfghijklnoprstw AB

ENTRY REQUIREMENTS Exam
SCHOLARSHIPS & BURSARIES Schol; Burs; Art; Mus; AP; VI Form; Sport
SPECIAL NEEDS abfghjklnqrstvx ACDEGHIJK   **DYSLEXIA** g   **DIET** abcd
ASSOCIATION GSA   **FOUNDED** 1877   **RELIGIOUS AFFILIATION** Inter-denom

OTHER SUBJECTS abcdefgh
FACILITIES ON SITE bceghi
EXAM BOARDS abc ABDEGH
RETAKES   NVQ COURSES

A-level: de ghi n p   v x
        BC GH K P R   W
        c ef j l
AS: h
GCSE: K U
      de no s v
      BC E G K NO R WX
      cdef j l
OTHER: l u
       O
       e

B — Stamford School Junior School; St. Paul's Street; Stamford; Lincs. PE9 2BS
Tel: 01780 64981 (Fax: 01780 480120) *D.R.Moss-Bowpitt*

	Boys	Age	Girls	Age	TOTAL
Day £1086	292	8-13			357
Weekly £2441					
Boarding £2441			65	8-13	

MAP 9 F 6
LOCATION Urban
DAY   RAIL b   AIR b
SPORT abcefgjlmstuvx AB
OTHER LANGUAGES
ACTIVITIES fghjlmot A

ENTRY REQUIREMENTS Exam
SCHOLARSHIPS & BURSARIES Burs; Teachers; AP
SPECIAL NEEDS bjklnqw BEGHI   **DYSLEXIA** cdef   **DIET** abcd
ASSOCIATION IAPS   **FOUNDED** 1532   **RELIGIOUS AFFILIATION** C of E

OTHER SUBJECTS bcfh
FACILITIES ON SITE acdhj
EXAM BOARDS
RETAKES   NVQ COURSES

OTHER: e g i l no v
       B G K   OP R
       cde j

B — Stamford School; Stamford; Lincs. PE9 2BS
Tel: 01780 62171 (Fax: 01780 480120) *G.J.Timm*

	Boys	Age	Girls	Age	TOTAL	SIXTH Boys	Girls
Day £1355	413	13-18			565	200	
Weekly £2710							
Boarding £2710	152	13-18					

MAP 9 F 6
LOCATION Urban
DAY   RAIL b   AIR b
SPORT abcdefghjkmsuwx AB
OTHER LANGUAGES a
ACTIVITIES efghijklnoqst ABD

ENTRY REQUIREMENTS CEE; Exam
SCHOLARSHIPS & BURSARIES Schol; Burs; Mus; Teachers; AP; VI Form
SPECIAL NEEDS bjklnqw EGHI   **DYSLEXIA** cdef   **DIET** abcd
ASSOCIATION HMC   **FOUNDED** 1532   **RELIGIOUS AFFILIATION** C of E

OTHER SUBJECTS abcdfh
FACILITIES ON SITE abcdhj
EXAM BOARDS abc AEGH
RETAKES   NVQ COURSES

A-level: cd ghi op   v x
         B GH K   P R   W
         c ef jk
AS:
GCSE: u
      cd   l o   v
      B G K O R   X
      cdefg jk
OTHER:
k

LINCOLNSHIRE *continued*

Stonefield House School; Church Lane; Lincoln LN2 1QR
Tel: 01522 541741 *J.P.S.Child*

		Boys	Age	Girls	Age	TOTAL		Boys	Girls
Day	£900-£1510	81	3-16	53	3-16	134	SIXTH		
Weekly									
Boarding									

ENTRY REQUIREMENTS CEE; Report & Interview
SCHOLARSHIPS & BURSARIES Schol; Siblings
SPECIAL NEEDS alnq   **DYSLEXIA** g   **DIET** abcd
ASSOCIATION ISAI   **FOUNDED** 1980   **RELIGIOUS AFFILIATION** Christian

MAP 9 E 3
LOCATION Urban
DAY   **RAIL** a   **AIR** a
SPORT abefjmpqsx B
OTHER LANGUAGES
ACTIVITIES fghijko A
OTHER SUBJECTS abch
FACILITIES ON SITE
EXAM BOARDS bc
RETAKES   **NVQ COURSES**

A-level   AS G   GCSE cd g i / B E G K P R v / cdef j   OTHER

Witham Hall; Bourne; Lincs. PE10 0JJ
Tel: 01778 590222 (Fax: 01778 590606) *D.H.Burston*

		Boys	Age	Girls	Age	TOTAL		Boys	Girls
Day	£990-£1830	58	3-13	41	3-13	151	SIXTH		
Weekly	£2450	23	7-13	7	7-13				
Boarding	£2450	17	7-13	5	7-13				

ENTRY REQUIREMENTS Test & Interview
SCHOLARSHIPS & BURSARIES Schol; Mus; Clergy
SPECIAL NEEDS n   **DYSLEXIA** c   **DIET** acd
ASSOCIATION IAPS   **FOUNDED** 1960   **RELIGIOUS AFFILIATION** C of E

MAP 9 F 5
LOCATION Rural
DAY ✓   **RAIL** b   **AIR** b
SPORT abcefjklmopqsvwx ABC
OTHER LANGUAGES a
ACTIVITIES cfghjlmortvw A
OTHER SUBJECTS bcfh
FACILITIES ON SITE bchjk
EXAM BOARDS
RETAKES   **NVQ COURSES**

A-level   AS   GCSE   OTHER cde g i l no q v / B G K OP R / cde j

Alleyn's Junior School; Townley Road; Dulwich; London SE22 8SU
Tel: 0181 693 3457 (Fax: 0181 693 3597) *Mrs B.E.Weir*

		Boys	Age	Girls	Age	TOTAL		Boys	Girls
Day	£1530-£1587	87	5-11	100	5-11	187	SIXTH		
Weekly									
Boarding									

ENTRY REQUIREMENTS Assessment & Interview
SCHOLARSHIPS & BURSARIES
SPECIAL NEEDS abghlnq   **DYSLEXIA** g   **DIET** acd
ASSOCIATION IAPS   **FOUNDED** 1619   **RELIGIOUS AFFILIATION** C of E

MAP 5 F 5
LOCATION Urban
DAY   **RAIL** a   **AIR** b
SPORT aejlmpqx B
OTHER LANGUAGES
ACTIVITIES
OTHER SUBJECTS bc
FACILITIES ON SITE bcdhi
EXAM BOARDS
RETAKES   **NVQ COURSES**

A-level   AS   GCSE   OTHER e lm o v / B E G K O R / cde

Alleyn's School; Townley Road; Dulwich; London SE22 8SU
Tel: 0181 693 3422 (Fax: 0181 299 3671) *Dr C.H.R.Niven*

		Boys	Age	Girls	Age	TOTAL		Boys	Girls
Day	£1530-£1880	459	11-18	456	11-18	915	SIXTH	116	122
Weekly									
Boarding									

ENTRY REQUIREMENTS Report & Exam & Interview
SCHOLARSHIPS & BURSARIES Schol; Art; Mus; AP
SPECIAL NEEDS ejn   **DYSLEXIA** g   **DIET** abcd
ASSOCIATION HMC   **FOUNDED** 1619   **RELIGIOUS AFFILIATION** C of E

MAP 5 F 5
LOCATION Inner City
DAY   **RAIL** a   **AIR** a
SPORT abcdefghijklmopquwx AB
OTHER LANGUAGES
ACTIVITIES cefghijklnopqst AB
OTHER SUBJECTS abcdfh
FACILITIES ON SITE bcdghi
EXAM BOARDS abc ABDEGH
RETAKES a   **NVQ COURSES**

A-level c e ghi l nop uv / B GH K P R U W / c efg j   AS fg FG K / e g l   GCSE pq x / c e g i l o st v / ABC G K N PQR U W / cdefgh l   OTHER l

Alpha Prep. School; 21 Hindes Road; Harrow; Middx. HA1 1SH
Tel: 0181 427 1471 (Fax: 0181 424 9324) *P.J.Wylie*

		Boys	Age	Girls	Age	TOTAL		Boys	Girls
Day	£1000-£1350	151	4-13	13	4-13	164	SIXTH		
Weekly									
Boarding									

ENTRY REQUIREMENTS
SCHOLARSHIPS & BURSARIES Teachers
SPECIAL NEEDS blqx l   **DYSLEXIA** g   **DIET** acd
ASSOCIATION IAPS   **FOUNDED** 1895   **RELIGIOUS AFFILIATION** C of E

MAP 5 D 3
LOCATION Urban
DAY   **RAIL** a   **AIR** a
SPORT abefjlmox AB
OTHER LANGUAGES
ACTIVITIES fghijo
OTHER SUBJECTS ch
FACILITIES ON SITE c
EXAM BOARDS
RETAKES   **NVQ COURSES**

A-level   AS   GCSE   OTHER egil o v / B G K OP R / cde j

LONDON (GREATER)

LONDON (GREATER) continued

C — American Community School; Hillingdon Court; 108 Vine Lane; Hillingdon; Middx UB10 0BE Tel: 01895 259771 (Fax: 01895 256974) B.W.Duncan

| Day Weekly Boarding | £2375-£4370 | Boys 303 | Age 4-18 | Girls 276 | Age 4-18 | TOTAL 579 | SIXTH Boys | Girls |

MAP 5 E 4
LOCATION Rural
DAY **RAIL** b **AIR** a
SPORT abcfjlmsu ABC
OTHER LANGUAGES ack
ACTIVITIES gjot
OTHER SUBJECTS abch
FACILITIES ON SITE hk
EXAM BOARDS C
RETAKES **NVQ COURSES**

ENTRY REQUIREMENTS Assessment
SCHOLARSHIPS & BURSARIES Burs; Clergy; Teachers
SPECIAL NEEDS beghjklstuw ABCDGHIK
DYSLEXIA **DIET**
ASSOCIATION ISAI **FOUNDED** 1978 **RELIGIOUS AFFILIATION** Non-denom

A-level — **AS** — **GCSE** e ghi l p v / B G M Q / cdef hi l — **OTHER**

B — Arnold House School; 3 Loudoun Road; St. John's Wood; London NW8 0LH Tel: 0171 286 1100 (Fax: 0171 266 0655) N.M.Allen

| Day Weekly Boarding | £1835 | Boys 223 | Age 5-13 | Girls | Age | TOTAL 223 | SIXTH Boys | Girls |

MAP 5 E 3
LOCATION Inner City
DAY **RAIL** a **AIR** a
SPORT abcefgjlmosx ABC
OTHER LANGUAGES
ACTIVITIES fghijot A
OTHER SUBJECTS cfh
FACILITIES ON SITE h
EXAM BOARDS
RETAKES **NVQ COURSES**

ENTRY REQUIREMENTS Interview
SCHOLARSHIPS & BURSARIES
SPECIAL NEEDS ejknqw BGI
DYSLEXIA e **DIET**
ASSOCIATION IAPS **FOUNDED** 1905 **RELIGIOUS AFFILIATION** C of E

A-level — **AS** — **GCSE** e gi l v / B G K P R / cde g j — **OTHER**

C — Arts Educational London Schools,The; Cone Ripman House; 14 Bath Road; Chiswick; London W4 1LY Tel: 0181 994 9366 (Fax: 0181 994 9274) P A Fowler

| Day Weekly Boarding | £1854-£2349 | Boys 31 | Age 8-16 | Girls 90 | Age 8-16 | TOTAL 121 | SIXTH Boys | Girls |

MAP 5 D 4
LOCATION Urban
DAY **RAIL** a **AIR** a
SPORT h
OTHER LANGUAGES
ACTIVITIES cghij
OTHER SUBJECTS abcdfh
FACILITIES ON SITE k
EXAM BOARDS acd
RETAKES **NVQ COURSES**

ENTRY REQUIREMENTS Report & Exam & Interview
SCHOLARSHIPS & BURSARIES Burs
SPECIAL NEEDS jnu
DYSLEXIA e **DIET** abcd
ASSOCIATION ISAI **FOUNDED** 1919 **RELIGIOUS AFFILIATION** Non-denom

A-level — **AS** — **GCSE** e g klmn v / B G K / cde — **OTHER**

C — Ashton House School; 50/52 Eversley Crescent; Isleworth; Middx. TW7 4LW Tel: 0181 560 3902 (Fax: 0181 568 1097) P.Turner

| Day Weekly Boarding | £1150-£1223 | Boys 63 | Age 3-11 | Girls 79 | Age 3-11 | TOTAL 142 | SIXTH Boys | Girls |

MAP 5 D 5
LOCATION Urban
DAY **RAIL** **AIR**
SPORT ejpqx BC
OTHER LANGUAGES
ACTIVITIES cf
OTHER SUBJECTS ch
FACILITIES ON SITE
EXAM BOARDS
RETAKES **NVQ COURSES**

ENTRY REQUIREMENTS Interview
SCHOLARSHIPS & BURSARIES Teachers; Siblings
SPECIAL NEEDS
DYSLEXIA **DIET**
ASSOCIATION ISAI **FOUNDED** 1930 **RELIGIOUS AFFILIATION** Non-denom

A-level — **AS** — **GCSE** e lm o v / B E G K O R / cde — **OTHER**

B — Belmont; Mill Hill; London NW7 4ED Tel: 0181 959 1431 (Fax: 0181 906 3519) John R.Hawkins

| Day Weekly Boarding | £1945 ✗ | Boys 303 | Age 7-13 | Girls | Age | TOTAL 303 | SIXTH Boys | Girls |

MAP 5 D 2
LOCATION Rural
DAY **RAIL** b **AIR** a
SPORT abcefgijlmsuwx ABC
OTHER LANGUAGES a
ACTIVITIES fghijlmopqst A
OTHER SUBJECTS bch
FACILITIES ON SITE acdhi
EXAM BOARDS
RETAKES **NVQ COURSES**

ENTRY REQUIREMENTS Test; Interview; Report
SCHOLARSHIPS & BURSARIES Mus; AP
SPECIAL NEEDS kn Bl
DYSLEXIA def **DIET** abcd
ASSOCIATION IAPS **FOUNDED** 1912 **RELIGIOUS AFFILIATION** Christian

A-level — **AS** — **GCSE** cde g i l no v / B E G K OP R / cde j — **OTHER**

LONDON (GREATER) *continued*

Bickley Park School; Bickley; Kent BR1 2DY
Bg
Tel: 0181 467 2195 (Fax: 0181 467 2195) *D.J.A.Cassell*

Day £530-£1830 | Boys 354 | Age 3-14 | Girls 15 | Age 3-5 | TOTAL 369 | SIXTH Boys — Girls —
Weekly
Boarding

MAP 6 G 6
LOCATION Urban
DAY **RAIL** b **AIR** a
SPORT abcdefjklsux AB
OTHER LANGUAGES
ACTIVITIES fghjqr A
OTHER SUBJECTS bch
FACILITIES ON SITE bhj
EXAM BOARDS
RETAKES   **NVQ COURSES**

ENTRY REQUIREMENTS Test & Interview
SCHOLARSHIPS & BURSARIES Burs
SPECIAL NEEDS bjnpquw CI
ASSOCIATION IAPS **FOUNDED** 1918
DYSLEXIA e   **DIET** acd
RELIGIOUS AFFILIATION Non-denom

A-level — | AS — | GCSE — | OTHER e g i l o q v / B G K OP R / cde j

Bishop Challoner School; Bromley Road; Shortlands; Kent BR2 0BS
C
Tel: 0181 460 3546 (Fax: 0181 466 8885) *T.Robinson*

Day £785-£1240 | Boys 308 | Age 2-18 | Girls 38 | Age 2-18 | TOTAL 346 | SIXTH Boys 37 Girls 1
Weekly
Boarding

MAP 6 G 6
LOCATION Urban
DAY **RAIL** a **AIR** a
SPORT abcefgjsx BC
OTHER LANGUAGES
ACTIVITIES fghijm A
OTHER SUBJECTS bch
FACILITIES ON SITE cdgh
EXAM BOARDS abd EG
RETAKES ab   **NVQ COURSES**

ENTRY REQUIREMENTS Exam & Interview
SCHOLARSHIPS & BURSARIES Schol
SPECIAL NEEDS bjn
ASSOCIATION ISAI **FOUNDED** 1953
DYSLEXIA e   **DIET** acd
RELIGIOUS AFFILIATION R C

A-level c e g i op v x / B G P R / cde j | AS G / c | GCSE e g i l o v / B E G K OP R / cde j | OTHER

Blackheath High School GPDST; Vanbrugh Park; Blackheath; London SE3 7AG
G
Tel: 0181 853 2929 (Fax: 0181 853 3663) *Miss R.K.Musgrave*

Day £1192-£1548 ✗ | Boys — | Age — | Girls 596 | Age 4-18 | TOTAL 596 | SIXTH Boys — Girls 72
Weekly
Boarding

MAP 6 G 4
LOCATION Inner City
DAY **RAIL** b **AIR** b
SPORT achlmpqrx BC
OTHER LANGUAGES
ACTIVITIES cfghijkost
OTHER SUBJECTS abcfh
FACILITIES ON SITE bcgh
EXAM BOARDS abcd ABEHJ
RETAKES   **NVQ COURSES**

ENTRY REQUIREMENTS Test & Interview
SCHOLARSHIPS & BURSARIES Schol; Burs; AP; VI Form
SPECIAL NEEDS
ASSOCIATION GSA **FOUNDED** 1880
DYSLEXIA   **DIET** a
RELIGIOUS AFFILIATION Non-denom

A-level cde g i p v / B GH K P U / cdefg | AS f | GCSE de g i l no v / B G K NPR U / cdefg j l | OTHER l m o u / NO

Bretby House School; 39 Woodlands Avenue; New Malden; Surrey KT3 3UL
C
Tel: 0181 942 5779 (Fax: 0181 336 0294) *Mrs S.M.Mallin*

Day £573-£1249 ✗ | Boys 72 | Age 3-8 | Girls 59 | Age 3-8 | TOTAL 131 | SIXTH Boys — Girls —
Weekly
Boarding

MAP 5 D 6
LOCATION
DAY **RAIL** **AIR**
SPORT
OTHER LANGUAGES
ACTIVITIES
OTHER SUBJECTS
FACILITIES ON SITE
EXAM BOARDS
RETAKES   **NVQ COURSES**

ENTRY REQUIREMENTS Interview
SCHOLARSHIPS & BURSARIES
SPECIAL NEEDS
ASSOCIATION ISAI **FOUNDED** 1936
DYSLEXIA   **DIET**
RELIGIOUS AFFILIATION

A-level | AS | GCSE | OTHER e v / B G / cd

Buckingham College; Hindes Road; Harrow HA1 1SH
Bg
Tel: 0181 427 1220 (Fax: 0181 861 4767) *D.F.T.Bell*

Day £1275-£1490 | Boys 162 | Age 11-18 | Girls 3 | Age 16-18 | TOTAL 165 | SIXTH Boys 23 Girls 3
Weekly
Boarding

MAP 5 D 3
LOCATION Urban
DAY **RAIL** a **AIR** a
SPORT abcefjlmwx AB
OTHER LANGUAGES
ACTIVITIES fghijkq A
OTHER SUBJECTS ach
FACILITIES ON SITE cgh
EXAM BOARDS abd AEG
RETAKES ab   **NVQ COURSES**

ENTRY REQUIREMENTS Exam & Interview
SCHOLARSHIPS & BURSARIES Burs
SPECIAL NEEDS bfjklnw AB
ASSOCIATION ISAI **FOUNDED** 1936
DYSLEXIA f   **DIET** abd
RELIGIOUS AFFILIATION Inter-denom

A-level a ghi p / B FG P / cdef | AS g l u / G U | GCSE a e ghi l opq uv / B E G P R U / cdef l | OTHER K O

LONDON (GREATER) continued

G | **Bute House Preparatory School for Girls; Bute House; Luxemburg Gardens; London W6 7EA Tel: 0171 603 7381 (Fax: 0171 371 3446)** *Mrs S.C.Salvidant*

MAP 5 E 4
LOCATION Inner City
DAY   RAIL b   AIR b

| Day Weekly Boarding | £1350 ✗ | Boys | Age | Girls 268 | Age 4-11 | TOTAL 268 | SIXTH | Boys | Girls |

SPORT lpqx B
OTHER LANGUAGES
ACTIVITIES cfgijno

ENTRY REQUIREMENTS
SCHOLARSHIPS & BURSARIES
SPECIAL NEEDS bej   DYSLEXIA   DIET acd
ASSOCIATION IAPS   FOUNDED 1958   RELIGIOUS AFFILIATION

OTHER SUBJECTS cfh
FACILITIES ON SITE h
EXAM BOARDS
RETAKES   NVQ COURSES

A-level | AS | GCSE | OTHER
| | | | e g i l   no   v
| | | | B   G   K   O P R
| | | | cde

C | **Cameron House; 4 The Vale; Chelsea; London SW3 4AH Tel: 0171 352 4040 (Fax: 0171 352 2349)** *Mrs F.N.Stack*

MAP 5 E 4
LOCATION Inner City
DAY   RAIL   AIR

| Day Weekly Boarding | £1860-£1925 | Boys 44 | Age 4-11 | Girls 55 | Age 4-11 | TOTAL 99 | SIXTH | Boys | Girls |

SPORT eghjlopqx
OTHER LANGUAGES
ACTIVITIES cfgijt

ENTRY REQUIREMENTS Assessment & Interview
SCHOLARSHIPS & BURSARIES
SPECIAL NEEDS nw   DYSLEXIA de   DIET
ASSOCIATION IAPS   FOUNDED 1980   RELIGIOUS AFFILIATION Non-denom

OTHER SUBJECTS afh
FACILITIES ON SITE c
EXAM BOARDS
RETAKES   NVQ COURSES

A-level | AS | GCSE | OTHER
| | | | e   o   v
| | | | B E G K   O R
| | | | cde   j

Gb | **Cavendish School; 179 Arlington Road; London NW1 7EY Tel: 0171 485 1958 (Fax: 0171 267 0098)** *Mrs L.J.Harris*

MAP 5 F 4
LOCATION
DAY   RAIL a   AIR b

| Day Weekly Boarding | £1225-£1312 | Boys 10 | Age 3-7 | Girls 153 | Age 3-11 | TOTAL 163 | SIXTH | Boys | Girls |

SPORT hpqx
OTHER LANGUAGES
ACTIVITIES cfghijnot

ENTRY REQUIREMENTS Test & Interview
SCHOLARSHIPS & BURSARIES
SPECIAL NEEDS aeghklnw BG   DYSLEXIA e   DIET acd
ASSOCIATION IAPS   FOUNDED 1875   RELIGIOUS AFFILIATION R C

OTHER SUBJECTS acfh
FACILITIES ON SITE dh
EXAM BOARDS
RETAKES   NVQ COURSES

A-level | AS | GCSE | OTHER
| | | | e   o   v
| | | | B E G K   O R
| | | | cde   l

G | **Channing School; Highgate; London N6 5HF Tel: 0181 340 2328 (Fax: 0181 341 5698)** *Mrs I.R.Raphael*

MAP 5 E 3
LOCATION Urban
DAY   RAIL b   AIR b

| Day Weekly Boarding | £1620-£1900 | Boys | Age | Girls 478 | Age 5-18 | TOTAL 478 | SIXTH | Boys | Girls 74 |

SPORT abcghjlmpqwx ABC
OTHER LANGUAGES
ACTIVITIES acfgijkopqrst AB

ENTRY REQUIREMENTS Report & Exam & Interview
SCHOLARSHIPS & BURSARIES Schol; Burs; VI Form
SPECIAL NEEDS abijq   DYSLEXIA   DIET ab
ASSOCIATION GSA   FOUNDED 1885   RELIGIOUS AFFILIATION Unitarian

OTHER SUBJECTS bcfh
FACILITIES ON SITE agh
EXAM BOARDS abcd ABDEGH
RETAKES   NVQ COURSES

A-level | AS | GCSE | OTHER
cd g i   p   v x | d | cd   v | l
B   G K   P | | B E G K   O |
  c efg j l | | cdefg j l | l

B | **City of London School; Queen Victoria Street; London EC4V 3AL Tel: 0171 489 0291 (Fax: 0171 329 6887)** *R.M.Dancey*

MAP 5 F 4
LOCATION Inner City
DAY   RAIL a   AIR a

| Day Weekly Boarding | £1944 | Boys 877 | Age 10-18 | Girls | Age | TOTAL 877 | SIXTH | Boys 248 | Girls |

SPORT abcefghjklmopstuwx ABC
OTHER LANGUAGES
ACTIVITIES aefghijklnoqstv AB

ENTRY REQUIREMENTS Report & Exam & Interview
SCHOLARSHIPS & BURSARIES Schol; Burs; Mus; Chor; AP; VI Form
SPECIAL NEEDS befghijklnqrstx ACDFGIJKL   DYSLEXIA   DIET acd
ASSOCIATION HMC   FOUNDED 1834   RELIGIOUS AFFILIATION Inter-denom

OTHER SUBJECTS cfh
FACILITIES ON SITE bceghik
EXAM BOARDS abcd DEGHJ
RETAKES   NVQ COURSES

A-level | AS | GCSE | OTHER
c efg i   opq   v x | o   vw | c eg i   o q   v | l n
AB   GH K   P | G | AB   G K   P R |
c efg jkl | cd   g | cdefghijkl | i

LONDON (GREATER) *continued*

G | **City of London School For Girls; Barbican; London EC2Y 8BB**
Tel: 0171 628 0841 (Fax: 0171 638 3212) *Dr Y.Burne*

		Boys	Age	Girls	Age	TOTAL	SIXTH	Boys	Girls
Day	£1698			640	7-18	640			149
Weekly									
Boarding									

MAP 5 g 4
LOCATION Inner City
DAY ✓ **RAIL** a **AIR** a
SPORT abcghjlmpqx ABC
OTHER LANGUAGES
ACTIVITIES ghijknot AB

ENTRY REQUIREMENTS Report & Exam & Interview
SCHOLARSHIPS & BURSARIES Schol; Burs; Mus; AP; VI Form
SPECIAL NEEDS bjlnq   **DYSLEXIA** g   **DIET** a
ASSOCIATION GSA   **FOUNDED** 1894   **RELIGIOUS AFFILIATION** Non-denom

OTHER SUBJECTS bcdfh
FACILITIES ON SITE chi
EXAM BOARDS abcd EH
RETAKES   **NVQ COURSES**

A-level: c efg i   nop   v
BC GH K   P R
c efg jkl

AS: c e   o
GH K   R
ef

GCSE: e g i   o   v
BC G K   P R
cdefg jkl

OTHER: l   u

B | **Colfe's Prep. School; Horn Park Lane; London SE12 8AW**
Tel: 0181 852 2283 (Fax: 0181 297 1216) *Mrs J.M.Fisher*

		Boys	Age	Girls	Age	TOTAL	SIXTH	Boys	Girls
Day	£1075-£1265	247	3-11	12	3-7	259			
Weekly									
Boarding									

MAP 6 G 5
LOCATION Urban
DAY ✓ **RAIL** b **AIR** a
SPORT aefjsx AB
OTHER LANGUAGES
ACTIVITIES fghijoqrt A

ENTRY REQUIREMENTS Report & Exam & Interview
SCHOLARSHIPS & BURSARIES Schol; Burs
SPECIAL NEEDS n   **DYSLEXIA** e   **DIET** a
ASSOCIATION IAPS   **FOUNDED**   **RELIGIOUS AFFILIATION** C of E

OTHER SUBJECTS cfh
FACILITIES ON SITE cehik
EXAM BOARDS
RETAKES   **NVQ COURSES**

A-level:

AS:

GCSE:

OTHER: e g i   o   v
B G K   O R
cde

B | **Colfe's School; Horn Park Lane; London SE12 8AW**
Tel: 0181 852 2283 (Fax: 0181 297 1216) *Dr D.J.Richardson*

		Boys	Age	Girls	Age	TOTAL	SIXTH	Boys	Girls
Day	£1675	706	11-18	39	16-18	745		174	39
Weekly									
Boarding									

MAP 6 G 5
LOCATION Urban
DAY **RAIL** a **AIR** b
SPORT abcefhjklmopqstuwx ABC
OTHER LANGUAGES
ACTIVITIES abcefghijklnopqstu A

ENTRY REQUIREMENTS Report & Exam & Interview
SCHOLARSHIPS & BURSARIES Schol; Burs; Mus; AP; VI Form
SPECIAL NEEDS abjlnq   **DYSLEXIA** e   **DIET** abcd
ASSOCIATION HMC   **FOUNDED** 1652   **RELIGIOUS AFFILIATION** C of E

OTHER SUBJECTS abcdfh
FACILITIES ON SITE bchik
EXAM BOARDS abd ABDEGH
RETAKES   **NVQ COURSES**

A-level: cd ghi l nop   uv x
B   GH K   P   U
c ef j l

AS: cd   h l n p   x
G K   U
ef j l

GCSE: d g i   no   v
B G K   P
cdef j l

OTHER: u
NO
g

C | **Collingwood School; Springfield Road; Wallington; Surrey SM6 0BD**
Tel: 0181 647 4607 *D.W.Sweet*

		Boys	Age	Girls	Age	TOTAL	SIXTH	Boys	Girls
Day	£300- £955	111	3-11	19	3-11	130			
Weekly									
Boarding									

MAP 5 F 6
LOCATION Urban
DAY **RAIL** a **AIR** a
SPORT acefjmpqx AB
OTHER LANGUAGES
ACTIVITIES cfghj

ENTRY REQUIREMENTS Test & Interview
SCHOLARSHIPS & BURSARIES
SPECIAL NEEDS n   **DYSLEXIA** e   **DIET** ad
ASSOCIATION ISAI   **FOUNDED** 1929   **RELIGIOUS AFFILIATION** Inter-denom

OTHER SUBJECTS ch
FACILITIES ON SITE
EXAM BOARDS
RETAKES   **NVQ COURSES**

A-level:

AS:

GCSE:

OTHER: e   l   v
B E G K   O R
cde

G | **Commonweal Lodge School; Woodcote Lane; Purley CR8 3HB**
Tel: 0181 660 3179 (Fax: 0181 660 1385) *Miss J.M.Brown*

		Boys	Age	Girls	Age	TOTAL	SIXTH	Boys	Girls
Day	£485-£1505			182	4-18	182			2
Weekly									
Boarding									

MAP 5 F 7
LOCATION Rural
DAY **RAIL** a **AIR** a
SPORT clnpqwx ABC
OTHER LANGUAGES a
ACTIVITIES gjot

ENTRY REQUIREMENTS Test; Report
SCHOLARSHIPS & BURSARIES Schol; Burs; Mus
SPECIAL NEEDS   **DYSLEXIA**   **DIET** acd
ASSOCIATION GSA   **FOUNDED** 1916   **RELIGIOUS AFFILIATION**

OTHER SUBJECTS bcdefgh
FACILITIES ON SITE hj
EXAM BOARDS ad E
RETAKES a   **NVQ COURSES**

A-level: de ghi l n   v x
BC   G K   P R U W
cdef

AS: d g i   n
K   R U W

GCSE: d e g i l n   v
BC   G K   P R U WX
cdef

OTHER: o
l   O   X

LONDON (GREATER) continued

B — Cranbrook College; Mansfield Road; Ilford IG1 3BD
Tel: 0181 554 1757 (Fax: 0181 518 0317) *G.T.Reading*

	Boys	Age	Girls	Age	TOTAL	SIXTH Boys	Girls
Day £950-£1220	198	4-16			198		
Weekly Boarding							

ENTRY REQUIREMENTS Test
SCHOLARSHIPS & BURSARIES Siblings
SPECIAL NEEDS b l   **DYSLEXIA**   **DIET** abcd
ASSOCIATION ISAI   **FOUNDED** 1896   **RELIGIOUS AFFILIATION** Non-denom

MAP 6 H 3
LOCATION Urban
DAY   RAIL b   **AIR** a
SPORT abcefjmswx AB
OTHER LANGUAGES
ACTIVITIES fhijk A
OTHER SUBJECTS ch
FACILITIES ON SITE
EXAM BOARDS ab
RETAKES   NVQ COURSES

A-level:
AS:
GCSE: e g i l B G P R v
cde
OTHER: K O

G — Croham Hurst School; 79 Croham Road; South Croydon CR2 7YN
Tel: 0181 680 3064 (Fax: 0181 688 1142) *Miss S.C.Budgen*

	Boys	Age	Girls	Age	TOTAL	SIXTH Boys	Girls
Day £740-£1530			496	4-18	496		59
Weekly Boarding							

ENTRY REQUIREMENTS Exam; Test & Interview
SCHOLARSHIPS & BURSARIES Schol; Burs; AP; VI Form
SPECIAL NEEDS hl   **DYSLEXIA**   **DIET** a
ASSOCIATION GSA   **FOUNDED** 1899   **RELIGIOUS AFFILIATION** Inter-denom

MAP 5 F 6
LOCATION Urban
DAY   RAIL b   **AIR** a
SPORT abcghjlmnpqsx ABC
OTHER LANGUAGES a
ACTIVITIES cghijops AB
OTHER SUBJECTS abch
FACILITIES ON SITE hj
EXAM BOARDS abd ABEGI
RETAKES a   **NVQ COURSES**

A-level: e ghi n p v BC GH K P R W c ef j l
AS: i p G c j
GCSE: e g i n v BC E G K O P R U W cdef j l
OTHER: l n

G — Croydon High School GPDST; Old Farleigh Road; Selsdon; South Croydon CR2 8YB
Tel: 0181 651 5020 (Fax: 0181 657 5413) *Mrs P.E.Davies*

	Boys	Age	Girls	Age	TOTAL	SIXTH Boys	Girls
Day £1192-£1548			1029	4-18	1029		174
Weekly Boarding							

ENTRY REQUIREMENTS Test
SCHOLARSHIPS & BURSARIES Schol; AP
SPECIAL NEEDS bglq   **DYSLEXIA**   **DIET** acd
ASSOCIATION GSA   **FOUNDED** 1874   **RELIGIOUS AFFILIATION** Non-denom

MAP 5 F 6
LOCATION Urban
DAY   RAIL b   **AIR** a
SPORT abcefklmpqwx AB
OTHER LANGUAGES
ACTIVITIES cfghijklostw AB
OTHER SUBJECTS abcdfh
FACILITIES ON SITE bchi
EXAM BOARDS abd ABE
RETAKES   NVQ COURSES

A-level: d g i l p uv x B GH K P R U cdefg j l
AS: d l u x GH K R U c j
GCSE: d ghi l no vw B G K P R WX cdefg j l
OTHER: kl C O

B — Cumnor House School; 168 Pampisford Road; South Croydon; Surrey CR2 6DA
Tel: 0181 660 3445 (Fax: 0181 660 3445) *A.A.Jeans*

	Boys	Age	Girls	Age	TOTAL	SIXTH Boys	Girls
Day £1250-£1420 ✗	349	4-13			349		
Weekly Boarding							

ENTRY REQUIREMENTS Test & Interview
SCHOLARSHIPS & BURSARIES Schol; Mus; Sport
SPECIAL NEEDS ab l   **DYSLEXIA**   **DIET** acd
ASSOCIATION IAPS   **FOUNDED** 1931   **RELIGIOUS AFFILIATION** C of E

MAP 5 F 6
LOCATION Urban
DAY   RAIL a   **AIR** a
SPORT abejsx A
OTHER LANGUAGES
ACTIVITIES fghjo A
OTHER SUBJECTS ch
FACILITIES ON SITE i
EXAM BOARDS
RETAKES   NVQ COURSES

A-level:
AS:
GCSE:
OTHER: e g i l no q v B G K O P R cde

B — Denmead School; 41-43 Wensleydale Road; Hampton; Middlesex TW12 2LP
Tel: 0181 979 1844 (Fax: 0181 941 8773) *R.Jeynes*

	Boys	Age	Girls	Age	TOTAL	SIXTH Boys	Girls
Day £1225-£1315	202	3-13			202		
Weekly Boarding							

ENTRY REQUIREMENTS Test & Interview
SCHOLARSHIPS & BURSARIES
SPECIAL NEEDS bw l   **DYSLEXIA**   **DIET** acd
ASSOCIATION IAPS   **FOUNDED** 1924   **RELIGIOUS AFFILIATION** C of E

MAP 5 D 6
LOCATION Urban
DAY   RAIL a   **AIR** a
SPORT abcefjmsux AC
OTHER LANGUAGES
ACTIVITIES fghijoq A
OTHER SUBJECTS bch
FACILITIES ON SITE ch
EXAM BOARDS
RETAKES   NVQ COURSES

A-level:
AS:
GCSE:
OTHER: e l o q v B E G K O R cde j

LONDON (GREATER) *continued*

C | **Devonshire House Preparatory School; 2 Arkwright Road; Hampstead; London NW3 6AD Tel: 0171 435 1916** *Mrs S.P.T.Donovan*

	Boys	Age	Girls	Age	TOTAL		Boys	Girls
Day £1475-£1660	160	3-13	112	3-11	272	SIXTH		
Weekly								
Boarding								

ENTRY REQUIREMENTS Test; Interview
SCHOLARSHIPS & BURSARIES Mus
SPECIAL NEEDS al GI   **DYSLEXIA**   **DIET** a
ASSOCIATION ISAI   **FOUNDED** 1989   **RELIGIOUS AFFILIATION** Inter-denom

MAP 5 E 3
LOCATION Urban
DAY   **RAIL** a   **AIR** a
SPORT aefghjlmopqsx B
OTHER LANGUAGES
ACTIVITIES cfghjost
OTHER SUBJECTS abcdfh
FACILITIES ON SITE bc
EXAM BOARDS
RETAKES   **NVQ COURSES**

A-level | AS | GCSE | OTHER: g i l   v / B G K   P R / cde j

B | **Downside School; Woodcote Lane; Purley; Surrey CR8 3HB Tel: 0181 660 0558** *T.M.Andrews*

	Boys	Age	Girls	Age	TOTAL		Boys	Girls
Day £560-£1425 ✗	222	3-13			222	SIXTH		
Weekly								
Boarding								

ENTRY REQUIREMENTS Assessment & Interview
SCHOLARSHIPS & BURSARIES Clergy; Teachers
SPECIAL NEEDS   **DYSLEXIA** g   **DIET** acd
ASSOCIATION IAPS   **FOUNDED** 1920   **RELIGIOUS AFFILIATION** Inter-denom

MAP 5 F 7
LOCATION Urban
DAY   **RAIL** a   **AIR** a
SPORT abefjlosx A
OTHER LANGUAGES a
ACTIVITIES fghjot A
OTHER SUBJECTS cfh
FACILITIES ON SITE hjk
EXAM BOARDS
RETAKES   **NVQ COURSES**

A-level | AS | GCSE | OTHER: e g i l   o q   uv / B G K   OP R / cde j

---

B g | **Dulwich College Prep. School; 42 Alleyn Park; Dulwich SE21 7AA Tel: 0181 670 3217 (Fax: 0181 766 7586)** *G.Marsh*

	Boys	Age	Girls	Age	TOTAL		Boys	Girls
Day £1210-£1960 ✗	701	3-13	12	3-5	735	SIXTH		
Weekly £2180-£2930	22	8-13						
Boarding								

ENTRY REQUIREMENTS Assessment
SCHOLARSHIPS & BURSARIES Burs
SPECIAL NEEDS abeghjlnpqstvwx ACDGHIJK   **DYSLEXIA** e   **DIET** abcd
ASSOCIATION IAPS   **FOUNDED** 1885   **RELIGIOUS AFFILIATION** C of E

MAP 5 F 5
LOCATION Urban
DAY   **RAIL** a   **AIR** a
SPORT abdefghjklmoswx AB
OTHER LANGUAGES
ACTIVITIES fghijloqst
OTHER SUBJECTS bcfh
FACILITIES ON SITE bci
EXAM BOARDS
RETAKES   **NVQ COURSES**

A-level | AS | GCSE | OTHER: e g i l   no   v / B G K   OP R / cdefg j

---

B | **Dulwich College; London SE21 7LD; Tel: 0181 693 3601 (Fax: 0181 693 6319)** *A.C.F.Verity*

	Boys	Age	Girls	Age	TOTAL		Boys	Girls
Day £1937-£2045	1316	7-18			1406	SIXTH	365	
Weekly £3925	34	10-18						
Boarding £4090	56	10-18						

ENTRY REQUIREMENTS Exam & Interview; Assessment & Interview; CEE & Interview
SCHOLARSHIPS & BURSARIES Schol; Burs; Art; Mus; Teachers; AP; VI Form
SPECIAL NEEDS abeijlnqt G   **DYSLEXIA** f   **DIET** acd
ASSOCIATION HMC   **FOUNDED** 1619   **RELIGIOUS AFFILIATION** C of E

MAP 5 F 5
LOCATION Urban
DAY ✓   **RAIL** b   **AIR** a
SPORT abcefghjkmorstuwx AB
OTHER LANGUAGES
ACTIVITIES befghijklnoqrstwx A
OTHER SUBJECTS abcfh
FACILITIES ON SITE abcdghik
EXAM BOARDS abd ADEH
RETAKES   **NVQ COURSES**

A-level: d fg i   op   v / B GH K   P R / cdefgh j l
AS: c   l   q / G
GCSE: d g i   no   v / B G K   P R / cdefgh j   l
OTHER: e   l n q   u wx / a   MNO / a   hi k

B | **Durston House; 12 Castlebar Road; Ealing; London W5 2DR Tel: 0181 810 6545 (Fax: 0181 810 9015)** *P.D.Craze*

	Boys	Age	Girls	Age	TOTAL		Boys	Girls
Day £1480-£1780	364	4-13			364	SIXTH		
Weekly								
Boarding								

ENTRY REQUIREMENTS Assessment & Interview
SCHOLARSHIPS & BURSARIES Schol; Burs
SPECIAL NEEDS bhjnp AI   **DYSLEXIA** de   **DIET**
ASSOCIATION IAPS   **FOUNDED** 1886   **RELIGIOUS AFFILIATION** Inter-denom

MAP 5 D 4
LOCATION Urban
DAY   **RAIL** a   **AIR** a
SPORT abcefgjmosx AB
OTHER LANGUAGES
ACTIVITIES fghjos A
OTHER SUBJECTS bch
FACILITIES ON SITE ab
EXAM BOARDS
RETAKES   **NVQ COURSES**

A-level | AS | GCSE | OTHER: c efg i l   o   v / B E G K   OP R / cde

LONDON (GREATER) continued

Bg Ealing College Upper School; 83 The Avenue; London W13 8JS
Tel: 0181 997 4346 *B.Webb*

		Boys	Age	Girls	Age	TOTAL		Boys	Girls
Day	£1300	144	10-19	2	16-19	146	SIXTH	43	2
Weekly									
Boarding									

ENTRY REQUIREMENTS Report; Test & Interview
SCHOLARSHIPS & BURSARIES VI Form
SPECIAL NEEDS bn   **DYSLEXIA** e   **DIET**
ASSOCIATION ISAI   **FOUNDED** 1820   **RELIGIOUS AFFILIATION** Non-denom

MAP 5 D 4
LOCATION Urban
DAY   **RAIL** a   **AIR** a
SPORT abcefjwx AB
OTHER LANGUAGES
ACTIVITIES fhijklqt A
OTHER SUBJECTS cf
FACILITIES ON SITE h
EXAM BOARDS abcd ADEH
RETAKES ab   **NVQ COURSES**

A-level: d g i l p v x   B G   P   cde
AS:
GCSE: d ghij l p v   AB E G   P R   cde
OTHER:

B Elmhurst School; 44/48 South Park Hill Road; South Croydon CR2 7DW
Tel: 0181 688 0661 (Fax: 0181 686 7675) *R.E.Anderson & B.K.Dighton*

		Boys	Age	Girls	Age	TOTAL		Boys	Girls
Day	£1050-£1250	245	4-11			245	SIXTH		
Weekly									
Boarding									

ENTRY REQUIREMENTS Test & Interview
SCHOLARSHIPS & BURSARIES Schol; Teachers; Sport
SPECIAL NEEDS   **DYSLEXIA**   **DIET** a
ASSOCIATION ISAI   **FOUNDED** 1879   **RELIGIOUS AFFILIATION** Inter-denom

MAP 5 F 6
LOCATION Urban
DAY   **RAIL** a   **AIR** a
SPORT aefjlx AB
OTHER LANGUAGES
ACTIVITIES fghj
OTHER SUBJECTS ch
FACILITIES ON SITE
EXAM BOARDS
RETAKES   **NVQ COURSES**

A-level:
AS:
GCSE:
OTHER: e l v   B E G K O   cde

Bg Eltham College; London SE9 4QF
Tel: 0181 857 1455 (Fax: 0181 857 1913) *D.M.Green*

		Boys	Age	Girls	Age	TOTAL		Boys	Girls
Day	£1400-£1817	707	7-18	52	16-18	768	SIXTH	143	52
Weekly	£1899		11-18						
Boarding	£3835	9	11-18						

ENTRY REQUIREMENTS Report & Exam & Interview
SCHOLARSHIPS & BURSARIES Schol; Burs; Mus; AP
SPECIAL NEEDS bgjklnqst AGH   **DYSLEXIA**   **DIET** abcd
ASSOCIATION HMC   **FOUNDED** 1842   **RELIGIOUS AFFILIATION** Inter-denom

MAP 6 H 5
LOCATION Urban
DAY ✓   **RAIL** a   **AIR** a
SPORT abcdefhjkmnpqrswx ABC
OTHER LANGUAGES
ACTIVITIES bfghijkloqstv AB
OTHER SUBJECTS bcdfh
FACILITIES ON SITE bcdghik
EXAM BOARDS abcd ABDEGH
RETAKES   **NVQ COURSES**

A-level: e g i l op vw   B GH K   P R U   cdef jk
AS: e   o   w   G K   f
GCSE: e g i l nop v   B GHI K N P R U   cdef jkl
OTHER:

Bg Emanuel School; Battersea Rise; London SW11 1HS
Tel: 0181 870 4171 (Fax: 0181 875 0267) *T.Jones-Parry*

		Boys	Age	Girls	Age	TOTAL		Boys	Girls
Day	£1429-£1529	702	10-18		10-18	702	SIXTH	124	
Weekly									
Boarding									

ENTRY REQUIREMENTS CEE; Exam & Interview
SCHOLARSHIPS & BURSARIES Schol; Burs; Mus; AP; VI Form
SPECIAL NEEDS ejklnpqsw GI   **DYSLEXIA** g   **DIET** acd
ASSOCIATION HMC   **FOUNDED** 1594   **RELIGIOUS AFFILIATION** C of E

MAP 5 E 4
LOCATION Urban
DAY   **RAIL** a   **AIR** a
SPORT abcefhjklorsuwx ABC
OTHER LANGUAGES
ACTIVITIES efghijlmnoqrst AB
OTHER SUBJECTS abcdfh
FACILITIES ON SITE cdghik
EXAM BOARDS abd ABE
RETAKES   **NVQ COURSES**

A-level: c e ghi l opq uvwx   B GHI K   PQR   cdefg jk
AS: c g l o   G I   Q
GCSE: c e ghi op vw   B E G K OP R   cdefg jkl
OTHER: u X

G Falkner House; 19 Brechin Place; London SW7 4QB
Tel: 0171 373 4501 (Fax: 0171 835 0073) *Mrs J.Bird*

		Boys	Age	Girls	Age	TOTAL		Boys	Girls
Day	£1750			135	4-11	135	SIXTH		
Weekly									
Boarding									

ENTRY REQUIREMENTS Test & Interview
SCHOLARSHIPS & BURSARIES
SPECIAL NEEDS behjlnt I   **DYSLEXIA** e   **DIET**
ASSOCIATION IAPS   **FOUNDED** 1954   **RELIGIOUS AFFILIATION** Christian

MAP 5 E 4
LOCATION Inner City
DAY   **RAIL**   **AIR**
SPORT lopqx B
OTHER LANGUAGES
ACTIVITIES cfghjo
OTHER SUBJECTS ch
FACILITIES ON SITE
EXAM BOARDS
RETAKES   **NVQ COURSES**

A-level:
AS:
GCSE:
OTHER: cde l v   B G K O R W   cde j

LONDON (GREATER) *continued*

Finton House School; 171 Trinity Road; London SW17 7HL
Tel: 0181 682 0921 (Fax: 0181 767 5017) *Miss T.M.O'Neill*

		Boys	Age	Girls	Age	TOTAL		Boys	Girls
Day	£1050-£1750	71	4-11	123	4-11	194	SIXTH		
Weekly									
Boarding									

ENTRY REQUIREMENTS None
SCHOLARSHIPS & BURSARIES Burs
SPECIAL NEEDS abcefhijklmnpqtux ABCGIJK
ASSOCIATION IAPS **FOUNDED** 1987 **RELIGIOUS AFFILIATION** **DYSLEXIA** de **DIET** a

MAP 5 E 5
LOCATION Inner City
DAY   **RAIL** a   **AIR** a
SPORT aejlmnpqsx B
OTHER LANGUAGES
ACTIVITIES cfhjot
OTHER SUBJECTS abcdfh
FACILITIES ON SITE c
EXAM BOARDS
RETAKES   **NVQ COURSES**

A-level | **AS** | **GCSE** | **OTHER** de g   l mno   s v
BCDE G K O
cde

Forest Girls' School; Nr Snaresbrook; London E17 3PY
Tel: 0181 521 7477 (Fax: 0181 520 7381) *A.G.Boggis*

		Boys	Age	Girls	Age	TOTAL		Boys	Girls
Day	£1828			360	11-18	360	SIXTH		93
Weekly									
Boarding									

ENTRY REQUIREMENTS CEE
SCHOLARSHIPS & BURSARIES Schol; Mus; Chor; Forces; Clergy; AP; VI Form
SPECIAL NEEDS   **DYSLEXIA**   **DIET** acd
ASSOCIATION GBA **FOUNDED** 1834 **RELIGIOUS AFFILIATION** C of E

MAP 6 G 3
LOCATION Urban
DAY ✓   **RAIL** b   **AIR** ab
SPORT abcghlmopqruwx AB
OTHER LANGUAGES
ACTIVITIES cefghijklnostw
OTHER SUBJECTS bcdh
FACILITIES ON SITE bcdghik
EXAM BOARDS abd ABDEH
RETAKES   **NVQ COURSES**

A-level de ghi l opq uv x
ABC GH K   P R
cdef j
AS c   g   l   o   v
B GH K M   R
cde
GCSE de ghi l   op   v
ABC E G K   P R
cdef j l
OTHER

Forest Preparatory School; Snaresbrook; London E17 3PY
Tel: 0181 520 1744 (Fax: 0181 520 3656) *R T Cryer*

		Boys	Age	Girls	Age	TOTAL		Boys	Girls
Day	£1251-£1828	329	7-13	64	7-11	395	SIXTH		
Weekly	£1912-£2870	2	9-13						
Boarding	£2011-£2870		9-13						

ENTRY REQUIREMENTS Exam & Interview
SCHOLARSHIPS & BURSARIES Schol; Mus; Forces; Clergy; AP
SPECIAL NEEDS   **DYSLEXIA**   **DIET** a
ASSOCIATION IAPS **FOUNDED** 1834 **RELIGIOUS AFFILIATION** C of E

MAP 6 G 3
LOCATION Urban
DAY ✓   **RAIL** b   **AIR** b
SPORT abcefjlmpqwx AB
OTHER LANGUAGES
ACTIVITIES fghijort
OTHER SUBJECTS bch
FACILITIES ON SITE cdghik
EXAM BOARDS
RETAKES   **NVQ COURSES**

A-level | **AS** | **GCSE** | **OTHER** e   l no   v
B E G K   O R
cde   j

Forest School; Nr. Snaresbrook; London E17 3PY
Tel: 0181 520 1744 (Fax: 0181 520 3656) *A.G.Boggis*

		Boys	Age	Girls	Age	TOTAL		Boys	Girls
Day	£1828	445	13-18			474	SIXTH	169	
Weekly	£2870		13-18						
Boarding	£2870	29	13-18						

ENTRY REQUIREMENTS CEE & Interview
SCHOLARSHIPS & BURSARIES Schol; Mus; Forces; Clergy; AP
SPECIAL NEEDS   **DYSLEXIA**   **DIET** a
ASSOCIATION HMC **FOUNDED** 1834 **RELIGIOUS AFFILIATION** C of E

MAP 6 G 3
LOCATION Urban
DAY ✓   **RAIL** b   **AIR** ab
SPORT abcefghjklmoqruwx ABC
OTHER LANGUAGES
ACTIVITIES efghijklmnoqstw
OTHER SUBJECTS bcdh
FACILITIES ON SITE cdghik
EXAM BOARDS ab ABDEH
RETAKES   **NVQ COURSES**

A-level de ghi l   op   uv   x
BC GH K   P R
c ef j
AS o   v
GH K M   R
c e
GCSE de ghi l   o q   v
ABC E G K   P R
cdef j
OTHER

Francis Holland School Clarence Gate; Ivor Place; London NW1 6XR
Tel: 0171 723 0176 (Fax: 0171 706 1522) *Mrs P.H.Parsonson*

		Boys	Age	Girls	Age	TOTAL		Boys	Girls
Day	£1765			376	11-18	376	SIXTH		89
Weekly									
Boarding									

ENTRY REQUIREMENTS Report & Exam & Interview
SCHOLARSHIPS & BURSARIES Burs; Mus; Clergy; AP; VI Form
SPECIAL NEEDS ehjklw A   **DYSLEXIA**   **DIET** abcd
ASSOCIATION GSA **FOUNDED** 1878 **RELIGIOUS AFFILIATION** C of E

MAP 5 F 4
LOCATION Inner City
DAY   **RAIL** a   **AIR** a
SPORT cghlmpqx ABC
OTHER LANGUAGES
ACTIVITIES cfghijkoqst AB
OTHER SUBJECTS abcdfh
FACILITIES ON SITE g
EXAM BOARDS abc DEH
RETAKES   **NVQ COURSES**

A-level c efg i   p   v x
B   GH   P R U
cdefgh j
AS c g   x
GH M   R U
c ef
GCSE cde g i   n   v
B G   K   P R
cdefgh j l
OTHER l n q u x
K M O R

LONDON (GREATER) continued

G — Francis Holland School; 39 Graham Terrace; London SW1W 8JF
Tel: 0171 730 2971 (Fax: 0171 823 4066) Mrs J.A.Anderson

	Boys	Age	Girls	Age	TOTAL	SIXTH Boys	Girls
Day Weekly Boarding	£1680-£1980		334	4-18	334		36

MAP 5 F 4
LOCATION Inner City
DAY RAIL b AIR b
SPORT dglmpqtwx AB
OTHER LANGUAGES
ACTIVITIES cghijknostw AB
OTHER SUBJECTS cfh
FACILITIES ON SITE
EXAM BOARDS abcd ABDEL
RETAKES a   NVQ COURSES

ENTRY REQUIREMENTS Test & Interview; Exam & Interview
SCHOLARSHIPS & BURSARIES Schol; Burs; Clergy; VI Form
SPECIAL NEEDS bgl   DYSLEXIA   DIET acd
ASSOCIATION GSA   FOUNDED 1881   RELIGIOUS AFFILIATION C of E

A-level: c efg i n p v
B G K   P   U
cdefg j l

AS: u

GCSE: c e g i
B E G K   P   X
cdefg j l

OTHER: l q w
O R
h

Gb — Garden House School; 53 Sloane Gardens; London SW1W 8ED
Tel: 0171 730 1652 (Fax: 0171 730 0470) Mrs R.Whaley & Mrs W.Challen

	Boys	Age	Girls	Age	TOTAL	SIXTH Boys	Girls
Day Weekly Boarding	£900-£2050 ✗	68	3-8	237	3-11	305	

MAP 5 F 4
LOCATION Inner City
DAY RAIL a AIR a
SPORT aegjlpqx B
OTHER LANGUAGES
ACTIVITIES cghjoqt
OTHER SUBJECTS abcfh
FACILITIES ON SITE c
EXAM BOARDS
RETAKES   NVQ COURSES

ENTRY REQUIREMENTS Test & Interview
SCHOLARSHIPS & BURSARIES Burs
SPECIAL NEEDS   DYSLEXIA   DIET acd
ASSOCIATION IAPS   FOUNDED 1951   RELIGIOUS AFFILIATION C of E

A-level:
AS:
GCSE:
OTHER: d e g l m n o s v
B G K O R
cde j

C — Glaisdale School; 14 Arundel Road; Cheam; Surrey SM2 7AD
Tel: 0181 642 4266 Mrs H.Steel

	Boys	Age	Girls	Age	TOTAL	SIXTH Boys	Girls
Day Weekly Boarding	£300-£840	54	3-11	105	3-11	159	

MAP 5 E 6
LOCATION Urban
DAY RAIL a AIR a
SPORT aefjlpqx
OTHER LANGUAGES
ACTIVITIES gj
OTHER SUBJECTS ch
FACILITIES ON SITE
EXAM BOARDS
RETAKES   NVQ COURSES

ENTRY REQUIREMENTS Interview
SCHOLARSHIPS & BURSARIES
SPECIAL NEEDS   DYSLEXIA   DIET acd
ASSOCIATION ISAI   FOUNDED 1925   RELIGIOUS AFFILIATION Inter-denom

A-level:
AS:
GCSE:
OTHER: e l o   v
B G K O
cde

Gb — Glenarm College; 20 Coventry Road; Ilford IG1 4QR
Tel: 0181 554 1760 (Fax: 01277 234591) Mrs V.Mullooly

	Boys	Age	Girls	Age	TOTAL	SIXTH Boys	Girls
Day Weekly Boarding	£825	9	4-7	115	4-11	124	

MAP 6 H 3
LOCATION Inner City
DAY RAIL b AIR b
SPORT celopqx AB
OTHER LANGUAGES
ACTIVITIES cgjt
OTHER SUBJECTS h
FACILITIES ON SITE
EXAM BOARDS
RETAKES   NVQ COURSES

ENTRY REQUIREMENTS Interview
SCHOLARSHIPS & BURSARIES
SPECIAL NEEDS abeklntuwx Hl   DYSLEXIA   DIET abcd
ASSOCIATION ISAI   FOUNDED 1893   RELIGIOUS AFFILIATION

A-level:
AS:
GCSE:
OTHER: e l n   v
B G   O R   X
cde

G — Glendower Prep. School; 87 Queen's Gate; London SW7 5JX
Tel: 0171 370 1927 (Fax: 0171 244 8308) Mrs B.Humber

	Boys	Age	Girls	Age	TOTAL	SIXTH Boys	Girls
Day Weekly Boarding	£1600 ✗			176	4-12	176	

MAP 5 E 4
LOCATION Inner City
DAY ✓ RAIL b AIR a
SPORT alpx B
OTHER LANGUAGES
ACTIVITIES cghjo
OTHER SUBJECTS abch
FACILITIES ON SITE bi
EXAM BOARDS
RETAKES   NVQ COURSES

ENTRY REQUIREMENTS Test; Test & Interview
SCHOLARSHIPS & BURSARIES
SPECIAL NEEDS ejkw l   DYSLEXIA   DIET abcd
ASSOCIATION IAPS   FOUNDED 1899   RELIGIOUS AFFILIATION Inter-denom

A-level:
AS:
GCSE:
OTHER: d e g   l n o q   v
B E G K O R
cde   j

LONDON (GREATER) continued

G | Godolphin & Latymer School, The; Iffley Road; Hammersmith; London W6 0PG
Tel: 0181 741 1936 (Fax: 0181 746 3352) *Miss Margaret Rudland*

Day	£1875	Boys	Age	Girls 706	Age 11-18	TOTAL 706	SIXTH	Boys	Girls 187
Weekly									
Boarding									

ENTRY REQUIREMENTS Exam & Interview
SCHOLARSHIPS & BURSARIES Burs; Mus; AP
SPECIAL NEEDS abfgjklqux AI
ASSOCIATION GSA   **FOUNDED** 1905   **RELIGIOUS AFFILIATION** Inter-denom   **DYSLEXIA**   **DIET** a

MAP 5 E 4
LOCATION Inner City
DAY   **RAIL** b   **AIR** a
SPORT bghjlmqrwx ABC
OTHER LANGUAGES
ACTIVITIES cfghijkost A
OTHER SUBJECTS abcfh
FACILITIES ON SITE ac
EXAM BOARDS abd BEH
RETAKES   **NVQ COURSES**

A-level: c efg i   p   v   BC GH K   P R   cdefg jkl
AS: bc f   G K   cdefg j   q   R
GCSE: c e   BC G K   cdefg jkl   v   R   X
OTHER: e   ef   l no   K MNO   u   R

B | Hall School; Crossfield Road; Hampstead; London NW3 4NU
Tel: 0171 722 1700 (Fax: 0171 483 0181) *Paul Ramage*

Day	£1840-£1890 ✗	Boys 400	Age 5-13	Girls	Age	TOTAL 400	SIXTH	Boys	Girls
Weekly									
Boarding									

ENTRY REQUIREMENTS
SCHOLARSHIPS & BURSARIES
SPECIAL NEEDS   **DYSLEXIA**   **DIET** a
ASSOCIATION IAPS   **FOUNDED** 1889   **RELIGIOUS AFFILIATION** C of E

MAP 5 E 3
LOCATION Inner City
DAY   **RAIL**   **AIR**
SPORT acefgjmosuwx B
OTHER LANGUAGES
ACTIVITIES fghijloqstx A
OTHER SUBJECTS cfh
FACILITIES ON SITE ch
EXAM BOARDS
RETAKES   **NVQ COURSES**

A-level:
AS:
GCSE:
OTHER: e g i l no   B G K OP R   cde j   v

B | Halliford School; Russell Road; Shepperton; Middx. TW17 9HX
Tel: 01932 223593 (Fax: 01932 229781) *J.R.Crook*

Day	£1480	Boys 273	Age 11-19	Girls 1	Age 16-19	TOTAL 274	SIXTH	Boys 40	Girls
Weekly									
Boarding									

ENTRY REQUIREMENTS Test
SCHOLARSHIPS & BURSARIES Burs
SPECIAL NEEDS bejklpquw DIK   **DYSLEXIA**   **DIET** abcd
ASSOCIATION SHMIS   **FOUNDED** 1921   **RELIGIOUS AFFILIATION** Inter-denom

MAP 5 C 6
LOCATION Rural
DAY   **RAIL** b   **AIR** a
SPORT abcefhjkrswx A
OTHER LANGUAGES
ACTIVITIES dfghijknostu A
OTHER SUBJECTS bcdefh
FACILITIES ON SITE abcgjk
EXAM BOARDS acd ABDE
RETAKES ab   **NVQ COURSES**

A-level: cde ghij   nop   v   AB GH K   P U   cde j l
AS: g i   P
GCSE: de ghij   nop   v   AB E G K   OP R U   cdef j l
OTHER: kl   N

C | Hampshire School, The; 63 Ennismore Gardens; Knightsbridge; London SW7 1NH
Tel: 0171 584 3297 *A.G.Bray*

Day	£700-£2208 ✗	Boys 58	Age 3-13	Girls 103	Age 3-13	TOTAL 161	SIXTH	Boys	Girls
Weekly									
Boarding									

ENTRY REQUIREMENTS Report & Interview
SCHOLARSHIPS & BURSARIES Schol; Burs; Mus
SPECIAL NEEDS bekntuvwx HI   **DYSLEXIA**   **DIET** abcd
ASSOCIATION ISAI   **FOUNDED** 1928   **RELIGIOUS AFFILIATION**

MAP 5 E 4
LOCATION Inner City
DAY ✓   **RAIL** a   **AIR** a
SPORT abcdejlmpqwx BC
OTHER LANGUAGES a
ACTIVITIES cfghjoqrt A
OTHER SUBJECTS abcdfh
FACILITIES ON SITE c
EXAM BOARDS
RETAKES   **NVQ COURSES**

A-level:
AS:
GCSE:
OTHER: defg i lmno q s uv   B G K OP R   cdef j l

B | Hampton School; Hanworth Road; Hampton TW12 3HD
Tel: 0181 979 5526 (Fax: 0181 941 7368) *G.G.Able*

Day	£1640	Boys 947	Age 11-18	Girls	Age	TOTAL 947	SIXTH	Boys 281	Girls
Weekly									
Boarding									

ENTRY REQUIREMENTS CEE; Exam
SCHOLARSHIPS & BURSARIES Schol; Burs; Mus; Chor; AP
SPECIAL NEEDS bit   **DYSLEXIA**   **DIET** abcd
ASSOCIATION HMC   **FOUNDED** 1557   **RELIGIOUS AFFILIATION**

MAP 5 C 5
LOCATION Urban
DAY ✓   **RAIL** a   **AIR** a
SPORT abcefhjkrstwx ABC
OTHER LANGUAGES
ACTIVITIES befghijklnopqrsu AB
OTHER SUBJECTS abcdh
FACILITIES ON SITE cghk
EXAM BOARDS abcd ABDEGHI
RETAKES   **NVQ COURSES**

A-level: efghi   nop   uv   B GH K   P R U   cdefg jkl
AS: c efgh l   op   v x   G K   cdefg j l
GCSE: e g i   no   v   B G K   P R   cdefg jkl
OTHER: e

LONDON (GREATER) continued

B — Harrow School; Harrow on the Hill HA1 3HW
Tel: 0181 869 1200 (Fax: 0181 864 5352) N.R.Bomford

MAP 5 D 3
LOCATION Urban
DAY   RAIL a   AIR a

		Boys	Age	Girls	Age	TOTAL		Boys	Girls
Day						780	SIXTH	311	2
Weekly									
Boarding	£4475	778	13-18	2					

SPORT abcdefghijklmostuvwx ABC
OTHER LANGUAGES
ACTIVITIES abdefghijlmnopqrstuvw ABC

ENTRY REQUIREMENTS CEE; Scholarship Exam
SCHOLARSHIPS & BURSARIES Schol; Art; Mus; Clergy
SPECIAL NEEDS ejklqsx EG
ASSOCIATION HMC   FOUNDED 1572   RELIGIOUS AFFILIATION C of E
DYSLEXIA   DIET abcd

OTHER SUBJECTS abcdfh
FACILITIES ON SITE bcdefghikl
EXAM BOARDS abd ABEGHJ
RETAKES   NVQ COURSES

A-level: cdefg i l nopq v x / AB GH K P R U / cdefg j l
AS: l / c
GCSE: cdefg i l opq vwx / AB GH K N P R U / cdefgh j l
OTHER: a   i

Gb — Harvington School; 20 Castle Bar Road; Ealing; London W5 2DS
Tel: 0181 997 1583 (Fax: 0181 810 4756) Mrs A.Fookes

MAP 5 D 4
LOCATION Urban
DAY   RAIL b   AIR a

		Boys	Age	Girls	Age	TOTAL		Boys	Girls
Day	£1050-£1312	2	3-5	191	3-16	193	SIXTH		
Weekly									
Boarding									

SPORT clmpqx ABC
OTHER LANGUAGES
ACTIVITIES ghjn

ENTRY REQUIREMENTS Test; Assessment
SCHOLARSHIPS & BURSARIES Mus; Teachers; Drama; Siblings
SPECIAL NEEDS bklqw B
ASSOCIATION ISAI   FOUNDED 1890   RELIGIOUS AFFILIATION Inter-denom
DYSLEXIA   DIET abcd

OTHER SUBJECTS bch
FACILITIES ON SITE
EXAM BOARDS acd
RETAKES   NVQ COURSES

A-level:
AS:
GCSE: e v / B E G / cde l
OTHER: l n / K O R

Gb — Hazelhurst School; 17 The Downs; Wimbledon SW20 8HF
Tel: 0181 946 1704 (Fax: 0181 944 7050) Mrs C.W.Milner-Williams

MAP 5 E 5
LOCATION Urban
DAY   RAIL a   AIR a

		Boys	Age	Girls	Age	TOTAL		Boys	Girls
Day	£1030-£1540	3	4-7	120	4-16	123	SIXTH		1
Weekly									
Boarding									

SPORT acfjlmpqx ABC
OTHER LANGUAGES a
ACTIVITIES cghjkn A

ENTRY REQUIREMENTS Exam; Interview
SCHOLARSHIPS & BURSARIES Schol
SPECIAL NEEDS bjnw Gl
ASSOCIATION ISAI   FOUNDED 1882   RELIGIOUS AFFILIATION Inter-denom
DYSLEXIA fg   DIET acd

OTHER SUBJECTS bch
FACILITIES ON SITE b
EXAM BOARDS ab
RETAKES   NVQ COURSES

A-level:
AS:
GCSE: de g i v / BC G P R W / cdef
OTHER: lmno / A K O

G — Heathfield School GPDST; Beaulieu Drive; Pinner; Middx. HA5 1NB
Tel: 0181 868 2346 (Fax: 0181 868 4405) Mrs Jean Merritt

MAP 5 D 3
LOCATION Urban
DAY ✓   RAIL b   AIR a

		Boys	Age	Girls	Age	TOTAL		Boys	Girls
Day	£1054-£1548			469	3-18	469	SIXTH		68
Weekly									
Boarding									

SPORT abchlnopqwx BC
OTHER LANGUAGES
ACTIVITIES cfghijnost AB

ENTRY REQUIREMENTS Report & Exam & Interview
SCHOLARSHIPS & BURSARIES Schol; Burs; AP; VI Form
SPECIAL NEEDS abgjnqt
ASSOCIATION GSA   FOUNDED 1900   RELIGIOUS AFFILIATION Non-denom
DYSLEXIA   DIET ab

OTHER SUBJECTS abcdfh
FACILITIES ON SITE bch
EXAM BOARDS abd BE
RETAKES ab   NVQ COURSES

A-level: cdefg i p v / B G K P R U W / c e jl
AS: de / G / c e l
GCSE: cde g i no v / B G K P R WX / cdef j l
OTHER: lmno u / NO

C — Hellenic College of London; 67 Pont Street; London SW1X 0BD
Tel: 0171 581 5044 (Fax: 0171 589 9055) J.W.Wardrobe

MAP 5 F 4
LOCATION Urban
DAY ✓   RAIL a   AIR a

		Boys	Age	Girls	Age	TOTAL		Boys	Girls
Day	£1335-£1705 ✗	81	2-18	88	2-18	169	SIXTH	12	10
Weekly									
Boarding									

SPORT abchjlmopy ABC
OTHER LANGUAGES a
ACTIVITIES cfghijos

ENTRY REQUIREMENTS Test & Interview; Assessment & Interview; Report & Exam & Interview
SCHOLARSHIPS & BURSARIES Schol; Burs; Teachers; VI Form
SPECIAL NEEDS j
ASSOCIATION ISAI   FOUNDED 1980   • RELIGIOUS AFFILIATION Orthodox
DYSLEXIA   DIET a

OTHER SUBJECTS ach
FACILITIES ON SITE h
EXAM BOARDS abcd ADEH
RETAKES   NVQ COURSES

A-level: cd ghi p x / B GH P / c e g
AS: cd g i / G P / e g
GCSE: cd ghi l n v / B G P T / cde g
OTHER: cde g i m v / B G K OP R / cde g

LONDON (GREATER) continued

C — Hendon Preparatory School; 20 Tenterden Grove; London NW4 1TD
Tel: 0181 203 7727 (Fax: 0181 203 3465) *Trevor Lee*

		Boys	Age	Girls	Age	TOTAL		Boys	Girls
Day	£1780 ✗	205	3-13	117	3-13	322	SIXTH		
Weekly									
Boarding									

ENTRY REQUIREMENTS Test & Interview
SCHOLARSHIPS & BURSARIES
SPECIAL NEEDS B   **DYSLEXIA** f   **DIET** acd
ASSOCIATION IAPS   **FOUNDED** 1873   **RELIGIOUS AFFILIATION** Non-denom

MAP 5 E 3
LOCATION Urban
DAY   **RAIL** a   **AIR** a
SPORT aefhjnopqsx AB
OTHER LANGUAGES
ACTIVITIES fghjoq
OTHER SUBJECTS abch
FACILITIES ON SITE ac
EXAM BOARDS
RETAKES   **NVQ COURSES**

A-level | AS | GCSE | OTHER: cde lm o v B G K R cde j

B — Hereward House School; 14 Strathray Gardens; Hampstead; London NW3 4NY
Tel: 0171 794 4820 *Mrs L.Sampson*

		Boys	Age	Girls	Age	TOTAL		Boys	Girls
Day	£1550-£1715	174	4-13			174	SIXTH		
Weekly									
Boarding									

ENTRY REQUIREMENTS Interview
SCHOLARSHIPS & BURSARIES Teachers
SPECIAL NEEDS   **DYSLEXIA**   **DIET** a
ASSOCIATION ISAI   **FOUNDED** 1950   **RELIGIOUS AFFILIATION** Inter-denom

MAP 5 E 3
LOCATION Urban
DAY   **RAIL** b   **AIR** b
SPORT aefjx A
OTHER LANGUAGES
ACTIVITIES fgh
OTHER SUBJECTS cfh
FACILITIES ON SITE c
EXAM BOARDS
RETAKES   **NVQ COURSES**

A-level | AS | GCSE | OTHER: de g i l v B G K P R cde g j

C — Highfield School and Nursery; 256 Trinity Road; London SW18 3RQ
Tel: 0181 874 2778 (Fax: 0181 874 2778) *Mrs V.J.F.Lowe*

		Boys	Age	Girls	Age	TOTAL		Boys	Girls
Day	£510-£1220	78	2-11	37	2-11	115	SIXTH		
Weekly									
Boarding									

ENTRY REQUIREMENTS Interview
SCHOLARSHIPS & BURSARIES
SPECIAL NEEDS fn   **DYSLEXIA** ef   **DIET**
ASSOCIATION ISAI   **FOUNDED** 1888   **RELIGIOUS AFFILIATION** Inter-denom

MAP 5 E 5
LOCATION Urban
DAY   **RAIL** a   **AIR**
SPORT ejpqsx AB
OTHER LANGUAGES
ACTIVITIES cfgh A
OTHER SUBJECTS
FACILITIES ON SITE
EXAM BOARDS
RETAKES   **NVQ COURSES**

A-level | AS | GCSE | OTHER: e v B G K cde j

C — Highfield School; 1 Bloomfield Road; Highgate N6 4ET
Tel: 0181 340 5981 (Fax: 0181 348 2709) *Mrs L.Hayes*

		Boys	Age	Girls	Age	TOTAL		Boys	Girls
Day	£615-£1230	63	3-8	74	3-11	137	SIXTH		
Weekly									
Boarding									

ENTRY REQUIREMENTS Assessment & Interview
SCHOLARSHIPS & BURSARIES
SPECIAL NEEDS bft   **DYSLEXIA**   **DIET** acd
ASSOCIATION ISAI   **FOUNDED** 1947   **RELIGIOUS AFFILIATION**

MAP 5 E 3
LOCATION Urban
DAY   **RAIL** b   **AIR** b
SPORT ahjlopqx
OTHER LANGUAGES
ACTIVITIES ghjt
OTHER SUBJECTS abcfh
FACILITIES ON SITE
EXAM BOARDS
RETAKES   **NVQ COURSES**

A-level | AS | GCSE | OTHER: b e mno v B G K O R cde

3g — Highgate Junior School; 3 Bishopswood Road; Highgate; London N6 4PL
Tel: 0181 340 9193 (Fax: 0181 342 8225) *H.S.Evers*

		Boys	Age	Girls	Age	TOTAL		Boys	Girls
Day	£2125 ✗	438	3-13	28	3-7	466	SIXTH		
Weekly									
Boarding									

ENTRY REQUIREMENTS Test & Interview
SCHOLARSHIPS & BURSARIES AP
SPECIAL NEEDS bhjklnqstu DHI   **DYSLEXIA** e   **DIET** ac
ASSOCIATION IAPS   **FOUNDED** 1889   **RELIGIOUS AFFILIATION** C of E

MAP 5 E 3
LOCATION Urban
DAY   **RAIL** b   **AIR** a
SPORT abcefgijklmswx B
OTHER LANGUAGES
ACTIVITIES fghijoqst A
OTHER SUBJECTS bcfh
FACILITIES ON SITE bcdehik
EXAM BOARDS
RETAKES   **NVQ COURSES**

A-level | AS | GCSE | OTHER: e l no v B E G K O R cde j

LONDON (GREATER) continued

B **Highgate School; North Road; Highgate; London N6 4AY**
Tel: 0181 340 1524 (Fax: 0181 340 7674) *R.P.Kennedy*

		Boys	Age	Girls	Age	TOTAL		Boys	Girls
Day	£2375 ✗	571	13-18			609	SIXTH	202	
Weekly		38							
Boarding									

MAP 5 E 3
LOCATION Urban
DAY   RAIL b   AIR a
SPORT abcdefghijklmostuwx ABC
OTHER LANGUAGES
ACTIVITIES efghijklnoqrst AB

ENTRY REQUIREMENTS CEE; Test & Interview
SCHOLARSHIPS & BURSARIES Schol; Mus; Clergy; Teachers; AP; VI Form
SPECIAL NEEDS ejnqw Gl   **DYSLEXIA**   **DIET** acd
ASSOCIATION HMC   **FOUNDED** 1565   **RELIGIOUS AFFILIATION** C of E

OTHER SUBJECTS bcfh
FACILITIES ON SITE bcdghik
EXAM BOARDS abcd BEH
RETAKES   NVQ COURSES

A-level	cde g i op v x	AS	e u	GCSE	c e no v	OTHER	l n t
	B GH K P		G K		B G K X		O R
	c efg jkl		e		cdefg jkl		

B **Homefield School; Western Road; Sutton; Surrey SM1 2TE**
Tel: 0181 642 0965 (Fax: 0181 770 1668) *P.R.Mowbray*

		Boys	Age	Girls	Age	TOTAL		Boys	Girls
Day	£820-£1360	292	3-13			292	SIXTH		
Weekly									
Boarding									

MAP 5 E 6
LOCATION Urban
DAY ✓   RAIL a   AIR a
SPORT abcefjloswx AC
OTHER LANGUAGES
ACTIVITIES fghijo

ENTRY REQUIREMENTS Test & Interview; Assessment & Interview
SCHOLARSHIPS & BURSARIES Schol
SPECIAL NEEDS abegjklqw Gl   **DYSLEXIA**   **DIET** acd
ASSOCIATION IAPS   **FOUNDED** 1870   **RELIGIOUS AFFILIATION** Non-denom

OTHER SUBJECTS abch
FACILITIES ON SITE ach
EXAM BOARDS
RETAKES   NVQ COURSES

A-level		AS		GCSE		OTHER	bcde g i l nopq s v
							B G K OP R
							cde g j

C **Ibstock Place - The Froebel School; Clarence Lane; Roehampton; London SW15 5PY**
Tel: 0181 876 9991 (Fax: 0181 878 4897) *Mrs F.Bayliss*

		Boys	Age	Girls	Age	TOTAL		Boys	Girls
Day	£550-£1750	199	3-16	255	3-16	454	SIXTH		
Weekly									
Boarding									

MAP 5 E 5
LOCATION Urban
DAY   RAIL b   AIR a
SPORT abcegjklmnopqswx AB
OTHER LANGUAGES a
ACTIVITIES cfghjknoqst A

ENTRY REQUIREMENTS Exam; Interview; Assessment
SCHOLARSHIPS & BURSARIES Burs; Mus; Teachers
SPECIAL NEEDS abejlnq Bl   **DYSLEXIA**   **DIET** acd
ASSOCIATION ISAI   **FOUNDED** 1894   **RELIGIOUS AFFILIATION** Non-denom

OTHER SUBJECTS bcdfh
FACILITIES ON SITE bcehi
EXAM BOARDS abc E
RETAKES   NVQ COURSES

A-level		AS		GCSE	d g i l no v	OTHER	N
					BC G K OP		
					cdef l		

G **Ilford Ursuline High School; Morland Road; Ilford; Essex IG1 4QS**
Tel: 0181 554 1995 (Fax: 0181 554 9537) *Miss J.Reddington*

		Boys	Age	Girls	Age	TOTAL		Boys	Girls
Day	£1433			368	11-18	368	SIXTH		55
Weekly									
Boarding									

MAP 6 H 3
LOCATION Urban
DAY   RAIL a   AIR a
SPORT cghlmpqtuvwx ABC
OTHER LANGUAGES
ACTIVITIES fghijoq

ENTRY REQUIREMENTS Exam; Report & Interview
SCHOLARSHIPS & BURSARIES Schol; Burs; AP
SPECIAL NEEDS b   **DYSLEXIA**   **DIET** abd
ASSOCIATION GSA   **FOUNDED** 1903   **RELIGIOUS AFFILIATION** R C

OTHER SUBJECTS abcdefgh
FACILITIES ON SITE acgh
EXAM BOARDS abcd ABDEH
RETAKES b   NVQ COURSES

A-level	c e ghi l v	AS	e ghi v x	GCSE	c e g i lmn q v x	OTHER	K
	B GH K P R		B G K PRT		B G K OP R WX		
	cdef hj		bcdef		cdefgh j l		

C **Innellan House St. Andrew's School Group; 44 Love Lane; Pinner; Middx. HA5 3EX**
Tel: 0181 866 1855 *Mrs R.Edwards*

		Boys	Age	Girls	Age	TOTAL		Boys	Girls
Day	£765- £830	37	3- 8	55	3- 8	92	SIXTH		
Weekly									
Boarding									

MAP 5 C 3
LOCATION Urban
DAY   RAIL a   AIR a
SPORT lx
OTHER LANGUAGES
ACTIVITIES

ENTRY REQUIREMENTS Interview
SCHOLARSHIPS & BURSARIES
SPECIAL NEEDS   **DYSLEXIA**   **DIET** acd
ASSOCIATION ISAI   **FOUNDED** 1923   **RELIGIOUS AFFILIATION** C of E

OTHER SUBJECTS ch
FACILITIES ON SITE
EXAM BOARDS
RETAKES   NVQ COURSES

A-level		AS		GCSE		OTHER	e o s v
							B E G K O R
							cde

LONDON (GREATER) *continued*

C — Italia Conti Academy Of Theatre Arts Ltd.; Italia Conti House; 23 Goswell Road; London EC1M 7AJ Tel: 0171 608 0047 (Fax: 0171 253 1430) *C.K.Vote*

		Boys	Age	Girls	Age	TOTAL	SIXTH	Boys	Girls
Day	£1550-£2300	– 30	10-21	146	10-21	176		20	100
Weekly									
Boarding									

ENTRY REQUIREMENTS Assessment & Interview
SCHOLARSHIPS & BURSARIES
SPECIAL NEEDS   **DYSLEXIA**   **DIET** ac
ASSOCIATION ISAI   **FOUNDED** 1911   **RELIGIOUS AFFILIATION** Inter-denom

MAP 5 F 4
LOCATION Inner City
DAY   **RAIL** a   **AIR** a
SPORT
OTHER LANGUAGES
ACTIVITIES cgj
OTHER SUBJECTS h
FACILITIES ON SITE k
EXAM BOARDS ad AE
RETAKES   **NVQ COURSES**

A-level d n cd
AS
GCSE e g n v / B G l / cde
OTHER

C — James Allen's Preparatory School; East Dulwich Grove; London SE22 8TE
Tel: 0181 693 0374 (Fax: 0181 693 8031) *P Heyworth*

		Boys	Age	Girls	Age	TOTAL	SIXTH	Boys	Girls
Day	£1445-£1505		4-11		4-11				
Weekly									
Boarding									

ENTRY REQUIREMENTS
SCHOLARSHIPS & BURSARIES
SPECIAL NEEDS abjklnpqtw BGH   **DYSLEXIA**   **DIET**
ASSOCIATION IAPS   **FOUNDED**   **RELIGIOUS AFFILIATION**

MAP 5 F 5
LOCATION Urban
DAY   **RAIL** a   **AIR** c
SPORT abcefhjlmopqstvx ABC
OTHER LANGUAGES a
ACTIVITIES fghijkoqstv A
OTHER SUBJECTS bcdefh
FACILITIES ON SITE bhi
EXAM BOARDS bd A
RETAKES a   **NVQ COURSES**

A-level
AS
GCSE b d e g i l v / AB DE G K P T / cde l
OTHER e v / B G X / cd

Gb — James Allen's Girls' School; East Dulwich Grove; London SE22 8TE
Tel: 0181 693 1181 (Fax: 0181 693 7842) *Mrs Marion Gibbs*

		Boys	Age	Girls	Age	TOTAL	SIXTH	Boys	Girls
Day	£1445-£1900	68	4-11	954	4-18	1023			190
Weekly				1					
Boarding									

ENTRY REQUIREMENTS Report & Exam & Interview
SCHOLARSHIPS & BURSARIES Schol; Art; Mus; AP
SPECIAL NEEDS abjklqtw ADGI   **DYSLEXIA**   **DIET** abcd
ASSOCIATION GSA   **FOUNDED** 1741   **RELIGIOUS AFFILIATION** C of E

MAP 5 F 5
LOCATION Inner City
DAY ✓   **RAIL** a   **AIR** a
SPORT abcdfghjlmpqtvwx ABC
OTHER LANGUAGES
ACTIVITIES cfghijklnopqstvw A
OTHER SUBJECTS abcdfh
FACILITIES ON SITE cdghik
EXAM BOARDS abcd ABEGH
RETAKES   **NVQ COURSES**

A-level c efg i l nop v x / B GH K M P R / c efgh jkl
AS c f h l op x / GH K / ef
GCSE c e g i l no v / AB G K OP R X / cdefgh jkl
OTHER c efg i l nop tuv x / K NOP R / a cdefghijkl

B — John Lyon School,The; Middle Road; Harrow; Middlesex HA2 0HN
Tel: 0181 422 2046 (Fax: 0181 422 5008) *The Revd.T.J.Wright*

		Boys	Age	Girls	Age	TOTAL	SIXTH	Boys	Girls
Day	£1785	503	11-18			503		126	
Weekly									
Boarding									

ENTRY REQUIREMENTS Exam & Interview
SCHOLARSHIPS & BURSARIES Schol; Mus; AP
SPECIAL NEEDS bfjklnqw ADGHI   **DYSLEXIA** g   **DIET** abcd
ASSOCIATION HMC   **FOUNDED** 1876   **RELIGIOUS AFFILIATION** Non-denom

MAP 5 D 3
LOCATION Urban
DAY   **RAIL** a   **AIR** a
SPORT abcefhjklotwx ABC
OTHER LANGUAGES
ACTIVITIES aefghijklnoqrstu AB
OTHER SUBJECTS bcdfh
FACILITIES ON SITE abchik
EXAM BOARDS ab EH
RETAKES   **NVQ COURSES**

A-level d e g i op v / AB GH K P R / c ef j
AS de K / e
GCSE d e g i no v / AB G K P R / cdef j
OTHER l u / l

B — Keble Prep. School; Wades Hill; Winchmore Hill; London N21 1BG
Tel: 0181 360 3359 (Fax: 0181 360 4000) *G.C.Waite*

		Boys	Age	Girls	Age	TOTAL	SIXTH	Boys	Girls
Day	£690-£1590	188	4-13			188			
Weekly									
Boarding									

ENTRY REQUIREMENTS Test & Interview
SCHOLARSHIPS & BURSARIES Schol; Burs
SPECIAL NEEDS hjlnw l   **DYSLEXIA** e   **DIET**
ASSOCIATION IAPS   **FOUNDED** 1929   **RELIGIOUS AFFILIATION** Non-denom

MAP 5 F 2
LOCATION Urban
DAY   **RAIL** b   **AIR** a
SPORT abefhjlsx AB
OTHER LANGUAGES
ACTIVITIES fghijrs A
OTHER SUBJECTS bc
FACILITIES ON SITE c
EXAM BOARDS
RETAKES   **NVQ COURSES**

A-level
AS
GCSE
OTHER cde g i l no q y / B G K OP R / cde j

191

LONDON (GREATER) continued

G | Kensington Prep. School for Girls GPDST; 17 Upper Phillimore Gardens; London W8 7HF Tel: 0171 937 0108 (Fax: 0171 937 0797) *Mrs G.Lumsdon*

		Boys	Age	Girls	Age	TOTAL	Boys	Girls
Day	£1568			181	4-11	181		
Weekly								
Boarding								

MAP 5 F 4
LOCATION Inner City
DAY   **RAIL** b   **AIR** a
SPORT lpqx B
OTHER LANGUAGES
ACTIVITIES cfghjo
OTHER SUBJECTS abch
FACILITIES ON SITE
EXAM BOARDS
RETAKES   **NVQ COURSES**

ENTRY REQUIREMENTS Assessment & Interview
SCHOLARSHIPS & BURSARIES
SPECIAL NEEDS aejn
ASSOCIATION IAPS   **FOUNDED** 1873   **RELIGIOUS AFFILIATION** Inter-denom
DYSLEXIA e   **DIET** a

A-level
AS
GCSE
OTHER: e   lmno   v   B E G K O R   cde

C | King Alfred School, The; North End Road; Manor Wood; London NW11 7HY Tel: 0181 905 5599 (Fax: 0181 455 1503) *F.P.Moran*

		Boys	Age	Girls	Age	TOTAL	Boys	Girls
Day	£1165-£2150	238	4-18	247	4-18	485	23	23
Weekly								
Boarding								

MAP 5 E 3
LOCATION Urban
DAY   **RAIL** b   **AIR** b
SPORT abcefhjlmpqwx ABC
OTHER LANGUAGES a
ACTIVITIES cghjoqst A
OTHER SUBJECTS bcdfh
FACILITIES ON SITE ch
EXAM BOARDS abcd ABDE
RETAKES   **NVQ COURSES**

ENTRY REQUIREMENTS Assessment & Interview
SCHOLARSHIPS & BURSARIES
SPECIAL NEEDS bn B
ASSOCIATION GBA   **FOUNDED** 1898   **RELIGIOUS AFFILIATION** Non-denom
DYSLEXIA ce   **DIET** a

A-level: d g i l   nop   v   B   GH K   N P   c ef
AS: K
GCSE: d   l no   v   AB E G   K   NO   cdef   l
OTHER

B | King's College Junior School; Southside; Wimbledon Common SW19 4TT Tel: 0181 946 2503 (Fax: 0181 944 6892) *C.Holloway*

		Boys	Age	Girls	Age	TOTAL	Boys	Girls
Day	£1965-£2076	461	7-13			461		
Weekly								
Boarding								

MAP 5 E 5
LOCATION Urban
DAY   **RAIL** a   **AIR** a
SPORT abcdefgjlmorsuwx ABC
OTHER LANGUAGES
ACTIVITIES afghijnost A
OTHER SUBJECTS cfh
FACILITIES ON SITE achik
EXAM BOARDS
RETAKES   **NVQ COURSES**

ENTRY REQUIREMENTS Report & Exam & Interview
SCHOLARSHIPS & BURSARIES Schol; Burs; AP
SPECIAL NEEDS jlq G
ASSOCIATION IAPS   **FOUNDED** 1912   **RELIGIOUS AFFILIATION** C of E
DYSLEXIA   **DIET** acd

A-level
AS
GCSE
OTHER: c e g i l   o q   v   B   G K   OP R   cdefg j l

B | King's College School; Southside; Wimbledon Common; London SW19 4TT Tel: 0181 947 9311 (Fax: 0181 947 1712) *R.M.Reeve*

		Boys	Age	Girls	Age	TOTAL	Boys	Girls
Day	£2090	720	13-18			720	269	
Weekly								
Boarding								

MAP 5 E 5
LOCATION Urban
DAY   **RAIL** a   **AIR** a
SPORT abcdefghjkmorstuwx AB
OTHER LANGUAGES
ACTIVITIES aefghijklnopqstuvw
OTHER SUBJECTS abcfh
FACILITIES ON SITE acdghik
EXAM BOARDS abcd BEHL
RETAKES   **NVQ COURSES**

ENTRY REQUIREMENTS CEE
SCHOLARSHIPS & BURSARIES Schol; Mus; Clergy; AP
SPECIAL NEEDS abefjklnpqs AGHI
ASSOCIATION HMC   **FOUNDED** 1829   **RELIGIOUS AFFILIATION** C of E
DYSLEXIA   **DIET** ab

A-level: cde g i l   op   v   B   GH K   P   U   c efgh j l
AS: h l   G K   ef   kl   x
GCSE: cde g i l   o   v   B   G K   P   x   cdefgh jkl
OTHER: q u   F   JKLMNO QR   i

B | King's House; 68 King's Road; Richmond; Surrey TW10 6ES Tel: 0181 940 1878 *R.H.L.Armitage*

		Boys	Age	Girls	Age	TOTAL	Boys	Girls
Day	£1120-£1575	324	4-13			324		
Weekly								
Boarding								

MAP 5 D 5
LOCATION Urban
DAY   **RAIL** b   **AIR** a
SPORT abcefhjkmswx AB
OTHER LANGUAGES
ACTIVITIES fghjo A
OTHER SUBJECTS ch
FACILITIES ON SITE ck
EXAM BOARDS
RETAKES   **NVQ COURSES**

ENTRY REQUIREMENTS Test; Interview
SCHOLARSHIPS & BURSARIES
SPECIAL NEEDS ejk BGI
ASSOCIATION IAPS   **FOUNDED** 1946   **RELIGIOUS AFFILIATION** Inter-denom
DYSLEXIA   **DIET** abcd

A-level
AS
GCSE
OTHER: e g i l   o   v   B   G K   OP R   cde   j

LONDON (GREATER) *continued*

Kingston Grammar School; 70 London Road; Kingston upon Thames; Surrey KT2 6PY Tel: 0181 546 5875 (Fax: 0181 547 1499) *C.D.Baxter*

		Boys	Age	Girls	Age	TOTAL		Boys	Girls
Day Weekly Boarding	£1710-£1795	383	10-18	214	10-18	597	SIXTH	90	54

ENTRY REQUIREMENTS CEE; Exam; Scholarship Exam
SCHOLARSHIPS & BURSARIES Schol; Burs; Art; Mus; Teachers; AP; VI Form; Sport
SPECIAL NEEDS abjklqtwx G **DYSLEXIA** **DIET** abcd
ASSOCIATION HMC **FOUNDED** 1561 **RELIGIOUS AFFILIATION** C of E

MAP 5 D 5
LOCATION Urban
DAY   RAIL a   **AIR** a
SPORT abcefhlmpruwx AB
OTHER LANGUAGES
ACTIVITIES efghijklopqrsv AB
OTHER SUBJECTS abcd
FACILITIES ON SITE abck
EXAM BOARDS abcd ABDEGH
RETAKES a   **NVQ COURSES**

| A-level | c e g i   n p   v x
B   GH K   OP R   U
cdef   j | AS | e
G   K | GCSE | e g i   o   v
B   FG   K   N P R   U
cdef   j l | OTHER | l   o   u
O |

Lady Eden's School; 39-41 Victoria Road; London W8 5RJ Tel: 0171 937 0583 (Fax: 0171 376 0515) *Mrs G.A.Wayne*

		Boys	Age	Girls	Age	TOTAL		Boys	Girls
Day Weekly Boarding	£825-£1895 ✗			153	3-11	153	SIXTH		

ENTRY REQUIREMENTS Test & Interview
SCHOLARSHIPS & BURSARIES
SPECIAL NEEDS **DYSLEXIA** **DIET** acd
ASSOCIATION IAPS **FOUNDED** 1947 **RELIGIOUS AFFILIATION** Non-denom

MAP 5 E 4
LOCATION Inner City
DAY   RAIL b   **AIR** a
SPORT aglpqvx B
OTHER LANGUAGES
ACTIVITIES cfghjq A
OTHER SUBJECTS ach
FACILITIES ON SITE
EXAM BOARDS
RETAKES   **NVQ COURSES**

| A-level | | AS | | GCSE | | OTHER | ef   lmno   v
B   G   K   O R
cde   j |

Lady Eleanor Holles School,The; Hanworth Road; Hampton; Middlesex TW12 3HF Tel: 0181 979 1601 (Fax: 0181 941 8291) *Miss E.M.Candy*

		Boys	Age	Girls	Age	TOTAL		Boys	Girls
Day Weekly Boarding	£1450-£1680			867	7-18	867	SIXTH		171

ENTRY REQUIREMENTS Exam & Interview
SCHOLARSHIPS & BURSARIES Schol; Burs; Mus; AP; VI Form
SPECIAL NEEDS bh **DYSLEXIA** **DIET** abc
ASSOCIATION GSA **FOUNDED** 1711 **RELIGIOUS AFFILIATION** C of E

MAP 5 C 5
LOCATION Urban
DAY   RAIL a   **AIR** a
SPORT acglmnpqrx AB
OTHER LANGUAGES
ACTIVITIES fghijknost AB
OTHER SUBJECTS abcdefgh
FACILITIES ON SITE bcdgik
EXAM BOARDS abcd ABDEGH
RETAKES   **NVQ COURSES**

| A-level | c e g i   n p   uv
BC   GH K   PQR   W
cdefg   jkl | AS | c   f h
G   K
def   l | p
QR | wx
U | GCSE | e g i   q   v
BC   G   K   P R   W
cdefg   jkl | OTHER | o
N |

Latymer Upper School; King Street; London W6 9LR Tel: 0181 741 1851 (Fax: 0181 748 5212) *C.Diggory*

		Boys	Age	Girls	Age	TOTAL		Boys	Girls
Day Weekly Boarding	£1697-£1934	1065	7-18			1065	SIXTH	244	

ENTRY REQUIREMENTS Exam & Interview
SCHOLARSHIPS & BURSARIES Schol; Burs; Mus; AP
SPECIAL NEEDS bfhijlnqs A **DYSLEXIA** g **DIET** abcd
ASSOCIATION HMC **FOUNDED** 1624 **RELIGIOUS AFFILIATION** Non-denom

MAP 5 E 4
LOCATION Urban
DAY   RAIL b   **AIR** a
SPORT abcefghjklorstwx AB
OTHER LANGUAGES
ACTIVITIES fghijklnoqrstx A
OTHER SUBJECTS abcfh
FACILITIES ON SITE cdhi
EXAM BOARDS abcdf ABEGHI
RETAKES   **NVQ COURSES**

| A-level | cdefg i   op   v x
B   GH K   P R
c efg   j | AS | f l   p   v
G K | GCSE | e g i   o   v x
B E G   K   P R
cdefgh   skl | OTHER | l   u |

Lyndhurst House Prep. School; 24 Lyndhurst Gardens; Hampstead; London NW3 5NW Tel: 0171 435 4936 *M.O.Spilberg*

		Boys	Age	Girls	Age	TOTAL		Boys	Girls
Day Weekly Boarding	£1810 ✗	143	7-13			143	SIXTH		

ENTRY REQUIREMENTS Test
SCHOLARSHIPS & BURSARIES
SPECIAL NEEDS bjw l **DYSLEXIA** **DIET** a
ASSOCIATION IAPS **FOUNDED** 1952 **RELIGIOUS AFFILIATION** Inter-denom

MAP 5 E 3
LOCATION Inner City
DAY   RAIL b   **AIR** b
SPORT abefjq AB
OTHER LANGUAGES
ACTIVITIES fghjot A
OTHER SUBJECTS fh
FACILITIES ON SITE
EXAM BOARDS
RETAKES   **NVQ COURSES**

| A-level | | AS | | GCSE | | OTHER | defg i l   v
B   G   K   OP R
cde g   j |

193

LONDON (GREATER) continued

B — Mall School; 185 Hampton Road; Twickenham; Middlesex TW2 5NQ
Tel: 0181 977 2523 *T.P.A.Mac Donogh*

		Boys	Age	Girls	Age	TOTAL		Boys	Girls
Day	£1250–£1450 ✗	291	4–13			291	SIXTH		
Weekly									
Boarding									

MAP 5 D 5
LOCATION Urban
DAY **RAIL** a **AIR** a
SPORT abefgjosx AB
OTHER LANGUAGES
ACTIVITIES fghjot A
OTHER SUBJECTS cfh
FACILITIES ON SITE cik
EXAM BOARDS
RETAKES **NVQ COURSES**

ENTRY REQUIREMENTS
SCHOLARSHIPS & BURSARIES Burs; Clergy
SPECIAL NEEDS knp Gl **DYSLEXIA** **DIET** acd
ASSOCIATION IAPS **FOUNDED** 1872 **RELIGIOUS AFFILIATION** C of E

A-level: e g i l o v / B G K OP R / cde g j
AS:
GCSE:
OTHER:

G — Marymount International School; George Road; Kingston upon Thames; Surrey KT2 7PE
Tel: 0181 949 0571 (Fax: 0181 336 2485) *Sister Rosaleen Sheridan*

		Boys	Age	Girls	Age	TOTAL		Boys	Girls
Day	£2300–£2567			90	11–18	190	SIXTH		109
Weekly	£4116–£4383			5	11–18				
Boarding	£4183–£4450			95	11–18				

MAP 5 D 5
LOCATION Urban
DAY **RAIL** a **AIR** a
SPORT bc BC
OTHER LANGUAGES a
ACTIVITIES gj
OTHER SUBJECTS bcdh
FACILITIES ON SITE dhk
EXAM BOARDS C
RETAKES **NVQ COURSES**

ENTRY REQUIREMENTS Report & Interview
SCHOLARSHIPS & BURSARIES Burs
SPECIAL NEEDS **DYSLEXIA** **DIET** ad
ASSOCIATION GSA **FOUNDED** 1955 **RELIGIOUS AFFILIATION** R C

A-level: efg i l n p / B GH K PQR / a cde i l
AS:
GCSE:
OTHER:

B — Merchant Taylors' School; Sandy Lodge; Northwood; Middlesex HA6 2HT
Tel: 01923 821850 (Fax: 01923 835110) *J.R.Gabitass*

		Boys	Age	Girls	Age	TOTAL		Boys	Girls
Day	£1917	689	11–18			748	SIXTH	255	
Weekly			11–18						
Boarding	£3674	59	11–18						

MAP 5 C 3
LOCATION Rural
DAY **RAIL** a **AIR** a
SPORT abcdefghijkmostuwx AB
OTHER LANGUAGES
ACTIVITIES befghijklmnoqrst ABD
OTHER SUBJECTS abcdfh
FACILITIES ON SITE bcdeghik
EXAM BOARDS abd EGH
RETAKES **NVQ COURSES**

ENTRY REQUIREMENTS CEE; Exam
SCHOLARSHIPS & BURSARIES Schol; Art; Mus; AP; VI Form
SPECIAL NEEDS behjklqst ACDGHIKL **DYSLEXIA** **DIET** abcd
ASSOCIATION HMC **FOUNDED** 1561 **RELIGIOUS AFFILIATION** C of E

A-level: de g i nopq uv x / B GH K N P R / c efg jk
AS:
GCSE: de g i l op v / B GH K P R / cdefg jkl
OTHER: o / hi l

Bg — Mill Hill School; The Ridgeway; London NW7 1QS
Tel: 0181 959 1176 (Fax: 0181 201 0663)

		Boys	Age	Girls	Age	TOTAL		Boys	Girls
Day	£2510 ✗	335	13–18	10	16–18	527	SIXTH	175	28
Weekly			13–18		16–18				
Boarding	£3880	160	13–18	22	16–18				

MAP 5 D 2
LOCATION Urban
DAY **RAIL** a **AIR** a
SPORT abcdefghijklmopstuwx ABC
OTHER LANGUAGES a
ACTIVITIES efghijklnopqstvw AB
OTHER SUBJECTS abcdfh
FACILITIES ON SITE abcdeghijk
EXAM BOARDS abcd ABDEH
RETAKES **NVQ COURSES**

ENTRY REQUIREMENTS Scholarship Exam; CEE & Interview; Report & Exam & Interview
SCHOLARSHIPS & BURSARIES Schol; Mus; Forces; Clergy; AP
SPECIAL NEEDS **DYSLEXIA** g **DIET** acd
ASSOCIATION HMC **FOUNDED** 1807 **RELIGIOUS AFFILIATION** Non-denom

A-level: cde ghi l nop v x / B GH K P / cdef j l
AS: l / e
GCSE: cde ghi l nopq v / B E G I K OP / cdef j l
OTHER: M O R / cd

G — More House School; 22-24 Pont Street; London SW1X 0AA
Tel: 0171 235 2855 (Fax: 0171 259 6782) *Miss M.Connell*

		Boys	Age	Girls	Age	TOTAL		Boys	Girls
Day	£1820 ✗			227	10–18	227	SIXTH		50
Weekly									
Boarding									

MAP 5 F 4
LOCATION Inner City
DAY **RAIL** a **AIR** a
SPORT bcegjlmpqwx ABC
OTHER LANGUAGES a
ACTIVITIES cfghijnoqs A
OTHER SUBJECTS ach
FACILITIES ON SITE d
EXAM BOARDS abcd AEH
RETAKES **NVQ COURSES**

ENTRY REQUIREMENTS Exam & Interview
SCHOLARSHIPS & BURSARIES Schol; Burs
SPECIAL NEEDS ejkn Gl **DYSLEXIA** g **DIET** a
ASSOCIATION GSA **FOUNDED** 1953 **RELIGIOUS AFFILIATION** R C

A-level: d fg i p v / B G K P R / cdef l
AS: G
GCSE: d g i n v / B G K P R / cdef j l
OTHER:

LONDON (GREATER) continued

Mount School; Milespit Hill; Mill Hill; London NW7 2RX
Tel: 0181 959 3403 (Fax: 0181 959 1503) Mrs M.Pond

	Boys	Age	Girls	Age	TOTAL		Boys	Girls
Day £1060-£1185			434	5-18	434	SIXTH		84
Weekly Boarding								

ENTRY REQUIREMENTS Test & Interview
SCHOLARSHIPS & BURSARIES Schol; Burs; VI Form
SPECIAL NEEDS ghijklnpqtw AHI
DYSLEXIA g   **DIET** a
ASSOCIATION ISAI   **FOUNDED** 1925   **RELIGIOUS AFFILIATION** Inter-denom

MAP 5 E 2
LOCATION Rural
DAY ✓   **RAIL** b   **AIR** b
SPORT abchlmpqwx BC
OTHER LANGUAGES a
ACTIVITIES ghijnow A
OTHER SUBJECTS bcdegh
FACILITIES ON SITE cg
EXAM BOARDS abcd ABDEFGI
RETAKES ab   **NVQ COURSES**

| A-level | cdefghij l n p v x
B GH K P R TU
cdef hij l | AS | cde ghi x
G K P R U W
cde | GCSE | cde ghij l nop v
B E G K OP R UV
cde hij l | OTHER | q u
I K OP R
cde |

Newland House School; Waldegrave Park; Twickenham; Middx. TW1 4TQ
Tel: 0181 892 7479 (Fax: 0181 744 0399) D.J.Ott

	Boys	Age	Girls	Age	TOTAL		Boys	Girls
Day £990-£1480 ✗	278	4-12	151	4-10	429	SIXTH		

ENTRY REQUIREMENTS
SCHOLARSHIPS & BURSARIES
SPECIAL NEEDS bejlnq GI
DYSLEXIA   **DIET** a
ASSOCIATION IAPS   **FOUNDED** 1897   **RELIGIOUS AFFILIATION** C of E

MAP 5 D 5
LOCATION Urban
DAY ✓   **RAIL** a   **AIR** a
SPORT acefjlmpqswx AB
OTHER LANGUAGES
ACTIVITIES fghijoqst A
OTHER SUBJECTS cfh
FACILITIES ON SITE chk
EXAM BOARDS
RETAKES   **NVQ COURSES**

| A-level | | AS | | GCSE | | OTHER | e l o uv
B G K O R
cde g j |

Norland Place School; 162-166 Holland Park Avenue; London W11 4UH
Tel: 0171 603 9103 (Fax: 0171 603 0648) Mrs S.J.Garnsey

	Boys	Age	Girls	Age	TOTAL		Boys	Girls
Day £1170-£1860	91	4- 8	153	4-11	244	SIXTH		
Weekly Boarding								

ENTRY REQUIREMENTS
SCHOLARSHIPS & BURSARIES
SPECIAL NEEDS
DYSLEXIA   **DIET** acd
ASSOCIATION IAPS   **FOUNDED** 1876   **RELIGIOUS AFFILIATION** Inter-denom

MAP 5 E 4
LOCATION Urban
DAY ✓   **RAIL** b   **AIR** a
SPORT jpqx B
OTHER LANGUAGES
ACTIVITIES gjot
OTHER SUBJECTS c
FACILITIES ON SITE c
EXAM BOARDS
RETAKES   **NVQ COURSES**

| A-level | | AS | | GCSE | | OTHER | e o v
B G K O
cde |

North London Collegiate School,The; Canons; Edgware HA8 7RJ
Tel: 0181 952 0912 (Fax: 0181 951 1391) Mrs J.L.Clanchy

	Boys	Age	Girls	Age	TOTAL		Boys	Girls
Day £1304-£1616			971	4-18	971	SIXTH		220
Weekly Boarding								

ENTRY REQUIREMENTS Exam & Interview
SCHOLARSHIPS & BURSARIES Schol; Burs; Mus; AP
SPECIAL NEEDS aijklnqtx G
DYSLEXIA   **DIET** a
ASSOCIATION GSA   **FOUNDED** 1850   **RELIGIOUS AFFILIATION** Non-denom

MAP 5 D 2
LOCATION Urban
DAY ✓   **RAIL** ✓   **AIR** ✓
SPORT acdfghlnpqtx ABC
OTHER LANGUAGES
ACTIVITIES fghijklnoqrst AB
OTHER SUBJECTS abcdfh
FACILITIES ON SITE abcgik
EXAM BOARDS ab BEH
RETAKES   **NVQ COURSES**

| A-level | cdef i l op v x
B GH K P R U
cdefg jkl | AS | G K
c ef | GCSE | de g i l no v
B G K P R
cdefgh jkl | OTHER | q s u
MNO Q
a |

Northwood College; Maxwell Road; Northwood; Middx. HA6 2YE
Tel: 01923 825446 (Fax: 01923 836526) Mrs A.Mayou

	Boys	Age	Girls	Age	TOTAL		Boys	Girls
Day £1099-£1612 ✗			617	4-18	617	SIXTH		77
Weekly Boarding								

ENTRY REQUIREMENTS Report & Exam & Interview
SCHOLARSHIPS & BURSARIES VI Form
SPECIAL NEEDS abjlnqtx ABGI
DYSLEXIA f   **DIET** acd
ASSOCIATION GSA   **FOUNDED** 1878   **RELIGIOUS AFFILIATION** Non-denom

MAP 5 C 3
LOCATION Urban
DAY ✓   **RAIL** b   **AIR** a
SPORT cklmopqwx ABC
OTHER LANGUAGES a
ACTIVITIES cefghijknor ABD
OTHER SUBJECTS abch
FACILITIES ON SITE cghik
EXAM BOARDS abcd BDEGL
RETAKES   **NVQ COURSES**

| A-level | cd ghi n p v x
ABC GH K P R U W
cdefg j l | AS | d g
G K R W
cdefg j | GCSE | cd g i no v
BCD G K OP R
cdefg j l | OTHER | klm u
A O R
ef hi l |

LONDON (GREATER) continued

G | Notting Hill & Ealing High School GPDST; 2 Cleveland Road; London W13 8AX
Tel: 0181 997 5744 (Fax: 0181 810 6891) *Mrs S.M.Whitfield*

	Boys	Age	Girls	Age	TOTAL	Boys	Girls
Day £1192-£1548			840	5-18	840	SIXTH	147
Weekly							
Boarding							

MAP 5 D 4
LOCATION Urban
DAY   **RAIL** a   **AIR** a
SPORT acklmpqwx AB
OTHER LANGUAGES
ACTIVITIES ghijkosv A

ENTRY REQUIREMENTS Test & Interview; Exam & Interview
SCHOLARSHIPS & BURSARIES Burs; AP
SPECIAL NEEDS ejlnpq   **DYSLEXIA** e   **DIET** ac
ASSOCIATION GSA   **FOUNDED** 1873   **RELIGIOUS AFFILIATION**
OTHER SUBJECTS bch
FACILITIES ON SITE k
EXAM BOARDS abc E
RETAKES   **NVQ COURSES**

A-level: efg i n v x   B GH K P R   cdefg j l
AS: G
GCSE: c e o v   B E G K R   cdefgh j l
OTHER: l n u   O T   h

C | Oakfield Preparatory School; 125-128 Thurlow Park Road; Dulwich; London SE21 8HP
Tel: 0181 670 4206 (Fax: 0181 766 6744) *Mrs Anne Tomkins*

	Boys	Age	Girls	Age	TOTAL	Boys	Girls
Day £600-£1200 ✗	249	2-11	218	2-11	467	SIXTH	
Weekly							
Boarding							

MAP 5 F 5
LOCATION Urban
DAY a   **RAIL** a   **AIR** c
SPORT abefhjlmpqx AB
OTHER LANGUAGES
ACTIVITIES cfghijnot A

ENTRY REQUIREMENTS Test; Assessment
SCHOLARSHIPS & BURSARIES
SPECIAL NEEDS   **DYSLEXIA**   **DIET**
ASSOCIATION ISAI   **FOUNDED** 1887   **RELIGIOUS AFFILIATION** Non-denom
OTHER SUBJECTS
FACILITIES ON SITE bh
EXAM BOARDS
RETAKES   **NVQ COURSES**

A-level:
AS:
GCSE:
OTHER: e lmn v   B D E G K O R   cde

G | Old Palace School of John Whitgift; Old Palace Road; Croydon CR0 1AX
Tel: 0181 688 2027 (Fax: 0181 680 5877) *Miss K.L.Hilton*

	Boys	Age	Girls	Age	TOTAL	Boys	Girls
Day £975-£1326			817	4-18	817	SIXTH	160
Weekly							
Boarding							

MAP 5 F 6
LOCATION Urban
DAY   **RAIL** a   **AIR** ab
SPORT afhlmpx AB
OTHER LANGUAGES o
ACTIVITIES fgijknoq AB

ENTRY REQUIREMENTS Exam
SCHOLARSHIPS & BURSARIES Schol; Burs; Mus; Clergy; Teachers; AP
SPECIAL NEEDS l   **DYSLEXIA**   **DIET**
ASSOCIATION GSA   **FOUNDED** 1889   **RELIGIOUS AFFILIATION** C of E
OTHER SUBJECTS abcdh
FACILITIES ON SITE cdg
EXAM BOARDS abcd ADEG
RETAKES   **NVQ COURSES**

A-level: cde g i l op uv x   BC GH K P R U W   cdefgh j l
AS: g i u   G   ef h l
GCSE: cdefg i l nopq uv x   BC E G K P R U W   cdefgh jkl
OTHER:

G | Old Vicarage School; 48 Richmond Hill; Richmond; Surrey TW10 6QX
Tel: 0181 940 0922 *Miss J.Reynolds*

	Boys	Age	Girls	Age	TOTAL	Boys	Girls
Day £1100-£1340			164	4-11	164	SIXTH	
Weekly							
Boarding							

MAP 5 D 5
LOCATION Inner City
DAY   **RAIL** a   **AIR** b
SPORT aglpqx
OTHER LANGUAGES
ACTIVITIES gjotv

ENTRY REQUIREMENTS None
SCHOLARSHIPS & BURSARIES
SPECIAL NEEDS jw l   **DYSLEXIA**   **DIET** acd
ASSOCIATION IAPS   **FOUNDED** 1881   **RELIGIOUS AFFILIATION** Non-denom
OTHER SUBJECTS ch
FACILITIES ON SITE
EXAM BOARDS
RETAKES   **NVQ COURSES**

A-level:
AS:
GCSE:
OTHER: de lmn s v   B G K O R   cde

C | Orley Farm School; South Hill Avenue; Harrow On The Hill; Middx. HA1 3NU
Tel: 0181 422 1525 (Fax: 0181 422 2479) *I.S.Elliott*

	Boys	Age	Girls	Age	TOTAL	Boys	Girls
Day £1159-£1648 ✗	432	4-13	24	4-13	456	SIXTH	
Weekly							
Boarding							

MAP 5 D 3
LOCATION Rural
DAY   **RAIL** b   **AIR** a
SPORT abcefhijklosuwx AB
OTHER LANGUAGES
ACTIVITIES fghijoqst

ENTRY REQUIREMENTS Test & Interview
SCHOLARSHIPS & BURSARIES Burs
SPECIAL NEEDS bejls   **DYSLEXIA**   **DIET** acd
ASSOCIATION IAPS   **FOUNDED** 1850   **RELIGIOUS AFFILIATION** C of E
OTHER SUBJECTS bcfh
FACILITIES ON SITE bchjk
EXAM BOARDS
RETAKES   **NVQ COURSES**

A-level:
AS:
GCSE:
OTHER: e l o q v   B G K R   cde j

LONDON (GREATER) *continued*

Palmers Green High School; Hoppers Road; Winchmore Hill; London N21 3LJ
Tel: 0181 886 1135 (Fax: 0181 882 9473) *Mrs S.Grant*

	Boys	Age	Girls 292	Age 3-16	TOTAL 292	SIXTH Boys	Girls
Day £512-£1340							
Weekly							
Boarding							

ENTRY REQUIREMENTS Test & Interview
SCHOLARSHIPS & BURSARIES Schol; Burs; Mus
SPECIAL NEEDS b   **DYSLEXIA**   **DIET** acd
ASSOCIATION GSA   **FOUNDED** 1905   **RELIGIOUS AFFILIATION** Inter-denom

MAP 5 F 2
LOCATION Urban
DAY ✓   **RAIL** b   **AIR** a
SPORT abclmpqvwx ABC
OTHER LANGUAGES
ACTIVITIES cfghijkopqst A
OTHER SUBJECTS bcf
FACILITIES ON SITE chk
EXAM BOARDS abcd
RETAKES   **NVQ COURSES**

A-level | AS | GCSE B E G K d h l no s v cdef O | OTHER l NO R

Parayhouse School; St. John's; World's End; King's Road; London SW10 0LU
Tel: 0171 352 2882 (Fax: 0171 352 2882) *Mrs S.L.Jackson*

	Boys 24	Age 4-17	Girls 19	Age 4-17	TOTAL 43	SIXTH Boys 4	Girls 3
Day £2100-£3100							
Weekly							
Boarding							

ENTRY REQUIREMENTS Assessment & Interview
SCHOLARSHIPS & BURSARIES
SPECIAL NEEDS bcefhijklmnoqtu BGHIL   **DYSLEXIA**   **DIET**
ASSOCIATION ISAI   **FOUNDED** 1964   **RELIGIOUS AFFILIATION** Non-denom

MAP 5 E 4
LOCATION Inner City
DAY   **RAIL** a   **AIR** a
SPORT bhjmpqx
OTHER LANGUAGES
ACTIVITIES jkt
OTHER SUBJECTS bcdfh
FACILITIES ON SITE
EXAM BOARDS L
RETAKES   **NVQ COURSES**

A-level | AS | GCSE BC G e kl cde | OTHER uv

Pembridge Hall School; 18 Pembridge Square; London W2 4EH
Tel: 0171 229 0121 (Fax: 0171 792 1086) *Mrs L.Marani*

	Boys	Age	Girls 232	Age 5-11	TOTAL 232	SIXTH Boys	Girls
Day £1565							
Weekly							
Boarding							

ENTRY REQUIREMENTS None
SCHOLARSHIPS & BURSARIES
SPECIAL NEEDS bjklnq BG   **DYSLEXIA** cde   **DIET**
ASSOCIATION IAPS   **FOUNDED** 1979   **RELIGIOUS AFFILIATION** Non-denom

MAP 5 E 4
LOCATION Inner City
DAY   **RAIL** a   **AIR** a
SPORT aclpqx B
OTHER LANGUAGES
ACTIVITIES cghjot
OTHER SUBJECTS cfh
FACILITIES ON SITE
EXAM BOARDS
RETAKES   **NVQ COURSES**

A-level | AS | GCSE B e lmno v cde G K O | OTHER

Peterborough & St. Margarets; School For Girls; Tanglewood; Common Road; Stanmore; Middlesex HA7 3JB
Tel: 0181 950 3600 (Fax: 0181 861 4767) *Mrs D.M.Tomlinson*

	Boys	Age	Girls 203	Age 4-16	TOTAL 203	SIXTH Boys	Girls
Day £960-£1420							
Weekly							
Boarding							

ENTRY REQUIREMENTS Exam; Interview   **SCHOLARSHIPS & BURSARIES** Burs
SPECIAL NEEDS abfhjklnqt GH   **DYSLEXIA**   **DIET** abcd
ASSOCIATION ISAI   **FOUNDED** 1902   **RELIGIOUS AFFILIATION** C of E

MAP 5 D 2
LOCATION Rural
DAY ✓   **RAIL** b   **AIR** a
SPORT afhlpqx ABC
OTHER LANGUAGES
ACTIVITIES cfgijnos A
OTHER SUBJECTS abch
FACILITIES ON SITE ahk
EXAM BOARDS abd
RETAKES   **NVQ COURSES**

A-level | AS | GCSE BC G K d g i l v cdef P R W | OTHER

Prospect House School; 75 Putney Hill; London SW15 3NT
Tel: 0181 780 0456 (Fax: 0181 940 5007) *Mrs S.C.Eley & Mrs H.M.Gerry*

	Boys 88	Age 3-11	Girls 107	Age 3-11	TOTAL 195	SIXTH Boys	Girls
Day £720-£1588							
Weekly							
Boarding							

ENTRY REQUIREMENTS
SCHOLARSHIPS & BURSARIES
SPECIAL NEEDS an B   **DYSLEXIA**   **DIET**
ASSOCIATION IAPS   **FOUNDED** 1991   **RELIGIOUS AFFILIATION** Christian

MAP 5 E 5
LOCATION Urban
DAY   **RAIL** b   **AIR** a
SPORT acejlmpqx B
OTHER LANGUAGES
ACTIVITIES cfghjt
OTHER SUBJECTS c
FACILITIES ON SITE a
EXAM BOARDS
RETAKES   **NVQ COURSES**

A-level | AS | GCSE B e lmno v K O R e | OTHER

LONDON (GREATER) *continued*

C | **Purcell School of Music; Mount Park Road; Harrow On The Hill; Middx. HA1 3JS**
Tel: 0181 422 1284 (Fax: 0181 423 0526) *K.J.Bain*

MAP 5 D 3
LOCATION Rural
DAY ✓ RAIL b AIR a

		Boys	Age	Girls	Age	TOTAL		Boys	Girls
Day	£3136-£3651	18	8-18	34	8-18	154	SIXTH	23	41
Weekly									
Boarding	£5046-£5613	41	8-18	61	8-18				

SPORT bcdjwx A
OTHER LANGUAGES a
ACTIVITIES fgjo

ENTRY REQUIREMENTS
SCHOLARSHIPS & BURSARIES Burs; Mus
SPECIAL NEEDS bdefghjklnopqstuvwx ABDEGHIJ   **DYSLEXIA** g   **DIET** a
ASSOCIATION SHMIS   **FOUNDED** 1962   **RELIGIOUS AFFILIATION**

OTHER SUBJECTS bcdh
FACILITIES ON SITE
EXAM BOARDS abd ABE
RETAKES a   NVQ COURSES

A-level: B G K e l v K cdef
AS: e G
GCSE: B G K e l n v X cdef
OTHER:

G | **Putney High School GPDST; 35 Putney Hill; London SW15 6BH**
Tel: 0181 788 4886 (Fax: 0181 789 8068) *Mrs E.Merchant*

MAP 5 E 5
LOCATION Urban
DAY RAIL a AIR b

		Boys	Age	Girls	Age	TOTAL		Boys	Girls
Day	£1192-£1548			849	4-18	849	SIXTH		153
Weekly									
Boarding									

SPORT acghjlmpqrsx BC
OTHER LANGUAGES
ACTIVITIES cfghijknopqs AB

ENTRY REQUIREMENTS Report & Exam & Interview
SCHOLARSHIPS & BURSARIES Schol; Burs; Mus; AP
SPECIAL NEEDS n   **DYSLEXIA**   **DIET** acd
ASSOCIATION GSA   **FOUNDED** 1893   **RELIGIOUS AFFILIATION** Inter-denom

OTHER SUBJECTS abch
FACILITIES ON SITE
EXAM BOARDS abd BEH
RETAKES   NVQ COURSES

A-level: B GH K c efg i l op v P R W c efgh j l
AS: GH g P
GCSE: BC G K c e g i l o v P R W cdefgh j l
OTHER:

Gb | **Putney Park School; Woodborough Road; London SW15 6PY**
Tel: 0181 788 8316 *P.F.Thomson*

MAP 5 E 5
LOCATION Urban
DAY ✓ RAIL b AIR a

		Boys	Age	Girls	Age	TOTAL		Boys	Girls
Day	£1270-£1460	93	4-9	234	4-16	327	SIXTH		
Weekly									
Boarding									

SPORT abclmpqwx BC
OTHER LANGUAGES a
ACTIVITIES cfghjt A

ENTRY REQUIREMENTS
SCHOLARSHIPS & BURSARIES Burs
SPECIAL NEEDS   **DYSLEXIA** g   **DIET**
ASSOCIATION ISAI   **FOUNDED** 1953   **RELIGIOUS AFFILIATION** Christian

OTHER SUBJECTS cfh
FACILITIES ON SITE
EXAM BOARDS abd EG
RETAKES   NVQ COURSES

A-level:
AS:
GCSE: BC E G K de v cdef
OTHER:

B | **Quainton Hall School; Hindes Road; Harrow; Middlesex HA1 1RX**
Tel: 0181 427 1304 (Fax: 0181 424 0914) *P.J.Milner*

MAP 5 D 3
LOCATION Urban
DAY RAIL AIR a

		Boys	Age	Girls	Age	TOTAL		Boys	Girls
Day	£1080-£1446 ✗	221	4-13			221	SIXTH		
Weekly									
Boarding									

SPORT abcefhjosx ABC
OTHER LANGUAGES
ACTIVITIES fghijnoq

ENTRY REQUIREMENTS Assessment & Interview
SCHOLARSHIPS & BURSARIES Burs; Clergy; Teachers
SPECIAL NEEDS bejnuw G   **DYSLEXIA** e   **DIET** a
ASSOCIATION IAPS   **FOUNDED** 1897   **RELIGIOUS AFFILIATION** C of E

OTHER SUBJECTS bch
FACILITIES ON SITE acdhi
EXAM BOARDS
RETAKES   NVQ COURSES

A-level:
AS:
GCSE:
OTHER: B G K c e g i l no q s v OP R cdef j

G | **Queen's College London; 43 Harley Street; London W1N 2BT;**
Tel: 0171 580 1533 (Fax: 0171 436 7607) *The Hon Lady Goodhart*

MAP 5 F 4
LOCATION Inner City
DAY RAIL a AIR a

		Boys	Age	Girls	Age	TOTAL		Boys	Girls
Day	£1940			368	11-18	368	SIXTH		95
Weekly									
Boarding									

SPORT ghlmpqx B
OTHER LANGUAGES
ACTIVITIES cghijnostu

ENTRY REQUIREMENTS Exam & Interview
SCHOLARSHIPS & BURSARIES Schol; Art; Mus; AP; VI Form
SPECIAL NEEDS   **DYSLEXIA**   **DIET** acd
ASSOCIATION GSA   **FOUNDED** 1848   **RELIGIOUS AFFILIATION** C of E

OTHER SUBJECTS abcfh
FACILITIES ON SITE
EXAM BOARDS abd ABEH
RETAKES   NVQ COURSES

A-level: B G K c efg i l n v P R cdefgh jkl
AS: G e U e
GCSE: B G K N cde l n p v x R X cdefgh jkl
OTHER:

LONDON (GREATER) *continued*

Queen's Gate School; 133 Queen's Gate; London SW7 5LE
Tel: 0171 589 3587 (Fax: 0171 584 7691) *Mrs A.Holyoak*

		Boys	Age	Girls	Age	TOTAL	SIXTH	Boys	Girls
Day	£1160–£1800			341	4-18	341			24
Weekly									
Boarding									

ENTRY REQUIREMENTS Test & Interview; Report & Exam & Interview
SCHOLARSHIPS & BURSARIES Schol
SPECIAL NEEDS **DYSLEXIA** **DIET** abcd
ASSOCIATION GSA **FOUNDED** 1891 **RELIGIOUS AFFILIATION** Non-denom

MAP 5 E 4
LOCATION
DAY **RAIL** b **AIR** a
SPORT abcglmnopqwx ABC
OTHER LANGUAGES
ACTIVITIES fghijlorstv
OTHER SUBJECTS abcgh
FACILITIES ON SITE c
EXAM BOARDS abcd ABDEGH
RETAKES a **NVQ COURSES**

A-level	AS	GCSE	OTHER
cd fg i n v B GH K P R T cdef hj l	cd fg B G e	cd ghi n v AB GH K P R cdef hj l	l v

Redcliffe School; 47 Redcliffe Gardens; London SW10 9JH
Tel: 0171 352 9247 (Fax: 0171 352 6936) *Miss R.E.Cunnah*

		Boys	Age	Girls	Age	TOTAL	SIXTH	Boys	Girls
Day	£1540 X	31	4-8	54	4-11	85			
Weekly									
Boarding									

ENTRY REQUIREMENTS Test & Interview
SCHOLARSHIPS & BURSARIES Schol
SPECIAL NEEDS n **DYSLEXIA** **DIET** acd
ASSOCIATION IAPS **FOUNDED** 1948 **RELIGIOUS AFFILIATION** Inter-denom

MAP 5 E 4
LOCATION Inner City
DAY **RAIL** b **AIR** a
SPORT ejlpqv
OTHER LANGUAGES
ACTIVITIES fghjo
OTHER SUBJECTS abch
FACILITIES ON SITE
EXAM BOARDS
RETAKES **NVQ COURSES**

A-level	AS	GCSE	OTHER
			e l o v B E G K O R cde

Reddiford School; 38 Cecil Park; Pinner; Middlesex HA5 5HH
Tel: 0181 866 0660 (Fax: 0181 866 4847) *B.J.Hembry*

		Boys	Age	Girls	Age	TOTAL	SIXTH	Boys	Girls
Day	£450–£1100	103	3-11	76	3-11	179			
Weekly									
Boarding									

ENTRY REQUIREMENTS Report & Exam & Interview
SCHOLARSHIPS & BURSARIES
SPECIAL NEEDS **DYSLEXIA** **DIET**
ASSOCIATION ISAI **FOUNDED** 1913 **RELIGIOUS AFFILIATION** C of E

MAP 5 C 3
LOCATION Urban
DAY **RAIL** a **AIR** a
SPORT aefjlopqx B
OTHER LANGUAGES
ACTIVITIES cfghj
OTHER SUBJECTS ach
FACILITIES ON SITE hi
EXAM BOARDS
RETAKES **NVQ COURSES**

A-level	AS	GCSE	OTHER
			e lmno v B E G K O R cde

Riverston School; Eltham Road; Lee; London SE12 8UF
Tel: 0181 318 4327 (Fax: 0181 297 0514) *D.M.Lewis*

		Boys	Age	Girls	Age	TOTAL	SIXTH	Boys	Girls
Day	£937–£1243	208	2-16	177	2-16	385			
Weekly									
Boarding									

ENTRY REQUIREMENTS Exam & Interview
SCHOLARSHIPS & BURSARIES Schol; Burs
SPECIAL NEEDS bnw AB **DYSLEXIA** def **DIET** abcd
ASSOCIATION ISAI **FOUNDED** 1927 **RELIGIOUS AFFILIATION** C of E

MAP 6 G 5
LOCATION Urban
DAY ✓ **RAIL** a **AIR** b
SPORT abcdefhjlopqstux ABC
OTHER LANGUAGES a
ACTIVITIES cfghjkmnopqtvw A
OTHER SUBJECTS abcdh
FACILITIES ON SITE fh
EXAM BOARDS ad AEI
RETAKES a **NVQ COURSES**

A-level	AS	GCSE	OTHER
		de ghijklmnopq st vwx BCDE G K OP S UV cdef l	

Rokeby; George Road; Kingston; Surrey KT2 7PB
Tel: 0181 942 2247 (Fax: 0181 942 5707) *R.M.Moody*

		Boys	Age	Girls	Age	TOTAL	SIXTH	Boys	Girls
Day	£1007–£1756 X	373	4-13			373			
Weekly									
Boarding									

ENTRY REQUIREMENTS Report & Test
SCHOLARSHIPS & BURSARIES Schol; Art; Mus; Sport
SPECIAL NEEDS ejn **DYSLEXIA** ef **DIET** acd
ASSOCIATION IAPS **FOUNDED** 1877 **RELIGIOUS AFFILIATION** Non-denom

MAP 5 D 5
LOCATION Urban
DAY ✓ **RAIL** a **AIR** a
SPORT abcefjkmosx AB
OTHER LANGUAGES
ACTIVITIES fghijost A
OTHER SUBJECTS cfh
FACILITIES ON SITE ach
EXAM BOARDS
RETAKES **NVQ COURSES**

A-level	AS	GCSE	OTHER
			e gil o v B G K OP R cde g j

LONDON (GREATER) continued

C — Rosemead Preparatory School; 70 Thurlow Park Road; London SE21 8HZ
Tel: 0181 670 5865 (Fax: 0181 761 9159) Mrs R.L.Lait

		Boys	Age	Girls	Age	TOTAL		Boys	Girls
Day	£1000-£1190 ✗	129	3-11	132	3-11	261	SIXTH		
Weekly									
Boarding									

ENTRY REQUIREMENTS Interview; Assessment
SCHOLARSHIPS & BURSARIES Schol
SPECIAL NEEDS b
ASSOCIATION ISAI   **FOUNDED** 1942   **RELIGIOUS AFFILIATION** Non-denom
DYSLEXIA   **DIET** acd

MAP 5 F 5
LOCATION Inner City
DAY RAIL a   AIR a
SPORT abcefjlmpqx B
OTHER LANGUAGES
ACTIVITIES cfghjo
OTHER SUBJECTS bch
FACILITIES ON SITE hk
EXAM BOARDS
RETAKES   **NVQ COURSES**

A-level: B D E G e lmno s v   K O R   X   cde   n
AS
GCSE
OTHER: B D E G   K O R   X   cde

C — Royal Russell Preparatory School; Coombe Lane; Croydon; Surrey CR9 5BX
Tel: 0181 651 5884 (Fax: 0181 657 0207) C.L.Hedges

		Boys	Age	Girls	Age	TOTAL		Boys	Girls
Day	£415-£1255 ✗	140	3-11	99	3-11	239	SIXTH		
Weekly									
Boarding									

ENTRY REQUIREMENTS Report & Exam & Interview
SCHOLARSHIPS & BURSARIES
SPECIAL NEEDS abejklnqtx ABI
ASSOCIATION IAPS   **FOUNDED** 1853   **RELIGIOUS AFFILIATION** C of E
DYSLEXIA e   **DIET** abcd

MAP 5 F 6
LOCATION Rural
DAY RAIL a   AIR a
SPORT abefhjlmpqx ABC
OTHER LANGUAGES a
ACTIVITIES cfghjot
OTHER SUBJECTS bcfh
FACILITIES ON SITE bcdehik
EXAM BOARDS
RETAKES   **NVQ COURSES**

A-level
AS
GCSE
OTHER: cde lmno s v   ABCDE G K O R   cde

C — Royal Russell School; Coombe Lane; Croydon CR9 5BX
Tel: 0181 657 4433 (Fax: 0181 657 0207) R.D.Balaam

		Boys	Age	Girls	Age	TOTAL		Boys	Girls
Day	£1765 ✗	218	3-18	89	3-18	445	SIXTH	57	47
Weekly	£3345	16	10-18	16	10-18				
Boarding	£3345	62	11-18	44	11-18				

ENTRY REQUIREMENTS Report & Exam & Interview
SCHOLARSHIPS & BURSARIES Schol; Mus; VI Form
SPECIAL NEEDS bejlnq GHI
ASSOCIATION SHMIS   **FOUNDED** 1853   **RELIGIOUS AFFILIATION** C of E
DYSLEXIA e   **DIET** abcd

MAP 5 F 6
LOCATION Rural
DAY RAIL a   AIR a
SPORT abcefghjklmopquwx ABC
OTHER LANGUAGES a
ACTIVITIES abcefghijklopqstw AB
OTHER SUBJECTS bcdfh
FACILITIES ON SITE bdehik
EXAM BOARDS abcde ABEH
RETAKES ab   **NVQ COURSES**

A-level: de ghi n vwx   B GH K P U   cdef l
AS: d   ef
GCSE: de ghij l n p v   B GH K P U X   cdef l
OTHER: C

B — St. Anthony's; 90 Fitzjohns Ave.; London NW3 6NP
Tel: 0171 435 0316 Nigel Pitel

		Boys	Age	Girls	Age	TOTAL		Boys	Girls
Day	£1680-£1720 ✗	257	6-13			257	SIXTH		
Weekly									
Boarding									

ENTRY REQUIREMENTS Assessment
SCHOLARSHIPS & BURSARIES
SPECIAL NEEDS jn
ASSOCIATION IAPS   **FOUNDED** 1952   **RELIGIOUS AFFILIATION** R C
DYSLEXIA e   **DIET** acd

MAP 5 E 3
LOCATION Urban
DAY RAIL   AIR
SPORT aefjsx B
OTHER LANGUAGES
ACTIVITIES fghijot A
OTHER SUBJECTS bch
FACILITIES ON SITE ci
EXAM BOARDS
RETAKES   **NVQ COURSES**

A-level
AS
GCSE
OTHER: B e g i l no s v   G K   P R   cde   j

Bg — St. Benedict's School; Ealing; London W5 2ES
Tel: 0181 997 9828 (Fax: 0181 566 7996) Dr A.J.Dachs

		Boys	Age	Girls	Age	TOTAL		Boys	Girls
Day	£1130-£1620	741	4-18	25	16-18	766	SIXTH	116	25
Weekly									
Boarding									

ENTRY REQUIREMENTS CEE; Test & Interview
SCHOLARSHIPS & BURSARIES AP
SPECIAL NEEDS bejklnqtw DGHI
ASSOCIATION HMC   **FOUNDED** 1902   **RELIGIOUS AFFILIATION** R C
DYSLEXIA g   **DIET**

MAP 5 D 4
LOCATION Urban
DAY ✓   RAIL a   AIR a
SPORT abcefghjkopsuwx ABC
OTHER LANGUAGES
ACTIVITIES efghijknoq A
OTHER SUBJECTS c
FACILITIES ON SITE cdhk
EXAM BOARDS abd EH
RETAKES   **NVQ COURSES**

A-level: cde g i p v   B GH K.   P R   c efg j l
AS: c   G K   R   g
GCSE: c e g i nop v   B G K   P R   cdefg j l
OTHER: l u   O

LONDON (GREATER) *continued*

G | **St. Catherine's School; Cross Deep; Twickenham; Middx. TW1 4QJ**
Tel: 0181 891 2898 (Fax: 0181 744 9629) *Miss D.Wynter*

Day	£895-£1250	Boys	Age	Girls	Age	TOTAL	SIXTH	Boys	Girls
Weekly		2	3-5	250	3-16	252			
Boarding									

MAP 5 D 5
LOCATION Urban
DAY   RAIL a   AIR a
SPORT acefhklmopqwx ABC
OTHER LANGUAGES
ACTIVITIES fghjnost
OTHER SUBJECTS cdfh
FACILITIES ON SITE bhik
EXAM BOARDS acd
RETAKES   NVQ COURSES

ENTRY REQUIREMENTS Exam
SCHOLARSHIPS & BURSARIES Burs
SPECIAL NEEDS B   DYSLEXIA   DIET
ASSOCIATION ISAI   FOUNDED 1914   RELIGIOUS AFFILIATION R C

A-level | AS | GCSE: de g i / BC E G K P R / cdef | OTHER: v / l n / NO

G | **St. Christopher's School; 32 Belsize Lane; Hampstead; London NW3 5AE**
Tel: 0171 435 1521 (Fax: 0171 431 6694) *Mrs F.Cook*

Day	£1470-£1560	Boys	Age	Girls	Age	TOTAL	SIXTH	Boys	Girls
Weekly				233	4-11	233			
Boarding									

MAP 5 E 3
LOCATION Urban
DAY   RAIL b   AIR b
SPORT lpqx
OTHER LANGUAGES
ACTIVITIES ghjot A
OTHER SUBJECTS acfh
FACILITIES ON SITE
EXAM BOARDS
RETAKES   NVQ COURSES

ENTRY REQUIREMENTS Assessment & Interview
SCHOLARSHIPS & BURSARIES
SPECIAL NEEDS   DYSLEXIA   DIET acd
ASSOCIATION IAPS   FOUNDED 1883   RELIGIOUS AFFILIATION Non-denom

A-level | AS | GCSE | OTHER: ef l no s v / B E G K O R / cde

C | **St. Christopher's School; 71 Wembley Park Drive; Wembley; Middx. HA9 8HE**
Tel: 0181 902 5069 *Mrs S.Morley*

Day	£880-£998	Boys	Age	Girls	Age	TOTAL	SIXTH	Boys	Girls
Weekly		53	4-11	53	4-11	106			
Boarding									

MAP 5 C 3
LOCATION Urban
DAY   RAIL b   AIR a
SPORT acejpq AB
OTHER LANGUAGES
ACTIVITIES fghjr
OTHER SUBJECTS
FACILITIES ON SITE
EXAM BOARDS
RETAKES   NVQ COURSES

ENTRY REQUIREMENTS Test; Interview
SCHOLARSHIPS & BURSARIES
SPECIAL NEEDS   DYSLEXIA   DIET
ASSOCIATION ISAI   FOUNDED 1928   RELIGIOUS AFFILIATION C of E

A-level | AS | GCSE | OTHER: e no v / B G K O R / cde j

C | **St. David's College; Justin Hall; West Wickham; Kent BR4 0QS;**
Tel: 0181 777 5852 (Fax: 0181 777 9549) *Mrs F.V.Schove & Mrs A.Wagstaff*

Day	£805-£855	Boys	Age	Girls	Age	TOTAL	SIXTH	Boys	Girls
Weekly		104	4-11	93	4-11	197			
Boarding									

MAP 6 G 6
LOCATION Urban
DAY   RAIL a   AIR a
SPORT aefjlmpqx B
OTHER LANGUAGES
ACTIVITIES cfgjo
OTHER SUBJECTS ch
FACILITIES ON SITE
EXAM BOARDS
RETAKES   NVQ COURSES

ENTRY REQUIREMENTS Test & Interview
SCHOLARSHIPS & BURSARIES Siblings
SPECIAL NEEDS I   DYSLEXIA   DIET a
ASSOCIATION ISAI   FOUNDED 1926   RELIGIOUS AFFILIATION Inter-denom

A-level | AS | GCSE | OTHER: e lm o v / B E G K O R / cde

C | **St. David's School; 23/25 Woodcote Valley Road; Purley CR8 3AL**
Tel: 0181 660 0723 *Mrs L.Randall*

Day	£505-£892	Boys	Age	Girls	Age	TOTAL	SIXTH	Boys	Girls
Weekly		90	3-11	85	3-11	175			
Boarding									

MAP 5 F 7
LOCATION Urban
DAY   RAIL b   AIR a
SPORT aefjlpqsx AB
OTHER LANGUAGES
ACTIVITIES fghjx
OTHER SUBJECTS abch
FACILITIES ON SITE
EXAM BOARDS
RETAKES   NVQ COURSES

ENTRY REQUIREMENTS Interview
SCHOLARSHIPS & BURSARIES Burs
SPECIAL NEEDS jklntw   DYSLEXIA g   DIET acd
ASSOCIATION ISAI   FOUNDED 1912   RELIGIOUS AFFILIATION C of E

A-level | AS | GCSE | OTHER: e lmno uv / B E G K O R / cde j

LONDON (GREATER) *continued*

C | **St. Dunstan's College; Stanstead Road; Catford; London SE6 4TY**
Tel: 0181 690 1274 (Fax: 0181 314 0242) *J.D.Moore*

		Boys	Age	Girls	Age	TOTAL		Boys	Girls
Day	£1155–£1790	784	4-18	126	4-18	910	SIXTH	155	36
Weekly									
Boarding									

MAP 6 G 5
LOCATION Urban
DAY ✓   **RAIL** a   **AIR** a
SPORT abcefhijklmpstuwx AB
OTHER LANGUAGES
ACTIVITIES efghijkno AD

ENTRY REQUIREMENTS Report & Exam & Interview
SCHOLARSHIPS & BURSARIES Schol; Burs; AP; VI Form
SPECIAL NEEDS n   **DYSLEXIA** e   **DIET** acd
ASSOCIATION HMC   **FOUNDED** 1888   **RELIGIOUS AFFILIATION** C of E
OTHER SUBJECTS abch
FACILITIES ON SITE cgik
EXAM BOARDS abcd ABEGH
RETAKES   **NVQ COURSES**

A-level: c efghi   n p   v x / B   GH K   OP R / c ef   j
AS: GH / ef
GCSE: de g i   o   v / B   G K   OP R   X / cdefg   j
OTHER: l   u / O R

G | **St. Helen's School; Eastbury Road; Northwood; Middx. HA6 3AS;**
Tel: 01923 828511 (Fax: 01923 835824) *Mrs Diana Jefkins*

		Boys	Age	Girls	Age	TOTAL		Boys	Girls
Day	£1012–£1591			877	4-18	939	SIXTH		153
Weekly	£2536–£2891			14	8-18				
Boarding	£2643–£2998			48	8-18				

MAP 5 C 3
LOCATION Urban
DAY ✓   **RAIL** a   **AIR** a
SPORT acghklnpqtwx ABC
OTHER LANGUAGES a
ACTIVITIES cefghijknoqswx ABD

ENTRY REQUIREMENTS Exam & Interview
SCHOLARSHIPS & BURSARIES Schol; Burs; Art; Mus; AP; VI Form
SPECIAL NEEDS   **DYSLEXIA** e   **DIET** a
ASSOCIATION GSA   **FOUNDED** 1899   **RELIGIOUS AFFILIATION** C of E
OTHER SUBJECTS abcdfh
FACILITIES ON SITE cdgi
EXAM BOARDS abd ABEGH
RETAKES a   **NVQ COURSES**

A-level: c e ghi   nop   v x / B   GH K   · P R / c efg   j l
AS: c   f   x / G   R / e
GCSE: c e g i l   no   v / B   G K   P R / cdefgh j l
OTHER: i kl

B | **St. James Independent Sch.for Boys; 61 Eccleston Square; London SW1V 1PH**
Tel: 0171 834 0471 (Fax: 0171 976 6012) *N.Debenham*

		Boys	Age	Girls	Age	TOTAL		Boys	Girls
Day	£1540–£1585	176	10-18			176	SIXTH	29	
Weekly									
Boarding									

MAP 5 F 4
LOCATION Inner City
DAY   **RAIL** a   **AIR** a
SPORT abefstwx AB
OTHER LANGUAGES
ACTIVITIES efghijkoq

ENTRY REQUIREMENTS Interview; Test & Interview
SCHOLARSHIPS & BURSARIES Teachers
SPECIAL NEEDS n   **DYSLEXIA**   **DIET** a
ASSOCIATION ISAI   **FOUNDED** 1975   **RELIGIOUS AFFILIATION** Inter-denom
OTHER SUBJECTS ach
FACILITIES ON SITE
EXAM BOARDS ab EH
RETAKES   **NVQ COURSES**

A-level: c e g i l / B   FGH   P / cd   g   j
AS:
GCSE: e g i l / B   FG   P / cde g   j
OTHER: n p / K M O R

G | **St. James Independent Sch.for Girls; 19 Pembridge Villas; London W11 3EP**
Tel: 0171 229 2253 (Fax: 0171 792 1002) *Mrs L.A.Hyde*

		Boys	Age	Girls	Age	TOTAL		Boys	Girls
Day	£1100–£1585			138	10-19	138	SIXTH		15
Weekly									
Boarding									

MAP 5 E 4
LOCATION Inner City
DAY   **RAIL** a   **AIR** a
SPORT afnopqx AB
OTHER LANGUAGES
ACTIVITIES cgjko

ENTRY REQUIREMENTS Interview; Test & Interview
SCHOLARSHIPS & BURSARIES Teachers; Siblings
SPECIAL NEEDS n   **DYSLEXIA**   **DIET** a
ASSOCIATION ISAI   **FOUNDED** 1975   **RELIGIOUS AFFILIATION** Inter-denom
OTHER SUBJECTS cgh
FACILITIES ON SITE
EXAM BOARDS abd AEH
RETAKES ab   **NVQ COURSES**

A-level: cde g i / B   FGH K   P / cde g   j
AS: G
GCSE: c e g i   o / B   FG K   P R / cde g   j
OTHER: h m n   v / K M O R   W

B | **St James Independent School Jnr Boys Dept; 91 Queen's Gate; London SW7 5AB**
Tel: 0171 373 5638 (Fax: 0171 835 0771) *P.Moss*

		Boys	Age	Girls	Age	TOTAL		Boys	Girls
Day	£1100–£1250	134	4-10			134	SIXTH		
Weekly									
Boarding									

MAP 5 E 4
LOCATION Inner City
DAY   **RAIL** a   **AIR** a
SPORT aeflx
OTHER LANGUAGES
ACTIVITIES fjo

ENTRY REQUIREMENTS Interview; Test & Interview
SCHOLARSHIPS & BURSARIES Teachers
SPECIAL NEEDS n   **DYSLEXIA**   **DIET** a
ASSOCIATION ISAI   **FOUNDED** 1975   **RELIGIOUS AFFILIATION** Inter-denom
OTHER SUBJECTS ch
FACILITIES ON SITE
EXAM BOARDS
RETAKES   **NVQ COURSES**

A-level:
AS:
GCSE:
OTHER: c ef   n / B   G   K M O / cd   g

LONDON (GREATER) continued

G — St James Independent School Jnr Girls Dept; 91 Queen's Gate; London SW7 5AB
Tel: 0171 373 5638 (Fax: 0171 835 0771) *P.Moss*

- Day £1100-£1250 ✗
- Weekly
- Boarding
- Boys — | Age — | Girls 124 | Age 4-10 | TOTAL 124 | SIXTH Boys — | Girls —

ENTRY REQUIREMENTS Interview; Test & Interview
SCHOLARSHIPS & BURSARIES Teachers
SPECIAL NEEDS n
DYSLEXIA — **DIET** a
ASSOCIATION ISAI **FOUNDED** 1975 **RELIGIOUS AFFILIATION** Inter-denom

MAP 5 E 4
LOCATION Inner City
DAY — **RAIL** a **AIR** a
SPORT afinpqx
OTHER LANGUAGES
ACTIVITIES cgjoqwx
OTHER SUBJECTS ch
FACILITIES ON SITE
EXAM BOARDS
RETAKES **NVQ COURSES**

- A-level —
- AS —
- GCSE: c ef mn v / B G K M O / cd g
- OTHER —

B — St. John's School; Potter Street Hill; Northwood HA6 3QY
Tel: 0181 866 0067 (Fax: 0181 868 8770) *C.R.Kelly*

- Day £1200-£1480 ✗
- Weekly
- Boarding
- Boys 317 | Age 4-13 | Girls — | Age — | TOTAL 317 | SIXTH Boys — | Girls —

ENTRY REQUIREMENTS Test & Interview
SCHOLARSHIPS & BURSARIES
SPECIAL NEEDS abhjlst H
DYSLEXIA — **DIET** abcd
ASSOCIATION IAPS **FOUNDED** 1920 **RELIGIOUS AFFILIATION** C of E

MAP 5 C 3
LOCATION Urban
DAY — **RAIL** b **AIR** a
SPORT abcdefghlosx ABC
OTHER LANGUAGES
ACTIVITIES fghijort A
OTHER SUBJECTS cfh
FACILITIES ON SITE bchk
EXAM BOARDS
RETAKES **NVQ COURSES**

- A-level —
- AS —
- GCSE —
- OTHER: d e g i l o v / B G K OP R / cde j

G — St. Margaret's School; 18 Kidderpore Gardens; London NW3 7SR
Tel: 0171 435 2439 *Mrs S.J.Meaden*

- Day £1170-£1385
- Weekly
- Boarding
- Boys — | Age — | Girls 138 | Age 5-16 | TOTAL 138 | SIXTH Boys — | Girls —

ENTRY REQUIREMENTS Test & Interview
SCHOLARSHIPS & BURSARIES
SPECIAL NEEDS n
DYSLEXIA fg **DIET** —
ASSOCIATION ISAI **FOUNDED** 1884 **RELIGIOUS AFFILIATION** C of E

MAP 5 E 3
LOCATION Inner City
DAY — **RAIL** b **AIR** a
SPORT dlmpqx B
OTHER LANGUAGES
ACTIVITIES cghjnw A
OTHER SUBJECTS abcdeh
FACILITIES ON SITE
EXAM BOARDS abc
RETAKES **NVQ COURSES**

- A-level —
- AS —
- GCSE: c e g i n v / B G K P / cde kl
- OTHER: l

B — St. Martin's School; 40 Moor Park Road; Northwood; Middx. HA6 2DJ
Tel: 01923 825740 (Fax: 01923 835452) *M.J.Hodgson*

- Day £475-£1590 ✗
- Weekly
- Boarding
- Boys 351 | Age 3-13 | Girls 1 | Age — | TOTAL 352 | SIXTH Boys — | Girls —

ENTRY REQUIREMENTS Assessment & Interview
SCHOLARSHIPS & BURSARIES Burs; Forces; Teachers
SPECIAL NEEDS n
DYSLEXIA e **DIET** abcd
ASSOCIATION IAPS **FOUNDED** 1922 **RELIGIOUS AFFILIATION** C of E

MAP 5 C 3
LOCATION Urban
DAY — **RAIL** a **AIR** a
SPORT abcefjkmoqsuwx AB
OTHER LANGUAGES
ACTIVITIES fghjloqrtx A
OTHER SUBJECTS bcfh
FACILITIES ON SITE i
EXAM BOARDS
RETAKES **NVQ COURSES**

- A-level —
- AS —
- GCSE —
- OTHER: e g i l o v / AB G K OP R / cde g j

C — St. Olave's Preparatory School; 106/110 Southwood Road; New Eltham; London SE9 3QS
Tel: 0181 850 9175 *P.D.Stradling*

- Day £536-£1064
- Weekly
- Boarding
- Boys 105 | Age 3-11 | Girls 91 | Age 3-11 | TOTAL 196 | SIXTH Boys — | Girls —

ENTRY REQUIREMENTS Assessment
SCHOLARSHIPS & BURSARIES
SPECIAL NEEDS n B
DYSLEXIA e **DIET** acd
ASSOCIATION IAPS **FOUNDED** 1932 **RELIGIOUS AFFILIATION** C of E

MAP 6 H 5
LOCATION Urban
DAY — **RAIL** a **AIR** a
SPORT aejlmpqx
OTHER LANGUAGES
ACTIVITIES cfgjo
OTHER SUBJECTS bcdh
FACILITIES ON SITE h
EXAM BOARDS
RETAKES **NVQ COURSES**

- A-level —
- AS —
- GCSE —
- OTHER: e l o v / B E G K O R / de

LONDON (GREATER) *continued*

B — St. Paul's Cathedral Choir School; New Change; London EC4M 9AD
Tel: 0171 248 5156 (Fax: 0171 329 6568) *S A Sides*

		Boys	Age	Girls	Age	TOTAL	SIXTH	Boys	Girls
Day	£1640	61	7-13			103			
Weekly	£0- £990								
Boarding		42	7-13						

MAP 5 F 4
LOCATION Inner City
DAY   **RAIL** b   **AIR** b
SPORT acejx AB
OTHER LANGUAGES
ACTIVITIES fghjlort
OTHER SUBJECTS cfh
FACILITIES ON SITE
EXAM BOARDS
RETAKES   **NVQ COURSES**

ENTRY REQUIREMENTS
SCHOLARSHIPS & BURSARIES Chor
SPECIAL NEEDS   **DYSLEXIA**   **DIET**
ASSOCIATION IAPS   **FOUNDED**   **RELIGIOUS AFFILIATION** C of E

A-level: **AS**   **GCSE**   **OTHER**: e g i lmno q v / B G K OP R / cde g j

---

G — St. Paul's Girls' School; Brook Green; London W6 7BS
Tel: 0171 603 2288 (Fax: 0171 602 9932) *Miss Janet Gough*

		Boys	Age	Girls	Age	TOTAL	SIXTH	Boys	Girls
Day	£2094			604	11-18	604			194
Weekly									
Boarding									

MAP 5 E 4
LOCATION Inner City
DAY   **RAIL** b   **AIR** a
SPORT acfghklnprwx ABC
OTHER LANGUAGES
ACTIVITIES bcfghijklnostv A
OTHER SUBJECTS abcdfh
FACILITIES ON SITE bchik
EXAM BOARDS abd BDEH
RETAKES   **NVQ COURSES**

ENTRY REQUIREMENTS Exam
SCHOLARSHIPS & BURSARIES Schol; Burs; Art; Mus; AP; VI Form
SPECIAL NEEDS agnq   **DYSLEXIA** g   **DIET** acd
ASSOCIATION GSA   **FOUNDED** 1904   **RELIGIOUS AFFILIATION** C of E

A-level: efg i p v / B GH K P / c efgh jkl   **AS**   **GCSE**: B G v X / cdef j   **OTHER**: ef lm o q u / G K O R / cdefghijkl

---

B — St. Paul's Prep.School; Colet Court; Lonsdale Road; Barnes; London SW13 9JT
Tel: 0181 748 3461 (Fax: 0181 563 7361) *G.J.Thompson*

		Boys	Age	Girls	Age	TOTAL	SIXTH	Boys	Girls
Day	£2066 X	426	7-13			436			
Weekly	£3181	9	7-13						
Boarding	£3181	1	7-13						

MAP 5 E 4
LOCATION Urban
DAY   **RAIL** b   **AIR** a
SPORT abcefghijklmoqrswx ABC
OTHER LANGUAGES
ACTIVITIES fghijoqtx A
OTHER SUBJECTS bcfh
FACILITIES ON SITE bcdhik
EXAM BOARDS
RETAKES   **NVQ COURSES**

ENTRY REQUIREMENTS Report & Exam & Interview
SCHOLARSHIPS & BURSARIES Schol; Burs; Mus; Chor; AP
SPECIAL NEEDS ejklpqt EGI   **DYSLEXIA**   **DIET** acd
ASSOCIATION IAPS   **FOUNDED** 1881   **RELIGIOUS AFFILIATION** C of E

A-level   **AS**   **GCSE**   **OTHER**: e g i l no q v / B G K OP R / cde g j

---

B — St. Paul's School; Lonsdale Road; Barnes; London SW13 9JT
Tel: 0181 748 9162 (Fax: 0181 748 9557) *R.S.Baldock*

		Boys	Age	Girls	Age	TOTAL	SIXTH	Boys	Girls
Day	£2694 X	713	13-18			777		303	
Weekly	£4119		13-18						
Boarding	£4119	64	13-18						

MAP 5 E 4
LOCATION Urban
DAY ✓   **RAIL** b   **AIR** a
SPORT abcefghijklorstwx ABC
OTHER LANGUAGES
ACTIVITIES fghijklnopqstuw AB
OTHER SUBJECTS bcdfh
FACILITIES ON SITE bcdhik
EXAM BOARDS abd BDEH
RETAKES   **NVQ COURSES**

ENTRY REQUIREMENTS CEE; Scholarship Exam; Report & Exam & Interview
SCHOLARSHIPS & BURSARIES Schol; Burs; Mus; AP; VI Form
SPECIAL NEEDS bjkl E   **DYSLEXIA**   **DIET** abcd
ASSOCIATION HMC   **FOUNDED** 1509   **RELIGIOUS AFFILIATION** C of E

A-level: cd g i l pq v x / B GH K P R / c efgh j   **AS**: cd g i l opq w / B GH K M P R / c efgh j l   **GCSE**: cd g i l no v / B G K P R X / cdefgh j   **OTHER**: i

---

C — Salcombe Preparatory School; 224/226 Chase Side; Southgate; London N14 4PL
Tel: 0181 441 5282 (Fax: 0181 441 5282) *A.J.Blackhurst*

		Boys	Age	Girls	Age	TOTAL	SIXTH	Boys	Girls
Day	£1095	202	2-11	137	2-11	339			
Weekly									
Boarding									

MAP 5 F 2
LOCATION Urban
DAY   **RAIL** b   **AIR** a
SPORT aefhjlopqx B
OTHER LANGUAGES
ACTIVITIES cfghijr
OTHER SUBJECTS ach
FACILITIES ON SITE
EXAM BOARDS
RETAKES   **NVQ COURSES**

ENTRY REQUIREMENTS Test & Interview
SCHOLARSHIPS & BURSARIES
SPECIAL NEEDS abegjklnquw l   **DYSLEXIA** g   **DIET** acd
ASSOCIATION ISAI   **FOUNDED** 1918   **RELIGIOUS AFFILIATION**

A-level   **AS**   **GCSE**   **OTHER**: def lmno s uv / B E G K O / cde

LONDON (GREATER) *continued*

Gb Sarum Hall; 15 Eton Avenue; London NW3 3EL
Tel: 0171 794 2261 (Fax: 0171 431 7501) *Lady Smith-Gordon*

	Boys	Age	Girls	Age	TOTAL		Boys	Girls
Day £1625 ✗	10	3-5	150	3-11	160	SIXTH		
Weekly								
Boarding								

MAP 5 E 3
LOCATION Inner City
DAY RAIL AIR
SPORT glpq B
OTHER LANGUAGES
ACTIVITIES cfghjno
OTHER SUBJECTS ach
FACILITIES ON SITE
EXAM BOARDS
RETAKES   NVQ COURSES

ENTRY REQUIREMENTS Interview
SCHOLARSHIPS & BURSARIES Burs; Siblings
SPECIAL NEEDS egjklnt GIL   **DYSLEXIA** g   **DIET** a
ASSOCIATION IAPS   **FOUNDED** 1929   **RELIGIOUS AFFILIATION** C of E

A-level	AS	GCSE	OTHER
			ef Imno v B EG K O R cde

C Shaftesbury Independent School; Godstone Road; Purley; Surrey CR8 2AN
Tel: 0181 668 8080 *P.A.B.Gowlland*

	Boys	Age	Girls	Age	TOTAL		Boys	Girls
Day £880-£1425	31	3-18	24	3-18	55	SIXTH		
Weekly								
Boarding								

MAP 5 F 7
LOCATION Urban
DAY ✓ RAIL a AIR a
SPORT acefjlpqvwx ABC
OTHER LANGUAGES a
ACTIVITIES cfghij
OTHER SUBJECTS bch
FACILITIES ON SITE k
EXAM BOARDS abd BE
RETAKES a   NVQ COURSES

ENTRY REQUIREMENTS Test & Interview
SCHOLARSHIPS & BURSARIES Burs; Clergy; VI Form; Siblings
SPECIAL NEEDS abcegjklnpqstuw BHI   **DYSLEXIA** eg   **DIET** abcd
ASSOCIATION ISAI   **FOUNDED** 1976   **RELIGIOUS AFFILIATION** Christian

A-level: e g i p v / BC GH P R W / cde
GCSE: e ghi p v / BC G K P R W / cdef
OTHER: c lmn q / o

B Shrewsbury House School; 107 Ditton Road; Surbiton; Surrey KT6 6RL
Tel: 0181 399 3066 (Fax: 0181 339 9529) *C.M.Ross*

	Boys	Age	Girls	Age	TOTAL		Boys	Girls
Day £1722	252	7-14			252	SIXTH		
Weekly								
Boarding								

MAP 5 D 6
LOCATION Urban
DAY RAIL a AIR
SPORT abcdefjkmstuwx AB
OTHER LANGUAGES
ACTIVITIES fghjoqt A
OTHER SUBJECTS cfh
FACILITIES ON SITE ahi
EXAM BOARDS
RETAKES   NVQ COURSES

ENTRY REQUIREMENTS Test
SCHOLARSHIPS & BURSARIES
SPECIAL NEEDS b GI   **DYSLEXIA**   **DIET** cd
ASSOCIATION IAPS   **FOUNDED** 1865   **RELIGIOUS AFFILIATION** C of E

OTHER: e l v / B G o / cde j

G South Hampstead High School GPDST; 3 Maresfield Gardens; London NW3 5SS
Tel: 0171 435 2899 (Fax: 0171 431 8022) *Mrs J.G.Scott*

	Boys	Age	Girls	Age	TOTAL		Boys	Girls
Day £1248-£1548			884	4-18	884	SIXTH		147
Weekly								
Boarding								

MAP 5 E 3
LOCATION Inner City
DAY RAIL a AIR a
SPORT bcghlmpqwx BC
OTHER LANGUAGES
ACTIVITIES cfghijkos AB
OTHER SUBJECTS abch
FACILITIES ON SITE ghk
EXAM BOARDS abc DE
RETAKES   NVQ COURSES

ENTRY REQUIREMENTS Exam & Interview
SCHOLARSHIPS & BURSARIES Schol; AP
SPECIAL NEEDS bjlqt I   **DYSLEXIA**   **DIET** a
ASSOCIATION GSA   **FOUNDED** 1876   **RELIGIOUS AFFILIATION** Non-denom

A-level: efg i p v x / B GH K P R U / cdefg j l
AS: c x / G K / e
GCSE: e g i o v / B G K P R U / cdefgh j l
OTHER: l / o

C Southbank International School; 36-38 Kensington Park Road; London W11 3BU
Tel: 0171 229 8230 (Fax: 0171 229 3784) *M.E.Toubkin*

	Boys	Age	Girls	Age	TOTAL		Boys	Girls
Day £2000-£3160	134	4-18	108	4-18	242	SIXTH	45	37
Weekly								
Boarding								

MAP 5 E 4
LOCATION Inner City
DAY ✓ RAIL a AIR a
SPORT bcjopvwx BC
OTHER LANGUAGES abcfhikl
ACTIVITIES fghjoqstx A
OTHER SUBJECTS bcd
FACILITIES ON SITE k
EXAM BOARDS C
RETAKES   NVQ COURSES

ENTRY REQUIREMENTS Report & Interview
SCHOLARSHIPS & BURSARIES Schol; Burs; Teachers; VI Form
SPECIAL NEEDS n   **DYSLEXIA** g   **DIET**
ASSOCIATION ISAI   **FOUNDED** 1979   **RELIGIOUS AFFILIATION**

OTHER: de ghi l n / B GH K M OP / a cdef hi kl

LONDON (GREATER) *continued*

C — Stowford; 95 Brighton Road; Sutton; Surrey SM2 5SJ
Tel: 0181 661 9444 *R.J.Shakespeare*

		Boys	Age	Girls	Age	TOTAL		Boys	Girls
Day	£966-£1549	42	7-17	10	7-17	52	SIXTH		1
Weekly									
Boarding									

ENTRY REQUIREMENTS Report & Exam & Interview
SCHOLARSHIPS & BURSARIES
SPECIAL NEEDS bghjklnstuw ADGH
DYSLEXIA cde **DIET**
ASSOCIATION ISAI **FOUNDED** 1975 **RELIGIOUS AFFILIATION** Christian

MAP 5 E 6
LOCATION Urban
DAY **RAIL** a **AIR** a
SPORT abcefhjlpqwx ABC
OTHER LANGUAGES a
ACTIVITIES fhjqt A
OTHER SUBJECTS
FACILITIES ON SITE
EXAM BOARDS abd D
RETAKES a **NVQ COURSES**

- **A-level**
- **AS**
- **GCSE** de ghi l / B G OP R v
- **OTHER** o / K O R

G — Streatham Hill & Clapham High School GPDST; Abbotswood Road; London SW16 1AW
Tel: 0181 677 8400 (Fax: 0181 677 2001) *Miss G.M.Ellis*

		Boys	Age	Girls	Age	TOTAL		Boys	Girls
Day	£1192-£1548			609	4-18	609	SIXTH		89
Weekly									
Boarding									

ENTRY REQUIREMENTS Test; Exam & Interview
SCHOLARSHIPS & BURSARIES Schol; AP; VI Form
SPECIAL NEEDS l
DYSLEXIA **DIET** a
ASSOCIATION GSA **FOUNDED** 1887 **RELIGIOUS AFFILIATION** Non-denom

MAP 5 E 5
LOCATION Rural
DAY **RAIL** ab **AIR** b
SPORT abcehlmopqrvwx ABC
OTHER LANGUAGES
ACTIVITIES bcfghijklnorstw AB
OTHER SUBJECTS bcdfh
FACILITIES ON SITE cghk
EXAM BOARDS abcd AEH
RETAKES **NVQ COURSES**

- **A-level** cdefg i op v / B GH K P R / cdefgh j l
- **AS** c / G K R / def
- **GCSE** d g i no v / B E G K P R / cdefgh jkl
- **OTHER** lm qr tu / K NO R / def ijkl

C — Study School,The; 57 Thetford Road; New Malden; Surrey KT3 5DP
Tel: 0181 942 0754 *J.H.N.Hudson*

		Boys	Age	Girls	Age	TOTAL		Boys	Girls
Day	£515-£1230	69	3-11	52	3-11	121	SIXTH		
Weekly									
Boarding									

ENTRY REQUIREMENTS Assessment & Interview
SCHOLARSHIPS & BURSARIES
SPECIAL NEEDS jkln B
DYSLEXIA g **DIET** a
ASSOCIATION ISAI **FOUNDED** 1923 **RELIGIOUS AFFILIATION** C of E

MAP 5 D 6
LOCATION Urban
DAY **RAIL** a **AIR** a
SPORT aejpqx
OTHER LANGUAGES
ACTIVITIES gh
OTHER SUBJECTS bch
FACILITIES ON SITE
EXAM BOARDS
RETAKES **NVQ COURSES**

- **A-level**
- **AS**
- **GCSE**
- **OTHER** e l v / B G K / cde

G — Study Preparatory School,The; Wilberforce House; Camp Road; Wimbledon Common; London SW19 4UN
Tel: 0181 947 6969 (Fax: 0181 944 5975) *Mrs L.Bond*

		Boys	Age	Girls	Age	TOTAL		Boys	Girls
Day	£1320-£1500			303	4-11	303	SIXTH		
Weekly									
Boarding									

ENTRY REQUIREMENTS Test & Interview
SCHOLARSHIPS & BURSARIES
SPECIAL NEEDS abgjklnqtw DGHIL
DYSLEXIA e **DIET**
ASSOCIATION ISAI **FOUNDED** 1893 **RELIGIOUS AFFILIATION** Non-denom

MAP 5 E 5
LOCATION Urban
DAY **RAIL** a **AIR** b
SPORT alpqx B
OTHER LANGUAGES
ACTIVITIES cfghijt A
OTHER SUBJECTS ch
FACILITIES ON SITE
EXAM BOARDS
RETAKES **NVQ COURSES**

- **A-level**
- **AS**
- **GCSE**
- **OTHER** e lmno v / B E G K O R / cde

Gb — Surbiton High School; Surbiton Crescent; Kingston Upon Thames KT1 2JT
Tel: 0181 546 5245 (Fax: 0181 547 0026) *Miss M.G.Perry*

		Boys	Age	Girls	Age	TOTAL		Boys	Girls
Day	£972-£1620	105	4-11	781	4-18	886	SIXTH		103
Weekly									
Boarding									

ENTRY REQUIREMENTS Exam & Interview
SCHOLARSHIPS & BURSARIES Schol; Mus; Clergy; AP; VI Form; Sport; Siblings
SPECIAL NEEDS G
DYSLEXIA **DIET** a
ASSOCIATION GSA **FOUNDED** 1884 **RELIGIOUS AFFILIATION** C of E

MAP 5 D 6
LOCATION Urban
DAY ✓ **RAIL** a **AIR** a
SPORT abcehjlmopqrsvwx ABC
OTHER LANGUAGES
ACTIVITIES cfghijknoqrst AB
OTHER SUBJECTS acf
FACILITIES ON SITE cgh
EXAM BOARDS abcd ABEHIL
RETAKES **NVQ COURSES**

- **A-level** cdefg i n p v / BC GH K PQR U / cdefg j l
- **AS** cde / G KM / c e j v
- **GCSE** de g i no v / BC E G K N P R U / cdefg j l
- **OTHER** i u / O Q / hi

LONDON (GREATER) continued

B | Sussex House; 68 Cadogan Square; London SW1X 0EA
Tel: 0171 584 1741 (Fax: 0171 589 2300) *N.P.Kaye*

Day	£1915 ✗	Boys 157	Age 8-13	Girls	Age	TOTAL 157	SIXTH	Boys	Girls
Weekly									
Boarding									

MAP 5 F 4
LOCATION Urban
DAY   RAIL a   AIR a
SPORT abefgjlx BC
OTHER LANGUAGES
ACTIVITIES fghijlot A
OTHER SUBJECTS cfh
FACILITIES ON SITE hk
EXAM BOARDS
RETAKES   NVQ COURSES

ENTRY REQUIREMENTS Test
SCHOLARSHIPS & BURSARIES Burs
SPECIAL NEEDS
ASSOCIATION IAPS   **FOUNDED** 1952   **DYSLEXIA**   **DIET**
RELIGIOUS AFFILIATION Non-denom

A-level   AS   GCSE   OTHER e g i l o v
                              B G K O R
                              cdefg j

G | Sutton High School GPDST; 55 Cheam Road; Sutton; Surrey SM1 2AX
Tel: 0181 642 0594 (Fax: 0181 642 2014) *Mrs A.Coutts*

Day	£1192-£1548	Boys	Age	Girls 755	Age 4-18	TOTAL 755	SIXTH	Boys	Girls 106
Weekly									
Boarding									

MAP 3 F 3
LOCATION Urban
DAY   RAIL a   AIR a
SPORT clmpqwx BC
OTHER LANGUAGES
ACTIVITIES fghijknot
OTHER SUBJECTS abcfh
FACILITIES ON SITE chi
EXAM BOARDS abcd DEH
RETAKES   NVQ COURSES

ENTRY REQUIREMENTS Test
SCHOLARSHIPS & BURSARIES Schol; AP
SPECIAL NEEDS begjlu GH
ASSOCIATION GSA   **FOUNDED** 1884   **DYSLEXIA** g   **DIET** a
RELIGIOUS AFFILIATION Non-denom

A-level c e g i   p   v x   AS   l o   x   GCSE d e g i   o v   OTHER f   l no
        BC GH K P R   W   G K   W   BC G K OP R W   NO
        c efg j   e   cdefg j l

G | Sydenham High School GPDST; 19 Westwood Hill; London SE26 6BL
Tel: 0181 778 8737 (Fax: 0181 776 8830) *Mrs Geraldine Baker*

Day	£1192-£1548	Boys	Age	Girls 699	Age 4-18	TOTAL 699	SIXTH	Boys	Girls 82
Weekly									
Boarding									

MAP 5 F 5
LOCATION Urban
DAY   RAIL a   AIR b
SPORT abcghlmopqwx ABC
OTHER LANGUAGES
ACTIVITIES acfghijklost A
OTHER SUBJECTS abcdfh
FACILITIES ON SITE bcghk
EXAM BOARDS abcd ABEI
RETAKES a   NVQ COURSES

ENTRY REQUIREMENTS Test & Interview
SCHOLARSHIPS & BURSARIES Schol; Burs; Mus; AP
SPECIAL NEEDS jl
ASSOCIATION GSA   **FOUNDED** 1887   **DYSLEXIA** g   **DIET** abcd
RELIGIOUS AFFILIATION Non-denom

A-level cde ghi n pq v x   AS c   v   GCSE cde g i lmno q v   OTHER cde g i lmno q uv
        BC GH K   P R TU   C G K   R   BC E G K   OP R W   BC E G K NOP R W
        cdef j l   ef   cdef j l   cdef j l

C | Sylvia Young Theatre School; Rossmore Road; London NW1 6NJ
Tel: 0171 402 0673 (Fax: 0171 723 1040) *Miss M.T.Melville*

Day	£990-£1280	Boys 44	Age 7-16	Girls 86	Age 7-16	TOTAL 130	SIXTH	Boys	Girls
Weekly									
Boarding									

MAP 5 F 4
LOCATION Inner City
DAY   RAIL a   AIR b
SPORT x
OTHER LANGUAGES
ACTIVITIES cgij
OTHER SUBJECTS bh
FACILITIES ON SITE k
EXAM BOARDS ad A
RETAKES   NVQ COURSES

ENTRY REQUIREMENTS Assessment & Interview
SCHOLARSHIPS & BURSARIES Burs; Siblings
SPECIAL NEEDS bln
ASSOCIATION ISAI   **FOUNDED** 1981   **DYSLEXIA** g   **DIET** a
RELIGIOUS AFFILIATION Non-denom

A-level   AS   GCSE e   n   OTHER   m
                    DE G   E G
                    cde   d

C | Thomas's Preparatory School; 28-40 Battersea High Street; London SW11 3JB
Tel: 0171 978 4224 (Fax: 0171 585 0463) *Miss J.Kelham*

Day	£1755-£2050 ✗	Boys 224	Age 4-13	Girls 192	Age 4-13	TOTAL 416	SIXTH	Boys	Girls
Weekly									
Boarding									

MAP 5 E 5
LOCATION Urban
DAY ✓   RAIL a   AIR a
SPORT aefjlmopsx
OTHER LANGUAGES
ACTIVITIES cghjot A
OTHER SUBJECTS acfh
FACILITIES ON SITE h
EXAM BOARDS
RETAKES   NVQ COURSES

ENTRY REQUIREMENTS Test & Interview; Exam & Interview
SCHOLARSHIPS & BURSARIES
SPECIAL NEEDS an
ASSOCIATION IAPS   **FOUNDED** 1977   **DYSLEXIA** e   **DIET** ab
RELIGIOUS AFFILIATION C of E

A-level   AS   GCSE   OTHER e g i l no   v
                            B   G K OP R
                            cde   j

LONDON (GREATER) continued

B — Tower House School; 188 Sheen Lane; London SW14 8LF
Tel: 0181 876 3323 *J.D.T.Wall*

- Day
- Weekly
- Boarding

£1595 ✗ | Boys 174 | Age 4-13 | Girls — | Age — | TOTAL 174 | SIXTH Boys — | Girls —

MAP 5 E 5
LOCATION Urban
DAY ✓   **RAIL** b   **AIR** a
SPORT aeijswx B
OTHER LANGUAGES
ACTIVITIES fghjos
OTHER SUBJECTS cfh
FACILITIES ON SITE
EXAM BOARDS
RETAKES   **NVQ COURSES**

ENTRY REQUIREMENTS Interview
SCHOLARSHIPS & BURSARIES Burs
SPECIAL NEEDS   **DYSLEXIA**   **DIET**
ASSOCIATION IAPS   **FOUNDED** 1931   **RELIGIOUS AFFILIATION**

A-level | AS | GCSE | OTHER: e l o v   B D G K O   cde g j

B — Trinity School; Shirley Park; Croydon CR9 7AT
Tel: 0181 656 9541 (Fax: 0181 655 0522) *B.J.Lenon*

- Day
- Weekly
- Boarding

£1768 | Boys 854 | Age 10-18 | Girls — | Age — | TOTAL 854 | SIXTH Boys 217 | Girls —

MAP 5 F 6
LOCATION Urban
DAY ✓   **RAIL** b   **AIR** a
SPORT abcdefhkmstuwx ABC
OTHER LANGUAGES
ACTIVITIES befghijklnopqrst AB
OTHER SUBJECTS abcdfh
FACILITIES ON SITE acghik
EXAM BOARDS abcd ABEH
RETAKES   **NVQ COURSES**

ENTRY REQUIREMENTS Report & Exam & Interview
SCHOLARSHIPS & BURSARIES Schol; Burs; Mus; Clergy; AP
SPECIAL NEEDS ejn GL   **DYSLEXIA** e   **DIET**
ASSOCIATION HMC   **FOUNDED** 1596   **RELIGIOUS AFFILIATION** C of E

A-level: de ghi opq v   B GH K N P R U   c ef l
AS: de G P R w ef
GCSE: de g i o v   B G K N P R   cdef j l
OTHER: l

C — Twickenham Prep.School; Beveree; 43 High Street; Hampton; Middx. TW12 2SA
Tel: 0181 979 6216 *G.D.Malcolm*

- Day
- Weekly
- Boarding

£845-£1350 | Boys 59 | Age 4-13 | Girls 76 | Age 4-11 | TOTAL 135 | SIXTH Boys — | Girls —

MAP 5 C 5
LOCATION Urban
DAY ✓   **RAIL** b   **AIR** a
SPORT aefjpqx AB
OTHER LANGUAGES
ACTIVITIES fghj
OTHER SUBJECTS ch
FACILITIES ON SITE
EXAM BOARDS
RETAKES   **NVQ COURSES**

ENTRY REQUIREMENTS Test & Interview; Assessment & Interview
SCHOLARSHIPS & BURSARIES
SPECIAL NEEDS in GL   **DYSLEXIA** g   **DIET** acd
ASSOCIATION IAPS   **FOUNDED** 1932   **RELIGIOUS AFFILIATION** Inter-denom

A-level | AS | GCSE | OTHER: c e g i   v   B G K OP R   cde g j

---

C — Unicorn School; 238 Kew Road; Richmond; Surrey TW9 3JX
Tel: 0181 948 3926 (Fax: 0181 332 6814) *Mrs F.C.Timmis*

- Day
- Weekly
- Boarding

£710-£1320 | Boys 74 | Age 3-11 | Girls 90 | Age 3-11 | TOTAL 164 | SIXTH Boys — | Girls —

MAP 5 D 5
LOCATION Urban
DAY ✓   **RAIL** b   **AIR** a
SPORT cejlpqwx B
OTHER LANGUAGES
ACTIVITIES ghjostw
OTHER SUBJECTS abcfh
FACILITIES ON SITE
EXAM BOARDS
RETAKES   **NVQ COURSES**

ENTRY REQUIREMENTS Interview
SCHOLARSHIPS & BURSARIES
SPECIAL NEEDS n   **DYSLEXIA** e   **DIET** abcd
ASSOCIATION IAPS   **FOUNDED** 1970   **RELIGIOUS AFFILIATION** Non-denom

A-level | AS | GCSE | OTHER: e l no v   B G K   cde

B — University College School Jnr.Br; Holly Hill; Hampstead; London NW3 6QN
Tel: 0171 435 3068 (Fax: 0171 435 7332) *J.F.Hubbard*

- Day
- Weekly
- Boarding

£2130 ✗ | Boys 231 | Age 7-11 | Girls — | Age — | TOTAL 231 | SIXTH Boys — | Girls —

MAP 5 E 3
LOCATION Urban
DAY ✓   **RAIL** a   **AIR** b
SPORT abefgjlmoswx AB
OTHER LANGUAGES
ACTIVITIES fghjorst A
OTHER SUBJECTS bch
FACILITIES ON SITE acik
EXAM BOARDS
RETAKES   **NVQ COURSES**

ENTRY REQUIREMENTS Report & Exam & Interview
SCHOLARSHIPS & BURSARIES
SPECIAL NEEDS bl   **DYSLEXIA**   **DIET** ac
ASSOCIATION IAPS   **FOUNDED** 1891   **RELIGIOUS AFFILIATION** Non-denom

A-level | AS | GCSE | OTHER: e l no v   B E G K NO   cde

LONDON (GREATER) *continued*

B | University College School; Frognal; London NW3 6XH
Tel: 0171 435 2215 (Fax: 0171 431 4385) *G.D.Slaughter*

		Boys	Age	Girls	Age	TOTAL		Boys	Girls
Day	£2130-£2275 ✗	690	11-18			690	SIXTH	200	
Weekly									
Boarding									

ENTRY REQUIREMENTS CEE; Exam & Interview
SCHOLARSHIPS & BURSARIES Schol; Burs; AP
SPECIAL NEEDS bej GL   **DYSLEXIA**   **DIET** ac
ASSOCIATION HMC   **FOUNDED** 1830   **RELIGIOUS AFFILIATION** Non-denom

MAP 5 E 3
LOCATION Urban
DAY   **RAIL** a   **AIR** b
SPORT abcdefghijklmostwx ABC
OTHER LANGUAGES
ACTIVITIES fghijlnoqrst AB
OTHER SUBJECTS cfh
FACILITIES ON SITE acghik
EXAM BOARDS bd BEGH
RETAKES   **NVQ COURSES**

A-level	de g i nop v x˙	AS		K	GCSE	de g i k nop v	OTHER	l u
	AB GH K N P					AB G K N P		o
	cdefg j					cdefg j l		kl

Gb | Virgo Fidelis School; Central Hill; Upper Norwood; London SE19 1RS
Tel: 0181 670 6917 (Fax: 0181 761 7459) *Sister Mary Teresa O'Sullivan*

		Boys	Age	Girls	Age	TOTAL		Boys	Girls
Day	£370-£1425	26	3- 8	333	3-18	359	SIXTH		14
Weekly									
Boarding									

ENTRY REQUIREMENTS Report; Exam & Interview
SCHOLARSHIPS & BURSARIES Schol; Burs
SPECIAL NEEDS befhjklq   **DYSLEXIA**   **DIET**
ASSOCIATION ISAI   **FOUNDED** 1848   **RELIGIOUS AFFILIATION** R C

MAP 5 F 5
LOCATION Urban
DAY   **RAIL** b   **AIR** b
SPORT aclmpqx AB
OTHER LANGUAGES a
ACTIVITIES cfghjot
OTHER SUBJECTS bcefh
FACILITIES ON SITE bdgh
EXAM BOARDS abcd ABEGL
RETAKES ab   **NVQ COURSES**

A-level	e ghij l p v	AS	g i p v	GCSE	e ghij l p v	OTHER	
	BC GH K M P R T		B G K P R		BC G K P R		
	cdefg j		e g j		cdefg j		

C | West Dene School; 167 Brighton Road; Purley CR8 4HE
Tel: 0181 660 2404 (Fax: 0181 660 2404) *Mrs G.Charkin*

		Boys	Age	Girls	Age	TOTAL		Boys	Girls
Day	£520- £830	38	3- 8	91	3- 8	129	SIXTH		
Weekly									
Boarding									

ENTRY REQUIREMENTS Interview
SCHOLARSHIPS & BURSARIES
SPECIAL NEEDS bjknpqtuw BGHI   **DYSLEXIA** g   **DIET** acd
ASSOCIATION ISAI   **FOUNDED** 1927   **RELIGIOUS AFFILIATION** Inter-denom

MAP 5 F 7
LOCATION Urban
DAY   **RAIL** a   **AIR** a
SPORT aejlqx
OTHER LANGUAGES
ACTIVITIES j
OTHER SUBJECTS ch
FACILITIES ON SITE h
EXAM BOARDS
RETAKES   **NVQ COURSES**

A-level		AS		GCSE		OTHER	e l o v
							B G K O R
							cde

B | Westminster Abbey Choir School; Deans Yard; London SW1P 3NY
Tel: 0171 222 6151 *L.G.Roland-Adams*

		Boys	Age	Girls	Age	TOTAL		Boys	Girls
Day						30	SIXTH		
Weekly									
Boarding	£873	30	7-13						

ENTRY REQUIREMENTS Test & Interview
SCHOLARSHIPS & BURSARIES Burs; Chor
SPECIAL NEEDS b   **DYSLEXIA**   **DIET** a
ASSOCIATION IAPS   **FOUNDED**   **RELIGIOUS AFFILIATION** C of E

MAP 5 F 4
LOCATION Inner City
DAY   **RAIL** a   **AIR** a
SPORT ejx AB
OTHER LANGUAGES
ACTIVITIES fghjo
OTHER SUBJECTS abch
FACILITIES ON SITE
EXAM BOARDS
RETAKES   **NVQ COURSES**

A-level		AS		GCSE		OTHER	c e l no v
							B E G K R
							cde j

B | Westminster Cathedral Choir School; Ambrosden Avenue; London SW1P 1QH
Tel: 0171 798 9081 (Fax: 0171 798 9090) *C.Foulds*

		Boys	Age	Girls	Age	TOTAL		Boys	Girls
Day	£1960	68	8-13			94	SIXTH		
Weekly									
Boarding	£970-£1080	26	8-13						

ENTRY REQUIREMENTS Test & Interview
SCHOLARSHIPS & BURSARIES Chor
SPECIAL NEEDS   **DYSLEXIA**   **DIET**
ASSOCIATION IAPS   **FOUNDED** 1901   **RELIGIOUS AFFILIATION** R C

MAP 5 F 4
LOCATION Urban
DAY   **RAIL** a   **AIR**
SPORT cejsx AB
OTHER LANGUAGES
ACTIVITIES gho
OTHER SUBJECTS ch
FACILITIES ON SITE
EXAM BOARDS
RETAKES   **NVQ COURSES**

A-level		AS		GCSE		OTHER	e l o v
							B E G K R
							cde g j

LONDON (GREATER) *continued*

Bg Westminster School; 17 Dean's Yard; London SW1P 3PB
Tel: 0171 963 1003 (Fax: 0171 963 1006) *D.M.Summerscale*

			Boys	Age	Girls	Age	TOTAL		Boys	Girls
Day	£2950-£3225	✗	421	12-18	42	16-18	665	SIXTH	216	70*
Weekly	£4300		1	12-18		16-18				
Boarding			173		28					

ENTRY REQUIREMENTS CEE; Scholarship Exam
SCHOLARSHIPS & BURSARIES Schol; Mus
SPECIAL NEEDS hjlns **DYSLEXIA** f **DIET** abcd
ASSOCIATION HMC **FOUNDED** 1560 **RELIGIOUS AFFILIATION** C of E

MAP 5 F 4
LOCATION Inner City
DAY **RAIL** a **AIR** a
SPORT acefghijoprsuwx B
OTHER LANGUAGES
ACTIVITIES fghijloqstu
OTHER SUBJECTS bcfh
FACILITIES ON SITE cd
EXAM BOARDS abcd BDEGHI
RETAKES **NVQ COURSES**

A-level: d fg i l opq v   B GH K P cdefg jkl
AS
GCSE: l q   GH K M   e l   bcdefg ijkl
GCSE (continued): d g i no q v   B G K P R
OTHER: h

B Westminster Under School; Adrian House; 27 Vincent Square; London SW1P 2NN
Tel: 0171 821 5788 (Fax: 0171 821 0458) *G.Ashton*

		Boys	Age	Girls	Age	TOTAL		Boys	Girls
Day	£2055	269	8-13			269	SIXTH		
Weekly									
Boarding									

ENTRY REQUIREMENTS Test
SCHOLARSHIPS & BURSARIES Schol; Burs; Mus; AP
SPECIAL NEEDS behjklnpt l **DYSLEXIA** e **DIET** acd
ASSOCIATION IAPS **FOUNDED** 1943 **RELIGIOUS AFFILIATION** C of E

MAP 5 F 4
LOCATION Inner City
DAY **RAIL** a **AIR** a
SPORT abdefgjmox AB
OTHER LANGUAGES
ACTIVITIES fghijoqrt A
OTHER SUBJECTS bcdfh
FACILITIES ON SITE h
EXAM BOARDS
RETAKES **NVQ COURSES**

OTHER: e g i l n v   B G K OP R   cde g j

B Whitgift School; Haling Park; South Croydon CR2 6YT
Tel: 0181 688 9222 (Fax: 0181 760 0682) *Dr C.A.Barnett*

		Boys	Age	Girls	Age	TOTAL		Boys	Girls
Day	£1832	1056	10-18			1056	SIXTH	268	
Weekly									
Boarding									

ENTRY REQUIREMENTS Exam & Interview; CEE & Interview
SCHOLARSHIPS & BURSARIES Schol; Burs; Mus; Clergy; AP
SPECIAL NEEDS abejlnw Al **DYSLEXIA** **DIET** a
ASSOCIATION HMC **FOUNDED** 1596 **RELIGIOUS AFFILIATION** C of E

MAP 5 F 6
LOCATION Urban
DAY **RAIL** a **AIR** a
SPORT abcdefghijkmstuwx AB
OTHER LANGUAGES
ACTIVITIES efghijklnopqrstuv AB
OTHER SUBJECTS bcfh
FACILITIES ON SITE abcdghik
EXAM BOARDS abcde ABDEGH
RETAKES **NVQ COURSES**

A-level: cd fghi l opq v x   B GH K N P R U   c efgh j
AS: cd g l pq   G   efgh
GCSE: cd g i l no vw   B G I K P R   cdefghijkl
OTHER: C MN

B Willington School; Worcester Road; Wimbledon; London SW19 7QQ
Tel: 0181 944 7020 (Fax: 0181 944 9596) *J.Hey*

			Boys	Age	Girls	Age	TOTAL		Boys	Girls
Day	£1250-£1495	✗	198	4-13			198	SIXTH		
Weekly										
Boarding										

ENTRY REQUIREMENTS
SCHOLARSHIPS & BURSARIES Burs
SPECIAL NEEDS B **DYSLEXIA** **DIET**
ASSOCIATION IAPS **FOUNDED** 1885 **RELIGIOUS AFFILIATION** Inter-denom

MAP 5 E 5
LOCATION Urban
DAY ✓ **RAIL** a **AIR** a
SPORT abefjswx B
OTHER LANGUAGES
ACTIVITIES fghjru
OTHER SUBJECTS ch
FACILITIES ON SITE c
EXAM BOARDS A
RETAKES **NVQ COURSES**

G Wimbledon High School GPDST; Mansel Road; London SW19 4AB
Tel: 0181 946 1756 (Fax: 0181 944 1989) *Dr J.Clough*

		Boys	Age	Girls	Age	TOTAL		Boys	Girls
Day	£1192-£1548			810	5-18	810	SIXTH		146
Weekly									
Boarding									

ENTRY REQUIREMENTS Report & Exam & Interview
SCHOLARSHIPS & BURSARIES Schol; Burs; AP
SPECIAL NEEDS efjknqt BGI **DYSLEXIA** e **DIET**
ASSOCIATION GSA **FOUNDED** 1880 **RELIGIOUS AFFILIATION** Non-denom

MAP 5 E 5
LOCATION Urban
DAY **RAIL** a **AIR** a
SPORT acklmpqwx ABC
OTHER LANGUAGES
ACTIVITIES cghijknost A
OTHER SUBJECTS abcdfh
FACILITIES ON SITE bcghi
EXAM BOARDS abcd AEH
RETAKES **NVQ COURSES**

A-level: efghi p vw   B GH K P R   cdefg j
AS
GCSE: e g i l no v   BC G K P R   cdefg j l
OTHER: m u   k

LONDON (GREATER) *continued*

C | **Woodside Park School; Woodside Lane; London N12 8SY**
Tel: 0181 445 2333 (Fax: 0181 445 0835) *R.F.Metters*

		Boys	Age	Girls	Age	TOTAL		Boys	Girls
Day	£675–£1600	239	3-16	98	3-16	337	SIXTH		
Weekly									
Boarding									

MAP 5 F 2
LOCATION Urban
DAY   **RAIL** b   **AIR** b
SPORT abefjkmpqx AB
OTHER LANGUAGES
ACTIVITIES fghjlot

ENTRY REQUIREMENTS Test & Interview
SCHOLARSHIPS & BURSARIES Schol; Burs
SPECIAL NEEDS j
ASSOCIATION IAPS   **FOUNDED** 1885
DYSLEXIA   **DIET** abcd
RELIGIOUS AFFILIATION Non-denom
OTHER SUBJECTS bch
FACILITIES ON SITE
EXAM BOARDS
RETAKES   **NVQ COURSES**

A-level   **AS**   **GCSE**   **OTHER** de g i l no   v   B   G   K   OP R   cde   j

---

C | **Amberleigh Prep. School; 398 Wilbraham Road; Chorlton-cum-Hardy; Manchester M21 0UH** Tel: 0161 881 1593 *P.F.Hayden*

		Boys	Age	Girls	Age	TOTAL		Boys	Girls
Day	£568–£842	75	4-11	40	4-11	115	SIXTH		
Weekly									
Boarding									

MAP 11 E 8
LOCATION Urban
DAY   **RAIL** b   **AIR** a
SPORT aefjpqx
OTHER LANGUAGES
ACTIVITIES cfghjo

ENTRY REQUIREMENTS Test & Interview
SCHOLARSHIPS & BURSARIES
SPECIAL NEEDS alnw A
ASSOCIATION ISAI   **FOUNDED** 1925
DYSLEXIA e   **DIET** abcd
RELIGIOUS AFFILIATION Non-denom
OTHER SUBJECTS ch
FACILITIES ON SITE hik
EXAM BOARDS
RETAKES   **NVQ COURSES**

A-level   **AS**   **GCSE**   **OTHER** e   mno   v   B E G   K   O R   X   cde

---

C | **Bridgewater School; Drywood Hall; Worsley Road; Worsley; Manchester M28 2WQ**
Tel: 0161 794 1463 (Fax: 0161 794 3519) *Dr B.J.Blundell*

		Boys	Age	Girls	Age	TOTAL		Boys	Girls
Day	£845–£1332 ✗	266	3-18	202	3-18	468	SIXTH	15	10
Weekly									
Boarding									

MAP 11 E 8
LOCATION Urban
DAY ✓   **RAIL** b   **AIR** a
SPORT abcefjlmnpqwx A
OTHER LANGUAGES a
ACTIVITIES bfghijqst

ENTRY REQUIREMENTS Test & Interview
SCHOLARSHIPS & BURSARIES Schol
SPECIAL NEEDS
ASSOCIATION ISAI   **FOUNDED** 1950
DYSLEXIA   **DIET** abcd
RELIGIOUS AFFILIATION Non-denom
OTHER SUBJECTS bcdfh
FACILITIES ON SITE b
EXAM BOARDS cd DG
RETAKES ab   **NVQ COURSES**

A-level d g i l   p   uv   G   P   U   def   **AS**   **GCSE** de g i l n   t v   BC E G   P   cdef   j   **OTHER**   O R

C | **Caius House School; 99 Church Road; Urmston M41 9FJ**
Tel: 0161 748 3261 (Fax: 0161 748 3261) *N.A.Ricketts*

		Boys	Age	Girls	Age	TOTAL		Boys	Girls
Day	£500–£680	61	3-11	53	3-11	114	SIXTH		
Weekly									
Boarding									

MAP 11 E 8
LOCATION Urban
DAY   **RAIL**   **AIR**
SPORT aefjpqx
OTHER LANGUAGES
ACTIVITIES bfghjq A

ENTRY REQUIREMENTS Assessment & Interview
SCHOLARSHIPS & BURSARIES
SPECIAL NEEDS bhi l
ASSOCIATION ISAI   **FOUNDED** 1908
DYSLEXIA   **DIET** d
RELIGIOUS AFFILIATION Inter-denom
OTHER SUBJECTS ch
FACILITIES ON SITE
EXAM BOARDS
RETAKES   **NVQ COURSES**

A-level   **AS**   **GCSE**   **OTHER** e   l o   v   B E G   K   O R   cde

---

C | **Chetham's School of Music; Long Millgate; Manchester M3 1SB**
Tel: 0161 834 9644 (Fax: 0161 839 3609) *Revd.P.F.Hullah*

		Boys	Age	Girls	Age	TOTAL		Boys	Girls
Day	£1610–£4025 ✗	37	8-18	18	8-18	281	SIXTH	51	72
Weekly									
Boarding	£5200	82	8-18	144	8-18				

MAP 11 E 8
LOCATION Inner City
DAY   **RAIL** a   **AIR** a
SPORT bhptwx A
OTHER LANGUAGES a
ACTIVITIES fghjoqt A

ENTRY REQUIREMENTS
SCHOLARSHIPS & BURSARIES Burs; Mus; Chor; AP
SPECIAL NEEDS beln
ASSOCIATION HMC   **FOUNDED** 1653
DYSLEXIA   **DIET** a
RELIGIOUS AFFILIATION Non-denom
OTHER SUBJECTS bcfh
FACILITIES ON SITE ei
EXAM BOARDS cd ADEL
RETAKES   **NVQ COURSES**

A-level e g i   uv   GH K   P   c ef   **AS**   B   GH   u   R   c   f   **GCSE** e   l n   v   B G K   P   cdef   j   X   **OTHER** e   l n   O R

MANCHESTER (GREATER)

211

MANCHESTER (GREATER) *continued*

B — Manchester Grammar School; Old Hall Lane; Manchester M13 0XT
Tel: 0161 224 7201 (Fax: 0161 257 2446) *G.M.Stephen*

Day	£1380	Boys 1414	Age 10-18	Girls	Age	TOTAL 1414	SIXTH	Boys 392	Girls
Weekly									
Boarding									

ENTRY REQUIREMENTS CEE; Exam
SCHOLARSHIPS & BURSARIES Burs; Teachers; AP; Siblings
SPECIAL NEEDS abegjlnpqstuw ADGHIL   **DYSLEXIA**   **DIET** abcd
ASSOCIATION HMC   **FOUNDED** 1515   **RELIGIOUS AFFILIATION** Inter-denom

MAP11 E 8
LOCATION Urban
DAY   **RAIL** b   **AIR** a
SPORT abcefjklmostvwx AB
OTHER LANGUAGES n
ACTIVITIES bfghijlnopqrstuvx A
OTHER SUBJECTS abcdefh
FACILITIES ON SITE abcgik
EXAM BOARDS abcd DH
RETAKES   **NVQ COURSES**

A-level	c e g i v x B GH K P R c efg jkl	AS	GH	GCSE	d e g i o v B GH K P R cdefg jkl	OTHER	f h l nopq stu F IJ MNO Q TU h

G — Manchester High School for Girls; Grangethorpe Road; Manchester M14 6HS
Tel: 0161 224 0447 (Fax: 0161 224 6192) *Miss E.M.Diggory*

Day	£875-£1305	Boys	Age	Girls 934	Age 4-18	TOTAL 934	SIXTH	Boys	Girls 189
Weekly									
Boarding									

ENTRY REQUIREMENTS Exam & Interview; Report & Interview
SCHOLARSHIPS & BURSARIES Schol; Burs; AP
SPECIAL NEEDS bgijklqt AGHJ   **DYSLEXIA**   **DIET** a
ASSOCIATION GSA   **FOUNDED** 1874   **RELIGIOUS AFFILIATION** Non-denom

MAP11 E 8
LOCATION Urban
DAY   **RAIL** b   **AIR** a
SPORT aflmpqx B
OTHER LANGUAGES
ACTIVITIES ghijknost AB
OTHER SUBJECTS abcfh
FACILITIES ON SITE cgi
EXAM BOARDS abcd AD
RETAKES   **NVQ COURSES**

A-level	c e g i p uv BC GH K P R U W cdefg jkl	AS	g l G e l	GCSE	d g i o v BC G K P R W cdefg jkl	OTHER	n

C — Moor Allerton School; 131 Barlow Moor Road; West Didsbury; Manchester M20 2PW
Tel: 0161 445 4521 *M.J.Clarke*

Day	£500-£1050	Boys 93	Age 3-11	Girls 51	Age 3-11	TOTAL 144	SIXTH	Boys	Girls
Weekly									
Boarding									

ENTRY REQUIREMENTS Assessment
SCHOLARSHIPS & BURSARIES
SPECIAL NEEDS bejknpqw GI   **DYSLEXIA** g   **DIET** acd
ASSOCIATION IAPS   **FOUNDED** 1914   **RELIGIOUS AFFILIATION** Non-denom

MAP11 E 8
LOCATION Urban
DAY   **RAIL** b   **AIR**
SPORT aejlmpqx A
OTHER LANGUAGES
ACTIVITIES cfghjoq
OTHER SUBJECTS bch
FACILITIES ON SITE a
EXAM BOARDS
RETAKES   **NVQ COURSES**

A-level		AS		GCSE		OTHER	e g i o v B G K OP R cde

C — Oaklands Preparatory School; 643 Wilbraham Road; Chorlton-cum-Hardy;
Manchester M21 9JT Tel: 0161 881 4702 *Mrs C.S.Whalley*

Day	£690-£835	Boys 78	Age 3-11	Girls 23	Age 3-11	TOTAL 101	SIXTH	Boys	Girls
Weekly									
Boarding									

ENTRY REQUIREMENTS Assessment & Interview
SCHOLARSHIPS & BURSARIES
SPECIAL NEEDS   **DYSLEXIA**   **DIET** acd
ASSOCIATION ISAI   **FOUNDED** 1976   **RELIGIOUS AFFILIATION**

MAP11 E 8
LOCATION Urban
DAY   **RAIL** b   **AIR** a
SPORT afjmpqx
OTHER LANGUAGES
ACTIVITIES fj
OTHER SUBJECTS
FACILITIES ON SITE
EXAM BOARDS
RETAKES   **NVQ COURSES**

A-level		AS		GCSE		OTHER	e v B E G K cde

Gb — Rosecroft School Didsbury; 826 Wilmslow Road; Didsbury; Manchester M20 2RN
Tel. 0161 434 2616 *Miss M.Mullins*

Day	£600-£1140	Boys 17	Age 3-7	Girls 94	Age 3-16	TOTAL 111	SIXTH	Boys	Girls
Weekly									
Boarding									

ENTRY REQUIREMENTS Assessment & Interview
SCHOLARSHIPS & BURSARIES Burs; Teachers
SPECIAL NEEDS bfknqtw GIL   **DYSLEXIA** eg   **DIET** ad
ASSOCIATION ISAI   **FOUNDED** 1979   **RELIGIOUS AFFILIATION** R C

MAP11 E 8
LOCATION Urban
DAY   **RAIL** b   **AIR** a
SPORT aflmpqx AB
OTHER LANGUAGES a
ACTIVITIES cfgjkloq
OTHER SUBJECTS ch
FACILITIES ON SITE d
EXAM BOARDS c
RETAKES   **NVQ COURSES**

A-level		AS		GCSE	d e g i t v BC E G K P R cde j l	OTHER	c e g i lmno v BC E G K OP R cde j l

MANCHESTER (GREATER) continued

C — St. Bede's College; Alexandra Park; Manchester M16 8HX
Tel: 0161 226 3323 (Fax: 0161 226 3813) *J.Byrne*

		Boys	Age	Girls	Age	TOTAL		Boys	Girls
Day	£848-£1290	644	5-18	525	5-18	1169	SIXTH	148	145
Weekly									
Boarding									

MAP11 E 8
LOCATION Urban
DAY ✓   RAIL b   AIR a
SPORT abcdefhjmopqsvwx ABC
OTHER LANGUAGES a
ACTIVITIES fghijopqtw A
OTHER SUBJECTS bcfh
FACILITIES ON SITE bcdegh
EXAM BOARDS abc ABDEGH
RETAKES ab   NVQ COURSES

ENTRY REQUIREMENTS Exam & Interview
SCHOLARSHIPS & BURSARIES Schol; Burs; Mus; AP; VI Form
SPECIAL NEEDS abcegjlnpqstu AHI   DYSLEXIA   DIET a
ASSOCIATION HMC   FOUNDED 1876   RELIGIOUS AFFILIATION R C

A-level: cdefghi l nop uvwx / B GH K P R U / cdefg j l
AS
GCSE: defghi l op uv / B GH K N P R U / cdefg j l
OTHER

C — William Hulme's Grammar School; Spring Bridge Road; Manchester M16 8PR
Tel: 0161 226 2054 (Fax: 0161 226 8922) *P.D.Briggs*

		Boys	Age	Girls	Age	TOTAL		Boys	Girls
Day	£1357	531	11-18	258	11-18	789	SIXTH	144	67
Weekly									
Boarding									

MAP11 E 8
LOCATION Urban
DAY   RAIL b   AIR a
SPORT abcefhlmnpqstuwx AB
OTHER LANGUAGES
ACTIVITIES efghijkloqrst A
OTHER SUBJECTS acfh
FACILITIES ON SITE bcghi
EXAM BOARDS ace ADEL
RETAKES   NVQ COURSES

ENTRY REQUIREMENTS Exam & Interview
SCHOLARSHIPS & BURSARIES Burs; Mus; Teachers; AP; VI Form; Siblings
SPECIAL NEEDS   DYSLEXIA   DIET acd
ASSOCIATION HMC   FOUNDED 1887   RELIGIOUS AFFILIATION Non-denom

A-level: c eghi op uvwx / B GH K P R / cdefg j l
AS
GCSE: egi o vw / B GH K P R / cdefg jkl
OTHER: f lm q o

G — Withington Girls School; 100 Wellington Road; Fallowfield; Manchester M14 6BL
Tel: 0161 224 1077 (Fax: 0161 248 5377) *Mrs M.Kenyon*

		Boys	Age	Girls	Age	TOTAL		Boys	Girls
Day	£865-£1250			593	7-18	593	SIXTH		119
Weekly									
Boarding									

MAP11 E 8
LOCATION Urban
DAY   RAIL a   AIR a
SPORT abcelmnpqtwx ABC
OTHER LANGUAGES
ACTIVITIES cghijkoqt A
OTHER SUBJECTS abcdfh
FACILITIES ON SITE chk
EXAM BOARDS bc D
RETAKES   NVQ COURSES

ENTRY REQUIREMENTS Exam & Interview
SCHOLARSHIPS & BURSARIES Burs; AP
SPECIAL NEEDS bgjklqt H   DYSLEXIA   DIET ac
ASSOCIATION GSA   FOUNDED 1890   RELIGIOUS AFFILIATION Non-denom

A-level: egi uv / BC GH K P R U / cdefgh j
AS: g G
GCSE: egi v / BC G K OP R / cdefg j l
OTHER: l no q s x K

G — Belvedere School GPDST,The; 17 Belvidere Road; Princes Park; Liverpool L8 3TF
Tel: 0151 727 1284 (Fax: 0151 727 0602) *Mrs C.H.Evans*

		Boys	Age	Girls	Age	TOTAL		Boys	Girls
Day	£850-£1328			653	3-18	653	SIXTH		104
Weekly									
Boarding									

MAP 8 G 1
LOCATION Urban
DAY ✓   RAIL a   AIR a
SPORT bchlnopqx ABC
OTHER LANGUAGES
ACTIVITIES fghijknost AB
OTHER SUBJECTS abcefh
FACILITIES ON SITE cg
EXAM BOARDS cd ADE
RETAKES   NVQ COURSES

ENTRY REQUIREMENTS Exam
SCHOLARSHIPS & BURSARIES Schol; Burs; AP
SPECIAL NEEDS bjiqs AHI   DYSLEXIA   DIET abcd
ASSOCIATION GSA   FOUNDED 1880   RELIGIOUS AFFILIATION Non-denom

A-level: eghi l n p uv / B GH K P R U / cdefg j l
AS: l G K P R / g
GCSE: egi l n v / B E G K P R X / cdefg j l
OTHER: g

G — Birkenhead High School GPDST; 86 Devonshire Place; Birkenhead L43 1TY
Tel: 0151 652 5777 (Fax: 0151 670 0639) *Mrs K.R.Irving*

		Boys	Age	Girls	Age	TOTAL		Boys	Girls
Day	£976-£1328			973	4-18	973	SIXTH		191
Weekly									
Boarding									

MAP 8 G 1
LOCATION Urban
DAY   RAIL b   AIR b
SPORT achlmnpqwx ABC
OTHER LANGUAGES
ACTIVITIES acfghjkno
OTHER SUBJECTS bch
FACILITIES ON SITE cghi
EXAM BOARDS ac AD
RETAKES   NVQ COURSES

ENTRY REQUIREMENTS Exam
SCHOLARSHIPS & BURSARIES Schol; AP
SPECIAL NEEDS q G   DYSLEXIA   DIET
ASSOCIATION GSA   FOUNDED 1901   RELIGIOUS AFFILIATION Inter-denom

A-level: c eghi l n p uvw / B GH K P R U / cdefg jkl
AS: B G K P / efg j l
GCSE: egi l no vw / B G K OP R / cdefg jkl
OTHER: s

MERSEYSIDE

MERSEYSIDE *continued*

B — Birkenhead School; 58 Beresford Road; Birkenhead L43 2JD
Tel: 0151 652 4014 (Fax: 0151 653 7412) *S.J.Haggett*

		Boys 1087	Age 3-18	Girls	Age	TOTAL 1087	SIXTH	Boys 193	Girls
Day	£916-£1221								
Weekly									
Boarding									

ENTRY REQUIREMENTS Exam
SCHOLARSHIPS & BURSARIES Schol; AP
SPECIAL NEEDS ejk L   **DYSLEXIA**   **DIET** a
ASSOCIATION HMC   **FOUNDED** 1860   **RELIGIOUS AFFILIATION** C of E

MAP 8 G 1
LOCATION Urban
DAY   **RAIL** a   **AIR** b
SPORT abcefijklmstuwx AB
OTHER LANGUAGES
ACTIVITIES efghijkloqrtx
OTHER SUBJECTS abcdfh
FACILITIES ON SITE abcdghk
EXAM BOARDS abce BDEH
RETAKES   **NVQ COURSES**

A-level: c e g i   p   uv
B   GH   P
c efg j l

AS: ef   q

GCSE: c e g i l   op   v
B   G   K   P
cdefg jkl

OTHER:

C — Carleton House Preparatory School; Lyndhurst Road; Mossley Hill; Liverpool L18 8AQ
Tel: 0151 724 4880 *Mrs C.Line*

		Boys 83	Age 4-11	Girls 58	Age 4-11	TOTAL 141	SIXTH	Boys	Girls
Day	£780								
Weekly									
Boarding									

ENTRY REQUIREMENTS Assessment & Interview
SCHOLARSHIPS & BURSARIES
SPECIAL NEEDS n   **DYSLEXIA** d   **DIET**
ASSOCIATION ISAI   **FOUNDED** 1975   **RELIGIOUS AFFILIATION** R C

MAP 8 G 1
LOCATION Urban
DAY   **RAIL** a   **AIR** a
SPORT aejpqx
OTHER LANGUAGES
ACTIVITIES cfgq
OTHER SUBJECTS bh
FACILITIES ON SITE
EXAM BOARDS E
RETAKES   **NVQ COURSES**

OTHER: e

C — Kingsmead School; Bertram Drive; Hoylake; Wirral L47 0LL
Tel: 0151 632 3156 (Fax: 0151 632 0302) *E.H.Bradby*

		Boys	Age	Girls	Age	TOTAL 182	SIXTH	Boys	Girls
Day	£550-£1645	103	3-13	58	3-13				
Weekly	£2085-£2295	4	7-13	1	7-13				
Boarding	£2185-£2395	9	7-13	7	7-13				

ENTRY REQUIREMENTS Interview
SCHOLARSHIPS & BURSARIES Schol; Burs; Mus; Forces; Clergy; Teachers
SPECIAL NEEDS abcefjklnpqtuvwx BEGHI   **DYSLEXIA** cde   **DIET** abcd
ASSOCIATION IAPS   **FOUNDED** 1904   **RELIGIOUS AFFILIATION** Evang'l

MAP 8 G 1
LOCATION Urban
DAY   **RAIL** b   **AIR** a
SPORT abcefjmpqstx ABC
OTHER LANGUAGES
ACTIVITIES cfghjot
OTHER SUBJECTS bch
FACILITIES ON SITE ehik
EXAM BOARDS
RETAKES   **NVQ COURSES**

OTHER: cde g i   lmno   v
BC   G   K   OP R
cde g j

C — Kingswood Schools; 26 Westcliffe Road; Birkdale; Southport; Merseyside PR8 2BU
Tel: 01704 563211 (Fax: 01704 550399) *E.J.Borowski*

		Boys 189	Age 2-18	Girls 210	Age 2-18	TOTAL 399	SIXTH	Boys 6	Girls 14
Day	£457-£1008								
Weekly									
Boarding									

ENTRY REQUIREMENTS Assessment & Interview
SCHOLARSHIPS & BURSARIES Schol; Burs
SPECIAL NEEDS ln B   **DYSLEXIA** ce   **DIET**
ASSOCIATION ISAI   **FOUNDED**   **RELIGIOUS AFFILIATION** Inter-denom

MAP 11 C 7
LOCATION Urban
DAY ✓   **RAIL** a   **AIR** a
SPORT abcdefjklmpqswx ABC
OTHER LANGUAGES a
ACTIVITIES cfghijklnopqstw A
OTHER SUBJECTS bcdh
FACILITIES ON SITE g
EXAM BOARDS c AD
RETAKES ab   **NVQ COURSES**

A-level: e ghi   p suv x
BC   G K   P R U
cde   l

AS: g i l   s uv
B   G K   P
e

GCSE: e ghi l   p   v x
BC E G   K   P R U
cdef   l

OTHER:

C — Liverpool College; Mossley Hill; Liverpool L18 8BE
Tel: 0151 724 4000 (Fax: 0151 729 0105) *B.R.Martin*

		Boys 716	Age 3-18	Girls 281	Age 3-18	TOTAL 997	SIXTH	Boys 103	Girls 40
Day	£830-£1360								
Weekly									
Boarding									

ENTRY REQUIREMENTS CEE; Exam; Report & Exam & Interview
SCHOLARSHIPS & BURSARIES Schol; Mus; Forces; Clergy; Teachers; AP; VI Form; Siblings
SPECIAL NEEDS kn   **DYSLEXIA**   **DIET** a
ASSOCIATION HMC   **FOUNDED** 1840   **RELIGIOUS AFFILIATION** C of E

MAP 8 G 1
LOCATION Urban
DAY ✓   **RAIL** a   **AIR** a
SPORT abcdefhijkmnpqsuwx ABC
OTHER LANGUAGES
ACTIVITIES cefghijklopqstvx AD
OTHER SUBJECTS abcfh
FACILITIES ON SITE acdgj
EXAM BOARDS c ABDGH
RETAKES   **NVQ COURSES**

A-level: cde ghi   l nop   uvw
B   GH K   P
cdefg j l

AS: ef   q

GCSE: cde g i l   nop   v
B   G   K   OP R
cdefg j l

OTHER: O R

MERSEYSIDE *continued*

Merchant Taylors' School for Girls; Crosby; Liverpool L23 5SP
Tel: 0151 924 3140 (Fax: 0151 932 1461) Mrs J.I.Mills

		Boys	Age	Girls	Age	TOTAL		Boys	Girls
Day	£807-£1248	65	4-7	849	4-18	914	SIXTH		143
Weekly									
Boarding									

ENTRY REQUIREMENTS Report & Exam & Interview
SCHOLARSHIPS & BURSARIES Schol; Burs; Teachers; AP; VI Form
SPECIAL NEEDS bgkln **DYSLEXIA** g **DIET** a
ASSOCIATION GSA **FOUNDED** 1888 **RELIGIOUS AFFILIATION** Inter-denom

MAP 8 G 1
LOCATION Urban
DAY ✓ **RAIL** b **AIR** b
SPORT abcfhlmnpqrwx ABC
OTHER LANGUAGES
ACTIVITIES cefghijknoqtx A
OTHER SUBJECTS abcdfh
FACILITIES ON SITE abghi
EXAM BOARDS c ABDEG
RETAKES **NVQ COURSES**

A-level: cd ghi n p uv / BC GH K OP / c ef jkl
AS: d
GCSE: cd g i v / BC E G K P R / cdef jkl
OTHER: d g i l nop uv x / BC G K OP R W / cdef jkl

Merchant Taylors' School; Crosby; Liverpool L23 0QP
Tel: 0151 928 3308 (Fax: 0151 928 0434) S.J.R.Dawkins

		Boys	Age	Girls	Age	TOTAL		Boys	Girls
Day	£843-£1248	823	7-18			823	SIXTH	177	
Weekly									
Boarding									

ENTRY REQUIREMENTS Test
SCHOLARSHIPS & BURSARIES Burs; AP; VI Form
SPECIAL NEEDS bklnq G **DYSLEXIA** g **DIET** acd
ASSOCIATION HMC **FOUNDED** 1620 **RELIGIOUS AFFILIATION** Non-denom

MAP 8 G 1
LOCATION Urban
DAY **RAIL** b **AIR** a
SPORT abcefhklmorstux AB
OTHER LANGUAGES
ACTIVITIES efghijklnopqrstvx A
OTHER SUBJECTS abcfh
FACILITIES ON SITE acgi
EXAM BOARDS c ADHL
RETAKES a **NVQ COURSES**

A-level: c e g i nop uv / B GH K M OP R U / c efg jkl
AS: G
GCSE: e g i o v / B G K P R / cdefg j l
OTHER:

Prenton Preparatory School; Mount Pleasant; Birkenhead; Merseyside L43 5SY
Tel: 0151 652 3182 (Fax: 0151 653 7428) Mrs N.M.Aloe

		Boys	Age	Girls	Age	TOTAL		Boys	Girls
Day	£700-£736	61	3-11	85	3-11	146	SIXTH		
Weekly									
Boarding									

ENTRY REQUIREMENTS Interview
SCHOLARSHIPS & BURSARIES Schol; Clergy; Teachers; Siblings
SPECIAL NEEDS ben B **DYSLEXIA** e **DIET**
ASSOCIATION ISAI **FOUNDED** 1935 **RELIGIOUS AFFILIATION** Non-denom

MAP 8 G 1
LOCATION Urban
DAY **RAIL** a **AIR** a
SPORT aejlpqx B
OTHER LANGUAGES a
ACTIVITIES cdfghj
OTHER SUBJECTS bch
FACILITIES ON SITE
EXAM BOARDS
RETAKES **NVQ COURSES**

A-level:
AS:
GCSE:
OTHER: e lmno v / B E G K O R / cde

St. Edward's College; North Drive; Sandfield Park; Liverpool; Merseyside L12 1LF
Tel: 0151 228 3376 (Fax: 0151 252 0219) J.E.Waszek

		Boys	Age	Girls	Age	TOTAL		Boys	Girls
Day	£800-£1166	701	3-18	356	3-18	1057	SIXTH	146	27
Weekly									
Boarding	£800-£1166								

ENTRY REQUIREMENTS Report & Exam & Interview
SCHOLARSHIPS & BURSARIES Burs; Mus; AP; VI Form; ARA
SPECIAL NEEDS abeghjlnsx J **DYSLEXIA** cef **DIET** a
ASSOCIATION HMC **FOUNDED** 1900 **RELIGIOUS AFFILIATION** R C

MAP 8 G 1
LOCATION Urban
DAY **RAIL** b **AIR** a
SPORT abcdefhjklmpstx BC
OTHER LANGUAGES i
ACTIVITIES cfghjknopqrst
OTHER SUBJECTS abcfh
FACILITIES ON SITE bcdghi
EXAM BOARDS abce ABDEGL
RETAKES **NVQ COURSES**

A-level: de ghi no uv / B GH K OP R / cde j l
AS: d g i / B G P R
GCSE: v x / cde j l
OTHER: de g i l no v / B E G K P R X / cde j l

St. Mary's College; Liverpool Road; Crosby; Merseyside L23 3AB
Tel: 0151 924 3926 (Fax: 0151 932 0363) W.Hammond

		Boys	Age	Girls	Age	TOTAL		Boys	Girls
Day	£674-£1248	521	3-18	358	3-18	879	SIXTH	90	42
Weekly									
Boarding									

ENTRY REQUIREMENTS Exam & Interview
SCHOLARSHIPS & BURSARIES Burs; AP; VI Form
SPECIAL NEEDS **DYSLEXIA** **DIET** acd
ASSOCIATION HMC **FOUNDED** 1919 **RELIGIOUS AFFILIATION** R C

MAP 8 G 1
LOCATION Urban
DAY **RAIL** b **AIR** a
SPORT abcfhklmpqsuwx ABC
OTHER LANGUAGES
ACTIVITIES cefghijkno ABD
OTHER SUBJECTS abcdh
FACILITIES ON SITE bcdghk
EXAM BOARDS bcd DL
RETAKES **NVQ COURSES**

A-level: cde ghi op uv / B GH K P R U / c efg j l
AS:
GCSE: l / R
OTHER: cde g i l nop v / AB E G K P R U / cdef j l

MERSEYSIDE continued

Sunnymede School; 4 Westcliffe Road; Birkdale; Southport PR8 2BN
Tel: 01704 568593 *S.J.Pattinson*

		Boys	Age	Girls	Age	TOTAL		Boys	Girls
Day	£575-£1275	109	3-13	60	3-13	169	SIXTH		
Weekly									
Boarding									

ENTRY REQUIREMENTS Interview
SCHOLARSHIPS & BURSARIES Schol; Teachers
SPECIAL NEEDS bginpqw B
DYSLEXIA   **DIET** abcd
ASSOCIATION IAPS   **FOUNDED** 1937   **RELIGIOUS AFFILIATION** Non-denom

MAP 11 C 7
LOCATION Urban
DAY √   **RAIL** a   **AIR** b
SPORT abefjkmpqsuwx ABC
OTHER LANGUAGES
ACTIVITIES cfghijoqrt A
OTHER SUBJECTS abcfh
FACILITIES ON SITE j
EXAM BOARDS
RETAKES   **NVQ COURSES**

A-level   **AS**   **GCSE**   **OTHER** e g i l no q v
ABC G K OP R
cde j

Tower College; Rainhill; Merseyside L35 6NE
Tel: 0151 426 4333 (Fax: 0151 426 3338) *Miss R.J.Oxley*

		Boys	Age	Girls	Age	TOTAL		Boys	Girls
Day	£582- £704	220	4-16	218	4-16	438	SIXTH		
Weekly									
Boarding									

ENTRY REQUIREMENTS Test
SCHOLARSHIPS & BURSARIES
SPECIAL NEEDS
DYSLEXIA   **DIET**
ASSOCIATION ISAI   **FOUNDED** 1948   **RELIGIOUS AFFILIATION** Inter-denom

MAP 8 H 1
LOCATION Urban
DAY   **RAIL** a   **AIR** a
SPORT abcfjlpqx ABC
OTHER LANGUAGES
ACTIVITIES cgio
OTHER SUBJECTS bch
FACILITIES ON SITE
EXAM BOARDS c
RETAKES   **NVQ COURSES**

A-level   **AS**   **GCSE** b d g i   v
B G   P R
cde
OTHER l

NORFOLK

Beeston Hall; West Runton; Cromer; Norfolk NR27 9NQ
Tel: 01263 837324 (Fax: 01263 838177) *J.M.Elder*

		Boys	Age	Girls	Age	TOTAL		Boys	Girls
Day	£2030	36	7-13	30	7-13	166	SIXTH		
Weekly		57	8-13	43	8-13				
Boarding	£2700								

ENTRY REQUIREMENTS Test & Interview
SCHOLARSHIPS & BURSARIES
SPECIAL NEEDS abejlnquw DGIL
DYSLEXIA d   **DIET**
ASSOCIATION IAPS   **FOUNDED** 1948   **RELIGIOUS AFFILIATION** C of E

MAP 10 J 4
LOCATION Rural
DAY   **RAIL** b   **AIR** a
SPORT abcefjklmopqstuwx AB
OTHER LANGUAGES c
ACTIVITIES acfghijlopqrstw DEFGHIJ
OTHER SUBJECTS acfh
FACILITIES ON SITE bdehjk
EXAM BOARDS
RETAKES   **NVQ COURSES**

A-level   **AS**   **GCSE**   **OTHER** d e g i l no   v
B G   P R U
cdefg jk

Cawston College; Cawston; Norwich; Norfolk NR10 4JD
Tel: 01603 871204 (Fax: 01603 871341) *Mrs B.Harrison*

		Boys	Age	Girls	Age	TOTAL		Boys	Girls
Day	£742-£1499	51	5-17	6	5-17	116	SIXTH	3	
Weekly	£2127-£2683	5	8-17		8-17				
Boarding	£2178-£2735	49	9-17	5	9-17				

ENTRY REQUIREMENTS Assessment & Interview
SCHOLARSHIPS & BURSARIES
SPECIAL NEEDS ablnquw B
DYSLEXIA ce   **DIET** a
ASSOCIATION ISAI   **FOUNDED** 1964   **RELIGIOUS AFFILIATION** C of E

MAP 10 J 5
LOCATION Rural
DAY   **RAIL** b   **AIR** c
SPORT abcdefhjkmopqsuwx BC
OTHER LANGUAGES a
ACTIVITIES aefghjklmnopqstw A
OTHER SUBJECTS abcdef
FACILITIES ON SITE bcdhkl
EXAM BOARDS abd AE
RETAKES a   **NVQ COURSES**

A-level   **AS** d   **GCSE** de ghi l o   v
BC E G K   P R
cdef
OTHER l
K   O
d

The New Eccles Hall School; Quidenham; Norwich NR16 2NZ
Tel: 01953 887217 (Fax: 01953 887397) *S.A.Simington*

		Boys	Age	Girls	Age	TOTAL		Boys	Girls
Day	£420-£1575		3-16		3-16	150	SIXTH		
Weekly	£2895		3-16		3-16				
Boarding	£2612-£2995		3-16		3-16				

ENTRY REQUIREMENTS Assessment & Interview
SCHOLARSHIPS & BURSARIES Mus; Chor; Forces
SPECIAL NEEDS bcejlnpquvwx ABEHI
DYSLEXIA c   **DIET** abcd
ASSOCIATION ISAI   **FOUNDED** 1944   **RELIGIOUS AFFILIATION** Inter-denom

MAP 10 J 6
LOCATION Rural
DAY   **RAIL** a   **AIR** b
SPORT abcdefhjkmopqstuwx ABC
OTHER LANGUAGES
ACTIVITIES aefghjkmnoqstwx AB
OTHER SUBJECTS bcdfh
FACILITIES ON SITE cdeik
EXAM BOARDS ad
RETAKES a   **NVQ COURSES**

A-level   **AS**   **GCSE** e l no   v
AB D G K O   X
cdef l
OTHER g i l
K OP R

NORFOLK *continued*

Glebe House; 2 Cromer Road; Hunstanton; Norfolk PE36 6HW
Tel: 01485 532809 (Fax: 01485 533900) *M.W.Spinney*

		Boys	Age	Girls	Age	TOTAL
Day	£995-£1895	46	4-13	28	4-13	79
Weekly	£2245-£2445	3	7-13	2	7-13	
Boarding						

SIXTH: Boys / Girls

ENTRY REQUIREMENTS Assessment & Interview
SCHOLARSHIPS & BURSARIES Schol; Burs; Mus; Forces; Sport; ARA; Siblings
SPECIAL NEEDS bn B **DYSLEXIA** cef **DIET** ad
ASSOCIATION IAPS **FOUNDED** 1879 **RELIGIOUS AFFILIATION** C of E

MAP10 H 4
LOCATION Rural
DAY √ **RAIL** b **AIR** c
SPORT abcefjklmopqsuwx AB
OTHER LANGUAGES
ACTIVITIES acfghijlmnoqswx A
OTHER SUBJECTS abch
FACILITIES ON SITE bcik
EXAM BOARDS
RETAKES **NVQ COURSES**

A-level:
AS:
GCSE:
OTHER: defg i l no v BC G K OP R cde j

Gresham's Preparatory School; Holt; Norfolk NR25 6EY
Tel: 01263 712227 (Fax: 01263 712028) *A.H.Cuff*

		Boys	Age	Girls	Age	TOTAL
Day	£955-£2005	118	4-13	83	4-13	266
Weekly	£2580	10	8-13	7	8-13	
Boarding	£2870	30	8-13	18	8-13	

SIXTH: Boys / Girls

ENTRY REQUIREMENTS Interview; Report; Assessment
SCHOLARSHIPS & BURSARIES Schol; Burs
SPECIAL NEEDS behjklnqw Gl **DYSLEXIA** ce **DIET** ad
ASSOCIATION IAPS **FOUNDED** 1555 **RELIGIOUS AFFILIATION** C of E

MAP10 J 4
LOCATION Rural
DAY √ **RAIL** b **AIR** b
SPORT abcefjklmpqswx AB
OTHER LANGUAGES
ACTIVITIES cfghjlopqrsw A
OTHER SUBJECTS abch
FACILITIES ON SITE abcdhi
EXAM BOARDS
RETAKES **NVQ COURSES**

A-level:
AS:
GCSE:
OTHER: e g i lmno q s uv ABC G K OP R cdef j

Gresham's School; Holt; Norfolk NR25 6EA
Tel: 01263 713271 (Fax: 01263 712028) *J.H.Arkell*

		Boys	Age	Girls	Age	TOTAL
Day	£2750	106	13-18	63	13-18	482
Weekly	£3535					
Boarding	£3930	203	13-18	110	13-18	

SIXTH: Boys 123 / Girls 71

ENTRY REQUIREMENTS CEE; Test; Scholarship Exam; Report & Interview
SCHOLARSHIPS & BURSARIES Schol; Art; Mus; AP; Sport; Drama
SPECIAL NEEDS n **DYSLEXIA** ce **DIET** a
ASSOCIATION HMC **FOUNDED** 1555 **RELIGIOUS AFFILIATION** C of E

MAP10 J 4
LOCATION Rural
DAY **RAIL** b **AIR** a
SPORT abcdefghjkmopqstuwx B
OTHER LANGUAGES a
ACTIVITIES efghijknoqstw AC
OTHER SUBJECTS abch
FACILITIES ON SITE cdghik
EXAM BOARDS abcde ABDEGH
RETAKES **NVQ COURSES**

A-level: c e g i l nopq v ABC GH K P R U cdef j
AS: C G K
GCSE: l o q u de g i l no q v ABC G K P R cdef hij l
OTHER: f l a ef i kl

Hethersett Old Hall School; Hethersett; Norwich NR9 3DW
Tel: 01603 810390 (Fax: 01603 812094) *Mrs V.M.Redington*

		Boys	Age	Girls	Age	TOTAL
Day	£1110-£1450			165	7-18	229
Weekly					7-18	
Boarding	£2285-£2850			64	7-18	

SIXTH: Boys / Girls 39

ENTRY REQUIREMENTS Report & Exam & Interview
SCHOLARSHIPS & BURSARIES Schol; Burs; Mus; Forces; Clergy; VI Form
SPECIAL NEEDS abfgjlnqtx EGHI **DYSLEXIA** ef **DIET** a
ASSOCIATION GSA **FOUNDED** 1924 **RELIGIOUS AFFILIATION** C of E

MAP10 J 6
LOCATION Rural
DAY √ **RAIL** a **AIR** a
SPORT abcfhlmopqtuwx ABC
OTHER LANGUAGES a
ACTIVITIES cghijklnopqstvwx BD
OTHER SUBJECTS abcefgh
FACILITIES ON SITE bghik
EXAM BOARDS abd ABE
RETAKES b **NVQ COURSES**

A-level: defghi l n uv x B G K N P R W bcdef l
AS: b defghi uv G K NOP R ef l
GCSE: de ghij l n uv BC G K N P R W bcdef l
OTHER: l no uv BC G K NO R T W cd jk

Langley Preparatory School and Nursery; Beech Hill; Yarmouth Rd.; Thorpe St. Andrew; Norwich NR7 0EA Tel: 01603 33861 (Fax: 01603 702639) *P.J.Weeks*

		Boys	Age	Girls	Age	TOTAL
Day	£670-£1315	82	2-12	17	2-12	99
Weekly						
Boarding						

SIXTH: Boys / Girls

ENTRY REQUIREMENTS Report & Interview
SCHOLARSHIPS & BURSARIES Schol; Burs
SPECIAL NEEDS ehjklnw Bl **DYSLEXIA** cef **DIET** acd
ASSOCIATION IAPS **FOUNDED** 1910 **RELIGIOUS AFFILIATION** Non-denom

MAP10 J 5
LOCATION Urban
DAY **RAIL** a **AIR** a
SPORT abefjlmqsx AC
OTHER LANGUAGES
ACTIVITIES cfghijlnopqt
OTHER SUBJECTS cfh
FACILITIES ON SITE chj
EXAM BOARDS
RETAKES **NVQ COURSES** 12

A-level:
AS:
GCSE:
OTHER: cde g i lmno q s v B E G K OP R cdef

NORFOLK *continued*

C — Langley School; Langley Park; Near Loddon; Norwich NR14 6BJ
Tel: 01508 520210 (Fax: 01508 528058) *S.J.W.Mc Arthur*

	Boys	Age	Girls	Age	TOTAL		Boys	Girls
Day	£1400-£1720	151	10-18	37	10-18	266	SIXTH	49	12
Weekly	£2330-£2680	25	10-18	10	10-18				
Boarding	£2695-£3270	36	10-18	7	10-18				

ENTRY REQUIREMENTS Test & Interview; Exam & Interview; Report & Interview; CEE & Interview
SCHOLARSHIPS & BURSARIES Schol; Burs; Art; Mus; Forces; VI Form; Sport; Siblings
SPECIAL NEEDS abegjklnqtuw BCDEGHI **DYSLEXIA** e **DIET** acd
ASSOCIATION SHMIS **FOUNDED** 1910 **RELIGIOUS AFFILIATION** Inter-denom

MAP10 J 5
LOCATION Rural
DAY ✓ **RAIL** b **AIR** c
SPORT abcdefghijklmopqstuwx ABC
OTHER LANGUAGES a
ACTIVITIES efghijklnopqstx A
OTHER SUBJECTS abcdfh
FACILITIES ON SITE abcdghkl
EXAM BOARDS abcd ABDEHIL
RETAKES a **NVQ COURSES**

- **A-level**: e ghi l op v ABC GH K P R c ef jl
- **AS**: gh l op v B G QR
- **GCSE**: de ghi l nop v ABC E G K NOP R cdef jl
- **OTHER**: o

G — Norwich High School for Girls GPDST; 95 Newmarket Road; Norwich; Norfolk NR2 2HU
Tel: 01603 453265 (Fax: 01603 259891) *Mrs V.C.Bidwell*

	Boys	Age	Girls	Age	TOTAL		Boys	Girls
Day	£976-£1328			894	4-18	894	SIXTH		154
Weekly									
Boarding									

ENTRY REQUIREMENTS Report & Exam & Interview
SCHOLARSHIPS & BURSARIES Schol; Burs; Mus; AP
SPECIAL NEEDS bjlq l **DYSLEXIA**   **DIET** a
ASSOCIATION GSA **FOUNDED** 1875 **RELIGIOUS AFFILIATION** Non-denom

MAP10 J 5
LOCATION Urban
DAY **RAIL** b **AIR** c
SPORT abcgklnpqrwx BC
OTHER LANGUAGES
ACTIVITIES cfghijknoqrs AB
OTHER SUBJECTS abch
FACILITIES ON SITE bcgi
EXAM BOARDS b B
RETAKES **NVQ COURSES**

- **A-level**: cd g i op uv B GH K P R cdefg j
- **AS**: d ef
- **GCSE**: cd g i l no vw B G K P R T cdefg jl
- **OTHER**: x K MNO R

B — Norwich School; 70 The Close; Norwich NR1 4DQ
Tel: 01603 623194 (Fax: 01603 623194) *C.D.Brown*

	Boys	Age	Girls	Age	TOTAL		Boys	Girls
Day	£1451-£1510	738	8-18	24	16-18	762	SIXTH	187	24
Weekly									
Boarding									

ENTRY REQUIREMENTS Exam & Interview
SCHOLARSHIPS & BURSARIES Schol; Mus; Chor; AP
SPECIAL NEEDS behlq AGI **DYSLEXIA**   **DIET** a
ASSOCIATION HMC **FOUNDED** 1547 **RELIGIOUS AFFILIATION** Non-denom

MAP10 J 5
LOCATION Inner City
DAY **RAIL** a **AIR** a
SPORT abcefghjkmopqrstuwx ABC
OTHER LANGUAGES
ACTIVITIES abfghijkmnopqstux AB
OTHER SUBJECTS bcdfh
FACILITIES ON SITE bcdg
EXAM BOARDS ab ABDEGH
RETAKES ab **NVQ COURSES**

- **A-level**: c efg i op v x B GH K P R cdef j
- **AS**: e o K g
- **GCSE**: c e l o v B G K R X cdefg jl
- **OTHER**: l q

Gb — Riddlesworth Hall; Diss; Norfolk IP22 2TA
Tel: 0195 368 1246 (Fax: 0195 368 8124) *Miss S.A.Smith*

	Boys	Age	Girls	Age	TOTAL		Boys	Girls
Day	£900-£1860 ✗	2	2-7	24	2-13	108	SIXTH		
Weekly	£2890			31	7-13				
Boarding	£2940			51	7-13				

ENTRY REQUIREMENTS Test & Interview
SCHOLARSHIPS & BURSARIES Schol; Burs; Art; Mus
SPECIAL NEEDS abjn B **DYSLEXIA** e **DIET** acd
ASSOCIATION IAPS **FOUNDED** 1946 **RELIGIOUS AFFILIATION** C of E

MAP10 J 7
LOCATION Rural
DAY ✓ **RAIL** b **AIR** c
SPORT almpqtux AB
OTHER LANGUAGES a
ACTIVITIES acfghijlmnopstwx A
OTHER SUBJECTS abcdfh
FACILITIES ON SITE bdi
EXAM BOARDS
RETAKES **NVQ COURSES**

- **A-level**:
- **AS**:
- **GCSE**:
- **OTHER**: c efg i lmno v B G K OP R cdef j

C — St. Christopher's School; George Hill; Old Catton; Norwich; Norfolk. NR6 7DE
Tel: 01603 425179 (Fax: 01603 622542) *Mrs C.Cunningham & Mrs D.Arthur*

	Boys	Age	Girls	Age	TOTAL		Boys	Girls
Day	£135-£823	74	2-12	48	2-12	122	SIXTH		
Weekly									
Boarding									

ENTRY REQUIREMENTS Interview
SCHOLARSHIPS & BURSARIES
SPECIAL NEEDS bntuw l **DYSLEXIA** g **DIET** acd
ASSOCIATION ISAI **FOUNDED** 1947 **RELIGIOUS AFFILIATION** Inter-denom

MAP10 J 5
LOCATION Urban
DAY **RAIL** b **AIR** b
SPORT abelmqx BC
OTHER LANGUAGES
ACTIVITIES fghj
OTHER SUBJECTS ch
FACILITIES ON SITE
EXAM BOARDS
RETAKES **NVQ COURSES**

- **A-level**:
- **AS**:
- **GCSE**:
- **OTHER**: e lmno s v B E G K O cde

NORFOLK *continued*

C **Taverham Hall School; Norwich NR8 6HU**
Tel: 01603 868206 (Fax: 01603 861061) *W.D.Lawton*

		Boys	Age	Girls	Age	TOTAL		Boys	Girls
Day	£935-£2070	✗	109	3-13	43	3-13	187	SIXTH	
Weekly	£2700		13	8-13	5	8-13			
Boarding	£2700		11	8-13	6	8-13			

ENTRY REQUIREMENTS Report & Interview
SCHOLARSHIPS & BURSARIES Schol; Mus; Forces; Clergy
SPECIAL NEEDS begjklnqstwx El   **DYSLEXIA** ce   **DIET** ad
ASSOCIATION IAPS   **FOUNDED** 1921   **RELIGIOUS AFFILIATION** C of E

MAP10 J 5
LOCATION Rural
DAY   **RAIL** b   **AIR** a
SPORT abcdefgjklmopqstuwx AB
OTHER LANGUAGES
ACTIVITIES abcfghjmorstw A
OTHER SUBJECTS cfh
FACILITIES ON SITE i
EXAM BOARDS
RETAKES   **NVQ COURSES**

A-level   AS   GCSE   OTHER:
                              e   l   o   v
                           B E G   K   O R
                              cdef j

C **Thetford Grammar School; 19 Bridge Street; Thetford; Norfolk; IP24 3AF**
Tel: 01842 752840 (Fax: 01842 750220) *J.R.Weeks*

		Boys	Age	Girls	Age	TOTAL		Boys	Girls
Day	£1277-£1387		148	7-18	122	7-18	270	SIXTH	20	20
Weekly									
Boarding									

ENTRY REQUIREMENTS Report & Exam & Interview
SCHOLARSHIPS & BURSARIES Schol; Burs; VI Form
SPECIAL NEEDS blntw Hl   **DYSLEXIA** e   **DIET** abcd
ASSOCIATION GBA   **FOUNDED**   **RELIGIOUS AFFILIATION** C of E

MAP10 I 6
LOCATION Rural
DAY ✓   **RAIL** a   **AIR** b
SPORT abcefjklmpqs ABC
OTHER LANGUAGES
ACTIVITIES cfghijkosu
OTHER SUBJECTS abch
FACILITIES ON SITE g
EXAM BOARDS ab ABDE
RETAKES   **NVQ COURSES**

A-level   e g i l   op   v x   AS   e g i   op   uv x   GCSE   e   l   op   v   OTHER: n
       BC GH K N P   c ef   K   BC GH K NO   X   R
          c ef   cdef

G **Thorpe House School; 7 Yarmouth Road; Norwich NR7 0EA**
Tel: 01603 433055 *Mrs F.M.Hunt*

		Boys	Age	Girls	Age	TOTAL		Boys	Girls
Day	£530- £825				322	3-16	322	SIXTH		
Weekly									
Boarding									

ENTRY REQUIREMENTS Test & Interview; Assessment & Interview
SCHOLARSHIPS & BURSARIES
SPECIAL NEEDS ablnt A   **DYSLEXIA** e   **DIET** a
ASSOCIATION ISAI   **FOUNDED** 1897   **RELIGIOUS AFFILIATION** C of E

MAP10 J 5
LOCATION Rural
DAY   **RAIL** a   **AIR** c
SPORT abcflmpqwx B
OTHER LANGUAGES
ACTIVITIES cgjnopsw A
OTHER SUBJECTS bch
FACILITIES ON SITE chi
EXAM BOARDS a L
RETAKES   **NVQ COURSES**

A-level   AS   GCSE: d g i l   v   OTHER: d g i   lmno   v
                                      B   N P   U   BC E G   K   OP R   W
                                    cde   cde   l

C **Town Close House Prep.School; 14 Ipswich Road; Norwich NR2 2LR**
Tel: 01603 620180 (Fax: 01603 618256) *S Higginson*

		Boys	Age	Girls	Age	TOTAL		Boys	Girls
Day	£350-£1465	✗	270	3-13	45	3- 9	324	SIXTH		
Weekly	£2128		8	8-13	1				
Boarding									

ENTRY REQUIREMENTS Assessment & Interview
SCHOLARSHIPS & BURSARIES Teachers; Siblings
SPECIAL NEEDS n   **DYSLEXIA** de   **DIET** acd
ASSOCIATION IAPS   **FOUNDED** 1932   **RELIGIOUS AFFILIATION** C of E

MAP10 J 5
LOCATION Urban
DAY   **RAIL** a   **AIR** a
SPORT abefgjlmpqstux
OTHER LANGUAGES
ACTIVITIES fghjost A
OTHER SUBJECTS cfh
FACILITIES ON SITE chi
EXAM BOARDS
RETAKES   **NVQ COURSES**

A-level   AS   GCSE   OTHER: e g i l   no   v
                                B   G   K   OP R
                                   cde   j

C **Falcon Manor School; Greens Norton; Towcester; Northants.; NN12 8BN**
Tel: 01327 350544 (Fax: 01327 359203) *G.D.Priest*

		Boys	Age	Girls	Age	TOTAL		Boys	Girls
Day	£1000-£1525	✗	14	8-18	3	8-18	105	SIXTH		
Weekly			14		1				
Boarding	£2318-£2575		46	9-18	27	9-18			

ENTRY REQUIREMENTS Report & Interview
SCHOLARSHIPS & BURSARIES Forces; Teachers
SPECIAL NEEDS abcklnpquw Bl   **DYSLEXIA** eg   **DIET** acd
ASSOCIATION ISAI   **FOUNDED** 1891   **RELIGIOUS AFFILIATION** Inter-denom

MAP 9 D 8
LOCATION Rural
DAY ✓   **RAIL** b   **AIR** a
SPORT abcdefhjkmopqstuvx ABC
OTHER LANGUAGES a
ACTIVITIES cdefhjklmnopqstwx
OTHER SUBJECTS abcdefh
FACILITIES ON SITE behi
EXAM BOARDS abcd ABL
RETAKES ab   **NVQ COURSES** 123

A-level: abcdefghi kl nopq s uvwx   AS: ab de g i   pq tuv   GCSE: de ghi l   p tuv   OTHER: a de ghijklmn   r v
         B E GHI K   OPQ T   W   B   G   P   T   W   B DEFG   OP R T   A   G K   OP
            c ef h l   c ef h l   bcdef h   l   def h l

N'HANTS

NORTHAMPTONSHIRE continued

Great Houghton Prep. School; Great Houghton Hall; Northampton NN4 7AG
Tel: 01604 761907 *M.T.E.Street*

C

		Boys	Age	Girls	Age	TOTAL
Day	£775-£1625	209	4-13	50	4-13	259
Weekly						
Boarding						

SIXTH: Boys | Girls

MAP 9 D 8
LOCATION Rural
DAY **RAIL** a **AIR** b
SPORT abcefhjlmpqsx AB
OTHER LANGUAGES
ACTIVITIES cfghijot A

ENTRY REQUIREMENTS Test & Interview
SCHOLARSHIPS & BURSARIES Schol; Burs; Clergy; Teachers
SPECIAL NEEDS ahjklnpw ABGI   **DYSLEXIA** de   **DIET** acd
ASSOCIATION IAPS   **FOUNDED** 1955   **RELIGIOUS AFFILIATION** C of E
OTHER SUBJECTS bcfh
FACILITIES ON SITE bchk
EXAM BOARDS
RETAKES   **NVQ COURSES**

A-level
AS
GCSE
OTHER: e g i l o q v
AB G K OP R
cde g j

Laxton Junior School; North Street; Oundle; Peterborough PE8 4AL
Tel: 01832 273673 (Fax: 01832 273564) *Miss S.C.A.Thomas*

C

		Boys	Age	Girls	Age	TOTAL
Day	£985-£1668	79	4-11	60	4-11	139
Weekly						
Boarding						

SIXTH: Boys | Girls

MAP 9 F 6
LOCATION Rural
DAY **RAIL** b **AIR** c
SPORT aefjlpqx B
OTHER LANGUAGES
ACTIVITIES cfghjo

ENTRY REQUIREMENTS Test & Interview; Assessment & Interview
SCHOLARSHIPS & BURSARIES
SPECIAL NEEDS bekn l   **DYSLEXIA** ce   **DIET** acd
ASSOCIATION IAPS   **FOUNDED** 1973   **RELIGIOUS AFFILIATION** Inter-denom
OTHER SUBJECTS ch
FACILITIES ON SITE i
EXAM BOARDS
RETAKES   **NVQ COURSES**

A-level
AS
GCSE
OTHER: de l no v
B E G K O R
cde

Maidwell Hall; Northampton NN6 9JG
Tel: 01604 686234 (Fax: 01604 686659) *P.R.Whitton*

C

			Boys	Age	Girls	Age	TOTAL
Day	£625-£1850	X	41	3-13	23	3-13	104
Weekly							
Boarding	£3100		40	8-13			

SIXTH: Boys | Girls

MAP 9 D 7
LOCATION Rural
DAY **RAIL** b **AIR** b
SPORT abcefjklmpqstuwx ABC
OTHER LANGUAGES
ACTIVITIES acdfghijmnopqrtvw A

ENTRY REQUIREMENTS Test & Interview
SCHOLARSHIPS & BURSARIES Schol; Burs; Mus; Chor; Teachers
SPECIAL NEEDS abejlntuw BEHI   **DYSLEXIA** ce   **DIET** ac
ASSOCIATION IAPS   **FOUNDED** 1932   **RELIGIOUS AFFILIATION** C of E
OTHER SUBJECTS abcdgh
FACILITIES ON SITE hjl
EXAM BOARDS
RETAKES   **NVQ COURSES**

A-level
AS
GCSE
OTHER: de g i lm o q v
B G JK OP R
cde j

Northampton High School; Newport Pagnell Road; Hardingstone; Northampton NN4 6UU
Tel: 01604 765765 (Fax: 01604 709418) *Mrs L.A.Mayne*

G

		Boys	Age	Girls	Age	TOTAL
Day	£805-£1370			856	3-18	856
Weekly						
Boarding						

SIXTH: Boys | Girls 109

MAP 9 D 8
LOCATION Urban
DAY ✓ **RAIL** a **AIR** b
SPORT abcdhjlmopqwx ABC
OTHER LANGUAGES
ACTIVITIES cghijknoqst BD

ENTRY REQUIREMENTS Exam; Report & Interview
SCHOLARSHIPS & BURSARIES Schol; Clergy; AP; VI Form
SPECIAL NEEDS ehjlq L   **DYSLEXIA**   **DIET** acd
ASSOCIATION GSA   **FOUNDED** 1878   **RELIGIOUS AFFILIATION** C of E
OTHER SUBJECTS abcdfh
FACILITIES ON SITE bchi
EXAM BOARDS abc ABDE
RETAKES   **NVQ COURSES**

A-level: cde g i   op   uv
BC   GH K   P R
c efg j l

AS: cde g   x
       G K
       ef j l

GCSE: de g i   o   v
BC E G K   P R
cdefg jkl

OTHER: l n
          NO   W

Oundle School; Oundle; Peterborough PE8 4EN
Tel: 01832 273536 (Fax: 01832 274967) *D.B.Mc Murray*

C

		Boys	Age	Girls	Age	TOTAL
Day	£1668	664	11-18	190	11-18	854
Weekly						
Boarding	£3275-£4285					

SIXTH: Boys 275 | Girls 76

MAP 9 F 6
LOCATION Rural
DAY **RAIL** b **AIR** b
SPORT abcdefghijkmopqrstuwx ABC
OTHER LANGUAGES
ACTIVITIES abcdefghijklmnopqstuvw ABD

ENTRY REQUIREMENTS CEE; Scholarship Exam; Report & Exam & Interview
SCHOLARSHIPS & BURSARIES Schol; Art; Mus; VI Form; ARA
SPECIAL NEEDS n   **DYSLEXIA** e   **DIET** acd
ASSOCIATION HMC   **FOUNDED** 1556   **RELIGIOUS AFFILIATION** C of E
OTHER SUBJECTS abcdfh
FACILITIES ON SITE abcdeghikl
EXAM BOARDS abcd ABDEGHL
RETAKES   **NVQ COURSES**

A-level: cdefg   nop   v
B GH K   P R   X
c efg j l

AS: fg   pq
B   GH K
      ef   l

GCSE: de ghi l no q v
B   G K   P R
defg jkl

OTHER: ef   l no r tu
A   F IJ M O QR

NORTHAMPTONSHIRE continued

C — Quinton House School; Upton; Northampton NN5 4UX
Tel: 01604 752050 (Fax: 01604 581707) *G.H.Griffiths*

	Boys	Age	Girls	Age	TOTAL	Boys (Sixth)	Girls (Sixth)
Day £724-£1231	170	3-18	162	3-18	332	10	5
Weekly							
Boarding							

ENTRY REQUIREMENTS Exam & Interview
SCHOLARSHIPS & BURSARIES Burs
SPECIAL NEEDS **DYSLEXIA** **DIET** abcd
ASSOCIATION ISAI **FOUNDED** 1963 **RELIGIOUS AFFILIATION** Non-denom

MAP 9 D 8
LOCATION
DAY **RAIL** a **AIR** b
SPORT abcefijmpqs ABC
OTHER LANGUAGES
ACTIVITIES cfghijknoqr
OTHER SUBJECTS abcdegh
FACILITIES ON SITE bdeg
EXAM BOARDS bd AEL
RETAKES ab **NVQ COURSES**

- **A-level**: e ghi lm o uv BC G PQ cde
- **AS**:
- **GCSE**: e ghi lm opq v BC G K P a cdef l
- **OTHER**: l p

Gb — St. Peter's School; 52 Headlands; Kettering; Northants. NN15 6DJ
Tel: 01536 512066 *Mrs B.Blakeley*

	Boys	Age	Girls	Age	TOTAL	Boys (Sixth)	Girls (Sixth)
Day £806-£1303	55	3-11	117	3-16	172		
Weekly							
Boarding							

ENTRY REQUIREMENTS Test & Interview
SCHOLARSHIPS & BURSARIES Schol; Burs
SPECIAL NEEDS abehjklnqstuw BHI **DYSLEXIA** ef **DIET** a
ASSOCIATION ISAI **FOUNDED** 1946 **RELIGIOUS AFFILIATION** C of E

MAP 9 E 7
LOCATION Urban
DAY **RAIL** a **AIR** b
SPORT acejlmpqwx AB
OTHER LANGUAGES
ACTIVITIES cghio
OTHER SUBJECTS abcdh
FACILITIES ON SITE a
EXAM BOARDS b
RETAKES **NVQ COURSES**

- **A-level**:
- **AS**:
- **GCSE**: e v BC E G R W cde
- **OTHER**: l K O

C — Spratton Hall School; Spratton; Northampton NN6 8HP
Tel: 01604 847292 (Fax: 01604 820844) *A.P.Bickley*

	Boys	Age	Girls	Age	TOTAL	Boys (Sixth)	Girls (Sixth)
Day £400-£1495 X	199	4-13	115	4-13	314		
Weekly							
Boarding							

ENTRY REQUIREMENTS
SCHOLARSHIPS & BURSARIES
SPECIAL NEEDS ejklnqw GIL **DYSLEXIA** ef **DIET** acd
ASSOCIATION IAPS **FOUNDED** 1951 **RELIGIOUS AFFILIATION** C of E

MAP 9 D 7
LOCATION Rural
DAY ✓ **RAIL** a **AIR** c
SPORT abcefgjklmpqsx AB
OTHER LANGUAGES
ACTIVITIES cfghjot
OTHER SUBJECTS abcfh
FACILITIES ON SITE abchj
EXAM BOARDS
RETAKES **NVQ COURSES**

- **A-level**:
- **AS**:
- **GCSE**:
- **OTHER**: de g i l o uv B G I K OP R X cde j

C — Wellingborough School; Wellingborough; Northamptonshire NN8 2BX
Tel: 01933 222427 (Fax: 01933 271 986) *F.R.Ullmann*

	Boys	Age	Girls	Age	TOTAL	Boys (Sixth)	Girls (Sixth)
Day £830-£1725	451	3-18	267	3-18	766	79	48
Weekly £2790	14	13-18	10	13-18			
Boarding £3100	15	13-18	9	13-18			

ENTRY REQUIREMENTS CEE; Test & Interview
SCHOLARSHIPS & BURSARIES Schol; Burs; Art; Mus; AP; VI Form
SPECIAL NEEDS beijln l **DYSLEXIA** ef **DIET** abcd
ASSOCIATION HMC **FOUNDED** 1595 **RELIGIOUS AFFILIATION** C of E

MAP 9 E 7
LOCATION Urban
DAY ✓ **RAIL** a **AIR** a
SPORT abcefhjkmopqstuwx ABC
OTHER LANGUAGES a
ACTIVITIES cefghijklmopqrstuv ABC
OTHER SUBJECTS abcdfh
FACILITIES ON SITE abcdhjkl
EXAM BOARDS bd BEG
RETAKES ab **NVQ COURSES**

- **A-level**: cde g i nop uv x B GH K OP c efg j
- **AS**: G
- **GCSE**: cde g i no v B G K P R bcdefg jk
- **OTHER**: c l tu K O R

C — Winchester House School; Brackley; Northants NN13 7AZ
Tel: 01280 702483 (Fax: 01280 706400) *D.R.Speight*

	Boys	Age	Girls	Age	TOTAL	Boys (Sixth)	Girls (Sixth)
Day £2700 X	99	3-14	55	3-14	254		
Weekly							
Boarding £2910	85	8-13	15	8-13			

ENTRY REQUIREMENTS Assessment & Interview
SCHOLARSHIPS & BURSARIES Schol; Art; Mus; Teachers
SPECIAL NEEDS aln **DYSLEXIA** cde **DIET** a
ASSOCIATION IAPS **FOUNDED** 1876 **RELIGIOUS AFFILIATION** C of E

MAP 3 D 1
LOCATION Urban
DAY **RAIL** b **AIR** a
SPORT abcdefgjklmpqstuvwx AB
OTHER LANGUAGES
ACTIVITIES cfghijoqrstwx A
OTHER SUBJECTS abcfh
FACILITIES ON SITE bcdjkl
EXAM BOARDS
RETAKES **NVQ COURSES**

- **A-level**:
- **AS**:
- **GCSE**:
- **OTHER**: de g i lmno q v B G JK NOP R X cde g j

NORTHUMBERLAND

C — Croft House School; West Quarter; Leazes Lane; Hexham; Northumberland NE46 3BB Tel: 01434 602082 *Mrs Janice M.Peers*

		Boys	Age	Girls	Age	TOTAL	SIXTH	Boys	Girls
Day	£1080-£1225 ✗	31	3-11	42	3-11	73			
Weekly									
Boarding									

ENTRY REQUIREMENTS None
SCHOLARSHIPS & BURSARIES Siblings
SPECIAL NEEDS n   **DYSLEXIA** e   **DIET** a
ASSOCIATION IAPS   **FOUNDED** 1971   **RELIGIOUS AFFILIATION** Non-denom

MAP 14 K 7
LOCATION Rural
DAY ✓   **RAIL** b   **AIR** a
SPORT acegjlpqsux AB
OTHER LANGUAGES
ACTIVITIES fgh
OTHER SUBJECTS ch
FACILITIES ON SITE a
EXAM BOARDS
RETAKES   **NVQ COURSES**

A-level   **AS**   **GCSE**   **OTHER**
  e   lm o
B D E G   K   O   R   X
cde

C — Longridge Towers School; Berwick-upon-Tweed; Northumberland; TD15 2XH Tel: 01289 307584 (Fax: 01289 302581) *Dr M.J.Barron*

		Boys	Age	Girls	Age	TOTAL	SIXTH	Boys	Girls
Day	£800-£1250	103	4-18	112	4-18	289		20	16
Weekly	£2345-£2550	5	8-18	4	8-18				
Boarding	£2495-£2700	31	8-18	34	8-18				

ENTRY REQUIREMENTS CEE; Report & Test
SCHOLARSHIPS & BURSARIES Schol; Burs; Mus; Forces; Clergy; VI Form
SPECIAL NEEDS bjklvw EGI   **DYSLEXIA**   **DIET** a
ASSOCIATION ISAI   **FOUNDED** 1983   **RELIGIOUS AFFILIATION** Inter-denom

MAP 14 K 4
LOCATION Rural
DAY ✓   **RAIL** a   **AIR** b
SPORT abcdefhlmpqrstuvwx ABC
OTHER LANGUAGES a
ACTIVITIES acfghijknopqrst A
OTHER SUBJECTS bcfh
FACILITIES ON SITE cdehik
EXAM BOARDS bcd DEGI
RETAKES a   **NVQ COURSES**

A-level   efg   i   v   **AS**   **GCSE**   e g i l   no   v   **OTHER**   c e   lmno q   v
BC GH K   P   U   BC   G K   PR U   BC E G K NO R
  cdef   cdef   k   cdef

C — Mowden Hall School; Stocksfield; Northumberland NE43 7TP Tel: 01661 842147 (Fax: 01661 842529) *A.P.Lewis*

		Boys	Age	Girls	Age	TOTAL	SIXTH	Boys	Girls
Day	£1150-£1895 ✗	53	4-10	25	4-10	174			
Weekly	£2660	3	8-11	3	8-11				
Boarding	£2660	66	8-13	24	8-13				

ENTRY REQUIREMENTS None
SCHOLARSHIPS & BURSARIES Burs
SPECIAL NEEDS abejklnqw BGI   **DYSLEXIA** e   **DIET** a
ASSOCIATION IAPS   **FOUNDED** 1935   **RELIGIOUS AFFILIATION** C of E

MAP 14 K 7
LOCATION Rural
DAY   **RAIL** b   **AIR** a
SPORT abcdefijklmnpqrstwx ABC
OTHER LANGUAGES
ACTIVITIES cfghijlnopqst
OTHER SUBJECTS c
FACILITIES ON SITE abehjk
EXAM BOARDS
RETAKES   **NVQ COURSES**

A-level   **AS**   **GCSE**   **OTHER**   egi l   o   v
                              B G   P R
                                 cde   j

C — Nunnykirk Hall School; Netherwitton; Morpeth; Northumberland NE61 4PB Tel: 01670 772685 *Mrs V.J.Hope*

		Boys	Age	Girls	Age	TOTAL	SIXTH	Boys	Girls
Day	£1960-£2170	5	9-16		9-16	38			
Weekly	£4250-£4710	14	9-16		9-16				
Boarding	£4450-£4900	16	9-16	3	9-16				

ENTRY REQUIREMENTS Interview
SCHOLARSHIPS & BURSARIES Burs
SPECIAL NEEDS n   **DYSLEXIA** a   **DIET** a
ASSOCIATION ISAI   **FOUNDED** 1977   **RELIGIOUS AFFILIATION** Inter-denom

MAP 14 L 6
LOCATION Rural
DAY ✓   **RAIL** b   **AIR** a
SPORT abcdefhjkmopqstux AB
OTHER LANGUAGES
ACTIVITIES acefkmnqsx
OTHER SUBJECTS bcdh
FACILITIES ON SITE acf
EXAM BOARDS c
RETAKES   **NVQ COURSES**

A-level   **AS**   **GCSE**   d   o   s   **OTHER**   lmn   v
                              C E G   N   S   B   K O R
                                cd

NOTTS

C — Bramcote School; Gamston; Nr. Retford; Notts. DN22 0QQ Tel: 01777 838636 (Fax: 01777 838633) *D.H.Fuller*

		Boys	Age	Girls	Age	TOTAL	SIXTH	Boys	Girls
Day	£850-£1800 ✗	80	2-13	39	2-13	169			
Weekly	£2350	4	7-13	1	7-13				
Boarding	£2350	30	7-13	15	7-13				

ENTRY REQUIREMENTS Interview
SCHOLARSHIPS & BURSARIES Forces; Clergy; Teachers
SPECIAL NEEDS abejklnquw ABEGHJ   **DYSLEXIA** de   **DIET** abcd
ASSOCIATION IAPS   **FOUNDED** 1922   **RELIGIOUS AFFILIATION** C of E

MAP 9 D 3
LOCATION Rural
DAY ✓   **RAIL** a   **AIR** a
SPORT abcdefhjklmopqswx ABC
OTHER LANGUAGES
ACTIVITIES cfgjmnopqrtw
OTHER SUBJECTS bcfh
FACILITIES ON SITE cehk
EXAM BOARDS
RETAKES   **NVQ COURSES**

A-level   **AS**   **GCSE**   **OTHER**   de g i l   no   v
                                          BC   G K   OP R
                                             cde   j

222

NOTTINGHAMSHIRE continued

C | Broadgate School; 1 Western Terrace; The Park; Nottingham NG7 1AF
Tel: 0115 947 4275 *T.Osgerby*

| Day Weekly Boarding | £750-£1200 | Boys 61 | Age 5-16 | Girls 27 | Age 5-16 | TOTAL 88 | SIXTH | Boys | Girls |

MAP 9 D 4
LOCATION Urban
DAY **RAIL** b **AIR** a
SPORT aefhjmpqx AB
OTHER LANGUAGES
ACTIVITIES fhij
OTHER SUBJECTS
FACILITIES ON SITE k
EXAM BOARDS abcd
RETAKES **NVQ COURSES**

ENTRY REQUIREMENTS Test & Interview
SCHOLARSHIPS & BURSARIES
SPECIAL NEEDS bn
ASSOCIATION ISAI **FOUNDED** 1900 **RELIGIOUS AFFILIATION** Non-denom **DYSLEXIA** ef **DIET**

A-level | AS | GCSE e g i l o v x
BC G P
cde j
OTHER R

C | Dagfa House School; Broadgate; Beeston; Nottingham NG9 2FU
Tel: 0115 925 4100 *A.Oatway*

| Day Weekly Boarding | £515-£1115 | Boys 136 | Age 2-16 | Girls 79 | Age 2-16 | TOTAL 215 | SIXTH | Boys | Girls |

MAP 9 C 4
LOCATION Urban
DAY **RAIL** a **AIR** a
SPORT abcefghjlmpqwx ABC
OTHER LANGUAGES
ACTIVITIES cfghijlo A
OTHER SUBJECTS abcdeh
FACILITIES ON SITE bch
EXAM BOARDS abcd
RETAKES a **NVQ COURSES**

ENTRY REQUIREMENTS Exam; Assessment & Interview
SCHOLARSHIPS & BURSARIES Schol
SPECIAL NEEDS abjlnqtuw BJ
ASSOCIATION ISAI **FOUNDED** 1969 **RELIGIOUS AFFILIATION** Inter-denom **DYSLEXIA** g **DIET** ad

A-level | AS | GCSE d e g i l o v
BC G OP W
cdef
OTHER d e g i lmno v
BC G K OP R W

C | Greenholme School; 392 Derby Road; Lenton; Nottingham NG7 2DX
Tel: 0115 978 7329 *Miss P.M.Breen*

| Day Weekly Boarding | £660-£1095 | Boys 156 | Age 3-11 | Girls 71 | Age 3-11 | TOTAL 227 | SIXTH | Boys | Girls |

MAP 9 D 4
LOCATION Urban
DAY **RAIL** a **AIR** a
SPORT aefjmpqx AB
OTHER LANGUAGES
ACTIVITIES cfghjo
OTHER SUBJECTS ch
FACILITIES ON SITE ah
EXAM BOARDS
RETAKES **NVQ COURSES**

ENTRY REQUIREMENTS Assessment & Interview
SCHOLARSHIPS & BURSARIES
SPECIAL NEEDS behjklnstw BGIL
ASSOCIATION ISAI **FOUNDED** 1935 **RELIGIOUS AFFILIATION** Inter-denom **DYSLEXIA** cde **DIET** acd

A-level | AS | GCSE | OTHER b e lmno v
B G K O R
cde

C | Grosvenor School; Edwalton; Nottingham NG12 4BS
Tel: 0115 923 1184 (Fax: 0115 923 5184) *C.G.J.Oldershaw*

| Day Weekly Boarding | £878- £968 | Boys 125 | Age 4-13 | Girls 56 | Age 4-13 | TOTAL 181 | SIXTH | Boys | Girls |

MAP 9 D 4
LOCATION Urban
DAY **RAIL** a **AIR** a
SPORT aefgjmpqtx AB
OTHER LANGUAGES
ACTIVITIES fghjqt A
OTHER SUBJECTS abcfh
FACILITIES ON SITE
EXAM BOARDS
RETAKES **NVQ COURSES**

ENTRY REQUIREMENTS Test & Interview
SCHOLARSHIPS & BURSARIES Clergy
SPECIAL NEEDS ehjklnw Bl
ASSOCIATION IAPS **FOUNDED** 1876 **RELIGIOUS AFFILIATION** Inter-denom **DYSLEXIA** e **DIET** acd

A-level | AS | GCSE | OTHER e g i l o v
B G K OP R
cde l

C | Highfields School; London Road; Newark-on-Trent; Notts. NG24 3AL
Tel: 01636 704103 (Fax: 01636 613048) *P.F.Smith*

| Day Weekly Boarding | £820- £836 ✗ | Boys 120 | Age 2-11 | Girls 92 | Age 2-11 | TOTAL 212 | SIXTH | Boys | Girls |

MAP 9 E 4
LOCATION Urban
DAY **RAIL** a **AIR** b
SPORT acefjmpqx B
OTHER LANGUAGES
ACTIVITIES got
OTHER SUBJECTS bcfh
FACILITIES ON SITE h
EXAM BOARDS
RETAKES **NVQ COURSES**

ENTRY REQUIREMENTS Interview; Assessment
SCHOLARSHIPS & BURSARIES
SPECIAL NEEDS bln
ASSOCIATION ISAI **FOUNDED** 1945 **RELIGIOUS AFFILIATION** Non-denom **DYSLEXIA** ef **DIET** a

A-level | AS | GCSE | OTHER e lmno v
B G K O
cde

NOTTINGHAMSHIRE *continued*

G | Hollygirt School; Elm Avenue; Nottingham NG3 4GF
Tel: 0115 958 0596 (Fax: 0115 924 0773) *Mrs M.R.Banks*

	Boys	Age	Girls	Age	TOTAL		Boys	Girls
Day £915-£1212			315	4-16	315	SIXTH		
Weekly								
Boarding								

ENTRY REQUIREMENTS Test & Interview; Report & Interview
SCHOLARSHIPS & BURSARIES Burs
SPECIAL NEEDS   **DYSLEXIA**   **DIET** a
ASSOCIATION GSA   **FOUNDED** 1877   **RELIGIOUS AFFILIATION** Inter-denom

MAP 9 D 4
LOCATION Inner City
DAY   **RAIL** b   **AIR** a
SPORT acflmpwx AB
OTHER LANGUAGES c
ACTIVITIES gijklno
OTHER SUBJECTS abcdh
FACILITIES ON SITE
EXAM BOARDS abcd ABDE
RETAKES   **NVQ COURSES**

A-level	AS	GCSE	e g i l o v B G K P R cdef	OTHER

C | Lorne House; London Road; Retford; Notts. DN22 7EB
Tel: 01777 703434 (Fax: 01777 838659) *A.N.Brownridge*

	Boys	Age	Girls	Age	TOTAL		Boys	Girls
Day £755-£1110	54	2-13	52	2-13	106	SIXTH		
Weekly								
Boarding								

ENTRY REQUIREMENTS Assessment & Interview
SCHOLARSHIPS & BURSARIES Schol; Burs
SPECIAL NEEDS jknw Bl   **DYSLEXIA** e   **DIET**
ASSOCIATION IAPS   **FOUNDED** 1937   **RELIGIOUS AFFILIATION** C of E

MAP 9 D 3
LOCATION Rural
DAY ✓   **RAIL** a   **AIR** b
SPORT abcdefhjklmpqx ABC
OTHER LANGUAGES
ACTIVITIES cfghijlopqt
OTHER SUBJECTS abcfh
FACILITIES ON SITE chjk
EXAM BOARDS
RETAKES   **NVQ COURSES**

A-level	AS	GCSE	OTHER	c e g i lmno q s uv BC G K NOP R cde

B | Nottingham High School Prep. School; Waverley Mount; Nottingham NG7 4ED
Tel: 0115 978 9411 (Fax: 0115 979 2202) *P.M.Pallant*

	Boys	Age	Girls	Age	TOTAL		Boys	Girls
Day £1299	185	7-10			185	SIXTH		
Weekly								
Boarding								

ENTRY REQUIREMENTS Exam
SCHOLARSHIPS & BURSARIES
SPECIAL NEEDS ahjklq   **DYSLEXIA**   **DIET** abcd
ASSOCIATION IAPS   **FOUNDED** 1905   **RELIGIOUS AFFILIATION** Non-denom

MAP 9 D 4
LOCATION Inner City
DAY ✓   **RAIL** a   **AIR** a
SPORT abcefjmqsx AB
OTHER LANGUAGES
ACTIVITIES fghijopt A
OTHER SUBJECTS bcfh
FACILITIES ON SITE chik
EXAM BOARDS
RETAKES   **NVQ COURSES**

A-level	AS	GCSE	OTHER	cdefg i l no s vwx B E G K OP R cdef

G | Nottingham High School for Girls GPDST; 9 Arboretum Street; Nottingham NG1 4JB
Tel: 0115 941 7663 (Fax: 0115 924 0757) *Mrs C.Bowering*

	Boys	Age	Girls	Age	TOTAL		Boys	Girls
Day £976-£1328			1091	4-18	1091	SIXTH		236
Weekly								
Boarding								

ENTRY REQUIREMENTS Exam & Interview
SCHOLARSHIPS & BURSARIES Schol; Burs; AP; VI Form
SPECIAL NEEDS abjl   **DYSLEXIA**   **DIET** abcd
ASSOCIATION GSA   **FOUNDED** 1875   **RELIGIOUS AFFILIATION** Non-denom

MAP 9 D 4
LOCATION Inner City
DAY   **RAIL** a   **AIR** a
SPORT abcefgklmpqvx ABC
OTHER LANGUAGES
ACTIVITIES cfghijknoqstu AB
OTHER SUBJECTS bcfh
FACILITIES ON SITE acghk
EXAM BOARDS abce ABDEG
RETAKES   **NVQ COURSES**

A-level	AS	GCSE	OTHER
defg i p uv BC GH K P R TU W cdefg j l	defg i op v B G K P R T W cdefg j l	de h l op vw BC G K O R WX cdefg jkl	lmn h

B | Nottingham High School; Waverley Mount; Nottingham NG7 4ED
Tel: 0115 978 6056 (Fax: 0115 979 2202) *Dr D.T.Witcombe*

	Boys	Age	Girls	Age	TOTAL		Boys	Girls
Day £1548-£1650	841	11-18			841	SIXTH	247	
Weekly								
Boarding								

ENTRY REQUIREMENTS Exam; Interview
SCHOLARSHIPS & BURSARIES Schol; Burs; AP
SPECIAL NEEDS   **DYSLEXIA**   **DIET** ab
ASSOCIATION HMC   **FOUNDED** 1513   **RELIGIOUS AFFILIATION** Inter-denom

MAP 9 D 4
LOCATION Urban
DAY   **RAIL** b   **AIR** a
SPORT abcdefghjkmsuwx BC
OTHER LANGUAGES
ACTIVITIES efghijklnopqstx AB
OTHER SUBJECTS bcd
FACILITIES ON SITE bcghi
EXAM BOARDS abcd AEH
RETAKES   **NVQ COURSES**

A-level	AS	GCSE	OTHER
c e g i p uv x B GH KM P R U cdef j	g i GH K M P def	e g i o q v B GH K P R U cdef h jk	h l FG M O g k

NOTTINGHAMSHIRE *continued*

C Plumtree School; Church Hill; Plumtree; Nottingham NG12 5ND
Tel: 0115 937 5859 *N.White*

		Boys	Age	Girls	Age	TOTAL		Boys	Girls
Day	£780-£790	59	3-11	52	3-11	111	SIXTH		
Weekly									
Boarding									

MAP 9 D 5
LOCATION Rural
DAY **RAIL** b **AIR** a
SPORT aejpqx
OTHER LANGUAGES
ACTIVITIES ghjo
OTHER SUBJECTS
FACILITIES ON SITE
EXAM BOARDS
RETAKES **NVQ COURSES**

ENTRY REQUIREMENTS Assessment & Interview
SCHOLARSHIPS & BURSARIES
SPECIAL NEEDS n   **DYSLEXIA** e   **DIET**
ASSOCIATION ISAI   **FOUNDED** 1974   **RELIGIOUS AFFILIATION** C of E

A-level   AS   GCSE   OTHER e l no v
                                    B E G K O R
                                    cde

C PNEU School; 13 Waverley Street; Nottingham NG7 4DX
Tel: 0115 978 3230 *T.J.Collins*

		Boys	Age	Girls	Age	TOTAL		Boys	Girls
Day	£890-£945	50	3-8	77	3-11	127	SIXTH		
Weekly									
Boarding									

MAP 9 D 4
LOCATION Urban
DAY **RAIL** a **AIR** a
SPORT aelpqx B
OTHER LANGUAGES
ACTIVITIES cj
OTHER SUBJECTS ch
FACILITIES ON SITE h
EXAM BOARDS
RETAKES **NVQ COURSES**

ENTRY REQUIREMENTS Interview
SCHOLARSHIPS & BURSARIES
SPECIAL NEEDS begjklntw ABI   **DYSLEXIA** e   **DIET** acd
ASSOCIATION IAPS   **FOUNDED** 1927   **RELIGIOUS AFFILIATION** Non-denom

A-level   AS   GCSE   OTHER e lm o   v
                                   B   G   O
                                   cde

C Ranby House; Retford; Notts. DN22 8HX
Tel: 01777 703138 (Fax: 01777 702813) *D.C.Wansey*

			Boys	Age	Girls	Age	TOTAL		Boys	Girls
Day	£950-£1785	X	141	3-13	106	3-13	305	SIXTH		
Weekly	£2355									
Boarding	£2355		44	7-13	14	7-13				

MAP 9 D 3
LOCATION Rural
DAY ✓ **RAIL** a **AIR** b
SPORT abcefjklmnopqsuwx ABC
OTHER LANGUAGES
ACTIVITIES acfghijnoqrstvw A
OTHER SUBJECTS abch
FACILITIES ON SITE bcdehjkl
EXAM BOARDS
RETAKES **NVQ COURSES**

ENTRY REQUIREMENTS Interview
SCHOLARSHIPS & BURSARIES Schol; Burs; Forces; Clergy; AP
SPECIAL NEEDS abjklnpqw BEGI   **DYSLEXIA** ce   **DIET** abcd
ASSOCIATION IAPS   **FOUNDED** 1948   **RELIGIOUS AFFILIATION** C of E

A-level   AS   GCSE   OTHER e g i lmno q   v
                                   BC E G   K   OP
                                   cdef   j

C Rodney School; Kirklington; Nr.Newark; Notts. NG22 8NB
Tel: 01636 813281 *Miss G.R.T.Howe*

		Boys	Age	Girls	Age	TOTAL		Boys	Girls
Day	£870-£1050	31	7-18	15	7-18	106	SIXTH	3	3
Weekly	£1850		7-18		7-18				
Boarding	£1850	29	7-18	31	7-18				

MAP 9 D 4
LOCATION Rural
DAY **RAIL** a **AIR** a
SPORT abcdefgjmpqswx ABC
OTHER LANGUAGES a
ACTIVITIES cfghijq A
OTHER SUBJECTS bch
FACILITIES ON SITE bch
EXAM BOARDS abd ABDE
RETAKES ab **NVQ COURSES**

ENTRY REQUIREMENTS CEE; Exam & Interview
SCHOLARSHIPS & BURSARIES
SPECIAL NEEDS   **DYSLEXIA**   **DIET** a
ASSOCIATION ISAI   **FOUNDED** 1944   **RELIGIOUS AFFILIATION** C of E

A-level e g i lmno   v   AS   GCSE e g i lmno   v   OTHER
         B   G   P R   B DE G K   P R
         cdef   cdef

C St. Joseph's School; 33 Derby Road; Nottingham NG1 5AW
Tel: 0115 941 8356 *Miss M.Mc Namara*

		Boys	Age	Girls	Age	TOTAL		Boys	Girls
Day	£880	117	1-11	91	1-11	208	SIXTH		
Weekly									
Boarding									

MAP 9 D 4
LOCATION Inner City
DAY **RAIL** **AIR**
SPORT ejlpqx B
OTHER LANGUAGES
ACTIVITIES fg
OTHER SUBJECTS
FACILITIES ON SITE
EXAM BOARDS
RETAKES **NVQ COURSES**

ENTRY REQUIREMENTS Test & Interview
SCHOLARSHIPS & BURSARIES Teachers
SPECIAL NEEDS   **DYSLEXIA**   **DIET**
ASSOCIATION ISAI   **FOUNDED**   **RELIGIOUS AFFILIATION** R C

A-level   AS   GCSE   OTHER e   m   v
                                   B G   K O R
                                   cde

NOTTINGHAMSHIRE continued

C — Salterford House School; Salterford Lane; Calverton; Nottingham NG14 6NZ
Tel: 0115 965 2127 (Fax: 0115 965 5627) Mrs M.Venables

		Boys	Age	Girls	Age	TOTAL		Boys	Girls
Day	£750-£770	97	2-11	88	2-11	185	SIXTH		
Weekly									
Boarding									

MAP 9 D 4
LOCATION Rural
DAY   RAIL   AIR

SPORT efjkpqx B
OTHER LANGUAGES
ACTIVITIES cgjop A

ENTRY REQUIREMENTS Interview
SCHOLARSHIPS & BURSARIES
SPECIAL NEEDS n   **DYSLEXIA** ef   **DIET**
ASSOCIATION ISAI   **FOUNDED** 1980   **RELIGIOUS AFFILIATION**

OTHER SUBJECTS c
FACILITIES ON SITE j
EXAM BOARDS
RETAKES   NVQ COURSES

A-level   AS   GCSE   OTHER
                          e   l no   s v
                          B G K O
                          cde

C — Wellow House School; Wellow; Near Newark; Notts. NG22 0EA
Tel: 01623 861054 (Fax: 01623 836665) Dr Malcolm Tozer

		Boys	Age	Girls	Age	TOTAL		Boys	Girls
Day	£1250-£1675 X	47	3-13	27	3-13	83	SIXTH		
Weekly	£2250	7	7-13	2	7-13				
Boarding									

MAP 9 D 3
LOCATION Rural
DAY   RAIL b   AIR a

SPORT abcdefjkmnopqsuwx ABC
OTHER LANGUAGES
ACTIVITIES acfgjlmnpqstw A

ENTRY REQUIREMENTS Scholarship Exam; Assessment & Interview
SCHOLARSHIPS & BURSARIES Schol; Art; Mus; Sport
SPECIAL NEEDS abfhjklnqstuwx ACEGHIJKL   **DYSLEXIA** g   **DIET** abcd
ASSOCIATION IAPS   **FOUNDED** 1971   **RELIGIOUS AFFILIATION** Inter-denom

OTHER SUBJECTS abcdfh
FACILITIES ON SITE bchik
EXAM BOARDS
RETAKES   NVQ COURSES

A-level   AS   GCSE   OTHER
                   de   j   de g i lmno   s v
                                 BC E G   K NOP R
                                 cde j

C — Worksop College; Worksop; Notts. S80 3AP
Tel: 01909 472391 (Fax: 01909 530161) R.A.Collard

		Boys	Age	Girls	Age	TOTAL		Boys	Girls
Day	£2480 X	75	13-18	52	13-18	326	SIXTH	90	43
Weekly	£3595	50	13-18	23	13-18				
Boarding	£3595	91	13-18	35	13-18				

MAP 9 D 3
LOCATION Rural
DAY ✓   RAIL a   AIR a

SPORT abcdefghjkmpqstuwx ABC
OTHER LANGUAGES ak
ACTIVITIES acefghjklmnopqstw AB

ENTRY REQUIREMENTS Scholarship Exam; Test & Interview; CEE & Interview
SCHOLARSHIPS & BURSARIES Schol; Burs; Art; Mus; Chor; Forces; Clergy; Sport; ARA
SPECIAL NEEDS klnqw BGHKL   **DYSLEXIA** e   **DIET** abcd
ASSOCIATION HMC   **FOUNDED** 1895   **RELIGIOUS AFFILIATION** C of E

OTHER SUBJECTS abcdh
FACILITIES ON SITE abcdehikl
EXAM BOARDS bcd ADGH
RETAKES ab   NVQ COURSES

A-level   AS   GCSE   OTHER
defghi l opq uv   q   defg i l   o   v   h
AB   GH K P   U   B   G K NOP R u WX   F
cde   j l   cde j l   k

OXFORDSHIRE

B — Abingdon School; Park Road; Abingdon OX14 1DE
Tel: 01235 521563 (Fax: 01235 534596) M.St.John Parker

		Boys	Age	Girls	Age	TOTAL		Boys	Girls
Day	£1754 X	643	11-18			761	SIXTH	235	
Weekly	£3283	71	11-18						
Boarding	£3283	47	11-18						

MAP 3 C 3
LOCATION Urban
DAY ✓   RAIL b   AIR b

SPORT abcefgijkmorstux ABC
OTHER LANGUAGES a
ACTIVITIES efghijklopqstu AB

ENTRY REQUIREMENTS CEE; Exam; Scholarship Exam
SCHOLARSHIPS & BURSARIES Schol; Burs; Art; Mus; AP; VI Form
SPECIAL NEEDS bhlnqu   **DYSLEXIA**   **DIET** acd
ASSOCIATION HMC   **FOUNDED** 1256   **RELIGIOUS AFFILIATION** C of E

OTHER SUBJECTS bcfh
FACILITIES ON SITE cdeghjk
EXAM BOARDS abcd ABDEGHK
RETAKES   NVQ COURSES

A-level   AS   GCSE   OTHER
c efghi   n p   v x   o q u   c e ghi   no   v x   kl no   u x
AB   GH K   P R U   AB   G K   P R U   B F I K O R
cdefg jk   cdefgh jkl   cd i

Bg — Bloxham School; Nr Banbury; Oxon. OX15 4PE
Tel: 01295 720206 (Fax: 01295 721897) D.K.Exham

		Boys	Age	Girls	Age	TOTAL		Boys	Girls
Day	£2095-£3085 X	78	11-18	10	16-18	339	SIXTH	126	35
Weekly		226	13-18	25	16-18				
Boarding	£3950								

MAP 3 C 1
LOCATION Rural
DAY   RAIL a   AIR a

SPORT abcdefghijkmpqstuwx ABC
OTHER LANGUAGES
ACTIVITIES adefghijklmopqrstuvn AB

ENTRY REQUIREMENTS CEE; Exam; Scholarship Exam; Report & Test
SCHOLARSHIPS & BURSARIES Schol; Burs; Art; Mus; Forces; Clergy; Teachers; AP; VI Form
SPECIAL NEEDS bdejklnq EGI   **DYSLEXIA** cef   **DIET** abcd
ASSOCIATION HMC   **FOUNDED** 1860   **RELIGIOUS AFFILIATION** C of E

OTHER SUBJECTS abcf
FACILITIES ON SITE abcdeghik
EXAM BOARDS abc ABEHL
RETAKES   NVQ COURSES

A-level   AS   GCSE   OTHER
 d ghi op uv x   l   d ghi   o q   v   l
B   GH K P   G   B E G K   P R   X   O R
 c ef   l   ef l   cdef   j l

226

OXFORDSHIRE continued

C — Carmel College; Mongewell Park; Wallingford OX10 8BT
Tel: 01491 837505 (Fax: 01491 825305) *Philip Skelker*

		Boys	Age	Girls	Age	TOTAL		Boys	Girls
Day	£2435	8	11-18	5	11-18	213	SIXTH	51	34
Weekly									
Boarding	£3000-£4355	127	11-18	73	11-18				

ENTRY REQUIREMENTS Report & Exam & Interview
SCHOLARSHIPS & BURSARIES Schol; Mus; AP; VI Form
SPECIAL NEEDS bjklnqw BGIL   **DYSLEXIA** ce   **DIET** ac
ASSOCIATION SHMIS   **FOUNDED** 1948   **RELIGIOUS AFFILIATION** Jewish

MAP 3 D 3
LOCATION Rural
DAY   **RAIL** b   **AIR** a
SPORT abcdefghjmoprtwx AB
OTHER LANGUAGES af
ACTIVITIES bcfghijklmorstw A
OTHER SUBJECTS bcdefh
FACILITIES ON SITE bhik
EXAM BOARDS abcd ABDEH
RETAKES a   **NVQ COURSES**

A-level: e ghij l opq v x / BC GH K P R U / cdef l
AS:
GCSE: e ghij l nopq v x / BC GH K P R U / cdef l
OTHER:

Gb — Carrdus School,The; Overthorpe Hall; Banbury; Oxfordshire OX17 2BS
Tel: 01295 263733 *Miss S.Carrdus*

		Boys	Age	Girls	Age	TOTAL		Boys	Girls
Day	£420-£1310	18	3-8	109	3-11	127	SIXTH		
Weekly									
Boarding									

ENTRY REQUIREMENTS Interview
SCHOLARSHIPS & BURSARIES Teachers
SPECIAL NEEDS n   **DYSLEXIA** e   **DIET**
ASSOCIATION IAPS   **FOUNDED** 1952   **RELIGIOUS AFFILIATION** Non-denom

MAP 3 C 1
LOCATION Rural
DAY   **RAIL** a   **AIR** b
SPORT afjlpqx B
OTHER LANGUAGES
ACTIVITIES h
OTHER SUBJECTS bch
FACILITIES ON SITE hj
EXAM BOARDS
RETAKES   **NVQ COURSES**

A-level:
AS:
GCSE:
OTHER: e l v / B G O / cde

B — Christ Church Cathedral School; 3 Brewer Street; Oxford OX1 1QW
Tel: 01865 242561 (Fax: 01865 202945) *A.H.Mottram*

		Boys	Age	Girls	Age	TOTAL		Boys	Girls
Day	£987-£1659	113	4-13			133	SIXTH		
Weekly									
Boarding	£2532	20	7-13						

ENTRY REQUIREMENTS Test & Interview
SCHOLARSHIPS & BURSARIES Chor
SPECIAL NEEDS aln   **DYSLEXIA** e   **DIET** abd
ASSOCIATION IAPS   **FOUNDED** 1540   **RELIGIOUS AFFILIATION** C of E

MAP 3 C 3
LOCATION Inner City
DAY   **RAIL** a   **AIR** b
SPORT aefjmswx A
OTHER LANGUAGES
ACTIVITIES fghjnot A
OTHER SUBJECTS ch
FACILITIES ON SITE
EXAM BOARDS
RETAKES   **NVQ COURSES**

A-level:
AS:
GCSE:
OTHER: c e g i lmno v / B G K OP R / cdef j

C — Cokethorpe School; Witney; Oxon. OX8 7PU
Tel: 01993 703921 (Fax: 01993 773499) *P.T.S.Cantwell*

		Boys	Age	Girls	Age	TOTAL		Boys	Girls
Day	£1350-£2620	116	9-18	28	9-18	205	SIXTH	24	2
Weekly	£3165-£3980	29	9-18						
Boarding	£3165-£3980	32	9-18						

ENTRY REQUIREMENTS CEE; Test & Interview
SCHOLARSHIPS & BURSARIES Schol; Burs; Siblings
SPECIAL NEEDS beijklnw BEGI   **DYSLEXIA** cde   **DIET** acd
ASSOCIATION SHMIS   **FOUNDED** 1957   **RELIGIOUS AFFILIATION**

MAP 3 C 3
LOCATION Rural
DAY ✓   **RAIL** b   **AIR** b
SPORT abcdefghjklmopqrstuwx ABC
OTHER LANGUAGES a
ACTIVITIES acdefghijklmoqstu ABC
OTHER SUBJECTS abcdfh
FACILITIES ON SITE bcdeghkl
EXAM BOARDS abcd AGHI
RETAKES ab   **NVQ COURSES**

A-level: cde g i l op v x / AB GH K OP R U / cdef
AS: G P
GCSE: e g i l op uvwx / AB E GHI K OP R U / cdef
OTHER:

B — Cothill House; Cothill; nr.Abingdon; Oxon OX13 6JL
Tel: 01865 390800 (Fax: 01865 390205) *A.D.Richardson*

		Boys	Age	Girls	Age	TOTAL		Boys	Girls
Day	£1100-£2020	100	4-13	50	4-11	401	SIXTH		
Weekly									
Boarding	£3200	251	8-13						

ENTRY REQUIREMENTS Assessment & Interview
SCHOLARSHIPS & BURSARIES Mus
SPECIAL NEEDS   **DYSLEXIA**   **DIET** a
ASSOCIATION IAPS   **FOUNDED** 1870   **RELIGIOUS AFFILIATION** C of E

MAP 3 C 3
LOCATION Rural
DAY   **RAIL** a   **AIR** b
SPORT aefjkmosuwx AB
OTHER LANGUAGES
ACTIVITIES fghijorst A
OTHER SUBJECTS cfh
FACILITIES ON SITE cjkl
EXAM BOARDS
RETAKES   **NVQ COURSES**

A-level:
AS:
GCSE:
OTHER: e g i o q v / B G K P R / cde g j

OXFORDSHIRE continued

Gb Cranford House School; Moulsford; Wallingford; Oxon. OX10 9HT
Tel: 01491 651218 (Fax: 01491 652557) Mrs A.B.Gray

		Boys	Age	Girls	Age	TOTAL		Boys	Girls
Day	£351-£1640 ✗	49	3-7	172	3-16	221	SIXTH		
Weekly									
Boarding									

ENTRY REQUIREMENTS Report & Interview
SCHOLARSHIPS & BURSARIES Schol; Burs; Mus; ARA
SPECIAL NEEDS knw B   **DYSLEXIA** e   **DIET** a
ASSOCIATION GSA   **FOUNDED** 1931   **RELIGIOUS AFFILIATION** C of E

MAP 3 D 3
LOCATION Rural
DAY ✓   **RAIL** a   **AIR** a
SPORT abcdjlmopqx ABC
OTHER LANGUAGES
ACTIVITIES cghijkoqrw
OTHER SUBJECTS bcdh
FACILITIES ON SITE bhj
EXAM BOARDS bd ABL
RETAKES   **NVQ COURSES**

A-level   AS   GCSE: e BC E G K cdef   v WX   OTHER: ghi lmno E OP R

C Dragon School; Bardwell Road; Oxford OX2 6SS
Tel: 01865 315400 (Fax: 01865 311664) R.S.Trafford

		Boys	Age	Girls	Age	TOTAL		Boys	Girls
Day	£1100-£2037	323	3-13	81	3-13	632	SIXTH		
Weekly									
Boarding	£3109	217	8-13	11	8-13				

ENTRY REQUIREMENTS Assessment
SCHOLARSHIPS & BURSARIES Schol
SPECIAL NEEDS aeghjklnq G   **DYSLEXIA** c   **DIET** ad
ASSOCIATION IAPS   **FOUNDED** 1877   **RELIGIOUS AFFILIATION** C of E

MAP 3 C 3
LOCATION Urban
DAY   **RAIL** a   **AIR** a
SPORT abcdefgjkmopqrstuwx B
OTHER LANGUAGES
ACTIVITIES cfghijlmopqst A
OTHER SUBJECTS bcfh
FACILITIES ON SITE achjk
EXAM BOARDS
RETAKES   **NVQ COURSES**

A-level   AS   GCSE   OTHER: cde g i lmno q uv B G K NOP R cdefgh j l

---

Gb Greycotes School; 1 Bardwell Road; Oxford OX2 6SU
Tel: 01865 515647 Mrs S.R.Hayward

		Boys	Age	Girls	Age	TOTAL		Boys	Girls
Day	£630-£1365	75	3-7	168	3-11	243	SIXTH		
Weekly									
Boarding									

ENTRY REQUIREMENTS Assessment & Interview
SCHOLARSHIPS & BURSARIES
SPECIAL NEEDS befhjkltuw ADHI   **DYSLEXIA**   **DIET**
ASSOCIATION IAPS   **FOUNDED** 1929   **RELIGIOUS AFFILIATION** Inter-denom

MAP 3 C 3
LOCATION Urban
DAY   **RAIL** a   **AIR** b
SPORT acjlpqx B
OTHER LANGUAGES
ACTIVITIES cfghjost
OTHER SUBJECTS bcfh
FACILITIES ON SITE bchk
EXAM BOARDS
RETAKES   **NVQ COURSES**

A-level   AS   GCSE   OTHER: def lmno s uv BC E G K O R cde

Gb Headington School; Oxford OX3 7TD
Tel: 01865 62711 (Fax: 01865 60268) Miss E.M.Tucker

		Boys	Age	Girls	Age	TOTAL		Boys	Girls
Day	£800-£1508	16	4-6	557	4-18	751	SIXTH		168
Weekly	£2510-£2980			77	9-18				
Boarding	£2540-£3010			101	9-18				

ENTRY REQUIREMENTS CEE; Test
SCHOLARSHIPS & BURSARIES Schol; Mus; Clergy; AP
SPECIAL NEEDS n   **DYSLEXIA** e   **DIET** abcd
ASSOCIATION GSA   **FOUNDED** 1915   **RELIGIOUS AFFILIATION** C of E

MAP 3 C 3
LOCATION Urban
DAY   **RAIL** a   **AIR** b
SPORT abcfghlmprtvwx ABC
OTHER LANGUAGES a
ACTIVITIES cghijknost B
OTHER SUBJECTS bcdfh
FACILITIES ON SITE bhi
EXAM BOARDS abcd ADEGH
RETAKES   **NVQ COURSES** 3

A-level: cd fg i n p s v x BC GH K   P R U W c efg j l
AS: G ef
GCSE: cd g i l BC G K P R W cdefgh j l   vw
OTHER: l O   u

Bg Josca's Prep.; Frilford House; Frilford; Abingdon; Oxon OX13 5NX
Tel: 01865 391570 A.Savin

		Boys	Age	Girls	Age	TOTAL		Boys	Girls
Day	£1095-£1550	159	4-13	3	4-7	162	SIXTH		
Weekly									
Boarding									

ENTRY REQUIREMENTS Test & Interview
SCHOLARSHIPS & BURSARIES
SPECIAL NEEDS n   **DYSLEXIA** e   **DIET**
ASSOCIATION IAPS   **FOUNDED** 1956   **RELIGIOUS AFFILIATION** C of E

MAP 3 C 3
LOCATION Rural
DAY   **RAIL** b   **AIR** c
SPORT aefjklosx B
OTHER LANGUAGES
ACTIVITIES aghjt A
OTHER SUBJECTS
FACILITIES ON SITE hi
EXAM BOARDS
RETAKES   **NVQ COURSES**

A-level   AS   GCSE   OTHER: e v B G cde j

OXFORDSHIRE *continued*

C — Kingham Hill School; Kingham; Oxfordshire OX7 6TH
Tel: 01608 658999 (Fax: 01608 658658) *M.H.Payne*

		Boys	Age	Girls	Age	TOTAL		Boys	Girls
Day	£1840-£1895	✗	7	11-18	1	11-18	183	SIXTH	17	3
Weekly	£3068-£3159		16	11-18	8	11-18				
Boarding	£3068-£3159		132	11-18	19	11-18				

ENTRY REQUIREMENTS Assessment & Interview
SCHOLARSHIPS & BURSARIES Burs; Art; Mus; Chor; Forces; Clergy
SPECIAL NEEDS aflnvw BEGI   **DYSLEXIA** c   **DIET** a
ASSOCIATION SHMIS **FOUNDED** 1886 **RELIGIOUS AFFILIATION** C of E

MAP 3 B 2
LOCATION Rural
DAY   **RAIL** a   **AIR** b
SPORT abcefhjlmpqstuwx AB
OTHER LANGUAGES a
ACTIVITIES adefghijknoqstuvwx A
OTHER SUBJECTS bcdfgh
FACILITIES ON SITE bcdghik
EXAM BOARDS abcd ADEGH
RETAKES ab   **NVQ COURSES** 23

A-level: e g i op v / G / ef P l
AS: g o v / G / ef j
GCSE: a e ghi l op v / AB E G K OP / cdef
OTHER: l

B — Magdalen College School; Oxford OX4 1DZ
Tel: 01865 242191 (Fax: 01865 240379) *P.M.Tinniswood*

		Boys	Age	Girls	Age	TOTAL		Boys	Girls
Day	£1603		495	9-18			513	SIXTH	146	
Weekly	Choristers only									
Boarding	£3042		18	9-18						

ENTRY REQUIREMENTS CEE; Report & Interview; Report & Exam & Interview
SCHOLARSHIPS & BURSARIES Schol; Mus; Chor; AP
SPECIAL NEEDS ehjklq l   **DYSLEXIA**   **DIET** a
ASSOCIATION HMC **FOUNDED** 1480 **RELIGIOUS AFFILIATION** C of E

MAP 3 C 3
LOCATION Urban
DAY   **RAIL** a   **AIR** a
SPORT abcdefgjkmrstux ABC
OTHER LANGUAGES a
ACTIVITIES efghijlorstv AD
OTHER SUBJECTS abcdfh
FACILITIES ON SITE cdk
EXAM BOARDS abcd HL
RETAKES   **NVQ COURSES**

A-level: cdefghi l v / B GH K P R / cdefg j
AS: j
GCSE: de g i l o v x / B G K NOP R / cdefg jk
OTHER: n p s x / J M O / e l

Gb — Manor Prep. School; Shippon Manor; Faringdon Road; Abingdon OX13 6LN
Tel: 01235 523789 (Fax: 01235 559593) *Mrs J.Hearnden*

		Boys	Age	Girls	Age	TOTAL		Boys	Girls
Day	£595-£1305	✗	45	3-7	327	3-11	372	SIXTH		
Weekly										
Boarding										

ENTRY REQUIREMENTS Assessment & Interview
SCHOLARSHIPS & BURSARIES
SPECIAL NEEDS beijklnpqt GIJK   **DYSLEXIA** e   **DIET** ac
ASSOCIATION IAPS **FOUNDED** 1947 **RELIGIOUS AFFILIATION** C of E

MAP 3 C 3
LOCATION Rural
DAY ✓ **RAIL** b **AIR** b
SPORT ajlnpqx AB
OTHER LANGUAGES
ACTIVITIES cfghjo
OTHER SUBJECTS ch
FACILITIES ON SITE bchk
EXAM BOARDS
RETAKES   **NVQ COURSES**

OTHER: de l no v / BC E G K O R / cde l

B — Moulsford Preparatory School; Moulsford; Nr.Wallingford; Oxon. OX10 9HR
Tel: 01491 651438 (Fax: 01491 651438) *M.J.Higham*

		Boys	Age	Girls	Age	TOTAL		Boys	Girls
Day	£1925	✗	122	7-13			164	SIXTH		
Weekly	£2435		42	7-13						
Boarding										

ENTRY REQUIREMENTS Report; Assessment & Interview
SCHOLARSHIPS & BURSARIES Burs
SPECIAL NEEDS n   **DYSLEXIA**   **DIET**
ASSOCIATION IAPS **FOUNDED** 1961 **RELIGIOUS AFFILIATION** C of E

MAP 3 D 3
LOCATION Rural
DAY ✓ **RAIL**   **AIR**
SPORT adefgjklrstx AB
OTHER LANGUAGES
ACTIVITIES afghjlmnost A
OTHER SUBJECTS
FACILITIES ON SITE cj
EXAM BOARDS
RETAKES   **NVQ COURSES**

OTHER: e g i l o v / B G K OP / cde

B — New College School; Savile Road; Oxford OX1 3UA
Tel: 01865 243657 *J.Edmunds*

		Boys	Age	Girls	Age	TOTAL		Boys	Girls
Day	£1360-£1490		136	7-13			136	SIXTH		
Weekly										
Boarding										

ENTRY REQUIREMENTS Report & Test
SCHOLARSHIPS & BURSARIES Chor
SPECIAL NEEDS   **DYSLEXIA**   **DIET** a
ASSOCIATION IAPS **FOUNDED** 1379 **RELIGIOUS AFFILIATION** C of E

MAP 3 C 3
LOCATION Urban
DAY   **RAIL** a   **AIR** b
SPORT aefjmo A
OTHER LANGUAGES
ACTIVITIES fghjoqtv
OTHER SUBJECTS ch
FACILITIES ON SITE d
EXAM BOARDS
RETAKES   **NVQ COURSES**

OTHER: e g i l n   v / B G K OP R / cdefg j

OXFORDSHIRE continued

G — Our Lady's Convent Senior School; Radley Road; Abingdon; Oxon OX14 3PS
Tel: 01235 524658 (Fax: 01235 535829) *Sister Monica Sheehy*

	Boys	Age	Girls	Age	TOTAL	SIXTH Boys	Girls
Day £1325			297	11-18	319		61
Weekly			7				
Boarding			15				

ENTRY REQUIREMENTS Exam & Interview
SCHOLARSHIPS & BURSARIES Schol; Burs; Art; Mus
SPECIAL NEEDS — **DYSLEXIA** — **DIET**
ASSOCIATION ISAI — **FOUNDED** 1860 — **RELIGIOUS AFFILIATION** R C

MAP 3 C 3
LOCATION Urban
DAY — **RAIL** b — **AIR** b
SPORT abcfmpqtwx BC
OTHER LANGUAGES
ACTIVITIES eghijknotw A
OTHER SUBJECTS bcfh
FACILITIES ON SITE bdhi
EXAM BOARDS bd AEG
RETAKES — **NVQ COURSES**

A-level: e g i lm p v x / BC G K OP R W / cdefg j l
AS: g
GCSE: R / e g i lm p v x / BC G K P R W / cdefg j l
OTHER:

G — Oxford High School GPDST; Belbroughton Road; Oxford OX2 6XA
Tel: 01865 59888 (Fax: 01865 52343) *Mrs J. Townsend*

	Boys	Age	Girls	Age	TOTAL	SIXTH Boys	Girls
Day £976-£1328			650	9-18	650		141
Weekly							
Boarding							

ENTRY REQUIREMENTS Exam & Interview; Assessment & Interview
SCHOLARSHIPS & BURSARIES Schol; Burs; Mus; AP
SPECIAL NEEDS j — **DYSLEXIA** — **DIET** ac
ASSOCIATION GSA — **FOUNDED** 1875 — **RELIGIOUS AFFILIATION**

MAP 3 C 3
LOCATION Urban
DAY — **RAIL** a — **AIR** b
SPORT acfhimopqrtwx ABC
OTHER LANGUAGES
ACTIVITIES afghijklnorst BD
OTHER SUBJECTS abcfh
FACILITIES ON SITE cghj
EXAM BOARDS abd BEGH
RETAKES — **NVQ COURSES**

A-level: cde g i n p v / B GH K P R W / cdefg jkl
AS: e l / G K / c ef k
GCSE: de g i l o v / B G K P R W / cdefgh jkl
OTHER:

B — Radley College; Abingdon; Oxon. OX14 2HR
Tel: 01235 543000 *R.M.Morgan*

	Boys	Age	Girls	Age	TOTAL	SIXTH Boys	Girls
Day					619	250	
Weekly							
Boarding £4100	619	13-18					

ENTRY REQUIREMENTS CEE
SCHOLARSHIPS & BURSARIES Schol; Art; Mus
SPECIAL NEEDS GL — **DYSLEXIA** — **DIET**
ASSOCIATION HMC — **FOUNDED** 1847 — **RELIGIOUS AFFILIATION** C of E

MAP 3 C 3
LOCATION Rural
DAY — **RAIL** b — **AIR** b
SPORT abefgijkmorstuwx B
OTHER LANGUAGES
ACTIVITIES efghijklmoqstv
OTHER SUBJECTS cf
FACILITIES ON SITE abcdeghikl
EXAM BOARDS abcd ABEGH
RETAKES — **NVQ COURSES**

A-level: cd fg i op vw / B GH K P R U / c efg j l
AS: q
GCSE: cd g i o vw / B G K OP R / cdefg j l
OTHER: l u / R / h k

Gb — Rupert House School; 90 Bell Street; Henley-on-Thames; Oxon RG9 2BN
Tel: 01491 574263 (Fax: 01491 573988) *Mrs G.Crane*

	Boys	Age	Girls	Age	TOTAL	SIXTH Boys	Girls
Day £595-£1460 X	62	4- 8	149	4-12	211		
Weekly							
Boarding							

ENTRY REQUIREMENTS Interview; Test & Interview
SCHOLARSHIPS & BURSARIES Burs
SPECIAL NEEDS ejkw l — **DYSLEXIA** — **DIET** a
ASSOCIATION IAPS — **FOUNDED** 1926 — **RELIGIOUS AFFILIATION** Inter-denom

MAP 3 D 4
LOCATION Urban
DAY — **RAIL** b — **AIR** a
SPORT aefjlmpqx AB
OTHER LANGUAGES
ACTIVITIES fghjlnos
OTHER SUBJECTS abcdh
FACILITIES ON SITE c
EXAM BOARDS
RETAKES — **NVQ COURSES**

A-level:
AS:
GCSE:
OTHER: e g i lmno v / B G K NOP R / cde

G — Rye St.Antony School; Pullen's Lane; Headington Hill; Oxford OX3 0BY
Tel: 01865 62802 (Fax: 01865 63611) *Miss A.M.Jones*

	Boys	Age	Girls	Age	TOTAL	SIXTH Boys	Girls
Day £960-£1695			250	8-18	373		87
Weekly £2295-£2625			40	8-18			
Boarding £2395-£2750			83	8-18			

ENTRY REQUIREMENTS Exam & Interview
SCHOLARSHIPS & BURSARIES
SPECIAL NEEDS abjl Bl — **DYSLEXIA** — **DIET** a
ASSOCIATION GSA — **FOUNDED** 1930 — **RELIGIOUS AFFILIATION** R C

MAP 3 C 3
LOCATION Urban
DAY — **RAIL** b — **AIR** b
SPORT acfglmpqwx AB
OTHER LANGUAGES an
ACTIVITIES cfghijknostw AB
OTHER SUBJECTS abcdfh
FACILITIES ON SITE acdeghj
EXAM BOARDS bd ABDEGHI
RETAKES — **NVQ COURSES**

A-level: cdefghi l n p v / BC G K P R U / bcdefghij l
AS: G / e
GCSE: R / cde g i l n v / BC G K P R TU X / bcdefghij l
OTHER:

OXFORDSHIRE *continued*

Bg St Edward's School; Woodstock Road; Oxford OX2 7NN
Tel: 01865 319204 (Fax: 01865 319206) *D.Christie*

		Boys	Age	Girls	Age	TOTAL		Boys	Girls
Day	£3070	127	13-18	12	16-18	573	SIXTH	215	59
Weekly									
Boarding	£4090	387	13-18	47	16-18				

ENTRY REQUIREMENTS CEE; Scholarship Exam; Report & Exam & Interview
SCHOLARSHIPS & BURSARIES Schol; Burs; Art; Mus; Chor; Forces; Clergy; VI Form; ARA
SPECIAL NEEDS ns G   **DYSLEXIA** e   **DIET** a
ASSOCIATION HMC   **FOUNDED** 1863   **RELIGIOUS AFFILIATION** C of E

MAP 3 C 3
LOCATION Urban
DAY   **RAIL** a   **AIR** a
SPORT abcdefghjkmoprstuwx ABC
OTHER LANGUAGES
ACTIVITIES acdefgijklmnoqrstuv B
OTHER SUBJECTS abcfh
FACILITIES ON SITE abcdeghjk
EXAM BOARDS bcd BEGH
RETAKES   **NVQ COURSES**

A-level: c efg i op v x / B GH K P R / c efg j l
AS: G / ef l
GCSE: c e g i o v / B GH K P R / cdefg j l
OTHER: l u / N / k

G St Helen & St Katharine, The School of; Faringdon Road; Abingdon OX14 1BE
Tel: 01235 520173 (Fax: 01235 532934) *Mrs C.L.Hall*

		Boys	Age	Girls	Age	TOTAL		Boys	Girls
Day	£1500			502	9-18	530	SIXTH		125
Weekly	£2750			28	17-18				
Boarding									

ENTRY REQUIREMENTS Exam
SCHOLARSHIPS & BURSARIES Schol; AP
SPECIAL NEEDS bhjklqx Gl   **DYSLEXIA**   **DIET** acd
ASSOCIATION GSA   **FOUNDED** 1903   **RELIGIOUS AFFILIATION** C of E

MAP 3 C 3
LOCATION Urban
DAY ✓   **RAIL** b   **AIR** b
SPORT abcfghjklnpqrtuwx ABC
OTHER LANGUAGES a
ACTIVITIES cfghijknost B
OTHER SUBJECTS bcfh
FACILITIES ON SITE abcdhjk
EXAM BOARDS abd BGH
RETAKES   **NVQ COURSES**

A-level: c efghi n p v x / BC GH K P R U / cdefgh j l
AS: de / C R / c efgh j
GCSE: e g i n v / BC G K P R / cdefgh jkl
OTHER: l / C   NO R

C St. Hugh's School; Carswell Manor; Faringdon; Oxon. SN7 8PT
Tel: 01367 870 223 (Fax: 01367 870 376) *D.Cannon*

		Boys	Age	Girls	Age	TOTAL		Boys	Girls
Day	£950-£2050	137	4-13	65	4-13	242	SIXTH		
Weekly	£2650	12	7-13	9	7-13				
Boarding	£2650	12	7-13	7	7-13				

ENTRY REQUIREMENTS Test & Interview
SCHOLARSHIPS & BURSARIES
SPECIAL NEEDS abegjlnt G   **DYSLEXIA** e   **DIET** abcd
ASSOCIATION IAPS   **FOUNDED** 1906   **RELIGIOUS AFFILIATION** C of E

MAP 3 C 3
LOCATION Rural
DAY   **RAIL** b   **AIR** b
SPORT abcfghjklmopqsx ABC
OTHER LANGUAGES
ACTIVITIES acfghjort A
OTHER SUBJECTS cfh
FACILITIES ON SITE chjk
EXAM BOARDS
RETAKES   **NVQ COURSES**

A-level:
AS:
GCSE:
OTHER: cde g i l no v / B G K OP R / cde g j

C St. Mary's Preparatory School; 13 St.Andrews Road; Henley-on-Thames; Oxon. RG9 1HS
Tel: 01491 573118 *Mrs S.Bradley*

		Boys	Age	Girls	Age	TOTAL		Boys	Girls
Day	£325-£1545	34	2-12	60	2-12	94	SIXTH		
Weekly									
Boarding									

ENTRY REQUIREMENTS Assessment & Interview
SCHOLARSHIPS & BURSARIES
SPECIAL NEEDS n   **DYSLEXIA** g   **DIET** a
ASSOCIATION ISAI   **FOUNDED** 1926   **RELIGIOUS AFFILIATION** Non-denom

MAP 3 D 4
LOCATION Urban
DAY   **RAIL** a   **AIR** a
SPORT ajlmpqx B
OTHER LANGUAGES
ACTIVITIES cfj
OTHER SUBJECTS bch
FACILITIES ON SITE h
EXAM BOARDS
RETAKES   **NVQ COURSES**

A-level:
AS:
GCSE:
OTHER: de g klmno s v / B E G K O R / cde

G St. Mary's School; Newbury Street; Wantage; Oxon OX12 8BZ
Tel: 01235 763571 (Fax: 01235 760467) *Mrs S.Bodinham*

		Boys	Age	Girls	Age	TOTAL		Boys	Girls
Day	£2400			237	16-18	237	SIXTH		63
Weekly	£3620			237	11-18				
Boarding									

ENTRY REQUIREMENTS CEE & Interview
SCHOLARSHIPS & BURSARIES Schol; VI Form
SPECIAL NEEDS abeghjklnqstuwx ABCDEGHIJK   **DYSLEXIA** ef   **DIET** acd
ASSOCIATION GSA   **FOUNDED** 1873   **RELIGIOUS AFFILIATION** C of E

MAP 3 C 3
LOCATION Urban
DAY   **RAIL** b   **AIR** b
SPORT abcfhklnopqwx ABC
OTHER LANGUAGES a
ACTIVITIES cfghijkmnoqstw A
OTHER SUBJECTS abcdefgh
FACILITIES ON SITE bdhik
EXAM BOARDS abd AEG
RETAKES a   **NVQ COURSES**

A-level: cdefghi nop v x / B GH K N P R U W / cdef j
AS: de / P
GCSE: cde g i l no v / B E G K N P R W / cdef j l
OTHER: l u / C   o

OXFORDSHIRE continued

B — Shiplake College; Henley-on-Thames RG9 4BW
Tel: 01734 402455 (Fax: 01734 402455) *N.V.Bevan*

		Boys	Age	Girls	Age	TOTAL	SIXTH	Boys	Girls
Day	£2510	73	13-18			306		116	
Weekly			13-18						
Boarding	£3725	233	13-18						

ENTRY REQUIREMENTS CEE & Interview
SCHOLARSHIPS & BURSARIES Art; Mus; Forces; Teachers; Siblings
SPECIAL NEEDS blnqstw BEGIJ **DYSLEXIA** c **DIET** a
ASSOCIATION SHMIS **FOUNDED** 1959 **RELIGIOUS AFFILIATION** C of E

MAP 3 D 4
LOCATION Rural
DAY **RAIL** a **AIR** a
SPORT abcdefhjkmrstuw AB
OTHER LANGUAGES a
ACTIVITIES efghijklmnoqstw AB
OTHER SUBJECTS bcfh
FACILITIES ON SITE aceghjk
EXAM BOARDS abd ABE
RETAKES ab **NVQ COURSES**

A-level: cde ghi o v / AB GHI K NOP R U / cdef l
AS: gh / G I / e
GCSE: AB e ghi op v / G I K P R / cdef l
OTHER: l n u

C — Sibford School; Sibford Ferris; Banbury OX15 5QL
Tel: 01295 780441 (Fax: 01295 788444) *John Dunston*

		Boys	Age	Girls	Age	TOTAL	SIXTH	Boys	Girls
Day	£1025-£1695	84	6-18	53	6-18	315		27	12
Weekly	£2295-£3200	37	9-18	20	9-18				
Boarding	£2295-£3200	82	9-18	39	9-18				

ENTRY REQUIREMENTS Report & Exam & Interview
SCHOLARSHIPS & BURSARIES Schol; Burs; Mus; VI Form
SPECIAL NEEDS begjklnqsw BEGI **DYSLEXIA** cd **DIET** a
ASSOCIATION SHMIS **FOUNDED** 1842 **RELIGIOUS AFFILIATION** Quaker

MAP 3 C 1
LOCATION Rural
DAY ✓ **RAIL** b **AIR** b
SPORT abcefhjklmopqstwx ABC
OTHER LANGUAGES a
ACTIVITIES acfghjklnopqstw AB
OTHER SUBJECTS abcdefgh
FACILITIES ON SITE bceghik
EXAM BOARDS bd ABEGH
RETAKES **NVQ COURSES**

A-level: defgh no v / G K W / cdef l
AS: n
GCSE: de h no v / ABCDE G I K O R W / bcdef l
OTHER: h jklm st / C E G NO S

B — Summer Fields; Mayfield Road; Summertown; Oxford OX2 7EN
Tel: 01865 54433 (Fax: 01865 510133) *N.Talbot-Rice*

		Boys	Age	Girls	Age	TOTAL	SIXTH	Boys	Girls
Day	£2100	14	8-13			254			
Weekly									
Boarding	£3230	240	8-13						

ENTRY REQUIREMENTS Test
SCHOLARSHIPS & BURSARIES Schol; Mus
SPECIAL NEEDS bejkl BGI **DYSLEXIA** **DIET**
ASSOCIATION IAPS **FOUNDED** 1864 **RELIGIOUS AFFILIATION** C of E

MAP 3 C 3
LOCATION
DAY **RAIL** a **AIR** a
SPORT abcejkmostuvx AB
OTHER LANGUAGES
ACTIVITIES fghijlmorstvw
OTHER SUBJECTS cfh
FACILITIES ON SITE bcdijkl
EXAM BOARDS
RETAKES **NVQ COURSES**

AS:
GCSE:
OTHER: de g i l no v / B G K OP RS / cde g j

G — Tudor Hall School; Banbury; Oxon OX16 9UR
Tel: 01295 263434 (Fax: 01295 262777) *Miss N.Godfrey*

		Boys	Age	Girls	Age	TOTAL	SIXTH	Boys	Girls
Day	£2106			26	11-18	267			78
Weekly									
Boarding	£3380			241	11-18				

ENTRY REQUIREMENTS CEE & Interview
SCHOLARSHIPS & BURSARIES Schol; Mus; VI Form
SPECIAL NEEDS ejkn EI **DYSLEXIA** g **DIET** acd
ASSOCIATION GSA **FOUNDED** 1850 **RELIGIOUS AFFILIATION** C of E

MAP 3 C 1
LOCATION Rural
DAY **RAIL** a **AIR** b
SPORT abcgklmnpqtwx ABC
OTHER LANGUAGES
ACTIVITIES cfgijklnostw B
OTHER SUBJECTS abcfgh
FACILITIES ON SITE bcdhj
EXAM BOARDS abd AEGK
RETAKES **NVQ COURSES**

A-level: defg i n p v / B GH K P R W / c efg l o
AS: de o uv x / B K R W / e
GCSE: de g i l o v / B E G K P R W / cdefgh j l
OTHER: C mno MNO / hi k

G — Wychwood School; 74 Banbury Road; Oxford OX2 6JR
Tel: 01865 57976 (Fax: 01865 56806) *Mrs M.L.Duffill*

		Boys	Age	Girls	Age	TOTAL	SIXTH	Boys	Girls
Day	£1450			88	11-18	151			34
Weekly	£2225			31	11-18				
Boarding	£2295			32	11-18				

ENTRY REQUIREMENTS Report & Exam & Interview
SCHOLARSHIPS & BURSARIES Schol; Art; Mus
SPECIAL NEEDS iln J **DYSLEXIA** efg **DIET** acd
ASSOCIATION GSA **FOUNDED** 1897 **RELIGIOUS AFFILIATION** Non-denom

MAP 3 C 3
LOCATION Urban
DAY **RAIL** a **AIR** b
SPORT cfglmopqwx AB
OTHER LANGUAGES a
ACTIVITIES cfghijknost A
OTHER SUBJECTS abcdfgh
FACILITIES ON SITE a
EXAM BOARDS bd AEGH
RETAKES **NVQ COURSES**

A-level: cdefg i p uv / B GH K N P U W / cdef h
AS:
GCSE: de g i l v / B E G K N P U W / cdef h l
OTHER: n / O R

SHROPSHIRE *continued*

G — Adcote School for Girls; Little Ness; Shrewsbury; Shropshire SY4 2JY
Tel: 01939 260202 (Fax: 01939 261300) *Mrs.S.B.Cecchet*

		Boys	Age	Girls	Age	TOTAL		Boys	Girls
Day	£950-£1700	✗		60	5-18	102	SIXTH		17
Weekly	£2135-£2780			11	8-18				
Boarding	£2420-£3065			31	8-18				

ENTRY REQUIREMENTS Interview; Report; Assessment & Interview
SCHOLARSHIPS & BURSARIES Forces; VI Form
SPECIAL NEEDS abejklnqtvw ABEGI   **DYSLEXIA** de   **DIET** abd
ASSOCIATION GSA   **FOUNDED** 1907   **RELIGIOUS AFFILIATION** C of E

MAP 8 H 4
LOCATION Rural
DAY ✓   **RAIL** a   **AIR** b
SPORT acfhlnpqx BC
OTHER LANGUAGES a
ACTIVITIES ghijknostw
OTHER SUBJECTS abcfh
FACILITIES ON SITE bgh
EXAM BOARDS bcd ABGL
RETAKES a   **NVQ COURSES**

A-level: defg i uv / BC G P R / cdef
AS: defghi uv / BC G P R U / cdef
GCSE: de ghi lm v / BC G K P R / cdef
OTHER: l u / K NO W

C — Bedstone College; Bucknell; Shropshire SY7 0BG
Tel: 01547 530303 (Fax: 01547 530740) *M.S.Symonds*

		Boys	Age	Girls	Age	TOTAL		Boys	Girls
Day	£1445-£2002	✗	13	7-19	12	7-19	188	SIXTH	19	10
Weekly	£2173-£3213			7-19		7-19				
Boarding	£2173-£3213		100	7-19	63	7-19				

ENTRY REQUIREMENTS Exam; Interview
SCHOLARSHIPS & BURSARIES Schol; Burs; Mus; Chor; Forces; VI Form
SPECIAL NEEDS ejlnqw I   **DYSLEXIA** ce   **DIET** a
ASSOCIATION SHMIS   **FOUNDED** 1948   **RELIGIOUS AFFILIATION** C of E

MAP 8 G 6
LOCATION Rural
DAY ✓   **RAIL** b   **AIR** b
SPORT abcefghklmpqstuwx ABC
OTHER LANGUAGES a
ACTIVITIES cfghijklmnopqrsuw A
OTHER SUBJECTS ch
FACILITIES ON SITE bcdegjkl
EXAM BOARDS b BD
RETAKES a   **NVQ COURSES**

A-level: e g i op uv / AB GH K OP / cdef l
AS: B G
GCSE: egil op v / ABC G K OP / cdef l
OTHER: C R

B — Birchfield School; Albrighton; Nr. Wolverhampton WV7 3AF
Tel: 01902 372534 (Fax: 01902 363516) *J.F.N.Benwell*

		Boys	Age	Girls	Age	TOTAL		Boys	Girls
Day	£995-£1575		179	4-13			195	SIXTH		
Weekly	£1885		16	8-13						
Boarding										

ENTRY REQUIREMENTS Assessment & Interview
SCHOLARSHIPS & BURSARIES Schol
SPECIAL NEEDS bijln BG   **DYSLEXIA** def   **DIET** a
ASSOCIATION IAPS   **FOUNDED** 1935   **RELIGIOUS AFFILIATION** C of E

MAP 8 J 5
LOCATION Rural
DAY   **RAIL** b   **AIR** a
SPORT abcefjlmosux ABC
OTHER LANGUAGES
ACTIVITIES fghjpq
OTHER SUBJECTS abch
FACILITIES ON SITE bcj
EXAM BOARDS
RETAKES   **NVQ COURSES**

OTHER: e i lm o q v / B G JK OP R / cde g j

C — Ellesmere College; Ellesmere; Shropshire SY12 9AB
Tel: 01691 622321 (Fax: 01691 623286) *D.R.Du Croz*

		Boys	Age	Girls	Age	TOTAL		Boys	Girls
Day	£1500-£2333	✗	104	9-18	20	9-18	352	SIXTH	92	29
Weekly										
Boarding	£3500		206	13-18	22	13-18				

ENTRY REQUIREMENTS CEE; Report & Exam & Interview
SCHOLARSHIPS & BURSARIES Schol; Burs; Art; Mus; Chor; Clergy; Teachers; AP; VI Form; Sport; ARA; Siblings
SPECIAL NEEDS jknpw l   **DYSLEXIA** e   **DIET** a
ASSOCIATION HMC   **FOUNDED** 1884   **RELIGIOUS AFFILIATION** C of E

MAP 8 H 2
LOCATION Rural
DAY ✓   **RAIL** b   **AIR** b
SPORT abcdefgjkmopqstuwx AB
OTHER LANGUAGES a
ACTIVITIES efghijklnopqstw A
OTHER SUBJECTS abcfgh
FACILITIES ON SITE abcdeghjkl
EXAM BOARDS b BDEH
RETAKES a   **NVQ COURSES**

A-level: cde ghi op uv / B GH K P R U / cdef j l
AS: u
GCSE: de ghi l no vw / AB E G K OPQR U / cdef j l
OTHER: l O

B — Kingsland Grange; Old Roman Road; Shrewsbury SY3 9AH
Tel: 01743 232132 *M.C.James*

		Boys	Age	Girls	Age	TOTAL		Boys	Girls
Day	£770-£1400	✗	151	4-13			163	SIXTH		
Weekly	£1700		12	7-13						
Boarding										

ENTRY REQUIREMENTS Interview
SCHOLARSHIPS & BURSARIES Burs; Clergy; Teachers
SPECIAL NEEDS bejklnsw BGI   **DYSLEXIA** def   **DIET** ad
ASSOCIATION IAPS   **FOUNDED** 1899   **RELIGIOUS AFFILIATION** Inter-denom

MAP 8 H 4
LOCATION Urban
DAY   **RAIL** a   **AIR** b
SPORT abdefhijksux AB
OTHER LANGUAGES
ACTIVITIES fghijnoqrw A
OTHER SUBJECTS bch
FACILITIES ON SITE cj
EXAM BOARDS
RETAKES   **NVQ COURSES**

OTHER: e g i l no q v / B G K OP R / cde j

SHROPSHIRE *continued*

Moor Park; Ludlow; Shropshire SY8 4EA
Tel: 01584 876061 (Fax: 01584 877311) *J.R.Badham*

		Boys	Age	Girls	Age	TOTAL		Boys	Girls
Day	£200-£1860	80	3-13	62	3-13	219	SIXTH		
Weekly	£2185-£2595	27	7-13	23	7-13				
Boarding	£2185-£2595	15	7-13	12	7-13				

ENTRY REQUIREMENTS Interview
SCHOLARSHIPS & BURSARIES Schol; Teachers
SPECIAL NEEDS bjlnptuvw BGI **DYSLEXIA** c **DIET** a
ASSOCIATION IAPS **FOUNDED** 1964 **RELIGIOUS AFFILIATION** R C

MAP 8 G 6
LOCATION Rural
DAY ✓ **RAIL** a **AIR** b
SPORT abcdefghjklmopqsuvwx AB
OTHER LANGUAGES
ACTIVITIES cfghijlmnopqstwx A
OTHER SUBJECTS abcfh
FACILITIES ON SITE bcdehjkl
EXAM BOARDS
RETAKES **NVQ COURSES**

A-level: e l o v / B G K O R / cde g j
AS:
GCSE:
OTHER:

Moreton Hall School; Weston Rhyn; Oswestry SY11 3EW
Tel: 01691 773 671 (Fax: 01691 778 552) *J.Forster*

		Boys	Age	Girls	Age	TOTAL		Boys	Girls
Day	£2530			20	10-18	279	SIXTH		102
Weekly									
Boarding	£3650			259	10-18				

ENTRY REQUIREMENTS CEE & Interview; Report & Exam & Interview
SCHOLARSHIPS & BURSARIES Schol; Mus; Forces; Clergy; Teachers; VI Form
SPECIAL NEEDS ajklnw BEGI **DYSLEXIA** c **DIET** abcd
ASSOCIATION GSA **FOUNDED** 1913 **RELIGIOUS AFFILIATION** C of E

MAP 8 G 4
LOCATION Rural
DAY ✓ **RAIL** a **AIR** C
SPORT abcdefhklmnpqtuvwx ABC
OTHER LANGUAGES an
ACTIVITIES acghijklnoqstw ABC
OTHER SUBJECTS abcdefgh
FACILITIES ON SITE acefghjkl
EXAM BOARDS abcd ADEGH
RETAKES ab **NVQ COURSES** 3

A-level: cdefghi no s u v x / BC GH K P R U W / cdefg jkl
AS: g n
GCSE: e ghi mno s v / BC GH I K OP R U W / cdefgh jkl
OTHER: d / C G / e

Old Hall School; Wellington.; Telford; Shropshire TF1 2DN
Tel: 01952 223117 (Fax: 01952 222674) *R.J.Ward*

		Boys	Age	Girls	Age	TOTAL		Boys	Girls
Day	£925-£1470	162	4-13	127	4-13	325	SIXTH		
Weekly	£1885	21	8-13	15	8-13				
Boarding									

ENTRY REQUIREMENTS Interview
SCHOLARSHIPS & BURSARIES Schol
SPECIAL NEEDS bjknqw BGI **DYSLEXIA** e **DIET** ad
ASSOCIATION IAPS **FOUNDED** 1830 **RELIGIOUS AFFILIATION** C of E

MAP 8 I 4
LOCATION Urban
DAY **RAIL** a **AIR** a
SPORT abcefhjlmpqsx AB
OTHER LANGUAGES a
ACTIVITIES fghijostu A
OTHER SUBJECTS bcfh
FACILITIES ON SITE cdhik
EXAM BOARDS
RETAKES **NVQ COURSES**

A-level:
AS:
GCSE:
OTHER: cdefg i l no q v / B G K NOP R / cdef j

Oswestry Junior School; The Quarry; Oswestry; Shropshire SY11 2TJ
Tel: 01691 653209 (Fax: 01691 671194) *C.J.Rickart*

		Boys	Age	Girls	Age	TOTAL		Boys	Girls
Day	£1625-£1772	67	8-13	61	8-13	162	SIXTH		
Weekly			8-13		8-13				
Boarding	£2872-£3030	24	8-13	10	8-13				

ENTRY REQUIREMENTS Exam & Interview
SCHOLARSHIPS & BURSARIES Schol; Forces; Teachers; Siblings
SPECIAL NEEDS abijknqw BEGI **DYSLEXIA** **DIET** abcd
ASSOCIATION IAPS **FOUNDED** 1960 **RELIGIOUS AFFILIATION**

MAP 8 G 4
LOCATION Rural
DAY ✓ **RAIL** a **AIR** b
SPORT acefhjlmopqsvx AB
OTHER LANGUAGES a
ACTIVITIES cfghijnoqw A
OTHER SUBJECTS abceh
FACILITIES ON SITE bcdeik
EXAM BOARDS
RETAKES **NVQ COURSES**

A-level:
AS:
GCSE:
OTHER: defg i lmno q s v / B G K OP R X / cde j

Oswestry School; Upper Brook Street; Oswestry SY11 2TL
Tel: 01691 655711 (Fax: 01691 671194) *P.K.Smith*

		Boys	Age	Girls	Age	TOTAL		Boys	Girls
Day	£1625-£1772	115	13-18	67	13-18	287	SIXTH	62	31
Weekly									
Boarding	£2872-£3030	65	13-19	40	13-18				

ENTRY REQUIREMENTS CEE; Exam; Scholarship Exam; Report & Interview
SCHOLARSHIPS & BURSARIES Schol; Forces; Teachers; VI Form
SPECIAL NEEDS beijklnqst DIK **DYSLEXIA** de **DIET** a
ASSOCIATION SHMIS **FOUNDED** 1407 **RELIGIOUS AFFILIATION**

MAP 8 G 4
LOCATION Urban
DAY **RAIL** a **AIR** b
SPORT aceijkmpstuwx AB
OTHER LANGUAGES a
ACTIVITIES cefghijmoqrtw A
OTHER SUBJECTS cef
FACILITIES ON SITE beik
EXAM BOARDS b BE
RETAKES **NVQ COURSES**

A-level: e hjl op v / ABC G U / cdef j
AS:
GCSE: e hjl op v / ABC G U / cdef j
OTHER:

SHROPSHIRE continued

C — Packwood Haugh; Ruyton-XI-Towns; Shrewsbury SY4 1HX
Tel: 01939 260217 (Fax: 01939 260051) *P.J.F.Jordan*

		Boys	Age	Girls	Age	TOTAL	SIXTH Boys	Girls
Day	£908-£2090 ✗	53	4-13	28	4-13	230		
Weekly								
Boarding	£2688	100	7-13	49	7-13			

ENTRY REQUIREMENTS Assessment & Interview
SCHOLARSHIPS & BURSARIES Schol; Clergy; Teachers
SPECIAL NEEDS bejkntuw EG   **DYSLEXIA** ef   **DIET** ac
ASSOCIATION IAPS   **FOUNDED** 1892   **RELIGIOUS AFFILIATION** C of E

MAP 8 H 4
LOCATION Rural
DAY ✓   **RAIL** b   **AIR** b
SPORT abcdefjklmnpqsuwx AB
OTHER LANGUAGES
ACTIVITIES cfghijlmnopqrtw
OTHER SUBJECTS cfh
FACILITIES ON SITE abchjl
EXAM BOARDS
RETAKES   **NVQ COURSES**

A-level   AS   GCSE   OTHER e g i l no v
B G K OP R
cde g j

Bg — Prestfelde; Shrewsbury SY2 6NZ
Tel: 01743 356500 (Fax: 01743 241434) *J.R.Bridgeland*

		Boys	Age	Girls	Age	TOTAL	SIXTH Boys	Girls
Day	£490-£1675 ✗	178	3-13	9	3-7	251		
Weekly			7-9					
Boarding	£2230	64	8-13					

ENTRY REQUIREMENTS Interview
SCHOLARSHIPS & BURSARIES Schol; Mus; Forces; Clergy; Teachers
SPECIAL NEEDS bn E   **DYSLEXIA** e   **DIET** a
ASSOCIATION IAPS   **FOUNDED** 1929   **RELIGIOUS AFFILIATION** C of E

MAP 8 H 4
LOCATION Urban
DAY   **RAIL** a   **AIR** b
SPORT abcefhjklmosux ABC
OTHER LANGUAGES
ACTIVITIES fghijmnoqsx
OTHER SUBJECTS ch
FACILITIES ON SITE cdhjl
EXAM BOARDS
RETAKES   **NVQ COURSES**

A-level   AS   GCSE   OTHER e g i l no v
B G K OP R
cde j

C — Queen's Park School; Queens Road; Oswestry; Shropshire SY11 2HZ
Tel: 01691 652416 (Fax: 01691 671439) *Mrs D.Baur*

		Boys	Age	Girls	Age	TOTAL	SIXTH Boys	Girls
Day	£2792-£2928 ✗	15	8-16	2	8-16	42		
Weekly	£3599-£3775	13	8-16	2	8-16			
Boarding	£3811-£3999	3	8-16	7	8-16			

ENTRY REQUIREMENTS Report; Assessment & Interview
SCHOLARSHIPS & BURSARIES Burs
SPECIAL NEEDS abknquvw BEI   **DYSLEXIA** a   **DIET** ab
ASSOCIATION ISAI   **FOUNDED** 1820   **RELIGIOUS AFFILIATION** Non-denom

MAP 8 G 4
LOCATION Urban
DAY ✓   **RAIL** a   **AIR** b
SPORT abcdefhjlmopqsvwx ABC
OTHER LANGUAGES n
ACTIVITIES cefghjklnqstwx
OTHER SUBJECTS bcdefgh
FACILITIES ON SITE bchik
EXAM BOARDS bd AL
RETAKES   **NVQ COURSES**

A-level   AS   GCSE def l no v
B DE G K R W
cdef l
OTHER ghi lm o s v
G K NO R WX
cdef

C — St. Winefride's Convent Jnr. Sch.; Belmont; Shrewsbury; Salop SY1 1LS
Tel: 01743 369883 *Sister Mary Felicity*

		Boys	Age	Girls	Age	TOTAL	SIXTH Boys	Girls
Day	£475-£490	48	4-11	71	3-11	119		
Weekly								
Boarding								

ENTRY REQUIREMENTS Interview
SCHOLARSHIPS & BURSARIES
SPECIAL NEEDS   **DYSLEXIA**   **DIET**
ASSOCIATION ISAI   **FOUNDED** 1868   **RELIGIOUS AFFILIATION** R C

MAP 8 H 4
LOCATION Inner City
DAY   **RAIL** a   **AIR**
SPORT ajlpqx AB
OTHER LANGUAGES
ACTIVITIES cfghr
OTHER SUBJECTS ch
FACILITIES ON SITE
EXAM BOARDS
RETAKES   **NVQ COURSES**

A-level   AS   GCSE   OTHER e v
B G K O
cde

G — Shrewsbury High School GPDST; 32 Town Walls; Shrewsbury SY1 1TN
Tel: 01743 362872 (Fax: 01743 364942) *Miss S.Gardner*

		Boys	Age	Girls	Age	TOTAL	SIXTH Boys	Girls
Day	£976-£1326			582	4-18	582		72
Weekly								
Boarding								

ENTRY REQUIREMENTS Test & Interview
SCHOLARSHIPS & BURSARIES Burs; AP
SPECIAL NEEDS   **DYSLEXIA**   **DIET** a
ASSOCIATION GSA   **FOUNDED** 1885   **RELIGIOUS AFFILIATION**

MAP 8 H 4
LOCATION Urban
DAY   **RAIL** a   **AIR** a
SPORT acfhlmpqrx ABC
OTHER LANGUAGES
ACTIVITIES fghijkost B
OTHER SUBJECTS bcdfh
FACILITIES ON SITE gh
EXAM BOARDS bd DEG
RETAKES   **NVQ COURSES**

A-level c efg i p uv
BC GH K N P R T
c efg j
AS K
ef
GCSE de g i l no v
BC G K P R
cdefgh j
OTHER

SHROPSHIRE *continued*

B — Shrewsbury School; The Schools; Shrewsbury SY3 7BA
Tel: 01743 344537 (Fax: 01743 243107) *F.E.Maidment*

		Boys	Age	Girls	Age	TOTAL		Boys	Girls
Day	£2900	143	13-18			698	SIXTH	265	
Weekly									
Boarding	£4125	555	13-18						

ENTRY REQUIREMENTS CEE; Scholarship Exam
SCHOLARSHIPS & BURSARIES Schol; Art; Mus; VI Form
SPECIAL NEEDS bejlqs   **DYSLEXIA**   **DIET** a
ASSOCIATION HMC   **FOUNDED** 1552   **RELIGIOUS AFFILIATION** C of E

MAP 8 H 4
LOCATION Urban
DAY   **RAIL** a   **AIR** a
SPORT abcdefghijkorsuwx ABC
OTHER LANGUAGES
ACTIVITIES efghijklnoqst ABD
OTHER SUBJECTS bcfh
FACILITIES ON SITE bcdghik
EXAM BOARDS bc BDEGH
RETAKES   **NVQ COURSES**

A-level: c efghi   o   v / B GH K   P R / cdefg jkl
AS: c   h   oq   v / G K / c efgh jkl
GCSE: B   cegilov / B G K   P R / cdefghijkl
OTHER: d   lnq u x / A   K MNO R U / c   h kl

C — Wrekin College; Wellington; Telford; Shropshire TF1 3BG
Tel: 01952 240131 (Fax: 01952 240338) *P.M.Johnson*

		Boys	Age	Girls	Age	TOTAL		Boys	Girls
Day	£1750-£2060	36	11-18	40	11-18	248	SIXTH	55	35
Weekly									
Boarding	£3770	112	13-18	60	13-18				

ENTRY REQUIREMENTS CEE; Test; Report & Interview
SCHOLARSHIPS & BURSARIES Schol; Burs; Art; Mus; Chor; Forces; Teachers; AP; VI Form; Sport; ARA
SPECIAL NEEDS bjklnqtu BDEGI   **DYSLEXIA** c   **DIET** abcd
ASSOCIATION HMC   **FOUNDED** 1880   **RELIGIOUS AFFILIATION** C of E

MAP 8 I 4
LOCATION Urban
DAY ✓   **RAIL** a   **AIR** a
SPORT abcdefghijklmpqstuvwx ABC
OTHER LANGUAGES a
ACTIVITIES bcefghijklmnopqstuw AC
OTHER SUBJECTS abcdfh
FACILITIES ON SITE bcdeghjk
EXAM BOARDS abcde ABDEGHK
RETAKES ab   **NVQ COURSES**

A-level: de ghi   nopq   v x / B GH K   OP R UW / cdef
AS: g i   u / G   P U
GCSE: de g i   o   v / B   G K   NOP R U X / cdef   j l
OTHER: l   n   q u / K NO   R

SOMERSET

C — All Hallows School; Cranmore Hall; East Cranmore; Shepton Mallet; Somerset BA4 4SF
Tel: 01749 880227 (Fax: 01749 880709) *C.J.Bird*

		Boys	Age	Girls	Age	TOTAL		Boys	Girls
Day	£900-£1800	64	4-14	49	4-14	194	SIXTH		
Weekly	£2760		4-14		4-14				
Boarding	£2760	44	4-14	37	4-14				

ENTRY REQUIREMENTS Interview; Report
SCHOLARSHIPS & BURSARIES
SPECIAL NEEDS abejlnqtuvwx BEGI   **DYSLEXIA** cdef   **DIET** a
ASSOCIATION IAPS   **FOUNDED** 1938   **RELIGIOUS AFFILIATION** RC/Christian

MAP 2 J 3
LOCATION Rural
DAY ✓   **RAIL** b   **AIR** b
SPORT abcefhlmopqsx ABC
OTHER LANGUAGES a
ACTIVITIES cfghjoqtw
OTHER SUBJECTS abcfh
FACILITIES ON SITE abcdhjk
EXAM BOARDS AB
RETAKES   **NVQ COURSES**

A-level:
AS:
GCSE:
OTHER: c e g i l   no q s   v / B   G JK   OP R / cde   j

G — Bruton School for Girls; Sunny Hill; Bruton; Somerset BA10 0NT
Tel: 01749 812277 (Fax: 01749 812537) *Mrs J.M.Wade*

		Boys	Age	Girls	Age	TOTAL		Boys	Girls
Day	£1050-£1262			314	8-18	538	SIXTH		87
Weekly	£2118-£2330			68	8-18				
Boarding	£2118-£2330			156	8-18				

ENTRY REQUIREMENTS Test; Report & Interview; Report & Test
SCHOLARSHIPS & BURSARIES Schol; Burs; AP; VI Form
SPECIAL NEEDS n   **DYSLEXIA** ef   **DIET** a
ASSOCIATION GSA   **FOUNDED** 1900   **RELIGIOUS AFFILIATION** C of E

MAP 2 J 4
LOCATION Rural
DAY   **RAIL** b   **AIR** c
SPORT adfgmpqx B
OTHER LANGUAGES a
ACTIVITIES cghijknopwx B
OTHER SUBJECTS bcdfh
FACILITIES ON SITE abcgj
EXAM BOARDS abcd ABDEGL
RETAKES   **NVQ COURSES**

A-level: cdefghi   n p   v / BC GH K   P R W / cdef   j l
AS: G   P R
GCSE: cde g i l   no   v / ABC   G K   P R W / cdef   j l
OTHER: u

C — Edgarley Hall; (Millfield Junior School); Glastonbury; Somerset BA6 8LD
Tel: 01458 832446 (Fax: 01458 833679) *R.J.Smyth*

		Boys	Age	Girls	Age	TOTAL		Boys	Girls
Day		100	8-13	82	8-13	436	SIXTH		
Weekly			8-13		8-13				
Boarding		162	8-13	92	8-13				

ENTRY REQUIREMENTS Scholarship Exam; Report & Interview
SCHOLARSHIPS & BURSARIES Schol; Burs
SPECIAL NEEDS abefgjklnqstuvwx ABDEGHI   **DYSLEXIA** cde   **DIET** acd
ASSOCIATION IAPS   **FOUNDED** 1946   **RELIGIOUS AFFILIATION** Inter-denom

MAP 2 I 4
LOCATION Rural
DAY   **RAIL** b   **AIR** a
SPORT abcdefghjklmopqstuwx AB
OTHER LANGUAGES a
ACTIVITIES acfghijmopqstw A
OTHER SUBJECTS abcdfh
FACILITIES ON SITE abcdehikl
EXAM BOARDS
RETAKES   **NVQ COURSES**

A-level:
AS:
GCSE:
OTHER: de g i lmno   v / BC E G   K   OP R / cdef   j l

236

SOMERSET continued

Edington and Shapwick School; Mark Road; Burtle; Bridgwater; Somerset TA7 8NJ
Tel: 01278 722012 (Fax: 01278 723312) *D.C.Walker & J.P.Whittock*

			Boys	Age	Girls	Age	TOTAL		Boys	Girls
Day	£2200-£2310	✗	37	8-13	8	8-13	171	SIXTH		
Weekly	£3047-£3432		9	8-13		8-13				
Boarding	£3234-£3432		108	8-13	9	8-13				

ENTRY REQUIREMENTS Assessment & Interview
SCHOLARSHIPS & BURSARIES Burs; Siblings
SPECIAL NEEDS ln B
DYSLEXIA a **DIET** ac
ASSOCIATION IAPS **FOUNDED** 1974 **RELIGIOUS AFFILIATION** Inter-denom

MAP 2 H 4
LOCATION Rural
DAY **RAIL** b **AIR** a
SPORT abcefhjlmoqswx ABC
OTHER LANGUAGES
ACTIVITIES fhjlmnoquwx A
OTHER SUBJECTS bcdh
FACILITIES ON SITE bch
EXAM BOARDS abd A
RETAKES a **NVQ COURSES**

A-level		AS		GCSE	de l o v	OTHER	e lmno v
				AB G cde	X	AB G K O cde	X

King's College; Taunton; Somerset TA1 3DX
Tel: 01823 272708 (Fax: 01823 334236) *R.S.Funnell*

			Boys	Age	Girls	Age	TOTAL		Boys	Girls
Day	£2520	✗	52	13-18	32	13-18	467	SIXTH	143	57
Weekly										
Boarding	£3830		282	13-18	101	13-18				

ENTRY REQUIREMENTS CEE
SCHOLARSHIPS & BURSARIES Schol; Burs; Art; Mus; Chor; Clergy; Teachers; VI Form; ARA; Siblings
SPECIAL NEEDS abgjklnqstuw ADEH **DYSLEXIA** e **DIET** ab
ASSOCIATION HMC **FOUNDED** 1880 **RELIGIOUS AFFILIATION** C of E

MAP 2 H 4
LOCATION Urban
DAY **RAIL** a **AIR** a
SPORT abcdefghijklmpstuwx BC
OTHER LANGUAGES a
ACTIVITIES abcefghijklmnopqrstuw AB
OTHER SUBJECTS abcdfh
FACILITIES ON SITE abcdhik
EXAM BOARDS abcd ABDEGH
RETAKES a **NVQ COURSES**

A-level	cde g i op v	AS	c	GCSE	de ghi o v	OTHER	l o q
	B GH K OP R				B E G K P R		F I K O
	cdefg j l		R g j		cdefg j l	X	

King's Hall; Pyrland; Kingston Road; Taunton; Somerset TA2 8AA
Tel: 01823 272431 (Fax: 01823 321189) *Mrs M.Willson*

		Boys	Age	Girls	Age	TOTAL		Boys	Girls
Day	£600-£1900	181	3-13	152	3-13	397	SIXTH		
Weekly	£1510-£2590	14	7-13	12	7-13				
Boarding	£1600-£2680	27	7-13	11	7-13				

ENTRY REQUIREMENTS Report & Interview
SCHOLARSHIPS & BURSARIES Schol; Mus; Forces; ARA; Siblings
SPECIAL NEEDS bglnq **DYSLEXIA** e **DIET** ab
ASSOCIATION IAPS **FOUNDED** 1987 **RELIGIOUS AFFILIATION** C of E

MAP 2 H 4
LOCATION Rural
DAY ✓ **RAIL** a **AIR** b
SPORT abcdefgjklmopqstwx AB
OTHER LANGUAGES
ACTIVITIES acfghijnopqrtwx A
OTHER SUBJECTS bcfh
FACILITIES ON SITE bcdhjk
EXAM BOARDS
RETAKES **NVQ COURSES**

A-level		AS		GCSE		OTHER	c e g i l no q v
							B G K OP R
							cdef j l

King's School Bruton Pre-Preparatory; Hazlegrove House; Sparkford; Yeovil; Somerset BA22 7JA
Tel: 01963 440822 (Fax: 01963 440569) *Mrs C.Riley*

		Boys	Age	Girls	Age	TOTAL		Boys	Girls
Day	£360-£940	64	3-9	43	3-9	107	SIXTH		
Weekly									
Boarding									

ENTRY REQUIREMENTS Interview
SCHOLARSHIPS & BURSARIES
SPECIAL NEEDS knpw L **DYSLEXIA** **DIET** a
ASSOCIATION IAPS **FOUNDED** 1953 **RELIGIOUS AFFILIATION** C of E

MAP 2 I 5
LOCATION Rural
DAY **RAIL** **AIR**
SPORT ajlmopsx
OTHER LANGUAGES
ACTIVITIES cghjnt
OTHER SUBJECTS cfh
FACILITIES ON SITE abchik
EXAM BOARDS
RETAKES **NVQ COURSES**

A-level		AS		GCSE		OTHER	e v
							B G K O
							cde

King's School Bruton Junior Sch.; Hazlegrove House; Sparkford; Yeovil; Somerset BA22 7JA
Tel: 01963 440314 (Fax: 01963 440569) *Revd.B.A.Bearcroft*

		Boys	Age	Girls	Age	TOTAL		Boys	Girls
Day	£1720-£2080	128	7-13	13		228	SIXTH		
Weekly			8-13						
Boarding	£2550-£2910	87	8-13						

ENTRY REQUIREMENTS Interview
SCHOLARSHIPS & BURSARIES Burs
SPECIAL NEEDS eghjklnw BGl **DYSLEXIA** cdef **DIET** acd
ASSOCIATION IAPS **FOUNDED** 1520 **RELIGIOUS AFFILIATION** C of E

MAP 2 I 5
LOCATION Rural
DAY **RAIL** a **AIR** b
SPORT abcdefgjklmopqstuwx ABC
OTHER LANGUAGES
ACTIVITIES afghijlmnoqrstwx A
OTHER SUBJECTS abcfh
FACILITIES ON SITE abcdehikl
EXAM BOARDS
RETAKES **NVQ COURSES**

A-level		AS		GCSE		OTHER	de g i l no q v
							B G JK NOP R
							cde g j

SOMERSET continued

Bg King's School; Bruton; Somerset BA10 0ED
Tel: 01749 813326 (Fax: 01749 813426) *R.I.Smyth*

		Boys	Age	Girls	Age	TOTAL	SIXTH	Boys	Girls
Day	£2590	62	13-18	2	16-18	312		119	20*
Weekly									
Boarding	£3655	230	13-18	18	16-18				

ENTRY REQUIREMENTS CEE; Assessment
SCHOLARSHIPS & BURSARIES Schol; Art; Mus; AP; ARA
SPECIAL NEEDS Ins B
DYSLEXIA e **DIET** ad
ASSOCIATION HMC **FOUNDED** 1519 **RELIGIOUS AFFILIATION** C of E

MAP 2 J 4
LOCATION Rural
DAY   **RAIL** a   **AIR** b
SPORT abcdefghijklmopstuwx BC
OTHER LANGUAGES
ACTIVITIES abefghijnoqstuvw AB
OTHER SUBJECTS abcfh
FACILITIES ON SITE abchjk
EXAM BOARDS bd AEGHL
RETAKES   **NVQ COURSES**

A-level: c e ghi l opq v x / AB GH K P R / cdefgh j l
AS: G
GCSE: c e g i l opq v x / AB G K P R / cdefgh j l
OTHER: o u

B Mark College; Mark; Highbridge; Somerset TA9 4NP
Tel: 01278 641632 (Fax: 01278 641426) *J.R.Ashcroft*

		Boys	Age	Girls	Age	TOTAL	SIXTH	Boys	Girls
Day	£3043	3	11-16			83			
Weekly	£3877-£4312	11	11-16						
Boarding	£3935-£4368	69	11-16						

ENTRY REQUIREMENTS Report; Assessment
SCHOLARSHIPS & BURSARIES
SPECIAL NEEDS aglnsvw EJ
DYSLEXIA a **DIET** ad
ASSOCIATION ISAI **FOUNDED** 1986 **RELIGIOUS AFFILIATION** C of E

MAP 2 H 4
LOCATION Rural
DAY   **RAIL** b   **AIR** a
SPORT abcdefghjlmosx ABC
OTHER LANGUAGES
ACTIVITIES fghijkmnopqstw A
OTHER SUBJECTS abd
FACILITIES ON SITE bch
EXAM BOARDS bcde AH
RETAKES   **NVQ COURSES**

A-level:
AS:
GCSE: d l no v / B E G U / cde l
OTHER: u / K NO

C Millfield School; Street; Somerset BA16 0YD
Tel: 01458 442291 (Fax: 01458 447276) *C.S.Martin*

		Boys	Age	Girls	Age	TOTAL	SIXTH	Boys	Girls
Day		177	13-18	132	13-18	1261		308	218
Weekly									
Boarding		580	13-18	372	13-18				

ENTRY REQUIREMENTS Report & Interview
SCHOLARSHIPS & BURSARIES Schol; Art; Mus; VI Form; ARA
SPECIAL NEEDS bjklnstw BCDEFGHIK
DYSLEXIA c **DIET** abd
ASSOCIATION HMC **FOUNDED** 1935 **RELIGIOUS AFFILIATION** Inter-denom

MAP 2 I 4
LOCATION Rural
DAY   **RAIL** b   **AIR** a
SPORT abcdefghjkmopqstuwx ABC
OTHER LANGUAGES a
ACTIVITIES abcfghjklmnopqrstw AB
OTHER SUBJECTS bcefgh
FACILITIES ON SITE abcdehikl
EXAM BOARDS abcd ABDEGHL
RETAKES ab   **NVQ COURSES**

A-level: a d fghi kl nop uv x / AB FGH K M P R / a cdef h j l
AS: u / GH K / e
GCSE: a d ghij lmno st v / ABC FG K N P R U W / a cdef hijkl
OTHER: C o u

C Park School,The; Yeovil BA20 1DH
Tel: 01935 23514 (Fax: 01935 411257) *Paul W.Bate*

		Boys	Age	Girls	Age	TOTAL	SIXTH	Boys	Girls
Day	£560-£1560	38	3-16	96	3-16	152			
Weekly	£2200-£2500	1	8-16	2	8-16				
Boarding	£2400-£2700		8-16	15	8-16				

ENTRY REQUIREMENTS Exam; Scholarship Exam; Interview
SCHOLARSHIPS & BURSARIES Schol; Burs; Art; Mus; Forces; Clergy; Teachers; AP
SPECIAL NEEDS w BE
DYSLEXIA   **DIET** a
ASSOCIATION ISAI **FOUNDED** 1851 **RELIGIOUS AFFILIATION** Christian

MAP 2 I 5
LOCATION Urban
DAY ✓   **RAIL** a   **AIR** c
SPORT abcefhjlmpqwx ABC
OTHER LANGUAGES
ACTIVITIES cdfghjknoqtwx AB
OTHER SUBJECTS bcdefgh
FACILITIES ON SITE ceh
EXAM BOARDS abcd
RETAKES   **NVQ COURSES**

A-level: e
AS: G
GCSE: d e g i l o v / BC E GH K P R U / cdef
OTHER: h n u / o

C Perrott Hill School; North Perrott; Crewkerne; Somerset TA18 7SL
Tel: 01460 72051 (Fax: 01460 78246) *J.E.A.Barnes*

		Boys	Age	Girls	Age	TOTAL	SIXTH	Boys	Girls
Day	£540-£1808	71	3-13	24	3-13	129			
Weekly	£2513	13	6-13	2	6-13				
Boarding	£2513	18	6-13	1	6-13				

ENTRY REQUIREMENTS Report & Interview
SCHOLARSHIPS & BURSARIES Schol; Burs; Mus; Forces; Clergy; Teachers; ARA; Siblings
SPECIAL NEEDS abfghjklnpqstuvw ABDEI
DYSLEXIA de **DIET** abcd
ASSOCIATION IAPS **FOUNDED** 1946 **RELIGIOUS AFFILIATION** C of E

MAP 2 I 5
LOCATION Rural
DAY ✓   **RAIL** a   **AIR** b
SPORT abcefghjklmopqstuwx ABC
OTHER LANGUAGES
ACTIVITIES cdfghijklmnoqrstw A
OTHER SUBJECTS abcfh
FACILITIES ON SITE cejk
EXAM BOARDS
RETAKES   **NVQ COURSES**

A-level:
AS:
GCSE:
OTHER: d e g i lmno v / B G I K OP R / cde g j

SOMERSET *continued*

C — Quantock School; Over-Stowey; Bridgwater; Somerset TA5 1HD
Tel: 01278 732252 *D.T.Peaster*

		Boys	Age	Girls	Age	TOTAL	SIXTH	Boys	Girls
Day	£700–£1200	1	7-18	2	7-18	82			
Weekly	£1900–£2500	1	7-18	1	7-18				
Boarding	£2000–£2600	51	7-18	26	7-18				

ENTRY REQUIREMENTS Report & Interview
SCHOLARSHIPS & BURSARIES Burs
SPECIAL NEEDS n B   **DYSLEXIA** eg   **DIET** a
ASSOCIATION ISAI   **FOUNDED** 1954   **RELIGIOUS AFFILIATION** Inter-denom

MAP 2 H 4
LOCATION Rural
DAY   **RAIL** b   **AIR** c
SPORT abcefhjkmpqstuwx ABC
OTHER LANGUAGES a
ACTIVITIES afghijklmoqrtuw AC
OTHER SUBJECTS cfh
FACILITIES ON SITE abcfhik
EXAM BOARDS bd B
RETAKES   **NVQ COURSES**

A-level: g i / GH P
AS
GCSE: e g i l o rs v / AB G OP / cde
OTHER

C — Queen's College Junior School; Trull Road; Taunton; Somerset TA1 4QR
Tel: 01823 272990 (Fax: 01823 323811) *P.N.Lee-Smith*

		Boys	Age	Girls	Age	TOTAL	SIXTH	Boys	Girls
Day	£660–£1725	74	4-12	74	4-12	182			
Weekly			8-12		8-12				
Boarding	£1440–£2610	17	8-12	17	8-12				

ENTRY REQUIREMENTS Report & Test
SCHOLARSHIPS & BURSARIES Schol; Mus; Forces; Clergy; Siblings
SPECIAL NEEDS abefgiklnpqstuw ABDEGHIJK   **DYSLEXIA** ce   **DIET** acd
ASSOCIATION IAPS   **FOUNDED** 1843   **RELIGIOUS AFFILIATION** Methodist

MAP 2 H 4
LOCATION Urban
DAY ✓   **RAIL** a   **AIR** a
SPORT abcefImpqswx AB
OTHER LANGUAGES
ACTIVITIES cfghijlnoqrtw A
OTHER SUBJECTS bch
FACILITIES ON SITE ahik
EXAM BOARDS
RETAKES   **NVQ COURSES**

A-level
AS
GCSE
OTHER: e g i l o v / B G K OP R / cde

C — Queen's College; Taunton; Somerset TA1 4QS
Tel: 01823 272559 (Fax: 01823 338430) *C.T.Bradnock*

		Boys	Age	Girls	Age	TOTAL	SIXTH	Boys	Girls
Day	£2025	132	12-18	145	12-18	441		66	54
Weekly									
Boarding	£3090	105	12-18	59	12-18				

ENTRY REQUIREMENTS CEE; Exam
SCHOLARSHIPS & BURSARIES Schol; Mus; Clergy; AP
SPECIAL NEEDS jn   **DYSLEXIA** cef   **DIET** a
ASSOCIATION HMC   **FOUNDED** 1843   **RELIGIOUS AFFILIATION** Methodist

MAP 2 H 4
LOCATION Rural
DAY   **RAIL** a   **AIR** b
SPORT abcdefgkmpqswx AB
OTHER LANGUAGES
ACTIVITIES dfghijknoqstw AB
OTHER SUBJECTS bcfh
FACILITIES ON SITE abcdhik
EXAM BOARDS abd AG
RETAKES   **NVQ COURSES**

A-level: c e ghij nop v x / AB GH K P R U / cdefg j l
AS
GCSE: e ghij nop v x / AB G OP R U / cde g j l
OTHER: l

Gb — St. Christopher's; 93 Berrow Road; Burnham-on-Sea; Somerset TA8 2NY
Tel: 01278 782234 *Mrs S.P.Morrell-Davies*

		Boys	Age	Girls	Age	TOTAL	SIXTH	Boys	Girls
Day	£750–£1470 ✗	24	3-11	81	3-13	122			
Weekly	£2450			5	7-13				
Boarding	£2450			12	7-13				

ENTRY REQUIREMENTS Test & Interview
SCHOLARSHIPS & BURSARIES Schol; Burs; Mus
SPECIAL NEEDS abghjklnq   **DYSLEXIA** e   **DIET** a
ASSOCIATION IAPS   **FOUNDED** 1930   **RELIGIOUS AFFILIATION** C of E

MAP 2 H 3
LOCATION Rural
DAY ✓   **RAIL** b   **AIR** b
SPORT acefImpqx AB
OTHER LANGUAGES
ACTIVITIES acfghjnortw A
OTHER SUBJECTS abcfh
FACILITIES ON SITE bcdhjk
EXAM BOARDS
RETAKES   **NVQ COURSES**

A-level
AS
GCSE
OTHER: e g i lm o v / B E G I K OP R / cde j l

C — Taunton Preparatory School; Staplegrove Road; Taunton; Somerset TA2 6AE
Tel: 01823 349250 (Fax: 01823 349202) *A.D.Wood*

		Boys	Age	Girls	Age	TOTAL	SIXTH	Boys	Girls
Day	£450–£1875	228	7-13	162	7-13	438			
Weekly			7-13		7-13				
Boarding	£1465–£2840	20	7-13	28	7-13				

ENTRY REQUIREMENTS Test; Report & Interview
SCHOLARSHIPS & BURSARIES Schol; Clergy
SPECIAL NEEDS gknnp Gl   **DYSLEXIA** def   **DIET** ab
ASSOCIATION IAPS   **FOUNDED** 1876   **RELIGIOUS AFFILIATION** Inter-denom

MAP 2 H 4
LOCATION Rural
DAY   **RAIL** a   **AIR** b
SPORT abcefhjkmopqswx AB
OTHER LANGUAGES a
ACTIVITIES afghjopqrstwx A
OTHER SUBJECTS c
FACILITIES ON SITE bcehi
EXAM BOARDS
RETAKES   **NVQ COURSES**

A-level
AS
GCSE
OTHER: e   l o v / B G / cde g j

SOMERSET continued

Taunton School; Taunton; Somerset TA2 6AD
Tel: 01823 349223 (Fax: 01823 349201) *B.B.Sutton*

		Boys	Age	Girls	Age	TOTAL		Boys	Girls
Day	£2420	151	13-18	134	13-18	506	SIXTH	103	104
Weekly									
Boarding	£3785	124	13-18	97	13-18				

MAP 2 H 4
LOCATION Rural
DAY ✓ **RAIL** a **AIR** b
SPORT abcdefghjklmopqstuwx AB
OTHER LANGUAGES a
ACTIVITIES abcdefghijklmnopqsw AB

ENTRY REQUIREMENTS CEE; Interview
SCHOLARSHIPS & BURSARIES Schol; Art; Mus; Forces; Clergy; AP; VI Form
SPECIAL NEEDS n   **DYSLEXIA**   **DIET** a
ASSOCIATION HMC   **FOUNDED** 1847   **RELIGIOUS AFFILIATION** Inter-denom
OTHER SUBJECTS abcegh
FACILITIES ON SITE abcdeghijk
EXAM BOARDS bd AG
RETAKES ab   **NVQ COURSES**

A-level: cdefghi l nop s uv / ABC GH KL OP U / cdefg j l
AS:
GCSE: de ghi nop v / ABC E G K OP R / cdefg j l
OTHER:

Wellington School; Wellington; Somerset TA21 8NT
Tel: 01823 668800 (Fax: 01823 668844) *A.J.Rogers*

		Boys	Age	Girls	Age	TOTAL		Boys	Girls
Day	£1466	324	10-19	285	10-19	778	SIXTH	119	75
Weekly									
Boarding	£2680	118	10-19	51	10-19				

MAP 2 H 4
LOCATION Urban
DAY   **RAIL** a   **AIR** b
SPORT abcefhklmopqstuwx AB
OTHER LANGUAGES a
ACTIVITIES efghijknoqstw A

ENTRY REQUIREMENTS CEE; Exam; Assessment & Interview
SCHOLARSHIPS & BURSARIES Schol; Burs; Forces; AP; VI Form
SPECIAL NEEDS kqw G   **DYSLEXIA**   **DIET** a
ASSOCIATION HMC   **FOUNDED** 1837   **RELIGIOUS AFFILIATION** C of E
OTHER SUBJECTS bcefh
FACILITIES ON SITE abcdegjk
EXAM BOARDS ab BEH
RETAKES ab   **NVQ COURSES**

A-level: cde ghi op v / ABC GH K P / c ef
AS:
GCSE: cde g i o q v / ABC G K P WX / cdef
OTHER: l n q / NO R U WX

Wells Cathedral Junior School; 10 New Street; Wells; Somerset BA5 2LQ
Tel: 01749 672291 (Fax: 01749 670724) *N.M.Wilson*

		Boys	Age	Girls	Age	TOTAL		Boys	Girls
Day	£852-£1637 ✗	93	4-10	71	4-10	194	SIXTH		
Weekly									
Boarding	£2654	14	7-10	16	7-10				

MAP 2 I 3
LOCATION Urban
DAY   **RAIL** b   **AIR** c
SPORT adefjlmpqsx
OTHER LANGUAGES
ACTIVITIES cfghjoqw A

ENTRY REQUIREMENTS Test
SCHOLARSHIPS & BURSARIES Schol; Mus; Chor
SPECIAL NEEDS   **DYSLEXIA**   **DIET** ab
ASSOCIATION IAPS   **FOUNDED** 1140   **RELIGIOUS AFFILIATION** C of E
OTHER SUBJECTS c
FACILITIES ON SITE adhjk
EXAM BOARDS
RETAKES   **NVQ COURSES**

A-level:
AS:
GCSE:
OTHER: e l no v / B G K O / cde

Wells Cathedral School; Wells BA5 2ST
Tel: 01749 672117 (Fax: 01749 670724) *J.S.Baxter*

		Boys	Age	Girls	Age	TOTAL		Boys	Girls
Day	£1784 ✗	181	11-18	158	11-18	612	SIXTH	91	92
Weekly									
Boarding	£3038	128	11-18	145	11-18				

MAP 2 I 3
LOCATION
DAY   **RAIL** b   **AIR** c
SPORT abcdefhjklmpqstuwx ABC
OTHER LANGUAGES a
ACTIVITIES cefghijklmnopqstuw AB

ENTRY REQUIREMENTS Test & Interview
SCHOLARSHIPS & BURSARIES Schol; Burs; Mus; Chor; Clergy; AP; VI Form; Siblings
SPECIAL NEEDS bejlnptx G   **DYSLEXIA** f   **DIET** ab
ASSOCIATION HMC   **FOUNDED** 909   **RELIGIOUS AFFILIATION** C of E
OTHER SUBJECTS abcdfh
FACILITIES ON SITE acdeghj
EXAM BOARDS abd ABEG
RETAKES a   **NVQ COURSES**

A-level: e g i nop vw / BC GH K P R U / cdef
AS: g / C GH K / cdef j
GCSE: p u / R / ij l
OTHER: e l no v / BC E G K NO R X / m pq R / ghi

STAFFS

Abbotsholme School; Rocester; Uttoxeter ST14 5BS
Tel: 01889 590217 (Fax: 01889 591001) *D.J.Farrant*

		Boys	Age	Girls	Age	TOTAL		Boys	Girls
Day	£2538 ✗	43	11-18	31	11-18	243	SIXTH	37	24
Weekly	£3797	16	11-18	6	11-18				
Boarding	£3797	99	11-18	48	11-18				

MAP 8 J 4
LOCATION Rural
DAY ✓ **RAIL** b   **AIR** b
SPORT abcdefghjklmopsuwx ABC
OTHER LANGUAGES a
ACTIVITIES fghijkmnopqstvw ABC

ENTRY REQUIREMENTS Test & Interview
SCHOLARSHIPS & BURSARIES Schol; Burs; Art; Mus; Forces; Clergy; Teachers; VI Form
SPECIAL NEEDS begjklnqstw DEGI   **DYSLEXIA** c   **DIET** abcd
ASSOCIATION HMC   **FOUNDED** 1889   **RELIGIOUS AFFILIATION** Inter-denom
OTHER SUBJECTS bcfh
FACILITIES ON SITE cdfhj
EXAM BOARDS abcd ABDEGH
RETAKES a   **NVQ COURSES**

A-level: defg i l opq uv / AB GH K OP R / c ef
AS: cd / G / c e j
GCSE: u / R / efghij l opq v / AB E G K OP RS / cdef j
OTHER:

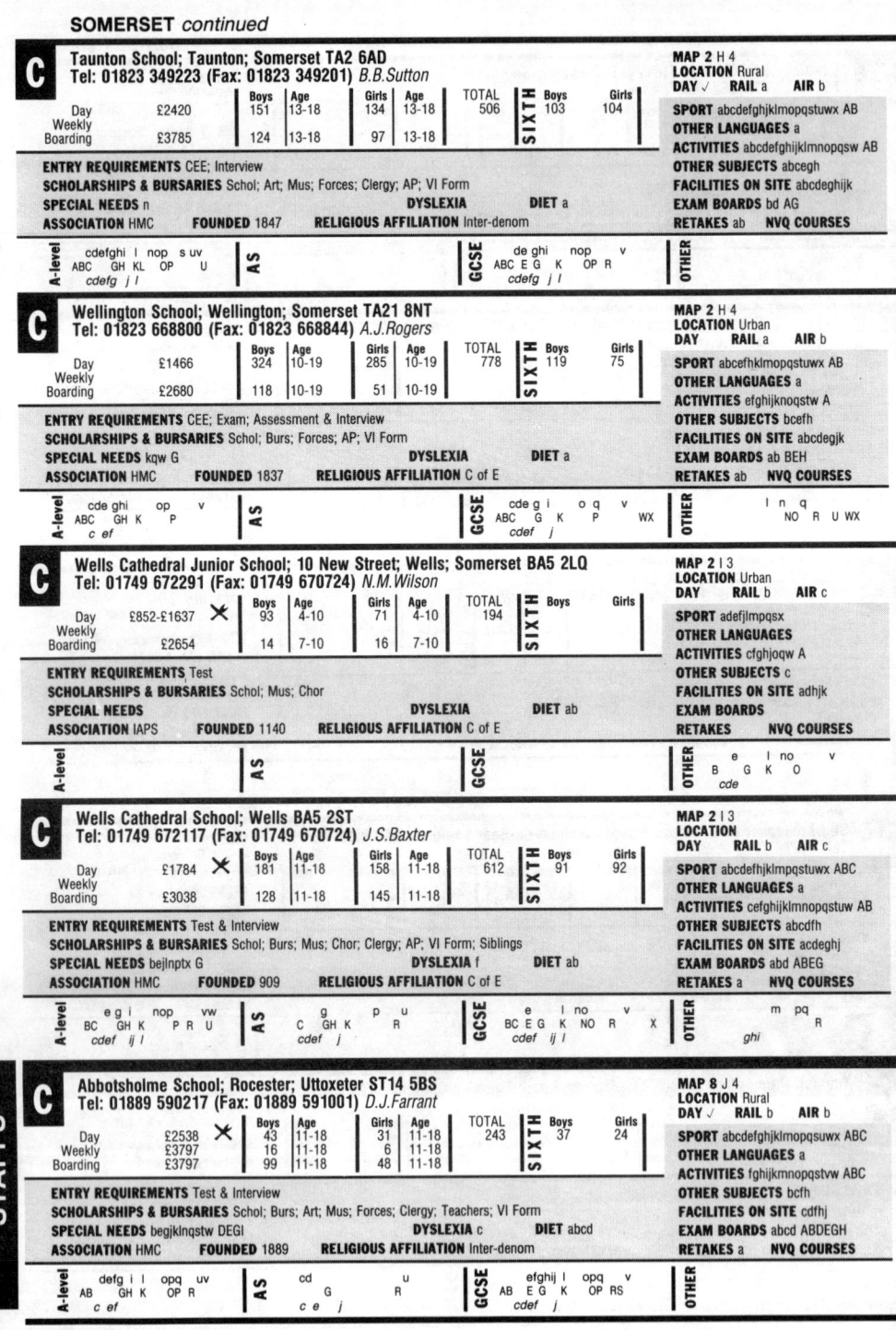

240

STAFFORDSHIRE *continued*

Brooklands School; 167 Eccleshall Road; Stafford ST16 1PD
Tel: 01785 51399 (Fax: 01785 51399) *C.T.O'Donnell*

		Boys	Age	Girls	Age	TOTAL		Boys	Girls
Day	£660-£1162	60	3-13	63	3-13	123	SIXTH		
Weekly									
Boarding									

MAP 8 J 4
LOCATION Urban
DAY **RAIL** a **AIR** a
SPORT abcefhjlmpqsx AB
OTHER LANGUAGES
ACTIVITIES cfghjot
OTHER SUBJECTS bcfh
FACILITIES ON SITE chk
EXAM BOARDS
RETAKES **NVQ COURSES**

ENTRY REQUIREMENTS Interview
SCHOLARSHIPS & BURSARIES Schol
SPECIAL NEEDS kn BGI
DYSLEXIA e **DIET** ad
ASSOCIATION IAPS **FOUNDED** 1946 **RELIGIOUS AFFILIATION** Non-denom

A-level — **AS** — **GCSE** — **OTHER** de g i lmno v / B G K OP R / cdef

Denstone College Prep. School; Smallwood Manor; Uttoxeter; Staffs. ST14 8NS
Tel: 01889 562083 (Fax: 01889 568682) *A.C.Ninham*

		Boys	Age	Girls	Age	TOTAL		Boys	Girls
Day	£806-£1771	81	3-13	57	3-13	182	SIXTH		
Weekly	£2221-£2373	4	8-13	1	8-13				
Boarding	£2221-£2373	27	8-13	12	8-13				

MAP 8 J 4
LOCATION Rural
DAY **RAIL** b **AIR** a
SPORT abcehjklmpqstux B
OTHER LANGUAGES a
ACTIVITIES acfghijotwx
OTHER SUBJECTS cfh
FACILITIES ON SITE cdikl
EXAM BOARDS
RETAKES **NVQ COURSES**

ENTRY REQUIREMENTS Test & Interview
SCHOLARSHIPS & BURSARIES Schol; Art; Mus; Chor; Forces; Clergy; Teachers
SPECIAL NEEDS bejknpqw BI
DYSLEXIA e **DIET** a
ASSOCIATION IAPS **FOUNDED** 1937 **RELIGIOUS AFFILIATION** C of E

A-level — **AS** — **GCSE** — **OTHER** e l o v / B G / cde j

Denstone College; Uttoxeter; Staffs ST14 5HN
Tel: 01889 590484 (Fax: 01889 591295) *H.C.K.Carson*

		Boys	Age	Girls	Age	TOTAL		Boys	Girls
Day	£1788-£2590	93	11-18	40	11-18	296	SIXTH	61	26
Weekly	£3630	57	11-18	15	11-18				
Boarding	£3630	61	11-18	30	11-18				

MAP 8 J 4
LOCATION Rural
DAY ✓ **RAIL** b **AIR** a
SPORT abcdefhijkmpqstuwx ABC
OTHER LANGUAGES
ACTIVITIES befghijklnopqrstuw AD
OTHER SUBJECTS abcdfh
FACILITIES ON SITE abcdehikl
EXAM BOARDS abcdf ABDEGH
RETAKES ab **NVQ COURSES**

ENTRY REQUIREMENTS CEE; Exam; Scholarship Exam
SCHOLARSHIPS & BURSARIES Schol; Art; Mus; Chor; Forces; Clergy; Teachers; AP
SPECIAL NEEDS bejlnqw EGI
DYSLEXIA de **DIET** acd
ASSOCIATION HMC **FOUNDED** 1868 **RELIGIOUS AFFILIATION** C of E

A-level efg i op uv v / B GH K P R U / c ef j **AS** G e **GCSE** egil op v x / B E G K OP R / cdef j **OTHER** M s

Edenhurst Preparatory School; Westlands Avenue; Newcastle-under-Lyme; Staffs ST5 2PU
Tel: 01782 619348 (Fax: 01782 662402) *N.H.F.Copestick*

		Boys	Age	Girls	Age	TOTAL		Boys	Girls
Day	£650-£1218	94	3-13	85	3-13	179	SIXTH		
Weekly									
Boarding									

MAP 8 I 3
LOCATION Urban
DAY ✓ **RAIL** a **AIR** b
SPORT abcefjklmopqswx AB
OTHER LANGUAGES
ACTIVITIES cfghijorst A
OTHER SUBJECTS cfh
FACILITIES ON SITE c
EXAM BOARDS
RETAKES **NVQ COURSES**

ENTRY REQUIREMENTS Test & Interview
SCHOLARSHIPS & BURSARIES Schol; Forces; Clergy; Teachers
SPECIAL NEEDS bejklnquw BGI
DYSLEXIA e **DIET** abcd
ASSOCIATION IAPS **FOUNDED** 1961 **RELIGIOUS AFFILIATION** C of E

A-level — **AS** — **GCSE** — **OTHER** de g i lmno q v / B G K OP R / cde j

Lichfield Cathedral Sch.(St.Chad's); The Palace; Lichfield; Staffs. WS13 7LH
Tel: 01543 263326 (Fax: 01543 263326) *The Rev.A.F.Walters*

		Boys	Age	Girls	Age	TOTAL		Boys	Girls
Day	£690-£1620	102	4-13	60	4-13	191	SIXTH		
Weekly	£2075-£2155	7	7-13	2	7-13				
Boarding	£2280-£2360	20	7-13		7-13				

MAP 8 K 4
LOCATION Urban
DAY **RAIL** a **AIR**
SPORT acefjlmopqx A
OTHER LANGUAGES
ACTIVITIES cfghijortw A
OTHER SUBJECTS bcfh
FACILITIES ON SITE abcdej
EXAM BOARDS
RETAKES **NVQ COURSES**

ENTRY REQUIREMENTS Report & Interview
SCHOLARSHIPS & BURSARIES Schol; Mus; Chor; Clergy
SPECIAL NEEDS behjkngstwx ACDGHIK
DYSLEXIA ef **DIET** acd
ASSOCIATION IAPS **FOUNDED** 1942 **RELIGIOUS AFFILIATION** C of E

A-level — **AS** — **GCSE** — **OTHER** e lm o v / B G K / cde j

STAFFORDSHIRE *continued*

C — Maple Hayes Hall School for Dyslexics; Abnalls Lane; Lichfield; Staffs WS13 8BL
Tel: 01543 264387 (Fax: 01543 262022) *Dr E.N.Brown*

		Boys	Age	Girls	Age	TOTAL	SIXTH	Boys	Girls
Day	£2575 ✗	22	7-16			7-16 83			
Weekly	£3250	15	7-16						
Boarding	£3700	46	7-16						

ENTRY REQUIREMENTS Assessment & Interview
SCHOLARSHIPS & BURSARIES Burs
SPECIAL NEEDS n B
DYSLEXIA a **DIET** acd
ASSOCIATION ISAI **FOUNDED** 1981 **RELIGIOUS AFFILIATION** C of E

MAP 8 K 4
LOCATION Rural
DAY   **RAIL** a   **AIR** a
SPORT abefghjlmox AB
OTHER LANGUAGES
ACTIVITIES bfghijklnoqrtw A
OTHER SUBJECTS acdfh
FACILITIES ON SITE abch
EXAM BOARDS bd AL
RETAKES a   **NVQ COURSES**

A-level: **AS**:   **GCSE** d e g i o v / AB G P / cd   **OTHER** A D o q / K O R V / c

C — Newcastle-under-Lyme School; Mount Pleasant; Newcastle-under-Lyme; Staffs. ST5 1DB
Tel: 01782 633604 (Fax: 01782 632765) *Dr R.M.Reynolds*

		Boys	Age	Girls	Age	TOTAL	SIXTH	Boys	Girls
Day	£1026-£1180	635	8-18	658	8-18	1293		150	157
Weekly									
Boarding									

ENTRY REQUIREMENTS Exam
SCHOLARSHIPS & BURSARIES Schol; AP
SPECIAL NEEDS behjklnqsu G
DYSLEXIA   **DIET** a
ASSOCIATION HMC **FOUNDED** 1874 **RELIGIOUS AFFILIATION**

MAP 8 I 3
LOCATION Urban
DAY   **RAIL**   **AIR**
SPORT abcefhkmpqsuwx AB
OTHER LANGUAGES
ACTIVITIES efghijknoqrstx AB
OTHER SUBJECTS bcdfh
FACILITIES ON SITE bchi
EXAM BOARDS abc DEH
RETAKES   **NVQ COURSES**

A-level: c e ghi p uv x / BC GH K P R U W / c efg jk   **AS**: c l / M / efg j   **GCSE**: e g i l o v / ABC G K NOP R U WX / cdefg jkl   **OTHER**

C — St. Bede's School; Bishton Hall; Wolseley Bridge; Nr. Stafford ST17 0XN
Tel: 01889 881277 (Fax: 01889 882749) *A.H.& H.C.Stafford Northcote*

		Boys	Age	Girls	Age	TOTAL	SIXTH	Boys	Girls
Day	£800-£1498 ✗	51	3-13	35	3-13	129			
Weekly	£1950	3	6-13	4	6-13				
Boarding	£1950	24	6-13	12	6-13				

ENTRY REQUIREMENTS Interview
SCHOLARSHIPS & BURSARIES Schol; Burs
SPECIAL NEEDS beijklnptuvw BHI
DYSLEXIA e   **DIET** a
ASSOCIATION IAPS **FOUNDED** 1936 **RELIGIOUS AFFILIATION** RC/Inter-denom

MAP 8 J 4
LOCATION Rural
DAY   **RAIL** a   **AIR** a
SPORT adefhjlmopqstux ABC
OTHER LANGUAGES
ACTIVITIES cfghjnrtx A
OTHER SUBJECTS bcfh
FACILITIES ON SITE cdfhik
EXAM BOARDS
RETAKES   **NVQ COURSES**

A-level: **AS**:   **GCSE**:   **OTHER** e g i lmno uv / BC E G K OP R / cdefg j

Gb — St. Dominic's Priory School; 21 Station Road; Stone; Staffs ST15 8EN
Tel: 01785 814181 (Fax: 01785 819361) *Mrs.J.Hildreth*

		Boys	Age	Girls	Age	TOTAL	SIXTH	Boys	Girls
Day	£690-£1098	27	3- 8	325	3-18	352			26
Weekly									
Boarding									

ENTRY REQUIREMENTS Exam; Report & Interview
SCHOLARSHIPS & BURSARIES Schol; Burs
SPECIAL NEEDS bln GH
DYSLEXIA e   **DIET**
ASSOCIATION ISAI **FOUNDED** 1934 **RELIGIOUS AFFILIATION** R C

MAP 8 J 4
LOCATION Urban
DAY   **RAIL** b   **AIR** b
SPORT cfjlmpqx ABC
OTHER LANGUAGES
ACTIVITIES cfghijknow AB
OTHER SUBJECTS bcegh
FACILITIES ON SITE dgh
EXAM BOARDS abcd ABDEGI
RETAKES ab   **NVQ COURSES**

A-level: e g i uv / B G K P T W / c e hj l   **AS**: e / c e g   **GCSE**: e g i l v / BC G K P R W / cdefg hj   **OTHER** l / c

Gb — St. Dominic's School; 32 Bargate Street; Brewood; Stafford ST19 9BA
Tel: 01902 850248 (Fax: 01902 851154) *Mrs K.S.Butwilowska*

		Boys	Age	Girls	Age	TOTAL	SIXTH	Boys	Girls
Day	£770-£1300	15	2- 7	403	2-18	418			34
Weekly									
Boarding									

ENTRY REQUIREMENTS Exam & Interview
SCHOLARSHIPS & BURSARIES Schol; VI Form
SPECIAL NEEDS ablnq
DYSLEXIA   **DIET** ad
ASSOCIATION GSA **FOUNDED** 1902 **RELIGIOUS AFFILIATION** R C

MAP 8 J 3
LOCATION Rural
DAY ✓   **RAIL** a   **AIR** a
SPORT abchklmpqvwx ABC
OTHER LANGUAGES
ACTIVITIES cghijknopqtw AB
OTHER SUBJECTS bcdfh
FACILITIES ON SITE cdgh
EXAM BOARDS abcd ABDEG
RETAKES ab   **NVQ COURSES**

A-level: defg ij l n p uv / BC GH K P R U / cdef   **AS**: u / P   **GCSE**: d e g ij l n p v / BC G K P R / cdef   **OTHER** o

STAFFORDSHIRE *continued*

C — St. Joseph's College; London Road; Trent Vale; Stoke on Trent; Staffs. ST4 5NT
Tel: 01782 48008 (Fax: 01782 745487) *J.E.Stoer*

Day £600-£1098
Weekly
Boarding

Boys	Age	Girls	Age	TOTAL	SIXTH Boys	Girls
335	4-18	135	4-18	470	57	

MAP 8 J 3
LOCATION Urban
DAY   RAIL a   AIR a
SPORT abcefjklmpqsx B
OTHER LANGUAGES
ACTIVITIES fghijkoq
OTHER SUBJECTS bch
FACILITIES ON SITE bcg
EXAM BOARDS bc D
RETAKES ab   NVQ COURSES 1

ENTRY REQUIREMENTS Exam & Interview
SCHOLARSHIPS & BURSARIES Schol; Burs; AP
SPECIAL NEEDS jn
ASSOCIATION ISAI   **FOUNDED** 1932   **RELIGIOUS AFFILIATION** R C   **DYSLEXIA** g   **DIET** a

A-level: B e g i   G op   K OP   R uv   cde l
AS: g
GCSE: B e g i l   G op   K OP R   v   cde l
OTHER:

G — School of S.Mary & S.Anne; Abbots Bromley; Nr Rugeley; Staffs. WS15 3BW
Tel: 01283 840232 (Fax: 01283 840988) *A.J.Grigg*

Day £840-£2370
Weekly £3005-£3555
Boarding £3005-£3555

Boys	Age	Girls	Age	TOTAL	SIXTH Boys	Girls
		127	5-18	281		73
		51	7-18			
		103	7-18			

MAP 8 J 4
LOCATION Rural
DAY ✓   RAIL b   AIR a
SPORT abcdfghklmopqtuwx ABC
OTHER LANGUAGES a
ACTIVITIES cdfghijklnoqstwx AB
OTHER SUBJECTS bcfh
FACILITIES ON SITE dehik
EXAM BOARDS abcd BDEGH
RETAKES   NVQ COURSES

ENTRY REQUIREMENTS Test & Interview
SCHOLARSHIPS & BURSARIES Schol; Art; Mus; Forces; Clergy; Teachers; AP; VI Form; Sport; ARA
SPECIAL NEEDS bjlnqw
ASSOCIATION GSA   **FOUNDED** 1874   **RELIGIOUS AFFILIATION** C of E   **DYSLEXIA**   **DIET** a

A-level: BC efghi GH K   p   P R TU   v   cdefg j l
AS: B e g   G l   K
GCSE: BC e ghi   G K   n   cdefg j l   OP R U WX   v
OTHER:

C — Stafford Grammar School; Burton Manor; Stafford ST18 9AT
Tel: 01785 49752 (Fax: 01785 55005) *M.S.James*

Day £1315
Weekly
Boarding

Boys	Age	Girls	Age	TOTAL	SIXTH Boys	Girls
161	11-18	127	11-18	288	38	22

MAP 8 J 4
LOCATION Rural
DAY   RAIL a   AIR a
SPORT abcefhjmpqswx ABC
OTHER LANGUAGES
ACTIVITIES fghijkoqst AB
OTHER SUBJECTS abcdh
FACILITIES ON SITE bcg
EXAM BOARDS bc ABDH
RETAKES   NVQ COURSES

ENTRY REQUIREMENTS Exam & Interview
SCHOLARSHIPS & BURSARIES Burs; AP; Siblings
SPECIAL NEEDS abghjklnqstw AGHI
ASSOCIATION SHMIS   **FOUNDED** 1982   **RELIGIOUS AFFILIATION**   **DYSLEXIA** ef   **DIET**

A-level: B d ghi l no GH K   uv   PQ   c ef
AS: d g i l   G K
GCSE: AB e g i l no   G K OP R   v   cdef   X
OTHER: l   o

C — Vernon Lodge Preparatory School; School Lane; Stretton; Near Brewood; Staffs. ST19 9LQ
Tel: 01902 850568 *Mrs D.Lodge*

Day £848-£1000
Weekly
Boarding

Boys	Age	Girls	Age	TOTAL	SIXTH Boys	Girls
45	2-11	35	2-11	80		

MAP 8 J 4
LOCATION Rural
DAY   RAIL b   AIR b
SPORT aehjlpqx
OTHER LANGUAGES
ACTIVITIES cfghijnqt
OTHER SUBJECTS acfh
FACILITIES ON SITE dfhk
EXAM BOARDS
RETAKES   NVQ COURSES

ENTRY REQUIREMENTS Test
SCHOLARSHIPS & BURSARIES
SPECIAL NEEDS an Bl
ASSOCIATION ISAI   **FOUNDED** 1981   **RELIGIOUS AFFILIATION** Non-denom   **DYSLEXIA**   **DIET**

A-level:
AS:
GCSE:
OTHER: e

C — Wolstanton Preparatory School; 30 Woodland Avenue; Newcastle; Staffs. ST5 8AZ
Tel: 01782 626675 *Mrs.E.A.Cooper*

Day £759
Weekly
Boarding

Boys	Age	Girls	Age	TOTAL	SIXTH Boys	Girls
25	3-11	20	3-11	45		

MAP 8 I 3
LOCATION Urban
DAY ✓   RAIL b   AIR a
SPORT jx
OTHER LANGUAGES
ACTIVITIES gho
OTHER SUBJECTS
FACILITIES ON SITE
EXAM BOARDS
RETAKES   NVQ COURSES

ENTRY REQUIREMENTS Test & Interview
SCHOLARSHIPS & BURSARIES Schol
SPECIAL NEEDS
ASSOCIATION ISAI   **FOUNDED** 1922   **RELIGIOUS AFFILIATION** Non-denom   **DYSLEXIA**   **DIET**

A-level:
AS:
GCSE:
OTHER:

STAFFORDSHIRE *continued*

Yarlet Schools,The; Stafford; Staffordshire ST18 9SU
Tel: 01889 508240 *R.S.Plant*

		Boys	Age	Girls	Age	TOTAL			
Day	£905-£1950	45	3-13	5	3-13	97	SIXTH	Boys	Girls
Weekly									
Boarding	£2390	47	7-13		7-13				

ENTRY REQUIREMENTS None
SCHOLARSHIPS & BURSARIES Forces
SPECIAL NEEDS beghjklnptuvw ABCDEGHIKL   **DYSLEXIA** e   **DIET** acd
ASSOCIATION IAPS   **FOUNDED** 1873   **RELIGIOUS AFFILIATION** C of E

MAP 8 J 4
LOCATION Rural
DAY   **RAIL** a   **AIR** a
SPORT acefjmpqsux AB
OTHER LANGUAGES
ACTIVITIES bcfghjmort
OTHER SUBJECTS acfh
FACILITIES ON SITE abcdhjk
EXAM BOARDS
RETAKES   **NVQ COURSES**

A-level | AS | GCSE | OTHER: e l o v / B G / cde j

Abbey School Woodbridge,The; Woodbridge; Suffolk IP12 1DS
Tel: 01394 382673 (Fax: 01394 383880) *M.S.Booth*

		Boys	Age	Girls	Age	TOTAL			
Day	£875-£1461	140	4-11	102	4-11	242	SIXTH	Boys	Girls
Weekly									
Boarding									

ENTRY REQUIREMENTS Exam & Interview; Assessment & Interview
SCHOLARSHIPS & BURSARIES
SPECIAL NEEDS   **DYSLEXIA**   **DIET** a
ASSOCIATION IAPS   **FOUNDED** 1950   **RELIGIOUS AFFILIATION** C of E

MAP 4 K 1
LOCATION Urban
DAY   **RAIL** b   **AIR** b
SPORT aefjlmopqsx ABC
OTHER LANGUAGES
ACTIVITIES cfghjorswx A
OTHER SUBJECTS c
FACILITIES ON SITE abh
EXAM BOARDS
RETAKES   **NVQ COURSES**

A-level | AS | GCSE | OTHER: e l o t v / BC EG K O R / cde

SUFFOLK

Amberfield School; Nacton; Nr. Ipswich IP10 0HL
Tel: 01473 659265 (Fax: 01473 659843) *Mrs M.L.Amphlett Lewis*

		Boys	Age	Girls	Age	TOTAL			
Day	£860-£1270	15	3-7	266	3-16	281	SIXTH	Boys	Girls
Weekly									
Boarding									

ENTRY REQUIREMENTS Test & Interview
SCHOLARSHIPS & BURSARIES Schol; Art; Mus; Siblings
SPECIAL NEEDS abegjklnoqstux ABCDGHIK   **DYSLEXIA** cde   **DIET** abcd
ASSOCIATION GSA   **FOUNDED** 1952   **RELIGIOUS AFFILIATION** Christian

MAP 4 K 1
LOCATION Rural
DAY ✓   **RAIL** b   **AIR** b
SPORT acflmpqwx AB
OTHER LANGUAGES
ACTIVITIES cfghijkot A
OTHER SUBJECTS bcdfh
FACILITIES ON SITE
EXAM BOARDS abcd
RETAKES   **NVQ COURSES**

A-level | AS | GCSE: e g i l n v / B G K PR W / cdef | OTHER: C

Barnardiston Hall Preparatory School; Barnardiston; Nr.Haverhill; Suffolk CB9 7TG
Tel: 01440 786316 (Fax: 01440 786355) *Lt.Col.K.A.Boulter*

		Boys	Age	Girls	Age	TOTAL			
Day	£1040-£1290	69	2-13	93	2-13	217	SIXTH	Boys	Girls
Weekly	£2100	6	6-13	3	6-13				
Boarding	£2350	28	6-13	18	6-13				

ENTRY REQUIREMENTS Assessment & Interview
SCHOLARSHIPS & BURSARIES Forces; Teachers; Siblings
SPECIAL NEEDS bghnqsuw B   **DYSLEXIA** cdef   **DIET** ac
ASSOCIATION IAPS   **FOUNDED** 1959   **RELIGIOUS AFFILIATION** Inter-denom

MAP 10 H 1
LOCATION Rural
DAY   **RAIL** b   **AIR** a
SPORT acdefhjlmopqstx ABC
OTHER LANGUAGES a
ACTIVITIES cdfghjlopqtwx
OTHER SUBJECTS abcfh
FACILITIES ON SITE ceh
EXAM BOARDS
RETAKES   **NVQ COURSES**

A-level | AS | GCSE | OTHER: efj i lmno q v / BC G K OP R / cdef j

---

Cherry Trees School; Flempton Road; Risby; Bury St Edmunds; Suffolk IP28 6QJ
Tel: 01284 760531 (Fax: 01284 750177) *Mrs.W.E.S.Compson*

		Boys	Age	Girls	Age	TOTAL			
Day	£220-£1400	109	2-13	92	2-13	201	SIXTH	Boys	Girls
Weekly	£1910-£2170		7-13		7-13				
Boarding									

ENTRY REQUIREMENTS Assessment & Interview
SCHOLARSHIPS & BURSARIES Burs
SPECIAL NEEDS abfijklnq B   **DYSLEXIA** cde   **DIET** a
ASSOCIATION ISAI   **FOUNDED** 1984   **RELIGIOUS AFFILIATION** Inter-denom

MAP 10 I 7
LOCATION Rural
DAY   **RAIL** a   **AIR** b
SPORT acefjlmopqsx ABC
OTHER LANGUAGES
ACTIVITIES cfghjknost B
OTHER SUBJECTS bcfgh
FACILITIES ON SITE ceh
EXAM BOARDS
RETAKES   **NVQ COURSES**

A-level | AS | GCSE | OTHER: e ghi lmno s v / BC EG K OP R / cdef j

SUFFOLK continued

Culford School; Bury St.Edmunds; Suffolk; IP28 6TX
Tel: 01284 728615 (Fax: 01284 728631) *J.S.Richardson*

		Boys	Age	Girls	Age	TOTAL		Boys	Girls
Day	£1758-£2257	226	2-18	170	2-18	621	SIXTH	68	61
Weekly	£2437-£2695	11	8-18	5	8-18				
Boarding	£2737-£3467	118	8-18	91	8-18				

ENTRY REQUIREMENTS CEE; Scholarship Exam; Exam & Interview; Report & Interview
SCHOLARSHIPS & BURSARIES Schol; Mus; Forces; AP; VI Form; Siblings
SPECIAL NEEDS befjnqs EGL **DYSLEXIA** e **DIET** acd
ASSOCIATION HMC **FOUNDED** 1881 **RELIGIOUS AFFILIATION** Methodist

MAP10 I 7
LOCATION Rural
DAY ✓ **RAIL** a **AIR** a
SPORT abcdefgklmopqstuwx ABC
OTHER LANGUAGES a
ACTIVITIES acfghijklmnorstw ABDE
OTHER SUBJECTS bcfh
FACILITIES ON SITE cdeghik
EXAM BOARDS abd ABDEH
RETAKES a   **NVQ COURSES**

A-level: cd g i nop uv / AB GH K P R / cdef j l
AS: fgh / C G K / ef l
GCSE: opq s uvw / P R T W
OTHER: cd g i no v / ABC G K OP R WX / cdefg j l
lm q

Fairstead House School; Fordham Road; Newmarket; Suffolk CB8 7AA
Tel: 01638 662318 (Fax: 01638 662318) *D.J.Wedgwood*

		Boys	Age	Girls	Age	TOTAL		Boys	Girls
Day	£770-£900	50	4-11	67	4-11	117	SIXTH		
Weekly									
Boarding									

ENTRY REQUIREMENTS None
SCHOLARSHIPS & BURSARIES Schol
SPECIAL NEEDS abegklnqstvw AGIK **DYSLEXIA** e **DIET** a
ASSOCIATION ISAI **FOUNDED** 1950 **RELIGIOUS AFFILIATION** Non-denom

MAP10 H 7
LOCATION Urban
DAY   **RAIL** b **AIR** a
SPORT aefjmpqs A
OTHER LANGUAGES
ACTIVITIES cdfgj
OTHER SUBJECTS ch
FACILITIES ON SITE
EXAM BOARDS
RETAKES   **NVQ COURSES**

A-level:
AS:
GCSE:
OTHER: e l no s v / B E G K O R / cde

Finborough School; The Hall; Great Finborough; Stowmarket; Suffolk IP14 3EF
Tel: 01449 674479 (Fax: 01449 770908) *J.Sinclair*

		Boys	Age	Girls	Age	TOTAL		Boys	Girls
Day	£525-£1210	29	2-18	30	2-18	227	SIXTH	12	13
Weekly	£1440-£1800		6-18	5	6-18				
Boarding	£2130-£2660	100	6-18	63	6-18				

ENTRY REQUIREMENTS Report; Report & Interview
SCHOLARSHIPS & BURSARIES Burs; Forces; Siblings
SPECIAL NEEDS nw BE **DYSLEXIA**   **DIET** abcd
ASSOCIATION ISAI **FOUNDED** 1978 **RELIGIOUS AFFILIATION** Non-denom

MAP10 J 7
LOCATION Rural
DAY   **RAIL** a **AIR** b
SPORT abcdefhjklmopsuwx ABC
OTHER LANGUAGES a
ACTIVITIES acdfghijklmnopqrstwx ABD
OTHER SUBJECTS bcdefgh
FACILITIES ON SITE abcd
EXAM BOARDS ab ABDEL
RETAKES ab   **NVQ COURSES**

A-level: d ghi op v / ABC K P / cdef l
AS: d ghi o v / ABC E G K P / cdef
GCSE: d h o v / ABC E G K O / cdef
OTHER: E G I O R / d h l

Framlingham College Junior School; Branderston Hall; Woodbridge IP13 7AQ
Tel: 01728 685331 (Fax: 01728 685437) *N.Johnson*

		Boys	Age	Girls	Age	TOTAL		Boys	Girls
Day	£900-£1579	134	4-13	98	4-13	293	SIXTH		
Weekly	£2546	5	7-13	3	7-13				
Boarding	£2546	31	7-13	22	7-13				

ENTRY REQUIREMENTS Exam; Report
SCHOLARSHIPS & BURSARIES Schol; Mus
SPECIAL NEEDS bjnw H **DYSLEXIA** de **DIET** a
ASSOCIATION IAPS **FOUNDED** 1949 **RELIGIOUS AFFILIATION** C of E

MAP10 K 8
LOCATION Rural
DAY   **RAIL** a **AIR** c
SPORT abefjklmopqswx AB
OTHER LANGUAGES
ACTIVITIES acfghjmoqrtwx A
OTHER SUBJECTS abcdh
FACILITIES ON SITE acdehil
EXAM BOARDS
RETAKES   **NVQ COURSES**

A-level:
AS:
GCSE:
OTHER: egi l no v / B G K OP R / cdef

Framlingham College; Nr.Woodbridge; Suffolk IP13 9EY
Tel: 01728 723789 (Fax: 01728 724546) *Mrs G.M.Randall*

		Boys	Age	Girls	Age	TOTAL		Boys	Girls
Day	£2072	77	13-18	57	13-18	435	SIXTH	102	65
Weekly			13-18		13-18				
Boarding	£3229	203	13-18	98	13-18				

ENTRY REQUIREMENTS CEE; Scholarship Exam; Report & Interview
SCHOLARSHIPS & BURSARIES Schol; Art; Mus; AP; VI Form; ARA; Drama
SPECIAL NEEDS bghjklnpqstvw BCDEGHIK **DYSLEXIA** f **DIET** abcd
ASSOCIATION HMC **FOUNDED** 1864 **RELIGIOUS AFFILIATION** C of E

MAP10 K 8
LOCATION Rural
DAY   **RAIL** b **AIR** b
SPORT abcdefhjklmopqstuwx ABC
OTHER LANGUAGES
ACTIVITIES acdefghijklnopqrstuvw ABCD
OTHER SUBJECTS abcdefgh
FACILITIES ON SITE abcdeghjkl
EXAM BOARDS abcd ABDEGH
RETAKES a   **NVQ COURSES** 2

A-level: efghi l nop s vwx / AB FGH K NOPQ T X / cdef h l
AS: e ghi l op s uvw / A FGH K MN PQR TU X / c ef h l
GCSE: e h l no v x / AB G K NO R X / cdef hj l
OTHER: l / N / ef i l

SUFFOLK continued

C — Hillcroft Preparatory School; Walnutree Manor; Haughley Green; near Stowmarket; Suffolk IP14 3RQ Tel: 01449 673003 (Fax: 01449 613072) *Frederick Rapsey & Mrs Gwyneth Rapsey*

MAP 4 J 7
LOCATION Rural
DAY ✓ RAIL a AIR b

		Boys	Age	Girls	Age	TOTAL		Boys	Girls
Day	£350-£1250 ✗	41	2-13	40	2-13	81	SIXTH		
Weekly									
Boarding									

SPORT acefhjklmpqtux ABC
OTHER LANGUAGES a
ACTIVITIES bcfghjnux A
OTHER SUBJECTS abcdh
FACILITIES ON SITE bcehk
EXAM BOARDS L
RETAKES   NVQ COURSES

ENTRY REQUIREMENTS Assessment
SCHOLARSHIPS & BURSARIES Burs; Mus; Chor; ARA; Siblings
SPECIAL NEEDS abcjknopuw BI   DYSLEXIA cdef   DIET abcd
ASSOCIATION ISAI   FOUNDED 1911   RELIGIOUS AFFILIATION Inter-denom

A-level   AS   GCSE
OTHER bcdefg i lmno q stuv
       B DE G   K   OP R
       cde   ij

Gb — Ipswich High School GPDST; Woolverstone; Ipswich IP9 1AZ
Tel: 01473 780201 (Fax: 01473 780985) *Miss V.C.Mac Cuish*

MAP10 J 8
LOCATION Rural
DAY   RAIL b   AIR b

		Boys	Age	Girls	Age	TOTAL		Boys	Girls
Day	£976-£1328	18	4-7	653	4-18	671	SIXTH		107
Weekly									
Boarding									

SPORT cfglmpqtx ABC
OTHER LANGUAGES
ACTIVITIES fghijknot B
OTHER SUBJECTS bcfh
FACILITIES ON SITE ghjk
EXAM BOARDS abcd BEG
RETAKES   NVQ COURSES

ENTRY REQUIREMENTS Exam
SCHOLARSHIPS & BURSARIES Schol; AP
SPECIAL NEEDS hl   DYSLEXIA   DIET
ASSOCIATION GSA   FOUNDED 1878   RELIGIOUS AFFILIATION Non-denom

A-level cd fg i   p   v   AS d   p   v   GCSE de g i l   v   OTHER   l no   u
        BC GH K   P R U   G K   R   BC E G K   P R   O
        c efg j   f   cdefgh j

B — Ipswich Prep. School; 35 Henley Road; Ipswich; Suffolk IP1 3SQ
Tel: 01473 255730 (Fax: 01473 213831) *David Williams*

MAP10 J 8
LOCATION Urban
DAY   RAIL a   AIR b

		Boys	Age	Girls	Age	TOTAL		Boys	Girls
Day	£1090-£1134	129	7-11			129	SIXTH		
Weekly									
Boarding									

SPORT abcefgjlmqsx AB
OTHER LANGUAGES
ACTIVITIES bfghjoqrt
OTHER SUBJECTS ch
FACILITIES ON SITE abdhik
EXAM BOARDS
RETAKES   NVQ COURSES

ENTRY REQUIREMENTS Test
SCHOLARSHIPS & BURSARIES
SPECIAL NEEDS   DYSLEXIA   DIET
ASSOCIATION IAPS   FOUNDED   RELIGIOUS AFFILIATION C of E

A-level   AS   GCSE
OTHER   e l o   v
          B   G K O R
          cd

Bg — Ipswich School; Ipswich IP1 3SG
Tel: 01473 255313 (Fax: 01473 213831) *Ian Galbraith*

MAP10 J 8
LOCATION Urban
DAY   RAIL b   AIR b

		Boys	Age	Girls	Age	TOTAL		Boys	Girls
Day	£1597-£1684	523	11-18	44	16-18	602	SIXTH	153	44
Weekly	£2511-£2802	10	11-18						
Boarding	£2555-£2884	25	11-18						

SPORT abcdefghijklmpqstuvwx ABC
OTHER LANGUAGES
ACTIVITIES aefghijklmnopqrstuvw AB
OTHER SUBJECTS abcdfh
FACILITIES ON SITE acdeghik
EXAM BOARDS abd ABDEH
RETAKES   NVQ COURSES

ENTRY REQUIREMENTS CEE; Exam; Scholarship Exam
SCHOLARSHIPS & BURSARIES Schol; Art; Mus; AP
SPECIAL NEEDS abejklnpquw CEGI   DYSLEXIA   DIET acd
ASSOCIATION HMC   FOUNDED 1390   RELIGIOUS AFFILIATION C of E

A-level cd g i l   opq   v   AS d   i   q   GCSE cd g i l o   v   OTHER   u
        B   GH K   P   GH K   B   G K   P   X   NO R
        c efg jk   ef k   cdefgh jkl

C — Moreton Hall; Mount Road; Bury St. Edmunds IP32 7BJ
Tel: 01284 753532 (Fax: 01284 769197) *M.E.Higgins*

MAP10 I 7
LOCATION Rural
DAY   RAIL a   AIR b

		Boys	Age	Girls	Age	TOTAL		Boys	Girls
Day	£1035-£2025 ✗	43	2-13	23	2-13	79	SIXTH		
Weekly	£2400	3	8-13	3	8-13				
Boarding	£2700	4	8-13	3	8-13				

SPORT abcfgjklmpqstuwx ABC
OTHER LANGUAGES a
ACTIVITIES cefghijnoqstw A
OTHER SUBJECTS abcfh
FACILITIES ON SITE bcdehik
EXAM BOARDS
RETAKES   NVQ COURSES

ENTRY REQUIREMENTS Interview; Report
SCHOLARSHIPS & BURSARIES Schol; Burs; Mus; Chor; Forces; Siblings
SPECIAL NEEDS bn   DYSLEXIA ef   DIET a
ASSOCIATION IAPS   FOUNDED 1962   RELIGIOUS AFFILIATION R C

A-level   AS   GCSE
OTHER   cde g i lmno   v
        B   G   K NOP R
        cde gh j

SUFFOLK *continued*

Old Buckenham Hall School; Brettenham Park; Ipswich; Suffolk IP7 7PH
Tel: 01449 740252 (Fax: 01449 740955) *H.D.Cocke*

		Boys	Age	Girls	Age	TOTAL		Boys	Girls
Day	£1025-£2175	71	3-13	8	3-7	161	SIXTH		
Weekly	£2700	21	7-13						
Boarding	£2800	61	7-13						

ENTRY REQUIREMENTS Report & Interview
SCHOLARSHIPS & BURSARIES Schol; Burs; Art; Mus; Clergy
SPECIAL NEEDS bejknpw GI **DYSLEXIA** ce **DIET** a
ASSOCIATION IAPS **FOUNDED** 1862 **RELIGIOUS AFFILIATION** C of E

MAP 10 J 8
LOCATION Rural
DAY **RAIL** b **AIR** b
SPORT abcefjklmstuwx AB
OTHER LANGUAGES
ACTIVITIES fghijmopqrw A
OTHER SUBJECTS ach
FACILITIES ON SITE bcjkl
EXAM BOARDS
RETAKES **NVQ COURSES**

A-level: AS: GCSE: OTHER: e l o q v B E G K R cde j

Old School,The; Toad Row; Henstead; Beccles; Suffolk NR34 7LG
Tel: 01502 741150 *M.J.Hewett*

		Boys	Age	Girls	Age	TOTAL		Boys	Girls
Day	£690-£930	65	4-13	65	4-13	130	SIXTH		
Weekly									
Boarding									

ENTRY REQUIREMENTS Interview
SCHOLARSHIPS & BURSARIES
SPECIAL NEEDS bn BCL **DYSLEXIA** ef **DIET**
ASSOCIATION ISAI **FOUNDED** 1979 **RELIGIOUS AFFILIATION** C of E

MAP 10 K 6
LOCATION Rural
DAY **RAIL** b **AIR** a
SPORT aefjlmpqsx B
OTHER LANGUAGES
ACTIVITIES fghjlotw A
OTHER SUBJECTS cfh
FACILITIES ON SITE bk
EXAM BOARDS
RETAKES **NVQ COURSES**

A-level: AS: GCSE: OTHER: e g i l no v B E G K OP R W cde

Orwell Park School; Nacton; Ipswich; Suffolk IP10 0ER
Tel: 01473 659225 (Fax: 01473 659822) *A.H.Auster*

		Boys	Age	Girls	Age	TOTAL		Boys	Girls
Day	£2080-£2200 ×	24	7-13	7	7-13	183	SIXTH		
Weekly		83	7-11	11	7-11				
Boarding	£2750-£3050	51	7-13	7	7-13				

ENTRY REQUIREMENTS Scholarship Exam; Test & Interview
SCHOLARSHIPS & BURSARIES Schol; Mus
SPECIAL NEEDS abejklnpqstuvwx ABEGHI **DYSLEXIA** ce **DIET** abcd
ASSOCIATION IAPS **FOUNDED** 1867 **RELIGIOUS AFFILIATION** Inter-denom

MAP 4 K 1
LOCATION Rural
DAY **RAIL** a **AIR** b
SPORT abcefhjklmopqstuwx AB
OTHER LANGUAGES a
ACTIVITIES bcfghijlmnopqrstuw A
OTHER SUBJECTS acfh
FACILITIES ON SITE bcehjkl
EXAM BOARDS
RETAKES **NVQ COURSES**

A-level: AS: GCSE: OTHER: cde g i lmno q uv ABC G K OP R cdefg j

---

Royal Hospital School; Holbrook; Ipswich; Suffolk IP9 2RX
Tel: 01473 328342 (Fax: 01473 328825) *N.K.D.Ward*

		Boys	Age	Girls	Age	TOTAL		Boys	Girls
Day	£1300 ×	1	16-18	3	16-18	584	SIXTH	89	26
Weekly									
Boarding	£2575	411	11-18	169	11-18				

ENTRY REQUIREMENTS CEE; Exam
SCHOLARSHIPS & BURSARIES Schol; Art; Mus; Forces
SPECIAL NEEDS bl BE **DYSLEXIA** **DIET** ad
ASSOCIATION SHMIS **FOUNDED** 1712 **RELIGIOUS AFFILIATION** RC/C of E

MAP 10 J 8
LOCATION Rural
DAY ✓ **RAIL** a **AIR** a
SPORT abcdefhjklmopqstuwx ABC
OTHER LANGUAGES a
ACTIVITIES bcdefghijklmnopqstw AB
OTHER SUBJECTS abcdfh
FACILITIES ON SITE bcdeghikl
EXAM BOARDS abcd ABDEGHI
RETAKES ab **NVQ COURSES**

A-level: de ghi l o uv x AB GH K P R U c ef j
AS: i l o uv x AB G K P R cdef
GCSE: de g i no v AB E G I K OP R WX cdef j
OTHER: h lm q KL

Saint Felix School; Southwold; Suffolk IP18 6SD;
Tel: 01502 722175 (Fax: 01502 722641) *Mrs S.R.Campion*

		Boys	Age	Girls	Age	TOTAL		Boys	Girls
Day	£2235-£2250 ×			87	11-18	232	SIXTH		61
Weekly	£3435-£3450			20	11-18				
Boarding	£3435-£3450			125	11-18				

ENTRY REQUIREMENTS CEE & Interview; Report & Exam & Interview
SCHOLARSHIPS & BURSARIES Schol; Mus
SPECIAL NEEDS ln **DYSLEXIA** f **DIET** abcd
ASSOCIATION GSA **FOUNDED** 1897 **RELIGIOUS AFFILIATION** Non-denom

MAP 10 L 7
LOCATION Rural
DAY ✓ **RAIL** b **AIR** b
SPORT acdfghklmopqtuwx AB
OTHER LANGUAGES a
ACTIVITIES acfghijklnoqstwx AB
OTHER SUBJECTS bcdefh
FACILITIES ON SITE bcdegjk
EXAM BOARDS abc ABDEG
RETAKES ab **NVQ COURSES**

A-level: cdefghi l no v B GH K P R U cdefg j l
AS: de h l o u B K R e
GCSE: de ghi no v BC G K N P R cdefgh jkl
OTHER: l

SUFFOLK continued

C | St. George's School; (Junior School of St.Felix); Southwold; Suffolk IP18 6SD
Tel: 01502 723314 (Fax: 01502 722641) *Mrs.W.Holland*

		Boys	Age	Girls	Age	TOTAL
Day	£820-£1395	34	2-11	64	2-11	103
Weekly	£2400			1	7-11	
Boarding	£2400			4	7-11	

SIXTH Boys Girls

ENTRY REQUIREMENTS Interview
SCHOLARSHIPS & BURSARIES Schol; Mus
SPECIAL NEEDS abgjklnqw BI   **DYSLEXIA** e   **DIET** abcd
ASSOCIATION IAPS   **FOUNDED** 1943   **RELIGIOUS AFFILIATION** Inter-denom

MAP 10 L 7
LOCATION Rural
DAY ✓   **RAIL** c   **AIR** c
SPORT acefghjklmpqsx B
OTHER LANGUAGES
ACTIVITIES cghijowx A .
OTHER SUBJECTS abch
FACILITIES ON SITE dj
EXAM BOARDS
RETAKES   **NVQ COURSES**

A-level
AS
GCSE
OTHER: e g i l m o s u v / BCDE G K OP R / cde

Bg | St. Joseph's College with the School of Jesus and Mary; Birkfield; Ipswich; Suffolk IP2 9DR Tel: 01473 690281 (Fax: 01473 602409) *John Regan*

		Boys	Age	Girls	Age	TOTAL		Boys	Girls
Day	£925-£1610	635	3-18	160	3-18	872	SIXTH	140	16
Weekly	£2270-£2531	3	11-19						
Boarding	£2522-£2812	74	11-19						

ENTRY REQUIREMENTS Test; Report
SCHOLARSHIPS & BURSARIES Schol; Burs; AP
SPECIAL NEEDS n BEL   **DYSLEXIA** e   **DIET** abcd
ASSOCIATION GBA   **FOUNDED** 1937   **RELIGIOUS AFFILIATION** RC/C of E

MAP 10 J 8
LOCATION Rural
DAY ✓   **RAIL** a   **AIR** b
SPORT abcefhjklmpqstwx AB
OTHER LANGUAGES a
ACTIVITIES fghijkoqrst AB
OTHER SUBJECTS bcdfh
FACILITIES ON SITE cdeghi
EXAM BOARDS abcd AGI
RETAKES   **NVQ COURSES**

A-level: e ghij l op v x / AB GH K OP R U / cdef l
AS: i p / GH R / e
GCSE: e ghij l op v x / ABC E G K P R U WX / cdef j l
OTHER: o

C | South Lee; Nowton Road; Bury St.Edmunds; Suffolk IP33 2BT
Tel: 01284 754654 (Fax: 01284 706178) *Mrs R.Williamson*

		Boys	Age	Girls	Age	TOTAL
Day	£1180-£1480	118	2-13	163	2-13	281
Weekly						
Boarding						

ENTRY REQUIREMENTS Assessment
SCHOLARSHIPS & BURSARIES Schol
SPECIAL NEEDS bjn B   **DYSLEXIA** def   **DIET** a
ASSOCIATION IAPS   **FOUNDED** 1961   **RELIGIOUS AFFILIATION** Inter-denom

MAP 10 I 7
LOCATION Rural
DAY ✓   **RAIL** a   **AIR** b
SPORT acefhjklmpqswx AB
OTHER LANGUAGES
ACTIVITIES cfghjlnopqtv
OTHER SUBJECTS bcdfh
FACILITIES ON SITE
EXAM BOARDS
RETAKES   **NVQ COURSES**

A-level
AS
GCSE
OTHER: d e g i l n o q t v / B G K OP R / cdef

C | Stoke College; Stoke-by-Clare; Sudbury; Suffolk CO10 8JE
Tel: 01787 278141 (Fax: 01787 277904) *D.Marshall*

		Boys	Age	Girls	Age	TOTAL
Day	£1088-£1621	101	3-16	87	3-16	217
Weekly	£2445-£2706	20	9-16	9	9-16	
Boarding						

ENTRY REQUIREMENTS Report & Interview
SCHOLARSHIPS & BURSARIES Schol; Mus; Siblings
SPECIAL NEEDS n   **DYSLEXIA** ce   **DIET** a
ASSOCIATION ISAI   **FOUNDED** 1951   **RELIGIOUS AFFILIATION** Non-denom

MAP 4 I 1
LOCATION Rural
DAY ✓   **RAIL** b   **AIR** a
SPORT abcdefjlmopqswx ABC
OTHER LANGUAGES
ACTIVITIES fghjmoqt AB
OTHER SUBJECTS bcdfh
FACILITIES ON SITE abcehj
EXAM BOARDS ab A
RETAKES   **NVQ COURSES**

A-level
AS
GCSE: e g i l n o v / ABC E G K P / cde j l
OTHER: l n / K

C | Woodbridge School; Woodbridge; Suffolk IP12 4JH
Tel: 01394 385547 (Fax: 01394 380944) *S.H.Cole*

		Boys	Age	Girls	Age	TOTAL		Boys	Girls
Day	£1784	212	11-18	251	11-18	499	SIXTH	73	87
Weekly			11-18		11-18				
Boarding	£2932	12	11-18	24	11-18				

ENTRY REQUIREMENTS CEE; Report & Exam & Interview
SCHOLARSHIPS & BURSARIES Schol; Burs; Art; Mus; AP
SPECIAL NEEDS abegijklnqstw DHI   **DYSLEXIA** f   **DIET** abcd
ASSOCIATION HMC   **FOUNDED** 1662   **RELIGIOUS AFFILIATION** C of E

MAP 10 K 8
LOCATION Rural
DAY ✓   **RAIL** a   **AIR** b
SPORT abcdefghjklmopqstuwx ABC
OTHER LANGUAGES a
ACTIVITIES acdefghijknopqsvw AB
OTHER SUBJECTS bcdh
FACILITIES ON SITE abcdghjk
EXAM BOARDS abcd ABDEGH
RETAKES   **NVQ COURSES**

A-level: de ghi op v / B GH K PQR U / cdef j
AS: e / G / ef
GCSE: de ghi no v / B G K OP R U / cdef hj l
OTHER: lm u / l NO R

SURREY

C — Aberdour School; Brighton Rd.; Burgh Heath; Tadworth; Surrey KT20 6AJ
Tel: 01737 354119 (Fax: 01737 363044) *A.Barraclough*

		Boys	Age	Girls	Age	TOTAL		Boys	Girls
Day	£550-£1470 ✗	219	3-13	6	3-5	225	SIXTH		
Weekly									
Boarding									

ENTRY REQUIREMENTS
SCHOLARSHIPS & BURSARIES Schol; Clergy
SPECIAL NEEDS beijkw GI   **DYSLEXIA**   **DIET** abcd
ASSOCIATION IAPS **FOUNDED** 1933 **RELIGIOUS AFFILIATION** C of E

MAP 5 E 7
LOCATION Rural
DAY   **RAIL** a   **AIR** a
SPORT abcefjkmsuwx ABC
OTHER LANGUAGES
ACTIVITIES fghijox A
OTHER SUBJECTS ch
FACILITIES ON SITE bhi
EXAM BOARDS
RETAKES   **NVQ COURSES**

A-level | AS | GCSE | OTHER: e g i l no v / B G K P R / cde g j

B — Aldro School; Shackleford; Godalming; Surrey GU8 6AS
Tel: 01483 810266 (Fax: 01483 811699) *I.M.Argyle*

		Boys	Age	Girls	Age	TOTAL		Boys	Girls
Day	£2190	127	7-13			215	SIXTH		
Weekly									
Boarding	£2835	88	7-13						

ENTRY REQUIREMENTS Report & Exam & Interview
SCHOLARSHIPS & BURSARIES
SPECIAL NEEDS bejklnpqw GI   **DYSLEXIA** e   **DIET** acd
ASSOCIATION IAPS **FOUNDED** 1898 **RELIGIOUS AFFILIATION** C of E

MAP 3 E 5
LOCATION Rural
DAY   **RAIL** a   **AIR** a
SPORT abcdefgjklmorstuwx ABC
OTHER LANGUAGES
ACTIVITIES afghijmorstvwx A
OTHER SUBJECTS bch
FACILITIES ON SITE acdhjk
EXAM BOARDS
RETAKES   **NVQ COURSES**

A-level | AS | GCSE | OTHER: de g i l no s v / B G K OP R / cde g j

C — American Community School; Heywood; Portsmouth Road; Cobham; Surrey KT11 1BL
Tel: 01932 867251 (Fax: 01932 869790) *T.Lehman*

		Boys	Age	Girls	Age	TOTAL		Boys	Girls
Day	£2375-£4370	608	3-18	518	3-18	1239	SIXTH	112	84
Weekly	£6375	13	12-18	10	12-18				
Boarding	£7155	50	12-18	40	12-18				

ENTRY REQUIREMENTS Assessment
SCHOLARSHIPS & BURSARIES Burs; Teachers
SPECIAL NEEDS beghjklnqstuw ABCDGIK   **DYSLEXIA** e   **DIET** a
ASSOCIATION ISAI **FOUNDED** 1975 **RELIGIOUS AFFILIATION** Non-denom

MAP 5 C 7
LOCATION Rural
DAY ✓   **RAIL** a   **AIR** a
SPORT abcfjklmnpsx ABC
OTHER LANGUAGES abchk
ACTIVITIES bfghijklopstwx
OTHER SUBJECTS bcfh
FACILITIES ON SITE bhkl
EXAM BOARDS CL
RETAKES   **NVQ COURSES**

A-level | AS | GCSE | OTHER: e g i l no v x / B G M OPQ T / cdef i l

C — Amesbury School; Hindhead; Surrey GU26 6BL
Tel: 01428 604322 *N.G.Taylor*

		Boys	Age	Girls	Age	TOTAL		Boys	Girls
Day	£800-£1975 ✗	120	3-13	34	3-13	170	SIXTH		
Weekly	£2435	16	7-13						
Boarding			7-13						

ENTRY REQUIREMENTS Assessment & Interview
SCHOLARSHIPS & BURSARIES Schol
SPECIAL NEEDS ijn   **DYSLEXIA**   **DIET** ac
ASSOCIATION IAPS **FOUNDED** 1870 **RELIGIOUS AFFILIATION** C of E

MAP 3 E 6
LOCATION Rural
DAY   **RAIL** a   **AIR** a
SPORT abcefjklmopswx AB
OTHER LANGUAGES
ACTIVITIES cfghjlorst A
OTHER SUBJECTS bcfh
FACILITIES ON SITE acdejk
EXAM BOARDS
RETAKES   **NVQ COURSES**

A-level | AS | GCSE | OTHER: e l o v x / B E G K OP R / cde g j

C — Barfield School; Runfold; Farnham; Surrey GU10 1PB
Tel: 01252 782271 (Fax: 01252 782505) *B.J.Hoar*

		Boys	Age	Girls	Age	TOTAL		Boys	Girls
Day	£1145-£1795 ✗	142	3-13	71	3-13	213	SIXTH		
Weekly									
Boarding									

ENTRY REQUIREMENTS Report & Interview
SCHOLARSHIPS & BURSARIES Schol
SPECIAL NEEDS abjknqstw BDHI   **DYSLEXIA** cef   **DIET** abcd
ASSOCIATION IAPS **FOUNDED** 1933 **RELIGIOUS AFFILIATION** Non-denom

MAP 3 E 5
LOCATION Rural
DAY   **RAIL** a   **AIR** a
SPORT aefhjkmnopqsuwx ABC
OTHER LANGUAGES
ACTIVITIES acfghijlnopqrsuw A
OTHER SUBJECTS ach
FACILITIES ON SITE cfi
EXAM BOARDS
RETAKES   **NVQ COURSES**

A-level | AS | GCSE | OTHER: e g i lmno q v / B G JK OP R / cde j

SURREY *continued*

C — Barrow Hills; Witley; Godalming; Surrey GU8 5NY
Tel: 01428 683639 (Fax: 01428 682634) *Michael Connolly*

		Boys	Age	Girls	Age	TOTAL		Boys	Girls
Day	£1155-£1935	128	4-13	25	4-13	153	SIXTH		
Weekly									
Boarding									

ENTRY REQUIREMENTS Assessment & Interview
SCHOLARSHIPS & BURSARIES Teachers
SPECIAL NEEDS bejklnpqw BGI **DYSLEXIA** e **DIET** a
ASSOCIATION IAPS **FOUNDED** 1950 **RELIGIOUS AFFILIATION** R C

MAP 3 E 5
LOCATION Rural
DAY **RAIL** a **AIR** a
SPORT acefjmopqsx AB
OTHER LANGUAGES a
ACTIVITIES afghjoqrtx A
OTHER SUBJECTS bcfh
FACILITIES ON SITE bcdeik
EXAM BOARDS
RETAKES **NVQ COURSES**

A-level AS GCSE OTHER e g i l no v
B E G K OP R
cde j

C — Belmont School; Feldemore; Holmbury St. Mary; Nr Dorking; Surrey RH5 6LQ
Tel: 01306 730852 (Fax: 01306 731220) *D.Gainer*

		Boys	Age	Girls	Age	TOTAL		Boys	Girls
Day	£890-£1725 ×	155	4-13	52	4-13	247	SIXTH		
Weekly	£2515	36	7-13	4	7-13				
Boarding									

ENTRY REQUIREMENTS Assessment & Interview
SCHOLARSHIPS & BURSARIES Schol; Teachers
SPECIAL NEEDS lnw E **DYSLEXIA** ce **DIET** acd
ASSOCIATION IAPS **FOUNDED** 1880 **RELIGIOUS AFFILIATION** C of E

MAP 3 F 5
LOCATION Rural
DAY √ **RAIL** b **AIR** a
SPORT abcdefjlmnpqstwx ABC
OTHER LANGUAGES a
ACTIVITIES cfghjloqtwx A
OTHER SUBJECTS ch
FACILITIES ON SITE abchj
EXAM BOARDS
RETAKES **NVQ COURSES**

A-level AS GCSE OTHER e lmno v
B E G K O R
cde j

C — Box Hill School; Mickleham; Dorking; Surrey RH5 6EA
Tel: 01372 373382 (Fax: 01372 363942) *Dr R.A.S.Atwood*

		Boys	Age	Girls	Age	TOTAL		Boys	Girls
Day	£2050 ×	57	11-18	33	11-18	233	SIXTH	53	17
Weekly	£3280	29	11-18	8	11-18				
Boarding	£3400	78	11-18	28	11-18				

ENTRY REQUIREMENTS Report & Exam & Interview
SCHOLARSHIPS & BURSARIES Schol; Burs; VI Form
SPECIAL NEEDS jn **DYSLEXIA** e **DIET** acd
ASSOCIATION SHMIS **FOUNDED** 1959 **RELIGIOUS AFFILIATION** Inter-denom

MAP 3 F 5
LOCATION Rural
DAY **RAIL** a **AIR** a
SPORT abcdefghjklmopstwx ABC
OTHER LANGUAGES a
ACTIVITIES abfghijklnoqsw AB
OTHER SUBJECTS abceh
FACILITIES ON SITE bceghjl
EXAM BOARDS bcd ABEGH
RETAKES a **NVQ COURSES**

A-level efghi p v x AS GCSE e l no v OTHER
BC G P BC G K O X
c ef l cdef l

G — Bramley School; Walton on the Hill; Surrey KT20 7ST
Tel: 0173 781 2004 *Mrs B.Johns*

		Boys	Age	Girls	Age	TOTAL		Boys	Girls
Day	£525-£1150			116	3-12	116	SIXTH		
Weekly									
Boarding									

ENTRY REQUIREMENTS Exam; Interview
SCHOLARSHIPS & BURSARIES
SPECIAL NEEDS **DYSLEXIA** **DIET** abcd
ASSOCIATION IAPS **FOUNDED** 1945 **RELIGIOUS AFFILIATION** C of E

MAP 5 E 8
LOCATION Rural
DAY **RAIL** b **AIR** a
SPORT alpq AB
OTHER LANGUAGES
ACTIVITIES cghj
OTHER SUBJECTS
FACILITIES ON SITE
EXAM BOARDS
RETAKES **NVQ COURSES**

A-level AS GCSE OTHER c e lm o s v
B E G K O R
cde

C — Burys Court; Leigh; Reigate; Surrey RH2 8RE
Tel: 01306 611372 *D.V.W.White*

		Boys	Age	Girls	Age	TOTAL		Boys	Girls
Day	£595	78	3-14	38	3-14	116	SIXTH		
Weekly									
Boarding									

ENTRY REQUIREMENTS Interview
SCHOLARSHIPS & BURSARIES
SPECIAL NEEDS w **DYSLEXIA** **DIET**
ASSOCIATION IAPS **FOUNDED** 1953 **RELIGIOUS AFFILIATION** C of E

MAP 4 G 5
LOCATION Rural
DAY √ **RAIL** a **AIR** a
SPORT abcefhjlmox AB
OTHER LANGUAGES
ACTIVITIES cfghjor A
OTHER SUBJECTS abch
FACILITIES ON SITE hj
EXAM BOARDS
RETAKES **NVQ COURSES**

A-level AS GCSE OTHER e l o q v
B G
cde

SURREY continued

C | Canbury School; Kingston Hill; Kingston-upon-Thames; Surrey KT2 7LN
Tel: 0181 549 8622 (Fax: 0181 974 6018) *J.G.Wyatt*

		Boys	Age	Girls	Age	TOTAL		Boys	Girls
Day	£1575	42	10-16	11	10-16	53	SIXTH		
Weekly									
Boarding									

ENTRY REQUIREMENTS Report & Exam & Interview
SCHOLARSHIPS & BURSARIES Schol; Burs
SPECIAL NEEDS b **DYSLEXIA** **DIET**
ASSOCIATION ISAI **FOUNDED** 1982 **RELIGIOUS AFFILIATION** Non-denom

MAP 5 D 5
LOCATION Urban
DAY **RAIL** b **AIR** a
SPORT abdfhjptwx ABC
OTHER LANGUAGES a
ACTIVITIES fghjo
OTHER SUBJECTS abdh
FACILITIES ON SITE
EXAM BOARDS a
RETAKES a **NVQ COURSES**

A-level	AS	GCSE	OTHER
		e g i n v	l n u
		G P	B K O R
		de	f k

C | Caterham Preparatory School; Mottrams; Harestone Valley Road; Caterham; Surrey CR3 6YB
Tel: 01883 342097 (Fax: 01883 341230) *A.D.Moy*

		Boys	Age	Girls	Age	TOTAL		Boys	Girls
Day	£550-£1840	194	3-11	37	3-11	254	SIXTH		
Weekly	£3364		11-13		11-13				
Boarding	£3364	23	11-13		11-13				

ENTRY REQUIREMENTS Test & Interview
SCHOLARSHIPS & BURSARIES Schol; Burs; Mus; Forces; Clergy; AP
SPECIAL NEEDS Intw E **DYSLEXIA** de **DIET** acd
ASSOCIATION IAPS **FOUNDED** 1811 **RELIGIOUS AFFILIATION** U R C

MAP 5 F 7
LOCATION Rural
DAY **RAIL** b **AIR** a
SPORT abcefjlmopqstwx AB
OTHER LANGUAGES
ACTIVITIES cfghijloqst A
OTHER SUBJECTS bcfh
FACILITIES ON SITE abcdik
EXAM BOARDS
RETAKES **NVQ COURSES**

A-level	AS	GCSE	OTHER
		e g i l o v	AB G K OP R
			cde j

C | Caterham School; Harestone Valley; Caterham; Surrey CR3 6YA
Tel: 01883 343028 (Fax: 01883 347795) *R.A.E.Davey*

		Boys	Age	Girls	Age	TOTAL		Boys	Girls
Day	£1840-£1932	430	11-18	150	11-18	730	SIXTH	170	50
Weekly			11-18		11-18				
Boarding	£3532-£3732	130	11-18	20	11-18				

ENTRY REQUIREMENTS Test & Interview; Report & Interview; CEE & Interview
SCHOLARSHIPS & BURSARIES Schol; Burs; Mus; Forces; AP; VI Form
SPECIAL NEEDS abejlnt AE **DYSLEXIA** e **DIET** acd
ASSOCIATION HMC **FOUNDED** 1811 **RELIGIOUS AFFILIATION** U R C

MAP 5 F 7
LOCATION Rural
DAY ✓ **RAIL** a **AIR** a
SPORT abcdefhjklmnpqsuwx ABC
OTHER LANGUAGES a
ACTIVITIES cefghijklnopqstw AB
OTHER SUBJECTS abcdfh
FACILITIES ON SITE abcdek
EXAM BOARDS abd ADEH
RETAKES **NVQ COURSES**

A-level	AS	GCSE	OTHER
cd fghi op v	cd g l q	d g i o v	l n su
B GH K P R		B G K OP R X	C F J MNO QR
c efg j l		cdefg j l	d i l

3g | Charterhouse; Godalming GU7 2DJ
Tel: 01483 291500 (Fax: 01483 291647) *P.Hobson*

		Boys	Age	Girls	Age	TOTAL		Boys	Girls
Day	£3516	17	13-18	5	16-18	700	SIXTH	231	77
Weekly									
Boarding	£4255	606	13-18	72	16-18				

ENTRY REQUIREMENTS CEE; Scholarship Exam
SCHOLARSHIPS & BURSARIES Schol; Burs; Art; Mus; AP; VI Form
SPECIAL NEEDS ejl **DYSLEXIA** **DIET** abcd
ASSOCIATION HMC **FOUNDED** 1611 **RELIGIOUS AFFILIATION** C of E

MAP 3 E 5
LOCATION Rural
DAY **RAIL** a **AIR** a
SPORT abcdefghjkmnoprstuwx ABC
OTHER LANGUAGES
ACTIVITIES abcefghijklnopqrstuwx AB
OTHER SUBJECTS abcfh
FACILITIES ON SITE abcdefhiki
EXAM BOARDS abd BEGH
RETAKES **NVQ COURSES**

A-level	AS	GCSE	OTHER
efg i op v x	B g q	e g i l o v	u
B GH K P R	ef	B G K M OPQR X	H M U
cdefg j l		cdefgh j l	e k

B | Chinthurst School; Tadworth; Surrey KT20 5QZ
Tel: 01737 812011 (Fax: 01737 814835) *T.J.Egan*

		Boys	Age	Girls	Age	TOTAL		Boys	Girls
Day	£420-£1225	375	3-13			375	SIXTH		
Weekly									
Boarding									

ENTRY REQUIREMENTS Assessment
SCHOLARSHIPS & BURSARIES
SPECIAL NEEDS blnq **DYSLEXIA** e **DIET** acd
ASSOCIATION IAPS **FOUNDED** 1911 **RELIGIOUS AFFILIATION**

MAP 5 E 7
LOCATION Rural
DAY **RAIL** a **AIR** a
SPORT abcefjklmosuwx ABC
OTHER LANGUAGES
ACTIVITIES fghijoqrtw A
OTHER SUBJECTS bcfh
FACILITIES ON SITE bhik
EXAM BOARDS
RETAKES **NVQ COURSES**

A-level	AS	GCSE	OTHER
		b e g i l no v	B G K OP R
			cde j

SURREY continued

City of London Freemen's School; Ashtead Park; Surrey KT21 1ET
Tel: 01372 277933 (Fax: 01372 276165) *D.C.Haywood*

		Boys	Age	Girls	Age	TOTAL	Boys	Girls
Day	£1446-£1941	301	7-18	370	7-18	707	42	71
Weekly	£2442-£2937	13	7-18	7	7-18			
Boarding	£2535-£3030	9	7-18	7	7-18			

SIXTH

MAP 5 D 7
LOCATION Rural
DAY **RAIL** a **AIR** a
SPORT abcdefghklmnopqswx AB
OTHER LANGUAGES
ACTIVITIES ghijknost AD

ENTRY REQUIREMENTS CEE; Scholarship Exam; Report & Exam & Interview
SCHOLARSHIPS & BURSARIES Schol; Burs; Mus; AP; VI Form
SPECIAL NEEDS bgjl G
DYSLEXIA **DIET** a
ASSOCIATION HMC **FOUNDED** 1854 **RELIGIOUS AFFILIATION** C of E
OTHER SUBJECTS bcfh
FACILITIES ON SITE abhik
EXAM BOARDS abd ABDEGH
RETAKES **NVQ COURSES**

A-level: d ghi l no q uv x   B GH K P   c ef l
AS: f l q vw   G K U   ef l
GCSE: de g i l n q v x   ABC G K P R W   cdef j l
OTHER: o

Claremont Fan Court School; Claremont Drive; Esher; Surrey KT10 9LY
Tel: 01372 467841 (Fax: 01372 471109) *Mrs P.B.Farrar*

		Boys	Age	Girls	Age	TOTAL	Boys	Girls
Day	£555-£1895	297	3-18	333	3-18	646	24	48
Weekly								
Boarding	£2880-£2995	7	11-18	9	11-18			

SIXTH

MAP 5 D 6
LOCATION Urban
DAY ✓ **RAIL** a **AIR** a
SPORT abcdefjklmnopqstwx BC
OTHER LANGUAGES
ACTIVITIES cfghijkoqs AB

ENTRY REQUIREMENTS Report & Exam & Interview
SCHOLARSHIPS & BURSARIES Schol; Burs
SPECIAL NEEDS
DYSLEXIA **DIET** a
ASSOCIATION SHMIS **FOUNDED** **RELIGIOUS AFFILIATION** Chr Sci
OTHER SUBJECTS abcdefgh
FACILITIES ON SITE bcgjk
EXAM BOARDS abcd ADEGL
RETAKES **NVQ COURSES**

A-level: efghi nopq v x   B GH K P U   cdef j
AS: C
GCSE: e g i l no q v   BC G K OP R W   cdef j l
OTHER: u   O R

Clewborough House Prep. School; Camberley; Surrey GU15 1NX
Tel: 01276 64799 (Fax: 01276 24424) *Commander M.F.Clarke*

		Boys	Age	Girls	Age	TOTAL	Boys	Girls
Day	£545-£1440 X	121	2-13	70	2-13	191		
Weekly								
Boarding								

SIXTH

MAP 3 E 5
LOCATION Rural
DAY **RAIL** a **AIR** a
SPORT acdefhjlmopqtuvwx AB
OTHER LANGUAGES
ACTIVITIES actghjqwx A

ENTRY REQUIREMENTS Test & Interview
SCHOLARSHIPS & BURSARIES Schol; Burs; Forces; Teachers; Siblings
SPECIAL NEEDS an
DYSLEXIA **DIET** abd
ASSOCIATION ISAI **FOUNDED** 1969 **RELIGIOUS AFFILIATION** Inter-denom
OTHER SUBJECTS abch
FACILITIES ON SITE jk
EXAM BOARDS
RETAKES **NVQ COURSES**

A-level:
AS:
GCSE:
OTHER: de l no v   B E G K O R   cde j l

Coworth Park School; Valley End; Chobham; Woking; Surrey GU24 8TE
Tel: 01276 855707 (Fax: 01276 856043) *Mrs P.S.Middleton*

		Boys	Age	Girls	Age	TOTAL	Boys	Girls
Day	£620-£1365	24	3-7	133	3-11	157		
Weekly								
Boarding								

SIXTH

MAP 3 E 4
LOCATION Rural
DAY **RAIL** a **AIR** a
SPORT jlmpqx B
OTHER LANGUAGES
ACTIVITIES cghjx

ENTRY REQUIREMENTS Test & Interview
SCHOLARSHIPS & BURSARIES
SPECIAL NEEDS bgjknw B
DYSLEXIA ef **DIET**
ASSOCIATION IAPS **FOUNDED** 1963 **RELIGIOUS AFFILIATION** Inter-denom
OTHER SUBJECTS bch
FACILITIES ON SITE hj
EXAM BOARDS
RETAKES **NVQ COURSES**

A-level:
AS:
GCSE:
OTHER: e lm v   B G   cde

Cranleigh Preparatory School; Cranleigh; Surrey GU6 8QH
Tel: 01483 274199 (Fax: 01483 277136) *M.R.Keppie*

		Boys	Age	Girls	Age	TOTAL	Boys	Girls
Day	£2090 X	99	7-13			178		
Weekly								
Boarding	£2770	79	7-13					

SIXTH

MAP 3 F 5
LOCATION Rural
DAY **RAIL** b **AIR** a
SPORT abcefgijklmqsuwx AB
OTHER LANGUAGES
ACTIVITIES fghijlmopqstw A

ENTRY REQUIREMENTS Report & Exam & Interview
SCHOLARSHIPS & BURSARIES Schol; AP
SPECIAL NEEDS ajkpqw Gl
DYSLEXIA **DIET** d
ASSOCIATION IAPS **FOUNDED** 1881 . **RELIGIOUS AFFILIATION** C of E
OTHER SUBJECTS acfh
FACILITIES ON SITE abcdhijk
EXAM BOARDS
RETAKES **NVQ COURSES**

A-level:
AS:
GCSE:
OTHER: cde g i l o s uv   B G K OP R   cde g j

SURREY *continued*

Cranleigh School; Cranleigh; Surrey GU6 8QQ
Tel: 01483 273997 (Fax: 01483 267398) *T.A.A.Hart*

		Boys	Age	Girls	Age	TOTAL		Boys	Girls
Day	£3110	- 78	13-18	4	16-18	513	SIXTH	176	76
Weekly Boarding	£4140	359	13-18	72	16-18				

ENTRY REQUIREMENTS CEE; Exam & Interview
SCHOLARSHIPS & BURSARIES Schol; Mus; Forces; Clergy; AP
SPECIAL NEEDS eijl E **DYSLEXIA** **DIET** acd
ASSOCIATION HMC **FOUNDED** 1865 **RELIGIOUS AFFILIATION** C of E

MAP 3 F 5
LOCATION Rural
DAY **RAIL** b **AIR** a
SPORT abcdefgijkmnopqstuwx B
OTHER LANGUAGES a
ACTIVITIES efghijklmnopqstuw A
OTHER SUBJECTS bcfh
FACILITIES ON SITE abcdegijkl
EXAM BOARDS abd ABEGHL
RETAKES **NVQ COURSES**

A-level: B GH K P R e g i l n pq v x c ef l
AS: B G K R l q ef l
GCSE: B G K e g i l o v cdef hj l
OTHER: B G K P e g i l o v cdef j l

Cranmore School; W.Horsley; Leatherhead; Surrey KT24 6AT;
Tel: 01483 284137 (Fax: 01483 281277) *K.A.Cheney*

		Boys	Age	Girls	Age	TOTAL		Boys	Girls
Day	£160-£1430	457	3-13			457	SIXTH		
Weekly Boarding									

ENTRY REQUIREMENTS Test & Interview
SCHOLARSHIPS & BURSARIES
SPECIAL NEEDS beijklntuw I **DYSLEXIA** **DIET**
ASSOCIATION IAPS **FOUNDED** 1968 **RELIGIOUS AFFILIATION** R C

MAP 3 F 5
LOCATION Rural
DAY **RAIL** b **AIR** a
SPORT abcdefghjklrswx AB
OTHER LANGUAGES
ACTIVITIES fghjoqtx A
OTHER SUBJECTS cfh
FACILITIES ON SITE bchikl
EXAM BOARDS
RETAKES **NVQ COURSES**

OTHER: B G K OP R de g i l o v cde j

Danes Hill; Oxshott; Surrey KT22 0JG
Tel: 01372 842509 (Fax: 01372 844452) *R.Parfitt*

		Boys	Age	Girls	Age	TOTAL		Boys	Girls
Day	£244-£1702	401	2-13	277	2-13	678	SIXTH		
Weekly Boarding									

ENTRY REQUIREMENTS Test & Interview
SCHOLARSHIPS & BURSARIES Schol; Mus
SPECIAL NEEDS bj i **DYSLEXIA** **DIET** ab
ASSOCIATION IAPS **FOUNDED** **RELIGIOUS AFFILIATION** Non-denom

MAP 3 F 5
LOCATION Rural
DAY ✓ **RAIL** b **AIR** a
SPORT abcefjklmnopqstuwx ABC
OTHER LANGUAGES a
ACTIVITIES acfghijnoqw A
OTHER SUBJECTS ch
FACILITIES ON SITE bhijk
EXAM BOARDS
RETAKES **NVQ COURSES**

OTHER: B EG K OP R de g i lmno v cdef j

Downsend Girls Preparatory School; 1 Leatherhead Road; Leatherhead; Surrey KT22 8TJ
Tel: 01372 362668 (Fax: 01372 363367) *Mrs.Harvey*

		Boys	Age	Girls	Age	TOTAL		Boys	Girls
Day	£295-£1425	79	2-7	155	2-11	234	SIXTH		
Weekly Boarding									

ENTRY REQUIREMENTS Interview
SCHOLARSHIPS & BURSARIES
SPECIAL NEEDS abln Bl **DYSLEXIA** **DIET** a
ASSOCIATION IAPS **FOUNDED** 1979 **RELIGIOUS AFFILIATION** Inter-denom

MAP 3 F 5
LOCATION Urban
DAY **RAIL** a **AIR** a
SPORT acejlmnopqx B
OTHER LANGUAGES
ACTIVITIES cghjot A
OTHER SUBJECTS ch
FACILITIES ON SITE bchi
EXAM BOARDS
RETAKES **NVQ COURSES**

OTHER: B G K OP R e g i lmno v cde

Downsend School; Leatherhead; Surrey KT22 8TJ
Tel: 01372 372197 (Fax: 01372 363367) *A.D.White*

		Boys	Age	Girls	Age	TOTAL		Boys	Girls
Day	£1425	309	7-13			309	SIXTH		
Weekly Boarding									

ENTRY REQUIREMENTS Assessment & Interview
SCHOLARSHIPS & BURSARIES
SPECIAL NEEDS ej Gl **DYSLEXIA** **DIET** a
ASSOCIATION IAPS **FOUNDED** 1891 **RELIGIOUS AFFILIATION** Non-denom

MAP 3 F 5
LOCATION Rural
DAY **RAIL** a **AIR** a
SPORT abcefjlsx AB
OTHER LANGUAGES
ACTIVITIES fghjot
OTHER SUBJECTS bcfh
FACILITIES ON SITE bchi
EXAM BOARDS
RETAKES **NVQ COURSES**

OTHER: B G K OP R e g i l no v cde j

SURREY continued

Duke of Kent School; Woolpit; Ewhurst; Cranleigh; Surrey GU6 7NS
Tel: 01483 277 313 (Fax: 01483 273 862) *R.K.Wilson*

		Boys	Age	Girls	Age	TOTAL		Boys	Girls
Day	£750-£1920	37	4-13	12	4-13	160	SIXTH		
Weekly			7-13		7-13				
Boarding	£2455-£2745	63	7-13	48	7-13				

MAP 3 E 5
LOCATION Rural
DAY RAIL b AIR a
SPORT acefjlmnopqsuwx AB
OTHER LANGUAGES
ACTIVITIES cfghjnoprst
OTHER SUBJECTS bcfh
FACILITIES ON SITE achi
EXAM BOARDS
RETAKES NVQ COURSES

ENTRY REQUIREMENTS Assessment & Interview
SCHOLARSHIPS & BURSARIES Burs; Siblings
SPECIAL NEEDS abjlnw BE   **DYSLEXIA** cef   **DIET** ad
ASSOCIATION IAPS   **FOUNDED** 1976   **RELIGIOUS AFFILIATION** C of E

A-level: de g i lmno q v
          BC G K NOP R
          cdef j l

AS

GCSE

OTHER

Dunottar School; High Trees Road; Reigate; Surrey RH2 7EL
Tel: 01737 761945 (Fax: 01737 779450) *Miss J.Burnell*

		Boys	Age	Girls	Age	TOTAL		Boys	Girls
Day	£840-£1510			442	5-18	442	SIXTH		39
Weekly									
Boarding									

MAP 4 G 5
LOCATION Rural
DAY ✓ RAIL a AIR a
SPORT abcefhjlmnpqwx ABC
OTHER LANGUAGES
ACTIVITIES cghijknopqrst A
OTHER SUBJECTS bcfh
FACILITIES ON SITE bchi
EXAM BOARDS abcd AEGH
RETAKES NVQ COURSES

ENTRY REQUIREMENTS CEE; Exam
SCHOLARSHIPS & BURSARIES Schol; Mus; VI Form
SPECIAL NEEDS bkl G   **DYSLEXIA**   **DIET** a
ASSOCIATION GSA   **FOUNDED** 1926   **RELIGIOUS AFFILIATION** Inter-denom

A-level: defghi l n p   v
         B GH K   PRT W
         cdef kl

AS: G
     c

GCSE: defghi l   p   v
      BC GH K   OP R T
      cdef kl

OTHER: mn   u
        K
        h

Eagle House; Sandhurst; Camberley; Surrey GU17 8PH
Tel: 01344 772134 (Fax: 01344 779039) *S.J.Carder*

		Boys	Age	Girls	Age	TOTAL		Boys	Girls
Day	£1235-£2125	131	4-13			183	SIXTH		
Weekly	£3020	28	8-13						
Boarding	£3020	24	8-13						

MAP 3 E 5
LOCATION Rural
DAY RAIL b AIR a
SPORT abcefijklmosuwx ABC
OTHER LANGUAGES
ACTIVITIES afghijorstw
OTHER SUBJECTS cfh
FACILITIES ON SITE abcdhi
EXAM BOARDS
RETAKES NVQ COURSES

ENTRY REQUIREMENTS Test
SCHOLARSHIPS & BURSARIES Schol; Mus
SPECIAL NEEDS bjlnqs AH   **DYSLEXIA** e   **DIET** ad
ASSOCIATION IAPS   **FOUNDED** 1820   **RELIGIOUS AFFILIATION** C of E

A-level

AS

GCSE

OTHER: e g i   no q v
        B G K   OP R
        cde j

Edgeborough; Frensham; Surrey GU10 3AH
Tel: 01252 792495 (Fax: 01252 795156) *R.A.Jackson*

		Boys	Age	Girls	Age	TOTAL		Boys	Girls
Day	£1235-£2285	118	3-13	60	3-13	214	SIXTH		
Weekly	£2705-£2990	22	7-13	6	7-13				
Boarding	£2705-£2990	8	7-13		7-13				

MAP 3 E 5
LOCATION Rural
DAY RAIL a AIR a
SPORT abcefklmpqstuwx ABC
OTHER LANGUAGES
ACTIVITIES acfghijoqrstwx A
OTHER SUBJECTS abcfh
FACILITIES ON SITE abcdhjkl
EXAM BOARDS
RETAKES NVQ COURSES

ENTRY REQUIREMENTS Assessment & Interview
SCHOLARSHIPS & BURSARIES Burs; Forces; ARA; Siblings
SPECIAL NEEDS g   **DYSLEXIA**   **DIET** ad
ASSOCIATION IAPS   **FOUNDED** 1906   **RELIGIOUS AFFILIATION** C of E

A-level

AS

GCSE

OTHER: e g i l o   v
        B G K   OP R
        cde g j

Elmhurst Ballet School; Heathcote Road; Camberley; Surrey GU15 2EU
Tel: 01276 65301 (Fax: 01276 670320) *J.Mc Namara*

		Boys	Age	Girls	Age	TOTAL		Boys	Girls
Day	£2005-£2230	6	8-19	28	8-19	235	SIXTH		
Weekly			8-19		8-19				
Boarding	£2860-£3040	21	8-19	180	8-19				

MAP 3 E 5
LOCATION Urban
DAY RAIL a AIR a
SPORT bchpqx AC
OTHER LANGUAGES ac
ACTIVITIES cfghjlno
OTHER SUBJECTS bcegh
FACILITIES ON SITE dgk
EXAM BOARDS d ABEGL
RETAKES NVQ COURSES

ENTRY REQUIREMENTS Interview
SCHOLARSHIPS & BURSARIES
SPECIAL NEEDS ajnqu BEGI   **DYSLEXIA** de   **DIET** ab
ASSOCIATION SHMIS   **FOUNDED** 1911   **RELIGIOUS AFFILIATION** C of E

A-level: d   n   v
           B G K
           c ef l

AS

GCSE: d   n   v
       B E G K   R
       def   l

OTHER: d   lmn   v
        BC E G K O R W
        cdef   l

SURREY continued

Epsom College; Epsom; Surrey KT17 4JQ
Tel: 01372 723621 (Fax: 01372 726277) *A.H.Beadles*

		Boys	Age	Girls	Age	TOTAL		Boys	Girls
Day	£2872	283	13-18	16	15-18	657	SIXTH	246	61
Weekly	£3812	185	13-18	27	15-18				
Boarding	£3865	128	13-18	18	15-18				

ENTRY REQUIREMENTS CEE; Exam; Scholarship Exam
SCHOLARSHIPS & BURSARIES Schol; Art; Mus; AP; VI Form; ARA
SPECIAL NEEDS bejqstw AEGHI
DYSLEXIA   **DIET** acd
ASSOCIATION HMC   **FOUNDED** 1853   **RELIGIOUS AFFILIATION** C of E

MAP 5 E 6
LOCATION Urban
DAY   **RAIL** a   **AIR** a
SPORT abcdefghjkmnopqstuwx ABC
OTHER LANGUAGES
ACTIVITIES aefghijknopqrstvw AB
OTHER SUBJECTS bcfh
FACILITIES ON SITE abcdghik
EXAM BOARDS abcd AEH
RETAKES   **NVQ COURSES**

A-level e g i   op   v x
B GH K   P R U
c ef j
AS
GCSE e g i   o   v
B   G K   P R
cdef j l
OTHER l no q   u
K   NO
e

Ewell Castle Junior School; Spring Street; Ewell; Surrey KT17 1UH
Tel: 0181 393 3952 (Fax: 0181 786 8218) *Mrs V.A.Goode*

		Boys	Age	Girls	Age	TOTAL		Boys	Girls
Day	£784- £990	103	3-11	25	3-11	128	SIXTH		
Weekly									
Boarding									

ENTRY REQUIREMENTS Test; Interview; Assessment
SCHOLARSHIPS & BURSARIES
SPECIAL NEEDS   **DYSLEXIA**   **DIET**
ASSOCIATION IAPS   **FOUNDED** 1926   **RELIGIOUS AFFILIATION** C of E

MAP 5 E 6
LOCATION
DAY   **RAIL** a   **AIR** a
SPORT abcefhjlmpqwx B
OTHER LANGUAGES
ACTIVITIES fghnpwx
OTHER SUBJECTS bch
FACILITIES ON SITE abch
EXAM BOARDS
RETAKES   **NVQ COURSES**

A-level
AS
GCSE
OTHER de g   lmno   s v
B E G K   O R
cde

Ewell Castle School; Church Street; Ewell; Surrey KT17 2AW
Tel: 0181 393 1413 (Fax: 0181 786 8218) *R.A.Fewtrell*

		Boys	Age	Girls	Age	TOTAL		Boys	Girls
Day	£1405-£1475	296	11-19	1	16-19	297	SIXTH	57	1
Weekly									
Boarding									

ENTRY REQUIREMENTS CEE; Test & Interview
SCHOLARSHIPS & BURSARIES Schol; VI Form
SPECIAL NEEDS beijlnqtw GHI   **DYSLEXIA** def   **DIET** abcd
ASSOCIATION SHMIS   **FOUNDED** 1926   **RELIGIOUS AFFILIATION** C of E

MAP 5 E 6
LOCATION Urban
DAY   **RAIL** a   **AIR** a
SPORT abcdefghjklmsuwx ABC
OTHER LANGUAGES
ACTIVITIES efghijkopstuwx A
OTHER SUBJECTS abcfh
FACILITIES ON SITE bch
EXAM BOARDS abd BDEI
RETAKES a   **NVQ COURSES**

A-level e g i   opq uv
AB   GH K   OP R
cdef   l
AS g l   u
G
e
GCSE e ghi   o q   v
AB E G K   OP R
cdef   l
OTHER h l no   uv
AB E G K   OP R
bcd f

Feltonfleet School; Cobham; Surrey KT11 1DR
Tel: 01932 862264 (Fax: 01932 860280) *D.T.Cherry*

		Boys	Age	Girls	Age	TOTAL		Boys	Girls
Day	£600-£1895	115	3-13	9	3-7	166	SIXTH		
Weekly	£2550	20	7-13		7-13				
Boarding	£2550	22	7-13		7-13				

ENTRY REQUIREMENTS Scholarship Exam; Report; Test & Interview
SCHOLARSHIPS & BURSARIES Schol; Burs; Mus; ARA
SPECIAL NEEDS   **DYSLEXIA**   **DIET**
ASSOCIATION IAPS   **FOUNDED** 1903   **RELIGIOUS AFFILIATION** C of E

MAP 5 C 7
LOCATION Rural
DAY   **RAIL** a   **AIR** a
SPORT abefjklmostuwx ABC
OTHER LANGUAGES
ACTIVITIES afghijlnorstwx A
OTHER SUBJECTS cdfh
FACILITIES ON SITE cehik
EXAM BOARDS
RETAKES   **NVQ COURSES**

A-level
AS
GCSE
OTHER e g i l o   v
B   G   P
cdef j

Flexlands School Educational Trust Ltd; Station Road; Chobham; Surrey GU24 8AG
Tel: 01276 858841 (Fax: 01276 856554) *Mrs S.J.Shaw*

		Boys	Age	Girls	Age	TOTAL		Boys	Girls
Day	£538-£1406	10	3-4	153	3-11	163	SIXTH		
Weekly									
Boarding									

ENTRY REQUIREMENTS Interview
SCHOLARSHIPS & BURSARIES
SPECIAL NEEDS nw I   **DYSLEXIA** e   **DIET** a
ASSOCIATION IAPS   **FOUNDED** 1935   **RELIGIOUS AFFILIATION** C of E

MAP 3 E 5
LOCATION Rural
DAY   **RAIL** a   **AIR** a
SPORT acflmopqx B
OTHER LANGUAGES
ACTIVITIES cgjox
OTHER SUBJECTS bch
FACILITIES ON SITE
EXAM BOARDS
RETAKES   **NVQ COURSES**

A-level
AS
GCSE
OTHER ef   l o   v
B   G K   O R
cde

255

SURREY continued

C — Frensham Heights; Rowledge; Farnham GU10 4EA
Tel: 01252 792134 (Fax: 01252 794335) *P.M.de Voil*

		Boys	Age	Girls	Age	TOTAL		Boys	Girls
Day	£2490	92	11-18	83	11-18	290	SIXTH	40	36
Weekly	£3890		11-18		11-18				
Boarding	£3890	48	11-18	67	11-18				

MAP 3 E 5
LOCATION Rural
DAY ✓ RAIL a AIR a
SPORT abcdefghjklmnopqstuwx ABC
OTHER LANGUAGES a
ACTIVITIES cfghjkoqstw AB
OTHER SUBJECTS bcdfgh
FACILITIES ON SITE bceghjk
EXAM BOARDS abcd ABDEHI
RETAKES a   NVQ COURSES

ENTRY REQUIREMENTS CEE; Exam & Interview; Report & Interview; Report & Exam & Interview
SCHOLARSHIPS & BURSARIES Schol; Burs; Art; Mus; Chor; VI Form
SPECIAL NEEDS abeghijklnqtuvw H **DYSLEXIA** **DIET** abcd
ASSOCIATION HMC **FOUNDED** 1925 **RELIGIOUS AFFILIATION** Inter-denom

A-level: de ghi mno v / B G K PQ / c ef
AS:
GCSE: de g i mnop v / B G K NOP / cdef l
OTHER: f l u / R

C — Glenesk School; East Horsley; Surrey KT24 6NS
Tel: 01483 282329 *Mrs S.Johnson*

		Boys	Age	Girls	Age	TOTAL		Boys	Girls
Day	£450-£1250	73	2-8	92	2-8	165	SIXTH		
Weekly									
Boarding									

MAP 3 F 5
LOCATION Urban
DAY   RAIL b AIR a
SPORT aefjlmsx
OTHER LANGUAGES
ACTIVITIES
OTHER SUBJECTS ch
FACILITIES ON SITE hi
EXAM BOARDS
RETAKES   NVQ COURSES

ENTRY REQUIREMENTS
SCHOLARSHIPS & BURSARIES
SPECIAL NEEDS n **DYSLEXIA** g **DIET**
ASSOCIATION ISAI **FOUNDED** 1926 **RELIGIOUS AFFILIATION** C of E

A-level:
AS:
GCSE:
OTHER: e lmno s v / B G K O R / cde

G — Greenacre School; Sutton Lane; Banstead; Surrey SM7 3RA
Tel: 01737 352114 (Fax: 01737 352114) *Mrs P.M.Wood*

		Boys	Age	Girls	Age	TOTAL		Boys	Girls
Day	£420-£1650	3		387	3-18	390	SIXTH		40
Weekly									
Boarding									

MAP 5 E 7
LOCATION Rural
DAY   RAIL c AIR a
SPORT abchilnopqwx ABC
OTHER LANGUAGES a
ACTIVITIES fghijknoqs
OTHER SUBJECTS abcdeh
FACILITIES ON SITE bcghi
EXAM BOARDS abd ABEG
RETAKES ab NVQ COURSES

ENTRY REQUIREMENTS Report & Exam & Interview
SCHOLARSHIPS & BURSARIES Schol; Forces; VI Form
SPECIAL NEEDS bgjlnqw GL **DYSLEXIA** g **DIET** acd
ASSOCIATION GSA **FOUNDED** 1933 **RELIGIOUS AFFILIATION** Inter-denom

A-level: cdefghi n p uv / B G K N P R U W / cdef j l
AS: i
GCSE: cde g i l no q v / B E G K NOP R U W / cdef j l
OTHER: l o q / O

G — Guildford High School for Girls; London Road; Guildford; Surrey GU1 1SJ
Tel: 01483 61440 (Fax: 01483 306516) *Mrs S.H.Singer*

		Boys	Age	Girls	Age	TOTAL		Boys	Girls
Day	£1008-£1700			730	4-18	730	SIXTH		120
Weekly									
Boarding									

MAP 3 E 5
LOCATION Urban
DAY   RAIL a AIR b
SPORT abcflnpqx AB
OTHER LANGUAGES
ACTIVITIES fghijkot BD
OTHER SUBJECTS bcdfh
FACILITIES ON SITE cgi
EXAM BOARDS abd ABEH
RETAKES   NVQ COURSES

ENTRY REQUIREMENTS Report & Exam & Interview
SCHOLARSHIPS & BURSARIES Schol; Mus; Clergy; AP; VI Form
SPECIAL NEEDS bl **DYSLEXIA** **DIET** a
ASSOCIATION GSA **FOUNDED** 1888 **RELIGIOUS AFFILIATION** C of E

A-level: d fgi n p v / BC GH K P R / c efg j l
AS: d / G K / j
GCSE: d g i v / BC G K P R X / cdefgh jkl
OTHER: lmno q / K O R

B — Hall Grove; London Road; Bagshot; Surrey GU19 5HZ
Tel: 01276 473059 (Fax: 01276 452003) *A.R.Graham*

		Boys	Age	Girls	Age	TOTAL		Boys	Girls
Day	£1205-£1510	227	4-13			227	SIXTH		
Weekly									
Boarding									

MAP 3 E 4
LOCATION Rural
DAY   RAIL a AIR a
SPORT abefhjklmoqsx AB
OTHER LANGUAGES
ACTIVITIES fghjoqrst A
OTHER SUBJECTS abcfh
FACILITIES ON SITE abcjl
EXAM BOARDS
RETAKES   NVQ COURSES

ENTRY REQUIREMENTS Test; Interview
SCHOLARSHIPS & BURSARIES
SPECIAL NEEDS abnr GL **DYSLEXIA** **DIET**
ASSOCIATION IAPS **FOUNDED** 1957 **RELIGIOUS AFFILIATION** Inter-denom

A-level:
AS:
GCSE:
OTHER: e l o q uv / AB E G K R / cde g j l

SURREY *continued*

G — Halstead Prep. School for Girls; Woodham Rise; Woking; Surrey GU21 4EE
Tel: 01483 772682 (Fax: 01483 757611) *Mrs A.Hancock*

	Boys	Age	Girls	Age	TOTAL	SIXTH	Boys	Girls
Day £615-£1275			207	3-11	207			
Weekly								
Boarding								

ENTRY REQUIREMENTS Assessment & Interview
SCHOLARSHIPS & BURSARIES
SPECIAL NEEDS bkt A **DYSLEXIA** **DIET** abcd
ASSOCIATION IAPS **FOUNDED** 1927 **RELIGIOUS AFFILIATION** C of E

MAP 3 F 5
LOCATION Urban
DAY **RAIL** a **AIR** a
SPORT apqx B
OTHER LANGUAGES
ACTIVITIES gj
OTHER SUBJECTS bcfh
FACILITIES ON SITE
EXAM BOARDS
RETAKES **NVQ COURSES**

A-level | AS | GCSE | OTHER: e lmno v / B E G K O R / cde

B — Haslemere Prep. School; The Heights; Hill Road; Haslemere; Surrey GU27 2JP
Tel: 01428 642350 (Fax: 01428 645314) *A.C.Morrison*

	Boys	Age	Girls	Age	TOTAL	SIXTH	Boys	Girls
Day £1280-£1650 X	178	5-14			178			
Weekly								
Boarding								

ENTRY REQUIREMENTS Test; Interview
SCHOLARSHIPS & BURSARIES
SPECIAL NEEDS bjkln I **DYSLEXIA** **DIET** acd
ASSOCIATION IAPS **FOUNDED** 1954 **RELIGIOUS AFFILIATION** Inter-denom

MAP 3 E 6
LOCATION Urban
DAY ✓ **RAIL** a **AIR** a
SPORT abcefhjlqstwx ABC
OTHER LANGUAGES
ACTIVITIES afghijlopqt A
OTHER SUBJECTS cfh
FACILITIES ON SITE ach
EXAM BOARDS
RETAKES **NVQ COURSES**

A-level | AS | GCSE | OTHER: cde g i l no q v / AB B G K OP R / cde j

---

C — Hawthorns,The; Pendell Court; Bletchingley; Surrey RH1 4QJ
Tel: 01883 743048 (Fax: 01883 744256) *T.R.Johns*

	Boys	Age	Girls	Age	TOTAL	SIXTH	Boys	Girls
Day £345-£1490 X	252	3-13	79	3-13	331			
Weekly								
Boarding								

ENTRY REQUIREMENTS Assessment & Interview
SCHOLARSHIPS & BURSARIES Burs; Clergy; Siblings
SPECIAL NEEDS n **DYSLEXIA** e **DIET** a
ASSOCIATION IAPS **FOUNDED** 1926 **RELIGIOUS AFFILIATION** C of E

MAP 4 G 5
LOCATION Rural
DAY **RAIL** a **AIR** a
SPORT abcefjklmnpqstuwx AB
OTHER LANGUAGES
ACTIVITIES cfghijloqtw A
OTHER SUBJECTS abc
FACILITIES ON SITE i
EXAM BOARDS
RETAKES **NVQ COURSES**

A-level | AS | GCSE | OTHER: e g i lmno st v / B G K OP R / cde j

---

C — Hazelwood School; Wolfs Hill; Limpsfield; Oxted; Surrey RH8 0QU
Tel: 01883 712194 (Fax: 01883 716135) *A.M.Synge*

	Boys	Age	Girls	Age	TOTAL	SIXTH	Boys	Girls
Day £515-£1840 X	218	3-13	59	3-13	297			
Weekly £2415	20	10-13		10-13				
Boarding								

ENTRY REQUIREMENTS Report; Assessment
SCHOLARSHIPS & BURSARIES
SPECIAL NEEDS ln B **DYSLEXIA** e **DIET**
ASSOCIATION IAPS **FOUNDED** 1890 **RELIGIOUS AFFILIATION** C of E

MAP 6 G 8
LOCATION Rural
DAY **RAIL** a **AIR** a
SPORT acefjklpqswx AB
OTHER LANGUAGES
ACTIVITIES cfghjlo
OTHER SUBJECTS abch
FACILITIES ON SITE abcdhik
EXAM BOARDS
RETAKES **NVQ COURSES**

A-level | AS | GCSE | OTHER: e g i lmno v / B G JK OP R / cde j

---

C — Hoe Bridge School; Hoe Place; Woking; Surrey GU22 8JE
Tel: 01483 760065 (Fax: 01483 757560) *R.W.K.Barr*

	Boys	Age	Girls	Age	TOTAL	SIXTH	Boys	Girls
Day £1650-£1895 X	165	7-14	5	7-14	179			
Weekly £2475-£2720	9	7-14						
Boarding								

ENTRY REQUIREMENTS Test & Interview
SCHOLARSHIPS & BURSARIES
SPECIAL NEEDS abejklnqtw AEGI **DYSLEXIA** e **DIET** acd
ASSOCIATION IAPS **FOUNDED** 1871 **RELIGIOUS AFFILIATION** C of E

MAP 3 F 5
LOCATION Rural
DAY **RAIL** a **AIR** a
SPORT abcdefgjkmopqrstuwx AB
OTHER LANGUAGES
ACTIVITIES acfghijloqrtw A
OTHER SUBJECTS bcfh
FACILITIES ON SITE behjk
EXAM BOARDS
RETAKES **NVQ COURSES**

A-level | AS | GCSE | OTHER: cdefg i l no v / BC G K OP R / cdefg j l

SURREY continued

C — Holy Cross Preparatory School; George Road; Kingston-upon-Thames; Surrey KT2 7NU Tel: 0181 942 0729 (Fax: 0181 336 0764) Mrs M.K.Hayes

Day £995-£1025
Weekly
Boarding

Boys 9 | Age 4-7 | Girls 225 | Age 4-11 | TOTAL 234 | SIXTH Boys | Girls

ENTRY REQUIREMENTS Assessment & Interview
SCHOLARSHIPS & BURSARIES Teachers
SPECIAL NEEDS aln A
ASSOCIATION IAPS FOUNDED 1930 RELIGIOUS AFFILIATION R C DYSLEXIA DIET

MAP 5 D 5
LOCATION Urban
DAY RAIL a AIR a
SPORT abcflmpq AB
OTHER LANGUAGES
ACTIVITIES cgo
OTHER SUBJECTS bch
FACILITIES ON SITE bch
EXAM BOARDS
RETAKES NVQ COURSES

A-level
AS
GCSE
OTHER: d lm o v
B E G K O R
cdef

C — King Edward's School; Witley; Nr. Godalming GU8 5SG Tel: 01428 682572 (Fax: 01428 685260) R.J.Fox

Day £2990
Weekly
Boarding £2080

Boys 77 / 216 | Age 11-18 / 11-18 | Girls 35 / 187 | Age 11-18 / 11-18 | TOTAL 515 | SIXTH Boys 82 | Girls 68

ENTRY REQUIREMENTS CEE; Exam
SCHOLARSHIPS & BURSARIES Schol; Burs; Forces; AP; VI Form
SPECIAL NEEDS abhijnot EGI
ASSOCIATION HMC FOUNDED 1553 RELIGIOUS AFFILIATION C of E DYSLEXIA DIET a

MAP 3 E 5
LOCATION Rural
DAY RAIL a AIR b
SPORT abcefghjklmopqstuvwx ABC
OTHER LANGUAGES
ACTIVITIES cfghijklnoqstuvw ABD
OTHER SUBJECTS abcfh
FACILITIES ON SITE bcdghi
EXAM BOARDS abcd ABDEGH
RETAKES NVQ COURSES

A-level: c efghi nop uv
ABC GH K N P R U W
cdef j l
AS: c e gh p v
GH P R U
ef j
GCSE: e g i no v
ABC E G K P R U
cdef j l
OTHER: l
o

B — Kingswood House; 56 West Hill; Epsom; Surrey KT19 8LG Tel: 01372 723590 (Fax: 01372 749081) G.F.M.Harvey

Day £980-£1435
Weekly
Boarding

Boys 201 | Age 4-13 | Girls | Age | TOTAL 201 | SIXTH Boys | Girls

ENTRY REQUIREMENTS Test & Interview
SCHOLARSHIPS & BURSARIES Schol; Burs; Clergy; Teachers; AP
SPECIAL NEEDS abgjln l
ASSOCIATION IAPS FOUNDED 1899 RELIGIOUS AFFILIATION Inter-denom DYSLEXIA ce DIET abcd

MAP 5 D 7
LOCATION Urban
DAY RAIL b AIR a
SPORT abefhjklmoqsx AB
OTHER LANGUAGES
ACTIVITIES fghjow A
OTHER SUBJECTS bch
FACILITIES ON SITE aj
EXAM BOARDS
RETAKES NVQ COURSES

A-level
AS
GCSE
OTHER: c efg i l o v
B G K OP R
cde j

B — Lanesborough School; Maori Road; Guildford; Surrey GU1 2EL Tel: 01483 502060 (Fax: 01483 306127) S.Deller

Day £585-£1540
Weekly
Boarding

Boys 314 | Age 4-14 | Girls | Age | TOTAL 314 | SIXTH Boys | Girls

ENTRY REQUIREMENTS Test & Interview
SCHOLARSHIPS & BURSARIES Chor
SPECIAL NEEDS ejkn Gl
ASSOCIATION IAPS FOUNDED 1930 RELIGIOUS AFFILIATION C of E DYSLEXIA e DIET abcd

MAP 3 E 5
LOCATION Urban
DAY RAIL a AIR a
SPORT abcefjlmostwx A
OTHER LANGUAGES
ACTIVITIES fghjort A
OTHER SUBJECTS bcfh
FACILITIES ON SITE
EXAM BOARDS
RETAKES NVQ COURSES

A-level
AS
GCSE
OTHER: c e g i l v
B G K OP R
cde j

G — Laverock School; Bluehouse Lane; Oxted; Surrey RH8 0AA Tel: 01883 714171 Mrs A.C.Paterson

Day £495-£1140
Weekly
Boarding

Boys | Age | Girls 155 | Age 3-11 | TOTAL 155 | SIXTH Boys | Girls

ENTRY REQUIREMENTS Interview; Assessment
SCHOLARSHIPS & BURSARIES
SPECIAL NEEDS ejkn Gl
ASSOCIATION IAPS FOUNDED 1929 RELIGIOUS AFFILIATION Inter-denom DYSLEXIA e DIET a

MAP 6 G 8
LOCATION Rural
DAY RAIL a AIR a
SPORT alpqx B
OTHER LANGUAGES
ACTIVITIES cgo
OTHER SUBJECTS ch
FACILITIES ON SITE j
EXAM BOARDS
RETAKES NVQ COURSES

A-level
AS
GCSE
OTHER: e l v
B G
cde

SURREY continued

C · Longacre Preparatory School; Shamley Green; Guildford GU5 0NQ
Tel: 0148 389 3225 *Mrs.L.Prince*

Day / Weekly Boarding — £280-£1300 ✗ | Boys 57 | Age 3-11 | Girls 93 | Age 3-11 | TOTAL 150 | SIXTH — Boys / Girls

ENTRY REQUIREMENTS Assessment & Interview
SCHOLARSHIPS & BURSARIES Schol; Burs; Mus; Teachers
SPECIAL NEEDS n
ASSOCIATION ISAI   **FOUNDED** 1940   **DYSLEXIA** de   **DIET** acd
RELIGIOUS AFFILIATION Inter-denom

MAP 3 E 5
LOCATION Rural
DAY ✓   **RAIL** b   **AIR** a
SPORT aefhjlmpqsx B
OTHER LANGUAGES
ACTIVITIES cfgjo
OTHER SUBJECTS abch
FACILITIES ON SITE hk
EXAM BOARDS
RETAKES   **NVQ COURSES**

A-level | AS | GCSE | OTHER e Imno q v / B EG K O R / cdef j

C · Lyndhurst School; 36 The Avenue; Camberley; Surrey GU15 3NE
Tel: 01276 22895 *R.L.Cunliffe*

Day / Weekly Boarding — £470-£1200 | Boys 107 | Age 3-12 | Girls 91 | Age 3-12 | TOTAL 198 | SIXTH — Boys / Girls

ENTRY REQUIREMENTS Assessment & Interview
SCHOLARSHIPS & BURSARIES Schol; Burs; Teachers
SPECIAL NEEDS aejknqw GHI
ASSOCIATION ISAI   **FOUNDED** 1895   **DYSLEXIA** e   **DIET**
RELIGIOUS AFFILIATION C of E

MAP 3 E 5
LOCATION Urban
DAY   **RAIL** a   **AIR** a
SPORT acejlmopqx AB
OTHER LANGUAGES
ACTIVITIES cfghtx
OTHER SUBJECTS fh
FACILITIES ON SITE
EXAM BOARDS
RETAKES   **NVQ COURSES**

A-level | AS | GCSE | OTHER e l v / B EG K O R / cde

Gb · Manor House School; Manor House Lane; Little Bookham; Surrey KT23 4EN
Tel: 01372 458538 (Fax: 01372 450514) *Mrs L.A.Mendes*

Day / Weekly Boarding — £425-£1800 £2055-£2615 ✗ | Boys 32 | Age 3-7 | Girls 282 / 8 | Age 3-16 / 6-16 | TOTAL 322 | SIXTH — Boys / Girls

ENTRY REQUIREMENTS Exam & Interview
SCHOLARSHIPS & BURSARIES Schol; Art; Mus
SPECIAL NEEDS
ASSOCIATION GSA   **FOUNDED** 1927   **DYSLEXIA**   **DIET** a
RELIGIOUS AFFILIATION C of E

MAP 3 F 5
LOCATION Rural
DAY ✓   **RAIL** a   **AIR** a
SPORT aflmnopqwx BC
OTHER LANGUAGES
ACTIVITIES cfghijknosw A
OTHER SUBJECTS bcfgh
FACILITIES ON SITE abj
EXAM BOARDS abcd
RETAKES   **NVQ COURSES**

A-level | AS | GCSE de g i n v / BC E G K OP R W / cdef j | OTHER l no / o

---

Gb · Micklefield School; 10-12 Somers Road; Reigate; Surrey RH2 9DU
Tel: 01737 242615 (Fax: 01737 248889) *Mrs C.M.Belton*

Day / Weekly Boarding — £249-£1252 | Boys 42 | Age 2-7 | Girls 200 | Age 2-12 | TOTAL 242 | SIXTH — Boys / Girls

ENTRY REQUIREMENTS Test; Interview
SCHOLARSHIPS & BURSARIES
SPECIAL NEEDS abjln
ASSOCIATION IAPS   **FOUNDED** 1910   **DYSLEXIA** de   **DIET** acd
RELIGIOUS AFFILIATION Non-denom

MAP 4 G 5
LOCATION Urban
DAY   **RAIL** b   **AIR** a
SPORT aejlpqx B
OTHER LANGUAGES
ACTIVITIES cghjot A
OTHER SUBJECTS acfh
FACILITIES ON SITE ch
EXAM BOARDS
RETAKES   **NVQ COURSES**

A-level | AS | GCSE | OTHER e Imno v / B EG K O R / cde j

---

g · Milbourne Lodge Junior School; 22 Milbourne Lane; Esher; Surrey KT10 9EA
Tel: 01372 462781 (Fax: 01372 469914) *Mrs J.Hinchliffe*

Day / Weekly Boarding — £575-£1310 ✗ | Boys 147 | Age 3-8 | Girls 8 | Age 3-8 | TOTAL 155 | SIXTH — Boys / Girls

ENTRY REQUIREMENTS
SCHOLARSHIPS & BURSARIES
SPECIAL NEEDS
ASSOCIATION ISAI   **FOUNDED** 1912   **DYSLEXIA**   **DIET**
RELIGIOUS AFFILIATION C of E

MAP 5 D 6
LOCATION Urban
DAY   **RAIL** b   **AIR** a
SPORT ajlosx
OTHER LANGUAGES
ACTIVITIES fg
OTHER SUBJECTS h
FACILITIES ON SITE bhj
EXAM BOARDS
RETAKES   **NVQ COURSES**

A-level | AS | GCSE | OTHER e s v / B G K O / cd

SURREY *continued*

Bg Milbourne Lodge School; Esher; Surrey KT10 9EG
Tel: 01372 462737 (Fax: 01372 471164) *N.R.Hale*

		Boys	Age	Girls	Age	TOTAL	SIXTH	Boys	Girls
Day	£1400-£1500 ✗	179	7-13	18	7-13	197			
Weekly									
Boarding									

ENTRY REQUIREMENTS Test
SCHOLARSHIPS & BURSARIES Schol
SPECIAL NEEDS   **DYSLEXIA**   **DIET**
ASSOCIATION IAPS   **FOUNDED**   **RELIGIOUS AFFILIATION** C of E

LOCATION
DAY **RAIL** **AIR** a
SPORT aejopsx AB
OTHER LANGUAGES
ACTIVITIES f
OTHER SUBJECTS h
FACILITIES ON SITE bj
EXAM BOARDS
RETAKES **NVQ COURSES**

MAP 5 D 6

A-level | **AS** | **GCSE** | **OTHER**
e l   v
B G
cde g j

B More House School; Frensham; Farnham; Surrey GU10 3AW
Tel: 01252 792303 (Fax: 01252 794397) *B.G.Huggett*

		Boys	Age	Girls	Age	TOTAL	SIXTH	Boys	Girls
Day	£2050 ✗	39	10-16			93			
Weekly	£3350		10-16						
Boarding	£3350	54	10-16						

ENTRY REQUIREMENTS Interview; Report; Assessment
SCHOLARSHIPS & BURSARIES
SPECIAL NEEDS Inqw BE   **DYSLEXIA** cdef   **DIET** ab
ASSOCIATION ISAI **FOUNDED** 1939 **RELIGIOUS AFFILIATION** R C

MAP 3 E 5
LOCATION Rural
DAY **RAIL** a **AIR** a
SPORT abcdefhjlmoswx ABC
OTHER LANGUAGES a
ACTIVITIES fghjklnopqtw A
OTHER SUBJECTS cdfh
FACILITIES ON SITE cdfj
EXAM BOARDS acd AL
RETAKES a **NVQ COURSES**

A-level | **AS** | **GCSE** de g i l o uv | **OTHER**
                    B E G   OP   X
                    cde

Gb Notre Dame School; Lingfield; Surrey; RH7 6PH
Tel: 01342 833176 (Fax: 01342 836048) *Mrs N.E.Shepley*

		Boys	Age	Girls	Age	TOTAL	SIXTH	Boys	Girls
Day	£420-£1425	17	3-8	337	3-18	354		6	23
Weekly									
Boarding									

ENTRY REQUIREMENTS Report & Exam & Interview
SCHOLARSHIPS & BURSARIES Schol
SPECIAL NEEDS n   **DYSLEXIA** de   **DIET** a
ASSOCIATION ISAI **FOUNDED** 1940 **RELIGIOUS AFFILIATION** R C

MAP 4 G 5
LOCATION Rural
DAY ✓ **RAIL** a **AIR** a
SPORT acdefhjklmpqtuwx BC
OTHER LANGUAGES
ACTIVITIES acghjkopq AD
OTHER SUBJECTS abch
FACILITIES ON SITE ghk
EXAM BOARDS abde ABEKL
RETAKES **NVQ COURSES**

A-level e ghi n v | **AS** u | **GCSE** de l n v | **OTHER** m o   W
B G K P   BC G K O R   X
c ef   cdef

C Notre Dame Prep. School; Burwood House; Cobham; Surrey KT11 1HA
Tel: 01932 862152 (Fax: 01932 868042) *Sister Julia Lanaghan*

		Boys	Age	Girls	Age	TOTAL	SIXTH	Boys	Girls
Day	£375-£1200	12	3-7	292	3-11	304			
Weekly									
Boarding									

ENTRY REQUIREMENTS
SCHOLARSHIPS & BURSARIES
SPECIAL NEEDS j   **DYSLEXIA**   **DIET**
ASSOCIATION IAPS **FOUNDED** 1937 **RELIGIOUS AFFILIATION** R C

MAP 5 C 7
LOCATION Rural
DAY **RAIL** b **AIR** a
SPORT pqx
OTHER LANGUAGES
ACTIVITIES cgj
OTHER SUBJECTS ch
FACILITIES ON SITE di
EXAM BOARDS
RETAKES **NVQ COURSES**

A-level | **AS** | **GCSE** | **OTHER** e m   v
                              B G   O R
                              cde

G Notre Dame Senior School; Burwood House; Cobham; Surrey KT11 1HA
Tel: 01932 863560 (Fax: 01932 860992) *Sister Faith Ede*

		Boys	Age	Girls	Age	TOTAL	SIXTH	Boys	Girls
Day	£1440-£1500 ✗			264	11-18	264			25
Weekly									
Boarding									

ENTRY REQUIREMENTS Exam & Interview
SCHOLARSHIPS & BURSARIES Schol; Burs
SPECIAL NEEDS bl   **DYSLEXIA**   **DIET** a
ASSOCIATION GSA **FOUNDED** 1937 **RELIGIOUS AFFILIATION** R C

MAP 5 C 7
LOCATION Rural
DAY ✓ **RAIL** a **AIR** a
SPORT abcflmpqwx ABC
OTHER LANGUAGES c
ACTIVITIES ghijko A
OTHER SUBJECTS acegh
FACILITIES ON SITE bcdghik
EXAM BOARDS abcd ABEG
RETAKES ab **NVQ COURSES**

A-level cdefghij lmn p v x | **AS** d | **GCSE** de g ij lmno v | **OTHER**
BC GH K OP RST   BC G K OP R
cdef j l   cdef j l

SURREY *continued*

C — Nower Lodge School; Dorking; Surrey RH4 3BT
Tel: 01306 882448 Mrs S.Watt

		Boys	Age	Girls	Age	TOTAL		Boys	Girls
Day	£950-£1325	76	3-13	44	3-13	120	SIXTH		
Weekly									
Boarding									

ENTRY REQUIREMENTS Assessment
SCHOLARSHIPS & BURSARIES Teachers
SPECIAL NEEDS nw B
ASSOCIATION IAPS **FOUNDED** 1962 **DYSLEXIA** de **DIET** abcd **RELIGIOUS AFFILIATION** Inter-denom

MAP 3 F 5
LOCATION Rural
DAY **RAIL** a **AIR** a
SPORT aefjkmpquwx B
OTHER LANGUAGES
ACTIVITIES afghijq A
OTHER SUBJECTS c
FACILITIES ON SITE
EXAM BOARDS
RETAKES **NVQ COURSES**

A-level | AS | GCSE | OTHER: e l o v B E G K O R cde

B — Oakhyrst Grange School; Stanstead Road; Caterham; Surrey CR3 6AF
Tel: 01883 343344 (Fax: 01883 342021) Mrs D.F.Cooper

		Boys	Age	Girls	Age	TOTAL		Boys	Girls
Day	£160-£960	123	3-12			123	SIXTH		
Weekly									
Boarding									

ENTRY REQUIREMENTS Interview
SCHOLARSHIPS & BURSARIES
SPECIAL NEEDS
ASSOCIATION ISAI **FOUNDED** 1950 **DYSLEXIA** **DIET** a **RELIGIOUS AFFILIATION** Non-denom

MAP 5 F 7
LOCATION Rural
DAY **RAIL** a **AIR** a
SPORT abcefjlox A
OTHER LANGUAGES
ACTIVITIES go
OTHER SUBJECTS ch
FACILITIES ON SITE hi
EXAM BOARDS
RETAKES **NVQ COURSES**

A-level | AS | GCSE | OTHER: e v B G K O R cde

3g — Parkside School; The Manor; Stoke d'Abernon; Cobham; Surrey KT11 3PX
Tel: 01932 862749 (Fax: 01932 860251) R.Shipp

		Boys	Age	Girls	Age	TOTAL		Boys	Girls
Day	£900-£1810	259	4-13	10	2-5	292	SIXTH		
Weekly	£2616	17	7-14						
Boarding	£2775	6	7-14						

ENTRY REQUIREMENTS Test & Interview
SCHOLARSHIPS & BURSARIES Burs; Forces; Teachers; Siblings
SPECIAL NEEDS ejknw Gl
ASSOCIATION IAPS **FOUNDED** 1879 **DYSLEXIA** e **DIET** cd **RELIGIOUS AFFILIATION** C of E

MAP 5 C 7
LOCATION Rural
DAY **RAIL** a **AIR** a
SPORT abcdefjklmostwx ABC
OTHER LANGUAGES
ACTIVITIES fghijmoqrstw A
OTHER SUBJECTS cfh
FACILITIES ON SITE bhil
EXAM BOARDS
RETAKES **NVQ COURSES**

A-level | AS | GCSE | OTHER: e l o v B G cdefg j l

G — Parsons Mead School; Ottways Lane; Ashtead; Surrey KT21 2PE
Tel: 01372 276401 (Fax: 01372 278796) Miss E.B.Plant

		Boys	Age	Girls	Age	TOTAL		Boys	Girls
Day	£982-£1675			337	3-18	343	SIXTH		31
Weekly	£2723-£2943			6	8-18				
Boarding									

ENTRY REQUIREMENTS Exam
SCHOLARSHIPS & BURSARIES Schol; Forces; Clergy
SPECIAL NEEDS ijlntw D
ASSOCIATION GSA **FOUNDED** 1897 **DYSLEXIA** **DIET** acd **RELIGIOUS AFFILIATION** C of E

MAP 5 D 7
LOCATION Urban
DAY ✓ **RAIL** a **AIR** a
SPORT abcflmpqwx ABC
OTHER LANGUAGES
ACTIVITIES ceghijkoqwx AB
OTHER SUBJECTS bcegh
FACILITIES ON SITE bhj
EXAM BOARDS abd AEL
RETAKES **NVQ COURSES**

A-level: c e ghi n p uv BC G K PQR U W c ef j
AS: H u
GCSE: c e g i l n p v BC G K OP R U W cdef j l
OTHER: l

G — Prior's Field; Godalming; Surrey GU7 2RH
Tel: 01483 810551 (Fax: 01483 810180) Mrs J.Mc Callum

		Boys	Age	Girls	Age	TOTAL		Boys	Girls
Day	£2185			101	11-18	211	SIXTH		41
Weekly	£3270			77	11-18				
Boarding	£3270			33	11-18				

ENTRY REQUIREMENTS CEE & Interview; Report & Exam & Interview
SCHOLARSHIPS & BURSARIES Schol; Burs; Art; Mus; Forces; VI Form; Drama
SPECIAL NEEDS jlnw
ASSOCIATION GSA **FOUNDED** 1902 **DYSLEXIA** ef **DIET** acd **RELIGIOUS AFFILIATION** Inter-denom

MAP 3 E 5
LOCATION Rural
DAY **RAIL** b **AIR** a
SPORT acfklmnopqvwx AB
OTHER LANGUAGES a
ACTIVITIES cfghijklnostw AB
OTHER SUBJECTS abcdefgh
FACILITIES ON SITE bceghj
EXAM BOARDS abde ABEG
RETAKES a **NVQ COURSES**

A-level: efg i l n p v BC GHI K N P R W c e i l
AS: g G
GCSE: e g i l no vw BC G I K N P R W cde j l
OTHER: h o

SURREY continued

B — Priory School; Bolters Lane; Banstead; Surrey SM7 2AJ
Tel: 01737 354479 (Fax: 01737 370537) *I.R.Chapman*

		Boys	Age	Girls	Age	TOTAL		Boys	Girls
Day	£540-£1430	175	3-13			175	SIXTH		
Weekly									
Boarding									

MAP 5 E 7
LOCATION Urban
DAY **RAIL** a **AIR** a
SPORT abcefjlmosx AB
OTHER LANGUAGES
ACTIVITIES fghjoq A

ENTRY REQUIREMENTS Interview
SCHOLARSHIPS & BURSARIES Teachers
SPECIAL NEEDS bjlnq A **DYSLEXIA** fg **DIET** ad
ASSOCIATION IAPS **FOUNDED** 1921 **RELIGIOUS AFFILIATION**

OTHER SUBJECTS bch
FACILITIES ON SITE bh
EXAM BOARDS
RETAKES **NVQ COURSES**

A-level
AS
GCSE
OTHER c e l v / B EG K O R / cde j

Bg — Reed's School; Cobham; Surrey KT11 2ES
Tel: 01932 863076 (Fax: 01932 869046) *D.E.Prince*

		Boys	Age	Girls	Age	TOTAL		Boys	Girls
Day	£2163-£2580	196	11-18	15	16-18	351	SIXTH	67	
Weekly									
Boarding	£2884-£3414	140	11-18		16-18				

MAP 5 C 7
LOCATION Rural
DAY ✓ **RAIL** b **AIR** a
SPORT abcdefhkmostuwx B
OTHER LANGUAGES ac
ACTIVITIES befghijkmnostv ABD

ENTRY REQUIREMENTS CEE; Test & Interview
SCHOLARSHIPS & BURSARIES Schol; Burs; Mus; AP; VI Form
SPECIAL NEEDS n **DYSLEXIA** cde **DIET** a
ASSOCIATION HMC **FOUNDED** 1813 **RELIGIOUS AFFILIATION** C of E

OTHER SUBJECTS abcdfh
FACILITIES ON SITE acdghik
EXAM BOARDS abcd ABDE
RETAKES **NVQ COURSES**

A-level e g i op uv / B GHI K P R / cdef
AS p / B G K / c ef l
GCSE e g i nop v / B GI K N P R / cdef j
OTHER l q u / NO X

C — Reigate Grammar School; Reigate; Surrey RH2 0QS
Tel: 01737 222231 (Fax: 01737 224201) *J.G.Hamlin*

		Boys	Age	Girls	Age	TOTAL		Boys	Girls
Day	£1624	680	10-18	95	10-18	775	SIXTH	159	36
Weekly									
Boarding									

MAP 4 G 5
LOCATION Urban
DAY **RAIL** a **AIR** a
SPORT abcdefghjklmpqstuwx BC
OTHER LANGUAGES
ACTIVITIES acefghijklnopqrstuvx A

ENTRY REQUIREMENTS CEE; Exam
SCHOLARSHIPS & BURSARIES Schol; Burs; Mus; AP
SPECIAL NEEDS kq G **DYSLEXIA** **DIET** a
ASSOCIATION HMC **FOUNDED** 1675 **RELIGIOUS AFFILIATION** Inter-denom

OTHER SUBJECTS abcfh
FACILITIES ON SITE aghjkl
EXAM BOARDS abd ABEH
RETAKES **NVQ COURSES**

A-level cde ghi n p v x / B GH K P R U / c ef j l
AS de u / G K / c eg
GCSE cde g i l o v / B G K OP R / cdef j l
OTHER de l n q u / B E K NO R / hi k

B — Reigate St.Mary's Prep.& Choir Sch; Chart Lane; Reigate; Surrey RH2 7RN
Tel: 01737 244880 (Fax: 01737 221540) *J.A.Hart*

		Boys	Age	Girls	Age	TOTAL		Boys	Girls
Day	£275-£1371	226	3-13			226	SIXTH		
Weekly									
Boarding									

MAP 4 G 5
LOCATION Urban
DAY **RAIL** a **AIR** a
SPORT abcefgjlmqswx AB
OTHER LANGUAGES
ACTIVITIES fghijnoq A

ENTRY REQUIREMENTS Assessment; Test & Interview
SCHOLARSHIPS & BURSARIES Schol; Burs; Chor; Siblings
SPECIAL NEEDS bklnw l **DYSLEXIA** e **DIET** a
ASSOCIATION IAPS **FOUNDED** 1950 **RELIGIOUS AFFILIATION** C of E

OTHER SUBJECTS abcdh
FACILITIES ON SITE b
EXAM BOARDS
RETAKES **NVQ COURSES**

A-level
AS
GCSE
OTHER e g i no q uv / B G K OP R

C — Ripley Court School; Rose Lane; Ripley; Surrey GU23 6NE
Tel: 01483 225217 *J.W.N.Dudgeon*

		Boys	Age	Girls	Age	TOTAL		Boys	Girls
Day	£896-£1441	208	4-13	25	4-13	253	SIXTH		
Weekly	£2213	8	8-13						
Boarding	£2213	12	8-13						

MAP 3 F 5
LOCATION Rural
DAY **RAIL** a **AIR** a
SPORT abcefjklmopqsux ABC
OTHER LANGUAGES
ACTIVITIES acfghijlorst A

ENTRY REQUIREMENTS Test & Interview
SCHOLARSHIPS & BURSARIES Burs
SPECIAL NEEDS jnw l **DYSLEXIA** e **DIET** abcd
ASSOCIATION IAPS **FOUNDED** 1893 **RELIGIOUS AFFILIATION** Inter-denom

OTHER SUBJECTS bcfh
FACILITIES ON SITE bhik
EXAM BOARDS
RETAKES **NVQ COURSES**

A-level
AS
GCSE
OTHER c e g i lm o q v / B G K OP R / cdefg j

SURREY *continued*

Rowan Prep. School; 6 Fitzalan Road; Claygate; Esher; Surrey KT10 0LX
Tel: 01372 462627 (Fax: 01372 470782) *Mrs E.Brown*

	Fees		Boys	Age	Girls	Age	TOTAL		Boys	Girls
Day	£475-£1545	✗			294	3-11	294	SIXTH		
Weekly										
Boarding										

ENTRY REQUIREMENTS Test & Interview
SCHOLARSHIPS & BURSARIES
SPECIAL NEEDS   **DYSLEXIA**   **DIET**
ASSOCIATION IAPS   **FOUNDED** 1936   **RELIGIOUS AFFILIATION** Inter-denom

MAP 5 D 6
LOCATION Urban
DAY   **RAIL** b   **AIR** a
SPORT alpqx B
OTHER LANGUAGES
ACTIVITIES fghijo
OTHER SUBJECTS abch
FACILITIES ON SITE
EXAM BOARDS
RETAKES   **NVQ COURSES**

A-level   AS   GCSE   OTHER: e g i lm o v / B G K OP R / cde

Royal Grammar School; High Street; Guildford GU1 3BB
Tel: 01483 502424 (Fax: 01483 306127) *T.M.S.Young*

	Fees	Boys	Age	Girls	Age	TOTAL		Boys	Girls
Day	£1905-£1995	834	11-18			834	SIXTH	223	
Weekly									
Boarding									

ENTRY REQUIREMENTS Report & Interview; CEE & Interview; Report & Exam & Interview
SCHOLARSHIPS & BURSARIES Schol; Mus; AP
SPECIAL NEEDS bejklqst   **DYSLEXIA**   **DIET** a
ASSOCIATION HMC   **FOUNDED** 1509   **RELIGIOUS AFFILIATION** Non-denom

MAP 3 E 5
LOCATION Urban
DAY   **RAIL** a   **AIR** a
SPORT abcefhkmstuwx ABC
OTHER LANGUAGES
ACTIVITIES befghijklnopqrstx AB
OTHER SUBJECTS bch
FACILITIES ON SITE cg
EXAM BOARDS abd ABEH
RETAKES   **NVQ COURSES**

A-level: cd g i opq v / B GH K P R U / c efg j
AS: q / c
GCSE: d g i o v / B G K P R U / cdefg jkl
OTHER: f l n u w / EF K M O R / e

Royal School Hindhead; Portsmouth Road; Hindhead; Surrey GU26 6BW
Tel: 01428 605407 (Fax: 01428 607977) *C.Brooks*

	Fees		Boys	Age	Girls	Age	TOTAL		Boys	Girls
Day	£1155-£2019	✗			264	4-18	409	SIXTH		50
Weekly	£2590-£3169				70	8-18				
Boarding	£2590-£3169				75	11-18				

ENTRY REQUIREMENTS CEE; Report & Exam & Interview
SCHOLARSHIPS & BURSARIES Schol; Burs
SPECIAL NEEDS beghjlnqw BEG   **DYSLEXIA** ef   **DIET** abcd
ASSOCIATION GSA   **FOUNDED** 1995   **RELIGIOUS AFFILIATION** C of E

MAP 3 E 6
LOCATION Rural
DAY ✓   **RAIL** a   **AIR** a
SPORT abcfghklmnopqtwx ABC
OTHER LANGUAGES af
ACTIVITIES bcfghijklnopqstuwx ABD
OTHER SUBJECTS abcdefgh
FACILITIES ON SITE bcdeghjk
EXAM BOARDS abcd ABDEGIJ
RETAKES ab   **NVQ COURSES**

A-level: c efghij p uv / BC GHI K PQR U / cdef ij l
AS: ef / G K U
GCSE: de o v / BC E G K QR U W / cdef hj l
OTHER: j lmn u / K NO R / i

Rydes Hill Preparatory; Rydes Hill House; Aldershot Road; Guildford; Surrey GU2 6BP
Tel: 01483 63160 *Mrs Joan Lenahan*

	Fees	Boys	Age	Girls	Age	TOTAL		Boys	Girls
Day	£380-£1180	18	3-7	136	3-11	154	SIXTH		
Weekly									
Boarding									

ENTRY REQUIREMENTS Interview; Exam & Interview
SCHOLARSHIPS & BURSARIES
SPECIAL NEEDS alnq   **DYSLEXIA**   **DIET** abc
ASSOCIATION IAPS   **FOUNDED** 1945   **RELIGIOUS AFFILIATION** R C

MAP 3 E 5
LOCATION Rural
DAY   **RAIL** a   **AIR**
SPORT aclmpqx AB
OTHER LANGUAGES
ACTIVITIES cg
OTHER SUBJECTS ch
FACILITIES ON SITE abc
EXAM BOARDS
RETAKES   **NVQ COURSES**

A-level   AS   GCSE   OTHER: de lmno v / BC G K O R / c e

St. Andrew's School; Horsell; Woking; Surrey GU21 4QW
Tel: 01483 760943 (Fax: 01483 740314) *A.Brownridge*

	Fees		Boys	Age	Girls	Age	TOTAL		Boys	Girls
Day	£900-£2000	✗	144	3-13	3	3-6	147	SIXTH		
Weekly										
Boarding										

ENTRY REQUIREMENTS Exam & Interview; Assessment & Interview
SCHOLARSHIPS & BURSARIES Schol; Teachers; Sport; ARA
SPECIAL NEEDS abjklnq BG   **DYSLEXIA** e   **DIET** acd
ASSOCIATION IAPS   **FOUNDED** 1937   **RELIGIOUS AFFILIATION** C of E

MAP 3 F 5
LOCATION Urban
DAY   **RAIL** a   **AIR** a
SPORT acefjklmsx AB
OTHER LANGUAGES
ACTIVITIES fghjnort A
OTHER SUBJECTS abcdfh
FACILITIES ON SITE bhjk
EXAM BOARDS
RETAKES   **NVQ COURSES**

A-level   AS   GCSE   OTHER: cdefg i l v / B G K OP R / cdefg j

SURREY *continued*

G | St. Catherine's Junior School; Bramley; Guildford; Surrey GU5 0AY
Tel: 01483 893363 (Fax: 01483 893003) *Mrs J.D.Lowe*

		Boys	Age	Girls	Age	TOTAL		Boys	Girls
Day	£980-£1555	X		146	4-11	153	SIXTH		
Weekly	£2785			5	9-11				
Boarding	£2785			2	9-11				

ENTRY REQUIREMENTS Assessment & Interview
SCHOLARSHIPS & BURSARIES
SPECIAL NEEDS   **DYSLEXIA**   **DIET** a
ASSOCIATION IAPS   **FOUNDED** 1885   **RELIGIOUS AFFILIATION** C of E

MAP 3 E 5
LOCATION Rural
DAY   **RAIL** a   **AIR** a
SPORT alpqx B
OTHER LANGUAGES
ACTIVITIES cghjot
OTHER SUBJECTS bcfh
FACILITIES ON SITE bdhik
EXAM BOARDS
RETAKES   **NVQ COURSES**

A-level | **AS** | **GCSE** d | **OTHER** e lmno v
                                              B G K O R
                                              cde

G | St. Catherine's School; Bramley; Guildford GU5 0DF
Tel: 01483 893363 (Fax: 01483 893003) *Mrs C.M.Oulton*

		Boys	Age	Girls	Age	TOTAL		Boys	Girls
Day	£1885	X		316	11-18	450	SIXTH		81
Weekly	£3085			68	11-18				
Boarding	£3085			66	11-18				

ENTRY REQUIREMENTS Exam
SCHOLARSHIPS & BURSARIES Schol; Mus; AP; VI Form
SPECIAL NEEDS j EGL   **DYSLEXIA**   **DIET** a
ASSOCIATION GSA   **FOUNDED** 1885   **RELIGIOUS AFFILIATION** C of E

MAP 3 E 5
LOCATION Rural
DAY ✓   **RAIL** a   **AIR** a
SPORT abcfhlnopqwx ABC
OTHER LANGUAGES a
ACTIVITIES cfghijklnopqstw AB
OTHER SUBJECTS abcdefh
FACILITIES ON SITE bcdeghik
EXAM BOARDS abd ABDEG
RETAKES a   **NVQ COURSES**

A-level cd fghi l   p   v   **AS**   d   **GCSE** d gi l   o   v   **OTHER**   u
            BC GH K   P R   G K   R   BC E G K   NOP R   W
            c efghj l   c e   j   cdefghj l

C | St. Christopher's; 6 Downs Road; Epsom; Surrey KT18 5HE
Tel: 01372 721807 *Miss J.Luckman*

		Boys	Age	Girls	Age	TOTAL		Boys	Girls
Day	£492-£952	X	65	3-7	76	3-7	141	SIXTH		
Weekly										
Boarding										

ENTRY REQUIREMENTS None
SCHOLARSHIPS & BURSARIES
SPECIAL NEEDS amw   **DYSLEXIA**   **DIET** acd
ASSOCIATION ISAI   **FOUNDED** 1938   **RELIGIOUS AFFILIATION** C of E

MAP 5 D 7
LOCATION Urban
DAY   **RAIL** a   **AIR** a
SPORT jlq
OTHER LANGUAGES
ACTIVITIES cjoq
OTHER SUBJECTS ch
FACILITIES ON SITE
EXAM BOARDS
RETAKES   **NVQ COURSES**

A-level | **AS** | **GCSE** | **OTHER** de g   no   v
                                            B G K   O RS
                                            cde

G | St. David's Junior School for Girls; Church Road; Ashford; Middlesex TW15 3DZ
Tel: 01784 240434 (Fax: 01784 248652) *Mrs P.Green*

		Boys	Age	Girls	Age	TOTAL		Boys	Girls
Day	£490-£1290	X	1	3-4	151	3-11	152	SIXTH		
Weekly										
Boarding										

ENTRY REQUIREMENTS Assessment & Interview
SCHOLARSHIPS & BURSARIES
SPECIAL NEEDS bijn   **DYSLEXIA** ce   **DIET** acd
ASSOCIATION IAPS   **FOUNDED** 1715   **RELIGIOUS AFFILIATION** C of E

MAP 5 B 5
LOCATION Urban
DAY ✓   **RAIL** a   **AIR** a
SPORT cdflmpqx ABC
OTHER LANGUAGES
ACTIVITIES cghjnoqt A
OTHER SUBJECTS bcfh
FACILITIES ON SITE d
EXAM BOARDS
RETAKES   **NVQ COURSES**

A-level | **AS** | **GCSE** | **OTHER** e lmno v
                                              B G K O R
                                              cde

G | St. David's Senior School; Ashford; Middx. TW15 3DZ
Tel: 01784 252494 (Fax: 01784 248652) *Mrs J.G.Osborne*

		Boys	Age	Girls	Age	TOTAL		Boys	Girls
Day	£1725	X		206	11-18	238	SIXTH		32
Weekly	£2820			9	11-18				
Boarding	£2995			23	11-18				

ENTRY REQUIREMENTS Report & Exam & Interview
SCHOLARSHIPS & BURSARIES Schol; Burs; Art; Mus; Forces
SPECIAL NEEDS AGHI jlnqtw   **DYSLEXIA** ce   **DIET** abcd
ASSOCIATION GSA   **FOUNDED** 1716   **RELIGIOUS AFFILIATION** C of E

MAP 5 B 5
LOCATION Rural
DAY ✓   **RAIL** a   **AIR** a
SPORT acdfklmpqtx ABC
OTHER LANGUAGES a
ACTIVITIES cfghijkmnot AD
OTHER SUBJECTS cefgh
FACILITIES ON SITE cdegk
EXAM BOARDS abd ABDEIL
RETAKES ab   **NVQ COURSES**

A-level cd ghi n p   v x   **AS**   d fghi   v x   **GCSE** cde ghi   n   v   **OTHER**   lm
            BC GH K PQ   U   B   G K PQR U   BC   G K   P R   C
            cdef j l   ef   cdef j l   f

264

SURREY *continued*

B · St. Edmund's School; Hindhead; Surrey GU26 6BH
Tel: 01428 604808 (Fax: 01428 607898)

		Boys	Age	Girls	Age	TOTAL		Boys	Girls
Day	£1225-£2125	84	2-13	22	2-7	152	SIXTH		
Weekly									
Boarding	£2750-£2825	46	7-13						

ENTRY REQUIREMENTS Assessment & Interview
SCHOLARSHIPS & BURSARIES Schol
SPECIAL NEEDS n B   **DYSLEXIA**   **DIET** ad
ASSOCIATION IAPS   **FOUNDED** 1874   **RELIGIOUS AFFILIATION** C of E

MAP 3 E 6
LOCATION Rural
DAY   **RAIL** a   **AIR** a
SPORT abcefjklmorstuwx AB
OTHER LANGUAGES
ACTIVITIES acfghijlnorstw A
OTHER SUBJECTS cfh
FACILITIES ON SITE abdhil
EXAM BOARDS
RETAKES   **NVQ COURSES**

A-level   **AS**   **GCSE** d g i   **OTHER** e i lmno v
 B E G K OP R
 cdefg j

C · St. George's College; Weybridge KT15 2QS
Tel: 01932 854811 (Fax: 01932 851829) *J.A.Peake*

		Boys	Age	Girls	Age	TOTAL		Boys	Girls
Day	£1915-£2165	450	11-18	49	16-18	499	SIXTH	92	76
Weekly									
Boarding									

ENTRY REQUIREMENTS CEE; Exam
SCHOLARSHIPS & BURSARIES Schol; Burs; Mus; AP; VI Form; Sport; ARA
SPECIAL NEEDS In   **DYSLEXIA** e   **DIET** a
ASSOCIATION HMC   **FOUNDED** 1869   **RELIGIOUS AFFILIATION** R C

MAP 5 B 6
LOCATION Urban
DAY ✓   **RAIL** a   **AIR** a
SPORT abcefhjkmnpqrstw AB
OTHER LANGUAGES
ACTIVITIES fghijklogrst B
OTHER SUBJECTS cf
FACILITIES ON SITE abcdghjk
EXAM BOARDS abcdf ABEGH
RETAKES   **NVQ COURSES**

A-level d f g i l n p   v x
 BC   GH K M P R   W
 c ef   j l
AS c
GCSE d g i   v
 B   G K   P R
 cdef hj l
OTHER o u
 R

B g · St. George's College Junior School; Weybridge Road; Addlestone; Weybridge; Surrey KT15 2QS Tel: 01932 845784 (Fax: 01932 843689) *Rev.M.D.Ashcroft C.J.*

			Boys	Age	Girls	Age	TOTAL		Boys	Girls
Day	£775-£1537	✗	194	2-11	3	2-11	197	SIXTH		
Weekly										
Boarding										

ENTRY REQUIREMENTS Interview; Report; Assessment
SCHOLARSHIPS & BURSARIES Teachers
SPECIAL NEEDS w   **DYSLEXIA**   **DIET** a
ASSOCIATION IAPS   **FOUNDED** 1952   **RELIGIOUS AFFILIATION** R C

MAP 5 B 6
LOCATION Urban
DAY   **RAIL** a   **AIR** a
SPORT abcefhjlmosx ABC
OTHER LANGUAGES
ACTIVITIES fghijnoqt
OTHER SUBJECTS abcdfh
FACILITIES ON SITE abdhjk
EXAM BOARDS
RETAKES   **NVQ COURSES**

A-level   **AS**   **GCSE**   **OTHER** e klmno s v
 B E G K   O R
 cde

G b · St. Hilary's School; Holloway Hill; Godalming; Surrey GU7 1RZ
Tel: 01483 416551 (Fax: 01483 418325) *Mrs M.I.Thomas*

		Boys	Age	Girls	Age	TOTAL		Boys	Girls
Day	£800-£1250	79	3-8	262	3-12	341	SIXTH		
Weekly									
Boarding									

ENTRY REQUIREMENTS Test & Interview
SCHOLARSHIPS & BURSARIES Schol; Burs; Mus; Siblings
SPECIAL NEEDS jkn BGI   **DYSLEXIA** de   **DIET** abcd
ASSOCIATION IAPS   **FOUNDED** 1927   **RELIGIOUS AFFILIATION** Non-denom

MAP 3 E 5
LOCATION Urban
DAY   **RAIL** a   **AIR** a
SPORT abefjlpqx AB
OTHER LANGUAGES
ACTIVITIES cfghjo A
OTHER SUBJECTS abcfh
FACILITIES ON SITE bch
EXAM BOARDS
RETAKES   **NVQ COURSES**

A-level   **AS**   **GCSE**   **OTHER** e g i lmno v
 B   G K OP R
 cde j

G · St. Ives School; Three Gates Lane; Haslemere; Surrey GU27 2ES
Tel: 01428 643734 (Fax: 01428 644788) *Mrs M.S.Greenway*

			Boys	Age	Girls	Age	TOTAL		Boys	Girls
Day	£1180-£1525	✗			127	4-11	127	SIXTH		
Weekly										
Boarding										

ENTRY REQUIREMENTS Assessment & Interview
SCHOLARSHIPS & BURSARIES
SPECIAL NEEDS bghjklnstwx ABHI   **DYSLEXIA**   **DIET** a
ASSOCIATION IAPS   **FOUNDED** 1962   **RELIGIOUS AFFILIATION** C of E

MAP 3 E 6
LOCATION Rural
DAY ✓   **RAIL** a   **AIR** b
SPORT aflmnopqx BC
OTHER LANGUAGES
ACTIVITIES cghijoqt A
OTHER SUBJECTS abcfh
FACILITIES ON SITE ch
EXAM BOARDS
RETAKES   **NVQ COURSES**

A-level   **AS**   **GCSE**   **OTHER** de   lmno   s v
 B DE G K   O R
 cde

SURREY continued

St. John's School; Leatherhead KT22 8SP
Tel: 01372 372021 (Fax: 01372 386606) *C.H.Tongue*

			Boys	Age	Girls	Age	TOTAL		Boys	Girls
Day	£2400	X	253	13-18	13	16-18	383	SIXTH	138	32
Weekly	£3500		61	13-18	18	16-18				
Boarding	£3500		37	13-18	1	16-18				

ENTRY REQUIREMENTS CEE
SCHOLARSHIPS & BURSARIES Schol; Art; Mus; Clergy; Teachers; AP; VI Form; ARA
SPECIAL NEEDS begiklnqtuw ADGHIJ   **DYSLEXIA** e   **DIET** acd
ASSOCIATION HMC   **FOUNDED** 1851   **RELIGIOUS AFFILIATION** C of E

MAP 3 F 5
LOCATION Urban
DAY   **RAIL** a   **AIR** a
SPORT abcdefghijklmnopqstuwx ABC
OTHER LANGUAGES a
ACTIVITIES efghijklnopqstv AB
OTHER SUBJECTS abcdfh
FACILITIES ON SITE cdghik
EXAM BOARDS ab ADEH
RETAKES   **NVQ COURSES**

A-level: cd ghi op v x / B GH K M P R / cdef j l
AS: d h / G K / ef
GCSE: w
GCSE: cd g i l o v / B E G K P R / cdef j l
OTHER: u / M O R

St. Maur's School; Weybridge; Surrey KT13 8NL
Tel: 01932 851411 (Fax: 01932 842037) *Mrs Maureen Dodds*

		Boys	Age	Girls	Age	TOTAL		Boys	Girls
Day	£755-£1575			7	3- 5	599	4-18	606	SIXTH		38
Weekly									
Boarding									

ENTRY REQUIREMENTS Report & Exam & Interview
SCHOLARSHIPS & BURSARIES Schol; Burs; AP; VI Form
SPECIAL NEEDS bhlntwx ACDGHJ   **DYSLEXIA**   **DIET** a
ASSOCIATION GSA   **FOUNDED** 1899   **RELIGIOUS AFFILIATION** R C

MAP 5 B 6
LOCATION Urban
DAY ✓   **RAIL** a   **AIR** a
SPORT acefhlnpqx BC
OTHER LANGUAGES
ACTIVITIES cghijknost AB
OTHER SUBJECTS ceh
FACILITIES ON SITE bdgjk
EXAM BOARDS abcd ABDEGH
RETAKES   **NVQ COURSES**

A-level: cdefghi l n uv x / BC GH K P W / cdefghj j l
AS: B
GCSE: u / ef j / W
GCSE: de ghi l n v / BC G K NOP R W / cdefghj l
OTHER:

St. Michael's School; Limpsfield; Oxted RH8 0QR
Tel: 01883 712311 (Fax: 01883 730720) *Dr.Margaret J.Hustler*

		Boys	Age	Girls	Age	TOTAL		Boys	Girls
Day	£990-£1995	14	3- 8	95	3-18	192	SIXTH		25
Weekly	£2650-£3500			8	7-18				
Boarding	£2650-£3500			75	7-18				

ENTRY REQUIREMENTS Report & Interview
SCHOLARSHIPS & BURSARIES Schol; Forces; Clergy
SPECIAL NEEDS bknq   **DYSLEXIA** cde   **DIET** acd
ASSOCIATION GSA   **FOUNDED** 1850   **RELIGIOUS AFFILIATION** C of E

MAP 6 G 8
LOCATION Rural
DAY   **RAIL** a   **AIR** a
SPORT acdhlpqvwx ABC
OTHER LANGUAGES a
ACTIVITIES acghijkloqwx AB
OTHER SUBJECTS abcdegh
FACILITIES ON SITE bcdghj
EXAM BOARDS abd DEG
RETAKES   **NVQ COURSES**

A-level: efghi l op uv / BC GH K P R / abcdef ij l
AS: fghi / G K P R
GCSE: u
GCSE: e ghi l nop v / BC E G K OP R W / abcdefghij l
OTHER:

St. Teresa's Preparatory School; Grove House; Guildford Road; Effingham; Surrey KT24 5QA
Tel: 01372 453456 (Fax: 01372 451562) *Mrs M.Head*

			Boys	Age	Girls	Age	TOTAL		Boys	Girls
Day	£995-£1410	X			177	2-11	183	SIXTH		
Weekly	£3195					8-11				
Boarding	£3195				6	8-11				

ENTRY REQUIREMENTS Test & Interview
SCHOLARSHIPS & BURSARIES
SPECIAL NEEDS abjklnquw B   **DYSLEXIA**   **DIET** abcd
ASSOCIATION IAPS   **FOUNDED** 1953   **RELIGIOUS AFFILIATION** R C

MAP 3 F 5
LOCATION Rural
DAY ✓   **RAIL** a   **AIR** a
SPORT afghklmpqx B
OTHER LANGUAGES a
ACTIVITIES cfghjnoqwx
OTHER SUBJECTS abch
FACILITIES ON SITE bchjkl
EXAM BOARDS
RETAKES   **NVQ COURSES**

A-level:
AS:
GCSE:
OTHER: ef l v / B E G K O R / cde

St. Teresa's School; Effingham Hill; Dorking; Surrey RH5 6ST
Tel: 01372 452037 (Fax: 01372 450311) *L.Allan*

		Boys	Age	Girls	Age	TOTAL		Boys	Girls
Day	£1690			213	11-18	335	SIXTH		65
Weekly				23	11-18				
Boarding	£3595			99	11-18				

ENTRY REQUIREMENTS Report & Exam & Interview
SCHOLARSHIPS & BURSARIES Schol; Burs; Art; Mus; Teachers; VI Form; Sport
SPECIAL NEEDS   **DYSLEXIA**   **DIET** a
ASSOCIATION GSA   **FOUNDED** 1928   **RELIGIOUS AFFILIATION** R C

MAP 3 F 5
LOCATION Rural
DAY ✓   **RAIL** a   **AIR** a
SPORT abcfghklmpqwx ABC
OTHER LANGUAGES a
ACTIVITIES cghijknoqstwx A
OTHER SUBJECTS abcdefgh
FACILITIES ON SITE abcdghj
EXAM BOARDS abd ABDEG
RETAKES a   **NVQ COURSES**

A-level: de ghi p v / BC GH K P R U W / c ef ij l
AS: d ghi p v / BC GH K P R U W / c ef j l
GCSE: e g i v / BC E G K OP R W / cdef ij l
OTHER: lmno t / K N / d

SURREY *continued*

C — Sanderstead Junior School; 29 Purley Oaks Road; Sanderstead; Surrey CR2 0NW
Tel: 0181 660 0801 *Mrs A.Barns*

| Day Weekly Boarding | £860-£1030 | Boys 32 | Age 3-11 | Girls 58 | Age 3-11 | TOTAL 90 | SIXTH | Boys | Girls |

ENTRY REQUIREMENTS Assessment & Interview
SCHOLARSHIPS & BURSARIES Clergy; Teachers
SPECIAL NEEDS n   **DYSLEXIA** e   **DIET** a
ASSOCIATION ISAI   **FOUNDED** 1906   **RELIGIOUS AFFILIATION** C of E

MAP 5 F 6
LOCATION Rural
DAY   **RAIL** a   **AIR** a
SPORT cejlmpqsx B
OTHER LANGUAGES a
ACTIVITIES c
OTHER SUBJECTS ch
FACILITIES ON SITE i
EXAM BOARDS
RETAKES   **NVQ COURSES**

A-level | AS | GCSE | OTHER
e   lm o   v
B EG   K   O R
cde

B — Scaitcliffe; Englefield Green; Egham; Surrey TW20 0YJ
Tel: 01784 432109 (Fax: 01784 430460) *W.A.Constable*

| Day Weekly Boarding | £600-£1932 £2613 | Boys 89 16 | Age 3-13 7-13 | Girls 1 | Age 3- 7 | TOTAL 106 | SIXTH | Boys | Girls |

ENTRY REQUIREMENTS Interview; Assessment
SCHOLARSHIPS & BURSARIES Burs
SPECIAL NEEDS abjklnqw BG   **DYSLEXIA** e   **DIET** acd
ASSOCIATION IAPS   **FOUNDED** 1896   **RELIGIOUS AFFILIATION** C of E

MAP 3 F 4
LOCATION Rural
DAY   **RAIL** a   **AIR** a
SPORT abcefgjlmosuwx ABC
OTHER LANGUAGES
ACTIVITIES fghijopqr A
OTHER SUBJECTS abch
FACILITIES ON SITE bdhjk
EXAM BOARDS
RETAKES   **NVQ COURSES**

A-level | AS | GCSE | OTHER
cde g i l   no q s   v
B   G   K   OP R
cde g   j

G — Sir William Perkins's School; Guildford Road; Chertsey KT16 9BN
Tel: 01932 562161 (Fax: 01932 570841) *Miss S.Ross*

| Day Weekly Boarding | £1315 | Boys | Age | Girls 591 | Age 11-18 | TOTAL 591 | SIXTH | Boys | Girls 140 |

ENTRY REQUIREMENTS Report & Exam & Interview
SCHOLARSHIPS & BURSARIES Schol; Burs; Mus; AP; VI Form
SPECIAL NEEDS abgjlqt GHJ   **DYSLEXIA**   **DIET** acd
ASSOCIATION GSA   **FOUNDED** 1725   **RELIGIOUS AFFILIATION** Non-denom

MAP 5 B 6
LOCATION Urban
DAY   **RAIL** b   **AIR** a
SPORT abcfhlmpqwx ABC
OTHER LANGUAGES
ACTIVITIES ghijkosu ABD
OTHER SUBJECTS abcdh
FACILITIES ON SITE bcgh
EXAM BOARDS abd BEG
RETAKES   **NVQ COURSES**

A-level: e g i   p   v
B   GH K   P R U
c ef   j
AS: e g   u
B   G   K
efg   j l
GCSE: e g i   v
BC   G   K   P   X
cdefg   j l
OTHER: cd   lmno q
NO   R

Gb — Stanway School; Chichester Road; Dorking; Surrey RH4 1LR
Tel: 01306 882151 *Mrs C.A.Belk*

| Day Weekly Boarding | £213-£1350 | Boys 51 | Age 3- 8 | Girls 168 | Age 3-12 | TOTAL 219 | SIXTH | Boys | Girls |

ENTRY REQUIREMENTS Interview; Test & Interview
SCHOLARSHIPS & BURSARIES
SPECIAL NEEDS ejpqw GI   **DYSLEXIA**   **DIET**
ASSOCIATION IAPS   **FOUNDED** 1934   **RELIGIOUS AFFILIATION** C of E

MAP 3 F 5
LOCATION Urban
DAY   **RAIL** a   **AIR** a
SPORT aejlmpx AB
OTHER LANGUAGES
ACTIVITIES cghijnr
OTHER SUBJECTS abch
FACILITIES ON SITE bcj
EXAM BOARDS
RETAKES   **NVQ COURSES**

A-level | AS | GCSE | OTHER
e g i l   no q s   v
B   G I K   OP R
cdef   j

G — Tormead School; Cranley Road; Guildford; Surrey GU1 2JD
Tel: 01483 575101 (Fax: 01483 450592) *Mrs H.E.M.Alleyne*

| Day Weekly Boarding | £890-£1700 | Boys | Age | Girls 610 | Age 5-18 | TOTAL 610 | SIXTH | Boys | Girls 77 |

ENTRY REQUIREMENTS Exam
SCHOLARSHIPS & BURSARIES Schol; Burs; Mus; Teachers; AP; VI Form
SPECIAL NEEDS   **DYSLEXIA**   **DIET** abcd
ASSOCIATION GSA   **FOUNDED** 1905   **RELIGIOUS AFFILIATION** Inter-denom

MAP 3 E 5
LOCATION Urban
DAY   **RAIL** a   **AIR** a
SPORT abcfghklmpqvwx ABC
OTHER LANGUAGES
ACTIVITIES cfghijknoqstu AB
OTHER SUBJECTS bcdefh
FACILITIES ON SITE gh
EXAM BOARDS abd ABE
RETAKES   **NVQ COURSES**

A-level: c efg i   n p   v x
BC   GH K   P R T W
cdef   j l
AS: e g   p   x
G   T W
ef   j l
GCSE: e g i   p   v
BC E G   K   P R   WX
cdef   j l
OTHER: d   l   u
I   MNO Q
i

267

SURREY continued

C — Virginia Water Prep School; Gorse Hill Road; Virginia Water; Surrey GU25 4AU
Tel: 01344 843138 (Fax: 01344 842927) *Mrs S.M.Winson*

MAP 3 E 4
LOCATION Rural
DAY   RAIL b   AIR a

		Boys	Age	Girls	Age	TOTAL	SIXTH Boys	Girls
Day	£1095–£1195	45	2–8	58	2–11	103		
Weekly								
Boarding								

SPORT ajpx B
OTHER LANGUAGES
ACTIVITIES cj

ENTRY REQUIREMENTS None
SCHOLARSHIPS & BURSARIES
SPECIAL NEEDS   DYSLEXIA   DIET
ASSOCIATION ISAI   FOUNDED 1933   RELIGIOUS AFFILIATION

OTHER SUBJECTS ch
FACILITIES ON SITE
EXAM BOARDS
RETAKES   NVQ COURSES

A-level | AS | GCSE | OTHER e   l o   v
                                 B   G
                                  cde

B g — Wallop School; 28 Hanger Hill; Weybridge; Surrey KT13 9YD
Tel: 01932 852885 (Fax: 01932 840093) *P.D.Westcombe*

MAP 5 B 6
LOCATION Urban
DAY   RAIL a   AIR a

		Boys	Age	Girls	Age	TOTAL	SIXTH Boys	Girls
Day	£932–£1576	123	3–13	17	3–11	140		
Weekly								
Boarding								

SPORT abefhjlmopqsx ABC
OTHER LANGUAGES
ACTIVITIES fghijoq A

ENTRY REQUIREMENTS Assessment & Interview
SCHOLARSHIPS & BURSARIES
SPECIAL NEEDS abegjklnqstw HI   DYSLEXIA e   DIET
ASSOCIATION IAPS   FOUNDED 1904   RELIGIOUS AFFILIATION Inter-denom

OTHER SUBJECTS bch
FACILITIES ON SITE abk
EXAM BOARDS
RETAKES   NVQ COURSES

A-level | AS | GCSE | OTHER c e g i k l   no   v
                              B   G K   OP R
                              cde g j

G — Wispers School; High Lane; Haslemere; Surrey GU27 1AD
Tel: 01428 643646 (Fax: 01428 641120) *L.H.Beltran*

MAP 3 E 6
LOCATION Rural
DAY ✓   RAIL a   AIR a

		Boys	Age	Girls	Age	TOTAL	SIXTH Boys	Girls
Day	£1960 X			45	11–18	104		9
Weekly	£3045			20	11–18			
Boarding	£3045			39	11–18			

SPORT abcfhklmopqtvwx ABC
OTHER LANGUAGES a
ACTIVITIES cdfghijklnopqtw A

ENTRY REQUIREMENTS CEE & Interview; Report & Exam & Interview
SCHOLARSHIPS & BURSARIES Schol; VI Form
SPECIAL NEEDS beijklqtvw AGI   DYSLEXIA   DIET abcd
ASSOCIATION GSA   FOUNDED 1946   RELIGIOUS AFFILIATION C of E

OTHER SUBJECTS abcdefgh
FACILITIES ON SITE beghjk
EXAM BOARDS abd ABEGH
RETAKES a   NVQ COURSES

A-level defghi   n   s   v | AS defghi   n   s   v | GCSE de g i l   n   s   v | OTHER de g   lmn   s   v
         BC   G K   P R   W   BC   G   K   P R W   BC   G K   P R   W   C G K M O R   W
         cdef hi l   cdef i l   cdef hi l   cdef   l

G — Woldingham School; Marden Park; Woldingham CR3 7YA
Tel: 01883 349431 (Fax: 01883 348 653) *Dr P.Dineen*

MAP 5 F 7
LOCATION Rural
DAY   RAIL b   AIR a

		Boys	Age	Girls	Age	TOTAL	SIXTH Boys	Girls
Day	£2309 X			103	11–18	537		133
Weekly								
Boarding	£3802			434	11–18			

SPORT abcefhjlmnopqsx B
OTHER LANGUAGES
ACTIVITIES gijknostw ABC

ENTRY REQUIREMENTS CEE; Report & Exam & Interview
SCHOLARSHIPS & BURSARIES
SPECIAL NEEDS n   DYSLEXIA   DIET a
ASSOCIATION GSA   FOUNDED 1842   RELIGIOUS AFFILIATION R C

OTHER SUBJECTS bcfh
FACILITIES ON SITE bcdeghik
EXAM BOARDS abcd ABEGH
RETAKES   NVQ COURSES

A-level efghi   l n p   v | AS   h   n | GCSE   egi l   v | OTHER
         B GH K   P R U   G   R   U   B E G K   P R   E   K   O
         c efg j l   cdefg j l   i

B — Woodcote House School; Windlesham; Surrey GU20 6PF
Tel: 01276 472115 (Fax: 01276 472890) *N.H.K.Paterson*

MAP 3 E 4
LOCATION Rural
DAY   RAIL a   AIR a

		Boys	Age	Girls	Age	TOTAL	SIXTH Boys	Girls
Day	£1685–£1710 X	16	8–13			93		
Weekly								
Boarding	£2415–£2435	77	8–13					

SPORT abcefjklmosuwx AB
OTHER LANGUAGES
ACTIVITIES fghijlmoqrw A

ENTRY REQUIREMENTS Test & Interview
SCHOLARSHIPS & BURSARIES
SPECIAL NEEDS abijklnpqw BG   DYSLEXIA   DIET a
ASSOCIATION IAPS   FOUNDED 1852   RELIGIOUS AFFILIATION Inter-denom

OTHER SUBJECTS ach
FACILITIES ON SITE abcdhjkl
EXAM BOARDS
RETAKES   NVQ COURSES

A-level | AS | GCSE | OTHER defg i l   no   v
                              B   G K   OP R
                              cdefg j l

SURREY *continued*

Yateley Manor School; 51 Reading Road; Yateley; Camberley; Surrey GU17 7UQ
Tel: 01252 873298 (Fax: 01252 860029) *F.G.F.Howard*

		Boys	Age	Girls	Age	TOTAL		Boys	Girls
Day	£469–£1569	323	3-13	161	3-13	484	SIXTH		
Weekly									
Boarding									

ENTRY REQUIREMENTS Report & Exam & Interview
SCHOLARSHIPS & BURSARIES Schol; Mus
SPECIAL NEEDS bjklnpqtuw Gl   **DYSLEXIA** e   **DIET** abcd
ASSOCIATION IAPS   **FOUNDED** 1947   **RELIGIOUS AFFILIATION** C of E

MAP 3 E 5
LOCATION Rural
DAY ✓   **RAIL** b   **AIR** b
SPORT abcegjklmopqsx AB
OTHER LANGUAGES
ACTIVITIES acdfghijoprst A
OTHER SUBJECTS bch
FACILITIES ON SITE bchik
EXAM BOARDS
RETAKES   **NVQ COURSES**

A-level / **AS** / **GCSE** / **OTHER** de g i lm o v BC E G K OP R cdef j l

---

Yehudi Menuhin School; Stoke d'Abernon; Cobham; Surrey KT11 3QQ
Tel: 01932 864739 (Fax: 01932 864633) *N.Chisholm*

		Boys	Age	Girls	Age	TOTAL		Boys	Girls
Day						48	SIXTH	5	6
Weekly									
Boarding	£6481	19	8-18	29	8-18				

ENTRY REQUIREMENTS Assessment & Interview
SCHOLARSHIPS & BURSARIES Burs
SPECIAL NEEDS anpuw J   **DYSLEXIA**   **DIET** abc
ASSOCIATION SHMIS   **FOUNDED** 1963   **RELIGIOUS AFFILIATION** Non-denom

MAP 5 C 7
LOCATION Rural
DAY   **RAIL** a   **AIR** a
SPORT chjqx ABC
OTHER LANGUAGES
ACTIVITIES cfghijot
OTHER SUBJECTS abcdfh
FACILITIES ON SITE ejk
EXAM BOARDS abcd ABEHI
RETAKES a   **NVQ COURSES**

A-level g B G K c ef ijk / **AS** f / **GCSE** g B E G K cdef ijk / **OTHER** e l n u M O R

Ashdown House; Forest Row; Sussex RH18 5JY
Tel: 0134 282 2574 (Fax: 0134 282 4380) *M.V.C.Williams*

		Boys	Age	Girls	Age	TOTAL		Boys	Girls
Day	£2500	13	8-9	5	8-10	202	SIXTH		
Weekly									
Boarding	£3110	135	8-13	49	8-13				

ENTRY REQUIREMENTS Interview
SCHOLARSHIPS & BURSARIES Forces
SPECIAL NEEDS jknpw Gl   **DYSLEXIA** e   **DIET**
ASSOCIATION IAPS   **FOUNDED** 1886   **RELIGIOUS AFFILIATION** C of E

MAP 4 H 6
LOCATION Rural
DAY   **RAIL** a   **AIR** a
SPORT acegjkmopqsux AB
OTHER LANGUAGES
ACTIVITIES cfghijorstw A
OTHER SUBJECTS bch
FACILITIES ON SITE cdehikl
EXAM BOARDS
RETAKES   **NVQ COURSES**

A-level / **AS** / **GCSE** / **OTHER** e g i lm o v BC G K OP R cde g j

---

Battle Abbey School; Battle; East Sussex TN33 0AD
Tel: 01424 772385 (Fax: 01424 773573) *D.J.A.Teall*

		Boys	Age	Girls	Age	TOTAL		Boys	Girls
Day	£1030–£1875	76	2-18	71	2-18	201	SIXTH	2	11
Weekly	£2430–£3030	1	8-18	3	8-18				
Boarding	£2430–£3030	23	8-18	27	8-18				

ENTRY REQUIREMENTS CEE; Exam; Scholarship Exam; Report & Interview
SCHOLARSHIPS & BURSARIES Schol; Forces; VI Form; ARA
SPECIAL NEEDS abejklnpqtw BEI   **DYSLEXIA** def   **DIET** acd
ASSOCIATION GSA   **FOUNDED** 1912   **RELIGIOUS AFFILIATION** Inter-denom

MAP 4 I 6
LOCATION Rural
DAY ✓   **RAIL** a   **AIR** b
SPORT abcdefhjklmopqstvwx ABC
OTHER LANGUAGES a
ACTIVITIES acdefghijklnoqrstwx A
OTHER SUBJECTS abcdefgh
FACILITIES ON SITE abcdik
EXAM BOARDS abcd ABDE
RETAKES ab   **NVQ COURSES**

A-level defg v B G PQ c ef / **AS** / **GCSE** defg i l o v BC E GH K P WX cdef / **OTHER** mn q stu C O R U W

Bodiam Manor; Bodiam; Robertsbridge; E.Sussex TN32 5UJ
Tel: 01580 830225 *Mr & Mrs P.L.Northen*

		Boys	Age	Girls	Age	TOTAL		Boys	Girls
Day	£869–£1588	75	2-13	75	2-13	150	SIXTH		
Weekly									
Boarding									

ENTRY REQUIREMENTS Assessment & Interview
SCHOLARSHIPS & BURSARIES Schol; Burs
SPECIAL NEEDS n   **DYSLEXIA** e   **DIET** a
ASSOCIATION IAPS   **FOUNDED** 1955   **RELIGIOUS AFFILIATION** C of E

MAP 4 I 6
LOCATION Rural
DAY   **RAIL** a   **AIR** b
SPORT acefjlmpqx AB
OTHER LANGUAGES
ACTIVITIES acfghjnoqt A
OTHER SUBJECTS cfh
FACILITIES ON SITE achi
EXAM BOARDS
RETAKES   **NVQ COURSES**

A-level / **AS** / **GCSE** / **OTHER** de lmno q uv B E G I K O R cde j

SUSSEX (EAST)

SUSSEX (EAST) continued

Gb Bricklehurst Manor; Stonegate; Wadhurst; Sussex TN5 7EL
Tel: 01580 200448 Mrs R.A.Lewis

MAP 4 H 6
LOCATION Rural
DAY   RAIL a   AIR a

		Boys	Age	Girls	Age	TOTAL		Boys	Girls
Day	£555-£1215	26	4-8	75	4-11	101	SIXTH		
Weekly									
Boarding									

SPORT aejlpqx B
OTHER LANGUAGES
ACTIVITIES cfhj
OTHER SUBJECTS ch
FACILITIES ON SITE i
EXAM BOARDS
RETAKES   NVQ COURSES

ENTRY REQUIREMENTS Interview
SCHOLARSHIPS & BURSARIES
SPECIAL NEEDS ejknqw Gl
DYSLEXIA f   **DIET** a
ASSOCIATION IAPS   **FOUNDED** 1959   **RELIGIOUS AFFILIATION** Non-denom

A-level: AS: GCSE:
OTHER: e lmno s v
        B E G K O R
        cde

G Brighton & Hove High School GPDST; The Temple; Montpelier Road; Brighton BN1 3AT
Tel: 01273 73 4112 (Fax: 01273 737120) Miss R.A.Woodbridge

MAP 4 G 7
LOCATION Urban
DAY   RAIL a   AIR a

		Boys	Age	Girls	Age	TOTAL		Boys	Girls
Day	£976-£1328			750	4-18	750	SIXTH		114
Weekly									
Boarding									

SPORT abcefgjlmopqvwx ABC
OTHER LANGUAGES
ACTIVITIES cfghijkoqrst AB
OTHER SUBJECTS bcdefh
FACILITIES ON SITE bcg
EXAM BOARDS abde ABDE
RETAKES   NVQ COURSES

ENTRY REQUIREMENTS Test
SCHOLARSHIPS & BURSARIES Schol; Burs; AP; VI Form
SPECIAL NEEDS bjlnqtu ADGHI   **DYSLEXIA**   **DIET** ab
ASSOCIATION GSA   **FOUNDED** 1876   **RELIGIOUS AFFILIATION** Inter-denom

A-level: c efg i   n pq v
          BC GH K   P R U
          cdefgh j
AS: e l
     GH
     ef
GCSE: de g i l n q   vw
        BC   G   K N P R
        cdefgh jkl
OTHER: w

C Brighton College; Eastern Road; Brighton BN2 2AL
Tel: 01273 697131 (Fax: 01273 682342) J.D.Leach

MAP 4 G 7
LOCATION Urban
DAY ✓   RAIL a   AIR a

		Boys	Age	Girls	Age	TOTAL		Boys	Girls
Day	£2618 ✗	280	13-18	90	13-18	472	SIXTH	125	43
Weekly	£3560	46	13-18	20	13-18				
Boarding	£3980	22	13-18	14	13-18				

SPORT abcdefgjkmopqrstuwx ABC
OTHER LANGUAGES
ACTIVITIES efghijklnopqrstw ABD
OTHER SUBJECTS abcdfh
FACILITIES ON SITE acdhik
EXAM BOARDS abcd ABEH
RETAKES   NVQ COURSES

ENTRY REQUIREMENTS CEE; Assessment & Interview
SCHOLARSHIPS & BURSARIES Schol; Burs; Art; Mus; Forces; Clergy; AP; VI Form; Sport
SPECIAL NEEDS bghjklnqt CEGHI   **DYSLEXIA** c   **DIET** acd
ASSOCIATION HMC   **FOUNDED** 1845   **RELIGIOUS AFFILIATION** C of E

A-level: cd ghi nop   vw
         BC GH K   P R U
         cdefg j l
AS: cd g   o q   wx
      C G K   P   U
      cdef
GCSE: d g i   o q   v
        BC G K   OP R U
        cdefg j
OTHER: e   l   q   u
        K M O R

C Brighton College Junior School; Walpole Lodge; Walpole Road; Brighton BN2 2EU
Tel: 01273 606845 (Fax: 01273 682342) G.H.Brown

MAP 4 G 7
LOCATION Urban
DAY   RAIL a   AIR a

		Boys	Age	Girls	Age	TOTAL		Boys	Girls
Day	£1972 ✗	150	8-13	54	8-13	204	SIXTH		
Weekly	£2410		8-13		8-13				
Boarding									

SPORT abcdefjklmopqsuwx ABC
OTHER LANGUAGES
ACTIVITIES afghijmorstw A
OTHER SUBJECTS ch
FACILITIES ON SITE abcdhi
EXAM BOARDS
RETAKES   NVQ COURSES

ENTRY REQUIREMENTS Report; Assessment
SCHOLARSHIPS & BURSARIES Forces; Clergy; AP
SPECIAL NEEDS   **DYSLEXIA**   **DIET**
ASSOCIATION IAPS   **FOUNDED** 1845   **RELIGIOUS AFFILIATION** C of E

A-level: AS: GCSE:
OTHER: efg i l   o q   v
          BC   G K   OP R
          cde   j

C Cumnor House School; Danehill; Haywards Heath; Sussex RH17 7HT
Tel: 01825 790347 (Fax: 01825 790910) N.J.Milner-Gulland

MAP 4 G 6
LOCATION Rural
DAY   RAIL a   AIR a

		Boys	Age	Girls	Age	TOTAL		Boys	Girls
Day	£880-£2195 ✗	67	4-13	53	4-13	196	SIXTH		
Weekly									
Boarding	£2720-£2860	42	8-13	34	8-13				

SPORT abcfjklmopqsvwx AB
OTHER LANGUAGES a
ACTIVITIES bcfghijoqrstvw A
OTHER SUBJECTS abcfh
FACILITIES ON SITE cfhjkl
EXAM BOARDS
RETAKES   NVQ COURSES

ENTRY REQUIREMENTS Interview
SCHOLARSHIPS & BURSARIES
SPECIAL NEEDS abegijklnqtuw BHI   **DYSLEXIA** e   **DIET** acd
ASSOCIATION IAPS   **FOUNDED** 1931   **RELIGIOUS AFFILIATION** C of E

A-level: AS: GCSE:
OTHER: cde g i lmno   v
        BC   G JK   NOP R
        cde   j

SUSSEX (EAST) continued

Bg Eastbourne College; Old Wish Road; Eastbourne BN21 4JX;
Tel: 01323 737655 (Fax: 01323 416137) *C.M.P.Bush*

		Boys	Age	Girls	Age	TOTAL		Boys	Girls
Day	£2864	159	13-18	24	16-18	478	SIXTH	162	69
Weekly									
Boarding	£3873	250	13-18	45	16-18				

ENTRY REQUIREMENTS CEE
SCHOLARSHIPS & BURSARIES Schol; Burs; Art; Mus; VI Form
SPECIAL NEEDS elqtu GHI
DYSLEXIA **DIET** ab
ASSOCIATION HMC **FOUNDED** 1867 **RELIGIOUS AFFILIATION** C of E

MAP 4 H 7
LOCATION Urban
DAY ✓ **RAIL** a **AIR** b
SPORT abcdefghijkmnoprstuwx ABC
OTHER LANGUAGES
ACTIVITIES aefghijklmnorstu B
OTHER SUBJECTS abcfh
FACILITIES ON SITE abcdeghik
EXAM BOARDS abcd AEH
RETAKES a **NVQ COURSES**

A-level	AS	GCSE	OTHER
c efghi l nopq v x AB GH K P cdefg j l	c g G j	c e g i l no q v AB B G K OP cdefg j l	

C Greenfields School; Priory Road; Forest Row; East Sussex RH18 5JD
Tel: 01342 822189 (Fax: 01342 825289) *Mrs M.I.Hodkin*

		Boys	Age	Girls	Age	TOTAL		Boys	Girls
Day	£640-£1749	68	3-18	58	3-18	157	SIXTH	4	7
Weekly	£2338-£2991		10-18		10-18				
Boarding	£2662-£3207	17	10-18	14	10-18				

ENTRY REQUIREMENTS Interview
SCHOLARSHIPS & BURSARIES Schol; Burs; Art; Mus; Sport
SPECIAL NEEDS bjknw B
DYSLEXIA e **DIET** abcd
ASSOCIATION ISAI **FOUNDED** 1981 **RELIGIOUS AFFILIATION** Inter-denom Scientology

MAP 4 H 6
LOCATION Rural
DAY ✓ **RAIL** a **AIR** a
SPORT befjmpqsx B
OTHER LANGUAGES a
ACTIVITIES cgjoqstw A
OTHER SUBJECTS bcdfh
FACILITIES ON SITE acgh
EXAM BOARDS ad ABEG
RETAKES ab **NVQ COURSES**

A-level	AS	GCSE	OTHER
c e g i l n v B E GH K N P cdef		de g i lmno q v BC E G K N P cdef	K

B Mayfield College; Mayfield; East Sussex TN20 6PL
Tel: 01435 872041 (Fax: 01435 873544) *C.P.Vroege*

		Boys	Age	Girls	Age	TOTAL		Boys	Girls
Day	£1000-£2140	30	11-18			90	SIXTH	26	
Weekly	£1965-£3105	13	11-18						
Boarding	£2025-£3950	47	11-18						

ENTRY REQUIREMENTS CEE; Test; Report & Interview; Report & Exam & Interview
SCHOLARSHIPS & BURSARIES Schol; Burs; Forces
SPECIAL NEEDS bjlnqwx BE
DYSLEXIA cdef **DIET** ad
ASSOCIATION ISAI **FOUNDED** 1868 **RELIGIOUS AFFILIATION** R C

MAP 4 H 6
LOCATION Rural
DAY ✓ **RAIL** a **AIR** a
SPORT abcdefghjkmosux ABC
OTHER LANGUAGES a
ACTIVITIES afghijopqt ABC
OTHER SUBJECTS abcdh
FACILITIES ON SITE bcdfh
EXAM BOARDS abcd ABDEGH
RETAKES ab **NVQ COURSES**

A-level	AS	GCSE	OTHER
de ghij l o v AB G K P R cdef	de K	de ghij l o v AB E G I K P R cdef	l K O S

Gb Micklefield Wadhurst; with the Legat School of Classical Ballet; Wadhurst TN5 6JA
Tel: 01892 783193 (Fax: 01892 783638) *E Reynolds*

		Boys	Age	Girls	Age	TOTAL		Boys	Girls
Day	£1625-£2140			60	11-18	169	SIXTH		21
Weekly	£3165-£3340			18	11-18				
Boarding	£3150-£3370	2	11-18	89	11-18				

ENTRY REQUIREMENTS CEE; Test; Report & Interview
SCHOLARSHIPS & BURSARIES Schol; Burs; Art; Mus; Forces; Clergy; VI Form; Sport; Drama
SPECIAL NEEDS abegijklnqstw BEGI
DYSLEXIA cde **DIET** abcd
ASSOCIATION GSA **FOUNDED** 1930 **RELIGIOUS AFFILIATION** C of E

MAP 4 H 6
LOCATION Rural
DAY ✓ **RAIL** a **AIR** a
SPORT abcflnpqtwx ABC
OTHER LANGUAGES a
ACTIVITIES cfghijknoqtw A
OTHER SUBJECTS abcdefgh
FACILITIES ON SITE deghik
EXAM BOARDS abcde ABDEGK
RETAKES ab **NVQ COURSES**

A-level	AS	GCSE	OTHER
c efg i n p v x BC G K OP R T W cdef i l		e g i l n p v x BC E GH K OP R W cdef i l	l

G Moira House School; Upper Carlisle Road; Eastbourne BN20 7TD
Tel: 01323 644144 (Fax: 01323 649720) *Adrian Underwood*

		Boys	Age	Girls	Age	TOTAL		Boys	Girls
Day	£1070-£2300			221	3-18	342	SIXTH		79
Weekly									
Boarding	£3420-£3570			121	8-18				

ENTRY REQUIREMENTS Scholarship Exam; Exam & Interview; CEE & Interview
SCHOLARSHIPS & BURSARIES Schol; Burs; Mus; Forces; VI Form
SPECIAL NEEDS bjklntw BE
DYSLEXIA de **DIET** acd
ASSOCIATION GSA **FOUNDED** 1875 **RELIGIOUS AFFILIATION** Inter-denom

MAP 4 H 7
LOCATION Rural
DAY ✓ **RAIL** a **AIR** a
SPORT acefghjklmopqtwx ABC
OTHER LANGUAGES a
ACTIVITIES cfghjklnopqstwx AB
OTHER SUBJECTS abcdfh
FACILITIES ON SITE abcdehik
EXAM BOARDS abcd ABDEGI
RETAKES ab **NVQ COURSES**

A-level	AS	GCSE	OTHER
de ghij n p v x BC FGH K P R U cdef j l	d ghi l n v BC FGH K OP R c ef l	de ghij l no v BC E GH K P R TU cdef j l	u Q

SUSSEX (EAST) continued

B — Mowden School; Droveway; Hove; E.Sussex BN3 6LU
Tel: 01273 503452 (Fax: 01273 503457) *C.E.M.Snell*

		Boys	Age	Girls	Age	TOTAL		Boys	Girls
Day	£1860	96	7-13			101	SIXTH		
Weekly	£2225	5	8-13						
Boarding									

ENTRY REQUIREMENTS Interview
SCHOLARSHIPS & BURSARIES Clergy; Teachers
SPECIAL NEEDS begklsw GI **DYSLEXIA** **DIET** abcd
ASSOCIATION IAPS **FOUNDED** 1896 **RELIGIOUS AFFILIATION** C of E

MAP 4 G 7
LOCATION Urban
DAY **RAIL** a **AIR** a
SPORT aefjmswx AB
OTHER LANGUAGES
ACTIVITIES fghijrt
OTHER SUBJECTS cfh
FACILITIES ON SITE chik
EXAM BOARDS
RETAKES **NVQ COURSES**

A-level	AS	GCSE	OTHER
		e g i l no v
		B G K OP R
		cde

C — Newlands Manor School; Sutton Place; Seaford; East Sussex BN25 3PL
Tel: 01323 890309 (Fax: 01323 490100) *B.F.Underwood*

		Boys	Age	Girls	Age	TOTAL		Boys	Girls
Day	£1890	61	13-18	29	13-18	264	SIXTH	47	19
Weekly	£2955-£3365		13-18		13-18				
Boarding	£2985-£3395	122	13-18	52	13-18				

ENTRY REQUIREMENTS CEE; Exam; Scholarship Exam; Interview; Report
SCHOLARSHIPS & BURSARIES Schol; Burs; Art; Mus; Chor; Forces; VI Form; Sport
SPECIAL NEEDS bjln B **DYSLEXIA** cde **DIET** abcd
ASSOCIATION ISAI **FOUNDED** 1978 **RELIGIOUS AFFILIATION** Inter-denom

MAP 4 H 7
LOCATION Rural
DAY **RAIL** a **AIR** b
SPORT abcefghjkmopqstwx ABC
OTHER LANGUAGES ai
ACTIVITIES adfghijkopqwx A
OTHER SUBJECTS bcdeh
FACILITIES ON SITE abdgi
EXAM BOARDS bc ABDEG
RETAKES ab **NVQ COURSES**

A-level	AS	GCSE	OTHER
e ghi l uv	a e gh l uv	e ghi l v
BC GH K P	B G K P	BC E G K N P U
cdef k	f	cdef jkl

C — Newlands Pre-Preparatory School; Eastbourne Road; Seaford; Sussex BN25 4NP
Tel: 01323 896461 (Fax: 01323 891599) *Mrs A.Morgan*

		Boys	Age	Girls	Age	TOTAL		Boys	Girls
Day	£780-£960	71	2-8	71	2-8	142	SIXTH		
Weekly									
Boarding									

ENTRY REQUIREMENTS
SCHOLARSHIPS & BURSARIES
SPECIAL NEEDS aegijlmn BGI **DYSLEXIA** **DIET** abcd
ASSOCIATION ISAI **FOUNDED** 1971 **RELIGIOUS AFFILIATION** Christian

MAP 4 H 7
LOCATION Urban
DAY ✓ **RAIL** a **AIR**
SPORT aejlpqx B
OTHER LANGUAGES
ACTIVITIES cfhjox
OTHER SUBJECTS c
FACILITIES ON SITE abdi
EXAM BOARDS
RETAKES **NVQ COURSES**

A-level	AS	GCSE	OTHER
		lmno v
		B G K O R
		cde

C — Newlands School; Eastbourne Road; Seaford; Sussex BN25 4NP
Tel: 01323 892334 (Fax: 01323 891599) *R.C.Clark*

		Boys	Age	Girls	Age	TOTAL		Boys	Girls
Day	£1390-£1710	85	7-13	43	7-13	232	SIXTH		
Weekly	£2780	1	7-13		7-13				
Boarding	£2810-£2860	63	7-13	40	7-13				

ENTRY REQUIREMENTS Interview
SCHOLARSHIPS & BURSARIES Schol; Burs; Art; Mus; Chor; Forces; Teachers; Sport
SPECIAL NEEDS bjklnpqtw BHI **DYSLEXIA** cde **DIET** abcd
ASSOCIATION IAPS **FOUNDED** 1854 **RELIGIOUS AFFILIATION** Non-denom

MAP 4 H 7
LOCATION Rural
DAY **RAIL** a **AIR** a
SPORT abcdefjlmopqsux AB
OTHER LANGUAGES a
ACTIVITIES cfghijnoqrwx A
OTHER SUBJECTS bch
FACILITIES ON SITE bcdik
EXAM BOARDS
RETAKES **NVQ COURSES**

A-level	AS	GCSE	OTHER
		c e g i lmno v
		BC G K OP R
		cde j

G — Roedean School; Roedean Way; Brighton; E.Sussex BN2 5RQ
Tel: 01273 603181 (Fax: 01273 676722) *Mrs A.R Longley*

		Boys	Age	Girls	Age	TOTAL		Boys	Girls
Day	£2455			4	16-18	429	SIXTH		167
Weekly									
Boarding	£4265			425	11-18				

ENTRY REQUIREMENTS CEE; Exam & Interview
SCHOLARSHIPS & BURSARIES Schol; Burs; Mus; VI Form
SPECIAL NEEDS jl E **DYSLEXIA** **DIET** a
ASSOCIATION GSA **FOUNDED** 1885 **RELIGIOUS AFFILIATION** C of E

MAP 4 G 7
LOCATION Urban
DAY **RAIL** a **AIR** a
SPORT abcegklmnopqtwx ABC
OTHER LANGUAGES
ACTIVITIES cfghijklnoqstuw AB
OTHER SUBJECTS abcdfh
FACILITIES ON SITE abcdghik
EXAM BOARDS abd ABDEH
RETAKES **NVQ COURSES**

A-level	AS	GCSE	OTHER
cd fghi nop v	cd fgh l o vwx	d ghi l no v
B GH K P	B GH K P	B E G K P R	C O W
c efg j l	cdefg j l	cdef j l

SUSSEX (EAST) *continued*

C **St. Andrews School; Meads; Eastbourne; Sussex BN20 7RP**
Tel: 01323 733203 (Fax: 01323 646860) *H.Davies Jones*

			Boys	Age	Girls	Age	TOTAL		Boys	Girls
Day	£500-£1780	✗	196	3-13	122	3-13	402			
Weekly	£2575							SIXTH		
Boarding	£2575		55	7-13	29	7-13				

ENTRY REQUIREMENTS Interview
SCHOLARSHIPS & BURSARIES Schol; Art; Mus; Forces; Sport
SPECIAL NEEDS ejknq l **DYSLEXIA** de **DIET** abcd
ASSOCIATION IAPS **FOUNDED** 1877 **RELIGIOUS AFFILIATION** C of E

MAP 4 H 7
LOCATION Urban
DAY ✓ **RAIL** a **AIR** a
SPORT abcdefjklmopqstuwx AB
OTHER LANGUAGES
ACTIVITIES cfghijnopqrstwx
OTHER SUBJECTS cfh
FACILITIES ON SITE cdhik
EXAM BOARDS
RETAKES **NVQ COURSES**

A-level	AS	GCSE	OTHER
			e l o v
			BC G
			cde j

B **St. Aubyns; Rottingdean; Brighton; E.Sussex BN2 7JN**
Tel: 01273 302170 (Fax: 01273 304004) *J.A.L.James*

		Boys	Age	Girls	Age	TOTAL		Boys	Girls
Day	£2175	33	7-13			114			
Weekly		11					SIXTH		
Boarding	£2935	70	7-13						

ENTRY REQUIREMENTS Assessment & Interview
SCHOLARSHIPS & BURSARIES Schol; Burs; Clergy; Teachers; Sport
SPECIAL NEEDS bgklntuw BDEGHI **DYSLEXIA** c **DIET** acd
ASSOCIATION IAPS **FOUNDED** 1895 **RELIGIOUS AFFILIATION** C of E

MAP 4 G 7
LOCATION Rural
DAY **RAIL** ab **AIR** a
SPORT abefgijlmoqsuwx ABC
OTHER LANGUAGES a
ACTIVITIES fghijlo
OTHER SUBJECTS cfh
FACILITIES ON SITE bcdhj
EXAM BOARDS
RETAKES **NVQ COURSES**

A-level	AS	GCSE	OTHER
			de g i l no v
			B G K OP R
			cde g j

C **St. Bede's School; The Dicker; Hailsham; East Sussex BN27 3QH**
Tel: 01323 843252 (Fax: 01323 442628) *R.Perrin*

		Boys	Age	Girls	Age	TOTAL		Boys	Girls
Day	£2350	91	13-19	40	13-19	396		84	64
Weekly	£3800	19	13-19	9	13-19		SIXTH		
Boarding	£3800	152	13-19	85	13-19				

ENTRY REQUIREMENTS CEE; Test; Scholarship Exam; Interview; Report; Test & Interview; Report & Interview; Report & Test **SCHOLARSHIPS & BURSARIES** Schol; Burs; Art; Mus; Forces; Teachers; VI Form; Sport; ARA; Drama **SPECIAL NEEDS** bjklnquw ABEGI **DYSLEXIA** de **DIET** acd
ASSOCIATION SHMIS **FOUNDED** 1978 **RELIGIOUS AFFILIATION** Inter-denom

MAP 4 H 7
LOCATION Rural
DAY ✓ **RAIL** a **AIR** a
SPORT abcdefghjklmopqstuwx ABC
OTHER LANGUAGES abchk
ACTIVITIES acefghijklmnopqstuvw ABC
OTHER SUBJECTS abcdfh
FACILITIES ON SITE acdefghijkl
EXAM BOARDS abd ADEG
RETAKES ab **NVQ COURSES** 23

A-level	AS	GCSE	OTHER
c efghi nop v	c ghi l o uvw	cdefghi l no v	b e h l s
ABC GHI K NOP R	B G I K PQR TU	BCDE G K NOP RS	F I NO
abcdef hij l		abcdefghij l	def i

C **St. Bede's School; Eastbourne BN20 7XL**
Tel: 01323 734222 (Fax: 01323 642445) *P.Pyemont*

		Boys	Age	Girls	Age	TOTAL		Boys	Girls
Day	£550-£1890	227	2-13	116	2-13	400			
Weekly	£2990		7-13		7-13		SIXTH		
Boarding	£2990	39	7-13	18	7-13				

ENTRY REQUIREMENTS Interview
SCHOLARSHIPS & BURSARIES Schol; Burs; Art; Mus; Sport
SPECIAL NEEDS bjlnw BE **DYSLEXIA** ce **DIET** acd
ASSOCIATION IAPS **FOUNDED** 1895 **RELIGIOUS AFFILIATION** C of E

MAP 4 H 7
LOCATION Rural
DAY ✓ **RAIL** a **AIR** b
SPORT abcefjklmopqstuwx AB
OTHER LANGUAGES a
ACTIVITIES acfghijlopqrstwx AB
OTHER SUBJECTS abcfh
FACILITIES ON SITE cdehik
EXAM BOARDS
RETAKES **NVQ COURSES**

A-level	AS	GCSE	OTHER
			cde g i lmno q s v
			BCDE G K NOP R
			cdefg j l

G **St. Leonards-Mayfield School; The Old Palace; Mayfield; East Sussex TN20 6PH**
Tel: 01435 873383 (Fax: 01435 872627) *Sister Jean Sinclair*

		Boys	Age	Girls	Age	TOTAL		Boys	Girls
Day	£2190	1		201	11-18	509		1	169
Weekly	£3260			56	11-18		SIXTH		
Boarding	£3285			251	11-18				

ENTRY REQUIREMENTS CEE
SCHOLARSHIPS & BURSARIES Schol; Burs; Art; Mus
SPECIAL NEEDS bejlntw H **DYSLEXIA** eg **DIET** a
ASSOCIATION GSA **FOUNDED** 1850 **RELIGIOUS AFFILIATION** R C

MAP 4 H 6
LOCATION Rural
DAY ✓ **RAIL** b **AIR** a
SPORT abcfgklmopqtwx ABC
OTHER LANGUAGES a
ACTIVITIES abcfghijklnopstw AB
OTHER SUBJECTS cefgh
FACILITIES ON SITE acdi
EXAM BOARDS abd ABEG
RETAKES **NVQ COURSES**

A-level	AS	GCSE	OTHER
cdefg i nop v	G	a cde g ij no v	lm q s u
BC GH K P R U W	cdefg j l	BC G K P R U WX	NO
cdefgh j l		cdefgh jkl	a i

SUSSEX (EAST) continued

Gb St. Mary's Hall; Eastern Road; Brighton BN2 5JF
Tel: 01273 606061 (Fax: 01273 620782) Mrs Pamela J.James

		Boys	Age	Girls	Age	TOTAL		Boys	Girls
Day	£390-£1980	7	3-8	328	3-19	431	SIXTH		56
Weekly	£2325-£2865			18	8-19				
Boarding	£2439-£2985			78	8-19				

ENTRY REQUIREMENTS CEE; Exam; Test
SCHOLARSHIPS & BURSARIES Schol; Burs; Mus; Forces; Clergy; Teachers; AP; VI Form; Siblings
SPECIAL NEEDS gjlnqw EH **DYSLEXIA** g **DIET** abcd
ASSOCIATION GSA **FOUNDED** 1836 **RELIGIOUS AFFILIATION** C of E

MAP 4 G 7
LOCATION Urban
DAY √ **RAIL** a **AIR** a
SPORT cklmpqwx ABC
OTHER LANGUAGES a
ACTIVITIES acdghijknopstw AB
OTHER SUBJECTS abcfh
FACILITIES ON SITE cdgi
EXAM BOARDS abd ABEGH
RETAKES   **NVQ COURSES**

A-level cdefghi nop v
B EFGH K   P R
c e hj l

AS   c e ghi   vw
G K   P R
e

GCSE   c e g i   o   v
B E G K   P R
cdefgh j l

OTHER   l n
NO

C Skippers Hill Prep. School; Five Ashes; Mayfield; East Sussex TN20 6HR
Tel: 01825 830234 (Fax: 01825 830234) T.W.Lewis

		Boys	Age	Girls	Age	TOTAL		Boys	Girls
Day	£545-£1655	92	2-13	64	2-13	156	SIXTH		
Weekly									
Boarding									

ENTRY REQUIREMENTS Test & Interview
SCHOLARSHIPS & BURSARIES Schol; Burs; Art; Mus; Sport; ARA
SPECIAL NEEDS w B **DYSLEXIA**   **DIET** a
ASSOCIATION IAPS **FOUNDED** 1945 **RELIGIOUS AFFILIATION** Inter-denom

MAP 4 H 6
LOCATION Rural
DAY   **RAIL** a **AIR** a
SPORT abcefjlmnopqsux ABC
OTHER LANGUAGES
ACTIVITIES cfghijnoqt A
OTHER SUBJECTS cfh
FACILITIES ON SITE chik
EXAM BOARDS
RETAKES   **NVQ COURSES**

A-level
AS
GCSE
OTHER   de g i lmno   v
B EG K   OP R
cde   j

C Temple Grove with St. Nicholas; Heron's Ghyll; Uckfield; Sussex TN22 4DA
Tel: 0182 571 2112 (Fax: 0182 571 3432) M.G.N.Lee & Mrs J.E.Lee

		Boys	Age	Girls	Age	TOTAL		Boys	Girls
Day	£575-£2230	83	3-13	100	3-13	207	SIXTH		
Weekly	£2273-£2295	10	7-13	6	7-13				
Boarding	£2273-£2295	2	7-13	6	7-13				

ENTRY REQUIREMENTS Test
SCHOLARSHIPS & BURSARIES Burs
SPECIAL NEEDS n B **DYSLEXIA**   **DIET** ad
ASSOCIATION IAPS **FOUNDED** 1810 **RELIGIOUS AFFILIATION** C of E

MAP 4 H 6
LOCATION Rural
DAY √ **RAIL** a **AIR** a
SPORT abcdefgjklmopqsux ABC
OTHER LANGUAGES a
ACTIVITIES acfghjmorstx A
OTHER SUBJECTS bcfh
FACILITIES ON SITE abcdhikl
EXAM BOARDS
RETAKES   **NVQ COURSES**

A-level
AS
GCSE
OTHER   de g i lmno q t v
ABC G K NOP R
cdef   j

C Vinehall; Robertsbridge; Sussex TN32 5JL
Tel: 01580 880413 (Fax: 01580 882119) D.C.Chaplin

		Boys	Age	Girls	Age	TOTAL		Boys	Girls
Day	£1120-£2750	143	4-13	85	4-13	310	SIXTH		
Weekly									
Boarding	£2750	54	7-13	28	7-13				

ENTRY REQUIREMENTS Interview
SCHOLARSHIPS & BURSARIES Forces; Clergy; Teachers
SPECIAL NEEDS bt **DYSLEXIA**   **DIET** abc
ASSOCIATION IAPS **FOUNDED** 1938 **RELIGIOUS AFFILIATION** RC/C of E

MAP 4 I 6
LOCATION Rural
DAY   **RAIL** a **AIR** b
SPORT abcefjklmpqstuwx AB
OTHER LANGUAGES
ACTIVITIES acfghijlmopqrtw A
OTHER SUBJECTS abcfh
FACILITIES ON SITE cdhikl
EXAM BOARDS
RETAKES   **NVQ COURSES**

A-level
AS
GCSE
OTHER   e g i lm o   v
B   G K   OP R
cde g   j

C Westerleigh; 17 Hollington Park Road; St.Leonards-on-Sea; Sussex TN38 0SE
Tel: 01424 440760 (Fax: 01424 440761) Mrs P.K.Wheeler

		Boys	Age	Girls	Age	TOTAL		Boys	Girls
Day	£1085-£1480	116	2-13	79	2-13	195	SIXTH		
Weekly									
Boarding									

ENTRY REQUIREMENTS Test & Interview
SCHOLARSHIPS & BURSARIES Schol; Burs; Teachers; ARA; Siblings
SPECIAL NEEDS bjn l **DYSLEXIA** ce **DIET** abcd
ASSOCIATION IAPS **FOUNDED** 1907 **RELIGIOUS AFFILIATION** C of E

MAP 4 I 7
LOCATION Urban
DAY √ **RAIL** a **AIR** b
SPORT abcefhjklmpqstuwx ABC
OTHER LANGUAGES a
ACTIVITIES abcfghjklmnopqstuvx A
OTHER SUBJECTS abcfh
FACILITIES ON SITE cfh
EXAM BOARDS
RETAKES   **NVQ COURSES**

A-level
AS
GCSE
OTHER   bcdefg i lmno q s v
BC   G K   OP R T
cdef   j

SUSSEX (WEST)

C — Ardingly College; Haywards Heath; West Sussex RH17 6SQ
Tel: 01444 892577 (Fax: 01444 892266) *J.W.Flecker*

			Boys	Age	Girls	Age	TOTAL		Boys	Girls
Day	£3065	X	97	13-18	59	13-18	474	SIXTH	85	86
Weekly Boarding	£3880		172	13-18	146	13-18				

ENTRY REQUIREMENTS CEE; Scholarship Exam; Report & Interview; Report & Test; Report & Exam & Interview **SCHOLARSHIPS & BURSARIES** Schol; Art; Mus; Chor; Forces; Clergy; AP; VI Form; Sport; ARA; Drama **SPECIAL NEEDS** begjlnqt AGH **DYSLEXIA** f **DIET** a
ASSOCIATION HMC **FOUNDED** 1858 **RELIGIOUS AFFILIATION** C of E

MAP 4 G 6
LOCATION Rural
DAY **RAIL** a **AIR** a
SPORT abcdefghjkmnopqrtuwx ABC
OTHER LANGUAGES a
ACTIVITIES cefghijklmnoqrstw A
OTHER SUBJECTS bcdfh
FACILITIES ON SITE abcdgik
EXAM BOARDS abd ABDEGH
RETAKES **NVQ COURSES**

A-level: cde ghi no v / B GH K OP U W / cdefgh jkl
AS: c fh l / G K PQR U / c e j
GCSE: e g i no v / B E G K P / cdefgh jkl
OTHER: c g i l / C K N P R / c ef h kl

C — Ardingly College Junior School; Haywards Heath; West Sussex RH17 6SQ
Tel: 01444 892279 (Fax: 01444 892266) *Peter E.J.Thwaites*

		Boys	Age	Girls	Age	TOTAL		Boys	Girls
Day	£360-£1800	73	3-13	57	3-13	194	SIXTH		
Weekly Boarding	£2400-£2665	33	7-13	31	7-13				

ENTRY REQUIREMENTS Assessment & Interview
SCHOLARSHIPS & BURSARIES Schol; Mus; Clergy; AP; Sport
SPECIAL NEEDS bltw **DYSLEXIA** **DIET** a
ASSOCIATION IAPS **FOUNDED** 1912 **RELIGIOUS AFFILIATION** C of E

MAP 4 G 6
LOCATION Rural
DAY **RAIL** a **AIR** a
SPORT abcefjmopqstuwx AB
OTHER LANGUAGES
ACTIVITIES dfghijmnoqrtwx A
OTHER SUBJECTS bcfh
FACILITIES ON SITE acdei
EXAM BOARDS
RETAKES **NVQ COURSES**

OTHER: e l o v / BC G K R / cdefg j l

C — Arundale School; Lower Street; Pulborough; West Sussex RH20 2BX
Tel: 01798 872520 *Miss K.M.Lovejoy*

			Boys	Age	Girls	Age	TOTAL		Boys	Girls
Day	£420-£1235	X	23	3-8	81	3-11	104	SIXTH		
Weekly Boarding										

ENTRY REQUIREMENTS Interview
SCHOLARSHIPS & BURSARIES Mus
SPECIAL NEEDS knw GI **DYSLEXIA** ef **DIET** a
ASSOCIATION IAPS **FOUNDED** 1953 **RELIGIOUS AFFILIATION** Christian

MAP 3 F 6
LOCATION Rural
DAY **RAIL** a **AIR** a
SPORT aehjlopqx B
OTHER LANGUAGES
ACTIVITIES cghjo
OTHER SUBJECTS ach
FACILITIES ON SITE
EXAM BOARDS
RETAKES **NVQ COURSES**

OTHER: egil o v / BC E G K OP R / cde j

B — Brambletye; East Grinstead; Sussex RH19 3PD
Tel: 01342 321004 (Fax: 01342 317562) *D.G.Fowler-Watt*

			Boys	Age	Girls	Age	TOTAL		Boys	Girls
Day	£2150	X	56	8-13			225	SIXTH		
Weekly Boarding	£2925		169	8-13						

ENTRY REQUIREMENTS Report
SCHOLARSHIPS & BURSARIES
SPECIAL NEEDS bgjklnpu BEI **DYSLEXIA** e **DIET** a
ASSOCIATION IAPS **FOUNDED** 1919 **RELIGIOUS AFFILIATION** C of E

MAP 4 G 5
LOCATION Rural
DAY **RAIL** a **AIR** a
SPORT acegjkosuwx AB
OTHER LANGUAGES
ACTIVITIES fghijmort A
OTHER SUBJECTS cfh
FACILITIES ON SITE cdikl
EXAM BOARDS
RETAKES **NVQ COURSES**

OTHER: c e l o v / B G K R / cdef j

C — Broadwater Manor School; Broadwater Road; Worthing; Sussex BN14 8HU
Tel: 01903 236687 (Fax: 01903 821777) *D Telfer*

			Boys	Age	Girls	Age	TOTAL		Boys	Girls
Day	£100-£1155	X	266	2-13	178	2-13	444	SIXTH		
Weekly Boarding										

ENTRY REQUIREMENTS Interview
SCHOLARSHIPS & BURSARIES
SPECIAL NEEDS **DYSLEXIA** **DIET** a
ASSOCIATION IAPS **FOUNDED** 1930 **RELIGIOUS AFFILIATION** Inter-denom

MAP 3 F 7
LOCATION Urban
DAY **RAIL** a **AIR** a
SPORT abefjlmopqsx AB
OTHER LANGUAGES
ACTIVITIES fghj
OTHER SUBJECTS abch
FACILITIES ON SITE ch
EXAM BOARDS
RETAKES **NVQ COURSES**

OTHER: de l o v / B E G K O R / cdef

SUSSEX (WEST) continued

G | Burgess Hill School; Keymer Road; Burgess Hill; West Sussex RH15 0EG
Tel: 01444 241050 (Fax: 01444 870314) *Mrs.Rosemary Lewis*

		Boys	Age	Girls	Age	TOTAL	SIXTH	Boys	Girls
Day	£855-£1840 ✗	43	3-4	562	3-18	662			82
Weekly									
Boarding	£2775-£3095			57	9-18				

ENTRY REQUIREMENTS Exam; Interview; Report & Interview
SCHOLARSHIPS & BURSARIES Schol; Mus; AP; VI Form
SPECIAL NEEDS behjklnqtw EGH   **DYSLEXIA** g   **DIET** acd
ASSOCIATION GSA   **FOUNDED** 1906   **RELIGIOUS AFFILIATION** Inter-denom

MAP 4 G 6
LOCATION Urban
DAY ✓   **RAIL** a   **AIR** a
SPORT abcfghlmopqtwx ABC
OTHER LANGUAGES a
ACTIVITIES cfghijknopqrstw AB
OTHER SUBJECTS abcdefgh
FACILITIES ON SITE bgh
EXAM BOARDS abcd ABEGJ
RETAKES ab   **NVQ COURSES**

A-level: cdefghi p v / B GH K P W / cdef j l
AS: h n / G K / ef j
GCSE: cde ghi n v / B G K P W / cdefgh j l
OTHER: lm o q s uv x / C E G H K M O R U

C | Christ's Hospital; Horsham; West Sussex RH13 7LS
Tel: 01403 252547 (Fax: 01403 255283) *R.C.Poulton*

		Boys	Age	Girls	Age	TOTAL	SIXTH	Boys	Girls
Day						818		133	81
Weekly									
Boarding	-£3563	496	11-18	322	11-18				

ENTRY REQUIREMENTS Assessment & Interview
SCHOLARSHIPS & BURSARIES Schol; Burs; AP
SPECIAL NEEDS bejlnq E   **DYSLEXIA** e   **DIET** acd
ASSOCIATION HMC   **FOUNDED** 1552   **RELIGIOUS AFFILIATION** C of E

MAP 3 F 6
LOCATION Rural
DAY   **RAIL** a   **AIR** a
SPORT abcdefghijklmopstuwx ABC
OTHER LANGUAGES
ACTIVITIES bcefghijklmnoqrstvx AB
OTHER SUBJECTS bcdefgh
FACILITIES ON SITE abcdehik
EXAM BOARDS abcd ABDEGH
RETAKES   **NVQ COURSES**

A-level: defghi opq v x / B GH K P R W / c efg jk
AS: q
GCSE: cde no q v / ABC G K O R WX / cdefg jk
OTHER: l / ef h l

C | Copthorne School Trust Ltd.; Effingham Lane; Copthorne; Sussex RH10 3HR
Tel: 01342 712311 (Fax: 01342 714014) *D.Newton*

		Boys	Age	Girls	Age	TOTAL	SIXTH	Boys	Girls
Day	£1095-£1990	144	4-13	65	4-13	218			
Weekly	£2420	6	9-13	3	9-13				
Boarding									

ENTRY REQUIREMENTS Test
SCHOLARSHIPS & BURSARIES Schol
SPECIAL NEEDS jw l   **DYSLEXIA**   **DIET** ad
ASSOCIATION IAPS   **FOUNDED** 1902   **RELIGIOUS AFFILIATION** C of E

MAP 4 G 6
LOCATION Rural
DAY   **RAIL**   **AIR** a
SPORT acejkmopqswx AB
OTHER LANGUAGES
ACTIVITIES cfghjosw A
OTHER SUBJECTS ch
FACILITIES ON SITE cdhijk
EXAM BOARDS
RETAKES   **NVQ COURSES**

OTHER: de g i lmno v / B G K OP R / cde j

C | Cottesmore School; Buchan Hill; Pease Pottage; West Sussex RH11 9AU
Tel: 01293 520648 (Fax: 01293 614784) *M.A.Rogerson*

		Boys	Age	Girls	Age	TOTAL	SIXTH	Boys	Girls
Day						140			
Weekly									
Boarding	£2910	100	7-13	40	7-13				

ENTRY REQUIREMENTS Report & Interview
SCHOLARSHIPS & BURSARIES Burs
SPECIAL NEEDS abeijlw B   **DYSLEXIA**   **DIET** acd
ASSOCIATION IAPS   **FOUNDED** 1894   **RELIGIOUS AFFILIATION** C of E

MAP 4 G 6
LOCATION Rural
DAY   **RAIL** a   **AIR** a
SPORT abdefijklmnopqrsuwx AB
OTHER LANGUAGES
ACTIVITIES acfghijlmoprstvw A
OTHER SUBJECTS abcfh
FACILITIES ON SITE dhikl
EXAM BOARDS
RETAKES   **NVQ COURSES**

OTHER: eg i l m o q v / B G K P R / cde j

B | Dorset House; The Manor; Bury; Pulborough; Sussex RH20 1PB
Tel: 01798 831456 (Fax: 01798 831141) *A.L.James*

		Boys	Age	Girls	Age	TOTAL	SIXTH	Boys	Girls
Day	£1110-£2235 ✗	72	4-13			115			
Weekly	£2680		7-13						
Boarding	£2680	43	7-13						

ENTRY REQUIREMENTS Interview
SCHOLARSHIPS & BURSARIES Burs; Forces
SPECIAL NEEDS bn   **DYSLEXIA** e   **DIET** a
ASSOCIATION IAPS   **FOUNDED** 1781   **RELIGIOUS AFFILIATION** Inter-denom

MAP 3 F 6
LOCATION Rural
DAY   **RAIL** a   **AIR** b
SPORT abdefjmosx AB
OTHER LANGUAGES
ACTIVITIES fghijmoqrst A
OTHER SUBJECTS cfh
FACILITIES ON SITE cjk
EXAM BOARDS
RETAKES   **NVQ COURSES**

OTHER: egi l o v / B E G K OP R / cde j

SUSSEX (WEST) *continued*

G — Farlington School; Strood Park; Horsham; W.Sussex RH12 3PN
Tel: 01403 254967 (Fax: 01403 272258) Mrs P.Mawer

	Boys	Age	Girls	Age	TOTAL		Boys	Girls
Day £840–£1930 ✗			268	4-18	309	SIXTH		45
Weekly £2720–£3080			31	9-18				
Boarding £3120			10	9-18				

ENTRY REQUIREMENTS Report & Exam & Interview
SCHOLARSHIPS & BURSARIES Schol; Burs; Mus; Chor; VI Form
SPECIAL NEEDS abjklnqwx E   **DYSLEXIA** e   **DIET** a
ASSOCIATION GSA   **FOUNDED** 1896   **RELIGIOUS AFFILIATION** C of E

MAP 3 F 6
LOCATION Rural
DAY   **RAIL** a   **AIR** a
SPORT abcfhlmopqwx ABC
OTHER LANGUAGES a
ACTIVITIES cfgijknopqstw AB
OTHER SUBJECTS bcdfh
FACILITIES ON SITE abfj
EXAM BOARDS abde ABEGHL
RETAKES   **NVQ COURSES**

A-level: cd ghi n v / BC GH K OP T / c ef l
AS: d i u / GH P
GCSE: d g i n vw / BC E G K P R T / cdef j l
OTHER: lm o / e k

C — Fonthill Lodge School; Coombe Hill Road; East Grinstead; West Sussex RH19 4LY
Tel: 01342 321635 (Fax: 01342 326844) Mrs J.M.Griffiths

	Boys	Age	Girls	Age	TOTAL		Boys	Girls
Day £394–£1499 ✗	49	2-8	109	2-11	158	SIXTH		
Weekly								
Boarding								

ENTRY REQUIREMENTS
SCHOLARSHIPS & BURSARIES Schol
SPECIAL NEEDS an   **DYSLEXIA** e   **DIET** acd
ASSOCIATION IAPS   **FOUNDED** 1808   **RELIGIOUS AFFILIATION** C of E

MAP 4 G 5
LOCATION Rural
DAY   **RAIL** a   **AIR** a
SPORT aejklmpqx B
OTHER LANGUAGES
ACTIVITIES cfgj
OTHER SUBJECTS ch
FACILITIES ON SITE
EXAM BOARDS
RETAKES   **NVQ COURSES**

OTHER: e

C — Great Ballard; Eartham; Chichester; W.Sussex PO18 0LR
Tel: 01243 814236 (Fax: 01243 814586) R.E.T.Jennings

	Boys	Age	Girls	Age	TOTAL		Boys	Girls
Day £541–£1704	73	3-13	40	3-13	161	SIXTH		
Weekly £2300–£2414	23	7-13	10	7-13				
Boarding £2300–£2414	11	7-13	4	7-13				

ENTRY REQUIREMENTS Test & Interview
SCHOLARSHIPS & BURSARIES Schol; Forces
SPECIAL NEEDS befjkls ABGH   **DYSLEXIA**   **DIET** a
ASSOCIATION IAPS   **FOUNDED** 1924   **RELIGIOUS AFFILIATION** C of E

MAP 3 E 7
LOCATION Rural
DAY   **RAIL** a   **AIR** a
SPORT abefgjklmnopqsuwx ABC
OTHER LANGUAGES a
ACTIVITIES acfghjnoprstwx A
OTHER SUBJECTS abcfh
FACILITIES ON SITE cjkl
EXAM BOARDS
RETAKES   **NVQ COURSES**

OTHER: de g i lmno q   v / BC G   K NOP R / cde j

C — Great Walstead; Lindfield; Haywards Heath; Sussex RH16 2QL
Tel: 01444 483528 (Fax: 01444 482122) H.J.Lowries

	Boys	Age	Girls	Age	TOTAL		Boys	Girls
Day £160–£1860 ✗	178	3-13	104	3-13	329	SIXTH		
Weekly								
Boarding £2300	30	7-13	17	7-13				

ENTRY REQUIREMENTS Assessment
SCHOLARSHIPS & BURSARIES Schol; Mus; Forces; Clergy; Teachers; Sport
SPECIAL NEEDS n E   **DYSLEXIA** c   **DIET**
ASSOCIATION IAPS   **FOUNDED** 1925   **RELIGIOUS AFFILIATION** Inter-denom

MAP 4 G 6
LOCATION Rural
DAY   **RAIL** a   **AIR** a
SPORT abcdefgjklmnopqsux ABC
OTHER LANGUAGES
ACTIVITIES fghijmoqtvwx A
OTHER SUBJECTS bcfh
FACILITIES ON SITE abcdhjk
EXAM BOARDS
RETAKES   **NVQ COURSES**

OTHER: e g i   o q   uv / ABC G   K   OP R / cde g j

C — Handcross Park School; Handcross; Haywards Heath; Sussex RH17 6HF
Tel: 01444 400526 (Fax: 01444 400527)

	Boys	Age	Girls	Age	TOTAL		Boys	Girls
Day £90–£2035	126	2-13	100	2-13	241	SIXTH		
Weekly								
Boarding £2460	12	7-13	3	7-13				

ENTRY REQUIREMENTS Interview; Report
SCHOLARSHIPS & BURSARIES Schol; Burs; Teachers
SPECIAL NEEDS ejknw l   **DYSLEXIA** e   **DIET** abcd
ASSOCIATION IAPS   **FOUNDED** 1887   **RELIGIOUS AFFILIATION** C of E

MAP 4 G 6
LOCATION Rural
DAY   **RAIL** a   **AIR** a
SPORT aefjklmopqsux ABC
OTHER LANGUAGES a
ACTIVITIES cfghjopqrtwx A
OTHER SUBJECTS acfh
FACILITIES ON SITE bcdejkl
EXAM BOARDS
RETAKES   **NVQ COURSES**

OTHER: de g i lmno q   v / BC E G K OP R / cde g j

277

SUSSEX (WEST) continued

C | Hurstpierpoint College; Hassocks; West Sussex BN6 9JS
Tel: 01273 833636 (Fax: 01273 835257) S.D.A.Meek

		Boys	Age	Girls	Age	TOTAL		Boys	Girls
Day	£3020	101	13-18		13-18	339	SIXTH	114	14
Weekly		230	13-18	8	13-18				
Boarding	£3790								

ENTRY REQUIREMENTS CEE; Scholarship Exam; Test & Interview
SCHOLARSHIPS & BURSARIES Schol; Art; Mus; Forces; Clergy; Teachers; AP; VI Form; Sport; ARA
SPECIAL NEEDS lnx l **DYSLEXIA** f **DIET** ad
ASSOCIATION HMC **FOUNDED** 1849 **RELIGIOUS AFFILIATION** C of E

MAP 4 G 6
LOCATION Rural
DAY ✓ **RAIL** a **AIR** a
SPORT abcdefghklmpqstuwx ABC
OTHER LANGUAGES a
ACTIVITIES aefghjklnopqstw ABD
OTHER SUBJECTS abcdefh
FACILITIES ON SITE abcdeghik
EXAM BOARDS abcd BDEFHL
RETAKES a **NVQ COURSES**

A-level: c e ghi l op v x / AB GH K P U / c ef j
AS: cde hi l op v / A G K U / c ef
GCSE: cde g i l o v / AB E G K OP U X / cdefg jkl
OTHER: R

C | Hurstpierpoint College Junior School; Hassocks; West Sussex BN6 9JS
Tel: 01273 834975 (Fax: 01273 835257) A.G.Gobat Esq

		Boys	Age	Girls	Age	TOTAL		Boys	Girls
Day	£1600-£1890	80	7-13	20	7-13	132	SIXTH		
Weekly			7-13						
Boarding	£2560	26	7-13	6					

ENTRY REQUIREMENTS Report & Interview; Report & Test
SCHOLARSHIPS & BURSARIES Schol; Burs; Mus; Forces; Clergy; AP
SPECIAL NEEDS bn B **DYSLEXIA** e **DIET** abcd
ASSOCIATION IAPS **FOUNDED** 1933 **RELIGIOUS AFFILIATION** C of E

MAP 4 G 7
LOCATION Rural
DAY a **AIR** a
SPORT abcefjklmopqsuwx ABC
OTHER LANGUAGES a
ACTIVITIES cfghjloprst A
OTHER SUBJECTS bcfh
FACILITIES ON SITE abcdhik
EXAM BOARDS
RETAKES **NVQ COURSES**

A-level:
AS:
GCSE:
OTHER: e g i l o v / AB G K P R / cde j

Bg | Lancing College; Lancing; West Sussex BN15 0RW
Tel: 01273 452213 (Fax: 01273 464720) C.J.Saunders

		Boys	Age	Girls	Age	TOTAL		Boys	Girls
Day	£3015	45	13-18	1	16-18	517	SIXTH	172	55
Weekly									
Boarding	£4010	417	13-18	54	16-18				

ENTRY REQUIREMENTS CEE; Scholarship Exam
SCHOLARSHIPS & BURSARIES Schol; Art; Mus; Clergy
SPECIAL NEEDS bhiklrs **DYSLEXIA** **DIET** ad
ASSOCIATION HMC **FOUNDED** 1848 **RELIGIOUS AFFILIATION** C of E

MAP 3 F 7
LOCATION Rural
DAY **RAIL** a **AIR** a
SPORT abcdefghijklmnopqstuwx ABC
OTHER LANGUAGES
ACTIVITIES bcefghijklmnopqstuv ABC
OTHER SUBJECTS abcfh
FACILITIES ON SITE bcdefghik
EXAM BOARDS abcd ABDEH
RETAKES a **NVQ COURSES**

A-level: cdefg i l op v / AB GH K P R U / cdefgh jkl
AS: G / ef h jkl
GCSE: cde g i l o q v x / AB GH K OP / cdefgh jkl
OTHER: a

Gb | Lavant House - Rosemead; Chichester; Sussex PO18 9AB
Tel: 01243 527211 (Fax: 01243 530490) Mrs Hylary Kingham

		Boys	Age	Girls	Age	TOTAL		Boys	Girls
Day	£450-£1850	14	3-18	125	3-18	199	SIXTH		28
Weekly	£2625-£3290			25	9-18				
Boarding	£2625-£3290			35	9-18				

ENTRY REQUIREMENTS CEE; Test & Interview
SCHOLARSHIPS & BURSARIES Schol; Burs; Art; VI Form
SPECIAL NEEDS bhjkn Gl **DYSLEXIA** e **DIET** acd
ASSOCIATION GSA **FOUNDED** 1952 **RELIGIOUS AFFILIATION** C of E

MAP 3 E 7
LOCATION Rural
DAY ✓ **RAIL** a **AIR** b
SPORT abclnpqwx ABC
OTHER LANGUAGES ac
ACTIVITIES cfghjklnoqtw A
OTHER SUBJECTS abcdefgh
FACILITIES ON SITE bcehj
EXAM BOARDS abd BEGH
RETAKES ab **NVQ COURSES**

A-level: c efg i v / BC G P / cdefg j l
AS: u
GCSE: e g i n v / BC E G P R / cdefg j l
OTHER: h l m o / K O

C | Oakwood; Chichester; West Sussex PO18 9AN
Tel: 01243 575209 (Fax: 01243 575433) S.J.Whittle

		Boys	Age	Girls	Age	TOTAL		Boys	Girls
Day	£436-£1708	80	3-13	46	3-13	154	SIXTH		
Weekly	£2266	14	7-13	4	7-13				
Boarding	£2450	8	7-13	2	7-13				

ENTRY REQUIREMENTS Test
SCHOLARSHIPS & BURSARIES Schol; Burs; Drama
SPECIAL NEEDS bklnqu BF **DYSLEXIA** e **DIET** abcd
ASSOCIATION IAPS **FOUNDED** 1912 **RELIGIOUS AFFILIATION** C of E

MAP 3 E 7
LOCATION Rural
DAY **RAIL** a **AIR** b
SPORT acefghjklmopqsuwx AB
OTHER LANGUAGES
ACTIVITIES cfghjopqrswx A
OTHER SUBJECTS ch
FACILITIES ON SITE achjk
EXAM BOARDS
RETAKES **NVQ COURSES**

A-level:
AS:
GCSE:
OTHER: de g i l mno q v / B G K OP R / cdef j

SUSSEX (WEST) continued

Our Lady of Sion School; Gratwicke Road; Worthing; W.Sussex BN11 4BL
Tel: 01903 204063 (Fax: 01903 214434) *B.Sexton*

		Boys	Age	Girls	Age	TOTAL		Boys	Girls
Day	£382-£1485	216	3-18	262	3-18	478	SIXTH	34	24
Weekly									
Boarding									

ENTRY REQUIREMENTS Exam; Interview; Report
SCHOLARSHIPS & BURSARIES Burs; VI Form
SPECIAL NEEDS n B
ASSOCIATION GBGSA **FOUNDED** 1862 **DYSLEXIA** g **DIET** a
RELIGIOUS AFFILIATION Inter-denom

MAP 3 F 7
LOCATION Urban
DAY ✓ **RAIL** a **AIR** b
SPORT abcehjlmopqswx ABC
OTHER LANGUAGES
ACTIVITIES cfghijnotv A
OTHER SUBJECTS bcdefh
FACILITIES ON SITE cdgh
EXAM BOARDS abd BEGH
RETAKES ab **NVQ COURSES**

A-level cde ghi op v
B GH K P R U
c ef j

AS G

GCSE de g i l no v
ABC E G K OP R
cdef j l

OTHER

Pennthorpe School; Rudgwick; Horsham; Sussex RH12 3HJ
Tel: 01403 822391 (Fax: 01403 822438) *The Rev.J.E.Spencer*

		Boys	Age	Girls	Age	TOTAL		Boys	Girls
Day	£725-£1885	✗	145	4-13	74	4-13	219	SIXTH	
Weekly									
Boarding									

ENTRY REQUIREMENTS Interview
SCHOLARSHIPS & BURSARIES Schol
SPECIAL NEEDS ejknpquw BGI
ASSOCIATION IAPS **FOUNDED** 1930 **DYSLEXIA** de **DIET** abcd
RELIGIOUS AFFILIATION C of E

MAP 3 F 6
LOCATION Rural
DAY ✓ **RAIL** a **AIR** a
SPORT abcdefijlmopqstuwx AB
OTHER LANGUAGES a
ACTIVITIES cfghjotx A
OTHER SUBJECTS bcfh
FACILITIES ON SITE bcdhik
EXAM BOARDS
RETAKES **NVQ COURSES**

A-level **AS** **GCSE**

OTHER de g i lm o q s v
BC G K OP R
cde j

Prebendal School; Chichester; West Sussex PO19 1RT
Tel: 01243 782026 *The Revd. Canon G.C.Hall*

		Boys	Age	Girls	Age	TOTAL		Boys	Girls
Day	£1660	✗	79	6-14	72	6-14	197	SIXTH	
Weekly	£2160		15	6-14	14	6-14			
Boarding	£2260		16	6-14	1	6-14			

ENTRY REQUIREMENTS Test
SCHOLARSHIPS & BURSARIES Mus; Chor; Siblings
SPECIAL NEEDS eijkn GI
ASSOCIATION IAPS **FOUNDED** 1497 **DYSLEXIA** e **DIET** a
RELIGIOUS AFFILIATION C of E

MAP 3 E 7
LOCATION Urban
DAY **RAIL** a **AIR** b
SPORT aefgjmpqx AB
OTHER LANGUAGES
ACTIVITIES fghjot
OTHER SUBJECTS cfh
FACILITIES ON SITE bcj
EXAM BOARDS
RETAKES **NVQ COURSES**

A-level **AS** **GCSE**

OTHER e g i o v
B G K P R
cde j

St. Margaret's Junior School; Convent of Mercy; Midhurst; Sussex GU29 9JN
Tel: 01730 813956 *Sister M Joan O'Dwyer*

		Boys	Age	Girls	Age	TOTAL		Boys	Girls
Day	£290-£625	176	3-11	266	3-11	442	SIXTH		
Weekly									
Boarding									

ENTRY REQUIREMENTS Assessment & Interview
SCHOLARSHIPS & BURSARIES
SPECIAL NEEDS abceghijklnpqstuw ABFGHIL
ASSOCIATION ISAI **FOUNDED** 1888 **DYSLEXIA** **DIET**
RELIGIOUS AFFILIATION R C

MAP 3 E 6
LOCATION Rural
DAY **RAIL** b **AIR** b
SPORT aefhjlmpq BC
OTHER LANGUAGES a
ACTIVITIES cfghijoqrt A
OTHER SUBJECTS bcdh
FACILITIES ON SITE bcdehk
EXAM BOARDS
RETAKES **NVQ COURSES**

A-level **AS** **GCSE**

OTHER cdefg klmno stuvw
B DE G JK O RS
cde j

Sandhurst School; 101 Brighton Road; Worthing; Sussex BN11 2EL
Tel: 01903 201933 *Mrs C.Skomski*

		Boys	Age	Girls	Age	TOTAL		Boys	Girls
Day	£470-£575	83	2-13	107	2-13	190	SIXTH		
Weekly									
Boarding									

ENTRY REQUIREMENTS Assessment & Interview
SCHOLARSHIPS & BURSARIES
SPECIAL NEEDS n
ASSOCIATION ISAI **FOUNDED** 1935 **DYSLEXIA** e **DIET**
RELIGIOUS AFFILIATION

MAP 3 F 7
LOCATION Urban
DAY **RAIL** b **AIR** b
SPORT ejmpqx
OTHER LANGUAGES
ACTIVITIES gj
OTHER SUBJECTS h
FACILITIES ON SITE
EXAM BOARDS
RETAKES **NVQ COURSES**

A-level **AS** **GCSE**

OTHER e v
B G K O R
cde

SUSSEX (WEST) continued

B g — Seaford College; Petworth GU28 0NB
Tel: 01798 867392 (Fax: 01798 867606) *R.C.Hannaford*

		Boys	Age	Girls	Age	TOTAL		Boys	Girls
Day	£1755-£1975	71	11-18	11	16-18	332	SIXTH	89	11
Weekly	£2750-£3210	72	11-18						
Boarding	£2750-£3210	178	11-18						

ENTRY REQUIREMENTS Assessment & Interview; CEE & Interview
SCHOLARSHIPS & BURSARIES Schol; Art; Mus; Chor; Forces; Clergy; VI Form; Sport; Siblings
SPECIAL NEEDS abegijklnqtuwx ABDGHIL   **DYSLEXIA** def   **DIET** abcd
ASSOCIATION SHMIS   **FOUNDED** 1884   **RELIGIOUS AFFILIATION** C of E

MAP 3 F 6
LOCATION Rural
DAY ✓   **RAIL** a   **AIR** a
SPORT abcdefghjklmopqstuwx ABC
OTHER LANGUAGES a
ACTIVITIES abefghijklmnopqrstuvw A
OTHER SUBJECTS abcfh
FACILITIES ON SITE abcdefghikl
EXAM BOARDS bd ADEH
RETAKES ab   **NVQ COURSES** 3

A-level: AB de ghi I op uv x / GH K NOP · U / cdef l
AS: AS de g i op U / GH K / cdef
GCSE: B de ghij l opq s uv / G K NOP R / cdef j l
OTHER: K

C — Shoreham College; St. Julian's Lane; Shoreham-by-Sea; Sussex BN43 6YW
Tel: 01273 592681 (Fax: 01273 591673) *D.R.Jarman*

		Boys	Age	Girls	Age	TOTAL		Boys	Girls
Day	£840-£1835	126	3-16	40	3-16	166	SIXTH	2	1
Weekly									
Boarding									

ENTRY REQUIREMENTS CEE; Test & Interview
SCHOLARSHIPS & BURSARIES Schol; Art; Mus; Forces; Clergy; Sport
SPECIAL NEEDS blnqt Gl   **DYSLEXIA** g   **DIET** acd
ASSOCIATION ISAI   **FOUNDED** 1842   **RELIGIOUS AFFILIATION** C of E

MAP 4 G 7
LOCATION Urban
DAY ✓   **RAIL** a   **AIR** a
SPORT abcefjopqtwx BC
OTHER LANGUAGES
ACTIVITIES efghijkorst A
OTHER SUBJECTS c
FACILITIES ON SITE hj
EXAM BOARDS bd ABE
RETAKES a   **NVQ COURSES**

A-level:
AS: h / G K
GCSE: u w / B d g i l p v / G K P / cde l
OTHER: n / O R

B — Slindon College; Slindon; Nr.Arundel; Sussex BN18 0RH
Tel: 01243 814320 (Fax: 01243 814647) *A.C.Baldwin*

		Boys	Age	Girls	Age	TOTAL		Boys	Girls
Day	£1995	22	11-18			89	SIXTH	16	
Weekly		38	11-18						
Boarding	£3050	29	11-18						

ENTRY REQUIREMENTS Report & Interview
SCHOLARSHIPS & BURSARIES Schol; Burs; Forces; Siblings
SPECIAL NEEDS bejlnpquw BE   **DYSLEXIA** de   **DIET** acd
ASSOCIATION ISAI   **FOUNDED** 1972   **RELIGIOUS AFFILIATION** Non-denom

MAP 3 F 7
LOCATION Rural
DAY ✓   **RAIL** a   **AIR** b
SPORT abcdefhjkmostwx ABC
OTHER LANGUAGES a
ACTIVITIES bfghjkmnopqstwx A
OTHER SUBJECTS bcdf
FACILITIES ON SITE bcj
EXAM BOARDS abcde ABEGL
RETAKES a   **NVQ COURSES**

A-level: AB e ghi l o v x / FG P / cde
AS: h / d
GCSE: ABC e h l no v x / EFG I K S / cdef
OTHER: l n t v / O R

B — Sompting Abbotts; Nr. Lancing; West Sussex BN15 0AZ
Tel: 01903 235960 *R.M.Johnson*

		Boys	Age	Girls	Age	TOTAL		Boys	Girls
Day	£675-£1295	133	3-13			147	SIXTH		
Weekly	£1595-£1895	14	8-13						
Boarding									

ENTRY REQUIREMENTS Test & Interview
SCHOLARSHIPS & BURSARIES
SPECIAL NEEDS abklpsw GHI   **DYSLEXIA**   **DIET** cd
ASSOCIATION IAPS   **FOUNDED** 1921   **RELIGIOUS AFFILIATION** C of E

MAP 3 F 7
LOCATION Rural
DAY ✓   **RAIL** a   **AIR** b
SPORT abefjlsuwx AB
OTHER LANGUAGES
ACTIVITIES fgjnt
OTHER SUBJECTS ch
FACILITIES ON SITE cjk
EXAM BOARDS
RETAKES   **NVQ COURSES**

A-level:
AS:
GCSE:
OTHER: B de g i no v / G K OP R / cde j

C — Stoke Brunswick; Ashurst Wood; East Grinstead; Sussex RH19 3PF
Tel: 01342 822233 (Fax: 01342 823854) *W.M.Ellerton*

		Boys	Age	Girls	Age	TOTAL		Boys	Girls
Day	£530-£2055	95	3-13	52	3-13	167	SIXTH		
Weekly	£2800	11	8-13	9	8-13				
Boarding	£2800		8-13		8-13				

ENTRY REQUIREMENTS Assessment & Interview
SCHOLARSHIPS & BURSARIES Schol; Burs; Mus; Forces
SPECIAL NEEDS n   **DYSLEXIA** e   **DIET**
ASSOCIATION IAPS   **FOUNDED** 1866   **RELIGIOUS AFFILIATION** C of E

MAP 4 G 5
LOCATION Rural
DAY ✓   **RAIL** a   **AIR** a
SPORT abcefjkmpqsuwx AB
OTHER LANGUAGES
ACTIVITIES cfghjlmotw
OTHER SUBJECTS cfh
FACILITIES ON SITE cdhijk
EXAM BOARDS
RETAKES   **NVQ COURSES**

A-level:
AS:
GCSE:
OTHER: B e gi lm o v / G K OP R / cde j

SUSSEX (WEST) *continued*

Gb Towers Convent School,The; Upper Beeding; Steyning; Sussex BN44 3TF
Tel: 01903 812185 (Fax: 01903 813858) *Sister Mary Andrew Fulgoney*

		Boys	Age	Girls	Age	TOTAL		Boys	Girls
Day	£600-£1065	2	3-8	141	3-16	210	SIXTH		
Weekly	£1710-£1800			14	8-16				
Boarding	£1810-£1910			53	8-16				

ENTRY REQUIREMENTS Report & Exam & Interview
SCHOLARSHIPS & BURSARIES
SPECIAL NEEDS   **DYSLEXIA** efg   **DIET** ad
ASSOCIATION ISAI   **FOUNDED** 1903   **RELIGIOUS AFFILIATION** R C

MAP 3 F 7
LOCATION Rural
DAY ✓   **RAIL** a   **AIR** b
SPORT acflopqx ABC
OTHER LANGUAGES
ACTIVITIES cegijknow A
OTHER SUBJECTS bcdeh
FACILITIES ON SITE cdhik
EXAM BOARDS abcd
RETAKES a   **NVQ COURSES**

A-level   AS   GCSE d g i l o v / BC G K OP R X / cdef h l   OTHER l h

C Westbourne House; Shopwyke; Chichester; Sussex PO20 6BH
Tel: 01243 782739 (Fax: 01243 539313) *S.L.Rigby*

		Boys	Age	Girls	Age	TOTAL		Boys	Girls
Day	£1040-£2080	93	3-13	46	3-13	231	SIXTH		
Weekly									
Boarding	£2575	88	7-13	4	7-13				

ENTRY REQUIREMENTS Assessment & Interview
SCHOLARSHIPS & BURSARIES Burs; Mus
SPECIAL NEEDS bejklnuw GHI   **DYSLEXIA**   **DIET** a
ASSOCIATION IAPS   **FOUNDED** 1907   **RELIGIOUS AFFILIATION** C of E

MAP 3 E 7
LOCATION Rural
DAY   **RAIL** a   **AIR** b
SPORT abcefgjklmopqstuwx AB
OTHER LANGUAGES
ACTIVITIES bcfghijlortw
OTHER SUBJECTS acfh
FACILITIES ON SITE abchijkl
EXAM BOARDS
RETAKES   **NVQ COURSES**

A-level   AS   GCSE   OTHER cde g i lmno q v / B G K OP R / cde g j

C Windlesham House School; Washington; Pulborough; West Sussex RH20 4AY
Tel: 01903 873207 (Fax: 01903 873017)

		Boys	Age	Girls	Age	TOTAL		Boys	Girls
Day		5		3		320	SIXTH		
Weekly									
Boarding	£2975	188	7-13	124	7-13				

ENTRY REQUIREMENTS Interview
SCHOLARSHIPS & BURSARIES
SPECIAL NEEDS bgjlnpstu AG   **DYSLEXIA** d   **DIET** acd
ASSOCIATION IAPS   **FOUNDED** 1837   **RELIGIOUS AFFILIATION** C of E

MAP 3 F 6
LOCATION Rural
DAY   **RAIL** b   **AIR** a
SPORT abcefgjklmnopqstuwx ABC
OTHER LANGUAGES a
ACTIVITIES acfghjlorstw A
OTHER SUBJECTS bcfh
FACILITIES ON SITE bcdehik
EXAM BOARDS
RETAKES   **NVQ COURSES**

A-level   AS   GCSE   OTHER de i lmnop v / BC G K NOP R W / cde g j l

B Worth School; Paddockhurst Road; Turners Hill; Crawley; West Sussex RH10 4SD
Tel: 01342 715911 (Fax: 01342 718298) *Fr.Christopher Jamison*

		Boys	Age	Girls	Age	TOTAL		Boys	Girls
Day	£1890-£2555	35	8-18			363	SIXTH	95	
Weekly									
Boarding	£2830-£3830	328	8-18						

ENTRY REQUIREMENTS CEE; Scholarship Exam; Assessment; Assessment & Interview
SCHOLARSHIPS & BURSARIES Schol; Mus; VI Form
SPECIAL NEEDS abeghjlnvwx BGI   **DYSLEXIA** e   **DIET** a
ASSOCIATION HMC   **FOUNDED** 1959   **RELIGIOUS AFFILIATION** RC/Christian

MAP 4 G 6
LOCATION Rural
DAY ✓   **RAIL** a   **AIR** a
SPORT abcefgjklmostuwx ABC
OTHER LANGUAGES a
ACTIVITIES fghijklmnopqstuw AD
OTHER SUBJECTS abcdfh
FACILITIES ON SITE bcdghikl
EXAM BOARDS abcd ABEGH
RETAKES   **NVQ COURSES**

A-level d ghi p v / B GHI K P R / c efgh j l   AS   GCSE h p v / GH R U / e l   GCSE d ghi l o v / AB G K P R X / cdefgh j l   OTHER l q

B Ascham House School; 30 West Avenue; Gosforth; Newcastle-upon-Tyne NE3 4ES
Tel: 0191 285 1619 (Fax: 0191 213 1105) *S.H.Reid*

		Boys	Age	Girls	Age	TOTAL		Boys	Girls
Day	£1075	286	4-13			286	SIXTH		
Weekly									
Boarding									

ENTRY REQUIREMENTS Interview
SCHOLARSHIPS & BURSARIES Schol
SPECIAL NEEDS   **DYSLEXIA**   **DIET** acd
ASSOCIATION IAPS   **FOUNDED** 1907   **RELIGIOUS AFFILIATION** Inter-denom

MAP 14 L 7
LOCATION Urban
DAY   **RAIL** a   **AIR** a
SPORT aelsx
OTHER LANGUAGES
ACTIVITIES ghjoq A
OTHER SUBJECTS cfh
FACILITIES ON SITE h
EXAM BOARDS
RETAKES   **NVQ COURSES**

A-level   AS   GCSE   OTHER e g i no v / B G K OP R / cde j

TYNE

TYNE AND WEAR continued

G — Central Newcastle High School GPDST; Eskdale Terr.; Newcastle-upon-Tyne NE2 4DS Tel: 0191 2811768 (Fax: 0191 2813267) Mrs A.M.Chapman

		Boys	Age	Girls	Age	TOTAL		Boys	Girls
Day	£976-£1328			886	4-18	886	SIXTH		158
Weekly									
Boarding									

MAP14 L 7
LOCATION Inner City
DAY **RAIL** a **AIR** a
SPORT acefghklmpqx ABC
OTHER LANGUAGES
ACTIVITIES cdefghijklnosw ABD
OTHER SUBJECTS bcdh
FACILITIES ON SITE bcghk
EXAM BOARDS abcd BDEH
RETAKES **NQV COURSES**

ENTRY REQUIREMENTS Exam & Interview
SCHOLARSHIPS & BURSARIES Schol; Burs; AP; VI Form
SPECIAL NEEDS bjlnqx G   **DYSLEXIA** e   **DIET** acd
ASSOCIATION GSA   **FOUNDED** 1895   **RELIGIOUS AFFILIATION** Non-denom

| A-level | cde g i p uv
B GH K P R U
cdefg jk | AS | c e l v
B G K R
c efg jkl | GCSE | a c e g i l n v
BC G K P R
cdefg jkl | OTHER | d lm o
C MNO W
a hi |

G — Dame Allan's Girls' School; Fowberry Crescent; Fenham; Newcastle-upon-Tyne NE4 9YJ Tel: 0191 2750708 (Fax: 0191 2747684) T.A.Willcocks

		Boys	Age	Girls	Age	TOTAL		Boys	Girls
Day	£939-£1190			443	8-18	443	SIXTH		99
Weekly									
Boarding									

MAP14 L 7
LOCATION Urban
DAY **RAIL** a **AIR** a
SPORT abcdfhjlmnopswx ABC
OTHER LANGUAGES
ACTIVITIES cfghijkopqst A
OTHER SUBJECTS bcdfh
FACILITIES ON SITE bhik
EXAM BOARDS bcd BDHL
RETAKES **NQV COURSES**

ENTRY REQUIREMENTS Exam & Interview
SCHOLARSHIPS & BURSARIES Schol; Burs; AP
SPECIAL NEEDS jln l   **DYSLEXIA** g   **DIET** abcd
ASSOCIATION GSA   **FOUNDED** 1705   **RELIGIOUS AFFILIATION** C of E

| A-level | de g i lm p uv
BC GH K PQR
cdef | AS | de
G R | GCSE | de g i lm p v
BC G K P R X
cdef j l | OTHER | e mn
O |

B — Dame Allan's Boys' School; Fowberry Crescent; Fenham; Newcastle-upon-Tyne NE4 9YJ Tel: 0191 275 0608 (Fax: 0191 274 7684) T.A.Willcocks

		Boys	Age	Girls	Age	TOTAL		Boys	Girls
Day	£939-£1190	458	8-18			458	SIXTH	103	
Weekly									
Boarding									

MAP14 L 7
LOCATION Urban
DAY **RAIL** a **AIR** a
SPORT abcdefhkmoswx ABC
OTHER LANGUAGES
ACTIVITIES fghijklopq AD
OTHER SUBJECTS bcfh
FACILITIES ON SITE bik
EXAM BOARDS abc BDE
RETAKES **NQV COURSES**

ENTRY REQUIREMENTS Interview; Exam & Interview
SCHOLARSHIPS & BURSARIES Schol; AP
SPECIAL NEEDS bejlntux AHI   **DYSLEXIA** g   **DIET** abcd
ASSOCIATION HMC   **FOUNDED** 1705   **RELIGIOUS AFFILIATION** C of E

| A-level | e g i l p uv
B GH K PQR
cdef | AS | e
G K
ef | GCSE | e g i l p v
B G K P R U X
cdef j l | OTHER | K |

C — Eastcliffe Grammar School; The Grove; Gosforth; Newcastle-upon-Tyne NE3 1NE Tel: 0191 2854873 G.D.Pearson

		Boys	Age	Girls	Age	TOTAL		Boys	Girls
Day	£800-£1360	150	3-18	47	3-18	197	SIXTH	21	5
Weekly									
Boarding									

MAP14 L 7
LOCATION Urban
DAY **RAIL** a **AIR** a
SPORT abcefghjkmopqstwx AB
OTHER LANGUAGES a
ACTIVITIES cfghijloqs A
OTHER SUBJECTS abcdeh
FACILITIES ON SITE cgk
EXAM BOARDS abc DE
RETAKES ab **NQV COURSES**

ENTRY REQUIREMENTS Report & Exam & Interview
SCHOLARSHIPS & BURSARIES Schol; Burs; VI Form
SPECIAL NEEDS ejn BG   **DYSLEXIA** ef   **DIET**
ASSOCIATION ISAI   **FOUNDED** 1946   **RELIGIOUS AFFILIATION** Inter-denom

| A-level | defghi l p v
ABC G K P R
c ef | AS | defghi l tuv
BC G K P R W
c e | GCSE | de ghi l no q t v
ABC E G K OP R W
cdef j | OTHER | defg i lmno q uv
BC G K OP R
cdef |

C — King's School,The; Tynemouth; North Shields NE30 4RF Tel: 0191 258 5995 (Fax: 0191 296 3826) Dr D.Younger

		Boys	Age	Girls	Age	TOTAL		Boys	Girls
Day	£657-£1240	748	4-18	146	4-18	894	SIXTH	130	24
Weekly									
Boarding									

MAP12 G 1
LOCATION Urban
DAY ✓ **RAIL** b **AIR** a
SPORT abcdefghjkmopqstwx ABC
OTHER LANGUAGES
ACTIVITIES acfghijklmnopqstuw AB
OTHER SUBJECTS abcdfh
FACILITIES ON SITE abcdghi
EXAM BOARDS ac ABDEG
RETAKES **NQV COURSES**

ENTRY REQUIREMENTS Report & Exam & Interview
SCHOLARSHIPS & BURSARIES Schol; Art; Mus; AP; VI Form
SPECIAL NEEDS I A   **DYSLEXIA**   **DIET** a
ASSOCIATION HMC   **FOUNDED** 1860   **RELIGIOUS AFFILIATION** C of E

| A-level | cd ghi l op v
AB GH K P R
c ef | AS | d
G K
ef | GCSE | d ghi l o v
AB G K P R X
cdef l | OTHER | c l
C E O |

TYNE AND WEAR continued

G — La Sagesse Convent High School; North Jesmond; Newcastle-upon-Tyne NE2 3RJ
Tel: 0191 281 3474 (Fax: 0191 281 2721) *Miss L.Clark*

	Boys	Age	Girls	Age	TOTAL	SIXTH Boys	Girls
Day £1220-£1240 Weekly Boarding			350	11-18	350		57

ENTRY REQUIREMENTS Exam & Interview
SCHOLARSHIPS & BURSARIES Schol; AP
SPECIAL NEEDS bjlnw G
ASSOCIATION GSA **FOUNDED** 1906 **RELIGIOUS AFFILIATION** R C **DYSLEXIA** e **DIET**

MAP 14 L 7
LOCATION Urban
DAY **RAIL** a **AIR** a
SPORT acfhlmpqtwx BC
OTHER LANGUAGES
ACTIVITIES cfghijoqrt ABD
OTHER SUBJECTS bcdefh
FACILITIES ON SITE abcdgh
EXAM BOARDS bcd ABDEG
RETAKES **NVQ COURSES**

A-level: defghi B G p uv P U cde l
AS: C G l e l
GCSE: v P de ghi l o v BC G K P R WX cde j l
OTHER: kl n f

G — La Sagesse Convent Junior School; North Jesmond; Newcastle-upon-Tyne NE2 3RJ
Tel: 0191 281 5308 *Mrs A.Ellis*

	Boys	Age	Girls	Age	TOTAL	SIXTH Boys	Girls
Day £600-£920 Weekly Boarding			121	3-11	121		

ENTRY REQUIREMENTS Exam & Interview
SCHOLARSHIPS & BURSARIES Teachers; Siblings
SPECIAL NEEDS jn G
ASSOCIATION GSA **FOUNDED** 1906 **RELIGIOUS AFFILIATION** R C **DYSLEXIA** e **DIET**

MAP 14 L 7
LOCATION Urban
DAY **RAIL** a **AIR** a
SPORT hlmpqx BC
OTHER LANGUAGES
ACTIVITIES cfghjo
OTHER SUBJECTS ch
FACILITIES ON SITE cdh
EXAM BOARDS
RETAKES **NVQ COURSES**

OTHER: e lm o v B E G K O R cde

C — Newcastle Prep. School; 6 Eslington Road; Newcastle-upon-Tyne NE2 4RH
Tel: 0191 281 1769 (Fax: 0191 281 5668) *G.Clayton*

	Boys	Age	Girls	Age	TOTAL	SIXTH Boys	Girls
Day £975-£1125 Weekly Boarding	166	2-13	71	2-13	237		

ENTRY REQUIREMENTS Interview
SCHOLARSHIPS & BURSARIES Schol
SPECIAL NEEDS abeijklnqstuwx ABDGHI
ASSOCIATION IAPS **FOUNDED** 1885 **RELIGIOUS AFFILIATION** **DYSLEXIA** de **DIET** ad

MAP 14 L 7
LOCATION Inner City
DAY **RAIL** a **AIR** a
SPORT acefjlmpqswx AB
OTHER LANGUAGES
ACTIVITIES cfghijloqsw A
OTHER SUBJECTS bch
FACILITIES ON SITE bchik
EXAM BOARDS
RETAKES **NVQ COURSES**

OTHER: c e g i lmno q s v BC G K OP R cde j

G — Newcastle U Tyne Church High Sch; Tankerville Terrace; Newcastle upon Tyne NE2 3BA
Tel: 0191 2814306 *Miss P.E.Davies*

	Boys	Age	Girls	Age	TOTAL	SIXTH Boys	Girls
Day £875-£1245 Weekly Boarding			667	3-18	667		85

ENTRY REQUIREMENTS Exam; Test & Interview
SCHOLARSHIPS & BURSARIES Schol; Mus; Clergy; AP; VI Form
SPECIAL NEEDS n
ASSOCIATION GSA **FOUNDED** 1885 **RELIGIOUS AFFILIATION** C of E **DYSLEXIA** **DIET** acd

MAP 14 L 7
LOCATION Urban
DAY **RAIL** b **AIR**
SPORT acfglmopqx ABC
OTHER LANGUAGES a
ACTIVITIES cfghijknop AD
OTHER SUBJECTS abch
FACILITIES ON SITE g
EXAM BOARDS bc ABD
RETAKES a **NVQ COURSES**

A-level: de g i l p v BC GH K PQR c ef j
AS: c C G K R ef
GCSE: cde ghi l v BC G K OPQR cdef j
OTHER: f o u o W

B — Newlands School; 34 The Grove; Gosforth; Newcastle-upon-Tyne NE3 1NH
Tel: 0191 285 2208 *N.R.Barton*

	Boys	Age	Girls	Age	TOTAL	SIXTH Boys	Girls
Day £865-£1135 ✗ Weekly Boarding	210	4-13			210		

ENTRY REQUIREMENTS Test & Interview
SCHOLARSHIPS & BURSARIES
SPECIAL NEEDS nqsw
ASSOCIATION IAPS **FOUNDED** 1900 **RELIGIOUS AFFILIATION** Inter-denom **DYSLEXIA** e **DIET** a

MAP 14 L 7
LOCATION Urban
DAY **RAIL** a **AIR** b
SPORT abcdeflosx AC
OTHER LANGUAGES
ACTIVITIES fghjpqtw
OTHER SUBJECTS bcfh
FACILITIES ON SITE ch
EXAM BOARDS
RETAKES **NVQ COURSES**

OTHER: e g i l o q v B G K OP R cde j

TYNE AND WEAR continued

B — Royal Grammar School; Eskdale Terrace; Newcastle-upon-Tyne NE2 4DX
Tel: 0191 2815711 (Fax: 0191 2120392) *J.F.X.Miller*

Day / Weekly Boarding £990-£1203
Boys 1098 | Age 8-18 | Girls — | Age — | TOTAL 1098 | SIXTH Boys 293 | Girls —

MAP14 L 7
LOCATION Urban
DAY ✓ RAIL a AIR a
SPORT abcefghlmorstuwx ABC
OTHER LANGUAGES
ACTIVITIES befghijlnopqstuv AB

ENTRY REQUIREMENTS Exam & Interview; CEE & Interview
SCHOLARSHIPS & BURSARIES AP
SPECIAL NEEDS abefghijklnpqstuwx ADFGHIK
ASSOCIATION HMC   FOUNDED 1525
DYSLEXIA   DIET ad
RELIGIOUS AFFILIATION Non-denom
OTHER SUBJECTS bcf
FACILITIES ON SITE cik
EXAM BOARDS bc DHL
RETAKES   NVQ COURSES

A-level: c e g i op uv x / B GH K P R / c efg j
AS: c e i l o q u / B G KM P R U / c efg j
GCSE: c e g i op v / B G K OP U / cdefg j
OTHER: n C N / a h l

C — Sunderland High School; Mowbray Road; Sunderland SR2 8HY
Tel: 01915 674984 (Fax: 01915 103953) *Ms Charlotte Rendle-Short*

Day / Weekly Boarding £785-£1305
Boys 216 | Age 3-18 | Girls 289 | Age 3-18 | TOTAL 505 | SIXTH Boys 7 | Girls 25

MAP12 G 1
LOCATION Urban
DAY ✓ RAIL a AIR
SPORT abcefhjlmopqswx BC
OTHER LANGUAGES
ACTIVITIES cfghijkmosx AD

ENTRY REQUIREMENTS Scholarship Exam; Assessment & Interview
SCHOLARSHIPS & BURSARIES Schol; Burs; VI Form; Siblings
SPECIAL NEEDS abejlq ACGH
ASSOCIATION SHMIS   FOUNDED 1884
DYSLEXIA   DIET abcd
RELIGIOUS AFFILIATION C of E
OTHER SUBJECTS abcdfh
FACILITIES ON SITE acgh
EXAM BOARDS c BDG
RETAKES ab   NVQ COURSES

A-level: e ghi p uv / BC GH K P R / c ef j
AS
GCSE: e g i l o v / BC G K P R / cdef j l
OTHER

G — Westfield School; Oakfield Road; Gosforth; Newcastle-upon-Tyne NE3 4HS
Tel: 0191 285 1948 (Fax: 0191 213 0734) *Mrs M.Farndale*

Day / Weekly Boarding £675-£1308
Boys — | Age — | Girls 345 | Age 3-18 | TOTAL 345 | SIXTH Boys — | Girls 38

MAP14 L 7
LOCATION Urban
DAY ✓ RAIL a AIR a
SPORT afghlnpqwx ABC
OTHER LANGUAGES
ACTIVITIES cfghijkoqtx AB

ENTRY REQUIREMENTS Exam & Interview
SCHOLARSHIPS & BURSARIES Schol; Burs; Art; Mus; VI Form; Siblings
SPECIAL NEEDS n
ASSOCIATION GSA   FOUNDED 1959
DYSLEXIA de   DIET a
RELIGIOUS AFFILIATION Inter-denom
OTHER SUBJECTS abcdegh
FACILITIES ON SITE gh
EXAM BOARDS bcd ABDEL
RETAKES   NVQ COURSES

A-level: e ghi n p v / BC G K P R / c ef
AS: G / ef
GCSE: e g i n uv / ABC G K P R W / cdef l
OTHER: h l o / O / ef

WARWICKSHIRE

C — Abbotsford School; Bridge Street; Kenilworth; Warwicks. CV8 1BP
Tel: 01926 52826 *Mrs B.Chitty*

Day / Weekly Boarding £780-£860
Boys 89 | Age 3-11 | Girls 37 | Age 3-11 | TOTAL 126 | SIXTH Boys — | Girls —

MAP 9 B 7
LOCATION Urban
DAY ✓ RAIL b AIR a
SPORT acefjlpqwx AB
OTHER LANGUAGES
ACTIVITIES cfghjt

ENTRY REQUIREMENTS Assessment & Interview
SCHOLARSHIPS & BURSARIES Schol; Burs
SPECIAL NEEDS bejklnqstw ABGHI
ASSOCIATION ISAI   FOUNDED 1909
DYSLEXIA e   DIET
RELIGIOUS AFFILIATION Inter-denom
OTHER SUBJECTS bcfh
FACILITIES ON SITE ch
EXAM BOARDS
RETAKES   NVQ COURSES

A-level
AS
GCSE
OTHER: e n / K R / e

C — Arnold Lodge School; Kenilworth Road; Leamington Spa; Warwicks. CV32 5TW
Tel: 01926 424737 (Fax: 01926 452679) *J.G.Hill*

Day / Weekly Boarding £405-£1360 / £2015
Boys 221 / 23 | Age 2-13 / 7-13 | Girls 89 / 5 | Age 2-13 / 7-13 | TOTAL 338 | SIXTH Boys — | Girls —

MAP 9 B 7
LOCATION Urban
DAY ✓ RAIL a AIR a
SPORT acejlmopqsx AB
OTHER LANGUAGES
ACTIVITIES cfghijlost A

ENTRY REQUIREMENTS Test & Interview
SCHOLARSHIPS & BURSARIES Schol; Mus
SPECIAL NEEDS B
ASSOCIATION IAPS   FOUNDED 1864
DYSLEXIA   DIET a
RELIGIOUS AFFILIATION C of E
OTHER SUBJECTS ch
FACILITIES ON SITE ik
EXAM BOARDS
RETAKES   NVQ COURSES

A-level
AS
GCSE
OTHER: B e g l o v / cde j

WARWICKSHIRE continued

C Bilton Grange; Dunchurch; Nr. Rugby CV22 6QU
Tel: 01788 810217 (Fax: 01788 816922) *Q.G.Edwards*

		Boys	Age	Girls	Age	TOTAL	SIXTH	Boys	Girls
Day	£787-£2292 ✕	129	4-13	72	4-13	284			
Weekly		21	7-13	8	7-13				
Boarding	£2865	41	7-13	13	7-13				

ENTRY REQUIREMENTS Report; Test & Interview
SCHOLARSHIPS & BURSARIES Schol; Burs; Mus; Forces; Clergy; Teachers; Sport; ARA; Siblings
SPECIAL NEEDS abehjklnpquw BEGI   **DYSLEXIA** ce   **DIET** a
ASSOCIATION IAPS   **FOUNDED** 1873   **RELIGIOUS AFFILIATION** C of E

MAP 9 C 7
LOCATION Rural
DAY   **RAIL** a   **AIR** a
SPORT abcdefhjklmpqstuvwx AB
OTHER LANGUAGES a
ACTIVITIES acfghjmnoqrstvwx A
OTHER SUBJECTS cfh
FACILITIES ON SITE bcdhik
EXAM BOARDS
RETAKES   **NVQ COURSES**

A-level: d e g i   lmno   q s   v
         B   G   K NOP R   W
         cdefg   j l
AS:
GCSE:
OTHER:

C Crescent School; Bawnmore Road; Bilton; Rugby; Warwicks. CV22 7QH
Tel: 01788 521595 *I.J.Wren*

		Boys	Age	Girls	Age	TOTAL	SIXTH	Boys	Girls
Day	£885- £955	86	2-12	96	2-12	182			
Weekly									
Boarding									

ENTRY REQUIREMENTS None
SCHOLARSHIPS & BURSARIES Burs
SPECIAL NEEDS lq   **DYSLEXIA**   **DIET** a
ASSOCIATION IAPS   **FOUNDED** 1947   **RELIGIOUS AFFILIATION** Inter-denom

MAP 9 C 7
LOCATION Urban
DAY   **RAIL** a   **AIR** a
SPORT aefjlmpqsx
OTHER LANGUAGES
ACTIVITIES cfghjoq
OTHER SUBJECTS bch
FACILITIES ON SITE
EXAM BOARDS
RETAKES   **NVQ COURSES**

A-level:
AS:
GCSE:
OTHER: e g i l   o   v
       B   G K   OP R
       cde   j

C Croft School,The; Alveston Hill; Stratford-on-Avon; Warwickshire
Tel: 01789 293795 (Fax: 01789 414960) *L.Wolfe*

		Boys	Age	Girls	Age	TOTAL	SIXTH	Boys	Girls
Day	£110-£1320	160	3-11	139	3-11	299			
Weekly									
Boarding									

ENTRY REQUIREMENTS Interview
SCHOLARSHIPS & BURSARIES Schol
SPECIAL NEEDS bejklnqsw Bl   **DYSLEXIA** cde   **DIET** a
ASSOCIATION IAPS   **FOUNDED** 1933   **RELIGIOUS AFFILIATION** Inter-denom

MAP 8 K 7
LOCATION Rural
DAY   **RAIL** a   **AIR** a
SPORT abcefjlmpqsx AB
OTHER LANGUAGES
ACTIVITIES acfghjnoqtx
OTHER SUBJECTS cfh
FACILITIES ON SITE bchik
EXAM BOARDS
RETAKES   **NVQ COURSES**

A-level:
AS:
GCSE:
OTHER: e g i   lmno   vw
       BC   G   K N P R
       cde   j

C Emscote Lawn; 21 Emscote Road; Warwick CV34 5QD
Tel: 01926 491961 (Fax: 01926 410376) *J.H.Riley*

		Boys	Age	Girls	Age	TOTAL	SIXTH	Boys	Girls
Day	£1140-£1429 ✕	250	3-13	148	3-11	410			
Weekly	£2108	12	8-13						
Boarding									

ENTRY REQUIREMENTS Test & Interview
SCHOLARSHIPS & BURSARIES Schol; Art; Mus; Forces; Clergy; Teachers
SPECIAL NEEDS abejklnqtw Gl   **DYSLEXIA**   **DIET** abcd
ASSOCIATION IAPS   **FOUNDED** 1919   **RELIGIOUS AFFILIATION** C of E

MAP 9 B 7
LOCATION Urban
DAY   **RAIL** a   **AIR** a
SPORT abejlmopqsx ABC
OTHER LANGUAGES
ACTIVITIES acfghijlnoqt A
OTHER SUBJECTS bcfh
FACILITIES ON SITE abcdik
EXAM BOARDS
RETAKES   **NVQ COURSES**

A-level:
AS:
GCSE:
OTHER: defg i kl   no   q   v
       BC   G   K   OP R
       cde g   j

G King's High School for Girls; Smith Street; Warwick CV34 4HJ
Tel: 01926 494485 (Fax: 01926 403089) *Mrs J.M.Anderson*

		Boys	Age	Girls	Age	TOTAL	SIXTH	Boys	Girls
Day	£1258-£1365			564	10-18	564			133
Weekly									
Boarding									

ENTRY REQUIREMENTS Report & Exam & Interview
SCHOLARSHIPS & BURSARIES Schol; Burs; Mus; Teachers; AP
SPECIAL NEEDS hjklqt G   **DYSLEXIA**   **DIET** a
ASSOCIATION GSA   **FOUNDED** 1879   **RELIGIOUS AFFILIATION** Inter-denom

MAP 9 B 7
LOCATION Urban
DAY   **RAIL** a   **AIR** a
SPORT abcfhklmpqwx ABC
OTHER LANGUAGES
ACTIVITIES fghijknos ABD
OTHER SUBJECTS abch
FACILITIES ON SITE abcgh
EXAM BOARDS abcd ABEGH
RETAKES   **NVQ COURSES**

A-level: d fghi   v
         BC   GH K   P R U
         c efg jkl
AS: e   j l
GCSE: d g i   no   v
      BC G   K   P R
      cdefg jkl
OTHER: lmno q   u   x
               K MNO QR   W
               de   j

WARWICKSHIRE continued

Kingsley School; Beauchamp Avenue; Leamington Spa CV32 5RD
Gb
Tel: 01926 425127 (Fax: 01926 831691) Mrs M.A.Webster

		Boys	Age	Girls	Age	TOTAL		Boys	Girls
Day	£950-£1415	8	2-7	575	2-18	583	SIXTH		85
Weekly									
Boarding									

ENTRY REQUIREMENTS Test; Test & Interview
SCHOLARSHIPS & BURSARIES Schol; VI Form
SPECIAL NEEDS behjlnqtw ABDGHJL **DYSLEXIA** e **DIET** ab
ASSOCIATION GSA **FOUNDED** 1884 **RELIGIOUS AFFILIATION** C of E

MAP 9 B 7
LOCATION Urban
DAY ✓ **RAIL** b **AIR** a
SPORT acfhklmopqwx ABC
OTHER LANGUAGES
ACTIVITIES cfghijklnoqstw AB
OTHER SUBJECTS abcdefgh
FACILITIES ON SITE bcg
EXAM BOARDS abd ADEG
RETAKES a **NVQ COURSES**

| A-level | c e ghi   n p   uv x
BC   GH K   P R U
cdefg j | AS | i
GH K
c ef | U | GCSE | c e g i lmno
BC   G   K   OP R   W
cdefg j l | v | OTHER | lm   q
o |

Princethorpe College; Leamington Road; Princethorpe; Rugby; Warwicks CV23 9PX
Bg
Tel: 01926 632147 (Fax: 01926 633365) The Rev A.Whelan

		Boys	Age	Girls	Age	TOTAL		Boys	Girls
Day	£1255	357	11-18	7	11-18	405	SIXTH	71	9
Weekly	£2365	10	11-18	1	16-18				
Boarding	£2535	28	11-18	2	16-18				

ENTRY REQUIREMENTS CEE; Report & Interview; Report & Test
SCHOLARSHIPS & BURSARIES Schol; Burs; Art; Mus; Chor; VI Form
SPECIAL NEEDS abejklnqtuv ABCDEGI **DYSLEXIA** ce **DIET** acd
ASSOCIATION ISAI **FOUNDED** 1966 **RELIGIOUS AFFILIATION** R C

MAP 9 C 7
LOCATION Rural
DAY ✓ **RAIL** a **AIR** a
SPORT abcefgjkmnopswx ABC
OTHER LANGUAGES a
ACTIVITIES afghijkmnost A
OTHER SUBJECTS abcfh
FACILITIES ON SITE bcdhk
EXAM BOARDS abcd ABDEI
RETAKES **NVQ COURSES**

| A-level | efghi   nop   v x
AB   GH K   P R
cde   l | AS | g
G
d | uv
R | GCSE | e g i   op
AB   G   K   OP R
cde   l | v x | OTHER | O |

Rugby School; Rugby; Warwickshire CV22 5EH
C
Tel: 01788 543465 (Fax: 01788 569124) M.B.Mavor

		Boys	Age	Girls	Age	TOTAL		Boys	Girls
Day	£1515-£3330 ✗	98	12-18	40	12-18	675	SIXTH	204	84
Weekly									
Boarding	£4240	407	13-18	130	13-18				

ENTRY REQUIREMENTS CEE; Scholarship Exam
SCHOLARSHIPS & BURSARIES Schol; Burs; Art; Mus; VI Form; ARA
SPECIAL NEEDS befjklnpquw DI **DYSLEXIA** cde **DIET** abcd
ASSOCIATION HMC **FOUNDED** 1567 **RELIGIOUS AFFILIATION** C of E

MAP 9 C 7
LOCATION Urban
DAY ✓ **RAIL** a **AIR** a
SPORT abcdefghjklmnopqstuwx ABC
OTHER LANGUAGES an
ACTIVITIES bcefghijklnoqrstuw A
OTHER SUBJECTS abcfh
FACILITIES ON SITE abcdghik
EXAM BOARDS abce ADEGHL
RETAKES **NVQ COURSES**

| A-level | efghi   op   v x
B   GH K   P   U
c efg jkl | AS | GH
d | u
j | U | GCSE | c e g i   no
B   G K   OP
cdefg jkl | v | X | OTHER | l
h |

St. Joseph's School; Coventry Road; Kenilworth; Warwickshire CV8 2FT
Gb
Tel: 01926 55348 Mrs L.P.A.Cox

		Boys	Age	Girls	Age	TOTAL		Boys	Girls
Day	£810-£1150	7	3-8	268	3-18	275	SIXTH		25
Weekly									
Boarding									

ENTRY REQUIREMENTS Exam & Interview; Assessment & Interview
SCHOLARSHIPS & BURSARIES Schol; Teachers; VI Form
SPECIAL NEEDS bjlnw L **DYSLEXIA** e **DIET** a
ASSOCIATION ISAI **FOUNDED** 1862 **RELIGIOUS AFFILIATION** R C

MAP 9 C 7
LOCATION Rural
DAY ✓ **RAIL** a **AIR** a
SPORT acfhlmpqwx B
OTHER LANGUAGES
ACTIVITIES cghijknoq A
OTHER SUBJECTS abcdegh
FACILITIES ON SITE abdh
EXAM BOARDS bc ABDG
RETAKES **NVQ COURSES**

| A-level | defg i   n p   uv
BC   GH K   P R   W
c e j | AS | h
C   G
d | p   u
R   W | GCSE | d e g i l
BC   G   K   OP R
cdef j | v | OTHER | lm
K   O
e |

Stratford Preparatory School; Church House; Old Town; Stratford-upon-Avon;
C
Warwickshire CV37 6BG Tel: 01789 297993 Mrs C.Quinn

		Boys	Age	Girls	Age	TOTAL		Boys	Girls
Day	£355-£1025	58	2-11	68	2-11	126	SIXTH		
Weekly									
Boarding									

ENTRY REQUIREMENTS Assessment & Interview
SCHOLARSHIPS & BURSARIES
SPECIAL NEEDS **DYSLEXIA** **DIET** abcd
ASSOCIATION ISAI **FOUNDED** 1989 **RELIGIOUS AFFILIATION** C of E

MAP 9 B 8
LOCATION Urban
DAY **RAIL** a **AIR**
SPORT cefjlmpqtx ABC
OTHER LANGUAGES
ACTIVITIES cfghijo
OTHER SUBJECTS ch
FACILITIES ON SITE h
EXAM BOARDS
RETAKES **NVQ COURSES**

| A-level | | AS | | GCSE | | OTHER | e |

WARWICKSHIRE continued

Gb Warwick Prep. School; Bridge Field; Banbury Road; Warwick CV34 6PL
Tel: 01926 491545 (Fax: 01926 403456) Mrs C.E.M.Prichard

		Boys	Age	Girls	Age	TOTAL	SIXTH	Boys	Girls
Day	£450-£1350 ✗	112	3-6	331	3-11	443			
Weekly									
Boarding									

ENTRY REQUIREMENTS Assessment & Interview
SCHOLARSHIPS & BURSARIES
SPECIAL NEEDS agjk G
ASSOCIATION IAPS   **FOUNDED**   **RELIGIOUS AFFILIATION** C of E   **DYSLEXIA**   **DIET** a

MAP 9 B 7
LOCATION Urban
DAY   **RAIL**   **AIR**
SPORT acflmpqx B
OTHER LANGUAGES
ACTIVITIES cghjo A
OTHER SUBJECTS c
FACILITIES ON SITE ch
EXAM BOARDS
RETAKES   **NVQ COURSES**

A-level: — | AS: — | GCSE: — | OTHER: e v / B G / cde

B Warwick School; Warwick CV34 6PP
Tel: 01926 492484 (Fax: 01926 401259) P.J.Cheshire

		Boys	Age	Girls	Age	TOTAL	SIXTH	Boys	Girls
Day	£1350-£1530	943	7-18			993		207	
Weekly	£2880-£3060	23	7-18						
Boarding	£3100-£3280	27	7-18						

ENTRY REQUIREMENTS Exam
SCHOLARSHIPS & BURSARIES Schol; Burs; AP
SPECIAL NEEDS bejklnpqtw AEGIL
ASSOCIATION HMC   **FOUNDED** 914   **RELIGIOUS AFFILIATION** C of E   **DYSLEXIA** g   **DIET** ad

MAP 9 B 7
LOCATION Urban
DAY   **RAIL** a   **AIR** a
SPORT abcdefghjklmorstuwx ABC
OTHER LANGUAGES a
ACTIVITIES adefghijklnopqrst AB
OTHER SUBJECTS bcfh
FACILITIES ON SITE bcdeghikl
EXAM BOARDS abcd BGH
RETAKES a   **NVQ COURSES**

A-level: c efghi l p uv x / B GH K P R U / cdefg j
AS: h l o v / c ef l
GCSE: P / egi l no v / B G K P R U / cdefg jkl
OTHER: l / i

G Wroxall Abbey; Warwick CV35 7NB
Tel: 01926 484220 (Fax: 01926 484531) Mrs.J.M.Gowen

		Boys	Age	Girls	Age	TOTAL	SIXTH	Boys	Girls
Day	£946-£1645 ✗		2-7	56	2-18	92			14
Weekly	£2693-£3220			12	10-18				
Boarding				24	10-18				

ENTRY REQUIREMENTS Scholarship Exam; Report & Test
SCHOLARSHIPS & BURSARIES Schol; Burs; Art; Mus; VI Form; Sport
SPECIAL NEEDS abejknqw EGJ
ASSOCIATION GSA   **FOUNDED** 1872   **RELIGIOUS AFFILIATION** C of E   **DYSLEXIA** e   **DIET** acd

MAP 9 B 7
LOCATION Rural
DAY ✓   **RAIL** a   **AIR** a
SPORT acdfhlmopqtvwx ABC
OTHER LANGUAGES a
ACTIVITIES acghijklmnostw AB
OTHER SUBJECTS abcdfh
FACILITIES ON SITE cdegi
EXAM BOARDS abcd ADEG
RETAKES ab   **NVQ COURSES**

A-level: defghi p uv x / BC G K P R U W / bcdef hj l
AS: de gi / C G
GCSE: bcde g i l o v x / BC G I K OP R W / bcdef hj
OTHER: cde ghi l no t v x / BC FG K OP R W / cdef h l

C Bablake Junior School; Coundon Road; Coventry CV1 4AU
Tel: 01203 634052 (Fax: 01203 633290) J.S.Dover

		Boys	Age	Girls	Age	TOTAL	SIXTH	Boys	Girls
Day	£925	93	7-11	96	7-11	189			
Weekly									
Boarding									

ENTRY REQUIREMENTS Report & Test
SCHOLARSHIPS & BURSARIES
SPECIAL NEEDS
ASSOCIATION IAPS   **FOUNDED** 1991   **RELIGIOUS AFFILIATION** Non-denom   **DYSLEXIA**   **DIET** abcd

MAP 9 C 7
LOCATION Inner City
DAY ✓   **RAIL** a   **AIR** a
SPORT abdefjlmpqstx B
OTHER LANGUAGES
ACTIVITIES fghjnop
OTHER SUBJECTS abcdfh
FACILITIES ON SITE abhi
EXAM BOARDS
RETAKES   **NVQ COURSES**

A-level: — | AS: — | GCSE: — | OTHER: de

C Bablake School; Coundon Road; Coventry CV1 4AU
Tel: 01203 228388 (Fax: 01203 631947) Dr S.Nuttall

		Boys	Age	Girls	Age	TOTAL	SIXTH	Boys	Girls
Day	£925-£1250	448	7-18	411	7-18	859		109	105
Weekly									
Boarding									

ENTRY REQUIREMENTS Report & Exam & Interview
SCHOLARSHIPS & BURSARIES Schol; Burs; AP; VI Form
SPECIAL NEEDS n
ASSOCIATION HMC   **FOUNDED** 1344   **RELIGIOUS AFFILIATION** Non-denom   **DYSLEXIA**   **DIET**

MAP 9 C 7
LOCATION Urban
DAY   **RAIL** a   **AIR** a
SPORT abcdefhklmopqsuvwx AB
OTHER LANGUAGES
ACTIVITIES acfghijkmnopst AB
OTHER SUBJECTS abcfh
FACILITIES ON SITE abghi
EXAM BOARDS cd ADG
RETAKES   **NVQ COURSES**

A-level: cd ghi p uv / B GH K P R / c ef j
AS: —
GCSE: cd g i l no vw / ABC G K P R / cdef h jkl
OTHER: —

WEST MIDLANDS

WEST MIDLANDS continued

C — Blue Coat School, The; Somerset Road; Edgbaston; Birmingham B17 0HR;
Tel: 0121 454 1425 (Fax: 0121 454 7757) *B.P.Bissell*

		Boys	Age	Girls	Age	TOTAL		Boys	Girls
Day	£960-£1460	202	3-13	128	3-13	401	SIXTH		
Weekly	£2230	14	7-13	24	7-13				
Boarding	£2230	16	7-13	17	7-13				

ENTRY REQUIREMENTS Test & Interview
SCHOLARSHIPS & BURSARIES Schol; Burs; Mus; Forces; Clergy; Teachers; AP
SPECIAL NEEDS afjlntu BEGI
ASSOCIATION IAPS   **FOUNDED** 1722   **DYSLEXIA** e   **DIET** abcd
RELIGIOUS AFFILIATION C of E

MAP 8 J 5
LOCATION Urban
DAY   **RAIL** a   **AIR** a
SPORT abdefjlmopqsx AB
OTHER LANGUAGES a
ACTIVITIES cfghijnoqstx A
OTHER SUBJECTS bcdfh
FACILITIES ON SITE bcdi
EXAM BOARDS
RETAKES   **NVQ COURSES**

A-level | **AS** | **GCSE** | **OTHER** c e g i lmno q v / BC G K NOP R / cdef j l

---

C — Coventry Prep. School; Kenilworth Road; Coventry CV3 6PT
Tel: 01203 675289 (Fax: 01203 672171) *David Clark*

		Boys	Age	Girls	Age	TOTAL		Boys	Girls
Day	£1025-£1375	118	3-13	42	3-13	160	SIXTH		
Weekly									
Boarding									

ENTRY REQUIREMENTS Test
SCHOLARSHIPS & BURSARIES
SPECIAL NEEDS knw GI
ASSOCIATION IAPS   **FOUNDED** 1920   **DYSLEXIA** g   **DIET** acd
RELIGIOUS AFFILIATION C of E

MAP 9 C 7
LOCATION Urban
DAY   **RAIL** a   **AIR** a
SPORT abcdefjlmopqsx A
OTHER LANGUAGES
ACTIVITIES cfghnopq A
OTHER SUBJECTS abch
FACILITIES ON SITE aj
EXAM BOARDS
RETAKES   **NVQ COURSES**

A-level | **AS** | **GCSE** | **OTHER** d e g i l o v / B G K OP R / cde j

---

C — Davenport Lodge School; 21 Davenport Road; Coventry CV5 6QA
Tel: 01203 675051 *Mrs M.D.Martin*

		Boys	Age	Girls	Age	TOTAL		Boys	Girls
Day	£690-£715	77	2-8	88	2-8	165	SIXTH		
Weekly									
Boarding									

ENTRY REQUIREMENTS Interview
SCHOLARSHIPS & BURSARIES
SPECIAL NEEDS n
ASSOCIATION ISAI   **FOUNDED** 1968   **DYSLEXIA** e   **DIET**
RELIGIOUS AFFILIATION Inter-denom

MAP 9 C 7
LOCATION Urban
DAY   **RAIL** a   **AIR** a
SPORT x B
OTHER LANGUAGES
ACTIVITIES g
OTHER SUBJECTS
FACILITIES ON SITE
EXAM BOARDS
RETAKES   **NVQ COURSES**

A-level | **AS** | **GCSE** | **OTHER**

C — Eastbourne House School; 111 Yardley Road; Acocks Green; Birmingham B27 6LL
Tel: 0121 706 2013 (Fax: 0121 706 2013) *P.J.Moynihan*

		Boys	Age	Girls	Age	TOTAL		Boys	Girls
Day	£680-£775	60	3-11	65	3-11	125	SIXTH		
Weekly									
Boarding									

ENTRY REQUIREMENTS Test & Interview
SCHOLARSHIPS & BURSARIES ARA
SPECIAL NEEDS
ASSOCIATION ISAI   **FOUNDED**   **DYSLEXIA**   **DIET**
RELIGIOUS AFFILIATION Non-denom

MAP 8 K 6
LOCATION Urban
DAY   **RAIL** a   **AIR** a
SPORT aejmpqx
OTHER LANGUAGES
ACTIVITIES fghjnoqt
OTHER SUBJECTS bch
FACILITIES ON SITE
EXAM BOARDS
RETAKES   **NVQ COURSES**

A-level | **AS** | **GCSE** | **OTHER** e lno s v / B G K O R / cde

---

G — Edgbaston C of E College; 31 Calthorpe Road; Birmingham B15 1RX
Tel: 0121 625 0398 (Fax: 0121 625 3340) *Mrs A.P.R.Varley-Tipton*

		Boys	Age	Girls	Age	TOTAL		Boys	Girls
Day	£820-£1425			319	3-18	319	SIXTH		29
Weekly									
Boarding									

ENTRY REQUIREMENTS Exam & Interview; Assessment & Interview
SCHOLARSHIPS & BURSARIES Schol; Clergy; AP; VI Form
SPECIAL NEEDS bejln H
ASSOCIATION GSA   **FOUNDED** 1886   **DYSLEXIA** e   **DIET** abcd
RELIGIOUS AFFILIATION C of E

MAP 8 J 5
LOCATION Urban
DAY   **RAIL** a   **AIR** a
SPORT acglmpqwx AB
OTHER LANGUAGES
ACTIVITIES cghijkost BD
OTHER SUBJECTS bcfh
FACILITIES ON SITE g
EXAM BOARDS bd AGHL
RETAKES   **NVQ COURSES**

A-level c efghi n v / BC G K P R W / c ef j
AS ef
GCSE d g i no v / B G K P R X / cdef j l
OTHER o u

WEST MIDLANDS continued

Edgbaston College; 249 Bristol Road; Edgbaston B5 7UH
Tel: 0121 472 1034 (Fax: 0121 414 0064) *Father A.W.D.Ledwich*

	Boys	Age	Girls	Age	TOTAL	SIXTH	Boys	Girls
Day £830-£1530	185	2-18	82	2-18	267		13	1
Weekly		16-18		16-18				
Boarding								

ENTRY REQUIREMENTS Exam; Assessment
SCHOLARSHIPS & BURSARIES Schol; Mus
SPECIAL NEEDS nw BL
DYSLEXIA ce **DIET** abcd
ASSOCIATION ISAI **FOUNDED** 1889 **RELIGIOUS AFFILIATION**

MAP 8 J 5
LOCATION Urban
DAY ✓ **RAIL** a **AIR** a
SPORT abcefhjlmpqswx AB
OTHER LANGUAGES a
ACTIVITIES cefghijkost
OTHER SUBJECTS cfh
FACILITIES ON SITE bcdh
EXAM BOARDS b GH
RETAKES a **NVQ COURSES** 13

A-level e ghi l n p uv / B G K R / cdef j
AS i
GCSE e ghi l nop v / BC E GH K R / cdefg j
OTHER

Edgbaston High School for Girls; Westbourne Road; Birmingham B15 3TS
Tel: 0121 454 5831 (Fax: 0121 454 2363) *Mrs S.J.Horsman*

	Boys	Age	Girls	Age	TOTAL	SIXTH	Boys	Girls
Day £560-£1405			930	3-18	930			126
Weekly								
Boarding								

ENTRY REQUIREMENTS Report & Exam & Interview
SCHOLARSHIPS & BURSARIES Schol; Burs; Mus; VI Form; Sport
SPECIAL NEEDS abegjlnu G
DYSLEXIA g **DIET** abcd
ASSOCIATION GSA **FOUNDED** 1876 **RELIGIOUS AFFILIATION** Non-denom

MAP 8 J 5
LOCATION Urban
DAY ✓ **RAIL** b **AIR** a
SPORT abcdefghlmopqtwx ABC
OTHER LANGUAGES
ACTIVITIES acghijklnopqst ABD
OTHER SUBJECTS abcdfh
FACILITIES ON SITE cgi
EXAM BOARDS abcd ABDGKL
RETAKES **NVQ COURSES**

A-level cde ghi p uv / BC GH K P R U W / cdef j l
AS de u / G K / c e
GCSE de g i no v / BC E G K P R WX / cdefg j l
OTHER d fg i lmno q v x / BC G K NOP R U W / cde j l

Eversfield Prep. School; Warwick Road; Solihull; West Midlands B91 1AT
Tel: 0121 705 0354 (Fax: 0121 709 0168) *K.Madden*

	Boys	Age	Girls	Age	TOTAL	SIXTH	Boys	Girls
Day £1437-£1640 ✗	176	3-13	2	3-4	178			
Weekly								
Boarding								

ENTRY REQUIREMENTS Test & Interview
SCHOLARSHIPS & BURSARIES Schol; Burs; Clergy; Siblings
SPECIAL NEEDS
DYSLEXIA **DIET**
ASSOCIATION IAPS **FOUNDED** 1931 **RELIGIOUS AFFILIATION** Christian

MAP 8 K 5
LOCATION Urban
DAY **RAIL** a **AIR** a
SPORT aejklosx AB
OTHER LANGUAGES
ACTIVITIES fgjot A
OTHER SUBJECTS cfh
FACILITIES ON SITE cj
EXAM BOARDS
RETAKES **NVQ COURSES**

A-level
AS
GCSE
OTHER e gi l o v / AB G K OP R / cde j

Haden Hill School; High Harcourt House; 154 Barrs Rd; Cradley Heath; Warley B64 7EX
Tel: 01384 569318 *Mrs B.M.Simons*

	Boys	Age	Girls	Age	TOTAL	SIXTH	Boys	Girls
Day £813-£1055	91	3-11	65	3-11	156			
Weekly								
Boarding								

ENTRY REQUIREMENTS Interview
SCHOLARSHIPS & BURSARIES
SPECIAL NEEDS
DYSLEXIA **DIET**
ASSOCIATION ISAI **FOUNDED** 1945 **RELIGIOUS AFFILIATION** Non-denom

MAP 8 J 5
LOCATION Urban
DAY **RAIL** a **AIR**
SPORT acefgjklmopqtwx ABC
OTHER LANGUAGES
ACTIVITIES cgo A
OTHER SUBJECTS ch
FACILITIES ON SITE
EXAM BOARDS
RETAKES **NVQ COURSES**

A-level
AS
GCSE
OTHER e v / B E G K O R / cde

Hallfield School; 48 Church Road; Edgbaston; Birmingham B15 3SJ
Tel: 0121 454 1496 (Fax: 0121 454 9182) *J.G.Cringle*

	Boys	Age	Girls	Age	TOTAL	SIXTH	Boys	Girls
Day £880-£1440 ✗	369	3-13			369			
Weekly								
Boarding								

ENTRY REQUIREMENTS Assessment & Interview
SCHOLARSHIPS & BURSARIES Schol; Mus; Clergy; Teachers
SPECIAL NEEDS abehjkltuvw BGHI
DYSLEXIA **DIET** abcd
ASSOCIATION IAPS **FOUNDED** 1879 **RELIGIOUS AFFILIATION** C of E

MAP 8 J 5
LOCATION Urban
DAY **RAIL** a **AIR** a
SPORT abcefjlsx AB
OTHER LANGUAGES
ACTIVITIES fghijnoqrt A
OTHER SUBJECTS cfh
FACILITIES ON SITE bchk
EXAM BOARDS
RETAKES **NVQ COURSES**

A-level
AS
GCSE
OTHER de g i l no s v / B G K OP R / cde j l

WEST MIDLANDS continued

Gb Highclare School; 10 Sutton Road; Erdington; Birmingham B23 6QL
Tel: 0121 373 7400 (Fax: 0121 373 7445) Mrs C.A.Hanson

| Day Weekly Boarding | £715-£1385 | Boys 19 | Age 16-18 | Girls 345 | Age 2-18 | TOTAL 364 | SIXTH | Boys 5 | Girls 27 |

MAP 8 K 5
LOCATION Urban
DAY RAIL a AIR a
SPORT aclmpqx AB
OTHER LANGUAGES
ACTIVITIES ghijot

ENTRY REQUIREMENTS Exam & Interview
SCHOLARSHIPS & BURSARIES Schol
SPECIAL NEEDS abgjlnq AH
ASSOCIATION GSA   FOUNDED 1932
DYSLEXIA def   DIET abcd
RELIGIOUS AFFILIATION Non-denom
OTHER SUBJECTS bcdfh
FACILITIES ON SITE
EXAM BOARDS abc ABDE
RETAKES   NVQ COURSES 3

- **A-level**: e ghi l uv   BC G K P R T W cdef
- **AS**: u
- **GCSE**: e ghi l v   BC G K P R T W cdef l
- **OTHER**:

Gb Holy Child School; Sir Harry's Road; Edgbaston; Birmingham B15 2UR
Tel: 0121 440 4103 (Fax: 0121 440 3639) Mrs Jean M.C.Hill

| Day Weekly Boarding | £795-£1500 | Boys 27 | Age 3-11 | Girls 268 | Age 3-18 | TOTAL 295 | SIXTH | Boys | Girls 19 |

MAP 8 J 5
LOCATION Urban
DAY a   AIR a
SPORT abcfghjlmopqswx ABC
OTHER LANGUAGES a
ACTIVITIES cghijkoq A

ENTRY REQUIREMENTS Exam; Report & Interview
SCHOLARSHIPS & BURSARIES Schol; Burs; AP; VI Form; Siblings
SPECIAL NEEDS abjn
ASSOCIATION GSA   FOUNDED 1933
DYSLEXIA   DIET acd
RELIGIOUS AFFILIATION R C
OTHER SUBJECTS abcdh
FACILITIES ON SITE adh
EXAM BOARDS abcd ABDEGH
RETAKES   NVQ COURSES

- **A-level**: efg i p uv   B GH K PQR bcdef j l
- **AS**: GH e R U l
- **GCSE**: e ghi n v   B G K P R cdef j l
- **OTHER**: C l o   O Q j l

C Hydesville Tower School; 25 Broadway North; Walsall WS1 2QG
Tel: 01922 24374 (Fax: 01922 746169) T.D.Farrell

| Day Weekly Boarding | £590-£1390 | Boys 207 | Age 3-17 | Girls 119 | Age 3-17 | TOTAL 326 | SIXTH | Boys | Girls |

MAP 8 J 5
LOCATION Urban
DAY ✓ RAIL a AIR a
SPORT abcefhjlmpqswx AB
OTHER LANGUAGES
ACTIVITIES cfghijknoqst A

ENTRY REQUIREMENTS Exam; Assessment & Interview
SCHOLARSHIPS & BURSARIES Schol; Burs; Mus; ARA
SPECIAL NEEDS bjlnqw Gl
ASSOCIATION ISAI   FOUNDED 1952
DYSLEXIA g   DIET acd
RELIGIOUS AFFILIATION Inter-denom
OTHER SUBJECTS bcdfh
FACILITIES ON SITE
EXAM BOARDS bc L
RETAKES a   NVQ COURSES

- **A-level**:
- **AS**:
- **GCSE**: de g i l v AB G K N P R T W cdef
- **OTHER**: de g i lmno v AB G K NOP R U W cdef

G King Edward VI High Sch. for Girls; Edgbaston Park Road; Birmingham B15 2UB
Tel: 0121 472 1834 (Fax: 0121 471 3808) Miss E.W.Evans

| Day Weekly Boarding | £1410 | Boys | Age | Girls 541 | Age 11-18 | TOTAL 541 | SIXTH | Boys | Girls 154 |

MAP 8 J 5
LOCATION Urban
DAY RAIL a AIR a
SPORT abcgklmnpquwx ABC
OTHER LANGUAGES
ACTIVITIES acdghijklnost ABD

ENTRY REQUIREMENTS Exam
SCHOLARSHIPS & BURSARIES Schol; Burs; AP
SPECIAL NEEDS begjlqstuwx ADHIJ
ASSOCIATION GSA   FOUNDED 1883
DYSLEXIA   DIET ab
RELIGIOUS AFFILIATION Inter-denom
OTHER SUBJECTS bcdfh
FACILITIES ON SITE bhi
EXAM BOARDS abc BDGHKL
RETAKES   NVQ COURSES

- **A-level**: cd g i p uv   B GH K P R U c efg j
- **AS**: d   G K
- **GCSE**: d g i v   B G K P R U cdefgh jkl
- **OTHER**: C   lmnop NO R W

B King Edward's School; Edgbaston Park Road; Birmingham B15 2UA
Tel: 0121 472 1672 (Fax: 0121 414 1897) H.R.Wright

| Day Weekly Boarding | £1480 | Boys 869 | Age 11-18 | Girls | Age | TOTAL 869 | SIXTH | Boys 237 | Girls |

MAP 8 J 5
LOCATION Urban
DAY RAIL a AIR a
SPORT abcefghiklmstuwx ABC
OTHER LANGUAGES
ACTIVITIES efghijknopqrst AB

ENTRY REQUIREMENTS Exam
SCHOLARSHIPS & BURSARIES Schol; Burs; Art; Mus; AP; VI Form
SPECIAL NEEDS
ASSOCIATION HMC   FOUNDED 1552
DYSLEXIA   DIET abc
RELIGIOUS AFFILIATION C of E
OTHER SUBJECTS abcfh
FACILITIES ON SITE bcdghik
EXAM BOARDS abcde BDEGHKL
RETAKES   NVQ COURSES

- **A-level**: c e ghi op uv   B GH K P c efg j l
- **AS**: d   G K de pq R
- **GCSE**: de g i no v   B G K P R cdefgh jkl
- **OTHER**: d   l no   O R

WEST MIDLANDS continued

King Henry VIII; Warwick Road; Coventry CV3 6AQ
Tel: 01203 673442 (Fax: 01203 677102) *T.J.Vardon*

		Boys	Age	Girls	Age	TOTAL		Boys	Girls
Day	£925-£1250	496	11-18	398	11-18	894	SIXTH	128	90
Weekly									
Boarding									

ENTRY REQUIREMENTS Exam
SCHOLARSHIPS & BURSARIES Schol; Burs; AP
SPECIAL NEEDS l **DYSLEXIA** **DIET** a
ASSOCIATION HMC **FOUNDED** 1545 **RELIGIOUS AFFILIATION** Non-denom

MAP 9 C 7
LOCATION Urban
DAY ✓ **RAIL** a **AIR** a
SPORT abcdefhklmpqsvwx B
OTHER LANGUAGES
ACTIVITIES cfghijkmopqst A
OTHER SUBJECTS abcfh
FACILITIES ON SITE aghi
EXAM BOARDS abcd DEGH
RETAKES **NVQ COURSES**

A-level: cdefghi l op uv BC GH K P R U c efg j l
AS: e l o K ef
GCSE: cde g i l nop v BC G K P R U cdefg j l
OTHER: u

King Henry VIII Junior School; Warwick Road; Coventry CV3 6AQ
Tel: 01203 717424 (Fax: 01203 677102) *Robert Waddington*

		Boys	Age	Girls	Age	TOTAL		Boys	Girls
Day	£925	101	7-11	126	7-11	227	SIXTH		
Weekly									
Boarding									

ENTRY REQUIREMENTS Exam & Interview
SCHOLARSHIPS & BURSARIES Burs; Teachers
SPECIAL NEEDS jkl l **DYSLEXIA** **DIET** a
ASSOCIATION IAPS **FOUNDED** 1545 **RELIGIOUS AFFILIATION** Non-denom

MAP 9 C 7
LOCATION Urban
DAY **RAIL** a **AIR** a
SPORT aefjlmpqsx B
OTHER LANGUAGES
ACTIVITIES fghijot A
OTHER SUBJECTS abcfh
FACILITIES ON SITE i
EXAM BOARDS
RETAKES **NVQ COURSES**

GCSE: e l no v
OTHER: B E G K O R cde

Mayfield Prep. School; Sutton Road; Walsall; West Midlands WS1 2PD
Tel: 01922 24107 (Fax: 01922 746908) *Mrs C.M.Jones*

		Boys	Age	Girls	Age	TOTAL		Boys	Girls
Day	£650- £925	121	3-11	94	3-11	215	SIXTH		
Weekly									
Boarding									

ENTRY REQUIREMENTS Test & Interview
SCHOLARSHIPS & BURSARIES
SPECIAL NEEDS b G **DYSLEXIA** **DIET**
ASSOCIATION IAPS **FOUNDED** 1922 **RELIGIOUS AFFILIATION** Inter-denom

MAP 8 J 5
LOCATION Urban
DAY **RAIL** b **AIR** a
SPORT aejlmpqsx
OTHER LANGUAGES
ACTIVITIES cgjo
OTHER SUBJECTS ach
FACILITIES ON SITE bci
EXAM BOARDS
RETAKES **NVQ COURSES**

OTHER: e lmno v B E G K O R cde j

Newbridge Preparatory School; 51 Newbridge Crescent; Wolverhampton; W.Midlands WV6 0LH
Tel: 01902 751088 (Fax: 01902 751088) *Miss M.j.Coulter*

		Boys	Age	Girls	Age	TOTAL		Boys	Girls
Day	£755-£1150	6	3- 4	139	3-11	145	SIXTH		
Weekly									
Boarding									

ENTRY REQUIREMENTS
SCHOLARSHIPS & BURSARIES Clergy
SPECIAL NEEDS bklnqw AG **DYSLEXIA** e **DIET** abcd
ASSOCIATION IAPS **FOUNDED** 1937 **RELIGIOUS AFFILIATION** Inter-denom

MAP 8 J 5
LOCATION Urban
DAY **RAIL** a **AIR** b
SPORT alpqx B
OTHER LANGUAGES
ACTIVITIES cgior
OTHER SUBJECTS bch
FACILITIES ON SITE c
EXAM BOARDS
RETAKES **NVQ COURSES**

OTHER: e g i l m o q s v B E G K OP R cde

Royal Wolverhampton Junior School; Penn Road; Wolverhampton WV3 0EF
Tel: 01902 341230 (Fax: 01902 344496) *Mrs M.Saunders*

		Boys	Age	Girls	Age	TOTAL		Boys	Girls
Day	£830-£1280	135	2-11	95	2-11	245	SIXTH		
Weekly	£2370	3	6-11	4	6-11				
Boarding	£2370	7	6-11	1	6-11				

ENTRY REQUIREMENTS Test; Interview; Report
SCHOLARSHIPS & BURSARIES Schol; Burs; Mus; Forces
SPECIAL NEEDS bgknq B **DYSLEXIA** ce **DIET** acd
ASSOCIATION IAPS **FOUNDED** 1850 **RELIGIOUS AFFILIATION** C of E

MAP 8 J 5
LOCATION Urban
DAY **RAIL** a **AIR** a
SPORT abcefhjlpqsx A
OTHER LANGUAGES
ACTIVITIES cfghjlot
OTHER SUBJECTS bcfh
FACILITIES ON SITE acdik
EXAM BOARDS
RETAKES **NVQ COURSES**

OTHER: de l no v B E G K O R cde

WEST MIDLANDS continued

C — Royal Wolverhampton School; Penn Road; Wolverhampton WV3 0EG
Tel: 01902 341230 (Fax: 01902 344496) Mrs B.A.Evans

		Boys	Age	Girls	Age	TOTAL		Boys	Girls
Day	£1725	94	11-18	59	11-18	302	SIXTH	45	33
Weekly	£2900	17	11-18	24	11-18				
Boarding	£3015	69	11-18	39	11-18				

ENTRY REQUIREMENTS Scholarship Exam; Exam & Interview
SCHOLARSHIPS & BURSARIES Schol; Burs; Mus; Forces
SPECIAL NEEDS bjlnpq Bl   **DYSLEXIA** e   **DIET** ad
ASSOCIATION SHMIS   **FOUNDED** 1850   **RELIGIOUS AFFILIATION** C of E

MAP 8 J 5
LOCATION Urban
DAY ✓   **RAIL** a   **AIR** a
SPORT abcefghjmopqsux ABC
OTHER LANGUAGES a
ACTIVITIES cefghijnoqrstw AB
OTHER SUBJECTS bcdfh
FACILITIES ON SITE acdeik
EXAM BOARDS bcd ABDEGH
RETAKES b   **NVQ COURSES**

A-level: e ghi l opq uv x   ABC GH K P R   bc ef   cdef
AS: g i   G   P
GCSE: e ghi l opq v x   ABC G K P R U   bcdef jk
OTHER: l

C — Ruckleigh School; 17 Lode Lane; Solihull; West Midlands; B91 2AB
Tel: 0121 705 2773 D.N.Carr-Smith

		Boys	Age	Girls	Age	TOTAL		Boys	Girls
Day	£625-£1286	134	3-11	95	3-11	229	SIXTH		
Weekly									
Boarding									

ENTRY REQUIREMENTS Interview
SCHOLARSHIPS & BURSARIES
SPECIAL NEEDS   **DYSLEXIA**   **DIET** acd
ASSOCIATION ISAI   **FOUNDED** 1909   **RELIGIOUS AFFILIATION**

MAP 8 K 5
LOCATION Urban
DAY ✓   **RAIL** a   **AIR** a
SPORT aejkmpq AB
OTHER LANGUAGES
ACTIVITIES fghio
OTHER SUBJECTS ch
FACILITIES ON SITE h
EXAM BOARDS
RETAKES   **NVQ COURSES**

A-level:
AS:
GCSE:
OTHER: R

G — St. Martin's; Malvern Hall; Brueton Avenue; Solihull B91 3EN
Tel: 0121 705 1265 (Fax: 0121 711 4529) Mrs S.J.Williams

		Boys	Age	Girls	Age	TOTAL		Boys	Girls
Day	£480-£1473			466	3-18	466	SIXTH		19
Weekly									
Boarding									

ENTRY REQUIREMENTS Exam; Assessment & Interview
SCHOLARSHIPS & BURSARIES Schol; Mus; VI Form; Siblings
SPECIAL NEEDS n   **DYSLEXIA** e   **DIET** acd
ASSOCIATION GSA   **FOUNDED** 1941   **RELIGIOUS AFFILIATION** Non-denom

MAP 8 K 5
LOCATION Urban
DAY ✓   **RAIL** b   **AIR** a
SPORT abcdfhklmopqvwx ABC
OTHER LANGUAGES
ACTIVITIES cfghijknoqst AB
OTHER SUBJECTS abcefgh
FACILITIES ON SITE gh
EXAM BOARDS abc ADEGH
RETAKES   **NVQ COURSES** 12

A-level: cde ghi n p uv   BC G K P R W   cdef
AS: l
GCSE: c e ghi l n v   BC G K P R WX   cdef j l
OTHER: m o O

Bg — Solihull School; Warwick Road; Solihull B91 3DJ
Tel: 0121 705 0958 (Fax: 0121 711 4439) A.Lee

		Boys	Age	Girls	Age	TOTAL		Boys	Girls
Day	£992-£1428	930	7-18	64	15-18	994	SIXTH	207	64
Weekly									
Boarding									

ENTRY REQUIREMENTS Exam
SCHOLARSHIPS & BURSARIES Schol; Mus; Chor; Clergy; AP; VI Form
SPECIAL NEEDS bejklnpqw Gl   **DYSLEXIA** g   **DIET** acd
ASSOCIATION HMC   **FOUNDED** 1560   **RELIGIOUS AFFILIATION** C of E

MAP 8 K 5
LOCATION Urban
DAY ✓   **RAIL** a   **AIR** a
SPORT abcdefgijmpstuwx AB
OTHER LANGUAGES
ACTIVITIES efghijknoqsx ABD
OTHER SUBJECTS ch
FACILITIES ON SITE cdghi
EXAM BOARDS bcd BDGH
RETAKES   **NVQ COURSES**

A-level: defghi l op uv   AB GH K P R   cdef j l
AS: e l
GCSE: defghi l nop v   AB GH K P R   cdef hj l
OTHER:

C — Tettenhall College; Wolverhampton WV6 8QX
Tel: 01902 751119 (Fax: 01902 741940) P.C.Bodkin

		Boys	Age	Girls	Age	TOTAL		Boys	Girls
Day	£1504-£1880	189	7-18	92	7-18	358	SIXTH	52	25
Weekly	£2030-£2537		7-18		7-18				
Boarding	£2503-£3049	45	7-18	32	7-18				

ENTRY REQUIREMENTS CEE; Test & Interview
SCHOLARSHIPS & BURSARIES Schol; Art; Mus; Chor; Forces; Clergy; Teachers
SPECIAL NEEDS bjlw E   **DYSLEXIA**   **DIET** acd
ASSOCIATION HMC   **FOUNDED** 1863   **RELIGIOUS AFFILIATION** Inter-denom

MAP 8 J 5
LOCATION Rural
DAY ✓   **RAIL** a   **AIR** a
SPORT abcdefijklmopqstuwx ABC
OTHER LANGUAGES a
ACTIVITIES cfghijkoqrstw A
OTHER SUBJECTS bcefh
FACILITIES ON SITE bcdhik
EXAM BOARDS ab BDEH
RETAKES ab   **NVQ COURSES**

A-level: e ghi l pq uv   ABC GH K P R U   cdef h l
AS: g i l pq u   G   P R U
GCSE: e ghi nop v   ABC G K P R U   cdef l
OTHER: lm   O

WEST MIDLANDS continued

West House School; 24 St.James Road; Edgbaston; Birmingham B15 2NX
Tel: 0121 440 4097 (Fax: 0121 440 5839) *G.K.Duce*

Day £495-£1546 | Boys 203 | Age 3-13 | Girls — | Age — | TOTAL 203 | SIXTH Boys — | Girls —
Weekly
Boarding

ENTRY REQUIREMENTS Test & Interview
SCHOLARSHIPS & BURSARIES Clergy; Teachers
SPECIAL NEEDS bjlnuw   **DYSLEXIA** e   **DIET** acd
ASSOCIATION IAPS   **FOUNDED** 1895   **RELIGIOUS AFFILIATION** Non-denom

MAP 8 J 5
LOCATION Urban
DAY **RAIL** a   **AIR** a
SPORT abcejlmqsux AB
OTHER LANGUAGES
ACTIVITIES fghjno
OTHER SUBJECTS ch
FACILITIES ON SITE ahj
EXAM BOARDS
RETAKES   **NVQ COURSES**

A-level — | AS — | GCSE — | OTHER: e g i l v / B G K OP R / cde j

---

Wolverhampton Grammar School; Compton Road; Wolverhampton; West Midlands
WV3 9RB Tel: 01902 21326 (Fax: 01902 21819) *B.St.J.Trafford*

Day £1600 | Boys 595 | Age 10-18 | Girls 140 | Age 10-18 | TOTAL 735 | SIXTH Boys 170 | Girls 40
Weekly
Boarding

ENTRY REQUIREMENTS Report & Exam & Interview
SCHOLARSHIPS & BURSARIES Schol; Burs; Mus; AP
SPECIAL NEEDS Inq   **DYSLEXIA**   **DIET** acd
ASSOCIATION HMC   **FOUNDED** 1512   **RELIGIOUS AFFILIATION** Non-denom

MAP 8 J 5
LOCATION Urban
DAY **RAIL** a   **AIR** a
SPORT abcdefhijlmpqstuwx ABC
OTHER LANGUAGES
ACTIVITIES cfghijkopqrtx AB
OTHER SUBJECTS bcdfh
FACILITIES ON SITE cgh
EXAM BOARDS bc BDEH
RETAKES   **NVQ COURSES**

A-level: cd g i nop uv x / B GH K M P R U / c ef j
AS: o / c
GCSE: K R
GCSE: d g i o q vw / B G K OP R / cdef hj
OTHER: lm u / ef h

Chafyn Grove School; Salisbury; Wilts. SP1 1LR
Tel: 01722 333423 (Fax: 01722 323114) *David Duff-Mitchell*

Day £880-£1878 | Boys 111 | Age 4-13 | Girls 59 | Age 4-13 | TOTAL 243 | SIXTH Boys — | Girls —
Weekly £2514 | | 7-13 | | 7-13
Boarding £2514 | 43 | 7-13 | 30 | 7-13

ENTRY REQUIREMENTS Interview
SCHOLARSHIPS & BURSARIES Schol
SPECIAL NEEDS bn   **DYSLEXIA** e   **DIET** a
ASSOCIATION IAPS   **FOUNDED** 1877   **RELIGIOUS AFFILIATION** C of E

MAP 3 B 6
LOCATION Urban
DAY **RAIL** a   **AIR** b
SPORT abcefhjklmopqswx ABC
OTHER LANGUAGES
ACTIVITIES acfghjoqtw A
OTHER SUBJECTS cfh
FACILITIES ON SITE cdehjk
EXAM BOARDS
RETAKES   **NVQ COURSES**

A-level — | AS — | GCSE — | OTHER: de lm o v / B E G K O R / cde j

WILTSHIRE

Dauntsey's School; West Lavington; Nr. Devizes SN10 4HE
Tel: 01380 812446 (Fax: 01380 813620) *C.R.Evans*

Day £2164 | Boys 180 | Age 11-18 | Girls 137 | Age 11-18 | TOTAL 620 | SIXTH Boys 98 | Girls 81
Weekly
Boarding £3514 | 161 | 11-18 | 142 | 11-18

ENTRY REQUIREMENTS CEE; Report; Report & Interview
SCHOLARSHIPS & BURSARIES Schol; Mus; AP
SPECIAL NEEDS bgjpqw BCEGL   **DYSLEXIA**   **DIET** abcd
ASSOCIATION HMC   **FOUNDED** 1542   **RELIGIOUS AFFILIATION** Inter-denom

MAP 3 A 5
LOCATION Rural
DAY ✓ **RAIL** b   **AIR** b
SPORT abcdefghklmnpqstuvwx ABC
OTHER LANGUAGES
ACTIVITIES cfghijklmnoqstw ABD
OTHER SUBJECTS cdfh
FACILITIES ON SITE abcdeghikl
EXAM BOARDS abcd ABDEGH
RETAKES   **NVQ COURSES**

A-level: cde g i op uv / B GH K P / c efg j
AS: c ghi l pq x / B K P R U / efg jk
GCSE: cde g i l op v / B G K N P R / cdefgh jk
OTHER: mn / KL NO R / e jk

Godolphin School, The; Milford Hill; Salisbury; Wilts. SP1 2RA
Tel: 01722 333059 (Fax: 01722 411700) *Mrs H.A.Fender*

Day £2152 | Boys — | Age — | Girls 227 | Age 7-18 | TOTAL 434 | SIXTH Boys — | Girls 92
Weekly | | | 5
Boarding £3593 | | | 202 | 11-18

ENTRY REQUIREMENTS CEE
SCHOLARSHIPS & BURSARIES Schol; Burs; Mus; AP; VI Form; Siblings
SPECIAL NEEDS bgln   **DYSLEXIA** ef   **DIET** ad
ASSOCIATION GSA   **FOUNDED** 1726   **RELIGIOUS AFFILIATION** C of E

MAP 3 B 6
LOCATION Urban
DAY ✓ **RAIL** a   **AIR** b
SPORT abcdfghlmnopqtwx ABC
OTHER LANGUAGES
ACTIVITIES abcfghijklnoqstw ABD
OTHER SUBJECTS abcdfh
FACILITIES ON SITE bchj
EXAM BOARDS abcd ABDEG
RETAKES   **NVQ COURSES**

A-level: cdefgh n uv / BC GH K M P R U / cdef j
AS: g i no v / G K M P R / ef
GCSE: de g i no v / BC E G K P R W / cdef j l
OTHER: l / e

WILTSHIRE continued

C — Heywood Preparatory School; The Priory; Corsham; Wilts. SN13 0AP
Tel: 01249 713379 (Fax: 01249 701757) Mrs.P.Hall

		Boys	Age	Girls	Age	TOTAL		Boys	Girls
Day	£715-£845	69	3-11	58	3-11	127	SIXTH		
Weekly									
Boarding									

ENTRY REQUIREMENTS Test & Interview
SCHOLARSHIPS & BURSARIES
SPECIAL NEEDS n   **DYSLEXIA**   **DIET** a
ASSOCIATION ISAI   **FOUNDED** 1940   **RELIGIOUS AFFILIATION** Non-denom

MAP 2 K 2
LOCATION Rural
DAY   **RAIL** a   **AIR**
SPORT adefjlmpqrvx A
OTHER LANGUAGES
ACTIVITIES cghjow
OTHER SUBJECTS ch
FACILITIES ON SITE
EXAM BOARDS
RETAKES   **NVQ COURSES**

A-level: — AS: — GCSE: — OTHER: e v B G K O R cde

Gb — La Retraite School; 19 Campbell Road; Salisbury; Wilts. SP1 3BQ
Tel: 01722 333094 (Fax: 01722 330868) Mrs.R.Simmons

		Boys	Age	Girls	Age	TOTAL		Boys	Girls
Day	£875-£1525	11	2-7	179	2-18	190	SIXTH		25
Weekly									
Boarding									

ENTRY REQUIREMENTS Exam; Interview
SCHOLARSHIPS & BURSARIES Schol; Burs
SPECIAL NEEDS bejklntw B   **DYSLEXIA**   **DIET** acd
ASSOCIATION GSA   **FOUNDED** 1953   **RELIGIOUS AFFILIATION** RC/Christian

MAP 3 B 6
LOCATION Urban
DAY ✓   **RAIL** a   **AIR** b
SPORT abcdfhlmopqtwx ABC
OTHER LANGUAGES
ACTIVITIES cfghijklnopqstw AB
OTHER SUBJECTS abcdefgh
FACILITIES ON SITE bcgh
EXAM BOARDS abcd ABGH
RETAKES ab   **NVQ COURSES**

A-level: defghij p v BC GH K N P U W cdef j
AS: g v K e j
GCSE: e g ij nop v BC E G K NOP U W cdef j l
OTHER: e lmno stu x C G K NO R W e

Gb — Leaden Hall School; 70 The Close; Salisbury; Wilts. SP1 2EP
Tel: 01722 334700 (Fax: 01722 410575) Mrs D.E.Watkins

		Boys	Age	Girls	Age	TOTAL		Boys	Girls
Day	£740-£1160	✗	2	163	3-13	189	SIXTH		
Weekly	£1770			13	7-13				
Boarding	£2080			11	7-13				

ENTRY REQUIREMENTS Assessment
SCHOLARSHIPS & BURSARIES Schol; Art; Mus; Clergy
SPECIAL NEEDS aijnqw l   **DYSLEXIA** e   **DIET** abcd
ASSOCIATION IAPS   **FOUNDED** 1947   **RELIGIOUS AFFILIATION** Inter-denom

MAP 3 B 6
LOCATION Urban
DAY   **RAIL** a   **AIR** b
SPORT alpqx B
OTHER LANGUAGES
ACTIVITIES cfgh
OTHER SUBJECTS bch
FACILITIES ON SITE j
EXAM BOARDS
RETAKES   **NVQ COURSES**

A-level: — AS: — GCSE: — OTHER: e m o v B E G K O R cde

C — Marlborough College; Marlborough; Wiltshire SN8 1PA
Tel: 01672 892200 (Fax: 01672 892207) E.J.H.Gould

		Boys	Age	Girls	Age	TOTAL		Boys	Girls
Day	£2995	✗	24	13-18	11	13-18	798	SIXTH	215	149
Weekly									
Boarding	£4250		501	13-18	262	13-18			

ENTRY REQUIREMENTS CEE; Scholarship Exam; Report & Interview; Report & Exam & Interview
SCHOLARSHIPS & BURSARIES Schol; Burs; Art; Mus; Chor; Forces; Clergy; VI Form; ARA
SPECIAL NEEDS bjlnqst GH   **DYSLEXIA** f   **DIET** a
ASSOCIATION HMC   **FOUNDED** 1843   **RELIGIOUS AFFILIATION** C of E

MAP 3 B 4
LOCATION Rural
DAY   **RAIL** b   **AIR** b
SPORT abcdefghijklmnopstuwx ABC
OTHER LANGUAGES
ACTIVITIES bcdefghijklmnopqrstvw A
OTHER SUBJECTS abcfh
FACILITIES ON SITE abcdhijk
EXAM BOARDS bd HL
RETAKES   **NVQ COURSES**

A-level: c efghi no v x B GH K P R cdefg jkl
AS: h U de
GCSE: c e g i no v B G K P R cdefg jkl
OTHER: l qr u w A J MNO QR U ab i

C — Pinewood School; Bourton; Swindon; Wilts. SN6 8HZ
Tel: 01793 782205 (Fax: 01793 783476) H.G.C.Boddington

		Boys	Age	Girls	Age	TOTAL		Boys	Girls
Day	£950-£2025	✗	93	4-13	50	4-13	179	SIXTH		
Weekly									
Boarding	£2650		29	7-13	7	7-13			

ENTRY REQUIREMENTS Assessment & Interview
SCHOLARSHIPS & BURSARIES Clergy; Teachers
SPECIAL NEEDS aw G   **DYSLEXIA**   **DIET** a
ASSOCIATION IAPS   **FOUNDED** 1875   **RELIGIOUS AFFILIATION** C of E

MAP 2 L 2
LOCATION Rural
DAY   **RAIL** b   **AIR** b
SPORT abcefgjklmnopqsuwx AB
OTHER LANGUAGES
ACTIVITIES cfghijoqrstvwx
OTHER SUBJECTS cf
FACILITIES ON SITE cdj
EXAM BOARDS
RETAKES   **NVQ COURSES**

A-level: — AS: — GCSE: — OTHER: e g i l o q v B G K OP R cde j

WILTSHIRE continued

C | Prior Park Preparatory School; Cricklade; Wiltshire SN6 6BB
Tel: 01793 750275 (Fax: 01793 750910) *G.B.Hobern*

		Boys	Age	Girls	Age	TOTAL
Day	£1555-£1565	46	7-13	32	7-13	194
Weekly	£2226-£2236	48	7-13	27	7-13	
Boarding	£2226-£2236	25	7-13	16	7-13	

SIXTH: Boys Girls

ENTRY REQUIREMENTS Interview; Report; Assessment
SCHOLARSHIPS & BURSARIES Burs; Mus
SPECIAL NEEDS npw   **DYSLEXIA** ce   **DIET** a
ASSOCIATION IAPS   **FOUNDED** 1946   **RELIGIOUS AFFILIATION** R C

MAP 3 B 3
LOCATION Rural
DAY ✓   **RAIL** a   **AIR** b
SPORT abcefhklmopqswx ABC
OTHER LANGUAGES
ACTIVITIES cfghijmnoqrsw A
OTHER SUBJECTS bch
FACILITIES ON SITE acdej
EXAM BOARDS
RETAKES   **NVQ COURSES**

A-level | AS | GCSE | OTHER: d e g i   lmno q s v   B   G   K NOP R   cde g j

---

C | St. Francis School; Marlborough Road; Pewsey SN9 5NT
Tel: 01672 563228 (Fax: 01672 564323) *P.W.Blundell*

		Boys	Age	Girls	Age	TOTAL
Day	£180-£1350	72	3-11	88	3-11	160
Weekly						
Boarding						

SIXTH: Boys Girls

ENTRY REQUIREMENTS Report & Interview
SCHOLARSHIPS & BURSARIES Schol; Sport; ARA; Drama
SPECIAL NEEDS abnx   **DYSLEXIA**   **DIET** a
ASSOCIATION IAPS   **FOUNDED** 1941   **RELIGIOUS AFFILIATION** Inter-denom

MAP 3 B 5
LOCATION Rural
DAY ✓   **RAIL** a   **AIR** b
SPORT acefjlmpqswx AB
OTHER LANGUAGES
ACTIVITIES cgjoqt
OTHER SUBJECTS bcdfh
FACILITIES ON SITE bc
EXAM BOARDS
RETAKES   **NVQ COURSES**

A-level | AS | GCSE | OTHER: d e g i   lmno s v   B   G   K   O   R   e

---

C | St. Margaret's School; Curzon Street; Calne; Wiltshire SN11 0DF
Tel: 01249 815197 (Fax: 01249 822 432) *Miss D.H.Burns*

		Boys	Age	Girls	Age	TOTAL
Day	£1065-£1125	19	4-11	51	4-11	70
Weekly						
Boarding						

SIXTH: Boys Girls

ENTRY REQUIREMENTS None
SCHOLARSHIPS & BURSARIES Teachers
SPECIAL NEEDS bghjlnqsx BCL   **DYSLEXIA** d   **DIET** ab
ASSOCIATION IAPS   **FOUNDED** 1873   **RELIGIOUS AFFILIATION** C of E

MAP 2 K 2
LOCATION Rural
DAY   **RAIL** a   **AIR** b
SPORT aefjlmopqsx B
OTHER LANGUAGES
ACTIVITIES cfghjno
OTHER SUBJECTS abch
FACILITIES ON SITE abdhjk
EXAM BOARDS
RETAKES   **NVQ COURSES**

A-level | AS | GCSE | OTHER: e   lmno   uv   B E G   K   O   R   cde

---

G | St. Mary's School; Calne SN11 0DF
Tel: 01249 815899 (Fax: 01249 822432) *Miss D.H.Burns*

		Boys	Age	Girls	Age	TOTAL
Day	£2275			37	11-18	304
Weekly						
Boarding	£3850			267	11-18	

SIXTH: Boys Girls 80

ENTRY REQUIREMENTS CEE
SCHOLARSHIPS & BURSARIES Schol; Burs
SPECIAL NEEDS bjiq   **DYSLEXIA**   **DIET** ad
ASSOCIATION GSA   **FOUNDED** 1873   **RELIGIOUS AFFILIATION** C of E

MAP 2 H 2
LOCATION Rural
DAY   **RAIL** a   **AIR** b
SPORT abcfghklmnopqvwx ABC
OTHER LANGUAGES
ACTIVITIES cghijklnostw B
OTHER SUBJECTS cfh
FACILITIES ON SITE adjk
EXAM BOARDS abd ABEH
RETAKES   **NVQ COURSES**

A-level: efg i   n p   v   B   GH K   P R U   c efg j l | AS | GCSE: d   l n   v   B   G   K   R   X   cdefgh j l | OTHER

C | Salisbury Cathedral School; 1 The Close; Salisbury; Wilts SP1 2EQ
Tel: 01722 322652 (Fax: 01722 410910) *C.J.A.Helyer*

		Boys	Age	Girls	Age	TOTAL
Day	£425-£1975	149	3-13	75	3-13	302
Weekly	£2625	20	8-13	8	8-13	
Boarding	£2625	25	8-13	25	8-13	

SIXTH: Boys Girls

ENTRY REQUIREMENTS Assessment & Interview
SCHOLARSHIPS & BURSARIES Chor
SPECIAL NEEDS jknw EGI   **DYSLEXIA**   **DIET** a
ASSOCIATION IAPS   **FOUNDED** 1091   **RELIGIOUS AFFILIATION** C of E

MAP 3 B 6
LOCATION Urban
DAY   **RAIL** a   **AIR** b
SPORT abcdefhjklmpqsx ABC
OTHER LANGUAGES
ACTIVITIES cfghijopqrst A
OTHER SUBJECTS bcfh
FACILITIES ON SITE acdej
EXAM BOARDS
RETAKES   **NVQ COURSES**

A-level | AS | GCSE | OTHER: e   lmno   v   B E G   K NO R   cdefg j

WILTSHIRE continued

B Sandroyd School; Tollard Royal; Salisbury SP5 5QD
Tel: 01725 516264 (Fax: 01725 516441) *Michael J Hatch*

		Boys	Age	Girls	Age	TOTAL		Boys	Girls
Day	£2450	5	7-11			135	SIXTH		
Weekly									
Boarding	£2970	130	7-13						

ENTRY REQUIREMENTS Assessment & Interview
SCHOLARSHIPS & BURSARIES Burs; Chor
SPECIAL NEEDS n   **DYSLEXIA** ce   **DIET** ad
ASSOCIATION IAPS   **FOUNDED** 1888   **RELIGIOUS AFFILIATION** C of E

MAP 3 K 2
LOCATION Rural
DAY b   **RAIL** b   **AIR** b
SPORT abcdefjlmostuwx AB
OTHER LANGUAGES
ACTIVITIES afghijloqrtw A
OTHER SUBJECTS abcfh
FACILITIES ON SITE bcdhi
EXAM BOARDS
RETAKES   **NVQ COURSES**

A-level   **AS**   **GCSE** cde g i l no q s v / B G K OP R / cde j
OTHER

Gb Stonar School; Cottles Park; Atworth; Melksham; Wilts. SN12 8NT
Tel: 01225 702309 (Fax: 01225 790830) *Mrs S.Hopkinson*

		Boys	Age	Girls	Age	TOTAL		Boys	Girls
Day	£780-£1763		2- 5	237	2-18	502	SIXTH		102
Weekly	£2914-£3182			35					
Boarding	£2914-£3182			230	8-18				

ENTRY REQUIREMENTS Report & Test
SCHOLARSHIPS & BURSARIES Schol; Burs; VI Form
SPECIAL NEEDS jn   **DYSLEXIA** e   **DIET** a
ASSOCIATION GSA   **FOUNDED** 1895   **RELIGIOUS AFFILIATION** C of E

MAP 2 K 2
LOCATION Rural
DAY ✓   **RAIL** b   **AIR** b
SPORT acdflmopqwx ABC
OTHER LANGUAGES a
ACTIVITIES bcfghijknoqstwx AB
OTHER SUBJECTS abcdefgh
FACILITIES ON SITE abcdeghi
EXAM BOARDS abcd ABDEGHIJ
RETAKES ab   **NVQ COURSES** 123

A-level cdefghi l nopq   vwx / BC E GH K NOPQR U W / cdef hj l
AS def o vw / BC GH K N P R U / ef l
GCSE cdefghi l nopq   vwx / BC E GH K NOPQR U WX / cdef hj l
OTHER l   u

C Warminster Junior School; Vicarage Street; Warminster; Wilts. BA12 8JG
Tel: 01985 213358 (Fax: 01985 214129) *A.M.T.Palmer*

		Boys	Age	Girls	Age	TOTAL		Boys	Girls
Day	£550-£1790	62	4-12	46	4-12	154	SIXTH		
Weekly	£2820-£3090								
Boarding	£2820-£3090	27	8-12	19	8-12				

ENTRY REQUIREMENTS Test & Interview
SCHOLARSHIPS & BURSARIES Schol; Burs
SPECIAL NEEDS abeijklntw BHI   **DYSLEXIA** ce   **DIET** abcd
ASSOCIATION IAPS   **FOUNDED** 1707   **RELIGIOUS AFFILIATION** C of E

MAP 2 K 3
LOCATION
DAY ✓   **RAIL** b   **AIR** a
SPORT aefjlmpqsx AB
OTHER LANGUAGES
ACTIVITIES cfghijlostwx
OTHER SUBJECTS bcfh
FACILITIES ON SITE abdehjk
EXAM BOARDS
RETAKES   **NVQ COURSES**

A-level   **AS**   **GCSE** e g i lmno v / BC G K NOP R W / cde
OTHER   l   u

C Warminster School; Warminster; Wilts. BA12 8PJ
Tel: 01985 213038 (Fax: 01985 214129) *T.D.Holgate*

		Boys	Age	Girls	Age	TOTAL		Boys	Girls
Day	£1790	79	12-18	47	12-18	310	SIXTH	43	35
Weekly	£3090		12-18		12-18				
Boarding	£3090	105	12-18	79	12-18				

ENTRY REQUIREMENTS CEE; Test & Interview
SCHOLARSHIPS & BURSARIES Schol; Burs; Forces; Clergy; VI Form; Siblings
SPECIAL NEEDS bejkIntw EGI   **DYSLEXIA** cdef   **DIET** ab
ASSOCIATION SHMIS   **FOUNDED** 1707   **RELIGIOUS AFFILIATION** C of E

MAP 2 K 3
LOCATION
DAY ✓   **RAIL** b   **AIR** b
SPORT abcefhjkmopqtuwx ABC
OTHER LANGUAGES a
ACTIVITIES cdefghijklmnopqrsw AD
OTHER SUBJECTS abcdegh
FACILITIES ON SITE acdeghjk
EXAM BOARDS bd ABEGH
RETAKES ab   **NVQ COURSES**

A-level e g i   op s v / ABC G K OP U / c ef   l
AS e g / BC G / c e
GCSE e ghi l no q s v / ABC G K P S W / cdef   l
OTHER   l   u / R

B Ampleforth College; York YO6 4ER
Tel: 01439 788224 (Fax: 01439 788330) *The Rev.G.F.L.Chamberlain OSB*

		Boys	Age	Girls	Age	TOTAL		Boys	Girls
Day	£2065-£3245	18	13-18			551	SIXTH	233	
Weekly									
Boarding	£4005	533	13-18						

ENTRY REQUIREMENTS CEE; Scholarship Exam; Report & Interview
SCHOLARSHIPS & BURSARIES Schol; Mus; Chor; VI Form; Siblings
SPECIAL NEEDS aegjkInqw EGI   **DYSLEXIA** de   **DIET** a
ASSOCIATION HMC   **FOUNDED** 1802   **RELIGIOUS AFFILIATION** R C

MAP 12 H 5
LOCATION Rural
DAY ✓   **RAIL** b   **AIR** c
SPORT abcdefghklmostuwx ABC
OTHER LANGUAGES a
ACTIVITIES efghijklmnopqrsw ABC
OTHER SUBJECTS bcfgh
FACILITIES ON SITE abcdefhikl
EXAM BOARDS abc ABDEH
RETAKES   **NVQ COURSES**

A-level cdefghi   op   v x / B GH k N P R / c efgh j l
AS c f   q / B GH K   R / c efgh j l
GCSE cde g i   o q   v / B   G K N P R / cdefgh j l
OTHER   l n u / I K   O R / b

N YORKS

296

YORKSHIRE (NORTH) continued

B **Ampleforth College Junior School; The Castle; Gilling East; York YO6 4HP**
Tel: 01439 788238 (Fax: 01439 788538) *Rev.J.A.Sierla*

		Boys	Age	Girls	Age	TOTAL		Boys	Girls
Day	£1725-£2180	9	8-13			106	SIXTH		
Weekly			8-13						
Boarding	£2805	97	8-13						

ENTRY REQUIREMENTS Assessment & Interview
SCHOLARSHIPS & BURSARIES Burs; Mus; Chor; Teachers; ARA; Siblings
SPECIAL NEEDS nw   **DYSLEXIA** def   **DIET** a
ASSOCIATION IAPS   **FOUNDED** 1914   **RELIGIOUS AFFILIATION** R C

MAP12 H 5
LOCATION Rural
DAY ✓   **RAIL** b   **AIR** b
SPORT abcefghjklmoqswx ABC
OTHER LANGUAGES a
ACTIVITIES abfghijmnoprtwx A
OTHER SUBJECTS abcfh
FACILITIES ON SITE bdhil
EXAM BOARDS
RETAKES   **NVQ COURSES**

A-level / AS / GCSE:
OTHER   e g i l   o q   v
B   G K   OP R
cde g j

C **Ashville College; Harrogate; N.Yorks. HG2 9JR**
Tel: 01423 566358 (Fax: 01423 505142) *M.H.Crosby*

		Boys	Age	Girls	Age	TOTAL		Boys	Girls
Day	£1050-£1560	328	7-18	246	7-18	725	SIXTH	67	62
Weekly	£2658-£2918		7-18		7-18				
Boarding	£2658-£2918	98	7-18	53	7-18				

ENTRY REQUIREMENTS CEE; Exam & Interview
SCHOLARSHIPS & BURSARIES Schol; Burs; Clergy
SPECIAL NEEDS abegjlnpquw GI   **DYSLEXIA** def   **DIET** a
ASSOCIATION HMC   **FOUNDED** 1877   **RELIGIOUS AFFILIATION** Methodist

MAP12 G 5
LOCATION Urban
DAY ✓   **RAIL** a   **AIR** a
SPORT abcdefhjkmpqstwx ABC
OTHER LANGUAGES a
ACTIVITIES fghijklmnopqrvw AB
OTHER SUBJECTS abcefgh
FACILITIES ON SITE abcghik
EXAM BOARDS abc ADEHL
RETAKES ab   **NVQ COURSES** 3

A-level: e ghi op uv AB GH K P R U cdef j
AS: q
GCSE: e ghi nop v ABC G K P R U cdef h j
OTHER: e h i v BC G K OP R cdef j

B **Aysgarth School Trust Ltd; Bedale; N.Yorks. DL8 1TF**
Tel: 01677 450240 (Fax: 01677 450736) *J.C.Hodgkinson*

		Boys	Age	Girls	Age	TOTAL		Boys	Girls
Day	£231-£1919	22	3-13	10	3-8	125	SIXTH		
Weekly	£2468-£2742	5	8-13						
Boarding	£2468-£2742	88	8-13						

ENTRY REQUIREMENTS Interview
SCHOLARSHIPS & BURSARIES Burs
SPECIAL NEEDS b   **DYSLEXIA**   **DIET** ab
ASSOCIATION IAPS   **FOUNDED** 1877   **RELIGIOUS AFFILIATION** C of E

MAP12 G 4
LOCATION Rural
DAY   **RAIL** b   **AIR** a
SPORT abcefijlmstuwx AB
OTHER LANGUAGES
ACTIVITIES acdfghjoqrst
OTHER SUBJECTS ach
FACILITIES ON SITE cdhik
EXAM BOARDS
RETAKES   **NVQ COURSES**

A-level / AS / GCSE:
OTHER   e g i l   o q   v
B   G K   OP R
cde g j

C **Ayton School; High Green; Great Ayton; North Yorkshire TS9 6BN**
Tel: 01642 722141 (Fax: 01642 724044) *Alice Meager*

		Boys	Age	Girls	Age	TOTAL		Boys	Girls
Day	£815-£1475	120	4-19	89	4-19	232	SIXTH	12	1
Weekly	£2785	5	11-19	2	11-19				
Boarding	£3165	13	11-19	3	11-19				

ENTRY REQUIREMENTS
SCHOLARSHIPS & BURSARIES Schol; Burs
SPECIAL NEEDS bjklnqstw EGHI   **DYSLEXIA** e   **DIET** acd
ASSOCIATION GBA   **FOUNDED** 1841   **RELIGIOUS AFFILIATION** Quaker

MAP12 H 3
LOCATION Rural
DAY ✓   **RAIL** b   **AIR** a
SPORT abcefjmpqx ABC
OTHER LANGUAGES a
ACTIVITIES fghjkmoqrt A
OTHER SUBJECTS abcdefh
FACILITIES ON SITE bcdeghjk
EXAM BOARDS abcd BDEH
RETAKES a   **NVQ COURSES**

A-level: de g i l nop uv B GH K P cdef
AS: i G e
GCSE: de ghi l no q v BC G K OP cdef l
OTHER: j

C **Bentham School; Bentham; nr.Lancaster LA2 7DB**
Tel: 015242 61275 (Fax: 015242 62944) *T.Halliwell*

		Boys	Age	Girls	Age	TOTAL		Boys	Girls
Day	£895-£1492	73	3-18	66	3-18	268	SIXTH	29	25
Weekly		3	7-18	1	7-18				
Boarding	£2485-£2995	79	7-18	46	7-18				

ENTRY REQUIREMENTS Test & Interview; Report & Interview
SCHOLARSHIPS & BURSARIES Schol; Burs; Art; Mus; Forces; VI Form; Siblings
SPECIAL NEEDS abefjklnpqtvw ABCEGHIJKL   **DYSLEXIA** e   **DIET** abd
ASSOCIATION SHMIS   **FOUNDED** 1726   **RELIGIOUS AFFILIATION** C of E

MAP11 D 5
LOCATION Rural
DAY ✓   **RAIL** b   **AIR** b
SPORT abcdefhjkmpqstwx ABC
OTHER LANGUAGES a
ACTIVITIES acdfghijklmnopqstuwx AB
OTHER SUBJECTS abcdefh
FACILITIES ON SITE bcdeghjk
EXAM BOARDS abcd ABDEGH
RETAKES ab   **NVQ COURSES**

A-level: de g i op uv ABC GH K P R cdef l
AS: de g i op v C GH K P c ef l
GCSE: de g i op v ABC G K N P R X cdef l
OTHER: lmn x F K O

297

YORKSHIRE (NORTH) continued

C — Bootham School; York YO3 7BU
Tel: 01904 623636 (Fax: 01904 652106) *I.M.Small*

			Boys	Age	Girls	Age	TOTAL		Boys	Girls
Day	£2147	✗	162	11-18	80	11-18	334	SIXTH	59	38
Weekly	£3308		17	11-18	18	11-18				
Boarding	£3308		46	11-18	11	11-18				

ENTRY REQUIREMENTS Report & Exam & Interview
SCHOLARSHIPS & BURSARIES Schol; Burs; Art; Mus; AP; VI Form
SPECIAL NEEDS abehjklnpqrstwx ADEGIKL   **DYSLEXIA** f   **DIET** a
ASSOCIATION HMC   **FOUNDED** 1823   **RELIGIOUS AFFILIATION** Quaker

MAP12 H 6
LOCATION Urban
DAY   **RAIL** a   **AIR** a
SPORT abcefghjmopqrwx ABC
OTHER LANGUAGES a
ACTIVITIES abcfghijklmnopqstuvw AB
OTHER SUBJECTS abcdfh
FACILITIES ON SITE abcegik
EXAM BOARDS abcd ABDEH
RETAKES a   **NVQ COURSES**

A-level: c e g i   uv   B   GH K   P   c ef   j
AS: gh   GH K   p   x   ef
GCSE: c e g i   o   v x   B E G K   P R U X   cdef   j l
OTHER: f   l n   t   gh k

B g — Bramcote School; Filey Road; Scarborough; North Yorkshire YO11 2TT
Tel: 01723 373086 (Fax: 01723 364186) *J.G.W.Walker*

		Boys	Age	Girls	Age	TOTAL		Boys	Girls
Day	£1860	5	7-10		7-10	97	SIXTH		
Weekly									
Boarding	£2650	92	7-13		7-13				

ENTRY REQUIREMENTS Assessment & Interview
SCHOLARSHIPS & BURSARIES Schol; Burs; Mus
SPECIAL NEEDS abejklnw Gl   **DYSLEXIA** e   **DIET** acd
ASSOCIATION IAPS   **FOUNDED** 1893   **RELIGIOUS AFFILIATION** C of E

MAP12 J 4
LOCATION Urban
DAY   **RAIL** b   **AIR** b
SPORT adefhjkmosuwx AB
OTHER LANGUAGES
ACTIVITIES afghijmnopqrstvw A
OTHER SUBJECTS acfh
FACILITIES ON SITE cdhik
EXAM BOARDS
RETAKES   **NVQ COURSES**

A-level:
AS:
GCSE:
OTHER: cde g i l   no q s v   B   G K   OP R   cde g   j

C — Catteral Hall; Giggleswick; Settle; N.Yorks. BD24 0DG
Tel: 01729 822527 (Fax: 01729 825505) *M.J.Morris*

			Boys	Age	Girls	Age	TOTAL		Boys	Girls
Day	£1956-£2104	✗	23	8-13	18	8-13	131	SIXTH		
Weekly										
Boarding	£2929-£3144		60	8-13	30	8-13				

ENTRY REQUIREMENTS Test; Report
SCHOLARSHIPS & BURSARIES Schol; Mus; AP
SPECIAL NEEDS bejklnqw Bl   **DYSLEXIA** ef   **DIET** ad
ASSOCIATION IAPS   **FOUNDED** 1934   **RELIGIOUS AFFILIATION** Inter-denom

MAP11 E 5
LOCATION Rural
DAY   **RAIL** c   **AIR** b
SPORT abcdefjklmpqsvwx AB
OTHER LANGUAGES
ACTIVITIES acdfghjloqtw A
OTHER SUBJECTS bcdh
FACILITIES ON SITE bcdhil
EXAM BOARDS
RETAKES   **NVQ COURSES**

A-level:
AS:
GCSE:
OTHER: e   o   v   BC E G   K   O R   cde   j

C — Cundall Manor; Helperby; York YO6 2RW
Tel: 01423 360200 (Fax: 01423 360754) *J.Napier*

			Boys	Age	Girls	Age	TOTAL		Boys	Girls
Day	£1050-£1650	✗	88	4-13	38	4-13	166	SIXTH		
Weekly	£2000-£2250			6-13		6-13				
Boarding	£2250-£2350		28	7-13	12	7-13				

ENTRY REQUIREMENTS Test & Interview
SCHOLARSHIPS & BURSARIES Schol; Burs; Mus; Forces; Sport
SPECIAL NEEDS n BG   **DYSLEXIA** de   **DIET** acd
ASSOCIATION IAPS   **FOUNDED** 1971   **RELIGIOUS AFFILIATION** C of E

MAP12 G 5
LOCATION Rural
DAY ✓   **RAIL** b   **AIR** a
SPORT abcefjkmopqstuwx ABC
OTHER LANGUAGES
ACTIVITIES acfghijmoqrstwx A
OTHER SUBJECTS cfh
FACILITIES ON SITE bdehil
EXAM BOARDS B
RETAKES   **NVQ COURSES**

A-level: cdefg j
AS:
GCSE:
OTHER:

C — Fyling Hall School; Robin Hood's Bay; Nr.Whitby; North Yorkshire YO22 4QD
Tel: 01947 880261 (Fax: 01947 880919) *Alex Gregg*

			Boys	Age	Girls	Age	TOTAL		Boys	Girls
Day	£795-£925	✗	31	5-18	21	5-18	206	SIXTH	13	11
Weekly										
Boarding	£1840-£2020		78	7-18	76	7-18				

ENTRY REQUIREMENTS Report & Interview
SCHOLARSHIPS & BURSARIES Schol; VI Form
SPECIAL NEEDS   **DYSLEXIA**   **DIET** a
ASSOCIATION ISAI   **FOUNDED** 1922   **RELIGIOUS AFFILIATION** Inter-denom

MAP12 J 3
LOCATION Rural
DAY ✓   **RAIL** b   **AIR** c
SPORT acdefmqstux AB
OTHER LANGUAGES
ACTIVITIES cefghjlmoqtwx A
OTHER SUBJECTS cdh
FACILITIES ON SITE c
EXAM BOARDS abcd DGI
RETAKES ab   **NVQ COURSES**

A-level: e g i l   o q   uv x   BC   G K   P   cdef   j
AS:
GCSE: e g i l   o q   v x   BC   G K   P R   W   cdef   j
OTHER:

298

YORKSHIRE (NORTH) *continued*

C | Giggleswick School; Settle; N.Yorks. BD24 0DE
Tel: 01729 82 3545 (Fax: 01729 82 4187) *A.P.Millard*

		Boys	Age	Girls	Age	TOTAL		Boys	Girls
Day	£2552	24	13-18	26	13-18	300	SIXTH	64	50
Weekly		162	13-18	88	13-18				
Boarding	£3848								

ENTRY REQUIREMENTS CEE; Test; Scholarship Exam; Test & Interview; Report & Exam & Interview
SCHOLARSHIPS & BURSARIES Schol; Burs; Art; Mus; Forces; Teachers; AP; VI Form; Sport; ARA; Drama; Siblings   **SPECIAL NEEDS** abgjlnq   **DYSLEXIA** e   **DIET** abcd
ASSOCIATION HMC   **FOUNDED** 1512   **RELIGIOUS AFFILIATION** C of E

MAP11 E 5
LOCATION Rural
DAY   **RAIL** a   **AIR** b
SPORT abcdefghijklmopqsuwx ABC
OTHER LANGUAGES a
ACTIVITIES bcdeghijkmnopqstw ABD
OTHER SUBJECTS abcdfh
FACILITIES ON SITE bcdeghikl
EXAM BOARDS abc ABDGH
RETAKES   **NVQ COURSES**

A-level ABC e ghi nop uv x GH K OP R c efg j
AS a eg i G ef
GCSE ABC eg i E G K o P v cdefg j l
OTHER l n O R

Bg | Grosvenor House School; Swarcliffe Hall; Birstwith; Harrogate; N.Yorks HG3 2JG
Tel: 01423 771029 *G.J.Raspin*

		Boys	Age	Girls	Age	TOTAL		Boys	Girls
Day	£470-£1380	166	3-13	10	4-11	187	SIXTH		
Weekly	£1985-£2200	4	8-13						
Boarding	£1985-£2200	7	8-13						

ENTRY REQUIREMENTS None
SCHOLARSHIPS & BURSARIES Forces; Clergy; Teachers
SPECIAL NEEDS hlnu   **DYSLEXIA** e   **DIET**
ASSOCIATION IAPS   **FOUNDED** 1905   **RELIGIOUS AFFILIATION** Inter-denom

MAP12 G 5
LOCATION Rural
DAY ✓   **RAIL** b   **AIR** a
SPORT cefjsx AB
OTHER LANGUAGES
ACTIVITIES fghjmrt
OTHER SUBJECTS cf
FACILITIES ON SITE bchijk
EXAM BOARDS
RETAKES   **NVQ COURSES**

A-level   **AS**   **GCSE**   **OTHER** B eg i G cde o j v P R

G | Harrogate Ladies' College; Clarence Drive; Harrogate; N.Yorks. HG1 2QG
Tel: 01423 504543 (Fax: 01423 568893)

		Boys	Age	Girls	Age	TOTAL		Boys	Girls
Day	£1995			136	10-18	342	SIXTH		91
Weekly	£2920			14	10-18				
Boarding	£2995			192	10-18				

ENTRY REQUIREMENTS Report & Test
SCHOLARSHIPS & BURSARIES Schol; Burs; Mus; AP
SPECIAL NEEDS abegijklnqwx AGHI   **DYSLEXIA** f   **DIET** a
ASSOCIATION GSA   **FOUNDED** 1893   **RELIGIOUS AFFILIATION** C of E

MAP12 G 5
LOCATION Urban
DAY ✓   **RAIL** a   **AIR** a
SPORT abchklnopqtwx ABC
OTHER LANGUAGES a
ACTIVITIES acfghijknopqstwx A
OTHER SUBJECTS abcefgh
FACILITIES ON SITE bcdeghik
EXAM BOARDS abcd ABDEH
RETAKES ab   **NVQ COURSES** 3

A-level ABC eg i op uv GH K P R W c efg j l
AS G n u
GCSE ABC de g i E G K op P R v W cdefg j l
OTHER c f j lmno K MNO R

Bg | Howsham Hall; York; YO6 7PJ
Tel: 01653 618374 *S.Knock*

		Boys	Age	Girls	Age	TOTAL		Boys	Girls
Day	£650-£1150	11	5-14	1		67	SIXTH		
Weekly									
Boarding	£1700-£1900	53	5-14	2					

ENTRY REQUIREMENTS None
SCHOLARSHIPS & BURSARIES Burs
SPECIAL NEEDS w E   **DYSLEXIA**   **DIET**
ASSOCIATION ISAI   **FOUNDED** 1958   **RELIGIOUS AFFILIATION** Inter-denom

MAP12 I 5
LOCATION Rural
DAY ✓   **RAIL** b   **AIR** a
SPORT adefqrstux A
OTHER LANGUAGES
ACTIVITIES fghjmqw
OTHER SUBJECTS ch
FACILITIES ON SITE cd
EXAM BOARDS
RETAKES   **NVQ COURSES**

A-level   **AS**   **GCSE**   **OTHER** ce l n s o

B | Malsis School; Cross Hills; N. Yorks BD20 8DT
Tel: 01535 633027 (Fax: 01535 630571) *N.Rowbotham*

		Boys	Age	Girls	Age	TOTAL		Boys	Girls
Day	£1985	23				159	SIXTH		
Weekly									
Boarding	£2650	136	7-14						

ENTRY REQUIREMENTS Interview
SCHOLARSHIPS & BURSARIES Clergy; Teachers
SPECIAL NEEDS eknpq Gl   **DYSLEXIA** ef   **DIET** ac
ASSOCIATION IAPS   **FOUNDED** 1920   **RELIGIOUS AFFILIATION** C of E

MAP11 F 6
LOCATION Rural
DAY   **RAIL** b   **AIR** b
SPORT abcefklmqstx ABC
OTHER LANGUAGES
ACTIVITIES cfghjmoqrst A
OTHER SUBJECTS abcfh
FACILITIES ON SITE bcdhikl
EXAM BOARDS
RETAKES   **NVQ COURSES**

A-level   **AS**   **GCSE**   **OTHER** B eg i l G K cde g j l o OP R uv

YORKSHIRE (NORTH) continued

C — Minster School York,The; Deangate; York YO1 2JA
Tel: 01904 625217 (Fax: 01904 632418) *R.J.Shephard*

		Boys	Age	Girls	Age	TOTAL		Boys	Girls
Day	£460-£1275	87	4-13	50	4-13	137	SIXTH		
Weekly									
Boarding									

ENTRY REQUIREMENTS Test & Interview
SCHOLARSHIPS & BURSARIES Chor
SPECIAL NEEDS bjn   **DYSLEXIA** g   **DIET**
ASSOCIATION IAPS   **FOUNDED** 627   **RELIGIOUS AFFILIATION** C of E

MAP12 H 6
LOCATION Urban
DAY   **RAIL** a   **AIR** b
SPORT abegjmpqx A
OTHER LANGUAGES
ACTIVITIES fghjotw
OTHER SUBJECTS ch
FACILITIES ON SITE
EXAM BOARDS
RETAKES   **NVQ COURSES**

A-level
AS
GCSE e   v
         B G K O R
         cde g j
OTHER

Gb — Mount School,The; Dalton Terrace; York YO2 4DD
Tel: 01904 622275 (Fax: 01904 627518) *Miss B.J.Windle*

		Boys	Age	Girls	Age	TOTAL		Boys	Girls
Day	£790-£1985 X	17	4-11	126	4-18	287	SIXTH		75
Weekly	£3230			20	11-18				
Boarding	£3230			124	11-18				

ENTRY REQUIREMENTS Report & Interview; Report & Exam & Interview
SCHOLARSHIPS & BURSARIES Schol; Burs; Mus; VI Form
SPECIAL NEEDS abehijklnpqruw EGHI   **DYSLEXIA** e   **DIET** abcd
ASSOCIATION GSA   **FOUNDED** 1831   **RELIGIOUS AFFILIATION** Quaker

MAP12 H 6
LOCATION Urban
DAY   **RAIL** a   **AIR** b
SPORT abcegjlmnpqrwx ABC
OTHER LANGUAGES a
ACTIVITIES cfghijklnoqstw
OTHER SUBJECTS bcdefh
FACILITIES ON SITE cegi
EXAM BOARDS abc ADEH
RETAKES a   **NVQ COURSES**

A-level cdefg i   op uv
BC   GH K   P R T
cdef   j
AS c   p
      G
      ef j
GCSE de g i no   v
BC E G   K   P R   W
cdefg j l
OTHER   lmn
                            MNO

Gb — Queen Ethelburga's College; Thorpe Underwood Hall; Thorpe Underwood; York YO5 9SZ
Tel: 01423 331480 (Fax: 01423 331007) *Mrs Gillian Richardson*

		Boys	Age	Girls	Age	TOTAL		Boys	Girls
Day	£499-£2259	24	2-11	108	2-18	260	SIXTH		33
Weekly	£2359-£3499		6-11	37	5-18				
Boarding	£2359-£3499		6-11	91	5-18				

ENTRY REQUIREMENTS CEE; Test & Interview
SCHOLARSHIPS & BURSARIES Schol; Forces; VI Form
SPECIAL NEEDS aejklntw BEGI   **DYSLEXIA** def   **DIET** abcd
ASSOCIATION GSA   **FOUNDED** 1912   **RELIGIOUS AFFILIATION** C of E

MAP12 H 5
LOCATION Rural
DAY   **RAIL** a   **AIR** a
SPORT acdefghjklnopqrx ABC
OTHER LANGUAGES a
ACTIVITIES acdfghijklmnopqrswx AB
OTHER SUBJECTS abcdefgh
FACILITIES ON SITE abcdeghik
EXAM BOARDS abc ABDE
RETAKES ab   **NVQ COURSES**

A-level c efghi n   v
B   GH   P R   U
cdef
AS c   g i   v
   B   GH K   P R U
   ef
GCSE c e g i no   v
BC   GH K   P R   U
cdef hj l
OTHER   h
                  P

G — Queen Margaret's School; Escrick Park; York YO4 6EU
Tel: 01904 728261 (Fax: 01904 728150) *Dr.G.A.H.Chapman*

		Boys	Age	Girls	Age	TOTAL		Boys	Girls
Day	£2158 X			27	11-18	366	SIXTH		102
Weekly	£3406			56	11-18				
Boarding	£3406			283	11-18				

ENTRY REQUIREMENTS CEE; Scholarship Exam; Report & Exam & Interview
SCHOLARSHIPS & BURSARIES Schol; Mus; Clergy; VI Form
SPECIAL NEEDS abghklq   **DYSLEXIA**   **DIET** a
ASSOCIATION GSA   **FOUNDED** 1901   **RELIGIOUS AFFILIATION** C of E

MAP12 H 6
LOCATION Rural
DAY   **RAIL** b   **AIR** b
SPORT abcdfgklmnopqruvwx ABC
OTHER LANGUAGES a
ACTIVITIES bcfghijklnopqstw ABD
OTHER SUBJECTS abcefgh
FACILITIES ON SITE bcdeghijkl
EXAM BOARDS abcd ABDE
RETAKES a   **NVQ COURSES**

A-level cd fghi nop uv x
BC   GH K   P R   W
c efg j l
AS c   p   uv x
   B   G
   ef
GCSE cd ghi no   v
BC   G   K   OP R   WX
bcdefg ij l
OTHER C   lmn
          K   O

G — Queen Mary's School; Baldersby Park; Topcliffe; Thirsk; Yorks YO7 3BZ
Tel: 01845 577425 (Fax: 01845 577368) *Mr & Mrs P.Belward*

		Boys	Age	Girls	Age	TOTAL		Boys	Girls
Day	£645-£1785 X	2	4-6	104	4-16	220	SIXTH		
Weekly	£2510-£2655			64	7-16				
Boarding	£2560-£2865			50	7-16				

ENTRY REQUIREMENTS Exam & Interview
SCHOLARSHIPS & BURSARIES Schol; Mus; Clergy
SPECIAL NEEDS bn B   **DYSLEXIA** e   **DIET** a
ASSOCIATION IAPS   **FOUNDED** 1925   **RELIGIOUS AFFILIATION** C of E

MAP12 G 4
LOCATION Rural
DAY ✓   **RAIL** a   **AIR** ac
SPORT abcdfglmnopqx AB
OTHER LANGUAGES
ACTIVITIES cdfghijklopqstw A
OTHER SUBJECTS bcfh
FACILITIES ON SITE bdhij
EXAM BOARDS abcd BDG
RETAKES   **NVQ COURSES**

A-level
AS
GCSE defg i   lmn   v
BC   G   K   P R
cdefg j
OTHER

YORKSHIRE (NORTH) continued

C — Read School; Drax; Selby; Yorks. YO8 8NL
Tel: 01757 618248 (Fax: 01757 617432) *A.J.Saddler*

		Boys	Age	Girls	Age	TOTAL		Boys	Girls
Day	£865–£1205	114	5-18	38	5-18	213	SIXTH	23	
Weekly	£2115–£2325	3	8-18		8-18				
Boarding	£2260–£2485	56	8-18	2	8-18				

ENTRY REQUIREMENTS Report & Interview
SCHOLARSHIPS & BURSARIES Schol; Burs; VI Form
SPECIAL NEEDS l   **DYSLEXIA**   **DIET**
ASSOCIATION ISAI   **FOUNDED** 1667   **RELIGIOUS AFFILIATION** C of E

MAP 12 I 7
LOCATION Rural
DAY ✓   **RAIL** b   **AIR** a
SPORT abcdefhjkmopstuwx ABC
OTHER LANGUAGES
ACTIVITIES efghijlmnoqrst C
OTHER SUBJECTS abcf
FACILITIES ON SITE cdegjk
EXAM BOARDS c AD
RETAKES ab   **NVQ COURSES**

A-level: e g i   n p   u v
B   G   OP R   U
cdef

AS: g i
ef   OP

GCSE: e ghi l   no   v
B   G   OP R   U
cdef   j

OTHER

C — Red House School; Moor Monkton; York YO5 8JQ
Tel: 01904 738256 (Fax: 01904 738256) *Major A.V.Gordon*

		Boys	Age	Girls	Age	TOTAL		Boys	Girls
Day	£536–£1544	24	4-13	14	4-13	49	SIXTH		
Weekly	£1966–£2184	3	7-13	1	7-13				
Boarding	£2060–£2289	4	7-13	3	7-13				

ENTRY REQUIREMENTS Test
SCHOLARSHIPS & BURSARIES Schol
SPECIAL NEEDS bijlnquw l   **DYSLEXIA**   **DIET**
ASSOCIATION ISAI   **FOUNDED** 1902   **RELIGIOUS AFFILIATION** C of E

MAP 12 H 5
LOCATION Rural
DAY ✓   **RAIL** b   **AIR** a
SPORT aefmpqstuwx AB
OTHER LANGUAGES
ACTIVITIES cfghjmw A
OTHER SUBJECTS ch
FACILITIES ON SITE bdfhjk
EXAM BOARDS
RETAKES   **NVQ COURSES**

A-level

AS

GCSE

OTHER: e g i   lmno   st vwx
B   E G   JK   OP R   UV
cdef   j

C — Ripon Cathedral Choir School; Ripon; N.Yorks.; HG4 2LA
Tel: 01765 602134 *R.H.Moore*

		Boys	Age	Girls	Age	TOTAL		Boys	Girls
Day	£1110–£1615	48	4-13	43	4-13	116	SIXTH		
Weekly	£2045	2	8-13	2	8-13				
Boarding	£2205	21	8-13		8-13				

ENTRY REQUIREMENTS Interview
SCHOLARSHIPS & BURSARIES Schol; Mus; Chor; Forces
SPECIAL NEEDS bn   **DYSLEXIA** e   **DIET** a
ASSOCIATION IAPS   **FOUNDED** 1960   **RELIGIOUS AFFILIATION** C of E

MAP 12 G 5
LOCATION Urban
DAY ✓   **RAIL** b   **AIR** a
SPORT abcefjmqswx AB
OTHER LANGUAGES
ACTIVITIES cfghijoqtw
OTHER SUBJECTS abch
FACILITIES ON SITE hk
EXAM BOARDS
RETAKES   **NVQ COURSES**

A-level

AS

GCSE

OTHER: d e g i l   o   vw
B   E G   K   OP R
cde   j

C — St. Hilda's School; Sneaton Castle; Whitby; N.Yorks. YO21 3QN
Tel: 01947 600051 (Fax: 01947 603490) *Mrs Mary E.Blain*

		Boys	Age	Girls	Age	TOTAL		Boys	Girls
Day	£925–£1525	46	3-18	105	3-18	237	SIXTH	10	24
Weekly	£2310–£2770		8-18	4	8-18				
Boarding	£2360–£2825	21	8-18	61	8-18				

ENTRY REQUIREMENTS Scholarship Exam; Exam & Interview
SCHOLARSHIPS & BURSARIES Schol; Burs; Art; Mus; Chor; Forces; Clergy; VI Form; Drama; Siblings
SPECIAL NEEDS abklnw BE   **DYSLEXIA** ef   **DIET** ad
ASSOCIATION ISAI   **FOUNDED** 1915   **RELIGIOUS AFFILIATION** C of E

MAP 12 I 3
LOCATION Rural
DAY ✓   **RAIL** b   **AIR** b
SPORT abcdefhjklmopqrsuvwx ABC
OTHER LANGUAGES a
ACTIVITIES abcdefghijklmnopqstwx AB
OTHER SUBJECTS abcdefgh
FACILITIES ON SITE bcdefgk
EXAM BOARDS abcd ADEGH
RETAKES a   **NVQ COURSES**

A-level: efg   i   uv x
BC   GH K   P R
b   ef   j

AS: g
B   G K   P
cde

GCSE: efg i l   no q   v
BC E G   K   OP R
bcdefg   j

OTHER: h   mno
K N

C — St. Martin's School; Kirkdale Manor; Nawton; York YO6 5UA
Tel: 01439 771215 (Fax: 01439 771153) *Stephen Mullen*

		Boys	Age	Girls	Age	TOTAL		Boys	Girls
Day	£709–£1487	39	3-13	35	3-13	118	SIXTH		
Weekly	£2091–£2145	9	7-13	7	7-13				
Boarding	£2091–£2145	23	7-13	5	7-13				

ENTRY REQUIREMENTS Interview
SCHOLARSHIPS & BURSARIES Schol; Forces
SPECIAL NEEDS abclnqw l   **DYSLEXIA** e   **DIET** acd
ASSOCIATION IAPS   **FOUNDED** 1946   **RELIGIOUS AFFILIATION** RC/C of E

MAP 12 H 5
LOCATION Rural
DAY   **RAIL** b   **AIR** a
SPORT acefjmpqsux AB
OTHER LANGUAGES
ACTIVITIES cfghijpqw
OTHER SUBJECTS ch
FACILITIES ON SITE bdhi
EXAM BOARDS
RETAKES   **NVQ COURSES**

A-level

AS

GCSE

OTHER: e g i   lmo   v
B   G   K   P R
cdefg   j

YORKSHIRE (NORTH) continued

St. Olave's School; The Junior School of St. Peter's; York YO3 6AB
Tel: 01904 623269 (Fax: 01904 670407) *T.Mulryne*

		Boys	Age	Girls	Age	TOTAL		Boys	Girls
Day	£1371-£1750	147	8-13	76	8-13	277	SIXTH		
Weekly									
Boarding	£2546-£2905	31	8-13	23	8-13				

ENTRY REQUIREMENTS Report & Test
SCHOLARSHIPS & BURSARIES Burs; Forces; Teachers; AP
SPECIAL NEEDS bgklqstx AGHIK
DYSLEXIA **DIET** abcd
ASSOCIATION IAPS **FOUNDED** 1876 **RELIGIOUS AFFILIATION** C of E

MAP12 H 6
LOCATION Urban
DAY **RAIL** a **AIR** c
SPORT abcefgklmpqsuwx AB
OTHER LANGUAGES
ACTIVITIES cfghijoqw A
OTHER SUBJECTS bcfh
FACILITIES ON SITE cdhik
EXAM BOARDS
RETAKES **NVQ COURSES**

A-level c e g i l o v
B G K OP R
cdef j

AS
GCSE
OTHER

St. Peter's School; York YO3 6AB
Tel: 01904 623213 (Fax: 01904 670407) *A.F.Trotman*

		Boys	Age	Girls	Age	TOTAL		Boys	Girls
Day	£1963-£2061	209	13-18	106	13-18	480	SIXTH	123	72
Weekly									
Boarding	£3372-£3462	102	13-18	63	13-18				

ENTRY REQUIREMENTS Exam; Scholarship Exam
SCHOLARSHIPS & BURSARIES Schol; Burs; Mus; Forces; Clergy; AP; VI Form
SPECIAL NEEDS blnqstx AGHIK
DYSLEXIA **DIET** abcd
ASSOCIATION HMC **FOUNDED** 627 **RELIGIOUS AFFILIATION** C of E

MAP12 H 6
LOCATION Urban
DAY **RAIL** a **AIR** b
SPORT abcefghjkmpqrsuwx AB
OTHER LANGUAGES
ACTIVITIES efghijkopqst AC
OTHER SUBJECTS bcdfh
FACILITIES ON SITE cdhik
EXAM BOARDS abc ABDEHL
RETAKES **NVQ COURSES**

A-level cde ghi op uv x
B GH K P R U
c efg j l

AS G
GCSE cde ghi o v
B G K P R U
cdefg j l
OTHER l

Lisvane - Scarborough College Junior School; Sandybed Lane; Scarborough; N. Yorks. YO12 5LJ Tel: 01723 361595 (Fax: 01723 377265) *R.N.Baird*

		Boys	Age	Girls	Age	TOTAL		Boys	Girls
Day	£849-£1214	81	3-11	77	3-11	162	SIXTH		
Weekly									
Boarding	£2300	1	7-11	3	7-11				

ENTRY REQUIREMENTS Test & Interview
SCHOLARSHIPS & BURSARIES Burs
SPECIAL NEEDS ejkpqw GI
DYSLEXIA **DIET** abcd
ASSOCIATION IAPS **FOUNDED** 1922 **RELIGIOUS AFFILIATION** Non-denom

MAP12 J 4
LOCATION Urban
DAY **RAIL** c **AIR** b
SPORT abcefjlmpqsx AB
OTHER LANGUAGES
ACTIVITIES cfghjlopr A
OTHER SUBJECTS bch
FACILITIES ON SITE chi
EXAM BOARDS
RETAKES **NVQ COURSES**

A-level
AS
GCSE
OTHER e g i lmno v
B G K OP R
cde

Scarborough College; Filey Road; Scarborough; North Yorkshire YO11 3BA
Tel: 01723 360620 (Fax: 01723 377265) *T.Kirkup*

		Boys	Age	Girls	Age	TOTAL		Boys	Girls
Day	£1702	189	11-18	147	11-18	381	SIXTH	50	33
Weekly	£3140		11-18		11-18				
Boarding	£3140	23	11-18	22	11-18				

ENTRY REQUIREMENTS CEE; Scholarship Exam; Assessment & Interview
SCHOLARSHIPS & BURSARIES Schol; Burs; Art; Mus; Forces; AP; VI Form; Siblings
SPECIAL NEEDS beijklnpqtw E
DYSLEXIA d **DIET** abcd
ASSOCIATION SHMIS **FOUNDED** 1898 **RELIGIOUS AFFILIATION** Inter-denom

MAP12 J 4
LOCATION Urban
DAY ✓ **RAIL** a **AIR** b
SPORT abcefhjklmpqstuwx AB
OTHER LANGUAGES
ACTIVITIES efghijklopqrs ABC
OTHER SUBJECTS abc
FACILITIES ON SITE cdegh
EXAM BOARDS cd ADEHL
RETAKES ab **NVQ COURSES**

A-level c e ghi o uv
ABC GH K OPQR
cdef j l
AS
GCSE e ghi o v
ABC G K NOP R
cdef j l
OTHER

Terrington Hall; York YO6 4PR
Tel: 01653 648227 (Fax: 01653 648458) *J.Desmond Gray*

		Boys	Age	Girls	Age	TOTAL		Boys	Girls
Day	£700-£1580	31	3-13	24	3-13	113	SIXTH		
Weekly	£2320	16	7-13	5	7-13				
Boarding	£2320	21	7-13	16	7-13				

ENTRY REQUIREMENTS Interview; Report
SCHOLARSHIPS & BURSARIES Schol; Burs; Forces; Clergy
SPECIAL NEEDS abegjklnqtuw BEGHIK
DYSLEXIA e **DIET** abc
ASSOCIATION IAPS **FOUNDED** 1921 **RELIGIOUS AFFILIATION** C of E

MAP12 H 5
LOCATION Rural
DAY ✓ **RAIL** b **AIR** a
SPORT abdefhjlmpqstuwx ABC
OTHER LANGUAGES a
ACTIVITIES cfghijmnopqrtuw A
OTHER SUBJECTS abcfh
FACILITIES ON SITE bcehi
EXAM BOARDS B
RETAKES **NVQ COURSES**

A-level f
AS
GCSE
OTHER de g i lmno q v
B GIK OP R
cde j l

302

YORKSHIRE (NORTH) continued

C — Woodleigh School; Langton; Malton; Yorks. YO17 9QN
Tel: 01653 658215 (Fax: 01653 658423) *D.M.England*

		Boys	Age	Girls	Age	TOTAL		Boys	Girls
Day	£240-£1250	16	3-13	10	3-13	53	SIXTH		
Weekly	£2110	9	7-13	1	7-13				
Boarding	£2110	15	7-13	2	7-13				

ENTRY REQUIREMENTS Interview
SCHOLARSHIPS & BURSARIES Schol; Forces
SPECIAL NEEDS bnw
ASSOCIATION IAPS **FOUNDED** 1929 **RELIGIOUS AFFILIATION** C of E
DYSLEXIA e **DIET**

MAP12 I 5
LOCATION Rural
DAY ✓ **RAIL** a **AIR** b
SPORT abcdefjlmopqsuwx ABC
OTHER LANGUAGES a
ACTIVITIES abcfghijoqstw A
OTHER SUBJECTS bcfh
FACILITIES ON SITE bcehj
EXAM BOARDS
RETAKES **NVQ COURSES**

A-level	AS	GCSE	OTHER
			e g i l m o q v
			AB E G K OP
			cdef j

Gb — York College for Girls; 62 Petergate; York YO1 2HZ
Tel: 01904 646421 (Fax: 01904 652191) *Mrs J.L.Clare*

		Boys	Age	Girls	Age	TOTAL		Boys	Girls
Day	£430-£1750			23	3-8	199	SIXTH		27
Weekly				176	3-18				
Boarding									

ENTRY REQUIREMENTS Exam; Test & Interview
SCHOLARSHIPS & BURSARIES Schol; Burs; VI Form
SPECIAL NEEDS bejklnqstuv Gl
ASSOCIATION GSA **FOUNDED** 1908 **RELIGIOUS AFFILIATION** C of E
DYSLEXIA g **DIET** abcd

MAP12 H 6
LOCATION Inner City
DAY **RAIL** a **AIR** b
SPORT achlmpqwx B
OTHER LANGUAGES
ACTIVITIES cfghijor A
OTHER SUBJECTS bch
FACILITIES ON SITE bdg
EXAM BOARDS bc BDH
RETAKES a **NVQ COURSES**

A-level	AS	GCSE	OTHER
d e g i l n uv	d e g i l n v	d e g i l n o v	c d e g i l m n o q v
BC GH K P R	BC G K R	BC G I K OP R	BC G K OP R
cdef j l		cdef l	cdef j

G — Ashdell Preparatory School; 266 Fulwood Road; Sheffield; S.Yorks. S10 3BL
Tel: 0114 266 3835 *Mrs J.Upton*

		Boys	Age	Girls	Age	TOTAL		Boys	Girls
Day	£1220-£1340			135	4-11	135	SIXTH		
Weekly									
Boarding									

ENTRY REQUIREMENTS Test & Interview
SCHOLARSHIPS & BURSARIES
SPECIAL NEEDS n
ASSOCIATION IAPS **FOUNDED** 1948 **RELIGIOUS AFFILIATION** C of E
DYSLEXIA e **DIET** acd

MAP 9 C 2
LOCATION Urban
DAY **RAIL** a **AIR** b
SPORT lmpqx B
OTHER LANGUAGES
ACTIVITIES cgjot
OTHER SUBJECTS cfh
FACILITIES ON SITE
EXAM BOARDS
RETAKES **NVQ COURSES**

A-level	AS	GCSE	OTHER
			e l n v
			B E G K R
			cde j

B — Birkdale School; Oakholme Road; Sheffield S10 3DH
Tel: 0114 266 8409 (Fax: 0114 267 1947) *The Revd.M.D.A.Hepworth*

		Boys	Age	Girls	Age	TOTAL		Boys	Girls
Day	£980-£1475	749	4-18	15	16-18	764	SIXTH	105	15
Weekly									
Boarding									

ENTRY REQUIREMENTS CEE; Test & Interview
SCHOLARSHIPS & BURSARIES Schol; Mus; Clergy; Teachers; VI Form
SPECIAL NEEDS nw B
ASSOCIATION SHMIS **FOUNDED** 1904 **RELIGIOUS AFFILIATION** Christian
DYSLEXIA ce **DIET** abcd

MAP 9 C 2
LOCATION Urban
DAY ✓ **RAIL** a **AIR** b
SPORT abcdefghjklmpqrstwx ABC
OTHER LANGUAGES
ACTIVITIES fghijknoqsu AB
OTHER SUBJECTS abch
FACILITIES ON SITE cgh
EXAM BOARDS bc DGHL
RETAKES a **NVQ COURSES**

A-level	AS	GCSE	OTHER
cde g i l op uv x	K	e ghi o v	l
B GH K P R U	ef j	B G K OP R	ef
cdefg j		cdefg j	

G — Brantwood Independent School for Girls; 1 Kenwood Bank; Sheffield S7 1NU
Tel: 0114 258 1747 (Fax: 0114 258 1847) *Mrs E.M.Swynnerton*

		Boys	Age	Girls	Age	TOTAL		Boys	Girls
Day	£910-£1125			181	4-16	181	SIXTH		
Weekly									
Boarding									

ENTRY REQUIREMENTS Test & Interview; Exam & Interview
SCHOLARSHIPS & BURSARIES
SPECIAL NEEDS n
ASSOCIATION ISAI **FOUNDED** **RELIGIOUS AFFILIATION** Non-denom
DYSLEXIA e **DIET** acd

MAP 9 C 2
LOCATION Urban
DAY **RAIL** a **AIR** b
SPORT acfhlmpqvwx B
OTHER LANGUAGES
ACTIVITIES cghjnot A
OTHER SUBJECTS bdfh
FACILITIES ON SITE bch
EXAM BOARDS abcd
RETAKES **NVQ COURSES**

A-level	AS	GCSE	OTHER
		d g i v	l m o
		B E G P R	C K O W
		cdef	

YORKSHIRE (SOUTH)

303

YORKSHIRE (SOUTH) continued

C — Hill House Prep School; Rutland Street; Doncaster DN1 2JD
Tel: 01302 323563 (Fax: 01302 761098) *Andrew Cruickshank*

		Boys	Age	Girls	Age	TOTAL	SIXTH	Boys	Girls
Day	£923-£1389	167	3-13	117	3-13	284			
Weekly									
Boarding									

- MAP 12 H 7
- LOCATION Urban
- DAY RAIL a AIR b
- SPORT acefhjklmpqswx ABC
- OTHER LANGUAGES
- ACTIVITIES dfghijoqstx A
- OTHER SUBJECTS cf
- FACILITIES ON SITE
- EXAM BOARDS
- RETAKES   NVQ COURSES

ENTRY REQUIREMENTS Test & Interview
SCHOLARSHIPS & BURSARIES
SPECIAL NEEDS   DYSLEXIA   DIET a
ASSOCIATION IAPS   FOUNDED 1912   RELIGIOUS AFFILIATION Inter-denom

- A-level: cde g i l no s v / B G K OP R / cdef j l
- AS:
- GCSE:
- OTHER:

C — Rudston Preparatory School; 59/63 Broom Road; Rotherham S60 2SW
Tel: 01709 837774 (Fax: 01709 837975) *Mrs A.W.Cartner*

		Boys	Age	Girls	Age	TOTAL	SIXTH	Boys	Girls
Day	£720	91	4-11	82	4-11	173			
Weekly									
Boarding									

- MAP 9 C 2
- LOCATION Urban
- DAY RAIL b AIR b
- SPORT aejmpqx A
- OTHER LANGUAGES
- ACTIVITIES cgi
- OTHER SUBJECTS acdh
- FACILITIES ON SITE
- EXAM BOARDS
- RETAKES   NVQ COURSES

ENTRY REQUIREMENTS Test & Interview
SCHOLARSHIPS & BURSARIES Burs
SPECIAL NEEDS   DYSLEXIA   DIET ad
ASSOCIATION IAPS   FOUNDED 1948   RELIGIOUS AFFILIATION

- A-level:
- AS:
- GCSE:
- OTHER: e lmno v / B E G K O R / cde

G — Sheffield High School GPDST; 10 Rutland Park; Sheffield S10 2PE
Tel: 0114 266 0324 (Fax: 0114 267 8520) *Mrs M.A.Houston*

		Boys	Age	Girls	Age	TOTAL	SIXTH	Boys	Girls
Day	£976-£1328			780	4-18	780			135
Weekly									
Boarding									

- MAP 9 C 2
- LOCATION Urban
- DAY RAIL a AIR b
- SPORT acfghjlmpqvx ABC
- OTHER LANGUAGES
- ACTIVITIES cfghijknot ABD
- OTHER SUBJECTS abcdfh
- FACILITIES ON SITE abcg
- EXAM BOARDS abcde DEG
- RETAKES   NVQ COURSES

ENTRY REQUIREMENTS Exam
SCHOLARSHIPS & BURSARIES Schol; Burs; AP
SPECIAL NEEDS bjlnq   DYSLEXIA   DIET abcd
ASSOCIATION GSA   FOUNDED 1878   RELIGIOUS AFFILIATION Non-denom

- A-level: cde g i p uvwx / B GH K OP R U / cdefg jkl
- AS: e u w / G K P / def
- GCSE: cde ghi   vw / B E G K PR X / cdefg jkl
- OTHER: l n

B — Westbourne Prep. School; 50-54 Westbourne Road; Sheffield S10 2QQ
Tel: 0114 266 0374 (Fax: 0114 267 0862) *C.R.Wilmshurst*

			Boys	Age	Girls	Age	TOTAL	SIXTH	Boys	Girls
Day	£895-£1405	X	177	4-13			177			
Weekly										
Boarding										

- MAP 9 C 2
- LOCATION Urban
- DAY RAIL a AIR b
- SPORT abcefjmswx ABC
- OTHER LANGUAGES
- ACTIVITIES fghijoqrst
- OTHER SUBJECTS abcfh
- FACILITIES ON SITE hk
- EXAM BOARDS
- RETAKES   NVQ COURSES

ENTRY REQUIREMENTS Interview
SCHOLARSHIPS & BURSARIES Burs
SPECIAL NEEDS abghjlntuvw ABDGI   DYSLEXIA de   DIET acd
ASSOCIATION IAPS   FOUNDED 1885   RELIGIOUS AFFILIATION Inter-denom

- A-level:
- AS:
- GCSE:
- OTHER: cde g i l no v / B G K NOP R / cdefg j

C — Ackworth School; Ackworth; Pontefract; W.Yorks. WF7 7LT
Tel: 01977 611401 (Fax: 01977 616225) *M.Dickinson*

			Boys	Age	Girls	Age	TOTAL	SIXTH	Boys	Girls
Day	£951-£1772	X	138	7-18	195	7-18	470		50	41
Weekly	£3111			11-18		11-18				
Boarding	£3111		71	11-18	66	11-18				

- MAP 12 H 7
- LOCATION Rural
- DAY RAIL b AIR a
- SPORT abcdefjlmopqtwx ABC
- OTHER LANGUAGES a
- ACTIVITIES bcfghijklmnoqstvw ADEFGHI
- OTHER SUBJECTS abcdfh
- FACILITIES ON SITE cdeghik
- EXAM BOARDS bcd BD
- RETAKES ab   NVQ COURSES

ENTRY REQUIREMENTS Test & Interview
SCHOLARSHIPS & BURSARIES Schol; Art; Mus; AP
SPECIAL NEEDS bgklnqtw El   DYSLEXIA e   DIET abd
ASSOCIATION HMC   FOUNDED 1779   RELIGIOUS AFFILIATION Quaker

- A-level: e ghi op uv / BC GH K P W / bcdef
- AS: G
- GCSE: o de g i o uvw / BC G K PRT W / bcdef hj l
- OTHER: lm n q u x / E K NO R

W YORKS

YORKSHIRE (WEST) continued

Bg — Batley Grammar School; Carlinghow Hill; Batley WF17 0AD
Tel: 01924 474980 (Fax: 01924 420513) *W.M.Duggan*

	Fees	Boys	Age	Girls	Age	TOTAL		Boys	Girls
Day	£1209	566	11-18	16	16-18	582	SIXTH	147	16
Weekly									
Boarding									

ENTRY REQUIREMENTS Exam
SCHOLARSHIPS & BURSARIES AP
SPECIAL NEEDS   **DYSLEXIA**   **DIET** ad
ASSOCIATION HMC   **FOUNDED** 1612   **RELIGIOUS AFFILIATION** C of E

MAP12 G 7
LOCATION Urban
DAY ✓   **RAIL** b   **AIR** a
SPORT abcdefjtuw AB
OTHER LANGUAGES
ACTIVITIES efghijknopqs A
OTHER SUBJECTS abcd
FACILITIES ON SITE cgh
EXAM BOARDS abcde DEH
RETAKES a   **NVQ COURSES**

A-level: cde g i l p uv x / B GH K P R / cdef j
AS: e
GCSE: cde g i l o vw / B G K P R / cdef j
OTHER:

Gb — Bradford Girls' Grammar School; Squire Lane; Bradford; W.Yorks. BD9 6RB;
Tel: 01274 545395 (Fax: 01274 482595) *Mrs L.J.Warrington*

	Fees	Boys	Age	Girls	Age	TOTAL		Boys	Girls
Day	£800-£1332	14	4-8	897	3-18	911	SIXTH		156
Weekly									
Boarding									

ENTRY REQUIREMENTS Exam & Interview
SCHOLARSHIPS & BURSARIES Burs; AP
SPECIAL NEEDS jklw   **DYSLEXIA**   **DIET**
ASSOCIATION GSA   **FOUNDED** 1875   **RELIGIOUS AFFILIATION** C of E

MAP11 F 6
LOCATION Urban
DAY   **RAIL** a   **AIR** b
SPORT acmopqtwx ABC
OTHER LANGUAGES
ACTIVITIES cghijknox BD
OTHER SUBJECTS bcegh
FACILITIES ON SITE cghi
EXAM BOARDS abcd ABDEHL
RETAKES   **NVQ COURSES**

A-level: cde ghi op uv x / BC GH K OPQ U / cdefg jkl
AS: g i l n u / BC G P / ef
GCSE: e g i l o v / BC G K P R / cdefg jkl
OTHER: hi

C — Bradford Grammar School; Bradford BD9 4JP
Tel: 01274 545461 (Fax: 01274 548129) *D.A.G.Smith*

	Fees	Boys	Age	Girls	Age	TOTAL		Boys	Girls
Day	£1078-£1307	1078	8-18	29	16-18	1107	SIXTH	253	29
Weekly									
Boarding									

ENTRY REQUIREMENTS Exam
SCHOLARSHIPS & BURSARIES AP
SPECIAL NEEDS abjklqsw AGI   **DYSLEXIA**   **DIET** ad
ASSOCIATION HMC   **FOUNDED** 1662   **RELIGIOUS AFFILIATION** Inter-denom

MAP11 F 6
LOCATION Urban
DAY   **RAIL** a   **AIR** a
SPORT abcefkmprstuwx AB
OTHER LANGUAGES
ACTIVITIES efghijkmoqtv A
OTHER SUBJECTS bcfh
FACILITIES ON SITE bchik
EXAM BOARDS abcd ABDEGH
RETAKES b   **NVQ COURSES**

A-level: e ghi opq uv x / B GH K M P R / c efg jk
AS: e GH K t w U / def
GCSE: d g i l no v / B G K OP / cdefg jkl
OTHER: G i

C — Bronte House School; (Woodhouse Grove Preparatory School); Apperley Bridge; Bradford; West Yorkshire BD10 0PQ
Tel: 0113 250 2811 (Fax: 0113 250 0666) *F.F.Watson*

	Fees	Boys	Age	Girls	Age	TOTAL		Boys	Girls
Day	£995-£1510 ✗	130	3-11	65	3-11	222	SIXTH		
Weekly	£2550	5	7-11		7-11				
Boarding	£2550	11	7-11	11	7-11				

ENTRY REQUIREMENTS Report & Test
SCHOLARSHIPS & BURSARIES Schol; Art; Mus; Forces
SPECIAL NEEDS bhjnuw EJ   **DYSLEXIA** ce   **DIET** acd
ASSOCIATION IAPS   **FOUNDED** 1934   **RELIGIOUS AFFILIATION** Methodist

MAP12 G 6
LOCATION Rural
DAY ✓   **RAIL** b   **AIR** a
SPORT abefjlpqsx AB
OTHER LANGUAGES
ACTIVITIES cfghjloqt A
OTHER SUBJECTS abcdh
FACILITIES ON SITE bdik
EXAM BOARDS
RETAKES   **NVQ COURSES**

A-level:
AS:
GCSE:
OTHER: d f l o t v / B E G K O R / cdef l

C — Cliff School; St. John's Lodge; 2 Leeds Road; Wakefield; West Yorks WF1 3JT
Tel: 01924 373 597 *E.J.C.Wallace*

	Fees	Boys	Age	Girls	Age	TOTAL		Boys	Girls
Day	£840	43	3-9	136	3-11	179	SIXTH		
Weekly									
Boarding									

ENTRY REQUIREMENTS Assessment; Assessment & Interview
SCHOLARSHIPS & BURSARIES
SPECIAL NEEDS n   **DYSLEXIA**   **DIET** a
ASSOCIATION ISAI   **FOUNDED** 1939   **RELIGIOUS AFFILIATION** Inter-denom

MAP12 G 7
LOCATION Urban
DAY   **RAIL** a   **AIR** a
SPORT acejlmopqx
OTHER LANGUAGES
ACTIVITIES cghjo
OTHER SUBJECTS bch
FACILITIES ON SITE a
EXAM BOARDS
RETAKES   **NVQ COURSES**

A-level:
AS:
GCSE:
OTHER: e g m o v / B E G K O R / cde

305

YORKSHIRE (WEST) continued

Froebelian School, The; Clarence Road; Horsforth; Leeds LS18 4LB
Tel: 0113 258 3047 *J.Tranmer*

MAP 12 G 6
LOCATION Urban
DAY RAIL a AIR a

		Boys	Age	Girls	Age	TOTAL		Boys	Girls
Day	£515-£785	89	3-11	95	3-11	184	SIXTH		
Weekly									
Boarding									

ENTRY REQUIREMENTS Test; Interview
SCHOLARSHIPS & BURSARIES
SPECIAL NEEDS abklnw DYSLEXIA DIET acd
ASSOCIATION IAPS FOUNDED 1913 RELIGIOUS AFFILIATION Non-denom

SPORT aefjlopqx C
OTHER LANGUAGES
ACTIVITIES cfghjnoq
OTHER SUBJECTS abcdh
FACILITIES ON SITE k
EXAM BOARDS
RETAKES NVQ COURSES

A-level: e lmn uv
AS:
GCSE:
OTHER: B E G K O R
      de

Fulneck School; Pudsey; W. Yorks. LS28 8DS
Tel: 0113 257 0235 (Fax: 0113 255 7316) *Mrs Bernice A.Heppell*

MAP 12 G 6
LOCATION Urban
DAY RAIL a AIR a

		Boys	Age	Girls	Age	TOTAL		Boys	Girls
Day	£580-£1540	264	3-18	248	3-18	563	SIXTH	41	48
Weekly	£2270-£2570	2	8-18	4	8-18				
Boarding	£2440-£2885	23	8-18	22	8-18				

ENTRY REQUIREMENTS Report & Exam & Interview
SCHOLARSHIPS & BURSARIES Schol; Burs; Forces; Clergy; Teachers; Siblings
SPECIAL NEEDS bijklnqstw AEGI DYSLEXIA e DIET abcd
ASSOCIATION GSA FOUNDED 1753 RELIGIOUS AFFILIATION Moravian

SPORT abcdefhjklmopqstwx ABC
OTHER LANGUAGES a
ACTIVITIES fghijklogstw AB
OTHER SUBJECTS abcdh
FACILITIES ON SITE bcdgk
EXAM BOARDS abc ABDEH
RETAKES NVQ COURSES

A-level: e ghi op uv   BC G K P R   cdef
AS: h G
GCSE: u U
      e ghi l nop v   BC G K P R   cdef l
OTHER: s G O R U W

Gateways School; Harewood; Leeds LS17 9LE
Tel: 0113 288 6345 (Fax: 0113 288 6148) *Mrs J.E.Stephen*

MAP 12 G 6
LOCATION Rural
DAY ✓ RAIL b AIR a

		Boys	Age	Girls	Age	TOTAL		Boys	Girls
Day	£760-£1180			276	3-18	276	SIXTH		35
Weekly									
Boarding									

ENTRY REQUIREMENTS Report & Exam & Interview
SCHOLARSHIPS & BURSARIES Schol; VI Form
SPECIAL NEEDS abejklnpqstwx BGHI DYSLEXIA g DIET acd
ASSOCIATION GSA FOUNDED 1941 RELIGIOUS AFFILIATION Inter-denom

SPORT acfhjlmpqx ABC
OTHER LANGUAGES
ACTIVITIES cfghijknoqst AB
OTHER SUBJECTS abcdefgh
FACILITIES ON SITE cg
EXAM BOARDS abc ABDEG
RETAKES ab NVQ COURSES 123

A-level: cde ghi uv BC G K P R c ef j l
AS: cd ghi BC G P R c ef j l
GCSE: cde l v BC G K R X cdef j l
OTHER: mno O X

Hipperholme Grammar School; Bramley Lane; Hipperholme; Halifax HX3 8JE
Tel: 01422 202256 (Fax: 01422 204592) *C.C.Robinson*

MAP 11 F 7
LOCATION Urban
DAY RAIL a AIR a

		Boys	Age	Girls	Age	TOTAL		Boys	Girls
Day	£1168	175	11-18	178	11-18	353	SIXTH	32	28
Weekly									
Boarding									

ENTRY REQUIREMENTS Exam
SCHOLARSHIPS & BURSARIES Schol; Burs; AP; VI Form
SPECIAL NEEDS In DYSLEXIA f DIET a
ASSOCIATION SHMIS FOUNDED 1648 RELIGIOUS AFFILIATION Non-denom

SPORT abcefhklmpqs ABC
OTHER LANGUAGES
ACTIVITIES fghijoqs A
OTHER SUBJECTS abcd
FACILITIES ON SITE ch
EXAM BOARDS abcde ABDEG
RETAKES ab NVQ COURSES

A-level: c egi op uv B G K P R c ef j
AS: e h G def
GCSE: c egi l nop v B G K P R cdef j
OTHER: l O

Lady Lane Park Preparatory School; Lady Lane; Bingley; West Yorkshire BD16 4AP
Tel: 01274 551168 (Fax: 01274 569732) *Mrs Kathleen L.Thornton*

MAP 11 F 6
LOCATION Rural
DAY RAIL c AIR a

		Boys	Age	Girls	Age	TOTAL		Boys	Girls
Day	£880-£930	122	2-11	85	2-11	207	SIXTH		
Weekly									
Boarding									

ENTRY REQUIREMENTS Assessment & Interview
SCHOLARSHIPS & BURSARIES
SPECIAL NEEDS DYSLEXIA DIET d
ASSOCIATION ISAI FOUNDED 1988 RELIGIOUS AFFILIATION Non-denom

SPORT aefhjlmpqx
OTHER LANGUAGES
ACTIVITIES cfghjlno A
OTHER SUBJECTS bc
FACILITIES ON SITE bc
EXAM BOARDS
RETAKES NVQ COURSES

YORKSHIRE (WEST) continued

Gb — Leeds Girls' High School; Headingley Lane; Leeds LS6 1BN;
Tel: 0113 274 4000 (Fax: 0113 275 2217) *Miss P.A.Randall*

| Day / Weekly / Boarding | £723–£1412 ✗ | Boys 26 | Age 3–7 | Girls 933 | Age 3–18 | TOTAL 959 | SIXTH | Boys | Girls 161 |

ENTRY REQUIREMENTS Report & Exam & Interview
SCHOLARSHIPS & BURSARIES Schol; Burs; Mus; AP
SPECIAL NEEDS hjlq A **DYSLEXIA** **DIET** a
ASSOCIATION GSA **FOUNDED** 1876 **RELIGIOUS AFFILIATION** Non-denom

MAP12 G 6
LOCATION Urban
DAY ✓ **RAIL** a **AIR** a
SPORT abcefhjlmpqwx BC
OTHER LANGUAGES
ACTIVITIES cfghijknoq ABD
OTHER SUBJECTS abcdh
FACILITIES ON SITE ghik
EXAM BOARDS ac ABDGHL
RETAKES **NVQ COURSES**

A-level: d ghi n p uv x / BC GH K P R / c efg j
AS: G
I
GCSE: d ghi l n v / BC E G K P R / cdefg j
OTHER: l o x / C G K M O QR U / h

B — Leeds Grammar School; Moorland Road; Leeds LS6 1AN
Tel: 0113 243 3417 (Fax: 0113 243 9906) *B.W.Collins*

| Day / Weekly / Boarding | £1206–£1456 | Boys 1178 | Age 7–18 | Girls | Age | TOTAL 1178 | SIXTH | Boys 238 | Girls |

ENTRY REQUIREMENTS Exam
SCHOLARSHIPS & BURSARIES AP
SPECIAL NEEDS abehilnx **DYSLEXIA** e **DIET** acd
ASSOCIATION HMC **FOUNDED** 1552 **RELIGIOUS AFFILIATION** C of E

MAP12 G 6
LOCATION Urban
DAY **RAIL** a **AIR** b
SPORT abcefhjklmrsuwx ABC
OTHER LANGUAGES f
ACTIVITIES befghijknopqstux AB
OTHER SUBJECTS bc
FACILITIES ON SITE abcdghik
EXAM BOARDS abcd BDEH
RETAKES **NVQ COURSES**

A-level: cde ghi l op uv x / B GH K P R / c efg
AS: c e g
o
R
GCSE: de g i l o vw / B G K P R / cdefg j
OTHER: o

G — Moorfield School; Wharfedale Lodge; 11 Ben Rhydding Road; Ilkley; West Yorks.
LS29 8RL Tel: 01943 607285 (Fax: 01943 603186) *Mrs.P.Brown*

| Day / Weekly / Boarding | £435–£950 | Boys | Age | Girls 153 | Age 2–11 | TOTAL 153 | SIXTH | Boys | Girls |

ENTRY REQUIREMENTS Assessment & Interview
SCHOLARSHIPS & BURSARIES
SPECIAL NEEDS bkln **DYSLEXIA** e **DIET** a
ASSOCIATION ISAI **FOUNDED** 1930 **RELIGIOUS AFFILIATION** Non-denom

MAP11 F 6
LOCATION Rural
DAY **RAIL** b **AIR** a
SPORT clpqx B
OTHER LANGUAGES
ACTIVITIES ghijo
OTHER SUBJECTS abch
FACILITIES ON SITE h
EXAM BOARDS
RETAKES **NVQ COURSES**

A-level:
AS:
GCSE:
OTHER: e lmn v / B E G K O R / cde

C — Moorlands School; Foxhill Drive; Weetwood Lane; Leeds LS16 5PF
Tel: 0113 278 5286 *N.Woolnough*

| Day / Weekly / Boarding | £540–£1210 | Boys 116 | Age 3–13 | Girls 61 | Age 3–13 | TOTAL 177 | SIXTH | Boys | Girls |

ENTRY REQUIREMENTS Exam & Interview
SCHOLARSHIPS & BURSARIES Schol; Art; Mus; Sport
SPECIAL NEEDS bfhln B **DYSLEXIA** ce **DIET** acd
ASSOCIATION IAPS **FOUNDED** 1898 **RELIGIOUS AFFILIATION** Non-denom

MAP12 G 6
LOCATION Urban
DAY **RAIL** b **AIR** b
SPORT abcefjlmopqsx ABC
OTHER LANGUAGES a
ACTIVITIES cfghijoqt
OTHER SUBJECTS cfh
FACILITIES ON SITE ch
EXAM BOARDS
RETAKES **NVQ COURSES**

A-level:
AS:
GCSE:
OTHER: e g i l m o s v / B G K OP R / cde j l

C — North Leeds and St. Edmund's Hall; North Park House; North Park Avenue;
Roundhay; Leeds LS8 1HS Tel: 0113 268 1830 *J.G.W.Lynch*

| Day / Weekly / Boarding | £880–£965 | Boys 99 | Age 3–11 | Girls 78 | Age 3–11 | TOTAL 177 | SIXTH | Boys | Girls |

ENTRY REQUIREMENTS Interview; Assessment & Interview
SCHOLARSHIPS & BURSARIES Schol
SPECIAL NEEDS bw **DYSLEXIA** **DIET**
ASSOCIATION ISAI **FOUNDED** 1960 **RELIGIOUS AFFILIATION** Non-denom

MAP12 G 6
LOCATION Urban
DAY **RAIL** b **AIR** b
SPORT cefjlmopqx AB
OTHER LANGUAGES
ACTIVITIES cfh
OTHER SUBJECTS ch
FACILITIES ON SITE h
EXAM BOARDS
RETAKES **NVQ COURSES**

A-level:
AS:
GCSE:
OTHER: e l v / B G K O / cde

YORKSHIRE (WEST) continued

B — Queen Elizabeth Grammar Jnr School; 158 Northgate; Wakefield WF1 3QX
Tel: 01924 373821 (Fax: 01924 366246) *M.M.Bisset*

		Boys	Age	Girls	Age	TOTAL	Boys	Girls
Day	£994-£1050 ✗	230	7-11			230		
Weekly								
Boarding								

SIXTH

ENTRY REQUIREMENTS Exam
SCHOLARSHIPS & BURSARIES Burs; Chor
SPECIAL NEEDS   **DYSLEXIA**   **DIET** ac
ASSOCIATION IAPS   **FOUNDED** 1591   **RELIGIOUS AFFILIATION** Non-denom

MAP12 G 7
LOCATION Urban
DAY ✓   **RAIL** a   **AIR** a
SPORT aeflsx
OTHER LANGUAGES
ACTIVITIES fghjnoq A
OTHER SUBJECTS bc
FACILITIES ON SITE bi
EXAM BOARDS
RETAKES   **NVQ COURSES**

A-level   **AS**   **GCSE**   **OTHER**: e h l no v / BC E G K O R / cde

---

B — Queen Elizabeth Grammar School; Northgate; Wakefield WF1 3QX
Tel: 01924 373943 (Fax: 01924 378871) *R.P.Mardling*

		Boys	Age	Girls	Age	TOTAL	Boys	Girls
Day	£1374	749	11-18			749	194	
Weekly								
Boarding								

SIXTH

ENTRY REQUIREMENTS Exam
SCHOLARSHIPS & BURSARIES Schol; Burs; Mus; AP; VI Form
SPECIAL NEEDS jlw Gl   **DYSLEXIA**   **DIET** acd
ASSOCIATION HMC   **FOUNDED** 1591   **RELIGIOUS AFFILIATION** Inter-denom

MAP12 G 7
LOCATION Urban
DAY   **RAIL** a   **AIR** a
SPORT abcdefhklmostuwx AB
OTHER LANGUAGES
ACTIVITIES dfghijkmopqrs A
OTHER SUBJECTS bcdh
FACILITIES ON SITE bcgk
EXAM BOARDS abc ADEGHL
RETAKES   **NVQ COURSES**

A-level: cd g i l op uv x / B GH K OP R / cdefg jkl   **AS**: K efg   **GCSE**: cd g i o q v / B G K P R / cdefgh jkl   **OTHER**: GH ef

---

C — Richmond House School; 168-172 Otley Road; Leeds LS16 5LG
Tel: 0113 275 2670 (Fax: 0113 230 4868) *J.F.Kellett*

		Boys	Age	Girls	Age	TOTAL	Boys	Girls
Day	£693-£1072	171	3-11	113	3-11	284		
Weekly								
Boarding								

SIXTH

ENTRY REQUIREMENTS Interview; Test & Interview
SCHOLARSHIPS & BURSARIES
SPECIAL NEEDS b G   **DYSLEXIA**   **DIET** a
ASSOCIATION IAPS   **FOUNDED** 1935   **RELIGIOUS AFFILIATION** Inter-denom

MAP12 G 6
LOCATION Urban
DAY   **RAIL** b   **AIR** a
SPORT adefjlmpqsx AB
OTHER LANGUAGES
ACTIVITIES fgjot A
OTHER SUBJECTS ch
FACILITIES ON SITE
EXAM BOARDS
RETAKES   **NVQ COURSES**

A-level   **AS**   **GCSE**   **OTHER**: e l o v / B G K O R / cde

---

C — Rishworth School; Rishworth; Sowerby Bridge; West Yorks. HX6 4QA
Tel: 01422 822217 (Fax: 01422 823231) *M.J.Elford*

		Boys	Age	Girls	Age	TOTAL	Boys	Girls
Day	£798-£1600	239	4-18	224	4-18	557	50	41
Weekly	£2852-£3096	6	11-18	4	11-18			
Boarding	£2852-£3096	56	11-18	28	11-18			

SIXTH

ENTRY REQUIREMENTS Exam; Report & Interview
SCHOLARSHIPS & BURSARIES Schol; Forces
SPECIAL NEEDS abejklnpqstw ADEHI   **DYSLEXIA** ef   **DIET** abcd
ASSOCIATION SHMIS   **FOUNDED** 1724   **RELIGIOUS AFFILIATION** C of E

MAP11 F 7
LOCATION Rural
DAY   **RAIL** a   **AIR** a
SPORT abcdefhjklmpqstwx AB
OTHER LANGUAGES a
ACTIVITIES cfghijklmoqstuw A
OTHER SUBJECTS abcdh
FACILITIES ON SITE cdhi
EXAM BOARDS abcd ABDEG
RETAKES ab   **NVQ COURSES**

A-level: de ghi l nop uv / BC GH K P R U / cdef j l   **AS**: G   **GCSE**: d ghi l nop uv / BC E G K P R U / cdef j l   **OTHER**

C — St. Agnes PNEU School; 25 Burton Crescent; Headingley; Leeds LS6 4DN
Tel: 0113 278 6722 *Mrs C.Burrows*

		Boys	Age	Girls	Age	TOTAL	Boys	Girls
Day	£375-£922	35	2-8	15	2-8	50		
Weekly								
Boarding								

SIXTH

ENTRY REQUIREMENTS Interview
SCHOLARSHIPS & BURSARIES
SPECIAL NEEDS   **DYSLEXIA**   **DIET**
ASSOCIATION ISAI   **FOUNDED** 1895   **RELIGIOUS AFFILIATION** C of E

MAP12 G 6
LOCATION Urban
DAY   **RAIL** b   **AIR** a
SPORT
OTHER LANGUAGES
ACTIVITIES c
OTHER SUBJECTS
FACILITIES ON SITE
EXAM BOARDS
RETAKES   **NVQ COURSES**

A-level   **AS**   **GCSE**   **OTHER**: e m v / B E G K O-R / cde

YORKSHIRE (WEST) continued

C — Silcoates School; Wrenthorpe; Wakefield WF2 0PD
Tel: 01924 291614 (Fax: 01924 368690) *A.P.Spillane*

	Fees		Boys	Age	Girls	Age	TOTAL		Boys	Girls
Day	£1042-£1748	X	439	7-18	151	7-18	595	SIXTH	63	10
Weekly			4							
Boarding			1							

ENTRY REQUIREMENTS Exam
SCHOLARSHIPS & BURSARIES Mus; Clergy; AP; VI Form
SPECIAL NEEDS aejklnqsw EGIJ **DYSLEXIA** e **DIET** abcd
ASSOCIATION HMC **FOUNDED** 1820 **RELIGIOUS AFFILIATION** U R C

MAP 12 G 7
LOCATION Urban
DAY ✓ **RAIL** a **AIR** a
SPORT abcdefkpqswx AB
OTHER LANGUAGES
ACTIVITIES fghijklnoqs A
OTHER SUBJECTS bch
FACILITIES ON SITE bcdehil
EXAM BOARDS abcd ABDEH
RETAKES a **NVQ COURSES**

A-level e g i l op uv
AB GH K P R
cdef l

AS M

GCSE e g i l op v
AB E G K OP R X
cdef l

OTHER

C — Sunny Hill House School; 7 Wrenthorpe Lane; Wrenthorpe; Wakefield; Yorks. WF2 0QB
Tel: 01924 291717 *Mrs C.Byrne*

	Fees	Boys	Age	Girls	Age	TOTAL		Boys	Girls
Day	£860	66	3-7	21	3-7	87	SIXTH		
Weekly									
Boarding									

ENTRY REQUIREMENTS Assessment & Interview
SCHOLARSHIPS & BURSARIES
SPECIAL NEEDS **DYSLEXIA** **DIET** a
ASSOCIATION ISAI **FOUNDED** 1982 **RELIGIOUS AFFILIATION** U R C

MAP 12 G 7
LOCATION Urban
DAY **RAIL** a **AIR** a
SPORT x
OTHER LANGUAGES
ACTIVITIES fghjn
OTHER SUBJECTS ch
FACILITIES ON SITE
EXAM BOARDS
RETAKES **NVQ COURSES**

A-level

AS

GCSE

OTHER e l v
B G K
cd

G — Wakefield Girls' High School; Wentworth Street; Wakefield WF1 2QS
Tel: 01924 372490 (Fax: 01924 382080) *Mrs P.A.Langham*

	Fees		Boys	Age	Girls	Age	TOTAL		Boys	Girls
Day	£1301-£1374	X			757	11-18	757	SIXTH		188
Weekly										
Boarding										

ENTRY REQUIREMENTS Exam
SCHOLARSHIPS & BURSARIES Burs; AP
SPECIAL NEEDS ejklq GI **DYSLEXIA** **DIET** abcd
ASSOCIATION GSA **FOUNDED** 1878 **RELIGIOUS AFFILIATION**

MAP 12 G 7
LOCATION Inner City
DAY **RAIL** a **AIR** a
SPORT abcefghjklmopqswx AB
OTHER LANGUAGES
ACTIVITIES cfghijkmnopqw BD
OTHER SUBJECTS bcfh
FACILITIES ON SITE bcgh
EXAM BOARDS cd ADEHL
RETAKES **NVQ COURSES**

A-level cd fg i l op uv x
BC GH K P R W
cdefg j l

AS h
G K
e jk

GCSE d g i l opq v
BC G K P R WX
cdefgh jkl

OTHER m

C — Wakefield Girls' High School Junior School; 2 St.John's Square; Wakefield WF1 2QX
Tel: 01924 374577 (Fax: 01924 368990) *Mrs D.M.Robinson*

	Fees		Boys	Age	Girls	Age	TOTAL		Boys	Girls
Day	£970-£984	X	51	4-7	253	4-11	304	SIXTH		
Weekly										
Boarding										

ENTRY REQUIREMENTS Exam & Interview
SCHOLARSHIPS & BURSARIES
SPECIAL NEEDS ablq **DYSLEXIA** **DIET** a
ASSOCIATION IAPS **FOUNDED** **RELIGIOUS AFFILIATION**

MAP 12 G 7
LOCATION Inner City
DAY **RAIL** a **AIR** a
SPORT almpx
OTHER LANGUAGES
ACTIVITIES fghjo
OTHER SUBJECTS ch
FACILITIES ON SITE c
EXAM BOARDS
RETAKES **NVQ COURSES**

A-level

AS

GCSE

OTHER e lm o v
B G K O R
cd

C — Woodhouse Grove School; Apperley Bridge; Yorks. BD10 0NR
Tel: 0113 250 2477 (Fax: 0113 250 5290) *D.W.Welsh*

	Fees		Boys	Age	Girls	Age	TOTAL		Boys	Girls
Day	£1755	X	276	11-18	143	11-18	546	SIXTH	80	33
Weekly	£2980		20	11-18	10	11-18				
Boarding	£2980		63	11-18	34	11-18				

ENTRY REQUIREMENTS Exam
SCHOLARSHIPS & BURSARIES Schol; Burs; Art; Mus; Forces; AP; VI Form; Sport
SPECIAL NEEDS befhijlnqstuw A **DYSLEXIA** cde **DIET** acd
ASSOCIATION HMC **FOUNDED** 1812 **RELIGIOUS AFFILIATION** Methodist

MAP 12 G 7
LOCATION Rural
DAY ✓ **RAIL** b **AIR** a
SPORT abcdefhmopqswx AB
OTHER LANGUAGES an
ACTIVITIES cfghiklnoqstwx AB
OTHER SUBJECTS bcfh
FACILITIES ON SITE bcdegik
EXAM BOARDS bcd ADEH
RETAKES ab **NVQ COURSES**

A-level a e ghi l op uv x
AB GH K P R
cdef

AS

GCSE e ghi l o v
AB G K P R
cdef

OTHER mn o
kl

309

WALES (NORTH) continued

C — Hillgrove School; Ffriddoedd Road; Bangor; Gwynedd LL57 2TW
Tel: 01248 353568 *J.G.J.Porter & Mrs S.P.Porter*

MAP 7 D 2
LOCATION Urban
DAY   RAIL a   AIR b

		Boys	Age	Girls	Age	TOTAL
Day	£550- £880	95	3-16	48	3-16	143
Weekly						
Boarding						

SIXTH: Boys   Girls

SPORT abcdefjlmpqswx AB
OTHER LANGUAGES n
ACTIVITIES fghjknopq A
OTHER SUBJECTS ch
FACILITIES ON SITE c
EXAM BOARDS e K
RETAKES a   NVQ COURSES

ENTRY REQUIREMENTS Test & Interview
SCHOLARSHIPS & BURSARIES
SPECIAL NEEDS bjklnqtuw BGHI   DYSLEXIA e   DIET
ASSOCIATION ISAI   FOUNDED 1934   RELIGIOUS AFFILIATION

A-level:
AS:
GCSE: B e g i o v G K OP R cde
OTHER: A   l

G — Howell's School; Denbigh; Clwyd LL16 3EN
Tel: 01745 813631 (Fax: 01745 814443) *Mrs M.Steel*

MAP 7 F 2
LOCATION Rural
DAY ✓   RAIL b   AIR b

		Boys	Age	Girls	Age	TOTAL
Day	£2145 ×			105	11-18	210
Weekly				105	11-18	
Boarding	£3282					

SIXTH: Boys   Girls 61

SPORT abcdefhklmnpqtwx ABC
OTHER LANGUAGES an
ACTIVITIES cghijknopqstw A
OTHER SUBJECTS abcdfgh
FACILITIES ON SITE adhj
EXAM BOARDS abce ABDEGHK
RETAKES a   NVQ COURSES

ENTRY REQUIREMENTS Scholarship Exam; Exam & Interview
SCHOLARSHIPS & BURSARIES Schol; Mus; Forces; AP; VI Form; Sport; Siblings
SPECIAL NEEDS bgjlnq GI   DYSLEXIA e   DIET abcd
ASSOCIATION GSA   FOUNDED 1859   RELIGIOUS AFFILIATION C in W

A-level: defghi uv   B GH K N P   c ef j l
AS: de h u   G K   c ef   l
GCSE: cde ghi n uv   BC E G K NOP R   cdef   j l
OTHER: l no   K   O R   X   h k

G — Howell's Preparatory School; Park Street; Denbigh; Clwyd LL16 3EN
Tel: 01745 815270 (Fax: 01745 814443) *Mrs.S.Gordon*

MAP 7 F 2
LOCATION Rural
DAY ✓   RAIL b   AIR a

		Boys	Age	Girls	Age	TOTAL
Day	£830-£1305 ×			83	3-11	92
Weekly	£1795-£1941			9	7-11	
Boarding	£1795-£1941				7-11	

SIXTH: Boys   Girls

SPORT lpqx B
OTHER LANGUAGES n
ACTIVITIES cgjlqwx
OTHER SUBJECTS bch
FACILITIES ON SITE bdhj
EXAM BOARDS
RETAKES   NVQ COURSES

ENTRY REQUIREMENTS Assessment & Interview
SCHOLARSHIPS & BURSARIES
SPECIAL NEEDS ajnw   DYSLEXIA   DIET abcd
ASSOCIATION IAPS   FOUNDED 1859   RELIGIOUS AFFILIATION C of E

A-level:
AS:
GCSE:
OTHER: e m v   B   K   O R   X   e

C — Lyndon School; Grosvenor Road; Colwyn Bay; Clwyd LL29 7YF
Tel: 01492 532347 *Mrs A.Ashworth*

MAP 7 F 2
LOCATION Urban
DAY   RAIL a   AIR b

		Boys	Age	Girls	Age	TOTAL
Day	£675- £910 ×	61	3-11	42	3-11	103
Weekly						
Boarding						

SIXTH: Boys   Girls

SPORT abejlpqx B
OTHER LANGUAGES n
ACTIVITIES fghjpt A
OTHER SUBJECTS
FACILITIES ON SITE
EXAM BOARDS
RETAKES   NVQ COURSES

ENTRY REQUIREMENTS
SCHOLARSHIPS & BURSARIES
SPECIAL NEEDS bno B   DYSLEXIA e   DIET a
ASSOCIATION ISAI   FOUNDED 1933   RELIGIOUS AFFILIATION C in W

A-level:
AS:
GCSE:
OTHER: e   o v   B   G   cde

C — Northgate School; Russell Road; Rhyl; Clwyd LL18 3DD
Tel: 01745 342510 *P.G.Orton*

MAP 7 F 2
LOCATION Urban
DAY ✓   RAIL a   AIR b

		Boys	Age	Girls	Age	TOTAL
Day	£500- £550	17	4-11	7	4-11	24
Weekly						
Boarding						

SIXTH: Boys   Girls

SPORT mqx
OTHER LANGUAGES n
ACTIVITIES cfhj
OTHER SUBJECTS h
FACILITIES ON SITE i
EXAM BOARDS
RETAKES   NVQ COURSES

ENTRY REQUIREMENTS Interview
SCHOLARSHIPS & BURSARIES
SPECIAL NEEDS bkn B   DYSLEXIA def   DIET a
ASSOCIATION ISAI   FOUNDED 1977   RELIGIOUS AFFILIATION

A-level:
AS:
GCSE:
OTHER: e   v   B   G   cd

WALES (NORTH) *continued*

C — Ruthin School; Ruthin; Clwyd LL15 1EE
Tel: 01824 702543 (Fax: 01824 707141) *John Rowlands*

	Boys	Age	Girls	Age	TOTAL		Boys	Girls
Day £650–£2075	108	3-18	53	3-18	248	SIXTH	38	6
Weekly £2225–£2715	22	7-18	7	7-18				
Boarding £2225–£3295	51	7-18	7	7-18				

ENTRY REQUIREMENTS Test & Interview; Report & Interview; CEE & Interview
SCHOLARSHIPS & BURSARIES Schol; Burs; Art; Mus; Chor; Forces; Clergy; VI Form; Sport; ARA
SPECIAL NEEDS blnptw E   **DYSLEXIA** e   **DIET** abd
ASSOCIATION SHMIS   **FOUNDED** 1284   **RELIGIOUS AFFILIATION** C of E

MAP 8 G 3
LOCATION Rural
DAY ✓   **RAIL** b   **AIR** a
SPORT abcdefhjmopqstuwx AB
OTHER LANGUAGES a
ACTIVITIES cefgijkmnopqs A
OTHER SUBJECTS acdh
FACILITIES ON SITE cegh
EXAM BOARDS bc ABDHK
RETAKES ab   **NVQ COURSES**

A-level defghi o v   B G K   cde l
AS defg i l o v   B G K P
GCSE cde l
OTHER mn   R

C — Rydal Penrhos Preparatory School; Pwllycrochan; Colwyn Bay; Clywd LL29 7BP
Tel: 01492 530381 (Fax: 01492 531872) *M.J.F.Andrews*

	Boys	Age	Girls	Age	TOTAL		Boys	Girls
Day £588–£2038	112	3-13	38	3-13	217	SIXTH		
Weekly £1403–£2800	6	7-13	2	7-13				
Boarding £1403–£2800	44	7-13	15	7-13				

ENTRY REQUIREMENTS Report & Interview
SCHOLARSHIPS & BURSARIES Schol; Forces
SPECIAL NEEDS ejlnqw Gl   **DYSLEXIA** e   **DIET** abcd
ASSOCIATION IAPS   **FOUNDED** 1885   **RELIGIOUS AFFILIATION** Methodist

MAP 7 F 2
LOCATION Urban
DAY ✓   **RAIL** a   **AIR** b
SPORT abcdefijkmpqswx ABC
OTHER LANGUAGES
ACTIVITIES acfghijklnopqrstx A
OTHER SUBJECTS bcdfh
FACILITIES ON SITE acdikl
EXAM BOARDS
RETAKES   **NVQ COURSES**

A-level
AS
GCSE
OTHER de g i l o v   BC G K   OP R   cde j

C — Rydal Penrhos Snr Sch (Co-ed Div); Colwyn Bay; Clwyd LL29 7BT
Tel: 01492 530155 (Fax: 01492 531872) *N.W.Thorne*

	Boys	Age	Girls	Age	TOTAL		Boys	Girls
Day £2368	90	13-18	57	13-18	302	SIXTH	80	35
Weekly		13-18		13-18				
Boarding £3283	111	13-18	44	13-18				

ENTRY REQUIREMENTS CEE; Exam; Test & Interview
SCHOLARSHIPS & BURSARIES Schol; Burs; Art; Mus; Forces; Clergy; AP; VI Form
SPECIAL NEEDS bejklnqtw ACGH   **DYSLEXIA** e   **DIET** a
ASSOCIATION HMC   **FOUNDED** 1885   **RELIGIOUS AFFILIATION** Methodist

MAP 7 F 2
LOCATION Urban
DAY ✓   **RAIL** a   **AIR** b
SPORT abcdefghjklmopqstuwx ABC
OTHER LANGUAGES an
ACTIVITIES cfghijklnopqrstw ABD
OTHER SUBJECTS abcdfh
FACILITIES ON SITE acdegik
EXAM BOARDS bcde ABDEHK
RETAKES ab   **NVQ COURSES**

A-level de ghi op v   BC GH K   P R U   c efg ij l
AS cd g   u   GH K   R
GCSE de ghij o v   BC G K   NOP R TU X   bcdefghij l
OTHER l   e

G — Rydal Penrhos Snr Sch (Girls' Div); Llannerch Road East; Colwyn Bay; Clwyd LL28 4DA
Tel: 01492 530333 (Fax: 01492 533198) *C.M.J.Allen*

	Boys	Age	Girls	Age	TOTAL		Boys	Girls
Day £1995–£2135		3-11	106	3-18	225	SIXTH		51
Weekly £2755–£3115			11	7-18				
Boarding £2755–£3115			108	7-18				

ENTRY REQUIREMENTS Test & Interview
SCHOLARSHIPS & BURSARIES Schol; Mus; AP; VI Form
SPECIAL NEEDS bjn   **DYSLEXIA** f   **DIET** a
ASSOCIATION GSA   **FOUNDED** 1880   **RELIGIOUS AFFILIATION** Inter-denom

MAP 7 F 2
LOCATION Urban
DAY   **RAIL** a   **AIR** b
SPORT abcdghklmopqtwx AB
OTHER LANGUAGES an
ACTIVITIES cfghijklnoqstuw A
OTHER SUBJECTS abcefgh
FACILITIES ON SITE abcdeik
EXAM BOARDS abcde ABDEGK
RETAKES b   **NVQ COURSES**

A-level defghij l op uv   ABC GH K   P TU U   cdef
AS de n   G   ef
GCSE de g ijkl nop   v x   ABC G K   NOP R U W   cdef
OTHER NO   .

B — St. David's College; Llandudno; Gwynedd LL30 1RD
Tel: 01492 875974 (Fax: 01492 870383) *W.G.Seymour*

	Boys	Age	Girls	Age	TOTAL		Boys	Girls
Day £1993–£2090	68	11-18			230	SIXTH	48	
Weekly		11-18						
Boarding £3065–£3214	162	11-18						

ENTRY REQUIREMENTS CEE; Exam & Interview
SCHOLARSHIPS & BURSARIES Schol; Art; Mus; Clergy; Sport
SPECIAL NEEDS blnqw G   **DYSLEXIA** cde   **DIET** acd
ASSOCIATION SHMIS   **FOUNDED** 1965   **RELIGIOUS AFFILIATION** Inter-denom

MAP 7 E 2
LOCATION Rural
DAY   **RAIL** a   **AIR** b
SPORT abcdefghjkmostuwx AB
OTHER LANGUAGES n
ACTIVITIES afghijklmnopqrstuw ABC
OTHER SUBJECTS bcdf
FACILITIES ON SITE bcdkl
EXAM BOARDS abcde ABDEIK
RETAKES ab   **NVQ COURSES**

A-level efghij l o v   AB GH MN P R   cdef
AS efg i o   G   P
GCSE e ghij l o v   AB E G K MN P R   cdef l
OTHER

WALES (NORTH) continued

C — St. Gerards School; Ffriddoedd Road; Bangor; Gwynedd LL57 2EL
Tel: 01248 351656 *Miss Anne Parkinson*

		Boys	Age	Girls	Age	TOTAL		Boys	Girls
Day	£585- £890	147	3-18	226	3-18	373	SIXTH	8	25
Weekly									
Boarding									

ENTRY REQUIREMENTS Interview; Assessment; Report & Interview
SCHOLARSHIPS & BURSARIES Burs
SPECIAL NEEDS bn   **DYSLEXIA** e   **DIET**
ASSOCIATION ISAI   **FOUNDED** 1915   **RELIGIOUS AFFILIATION** R C

MAP 7 D 2
LOCATION Urban
DAY   **RAIL** a   **AIR** c
SPORT bjmpqx BC
OTHER LANGUAGES n
ACTIVITIES cgjo
OTHER SUBJECTS bc
FACILITIES ON SITE ad
EXAM BOARDS e K
RETAKES ab   **NVQ COURSES**

A-level B e g i GH K P R v *cdef*
AS
GCSE BC G e g i l n K P R v W *cdef*
OTHER

C — Tower House; Barmouth; Gwynedd LL42 1RF
Tel: 01341 280127 *Mrs J.M.Pugh*

		Boys	Age	Girls	Age	TOTAL		Boys	Girls
Day	£698-£1000	23	4-16	43	4-16	66	SIXTH		
Weekly	£1418-£1720								
Boarding									

ENTRY REQUIREMENTS Test & Interview
SCHOLARSHIPS & BURSARIES
SPECIAL NEEDS bn BG   **DYSLEXIA** fg   **DIET**
ASSOCIATION ISAI   **FOUNDED** 1975   **RELIGIOUS AFFILIATION** Non-denom

MAP 7 E 4
LOCATION Rural
DAY   **RAIL** a   **AIR** c
SPORT abcefhjlmnpqwx ABC
OTHER LANGUAGES n
ACTIVITIES cfghijkrt A
OTHER SUBJECTS abcdfh
FACILITIES ON SITE ch
EXAM BOARDS abde
RETAKES a   **NVQ COURSES**

A-level
AS
GCSE B e g i G o P v *cde*
OTHER l

WALES (SOUTH)

C — Cathedral School Llandaff,The; Cardiff CF5 2YH
Tel: 01222 563179 (Fax: 01222 567752) *P.L.Gray*

		Boys	Age	Girls	Age	TOTAL		Boys	Girls
Day	£1015-£1530 ✗	212	4-13	61	4-13	294	SIXTH		
Weekly	£2450	4	8-13		8-13				
Boarding	£2500	17	8-13		8-13				

ENTRY REQUIREMENTS Test; Interview
SCHOLARSHIPS & BURSARIES Chor
SPECIAL NEEDS abjln AL   **DYSLEXIA** e   **DIET** abcd
ASSOCIATION IAPS   **FOUNDED** 1880   **RELIGIOUS AFFILIATION** C in W

MAP 2 H 2
LOCATION Urban
DAY   **RAIL** a   **AIR** a
SPORT abcefghjklmpqsx B
OTHER LANGUAGES n
ACTIVITIES cfghijlnoqswx A
OTHER SUBJECTS abch
FACILITIES ON SITE cdhjk
EXAM BOARDS
RETAKES   **NVQ COURSES**

A-level
AS
GCSE
OTHER B cde g i l G K no OP R uv *cdefg j*

Bg — Christ College; Brecon; Powys LD3 8AG
Tel: 01874 623359 (Fax: 01874 611478) *S.W.Hockey*

		Boys	Age	Girls	Age	TOTAL		Boys	Girls
Day	£2317	65	10-18	6	16-18	347	SIXTH	112	28
Weekly									
Boarding	£3135	254	10-18	22	16-18				

ENTRY REQUIREMENTS CEE; Report & Interview; Report & Test; Report & Exam & Interview
SCHOLARSHIPS & BURSARIES Schol; Burs; Mus; Forces; Clergy; Teachers; AP; VI Form; Sport
SPECIAL NEEDS abjklnqstw DEI   **DYSLEXIA** f   **DIET** a
ASSOCIATION HMC   **FOUNDED** 1541   **RELIGIOUS AFFILIATION** C in W

MAP 9 D 6
LOCATION Rural
DAY   **RAIL** b   **AIR** a
SPORT abcdefghjklmopqstuwx ABC
OTHER LANGUAGES an
ACTIVITIES aefghijklmnopqrstvw C
OTHER SUBJECTS bcdfh
FACILITIES ON SITE abcdeghjk
EXAM BOARDS abcde ABDEHIK
RETAKES b   **NVQ COURSES**

A-level B defghi GH K op NOP R v U *cdefg ij l*
AS c e G K o *ef j l*
GCSE B e g i G K OP R v *cdefgh j l*
OTHER

Gb — Elm Tree House School; 27 Palace Road; Llandaff; Cardiff CF5 2AG
Tel: 01222 563386 (Fax: 01222 563386) *Mrs C.M.L.Thomas*

		Boys	Age	Girls	Age	TOTAL		Boys	Girls
Day	£785- £929	6	3-7	121	3-11	127	SIXTH		
Weekly									
Boarding									

ENTRY REQUIREMENTS Test & Interview
SCHOLARSHIPS & BURSARIES Schol; Burs
SPECIAL NEEDS   **DYSLEXIA**   **DIET** abcd
ASSOCIATION ISAI   **FOUNDED** 1922   **RELIGIOUS AFFILIATION** Non-denom

MAP 2 H 2
LOCATION Urban
DAY   **RAIL** a   **AIR** a
SPORT lptx AB
OTHER LANGUAGES
ACTIVITIES cfgj
OTHER SUBJECTS h
FACILITIES ON SITE hi
EXAM BOARDS
RETAKES   **NVQ COURSES**

A-level
AS
GCSE
OTHER B e G K lmo O R v *cde*

WALES (SOUTH) *continued*

G — Haberdashers' Monmouth School for Girls; Hereford Road; Monmouth NP5 3XT
Tel: 01600 714214 (Fax: 01600 772244) *Mrs D.L.Newman*

	Boys	Age	Girls	Age	TOTAL	SIXTH	Boys	Girls
Day	£1167-£1407		521	7-18	648			151
Weekly	£2424-£2664		68	7-18				
Boarding	£2424-£2664		59	7-18				

ENTRY REQUIREMENTS Report & Exam & Interview
SCHOLARSHIPS & BURSARIES Schol; Mus; AP
SPECIAL NEEDS   **DYSLEXIA**   **DIET** ad
ASSOCIATION GSA   **FOUNDED** 1892   **RELIGIOUS AFFILIATION** C in W

MAP 2 I 1
LOCATION Rural
DAY   **RAIL** b   **AIR** c
SPORT abcdlnpqrx ABC
OTHER LANGUAGES a
ACTIVITIES cfghijknostwx AB
OTHER SUBJECTS bcdfgh
FACILITIES ON SITE bcehik
EXAM BOARDS bcde ADEGHK
RETAKES   **NVQ COURSES**

A-level: cd fg i nop vw / BC GH K PQR U W / c ef h jkl
AS: BC G / c ef   l q   w
GCSE: d ghi nop v / BC G K N P R W / cdefgh j l
OTHER: l   u / o

C — Haylett Grange School; Haverfordwest; Dyfed SA62 4LA
Tel: 01437 762472 *Mrs J.M.Sharpe & Mrs J.M.Hanby*

	Boys	Age	Girls	Age	TOTAL	SIXTH	Boys	Girls
Day	£500-£550	65	3-11	61	3-11	126		
Weekly								
Boarding								

ENTRY REQUIREMENTS Interview
SCHOLARSHIPS & BURSARIES
SPECIAL NEEDS   **DYSLEXIA**   **DIET** ad
ASSOCIATION ISAI   **FOUNDED** 1956   **RELIGIOUS AFFILIATION** Non-denom

MAP 7 B 8
LOCATION Rural
DAY   **RAIL** b   **AIR** c
SPORT aejlmpqx B
OTHER LANGUAGES n
ACTIVITIES cfgjox
OTHER SUBJECTS ch
FACILITIES ON SITE j
EXAM BOARDS
RETAKES   **NVQ COURSES**

A-level: (blank)
AS: (blank)
GCSE: (blank)
OTHER: e   l no   v / B G   O R / cde   j

G — Howell's School Llandaff GPDST; Cardiff CF5 2YD
Tel: 01222 562019 (Fax: 01222 578879) *Mrs C.Jane Fitz*

	Boys	Age	Girls	Age	TOTAL	SIXTH	Boys	Girls
Day	£976-£1328		691	4-18	691			133
Weekly								
Boarding								

ENTRY REQUIREMENTS Report & Exam & Interview
SCHOLARSHIPS & BURSARIES Schol; Burs; Mus; AP; VI Form
SPECIAL NEEDS bghlnqt BGH   **DYSLEXIA**   **DIET** abcd
ASSOCIATION GSA   **FOUNDED** 1860   **RELIGIOUS AFFILIATION** Inter-denom

MAP 2 H 2
LOCATION Urban
DAY   **RAIL** a   **AIR** a
SPORT aceghlmnpqrwx AB
OTHER LANGUAGES n
ACTIVITIES cghijklnoqstwx AB
OTHER SUBJECTS bcdfh
FACILITIES ON SITE cgi
EXAM BOARDS abcde BEHK
RETAKES   **NVQ COURSES**

A-level: c e g i   p   v / B GH K P R U / c ef c ef
AS: e   v / G K
GCSE: d   no   vw / BC E G K O R U X / cdefg j
OTHER: hi kl

C — Kings Monkton School; 18 The Parade; Cardiff CF2 3UA
Tel: 01222 483130 (Fax: 01222 457828) *R.Griffin*

	Boys	Age	Girls	Age	TOTAL	SIXTH	Boys	Girls
Day	£795-£1378	278	2-18	120	2-18	398		27	3

ENTRY REQUIREMENTS Exam; Interview
SCHOLARSHIPS & BURSARIES Schol; VI Form; Siblings
SPECIAL NEEDS bjnx BH   **DYSLEXIA** e   **DIET**
ASSOCIATION ISAI   **FOUNDED** 1870   **RELIGIOUS AFFILIATION** Inter-denom

MAP 2 H 2
LOCATION Inner City
DAY ✓   **RAIL** a   **AIR** a
SPORT abcefjklmpqsx ABC
OTHER LANGUAGES a
ACTIVITIES fghjlnoq ABD
OTHER SUBJECTS abcdh
FACILITIES ON SITE cdg
EXAM BOARDS abcde ADK
RETAKES ab   **NVQ COURSES**

A-level: e ghi l   p   v x / B G P / cde
AS: h
GCSE: e ghi l   op   v x / B E G K N P / cdef hj
OTHER: n / E   R

C — Llandovery College; Llandovery; Dyfed SA20 0EE
Tel: 01550 20315 (Fax: 01550 20168) *Dr Claude E.Evans*

	Boys	Age	Girls	Age	TOTAL	SIXTH	Boys	Girls
Day	£1840-£2068	47	11-18	31	11-18	238		55	27
Weekly	£2686-£3170	37	11-18	15	11-18				
Boarding	£2686-£3170	77	11-18	31	11-18				

ENTRY REQUIREMENTS CEE; Exam & Interview; Report & Interview
SCHOLARSHIPS & BURSARIES Schol; Burs; Mus; Forces; Clergy; AP; VI Form; Sport
SPECIAL NEEDS ln   **DYSLEXIA** c   **DIET** a
ASSOCIATION HMC   **FOUNDED** 1847   **RELIGIOUS AFFILIATION** C in W

MAP 7 E 8
LOCATION Rural
DAY ✓   **RAIL** b   **AIR** b
SPORT abcdefhklmopsuw ABC
OTHER LANGUAGES an
ACTIVITIES efghijklmnoqstw A
OTHER SUBJECTS bcfh
FACILITIES ON SITE bcdeghkl
EXAM BOARDS abce ABDEHK
RETAKES   **NVQ COURSES**

A-level: cde ghi l no   uv / B G K OP R / cde g j
AS: a de / e
GCSE: cde ghi l no   v / B E G K NOP R W / cde g j
OTHER:

313

WALES (SOUTH) continued

B — Monmouth School; Monmouth NP5 3XP
Tel: 01600 713143 (Fax: 01600 772701) *T.H.P.Haynes*

		Boys	Age	Girls	Age	TOTAL	SIXTH	Boys	Girls
Day	£1080-£1636	459	7-18			645		166	
Weekly	£2725		11-18						
Boarding	£2725	186	11-18						

ENTRY REQUIREMENTS CEE; Scholarship Exam; Report & Exam & Interview
SCHOLARSHIPS & BURSARIES Schol; Burs; Mus; AP; VI Form; Sport
SPECIAL NEEDS ejknpq EG   **DYSLEXIA** g   **DIET** ad
ASSOCIATION HMC   **FOUNDED** 1615   **RELIGIOUS AFFILIATION** C in W

MAP 2 I 1
LOCATION Rural
DAY ✓   **RAIL** b   **AIR** b
SPORT abcdefghjklorstuwx AB
OTHER LANGUAGES
ACTIVITIES befghijklmoqstw ABD
OTHER SUBJECTS bcfh
FACILITIES ON SITE cdhi
EXAM BOARDS bcde BDEGHK
RETAKES   **NVQ COURSES**

- **A-level**: c efg i nop vw / BC GH K PQR U / c efgh jkl
- **AS**: f l q / C G K / c ef l
- **GCSE**: d g i o v / B G K P R / cdefg jkl
- **OTHER**: l

C — Netherwood School; Saundersfoot; Dyfed SA69 9BE
Tel: 01834 811057 (Fax: 01834 813360) *D.Huw Morris*

		Boys	Age	Girls	Age	TOTAL	SIXTH	Boys	Girls
Day	£575-£995	63	3-16	64	3-16	176			
Weekly	£1575-£1825	13	7-16	9	7-16				
Boarding	£1875-£2100	18	7-16	9	8-16				

ENTRY REQUIREMENTS Interview
SCHOLARSHIPS & BURSARIES Schol
SPECIAL NEEDS eknw BGIL   **DYSLEXIA** ef   **DIET**
ASSOCIATION IAPS   **FOUNDED** 1947   **RELIGIOUS AFFILIATION** C of E

MAP 1 D 7
LOCATION Rural
DAY ✓   **RAIL** a   **AIR** b
SPORT abcdghjklmopqswx AB
OTHER LANGUAGES an
ACTIVITIES cefghjknoqrwx A
OTHER SUBJECTS abch
FACILITIES ON SITE h
EXAM BOARDS cde K
RETAKES a   **NVQ COURSES**

- **A-level**:
- **AS**:
- **GCSE**: e ghi v / B G P / cde
- **OTHER**: lmn / K O R / f j

C — Rougemont School; Llantarnam Hall; Malpas Road; Newport; Gwent NP9 6QB
Tel: 01633 855560 (Fax: 01633 855598) *I.Brown*

		Boys	Age	Girls	Age	TOTAL	SIXTH	Boys	Girls
Day	£946-£1478	242	3-18	239	3-18	481		27	27
Weekly									
Boarding									

ENTRY REQUIREMENTS CEE; Test & Interview
SCHOLARSHIPS & BURSARIES Schol; Burs; Teachers; VI Form
SPECIAL NEEDS abjlnqstuw GHI   **DYSLEXIA** de   **DIET** abd
ASSOCIATION GBA   **FOUNDED** 1927   **RELIGIOUS AFFILIATION** Inter-denom

MAP 2 H 1
LOCATION Urban
DAY ✓   **RAIL** a   **AIR** a
SPORT abcefhjmpqrswx ABC
OTHER LANGUAGES
ACTIVITIES cfghijknoqrs AB
OTHER SUBJECTS bc
FACILITIES ON SITE g
EXAM BOARDS bde GHL
RETAKES ab   **NVQ COURSES**

- **A-level**: egi np v / B GH PR / c ef
- **AS**: e u / B K R / ef
- **GCSE**: eghi l n v / B G K P R / cdef
- **OTHER**: lm q u / K M O

C — St. John's-on-the-Hill; Chepstow; Gwent NP6 7LE
Tel: 01291 622045 (Fax: 01291 623932) *I.K.Etchells*

		Boys	Age	Girls	Age	TOTAL	SIXTH	Boys	Girls
Day	£311-£1718	151	2-13	96	2-13	273			
Weekly	£2320	13	7-13	4	7-13				
Boarding	£2320	8	7-13	1	7-13				

ENTRY REQUIREMENTS Test & Interview
SCHOLARSHIPS & BURSARIES Schol; Burs; Art; Mus; Forces; Sport; ARA; Drama; Siblings
SPECIAL NEEDS bknuw BGI   **DYSLEXIA** de   **DIET** acd
ASSOCIATION IAPS   **FOUNDED** 1923   **RELIGIOUS AFFILIATION** C of E

MAP 2 I 1
LOCATION Rural
DAY ✓   **RAIL** b   **AIR** b
SPORT abcefjklmpqsux AB
OTHER LANGUAGES
ACTIVITIES acfghijlqw A
OTHER SUBJECTS abc
FACILITIES ON SITE chj
EXAM BOARDS
RETAKES   **NVQ COURSES**

- **A-level**:
- **AS**:
- **GCSE**:
- **OTHER**: e l o v / B E G R / cde

C — St. John's School; Newton; Porthcawl; Mid Glamorgan CF36 5NP
Tel: 01656 783404 (Fax: 01656 783404)

		Boys	Age	Girls	Age	TOTAL	SIXTH	Boys	Girls
Day	£910-£1560	112	3-16	66	3-16	229			
Weekly	£1925-£2135	24	7-16	14	7-16				
Boarding	£2235-£2450	7	7-16	6	7-16				

ENTRY REQUIREMENTS Assessment & Interview
SCHOLARSHIPS & BURSARIES Schol
SPECIAL NEEDS ejknw GI   **DYSLEXIA** e   **DIET** a
ASSOCIATION IAPS   **FOUNDED** 1921   **RELIGIOUS AFFILIATION**

MAP 2 G 2
LOCATION Rural
DAY ✓   **RAIL** a   **AIR** a
SPORT abcefjopqsx ABC
OTHER LANGUAGES a
ACTIVITIES acfghijknoq
OTHER SUBJECTS abcdh
FACILITIES ON SITE bhj
EXAM BOARDS abcde
RETAKES   **NVQ COURSES**

- **A-level**:
- **AS**:
- **GCSE**: d g i l vw / B E G P R / ef
- **OTHER**: e l v / B G / cde

WALES (SOUTH) continued

C — St. Michael's School; Bryn; Llanelli; Dyfed SA14 9TU
Tel: 01554 820325 (Fax: 01554 821716) *D.T.Sheehan*

		Boys	Age	Girls	Age	TOTAL		Boys	Girls
Day	£650-£1085	188	4-18	128	4-18	316	SIXTH	18	20
Weekly									
Boarding									

ENTRY REQUIREMENTS Exam; Test & Interview
SCHOLARSHIPS & BURSARIES Schol; Mus; VI Form; Sport
SPECIAL NEEDS   **DYSLEXIA**   **DIET** a
ASSOCIATION ISAI   **FOUNDED** 1923   **RELIGIOUS AFFILIATION** Non-denom

MAP 1 E 1
LOCATION Rural
DAY   **RAIL**   **AIR**
SPORT abdefjkmpqswx AB
OTHER LANGUAGES n
ACTIVITIES acdfghijknoptw A
OTHER SUBJECTS cfg
FACILITIES ON SITE bg
EXAM BOARDS de AEIK
RETAKES ab   **NVQ COURSES**

A-level: B e ghi l q v x / cdef l / G N P U
AS
GCSE: B e ghi l o q v x / cdefg l / BC G K P U
OTHER

C — Westbourne College; 4 Hickman Road; Penarth; S.Glam. CF64 2AJ
Tel: 01222 705705 (Fax: 01222 709988) *Dr B.Young*

		Boys	Age	Girls	Age	TOTAL		Boys	Girls
Day	£1455	32	14-16	6	14-16	38	SIXTH		
Weekly									
Boarding									

ENTRY REQUIREMENTS CEE; Test & Interview
SCHOLARSHIPS & BURSARIES
SPECIAL NEEDS blq G   **DYSLEXIA**   **DIET**
ASSOCIATION ISAI   **FOUNDED** 1976   **RELIGIOUS AFFILIATION** Non-denom

MAP 2 H 2
LOCATION Urban
DAY   **RAIL** a   **AIR** a
SPORT abcefhjlmpqsx B
OTHER LANGUAGES
ACTIVITIES h
OTHER SUBJECTS
FACILITIES ON SITE h
EXAM BOARDS ce
RETAKES   **NVQ COURSES**

A-level
AS: H
GCSE: B e ghi l v / cde g j / G P R
OTHER: B e G v / cd / R

C — Westbourne House; 4 Hickman Road; Penarth; S.Glam. CF64 2AJ
Tel: 01222 707861 (Fax: 01222 709988) *R.H.Haines & A.Swain*

		Boys	Age	Girls	Age	TOTAL		Boys	Girls
Day	£715-£1455	74	3-13	28	3-13	102	SIXTH		
Weekly									
Boarding									

ENTRY REQUIREMENTS Test & Interview
SCHOLARSHIPS & BURSARIES
SPECIAL NEEDS bjlq G   **DYSLEXIA**   **DIET**
ASSOCIATION IAPS   **FOUNDED** 1890   **RELIGIOUS AFFILIATION** Non-denom

MAP 2 H 2
LOCATION Urban
DAY   **RAIL** a   **AIR** a
SPORT abcefhjmpqsx B
OTHER LANGUAGES
ACTIVITIES hs
OTHER SUBJECTS h
FACILITIES ON SITE h
EXAM BOARDS
RETAKES   **NVQ COURSES**

A-level
AS
GCSE
OTHER: B e ghi l o v / cde g j / G OP R

C — Aberlour House; Aberlour; Banffshire AB38 9LJ
Tel: 01340 871267 (Fax: 01340 871238) *John Caithness*

		Boys	Age	Girls	Age	TOTAL		Boys	Girls
Day	£1880 ✗	7	7-13	8	7-13	111	SIXTH		
Weekly									
Boarding	£2745	59	7-13	37	7-13				

ENTRY REQUIREMENTS Report; Assessment & Interview
SCHOLARSHIPS & BURSARIES Schol; Burs; AP
SPECIAL NEEDS abgjlnuvw BEI   **DYSLEXIA** e   **DIET** ad
ASSOCIATION IAPS   **FOUNDED** 1937   **RELIGIOUS AFFILIATION** Non-denom

MAP 16 I 5
LOCATION Rural
DAY ✓   **RAIL** a   **AIR** b
SPORT abcdefjklmopqsx ABC
OTHER LANGUAGES a
ACTIVITIES acghjmoqtw A
OTHER SUBJECTS bcdh
FACILITIES ON SITE abchik
EXAM BOARDS
RETAKES   **NVQ COURSES**

A-level
AS
GCSE
OTHER: B e g i l o v / cdef j / G K OP R

G — Albyn School for Girls; 17-23 Queens Road; Aberdeen AB9 2PA
Tel: 01224 322408 (Fax: 01224 209173) *Miss N.Smith*

		Boys	Age	Girls	Age	TOTAL		Boys	Girls
Day	£403-£1308	11	2-5	400	2-18	411	SIXTH		73
Weekly									
Boarding									

ENTRY REQUIREMENTS Report; Test & Interview; Exam & Interview
SCHOLARSHIPS & BURSARIES Schol; Art; Mus; AP
SPECIAL NEEDS n   **DYSLEXIA** e   **DIET** a
ASSOCIATION GBGSA   **FOUNDED** 1867   **RELIGIOUS AFFILIATION** Non-denom

MAP 16 L 6
LOCATION Urban
DAY   **RAIL** a   **AIR** a
SPORT acmptwx BC
OTHER LANGUAGES a
ACTIVITIES gijklno B
OTHER SUBJECTS bch
FACILITIES ON SITE
EXAM BOARDS l
RETAKES   **NVQ COURSES**

A-level: B d g i v / c ef j / G K P
AS: BC cd g i v / c ef j / G K P
GCSE: BC d g i v / c ef j / G K OP
OTHER: C d k kl / cd l / G I K O R U W

SCOTLAND

SCOTLAND *continued*

C — Ardvreck School; Crieff; Perthshire; PH7 4EX
Tel: 01764 653112 (Fax: 01764 654920) *N.Gardner*

		Boys	Age	Girls	Age	TOTAL		Boys	Girls
Day	£1550-£1620	27	4-12	15	4-12	128	SIXTH		
Weekly									
Boarding	£2525-£2650	58	8-13	28	8-13				

ENTRY REQUIREMENTS Interview
SCHOLARSHIPS & BURSARIES Schol; Burs; AP
SPECIAL NEEDS ejklnuw Gl   **DYSLEXIA** df   **DIET** a
ASSOCIATION IAPS   **FOUNDED** 1883   **RELIGIOUS AFFILIATION** Inter-denom

MAP14 G 2
LOCATION Rural
DAY   **RAIL** b   **AIR** a
SPORT abdefhjkmnopqstux AB
OTHER LANGUAGES
ACTIVITIES cfghijmnoqstwx A
OTHER SUBJECTS abcfh
FACILITIES ON SITE abi
EXAM BOARDS
RETAKES   **NVQ COURSES**

A-level   AS   GCSE
OTHER   e   Imno   v
BC   G   K   R
cde   j

C — Beaconhurst Grange; 52 Kenilworth Road; Bridge-of-Allan; Stirling FK9 4RR
Tel: 01786 832146 (Fax: 01786 833415) *D.R.Clegg*

		Boys	Age	Girls	Age	TOTAL		Boys	Girls
Day	£349-£1413	127	3-16	114	3-16	241	SIXTH		
Weekly									
Boarding									

ENTRY REQUIREMENTS Interview
SCHOLARSHIPS & BURSARIES Schol; Mus
SPECIAL NEEDS   **DYSLEXIA**   **DIET** a
ASSOCIATION IAPS   **FOUNDED** 1919   **RELIGIOUS AFFILIATION** Inter-denom

MAP13 F 3
LOCATION Urban
DAY ✓   **RAIL** a   **AIR** a
SPORT acefjklmpswx AB
OTHER LANGUAGES a
ACTIVITIES cfghijoqw A
OTHER SUBJECTS bch
FACILITIES ON SITE h
EXAM BOARDS l
RETAKES   **NVQ COURSES**

A-level   AS   GCSE
OTHER   e g i   v
B   G   K   OP
cdef   j

C — Belhaven Hill; Dunbar; East Lothian EH42 1NN
Tel: 01368 862785 (Fax: 01368 865225) *I.M.Osborne*

		Boys	Age	Girls	Age	TOTAL		Boys	Girls
Day	£1950	3	8-13		8-13	73	SIXTH		
Weekly	£2770	16	8-13		8-13				
Boarding	£2795	54	8-13		8-13				

ENTRY REQUIREMENTS Interview
SCHOLARSHIPS & BURSARIES AP
SPECIAL NEEDS B   **DYSLEXIA**   **DIET**
ASSOCIATION IAPS   **FOUNDED** 1923   **RELIGIOUS AFFILIATION** Non-denom

MAP14 J 3
LOCATION Rural
DAY   **RAIL** a   **AIR** a
SPORT abcdefjklmqsuwx AB
OTHER LANGUAGES
ACTIVITIES afgijmoprw A
OTHER SUBJECTS ch
FACILITIES ON SITE hj
EXAM BOARDS
RETAKES   **NVQ COURSES**

A-level   AS   GCSE
OTHER   e g i   l
B   G   K   OP R
cde g   j

Gb — Butterstone School; Arthurstone; Meigle; Perthshire; Scotland PH12 8QY
Tel: 01828 640528 (Fax: 01828 640640) *C.G.Syers-Gibson*

		Boys	Age	Girls	Age	TOTAL		Boys	Girls
Day	£983-£1855	22	3- 9	31	3-13	82	SIXTH		
Weekly	£2988			1					
Boarding	£2988			28	8-13				

ENTRY REQUIREMENTS Interview
SCHOLARSHIPS & BURSARIES Schol; Burs; AP
SPECIAL NEEDS abcegjklnpqstw BEGHIKL   **DYSLEXIA** e   **DIET** abcd
ASSOCIATION IAPS   **FOUNDED** 1947   **RELIGIOUS AFFILIATION** C of S

MAP14 H 1
LOCATION Rural
DAY   **RAIL** b   **AIR** b
SPORT acmpqvx AB
OTHER LANGUAGES
ACTIVITIES acfghijoqstw A
OTHER SUBJECTS abch
FACILITIES ON SITE ae
EXAM BOARDS
RETAKES   **NVQ COURSES**

A-level   AS   GCSE
OTHER   e g i   lmn   v
BC   G   K   OP R
cde   j

C — Cargilfield; Barnton Avenue West; Edinburgh EH4 6HU
Tel: 0131 336 2207 (Fax: 0131 336 3179) *A.J.S.Bateman*

		Boys	Age	Girls	Age	TOTAL		Boys	Girls
Day	£465-£2050	71	3-13	40	3-13	191	SIXTH		
Weekly	£2880	25	8-13	8	8-13				
Boarding	£2880	27	8-13	20	8-13				

ENTRY REQUIREMENTS Test & Interview
SCHOLARSHIPS & BURSARIES Forces; AP; Siblings
SPECIAL NEEDS an BL   **DYSLEXIA** e   **DIET** ab
ASSOCIATION IAPS   **FOUNDED** 1873   • **RELIGIOUS AFFILIATION** Inter-denom

MAP14 H 3
LOCATION Urban
DAY   **RAIL** b   **AIR** a
SPORT abcefhjklm nopqstuwx AB
OTHER LANGUAGES
ACTIVITIES acfghijnoqrtw A
OTHER SUBJECTS abch
FACILITIES ON SITE acdhik
EXAM BOARDS
RETAKES   **NVQ COURSES**

A-level   AS   GCSE
OTHER   cde g i   lm o q s   v
AB   G   K   OP R
cdefg   j   l

SCOTLAND continued

Clifton Hall School; Newbridge; Edinburgh EH28 8LQ
Tel: 0131 333 1359 (Fax: 0131 333 4609) *M.A.M.Adams*

		Boys	Age	Girls	Age	TOTAL		Boys	Girls
Day	£180-£1800	- 68	3-11	51	3-11	125	SIXTH		
Weekly	£2475	5	7-11	1	7-11				
Boarding									

ENTRY REQUIREMENTS Assessment & Interview
SCHOLARSHIPS & BURSARIES Schol; Burs; Forces; AP
SPECIAL NEEDS abeijlnqvwx ABEGHI
ASSOCIATION IAPS   **FOUNDED** 1930

DYSLEXIA e   **DIET** ad
RELIGIOUS AFFILIATION Inter-denom

MAP14 H 3
LOCATION Rural
DAY ✓   **RAIL** b   **AIR** a
SPORT acdefgjklmopqsx ABD
OTHER LANGUAGES
ACTIVITIES cfghijnov A
OTHER SUBJECTS bcdh
FACILITIES ON SITE bhikl
EXAM BOARDS
RETAKES   **NVQ COURSES**

A-level — **AS** — **GCSE** e g i lmno q   uv   BC   G   K   OP R   cdef   j
OTHER

Craigclowan Prep. School; Edinburgh Road; Perth PH2 8PS
Tel: 01738 626310 (Fax: 01738 440349) *M.E.Beale*

		Boys	Age	Girls	Age	TOTAL		Boys	Girls
Day	£1345	125	3-13	115	3-13	240	SIXTH		
Weekly									
Boarding									

ENTRY REQUIREMENTS Interview
SCHOLARSHIPS & BURSARIES Burs; Teachers; AP; Siblings
SPECIAL NEEDS elnt B
ASSOCIATION IAPS   **FOUNDED** 1952

DYSLEXIA de   **DIET** ad
RELIGIOUS AFFILIATION Inter-denom

MAP14 H 2
LOCATION Rural
DAY   **RAIL** a   **AIR** a
SPORT acefgklmpqsx B
OTHER LANGUAGES
ACTIVITIES cfghijoq A
OTHER SUBJECTS bcfh
FACILITIES ON SITE bch
EXAM BOARDS
RETAKES   **NVQ COURSES**

A-level — **AS** — **GCSE** cde g i lmno   s v   B   G   K   P R   cde   j l
OTHER

Croftinloan School; Pitlochry; Perthshire PH16 5JR
Tel: 01796 472057 (Fax: 01796 473962) *Nicholas J Heuvel*

		Boys	Age	Girls	Age	TOTAL		Boys	Girls
Day	£1010-£1966	6	8-13	3	8-13	79	SIXTH		
Weekly			8-13		8-13				
Boarding	£2790	38	8-13	32	8-13				

ENTRY REQUIREMENTS Interview
SCHOLARSHIPS & BURSARIES Schol; Burs; Forces; Clergy; Teachers; AP; Siblings
SPECIAL NEEDS abejlnqtuw BEGI
ASSOCIATION IAPS   **FOUNDED** 1936

DYSLEXIA e   **DIET** a
RELIGIOUS AFFILIATION Inter-denom

MAP16 H 8
LOCATION Rural
DAY   **RAIL** a   **AIR** b
SPORT acdefjklmopqstuwx AB
OTHER LANGUAGES a
ACTIVITIES acfghijmnopqrstx A
OTHER SUBJECTS bcfh
FACILITIES ON SITE abdhik
EXAM BOARDS
RETAKES   **NVQ COURSES**

A-level — **AS** — **GCSE** de g i lmno q   v   B   G   K   NOP R   cde   j l
OTHER

Dollar Academy; Dollar; Clackmannanshire FK14 7DU
Tel: 01259 742511 (Fax: 01259 742867) *J.S.Robertson*

		Boys	Age	Girls	Age	TOTAL		Boys	Girls
Day	£1045-£1383	485	5-18	464	5-18	1110	SIXTH	127	112
Weekly	£2567-£2905	13	9-19	6	9-19				
Boarding	£2727-£3065	82	9-19	60	9-19				

ENTRY REQUIREMENTS
SCHOLARSHIPS & BURSARIES Schol; AP
SPECIAL NEEDS bejklnqtuw ABEHI
ASSOCIATION HMC   **FOUNDED** 1818

DYSLEXIA de   **DIET** acd
RELIGIOUS AFFILIATION Non-denom

MAP14 G 2
LOCATION Rural
DAY   **RAIL** b   **AIR** a
SPORT abcdefghjklmpqstuwx ABCD
OTHER LANGUAGES ae
ACTIVITIES cefghijklmnopqstuvwx ABD
OTHER SUBJECTS abcdefgh
FACILITIES ON SITE bcghikl
EXAM BOARDS EHI
RETAKES   **NVQ COURSES**

A-level a de ghij l   op r   v x   ABC   G I K   P   U   cdefg   j l
AS a cd fg ij l   nopqr   v   ABC   GHI K   P   U W   cdefg   j l
GCSE a cd fghi   l   op r   vw   ABC   G   K   P   W
OTHER f   lmn   u   C   K MNO   i

Drumley House School; Nr. Ayr; Ayrshire KA6 5AT
Tel: 01292 520340 (Fax: 01292 520340) *C.F.Robinson*

		Boys	Age	Girls	Age	TOTAL		Boys	Girls
Day	£410-£1498	85	3-13	28	3-13	113	SIXTH		
Weekly									
Boarding									

ENTRY REQUIREMENTS Test & Interview
SCHOLARSHIPS & BURSARIES Schol; Mus
SPECIAL NEEDS B
ASSOCIATION IAPS   **FOUNDED** 1960

DYSLEXIA   **DIET** a
RELIGIOUS AFFILIATION Inter-denom

MAP13 E 5
LOCATION Rural
DAY ✓   **RAIL** b   **AIR** b
SPORT abefjklmopqsux AB
OTHER LANGUAGES
ACTIVITIES cghjoptw A
OTHER SUBJECTS cfh
FACILITIES ON SITE ahk
EXAM BOARDS
RETAKES   **NVQ COURSES**

A-level — **AS** — **GCSE** e g i lmno   s v   B   G   K   OP R   cde
OTHER

317

SCOTLAND continued

C — Dundee High School; P.O.Box 16; Dundee DD1 9BP
Tel: 01382 202921 (Fax: 01382 229822) *R.Nimmo*

		Boys	Age	Girls	Age	TOTAL		Boys	Girls
Day	£915-£1303	596	5-18	547	5-18	1143	SIXTH	135	106
Weekly									
Boarding									

ENTRY REQUIREMENTS Interview
SCHOLARSHIPS & BURSARIES Burs; AP
SPECIAL NEEDS ejknqw **DYSLEXIA** e **DIET**
ASSOCIATION HMC **FOUNDED** 1239 **RELIGIOUS AFFILIATION** Inter-denom

MAP14 I 1
LOCATION Inner City
DAY **RAIL** a **AIR** b
SPORT abcegkmpsuwx AB
OTHER LANGUAGES
ACTIVITIES cefghijkmostx AB
OTHER SUBJECTS aceg
FACILITIES ON SITE ab
EXAM BOARDS I
RETAKES **NVQ COURSES**

A-level: de ghi l pq v BC G K P U cdefg jkl
AS: de ghi l n pqr v ABC G K OP U cdefg jkl
GCSE: a de ghi l pqr v x ABC G K OP R U cdefg jkl
OTHER: mn q t l O R

Bg — Edinburgh Academy,The; Henderson Row; Edinburgh EH3 5BL
Tel: 0131 556 4603 (Fax: 0131 556 9353) *J.V.Light*

		Boys	Age	Girls	Age	TOTAL		Boys	Girls
Day	£1695	445	10-18	12	16-18	500	SIXTH	123	32
Weekly	£3516		10-18		16-18				
Boarding	£3614	38	10-18	5	16-18				

ENTRY REQUIREMENTS CEE & Interview; Report & Exam & Interview
SCHOLARSHIPS & BURSARIES Schol; Burs; Art; Mus; Teachers; AP; VI Form
SPECIAL NEEDS bgjklnpqstuvwx AGHI **DYSLEXIA** def **DIET** abcd
ASSOCIATION HMC **FOUNDED** 1824 **RELIGIOUS AFFILIATION** Inter-denom

MAP14 H 3
LOCATION Urban
DAY ✓ **RAIL** a **AIR** a
SPORT abcdefghijkmopstuwx AB
OTHER LANGUAGES
ACTIVITIES efghijkloqrstw ABD
OTHER SUBJECTS bcfh
FACILITIES ON SITE bcgk
EXAM BOARDS b ABEHI
RETAKES ab **NVQ COURSES**

A-level: cde ghi l opq v x B GH K P R U c efg jk
AS: e ghi l p B G K P defg jk
GCSE: cde ghi l opq v B G K P U cdefg jk
OTHER: q K c

Bg — Edinburgh Academy Prep. School,The; 10 Arboretum Road; Edinburgh EH3 5PL
Tel: 0131 552 3690 (Fax: 0131 556 9353) *C.R.F.Paterson*

		Boys	Age	Girls	Age	TOTAL		Boys	Girls
Day	£725-£1189	347	3-11	12	3-5	359	SIXTH		
Weekly	£3010		8-11						
Boarding	£3108		8-11						

ENTRY REQUIREMENTS Report & Exam & Interview
SCHOLARSHIPS & BURSARIES Schol
SPECIAL NEEDS B **DYSLEXIA** **DIET** abcd
ASSOCIATION IAPS **FOUNDED** 1824 **RELIGIOUS AFFILIATION** Inter-denom

MAP14 H 3
LOCATION Urban
DAY ✓ **RAIL** a **AIR** a
SPORT abcefgjlmosw ABC
OTHER LANGUAGES
ACTIVITIES fghijoqr A
OTHER SUBJECTS ach
FACILITIES ON SITE bhk
EXAM BOARDS
RETAKES **NVQ COURSES**

OTHER: e l o uv B E G K O R cde j

C — Fettes College; Carrington Road; Edinburgh EH4 1QX
Tel: 0131 332 2281 (Fax: 0131 332 3081) *M.T.Thyne*

		Boys	Age	Girls	Age	TOTAL		Boys	Girls
Day	£1745-£2745	47	10-18	55	10-18	474	SIXTH	78	80
Weekly	£2745	6		1					
Boarding	£2785-£4085	204	10-18	161	10-18				

ENTRY REQUIREMENTS Report & Exam & Interview
SCHOLARSHIPS & BURSARIES Schol; Burs; Mus; Forces; Clergy; Teachers; AP; VI Form; Siblings
SPECIAL NEEDS bejklnqtw l **DYSLEXIA** **DIET** ab
ASSOCIATION HMC **FOUNDED** 1870 **RELIGIOUS AFFILIATION** Inter-denom

MAP14 H 3
LOCATION Urban
DAY **RAIL** a **AIR** a
SPORT abcdefgikmnpstuwx BC
OTHER LANGUAGES a
ACTIVITIES acdefghijklmnoqstw ABD
OTHER SUBJECTS bcfh
FACILITIES ON SITE abcdeghik
EXAM BOARDS abc AEHI
RETAKES b **NVQ COURSES**

A-level: a efghi l op v AB GH K P R U cdefg jkl
AS: e g i op v B G K P R cdef j l
GCSE: a e ghi l nop v AB G K P U cdefg jkl
OTHER:

C — George Heriot's School; Lauriston Place; Edinburgh EH3 9EQ
Tel: 0131 229 7263 (Fax: 0131 229 6363) *K.P.Pearson*

		Boys	Age	Girls	Age	TOTAL		Boys	Girls
Day	£715-£1250	891	3-18	654	3-18	1545	SIXTH	182	122
Weekly									
Boarding									

ENTRY REQUIREMENTS Test; Exam & Interview
SCHOLARSHIPS & BURSARIES Schol; Burs; AP
SPECIAL NEEDS begjlnqtw BH **DYSLEXIA** de **DIET** a
ASSOCIATION HMC **FOUNDED** 1628 * **RELIGIOUS AFFILIATION** Non-denom

MAP14 H 3
LOCATION Inner City
DAY **RAIL** a **AIR** a
SPORT abcefghklmpqrstuwx ABC
OTHER LANGUAGES e
ACTIVITIES aefghijklmnoqrstuvwx AB
OTHER SUBJECTS bcdefgh
FACILITIES ON SITE bdeik
EXAM BOARDS IL
RETAKES **NVQ COURSES**

A-level: a cde ghij l op v ABC G K P U cdefg j l
AS: a de gi l p vw ABC G K P R c efghi j l
GCSE: a de gi l p vw ABC G K P R efg j l
OTHER: c efghj l

SCOTLAND continued

C — George Watson's College; Colinton Road; Edinburgh EH10 5EG
Tel: 0131 447 7931 (Fax: 0131 452 8594) *F.E.Gerstenberg*

		Boys	Age	Girls	Age	TOTAL		Boys	Girls
Day	£308-£1380	1158	3-18	943	3-18	2144	SIXTH	219	183
Weekly			11-18		11-18				
Boarding	£2760	34	11-18	9	11-18				

ENTRY REQUIREMENTS Exam; Interview
SCHOLARSHIPS & BURSARIES Schol; Burs; Mus; AP; VI Form
SPECIAL NEEDS beghijklmnqstw BEGHI **DYSLEXIA** cde **DIET** abcd
ASSOCIATION HMC **FOUNDED** 1723 **RELIGIOUS AFFILIATION** Inter-denom

MAP14 H 3
LOCATION Urban
DAY ✓ **RAIL** a **AIR** a
SPORT abcefghklmprstuwx ABCD
OTHER LANGUAGES ae
ACTIVITIES cfghijklmnopqrstuwx AB
OTHER SUBJECTS abcefgh
FACILITIES ON SITE abcehik
EXAM BOARDS I
RETAKES **NVQ COURSES**

A-level
AS
GCSE
OTHER a de ghi l nopqr uvwx
ABC GHI K M OP R U W
bcdefgh jkl

C — Glasgow Academy, The; Colebrooke Street; Glasgow G12 8HE
Tel: 0141 334 8558 (Fax: 0141 337 3473) *D.Comins*

		Boys	Age	Girls	Age	TOTAL		Boys	Girls
Day	£915-£1430	729	4-18	314	4-18	1043	SIXTH	149	51
Weekly									
Boarding									

ENTRY REQUIREMENTS Exam & Interview
SCHOLARSHIPS & BURSARIES Schol; Burs; AP
SPECIAL NEEDS abklnq B **DYSLEXIA** e **DIET** acd
ASSOCIATION HMC **FOUNDED** 1846 **RELIGIOUS AFFILIATION** C of S

MAP13 F 4
LOCATION Inner City
DAY **RAIL** a **AIR** a
SPORT abcefghjklmopstuwx BCD
OTHER LANGUAGES
ACTIVITIES cefghijklnoqst AB
OTHER SUBJECTS cefgh
FACILITIES ON SITE abchk
EXAM BOARDS HI
RETAKES **NVQ COURSES**

A-level efg i v
B GH K P
c efg j
AS
GCSE d
OTHER d ghi l p v
BC G K NOP
cdefgh j l

C — Glasgow, The High School of; 637 Crow Road; Glasgow G13 1PL
Tel: 0141 954 9628 (Fax: 0141 959 0191) *Robin G.Easton*

		Boys	Age	Girls	Age	TOTAL		Boys	Girls
Day	£498-£1422	496	3-18	493	3-18	989	SIXTH	97	79
Weekly									
Boarding									

ENTRY REQUIREMENTS Report & Exam & Interview
SCHOLARSHIPS & BURSARIES Schol; Burs; AP
SPECIAL NEEDS begklnt CDGHL **DYSLEXIA** e **DIET** abcd
ASSOCIATION HMC **FOUNDED** 1124 **RELIGIOUS AFFILIATION** Inter-denom

MAP13 F 4
LOCATION Urban
DAY **RAIL** a **AIR** a
SPORT abcefghjklmopstwx ABC
OTHER LANGUAGES
ACTIVITIES bcfghijknopqrst AB
OTHER SUBJECTS abcdfgh
FACILITIES ON SITE bgh
EXAM BOARDS IL
RETAKES **NVQ COURSES**

A-level a defg i l p v x
B G K PQ U
cdef j
AS a d ghi l p v x
BC G K P R
cdefg j l
GCSE d g i l p v x
BC G K P R
cdefg j l
OTHER n q u
E I NO W

C — Glenalmond College; Perth PH1 3RY
Tel: 01738 880442 (Fax: 01738 880410) *I.G.Templeton*

		Boys	Age	Girls	Age	TOTAL		Boys	Girls
Day	£1995-£2660	✗	18	12-18		16-18	263	SIXTH	87	28
Weekly									
Boarding	£2995-£3990		217	12-18	28	16-18			

ENTRY REQUIREMENTS CEE; Scholarship Exam; Report & Exam & Interview
SCHOLARSHIPS & BURSARIES Schol; Burs; Art; Mus; Forces; Clergy; AP; VI Form
SPECIAL NEEDS bejkln EGI **DYSLEXIA** **DIET** acd
ASSOCIATION HMC **FOUNDED** 1841 **RELIGIOUS AFFILIATION**

MAP14 H 2
LOCATION Rural
DAY ✓ **RAIL** b **AIR** a
SPORT abcdefghjkmopqrstuwx ABC
OTHER LANGUAGES a
ACTIVITIES efghijkmnoqsuw AB
OTHER SUBJECTS abcdh
FACILITIES ON SITE abcdeghikl
EXAM BOARDS bcd DHIL
RETAKES **NVQ COURSES**

A-level c efg i l opq v
B GH K P R
cdefg j l
AS g i v
B G
cde
GCSE c e g i l o q vw
B G K P R U
cdefg j l
OTHER h

C — Gordonstoun School; Elgin; Moray IV30 2RF
Tel: 01343 830 445 (Fax: 01343 830 074) *M.C.S-R.Pyper*

		Boys	Age	Girls	Age	TOTAL		Boys	Girls
Day	£2603	✗	12	13-18	7	13-18	457	SIXTH	112	101
Weekly									
Boarding	£4035		254	13-18	184	13-18			

ENTRY REQUIREMENTS CEE; Exam; Scholarship Exam; Report; Report & Interview
SCHOLARSHIPS & BURSARIES Schol; Burs; Mus; Forces; Teachers; AP; VI Form
SPECIAL NEEDS ln EG **DYSLEXIA** e **DIET** a
ASSOCIATION HMC **FOUNDED** 1934 **RELIGIOUS AFFILIATION** Inter-denom

MAP16 I 5
LOCATION Rural
DAY **RAIL** a **AIR** b
SPORT abcdefghjkmopqstuvwx ABC
OTHER LANGUAGES a
ACTIVITIES abcefghijklmnopqstw A
OTHER SUBJECTS abcdefh
FACILITIES ON SITE abcdghi
EXAM BOARDS abde ABEGH
RETAKES ab **NVQ COURSES**

A-level defghi nop vwx
B GH K P U
c ef j l
AS G K
GCSE de h l no vw
B D GH K O X
cdef hj l
OTHER l u
O R
def h kl

SCOTLAND continued

C — Hutchesons' Grammar School; 21 Beaton Road; Glasgow G41 4NW
Tel: 0141 423 2933 (Fax: 0141 424 0251) *D.R.Ward*

		Boys	Age	Girls	Age	TOTAL		Boys	Girls
Day	£1038-£1279	951	5-19	862	5-19	1813	SIXTH	195	160
Weekly									
Boarding									

MAP 13 F 4
LOCATION Urban
DAY   **RAIL** a   **AIR** a
SPORT abcdefgjkmoprsx ABCD
OTHER LANGUAGES
ACTIVITIES acfghijkopqrs AB
OTHER SUBJECTS bch
FACILITIES ON SITE k
EXAM BOARDS BDEI
RETAKES b   **NVQ COURSES**

ENTRY REQUIREMENTS Exam & Interview
SCHOLARSHIPS & BURSARIES Schol; Burs; AP
SPECIAL NEEDS jlq GIJ   **DYSLEXIA**   **DIET** a
ASSOCIATION HMC   **FOUNDED** 1641   **RELIGIOUS AFFILIATION** Non-denom

A-level: a de ghij l   p   uv x   ABC GHI K M P   cdefg j l
AS:
GCSE: d g i l   p   v x   BC G K   P   cdefg jk
OTHER: a cde g i   mn pq   v x   BC G I K MNOP R   W   cdefg l

C — Keil School; Helenslee Road; Dumbarton G82 4AL
Tel: 01389 762003 (Fax: 01389 764267) *J.A.Cummings*

		Boys	Age	Girls	Age	TOTAL		Boys	Girls
Day	£1498-£1747	65	10-18	50	10-18	207	SIXTH	40	15
Weekly	£3065-£3119								
Boarding	£3065-£3119	71	10-18	21	10-18				

MAP 13 E 3
LOCATION Rural
DAY ✓   **RAIL** a   **AIR** a
SPORT abcefghjkmpstwx ABCD
OTHER LANGUAGES ae
ACTIVITIES fghijkmopqsw AB
OTHER SUBJECTS cdh
FACILITIES ON SITE abch
EXAM BOARDS DEHI
RETAKES b   **NVQ COURSES**

ENTRY REQUIREMENTS Test; Interview
SCHOLARSHIPS & BURSARIES Schol; Burs; Forces; AP; Siblings
SPECIAL NEEDS bejklnpw E   **DYSLEXIA** d   **DIET** ad
ASSOCIATION SHMIS   **FOUNDED** 1915   **RELIGIOUS AFFILIATION** C of S

A-level: e   v   B G   P   cdef
AS: e g i   op   v   AB G K   P   cde
GCSE: e g i   o   v   AB G K   P   cdef
OTHER: a   l   k

B — Kelvinside Academy; 33 Kirklee Road; Glasgow G12 0SW
Tel: 0141 357 3376 (Fax: 0141 357 5401) *J.H.Duff*

		Boys	Age	Girls	Age	TOTAL		Boys	Girls
Day	£795-£1485	546	4-18			546	SIXTH	118	
Weekly									
Boarding									

MAP 13 F 4
LOCATION Urban
DAY ✓   **RAIL** a   **AIR** a
SPORT abcdefghjklmostuwx ABCD
OTHER LANGUAGES
ACTIVITIES efghijklnopq AB
OTHER SUBJECTS abch
FACILITIES ON SITE abhk
EXAM BOARDS CF
RETAKES   **NVQ COURSES**

ENTRY REQUIREMENTS Test & Interview
SCHOLARSHIPS & BURSARIES Schol; AP
SPECIAL NEEDS bjklnpqstw Gl   **DYSLEXIA** de   **DIET** acd
ASSOCIATION HMC   **FOUNDED** 1878   **RELIGIOUS AFFILIATION** C of S

A-level: d g i   p   uv   B GH K M   P R U   cdef j
AS: d fg i l   p   tuv   B G I K   OP R   cdefg j
GCSE: d g i l   pq   uvw   B G K   OP R   cdefg j
OTHER: l n q   t   G I K   O   U   cde

G — Kilgraston School; Bridge of Earn; Perthshire PH2 9BQ
Tel: 01738 812257 (Fax: 01738 813410) *Mrs Juliet L Austin*

		Boys	Age	Girls	Age	TOTAL		Boys	Girls
Day	£1230-£1885			115	5-18	269	SIXTH		81
Weekly	£2965-£3275			63	8-18				
Boarding	£2965-£3275			91	8-18				

MAP 14 H 2
LOCATION Rural
DAY ✓   **RAIL** a   **AIR** a
SPORT acfghklmopquvwx ABCD
OTHER LANGUAGES ace
ACTIVITIES cfghijklmnopqstw A
OTHER SUBJECTS bcdefgh
FACILITIES ON SITE abdeghk
EXAM BOARDS BDGHI
RETAKES   **NVQ COURSES**

ENTRY REQUIREMENTS Report & Exam & Interview
SCHOLARSHIPS & BURSARIES Schol; Burs; Art; Mus; Teachers; AP; VI Form
SPECIAL NEEDS egjklnqtw GH   **DYSLEXIA** ef   **DIET** acd
ASSOCIATION GSA   **FOUNDED** 1930   **RELIGIOUS AFFILIATION** RC/Inter-denom

A-level: cd fg i   v   BC G   P   cdef l
AS: cd g i l n   v   BC G K   P R   cdef j l
GCSE: cd g i l   v   BC G K   P R   cdef hj l
OTHER: n   A   O   W

C — Lathallan School; Montrose; Angus DD10 0HN
Tel: 01561 362220 (Fax: 01561 361695) *P.F.Fawkes*

		Boys	Age	Girls	Age	TOTAL		Boys	Girls
Day	£1239-£1778	46	5-13	27	5-13	128	SIXTH		
Weekly	£2749	16	7-13	4	7-13				
Boarding	£2812	22	7-13	13	7-13				

MAP 14 K 8
LOCATION Rural
DAY ✓   **RAIL** a   **AIR** a
SPORT abcefkmopqsuvx AB
OTHER LANGUAGES
ACTIVITIES abcfghijlmnoqrtvw A
OTHER SUBJECTS acfh
FACILITIES ON SITE abchk
EXAM BOARDS
RETAKES   **NVQ COURSES**

ENTRY REQUIREMENTS Test & Interview
SCHOLARSHIPS & BURSARIES Schol; Burs; Art; Mus; Forces; Teachers; AP; Sport; Drama; Siblings
SPECIAL NEEDS an BE   **DYSLEXIA** e   **DIET** abcd
ASSOCIATION IAPS   **FOUNDED** 1930   **RELIGIOUS AFFILIATION** Inter-denom

A-level:
AS:
GCSE:
OTHER: e i l o   v   AB G K   OP S   cdef j

SCOTLAND *continued*

Gb Laurel Bank School; 4 Lilybank Terrace; Glasgow G12 8RX
Tel: 0141 339 9127 (Fax: 0141 357 5530) *Mrs E.Surber*

		Boys	Age	Girls	Age	TOTAL		Boys	Girls
Day	£861-£1422	13	3-5	376	3-18	389	SIXTH		66
Weekly									
Boarding									

ENTRY REQUIREMENTS Test & Interview
SCHOLARSHIPS & BURSARIES AP
SPECIAL NEEDS jknqw BGHI   **DYSLEXIA** de   **DIET** a
ASSOCIATION GSA   **FOUNDED** 1903   **RELIGIOUS AFFILIATION** Non-denom

MAP13 F 4
LOCATION Urban
DAY   **RAIL** a   **AIR** a
SPORT aclmpwx ABC
OTHER LANGUAGES
ACTIVITIES ghijko A
OTHER SUBJECTS bch
FACILITIES ON SITE bk
EXAM BOARDS I
RETAKES   **NVQ COURSES**

A-level: egi l v / BC GH P / cdefg j
AS: d gi l p v / BC G K P / cdefg j l
GCSE: d g i l n v / BC G K P / cdefg j l
OTHER: x / I M O U / k

C Lomond School; Stafford Street; Helensburgh; Dunbartonshire G84 9JX
Tel: 01436 672476 (Fax: 01436 678320) *A.D.Macdonald*

		Boys	Age	Girls	Age	TOTAL		Boys	Girls
Day	£430-£1515	221	2-18	205	2-18	501	SIXTH	47	50
Weekly	£3070-£3205	1	10-18	2	10-18				
Boarding	£3175-£3310	38	10-18	34	10-18				

ENTRY REQUIREMENTS Test & Interview
SCHOLARSHIPS & BURSARIES Schol; Mus; Forces; Teachers; AP; VI Form
SPECIAL NEEDS bjklnqstvwx ABGHI   **DYSLEXIA** ef   **DIET** a
ASSOCIATION GBA   **FOUNDED** 1977   **RELIGIOUS AFFILIATION** Non-denom

MAP13 E 3
LOCATION Urban
DAY   **RAIL** a   **AIR** a
SPORT abcdefghjklmopqrstuvwx ABCD
OTHER LANGUAGES ae
ACTIVITIES cfghijkmnopqrstuvwx AB
OTHER SUBJECTS abcdegh
FACILITIES ON SITE abgk
EXAM BOARDS EI
RETAKES b   **NVQ COURSES** 123

A-level: egi l v / AB G K P / cdef
AS:
GCSE:
OTHER: a e gi jl op* v / AB G K OP R W / cdef l

C Loretto Junior School; North Esk Lodge; Musselburgh; Midlothian; EH21 6JA
Tel: 0131 665 2628 (Fax: 0131 665 1815) *David P.Clark*

		Boys	Age	Girls	Age	TOTAL		Boys	Girls
Day	£1900-£1946	21	8-13	3	8-13	73	SIXTH		
Weekly	£2850-£2920	13	8-13	1	8-13				
Boarding	£2850-£2920	33	8-13	2	8-13				

ENTRY REQUIREMENTS Test & Interview
SCHOLARSHIPS & BURSARIES Schol; Burs; Forces; AP
SPECIAL NEEDS jn   **DYSLEXIA**   **DIET** a
ASSOCIATION IAPS   **FOUNDED** 1891   **RELIGIOUS AFFILIATION** Inter-denom

MAP14 H 3
LOCATION
DAY   **RAIL** b   **AIR** a
SPORT acefijklmnpqswx AB
OTHER LANGUAGES
ACTIVITIES cfgijoqtw A
OTHER SUBJECTS c
FACILITIES ON SITE acdhik
EXAM BOARDS
RETAKES   **NVQ COURSES**

A-level:
AS:
GCSE:
OTHER: e v / B G K O / cde j

C Loretto School; Musselburgh; Midlothian EH21 7RE
Tel: 0131 665 2567 (Fax: 0131 653 2773) *Keith J.Budge*

		Boys	Age	Girls	Age	TOTAL		Boys	Girls
Day	£2580	11	13-18		13-18	307	SIXTH	107	41
Weekly									
Boarding	£3870	255	13-18	41	13-18				

ENTRY REQUIREMENTS CEE; Scholarship Exam; Assessment & Interview
SCHOLARSHIPS & BURSARIES Schol; Burs; Art; Mus; AP; VI Form
SPECIAL NEEDS bhlns B   **DYSLEXIA** e   **DIET** a
ASSOCIATION HMC   **FOUNDED** 1827   **RELIGIOUS AFFILIATION** Ecum

MAP14 H 3
LOCATION Urban
DAY   **RAIL** b   **AIR** a
SPORT abcefghijkmnopstuwx ABC
OTHER LANGUAGES
ACTIVITIES abcefghijklmnopqstuw ACD
OTHER SUBJECTS abcdfh
FACILITIES ON SITE bcdeghik
EXAM BOARDS abc ABDEHI
RETAKES b   **NVQ COURSES**

A-level: cdefghi opq v x / AB GH K P R U / c efg j
AS:
GCSE: de gi o q v / AB E G K P R U X / cdefg j
OTHER: I NO / d

C Mary Erskine and Stewart's Melville Jnr School,The; Queensferry Road; Edinburgh EH4 3EZ Tel: 0131 332 0888 (Fax: 0131 332 0831) *Bryan Lewis*

		Boys	Age	Girls	Age	TOTAL		Boys	Girls
Day	£580-£1140	586	3-12	541	3-12	1141	SIXTH		
Weekly									
Boarding	£2430	7	10-12	7	10-12				

ENTRY REQUIREMENTS Exam & Interview
SCHOLARSHIPS & BURSARIES Schol; AP
SPECIAL NEEDS behjklnqtw BGI   **DYSLEXIA**   **DIET** abcd
ASSOCIATION IAPS   **FOUNDED**   **RELIGIOUS AFFILIATION**

MAP14 H 3
LOCATION Urban
DAY ✓   **RAIL** a   **AIR** a
SPORT abcefglmoqsx ABC
OTHER LANGUAGES
ACTIVITIES cfghijoqtw A
OTHER SUBJECTS abcfh
FACILITIES ON SITE abchik
EXAM BOARDS
RETAKES   **NVQ COURSES**

A-level:
AS:
GCSE:
OTHER: e lmno q st v / BC E G K O R / cdef

321

SCOTLAND continued

Mary Erskine School; Ravelston; Edinburgh EH4 3NT
Tel: 0131 337 2391 (Fax: 0131 346 1137) *P.F.J.Tobin*

		Boys	Age	Girls	Age	TOTAL		Boys	Girls
Day	£1380			628	12-18	658	SIXTH		194
Weekly	£2760			2	12-18				
Boarding	£2760			28	12-18				

ENTRY REQUIREMENTS Exam & Interview
SCHOLARSHIPS & BURSARIES Schol; Burs; Mus; AP
SPECIAL NEEDS befklnq BGJ   **DYSLEXIA** e   **DIET** a
ASSOCIATION GSA   **FOUNDED** 1694   **RELIGIOUS AFFILIATION** Non-denom

MAP 14 H 3
LOCATION Inner City
DAY   **RAIL** a   **AIR** a
SPORT abcfgklmqrtuwx ABCD
OTHER LANGUAGES
ACTIVITIES cefghjklopqstw AB
OTHER SUBJECTS bcefgh
FACILITIES ON SITE abchi
EXAM BOARDS c HI
RETAKES   **NVQ COURSES**

A-level	d fg i p v	AS	a d fghi op v	GCSE	a d g i op v	OTHER	l n u
	B G K P U		BC G K OP R		BC G K OP R		K O R
	cdefg j		cdefg j l		cdefg j l		i

Merchiston Castle School; Colinton; Edinburgh EH13 0PU
Tel: 0131 441 1722 (Fax: 0131 441 6060) *D.M.Spawforth*

		Boys	Age	Girls	Age	TOTAL		Boys	Girls
Day	£1770-£2480	98	10-18			387	SIXTH	139	
Weekly									
Boarding	£2770-£3835	289	10-18						

ENTRY REQUIREMENTS CEE; Exam
SCHOLARSHIPS & BURSARIES Schol; Burs; Mus; Forces; Clergy; Teachers; AP; VI Form
SPECIAL NEEDS abefghjlnqrst ACDEHIJK   **DYSLEXIA** f   **DIET** acd
ASSOCIATION HMC   **FOUNDED** 1833   **RELIGIOUS AFFILIATION** Inter-denom

MAP 14 H 3
LOCATION Urban
DAY   **RAIL** b   **AIR** a
SPORT abcfghijklmostuwx ABC
OTHER LANGUAGES ai
ACTIVITIES acefghijklmnopqrstw ABC
OTHER SUBJECTS abcfh
FACILITIES ON SITE abcdeghik
EXAM BOARDS abc BDEGHI
RETAKES b   **NVQ COURSES**

A-level	d e g i o q v x	AS	d e g i q v	GCSE	d e g i o q v x	OTHER	k l
	AB GH K P R		B G K P R		AB G K P R		K N R
	abcdefg ij l		cdef j l		abcdefg j l		

Morrison's Academy; Crieff; Perthshire PH7 3AN
Tel: 01764 653885 (Fax: 01764 655411) *H.A.Ashmall*

		Boys	Age	Girls	Age	TOTAL		Boys	Girls
Day	£750-£1215	248	8-19	217	8-19	583	SIXTH	127	100
Weekly									
Boarding	£3173-£3530	85	8-19	33	8-19				

ENTRY REQUIREMENTS Test
SCHOLARSHIPS & BURSARIES Schol; Burs; AP; VI Form
SPECIAL NEEDS bhjklnqt GI   **DYSLEXIA** e   **DIET** ad
ASSOCIATION HMC   **FOUNDED** 1860   **RELIGIOUS AFFILIATION** Inter-denom

MAP 14 G 2
LOCATION Rural
DAY   **RAIL** b   **AIR** b
SPORT abcfgkmpstwx AB
OTHER LANGUAGES a
ACTIVITIES efghijkopq AB
OTHER SUBJECTS ce
FACILITIES ON SITE bhik
EXAM BOARDS DEHI
RETAKES b   **NVQ COURSES**

A-level	a d g i p v	AS	a d g i l p v	GCSE	a d g i l p v	OTHER	
	B GH P		B G K P		B G K P		
	c ef l		cdef l		cdef l		

New Park School; Hepburn Gardens; St. Andrews; Fife KY16 9LN
Tel: 01334 472017 (Fax: 01334 472859) *A.R.M.Donald*

		Boys	Age	Girls	Age	TOTAL		Boys	Girls
Day	£275-£1475 ✗	77	4-13	42	4-13	127	SIXTH		
Weekly	£2020	2	7-13		7-13				
Boarding	£2620	4	7-13	2	7-13				

ENTRY REQUIREMENTS Scholarship Exam; Interview
SCHOLARSHIPS & BURSARIES Schol
SPECIAL NEEDS bijklnpvw BEI   **DYSLEXIA** e   **DIET** a
ASSOCIATION IAPS   **FOUNDED** 1933   **RELIGIOUS AFFILIATION** Non-denom

MAP 14 I 2
LOCATION
DAY   **RAIL** b   **AIR** a
SPORT acefgjklmpswx AB
OTHER LANGUAGES
ACTIVITIES cfghjoqtw A
OTHER SUBJECTS ch
FACILITIES ON SITE
EXAM BOARDS
RETAKES   **NVQ COURSES**

A-level		AS		GCSE		OTHER	e g i l no v
							B G K OP
							cde j

Park School; 25 Lynedoch Street; Glasgow G3 6EX
Tel: 0141 332 0426 (Fax: 0141 332 1056) *Mrs M.E.Myatt*

		Boys	Age	Girls	Age	TOTAL		Boys	Girls
Day	£438-£1323			291	3-17	291	SIXTH		66
Weekly									
Boarding									

ENTRY REQUIREMENTS Test & Interview
SCHOLARSHIPS & BURSARIES Burs; AP
SPECIAL NEEDS bln   **DYSLEXIA** de   **DIET**
ASSOCIATION GSA   **FOUNDED** 1880   **RELIGIOUS AFFILIATION**

MAP 13 F 4
LOCATION Inner City
DAY   **RAIL** a   **AIR** a
SPORT abcghklmnopwx B
OTHER LANGUAGES
ACTIVITIES acghijkos B
OTHER SUBJECTS bcdfh
FACILITIES ON SITE bch
EXAM BOARDS EI
RETAKES   **NVQ COURSES**

A-level	e g i v	AS	d g i l p v	GCSE	d g i l v	OTHER	q
	B G P		B G K P		BC G K P		C N
	cdefg j		cdefg j l		cdefg j l		

SCOTLAND *continued*

C Rannoch School; Rannoch; Perthshire PH17 2QQ
Tel: 01882 632332 (Fax: 01882 632443) *M.Barratt*

		Boys	Age	Girls	Age	TOTAL		Boys	Girls
Day	£1830	8	10-18	3	10-18	254	SIXTH	65	20
Weekly									
Boarding	£2900-£3450	180	10-18	63	10-18				

ENTRY REQUIREMENTS CEE; Scholarship Exam; Interview; Report
SCHOLARSHIPS & BURSARIES Schol; Art; Mus; Forces; Clergy; Teachers; AP; VI Form; Siblings
SPECIAL NEEDS abjklnqtw BE   **DYSLEXIA** def   **DIET** acd
ASSOCIATION SHMIS   **FOUNDED** 1959   **RELIGIOUS AFFILIATION** Inter-denom

MAP 16 G 8
LOCATION Rural
DAY   **RAIL** b   **AIR** b
SPORT abcdefhjklmopqrstuvwx ABC
OTHER LANGUAGES e
ACTIVITIES acfghijklmnopqrstuw A
OTHER SUBJECTS abcfh
FACILITIES ON SITE bcdghikl
EXAM BOARDS abcd ADEI
RETAKES a   **NVQ COURSES**

A-level: defghi lm o q vw / ABC G K P / cdef l
AS: de g i l op vwx / B G K P / cdef
GCSE: de g j lm o q v x / ABC G K OP R U / cdef l
OTHER: i w / NO R U

C Robert Gordon's College; Schoolhill; Aberdeen AB9 1FE
Tel: 01224 646346 (Fax: 01224 630301) *G.A.Allan*

		Boys	Age	Girls	Age	TOTAL		Boys	Girls
Day	£845-£1300	942	4-17	431	4-17	1390	SIXTH	208	70
Weekly									
Boarding		11		6					

ENTRY REQUIREMENTS Test & Interview; Report & Interview
SCHOLARSHIPS & BURSARIES Schol; Burs; Teachers; AP; VI Form
SPECIAL NEEDS befjklnqt l   **DYSLEXIA** e   **DIET** a
ASSOCIATION HMC   **FOUNDED** 1732   **RELIGIOUS AFFILIATION** C of S

MAP 16 L 6
LOCATION Inner City
DAY   **RAIL** a   **AIR** a
SPORT abcdefhjklmnpsx ABCD
OTHER LANGUAGES
ACTIVITIES efghijklmnopqrsu AB
OTHER SUBJECTS cdfh
FACILITIES ON SITE abgik
EXAM BOARDS I
RETAKES   **NVQ COURSES**

A-level: a de g i op r v / B G K P / cdefgh j
AS: a cdefghi l op r v / AB G K P R / cdefgh j
GCSE: a de g i l op r v / AB G K P R / cdefgh j
OTHER: G / f

C St. Aloysius' College; 45 Hill Street; Glasgow G3 6RJ
Tel: 0141 332 3190 (Fax: 0141 353 0426) *Rev Adrian Porter SJ*

		Boys	Age	Girls	Age	TOTAL		Boys	Girls
Day	£1053	644	8-18	437	8-18	1081	SIXTH	124	106
Weekly									
Boarding									

ENTRY REQUIREMENTS Report & Test
SCHOLARSHIPS & BURSARIES Burs
SPECIAL NEEDS n   **DYSLEXIA** df   **DIET** ad
ASSOCIATION HMC   **FOUNDED** 1906   **RELIGIOUS AFFILIATION** R C

MAP
LOCATION Inner City
DAY   **RAIL** a   **AIR** a
SPORT cehjmswx A
OTHER LANGUAGES a
ACTIVITIES fgiot A
OTHER SUBJECTS c
FACILITIES ON SITE dh
EXAM BOARDS abd EI
RETAKES b   **NVQ COURSES**

A-level: d g i l p v / BC G K P / c efgh j
AS: d g i l p v / B G K P / defgh j
GCSE: d g i l p v / B G K P / defgh j
OTHER: M O R

C St. Columba's School; Duchal Road; Kilmacolm; Renfrewshire PA13 4AU
Tel: 01505 872238 (Fax: 01505 873995) *A.H.Livingstone*

		Boys	Age	Girls	Age	TOTAL		Boys	Girls
Day	£375-£1263	249	3-17	319	3-17	568	SIXTH	32	49
Weekly									
Boarding									

ENTRY REQUIREMENTS Assessment & Interview
SCHOLARSHIPS & BURSARIES AP
SPECIAL NEEDS   **DYSLEXIA**   **DIET** a
ASSOCIATION GBGSA   **FOUNDED** 1897   **RELIGIOUS AFFILIATION**

MAP 13 E 3
LOCATION Rural
DAY   **RAIL** b   **AIR** a
SPORT abcdefhjklmpswx ABC
OTHER LANGUAGES
ACTIVITIES acfghjknoqrt AB
OTHER SUBJECTS abcefgh
FACILITIES ON SITE abch
EXAM BOARDS I
RETAKES   **NVQ COURSES**

A-level: e g i op v / AB G K P / cdef j l
AS: e g i k o q v / AB G K P / def j l
GCSE: a e g i o v / ABC G K P U / cdef j l
OTHER: j l u / C G

Gb St. Denis and Cranley School; Ettrick Road; Edinburgh EH10 5BJ
Tel: 0131 229 1500 (Fax: 0131 229 5753) *Mrs J.M.Munro*

		Boys	Age	Girls	Age	TOTAL		Boys	Girls
Day	£415-£1495	9	3-7	104	3-18	167	SIXTH		43
Weekly	£2380-£3050			6	8-18				
Boarding	£2380-£3050			48	8-18				

ENTRY REQUIREMENTS Test; Interview; Report
SCHOLARSHIPS & BURSARIES Schol; Forces; Clergy; AP; VI Form; Siblings
SPECIAL NEEDS egjlntw G   **DYSLEXIA** e   **DIET** ad
ASSOCIATION GSA   **FOUNDED** 1858   **RELIGIOUS AFFILIATION** Inter-denom

MAP 14 H 3
LOCATION Urban
DAY ✓   **RAIL** b   **AIR** a
SPORT abchklmoqvwx AB
OTHER LANGUAGES
ACTIVITIES cfghijklnoqrstwx AB
OTHER SUBJECTS abcdefgh
FACILITIES ON SITE ehk
EXAM BOARDS EGI
RETAKES b   **NVQ COURSES** 12

A-level: de g i q v / B G K P / cdef j l
AS: d fghi v / BC GH K P / cdef j l
GCSE: d ghi l o q v / BC G K N P W / cdefg j l
OTHER: f h lmno q stu x / C E K NO R U / c

323

SCOTLAND continued

St. George's School for Girls; Garscube Terrace; Edinburgh EH12 6BG
Gb
Tel: 0131 332 4575 (Fax: 0131 315 2035) *Dr.J.Mc Clure*

	Boys	Age	Girls	Age	TOTAL	SIXTH	Boys	Girls
Day	£450-£1495	2	3-5	806	3-18	889		160
Weekly								
Boarding	£2755-£2855			81	9-18			

ENTRY REQUIREMENTS Test & Interview
SCHOLARSHIPS & BURSARIES Clergy; Teachers; AP; VI Form
SPECIAL NEEDS abghjlnqst Al   **DYSLEXIA**   **DIET** a
ASSOCIATION GSA   **FOUNDED** 1888   **RELIGIOUS AFFILIATION** Non-denom

MAP14 H 3
LOCATION Urban
DAY **RAIL** a **AIR** a
SPORT abcfhjklmnpqvwx ABC
OTHER LANGUAGES
ACTIVITIES cfghijklnostw ABD
OTHER SUBJECTS abcdfh
FACILITIES ON SITE abch
EXAM BOARDS abc BDEI
RETAKES   **NVQ COURSES**

A-level: de g i p v   B GH K P   c efg j l
AS: de g i n p v   BC G K OP   c efg j l
GCSE: de g i no v   B G K P T   cdefg j l
OTHER: l   b ef h l   R U

St. Katharines School; The Pends; St. Andrews; Fife KY16 9RB
G
Tel: 01334 472446 (Fax: 01334 479196) *T.C.R.Bayley & Mrs G.J.Robson-Bayley*

	Boys	Age	Girls	Age	TOTAL	SIXTH	Boys	Girls
Day	£1100-£1688	✗		17	7-12	53		
Weekly	£2874			1	7-12			
Boarding	£2974			35	7-12			

ENTRY REQUIREMENTS Report & Interview
SCHOLARSHIPS & BURSARIES Schol; Burs; Forces; AP; Siblings
SPECIAL NEEDS abjn B   **DYSLEXIA**   **DIET** abcd
ASSOCIATION IAPS   **FOUNDED** 1894   **RELIGIOUS AFFILIATION** Non-denom

MAP14 I 2
LOCATION Rural
DAY **RAIL** a **AIR** a
SPORT acefklmnpqwx AB
OTHER LANGUAGES
ACTIVITIES cfghijopqrw AB
OTHER SUBJECTS abch
FACILITIES ON SITE bikl
EXAM BOARDS
RETAKES   **NVQ COURSES**

A-level:
AS:
GCSE:
OTHER: e g i lmn v   BC G K OP R   de j

St. Leonards School; St. Andrews; Fife KY16 9QU
G
Tel: 01334 472126 (Fax: 01334 476152) *Mrs Mary James*

	Boys	Age	Girls	Age	TOTAL	SIXTH	Boys	Girls
Day	£2075			52	13-18	277		98
Weekly					17-18			
Boarding	£3925			225	13-18			

ENTRY REQUIREMENTS Exam & Interview; CEE & Interview
SCHOLARSHIPS & BURSARIES Schol; Burs; Art; Mus; Forces; Clergy; Teachers; AP; VI Form; Sport; Siblings   **SPECIAL NEEDS** blnqw   **DYSLEXIA** d   **DIET** abcd
ASSOCIATION GSA   **FOUNDED** 1877   **RELIGIOUS AFFILIATION** Non-denom

MAP14 I 2
LOCATION Urban
DAY **RAIL** b **AIR** b
SPORT abcdefghjklmnopqtuwx ABC
OTHER LANGUAGES a
ACTIVITIES acfghijklnopqrstw AB
OTHER SUBJECTS abcdefgh
FACILITIES ON SITE abeghi
EXAM BOARDS abc ABDEHIL
RETAKES a   **NVQ COURSES**

A-level: cd fg i n p v   B GH K P U   a efg ij l
AS: e g i l   B G K P   cdef l
GCSE: d g i v   B G K P U   cdefghj l
OTHER: h lm o v   O R W

St. Margaret's School for Girls; 17 Albyn Place; Aberdeen AB9 1RH
Gb
Tel: 01224 584466 (Fax: 01224 585600) *Miss L.Ogilvie*

	Boys	Age	Girls	Age	TOTAL	SIXTH	Boys	Girls
Day	£232-£1234	4	3-5	412	3-18	416		73
Weekly								
Boarding								

ENTRY REQUIREMENTS Test & Interview
SCHOLARSHIPS & BURSARIES Schol; AP
SPECIAL NEEDS befghjklnqtuvw ABDGHIK   **DYSLEXIA** de   **DIET**
ASSOCIATION GSA   **FOUNDED** 1846   **RELIGIOUS AFFILIATION** Inter-denom

MAP16 L 6
LOCATION
DAY **RAIL** a **AIR** a
SPORT abcfklmpqrwx BCD
OTHER LANGUAGES
ACTIVITIES cfghijknoqu AB
OTHER SUBJECTS abcdegh
FACILITIES ON SITE bgh
EXAM BOARDS IL
RETAKES   **NVQ COURSES**

A-level: d g i v   B G K P   cdef
AS: cd fg i v   B G K P   cdef j
GCSE: d ghi l n v   B G K P   cdef j
OTHER: a m w   C   O R

St. Margaret's School; East Suffolk Road; Edinburgh EH16 5PJ
Gb
Tel: 0131 668 1986 (Fax: 0131 662 0957) *Miss Anne C.Mitchell*

	Boys	Age	Girls	Age	TOTAL	SIXTH	Boys	Girls
Day	£685-£1380	26	3-7	589	3-18	664		121
Weekly					9-18			
Boarding	£2035-£2785			49	9-18			

ENTRY REQUIREMENTS Report; Test & Interview
SCHOLARSHIPS & BURSARIES Schol; Mus; AP; VI Form
SPECIAL NEEDS ghjklnq B   **DYSLEXIA** e   **DIET** acd
ASSOCIATION GSA   **FOUNDED** 1890   **RELIGIOUS AFFILIATION** Non-denom

MAP14 H 3
LOCATION Urban
DAY **RAIL** a **AIR** a
SPORT acghlmnpqwx BC
OTHER LANGUAGES
ACTIVITIES cfghijklnoqstw ABD
OTHER SUBJECTS abcdefgh
FACILITIES ON SITE ceg
EXAM BOARDS GI
RETAKES   **NVQ COURSES**

A-level: de ghi p uv   B GH K P U   cdef j l
AS: a e ghi p v   BC G K P   cdef j l
GCSE: e ghi l p vw   BC G K P   cdef jkl
OTHER: a de ghi l n q   BC G NO R U   cdef

324

SCOTLAND continued

C — St. Mary's School; Abbey Park; Melrose; Roxburghshire TD6 9LN
Tel: 0189 682 2517 (Fax: 0189 682 3550) *R.M.Common*

		Boys	Age	Girls	Age	TOTAL	Boys	Girls
Day	£985-£1610	31	4-13	36	4-13	92		
Weekly	£2685	8	8-13	3	8-13			
Boarding	£2740	8	8-13	6	8-13			

SIXTH

ENTRY REQUIREMENTS Assessment & Interview
SCHOLARSHIPS & BURSARIES Schol; AP
SPECIAL NEEDS jq   **DYSLEXIA**   **DIET** a
ASSOCIATION IAPS **FOUNDED** 1895 **RELIGIOUS AFFILIATION** Inter-denom

MAP14 I 5
LOCATION Rural
DAY   **RAIL** c   **AIR** b
SPORT acefklmpqsx AB
OTHER LANGUAGES a
ACTIVITIES cfghijlmqrw A
OTHER SUBJECTS abc
FACILITIES ON SITE abk
EXAM BOARDS
RETAKES   **NVQ COURSES**

A-level:
AS:
GCSE:
OTHER: c e g i lmn s u v BC G K OP R cde j

B — Stewart's Melville College; Queensferry Rd; Edinburgh EH4 3EZ
Tel: 0131 332 7925 (Fax: 0131 343 2432) *P.F.J.Tobin*

		Boys	Age	Girls	Age	TOTAL	Boys	Girls
Day	£1470	723	11-18			756	225	
Weekly								
Boarding	£2850	33	11-18					

SIXTH

ENTRY REQUIREMENTS Exam; Interview; Report & Exam & Interview
SCHOLARSHIPS & BURSARIES Schol; Burs; Mus; AP
SPECIAL NEEDS ejknqw GI   **DYSLEXIA** d   **DIET** a
ASSOCIATION HMC **FOUNDED** 1832 **RELIGIOUS AFFILIATION** Inter-denom

MAP14 H 3
LOCATION Urban
DAY ✓   **RAIL** a   **AIR** b
SPORT abcdefgjkmrstuwx ABD
OTHER LANGUAGES
ACTIVITIES befghijkoqrtuv AB
OTHER SUBJECTS bcd
FACILITIES ON SITE abchi
EXAM BOARDS c AHIL
RETAKES   **NVQ COURSES**

A-level: g i l p v B GH K P R cdefg j
AS: cd h o A   O R l
GCSE: a
OTHER: C I M q tu w i

C — Strathallan School; Forgandenny; Perth PH2 9EG
Tel: 0173 881 2546 (Fax: 01738 812549) *A.W.Mc Phail*

		Boys	Age	Girls	Age	TOTAL	Boys	Girls
Day	£2115-£2570	11	10-18	20	10-18	492	101	55
Weekly								
Boarding	£2900-£3685	313	10-18	148	10-18			

SIXTH

ENTRY REQUIREMENTS CEE; Exam & Interview
SCHOLARSHIPS & BURSARIES Schol; Mus; Forces; VI Form
SPECIAL NEEDS abgln B   **DYSLEXIA** de   **DIET** acd
ASSOCIATION HMC **FOUNDED** 1912 **RELIGIOUS AFFILIATION** Inter-denom

MAP14 H 2
LOCATION Rural
DAY   **RAIL** b   **AIR** a
SPORT abcdefghjklmnopqstuwx ABCD
OTHER LANGUAGES
ACTIVITIES cefghijklmnopqrstuw ABC
OTHER SUBJECTS bcdefh
FACILITIES ON SITE abcdeghikl
EXAM BOARDS abcd ABDEHI
RETAKES ab   **NVQ COURSES**

A-level: defghi op v x B GH K M P U cdef j l
AS: H M c ef
GCSE: de ghi l o v B FG K M OP U X cdef j
OTHER: de ghi l op v B G K P cdef ij l

C — Wellington School; Carleton Turrets; Ayr KA7 2XH
Tel: 01292 269321 (Fax: 01292 282313) *Mrs D.A.Gardner*

		Boys	Age	Girls	Age	TOTAL	Boys	Girls
Day	£470-£1595	30	3-14	313	3-18	371		70
Weekly	£2390-£3180			4				
Boarding	£2390-£3180			24	7-18			

SIXTH

ENTRY REQUIREMENTS Report & Exam & Interview
SCHOLARSHIPS & BURSARIES Burs; AP
SPECIAL NEEDS bejklqtuwx BDGI   **DYSLEXIA**   **DIET** abcd
ASSOCIATION GSA **FOUNDED** 1836 **RELIGIOUS AFFILIATION** Non-denom

MAP13 E 5
LOCATION
DAY   **RAIL** a   **AIR** a
SPORT abcfjklmopqstuvwx BC
OTHER LANGUAGES
ACTIVITIES acefghijknoqstwx AB
OTHER SUBJECTS bcdefgh
FACILITIES ON SITE eh
EXAM BOARDS AEI
RETAKES   **NVQ COURSES**

A-level: a de ghij l p v B G K P cdefg jkl
AS: e ghi v B G P cdef jkl
GCSE: a e ghij l p v B E G K P U cdefg jkl
OTHER: lmnopq s E K N h

B — Bangor Grammar School; Bangor; County Down; Northern Ireland BT20 5HJ
Tel: 01247 473734 (Fax: 01247 273245) *T.W.Patton*

		Boys	Age	Girls	Age	TOTAL	Boys	Girls
Day	£30-£150	1059	4-18			1059	216	
Weekly								
Boarding								

SIXTH

ENTRY REQUIREMENTS Exam
SCHOLARSHIPS & BURSARIES
SPECIAL NEEDS abegjklnqstuw ACGHI   **DYSLEXIA**   **DIET** a
ASSOCIATION HMC **FOUNDED** 1856 **RELIGIOUS AFFILIATION** Inter-denom

MAP17 F 3
LOCATION Urban
DAY   **RAIL** a   **AIR** a
SPORT abcdefhklmqstuwx ABC
OTHER LANGUAGES
ACTIVITIES acefghijklmnopqstu AB
OTHER SUBJECTS abcdfh
FACILITIES ON SITE abceghkl
EXAM BOARDS f ABEFL
RETAKES ab   **NVQ COURSES**

N IRE

A-level: cdefghi o v B GHI K OP U cdef ij
AS: l
GCSE: cde ghi l o v B GH K P R U cdefg j
OTHER: mn s u x F NO R

NORTHERN IRELAND continued

C — Belfast Royal Academy; Belfast BT14 6JL
Tel: 01232 740423 (Fax: 01232 352737) *W.M.Sillery*

		Boys	Age	Girls	Age	TOTAL		Boys	Girls
Day	£460	814	4-19	860	4-19	1674	SIXTH	174	185
Weekly									
Boarding									

ENTRY REQUIREMENTS Interview
SCHOLARSHIPS & BURSARIES
SPECIAL NEEDS beghjklnqtuw BGHI   **DYSLEXIA** f   **DIET** acd
ASSOCIATION HMC   **FOUNDED** 1785   **RELIGIOUS AFFILIATION** Inter-denom

MAP17 E 3
LOCATION Urban
DAY   **RAIL** a   **AIR** a
SPORT abcdefkmpstuwx AB
OTHER LANGUAGES
ACTIVITIES efghijknopqst AB
OTHER SUBJECTS abcefh
FACILITIES ON SITE abcghi
EXAM BOARDS f L
RETAKES ab   **NVQ COURSES**

A-level c efg i   p   v x
 BC   GH K   P R   U
 defg j l

AS   K

GCSE   e g i l   no q   v
 ABC   G   K   P R
 cdefg ij l

OTHER   l
 f i kl

B — Cabin Hill; Knock; Belfast; N.Ireland BT4 3HJ
Tel: 01232 653368 (Fax: 01232 651966) *C.A.I.Dyer*

		Boys	Age	Girls	Age	TOTAL		Boys	Girls
Day	£287- £943	354	4-13	1		392	SIXTH		
Weekly	£1503-£2043	26	7-13						
Boarding	£1537-£2076	11	7-13						

ENTRY REQUIREMENTS Report & Test
SCHOLARSHIPS & BURSARIES Forces; Clergy
SPECIAL NEEDS abefghjklnqtuvw BCDEGHIJK   **DYSLEXIA** de   **DIET** abcd
ASSOCIATION IAPS   **FOUNDED** 1929   **RELIGIOUS AFFILIATION** Inter-denom

MAP17 E 3
LOCATION Urban
DAY   **RAIL** a   **AIR** a
SPORT abcdefjkmsuwx AB
OTHER LANGUAGES
ACTIVITIES afghijopqtw A
OTHER SUBJECTS cfh
FACILITIES ON SITE bchik
EXAM BOARDS
RETAKES   **NVQ COURSES**

A-level

AS

GCSE   e

OTHER   e   l o s v
 B E G K   O R
 cdefg j l

B — Coleraine Academical Institution; Castlerock Road; Coleraine; N.Ireland; BT51 3LA
Tel: 01265 44331 (Fax: 01265 52632) *R.S.Forsythe*

		Boys	Age	Girls	Age	TOTAL		Boys	Girls
Day	£910	790	11-19			859	SIXTH	178	
Weekly	£1080		11-19						
Boarding	£1080	69	11-19						

ENTRY REQUIREMENTS Interview
SCHOLARSHIPS & BURSARIES Burs
SPECIAL NEEDS eknpqw GI   **DYSLEXIA** g   **DIET** d
ASSOCIATION HMC   **FOUNDED** 1860   **RELIGIOUS AFFILIATION** Inter-denom

MAP17 C 1
LOCATION Rural
DAY   **RAIL**   **AIR** a
SPORT abcdefhjkrstwx AB
OTHER LANGUAGES a
ACTIVITIES fghijkmoqrst A
OTHER SUBJECTS abcdfh
FACILITIES ON SITE bcehik
EXAM BOARDS acdf AEF
RETAKES a   **NVQ COURSES**

A-level cdefg i l   opq   vwx
 AB   GH K   P
 cdef j l

AS   K
 e

GCSE   cde g i l   o q   vw
 AB   G   K   OP R U
 cdef   l

OTHER

C — Methodist College; 1 Malone Road; Belfast BT9 6BY; N.Ireland
Tel: 01232 669558 (Fax: 01232 669375) *T.W.Mulryne*

		Boys	Age	Girls	Age	TOTAL		Boys	Girls
Day	£50-£55	1217	4-18	1063	4-18	2430	SIXTH	225	293
Weekly									
Boarding	£1036-£1912	92	8-18	58	9-18				

ENTRY REQUIREMENTS Assessment & Interview
SCHOLARSHIPS & BURSARIES Schol; Clergy
SPECIAL NEEDS beghjklnqrstuvwx ABCDGHIKL   **DYSLEXIA** e   **DIET** ad
ASSOCIATION HMC   **FOUNDED** 1865   **RELIGIOUS AFFILIATION** Methodist

MAP17 E 3
LOCATION Urban
DAY   **RAIL** b   **AIR** a
SPORT abcefgkmprswx ABC
OTHER LANGUAGES
ACTIVITIES bfghijkosx AB
OTHER SUBJECTS bc
FACILITIES ON SITE abcdghik
EXAM BOARDS cf AEFL
RETAKES   **NVQ COURSES**

A-level c efg i   p   vwx
 BC   GH K   P R   U
 cdefg jkl

AS   l o
 c

GCSE   a cd g i l   no   vw
 BC   G   K   PQR
 cdefg jkl

OTHER

B — Portora Royal School; Enniskillen; Co. Fermanagh BT74 7HA; N.Ireland
Tel: 01365 322658 (Fax: 01365 328668) *R.L.Bennett*

		Boys	Age	Girls	Age	TOTAL		Boys	Girls
Day	£14	431	11-18			431	SIXTH	80	
Weekly									
Boarding									

ENTRY REQUIREMENTS Exam; Interview
SCHOLARSHIPS & BURSARIES
SPECIAL NEEDS elnqw   **DYSLEXIA** g   **DIET** a
ASSOCIATION HMC   **FOUNDED** 1608   **RELIGIOUS AFFILIATION** Inter-denom

MAP17 A 4
LOCATION Rural
DAY   **RAIL**   **AIR** b
SPORT abcdejrstwx AB
OTHER LANGUAGES
ACTIVITIES bfghijklmnopqst A
OTHER SUBJECTS bcdfh
FACILITIES ON SITE bcdeghj
EXAM BOARDS f BF
RETAKES ab   **NVQ COURSES**

A-level   e g i   op   v x
 AB   GH K   P
 c ef

AS   l o
 G   P

GCSE   e g i   o   v x
 AB   G   K   P
 cdef

OTHER

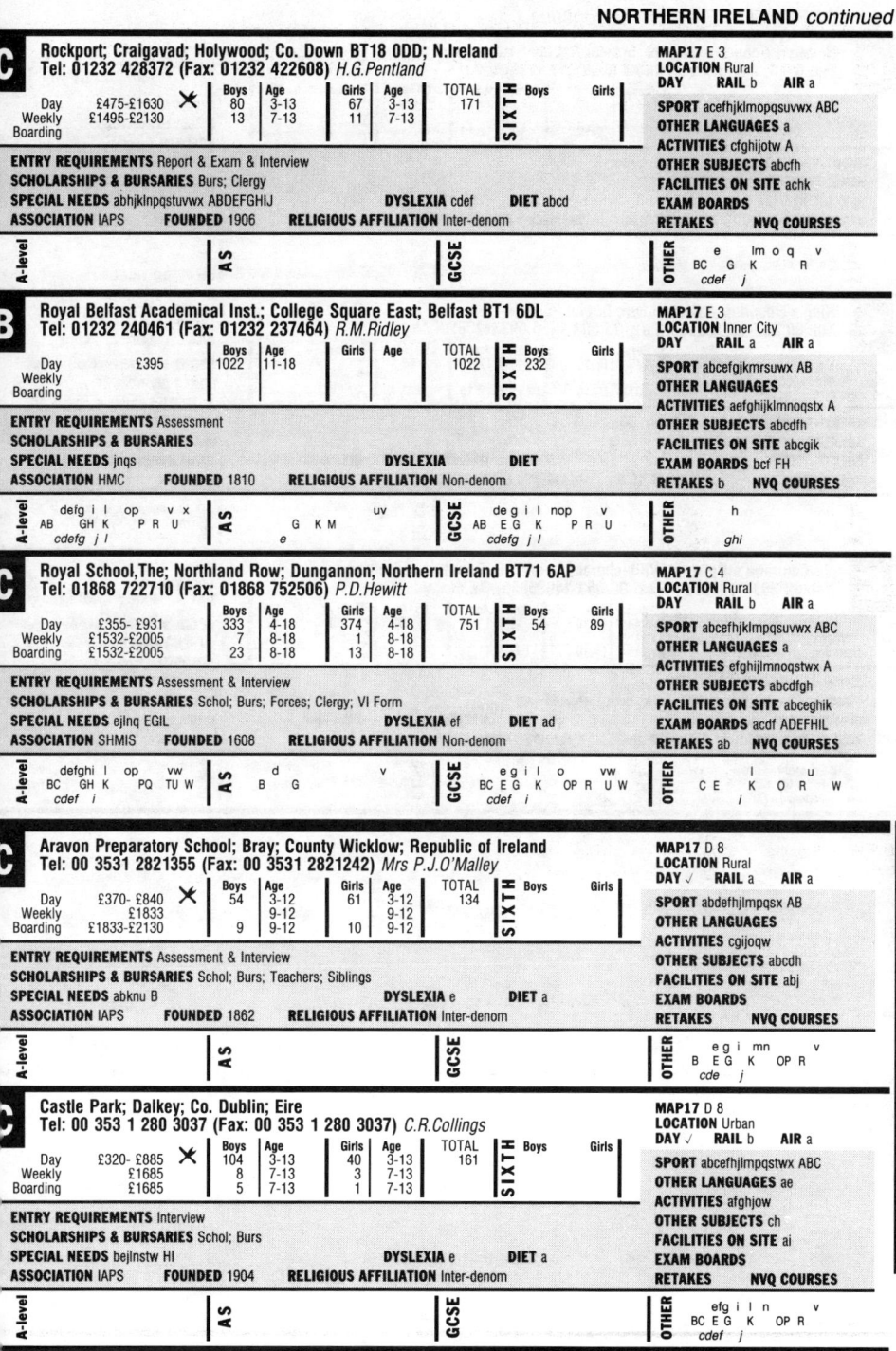

NORTHERN IRELAND *continued*

C — **Rockport; Craigavad; Holywood; Co. Down BT18 0DD; N.Ireland**
Tel: 01232 428372 (Fax: 01232 422608) *H.G.Pentland*

		Boys	Age	Girls	Age	TOTAL		Boys	Girls
Day	£475–£1630	80	3-13	67	3-13	171	SIXTH		
Weekly	£1495–£2130	13	7-13	11	7-13				
Boarding									

ENTRY REQUIREMENTS Report & Exam & Interview
SCHOLARSHIPS & BURSARIES Burs; Clergy
SPECIAL NEEDS abhjklnpqstuvwx ABDEFGHIJ   **DYSLEXIA** cdef   **DIET** abcd
ASSOCIATION IAPS   **FOUNDED** 1906   **RELIGIOUS AFFILIATION** Inter-denom

MAP17 E 3
LOCATION Rural
DAY   **RAIL** b   **AIR** a
SPORT acefhjklmopqsuvwx ABC
OTHER LANGUAGES a
ACTIVITIES cfghijotw A
OTHER SUBJECTS abcfh
FACILITIES ON SITE achk
EXAM BOARDS
RETAKES   **NVQ COURSES**

A-level defg i l op v x
BC GH K PQ R U
cdefg j l

AS

GCSE uv
B G K M
e

OTHER e lm o q v
BC G K   R
cdef j

B — **Royal Belfast Academical Inst.; College Square East; Belfast BT1 6DL**
Tel: 01232 240461 (Fax: 01232 237464) *R.M.Ridley*

		Boys	Age	Girls	Age	TOTAL		Boys	Girls
Day	£395	1022	11-18			1022	SIXTH	232	
Weekly									
Boarding									

ENTRY REQUIREMENTS Assessment
SCHOLARSHIPS & BURSARIES
SPECIAL NEEDS jnqs   **DYSLEXIA**   **DIET**
ASSOCIATION HMC   **FOUNDED** 1810   **RELIGIOUS AFFILIATION** Non-denom

MAP17 E 3
LOCATION Inner City
DAY   **RAIL** a   **AIR** a
SPORT abcefgjkmrsuwx AB
OTHER LANGUAGES
ACTIVITIES aefghijklmnoqstx A
OTHER SUBJECTS abcdfh
FACILITIES ON SITE abcgik
EXAM BOARDS bcf FH
RETAKES b   **NVQ COURSES**

A-level defg i l op v x
AB GH K P R U
cdefg j l

AS d
B G
e

GCSE de g i l nop v
AB E G K P R U
cdefg j l

OTHER h
ghi

C — **Royal School,The; Northland Row; Dungannon; Northern Ireland BT71 6AP**
Tel: 01868 722710 (Fax: 01868 752506) *P.D.Hewitt*

		Boys	Age	Girls	Age	TOTAL		Boys	Girls
Day	£355–£931	333	4-18	374	4-18	751	SIXTH	54	89
Weekly	£1532–£2005	7	8-18	1	8-18				
Boarding	£1532–£2005	23	8-18	13	8-18				

ENTRY REQUIREMENTS Assessment & Interview
SCHOLARSHIPS & BURSARIES Schol; Burs; Forces; Clergy; VI Form
SPECIAL NEEDS ejlnq EGIL   **DYSLEXIA** ef   **DIET** ad
ASSOCIATION SHMIS   **FOUNDED** 1608   **RELIGIOUS AFFILIATION** Non-denom

MAP17 C 4
LOCATION Rural
DAY   **RAIL** b   **AIR** a
SPORT abcefhjklmpqsuvwx ABC
OTHER LANGUAGES a
ACTIVITIES efghijlmnoqstwx A
OTHER SUBJECTS abcdfgh
FACILITIES ON SITE abceghik
EXAM BOARDS acdf ADEFHIL
RETAKES ab   **NVQ COURSES**

A-level defgh i op vw
BC GH K   PQ TU W
cdef i

AS d
B G

GCSE e g i l o vw
BC E G K   OP R U W
cdef i

OTHER l u
C E   K O R W
i

C — **Aravon Preparatory School; Bray; County Wicklow; Republic of Ireland**
Tel: 00 3531 2821355 (Fax: 00 3531 2821242) *Mrs P.J.O'Malley*

		Boys	Age	Girls	Age	TOTAL		Boys	Girls
Day	£370–£840	54	3-12	61	3-12	134	SIXTH		
Weekly	£1833		9-12		9-12				
Boarding	£1833–£2130	9	9-12	10	9-12				

ENTRY REQUIREMENTS Assessment & Interview
SCHOLARSHIPS & BURSARIES Schol; Burs; Teachers; Siblings
SPECIAL NEEDS abknu B   **DYSLEXIA** e   **DIET** a
ASSOCIATION IAPS   **FOUNDED** 1862   **RELIGIOUS AFFILIATION** Inter-denom

MAP17 D 8
LOCATION Rural
DAY ✓   **RAIL** a   **AIR** a
SPORT abdefhjlmpqsx AB
OTHER LANGUAGES
ACTIVITIES cgijoqw
OTHER SUBJECTS abcdh
FACILITIES ON SITE abj
EXAM BOARDS
RETAKES   **NVQ COURSES**

A-level

AS

GCSE

OTHER e g i mn   v
B E G K   OP R
cde   j

C — **Castle Park; Dalkey; Co. Dublin; Eire**
Tel: 00 353 1 280 3037 (Fax: 00 353 1 280 3037) *C.R.Collings*

		Boys	Age	Girls	Age	TOTAL		Boys	Girls
Day	£320–£885	104	3-13	40	3-13	161	SIXTH		
Weekly	£1685	8	7-13	3	7-13				
Boarding	£1685	5	7-13	1	7-13				

ENTRY REQUIREMENTS Interview
SCHOLARSHIPS & BURSARIES Schol; Burs
SPECIAL NEEDS bejlnstw HI   **DYSLEXIA** e   **DIET** a
ASSOCIATION IAPS   **FOUNDED** 1904   **RELIGIOUS AFFILIATION** Inter-denom

MAP17 D 8
LOCATION Urban
DAY ✓   **RAIL** a   **AIR** a
SPORT abcefhjlmpqstwx ABC
OTHER LANGUAGES ae
ACTIVITIES afghjow
OTHER SUBJECTS ch
FACILITIES ON SITE ai
EXAM BOARDS
RETAKES   **NVQ COURSES**

A-level

AS

GCSE

OTHER efg i l n   v
BC E G K   OP R
cdef j

REPUBLIC OF IRELAND

REPUBLIC OF IRELAND *continued*

C | Headfort School; Kells; Co. Meath; Republic of Ireland
Tel: 0146 40065 (Fax: 0146 41842) *W.L.W.Goulding*

		Boys	Age	Girls	Age	TOTAL	SIXTH	Boys	Girls
Day	£1925					65			
Weekly	£1925								
Boarding		52	7-13	13	7-13				

MAP17 D 3
LOCATION Rural
DAY   **RAIL** c   **AIR** a
SPORT adejmswx AB
OTHER LANGUAGES
ACTIVITIES cfghijow

ENTRY REQUIREMENTS Report & Interview
SCHOLARSHIPS & BURSARIES Schol
SPECIAL NEEDS   **DYSLEXIA**   **DIET**
ASSOCIATION IAPS   **FOUNDED** 1949   **RELIGIOUS AFFILIATION**

OTHER SUBJECTS ch
FACILITIES ON SITE hi
EXAM BOARDS
RETAKES   **NVQ COURSES**

A-level   **AS**   **GCSE**   **OTHER**   e   lm   v
                                                                                                       BC   G
                                                                                                       cd

---

C | King's Hospital; Palmerstown; Dublin 20; Eire
Tel: 00 353 1626 5933 (Fax: 00 353 1626 5933x236) *H Meyer*

		Boys	Age	Girls	Age	TOTAL	SIXTH	Boys	Girls
Day	£646	149	12-18	148	12-18	651			
Weekly									
Boarding	£1457	201	12-18	153	12-18				

MAP17 D 8
LOCATION Rural
DAY   **RAIL** a   **AIR** a
SPORT abcdefhmqrsx ABC
OTHER LANGUAGES ae
ACTIVITIES cfghijkmnopstvw AC

ENTRY REQUIREMENTS Exam; Report & Interview
SCHOLARSHIPS & BURSARIES Schol; Burs
SPECIAL NEEDS aghnq BEG   **DYSLEXIA** d   **DIET** a
ASSOCIATION GBA   **FOUNDED** 1669   **RELIGIOUS AFFILIATION** C of I

OTHER SUBJECTS abcdefgh
FACILITIES ON SITE abdeghik
EXAM BOARDS
RETAKES   **NVQ COURSES**

A-level   **AS**   **GCSE**   **OTHER**   a   defghij   l   n   pq s   v
                                                                                    ABC   GH   K   OP   RS
                                                                                        cdef   l

---

C | St. Columba's College; Whitechurch; Dublin 16; Republic of Ireland
Tel: 00 353 14906791 (Fax: 00 353 14936655) *T.E.Macey*

		Boys	Age	Girls	Age	TOTAL	SIXTH	Boys	Girls
Day	£945-£1125	44	11-18	12	11-18	303		60	50
Weekly									
Boarding	£1650-£1965	145	11-18	102	11-18				

MAP17 D 8
LOCATION Rural
DAY   **RAIL** b   **AIR** a
SPORT abcdefhjklmswx AB
OTHER LANGUAGES ae
ACTIVITIES cfghijlmnopqrstw C

ENTRY REQUIREMENTS CEE; Exam
SCHOLARSHIPS & BURSARIES Schol; Burs; Clergy; Siblings
SPECIAL NEEDS bgjklnqtw EGI   **DYSLEXIA** e   **DIET** abcd
ASSOCIATION HMC   **FOUNDED** 1843   **RELIGIOUS AFFILIATION** C of I

OTHER SUBJECTS bcefgh
FACILITIES ON SITE abcdefgjkl
EXAM BOARDS a BEL
RETAKES a   **NVQ COURSES**

A-level   c   efghi   op   vw   **AS**   **GCSE**   **OTHER**
         B   GH   K   P
         cdefgh j   l

KEY

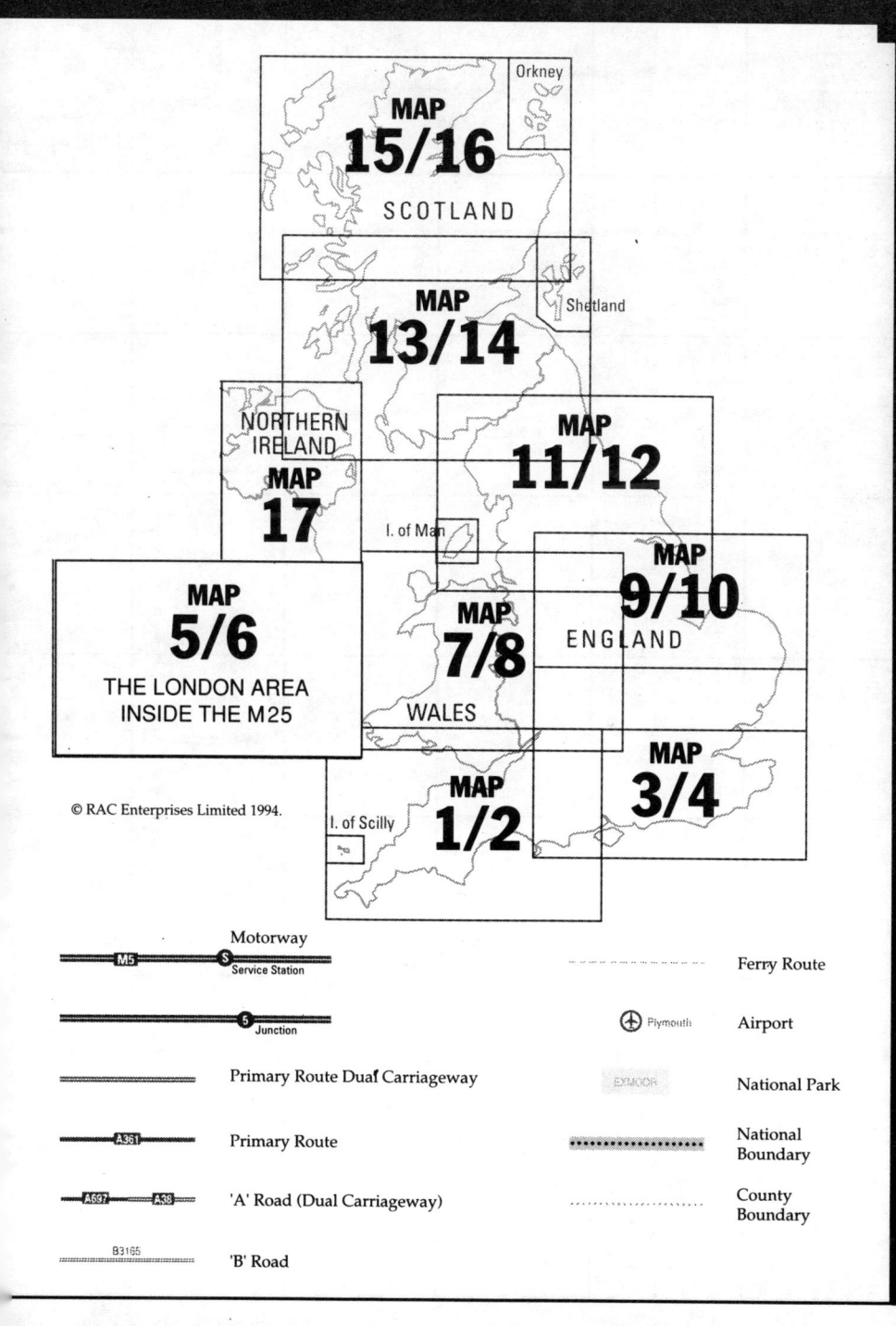

MAPS

MAP 15/16 SCOTLAND
Orkney

MAP 13/14
Shetland

NORTHERN IRELAND

MAP 17

I. of Man

MAP 11/12

MAP 5/6
THE LONDON AREA INSIDE THE M25

MAP 7/8

MAP 9/10 ENGLAND

WALES

© RAC Enterprises Limited 1994.

I. of Scilly

MAP 1/2

MAP 3/4

M5 / S Service Station	Motorway		Ferry Route
5 Junction		Plymouth	Airport
	Primary Route Dual Carriageway	EXMOOR	National Park
A361	Primary Route	••••••••••••	National Boundary
A697 — A38	'A' Road (Dual Carriageway)	....	County Boundary
B3165	'B' Road		

MAP 1

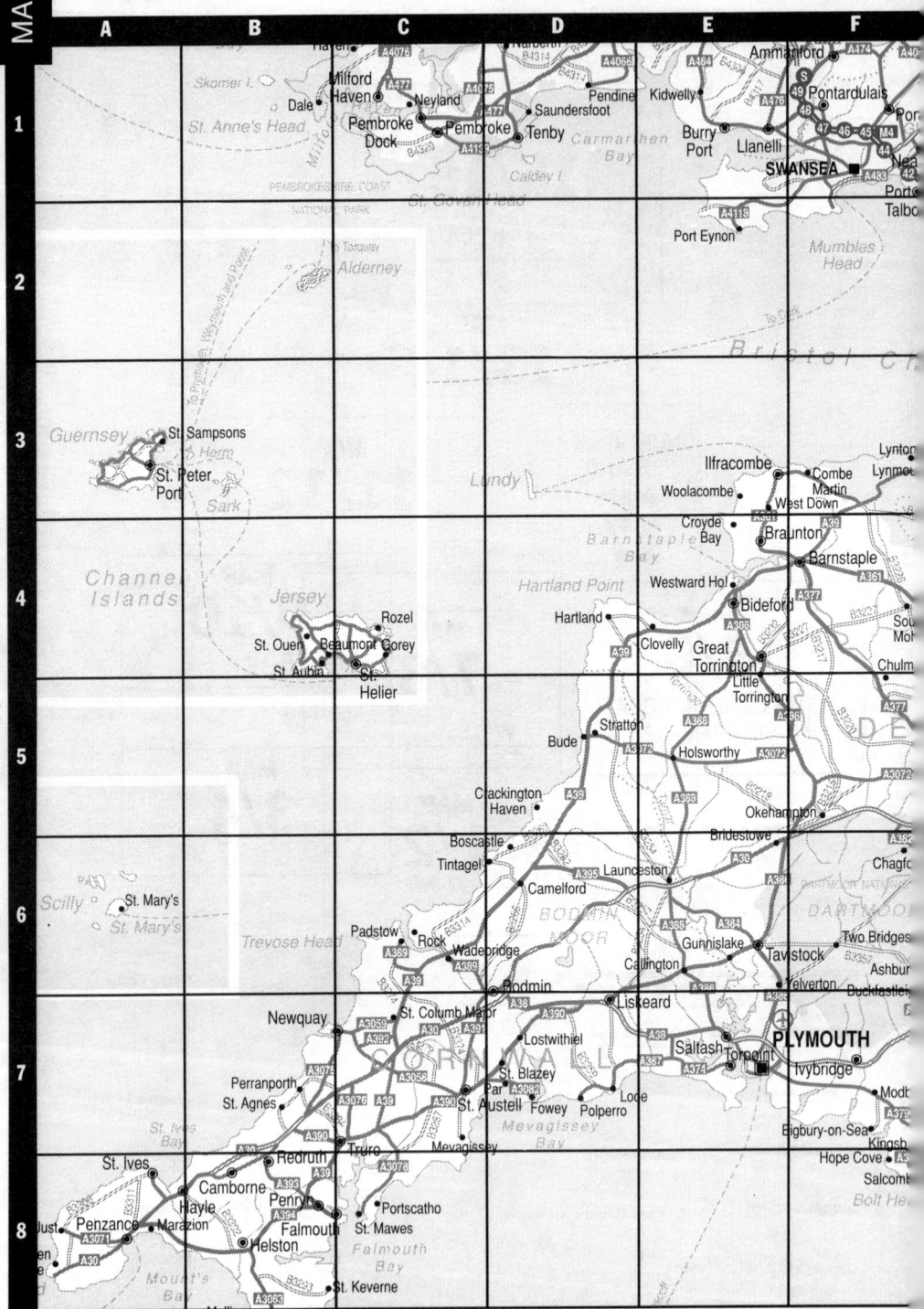

MAP 2

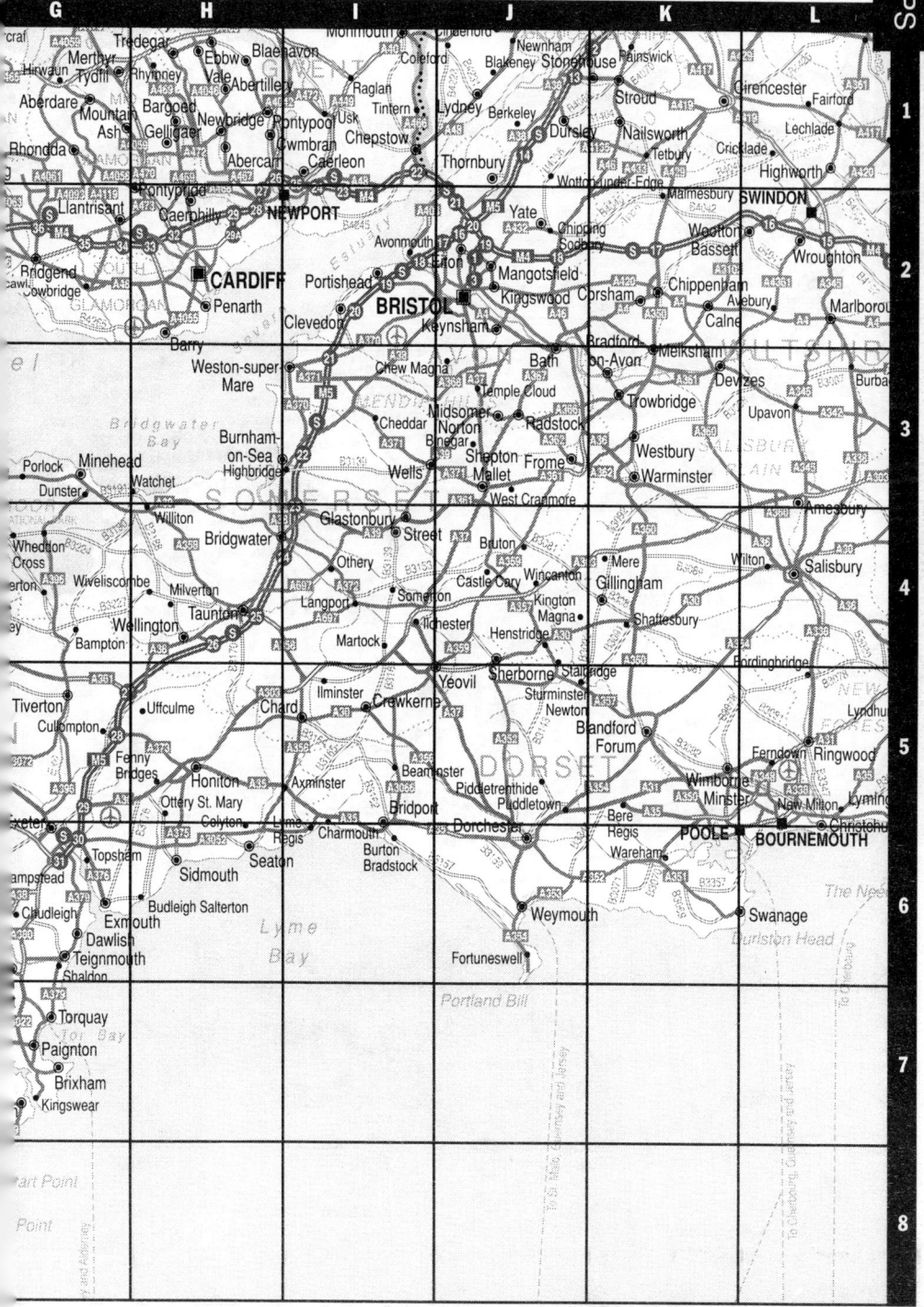

MAP 3

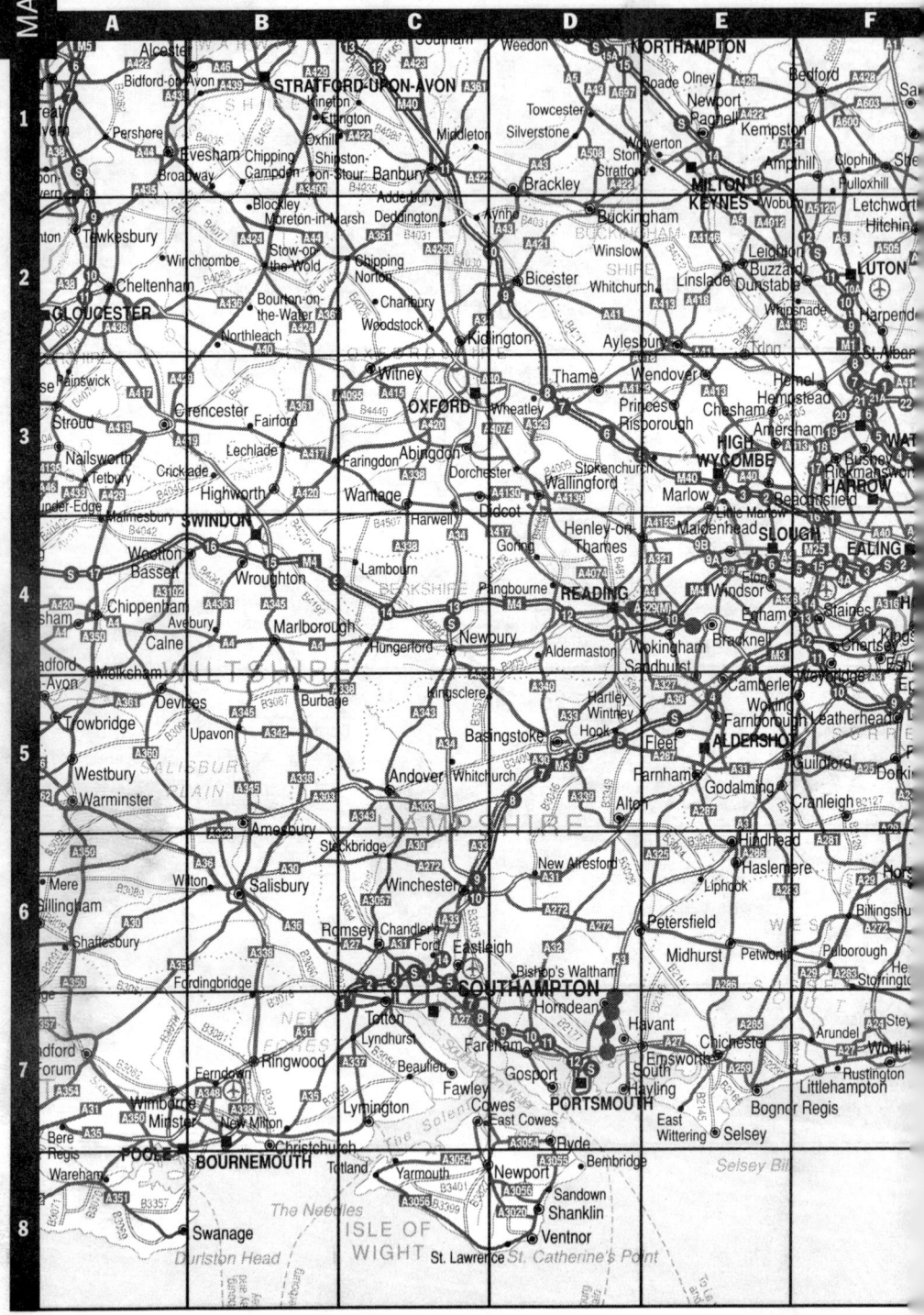

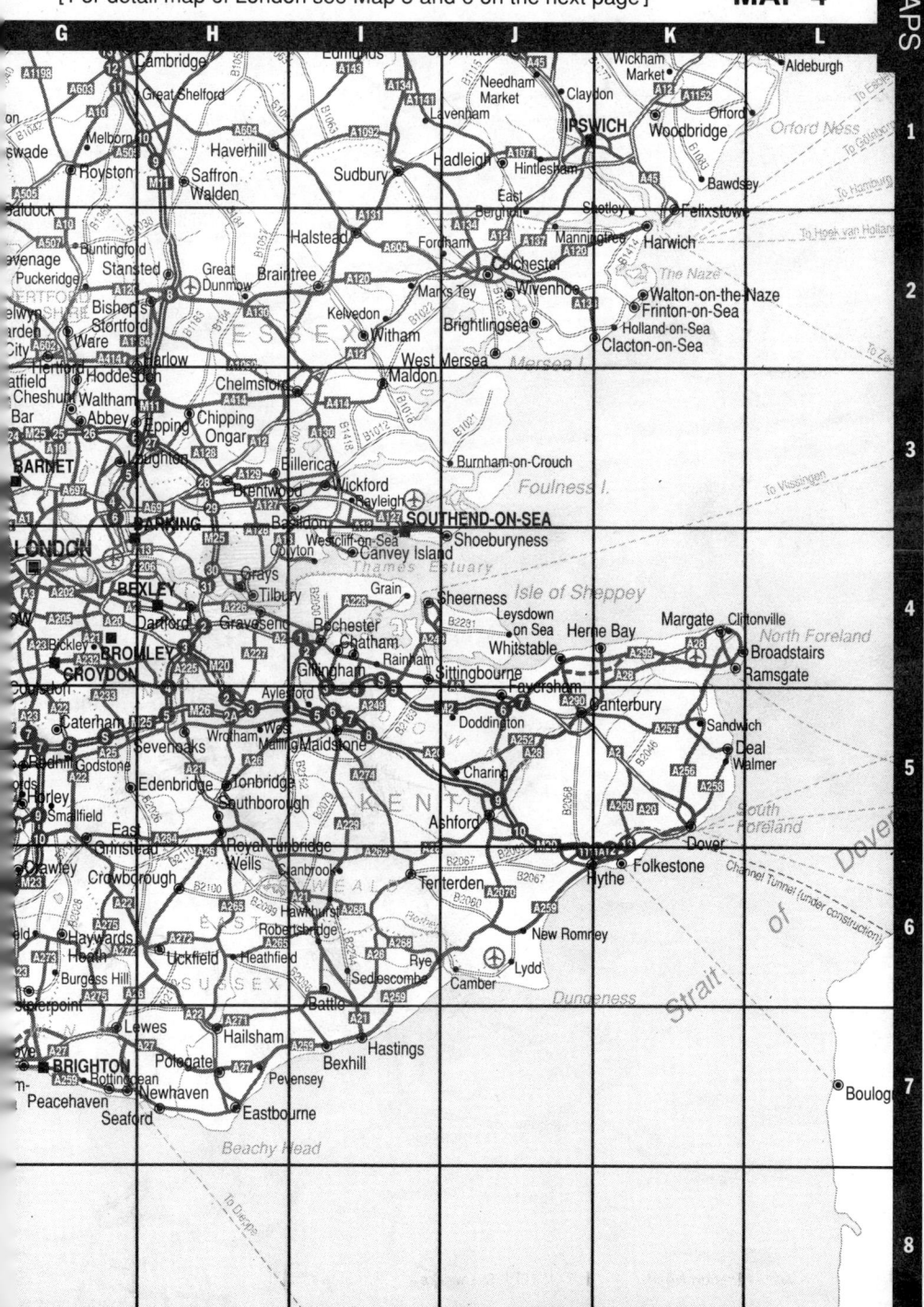

[For detail map of London see Map 5 and 6 on the next page] **MAP 4**

MAP 5

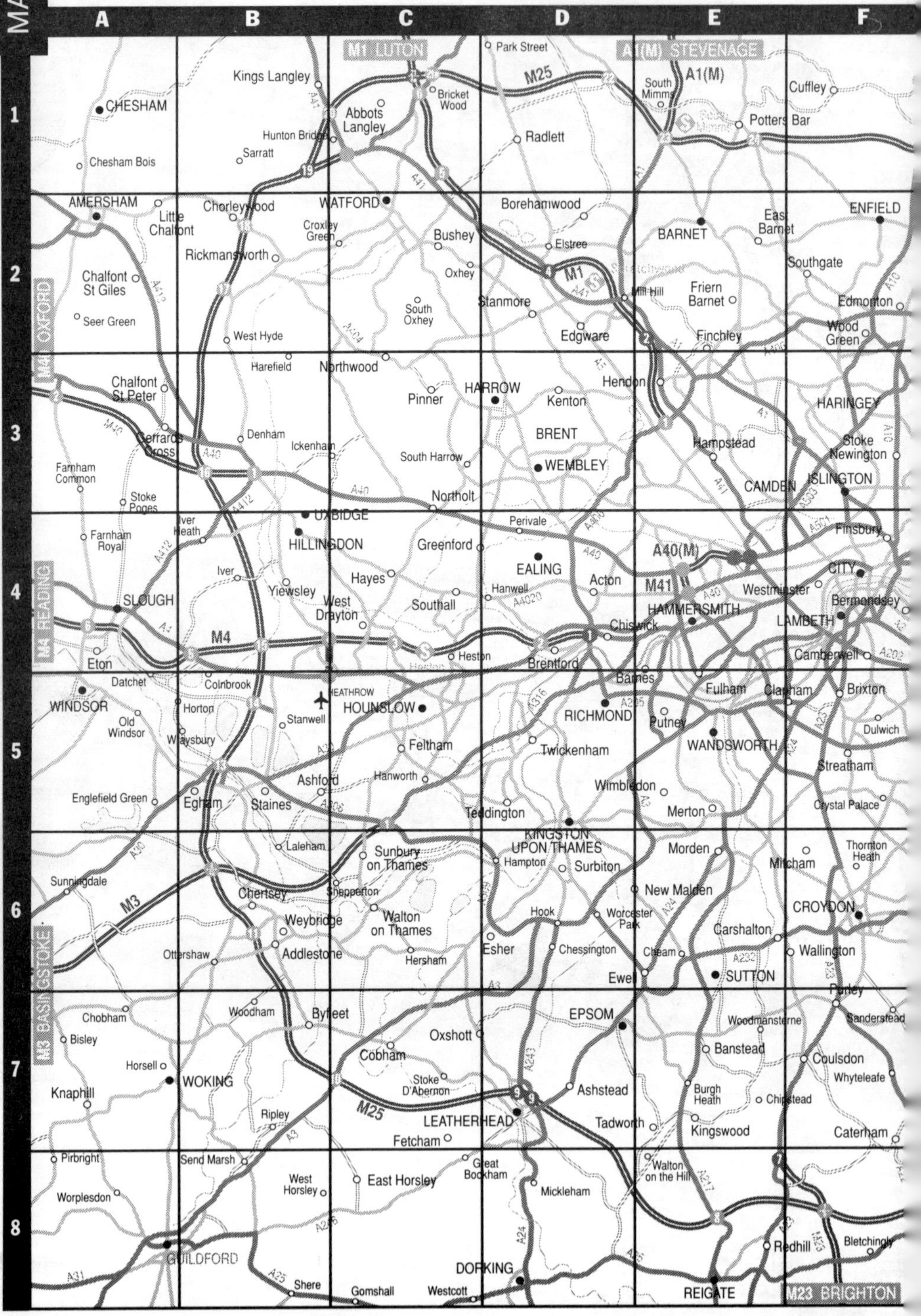

MAP 6

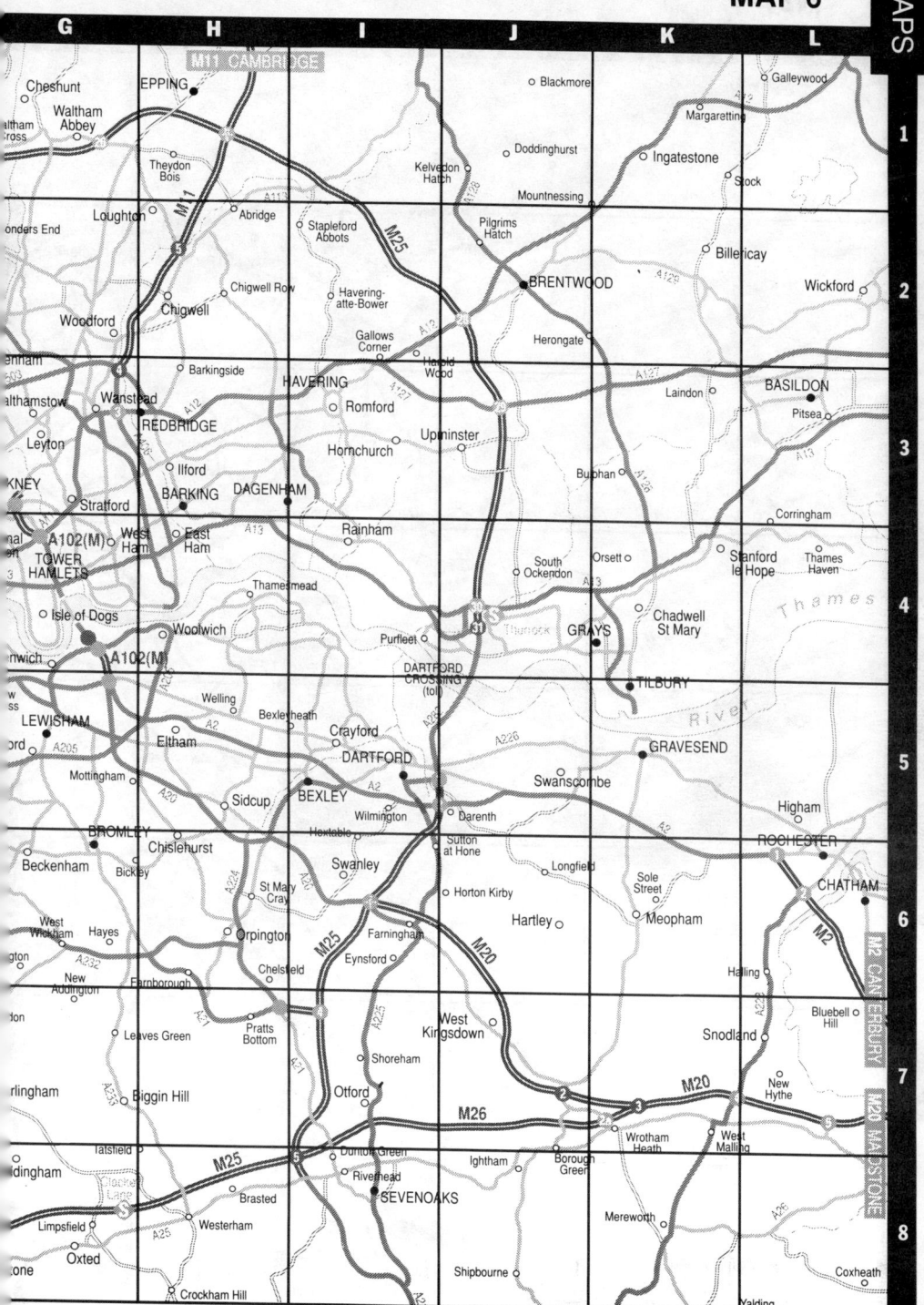

SCALE APPROXIMATELY 4.5 MILES TO THE SQUARE

MAP 7

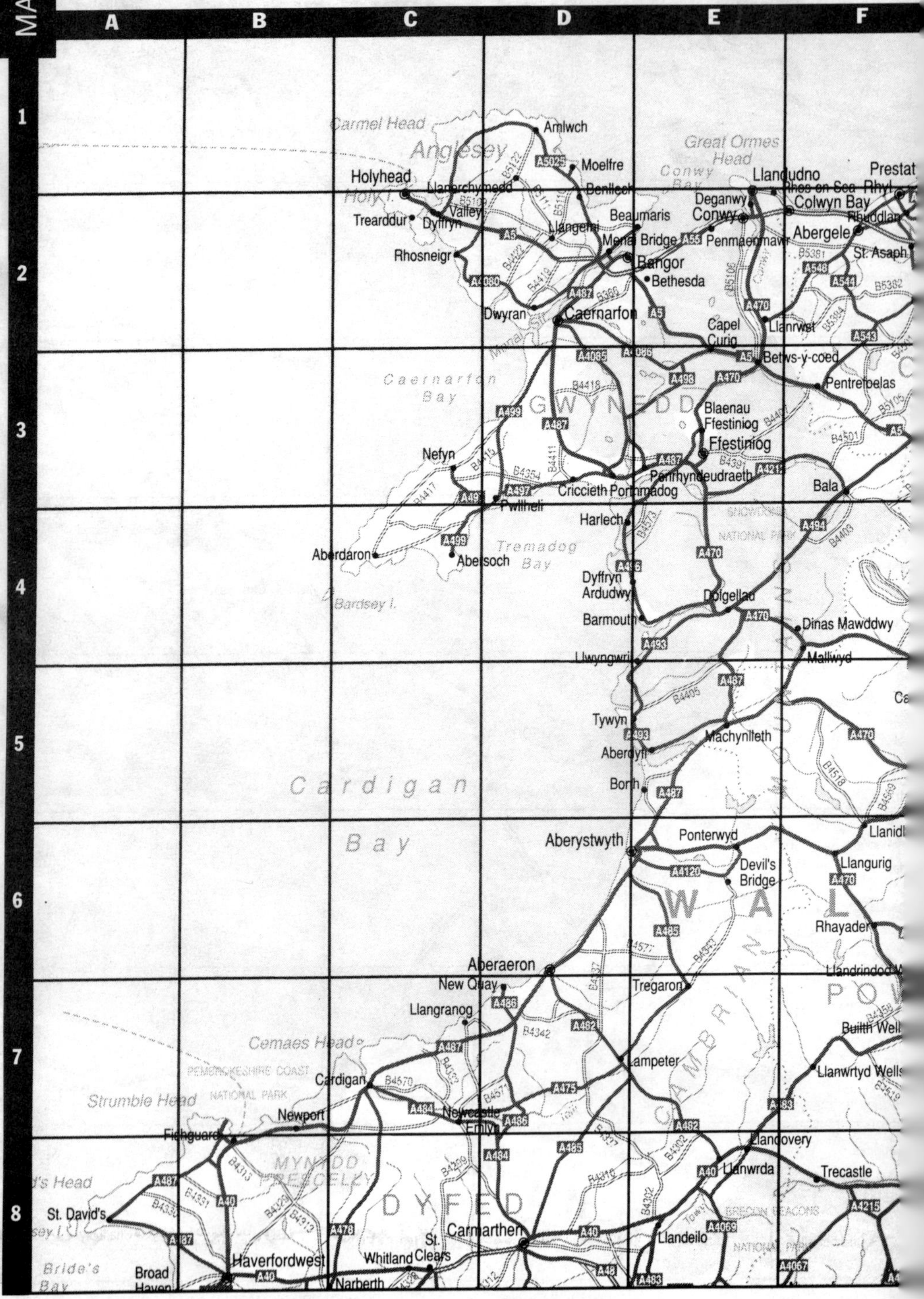

MAP 8

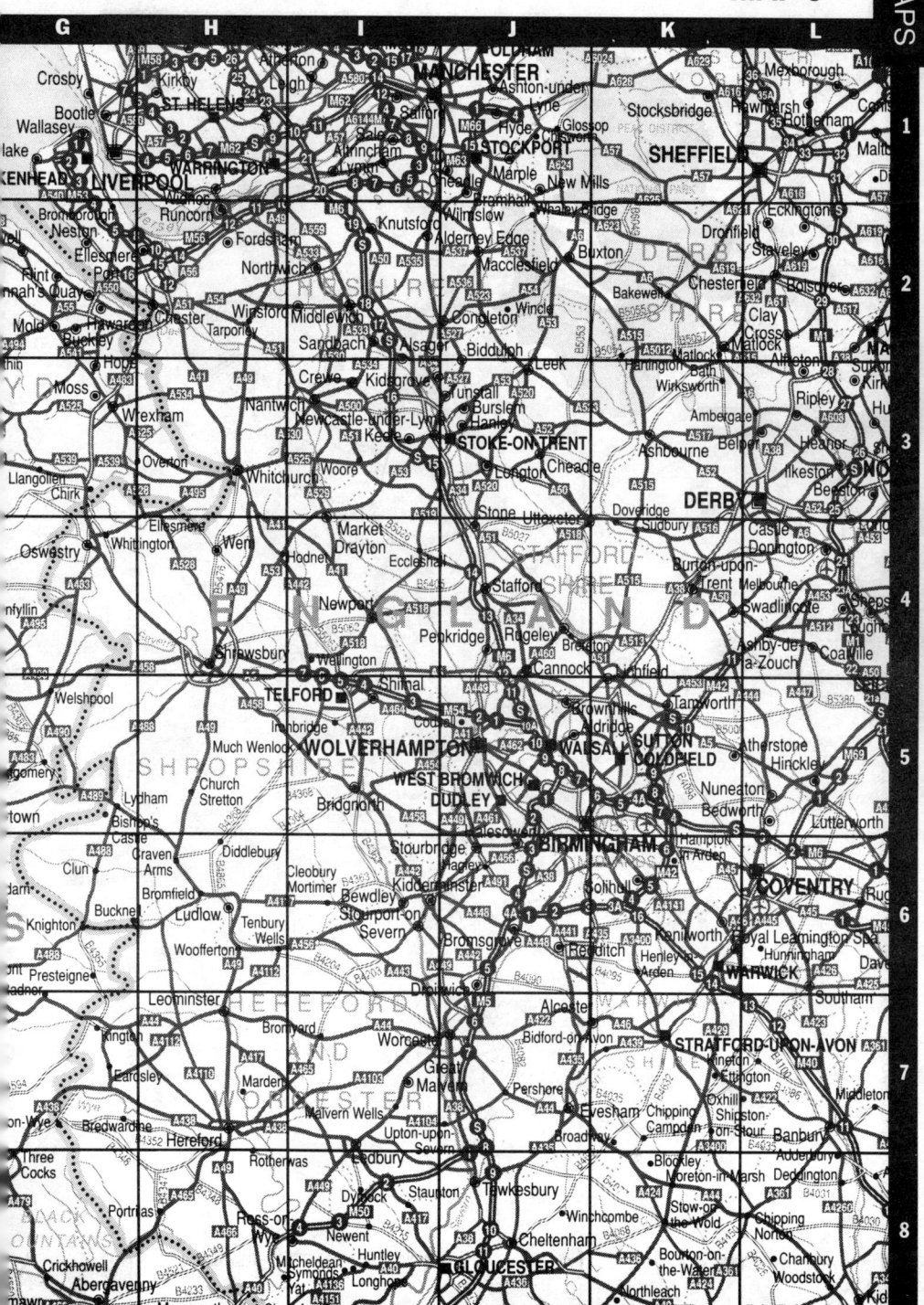

SCALE APPROXIMATELY 14 MILES TO THE SQUARE

MAP 9

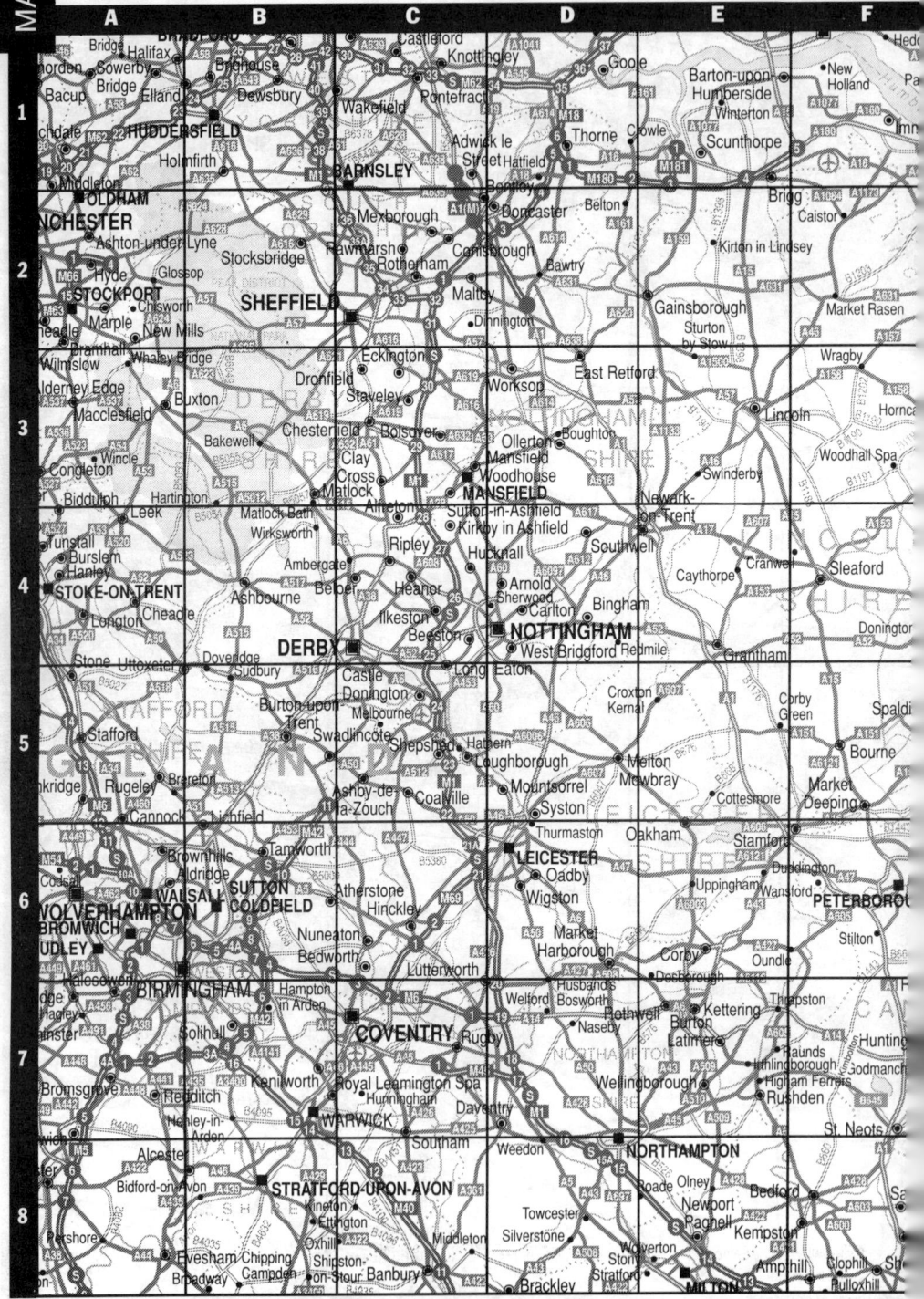

MAP 10

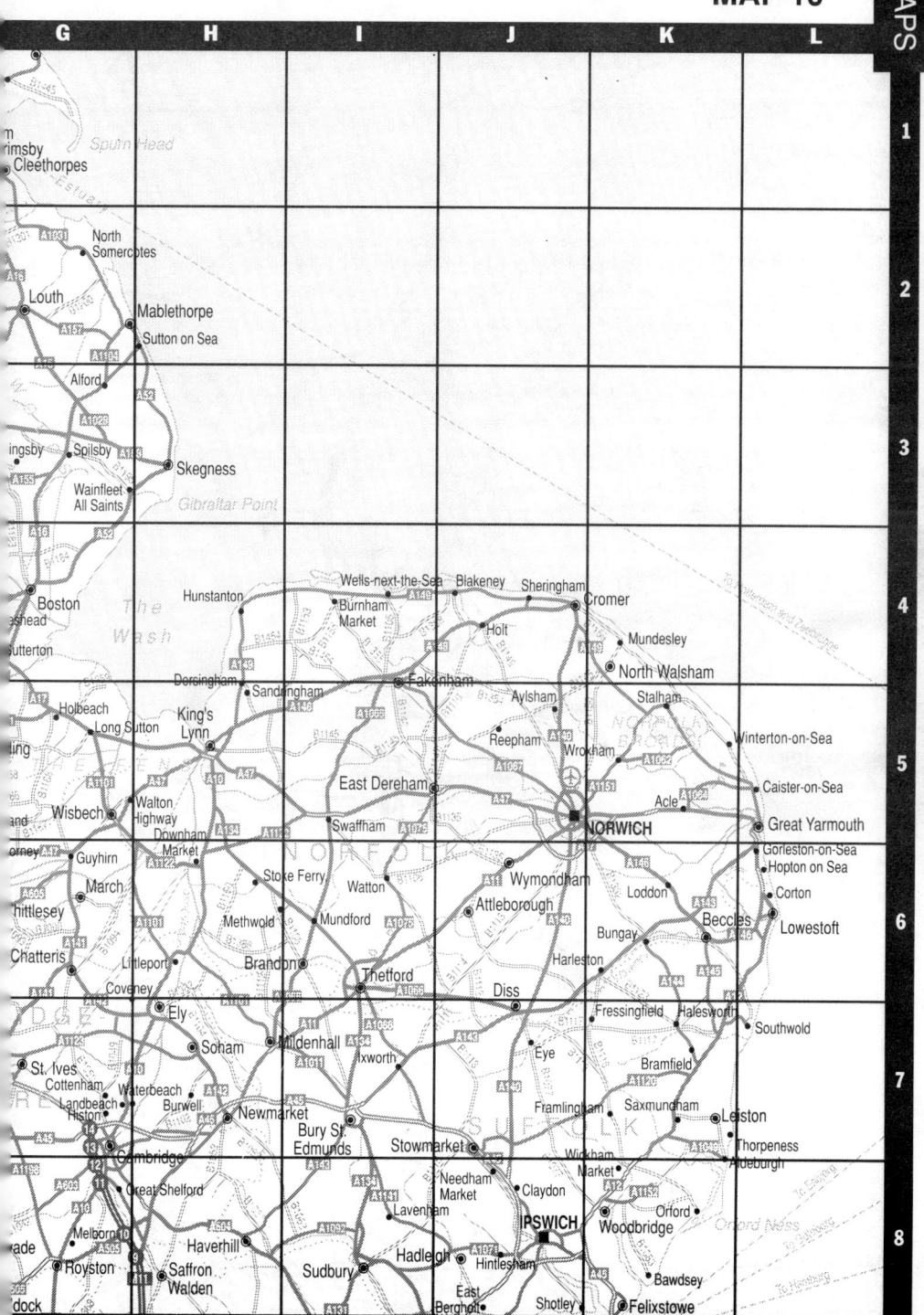

SCALE APPROXIMATELY 14 MILES TO THE SQUARE

MAP 11

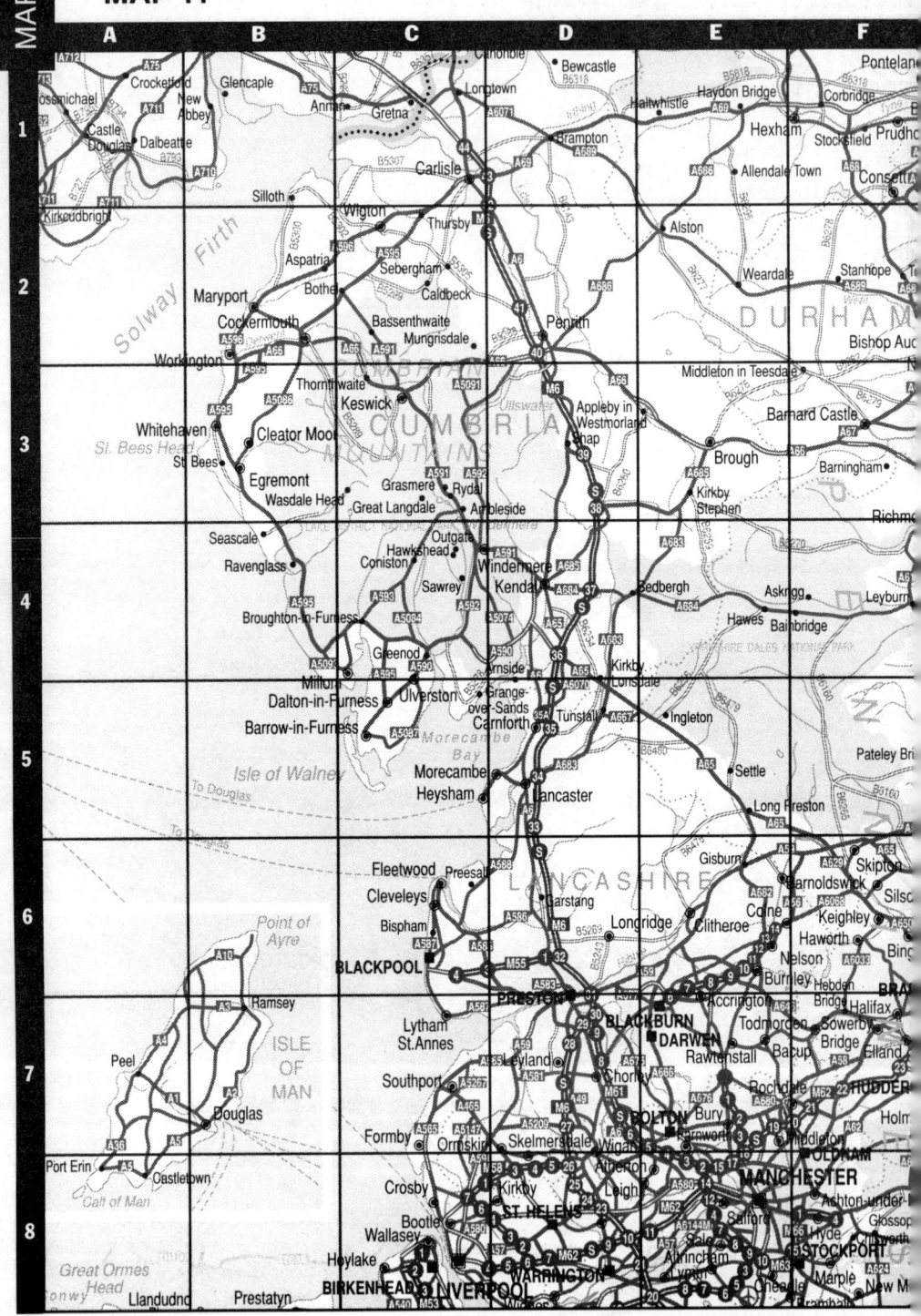

MAP 12

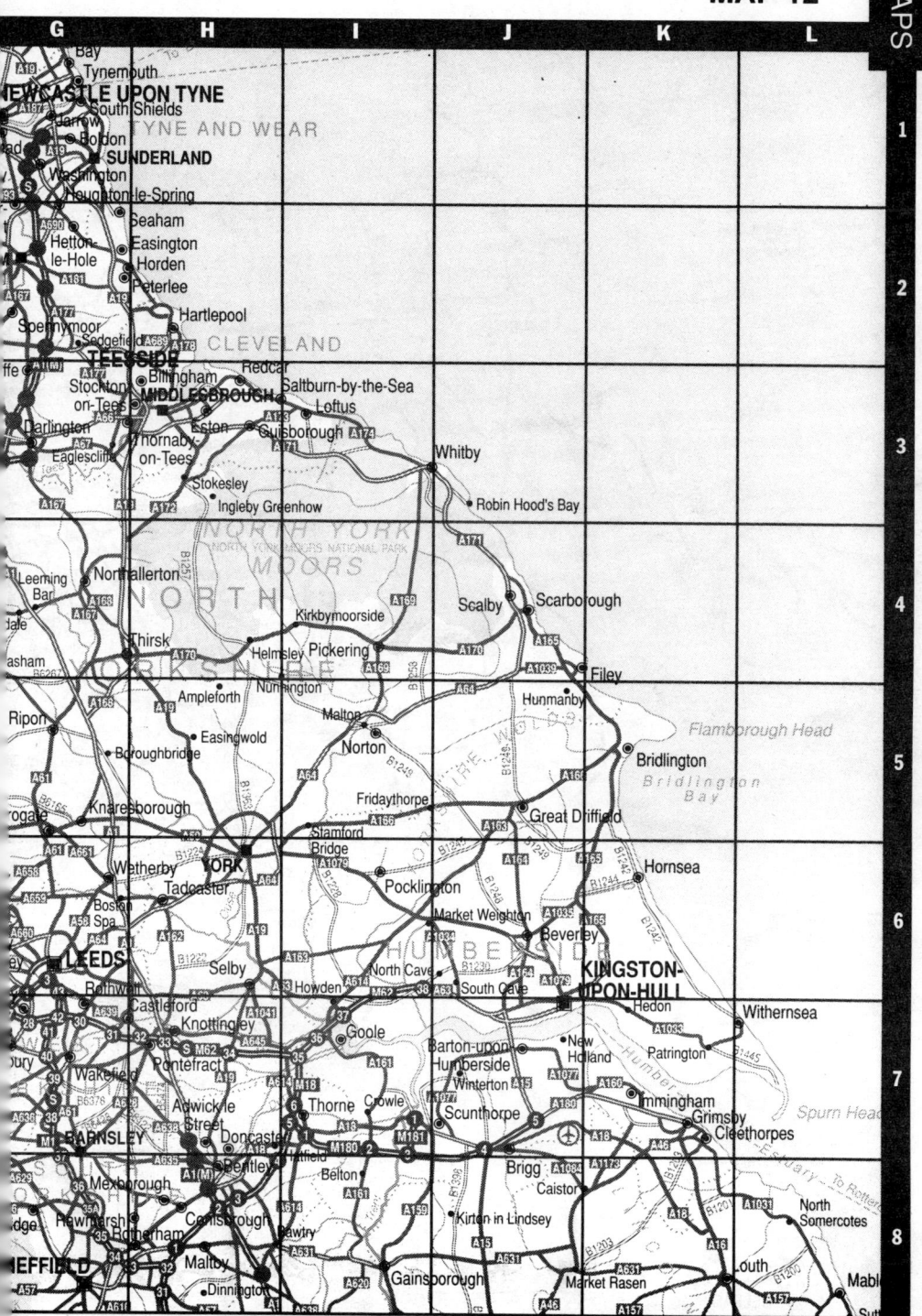

SCALE APPROXIMATELY 14 MILES TO THE SQUARE

MAP 13

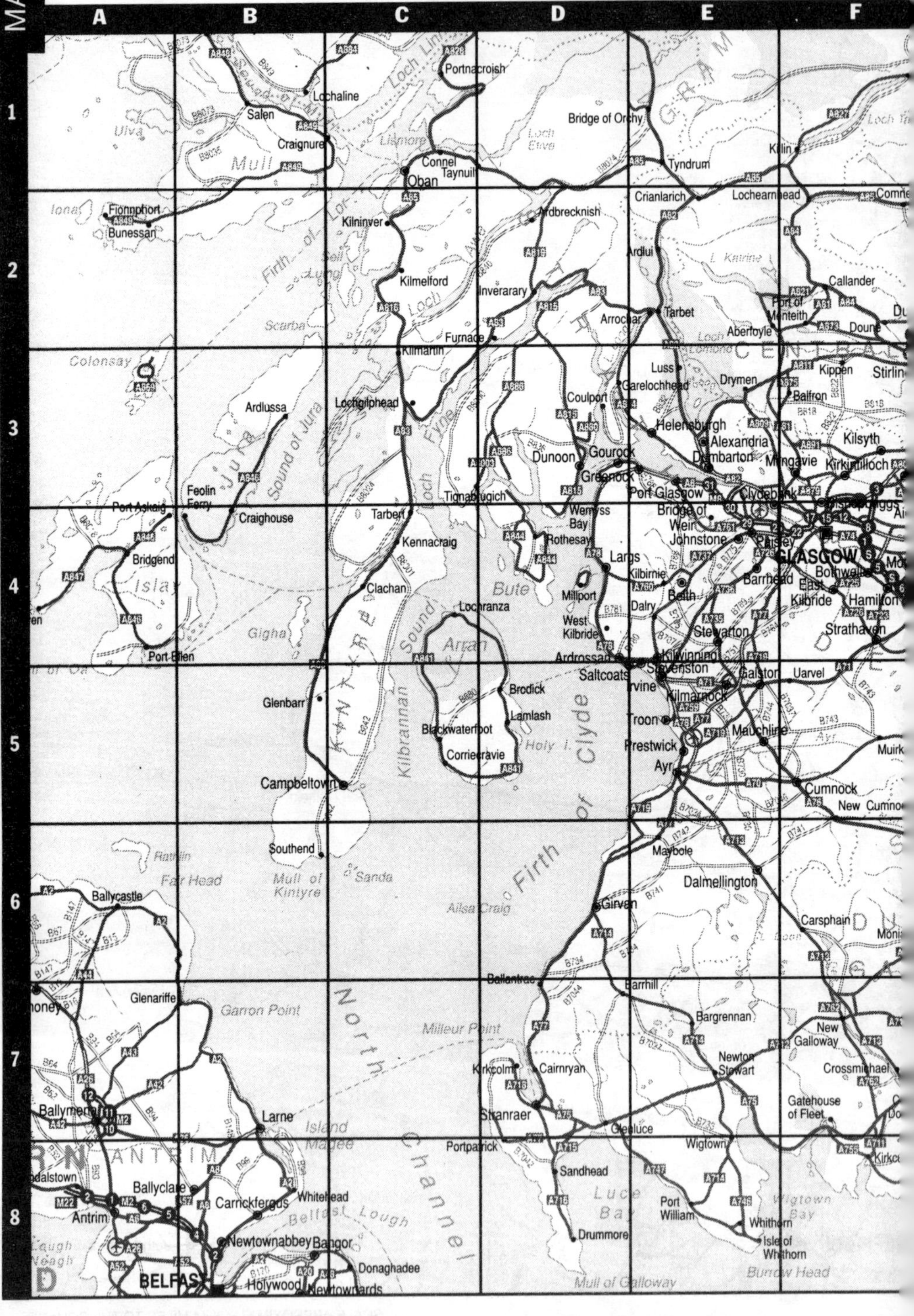

MAP 14

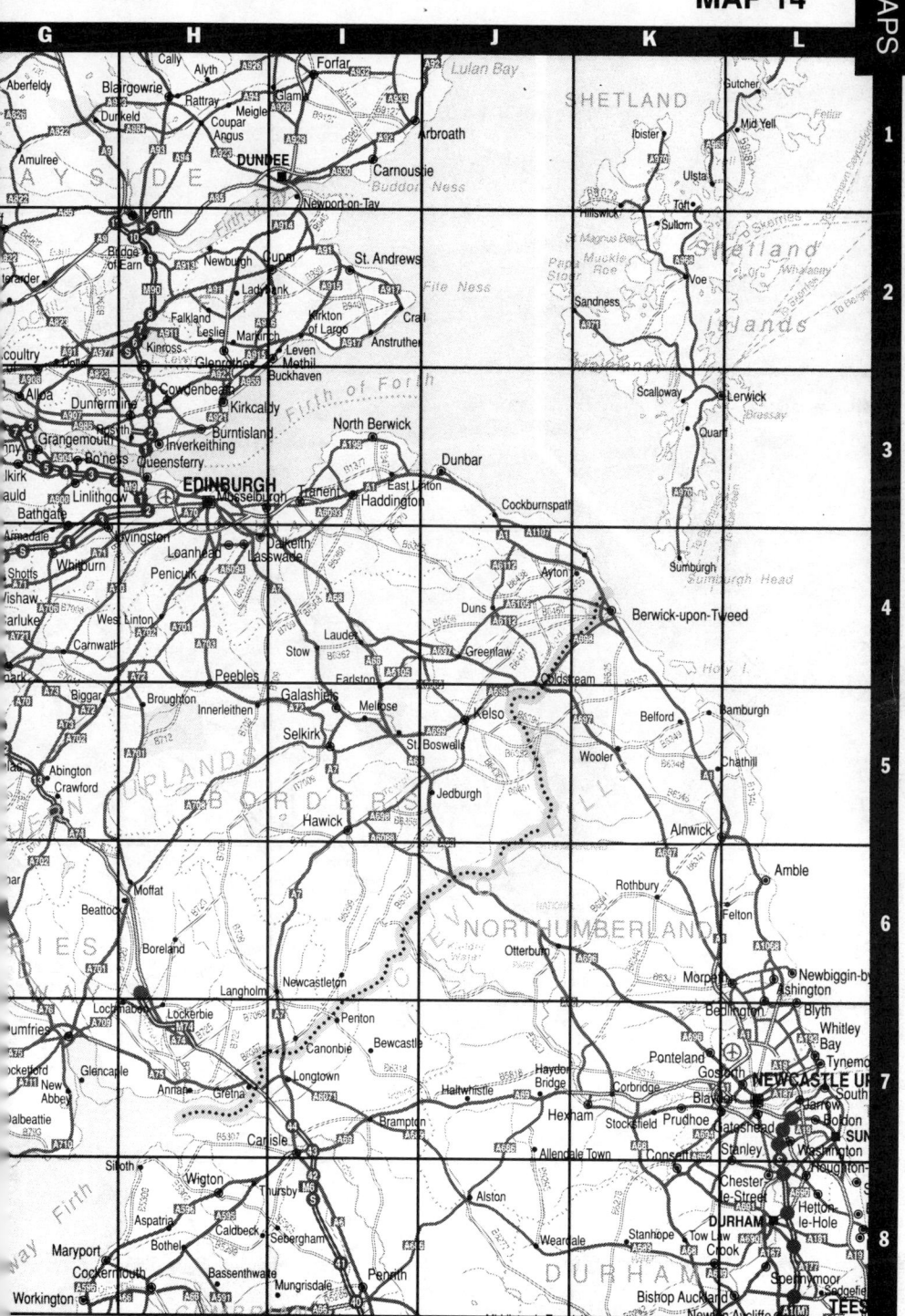

MAP 15

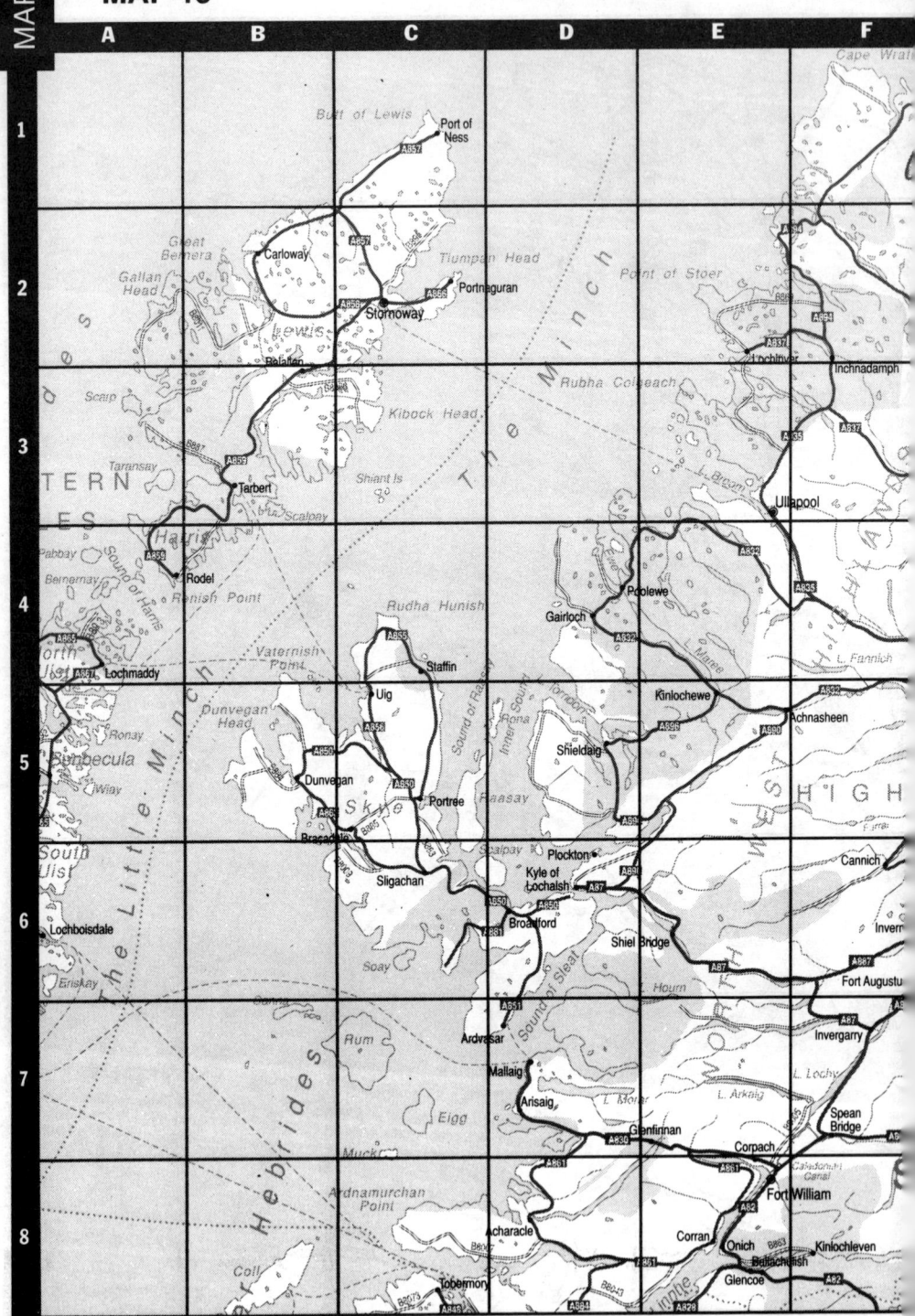

MAP 16

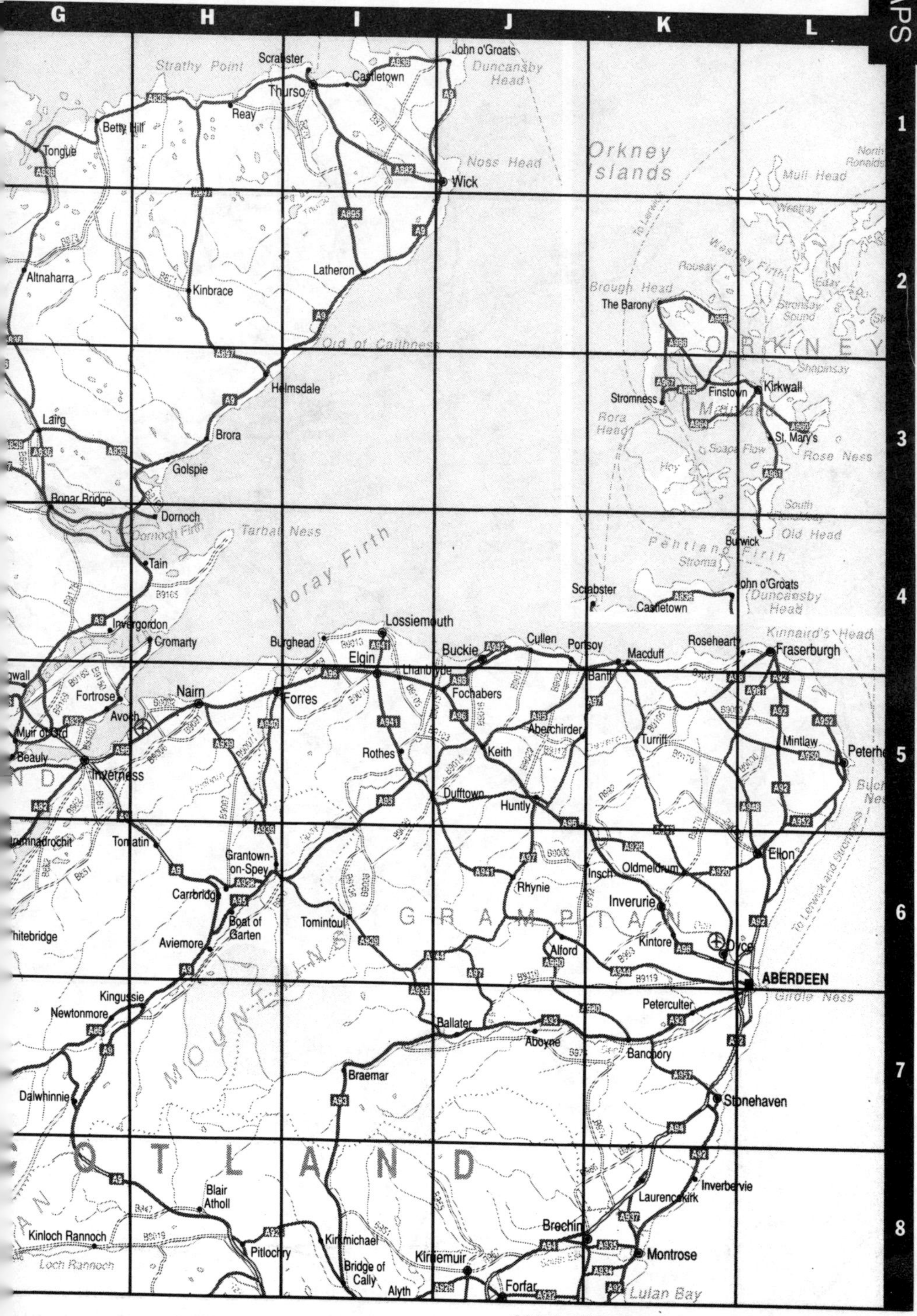

SCALE APPROXIMATELY 16.5 MILES TO THE SQUARE

MAP 17

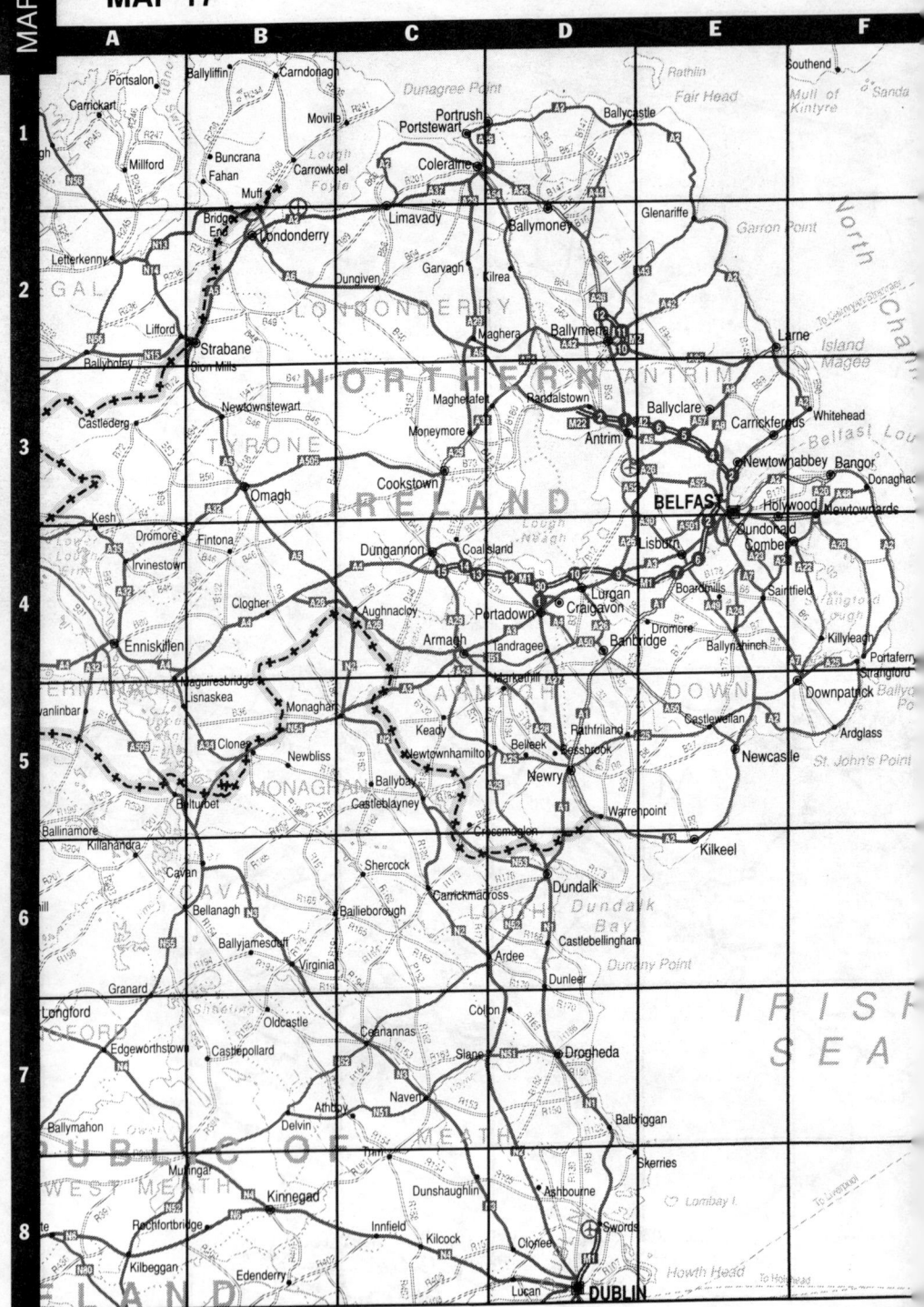

SCALE APPROXIMATELY 16 MILES TO THE SQU[ARE]

1995 EXAM RESULTS : AN INTRODUCTION AND A WARNING

The Introduction

The examination sections of *Choosing Your Independent School* include schools' A- and AS-level (Advanced and Advanced Supplementary), GCSE (General Certificate of Secondary Education) and Scottish results for 1995. *Full guidance on how to use them is given at the beginning of each list.*

A- and AS-level results of more than 500 schools include:

* the number of second year sixth-form examination candidates in 1995;
* the average number of subject entries per candidate in 1995;
* the average number of UCAS points (†) per subject entry in 1995, and
* the average number of UCAS points per candidate in 1995.

The last three appear between the bold vertical lines, with the corresponding aggregate figures for the five years 1990–94 immediately below.

† UCAS (Universities & Colleges Admissions Service) points are calculated thus: A-level grade $A=10$, $B=8$, $C=6$, $D=4$, $E=2$; AS-level grade $A=5$, $B=4$, $C=3$, $D=2$, $E=1$.

GCSE results of more than 600 schools include:

* the number of fifth year (ie main GCSE year 11) candidates in 1995;
* the average number of subject entries per candidate in 1995, and
* the percentage of candidates achieving 5 or more GCSEs at grades A–C in 1995.

These indices appear between the bold vertical lines, with the corresponding aggregate figures for 1990–94 below.

N.B. Percentages are cumulative across all grades: e.g. figures under C are the percentages of candidates achieving grades *A–C. The starred A grade was introduced in 1994. Fourth year candidates who took subjects a year early will have their results included when they reach the fifth year. If they retake subjects in their fifth year and achieve a higher grade, the latter will be counted. (Results are provisional.

Some are subject to revision, either through regrading by examination boards or because they are modular courses.)

The Warning

We are publishing alphabetical lists of schools' results, not league tables. But newspaper league tables are constructed from them and a school is likely to appear in different positions in different tables depending on the criteria used (eg UCAS points or A/B grades). That should not discredit the exercise. But it does reinforce the need for parents to understand the limitations of such lists and of league tables, which have been described as the worship of measurement over quality. We take the view that parents are entitled to have the information, in the context of a huge amount of other information about each school. But they should bear the following points in mind in interpreting it.

First, examination results are only one measure of a school's achievements – albeit a very important one. They should not be seen in isolation from all the other details and characteristics of schools.

Secondly, they are largely raw and therefore crude measurements, not moderated by factors affecting candidates (such as their backgrounds) or schools (such as catchment areas).

Thirdly, they do not tell you how academically selective the school is in admitting pupils at 11, 12, 13 or into the sixth-form at 16.

Fourthly, they do not tell you a school's examination entry policy: does it enter for examinations only those who are certain, or at least very likely, to pass and thereby score more highly than a school with a more liberal policy?

Fifthly, they tell you nothing about 'added value': the extent to which a school has enabled a boy or girl to achieve more than seemed possible three, five or seven years earlier.

Sixthly, they are aggregate results: is it sensible to choose or dismiss a school by the position which the sum of other children's performances have put it in a league table, rather than by the needs and potential of your own child?

Some of these factors are illustrated by the notes below on individual schools or types of schools.

Frankly, it is a foolish parent who chooses a school with only a league table for guidance. Fortunately, evidence of such foolishness is sparse – so far. In the ISIS/MORI survey of *Why & How Parents Choose an Independent School* (1993), the school's *league table position* was cited as an important factor in their choice by only 15% of parents; however, 80% mentioned its examination results.

Remember the milk test. School A takes only the academic cream. Rigorous selection procedures ensure that it recruits those pupils whose ability matches the highest expectations. It whips the cream into shape and with apparently effortless ease secures high pass marks and grades. School B takes silver rather than gold top. There is some cream but it is mostly pretty average milk with some distinctly watery stuff lower down. The cream get excellent results. Much of the milk and water do better than expected. But the overall pass and grade rates are pulled down by predictably weaker performers.

Which is the 'better' school? Conventional parental wisdom will conclude that, on the single measure of exam performance, School A is better. But which has had to work harder? Which has produced more pupils whose results exceed expectations? Which has achieved greater added value? And which has the harder job in educating the public in the sensible interpretation of exam results?

To say that School A has enabled its pupils to get the results at 16 and 18 which their abilities at 11 or 13 indicated were well within their grasp is not to disparage its achievement. Any school where such talent is nurtured and fulfilled is an educational jewel to be treasured. But, despite conventional wisdom, it may not be 'better' than School B.

One final caution: looking at one year's results in isolation can be misleading. Schools have variable intakes and 'off' years. That is why we publish average results over a five-year period as well as for the latest year.

David Woodhead

Notes affecting individual schools or types of school

Sixth-form provision is becoming more diverse as vocational courses – such as BTEC (Business & Technology Education Council), City & Guilds, GNVQ (General National Vocational Qualification) and RSA (Royal Society of Arts) – are added to the traditional A-levels. In some schools, such as Sibford in Oxfordshire, most sixth-form pupils are prepared for vocational qualifications (eg City & Guilds Diploma in Vocational Education or BTEC). Since A-levels form a small part of their provision, these schools are not included in the A-level results list.

The specialist music schools referred to in Chapter 7 (such as Chetham's, Purcell, Wells Cathedral and Yehudi Menuhin) are centres of musical excellence and also provide a mainstream academic education. However, pupils undertaking the schools' intensive musical programme take fewer GCSE and A-level subjects. This affects the average number of points obtained per candidate.

Another distortion affects schools with a substantial proportion of *dyslexic* pupils. For example, all pupils joining Shapwick School in Somerset at 13 are dyslexic and the majority have profound reading, spelling and numeracy problems. A typical profile of a 13+ student would show a reading age of 7.11, comprehension age of 9.10, spelling age of 7.2 and number age of 8.9. Yet in a typical year the average number of GCSEs taken is six and the majority are passed at grades A-D; all students continue into further education at 16, taking mainly A-levels and BTECs.

Cawston College in Norfolk, Grenville College in Devon, Maple Hayes Hall School in Staffordshire and Mark College in Somerset are also among schools catering strongly for dyslexic pupils.

Lord Mayor Treloar College in Hampshire has *severely disabled* students only.

Some pairs of schools publish *combined A-level results*, eg Dame Allan's Boys' & Dame Allan's Girls' in Newcastle upon Tyne, Forest & Forest Girls' in London E17 and Halliford & St David's in Middlesex, which have joint sixth-forms.

Merchant Taylors', Crosby, supplied results for the calculation of previous years' averages from 1991.

The sixth-form at St Martin's School, Solihull, has been operating since 1990.

HOW TO USE THIS SECTION

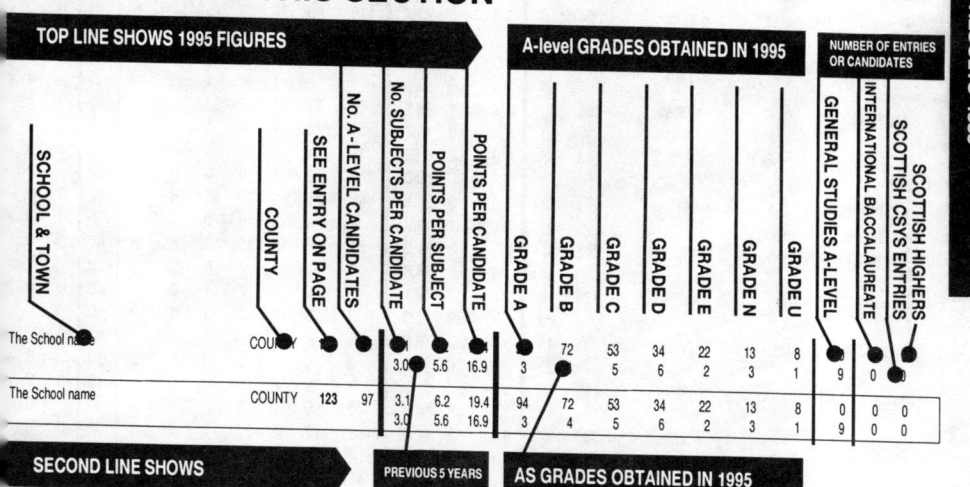

A & AS LEVEL RESULTS 1995

TOP LINE SHOWS 1995 FIGURES → A-level GRADES OBTAINED IN 1995 | NUMBER OF ENTRIES OR CANDIDATES

Column headings (left to right):
- SCHOOL & TOWN
- COUNTY
- SEE ENTRY ON PAGE
- No. A-LEVEL CANDIDATES
- No. SUBJECTS PER CANDIDATE
- POINTS PER SUBJECT
- POINTS PER CANDIDATE
- GRADE A
- GRADE B
- GRADE C
- GRADE D
- GRADE E
- GRADE N
- GRADE U
- GENERAL STUDIES A-LEVEL
- INTERNATIONAL BACCALAUREATE
- SCOTTISH HIGHERS
- SCOTTISH CSYS ENTRIES

Example entries:

School	County	Page	Cands	Subj/Cand	Pts/Subj	Pts/Cand	A	B	C	D	E	N	U	GS	IB	SH	CSYS
The School name	COUNTY			3.0	5.6	16.9	3	72 5	53 6	34 2	22 3	13 1	8	9	0	0	
The School name	COUNTY	123	97	3.1 / 3.0	6.2 / 5.6	19.4 / 16.9	94 / 3	72 / 4	53 / 5	34 / 6	22 / 2	13 / 3	8 / 1	0 / 9	0 / 0	0 / 0	

SECOND LINE SHOWS → PREVIOUS 5 YEARS | AS GRADES OBTAINED IN 1995

You are strongly advised to read school entries in this section in conjunction with the full descriptive entry in the county list.

Read also the introduction and warning on pages 347-350.

The figures show, reading left to right:
- The number of A-level candidates entered by the school in 1995.
- Between the **2 heavy vertical rules** is a Summary of A and AS level data.

The TOP LINE of each school's entry gives the 1995 figure for a) number of subject entries per candidate
b) average points score per subject entry and
c) average number of points per candidate.

The SECOND LINE gives the school's average number and points for (a), (b) and (c) over the previous 5 yrs.
- The next 7 columns after the thick vertical rules give the total number of 1995 results at each grade for A level (ABOVE) and AS level (BELOW) as well as N & U grades.
- The single column to the right between the two vertical thinner lines gives the number of candidates entered for General Studies at A level (ABOVE) and AS level (BELOW). General Studies results are not included in the points scores.
- The last two columns denote the number of candidates entering the International Baccalaureate and (final column) number entering Scottish Highers (ABOVE) and Scottish Certificate of Sixth Year Studies (BELOW).

School	County	P					A	B	C	D	E	N	U			
Abbey Gate College	CHESHIRE	88	20	2.9	5.5	15.9	6	10	22	6	5	5	1	19	0	0
			25	3.3	4.6	15.2	1	0	2	1	0	1	1	0		0
Abbey School, The	BERKS	68	93	3.2	7.1	22.4	89	79	53	33	18	10	4	0	0	0
			93	3.2	7.4	23.5	10	5	2	0	0	0	0	32		0
Abbotsholme School	STAFFS	238	30	3.0	5.6	16.5	14	18	25	10	11	4	7	22	0	0
			31	2.9	4.3	12.4	0	0	0	0	0	0	0	0		0
Abingdon School	OXON	224	117	3.3	7.6	25.3	153	100	62	32	21	6	5	0	0	0
			112	3.3	6.9	22.6	6	7	9	0	1	1	0	9		0
Ackworth School	W YORKS	302	29	2.9	4.7	13.6	4	11	22	27	12	1	5	13	0	0
			41	2.9	5.5	15.9	0	0	0	0	2	0	2	0		0
Adcote School for Girls	SALOP	231	4	3.0	5.0	15.0	0	4	3	1	3	1	0	0	0	0
			6	2.8	5.1	14.5	0	0	0	0	0	0	0	0		0
Aldenham School	HERTS	142	52	2.9	4.4	13.0	13	20	37	30	22	16	15	0	0	0
			64	3.0	4.2	12.7	0	0	0	0	0	0	0	0		0
Alice Ottley School, The	HERWORCS	136	66	2.9	7.8	22.7	91	36	28	22	6	4	1	64	0	0
			56	3.0	6.6	19.7	1	6	0	2	0	0	0	0		0
Alleyn's School	GR LON	175	112	3.2	7.3	23.0	139	79	52	34	22	13	5	8	0	0
			117	3.1	6.0	18.9	3	3	5	7	2	0	0	0		0
Allhallows College	DORSET	107	30	2.8	4.9	13.7	9	16	18	15	11	9	5	0	0	0
			44	2.7	4.5	12.2	0	0	0	1	0	0	0	0		0

A & AS LEVEL RESULTS 19

School	County	P					A	B	C	D	E	N	U		
Ampleforth College	N YORKS	294	116	3.5	6.8	23.7	119	89	71	60	25	14	6	0	0
			120	3.7	6.2	22.6	10	8	10	10	4	1	0	0	0
Ardingly College	W SUSSEX	273	67	3.0	5.7	17.0	50	29	30	42	24	14	9	0	4
			89	2.9	5.6	16.5	1	0	1	2	1	0	0	0	0
Arnold School	LANCS	166	87	3.1	6.4	19.7	65	63	47	52	29	7	1	85	0
			93	3.0	6.0	18.3	0	1	1	0	1	4	0	0	0
Arts Educational School	HERTS	143	25	2.3	5.8	13.2	15	4	16	9	7	4	2	0	0
				0.0	0.0	0.0	0	0	1	0	0	0	0	0	0
Ashford School	KENT	154	51	3.0	6.9	20.5	46	35	22	23	10	5	1	0	0
			61	3.0	6.1	18.2	4	4	6	4	0	1	0	0	0
Ashville College	N YORKS	295	57	3.1	6.8	21.2	61	36	28	25	15	6	6	49	0
			49	3.1	4.8	14.8	1	0	0	2	0	0	1	0	0
Atherley School,The	HANTS	126	8	2.5	7.7	19.1	7	5	5	2	1	0	0	0	0
			23	2.6	5.0	12.8	0	0	1	0	0	0	0	0	0
Austin Friars School	CUMBRIA	98	41	3.0	6.3	19.2	29	36	22	14	9	8	6	41	0
			35	3.0	5.6	16.5	0	0	1	0	0	0	0	0	0
Ayton School	N YORKS	295	12	3.0	5.7	17.0	3	12	8	5	4	2	1	10	0
			10	3.1	4.6	14.5	0	0	1	0	1	0	0	0	0
Bablake School	W MIDS	285	102	3.1	7.7	24.0	136	77	52	30	11	9	3	102	0
			101	3.1	6.9	21.7	1	1	3	0	0	0	0	0	0
Badminton School	AVON	61	46	3.2	7.3	23.5	46	41	31	13	12	0	1	0	0
			40	3.2	7.1	22.6	0	4	3	2	2	0	0	0	0
Fernhill Manor/Ballard College	HANTS	126	10	2.5	4.3	10.8	2	3	8	2	4	1	5	0	0
			7	2.8	4.0	11.1	0	0	0	0	0	0	1	0	0
Bancroft's School	ESSEX	115	101	3.2	7.2	23.1	102	89	60	35	16	7	7	0	0
			98	3.1	6.4	19.6	11	0	3	0	1	0	0	0	0
Barnard Castle School	DURHAM	113	72	3.1	5.3	16.7	50	31	36	48	19	22	18	46	0
			73	3.0	5.0	15.1	0	1	1	1	0	0	0	0	0
Baston School	KENT	154	15	2.6	2.8	7.2	3	2	4	3	13	8	5	0	0
			14	3.0	4.4	13.3	0	0	0	0	0	2	0	0	0
Bath High School GPDST	AVON	61	46	3.0	7.8	23.8	64	29	22	16	4	1	1	21	0
			46	3.0	6.9	20.5	1	1	2	1	1	0	0	0	0
Batley Grammar School	W YORKS	303	88	3.1	5.3	16.5	49	35	63	51	36	19	17	88	0
			79	3.1	5.5	16.7	4	1	0	1	3	1	1	0	0
Bearwood College	BERKS	69	14	2.9	2.4	6.9	1	0	5	8	12	5	9	0	0
			29	2.7	3.7	9.8	0	0	0	0	0	1	0	0	0
Bedales School	HANTS	126	66	3.0	6.3	18.9	47	48	39	27	22	9	6	0	0
			70	3.0	6.7	20.5	0	1	2	0	0	0	0	0	0
Bedford High School	BEDS	67	85	3.0	6.9	20.8	87	50	42	35	20	4	10	13	0
			105	3.0	6.1	18.4	7	4	5	0	1	0	0	0	0
Bedford Modern School	BEDS	67	129	3.3	6.7	21.7	116	93	72	66	30	14	9	0	0
			128	3.3	6.1	20.4	9	10	9	10	1	1	1	47	0
Bedford School	BEDS	68	127	3.1	7.5	23.1	156	93	73	37	20	8	3	0	0
			145	3.0	6.5	19.6	0	0	0	0	1	1	0	0	0
Bedgebury School	KENT	154	38	2.6	5.2	13.3	10	16	28	19	12	10	1	0	0
			39	2.5	4.5	11.2	1	0	1	1	1	0	0	7	0
Bedstone College	SALOP	231	10	2.7	4.0	10.7	1	4	5	5	6	3	1	8	0
			20	2.8	4.7	13.2	0	0	1	0	0	2	2	0	0
Beechwood School Sacred Heart	KENT	154	22	3.5	6.8	24.0	24	19	13	9	2	1	2	0	0
			20	2.9	5.4	15.8	0	1	2	3	3	1	7	0	0
Belvedere School GPDST,The	MERSEY	211	45	3.0	6.0	18.0	30	29	27	21	16	4	8	43	0
			45	2.9	5.6	16.2	0	0	0	0	1	0	0	0	0
Bembridge School	IOW	153	24	2.8	4.5	12.8	6	15	12	7	14	5	7	0	0
			25	2.8	4.0	11.2	0	0	0	0	0	2	2	5	0
Benenden School	KENT	155	63	3.2	8.1	25.5	76	70	25	13	4	0	0	0	0
			58	3.2	6.9	21.8	3	11	3	3	1	2	0	4	0
Bentham School	N YORKS	295	31	2.5	2.9	7.2	1	4	18	12	12	17	13	24	0
			26	2.8	4.3	11.9	0	0	0	0	0	0	0	0	0
Berkhamsted School for Girls	HERTS	143	61	3.1	7.2	22.5	55	43	43	31	5	3	1	0	0
			59	3.0	7.1	21.0	12	6	1	0	0	0	0	0	0

352

A & AS LEVEL RESULTS 1995

School	County	P					A	B	C	D	E	N	U		
Berkhamsted School	HERTS	143	70	3.4	6.8	23.0	64	63	43	36	13	12	0	2	0 0
			88	3.2	6.1	19.7	1	3	4	3	2	2	0	5	0
Bethany School	KENT	155	23	3.0	4.7	13.8	7	13	8	19	10	3	8	0	0 0
			23	2.8	4.3	12.0	0	0	0	0	0	0	0	0	0
Birkdale School	S YORKS	301	45	3.3	6.3	21.0	35	37	31	20	15	6	4	44	0 0
			34	2.9	5.8	17.1	0	0	1	0	2	1	0	0	0
Birkenhead High School GPDST	MERSEY	211	92	3.1	7.0	21.3	93	68	46	32	20	15	1	47	0 0
			93	3.1	6.6	20.3	5	3	1	2	1	0	0	0	0
Birkenhead School	MERSEY	212	93	3.2	6.7	21.2	96	55	45	42	31	12	4	93	0 0
			98	3.1	6.3	19.4	9	3	5	0	1	0	0	0	0
Bishop Challoner School	GR LON	177	17	2.8	4.5	12.5	3	6	14	11	3	5	5	0	0 0
			13	3.0	4.1	12.4	0	0	0	0	0	0	0	0	0
Bishop's Stortford College	HERTS	144	65	2.9	7.2	20.9	59	43	49	22	13	1	1	0	0 0
			71	3.0	6.1	18.5	2	1	1	0	0	0	0	0	0
Blackheath High School GPDST	GR LON	177	31	2.9	6.4	18.5	21	18	22	14	9	4	1	0	0 0
			33	3.0	6.5	19.5	3	0	0	0	0	0	0	0	0
Bloxham School	OXON	224	67	3.0	5.9	17.5	44	38	49	22	19	16	10	42	0 0
			81	3.0	5.4	16.5	0	1	0	0	2	0	0	0	0
Blundell's School	DEVON	102	78	3.2	6.1	19.5	56	47	50	49	30	10	5	0	0 0
			106	2.7	5.2	14.1	2	2	3	1	0	0	0	0	0
Bolitho School, The	CORNWALL	96	2	3.0	6.3	19.0	0	3	1	2	0	0	0	0	0 0
			4	2.5	3.5	8.5	0	0	0	0	0	0	0	0	0
Bolton School (Boys Div.)	LANCS	166	101	3.1	7.9	24.4	147	60	42	24	14	4	0	101	0 0
			118	3.0	7.0	21.0	11	13	4	7	5	0	1	0	0
Bolton School (Girls Div.)	LANCS	166	101	3.1	7.1	21.8	100	73	61	42	22	8	1	100	0 0
			107	3.1	6.9	21.1	5	1	2	0	0	0	0	0	0
Bootham School	N YORKS	296	40	3.1	6.1	19.1	25	25	30	14	15	5	1	30	0 0
			41	3.1	5.9	18.4	6	1	1	3	4	2	3	0	0
Box Hill School	SURREY	248	22	2.7	4.6	12.4	9	5	13	9	8	6	8	0	0 0
			23	2.8	4.0	11.2	1	1	0	2	0	0	1	0	0
Bradfield College	BERKS	69	125	3.0	6.8	20.4	103	96	71	58	34	8	3	0	0 0
			123	3.0	6.1	18.1	1	2	1	2	0	0	0	0	0
Bradford Girls' Grammar School	W YORKS	303	55	3.1	7.5	23.3	60	42	39	18	6	2	1	46	0 0
			86	3.0	6.8	20.2	3	2	1	0	0	0	0	0	0
Bradford Grammar School	W YORKS	303	149	3.2	7.6	24.1	174	130	76	49	21	7	1	10	0 0
			158	3.2	7.6	24.3	13	6	7	4	5	0	0	0	0
Bredon School	GLOS	122	2	1.0	9.0	9.0	1	1	0	0	0	0	0	0	0 0
			6	1.3	3.0	4.0	0	0	0	0	0	0	0	0	0
Brentwood School	ESSEX	115	130	3.3	6.5	21.5	116	90	88	69	37	18	2	0	0 0
			117	3.2	6.1	19.7	3	0	2	5	1	2	1	0	0
Bridgewater School	GR MANCH	209	8	3.1	5.0	15.7	2	6	7	3	2	1	4	7	0 0
			4	3.0	5.7	17.1	0	0	0	0	0	0	0	0	0
Brighton & Hove High School GPDST	E SUSSEX	268	61	3.1	6.7	20.5	54	49	29	24	18	6	3	0	0 0
			56	3.0	7.3	22.1	0	1	1	2	1	0	4	0	0
Brighton College	E SUSSEX	268	85	3.2	7.0	22.1	79	65	61	32	20	6	1	0	0 0
			92	3.0	6.5	19.6	5	1	0	0	3	0	1	0	0
Brigidine School, The	BERKS	69	16	2.8	4.6	13.0	6	5	6	13	8	4	2	0	0 0
			19	2.8	4.5	12.4	0	0	1	0	1	0	0	0	0
Bristol Cathedral School	AVON	61	50	2.9	7.2	21.2	56	33	25	14	11	6	1	0	0 0
			59	3.2	5.3	16.6	1	0	0	1	0	0	0	0	0
Bristol Grammar School	AVON	62	138	3.0	7.4	22.0	153	110	60	51	27	7	3	1	0 0
			123	3.1	7.0	21.5	1	1	0	0	0	0	0	0	0
British School in The Netherlands, The	OVERSEAS		57	3.4	6.1	20.9	35	39	41	40	16	5	4	0	0 0
			56	3.4	5.8	19.7	7	4	10	3	2	1	1	0	0
British School of Paris, The	OVERSEAS		33	2.9	5.8	17.2	21	23	15	15	11	7	5	2	0 0
				0.0	0.0	0.0	0	0	0	0	0	0	0	20	0
Bromley High School GPDST	KENT	155	60	3.0	7.6	22.6	67	43	42	22	2	1	1	0	0 0
			55	3.0	6.5	19.2	0	0	0	0	0	0	0	0	0
Bromsgrove School	HER WORCS	137	100	3.1	6.4	19.8	67	77	56	39	28	14	7	94	0 0
			93	3.0	5.6	16.7	12	10	9	8	2	2	2	0	0

353

A & AS LEVEL RESULTS 1995

School	County		P					A	B	C	D	E	N	U		
Bruton School for Girls	SOMERSET	234	44	3.0	6.7	19.8	40	29	18	28	8	4	2	0	0
			47	2.9	5.3	15.2	0	1	0	0	0	0	1	0	0
Bryanston School	DORSET	107	125	3.2	6.8	21.8	109	93	85	47	26	14	6	0	0
			126	3.2	6.7	21.5	14	7	11	4	2	0	1	0	0
Buckingham College	GR LON	177	17	3.1	5.7	17.9	13	9	7	12	6	3	3	0	0
				0.0	0.0	0.0	0	0	0	0	0	0	0	0	0
Burgess Hill School	W SUSSEX	274	38	3.0	6.9	20.4	33	25	27	15	7	5	0	0	0
			31	2.9	6.5	18.8	1	0	1	0	1	0	0	0	0
Bury Grammar School	LANCS	166	53	3.1	6.3	19.2	44	29	38	17	17	9	6	53	0
			74	3.0	6.2	18.7	2	0	1	1	0	0	0	0	0
Bury Grammar School (Girls)	LANCS	166	105	3.0	6.8	20.6	102	54	62	44	26	8	4	105	0
			95	3.0	6.1	18.4	13	3	6	4	7	0	1	0	0
Bury Lawn School	BUCKS	80	9	2.8	5.4	15.0	6	5	1	3	3	1	2	0	0
			10	2.4	3.7	8.9	0	0	2	1	3	2	0	0	0
Canford School	DORSET	108	99	3.1	7.2	22.1	103	60	85	31	12	5	4	0	0
			114	3.0	6.4	19.2	1	1	2	0	0	0	0	0	0
Carmel College	OXON	225	35	2.6	5.4	14.1	17	14	18	20	12	3	8	0	0
			38	2.9	6.2	18.1	0	0	0	0	0	0	0	0	0
Casterton School	CUMBRIA	98	41	3.0	6.9	21.2	38	26	30	19	11	1	0	38	0
			45	2.9	6.7	19.5	0	0	0	1	0	0	0	0	0
Caterham School	SURREY	249	84	3.2	7.7	25.1	108	74	49	27	11	1	1	0	0
			88	3.2	6.8	21.8	1	0	1	1	0	0	0	0	0
Central Newcastle High School GPDST	TYNE	280	69	3.0	7.4	22.3	64	53	46	29	2	3	1	32	0
			74	3.1	6.9	21.6	9	4	3	4	1	2	0	0	0
Channing School	GR LON	178	40	3.0	8.0	23.9	52	33	20	9	5	1	0	0	0
			29	3.0	6.9	20.3	1	0	0	0	0	0	0	0	0
Charterhouse	SURREY	249	144	3.1	7.8	24.5	180	125	79	41	12	6	0	0	0
			164	3.1	7.3	23.0	8	7	1	0	2	0	0	0	0
Cheadle Hulme School	CHESHIRE	89	116	3.0	6.4	19.5	93	69	77	65	26	13	6	116	0
			112	3.0	6.5	19.9	0	0	0	0	1	0	1	0	0
Cheltenham College (A-levels)	GLOS	123	132	3.1	6.9	21.2	119	102	84	53	22	15	8	27	7	0
			127	3.1	6.4	20.0	4	2	1	0	1	0	0	0	0

IB RESULT GRADES

							7	6	5	4	3	2	1		
IB results Higher Grade			7	3.4	5.5	19.0	3	5	4	1	3	4	1	0	0	0
IB results Subsidiary Grades			13	0.7	7.7	5.2	4	2	0	0	1	0	0	0	0
Cheltenham Ladies' College, The	GLOS	123	140	3.1	7.9	24.6	183	126	65	41	18	2	1	0	0
			131	3.1	7.6	23.5	1	2	1	0	0	0	0	0	0
Chetham's School of Music	GR MANCH	209	52	2.4	8.0	18.9	57	30	16	10	3	2	0	1	0	0
			53	2.4	7.2	17.1	2	1	5	1	1	0	1	0	0
Chigwell School	ESSEX	116	66	3.2	7.2	22.7	64	53	51	24	7	2	4	0	0
			65	3.0	6.5	19.5	3	0	1	1	0	0	2	0	0
Christ College	S WALES	310	64	3.1	6.0	18.4	36	44	46	30	16	8	8	0	0
			66	3.0	5.7	16.8	2	2	4	3	4	1	0	60	0
Christ's Hospital	W SUSSEX	274	99	3.2	6.9	22.0	90	78	69	32	18	10	5	0	0
			99	3.1	6.5	19.9	4	8	4	6	0	0	2	0	0
Churcher's College	HANTS	127	63	3.0	6.5	19.7	46	34	49	38	18	0	2	0	0
			50	3.0	5.6	16.9	3	0	2	1	1	0	0	0	0
City of London Freemen's School	SURREY	250	56	3.0	6.8	20.4	51	41	24	21	13	8	2	53	0
			57	3.1	5.6	17.4	3	3	4	5	0	4	0	0	0
City of London School	GR LON	178	121	3.2	7.8	25.2	157	107	53	23	18	5	4	0	0
			115	3.2	7.4	23.5	21	12	6	4	2	0	0	0	0
City of London School For Girls	GR LON	179	71	3.2	7.7	24.2	94	57	36	21	7	4	4	0	0
			75	3.1	7.3	22.7	0	2	0	0	0	0	0	0	0
Claremont Fan Court School	SURREY	250	35	2.9	5.6	16.2	21	18	20	15	17	7	4	1	0	0
			31	3.0	5.5	16.7	0	0	0	0	0	0	0	0	0
Claysmore School	DORSET	108	39	2.8	5.2	14.6	13	10	39	21	17	3	4	5	0	0
			43	2.8	4.9	13.7	0	0	0	2	2	1	0	0	0
Clifton College	AVON	62	128	3.2	7.5	24.0	155	99	73	41	20	6	3	6	0	0
			126	3.2	6.2	19.5	10	8	2	0	1	1	2	0	0

354

A & AS LEVEL RESULTS 1995

School	County	P					A	B	C	D	E	N	U			
Clifton High School	AVON	62	52	3.0	7.1	21.2	61	34	23	14	11	11	1	0	0	0
			51	3.0	6.4	19.0	1	0	0	0	0	0	1	0		0
Cobham Hall School	KENT	155	26	3.1	6.3	19.4	21	19	12	14	5	4	4	0	0	0
			31	3.0	5.1	15.3	0	0	1	0	1	0	0	0		0
Cokethorpe School	OXON	225	12	2.6	1.7	4.3	0	1	2	5	6	2	14	0	0	0
			15	2.3	2.5	5.7	0	0	0	0	0	1	1	0		0
Colfe's School	GR LON	179	102	3.3	6.4	20.8	78	73	69	49	35	8	6	4	0	0
			92	3.1	5.5	17.4	5	7	6	3	3	3	1	0		0
Colston's Girls' School	AVON	62	66	2.8	5.3	15.1	31	38	31	35	28	19	6	0	0	0
			54	2.8	5.8	16.4	0	0	0	0	0	0	0	0		0
Colston's Collegiate School	AVON	63	53	2.9	4.5	13.2	17	21	25	38	29	11	13	16	0	0
			53	2.9	4.6	13.6	0	0	0	0	0	0	0	37		0
Combe Bank School	KENT	156	24	2.9	4.5	13.2	7	12	15	10	11	7	8	0	0	0
			19	2.6	5.1	13.1	0	0	0	0	0	0	0	0		0
Cranleigh School	SURREY	251	115	3.1	6.0	18.7	58	81	86	72	35	15	6	0	0	0
			130	3.2	6.5	20.4	3	3	4	5	3	0	0	0		0
Croft House School	DORSET	108	20	2.5	4.5	10.9	6	5	12	6	8	7	3	0	0	0
			13	2.5	4.6	11.7	0	1	0	1	1	0	1	0		0
Croham Hurst School	GR LON	180	31	3.1	6.5	19.9	19	26	22	16	6	2	3	0	0	0
			31	2.9	5.9	17.3	2	0	0	0	0	0	0	0		0
Croydon High School GPDST	GR LON	180	75	3.2	7.6	23.9	87	63	46	16	11	4	1	21	0	0
			85	3.2	6.8	21.6	3	4	6	2	3	0	0	0		0
Culcheth Hall	CHESHIRE	90	11	2.6	3.6	9.5	1	1	7	8	6	4	1	7	0	0
			15	2.8	4.8	13.3	0	0	0	0	0	0	2	0		0
Culford School	SUFFOLK	243	59	3.0	6.2	18.5	42	31	38	24	12	9	5	10	0	0
			59	2.9	5.4	15.5	3	5	6	8	5	3	2	45		0
Dame Alice Harpur School	BEDS	68	88	3.0	6.5	19.6	60	62	61	43	15	12	5	33	0	0
			106	2.9	6.2	17.9	4	5	4	3	2	0	0	0		0
Dame Allan's Schools	TYNE	280	100	3.0	6.2	18.7	76	56	58	54	33	11	8	75	0	0
			102	3.0	5.8	17.1	3	3	2	1	1	0	0	0		0
Dauntsey's School	WILTS	291	91	3.2	6.8	22.0	69	79	57	51	14	1	3	22	0	0
			94	3.1	6.2	19.6	7	7	7	9	5	2	1	0		0
Dean Close School	GLOS	123	81	3.3	7.6	24.8	99	71	53	22	10	2	3	0	0	0
			84	3.2	6.4	20.5	2	1	1	4	1	0	0	0		0
Denstone College	STAFFS	239	50	3.0	5.0	15.2	17	24	35	29	31	6	4	27	0	0
			55	3.0	5.1	15.3	0	0	1	1	4	4	3	0		0
Derby High School	DERBYS	100	30	3.0	7.1	21.1	28	26	14	13	4	3	1	30	0	0
			22	2.8	6.4	18.0	0	0	0	0	0	0	0	0		0
Dixie Grammar & Wolstan Prep Schools	LEICS	170	14	2.9	6.4	18.3	7	13	6	9	4	0	1	11	0	0
				0.0	0.0	0.0	0	0	0	0	0	0	0	0		0
Douai School	BERKS	70	20	3.0	4.6	13.6	2	9	17	15	9	7	0	20	0	0
			40	3.1	5.3	16.6	0	0	0	0	1	0	0	0		0
Dover College	KENT	156	34	3.1	4.5	14.1	9	22	16	20	16	12	11	0	0	0
			49	2.9	4.5	13.2	0	1	1	0	0	0	0	0		0
Downe House	BERKS	70	71	3.2	8.3	26.3	97	71	34	13	1	0	0	71	0	0
			64	3.1	7.3	22.8	5	7	4	3	0	0	0	0		0
Downside School	AVON	63	72	3.0	6.1	18.6	53	41	47	32	27	13	3	0	0	0
			79	3.1	5.8	17.8	0	2	0	3	0	0	1	0		0
Duchy Grammar School,The	CORNWALL	97	3	3.0	4.0	12.0	0	1	2	3	2	1	0	0	0	0
			5	3.4	3.7	12.7	0	0	0	0	0	0	0	0		0
Duke of York's Royal Military School	KENT	156	34	2.9	5.4	15.6	6	29	26	15	10	10	2	23	0	0
			34	3.0	5.5	16.6	0	0	0	0	1	0	0	10		0
Dulwich College	GR LON	181	170	3.2	7.3	23.2	214	114	99	51	23	20	8	0	0	0
			192	3.1	7.0	21.7	4	3	1	2	3	0	2	0		0
Dunottar School	SURREY	252	16	3.0	6.2	18.7	8	14	11	9	3	1	2	0	0	0
			20	2.9	6.0	17.3	0	0	0	0	0	0	0	0		0
Durham High School for Girls	DURHAM	113	19	3.1	6.2	18.8	17	9	12	10	2	6	2	0	0	0
			28	3.0	6.7	19.9	0	0	0	0	0	0	0	0		0
Durham School	DURHAM	114	65	3.1	5.6	17.1	36	44	37	33	20	20	8	44	0	0
			77	2.9	5.6	16.4	0	0	1	1	0	0	0	0		0

A & AS LEVEL RESULTS 1995

School	County		P					A	B	C	D	E	N	U		
Ealing College Upper School	GR LON	182	11	3.0	4.8	14.5	4	10	3	3	5	2	6	0	0	0
			23	2.8	4.9	13.8	0	0	0	0	0	1	0	0	0	0
Eastbourne College	E SUSSEX	269	104	3.0	6.9	20.7	90	73	77	37	27	8	2	0	0	0
			116	3.0	6.2	18.8	2	0	0	0	0	0	0	0	0	0
Edgbaston C of E College	W MIDS	286	19	2.9	5.7	16.6	11	8	12	14	7	3	0	0	0	0
			18	3.0	4.8	14.4	0	0	0	0	0	0	0	0	0	0
Edgbaston High School for Girls	W MIDS	287	58	3.0	6.3	18.6	40	30	41	39	12	7	1	54	0	0
			54	3.0	6.2	18.2	1	2	0	1	0	1	0	4	0	0
Edgehill College	DEVON	102	43	2.7	3.6	9.7	8	11	19	19	21	16	19	0	0	0
			38	3.1	4.7	14.4	0	3	2	0	1	1	3	0	0	0
Elizabeth College	C.I.	87	78	3.0	5.8	17.6	55	39	46	47	24	16	9	0	0	0
			65	3.0	5.9	17.9	0	0	0	1	0	0	0	0	0	0
Ellesmere College	SALOP	231	51	2.8	4.7	13.2	19	15	30	32	26	14	6	31	0	0
			73	2.7	4.5	12.5	0	0	1	1	0	0	0	16	0	0
Elmhurst Ballet School	SURREY	252	16	1.6	5.6	9.1	4	6	5	4	5	1	1	0	0	0
			25	1.6	5.7	9.0	0	0	0	1	0	0	0	0	0	0
Elmslie Girls School	LANCS	167	10	2.6	3.8	10.0	1	2	7	5	6	5	0	0	0	0
			20	2.7	4.8	13.1	0	0	0	0	0	0	0	6	0	0
Eltham College	GR LON	182	91	3.3	7.4	24.0	109	75	40	42	16	8	0	0	0	0
			90	3.2	7.1	22.8	6	2	3	2	0	0	0	0	0	0
Emanuel School	GR LON	182	63	3.0	6.1	17.9	40	41	40	25	20	12	5	0	0	0
			71	2.8	4.8	13.6	1	1	1	2	2	0	0	5	0	0
Embley Park School	HANTS	128	19	2.8	4.4	12.5	8	3	10	12	8	6	3	0	0	0
			19	2.6	3.2	8.3	0	1	0	2	2	1	3	13	0	0
Eothen School	SURREY		7	3.1	5.5	17.4	2	7	2	5	2	2	0	0	0	0
			9	2.7	5.3	14.3	1	0	0	2	1	0	0	0	0	0
Epsom College	SURREY	253	148	3.2	7.5	23.9	194	97	91	56	21	7	3	0	0	0
			148	3.1	7.1	22.2	1	0	0	0	0	1	0	0	0	0
Eton College	BERKS	71	240	3.5	8.5	29.5	450	183	124	37	8	2	1	42	0	0
			257	3.4	8.3	27.9	18	17	11	3	0	1	0	0	0	0
Ewell Castle School	SURREY	253	29	2.7	4.4	11.8	4	14	9	26	13	4	7	0	0	0
			26	3.0	4.5	13.6	0	1	0	0	1	0	0	0	0	0
Exeter School	DEVON	103	130	3.1	6.6	20.4	113	83	85	45	34	17	7	81	0	0
			119	3.1	6.5	19.9	7	6	10	4	2	2	1	0	0	0
Farlington School	W SUSSEX	275	19	2.9	5.8	17.2	8	10	19	12	2	4	1	0	0	0
			23	2.8	5.8	15.9	0	0	0	0	1	0	0	15	0	0
Farnborough Hill	HANTS	128	54	3.0	6.8	20.2	45	37	35	26	12	4	1	0	0	0
			39	2.9	6.4	18.5	1	0	0	0	0	0	0	0	0	0
Farringtons and Stratford House	KENT	157	33	3.0	4.9	14.8	12	18	22	15	17	8	7	8	0	0
			32	3.0	4.4	13.0	0	0	0	0	0	1	0	0	0	0
Felsted School	ESSEX	117	86	3.1	7.0	21.8	87	69	52	28	14	15	4	0	0	0
			102	3.0	6.1	18.6	0	1	0	0	0	0	0	0	0	0
Forest Schools	GR LON	183	123	3.0	6.4	19.3	101	85	58	51	31	21	10	94	0	0
			117	3.0	6.0	18.3	3	1	6	11	5	2	1	0	0	0
Framlingham College	SUFFOLK	243	78	2.8	6.3	17.7	55	44	47	26	19	8	6	1	0	0
			71	2.8	4.9	14.0	3	3	2	7	7	3	2	54	0	0
Francis Holland School Clarence Gate	GR LON	183	49	3.1	7.4	22.9	45	52	27	14	8	2	0	0	0	0
			41	3.0	6.7	20.0	0	3	3	0	0	0	0	0	0	0
Francis Holland School	GR LON	184	18	2.7	6.4	17.6	11	10	12	10	6	0	0	0	0	0
			19	2.8	6.0	16.9	0	0	0	1	0	0	0	6	0	0
Frensham Heights	SURREY	254	28	3.2	6.7	21.4	25	23	15	11	6	1	5	0	0	0
			32	2.9	5.6	16.1	0	2	3	1	0	2	0	0	0	0
Friends School	ESSEX	117	14	2.9	5.1	14.5	4	7	8	8	6	1	2	11	0	0
			25	3.0	4.3	13.2	0	0	1	6	0	1	1	0	0	0
Fulneck School	W YORKS	304	44	2.9	3.8	11.0	8	20	17	20	30	18	13	39	0	0
			25	2.7	4.0	10.9	0	0	0	0	0	0	0	0	0	0
Fyling Hall School	N YORKS	296	10	2.7	2.3	6.1	0	1	5	4	3	6	7	10	0	0
			10	2.9	2.0	5.7	0	0	0	0	1	0	1	0	0	0
Gateways School	W YORKS	304	10	2.9	5.9	17.2	8	4	5	5	2	0	0	10	0	0
			16	2.8	4.6	13.2	0	0	0	0	0	0	0	0	0	0

A & AS LEVEL RESULTS 1995

School	County			P			A	B	C	D	E	N	U			
Giggleswick School	N YORKS	297	56	3.0	6.0	17.9	27	40	43	26	21	7	1	56	0	0
			59	2.8	5.6	16.0	1	1	0	0	2	0	1	0		0
Godolphin & Latymer School,The	GR LON	185	84	3.2	8.3	26.2	123	71	42	17	3	1	0	0	0	0
			96	3.1	7.6	23.5	11	3	3	1	0	0	0	0		0
Godolphin School,The	WILTS	291	41	3.1	6.0	18.5	27	25	28	25	10	12	0	26	0	0
			36	3.1	6.2	19.1	0	0	0	0	0	0	0	0		0
Gordonstoun School	SCOTLAND	317	105	3.0	5.5	16.8	42	69	75	64	36	19	8	0	0	0
			102	3.0	5.9	17.6	0	1	2	2	3	2	2	0		0
Grange School,The	CHESHIRE	90	62	2.8	6.9	19.4	52	40	37	28	12	2	3	61	0	0
			52	3.0	6.8	20.4	1	0	0	0	1	0	0	0		0
Greenacre School	SURREY	254	17	3.1	4.5	13.6	4	12	8	6	11	7	3	16	0	0
			24	2.8	4.9	13.5	0	0	0	1	0	1	0	0		0
Greenfields School	E SUSSEX	269	8	2.1	7.5	16.0	7	2	5	3	0	0	0	0	0	0
			2	1.8	5.9	10.7	0	0	0	0	0	0	0	0		0
Grenville College	DEVON	103	32	2.7	3.1	8.2	2	7	15	15	18	12	16	11	0	0
			27	2.6	3.9	10.3	0	0	0	0	0	0	0	0		0
Gresham's School	NORFOLK	215	89	3.1	6.8	21.3	83	54	58	47	26	2	2	0	0	0
			91	3.3	6.4	20.9	6	1	2	1	2	1	2	0		0
Guildford High School for Girls	SURREY	254	57	3.1	8.4	25.9	95	43	18	16	2	0	0	0	0	0
			49	3.1	7.5	23.4	1	0	0	1	0	0	0	0		0
Haberdashers' Aske's Sch. for Girls	HERTS	145	114	3.2	8.4	26.9	181	94	46	19	6	3	0	0	0	0
			116	3.0	7.9	24.1	20	5	5	4	0	0	0	0		0
Haberdashers' Aske's School,The	HERTS	145	152	3.4	8.4	28.2	267	111	69	31	8	3	1	1	0	0
			155	3.3	8.0	25.9	16	15	10	2	3	1	0	0		0
Haberdashers' Monmouth School for Girl	S WALES	311	70	2.9	6.9	20.2	55	54	48	30	11	7	1	0	0	0
			72	3.1	6.6	20.4	0	0	0	0	0	0	0	11		0
Haileybury	HERTS	145	116	3.1	6.9	21.8	118	75	79	44	28	10	5	44	0	0
			148	3.1	6.6	20.3	3	5	1	2	1	0	0	0		0
Halliford School/St David's School	GR LON	185	36	2.9	4.6	13.6	15	15	15	20	16	12	10	0	0	0
			38	2.9	4.0	11.4	1	0	4	1	0	1	0	0		0
Hampton School	GR LON	185	136	3.5	6.4	22.8	119	94	96	60	44	10	9	136	0	0
			119	3.5	6.2	21.3	8	23	25	18	14	6	7	0		0
Haresfoot Senior School	HERTS	145	2	2.5	2.8	7.0	0	0	0	2	3	0	0	2	0	0
			3	2.7	3.5	9.3	0	0	0	0	0	0	0	0		0
Harrogate Ladies' College	N YORKS	297	37	3.2	6.7	21.7	38	27	20	18	5	5	6	23	0	0
			47	3.2	5.7	18.0	0	1	0	0	0	0	0	0		0
Harrow School	GR LON	186	146	3.2	7.4	23.5	177	117	76	45	24	12	6	0	0	0
			149	3.1	7.4	22.7	3	3	5	1	0	0	0	0		0
Headington School	OXON	226	84	3.2	7.0	22.4	90	51	57	37	21	2	5	0	0	0
			65	3.0	6.8	20.9	4	1	4	1	0	0	0	0		0
Heathfield School	BERKS	72	18	3.0	7.7	23.0	19	18	8	7	2	0	0	0	0	0
			22	3.0	5.7	17.1	0	0	0	0	0	0	0	0		0
Heathfield School GPDST	GR LON	186	37	3.0	6.8	20.5	36	20	22	20	6	4	2	0	0	0
			30	3.0	6.1	18.2	0	2	1	1	1	0	0	0		0
Hellenic College of London	GR LON	186	8	4.0	6.1	24.2	7	4	8	7	3	1	1	0	0	0
				3.8	5.8	22.2	2	0	0	0	0	0	0	0		0
Hereford Cathedral School	HERWORCS	138	88	3.2	5.7	18.3	46	56	72	50	25	11	17	75	0	0
			79	3.1	6.2	19.0	0	1	3	2	3	0	0	0		0
Hethersett Old Hall School	NORFOLK	215	18	2.6	4.4	11.3	0	4	11	12	6	2	1	3	0	0
			19	2.6	5.7	15.0	2	3	5	2	5	0	4	4		0
Highclare School	W MIDS	288	10	2.6	5.9	15.3	4	5	6	6	4	0	1	2	0	0
			14	2.7	4.7	12.6	1	0	0	0	0	0	0	0		0
Highgate School	GR LON	188	101	3.2	7.3	23.0	96	91	69	36	15	4	3	0	0	0
			93	3.1	6.5	20.1	3	4	3	2	1	0	0	8		0
Hipperholme Grammar School	W YORKS	304	30	2.8	4.8	13.5	9	13	17	18	18	3	6	24	0	0
			28	2.9	4.8	13.8	0	0	0	1	0	2	0	0		0
Holy Child School	W MIDS	288	10	2.9	6.8	19.7	7	6	8	6	2	0	0	0	0	0
			20	3.0	4.7	13.9	0	0	1	0	0	0	0	0		0
Holy Trinity College	KENT	158	35	2.9	6.0	17.3	23	26	11	20	7	8	4	0	0	0
			28	2.8	6.0	16.6	0	1	0	1	0	0	0	0		0

357

A & AS LEVEL RESULTS 1995

School	County		P					A	B	C	D	E	N	U		
Holy Trinity School	HERWORCS	139	15	3.1	5.8	17.8	6	11	7	13	5	1	0	10	0	0
			13	2.8	4.8	13.6	1	1	1	1	0	1	0	0	0
Howell's School	N WALES	308	29	3.0	7.7	22.8	40	17	16	5	5	2	1	0	0	0
			30	3.0	5.9	17.4	0	0	0	0	0	0	1	0	0
Howell's School Llandaff GPDST	S WALES	311	67	3.0	6.8	20.2	56	47	42	30	13	7	3	0	0	0
			67	3.0	6.1	18.3	3	0	0	1	0	0	0	0	0
Hull Grammar School	HUMBER	151	39	3.0	3.7	11.3	13	5	18	30	20	12	14	38	0	0
			14	3.0	3.4	10.1	0	0	0	0	1	2	9	0	0
Hull High School	HUMBER	151	15	2.9	6.4	18.9	14	7	10	4	2	5	0	15	0	0
			17	2.9	6.2	18.0	0	1	1	0	0	0	2	0	0
Hulme Grammar School for Girls	LANCS	167	53	3.0	6.0	17.8	35	30	30	35	16	9	3	53	0	0
			53	3.0	6.6	19.5	0	0	0	0	1	0	0	0	0
Hulme Grammar School	LANCS	167	87	3.1	6.0	18.8	67	53	48	47	19	22	11	87	0	0
			85	3.0	5.9	17.8	3	1	0	2	1	0	0	0	0
Hurst Lodge School	BERKS	73	2	2.0	3.5	7.0	0	1	0	1	1	0	1	0	0	0
			7	2.9	4.1	11.7	0	0	0	0	0	0	0	0	0
Hurstpierpoint College	W SUSSEX	276	46	3.2	6.3	20.2	36	31	30	21	17	3	5	0	0	0
			69	3.0	5.7	17.0	1	0	5	2	1	0	1	0	0
Hymers College	HUMBER	152	91	3.2	6.8	21.8	90	66	56	30	21	12	5	56	0	0
			97	3.1	6.3	19.5	2	2	9	3	4	1	2	0	0
Ilford Ursuline High School	GR LON	188	30	3.0	5.9	17.4	11	25	18	15	8	3	2	0	0	0
			34	2.9	5.5	15.9	1	2	2	3	3	4	0	0	0
Ipswich High School GPDST	SUFFOLK	244	55	3.1	7.1	21.9	52	37	41	25	7	2	2	1	0	0
			45	3.0	6.7	20.1	2	2	1	2	2	0	0	0	0
Ipswich School	SUFFOLK	244	91	3.1	7.0	21.4	83	67	64	39	13	9	3	0	0	0
			95	3.1	6.6	20.8	1	1	0	1	0	0	0	0	0
James Allen's Girls' School	GR LON	189	97	3.1	8.0	25.1	137	79	47	18	12	3	1	0	0	0
			86	3.1	7.6	23.5	9	3	0	0	0	0	0	0	0
John Lyon School,The	GR LON	189	62	3.1	6.3	19.5	39	47	45	30	24	5	1	0	0	0
			68	3.1	6.4	20.0	0	0	0	1	1	0	0	0	0
Kelly College	DEVON	103	62	2.9	5.2	14.9	28	27	41	30	25	14	8	61	0	0
			54	2.9	5.0	14.5	0	1	2	1	2	1	1	1	0
Kent College	KENT	159	68	3.2	5.4	17.7	35	36	45	38	27	16	6	0	0	0
			74	3.1	6.0	18.9	5	6	8	4	6	3	4	8	0
Kent College Pembury	KENT	159	38	2.9	5.6	16.0	25	16	17	20	13	7	4	4	0	0
			31	3.0	5.0	14.8	0	1	3	3	4	2	1	0	0
Kimbolton School	CAMBS	84	69	2.9	6.3	18.7	59	42	31	28	25	12	4	53	0	0
			67	2.9	6.1	18.0	2	0	0	1	1	0	0	0	0
King Alfred School,The	GR LON	190	26	2.8	5.8	16.4	19	9	19	8	9	7	2	0	0	0
			19	2.9	6.0	17.4	0	0	0	0	0	0	0	0	0
King Edward VI High Sch. for Girls	W MIDS	288	73	3.1	8.8	27.4	132	54	29	6	1	0	0	73	0	0
			81	3.0	8.1	24.7	10	0	0	0	0	0	0	0	0
King Edward VI School	HANTS	129	120	3.1	7.8	24.2	170	84	66	24	18	9	3	0	0	0
			138	3.1	7.1	21.8	0	0	0	0	0	0	0	0	0
King Edward's School	AVON	64	112	3.1	6.1	19.1	77	75	66	59	45	12	4	0	0	0
			107	3.1	6.6	20.4	1	1	6	6	4	3	2	0	0
King Edward VII School	LANCS	167	43	3.0	5.5	16.3	17	24	31	32	12	10	1	43	0	0
			62	3.0	5.1	15.2	0	0	0	1	1	0	0	0	0
King Edward's School	W MIDS	288	122	3.2	8.1	26.1	195	81	63	25	9	3	0	122	0	0
			110	3.3	8.4	27.5	9	5	2	9	2	5	1	0	0
King Edward's School	SURREY	256	61	2.9	5.9	17.1	35	34	37	37	20	6	5	44	0	0
			60	2.9	5.2	15.2	0	1	0	4	2	2	0	0	0
King Henry VIII	W MIDS	289	108	3.2	7.3	23.3	115	95	66	32	18	8	3	91	0	0
			108	3.2	6.5	20.7	3	4	2	3	1	2	1	0	0
King William's College	IOM	153	42	3.0	6.0	18.4	25	26	35	19	15	4	4	19	0	0
			44	3.0	5.1	15.2	0	0	0	0	0	0	0	1	0
King's College School	GR LON	190	131	3.3	8.6	28.7	252	101	44	19	7	2	0	0	0	0
			127	3.2	7.8	25.4	6	4	7	4	1	0	1	0	0
King's College	SOMERSET	235	99	3.1	6.0	18.5	65	63	57	68	27	17	7	0	0	0
			99	2.9	5.7	16.7	1	0	0	0	0	0	0	0	0

School	Location	P					A	B	C	D	E	N	U		
King's High School for Girls	W'WICKS	283	58	3.1	7.6	23.7	65	44	39	15	7	3	0	0	0
			60	3.0	6.8	20.3	10	2	2	0	1	0	0	0	0
Kings Monkton School	S WALES	311	14	3.0	5.0	15.1	6	8	7	8	7	1	5	0	0
			11	2.6	5.1	13.4	0	0	0	0	0	0	0	0	0
King's School	SOMERSET	236	57	3.2	6.4	20.6	45	35	34	41	12	3	5	0	0
			59	3.0	5.5	16.7	3	4	4	3	2	0	0	0	0
King's School	KENT	160	139	3.3	8.0	26.5	205	108	70	35	16	4	1	22	0	0
			169	3.2	7.4	23.7	19	15	8	1	0	1	0	0	0
King's School	CHESHIRE	92	71	3.2	7.4	23.8	98	45	35	27	12	8	2	70	0	0
			63	3.2	7.3	23.2	2	0	0	0	0	0	0	0	0
King's School,The	TYNE	280	75	3.4	5.0	17.1	38	45	36	44	33	20	21	0	0	0
			80	3.3	5.2	17.5	3	4	7	10	9	3	5	0	0
King's School,The	CHESHIRE	92	132	3.0	5.9	17.8	82	85	81	57	47	19	17	5	0	0
			135	3.0	6.0	18.1	2	4	4	4	1	1	0	0	0
King's School	GLOS	124	47	3.0	6.1	18.2	28	37	30	17	10	6	5	0	0	0
			44	3.0	5.4	16.0	1	0	0	1	3	3	5	3	0
King's School Rochester	KENT	160	63	3.7	6.1	23.0	47	46	57	50	19	7	5	0	0	0
			74	3.1	5.7	17.6	1	3	2	3	1	0	0	0	0
King's School,The	HERWORCS	139	113	3.1	7.2	22.1	114	83	68	42	23	5	3	5	0	0
			135	3.0	6.6	20.2	9	4	2	4	1	0	0	0	0
King's School	CAMBS	85	44	3.3	5.7	18.9	25	29	33	21	17	8	6	0	0	0
			60	3.2	5.6	17.7	3	1	3	2	0	1	3	0	0
Kingham Hill School	OXON	227	7	2.6	1.9	4.9	0	1	0	4	3	2	6	0	0	0
			14	2.8	3.2	9.0	0	0	0	0	4	0	0	0	0
Kingsley School	W'WICKS	284	33	3.0	5.9	17.9	19	25	16	17	14	6	2	21	0	0
			37	3.0	5.7	17.2	0	2	0	0	1	0	0	0	0
Kingston Grammar School	GR LON	191	74	3.1	6.4	19.6	57	43	64	26	23	12	3	0	0	0
			74	3.1	6.0	18.4	0	0	0	0	0	0	0	0	0
Kingswood School	AVON	64	66	3.1	5.9	18.2	39	47	41	26	21	16	6	32	0	0
			76	3.2	5.3	16.9	1	4	3	4	4	1	0	0	0
Kingswood Schools	MERSEY	212	7	3.0	5.3	16.0	3	3	5	5	4	1	0	7	0	0
			12	2.9	3.2	9.1	0	0	0	0	0	0	0	0	0
Kirkham Grammar School	LANCS	168	65	2.9	5.4	15.5	25	41	40	28	15	14	13	56	0	0
			58	2.9	5.2	15.4	1	2	6	5	6	2	3	0	0
La Retraite School	WILTS	292	17	2.4	4.2	9.8	1	6	9	11	5	5	3	0	0	0
			17	2.5	4.1	10.5	0	0	0	0	0	1	0	0	0
La Sagesse Convent High School	TYNE	281	27	3.1	4.7	14.9	6	12	20	19	12	4	4	9	0	0
			26	2.8	4.9	13.6	1	3	2	1	2	4	4	0	0
Ladies College	C.I.	88	34	2.9	7.0	20.6	33	24	16	13	5	6	0	0	0	0
			40	3.1	6.4	19.6	1	1	2	2	0	0	0	0	0
Lady Eleanor Holles School,The	GR LON	191	87	3.4	8.3	28.3	139	78	29	14	11	0	0	87	0	0
			77	3.2	7.5	24.0	22	8	11	6	5	0	0	0	0
Lancing College	W SUSSEX	276	102	3.2	6.8	21.4	77	89	74	45	20	9	3	0	0	0
			129	3.2	6.6	20.8	4	1	2	0	2	2	0	0	0
Langley School	NORFOLK	216	27	2.6	3.1	8.1	2	10	6	11	17	7	15	0	0	0
			22	2.7	3.7	9.8	0	0	0	0	0	4	3	0	0
Latymer Upper School	GR LON	191	122	3.2	7.0	22.2	130	91	69	38	37	11	4	0	0	0
			111	3.1	6.6	20.5	6	2	1	2	1	0	0	0	0
Lavant House	W SUSSEX	276	2	3.0	8.3	25.0	1	5	0	0	0	0	0	0	0	0
			6	2.6	4.7	12.4	0	0	0	0	0	0	0	0	0
Lawnside School	HERWORCS		9	2.9	3.0	8.6	1	0	3	8	5	2	4	0	0	0
			11	3.0	4.2	8.9	0	0	2	0	1	2	1	0	0
Leeds Girls' High School	W YORKS	305	75	3.1	7.2	22.7	96	38	43	28	15	10	1	74	0	0
			76	3.1	7.1	21.7	6	0	2	1	0	0	0	0	0
Leeds Grammar School	W YORKS	305	117	3.1	6.8	21.3	114	77	71	51	25	18	4	116	0	0
			130	3.1	7.0	22.0	4	4	3	4	1	0	1	0	0
Leicester Grammar School	LEICS	170	63	3.1	6.8	21.3	55	50	35	31	14	8	1	4	0	0
			57	3.2	7.0	22.4	2	3	2	1	0	1	0	0	0
Leicester High School for Girls	LEICS	171	21	3.0	6.6	20.1	11	23	12	12	4	1	1	5	0	0
			22	3.0	6.4	19.0	0	0	0	0	0	0	0	0	0

359

A & AS LEVEL RESULTS 1995

School	County	P				A	B	C	D	E	N	U		
Leighton Park School	BERKS	73	63	3.2	6.4	20.5	54	44	42	24	16	10	8	0	0	0
			55	3.1	5.4	16.5	3	0	1	2	0	1	0	0	0
Leys School,The	CAMBS	85	94	3.0	6.0	18.3	62	56	63	46	32	10	12	0	0	0
			91	3.0	6.2	18.6	2	3	0	1	0	0	0	0	0
Licensed Victuallers' School	BERKS	74	28	3.0	4.7	13.9	7	9	24	13	15	3	7	0	0	0
			26	2.9	3.7	10.8	1	2	1	2	1	1	3	22	0
Liverpool College	MERSEY	212	70	3.0	5.3	16.0	26	45	45	43	30	17	4	64	0	0
			63	3.0	5.5	16.5	0	0	0	0	0	0	0	0	0
Llandovery College	S WALES	311	33	3.0	5.0	14.8	8	14	26	25	9	9	4	0	0	0
			33	2.8	5.0	14.1	1	3	1	1	0	0	0	0	0
Longridge Towers School	NORTHUMB	220	8	3.2	5.8	18.9	4	6	7	5	0	4	0	0	0	0
			8	3.6	5.1	18.3	0	0	0	0	1	0	0	0	0
Lord Mayor Treloar College	HANTS	130	3	2.0	5.7	11.3	1	1	2	0	2	0	0	0	0	0
			9	2.2	5.5	12.4	0	0	0	0	0	0	0	0	0
Lord Wandsworth College	HANTS	130	63	3.0	5.7	17.4	28	41	50	36	15	12	6	0	0	0
			59	2.9	5.9	17.3	0	1	2	1	2	0	0	0	0
Loughborough Grammar School	LEICS	171	134	3.1	6.7	20.6	134	85	75	55	35	21	10	128	0	0
			130	3.1	6.7	20.8	1	0	0	0	0	0	0	0	0
Loughborough High School	LEICS	171	76	3.1	7.8	24.2	101	58	45	20	7	2	2	75	0	0
			70	3.0	7.1	21.2	1	0	0	0	0	0	0	0	0
Luckley-Oakfield School	BERKS	74	35	2.7	3.7	9.9	3	14	10	26	16	14	10	8	0	0
			25	2.7	5.2	14.2	0	0	2	0	1	0	0	0	0
Magdalen College School	OXON	227	65	3.2	7.5	24.3	94	44	32	17	13	6	4	0	0	0
			71	3.2	7.1	22.6	0	0	1	0	0	0	0	0	0
Malvern College (A-levels)	HERWORCS	140	135	3.2	6.6	21.2	115	89	86	71	39	8	8	20	15	0
			132	3.1	6.6	20.7	6	12	9	5	2	2	0	0	0

IB RESULT GRADES

							7	6	5	4	3	2	1		
IB results Higher Grade			15	3.5	6.8	23.6	11	13	6	6	7	2	0	0	0	0
IB results Subsidiary Grades			6	3.5	6.9	24.2	8	5	2	0	0	0	0	0	0

School	County	P				A	B	C	D	E	N	U		
Malvern Girls' College	HERWORCS	140	96	3.2	8.1	25.7	137	83	43	20	6	4	2	52	0	0
			81	3.1	7.6	23.5	7	9	4	2	1	0	0	0	0
Manchester Grammar School	GR MANCH	210	200	3.3	8.4	27.8	357	155	79	31	9	7	3	0	0	0
			199	3.1	8.3	25.6	9	12	12	4	1	0	0	0	0
Manchester High School for Girls	GR MANCH	210	102	3.1	7.6	23.6	141	62	53	27	15	10	2	63	0	0
			92	3.2	6.9	22.0	4	3	3	4	1	0	0	0	0
Marlborough College	WILTS	292	165	3.1	6.9	21.5	151	136	89	76	37	16	5	2	0	0
			193	3.1	6.8	21.1	3	3	3	0	0	0	0	0	0
Mayfield College	E SUSSEX	269	13	2.8	3.3	9.4	0	3	9	7	8	4	6	0	0	0
			15	2.8	2.7	7.5	0	0	0	0	0	0	0	0	0
Maynard School	DEVON	104	54	3.0	6.9	20.9	46	48	26	23	9	6	2	14	0	0
			49	3.0	7.1	21.3	0	2	4	0	0	0	0	0	0
Merchant Taylors' School for Girls	MERSEY	213	71	3.1	7.5	23.1	91	57	30	20	8	9	3	71	0	0
			70	3.0	6.9	20.7	0	0	0	0	0	0	0	0	0
Merchant Taylors' School	MERSEY	213	77	3.1	7.3	22.5	86	59	47	24	12	7	2	77	0	0
			91	3.1	7.4	22.8	0	0	0	1	0	0	0	0	0
Merchant Taylors' School	GR LON	192	125	3.1	7.8	24.6	172	99	56	46	12	3	2	63	0	0
			119	3.1	7.2	22.2	4	0	0	0	0	0	0	0	0
Micklefield Wadhurst	E SUSSEX	269	21	2.4	4.1	10.0	2	10	9	7	12	8	2	0	0	0
			13	2.6	4.4	11.4	0	0	0	1	1	0	1	0	0
Mill Hill School	GR LON	192	100	3.2	6.2	20.0	69	72	81	47	26	9	16	0	0	0
			109	3.1	5.9	18.3	0	1	0	4	1	0	0	0	0
Millfield School	SOMERSET	236	238	3.0	6.4	18.9	199	132	144	106	61	32	24	210	0	0
			220	3.0	6.3	18.8	8	0	2	2	0	1	0	0	0
Milton Abbey School	DORSET	110	42	2.9	3.3	9.4	2	12	21	23	20	15	19	0	0	0
			40	2.7	3.5	9.4	0	3	0	3	3	6	3	25	0
Moira House School	E SUSSEX	269	33	3.0	6.4	19.1	16	29	27	14	5	4	2	0	0	0
			31	3.0	5.7	16.9	0	1	1	0	0	1	0	0	0
Monkton Combe School	AVON	64	65	3.0	6.5	19.6	52	44	42	27	12	8	9	0	0	0
			77	3.0	5.7	17.1	1	1	2	1	0	0	0	0	0

A & AS LEVEL RESULTS 1995

School	County	P					A	B	C	D	E	N	U		
Monmouth School	S WALES	312	84	3.1	7.1	22.3	79	66	59	25	11	6	1	0	0 0
			81	3.1	6.6	20.6	2	7	9	6	4	2	2	0	0
More House School	GR LON	192	26	3.1	6.7	21.0	23	21	17	10	3	4	3	0	0 0
			19	3.0	6.4	19.2	0	0	0	0	0	0	0	0	0
Moreton Hall School	SALOP	232	57	3.1	6.5	20.0	36	50	39	29	16	4	1	0	0 0
			41	3.0	5.6	16.7	0	0	0	0	0	0	0	0	0
Mostyn House School	CHESHIRE	92	27	2.6	3.0	7.7	3	5	13	11	7	15	16	22	0 0
				0.0	0.0	0.0	0	0	0	0	1	0	0	0	0
Mount Carmel School	CHESHIRE	93	43	3.0	4.5	13.5	11	18	20	32	30	9	7	31	0 0
			35	2.9	5.3	15.5	0	3	1	1	0	1	0	1	0
Mount School, The	N YORKS	298	39	3.1	7.3	22.6	45	27	19	18	7	1	0	26	0 0
			35	3.0	5.4	16.1	2	0	1	1	1	0	0	0	0
Mount School	GR LON	193	54	2.9	4.6	13.2	21	26	27	18	19	18	19	0	0 0
			28	3.1	5.0	15.4	0	2	2	2	3	1	5	0	0
Mount St. Mary's College	DERBYS	100	45	3.1	6.1	18.6	33	23	29	24	11	11	2	0	0 0
			51	3.2	4.5	14.5	3	2	1	3	1	0	0	0	0
New Hall School	ESSEX	119	60	3.0	6.8	20.5	44	46	48	27	8	2	2	0	0 0
			60	2.8	5.8	16.3	0	1	0	1	3	1	0	0	0
Newcastle-under-Lyme School	STAFFS	240	151	3.1	6.5	20.3	136	88	97	65	38	24	9	151	0 0
			156	3.1	6.4	19.8	8	6	1	3	3	2	3	0	0
Newcastle U Tyne Church High Sch	TYNE	281	47	3.0	6.0	17.9	31	20	32	29	14	4	3	0	0 0
			33	3.1	5.7	17.4	3	3	2	0	3	0	0	0	0
Newlands Manor School	E SUSSEX	270	26	2.8	4.6	13.1	15	6	11	12	10	5	10	0	0 0
			23	3.0	4.2	12.7	0	0	2	1	1	2	5	0	0
North Cestrian Grammar School	CHESHIRE	93	24	3.0	5.7	16.9	13	12	17	17	5	4	3	24	0 0
			34	2.9	4.0	11.9	0	0	0	0	0	0	0	0	0
North Foreland Lodge	HANTS	131	22	2.9	6.6	18.8	15	14	16	10	5	3	0	0	0 0
			21	2.9	5.9	17.4	1	0	0	0	0	0	0	0	0
North London Collegiate School, The	GR LON	193	106	3.3	8.6	28.6	188	85	48	15	4	0	0	0	0 0
			103	3.2	8.3	26.4	17	7	1	0	0	0	0	0	0
Northampton High School	N'HANTS	218	46	3.0	7.4	22.4	46	39	24	14	7	1	3	16	0 0
			56	3.0	6.0	18.0	3	3	6	0	1	0	0	0	0
Northfield School	HERTS	147	5	3.2	5.9	18.8	1	4	6	1	3	0	0	0	0 0
			3	2.4	4.1	9.5	0	0	0	3	0	0	0	0	0
Northwood College	GR LON	193	39	3.0	6.8	20.5	34	36	13	20	7	5	2	0	0 0
			31	2.9	6.0	17.4	0	0	0	0	0	0	0	0	0
Norwich High School for Girls GPDST	NORFOLK	216	87	3.0	7.3	22.3	92	62	55	41	13	1	1	87	0 0
			70	3.1	6.5	20.2	0	0	0	0	0	0	0	0	0
Norwich School	NORFOLK	216	93	3.1	7.1	22.0	97	64	57	40	20	6	2	0	0 0
			91	3.1	6.5	19.8	3	2	1	0	0	0	0	0	0
Notre Dame School	SURREY	258	15	2.8	5.7	15.9	6	13	8	4	4	6	0	0	0 0
			13	2.7	4.9	13.0	0	0	1	0	0	1	0	15	0
Notre Dame Senior School	SURREY	258	14	2.9	6.7	19.1	9	9	11	9	1	0	1	0	0 0
			20	2.6	5.6	14.6	0	0	0	0	1	0	0	0	0
Notting Hill & Ealing High School GPDS	GR LON	194	73	3.0	7.4	22.4	78	66	31	24	16	6	0	0	0 0
			70	2.9	7.1	21.1	2	1	0	0	0	0	0	0	0
Nottingham High School for Girls GPDST	NOTTS	222	118	3.2	7.6	24.2	148	85	73	33	13	4	2	69	0 0
			113	3.1	7.1	22.0	6	6	7	9	2	1	0	0	0
Nottingham High School	NOTTS	222	123	3.3	7.9	25.8	192	94	51	26	16	4	8	104	0 0
			116	3.0	7.4	22.5	4	3	3	8	6	0	0	0	0
Oakham School	LEICS	172	149	3.1	7.0	21.7	149	100	107	52	33	9	5	0	0 0
			143	3.0	6.9	19.6	0	3	0	4	1	0	0	0	0
Ockbrook School	DERBYS	100	13	3.0	6.0	18.0	8	10	8	3	7	2	1	0	0 0
			14	2.7	4.8	13.2	0	0	0	0	0	0	0	0	0
Old Palace School of John Whitgift	GR LON	194	72	3.1	7.6	23.2	89	53	42	21	6	5	3	44	0 0
			73	3.1	7.1	21.7	1	1	0	0	0	0	0	0	0
Oratory School, The	BERKS	75	57	3.2	7.2	22.9	66	30	39	23	6	7	2	0	0 0
			61	3.1	6.8	21.2	8	4	2	1	0	0	0	0	0
Oswestry School	SALOP	232	44	3.1	4.8	15.0	21	23	16	18	18	22	9	0	0 0
			40	2.8	4.9	13.6	5	2	6	3	3	2	0	0	0

361

A & AS LEVEL RESULTS 1995

School	County	P					A	B	C	D	E	N	U		
Oundle School	N'HANTS	218	198	3.5	7.5	26.4	248	183	108	49	27	11	4	0	0 0
			183	3.1	7.2	22.5	26	29	26	20	17	6	6	0	0
Our Lady of Sion School	W SUSSEX	277	27	2.9	5.5	15.8	11	15	17	17	12	5	1	0	0 0
			24	2.6	5.3	13.7	0	0	0	1	0	0	0	0	0
Our Lady's Convent Senior School	OXON	228	31	3.0	6.8	20.5	23	27	22	12	4	5	0	0	0 0
			27	2.8	5.5	15.2	0	0	0	0	0	0	0	0	0
Oxford High School GPDST	OXON	228	72	3.1	8.3	25.7	113	54	33	14	7	0	1	0	0 0
			74	3.1	7.4	22.8	1	3	1	0	0	0	0	0	0
Pangbourne College	BERKS	75	62	2.9	4.3	12.2	13	19	34	48	37	15	10	0	0 0
			56	3.1	4.6	14.5	0	0	0	3	0	1	0	0	0
Park School for Girls	ESSEX	119	6	2.5	4.8	12.0	2	3	2	3	2	0	3	0	0 0
			11	2.8	5.9	16.6	0	0	0	0	0	0	0	3	0
Parsons Mead School	SURREY	259	10	3.1	6.9	21.3	9	8	5	4	2	2	0	6	0 0
			19	2.7	4.4	12.0	1	1	0	0	0	0	0	0	0
Perse School for Girls	CAMBS	86	51	3.2	8.4	26.9	88	35	21	5	6	2	0	0	0 0
			65	3.0	7.3	22.1	7	2	3	1	0	0	0	0	0
Perse School, The	CAMBS	86	71	3.2	8.1	25.7	116	47	38	14	4	6	0	0	0 0
			65	3.1	7.9	24.4	0	0	0	0	0	0	0	0	0
Peterborough High School	CAMBS	86	18	2.8	5.9	16.8	11	11	9	8	6	3	2	0	0 0
			21	2.8	4.6	13.0	0	0	1	2	0	0	0	0	0
Pipers Corner School	BUCKS	83	23	2.7	5.2	13.9	7	12	17	9	8	8	1	5	0 0
			23	2.5	5.4	13.6	0	0	0	0	0	0	1	7	0
Plymouth College	DEVON	104	120	3.0	5.6	17.2	69	71	77	55	49	27	11	97	0 0
			102	3.1	6.0	18.5	1	2	2	3	3	3	1	0	0
Pocklington School	HUMBER	152	84	3.2	4.9	15.6	41	37	57	44	32	33	19	77	0 0
			87	3.1	5.3	16.2	2	0	1	2	3	1	1	0	0
Polam Hall School	DURHAM	114	16	3.3	8.0	26.4	25	12	10	2	3	1	0	14	0 0
			32	3.1	5.2	16.4	0	0	1	0	0	0	0	0	0
Portsmouth Grammar School, The	HANTS	132	93	3.2	7.7	24.6	117	68	61	31	10	4	0	0	0 0
			107	3.1	6.9	21.6	10	1	2	1	1	0	0	0	0
Portsmouth High School GPDST	HANTS	132	57	3.1	6.9	21.5	45	53	36	27	10	4	1	0	0 0
			54	3.2	7.7	24.7	0	1	2	0	0	0	0	0	0
Presentation College	BERKS	75	31	3.2	5.3	16.7	11	19	25	22	7	9	3	15	0 0
			33	3.0	5.5	16.5	0	0	0	1	3	0	0	0	0
Princess Helena College, The	HERTS	147	18	2.9	6.1	17.9	10	10	14	8	4	2	1	0	0 0
			14	3.1	5.5	16.9	0	2	2	1	1	0	0	0	0
Princethorpe College	W'WICKS	284	33	3.0	5.4	16.3	19	13	19	24	15	6	1	0	0 0
			53	2.9	4.8	13.8	0	0	1	1	0	1	2	12	0
Prior Park College	AVON	65	60	3.0	6.2	18.5	39	46	33	27	22	3	8	1	0 0
			60	3.0	5.5	16.6	0	0	0	0	2	1	0	0	0
Prior's Field	SURREY	259	16	2.6	4.7	12.4	1	9	10	9	3	3	4	0	0 0
			18	2.7	4.7	12.6	1	0	1	2	2	0	0	0	0
Purcell School of Music	GR LON	196	30	2.5	8.1	20.2	41	12	6	11	2	0	0	0	0 0
			25	2.3	7.2	16.4	0	2	1	1	2	0	0	0	0
Putney High School GPDST	GR LON	196	70	2.9	7.4	21.4	70	57	41	17	11	3	1	0	0 0
			69	2.9	6.9	19.9	0	1	0	0	1	0	0	0	0
Queen Anne's School	BERKS	76	29	3.4	6.3	21.1	27	19	18	12	9	6	3	0	0 0
			53	3.1	6.4	19.7	2	0	2	0	1	2	1	0	0
Queen Elizabeth Grammar School	W YORKS	306	89	3.1	6.3	19.5	81	60	43	33	26	19	13	89	0 0
			92	3.1	6.6	20.2	0	0	0	0	2	0	0	0	0
Queen Elizabeth's Grammar School	LANCS	168	153	3.1	6.4	19.5	133	99	87	57	49	29	12	152	0 0
			171	3.0	6.2	18.6	0	0	1	1	1	0	0	0	0
Queen Elizabeth's Hospital	AVON	65	59	3.2	6.3	20.0	42	41	48	27	14	2	10	0	0 0
			59	3.2	6.3	20.2	0	0	1	2	0	0	1	0	0
Queen Ethelburga's College	N YORKS	298	15	2.9	3.9	11.5	4	2	7	14	6	4	4	0	0 0
			12	2.7	3.5	9.2	0	0	1	1	2	1	1	0	0
Queen Margaret's School	N YORKS	298	44	3.0	7.1	21.0	34	38	30	17	6	3	0	5	0 0
			37	2.8	6.8	19.4	1	3	1	0	1	1	0	0	0
Queen Mary School	LANCS	168	49	3.0	6.0	17.9	35	27	20	29	17	4	9	49	0 0
			53	3.0	5.3	16.1	4	3	3	0	1	0	0	0	0

362

A & AS LEVEL RESULTS 1995

School	County	P					A	B	C	D	E	N	U			
Queen's College London	GR LON	196	33	3.0	7.0	21.3	20	33	27	15	3	0	0	0	0	0
			50	3.1	5.6	17.6	0	2	0	1	1	0	0	0		0
Queen's College	SOMERSET	237	57	3.1	5.7	17.3	35	24	41	35	23	11	4	0	0	0
			61	3.1	6.1	18.5	2	0	0	0	0	0	0	0		0
Queen's Gate School	GR LON	197	10	2.7	6.3	17.0	6	6	8	3	1	3	0	0	0	0
			17	2.7	5.5	14.8	0	0	0	0	0	0	0	0		0
Queen's School, The	CHESHIRE	94	53	3.1	7.5	23.2	58	44	32	20	2	4	1	49	0	0
			63	3.1	7.6	23.3	3	1	1	1	0	1	0	0		0
Queenswood School	HERTS	148	54	3.0	7.5	22.2	50	51	33	16	6	2	1	0	0	0
			54	3.0	5.9	17.7	3	0	1	0	0	0	1	0		0
Quinton House School	N'HANTS	219	9	3.0	4.3	12.8	1	5	5	4	2	5	2	0	0	0
			0	0.0	0.0	0.0	1	2	0	0	2	1	0	9		0
Radley College	OXON	228	127	3.5	7.7	27.2	182	116	84	31	8	1	3	0	0	0
			118	3.3	7.4	24.3	3	1	7	6	11	12	2	0		0
Ratcliffe College	LEICS	172	59	3.0	5.2	15.5	29	26	35	40	23	9	13	0	0	0
			54	3.0	5.2	15.6	0	0	0	1	0	0	0	0		0
Read School	N YORKS	299	13	2.3	5.1	11.7	7	3	2	8	7	0	2	12	0	0
			13	2.8	2.7	7.7	0	0	0	0	0	0	3	0		0
Reading Blue Coat School	BERKS	76	64	3.0	6.4	19.0	43	54	30	32	18	9	3	13	0	0
			69	2.9	5.8	16.7	1	1	0	0	0	1	1	51		0
Red Maids' School	AVON	65	57	3.1	7.6	23.3	64	58	18	18	9	4	1	0	0	0
			53	3.1	6.7	20.8	1	4	1	1	0	0	0	57		0
Redland High School	AVON	66	64	3.0	6.7	20.3	60	34	45	28	10	10	3	0	0	0
			49	3.0	6.4	19.5	2	4	0	0	0	0	0	0		0
Reed's School	SURREY	260	30	2.8	5.1	14.4	12	10	19	22	8	8	4	4	0	0
			37	2.9	4.0	11.7	1	1	1	1	0	1	0	0		0
Reigate Grammar School	SURREY	260	96	3.2	6.6	20.9	94	46	68	52	28	8	0	0	0	0
			119	3.1	6.3	19.2	1	0	5	1	4	2	3	21		0
Rendcomb College	GLOS	124	38	3.0	5.5	16.8	25	22	16	19	10	10	10	0	0	0
			44	2.9	5.2	15.2	1	3	0	0	2	0	0	0		0
Repton School	DERBYS	101	133	3.1	6.6	20.2	121	84	75	56	27	16	17	74	0	0
			130	3.2	6.2	20.0	5	3	6	6	3	0	0	0		0
Rickmansworth Masonic School	HERTS	148	46	2.8	5.4	15.2	24	23	21	26	18	11	6	0	0	0
			52	2.7	4.7	12.7	1	1	0	1	0	0	0	0		0
Rishworth School	W YORKS	306	41	2.8	3.3	9.0	7	14	9	22	23	15	23	34	0	0
			38	3.0	5.0	14.8	0	0	0	0	0	0	0	0		0
R.N.I.B. New College Worcester	HERWORCS	141	16	2.9	5.0	14.2	4	9	13	4	8	3	4	0	0	0
			15	2.8	5.5	15.5	0	0	2	0	0	0	0	0		0
Roedean School	E SUSSEX	270	83	3.3	7.3	24.0	109	44	35	31	24	3	2	0	0	0
			70	3.1	7.1	21.6	11	13	14	5	5	2	0	0		0
Rosemead	W SUSSEX		8	2.7	4.4	12.0	3	3	3	4	2	5	1	0	0	0
			14	3.1	5.5	17.2	0	0	0	1	2	0	0	0		0
Rossall School	LANCS	169	73	3.0	5.4	16.1	42	39	39	37	27	20	11	31	0	0
			72	3.1	5.0	15.4	0	1	1	0	0	1	1	0		0
Rougemont School	S WALES	312	33	3.0	7.1	21.0	36	17	23	12	4	4	1	0	0	0
			25	2.9	5.8	17.2	0	0	0	1	2	0	0	32		0
Royal Grammar School	TYNE	282	147	3.3	8.0	26.5	229	82	76	33	13	10	1	7	0	0
			151	3.2	7.3	23.1	40	18	14	11	1	0	0	0		0
Royal Grammar School	SURREY	261	107	3.3	8.8	29.0	218	76	31	12	4	4	0	0	0	0
			116	3.2	7.7	24.6	14	2	0	0	0	0	0	0		0
Royal Grammar School	HERWORCS	141	103	3.3	7.2	23.9	118	73	60	39	18	7	2	29	0	0
			89	3.2	6.5	20.7	7	9	14	10	9	3	0	0		0
Royal Hospital School	SUFFOLK	245	57	2.7	5.3	14.4	13	28	32	38	18	6	2	25	0	0
			59	2.9	4.4	12.8	0	1	5	4	1	2	1	0		0
Royal Naval School for Girls	SURREY	261	28	2.9	6.7	19.7	25	21	12	10	7	2	3	21	0	0
			27	2.8	5.6	15.6	0	0	2	1	1	0	0	0		0
Royal Russell School	GR LON	198	44	3.1	5.2	16.2	19	28	22	28	20	12	5	0	0	0
			38	2.9	4.5	13.0	1	1	2	0	0	1	1	0		0
Royal School, The	AVON	66	43	2.9	5.3	15.4	23	20	20	21	12	11	8	0	0	0
			36	2.9	4.7	13.4	1	4	3	6	4	3	1	23		0

School	County	P					A	B	C	D	E	N	U		
Royal School, The	N IRE	325	74	3.0	5.4	16.4	41	45	39	39	24	24	10	0	0 0
			63	3.0	5.5	16.6	0	0	1	1	0	0	0	0	0
Royal Wolverhampton School	W MIDS	290	40	3.1	4.4	13.6	19	14	18	28	12	10	23	12	0 0
			37	3.0	4.6	13.9	0	0	0	0	0	1	0	0	0
Rugby School	W'WICKS	284	140	3.4	7.5	25.5	194	104	85	47	25	9	4	0	0 0
			167	3.2	6.9	21.8	6	3	3	1	0	0	0	97	0
Ruthin School	N WALES	309	22	2.9	5.5	16.1	5	22	9	15	7	3	2	0	0 0
			24	2.6	4.3	11.5	0	0	0	0	0	3	0	0	0
Rydal School	N WALES	309	58	3.1	5.7	17.6	44	22	33	26	23	14	6	0	0 0
			66	2.9	5.3	15.5	4	3	4	5	2	1	1	38	0
Penrhos College	N WALES	309	24	2.8	5.4	15.2	9	16	13	11	9	2	4	13	0 0
			28	2.8	5.7	15.7	0	1	0	1	0	2	2	0	0
Ryde School	IOW	153	56	3.2	5.3	17.1	26	26	40	33	25	14	6	0	0 0
			51	3.1	5.5	17.1	3	5	5	7	3	0	1	9	0
Rye St.Antony School	OXON	228	41	3.1	5.1	15.9	19	19	24	24	23	8	6	0	0 0
			28	3.0	5.7	17.0	3	0	2	1	2	1	1	0	0
St. Albans High School for Girls	HERTS	148	56	3.1	7.8	24.4	75	42	31	15	4	2	1	11	0 0
			59	3.1	7.5	23.3	0	4	2	3	1	0	0	0	0
St. Albans School	HERTS	148	87	3.2	6.4	20.5	68	68	52	39	20	9	12	0	0 0
			98	3.2	6.0	19.3	1	5	4	8	1	0	0	78	0
St Ambrose College	CHESHIRE	94	77	3.0	5.0	15.1	32	41	44	42	42	25	4	77	0 0
			65	2.9	5.3	15.5	0	0	0	0	0	2	0	0	0
St. Anne's School	CUMBRIA	99	26	3.0	5.7	17.5	17	14	14	16	8	5	3	23	0 0
			35	2.8	5.3	15.2	0	0	1	2	1	0	0	0	0
St. Anselm's College	MERSEY		63	2.8	5.1	14.4	25	32	38	29	25	18	8	63	0 0
			71	3.0	5.2	15.6	0	0	0	3	0	3	1	0	0
St. Antony's-Leweston School	DORSET	111	28	2.8	5.7	16.2	11	20	16	17	7	7	1	0	0 0
			42	2.8	5.8	16.5	1	0	0	0	0	0	0	0	0
St. Augustine's College	KENT		14	3.0	5.5	16.6	7	9	11	3	5	4	2	9	0 0
			10	3.2	3.9	12.3	0	0	0	1	0	0	1	0	0
St. Bede's College	GR MANCH	211	147	3.0	6.3	18.6	89	106	101	81	32	21	4	140	0 0
			126	3.0	5.6	16.7	0	0	0	0	0	0	0	0	0
St. Bede's School	E SUSSEX	271	47	3.0	5.7	17.4	34	24	24	25	17	10	8	0	0 0
			46	2.8	4.2	11.7	1	1	0	0	0	0	0	0	0
St. Bees School	CUMBRIA	99	34	3.1	6.3	19.5	32	20	19	12	11	8	3	34	0 0
			53	2.9	5.3	15.6	0	0	0	0	0	0	0	0	0
St. Benedict's School	GR LON	198	57	3.1	6.8	21.4	53	44	36	20	11	6	5	0	0 0
			83	3.1	5.5	16.8	1	1	1	2	1	1	1	0	0
St. Catherine's School	SURREY	262	36	3.1	7.6	23.5	40	28	24	18	1	0	0	0	0 0
			47	3.1	6.7	20.9	0	0	1	0	0	0	0	1	0
St. Christopher School	HERTS	149	39	2.8	6.0	16.9	22	24	21	16	17	4	3	0	0 0
			38	3.0	5.2	15.9	3	0	3	0	1	0	1	0	0
St Clotilde's School	GLOS	125	9	2.9	6.8	19.7	7	6	6	4	2	0	1	0	0 0
			12	2.8	4.7	13.1	0	0	1	0	0	0	0	0	0
St. David's College	N WALES	309	25	2.5	5.0	12.5	7	9	14	13	5	2	6	0	0 0
			22	2.7	4.1	11.0	1	1	3	1	5	0	2	0	0
St David's School/Halliford School	SURREY	262	36	2.9	4.6	13.6	15	15	15	20	16	12	10	0	0 0
			38	2.9	4.0	11.4	1	0	4	1	0	1	0	0	0
St. Dominic's Priory School	STAFFS	240	10	3.0	5.8	17.4	5	6	5	10	3	1	0	8	0 0
			12	2.7	5.3	14.1	0	0	0	0	0	0	0	0	0
St. Dominic's School	STAFFS	240	20	3.1	4.3	13.3	4	10	9	18	9	8	3	3	0 0
			23	2.9	5.0	14.4	0	0	0	1	0	0	1	0	0
St. Dunstan's Abbey School	DEVON	105	23	3.0	6.5	19.5	21	13	14	9	6	4	2	0	0 0
			22	2.9	6.1	17.9	0	0	1	0	0	0	0	0	0
St. Dunstan's College	GR LON	200	61	3.1	6.7	21.0	51	41	42	33	19	1	3	0	0 0
			70	3.1	5.4	16.7	1	2	2	0	0	0	0	0	0
St. Edmund's College	HERTS	149	38	3.3	5.7	19.0	27	21	25	21	13	10	4	5	0 0
			48	3.3	4.8	16.1	1	1	2	3	3	0	0	0	0
St. Edmund's School	KENT	162	46	3.0	5.8	17.7	33	24	29	22	14	12	6	0	0 0
			53	2.9	5.0	14.3	0	0	0	0	0	0	0	0	0

A & AS LEVEL RESULTS 1995

School	County				P		A	B	C	D	E	N	U			
St. Edward's College	MERSEY	213	72	3.2	5.7	18.1	52	42	35	39	29	17	4	49	0	0
			84	3.1	5.5	16.8	0	3	1	0	9	4	1	0		0
St Edward's School	OXON	229	128	3.1	6.7	20.8	98	104	80	67	33	8	5	0	0	0
			123	3.1	6.6	20.3	3	3	2	2	0	0	0	0		0
St. Edward's School	GLOS	125	45	2.6	5.8	15.0	23	25	18	15	18	5	4	21	0	0
			46	2.8	5.0	13.8	2	2	5	2	4	1	0	0		0
St. Elphin's School	DERBYS	101	19	3.2	6.6	20.8	15	14	13	9	5	2	1	13	0	0
			26	2.9	5.1	14.8	1	0	1	1	0	0	0	0		0
Saint Felix School	SUFFOLK	245	25	3.1	6.5	19.9	15	22	19	9	8	2	1	0	0	0
			34	3.0	6.0	17.9	0	0	2	0	0	0	0	0		0
St. Francis' College	HERTS	149	24	2.8	5.1	14.3	9	14	14	8	9	7	5	0	0	0
			21	2.8	5.0	14.4	0	1	1	0	1	2	0	0		0
St. George's College	SURREY	263	65	3.0	5.9	17.9	36	53	32	33	25	12	7	0	0	0
			60	3.1	5.3	16.1	0	1	0	0	0	0	0	0		0
St. George's School	BERKS	77	30	3.0	7.6	22.6	27	32	17	11	1	0	1	0	0	0
			33	3.0	6.3	19.3	1	0	0	0	0	0	0	0		0
St. Gerards School	N WALES	310	17	3.0	5.6	16.9	4	11	18	6	6	3	1	0	0	0
			11	2.8	6.3	17.8	0	3	0	1	1	0	0	0		0
St Helen & St Katharine, The School of	OXON	229	60	3.1	7.6	23.5	75	52	26	17	10	4	2	0	0	0
			67	3.1	7.0	21.5	0	0	0	0	0	0	0	0		0
St. Helen's School	GR LON	200	71	3.1	8.0	24.3	96	55	30	22	6	2	0	0	0	0
			73	3.0	7.1	21.1	2	7	1	2	1	0	0	0		0
St. Hilary's School	CHESHIRE	95	10	3.1	6.3	19.6	10	4	7	4	3	0	3	4	0	0
			18	3.0	4.6	13.5	0	0	0	0	0	0	0	0		0
St. Hilda's School	N YORKS	299	14	3.0	3.4	10.1	6	1	3	7	14	6	5	5	0	0
			14	3.0	4.9	14.5	0	0	0	0	0	0	1	0		0
St. James Independent Sch.for Boys	GR LON	200	9	2.8	5.8	16.2	5	6	4	3	5	0	1	0	0	0
			17	3.0	6.3	18.7	0	0	0	1	0	0	1	0		0
St. James Independent Sch.for Girls	GR LON	200	1	4.0	10.0	40.0	4	0	0	0	0	0	0	0	0	0
			14	2.6	6.8	17.9	0	0	0	0	0	0	0	0		0
St. James School	HUMBER	152	20	2.7	4.3	11.5	6	8	6	10	11	4	4	16	0	0
			12	2.8	4.4	12.2	0	0	0	3	2	2	1	0		0
St. James's and The Abbey	HERWORCS	141	18	2.9	5.0	14.8	4	9	13	14	6	3	3	0	0	0
			20	2.8	5.1	14.4	0	1	1	0	0	0	0	0		0
St. John's College	HANTS	133	59	3.0	5.3	15.7	36	27	29	30	28	16	9	0	0	0
			51	3.0	4.9	14.7	0	0	0	0	0	0	0	0		0
St. John's School	SURREY	264	74	3.0	6.0	18.2	39	50	52	45	22	7	5	0	0	0
			87	3.0	5.6	16.7	1	0	1	4	2	1	0	0		0
St. Joseph's College with the School o	SUFFOLK	246	62	3.0	6.5	19.6	48	42	35	29	14	8	4	0	0	0
			74	3.0	5.3	16.0	2	6	2	1	1	0	0	0		0
St. Joseph's College	STAFFS	241	28	2.9	4.6	13.4	16	7	15	9	16	9	9	28	0	0
			21	3.3	4.3	14.3	0	0	0	0	0	0	0	0		0
St. Joseph's Convent School	BERKS	78	40	2.9	4.9	14.1	10	15	32	25	18	9	2	0	0	0
			36	2.9	5.0	14.4	0	2	2	0	2	3	0	0		0
St. Joseph's School	W'WICKS	284	10	2.7	4.3	11.5	1	5	5	5	4	1	3	5	0	0
				0.0	0.0	0.0	0	0	1	1	2	1	1	0		0
St. Joseph's School	LINCS	173	12	2.7	5.5	14.7	4	3	13	6	5	0	1	4	0	0
			12	2.5	4.8	12.2	0	0	0	0	0	0	0	0		0
St. Lawrence College	KENT	162	48	3.1	6.4	20.1	38	31	31	27	9	3	6	0	0	0
			56	3.0	5.8	17.2	2	1	1	2	2	1	1	0		0
St. Leonards-Mayfield School	E SUSSEX	271	80	3.2	6.4	20.3	58	65	52	33	24	12	6	0	0	0
			78	3.1	6.5	20.5	2	1	4	2	0	1	0	0		0
St. Margaret's School for Girls	DEVON	105	34	2.9	6.5	18.5	27	17	25	13	6	5	3	3	0	0
			39	2.9	6.1	17.9	1	0	1	0	0	0	0	0		0
St. Margaret's School	HERTS	150	34	2.8	6.6	18.1	24	20	21	18	7	3	1	1	0	0
			38	2.9	5.4	15.4	1	0	0	0	0	0	0	0		0
St. Martin's	W MIDS	290	10	2.9	6.4	18.6	10	4	4	5	5	1	0	5	0	0
			17	2.9	5.6	16.1	0	0	0	0	0	0	0	0		0
St. Mary's College	MERSEY	213	57	2.9	4.9	14.1	18	29	38	25	32	16	6	57	0	0
			63	3.0	5.1	15.1	0	0	0	1	0	0	0	0		0

365

School	County		P				A	B	C	D	E	N	U			
St. Mary's Convent School	HERWORCS	141	20	2.8	5.6	15.6	11	8	9	19	3	1	4	0	0	0
			20	2.9	5.5	15.8	0	0	0	0	1	0	1	0	0	0
St. Mary's Hall	E SUSSEX	272	27	2.7	4.4	11.7	9	11	12	11	11	7	10	0	0	0
			19	2.8	5.3	14.8	0	0	0	0	0	1	1	0	0	0
St. Mary's School	CAMBS	87	50	2.9	7.0	20.4	49	33	27	17	14	3	2	0	0	0
			54	2.9	6.4	18.7	1	0	1	0	0	0	0	0	0	0
St. Mary's School	BERKS	78	43	3.0	7.9	23.7	52	42	21	7	4	3	0	0	0	0
			42	3.1	7.3	22.4	0	0	0	0	0	0	0	0	0	0
St. Mary's School	WILTS	293	43	3.0	8.7	26.6	76	36	15	1	1	2	0	0	0	0
			40	3.0	7.6	23.2	0	0	0	0	0	0	0	0	0	0
St. Mary's School	DORSET	111	37	2.9	7.1	20.4	32	28	22	14	7	2	1	0	0	0
			32	2.8	6.1	17.2	0	0	3	0	0	0	0	0	0	0
St. Mary's School	OXON	229	36	2.8	5.3	15.0	15	24	20	9	18	9	5	0	0	0
			28	2.7	6.0	16.0	0	0	0	2	1	0	0	0	0	0
St. Mary's School	BUCKS	83	11	2.6	5.8	15.4	0	10	10	4	3	0	1	0	0	0
			17	2.7	4.7	12.6	0	1	1	0	0	0	1	0	0	0
St. Maur's School	SURREY	264	16	2.9	5.8	17.0	7	11	12	5	6	4	0	0	0	0
			43	3.0	5.9	17.6	1	0	1	0	2	0	0	9	0	0
St. Michael's School	SURREY	264	14	3.1	4.8	15.0	4	11	10	1	9	4	5	0	0	0
			9	3.3	3.6	11.8	0	0	0	0	0	1	0	0	0	0
St. Michael's School	S WALES	313	17	2.9	6.5	18.7	19	8	5	5	6	3	3	0	0	0
			14	2.8	6.3	17.4	0	0	0	1	0	0	0	0	0	0
St. Nicholas' School	HANTS	133	11	3.1	6.9	21.5	9	11	4	6	2	1	0	0	0	0
			15	2.9	5.1	14.5	0	0	2	0	0	0	0	0	0	0
St. Paul's Girls' School	GR LON	202	101	3.1	9.0	28.2	206	67	35	2	5	0	0	0	0	0
			105	3.2	8.3	26.2	3	2	0	0	0	0	0	0	0	0
St. Paul's School	GR LON	202	141	3.6	8.8	31.8	294	95	52	16	1	1	1	0	0	0
			145	3.4	8.6	28.9	47	32	10	3	2	1	0	0	0	0
St. Peter's School	N YORKS	300	97	3.1	7.0	21.9	95	73	64	35	25	7	3	97	0	0
			92	3.1	6.5	19.9	0	0	4	2	0	0	0	0	0	0
St. Swithun's School	HANTS	134	48	3.2	7.9	25.2	75	31	22	14	9	2	0	48	0	0
			47	3.0	7.3	22.0	0	1	0	0	0	0	0	0	0	0
St. Teresa's School	SURREY	264	28	3.1	5.0	15.5	12	13	15	24	8	6	7	0	0	0
			24	3.0	5.2	15.4	1	0	1	0	0	0	0	0	0	0
St. Ursula's High School	AVON	66	14	2.9	4.9	14.4	7	1	16	4	6	6	1	0	0	0
			17	2.6	4.5	11.7	0	0	0	0	0	0	0	0	0	0
Scarborough College	N YORKS	300	39	3.1	5.3	16.2	15	19	28	32	16	6	3	39	0	0
			41	2.7	5.1	13.8	0	0	1	0	0	0	0	0	0	0
Scarisbrick Hall School	LANCS	169	13	3.0	6.0	18.0	7	12	5	7	5	3	0	13	0	0
			13	2.9	5.8	16.7	0	0	0	0	0	0	0	0	0	0
School of S.Mary & S.Anne	STAFFS	241	29	2.8	7.2	20.3	26	25	12	11	7	0	1	0	0	0
			28	3.0	5.7	17.0	0	0	0	0	0	0	0	5	0	0
Seaford College	W SUSSEX	278	36	2.7	4.4	11.7	8	16	19	17	16	11	9	0	0	0
			44	2.6	3.0	8.0	0	0	0	0	1	0	0	0	0	0
Sedbergh School	CUMBRIA	99	71	3.2	6.2	19.5	53	49	39	42	22	12	5	29	0	0
			78	3.2	5.7	18.4	0	2	1	2	1	0	0	0	0	0
Selwyn School	GLOS	125	10	3.0	2.7	8.0	3	1	1	5	6	4	9	4	0	0
			14	2.4	3.8	9.1	0	0	1	0	1	0	1	0	0	0
Sevenoaks School (A-levels)	KENT	163	126	3.2	7.5	23.6	146	98	75	44	16	7	1	0	0	0
			186	3.1	7.0	21.6	5	5	7	1	0	1	1	0	0	0
Sevenoaks School (IB exams)	KENT	163	69	3.5	7.7	27.1	81	64	28	14	16	5	0	0	0	0
			71	3.5	8.1	28.7	33	23	9	2	2	0	0	0	0	0
IB RESULT GRADES							7	6	5	4	3	2	1			
IB results Higher Grade			19	3.0	5.9	17.6	5	14	17	11	7	0	0	0	0	0
IB results Subsidiary Grades			24	2.9	5.3	15.2	0	0	1	3	3	0	0	0	0	0
Sheffield High School GPDST	S YORKS	302	68	3.0	7.6	22.9	81	51	36	19	8	6	2	66	0	0
			58	3.0	6.1	18.6	6	0	1	0	0	0	0	0	0	0
Sherborne School For Girls	DORSET	111	79	3.1	7.6	23.2	85	74	42	27	8	2	1	0	0	0
			76	3.1	7.2	22.3	2	0	1	1	0	0	0	0	0	0

A & AS LEVEL RESULTS 1995

A & AS LEVEL RESULTS 1995

School	County	P		3 cols			A	B	C	D	E	N	U		
Sherborne School	DORSET	112	119	3.1	7.3	22.5	125	93	78	43	20	3	4	0	0	0
			126	3.1	6.8	21.0	0	0	0	4	1	0	0	0		
Sherrardswood School	HERTS	150	4	3.2	3.2	10.5	0	0	2	6	3	1	1	0	0	0
			9	2.9	3.4	9.8	0	0	0	0	1	0	0	0		
Shiplake College	OXON	230	48	2.7	3.7	10.1	15	7	17	21	26	15	16	0	0	0
			42	2.7	3.7	10.2	1	2	4	2	10	3	7	0		
Shoreham College	W SUSSEX	278	3	3.0	5.1	15.3	0	3	2	2	1	1	0	3	0	0
			6	2.9	4.2	12.2	0	0	0	0	0	0	0	0		
Shrewsbury High School GPDST	SALOP	233	32	3.1	6.7	20.8	27	26	19	13	10	4	0	20	0	0
			37	3.0	6.8	20.3	0	0	0	0	1	0	0	0		
Shrewsbury School	SALOP	234	126	3.2	7.9	25.6	196	87	61	36	14	5	6	17	0	0
			134	3.2	7.2	23.0	1	4	1	2	1	0	0	0		
Sidcot School	AVON	66	36	3.1	6.1	18.9	27	19	25	20	13	3	1	0	0	0
			23	2.8	5.2	14.5	0	0	1	0	1	3	1	0		
Silcoates School	W YORKS	307	30	3.0	5.0	15.0	16	15	14	11	16	8	8	13	0	0
			57	3.1	4.9	15.0	1	0	1	1	1	0	0	0		
Sir William Perkins's School	SURREY	265	74	3.0	7.5	22.7	91	50	41	21	12	6	1	0	0	0
			51	3.0	7.3	21.7	1	2	2	0	0	0	0	74		
Solihull School	W MIDS	290	131	3.1	6.9	21.4	110	107	85	53	26	12	6	125	0	0
			130	3.1	6.7	20.7	6	7	4	1	1	0	0	0		
South Hampstead High School GPDST	GR LON	203	74	3.1	7.9	24.4	104	55	36	20	9	3	1	0	0	0
			68	3.1	7.9	24.1	3	0	0	0	0	0	0	0		
Southbank International School (IB exa	GR LON	203	18	3.6	7.7	27.7	22	13	12	6	0	3	0	0	18	0
			21	3.5	6.8	23.9	10	5	2	1	0	0	0	0		
Stafford Grammar School	STAFFS	241	33	3.1	5.9	18.1	21	22	14	22	14	5	2	32	0	0
			24	3.0	4.9	14.5	2	0	0	0	1	0	0	0		
Stamford High School for Girls	LINCS	174	76	3.0	6.5	19.3	51	49	53	43	12	11	0	0	0	0
			85	3.0	6.2	18.4	4	6	1	1	2	0	0	0		
Stamford School	LINCS	174	93	3.0	6.6	20.0	78	61	60	46	21	12	3	0	0	0
			104	3.0	6.2	18.7	0	0	0	1	1	0	0	1		
Stanbridge Earls School	HANTS	134	13	2.0	2.2	4.4	0	1	3	3	7	5	4	0	0	0
			12	2.0	2.8	5.8	0	0	1	0	2	0	4	0		
Stockport Grammar School	CHESHIRE	95	133	3.0	7.3	22.0	146	97	75	48	22	8	2	133	0	0
			134	3.0	6.8	20.2	0	0	0	0	0	0	0	0		
Stonar School	WILTS	294	42	3.0	4.9	14.5	17	16	24	28	26	8	5	1	0	0
			42	2.7	4.9	13.1	0	0	1	0	1	0	0	0		
Stonyhurst College	LANCS	169	70	3.3	6.2	20.5	53	45	53	46	19	6	8	0	0	0
			83	3.1	6.0	18.9	1	0	0	0	0	0	0	0		
Stowe School	BUCKS	83	128	3.1	6.2	19.2	83	86	90	72	33	12	10	0	0	0
			123	2.9	5.9	17.4	2	4	6	1	2	1	1	22		
Streatham Hill & Clapham High School G	GR LON	204	42	2.9	5.5	15.7	21	22	26	13	19	9	6	0	0	0
			32	3.1	6.1	18.8	0	4	3	1	1	0	0	0		
Sunderland High School	TYNE	282	20	2.7	4.9	13.4	4	17	10	5	6	8	5	10	0	0
			27	2.7	4.4	12.1	0	0	0	0	0	0	0	0		
Surbiton High School	GR LON	204	51	3.1	7.3	22.9	62	28	29	26	13	0	0	0	0	0
			43	3.0	6.5	19.4	1	4	0	0	0	0	0	0		
Sutton High School GPDST	GR LON	205	53	3.2	7.9	25.7	81	30	29	16	5	3	1	0	0	0
			64	3.1	6.6	20.3	10	2	2	1	0	0	0	0		
Sutton Valence School	KENT	164	52	2.9	5.9	17.2	30	29	37	21	17	5	9	0	0	0
			54	3.0	4.5	13.4	2	2	0	0	2	0	2	0		
Sydenham High School GPDST	GR LON	205	41	2.9	5.6	16.4	23	19	28	20	18	8	3	0	0	0
			40	2.8	5.3	15.1	0	1	0	1	0	0	0	0		
Talbot Heath School	DORSET	112	30	3.0	7.4	22.3	35	21	16	11	5	2	0	0	0	0
			47	2.9	6.8	19.9	0	0	0	0	0	0	0	0		
Taunton School	SOMERSET	238	81	3.0	6.4	18.8	59	46	61	37	15	7	10	0	0	0
			100	3.0	5.6	16.9	0	2	3	1	0	1	1	0		
Teesside High School for Girls	CLEVE	96	39	2.9	5.2	15.2	15	19	28	24	10	12	4	30	0	0
			25	3.0	6.2	18.9	0	1	0	0	1	1	1	7		
Tettenhall College	W MIDS	290	35	2.9	5.1	14.8	5	23	27	23	12	5	5	23	0	0
			36	3.2	4.9	15.6	0	0	0	2	1	1	0	0		

367

School	County	P					A	B	C	D	E	N	U		
Thetford Grammar School	NORFOLK	217	16	3.4	7.1	24.1	20	9	10	9	3	2	0	0	0
			20	3.0	5.6	16.8	1	1	0	1	0	0	0	16	0
Tonbridge School	KENT	164	123	3.3	8.0	26.1	180	103	66	31	15	4	1	0	0
			127	3.2	7.7	24.8	6	1	1	1	0	0	0	0	0
Tormead School	SURREY	265	37	3.0	6.6	19.8	26	35	17	12	9	6	2	0	0
			33	3.0	7.1	21.0	1	2	3	0	2	0	0	0	0
Trent College	DERBYS	102	93	3.1	6.6	20.5	77	54	68	38	18	14	5	28	0
			120	3.1	6.1	18.8	4	13	7	7	2	1	0	0	0
Trinity School	DEVON	106	2	1.0	7.0	7.0	1	0	0	1	0	0	0	0	0
				0.0	0.0	0.0	0	0	0	0	0	0	0	0	0
Trinity School	GR LON	206	112	3.2	6.5	21.0	88	89	73	45	24	11	13	0	0
			98	3.2	6.4	20.4	8	7	3	7	5	4	1	0	0
Truro High School for Girls	CORNWALL	98	40	3.0	6.8	20.4	40	29	15	17	11	5	2	0	0
			31	3.0	6.0	17.7	0	0	0	1	1	0	0	0	0
Truro School	CORNWALL	98	105	3.2	7.3	23.3	127	78	42	38	19	9	7	0	0
			136	3.1	6.1	18.6	7	9	10	3	3	3	0	0	0
Tudor Hall School	OXON	230	36	2.9	7.0	20.4	28	27	26	10	10	1	1	0	0
			30	2.9	6.7	19.7	2	2	1	0	0	0	0	5	0
University College School	GR LON	207	101	3.1	7.7	23.6	129	75	58	31	11	4	1	0	0
			97	3.1	7.7	23.7	0	0	0	0	0	0	0	0	0
Uppingham School	LEICS	173	169	3.1	6.8	21.3	153	119	108	81	38	16	4	0	16
			148	3.0	6.2	18.4	6	4	7	2	5	3	0	0	0
Ursuline College	KENT	164	13	3.0	4.0	12.0	2	7	6	8	6	5	5	0	0
			29	3.1	5.0	15.4	0	0	0	0	0	0	0	4	0
Victoria College	C.I.	88	62	3.0	5.8	17.7	36	39	37	43	15	14	4	62	0
			64	2.9	5.5	15.8	0	0	0	0	0	0	0	0	0
Virgo Fidelis School	GR LON	207	9	3.6	4.1	14.4	1	4	8	7	6	2	4	0	0
			10	2.5	3.4	8.6	0	0	0	0	0	0	0	0	0
Wakefield Girls' High School	W YORKS	307	95	3.0	7.3	22.1	95	75	63	31	15	8	0	95	0
			89	3.1	6.2	19.0	1	2	0	0	1	0	0	0	0
Walthamstow Hall	KENT	164	47	3.1	6.7	20.7	41	38	18	23	13	6	3	0	0
			52	3.0	6.4	19.0	6	0	0	2	1	0	0	0	0
Warminster School	WILTS	294	41	2.7	4.8	13.0	7	22	25	25	18	9	5	0	0
			32	2.7	4.4	12.2	0	0	0	1	0	0	1	0	0
Warwick School	W'WICKS	285	92	3.3	7.9	26.0	138	57	40	25	10	6	0	90	0
			108	3.1	6.4	19.6	18	12	14	7	2	1	0	0	0
Wellingborough School	N'HANTS	219	66	2.9	7.3	21.5	73	41	41	25	6	2	5	21	0
			77	3.2	6.0	19.4	0	0	0	0	0	0	0	0	0
Wellington College	BERKS	79	186	3.3	7.5	24.9	206	175	118	60	12	13	3	0	0
			171	3.2	6.8	22.1	19	14	11	9	3	0	1	0	0
Wellington School	MERSEY		19	2.5	2.0	5.2	1	3	4	6	8	13	13	16	0
			17	3.0	2.3	7.0	0	0	0	0	0	0	0	0	0
Wellington School	SOMERSET	238	92	3.1	6.5	20.1	65	72	75	32	21	12	5	0	0
			80	3.0	6.0	18.0	0	0	0	0	3	0	0	0	0
Wells Cathedral School	SOMERSET	238	84	2.8	6.5	18.5	65	59	43	34	16	12	8	0	0
			79	2.9	6.3	18.6	0	1	1	0	0	2	0	0	0
Wentworth Milton Mount School	DORSET	113	35	3.0	5.1	15.0	14	18	24	17	15	9	7	0	0
			27	2.8	5.6	15.6	0	0	0	0	0	0	0	0	0
West Buckland School	DEVON	107	48	2.9	5.8	16.8	27	29	28	24	13	8	6	46	0
			42	2.9	5.4	15.4	0	2	1	1	4	1	0	0	0
West Heath School	KENT	165	11	2.8	4.3	12.2	0	3	11	8	5	4	0	0	0
			22	2.8	5.8	16.3	0	0	0	1	0	0	0	0	0
Westfield School	TYNE	282	15	2.7	5.7	15.2	5	10	9	9	4	2	1	1	0
			16	2.7	5.2	13.8	0	0	0	0	0	0	0	0	0
Westholme School	LANCS	170	49	2.9	7.0	20.2	40	41	27	18	12	1	2	46	0
			47	3.0	5.4	16.3	0	0	0	1	0	0	1	0	0
Westminster School	GR LON	208	132	3.6	8.8	31.4	288	101	50	16	5	2	0	0	0
			147	3.4	8.4	28.5	11	5	3	1	1	0	0	0	0
Westonbirt School	GLOS	125	37	2.9	6.1	17.6	17	25	33	17	5	5	4	0	0
			31	2.9	4.7	13.6	0	0	1	1	0	0	1	0	0

School	County	P		A	B	C	D	E	N	U			
Whitgift School	GR LON	208	125	3.2	7.3	23.7	150	98	58	46	21	13	5	0	0	0
			118	3.3	6.7	21.9	11	6	6	2	1	1	1	0	0
William Hulme's Grammar School	GR MANCH	211	112	3.0	5.5	16.5	59	68	60	61	54	22	11	110	0	0
			95	3.0	5.3	16.1	0	0	0	0	0	0	0	0	0
Wimbledon High School GPDST	GR LON	208	71	3.0	7.9	23.9	92	56	31	24	8	1	0	0	0	0
			57	3.0	7.5	22.6	1	4	3	0	1	0	0	0	0
Winchester College	HANTS	135	136	3.7	8.7	31.9	286	112	56	16	5	0	1	0	0	0
			132	3.4	8.4	28.8	15	11	12	3	5	1	0	0	0
Wisbech Grammar School	CAMBS	87	75	3.3	6.3	20.6	68	37	44	32	24	11	6	0	0	0
			60	3.0	5.5	16.5	14	4	9	6	5	5	4	0	0
Wispers School	SURREY	266	2	2.0	7.2	14.5	0	2	1	0	0	0	0	0	0	0
			10	2.7	4.5	12.2	0	0	2	0	1	0	0	0	0
Withington Girls School	GR MANCH	211	59	3.0	8.6	26.2	110	37	15	14	2	1	0	53	0	0
			60	3.1	7.9	24.6	0	0	0	0	0	0	0	0	0
Woldingham School	SURREY	266	59	3.2	6.6	21.1	40	53	34	29	10	9	1	0	0	0
			54	3.0	6.9	20.6	5	4	7	6	4	0	0	0	0
Wolverhampton Grammar School	W MIDS	291	94	3.2	7.5	23.8	120	67	51	33	14	5	2	94	0	0
			90	3.1	6.6	20.4	3	4	2	1	0	0	1	0	0
Woodbridge School	SUFFOLK	246	77	3.0	6.2	18.7	47	49	62	36	25	4	6	0	0	0
			71	3.0	5.7	17.5	0	2	1	0	2	0	1	0	0
Woodhouse Grove School	W YORKS	307	57	2.9	6.8	19.6	56	35	30	13	22	9	0	25	0	0
			73	2.9	4.2	12.3	0	0	0	0	0	0	0	0	0
Worksop College	NOTTS	224	59	2.8	5.2	14.9	25	34	26	33	26	10	10	47	0	0
			64	2.9	4.4	12.5	1	1	0	2	2	0	3	0	0
Worth School	W SUSSEX	279	44	3.0	6.5	19.8	37	27	28	17	13	5	5	0	0	0
			55	2.9	6.2	18.3	3	1	1	0	0	0	0	0	0
Wrekin College	SALOP	234	34	2.9	6.2	18.0	19	26	16	22	8	4	2	0	0	0
			68	2.9	4.4	13.0	0	2	2	0	1	0	0	0	0
Wroxall Abbey	W'WICKS	285	4	2.2	1.1	2.5	0	0	1	3	1	4	0	0	0	0
			5	2.6	2.1	5.4	0	0	0	0	0	0	0	0	0
Wychwood School	OXON	230	18	3.0	6.9	20.6	12	16	13	8	4	0	0	0	0	0
			12	2.8	5.9	16.2	0	0	1	0	1	0	0	0	0
Wycliffe College	GLOS	126	62	2.9	6.4	18.7	53	38	29	29	15	12	5	0	0	0
			70	2.9	5.4	16.0	0	1	0	1	0	0	0	0	0
Wycombe Abbey School	BUCKS	84	55	3.2	8.5	27.0	93	43	28	8	1	0	0	0	0	0
			83	3.0	8.0	23.8	1	0	0	1	0	0	0	0	0
Yarm School	CLEVE	96	65	3.2	6.5	20.7	50	56	31	31	23	8	0	60	0	0
			51	3.2	5.9	18.9	0	4	6	2	2	1	0	0	0
Yehudi Menuhin School	SURREY	267	6	1.8	6.4	11.7	6	0	0	2	1	2	0	0	0	0
			8	1.6	8.6	14.0	0	0	0	0	0	0	0	0	0
York College for Girls	N YORKS	301	11	3.0	7.2	21.6	15	5	5	4	1	2	1	7	0	0
			15	3.1	6.1	19.1	0	0	0	0	0	0	0	4	0

HOW TO USE THIS SECTION

TOP LINE SHOWS 1995 FIGURES → *A+% | A-U GRADE & % GRADE & ABOVE IN 1995

Column headings (left to right):
- SCHOOL & TOWN
- COUNTY
- SEE ENTRY ON PAGE
- No. OF GCSE CANDIDATES
- No. SUBJECTS PER CANDIDATE
- ACHIEVING 5+ *A-C GRADES % CANDIDATES
- GRADE *A & % GRADE *A †
- GRADE A & % GRADE A
- GRADE B & % GRADE B
- GRADE C & % GRADE C
- GRADE D & % GRADE D
- GRADE E & % GRADE E
- GRADE F & % GRADE F
- GRADE G & % GRADE G
- GRADE U & % GRADE U

Example rows:

The School	COUNTY				45 9.6	13 38.5	116 63.2	130 91.0	31 97.6	11 100.0			
					50 9.0 41	118 22.0	136 47.3	185 81.7	68 94.4	24 98.8	4 99.7	1 100.0	
The School	COUNTY	144	37 9.1	96.4	4 5.4	9 17.5	70 31.1	11 45.9	14 64.9	12 81.1	7 90.5	5 97.3	2 100.0
			53 8.2	98.2	3 5.1	32 16.4	95 34.3	48 58.8	38 78.8	23 90.5	13 97.2	4 99.2	1 100.0

SECOND LINE SHOWS PREVIOUS YEARS 1990-94 | **AVERAGE NUMBERS OF CANDIDATES, SUBJECTS AND GRADES** | † % *A in 1994 only | **A-U GRADE & % GRADE & ABOVE IN 1990-94**

You are strongly advised to read school entries in this section in conjunction with the full descriptive entry in the county list. Read also the introduction and warning on pages 347-350.

● The figures between the **2 heavy rules** show number of GCSE candidates, number of subjects per candidate and % passing 5 or more at *A-C.

● The next nine columns after the heavy rule give the 1995 results at each grade for *A, A, B, C, D, E, F, G and U grades, followed by the % at grade A and the cumulative % at other grades.

For example, the figures under C are the numbers of entries graded C and the percentage of entries graded *A-C.

GCSE ENGLAND & WALES RESULTS 1995

School	County	P		*A		A		B		C		D		E		F		G		U	
Abbey Gate College	CHESHIRE	88	50	7.9	92.0	6	1.5	88	23.9	179	69.5	87	91.6	27	98.5	5	99.7	1	100.0		
			52	8.2	96.4	29	6.5	99	24.6	132	55.5	129	85.7	41	95.3	16	99.0	4	100.0	0	100.0	0	100.0
Abbey School,The	BERKS	68	109	10.6	100	209	18.0	502	61.3	327	89.6	107	98.8	13	99.9	1	100.0				
			117	10.5	100	164	14.2	643	55.1	369	85.2	152	97.6	24	99.6	4	99.9	1	100.0	0	100.0	0	100.0
Abbot's Hill	HERTS	142	36	8.5	80.6	5	1.6	38	14.1	69	36.7	124	77.4	51	94.1	15	99.0	3	100.0		
			32	7.8	82.8	10	4.1	34	14.6	51	35.2	66	61.9	46	80.5	23	89.8	16	96.3	6	98.7	3	100.0
Abbotsholme School	STAFFS	238	41	8.3	78.0	31	9.1	65	28.3	84	53.1	81	77.0	44	90.0	26	97.6	4	98.8	3	99.7	1	100.0
			46	8.2	68.4	22	6.9	65	18.3	81	39.8	124	72.8	52	86.6	33	95.3	14	99.0	2	99.6	1	100.0
Abingdon School	OXON	224	141	9.8	100	199	14.4	490	50.0	427	80.9	220	96.9	31	99.1	11	99.9	1	100.0		
			115	10.7	99.1	145	13.4	521	44.7	388	76.3	218	94.0	57	98.7	13	99.7	2	99.9	1	100.0	0	100.0
Ackworth School	W YORKS	302	79	9.2	91.1	51	7.0	162	29.4	235	61.9	196	89.0	56	96.7	20	99.4	3	99.9	1	100.0		
			73	8.4	79.5	42	6.3	158	27.1	149	51.5	153	76.5	81	89.8	39	96.1	14	98.4	5	99.2	4	100.0
Aldenham School	HERTS	142	65	8.9	86.2	22	3.8	96	20.4	189	53.0	173	82.9	67	94.5	22	98.3	6	99.3	4	100.0		
			70	9.4	83.6	22	4.3	94	15.1	170	40.8	258	79.8	98	94.6	24	98.2	7	99.3	3	99.7	1	100.0
Alice Ottley School,The	HERWORCS	136	92	9.1	100	190	22.8	271	55.2	259	86.2	104	98.7	11	100.0						
			80	9.1	100	150	19.2	311	47.1	227	78.5	125	95.7	26	99.3	5	100.0					
Alleyn's School	GR LON	175	137	9.0	99.3	256	20.8	444	57.0	338	84.5	151	96.8	33	99.5	4	99.8	2	100.0			
			137	8.9	97.1	137	11.1	429	37.5	388	69.4	256	90.4	88	97.6	23	99.5	4	99.9	1	100.0	0	100.0
Allhallows College	DORSET	107	38	8.9	76.3	11	3.2	48	17.4	94	45.0	90	71.5	59	88.8	23	95.6	14	99.7	1	100.0		
			55	8.2	71.1	25	7.7	64	15.3	108	39.3	155	73.7	68	88.8	35	96.6	13	99.5	1	99.7	1	100.0
Amberfield School	SUFFOLK	242	23	8.5	95.7	25	12.8	56	41.3	61	72.4	39	92.3	12	98.5	2	99.5	1	100.0			
			30	8.4	97.2	20	6.5	85	35.6	81	68.0	52	88.8	17	95.6	7	98.4	3	99.6	1	100.0		
Ampleforth College	N YORKS	294	113	10.0	92.0	164	14.5	312	42.0	376	75.1	191	92.0	64	97.6	17	99.1	10	100.0			
			115	10.0	94.6	53	4.9	338	30.3	354	61.1	308	87.9	99	96.5	33	99.4	6	99.9	1	100.0	0	100.0
Ardingly College	W SUSSEX	273	107	8.6	88.8	46	5.0	158	22.2	329	58.0	269	87.3	84	96.4	26	99.2	6	99.9	0	99.9	1	100.0
			90	8.7	95.7	37	4.6	189	25.1	243	56.2	229	85.5	78	95.5	27	98.9	6	99.7	1	99.8	1	100.0
Arnold School	LANCS	166	131	8.3	87.0	174	15.9	306	44.0	298	71.3	215	91.0	72	97.6	24	99.8	2	100.0			
			124	8.1	94.9	113	11.9	374	39.6	276	67.1	198	86.9	88	95.7	29	98.6	12	99.8	2	100.0	0	100.0

GCSE ENGLAND & WALES RESULTS 1995

School	County		P	*A	A	B	C	D	E	F	G	U
Arts Educational School	HERTS	143	37 7.4 78.4	9 3.3	39 17.6	73 44.3	95 79.1	49 97.1	8 100.0			
			0 0.0 0.0	0 0.0	0 0.0	0 0.0	0 0.0	0 0.0	0 0.0	0 0.0	0 0.0	0 0.0
Arts Educational London Schools,The	GR LON	176	31 7.2 61.3	14 6.3	53 29.9	46 50.4	54 74.6	26 86.2	24 96.9	6 99.6	0 99.6	1 100.0
			29 6.1 66.7	12 7.1	28 16.7	35 36.2	54 66.3	32 84.2	16 93.1	8 97.5	3 99.2	1 100.0
Ashford School	KENT	154	57 8.9 98.2	146 28.6	174 62.7	126 87.5	54 98.0	7 99.4	1 99.6	0 99.6	0 99.6	2 100.0
			77 9.9 95.7	132 21.0	304 43.5	182 67.5	206 94.7	30 98.7	8 99.7	2 100.0	0 100.0	0 100.0
Ashville College	N YORKS	295	91 8.7 86.8	56 7.1	183 30.2	259 63.0	195 87.6	74 97.0	21 99.6	3 100.0		
			79 8.5 94.3	65 8.4	201 31.7	200 61.4	167 86.2	60 95.0	22 98.3	7 99.3	2 99.6	2 100.0
Atherley School,The	HANTS	126	47 8.9 87.2	36 8.6	110 34.8	152 71.0	77 89.3	31 96.7	10 99.0	4 100.0		
			55 8.9 98.1	24 5.1	148 31.7	157 64.1	120 89.0	36 96.4	12 98.9	5 99.9	0 99.9	0 100.0
Austin Friars School	CUMBRIA	98	53 9.9 88.7	24 4.6	114 26.2	170 58.6	133 83.8	60 95.2	19 98.9	3 99.4	2 99.8	1 100.0
			47 10.1 88.1	26 6.1	145 31.7	137 60.7	111 84.2	43 93.3	21 97.8	7 99.2	2 99.7	1 100.0
Ayton School	N YORKS	295	35 8.4 65.7	5 1.7	34 13.3	78 39.9	93 71.7	54 90.1	20 96.9	9 100.0		
			27 7.7 75.0	43 17.7	47 27.4	48 50.9	55 77.8	30 92.5	9 96.9	4 98.8	2 99.8	0 100.0
Babington House School	KENT	154	17 8.2 64.7	15 10.8	27 30.2	27 49.6	36 75.5	13 84.9	15 95.7	6 100.0		
			17 7.4 0.0	0 0.0	16 12.7	24 31.8	37 61.2	27 82.7	14 93.8	4 97.0	2 98.6	1 100.0
Bablake School	W MIDS	285	121 9.9 100	189 15.8	469 55.2	363 85.6	140 97.3	30 99.8	1 99.9	0 99.9	0 99.9	1 100.0
			121 9.0 99.2	178 15.8	533 57.4	319 86.9	116 97.6	21 99.5	5 100.0			
Badminton School	AVON	61	53 9.3 100	124 25.1	203 66.1	151 96.6	17 100.0					
			47 9.5 100	84 20.9	243 58.0	123 85.4	52 97.0	11 99.5	2 99.9	0 99.9	0 99.9	0 100.0
Fernhill Manor/Ballard College	HANTS	126	27 8.6 96.3	41 17.7	48 38.5	76 71.4	48 92.2	13 97.8	2 98.7	3 100.0		
			33 8.3 96.8	16 6.1	67 25.7	72 52.2	86 83.8	29 94.5	11 98.5	4 100.0		
Bancroft's School	ESSEX	115	106 9.0 99.1	335 35.1	366 73.5	198 94.2	41 98.5	11 99.7	3 100.0			
			104 8.9 100	190 20.4	413 48.7	284 79.3	143 94.8	35 98.6	9 99.5	4 100.0	0 100.0	0 100.0
Barnard Castle School	DURHAM	113	94 8.9 87.2	42 5.0	148 22.7	258 53.6	269 85.8	82 95.6	23 98.3	10 99.5	3 99.9	1 100.0
			77 8.7 86.8	59 9.0	156 25.0	176 51.2	177 77.6	87 90.5	40 96.5	17 99.0	6 99.9	0 100.0
Baston School	KENT	154	28 8.9 78.6	14 5.6	38 20.8	73 50.0	64 75.6	44 93.2	11 97.6	2 98.4	4 100.0	
			32 8.7 95.7	15 7.3	69 25.8	69 50.6	69 75.3	42 90.4	16 96.1	8 99.0	2 99.7	0 100.0
Bath High School GPDST	AVON	61	57 9.2 98.2	84 16.1	191 52.6	187 84.5	61 96.2	19 99.2	3 99.8	0 99.8	0 99.8	1 100.0
			61 8.6 100	69 11.9	268 54.2	168 86.5	55 97.1	13 99.6	2 100.0			
Batley Grammar School	W YORKS	303	93 10.2 98.9	83 8.8	268 37.2	301 69.1	214 91.7	50 97.0	18 98.9	1 99.0	0 99.0	9 100.0
			97 9.9 97.5	65 8.0	313 33.9	308 66.0	233 90.3	62 96.7	21 98.9	7 99.6	3 99.9	0 100.0
Battle Abbey School	E SUSSEX	267	22 8.6 68.2	8 4.2	33 21.6	33 38.9	56 68.4	30 84.2	17 93.2	10 98.4	1 98.9	2 100.0
			20 8.7 69.6	12 5.9	32 20.0	32 38.9	47 66.5	31 84.8	15 93.6	8 99.4	2 99.5	0 100.0
Bearwood College	BERKS	69	46 8.1 50.0	5 1.3	20 6.7	84 29.1	102 56.4	57 71.7	49 84.8	40 95.5	10 98.1	7 100.0
			60 7.5 48.9	6 1.6	44 9.9	80 27.4	123 54.4	92 74.6	63 88.5	37 96.6	10 98.8	5 100.0
Bedales School	HANTS	126	87 9.8 96.6	101 11.8	230 38.8	268 70.2	192 92.7	48 98.4	13 99.9	1 100.0		
			82 9.2 89.9	86 11.2	254 36.0	226 66.0	177 89.6	60 97.5	13 99.3	3 99.7	0 99.7	2 100.0
Bedford High School	BEDS	67	124 9.5 96.8	119 10.1	355 40.1	459 78.9	194 95.3	49 99.5	4 99.8	2 100.0		
			120 9.3 95.3	167 13.4	456 43.8	351 75.3	199 93.2	54 98.0	17 99.5	5 100.0	0 100.0	0 100.0
Bedford Modern School	BEDS	67	155 9.1 96.8	134 9.5	404 38.1	511 74.3	285 94.5	61 98.9	15 99.9	1 100.0		
			158 8.4 96.1	72 5.1	468 36.3	422 68.2	290 90.0	99 97.5	24 99.3	7 99.8	0 99.8	2 100.0
Bedford School	BEDS	68	155 9.2 96.8	118 8.3	395 35.9	601 78.0	259 96.1	49 99.6	5 99.9	0 99.9	0 99.2	1 100.0
			142 10.0 95.6	64 5.0	414 30.0	476 63.4	367 89.1	112 97.0	33 99.3	7 99.8	1 99.9	1 100.0
Bedgebury School	KENT	154	53 8.6 67.9	23 5.0	66 19.4	119 45.4	140 76.0	71 91.5	25 96.9	10 99.1	2 99.6	2 100.0
			53 8.9 74.4	7 1.9	96 20.6	122 46.6	121 72.3	79 89.1	38 97.2	9 99.1	3 99.8	1 100.0
Bedstone College	SALOP	231	23 8.0 43.5	5 2.7	12 9.2	48 35.1	48 61.1	39 82.2	23 94.6	5 97.3	3 98.9	2 100.0
			34 8.0 70.0	11 4.1	46 17.8	60 40.0	74 67.5	43 83.4	26 93.0	14 98.2	3 99.3	1 100.0
Beechwood School Sacred Heart	KENT	154	21 8.6 90.5	47 26.1	57 57.8	54 87.8	13 95.0	5 97.8	3 99.4	1 100.0		
			32 7.4 90.9	12 6.9	82 35.4	55 58.6	60 84.0	22 93.2	12 98.3	3 99.6	1 100.0	
Belvedere School GPDST,The	MERSEY	211	71 8.7 98.6	146 23.6	168 50.8	183 80.4	98 96.3	17 99.0	3 99.5	0 99.5	0 99.5	3 100.0
			65 8.6 100	105 16.8	255 49.8	182 82.7	76 96.4	17 99.5	3 100.0			
Bembridge School	IOW	153	32 7.3 50.0	4 1.7	32 15.3	55 28.7	68 67.7	47 87.7	19 95.7	6 98.3	3 99.1	2 100.0
			41 8.1 50.0	6 1.7	37 11.4	61 29.6	110 62.5	68 82.8	32 92.3	18 97.7	4 98.9	3 100.0
Benenden School	KENT	155	62 8.8 100	75 13.7	228 55.4	185 89.2	52 98.7	7 100.0				
			68 8.8 100	88 13.8	259 46.6	186 77.9	112 96.8	16 99.5	3 100.0			
Bentham School	N YORKS	295	35 7.9 60.0	9 3.3	49 21.1	80 50.2	59 71.6	41 86.5	20 93.8	13 98.5	0 98.5	4 100.0
			45 8.5 53.3	9 3.6	62 16.7	77 36.9	96 61.9	68 79.7	36 89.1	35 98.3	5 99.6	1 100.0
Berkhamsted School for Girls	HERTS	143	52 9.0 100	81 17.4	167 53.2	147 84.8	51 95.7	16 99.1	4 100.0			
			59 9.1 98.1	65 13.7	268 52.0	149 79.6	87 95.7	18 99.1	5 100.0			

GCSE ENGLAND & WALES RESULTS 1995

School	County	P	*A	A	B	C	D	E	F	G	U
Berkhamsted School	HERTS	143	94 10.6 98.9	75 7.6	266 34.3	354 70.0	241 94.3	50 99.3	7 100.0		
			98 9.8 98.0	50 4.9	285 30.5	366 68.4	239 93.1	55 98.8	10 99.8	2 100.0	
Bethany School	KENT	155	57 7.0 78.9	7 1.8	23 7.5	134 41.1	130 73.7	70 91.2	27 98.0	7 99.7	1 100.0
			50 7.5 68.2	14 4.1	34 9.8	83 31.8	115 62.2	74 81.8	39 92.2	21 97.7	6 99.3	2 100.0
Birkdale School	S YORKS	301	66 9.3 92.4	105 17.0	168 44.3	188 74.8	97 90.6	45 97.9	8 99.2	5 100.0	
			58 8.6 94.4	43 6.7	157 33.5	143 62.4	122 87.0	46 96.3	14 99.1	4 99.9	0 99.9	0 100.0
Birkenhead High School GPDST	MERSEY	211	121 8.6 100	262 25.0	448 67.9	255 92.3	76 99.5	4 99.9	1 100.0		
			110 8.7 100	232 23.9	543 61.6	253 88.1	98 98.3	13 99.7	3 100.0		
Birkenhead School	MERSEY	212	112 9.1 98.2	178 17.5	356 52.4	273 79.1	181 96.9	25 99.3	7 100.0		
			111 8.9 97.5	113 10.6	469 49.7	322 82.2	136 95.9	29 98.9	9 99.8	2 100.0	0 100.0	0 100.0
Bishop Challoner School	GR LON	177	30 8.6 70.0	6 2.3	13 7.4	59 30.4	97 68.1	60 91.4	18 98.4	4 100.0	
			40 8.1 70.3	5 1.5	31 9.9	56 27.3	84 53.3	73 76.0	41 88.7	24 96.2	9 98.9	3 100.0
Bishop's Stortford College	HERTS	144	80 9.9 96.2	138 17.4	238 47.5	236 77.4	136 94.6	32 98.6	8 99.6	3 100.0	
			71 10.0 96.9	83 13.0	239 36.1	194 63.4	168 87.0	66 96.3	19 99.0	6 99.9	1 100.0	
Blackheath High School GPDST	GR LON	177	55 9.3 92.7	51 9.9	186 46.2	173 79.9	74 94.3	26 99.4	3 100.0		
			51 8.2 96.3	45 10.2	163 41.3	122 70.6	83 90.5	27 97.0	10 99.4	2 99.9	0 99.9	0 100.0
Bloxham School	OXON	224	59 9.3 91.5	84 15.4	155 43.8	146 70.5	98 88.5	43 96.3	16 99.3	4 100.0	
			62 9.1 89.9	33 5.1	126 23.5	166 52.8	184 85.2	57 95.3	16 98.1	6 99.2	2 99.5	2 100.0
Blundell's School	DEVON	102	81 10.3 90.1	20 2.4	166 22.4	275 55.4	262 86.9	81 96.6	22 99.3	6 100.0	
			89 9.8 97.5	46 5.5	188 22.6	232 49.3	272 80.6	109 93.1	42 97.9	13 99.4	2 99.6	3 100.0
Bolitho School,The	CORNWALL	96	21 8.5 85.7	21 11.7	50 39.7	50 67.6	39 89.4	9 94.4	4 96.6	5 99.4	0 99.4	1 100.0
			23 8.4 79.2	9 4.6	43 22.8	55 50.8	47 74.6	28 88.8	14 95.9	6 99.0	2 100.0	
Bolton School (Boys Div.)	LANCS	166	108 10.3 100	222 19.9	448 60.0	312 87.9	108 97.6	25 99.8	2 100.0		
			117 10.2 100	164 13.2	595 52.9	323 80.2	182 95.5	39 98.8	11 99.7	2 99.9	1 100.0	0 100.0
Bolton School (Girls Div.)	LANCS	166	120 9.6 100	276 23.9	441 62.2	336 91.3	92 99.3	7 99.9	0 99.9	1 100.0	
			111 9.0 100	274 24.2	557 60.8	265 87.2	111 98.2	16 99.8	1 99.9	0 99.9	0 99.9	0 100.0
Bootham School	N YORKS	296	58 9.8 91.4	41 7.2	139 31.7	175 62.6	144 88.0	54 97.5	12 99.6	2 100.0	
			57 9.0 91.2	49 7.3	145 30.1	146 58.4	129 83.4	50 93.1	22 97.4	9 99.1	3 99.7	1 100.0
Bowbrook House School	HERWORCS	136	11 8.3 63.6	6 6.6	20 28.6	21 51.6	18 71.4	15 87.9	6 94.5	5 100.0	
			13 7.6 85.7	9 8.0	14 16.0	17 33.0	29 62.0	22 84.0	11 95.0	4 99.0	1 100.0	
Box Hill School	SURREY	248	61 7.5 63.9	9 2.0	23 7.0	111 31.3	170 68.5	78 85.6	40 94.3	19 98.5	6 99.8	
			52 7.7 55.6	6 1.8	56 15.0	68 32.2	127 64.4	65 80.9	50 93.5	21 98.9	9 99.6	1 100.0
Bradfield College	BERKS	69	115 9.5 98.3	72 6.6	258 30.4	440 70.8	265 95.2	47 99.5	5 100.0		
			103 9.9 85.6	37 3.6	294 29.6	307 59.7	291 88.3	91 97.2	20 99.2	7 99.9	1 100.0	0 100.0
Brantwood Independent School for Girls	S YORKS	301	18 9.4 94.4	0 0.0	33 20.5	67 62.1	46 90.7	12 98.1	3 100.0		
			23 9.1 85.7	1 0.8	38 18.2	55 44.5	61 73.7	33 89.5	18 98.1	4 100.0		
Bradford Girls' Grammar School	W YORKS	303	104 9.0 100	349 37.3	290 68.3	228 92.7	63 99.5	5 100.0			
			99 9.0 100	196 20.2	426 52.5	262 82.0	128 96.5	25 99.3	5 99.9	1 100.0	0 100.0	0 100.0
Bradford Grammar School	W YORKS	303	154 8.6 99.4	227 17.1	505 55.3	381 84.1	177 97.4	25 99.3	7 99.8	0 99.8	0 99.8	2 100.0
			139 8.7 97.1	151 11.4	740 63.4	287 87.0	113 96.3	35 99.1	8 99.8	2 100.0	0 100.0	0 100.0
Braeside School For Girls	ESSEX	115	24 7.4 66.7	3 1.7	26 16.4	51 45.2	51 74.0	29 90.4	10 96.0	5 98.9	2 100.0	
			23 8.3 70.0	4 2.5	14 7.9	32 24.8	64 58.7	43 81.4	25 94.6	9 99.4	1 99.9	0 100.0
Bredon School	GLOS	122	40 7.1 10.0	1 0.4	6 2.5	18 8.9	39 22.7	59 43.6	50 61.3	48 78.4	28 88.3	33 100.0
			50 5.9 16.3	0 0.0	5 1.7	18 7.8	44 22.7	61 43.4	71 67.4	53 85.4	33 96.5	10 100.0
Brentwood School	ESSEX	115	152 10.7 94.1	131 8.0	425 34.1	486 63.9	363 86.1	166 96.3	50 99.4	9 99.9	1 100.0	
			123 8.9 98.0	215 13.8	359 36.6	372 70.4	215 90.0	78 97.1	22 99.1	6 99.6	1 99.7	3 100.0
Bridgewater School	GR MANCH	209	39 8.3 84.6	8 2.5	47 17.0	102 48.5	111 82.7	40 95.1	16 100.0		
			32 8.4 90.0	5 2.0	59 22.7	79 52.0	89 85.1	30 96.8	9 99.6	1 100.0		
Brighton & Hove High School GPDST	E SUSSEX	268	76 8.9 100	149 21.9	276 62.5	189 90.3	56 98.5	10 100.0			
			80 8.8 100	94 14.7	348 51.9	218 82.7	95 96.2	21 99.1	5 99.8	1 100.0	0 100.0	0 100.0
Brighton College	E SUSSEX	268	97 10.0 89.7	113 11.7	264 39.0	301 70.1	209 91.7	58 97.7	16 99.4	4 99.8	0 99.8	2 100.0
			96 9.5 93.1	40 4.7	310 34.6	314 68.8	212 91.9	58 98.3	14 99.8	2 100.0		
Brigidine School,The	BERKS	69	38 8.9 86.4	30 8.8	59 26.2	118 60.9	91 85.6	35 95.7	10 99.7	1 100.0		
			53 9.2 80.9	24 5.8	93 20.3	121 45.3	132 72.6	77 88.5	35 95.7	12 98.2	7 99.7	1 100.0
Bristol Cathedral School	AVON	61	73 8.5 95.9	35 5.6	118 24.6	226 60.8	192 91.7	42 98.4	6 99.4	2 99.7	0 99.7	2 100.0
			70 8.9 89.5	26 4.0	156 25.9	204 58.7	182 87.9	54 96.6	17 99.4	3 99.8	0 99.8	1 100.0
Bristol Grammar School	AVON	62	148 9.9 100	285 19.5	540 56.4	460 87.9	144 97.7	21 99.2	9 99.8	0 99.8	0 99.8	3 100.0
			145 10.1 98.6	180 12.2	637 45.9	462 77.5	234 93.4	71 98.3	19 99.6	6 100.0	0 100.0	0 100.0
British School in The Netherlands,The	OVERSEAS		60 9.2 90.0	76 13.7	223 53.9	161 82.9	52 92.3	27 97.1	9 98.7	2 99.1	4 99.8	1 100.0
			70 8.8 89.7	73 12.1	210 36.6	163 63.1	142 86.2	57 95.5	19 98.6	6 99.5	1 99.7	1 100.0

372

GCSE ENGLAND & WALES RESULTS 1995

School	County	P				*A		A		B		C		D		E		F		G		U	
British School of Paris,The	OVERSEAS		40	8.7	82.5	37	10.7	88	36.0	84	60.2	72	81.0	39	92.2	19	97.7	4	98.8	3	99.7	1	100.0
			0	0.0	0.0	0	0.0	0	0.0	0	0.0	0	0.0	0	0.0	0	0.0	0	0.0	0	0.0	0	0.0
Broadgate School	NOTTS	221	23	7.7	60.9	2	1.1	16	10.1	33	28.7	64	64.6	35	84.3	19	94.9	7	98.9	2	100.0		
			22	8.3	61.1	0	0.0	47	25.8	53	54.9	56	85.7	21	97.3	5	100.0						
Bromley High School GPDST	KENT	155	85	8.9	98.8	71	9.4	286	47.1	301	86.8	87	98.3	13	100.0								
			82	8.9	98.8	55	7.3	321	45.8	252	80.6	116	96.6	22	99.6	3	100.0						
Bromsgrove School	HERWORCS	137	141	9.0	93.6	127	10.0	379	40.0	399	71.5	253	91.5	74	97.3	25	99.3	6	99.8	0	99.8	3	100.0
			120	9.4	88.6	60	4.9	221	20.6	331	49.9	348	80.6	157	94.5	51	99.0	10	99.9	1	100.0		
Bruton School for Girls	SOMERSET	234	84	8.8	96.4	84	11.4	206	39.4	284	78.0	120	94.3	33	98.8	9	100.0						
			80	8.4	91.5	29	4.8	232	35.1	214	66.6	147	88.2	56	96.5	18	99.1	5	99.9	1	100.0		
Bryanston School	DORSET	107	128	9.5	97.7	93	7.6	347	36.2	455	73.5	251	94.2	51	98.4	18	99.8	2	100.0				
			134	9.0	98.6	78	6.0	439	37.8	397	70.8	285	94.5	56	99.1	8	99.8	2	99.9	0	99.9	0	100.0
Buckingham College	GR LON	177	40	8.6	67.5	15	4.3	47	17.9	83	41.9	96	69.7	57	86.1	26	93.6	18	98.8	2	99.4	2	100.0
			0	0.0	0.0	0	0.0	0	0.0	0	0.0	0	0.0	0	0.0	0	0.0	0	0.0	0	0.0	0	0.0
Burgess Hill School	W SUSSEX	274	48	9.1	97.9	77	17.7	149	52.0	133	82.5	61	96.6	12	99.3	3	100.0						
			50	8.7	96.5	53	10.5	178	44.0	124	72.9	83	92.3	23	97.6	8	99.5	2	100.0	0	100.0	0	100.0
Bury Grammar School	LANCS	166	103	8.6	94.2	104	11.8	259	41.2	274	72.2	184	93.1	46	98.3	10	99.4	1	99.5	0	99.5	4	100.0
			95	8.8	95.4	62	6.7	339	41.9	260	72.9	163	92.4	46	97.9	14	99.5	3	99.9	1	100.0		
Bury Grammar School (Girls)	LANCS	166	128	9.0	98.4	296	25.8	452	65.3	303	91.7	83	99.0	12	100.0								
			123	8.9	97.5	217	20.3	556	55.0	332	85.4	126	97.0	26	99.4	4	99.7	2	99.9	0	99.9	0	100.0
Bury Lawn School	BUCKS	80	17	8.2	58.8	5	3.6	14	13.7	25	31.7	37	58.3	31	80.6	21	95.7	6	100.0				
			32	7.6	40.0	4	2.0	19	8.3	31	21.1	61	46.4	46	65.4	45	84.0	25	94.4	10	98.5	3	100.0
Canbury School	SURREY	249	10	7.3	40.0	2	2.7	3	6.8	16	28.8	25	63.0	15	83.6	7	93.2	4	98.6	1	100.0		
			10	7.0	40.0	3	4.3	6	10.0	7	20.1	21	50.1	16	73.1	8	84.5	7	94.6	3	98.9	0	100.0
Canford School	DORSET	108	81	11.0	100	117	13.2	289	45.8	303	79.9	146	96.4	26	99.3	4	99.8	2	100.0				
			92	10.4	100	101	9.8	387	42.4	322	75.9	197	96.4	27	99.3	6	99.9	1	100.0	0	100.0	0	100.0
Carmel College	OXON	225	37	8.3	64.9	4	1.3	54	18.8	89	47.7	88	76.3	39	89.0	29	98.4	4	99.7	1	100.0		
			43	8.1	78.4	10	3.3	65	19.3	92	45.7	100	74.4	54	89.9	24	96.8	9	99.4	2	100.0		
Casterton School	CUMBRIA	98	57	8.9	100	53	10.4	191	48.0	169	81.3	84	97.8	8	99.4	1	100.0						
			51	8.9	95.2	55	14.6	197	45.7	143	77.1	88	96.5	13	99.3	3	100.0						
Caterham School	SURREY	249	94	8.9	95.7	99	11.9	214	37.6	318	75.8	138	92.3	45	97.7	19	100.0						
			87	9.7	94.7	50	5.4	235	29.0	230	56.3	238	84.5	98	96.1	28	99.4	4	99.9	1	100.0	0	100.0
Cawston College	NORFOLK	214	29	6.1	20.7	0	0.0	1	0.6	13	8.0	47	34.7	45	60.2	43	84.7	19	95.5	6	98.9	2	100.0
			30	6.4	40.0	0	0.0	6	3.1	22	14.4	46	38.2	47	62.4	34	80.0	25	92.9	10	98.0	3	100.0
Central Newcastle High School GPDST	TYNE	280	86	9.4	100	175	21.6	321	61.2	249	91.9	60	99.3	4	99.8	2	100.0						
			80	9.3	100	140	18.9	393	57.1	206	85.1	86	96.7	19	99.3	5	100.0						
Channing School	GR LON	178	53	8.5	100	60	13.3	191	55.8	142	87.3	51	98.7	5	99.8	1	100.0						
			48	8.0	100	75	17.2	161	46.3	119	77.6	65	94.7	17	99.2	3	100.0						
Charterhouse	SURREY	249	126	9.4	100	274	23.2	440	60.4	312	86.8	128	97.6	25	99.7	3	100.0						
			118	9.2	100	193	19.9	486	48.5	334	79.3	194	97.2	27	99.7	3	100.0	0	100.0	0	100.0		
Cheadle Hulme School	CHESHIRE	89	134	9.0	98.5	175	14.5	413	48.9	392	81.5	181	96.5	33	99.3	7	99.8	2	100.0				
			125	9.0	100	113	10.4	523	48.2	338	78.0	186	94.4	46	98.5	13	99.6	3	99.9	1	100.0		
Cheltenham College	GLOS	123	91	9.8	96.7	110	12.3	260	41.5	296	74.7	173	94.2	44	99.1	7	99.9	1	100.0				
			100	9.7	98.9	90	10.1	329	35.6	313	67.8	227	91.1	63	97.6	19	99.5	3	99.8	1	99.9	0	100.0
Cheltenham Ladies' College,The	GLOS	123	126	9.6	100	299	24.8	539	69.5	263	91.4	93	99.1	10	99.9	1	100.0						
			127	9.8	99.2	299	24.1	730	63.4	307	88.0	122	97.8	23	99.6	3	99.8	1	99.9	0	99.9	1	100.0
Chetham's School of Music	GR MANCH	209	33	6.5	93.9	60	28.2	84	67.6	50	91.1	13	97.2	2	98.1	3	99.5	0	99.5	1	100.0		
			34	6.0	94.6	26	10.9	100	51.2	50	75.5	35	92.6	10	97.5	4	99.4	1	99.9	0	99.9	0	100.0
Chigwell School	ESSEX	116	84	8.9	96.4	78	10.4	188	35.5	262	70.4	163	92.1	50	98.8	9	100.0						
			64	9.2	97.4	37	5.4	188	33.4	209	69.3	135	92.4	34	98.3	7	99.5	3	100.0	0	100.0	0	100.0
Christ College	S WALES	310	53	9.4	88.7	31	6.2	112	28.7	127	54.2	149	84.1	62	96.6	15	99.6	2	100.0				
			56	10.3	92.5	26	3.9	127	22.9	155	49.7	185	81.8	70	93.9	25	98.3	8	99.7	2	100.0		
Christ's Hospital	W SUSSEX	274	120	9.0	98.3	99	9.2	324	39.3	385	75.2	195	93.3	58	98.7	12	99.8	2	100.0				
			118	9.6	99.1	98	9.7	447	41.3	350	72.3	236	93.2	62	98.7	13	99.9	1	99.9	0	99.9	0	100.0
Churcher's College	HANTS	127	94	8.9	97.9	81	9.6	181	31.2	325	69.9	201	93.8	48	99.5	4	100.0						
			80	9.0	96.7	63	8.1	188	28.2	233	60.9	195	88.3	59	96.5	15	98.7	7	99.6	2	99.9	0	100.0
City of London Freemen's School	SURREY	250	84	10.0	98.8	138	16.4	264	47.8	265	79.3	123	93.9	37	98.3	11	99.6	2	99.9	1	100.0		
			83	9.7	100	81	11.1	303	40.0	239	69.9	170	91.2	57	98.4	11	99.7	2	100.0				
City of London School	GR LON	178	134	10.1	98.5	235	17.4	537	57.1	388	85.9	156	97.4	25	99.3	3	99.5	0	99.5	0	99.5	7	100.0
			130	9.6	97.8	187	14.8	574	49.1	387	80.3	185	95.1	45	98.7	13	99.6	2	100.0	0	100.0	0	100.0

373

GCSE ENGLAND & WALES RESULTS 1995

School	County	P				*A		A		B		C		D		E		F		G		U
City of London School For Girls	GR LON	179	78	9.0	98.7	226	32.3	267	70.5	168	94.6	35	99.6	3	100.0						
			78	9.1	100	252	34.8	399	63.9	180	89.6	62	98.4	9	99.7	2	99.9	0	99.9	0	99.9	0	100.0
Claires Court School	BERKS	70	41	9.4	75.6	13	3.4	52	16.8	118	47.4	116	77.5	54	91.5	25	97.9	7	99.7	1	100.0	
			39	9.6	86.5	11	3.1	62	17.0	105	44.8	117	75.8	55	90.4	24	96.7	11	99.6	1	99.9	0	100.0
Claremont Fan Court School	SURREY	250	55	8.9	87.3	32	6.5	95	25.9	171	60.7	121	85.3	59	97.4	12	99.8	1	100.0			
			65	8.1	86.6	34	6.0	163	32.6	156	62.6	122	86.0	50	95.6	16	98.7	7	100.0			
Claysmore School	DORSET	108	65	8.2	63.1	25	4.7	77	19.2	130	43.7	151	72.1	83	87.8	45	96.2	15	99.1	1	99.2	4	100.0
			76	8.4	59.5	23	3.6	64	10.8	118	29.4	188	58.9	151	82.6	68	93.3	29	97.8	11	99.6	2	100.0
Clifton College	AVON	62	133	9.1	92.5	155	12.9	353	42.2	376	73.4	232	92.6	72	98.6	13	99.7	4	100.0			
			132	9.6	95.9	71	6.3	491	40.0	362	68.7	264	89.7	89	96.7	30	99.1	8	99.7	1	99.8	2	100.0
Clifton High School	AVON	62	87	9.0	97.7	152	19.5	211	46.5	286	83.2	111	97.4	15	99.4	5	100.0				
			75	8.9	100	97	12.7	255	40.9	224	74.3	127	93.3	35	98.5	8	99.7	2	100.0			
Cobham Hall School	KENT	155	28	7.5	71.4	15	7.1	40	26.2	72	60.5	48	83.3	28	96.7	6	99.5	1	100.0			
			44	8.9	63.3	10	4.3	77	20.4	98	45.7	108	73.6	66	90.6	26	97.3	7	99.1	2	99.6	1	100.0
Cokethorpe School	OXON	225	38	8.1	50.0	3	1.0	27	9.8	71	33.0	90	62.4	61	82.4	39	95.1	14	99.7	1	100.0	
			35	8.0	44.4	3	1.4	19	7.3	40	21.8	87	53.3	66	77.3	37	90.7	17	96.9	6	99.1	2	100.0
Colchester Boys High School	ESSEX	116	23	8.1	60.9	9	4.8	25	18.2	62	51.3	44	74.9	33	92.5	7	96.3	4	98.4	2	99.5	1	100.0
			34	7.6	63.3	16	7.4	33	14.1	51	34.1	84	67.0	45	84.6	24	94.0	11	98.3	4	99.8	0	100.0
Colfe's School	GR LON	179	96	8.8	94.8	49	5.8	181	27.3	339	67.4	206	91.8	57	98.6	11	99.9	1	100.0			
			100	9.0	93.1	68	7.6	277	32.4	276	63.1	220	87.6	83	96.8	21	99.1	4	99.6	1	99.7	2	100.0
Colston's Girls' School	AVON	62	68	9.1	0.0	59	9.5	200	41.8	228	78.7	94	93.9	33	99.2	2	99.5	3	100.0			
			99	8.5	94.6	71	8.4	238	30.1	264	61.5	229	88.8	66	96.7	22	99.3	5	99.9	0	99.9	0	100.0
Colston's Collegiate School	AVON	63	75	9.7	86.7	40	5.5	154	26.6	223	57.2	195	84.0	75	94.2	30	98.4	11	99.9	0	99.9	1	100.0
			72	9.2	72.3	12	1.9	102	15.8	151	38.6	217	71.5	109	88.1	54	96.2	19	99.1	3	99.6	2	100.0
Combe Bank School	KENT	156	31	9.4	87.1	6	2.1	69	25.8	118	66.3	62	87.6	30	97.9	6	100.0				
			42	9.0	86.8	2	0.5	97	25.9	121	58.2	101	85.2	37	95.1	14	98.8	4	99.9	0	99.9	0	100.0
Commonweal Lodge School	GR LON	179	21	8.6	76.2	10	5.6	30	22.2	65	58.3	41	81.1	31	98.3	3	100.0				
			23	8.0	73.7	8	5.3	27	15.5	43	38.5	61	71.1	35	89.8	13	96.8	5	99.5	1	100.0	
Cranbrook College	GR LON	180	23	8.2	65.2	7	3.7	27	18.1	61	50.5	45	74.5	34	92.6	10	97.9	3	99.5	1	100.0	
			21	7.8	79.2	6	3.0	21	13.2	47	41.5	57	75.8	25	90.9	10	96.9	4	99.3	1	99.9	0	100.0
Cranford House School	OXON	226	10	8.1	90.0	3	3.7	13	19.8	20	44.4	33	85.2	9	96.3	3	100.0				
			19	8.2	90.9	12	6.5	32	21.9	39	47.1	56	83.2	19	95.5	6	99.4	1	100.0			
Cranleigh School	SURREY	251	92	8.9	95.7	75	9.2	202	33.8	263	65.9	208	91.3	52	97.7	12	99.1	6	99.9	0	99.9	1	100.0
			98	9.7	97.3	112	11.2	304	34.5	283	64.4	242	89.9	59	96.2	23	98.6	9	99.6	1	99.7	3	100.0
Cransley School	CHESHIRE	90	21	7.9	90.5	16	9.7	39	33.3	55	66.7	36	88.5	9	93.9	9	99.4	1	100.0			
			19	7.8	100	8	6.1	46	31.8	47	62.9	45	92.7	9	98.7	2	100.0				
Croft House School	DORSET	108	18	8.0	61.1	5	3.5	14	13.2	35	37.5	41	66.0	25	83.3	12	91.7	5	95.1	2	96.5	5	100.0
			35	8.8	56.2	7	5.0	38	12.5	54	29.8	90	58.7	64	79.3	40	92.1	17	97.6	5	99.2	2	100.0
Croham Hurst School	GR LON	180	44	9.0	100	51	12.8	135	46.9	150	84.6	52	97.7	8	99.7	1	100.0				
			53	8.8	93.8	39	6.7	150	33.9	157	67.5	109	90.9	36	98.6	5	99.7	1	99.9	0	99.9	0	100.0
Croydon High School GPDST	GR LON	180	108	9.0	100	200	20.7	388	60.7	294	91.1	79	99.3	7	100.0						
			104	9.0	100	145	15.3	464	52.9	284	83.3	123	96.5	27	99.4	4	99.8	1	99.9	0	99.9	0	100.0
Culcheth Hall	CHESHIRE	90	26	7.7	84.6	5	2.5	37	21.1	70	56.3	56	84.4	22	95.5	8	99.5	1	100.0			
			39	7.6	87.1	8	3.2	69	23.9	81	51.1	92	82.0	32	92.7	13	97.1	6	99.1	2	99.8	0	100.0
Culford School	SUFFOLK	243	95	9.7	85.3	68	7.4	190	28.1	276	58.1	211	81.1	111	93.1	43	97.8	18	99.8	2	100.0	
			83	10.0	90.8	27	3.9	222	27.3	244	56.7	204	81.3	92	92.4	41	97.3	19	99.3	3	99.7	2	100.0
Dagfa House School	NOTTS	221	18	6.9	44.4	0	0.0	3	2.4	21	19.4	41	52.4	25	72.6	21	89.5	11	98.4	1	99.2	1	100.0
			13	7.9	0.0	0	0.0	21	20.7	30	50.4	24	74.1	17	90.9	3	93.8	4	97.8	1	98.8	1	100.0
Dame Alice Harpur School	BEDS	68	115	9.0	100	180	17.5	330	49.5	346	84.8	129	97.4	22	99.5	5	100.0				
			126	8.8	96.0	165	14.9	448	43.2	355	75.2	223	95.2	41	98.9	9	99.7	2	99.9	1	100.0	0	100.0
Dame Allan's Girls' School	TYNE	280	65	9.0	96.9	119	20.3	185	52.0	179	82.6	73	95.0	28	99.8	1	100.0				
			62	9.3	97.1	127	20.7	222	42.9	163	71.2	109	90.2	40	97.1	12	99.2	2	99.5	1	99.7	1	100.0
Dame Allan's Boys' School	TYNE	280	63	9.4	96.8	101	17.1	179	47.4	205	82.1	70	93.9	22	97.6	12	99.7	1	99.8	1	100.0	
			66	8.5	96.9	48	8.2	231	43.1	168	73.2	101	91.2	38	98.0	10	99.8	1	100.0			
Dauntsey's School	WILTS	291	101	9.6	99.0	130	13.4	278	42.0	378	80.6	152	96.6	26	99.3	6	99.9	1	100.0			
			96	9.4	98.0	56	5.6	275	31.7	281	62.9	241	89.7	68	97.2	20	99.4	4	99.9	0	99.9	1	100.0
Dean Close School	GLOS	123	90	10.9	95.6	91	9.3	246	34.5	311	66.3	244	91.3	68	98.3	14	99.7	2	99.9	0	99.9	1	100.0
			92	10.7	97.8	67	6.7	286	30.6	320	63.4	255	89.5	78	97.5	21	99.7	3	100.0	0	100.0	0	100.0
Denstone College	STAFFS	239	52	9.2	67.3	21	4.4	52	15.3	132	42.9	116	71.3	83	88.7	30	95.0	16	98.3	6	99.6	2	100.0
			60	8.2	71.1	16	3.9	77	16.3	126	42.1	152	73.1	77	88.8	32	95.4	16	98.7	3	99.3	3	100.0

374

GCSE ENGLAND & WALES RESULTS 1995

School	County	P		*A		A		B		C		D		E		F		G		U	
Derby High School	DERBYS	100	60	8.9	98.3	84	15.7	177	48.8	172	80.9	83	96.4	16	99.4	3	100.0				
			44	9.1	95.2	85	22.7	201	54.1	110	81.4	59	96.0	14	99.5	1	99.8	1	100.0		
Ditcham Park School	HANTS	127	38	8.9	89.5	54	16.0	80	39.6	109	71.9	60	89.6	23	96.4	10	99.4	0	99.4	0	99.4	2	100.0
			36	9.0	91.7	13	6.1	88	28.3	93	57.3	79	81.9	35	92.8	15	97.4	7	99.6	1	99.9	0	100.0
Dixie Grammar & Wolstan Prep Schools	LEICS	170	52	8.4	88.5	37	8.5	123	36.7	139	68.6	91	89.4	38	98.2	5	99.3	3	100.0			
			34	8.6	81.2	15	5.9	47	17.1	77	43.5	93	75.3	45	90.8	19	97.3	6	99.3	2	100.0	
Dodderhill School	HERWORCS	137	27	9.0	88.9	10	4.1	45	22.7	84	57.4	60	82.2	27	93.4	10	97.5	5	99.6	0	99.6	1	100.0
			20	8.0	91.3	4	2.3	32	20.6	46	49.4	51	81.3	20	93.8	7	98.1	3	100.0			
Douai School	BERKS	70	41	10.0	73.2	10	2.5	59	16.9	112	44.4	110	71.3	70	88.5	33	96.6	10	99.0	3	99.8	1	100.0
			42	9.7	77.8	3	0.8	60	15.1	99	39.6	138	73.8	62	89.2	35	97.8	7	99.6	1	99.8	1	100.0
Dover College	KENT	156	49	7.3	77.6	20	5.6	46	18.5	87	42.9	132	79.8	46	92.7	19	98.0	4	99.2	0	99.2	3	100.0
			52	6.5	48.8	7	2.8	47	14.1	69	34.4	105	65.3	64	84.2	28	92.4	15	96.8	6	98.6	4	100.0
Downe House	BERKS	70	87	10.4	100	228	25.2	423	72.1	219	96.3	33	100.0									
			75	10.3	100	88	12.6	424	57.2	236	87.7	75	97.4	17	99.6	3	100.0	0	100.0	0	100.0	0	100.0
Downside School	AVON	63	51	9.4	90.2	33	6.9	107	29.2	170	64.7	106	86.8	45	96.2	13	99.0	5	100.0			
			74	9.1	88.5	14	2.6	170	25.6	174	51.3	184	78.5	88	91.5	39	97.3	14	99.4	3	99.8	1	100.0
Duchy Grammar School, The	CORNWALL	97	23	9.8	60.9	5	2.2	23	12.4	45	32.4	50	54.7	42	73.3	32	87.6	20	96.4	7	99.6	1	100.0
			24	7.9	72.2	4	2.4	27	14.9	29	30.3	49	56.3	38	76.5	25	89.8	14	97.2	3	98.8	2	100.0
Duke of York's Royal Military School	KENT	156	64	9.5	79.7	29	4.8	76	17.3	173	45.7	201	78.8	88	93.3	35	99.0	6	100.0			
			75	9.7	77.6	10	1.5	110	15.4	198	42.5	250	76.8	108	91.6	41	97.2	12	98.8	4	99.4	4	100.0
Dulwich College	GR LON	181	198	10.7	100	248	11.7	775	48.4	781	85.3	267	98.0	39	99.8	3	100.0	1	100.0			
			192	10.2	100	190	10.4	872	46.5	637	79.0	313	95.0	75	98.9	18	99.8	3	99.9	0	99.9	1	100.0
Dunottar School	SURREY	252	35	8.6	100	55	18.2	108	54.0	110	90.4	25	98.7	4	100.0						
			49	8.5	97.6	28	7.9	154	38.7	134	71.2	83	91.3	27	97.8	8	99.8	1	100.0			
Durham High School for Girls	DURHAM	113	45	9.5	97.8	70	16.3	158	53.1	128	83.0	65	98.1	5	99.3	2	99.8	1	100.0			
			45	9.2	100	64	14.5	199	51.2	118	79.7	66	95.7	13	98.8	4	99.8	1	100.0			
Durham School	DURHAM	114	50	8.9	82.0	39	8.7	98	30.6	128	59.3	96	80.8	50	91.9	24	97.3	9	99.3	1	99.6	2	100.0
			61	9.3	81.4	33	6.5	137	25.4	145	50.9	154	78.1	77	91.6	30	96.9	13	99.2	2	99.6	2	100.0
Ealing College Upper School	GR LON	182	32	7.8	81.2	3	1.2	36	15.6	89	51.2	66	77.6	37	92.4	11	98.7	2	100.0			
			44	8.4	66.7	3	1.2	41	11.3	74	31.2	106	59.7	76	80.2	45	92.3	20	97.7	6	99.3	2	100.0
Eastbourne College	E SUSSEX	269	90	10.1	98.9	73	8.0	225	32.7	362	72.4	205	94.8	34	98.6	12	99.9	1	100.0			
			101	10.4	96.8	47	5.0	300	29.4	345	62.3	295	90.4	77	97.7	22	99.8	2	100.0			
Eastcliffe Grammar School	TYNE	280	28	7.5	53.6	0	0.0	12	5.7	37	23.3	68	55.7	56	82.4	22	92.9	14	99.5	1	100.0		
			0			0	0.0	0	0.0	0	0.0	0	0.0	0	0.0	0	0.0	0	0.0	0	0.0	0	0.0
Eccles Hall School	NORFOLK	214	30	9.2	36.7	1	0.4	10	4.0	35	16.6	65	40.1	76	67.5	52	86.3	25	95.3	12	99.6	1	100.0
			35	8.2	24.2	2	0.7	10	3.5	25	12.1	71	36.7	76	63.1	53	81.4	30	91.8	14	96.7	9	100.0
Edgbaston C of E College	W MIDS	286	42	9.8	95.2	14	3.4	73	21.2	129	52.7	136	85.9	34	94.1	21	99.3	1	99.5	0	99.5	2	100.0
			45	9.1	97.4	18	4.8	126	31.8	123	61.8	97	85.5	41	95.6	14	99.0	4	100.0	0	100.0	0	100.0
Edgbaston High School for Girls	W MIDS	287	80	8.9	96.7	137	19.3	210	48.9	231	81.5	110	97.0	18	99.6	3	100.0				
			84	8.8	100	113	13.8	328	47.5	220	77.4	124	94.1	31	98.3	11	99.8	1	100.0	0	100.0	0	100.0
Edgehill College	DEVON	102	59	8.5	81.4	13	2.6	82	18.9	158	50.4	142	78.7	56	89.8	38	97.4	7	98.8	5	99.8	1	100.0
			57	8.6	81.7	11	2.7	91	19.0	132	46.0	140	74.6	63	87.5	36	94.9	17	98.4	6	99.6	2	100.0
Egerton-Rothesay School Limited	HERTS	144	28	8.9	53.6	3	1.2	32	14.0	51	34.4	63	59.6	57	82.4	28	93.6	14	99.2	1	99.2	1	100.0
			20	8.4	62.9	5	1.7	17	10.9	36	32.6	43	58.5	31	77.2	23	91.1	8	95.9	6	99.5	0	100.0
Elizabeth College	C.I.	87	74	8.8	91.9	64	9.8	181	37.5	211	69.8	129	89.6	45	96.5	14	98.6	7	99.7	1	99.8	1	100.0
			84	9.2	90.2	59	8.0	205	28.1	206	54.8	206	81.4	90	93.1	36	97.7	14	99.5	2	99.8	1	100.0
Ellesmere College	SALOP	231	56	8.9	89.3	13	2.6	73	17.2	144	45.9	196	85.0	54	95.8	16	99.0	4	99.8	0	99.8	1	100.0
			62	7.7	84.2	18	3.7	99	21.3	128	47.8	158	80.4	54	91.6	29	97.6	9	99.5	1	99.7	1	100.0
Elmhurst Ballet School	SURREY	252	36	9.3	72.2	7	2.1	71	23.3	91	50.4	78	73.7	51	89.0	22	95.5	11	98.8	4	100.0		
			42	7.6	81.1	31	9.5	92	30.7	82	56.4	74	79.6	39	91.8	14	96.2	10	99.4	2	100.0		
Elmslie Girls School	LANCS	167	39	8.0	79.5	15	4.8	69	27.0	81	53.1	82	79.4	34	90.4	19	96.5	6	98.4	3	99.4	2	100.0
			34	7.8	82.8	39	16.2	66	27.7	65	52.1	71	78.7	35	91.5	15	97.5	5	99.3	1	99.6	1	100.0
Eltham College	GR LON	182	77	9.9	96.1	102	13.4	245	45.5	206	72.5	161	93.6	35	98.2	10	99.5	2	99.7	2	100.0		
			72	10.1	100	111	14.7	323	47.6	217	77.6	121	94.3	34	99.0	7	100.0	0	100.0	0	100.0	0	100.0
Emanuel School	GR LON	182	133	8.8	91.0	73	6.2	274	29.6	423	65.8	281	89.8	92	97.6	21	99.4	6	99.9	1	100.0		
			118	8.0	75.6	40	3.7	219	24.1	277	53.5	269	82.0	110	93.7	45	98.4	11	99.6	3	99.9	0	100.0
Embley Park School	HANTS	128	39	7.5	87.2	7	2.4	43	17.1	99	50.9	105	86.7	32	97.6	7	100.0					
			39	7.7	47.4	4	1.4	26	9.1	56	27.9	103	62.5	62	83.4	33	94.5	11	98.2	4	99.5	1	100.0
Eothen School	SURREY		38	8.6	84.2	31	9.5	55	26.4	95	55.5	100	86.2	33	96.3	8	98.8	3	99.7	1	100.0		
			31	7.8	85.2	9	4.6	67	28.5	63	54.5	67	82.2	27	93.3	11	97.9	3	99.1	2	99.9	0	100.0

375

GCSE ENGLAND & WALES RESULTS 1995

School	County	P				*A		A		B		C		D		E		F		G		U	
Epsom College	SURREY	253	125	10.0	100	176	14.1	382	44.6	443	80.0	205	96.4	36	99.3	3	99.5	1	99.6	0	99.6	5	100.0
			120	9.8	99.2	170	13.9	528	47.7	380	79.9	191	96.1	31	98.7	12	99.7	3	100.0				
Eton College	BERKS	71	254	9.6	100	563	23.1	1119	69.1	663	96.3	85	99.8	4	100.0								
			250	9.7	100	301	13.4	1373	59.3	717	88.9	233	98.6	31	99.8	3	100.0	0	100.0	0	100.0	1	100.0
Ewell Castle School	SURREY	253	42	7.6	73.8	4	1.3	33	11.6	84	37.9	112	73.0	62	92.5	15	97.2	8	99.7	1	100.0		
			59	7.9	53.0	5	1.0	66	14.3	96	34.9	141	65.1	96	85.7	41	94.4	22	99.1	4	100.0		
Exeter School	DEVON	103	122	9.5	98.4	149	12.9	401	47.5	378	80.1	175	95.2	45	99.1	10	99.9	0	99.9	0	99.9	1	100.0
			105	9.6	98.1	112	11.4	415	43.6	327	76.2	194	95.5	36	99.1	9	100.0						
Falcon Manor School	N'HANTS	217	15	7.2	40.0	0	0.0	7	6.5	30	34.3	25	57.4	9	65.7	17	81.5	12	92.6	5	97.2	3	100.0
			23	8.1	31.2	0	0.0	4	2.1	13	9.0	43	31.9	44	55.3	38	75.5	29	90.9	13	97.8	4	100.0
Farlington School	W SUSSEX	275	39	9.1	100	28	7.9	113	39.9	130	76.8	67	95.8	14	99.7	1	100.0						
			43	8.5	97.8	31	8.0	104	30.6	126	65.6	88	90.0	30	98.6	6	100.0						
Farnborough Hill	HANTS	128	85	9.6	98.8	115	14.1	293	50.1	299	86.9	88	97.7	17	99.8	2	100.0						
			84	9.1	95.3	101	12.5	299	41.5	246	73.5	141	91.9	47	98.0	13	99.7	1	99.8	1	100.0	0	100.0
Farringtons and Stratford House	KENT	157	66	9.3	90.9	28	4.6	129	25.7	211	60.2	174	88.7	50	96.9	12	98.9	6	99.8	1	100.0		
			54	8.8	77.3	30	4.6	93	20.7	133	48.5	125	74.6	75	90.3	28	96.1	15	99.2	3	99.9	0	100.0
Felsted School	ESSEX	117	65	9.0	96.9	77	13.2	177	43.6	203	78.5	96	95.0	21	98.6	8	100.0						
			77	8.6	95.3	62	11.5	284	44.4	186	72.4	134	92.5	40	98.5	8	99.7	2	100.0				
Forest Girls' School	GR LON	183	56	9.8	98.2	51	9.3	194	44.5	177	76.6	102	95.1	20	98.7	7	100.0						
			50	9.5	92.2	29	5.7	182	39.8	162	74.2	85	92.2	26	97.7	9	99.6	2	100.0				
Forest Boys' School	GR LON	183	103	9.8	93.2	51	5.1	225	27.4	326	59.8	299	89.5	89	98.3	16	99.9	1	100.0				
			97	9.4	97.0	39	4.0	236	26.8	290	58.6	241	85.0	98	95.8	29	99.0	8	99.8	1	100.0	0	100.0
Framlingham College	SUFFOLK	243	104	8.7	87.5	60	6.6	187	27.2	289	59.1	231	84.6	105	96.1	30	99.4	5	100.0				
			92	8.4	93.7	80	9.6	174	24.5	221	53.0	216	80.8	89	92.3	40	97.5	16	99.5	2	99.8	1	100.0
Francis Holland School Clarence Gate	GR LON	183	55	9.0	100	73	14.8	156	46.5	175	81.9	76	97.4	13	100.0								
			53	8.6	100	62	14.4	211	49.2	147	81.7	68	96.7	12	99.3	3	100.0						
Francis Holland School	GR LON	184	27	8.3	96.3	36	16.1	88	55.6	62	83.4	33	98.2	4	100.0								
			25	8.5	100	73	31.6	93	50.7	63	80.3	33	95.8	6	98.6	2	99.5	1	100.0				
Frensham Heights	SURREY	254	54	9.2	77.8	29	5.8	118	29.6	137	57.1	115	80.3	78	96.0	18	99.6	2	100.0				
			47	9.2	92.8	26	4.2	125	29.7	124	58.0	116	84.4	48	95.4	15	98.8	5	100.0	0	100.0	0	100.0
Friends School	ESSEX	117	56	8.1	62.5	24	5.3	62	19.0	102	41.6	117	67.5	74	83.8	43	93.4	19	97.6	3	98.2	8	100.0
			45	8.5	60.0	8	2.7	56	15.0	83	36.6	104	63.6	66	80.7	42	91.6	20	96.8	8	98.9	4	100.0
Fulneck School	W YORKS	304	76	8.8	84.2	23	3.4	121	21.5	224	55.0	175	81.2	76	92.5	30	97.0	14	99.1	5	99.9	1	100.0
			49	8.8	86.0	23	5.0	79	19.5	125	48.6	129	78.6	52	90.7	25	96.5	11	99.0	4	100.0	0	100.0
Fyling Hall School	N YORKS	296	26	9.2	53.8	3	1.3	14	7.1	42	24.7	81	58.6	50	79.5	32	92.9	11	97.5	6	100.0		
			32	9.2	55.6	1	0.4	22	7.4	39	20.6	105	56.1	71	80.1	34	91.6	18	97.7	5	99.4	1	100.0
Gateways School	W YORKS	304	28	9.3	92.9	35	13.4	59	36.0	96	72.8	49	91.6	16	97.7	4	99.2	2	100.0				
			33	8.7	91.7	17	5.4	65	23.7	82	52.4	78	79.6	32	90.8	18	97.1	6	99.2	2	99.9	0	100.0
Giggleswick School	N YORKS	297	62	8.6	93.5	59	11.0	120	33.4	194	69.6	127	93.3	30	98.9	5	99.8	1	100.0				
			60	8.2	92.7	42	8.9	159	34.2	132	61.2	126	87.1	42	95.7	15	98.7	5	99.8	1	100.0	0	100.0
Godolphin & Latymer School, The	GR LON	185	100	9.1	100	208	23.0	392	66.2	262	95.1	42	99.8	2	100.0								
			98	9.0	100	106	12.0	438	52.1	279	83.7	121	97.5	17	99.4	4	99.9	1	100.0	0	100.0	0	100.0
Godolphin School, The	WILTS	291	56	8.9	100	79	15.9	160	48.0	179	83.9	75	99.0	4	99.8	1	100.0						
			54	9.0	100	84	15.8	167	38.3	168	73.4	91	92.3	27	98.0	7	99.4	2	99.8	0	99.8	0	100.0
Gordonstoun School	SCOTLAND		74	8.9	85.1	25	3.8	140	25.0	227	59.3	161	83.7	91	97.4	14	99.5	3	100.0				
			85	8.4	94.3	27	4.4	194	27.7	235	60.4	205	88.9	60	97.2	16	99.5	3	99.9	0	99.9	0	100.0
Gosfield School	ESSEX	117	19	7.7	31.6	1	0.7	15	10.9	25	27.9	42	56.5	27	74.8	17	86.4	13	95.2	0	95.2	7	100.0
			17	9.0	10.5	2	1.1	5	4.1	21	18.2	34	41.2	37	66.2	23	81.8	17	93.2	5	96.6	5	100.0
Grange School, The	CHESHIRE	90	91	8.9	97.8	129	15.9	290	51.7	252	82.8	117	97.3	18	99.5	3	99.9	1	100.0				
			71	8.9	100	69	12.0	280	46.9	191	77.3	117	96.0	19	99.0	5	99.8	1	100.0	0	100.0	0	100.0
Greenacre School	SURREY	254	35	8.6	97.1	22	7.3	91	37.7	116	76.3	55	94.7	13	99.0	3	100.0						
			41	8.4	97.3	8	2.6	99	29.5	102	59.2	94	86.6	34	96.6	10	99.5	1	99.8	0	99.8	0	100.0
Greenfields School	E SUSSEX	269	12	4.1	25.0	0	0.0	14	28.6	19	67.3	6	79.6	7	93.2	2	98.0	0	98.0	1	98.0	1	100.0
			9	4.7	58.3	3	4.3	12	30.5	10	54.0	9	75.1	5	86.9	3	93.9	1	96.2	1	98.6	1	100.0
Grenville College	DEVON	103	88	8.5	63.6	21	2.8	92	15.2	169	37.9	201	64.8	125	81.6	76	91.8	40	97.2	15	99.2	6	100.0
			69	8.8	58.2	29	4.0	63	11.3	97	27.2	160	53.4	132	75.0	83	88.6	44	95.8	20	99.1	5	100.0
Gresham's School	NORFOLK	215	97	10.2	99.0	72	7.3	295	37.2	330	70.6	231	94.0	51	99.2	8	100.0						
			89	10.0	100	55	6.1	275	32.0	295	64.9	237	94.1	63	98.4	12	99.8	2	100.0				
Grove School, The	SURREY		34	8.4	97.1	22	7.7	94	40.4	107	77.7	52	95.8	6	97.9	5	99.7	1	100.0				
			30	9.0	95.5	7	3.1	74	27.9	83	58.7	66	83.2	30	94.4	12	98.8	2	99.6	1	99.9	0	100.0

376

School	County	P	*A	A	B	C	D	E	F	G	U
Guildford High School for Girls	SURREY	254	72 9.1 100	189 29.0	293 73.9	142 95.7	28 100.0				
			68 9.0 100	89 15.1	391 66.6	163 93.2	35 98.9	6 99.8	1 100.0		
Haberdashers' Aske's Sch. for Girls	HERTS	145	123 9.3 100	336 29.4	468 70.5	262 93.4	63 98.9	7 99.6	5 100.0		
			118 8.8 100	264 23.9	656 68.4	266 94.0	49 98.7	10 99.7	2 99.9	0 99.9	0 99.9	1 100.0
Haberdashers' Aske's School, The	HERTS	145	156 9.9 100	529 34.4	625 75.0	302 94.6	75 99.5	8 100.0			
			157 9.3 99.4	329 21.2	850 62.9	412 91.2	109 98.7	14 99.6	4 99.9	1 100.0	0 100.0	0 100.0
Haberdashers' Monmouth School for Girl	S WALES	311	89 9.1 100	162 20.1	320 59.7	225 87.6	85 98.1	13 99.8	2 100.0		
			77 9.2 100	90 12.2	320 47.6	218 78.3	122 95.5	26 99.2	5 99.9	1 100.0	
Haileybury	HERTS	145	121 9.0 97.5	91 8.3	289 34.7	402 71.4	243 93.6	60 99.1	10 100.0		
			98 9.3 98.9	65 7.9	300 34.4	304 67.7	218 91.7	57 97.9	15 99.6	4 100.0	
Halliford School	GR LON	185	49 8.8 85.7	21 4.9	80 23.4	146 57.3	109 82.6	45 93.0	20 97.7	8 99.5	2 100.0
			52 8.9 90.2	12 2.7	85 19.0	113 43.7	132 72.6	71 88.1	35 95.8	14 98.8	3 99.5	2 100.0
Hammond School	CHESHIRE	91	34 8.3 100	15 5.3	83 34.8	94 68.1	64 90.8	21 98.2	4 99.6	1 100.0	
			35 8.3 86.7	30 12.2	73 27.2	90 58.3	76 84.5	32 95.5	10 99.0	3 100.0	
Hampton School	GR LON	185	156 9.9 99.4	185 12.0	527 46.2	551 82.0	237 97.4	33 99.5	7 100.0		
			139 9.4 98.6	95 6.6	513 40.5	434 73.6	248 92.5	70 97.8	23 99.5	6 100.0	
Haresfoot Senior School	HERTS	145	11 8.9 63.6	2 2.0	5 7.1	23 30.6	24 55.1	25 80.6	12 95.9	3 95.9	3 99.0	1 100.0
			5 8.3 33.3	0 0.0	6 16.0	10 42.7	10 69.3	7 88.0	3 96.0	1 98.7	0 98.7	0 100.0
Harrogate Ladies' College	N YORKS	297	58 8.9 91.4	99 19.4	136 46.2	142 74.1	81 90.0	39 97.6	6 98.8	6 100.0	
			62 8.6 92.9	125 20.9	195 41.4	143 68.2	110 88.9	38 96.1	16 99.1	4 99.8	1 100.0
Harrow School	GR LON	186	161 9.4 100	299 19.8	584 58.5	461 89.1	133 97.9	30 99.9	2 100.0		
			150 9.0 99.4	153 10.3	621 48.3	431 80.2	224 96.7	38 99.5	6 100.0	0 100.0	0 100.0
Harvington School	GR LON	186	9 8.6 88.9	7 9.1	20 35.1	17 57.1	24 85.8	6 96.1	3 100.0		
			14 7.4 93.3	10 8.7	27 28.9	31 59.9	25 84.8	12 96.8	3 99.8	0 99.8	0 99.8
Hawley Place School	HANTS	129	13 7.9 84.6	6 5.8	23 28.2	42 68.9	17 85.4	11 96.1	2 98.1	2 100.0	
			19 7.7 72.7	2 2.4	21 14.2	33 36.5	42 64.9	29 84.5	17 95.9	5 99.3	1 100.0
Hazelhurst School	GR LON	186	14 10.1 92.9	5 3.5	30 24.8	41 53.9	41 83.0	17 95.0	6 99.3	1 100.0	
			12 9.3 60.0	1 1.0	16 14.1	26 37.0	30 63.5	20 81.1	10 89.9	7 96.1	2 97.9	2 100.0
Headington School	OXON	226	76 9.6 100	108 14.9	250 49.3	244 82.9	96 96.1	23 99.3	4 99.9	1 100.0	
			81 9.2 93.0	78 9.6	290 41.2	223 71.3	148 91.2	52 98.2	11 99.7	2 100.0	
Heathfield School	BERKS	72	39 9.0 100	33 9.4	124 44.9	139 84.6	50 98.9	3 99.7	1 100.0		
			34 8.5 100	29 7.6	102 37.2	104 73.1	63 94.8	12 99.0	2 99.7	1 100.0	
Heathfield School GPDST	GR LON	186	51 8.6 100	50 11.3	153 46.0	152 80.5	75 97.5	9 99.5	2 100.0		
			58 8.6 96.3	45 9.6	180 38.1	148 67.9	121 92.3	30 98.4	6 99.6	2 100.0	
Hellenic College of London	GR LON	186	15 9.5 86.7	9 6.3	35 31.0	34 54.9	41 83.8	15 94.4	8 100.0		
			14 9.4 100	0 0.0	33 24.3	28 45.0	37 72.3	19 86.3	9 92.9	6 97.3	2 98.8	1 100.0
Hemdean House School	BERKS	72	8 8.4 87.5	3 4.5	12 22.4	19 50.7	19 79.1	14 100.0			
			10 7.4 85.7	1 1.6	14 19.3	20 46.8	22 77.1	10 90.9	3 95.0	3 99.2	0 99.2	0 100.0
Hereford Cathedral School	HERWORCS	138	94 9.5 91.5	41 4.6	226 30.0	326 66.7	205 89.8	75 98.2	10 99.3	4 99.8	1 99.9	1 100.0
			91 9.8 98.9	55 6.2	262 30.5	296 63.5	211 87.1	75 95.5	27 98.5	9 99.5	2 99.7	2 100.0
Hethersett Old Hall School	NORFOLK	215	34 8.2 73.5	15 5.4	35 17.9	75 44.8	99 80.3	38 93.9	12 98.2	4 99.6	1 100.0	
			34 8.7 87.5	12 5.7	66 23.1	78 49.6	85 78.5	38 91.4	17 97.1	7 99.5	1 99.9	0 100.0
Highclare School	W MIDS	288	25 7.8 92.0	11 5.7	54 33.5	63 66.0	49 91.2	12 97.4	5 100.0		
			34 7.9 83.9	7 2.8	56 20.8	80 50.1	82 80.1	35 92.9	14 98.0	5 99.9	0 99.9	0 100.0
Highgate School	GR LON	188	124 9.0 99.2	180 16.1	406 52.3	343 82.9	160 97.1	27 99.6	5 100.0		
			119 8.7 99.2	107 9.6	384 38.9	355 73.0	208 93.0	58 98.6	13 99.8	1 99.9	0 99.9	0 100.0
Hillcrest Grammar School	CHESHIRE	91	38 8.6 68.4	15 4.6	52 20.5	78 44.3	97 74.0	61 92.7	17 97.9	6 99.7	1 100.0	
			14 8.1 71.4	2 1.8	11 9.4	31 35.9	35 65.8	25 87.2	11 96.6	3 99.1	1 100.0	
Hillgrove School	N WALES	308	14 8.0 57.1	1 0.9	16 15.2	35 46.4	25 68.8	15 82.1	16 96.4	4 100.0		
			8 8.1 33.3	0 0.0	9 14.2	11 31.5	18 59.9	17 86.8	7 97.8	1 99.4	0 99.4	0 100.0
Hipperholme Grammar School	W YORKS	304	65 9.3 73.8	9 1.5	92 16.7	153 42.1	193 74.1	99 90.5	38 96.8	16 99.5	3 100.0	
			56 9.5 79.4	13 2.0	103 20.0	140 46.3	152 75.0	77 89.5	38 96.6	14 99.3	3 99.8	0 100.0
Hollygirt School	NOTTS	222	26 8.9 80.8	4 1.7	45 21.1	80 55.6	59 81.0	27 92.7	11 99.6	1 100.0		
			39 8.8 86.8	7 2.3	84 27.0	104 60.0	79 85.1	31 94.9	12 98.7	3 99.7	1 100.0	
Holy Child School	W MIDS	288	34 9.7 88.2	49 14.8	78 38.5	97 67.9	56 84.8	31 94.2	14 98.5	2 99.1	0 99.1	3 100.0
			33 8.9 90.3	20 6.7	74 26.7	82 54.7	80 82.1	36 94.4	11 98.2	3 99.2	1 99.5	1 100.0
Holy Trinity College	KENT	158	47 9.8 100	32 6.9	89 26.2	197 68.8	122 95.2	21 99.8	1 100.0			
			52 9.7 97.8	37 8.3	176 36.6	154 67.4	121 91.6	30 97.6	10 99.6	2 100.0	0 100.0	0 100.0
Holy Trinity School	HERWORCS	139	41 9.2 92.7	29 7.7	103 34.9	125 68.0	78 88.4	32 96.8	10 99.5	2 100.0		
			37 8.8 84.8	16 5.6	84 26.3	93 54.4	83 79.5	42 92.2	16 97.0	6 98.9	3 99.8	0 100.0

377

GCSE ENGLAND & WALES RESULTS 1995

School		P			*A		A		B		C		D		E		F		G		U	
Homefield School	DORSET	109	51	7.9	58.8	9	2.2	24	8.2	84	29.2	133	62.3	73	80.5	51	93.3	21	98.5	2	99.0	4 100.0
			48	7.5	54.2	3	0.8	32	9.7	106	39.0	107	68.5	79	90.3	30	98.6	4	99.7	1 100.0	
Howell's School	N WALES	308	37	8.8	94.6	52	16.0	124	54.0	115	89.3	26	97.2	8	99.7	1 100.0				
			45	8.5	100	48	14.2	154	42.5	111	71.2	83	92.7	21	98.2	6	99.7	1 100.0		
Howell's School Llandaff GPDST	S WALES	311	85	9.1	100	276	35.6	286	72.5	169	94.3	36	99.0	7	99.9	1 100.0				
			90	8.8	97.7	277	33.0	381	55.1	195	79.8	115	94.4	34	98.7	8	99.7	1	99.8	1	99.9	0 100.0
Hull Grammar School	HUMBER	151	58	8.8	79.3	23	4.5	105	25.1	146	53.7	152	83.5	49	93.1	27	98.4	6	99.6	0	99.6	2 100.0
			55	8.4	83.3	24	4.9	85	19.7	96	40.7	129	68.9	75	85.3	44	94.9	14	97.9	5	99.0	4 100.0
Hull High School	HUMBER	151	33	9.3	97.0	43	14.0	65	35.2	111	71.3	63	91.9	14	96.4	8	99.0	3 100.0		
			33	9.0	96.2	45	19.2	114	41.7	84	70.2	53	88.1	21	95.3	11	99.0	3 100.0		
Hulme Grammar School for Girls	LANCS	167	89	9.0	100	239	29.9	274	64.1	200	89.1	78	98.9	7	99.8	2 100.0				
			71	8.7	100	94	13.4	299	51.6	182	81.2	92	96.1	19	99.2	4	99.8	1 100.0		
Hulme Grammar School	LANCS	167	84	10.5	98.8	83	9.5	255	38.5	285	71.0	197	93.4	40	97.9	11	99.2	5	99.8	1	99.9	1 100.0
			111	10.2	98.2	105	8.9	389	36.0	347	66.6	253	88.8	85	96.3	30	98.9	9	99.7	3 100.0	0 100.0
Hulme Hall Schools	CHESHIRE	91	79	7.3	62.0	22	3.8	62	14.6	160	42.3	166	71.1	99	88.2	45	96.0	15	98.6	6	99.7	2 100.0
			75	7.1	63.5	11	2.3	73	14.1	117	36.1	155	65.3	89	82.0	53	92.0	30	97.6	11	99.7	1 100.0
Hurst Lodge School	BERKS	73	8	8.9	87.5	0	0.0	12	16.9	30	59.2	19	85.9	9	98.6	1 100.0				
			18	8.8	75.0	0	0.0	23	14.8	42	41.9	51	74.7	25	90.9	9	96.6	4	99.2	1	99.9	0 100.0
Hurstpierpoint College	W SUSSEX	276	81	10.2	92.6	24	2.9	163	22.7	313	60.7	216	86.9	84	97.1	15	98.9	7	99.8	0	99.8	2 100.0
			79	10.7	95.9	27	3.5	165	20.0	258	50.3	302	85.8	88	96.1	25	99.1	8 100.0		
Hydesville Tower School	W MIDS	288	16	9.2	81.2	12	8.1	19	20.9	35	44.6	41	72.3	22	87.2	12	95.3	6	99.3	0	99.3	1 100.0
			21	8.3	82.6	3	1.5	21	12.5	42	36.4	52	65.9	34	83.2	17	94.9	7	98.9	1	99.4	1 100.0
Hymers College	HUMBER	152	105	9.5	100	191	19.2	358	55.2	333	88.7	96	98.4	14	99.8	2 100.0				
			99	9.4	100	214	21.9	349	42.3	288	73.3	184	93.2	47	98.2	12	99.5	4 100.0	0 100.0	0 100.0
Ibstock Place - The Froebel School	GR LON	188	36	8.5	83.3	11	3.6	67	25.5	110	61.4	81	87.9	29	97.4	6	99.3	2 100.0		
			22	8.3	75.0	8	5.1	30	17.5	44	41.6	52	70.0	27	84.8	17	94.1	7	97.9	3	99.6	0 100.0
Ilford Ursuline High School	GR LON	188	55	9.8	69.1	21	3.9	98	22.0	104	41.3	133	65.9	106	85.6	50	94.8	23	99.1	4	99.8	1 100.0
			65	9.0	84.0	43	6.4	146	26.3	161	53.6	149	78.9	76	91.8	31	97.0	12	99.1	3	99.6	2 100.0
Indefatigable School	N WALES		32	8.6	40.6	3	1.1	7	3.5	47	20.1	78	47.7	59	68.6	53	87.3	21	94.7	9	97.9	6 100.0
			34	8.0	53.7	1	0.3	8	2.9	29	13.5	72	39.8	70	65.4	50	83.6	27	93.5	14	98.6	3 100.C
Ipswich High School GPDST	SUFFOLK	244	66	9.0	100	190	32.0	249	74.0	129	95.8	23	99.7	2 100.0					
			60	8.6	100	95	18.1	256	53.1	154	82.8	75	97.3	11	99.4	3 100.0				
Ipswich School	SUFFOLK	244	91	10.0	96.7	60	6.6	290	38.4	327	74.2	184	94.4	37	98.5	12	99.8	1	99.9	1 100.0	
			86	10.1	96.6	90	10.1	307	37.4	256	66.9	208	90.9	60	97.8	14	99.4	4	99.8	1 100.0	0 100.C
Italia Conti Academy Of Theatre Arts L	GR LON	189	11	7.4	18.2	6	7.4	7	16.0	8	25.9	17	46.9	22	74.1	16	93.8	3	97.5	0	97.5	2 100.C
			29	7.9	41.2	7	2.7	17	7.9	29	20.5	55	44.5	49	65.9	38	82.5	23	92.6	13	98.3	4 100.C
James Allen's Girls' School	GR LON	189	112	9.6	99.1	350	32.4	436	72.8	226	93.8	53	98.7	10	99.6	2	99.8	2 100.0		
			107	9.7	100	219	20.4	535	56.1	300	85.2	111	95.9	32	99.0	8	99.8	2 100.0		
John Lyon School,The	GR LON	189	78	8.4	96.2	51	7.8	226	42.2	234	77.8	107	94.1	31	98.8	7	99.8	1 100.0		
			74	8.6	97.4	41	6.3	254	40.9	226	76.3	105	92.7	32	97.7	10	99.2	4	99.8	1 100.0	
Kelly College	DEVON	103	43	9.5	95.3	22	5.4	80	25.1	152	62.4	101	87.2	38	96.6	8	98.5	5	99.8	1 100.0	
			53	8.9	76.5	23	5.0	90	20.2	125	46.8	152	79.1	56	91.0	25	96.3	12	98.9	3	99.5	2 100.■
Kent College	KENT	159	90	8.7	93.3	54	6.9	187	30.9	277	66.5	177	89.2	58	96.7	21	99.4	4	99.9	0	99.9	1 100.0
			86	7.9	85.5	39	5.4	188	28.8	195	57.4	182	84.1	74	94.9	20	97.9	10	99.3	1	99.5	3 100.■
Kent College Pembury	KENT	159	33	7.9	87.9	21	8.1	76	37.3	89	71.5	61	95.0	12	99.6	1 100.0				
			43	8.0	86.5	22	7.5	100	30.1	98	58.5	91	84.8	34	94.7	13	98.4	5	99.0	0	99.0	1 100.■
Kimbolton School	CAMBS	84	93	9.0	95.7	112	13.4	216	39.3	278	72.7	177	93.9	45	99.3	4	99.8	1	99.9	0	99.9	1 100.0
			84	9.0	95.3	42	5.5	248	33.6	241	65.2	187	89.7	58	97.3	16	99.4	3	99.8	1	99.9	0 100.■
King Alfred School,The	GR LON	190	37	7.7	86.5	23	8.0	91	39.9	82	68.5	64	90.9	19	97.6	7 100.0				
			43	7.8	88.4	29	8.9	100	32.0	99	61.9	75	84.6	32	94.3	12	97.9	5	99.4	1	99.7	1 100.0
King Edward VI High Sch. for Girls	W MIDS	288	76	10.3	100	293	37.5	348	82.0	119	97.2	19	99.6	3 100.0					
			77	9.4	100	297	37.1	490	75.5	141	94.9	32	99.3	4	99.9	1 100.0				
King Edward VI School	HANTS	129	141	9.0	96.5	213	16.9	415	49.8	375	79.5	190	94.5	53	98.7	12	99.7	4 100.0		
			145	9.4	99.3	143	10.8	546	42.0	455	75.3	264	94.6	56	98.7	16	99.0	1	99.9	0	99.9	1 100.■
King Edward's School	AVON	64	102	9.0	100	123	13.4	293	45.3	303	78.3	167	96.5	25	99.2	5	99.8	0	99.8	0	99.8	2 100.0
			96	9.0	100	105	12.4	361	44.2	283	76.9	140	93.1	43	98.1	12	99.4	4	99.9	0	99.9	0 100.■
King Edward VII School	LANCS	167	78	9.0	100	103	14.7	195	42.6	263	80.1	116	96.7	16	99.0	6	99.9	0	99.9	1	99.9	1 100.■
			82	8.8	87.7	60	8.2	220	32.2	207	60.9	184	86.4	70	96.1	22	99.2	5	99.9	1 100.0	
King Edward's School	W MIDS	288	130	10.9	100	530	37.3	617	80.7	232	97.0	36	99.6	5	99.9	1 100.0				
			114	10.9	100	304	22.9	838	72.8	258	93.7	61	98.6	12	99.6	5 100.0	0 100.0	0 100.0	0 100.■

378

GCSE ENGLAND & WALES RESULTS 1995

School	Location	P			*A		A		B		C		D		E		F		G		U	
King Edward's School	SURREY	256	95	8.7	98.9	33	4.0	166	24.1	333	64.4	216	90.6	71	99.2	5	99.8	1	99.9	0	99.9	1	100.0
			94	8.0	89.2	34	3.4	195	26.8	233	57.7	208	85.2	83	96.2	22	99.2	5	99.8	1	99.9	0	100.0
King Henry VIII	W MIDS	289	131	9.0	100	179	15.2	495	57.4	364	88.3	103	97.1	26	99.3	7	99.9	0	99.9	0	99.9	1	100.0
			130	9.0	97.7	139	11.9	583	52.0	363	82.9	156	96.2	37	99.3	7	99.9	1	100.0				
King William's College	IOM	153	52	8.8	88.5	35	7.6	90	27.2	171	64.3	113	88.9	35	96.5	11	98.9	5	100.0				
			56	8.8	72.2	22	4.4	116	24.1	129	49.9	125	75.0	77	90.4	32	96.8	11	99.0	4	99.8	0	100.0
King's College School	GR LON	190	144	10.3	100	399	27.0	575	65.9	372	91.0	116	98.9	10	99.5	3	99.7	0	99.7	0	99.7	4	100.0
			135	10.5	100	190	13.0	703	52.6	417	82.2	204	96.7	36	99.3	7	99.8	2	99.9	1	100.0	0	100.0
King's College	SOMERSET	235	103	9.9	85.4	67	6.6	223	28.5	296	57.5	306	87.5	100	97.4	22	99.5	5	100.0				
			86	9.9	93.2	43	4.7	222	27.2	254	57.2	258	87.6	80	97.0	19	99.3	4	99.7	1	99.9	1	100.0
King's High School for Girls	W'WICKS	283	97	8.9	99.0	173	20.0	379	63.9	236	91.2	64	98.6	12	100.0								
			81	9.8	100	128	16.2	392	52.8	218	80.3	124	96.0	26	99.2	5	99.9	1	100.0				
Kings Monkton School	S WALES	311	31	8.5	77.4	15	5.7	42	21.8	78	51.5	62	75.2	35	88.5	20	96.2	6	98.5	2	99.2	2	100.0
			30	8.1	62.5	6	3.0	55	23.0	55	45.6	65	72.2	42	89.5	18	96.9	4	98.5	2	99.3	1	100.0
King's School	SOMERSET	236	54	9.2	96.3	65	13.1	123	37.8	141	66.2	126	91.5	34	98.4	6	99.6	2	100.0				
			70	8.7	91.8	53	7.9	144	25.5	178	54.5	179	84.3	70	95.8	20	99.1	5	99.9	0	99.9	0	100.0
King's School	KENT	160	129	10.4	100	193	14.4	528	54.0	471	89.2	127	98.7	14	99.8	3	100.0						
			119	10.4	100	125	8.2	577	48.5	363	77.8	202	94.1	59	98.9	12	99.8	2	100.0				
King's School	CHESHIRE	92	74	9.0	100	218	32.7	221	65.9	163	90.4	56	98.8	7	99.8	0	99.8	1	100.0				
			66	8.8	100	145	20.1	354	65.4	140	89.2	50	97.8	11	99.7	2	100.0						
King's School, The	TYNE	280	101	9.0	93.1	34	3.7	203	26.1	297	58.7	256	86.9	82	95.9	25	98.7	8	99.6	1	99.7	3	100.0
			100	8.9	85.6	32	3.4	205	23.5	273	53.9	251	81.8	109	94.0	39	98.3	13	99.8	2	100.0	0	100.0
King's School, The	CHESHIRE	92	121	8.6	94.2	101	9.7	270	35.7	344	68.8	245	92.4	63	98.5	16	100.0						
			118	8.5	95.3	156	14.3	345	37.5	298	67.3	235	90.7	70	97.7	19	99.6	3	99.9	1	100.0		
King's School	GLOS	124	74	9.1	90.5	67	10.0	173	35.8	217	68.2	137	88.7	60	97.2	13	99.6	3	100.0				
			73	8.9	83.9	24	4.8	171	27.1	179	54.6	163	79.7	82	92.4	31	97.1	14	99.3	3	99.9	1	100.0
King's School Rochester	KENT	160	52	9.3	96.2	26	5.4	79	21.7	191	61.2	141	90.3	36	97.7	10	99.8	1	100.0				
			65	9.7	98.4	24	4.2	158	25.9	174	53.6	175	81.4	80	94.1	27	98.4	8	99.7	1	99.9	0	100.0
King's School, The	HER/WORCS	139	96	10.2	97.9	69	7.1	286	36.4	371	74.4	181	92.9	55	98.6	14	100.0						
			99	9.4	93.9	88	9.4	292	33.5	307	66.7	225	91.1	64	98.0	16	99.7	1	99.8	0	99.8	1	100.0
King's School	CAMBS	85	86	9.4	87.2	47	5.8	165	26.2	272	59.8	234	88.8	77	98.0	19	99.5	3	99.9	0	99.9	1	100.0
			92	9.2	92.7	51	5.7	172	22.4	246	51.6	277	84.4	106	97.0	18	99.1	4	99.6	1	99.7	2	100.0
Kingham Hill School	OXON	227	42	8.5	61.9	2	0.6	34	10.1	98	37.5	99	65.3	59	81.8	41	93.3	14	97.2	5	98.6	5	100.0
			45	7.3	31.4	8	2.9	24	7.8	38	19.2	77	42.2	83	67.1	54	83.3	34	93.5	17	98.6	4	100.0
Kingsley School	W'WICKS	284	86	8.9	96.5	42	5.5	174	28.2	265	62.8	236	93.6	44	99.3	5	100.0						
			64	8.6	91.0	12	1.8	123	22.7	185	56.3	166	86.4	61	97.5	13	99.8	1	100.0				
Kingston Grammar School	GR LON	191	90	9.0	96.7	54	6.7	269	40.0	293	76.2	153	95.2	29	98.8	5	99.4	4	99.9	0	99.9	1	100.0
			86	8.5	95.4	26	3.3	278	38.7	209	67.2	164	89.6	51	96.6	18	99.0	7	100.0				
Kingswood School	AVON	64	74	9.1	87.8	95	14.1	188	42.1	196	71.2	119	88.9	54	96.9	21	100.0						
			78	10.2	100	23	3.4	203	26.0	232	55.0	215	81.9	92	93.4	33	97.5	14	99.2	3	99.6	3	100.0
Kingswood Schools	MERSEY	212	44	8.3	50.0	7	1.9	33	10.9	100	38.3	122	71.6	56	86.9	36	96.7	10	99.5	2	100.0		
			49	8.8	75.0	4	1.0	53	12.5	98	35.2	143	68.2	85	87.9	36	96.2	13	99.2	3	99.9	0	100.0
Kirkham Grammar School	LANCS	168	84	8.8	98.8	42	5.7	198	32.6	272	69.6	188	95.1	28	98.9	8	100.0						
			79	8.2	87.1	24	4.0	185	29.4	192	59.0	186	87.8	55	96.3	18	99.1	5	99.8	1	100.0		
Kirkstone House School	LINCS	173	26	7.4	42.3	6	3.1	5	5.7	26	19.2	66	53.4	44	76.2	27	90.2	19	100.0				
			28	8.0	59.4	5	1.9	22	10.4	39	28.1	65	57.6	43	77.1	31	91.1	16	98.4	3	99.7	0	100.0
La Retraite School	WILTS	292	23	9.2	96.7	10	4.7	39	23.1	82	61.8	57	88.7	20	98.1	4	100.0						
			30	8.5	73.7	6	3.7	54	21.3	71	48.8	77	78.7	37	93.0	13	98.1	4	99.6	0	99.6	1	100.0
La Sagesse Convent High School	TYNE	281	67	9.2	82.1	45	7.3	134	28.9	160	54.8	176	83.2	81	96.3	18	99.2	4	99.8	1	100.0		
			54	8.7	94.5	23	4.6	144	32.0	123	58.4	115	83.0	45	92.7	20	97.0	9	98.9	4	99.8	1	100.0
La Sagesse Convent School	HANTS		15	8.6	80.0	9	7.0	32	31.8	37	60.5	30	83.7	8	89.9	10	97.7	3	100.0				
			30	8.5	85.2	6	2.5	52	20.5	70	47.7	79	78.3	36	92.2	14	97.7	5	99.6	1	100.0		
Ladies College	C.I.	88	55	9.1	94.5	84	16.8	176	52.0	156	83.2	59	95.0	20	99.0	5	100.0						
			40	9.3	98.2	83	16.2	172	40.2	155	73.2	96	93.6	21	98.1	7	99.6	2	100.0				
Lady Eleanor Holles School, The	GR LON	191	95	10.0	100	293	30.9	382	71.3	210	93.5	53	99.0	6	99.7	2	99.9	0	99.9	0	99.9	1	100.0
			91	9.4	100	193	22.7	547	68.5	194	91.2	63	98.6	9	99.6	2	99.9	1	100.0				
Lancing College	W SUSSEX	276	107	10.5	94.4	98	8.7	313	36.5	389	71.1	219	90.6	76	97.3	27	99.7	3	100.0				
			94	8.8	94.7	82	8.4	240	30.8	245	60.4	226	87.6	78	97.0	18	99.2	6	99.9	0	99.9	1	100.0
Langley School	NORFOLK	216	53	7.5	54.7	2	0.5	42	11.1	55	24.9	158	64.7	109	92.2	23	98.0	8	100.0				
			44	7.5	60.7	7	1.7	30	9.3	64	28.6	117	63.7	75	86.3	29	95.0	11	98.3	4	99.5	1	100.0

379

GCSE ENGLAND & WALES RESULTS 1995

School	County	P	*A		A		B		C		D		E		F		G		U	
Latymer Upper School	GR LON	191	144	9.6	98.6	240	17.4	519	55.0	434	86.4	152	97.4	30	99.6	5	99.9	1	100.0		
			139	8.9	94.5	133	10.4	432	37.0	402	69.5	253	89.9	87	96.9	27	99.1	5	99.5	1	99.6	5	100.0
Lavant House	W SUSSEX	276	15	8.7	93.3	17	13.0	18	26.7	54	67.9	36	95.4	4	98.5	2	100.0				
			14	8.5	78.6	6	5.0	31	31.1	38	63.0	30	88.2	10	96.6	3	99.2	1	100.0		
Leeds Girls' High School	W YORKS	305	91	9.0	100	211	25.8	315	64.2	242	93.8	44	99.1	4	99.6	2	99.9	1	100.0		
			90	8.9	100	177	20.9	432	57.8	218	84.8	100	97.2	20	99.6	3	100.0				
Leeds Grammar School	W YORKS	305	129	11.0	99.2	142	10.0	454	41.8	481	75.6	282	95.4	52	99.0	11	99.8	2	99.9	0	99.9	1	100.0
			133	9.7	99.2	233	21.0	582	48.6	395	79.1	208	95.2	45	98.7	14	99.8	3	100.0			
Leicester Grammar School	LEICS	170	84	9.9	97.6	131	15.7	328	55.2	264	86.9	80	96.5	25	99.5	3	99.9	0	99.9	0	99.9	1	100.0
			78	9.6	100	131	15.9	347	49.8	234	81.0	108	95.5	26	98.9	7	99.9	1	100.0			
Leicester High School for Girls	LEICS	171	49	9.0	100	36	8.2	98	30.4	145	63.3	132	93.2	26	99.1	4	100.0				
			42	8.6	100	40	10.6	127	36.9	105	65.6	96	91.8	23	98.1	6	99.7	1	100.0			
Leighton Park School	BERKS	73	55	9.3	72.7	26	5.1	97	24.1	124	48.4	126	73.1	73	87.5	41	95.5	18	99.0	3	99.6	2	100.0
			52	9.6	86.0	20	4.3	139	28.5	138	56.0	125	80.8	57	92.2	27	97.6	9	99.4	2	99.8	1	100.0
Leys School,The	CAMBS	85	65	9.2	96.9	38	6.4	136	29.1	225	66.8	152	92.3	40	99.0	5	99.8	1	100.0			
			64	9.2	90.5	40	6.6	162	28.8	172	58.0	164	85.8	63	96.4	17	99.3	4	100.0			
Licensed Victuallers' School	BERKS	74	78	8.4	55.1	11	1.7	57	10.4	129	30.1	181	57.7	160	82.1	82	94.7	26	98.6	8	99.8	1	100.0
			84	8.7	68.1	6	0.7	75	10.4	139	29.5	194	56.2	140	75.4	101	89.2	48	95.8	23	99.0	7	100.0
Lime House School	CUMBRIA	99	25	7.4	28.0	3	1.6	13	8.7	19	19.0	45	43.5	52	71.7	39	92.9	10	98.4	0	98.4	3	100.0
			26	7.2	61.5	5	2.7	16	11.2	34	29.3	82	72.9	28	87.8	19	97.9	1	98.4	3	100.0		
Liverpool College	MERSEY	212	110	8.8	93.6	112	11.5	226	34.8	302	65.9	230	89.6	75	97.3	19	99.3	6	99.9	1	100.0		
			76	8.2	87.0	74	9.0	184	31.9	167	58.7	165	85.2	68	96.1	18	99.0	5	99.8	1	100.0		
Llandovery College	S WALES		30	9.7	76.7	8	2.7	33	14.0	83	42.5	81	70.2	60	90.8	17	96.6	6	98.6	3	99.7	1	100.0
			49	6.5	71.4	15	4.6	49	16.6	73	39.8	89	68.2	55	85.7	29	95.0	11	98.5	2	99.1	2	100.0
Longridge Towers School	NORTHUMB	220	38	8.7	81.6	14	4.3	54	20.7	105	52.6	95	81.5	45	95.1	13	99.1	1	99.4	0	99.4	2	100.0
			30	8.5	78.8	5	1.8	52	20.6	70	47.8	88	82.0	33	94.9	11	99.1	2	99.9	0	99.9	0	100.0
Lord Mayor Treloar College	HANTS	130	20	5.2	15.0	3	2.9	6	8.7	10	18.3	17	34.6	21	54.8	12	66.3	23	88.5	9	97.1	3	100.0
			29	4.6	28.6	6	7.8	12	9.7	14	20.2	32	44.1	29	65.8	23	83.0	15	94.2	5	97.9	2	100.0
Lord Wandsworth College	HANTS	130	77	9.8	97.4	55	7.3	197	33.4	264	68.3	183	92.6	42	98.1	11	99.6	2	99.9	1	100.0		
			76	9.4	92.7	29	3.7	177	25.4	204	53.8	212	83.3	87	95.4	25	98.9	6	99.7	1	99.8	1	100.0
Loughborough Grammar School	LEICS	171	144	9.0	97.2	172	13.2	445	47.4	415	79.3	214	95.8	35	98.5	15	99.6	3	99.8	0	99.8	2	100.0
			135	8.4	99.3	136	11.0	514	47.3	358	78.7	196	95.8	39	99.2	8	99.9	1	100.0			
Loughborough High School	LEICS	171	80	9.0	100	227	31.7	275	70.0	195	97.2	20	100.0								
			79	8.4	100	158	23.5	371	60.8	183	88.4	66	98.3	9	99.7	1	99.8	1	100.0			
Luckley-Oakfield School	BERKS	74	45	8.6	93.3	53	13.6	88	36.2	117	66.3	92	90.0	27	96.9	11	99.7	1	100.0			
			53	8.6	92.5	46	10.9	138	32.1	140	62.7	103	85.2	47	95.4	15	98.7	5	99.8	1	100.0		
Magdalen College School	OXON	227	72	10.3	98.6	119	16.0	279	53.4	214	82.1	99	95.4	28	99.2	6	100.0				
			75	9.6	100	151	18.9	339	51.4	203	79.7	106	94.4	28	98.3	8	99.4	2	99.7	1	99.9	1	100.0
Malvern College	HERWORCS	140	128	9.7	95.3	100	8.0	352	36.3	493	75.9	228	94.2	58	98.9	9	99.6	5	100.0			
			120	9.7	94.7	51	3.9	388	34.2	418	70.0	269	93.1	66	98.8	12	99.8	1	99.9	0	99.9	1	100.0
Malvern Girls' College	HERWORCS	140	78	9.1	98.7	159	22.4	276	61.3	214	91.4	50	98.5	9	99.7	2	100.0				
			79	9.1	100	49	7.5	358	51.3	232	83.7	94	96.8	19	99.4	4	100.0				
Manchester Grammar School	GR MANCH	210	202	9.6	100	633	32.5	848	76.0	397	96.4	67	99.8	4	100.0					
			206	9.6	100	325	16.8	1196	64.0	510	89.9	168	98.5	26	99.8	4	100.0				
Manchester High School for Girls	GR MANCH	210	94	10.0	100	228	24.3	342	60.7	268	89.2	87	98.5	12	99.8	2	100.0				
			109	9.4	100	188	17.9	583	60.7	265	86.6	108	97.2	25	99.6	4	100.0				
Manor House School	SURREY	257	26	9.0	96.2	5	2.1	69	31.6	84	67.5	54	90.6	19	98.7	3	100.0				
			22	8.7	85.7	7	3.8	33	17.5	53	44.7	57	73.9	29	88.8	12	95.0	6	98.0	2	99.1	1	100.0
Maple Hayes Hall School for Dyslexics	STAFFS	240	26	6.8	3.8	0	0.0	1	0.6	8	5.1	18	15.3	40	38.1	52	67.6	37	88.6	15	97.2	5	100.0
			18	6.0	16.7	0	0.0	1	0.9	8	8.2	20	26.4	21	45.5	22	65.5	19	82.7	13	94.5	6	100.0
Marlborough College	WILTS	292	162	9.1	99.4	251	16.9	517	51.9	451	82.3	217	97.0	40	99.7	5	100.0				
			153	9.2	98.8	133	9.2	533	39.6	488	74.2	282	94.1	69	99.0	12	99.9	2	100.0			
Mayfield College	E SUSSEX	269	16	8.7	62.5	4	2.9	30	24.3	29	45.0	36	70.7	19	84.3	12	92.7	7	97.9	1	98.6	2	100.0
			32	5.7	42.1	1	0.8	12	7.1	32	24.5	49	49.0	51	76.8	22	88.8	15	97.0	5	99.7	0	100.0
Maynard School	DEVON	104	67	9.8	100	157	23.9	270	64.9	175	91.5	47	98.6	6	99.5	2	99.8	1	100.0			
			66	9.6	98.6	114	18.2	349	58.5	152	82.4	86	96.0	23	99.6	2	99.9	0	99.9	0	99.9	0	100.0
Mayville High School	HANTS	130	16	8.4	87.5	1	0.7	18	14.2	51	52.2	46	86.6	12	95.5	6	100.0				
			17	7.6	0.0	7	7.2	22	18.0	35	45.3	34	71.9	21	88.3	11	96.9	3	99.2	1	100.0		
Merchant Taylors' School for Girls	MERSEY	213	109	9.0	99.1	254	25.9	393	66.1	254	92.0	67	98.9	11	100.0					
			85	8.9	100	150	19.9	421	60.1	202	87.0	80	97.6	13	99.3	4	99.9	1	100.0			

380

School	County	P				*A		A		B		C		D		E		F		G		U	
Merchant Taylors' School	MERSEY	213	113	9.0	99.1	200	19.6	362	55.2	258	80.5	153	95.5	36	99.0	7	99.7	0	99.7	0	99.7	3	100.0
			108	8.8	100	133	13.8	527	58.2	258	85.3	113	97.2	22	99.5	5	100.0						
Merchant Taylors' School	GR LON	192	136	9.4	100	296	23.3	513	63.6	307	87.7	135	98.3	15	99.5	4	99.8	1	99.9	0	99.9	1	100.0
			134	9.1	100	118	9.4	598	51.0	370	61.4	181	96.2	39	99.4	6	99.9	1	100.0	0	100.0	0	100.0
Micklefield Wadhurst	E SUSSEX	269	35	7.8	51.4	2	0.7	15	6.2	74	33.3	90	66.3	56	86.8	21	94.5	10	98.2	4	99.6	1	100.0
			36	8.2	54.8	5	2.1	48	16.4	64	37.9	89	67.7	55	86.1	27	95.2	8	97.9	4	99.2	1	100.0
Mill Hill School	GR LON	192	117	8.9	93.2	94	9.0	270	34.9	341	67.6	238	90.4	85	98.6	10	99.5	5	100.0				
			96	9.2	94.6	37	4.1	255	29.5	284	61.4	247	89.1	73	97.3	18	99.4	5	99.9	0	99.9	0	100.0
Millfield School	SOMERSET	236	258	8.8	83.3	157	6.9	548	31.0	696	61.6	521	84.4	239	94.9	92	99.0	21	99.9	2	100.0		
			234	8.8	75.7	94	4.2	619	32.3	558	60.6	434	82.5	205	92.9	90	97.5	37	99.3	9	99.8	4	100.0
Milton Abbey School	DORSET	110	40	8.6	70.0	5	1.5	28	9.6	82	33.6	125	70.2	76	92.4	15	96.8	7	98.8	1	99.1	3	100.0
			56	9.0	86.9	6	1.1	42	8.5	125	33.4	188	70.8	86	87.9	42	96.2	16	99.4	2	99.8	1	100.0
Moira House School	E SUSSEX	269	41	8.4	87.8	34	9.9	78	32.5	118	66.7	68	86.4	28	94.5	15	98.8	3	99.7	0	99.7	1	100.0
			47	8.7	86.7	28	5.4	152	38.7	125	69.4	79	88.7	35	97.3	8	99.3	3	100.0				
Monkton Combe School	AVON	64	55	8.6	87.3	38	8.1	119	33.3	174	70.1	105	92.4	28	98.3	5	99.4	2	99.8	1	100.0		
			56	8.8	81.5	14	2.8	123	25.5	138	53.4	147	83.1	58	94.9	19	98.7	5	99.7	1	99.9	0	100.0
Monmouth School	S WALES		86	10.0	100	134	15.6	317	52.5	284	85.6	101	97.3	18	99.4	5	100.0						
			82	9.8	100	131	16.5	331	44.2	265	77.1	135	93.8	39	98.6	8	99.6	3	100.0	0	100.0	0	100.0
More House School	GR LON	192	31	8.5	100	25	9.5	67	34.8	107	75.4	43	91.7	14	97.0	6	99.2	2	100.0				
			35	9.7	96.8	14	4.9	119	35.9	111	68.5	82	92.6	21	98.8	3	99.7	1	100.0				
Moreton Hall School	SALOP	232	45	9.1	93.3	79	19.2	113	46.7	113	74.2	76	92.7	16	96.6	11	99.3	1	99.5	1	99.8	1	100.0
			53	8.8	89.8	36	7.8	156	34.8	147	66.2	117	91.2	30	97.6	9	99.5	2	99.9	0	99.9	1	100.0
Mostyn House School	CHESHIRE	92	40	8.9	62.5	2	0.6	31	9.2	101	37.4	103	66.2	67	84.9	36	95.0	15	99.2	2	99.7	1	100.0
			41	8.8	78.7	9	2.2	57	16.3	96	42.8	112	73.8	57	89.6	26	96.7	8	98.9	3	99.8	0	100.0
Mount Carmel School	CHESHIRE	93	69	10.3	95.7	72	10.1	148	31.0	253	66.6	172	90.8	42	96.8	19	99.4	4	100.0				
			64	8.7	93.7	35	6.2	202	37.6	169	68.0	127	90.8	35	97.1	11	99.1	5	100.0				
Mount School, The	N YORKS	298	34	8.8	91.2	60	20.0	90	50.0	77	75.7	49	92.0	16	97.2	7	99.7	1	100.0				
			44	8.5	93.5	49	12.5	114	33.3	106	61.7	91	86.2	37	96.1	12	99.3	2	99.8	0	99.8	0	100.0
Mount School	GR LON	193	60	7.7	90.0	15	3.3	99	24.8	154	58.3	120	84.3	52	95.7	10	97.8	6	99.1	2	99.6	2	100.0
			58	8.1	77.8	21	4.1	111	24.3	136	53.0	133	81.0	57	93.1	20	97.3	7	98.8	3	99.4	2	100.0
Mount St. Mary's College	DERBYS	100	68	9.0	75.0	22	4.1	85	19.7	129	43.5	162	73.4	91	90.2	42	98.0	8	99.4	1	99.6	2	100.0
			60	10.3	82.1	16	2.9	103	17.2	143	40.4	182	69.9	108	87.4	53	96.0	19	99.1	4	99.7	1	100.0
Mount St. Mary's Convent	DEVON	104	48	8.7	70.8	10	2.4	61	17.0	125	46.9	114	74.2	64	89.5	37	98.7	7	100.0				
School			54	8.9	63.0	20	4.2	60	16.6	118	41.2	133	68.8	75	84.4	49	94.6	24	99.6	2	100.0		
Netherwood School	S WALES		17	7.4	70.6	6	4.8	22	22.2	36	50.8	36	79.4	19	94.4	5	98.4	2	100.0				
			16	8.6	53.8	1	0.9	14	10.4	25	29.1	36	55.9	28	76.8	20	91.7	9	98.4	1	99.1	1	100.0
New Hall School	ESSEX	119	70	9.5	94.3	51	7.6	139	28.4	233	63.3	154	86.4	71	97.0	15	99.3	4	99.9	1	100.0		
			81	8.8	92.5	42	6.7	195	28.4	228	60.3	178	85.2	69	94.8	28	98.7	7	99.7	2	100.0		
Newcastle-under-Lyme	STAFFS	240	173	9.1	100	345	22.0	584	59.1	440	87.1	176	98.3	24	99.9	2	100.0						
School			181	9.2	100	252	15.5	719	46.2	530	78.1	274	94.6	70	98.8	15	99.7	4	100.0	0	100.0	0	100.0
Newcastle U Tyne Church	TYNE	281	72	9.6	98.6	113	17.8	182	46.5	224	81.7	98	97.2	15	99.5	2	99.8	1	100.0				
High Sch			58	8.7	98.4	46	8.6	178	36.7	165	69.2	112	91.2	31	97.2	11	99.4	2	99.8	1	100.0		
Newlands Manor School	E SUSSEX	270	61	7.2	60.7	11	2.5	61	16.4	142	48.7	134	79.3	56	92.0	18	96.1	9	98.2	2	98.6	6	100.0
			60	8.2	61.0	18	3.9	61	13.3	92	32.1	161	65.0	89	83.2	51	93.6	24	98.5	4	99.3	3	100.0
North Cestrian Grammar	CHESHIRE	93	76	9.1	72.4	16	2.3	59	10.9	176	36.3	243	71.5	128	90.0	52	97.5	14	99.6	3	100.0		
School			71	9.0	83.8	6	1.0	91	14.3	174	41.5	233	77.8	92	92.1	35	97.6	12	99.5	3	99.9	0	100.0
North Foreland Lodge	HANTS	131	28	9.2	92.9	1	0.4	58	22.9	100	61.6	88	80.8	22	96.5	9	100.0						
			30	9.0	94.4	29	8.6	102	40.1	96	75.8	48	93.7	13	98.5	3	99.6	1	100.0				
North London Collegiate	GR LON	193	104	9.5	100	419	42.3	434	86.1	120	98.2	18	100.0										
School, The			98	9.5	100	265	27.2	591	69.2	213	92.2	58	98.4	10	99.5	5	100.0						
Northampton High School	N'HANTS	218	92	8.3	98.9	91	11.7	279	47.4	293	85.0	92	96.8	22	99.6	3	100.0						
			82	8.1	96.2	99	15.0	242	39.3	206	70.2	141	91.3	40	97.3	14	99.4	4	100.0				
Northfield School	HERTS	147	12	7.6	98.9	0	0.0	20	21.3	39	62.8	24	88.3	7	95.7	4	100.0						
			16	7.6	90.9	2	2.4	9	7.2	25	27.7	40	60.3	27	82.2	13	92.8	8	99.3	0	99.3	1	100.0
Northwood College	GR LON	193	53	9.1	100	46	9.6	231	57.6	156	90.0	40	98.3	8	100.0								
			47	8.8	97.7	33	8.3	141	35.9	159	74.5	81	94.2	16	98.1	6	99.5	2	100.0				
Norwich High School for	NORFOLK	216	102	9.0	100	147	16.0	412	61.0	285	92.1	64	99.1	8	100.0								
Girls GPDST			92	9.0	100	120	13.9	393	50.6	254	81.5	120	96.0	23	98.8	8	99.8	1	99.9	0	99.9	0	100.0
Norwich School	NORFOLK	216	104	9.0	100	162	17.3	352	54.7	292	85.8	103	96.8	24	99.4	6	100.0						
			101	9.0	100	105	11.3	359	42.0	317	77.1	164	95.2	35	99.1	7	99.9	1	100.0	0	100.0	0	100.0

GCSE ENGLAND & WALES RESULTS 1995

381

GCSE ENGLAND & WALES RESULTS 1995

School	County	P	*A		A		B		C		D		E		F		G		U	
Notre Dame School	SURREY	258	43	8.8	90.7	56	14.8	70	33.3	112	63.0	89	86.5	44	98.1	7	100.0		
			47	8.8	93.3	31	11.1	98	25.0	109	51.2	109	77.4	53	90.1	27	96.6	8	98.6	4 99.5	2 100.0
Notre Dame Senior School	SURREY	258	51	10.0	94.1	43	8.5	114	30.9	178	65.9	104	86.4	57	97.6	9	99.4	2 99.8	1 100.0	
			61	9.9	91.1	32	5.8	149	25.7	163	52.6	186	83.4	61	93.5	26	97.8	12 99.8	1 100.0	
Notting Hill & Ealing High School GPDS	GR LON	194	80	9.0	98.7	168	23.3	287	63.0	204	91.3	49	98.1	14	100.0					
			82	9.0	100	136	18.7	392	56.9	208	85.2	85	96.7	17	99.0	6 99.9	1 100.0			
Nottingham High School for Girls GPDST	NOTTS	222	115	9.1	100	235	22.5	438	64.4	276	90.8	90	99.4	6	100.0					
			116	8.9	97.4	168	16.0	577	58.9	300	87.7	106	98.0	18	99.7	3 100.0	0 100.0	0 100.0	0 100.0
Nottingham High School	NOTTS	222	115	10.0	100	342	29.8	439	68.0	275	92.0	78	98.8	12	99.8	1 99.9	0 99.9	0 99.9	1 100.0
			118	9.4	99.2	169	13.9	666	63.1	293	89.5	96	98.2	17	99.7	3 100.0				
Oakham School	LEICS	172	167	9.7	98.2	182	11.2	568	46.2	596	82.9	235	97.4	32	99.4	9 99.9	1 100.0		
			149	9.7	99.4	144	9.4	530	38.8	477	71.8	316	93.8	72	98.8	15 99.8	3 100.0			
Ockbrook School	DERBYS	100	32	9.1	96.9	24	8.3	74	33.8	101	68.6	71	93.1	16	98.6	4 100.0			
			34	8.6	79.3	3	1.2	59	20.5	84	49.1	93	80.9	35	92.8	16 98.3	5 100.0			
Old Palace School of John Whitgift	GR LON	194	87	9.6	100	223	26.8	319	65.1	221	91.6	66	99.5	4	100.0					
			86	9.4	98.9	167	19.2	425	56.2	272	89.6	75	98.8	8	99.8	1 100.0	0 100.0	0 100.0	0 100.0
Oratory School, The	BERKS	75	72	9.2	98.6	44	6.7	134	27.0	244	63.9	172	90.0	45	96.8	19 99.7	1 99.8	0 99.8	1 100.0
			69	9.4	92.1	30	4.2	171	27.3	216	60.6	174	87.5	56	96.1	18 98.9	4 99.5	0 99.5	3 100.0
Oriel Bank High School	CHESHIRE	93	36	8.3	80.6	14	4.7	63	25.8	91	56.4	84	84.6	26	93.3	8 96.0	8 98.7	1 99.9	3 100.0
			35	8.1	83.9	8	3.3	66	24.2	85	54.4	77	81.9	35	94.3	12 98.6	3 99.6	1 100.0	
Oswestry School	SALOP	232	69	8.3	82.6	23	4.0	128	26.4	178	57.6	130	80.4	61	91.1	33 96.8	13 99.1	2 99.5	3 100.0
			70	8.2	64.3	47	8.3	133	24.6	144	49.6	141	74.0	78	87.6	38 94.1	18 97.3	9 98.8	6 100.0
Oundle School	N'HANTS	218	185	8.5	99.5	225	14.3	669	56.8	492	88.1	165	98.5	21	99.9	2 100.0			
			170	8.8	99.8	155	9.0	691	47.9	479	79.7	235	95.4	56	99.1	10 99.8	1 99.8	0 99.9	2 100.0
Our Lady of Sion School	W SUSSEX	277	55	9.0	85.5	53	10.7	125	36.0	128	61.8	109	83.8	51	94.1	24 99.0	5 100.0		
			54	8.1	91.5	17	4.1	131	30.8	126	59.9	108	84.7	42	94.4	18 98.5	6 99.9	0 99.9	0 100.0
Our Lady's Convent Senior School	OXON	228	69	8.9	88.4	69	11.2	152	35.8	188	66.3	129	87.2	56	96.3	18 99.2	5 100.0		
			54	8.7	94.4	28	5.8	126	27.9	154	60.5	117	85.2	47	95.1	19 99.2	4 100.0			
Oxford High School GPDST	OXON	228	80	9.3	100	239	32.1	311	73.8	161	95.4	30	99.5	3	99.9	1 100.0			
			78	9.6	100	191	24.7	426	61.9	191	87.4	78	97.9	14	99.7	2 100.0				
Palmers Green High School	GR LON	195	25	9.2	100	27	11.7	55	35.7	80	70.4	47	90.9	20	99.6	1 100.0			
			0	0.0	0.0	0	0.0	0	0.0	0	0.0	0	0.0	0	0.0	0 0.0	0 0.0	0 0.0	0 0.0
Pangbourne College	BERKS	75	88	8.4	73.9	4	0.5	73	10.4	196	37.0	268	73.4	106	87.8	60 95.9	19 98.5	1 98.6	10 100.0
			75	9.6	71.6	9	1.3	86	12.2	170	35.7	272	73.3	121	90.0	49 96.8	15 98.9	4 99.4	4 100.0
Park School, The	SOMERSET	236	9	9.2	100	6	7.2	24	36.1	26	67.5	23	95.2	4	100.0					
			18	8.1	100	4	2.7	42	29.5	36	54.3	39	81.0	14	90.7	8 96.2	5 99.6	0 99.6	0 100.0
Park School for Girls	ESSEX	119	34	8.2	79.4	5	1.8	77	29.5	82	59.0	73	85.3	28	95.3	11 99.3	2 100.0		
			30	8.0	76.7	33	13.4	55	26.2	56	49.8	73	80.6	32	94.1	11 98.7	3 100.0			
Parsons Mead School	SURREY	259	44	8.6	84.1	14	3.7	75	23.6	164	67.1	75	87.0	35	96.3	12 99.5	2 100.0		
			49	8.6	89.8	19	4.4	101	25.0	138	57.7	112	84.4	50	96.2	11 98.9	3 99.6	1 99.9	0 100.0
Perse School for Girls	CAMBS	86	84	10.6	100	304	34.2	356	74.2	178	94.2	46	99.3	4	99.8	2 100.0			
			80	10.0	100	156	18.6	445	59.5	203	84.9	86	95.7	26	98.9	7 99.8	1 99.9	0 99.9	0 100.0
Perse School, The	CAMBS	86	75	10.1	100	112	14.7	275	50.9	258	84.9	94	97.2	13	98.9	6 99.7	2 100.0		
			77	10.3	100	105	13.6	357	47.9	242	78.5	132	95.2	30	99.0	6 99.8	1 99.9	0 99.9	0 100.0
Peterborough High School	CAMBS	86	26	8.8	80.8	19	8.3	53	31.4	73	63.3	50	85.2	18	93.0	11 97.8	4 99.6	0 99.6	1 100.0
			37	8.7	93.7	12	4.2	85	26.9	104	59.1	94	88.2	27	96.9	9 99.4	2 100.0			
Peterborough & St. Margarets	GR LON	195	19	8.4	68.4	3	1.9	31	21.3	36	43.8	51	75.6	32	95.6	5 88.1	1 99.4	1 100.0	
			20	8.0	77.8	1	0.7	32	20.4	39	45.2	39	70.0	26	86.5	15 96.1	5 99.2	1 99.9	0 100.0
Pipers Corner School	BUCKS	83	53	8.8	88.7	45	9.6	120	35.5	143	66.0	107	88.9	40	97.4	8 99.1	4 100.0		
			54	8.2	94.6	26	5.7	103	24.3	115	50.3	123	78.0	59	91.3	26 97.2	10 99.4	2 99.9	0 100.0
Plymouth College	DEVON	104	82	9.8	97.6	73	9.1	161	29.1	249	60.1	234	89.2	53	95.8	17 97.9	7 98.8	0 98.8	10 100.0
			98	9.4	95.6	65	7.6	300	33.7	298	65.8	213	88.8	72	96.5	26 99.3	5 99.8	1 100.0	0 100.0
Pocklington School	HUMBER	152	108	9.7	93.5	58	5.6	254	29.9	370	63.3	275	91.6	67	98.0	17 99.6	9 99.8	2 99.8	2 100.0
			88	9.5	89.4	30	3.5	182	22.5	264	54.0	250	83.9	83	93.8	33 97.8	14 99.4	3 99.8	1 100.0
Polam Hall School	DURHAM	114	55	8.9	89.1	33	6.8	118	30.9	174	66.6	121	91.4	29	97.3	10 99.4	3 100.0		
			57	8.4	89.4	99	16.6	150	35.5	119	60.4	96	80.5	54	91.8	28 97.7	7 99.1	2 99.5	2 100.0
Portsmouth Grammar School, The	HANTS	132	108	9.0	100	168	17.2	383	56.6	308	88.2	97	98.2	14	99.6	4 100.0			
			108	9.3	98.1	108	10.5	500	52.1	303	82.3	137	96.0	34	99.4	5 99.9	0 99.9	1 100.0	0 100.0
Portsmouth High School GPDST	HANTS	132	84	9.0	97.6	152	20.2	319	62.6	203	89.6	56	97.1	15	99.1	7 100.0			
			83	9.0	100	107	13.7	386	54.3	220	83.7	97	96.7	21	99.7	6 100.0				

382

			P			*A	A	B	C	D	E	F	G	U
Presentation College	BERKS	75	45	9.0	86.7	15	3.7	69	20.6	126	51.6	134	84.5	42	94.8	16	98.8	4	99.8	0	99.8	1	100.0
			59	9.0	86.5	19	3.7	148	28.5	151	56.8	142	83.5	60	94.7	23	99.0	5	100.0	0	100.0	0	100.0
Princess Helena College,The	HERTS	147	23	8.3	100	22	11.6	47	36.3	63	69.5	48	94.7	9	99.5	1	100.0				
			29	8.1	90.0	12	4.9	54	23.9	64	51.2	69	80.7	28	92.7	11	97.4	5	99.5	1	99.9	0	100.0
Princethorpe College	W'WICKS	284	94	8.3	75.5	25	3.2	78	13.0	217	40.5	251	72.2	129	88.5	58	95.8	29	99.5	3	99.9	1	100.0
			93	8.3	69.8	25	3.4	101	13.7	168	35.3	235	65.6	135	82.9	82	93.5	38	98.4	10	99.7	2	100.0
Prior Park College	AVON	65	77	9.7	85.7	72	9.7	187	34.7	215	63.5	166	85.8	67	94.8	25	98.1	10	99.5	2	99.7	2	100.0
			74	9.7	90.7	82	9.6	225	33.6	233	66.1	154	87.6	63	96.4	21	99.3	4	99.9	1	100.0		
Prior's Field	SURREY	259	36	8.5	97.2	18	5.9	57	24.6	109	60.3	91	90.2	16	95.4	12	99.3	1	99.7	0	99.7	1	100.0
			41	8.2	97.5	6	1.8	76	22.9	117	57.7	99	87.2	30	96.1	11	99.3	2	99.9	0	99.9	0	100.0
Purcell School of Music	GR LON	196	20	7.0	85.0	23	16.4	34	40.7	53	78.6	18	91.4	8	97.1	2	98.6	2	100.0				
			21	6.5	92.6	20	10.8	60	47.4	40	77.0	24	94.8	6	99.3	1	100.0						
Putney High School GPDST	GR LON	196	85	9.2	100	134	17.1	322	58.1	266	92.0	60	99.6	3	100.0								
			88	9.0	98.0	100	10.8	314	42.1	272	76.3	145	94.6	37	99.2	5	99.9	1	100.0				
Putney Park School	GR LON	196	29	8.0	93.1	7	3.0	44	22.0	105	67.2	50	88.8	20	97.4	5	99.6	0	99.6	1	100.0		
			22	7.8	85.7	14	8.3	35	21.6	40	44.4	47	71.1	26	85.9	17	95.6	4	97.8	2	99.0	1	100.0
Quantock School	SOMERSET	237	17	6.8	52.9	1	0.9	1	1.7	20	19.0	51	62.9	25	84.5	12	94.8	3	97.4	2	99.1	1	100.0
			36	7.3	0.0	0	0.0	43	16.1	62	39.4	78	68.6	42	84.4	22	92.6	14	97.9	4	99.4	1	100.0
Queen Anne's School	BERKS	76	65	9.3	98.5	38	6.3	188	37.3	247	78.1	109	96.0	18	99.0	5	99.8	1	100.0				
			62	8.8	98.2	22	4.3	226	42.7	179	75.9	109	96.1	17	99.2	4	100.0	0	100.0	0	100.0	1	100.0
Queen Elizabeth Grammar School	W YORKS	306	105	9.0	100	86	9.1	341	45.1	371	84.4	125	97.6	21	99.8	1	99.9	0	99.9	0	99.9	1	100.0
			108	9.1	99.1	161	16.0	438	47.8	270	75.2	185	94.0	46	98.7	11	99.8	2	100.0				
Queen Elizabeth's Grammar School	LANCS	168	160	9.9	96.9	138	8.7	370	32.0	559	67.3	382	91.4	99	97.6	31	99.6	5	99.9	2	100.0		
			144	9.4	98.6	149	10.1	529	41.4	413	72.1	261	91.4	77	97.1	27	99.1	7	99.6	2	99.8	3	100.0
Queen Elizabeth's Hospital	AVON	65	83	9.2	100	110	14.5	238	45.8	264	80.5	126	97.1	19	99.6	3	100.0						
			76	8.3	98.7	63	9.0	270	44.9	277	77.8	102	94.0	28	98.4	7	99.5	2	99.8	1	100.0		
Queen Ethelburga's College	N YORKS	298	29	8.0	82.8	16	6.9	48	27.5	88	65.2	50	86.7	25	97.4	5	99.6	1	100.0				
			20	8.7	84.0	11	4.9	47	28.3	43	53.1	46	79.6	22	92.3	9	97.5	3	99.2	1	99.8	0	100.0
Queen Margaret's School	N YORKS	298	57	9.1	100	66	12.7	175	46.3	174	79.8	81	95.4	21	99.4	3	100.0						
			61	8.0	98.4	102	19.7	224	50.0	133	77.3	83	94.3	21	98.6	6	99.8	1	100.0				
Queen Mary School	LANCS	168	84	9.0	97.6	80	10.6	201	37.2	256	71.0	169	93.4	44	99.2	6	100.0						
			93	8.8	97.9	82	9.6	255	33.4	267	66.3	202	91.1	51	97.4	16	99.4	4	99.9	1	100.0		
Queen Mary's School	N YORKS	298	25	8.6	80.0	24	11.2	45	32.2	69	64.5	44	85.0	23	95.8	6	98.6	2	99.5	1	100.0		
			29	8.3	78.4	25	7.8	72	32.6	66	60.5	54	83.4	26	94.4	9	98.2	3	99.5	1	99.9	0	100.0
Queen's College London	GR LON	196	54	9.0	100	38	7.8	162	41.2	200	82.5	68	96.5	16	99.8	1	100.0						
			59	8.6	98.2	21	4.4	129	26.5	155	57.3	137	84.6	50	94.5	19	98.3	6	99.5	2	99.9	0	100.0
Queen's College	SOMERSET	237	96	10.0	97.9	70	7.3	324	41.2	328	75.5	176	93.9	44	98.5	11	99.7	3	100.0				
			83	9.5	89.1	60	6.7	252	33.6	226	62.4	196	87.4	63	95.4	24	98.4	10	99.7	1	99.8	1	100.0
Queen's Gate School	GR LON	197	36	7.3	86.1	28	10.6	56	31.9	94	67.7	57	89.4	24	98.5	4	100.0						
			23	7.5	77.3	17	10.8	48	29.2	44	54.4	42	78.5	23	91.6	9	96.8	4	99.1	1	99.7	0	100.0
Queen's School,The	CHESHIRE	94	69	9.4	100	177	27.4	281	70.8	158	95.2	28	99.5	3	100.0								
			60	9.2	100	146	26.0	400	77.9	98	95.6	20	99.3	3	99.8	1	100.0						
Queenswood School	HERTS	148	51	9.1	98.0	49	10.6	164	45.9	176	83.8	68	98.5	5	99.6	2	100.0						
			65	9.8	100	63	12.6	270	46.9	201	80.3	93	95.7	22	99.4	3	99.9	0	99.9	0	99.9	0	100.0
Quinton House School	N'HANTS	219	23	9.4	78.3	4	1.9	31	16.2	49	38.9	87	79.2	31	93.5	10	98.1	4	100.0				
			20	8.7	85.0	10	5.7	35	25.9	42	50.0	55	81.6	19	92.5	12	99.4	1	100.0				
Radley College	OXON	228	120	9.0	100	283	26.1	410	63.9	287	90.4	97	99.4	6	99.9	1	100.0						
			120	10.5	100	176	15.9	557	46.7	436	81.1	197	96.6	36	99.4	6	99.9	1	100.0	0	100.0	0	100.0
Ratcliffe College	LEICS	172	74	8.8	91.9	18	2.8	108	19.3	199	49.8	232	85.3	80	97.5	13	99.2	2	99.8	1	100.0		
			83	8.5	73.9	34	4.6	139	20.7	183	46.5	228	78.8	91	91.7	40	97.3	14	99.3	2	99.6	2	100.0
Read School	N YORKS	299	31	8.4	67.7	0	0.0	9	9.6	71	36.9	91	71.9	44	88.8	20	96.5	6	98.8	3	100.0		
			36	8.4	50.0	3	1.1	24	8.3	44	23.0	93	53.9	70	77.2	45	92.1	17	97.8	5	99.5	1	100.0
Reading Blue Coat School	BERKS	76	92	9.2	96.7	60	7.1	213	32.3	291	66.7	225	93.3	42	98.2	11	99.5	1	99.8	2	100.0		
			85	8.2	96.4	50	6.6	205	30.7	233	64.1	169	88.2	62	97.1	16	99.4	4	99.9	0	99.9	0	100.0
Red House School Ltd	CLEVE	96	35	9.2	97.1	37	11.5	79	36.1	100	67.3	80	92.2	13	96.3	7	98.4	2	99.1	3	100.0		
			32	8.9	93.9	59	19.6	120	46.4	79	74.2	45	90.1	17	96.1	8	98.6	2	99.6	1	99.9	0	100.0
Red Maids' School	AVON	65	74	9.9	100	173	23.7	229	55.0	239	87.7	77	98.2	12	99.9	1	100.0						
			76	9.2	98.7	140	18.4	357	55.3	207	85.1	90	98.0	13	99.9	1	100.0						
Redland High School	AVON	66	75	9.4	98.7	143	20.3	236	53.9	215	84.5	82	96.2	23	99.4	4	100.0						
			71	9.0	100	66	11.5	279	45.8	199	77.0	118	95.5	24	99.2	4	99.8	1	100.0				

GCSE ENGLAND & WALES RESULTS 1995

383

GCSE ENGLAND & WALES RESULTS 1995

School	County	P				*A		A		B		C		D		E		F		G		U	
Reed's School	SURREY	260	69	8.9	84.1	22	3.6	108	21.1	194	52.5	196	84.3	71	95.8	17	98.5	8	99.8	1	100.0		
			62	9.6	88.1	14	2.3	90	15.7	161	42.7	197	75.9	102	93.1	30	98.1	9	99.6	1	99.8	1	100.0
Reigate Grammar School	SURREY	260	130	9.6	98.5	127	10.2	343	37.7	407	70.3	267	91.7	77	97.9	18	99.4	5	99.8	0	99.8	3	100.0
			117	9.6	96.3	75	7.0	403	37.2	364	69.6	249	91.8	65	97.6	22	99.5	5	100.0	0	100.0	0	100.0
Rendcomb College	GLOS	124	38	8.7	94.7	41	12.5	73	34.7	124	72.3	68	93.0	12	96.7	6	98.5	1	98.8	1	99.1	3	100.0
			37	8.6	92.5	5	1.4	76	23.9	95	53.5	92	82.1	38	93.9	14	98.3	4	99.5	1	99.8	0	100.0
Repton School	DERBYS	101	119	9.4	99.2	144	12.9	386	47.3	386	81.8	176	97.5	26	99.8	2	100.0						
			98	9.8	100	64	6.0	322	35.0	302	66.5	240	91.6	59	97.8	17	99.5	3	99.9	1	100.0	0	100.0
Rickmansworth Masonic School	HERTS	148	76	8.4	88.2	39	6.1	125	25.6	224	60.5	168	86.7	61	96.3	17	98.9	7	100.0				
			79	8.7	76.0	46	7.0	128	19.8	181	45.9	204	75.4	104	90.4	45	96.9	12	98.7	6	99.5	3	100.0
Rishworth School	W YORKS	306	88	9.0	59.1	30	3.6	87	14.8	186	38.3	200	63.5	138	80.9	95	92.9	44	98.5	8	99.9	4	100.0
			77	8.9	70.1	31	4.5	101	15.7	152	37.9	203	67.6	100	82.2	71	92.6	32	97.3	16	99.6	2	100.0
Riverston School	GR LON	197	32	7.0	43.7	4	1.8	27	13.8	45	33.9	75	67.4	40	85.3	22	95.1	9	99.1	2	100.0		
			26	7.2	43.5	6	4.0	11	6.3	33	23.7	57	53.6	44	76.8	25	89.9	14	97.3	4	99.4	1	100.0
R.N.I.B. New College Worcester	HERWORCS	141	20	9.6	55.0	6	3.1	17	11.9	48	36.8	48	61.7	47	86.0	21	96.9	5	99.5	1	100.0		
			14	8.3	62.5	7	5.5	27	26.7	28	50.9	26	73.3	16	87.1	11	96.6	3	99.1	1	100.0		
Rodney School	NOTTS	223	20	6.6	60.0	8	4.7	26	19.8	44	45.3	43	70.3	23	83.7	21	95.9	6	99.4	0	99.4	1	100.0
			37	8.1	69.4	10	3.5	23	9.4	82	36.9	89	66.7	66	88.8	27	97.8	4	99.2	2	99.8	0	100.0
Roedean School	E SUSSEX	270	68	9.3	100	124	19.6	252	59.4	193	89.9	58	99.1	4	99.7	2	100.0						
			76	9.1	100	121	16.9	334	51.7	220	83.4	98	97.5	14	99.6	3	100.0						
Rookwood School	HANTS	132	13	8.5	100	5	4.5	32	33.6	34	64.5	31	92.7	6	98.2	2	100.0						
			15	8.4	90.9	13	12.7	33	28.1	32	53.0	32	78.0	17	91.3	7	96.7	3	99.1	1	99.8	0	100.0
Rosemead	W SUSSEX		19	8.1	78.9	7	4.5	27	22.1	42	49.4	40	75.3	26	92.2	6	96.1	3	98.1	2	99.4	1	100.0
			28	8.4	83.3	16	7.2	69	30.8	60	56.6	55	80.1	29	92.5	12	97.7	4	99.4	1	99.8	0	100.0
Rossall School	LANCS	169	81	8.1	82.7	57	8.7	162	33.3	202	64.1	159	88.3	47	95.4	18	98.2	10	99.7	0	99.7	2	100.0
			84	8.5	76.6	38	6.1	149	22.0	199	49.8	195	77.1	93	90.2	46	96.6	18	99.1	2	99.4	4	100.0
Rougemont School	S WALES		37	8.9	100	29	8.8	82	33.7	98	63.5	100	93.9	15	98.5	4	99.7	1	100.0				
			43	8.9	78.4	33	10.6	93	26.5	91	50.6	103	77.9	49	90.8	23	96.9	7	98.8	2	99.3	2	100.0
Royal Grammar School	TYNE	282	136	10.2	100	325	23.4	510	60.1	339	84.5	174	97.0	35	99.6	6	100.0						
			136	10.4	100	319	22.6	706	54.6	393	82.4	204	96.9	37	99.5	7	100.0	0	100.0	0	100.0	0	100.0
Royal Grammar School	SURREY	261	149	9.0	100	358	26.7	626	73.4	285	94.7	67	99.7	4	100.0								
			130	9.5	100	364	26.8	725	64.2	326	90.4	97	98.2	18	99.7	3	99.9	0	99.9	0	99.9	0	100.0
Royal Grammar School	HERWORCS	141	127	9.1	97.6	151	13.0	287	37.8	414	73.5	254	95.4	45	99.3	7	99.9	0	99.9	0	99.9	1	100.0
			114	8.8	99.1	80	7.6	441	45.6	324	77.9	171	94.9	42	99.1	8	99.9	1	100.0				
Royal Hospital School	SUFFOLK	245	95	8.6	82.1	14	1.7	89	12.6	292	48.3	237	77.4	132	93.5	40	98.4	11	99.9	1	99.9	1	100.0
			109	8.9	70.8	6	0.6	68	7.1	184	26.2	303	57.5	252	83.6	114	95.3	37	99.2	6	99.8	2	100.0
Royal Naval School for Girls	SURREY	261	52	8.2	82.7	31	7.3	103	31.5	128	61.5	117	89.0	39	98.1	6	99.5	2	100.0				
			46	8.3	93.0	36	9.9	106	29.5	131	63.7	97	89.0	33	97.6	7	99.4	2	99.9	0	99.9	0	100.0
Royal Russell School	GR LON	198	94	7.3	51.1	12	1.7	58	10.2	197	38.8	199	67.6	131	86.6	56	94.8	27	98.7	4	99.3	5	100.0
			72	7.5	59.7	20	3.3	77	14.9	113	35.6	167	66.3	101	84.9	51	94.3	23	98.5	5	99.4	3	100.0
Royal School, The	AVON	66	51	8.9	92.2	37	8.2	117	34.1	157	68.8	101	91.2	28	97.3	10	99.6	2	100.0				
			48	8.8	83.7	9	2.4	83	20.2	134	52.1	109	78.0	59	92.1	23	97.5	8	99.4	2	99.9	0	100.0
Royal School, The	N IRE		115	9.0	90.4	20	1.9	203	21.5	385	58.7	295	87.2	80	94.9	32	98.0	13	99.2	3	99.5	5	100.0
			84	8.5	91.5	19	2.6	168	24.2	230	56.5	190	83.2	74	93.6	30	97.8	10	99.2	3	99.6	2	100.0
Royal Wolverhampton School	W MIDS	290	55	7.8	65.5	17	4.0	59	17.7	100	41.0	133	72.0	57	85.3	34	93.2	17	97.2	8	99.1	4	100.0
			47	7.6	66.7	1	0.4	54	15.1	75	36.1	118	69.0	65	87.2	28	95.0	12	98.4	3	99.2	2	100.0
Rugby School	W'WICKS	284	112	9.6	100	176	16.3	383	51.9	400	89.0	113	99.4	6	100.0								
			105	9.6	99.0	71	7.1	346	35.7	330	68.5	248	93.1	58	98.8	10	99.8	1	99.9	0	99.9	0	100.0
Rushmoor Independent School	HANTS	133	10	8.1	40.0	1	1.2	7	9.9	12	24.7	20	49.4	22	76.5	10	88.9	8	98.8	1	100.0		
			10	8.0	100	0	0.0	10	12.4	13	28.6	20	53.5	16	73.4	10	85.8	7	94.5	4	99.5	0	100.0
Rushmoor School	BEDS	68	17	8.6	82.4	0	0.0	16	11.0	50	45.2	43	74.7	22	89.7	12	97.9	2	99.3	0	99.3	1	100.0
			0	0.0		0	0.0	0	0.0	0	0.0	0	0.0	0	0.0	0	0.0	0	0.0	0	0.0	0	0.0
Ruthin School	N WALES	309	27	7.6	81.5	8	3.9	31	19.0	59	47.8	62	78.0	29	91.0	11	96.6	7	100.0				
			33	8.1	72.0	8	3.7	46	23.9	52	49.7	58	78.5	25	91.0	11	96.4	5	98.9	1	99.4	1	100.0
Rydal School	N WALES	309	71	10.4	93.0	91	12.3	178	36.5	221	66.5	175	90.2	51	97.2	17	99.5	4	100.0				
			68	9.1	88.1	36	5.9	171	28.9	171	56.7	167	83.8	68	94.9	21	98.3	7	99.4	2	99.7	1	100.0
Penrhos College	N WALES	309	31	8.9	100	72	26.0	83	56.0	73	82.3	40	96.8	6	98.9	2	99.6	0	99.6	1	100.0		
			47	8.6	93.9	36	12.2	125	33.1	118	62.7	96	86.8	29	94.1	16	98.1	5	99.3	1	99.6	1	100.0
Ryde School	IOW	153	109	9.0	85.3	57	5.8	176	23.7	339	58.1	282	86.8	88	95.7	26	98.4	10	99.4	4	99.8	2	100.0
			74	9.0	87.7	10	1.5	129	19.8	192	48.7	236	84.3	69	94.7	23	98.2	8	99.4	3	99.8	1	100.0

GCSE ENGLAND & WALES RESULTS 1995

School	County	P	*A	A	B	C	D	E	F	G	U
Rye St.Antony School	OXON	228	53 9.9 86.8	31 5.9	100 25.0	145 52.6	145 80.2	74 94.3	23 98.7	5 99.6	2 100.0
			52 9.3 93.3	39 6.6	130 28.7	151 60.2	116 84.3	46 93.9	21 98.3	6 99.5	2 99.9	0 100.0
Sackville School	KENT	161	34 7.7 64.7	8 3.1	16 9.2	58 31.4	99 69.3	48 87.7	26 97.7	5 99.6	0 99.6	1 100.0
			35 7.7 54.5	5 2.0	22 8.4	41 23.5	72 49.9	68 74.9	45 91.4	17 97.7	6 99.9	0 100.0
St. Albans High School for Girls	HERTS	148	79 9.0 100	133 18.8	325 64.6	191 91.5	54 99.2	4 99.7	0 99.7	2 100.0		
			76 9.0 100	95 13.7	361 55.6	215 87.0	80 98.7	8 99.9	1 100.0			
St. Albans School	HERTS	148	114 9.1 98.2	130 12.6	327 44.2	381 81.1	153 95.9	33 99.1	7 99.8	2 100.0		
			99 9.3 97.8	70 8.3	298 33.8	320 68.5	203 90.5	61 97.1	20 99.3	3 99.6	2 99.8	1 100.0
St Ambrose College	CHESHIRE	94	118 10.8 92.4	52 4.1	287 26.6	417 59.4	335 85.7	121 95.2	46 98.8	12 99.8	3 100.0	
			97 10.4 93.6	65 6.5	273 28.3	297 57.7	282 85.7	100 95.6	32 98.7	9 99.6	3 99.9	0 100.0
St. Andrew's School	BEDS	68	27 8.9 88.9	5 2.1	42 19.6	72 49.6	80 82.9	24 92.9	15 99.2	2 100.0		
			27 8.4 55.6	1 0.4	15 7.0	45 26.9	76 60.4	52 83.3	30 96.5	6 99.1	2 100.0	
St Anne's High School	DURHAM	114	13 8.5 92.3	14 12.7	38 47.3	22 67.3	26 90.9	8 98.2	2 100.0			
			25 8.7 81.0	5 2.7	45 21.6	59 49.3	53 74.2	32 89.3	14 95.9	6 98.7	2 99.6	0 100.0
St. Anne's School	CUMBRIA	99	43 8.7 93.0	57 15.2	89 39.0	125 72.5	77 93.0	20 98.4	5 99.7	1 100.0		
			45 8.2 92.5	21 6.0	120 33.8	119 66.2	82 88.6	29 96.5	8 98.7	4 99.8	0 99.8	0 100.0
St. Anselm's College	MERSEY		94 9.8 81.9	41 4.4	167 22.5	271 51.8	233 77.0	123 90.3	70 97.8	15 99.5	2 99.7	3 100.0
			101 9.9 80.8	57 5.6	216 22.7	286 51.4	259 77.3	128 90.1	65 96.6	24 99.0	6 99.6	3 100.0
St. Antony's-Leweston School	DORSET	111	49 8.6 89.8	32 7.6	104 32.5	141 66.1	89 87.4	31 94.7	13 97.9	5 99.0	4 100.0	
			62 7.9 87.0	38 8.6	145 31.3	143 60.5	117 84.5	47 94.1	15 97.5	8 98.8	2 99.2	4 100.0
St. Augustine's College	KENT		32 8.7 78.1	12 4.3	46 20.7	82 50.0	87 81.1	31 92.1	15 97.5	6 99.6	1 100.0	
			27 8.6 81.8	9 3.2	38 17.0	51 38.7	67 67.2	40 84.3	23 94.0	9 97.9	4 99.6	1 100.0
St. Bede's College	GR MANCH	211	131 8.7 97.7	223 19.5	421 56.2	310 83.3	151 96.5	31 99.2	9 100.0			
			125 8.7 95.4	98 8.8	449 43.0	331 73.3	203 91.9	67 98.1	16 99.5	5 100.0	0 100.0	0 100.0
St. Bede's School	E SUSSEX	271	85 8.1 58.8	32 4.7	114 21.3	175 46.9	170 71.7	105 87.0	59 95.6	28 99.7	1 99.9	1 100.0
			75 8.1 73.2	31 4.0	89 15.7	129 36.9	174 65.6	101 82.3	63 92.7	28 97.3	9 98.8	7 100.0
St. Bees School	CUMBRIA	99	44 9.1 86.4	29 7.3	85 28.6	103 54.4	120 84.5	42 95.0	15 98.7	2 99.2	0 99.2	3 100.0
			52 8.9 87.2	36 8.3	149 34.0	127 61.7	121 88.0	34 95.4	14 98.5	5 99.6	1 99.8	1 100.0
St. Benedict's Convent School	HANTS	133	6 9.2 100	6 10.9	10 29.1	24 72.7	15 100.0					
			10 8.2 42.9	3 5.2	13 17.1	18 39.0	21 64.6	16 84.1	7 92.7	5 98.8	1 100.0	
St. Benedict's School	GR LON	198	92 10.1 92.4	90 9.7	207 31.9	336 68.0	188 88.2	60 94.6	32 98.1	12 99.4	0 99.4	6 100.0
			83 9.8 96.6	57 5.9	196 25.4	263 57.6	185 80.3	102 92.8	47 98.7	16 99.6	3 100.0	
St. Catherine's School	GR LON	199	21 8.7 90.5	12 6.6	50 33.9	64 68.9	34 87.4	15 95.6	4 97.8	3 99.5	1 100.0	
			23 8.8 80.0	8 3.8	45 23.5	52 49.6	45 72.1	28 86.2	17 94.7	8 98.7	2 99.7	0 100.0
St. Catherine's School	SURREY	262	74 8.5 98.6	134 21.4	285 66.8	177 95.1	29 99.7	2 100.0				
			70 9.3 98.3	105 18.4	325 53.5	205 85.2	76 97.0	15 99.3	3 99.8	1 99.9	0 99.9	0 100.0
St. Christopher School	HERTS	149	65 8.4 76.9	36 6.6	117 27.9	158 56.8	120 78.6	66 90.7	26 95.4	18 98.7	3 99.3	4 100.0
			53 8.7 70.6	25 5.7	72 16.7	110 40.5	124 67.3	84 85.5	44 95.0	15 98.3	3 98.9	5 100.0
St Clotilde's School	GLOS	125	25 9.0 92.0	16 7.1	43 26.3	90 66.5	46 87.1	24 97.8	4 99.6	1 100.0		
			25 7.8 85.7	1 2.0	63 32.4	68 67.5	40 88.1	17 96.8	6 99.9	0 99.9	0 99.9	0 100.0
St. David's College	N WALES	309	46 7.3 37.0	6 1.8	18 7.1	49 21.7	119 57.0	76 79.5	49 94.1	19 99.7	1 100.0	
			41 7.9 38.9	0 0.0	41 12.6	61 31.4	103 63.1	74 85.8	33 96.0	10 99.1	2 99.7	1 100.0
St. David's Senior School	SURREY	262	50 8.8 98.0	29 6.6	123 34.6	164 72.0	87 91.8	23 97.0	10 99.3	3 100.0		
			40 8.5 87.8	21 6.4	73 22.8	104 53.6	88 79.6	43 92.4	19 98.0	5 99.5	1 99.8	0 100.0
St. Dominic's Priory School	STAFFS	240	46 8.9 91.3	27 6.6	98 30.5	133 62.9	111 90.0	34 98.3	7 100.0			
			49 8.9 97.6	0 0.0	106 24.3	123 52.5	129 82.0	46 92.5	21 97.3	9 99.4	2 99.9	0 100.0
St. Dominic's School	STAFFS	240	43 9.8 95.3	23 5.5	97 28.6	177 70.7	87 91.4	26 97.6	7 99.3	3 100.0		
			55 9.7 94.6	40 7.3	137 27.1	176 60.1	151 88.4	39 95.7	17 98.8	5 99.8	1 100.0	0 100.0
St. Dunstan's Abbey School	DEVON	105	33 8.7 90.9	30 10.5	86 40.4	86 70.4	57 90.2	20 97.2	7 99.7	1 100.0		
			41 8.4 97.6	34 9.4	144 43.6	102 73.1	67 92.5	21 98.6	4 99.7	1 100.0		
St. Dunstan's College	GR LON	200	103 9.1 97.1	70 7.5	235 32.5	317 66.2	235 91.3	70 98.7	10 99.8	2 100.0		
			98 8.4 93.6	35 4.4	201 25.3	241 54.5	240 83.7	97 95.4	29 99.0	8 99.9	0 99.9	0 100.0
St. Edmund's College	HERTS	149	82 10.4 74.4	35 4.1	125 18.8	236 46.4	219 72.1	148 89.4	60 96.5	24 99.3	6 100.0	
			81 10.2 76.5	38 4.4	136 17.4	220 44.0	227 71.4	136 87.8	60 95.1	30 98.7	8 99.7	2 100.0
St. Edmund's School	KENT	162	69 8.9 84.1	66 10.7	136 32.7	172 60.6	128 81.4	68 92.4	35 98.1	7 99.2	3 99.7	2 100.0
			66 8.6 76.1	13 2.4	118 21.3	148 47.3	164 76.1	80 90.1	40 97.2	11 99.1	3 99.6	2 100.0
St. Edward's College	MERSEY	213	90 9.4 92.2	84 9.9	191 32.4	296 67.3	217 92.9	45 98.2	12 99.6	2 99.9	1 100.0	
			89 9.4 88.9	52 6.1	237 29.4	271 61.7	220 87.9	77 97.1	19 99.4	3 99.7	1 99.8	1 100.0
St Edward's School	OXON	229	90 8.9 94.4	71 8.9	182 31.6	244 62.0	221 89.6	66 97.9	16 99.9	0 99.9	0 99.9	1 100.0
			106 10.0 96.4	61 5.6	376 36.8	336 68.8	245 92.0	64 98.1	17 99.7	3 100.0		

385

GCSE ENGLAND & WALES RESULTS 1995

School	County	P						A		A		B		C		D		E		F		G		U	
St. Edward's School	GLOS	125	98	9.2	81.6	22	2.4	160	20.2	340	57.9	229	83.4	93	93.7	45	98.7	12	100.0				
			106	9.2	68.9	51	6.1	176	18.9	232	42.6	270	70.1	175	87.9	77	95.7	29	98.7	10	99.7	2	100.0
St. Elphin's School	DERBYS	101	32	8.7	93.7	70	25.2	82	54.7	85	85.3	27	95.0	8	97.8	6	100.0						
			39	8.1	92.9	38	16.2	120	40.6	88	68.5	60	87.6	22	94.5	11	98.0	4	99.3	2	99.9	0	100.0
Saint Felix School	SUFFOLK	245	44	8.5	93.2	31	8.3	96	34.0	138	70.9	79	92.0	23	98.1	3	98.9	0	98.9	0	98.9	4	100.0
			50	8.4	95.8	50	12.0	141	36.0	127	66.3	98	89.7	30	96.9	11	99.5	2	100.0				
St. Francis' College	HERTS	149	36	9.6	94.4	61	17.6	125	53.6	90	79.5	51	94.2	15	98.6	5	100.0						
			35	8.5	92.7	35	9.9	106	37.4	95	68.9	69	91.7	19	98.0	5	99.7	1	100.0				
S. Gabriels School	BERKS	77	43	9.4	95.3	36	8.9	106	35.2	137	69.2	91	91.8	25	98.0	6	99.5	2	100.0				
			29	8.9	93.7	36	12.2	72	30.2	86	63.0	60	85.9	25	95.4	10	99.2	2	100.0				
St. George's College	SURREY	263	83	9.9	92.8	50	6.1	164	26.1	265	58.5	238	87.5	80	97.3	15	99.1	7	100.0				
			76	9.4	95.7	37	5.5	142	20.8	227	52.6	214	82.5	86	94.5	32	99.0	6	99.9	1	100.0		
St. George's School	BERKS	77	51	8.5	100	43	9.9	136	41.3	169	80.4	67	95.8	17	99.8	1	100.0						
			44	8.8	97.9	39	9.7	168	45.5	130	79.2	65	96.0	12	99.1	2	99.6	1	99.9	0	99.9	0	100.0
St. Gerards School	N WALES	310	35	9.0	77.1	28	8.9	66	29.8	106	63.5	69	85.4	36	96.8	8	99.4	2	100.0				
			29	8.8	70.0	16	5.9	57	23.3	65	48.6	74	77.3	38	92.1	14	97.5	5	99.5	1	99.8	0	100.0
St Helen & St Katharine, The School of	OXON	229	74	10.5	100	286	37.0	345	81.5	120	97.0	20	99.6	3	100.0								
			74	10.2	100	161	20.8	474	67.2	181	91.2	52	98.1	12	99.7	2	100.0	0	100.0	0	100.0	0	100.0
St. Helen's School	GR LON	200	87	9.2	98.9	138	17.3	358	62.0	259	94.4	38	99.1	6	99.9	0	99.9	0	99.9	0	99.9	1	100.0
			82	9.0	98.7	130	18.5	364	52.7	222	82.8	100	96.3	23	99.4	4	99.9	0	99.9	0	99.9	0	100.0
St. Hilary's School	CHESHIRE	95	33	8.6	93.9	12	4.2	56	24.0	70	48.8	104	85.5	31	96.5	8	99.3	2	100.0				
			33	8.8	77.5	20	5.9	90	32.1	86	61.4	80	88.7	25	97.3	6	99.3	1	99.7	1	100.0		
St. Hilda's School	ESSEX	120	24	8.0	79.2	4	2.1	35	20.2	52	47.2	64	80.3	24	92.7	11	98.4	3	100.0				
			29	7.9	91.7	2	2.0	26	11.5	58	37.0	89	76.2	40	92.1	13	97.8	4	99.6	1	100.0		
St. Hilda's School	N YORKS	299	19	9.0	94.7	16	9.4	35	29.8	59	64.3	42	88.9	12	95.9	7	100.0						
			24	8.6	82.4	12	7.8	57	29.1	53	55.3	45	77.5	31	92.8	10	97.7	3	99.2	1	99.7	0	100.0
St. James Independent Sch.for Boys	GR LON	200	17	10.2	100	18	10.3	61	45.4	57	78.2	32	96.6	5	99.4	1	100.0						
			21	8.9	83.3	14	6.6	35	20.7	48	46.8	56	77.3	24	90.3	11	96.3	4	98.5	2	99.6	0	100.0
St. James Independent Sch.for Girls	GR LON	200	15	9.3	93.3	14	10.1	37	36.7	47	70.5	30	92.1	7	97.1	2	98.6	2	100.0				
			15	7.7	100	2	22.2	24	20.8	37	52.8	29	77.9	18	93.4	5	97.8	2	99.5	0	99.5	0	100.0
St. James School	HUMBER	152	16	8.5	93.7	2	1.5	19	15.4	58	58.1	40	87.5	11	95.6	6	100.0						
			34	7.6	66.7	13	6.4	58	23.9	60	47.5	66	73.4	37	87.9	20	95.8	8	98.9	2	99.7	0	100.0
St. James's and The Abbey	HERWORCS	141	35	8.5	82.9	27	9.1	78	35.2	86	64.1	66	86.2	28	95.6	9	98.7	4	100.0				
			31	8.2	84.4	19	6.4	51	21.4	68	47.8	82	79.6	31	91.7	13	96.7	6	99.1	2	99.8	0	100.0
St. John's College	HANTS	133	79	8.7	82.3	39	5.7	136	25.4	170	50.1	233	83.9	88	96.7	19	99.4	3	99.9	1	100.0		
			101	8.9	85.1	29	3.8	168	19.4	242	46.4	251	74.3	138	89.7	63	96.7	20	99.0	8	99.9	1	100.0
St. John's School	ESSEX	120	33	8.2	66.7	15	5.5	34	18.1	79	47.2	77	75.6	46	12	97.0	4	98.5	3	99.6	1	100.0
			35	8.3	65.7	6	2.1	39	15.5	82	43.8	77	70.3	50	87.6	28	97.2	7	99.7	1	100.0		
St. John's School	SURREY	264	69	8.8	95.7	37	6.1	138	28.9	225	66.1	169	94.0	31	99.2	5	100.0						
			87	9.0	88.2	44	6.8	163	22.0	240	52.7	228	81.9	92	93.7	35	98.2	12	99.7	1	99.8	1	100.0
St. Joseph's College with the School o	SUFFOLK	246	105	9.2	89.5	47	4.9	176	23.1	350	59.4	235	83.7	111	95.2	36	99.0	9	99.9	1	100.0		
			102	9.2	88.2	68	6.8	238	26.8	252	53.7	227	77.9	116	90.2	57	96.3	26	99.1	6	99.7	2	100.0
St. Joseph's College	STAFFS	241	52	8.7	88.5	13	2.9	79	20.4	151	54.0	144	86.0	48	96.7	18	99.4	6	100.0				
			46	8.5	88.6	34	4.9	106	28.6	113	57.2	97	81.7	50	94.4	16	98.4	5	99.7	1	99.9	0	100.0
St. Joseph's Convent School	BERKS	78	61	8.9	82.0	18	3.3	91	20.1	179	53.0	141	79.0	85	94.7	23	98.9	6	100.0				
			85	9.0	75.0	21	3.1	175	23.4	220	52.1	224	81.4	100	94.5	33	98.8	7	99.7	2	100.0	0	100.0
St. Joseph's School	W'WICKS	284	34	8.6	85.3	12	4.1	65	26.2	100	60.2	85	89.1	30	99.3	1	99.7	1	100.0				
			0		0.0	0	0.0	0	0.0	0	0.0	0	0.0	0	0.0	0	0.0	0	0.0	0	0.0	0	0.0
St. Joseph's School	CORNWALL	97	25	9.0	96.0	15	6.7	62	34.2	68	64.4	59	90.7	16	97.8	3	99.1	2	100.0				
			27	8.6	97.0	16	5.6	61	27.4	70	57.3	68	86.3	23	96.2	7	99.1	2	100.0				
St. Joseph's School	LINCS	173	31	8.5	83.9	21	8.0	70	34.5	78	64.0	55	84.8	24	93.9	9	97.3	7	100.0				
			36	8.5	84.6	29	8.8	64	22.8	73	46.6	90	75.9	42	89.6	18	95.5	10	98.8	2	99.4	1	100.0
St. Lawrence College	KENT	132	50	9.9	92.0	51	10.3	114	33.4	154	64.6	113	87.4	47	97.0	13	99.6	2	100.0				
			63	9.5	94.8	23	4.1	182	31.4	172	60.2	149	85.2	58	94.9	21	98.5	8	99.8	1	100.0	0	100.0
St. Leonards-Mayfield School	E SUSSEX	271	78	9.6	96.2	77	10.3	237	42.1	248	75.4	149	95.4	21	98.3	11	99.7	2	100.0				
			79	9.8	98.7	58	7.6	333	42.5	263	74.9	151	93.5	39	98.3	11	99.6	3	100.0				
St. Margaret's School for Girls	DEVON	105	61	8.4	100	72	14.1	160	45.4	168	78.3	90	95.9	20	99.8	1	100.0						
			61	8.5	100	67	13.1	208	42.9	168	75.5	98	94.5	23	99.0	4	99.7	1	99.9	0	99.9	0	100.0
St. Margaret's School	HERTS	150	53	9.2	94.3	16	3.3	123	28.6	196	68.9	117	93.0	32	99.6	1	99.8	1	100.0				
			63	8.6	95.2	46	8.6	162	31.5	182	65.1	122	87.6	47	96.3	14	98.9	5	99.8	1	100.0	0	100

386

School	Location		P		*A		A		B		C		D		E		F		G		U	
St. Margaret's School	GR LON	201	20	9.0	85.0	16	8.9	35	28.3	76	70.6	28	86.1	20	97.2	3	98.9	2	100.0		
			16	8.1	71.4	11	9.3	20	16.6	27	37.1	40	67.3	26	87.0	12	96.1	4	99.1	1 99.8	0 100.0
St. Martin's	W MIDS	290	55	9.0	100	109	22.1	158	54.0	164	87.2	53	98.0	9	99.8	1	100.0				
			45	8.8	93.0	61	16.2	165	44.6	122	75.3	75	94.2	15	97.9	6	99.4	2 99.9		0 99.9	0 100.0
St. Mary's College	MERSEY	213	96	9.9	93.7	87	9.2	233	33.7	307	66.0	219	89.1	77	97.2	24	99.7	2 99.9		1 100.0	
			84	9.0	92.9	53	6.4	195	27.3	222	56.7	202	83.4	83	94.4	30	98.4	10 99.7		2 100.0	0 100.0
St. Mary's College	KENT	162	15	7.7	66.7	5	4.3	11	13.9	31	40.9	34	70.4	20	87.8	7	93.9	6 99.1		0 99.1	1 100.0
			20	8.0	63.6	5	5.8	24	15.6	37	38.7	42	64.8	26	81.0	18	92.3	9 97.9		3 99.8	0 100.0
St. Mary's Convent School	HERWORCS	141	58	8.3	93.1	79	16.5	138	45.3	163	79.3	72	94.4	18	98.1	8	99.8	1 100.0			
			53	9.3	89.1	64	14.4	155	34.0	134	61.0	113	83.9	53	94.6	20	98.6	6 99.8		0 99.8	0 100.0
St. Mary's Hall	E SUSSEX	272	47	8.4	89.4	16	4.1	59	19.1	140	54.7	134	88.8	38	98.5	6	100.0				
			41	9.0	91.9	19	6.1	99	28.1	126	62.4	91	87.2	33	96.2	10	98.9	3 99.7		1 100.0	
St. Mary's School	CAMBS	87	86	9.7	97.7	66	7.9	272	40.7	351	82.9	120	97.4	17	99.4	4	99.9	1 100.0			
			90	9.9	99.0	63	6.4	273	32.4	313	67.9	220	92.8	51	98.6	10	99.7	2 99.9		0 99.9	0 100.0
St. Mary's School	BERKS	78	46	9.6	100	51	11.6	201	57.1	152	91.6	36	99.8	1	100.0						
			47	9.7	100	38	8.3	210	47.9	145	79.7	72	95.6	17	99.3	3	100.0	0 100.0		0 100.0	0 100.0
St. Mary's School	WILTS	293	52	9.2	100	132	27.4	234	76.1	94	95.6	17	99.2	3	99.8	1	100.0				
			52	8.9	100	77	18.4	263	60.3	128	88.1	48	98.5	6	99.8	1	100.0				
St. Mary's School	DORSET	111	44	9.5	97.7	52	12.4	123	41.7	154	78.3	74	96.0	11	98.6	4	99.5	2 100.0			
			44	9.0	97.4	72	19.3	148	40.5	125	71.8	82	92.3	20	97.3	8	99.3	2 99.8		0 99.8	0 100.0
St. Mary's School	ESSEX	121	59	7.6	86.4	32	7.1	105	30.5	149	63.7	98	85.5	42	94.9	13	97.8	7 99.3		3 100.0	
			57	7.9	86.5	17	4.1	147	33.2	131	62.3	119	88.7	36	96.6	12	99.3	3 100.0		0 100.0	0 100.0
St. Mary's School	OXON	229	47	8.3	80.9	22	5.7	85	27.6	112	56.4	97	81.4	48	93.8	17	98.2	7 100.0			
			53	8.7	82.4	16	3.6	118	26.1	161	60.9	119	86.6	45	96.3	13	99.1	3 99.8		1 100.0	
St. Mary's School	BUCKS	83	28	8.6	92.9	34	14.1	72	44.0	84	78.8	39	95.0	11	99.6	1	100.0				
			30	7.7	92.3	21	10.8	62	28.3	77	61.4	61	87.6	21	96.6	7	99.6	1 100.0			
St. Maur's School	SURREY	264	70	9.7	98.6	43	6.3	200	35.7	277	76.5	134	96.2	23	99.6	3	100.0				
			68	8.8	93.8	17	2.9	192	32.4	187	63.5	156	89.5	49	97.6	12	99.6	2 100.0		0 100.0	0 100.0
St. Michael's School	SURREY	264	19	9.5	89.5	10	5.6	37	26.1	56	57.2	45	82.2	19	92.8	13	100.0				
			22	8.4	57.7	7	3.2	26	14.6	44	38.3	47	63.6	34	82.0	19	92.2	9 97.1		3 98.7	2 100.0
St. Michael's School	S WALES		41	8.9	80.5	32	8.8	74	29.1	103	57.4	98	84.3	42	95.9	14	99.7	0 99.7		0 99.7	1 100.0
			44	6.8	82.9	15	5.0	66	22.9	69	45.8	83	73.3	51	90.2	19	96.5	6 98.5		2 99.2	2 100.0
St. Nicholas School	ESSEX	121	17	8.9	82.4	2	1.3	18	13.2	42	40.8	56	77.6	19	90.1	9	96.1	2 97.4		0 97.4	4 100.0
			19	8.7	81.0	5	2.8	29	17.8	47	45.6	61	81.7	22	94.7	8	99.4	1 100.0			
St. Nicholas' School	HANTS	133	31	9.6	90.3	26	8.8	58	28.3	98	61.3	84	89.6	25	98.0	4	99.3	2 100.0			
			45	9.2	91.7	31	9.1	116	29.4	109	55.7	110	82.3	49	94.1	19	98.7	5 99.9		0 99.9	0 100.0
St. Paul's Girls' School	GR LON	202	81	8.4	100	252	36.8	334	85.7	85	98.1	12	99.9	1	100.0						
			83	8.9	100	186	32.9	541	77.8	121	94.1	36	98.9	7	99.9	1	100.0				
St. Paul's School	GR LON	202	154	10.5	100	402	24.9	793	73.9	356	96.0	60	99.7	3	99.9	2	100.0				
			151	10.6	100	359	22.0	1012	67.7	400	92.7	97	98.8	16	99.8	3	99.9	1 100.0			
St. Peter's School	N'HANTS	219	7	7.7	100	9	16.7	7	29.6	18	63.0	17	94.4	3	100.0						
			11	7.9	60.0	0	0.0	5	5.7	18	26.4	36	67.7	16	86.0	9	96.3	2 98.6		1 99.8	0 100.0
St. Peter's School	N YORKS	300	95	10.0	100	245	25.8	311	58.5	250	84.8	118	97.3	22	99.6	4	100.0				
			93	10.2	98.9	144	15.1	326	37.2	319	70.6	197	91.3	56	97.1	19	99.1	5 99.7		1 99.8	2 100.0
St. Swithun's School	HANTS	134	82	9.0	100	262	35.5	316	78.3	138	97.0	20	99.7	1	99.9	0	99.9	0 99.9		1 100.0	
			67	9.0	100	204	32.3	315	58.9	163	85.9	73	98.0	10	99.7	2	100.0				
St. Teresa's School	SURREY	264	63	8.7	93.7	49	8.9	141	34.7	180	67.5	110	87.6	51	96.9	16	99.8	1 100.0			
			53	8.2	100	53	11.6	127	31.8	136	63.2	99	86.0	38	94.8	14	98.0	6 99.4		2 99.9	0 100.0
St. Ursula's High School	AVON	66	29	9.3	79.3	3	1.1	58	22.5	81	52.4	74	79.7	34	92.3	12	96.7	6 98.9		3 100.0	
			35	8.7	88.5	2	0.8	42	14.1	77	39.5	85	67.4	56	85.9	26	94.4	11 98.0		5 98.7	1 100.0
Scarborough College	N YORKS	300	62	8.9	87.1	50	9.0	124	31.5	176	63.3	127	86.3	53	95.8	18	99.1	5 100.0			
			71	8.9	91.0	29	4.2	166	27.1	161	52.5	162	78.1	81	90.8	37	96.7	18 99.5		2 99.8	1 100.0
Scarisbrick Hall School	LANCS	169	37	9.8	89.2	24	6.6	90	31.3	129	66.8	74	87.1	39	97.8	7	99.7	1 100.0			
			47	8.9	100	25	5.8	132	33.1	135	65.7	91	87.7	33	95.7	15	99.3	3 100.0			
School of Jesus & Mary	SUFFOLK		32	9.0	84.4	1	0.3	45	16.0	104	52.3	77	79.1	39	92.7	13	97.2	7 99.7		1 100.0	
			34	8.7	94.3	16	5.1	53	18.8	89	48.7	84	76.8	39	90.8	24	96.6	7 99.0		2 99.7	0 100.0
School of S.Mary & S.Anne	STAFFS	241	29	8.5	96.6	9	3.6	57	26.7	97	66.0	60	90.3	21	98.8	3	100.0				
			35	9.6	88.9	28	9.2	90	28.6	90	55.4	87	81.3	41	93.5	15	98.0	5 99.5		1 99.8	0 100.0
Seaford College	W SUSSEX	278	63	7.9	50.8	9	1.8	39	9.6	122	34.1	134	60.9	97	80.4	68	94.0	22 98.4		5 99.4	3 100.0
			62	7.5	47.2	4	1.0	50	11.3	79	28.5	130	56.8	105	79.7	59	92.5	25 97.9		5 99.0	4 100.0

387

GCSE ENGLAND & WALES RESULTS 1995

School	County	P				*A		A		B		C		D		E		F		G		U	
Sedbergh School	CUMBRIA	99	65	8.4	95.4	34	6.2	113	26.9	206	64.7	135	89.4	44	97.4	12	99.6	2	100.0				
			86	10.1	94.9	44	5.7	261	30.9	262	61.0	235	87.9	78	96.9	22	99.4	5	100.0	0	100.0	0	100.0
Selwyn School	GLOS	125	18	9.3	61.1	8	4.8	27	21.0	36	42.5	47	70.7	30	88.6	13	96.4	5	99.4	1	100.0		
			32	8.0	71.4	18	6.2	54	22.3	74	50.7	72	78.4	37	92.6	14	98.0	5	99.9	0	99.9	0	100.0
Sevenoaks School	KENT	163	142	9.2	99.3	282	21.6	494	59.3	394	89.4	124	98.9	13	99.9	0	99.9	1	100.0				
			128	9.5	100	213	17.8	613	53.7	371	84.0	173	98.2	19	99.8	2	99.9	1	100.0				
Shaftesbury Independent School	GR LON	203	7	7.1	85.7	1	2.0	4	10.0	21	52.0	14	80.0	6	92.0	4	100.0						
			6	7.7	50.0	1	2.1	6	12.4	14	41.5	15	72.5	8	89.1	4	97.4	1	99.5	0	99.5	0	100.0
Shebbear College	DEVON	106	36	8.8	66.7	13	4.1	63	24.1	84	50.6	77	75.0	44	88.9	24	96.5	8	99.1	3	100.0		
			49	9.0	78.0	17	3.5	81	19.2	99	41.9	132	72.1	75	89.3	33	96.8	10	99.1	3	99.8	0	100.0
Sheffield High School GPDST	S YORKS	302	66	9.1	98.5	116	19.3	240	59.1	180	89.0	58	98.7	8	100.0								
			81	8.9	97.6	99	13.7	352	51.7	206	80.4	105	95.0	27	98.7	8	99.9	1	100.0				
Sherborne School For Girls	DORSET	111	85	9.9	100	173	20.5	290	55.0	223	81.5	122	96.0	28	99.3	6	100.0						
			83	10.0	100	89	10.9	399	50.6	279	84.5	109	97.7	17	99.8	2	100.0						
Sherborne School	DORSET	112	127	10.2	97.6	167	12.9	458	48.3	427	81.3	198	96.6	41	99.8	0	99.8	1	99.8	0	99.8	2	100.0
			131	8.8	100	71	6.0	493	44.3	409	80.1	195	97.1	29	99.7	4	100.0						
Sherrardswood School	HERTS	150	24	7.8	62.5	7	3.7	27	18.2	33	35.8	62	69.0	22	80.7	19	90.9	11	96.8	5	99.5	1	100.0
			23	8.0	66.7	3	1.8	30	17.2	41	40.0	54	69.9	30	86.6	14	94.3	8	98.8	2	99.9	0	100.0
Shiplake College	OXON	230	70	7.8	74.3	8	1.5	54	11.4	164	41.5	187	75.9	73	89.3	42	97.1	13	99.4	3	100.0		
			77	7.6	56.2	10	1.6	62	11.0	122	32.0	204	67.1	109	85.9	49	94.4	24	98.5	6	99.5	2	100.0
Shoreham College	W SUSSEX	278	23	7.4	30.4	1	0.6	19	11.8	14	20.0	47	47.6	40	71.2	25	85.9	17	95.9	7	100.0		
			32	8.2	56.7	3	1.2	28	11.2	54	31.9	82	63.5	48	82.0	27	92.4	13	97.4	5	99.3	1	100.0
Shrewsbury High School GPDST	SALOP	233	76	9.6	100	78	10.7	184	35.8	321	79.8	130	97.5	15	99.6	2	99.9	1	100.0				
			57	8.7	100	59	11.0	242	51.1	141	79.5	77	95.0	20	99.0	4	99.8	1	100.0				
Shrewsbury School	SALOP	234	138	10.1	100	210	15.0	462	48.1	452	80.5	244	97.9	25	99.7	3	99.9	1	100.0				
			134	10.1	100	150	10.4	547	42.4	434	74.3	280	94.9	58	99.2	9	99.9	2	100.0				
Sibford School	OXON	230	64	7.7	39.1	14	2.9	36	10.2	88	28.2	95	47.6	102	68.4	84	85.5	43	94.3	19	98.2	9	100.0
			58	6.3	38.0	5	1.5	34	9.6	56	25.0	89	49.5	71	69.0	53	83.6	38	94.0	17	98.7	4	100.0
Sidcot School	AVON	66	61	7.8	70.5	28	5.9	97	26.3	116	50.6	131	78.2	72	93.3	28	99.2	3	99.8	1	100.0		
			46	7.7	76.8	12	2.8	68	19.8	78	41.9	113	73.8	54	89.1	24	95.9	10	98.7	4	99.8	0	100.0
Silcoates School	W YORKS	307	70	9.0	80.0	22	3.5	89	17.7	203	50.1	182	79.1	85	92.7	38	98.7	8	100.0				
			58	8.5	95.1	13	2.4	95	20.1	151	51.0	151	81.9	54	92.9	21	97.2	8	98.9	4	99.7	1	100.0
Sir William Perkins's School	SURREY	265	82	9.7	100	197	24.7	327	65.7	230	94.5	40	99.5	4	100.0								
			78	9.1	98.7	112	14.7	337	50.1	208	79.1	118	95.5	27	99.3	4	99.9	1	100.0				
Slindon College	W SUSSEX	278	19	7.1	0.0	0	0.0	6	4.5	11	12.7	18	26.1	32	50.0	38	78.4	15	89.6	7	94.8	7	100.0
			31	7.3	25.0	0	0.0	13	5.8	32	20.0	51	42.6	45	62.6	30	75.9	29	88.7	14	94.9	1	100.0
Solihull School	W MIDS	290	115	10.0	99.1	167	14.5	400	49.4	353	80.1	180	95.8	38	99.1	9	99.9	1	100.0				
			122	9.3	100	185	14.9	437	42.0	379	75.7	216	94.8	46	98.9	11	99.9	1	100.0	0	100.0	0	100.0
South Hampstead High School GPDST	GR LON	203	87	9.0	100	195	24.9	360	70.8	191	95.2	38	100.0										
			77	8.7	100	125	18.5	394	62.5	181	89.6	64	99.1	5	99.9	1	100.0						
Stafford Grammar School	STAFFS	241	50	9.0	96.0	15	3.3	113	28.5	172	66.8	110	91.3	27	97.3	8	99.1	3	99.8	0	99.8	1	100.0
			47	8.8	88.1	14	3.7	79	19.8	110	46.3	127	77.0	57	90.7	27	97.2	10	99.7	1	99.9	0	100.0
Stamford High School for Girls	LINCS	174	115	9.1	97.4	125	11.9	357	45.9	396	83.6	133	96.3	31	99.2	6	99.8	2	100.0				
			114	9.1	94.8	91	8.7	346	34.9	361	69.6	245	93.1	59	98.7	10	99.7	3	100.0	0	100.0	0	100.0
Stamford School	LINCS	174	125	9.1	96.0	100	8.8	355	40.1	401	75.5	217	94.6	48	98.9	7	99.5	3	99.7	0	99.7	3	100.0
			120	9.4	98.4	63	5.7	376	34.7	395	70.0	247	92.1	65	97.9	20	99.6	4	100.0				
Stanbridge Earls School	HANTS	134	33	7.3	39.4	2	0.8	12	5.8	44	24.1	65	51.0	41	68.0	38	83.8	22	92.9	8	96.3	9	100.0
			41	6.2	13.8	0	0.0	13	5.2	30	17.1	72	45.7	58	68.8	41	85.1	23	94.3	10	98.2	4	100.0
Stockport Grammar School	CHESHIRE	95	143	8.0	100	379	33.1	409	68.9	265	92.0	82	99.2	6	99.9	3	100.0						
			147	8.0	100	272	23.0	649	59.8	322	87.2	128	98.1	17	99.6	4	99.9	1	100.0				
Stoke College	SUFFOLK	246	21	8.5	71.4	9	5.0	25	19.0	53	48.6	55	79.3	28	95.0	9	100.0						
			32	8.0	58.6	5	2.1	30	12.1	53	32.7	80	63.8	48	82.5	27	93.0	13	98.1	3	99.2	2	100.0
Stonar School	WILTS	294	71	9.7	84.5	26	3.8	116	20.7	233	54.6	202	84.0	75	94.9	25	98.5	10	100.0				
			64	8.9	76.4	40	5.9	105	19.9	139	44.3	175	75.0	84	89.8	41	97.0	12	99.1	4	99.8	1	100.0
Stonefield House School	LINCS	175	19	7.8	73.7	13	8.7	21	22.8	28	41.6	44	71.1	28	89.9	10	96.6	5	100.0				
			12	8.1	83.3	8	8.0	16	18.9	24	44.2	29	74.7	16	91.6	6	97.9	2	100.0				
Stonyhurst College	LANCS	169	83	9.6	96.4	35	4.5	246	35.4	264	68.6	175	90.7	59	98.1	10	99.4	4	99.9	0	99.9	1	100.0
			80	10.6	78.3	40	5.6	194	23.9	229	50.9	227	77.8	119	91.8	48	97.5	14	99.1	2	99.4	5	100.0
Stover School	DEVON	106	48	8.0	87.5	34	8.9	118	39.8	112	69.7	74	88.5	27	95.5	13	99.0	4	100.0				
			0	0.0	0.0	0	0.0	0	0.0	0	0.0	0	0.0	0	0.0	0	0.0	0	0.0	0	0.0	0	0.0

388

GCSE ENGLAND & WALES RESULTS 1995

School	County	P				*A		A		B		C		D		E		F		G		U	
Stowe School	BUCKS	83	103	8.7	94.2	65	7.3	212	31.0	294	63.9	256	92.6	49	98.1	11	99.3	3	99.7	0	99.7	3	100.0
			104	9.0	93.7	55	6.6	196	22.2	268	50.9	313	84.4	105	95.6	31	98.9	5	99.5	1	99.6	4	100.0
Stowford	GR LON	204	8	7.7	50.0	4	6.5	3	11.3	11	29.0	18	58.1	10	74.2	6	83.9	6	93.5	2	96.8	2	100.0
			13	6.0	0.0	0	0.0	3	3.9	9	15.6	18	39.0	22	67.5	14	85.7	6	93.5	3	97.4	2	100.0
Streatham Hill & Clapham	GR LON	204	59	9.0	100	46	8.6	169	40.4	209	79.7	83	95.3	24	99.8	1	100.0						
High School G			60	8.8	96.8	37	6.6	174	34.7	154	64.2	128	88.7	51	98.4	6	99.6	2	100.0	0	100.0	0	100.0
Sunderland High School	TYNE	282	31	9.6	96.8	34	11.4	66	33.4	108	69.6	70	93.0	20	99.7	1	100.0						
			35	8.7	94.3	25	7.7	92	31.5	77	56.5	78	81.8	38	94.2	13	98.4	5	100.0				
Surbiton High School	GR LON	204	78	9.8	98.7	56	7.3	244	39.3	294	77.9	140	96.2	21	99.0	7	99.9	1	100.0				
			65	9.6	100	75	12.1	234	39.7	204	72.2	128	92.7	36	98.4	8	99.7	2	100.0				
Sutton High School GPDST	GR LON	205	85	9.9	98.8	147	17.5	369	61.4	240	90.0	73	98.7	11	100.0								
			85	9.1	97.6	171	20.9	385	53.8	215	81.4	103	94.6	33	98.8	8	99.9	1	100.0				
Sutton Valence School	KENT	164	73	8.9	87.7	45	6.9	149	29.7	225	64.2	148	86.8	60	96.0	16	98.5	8	99.7	0	99.7	2	100.0
			69	9.0	87.5	18	3.4	128	21.2	189	51.6	192	82.4	77	94.8	21	98.1	10	99.7	1	99.9	0	100.0
Sydenham High School	GR LON	205	77	8.8	85.7	42	6.2	169	31.3	319	78.5	123	96.7	19	99.6	3	100.0						
GPDST			67	8.6	89.2	45	6.9	146	26.8	172	56.5	152	82.7	66	94.1	25	98.4	8	99.8	1	100.0		
Talbot Heath School	DORSET	112	79	8.8	98.7	83	12.0	266	50.3	256	87.2	84	99.3	5	100.0								
			76	8.9	95.8	92	15.0	261	41.1	221	73.6	132	93.1	34	98.1	11	99.7	2	100.0				
Taunton School	SOMERSET	238	106	8.6	84.9	82	9.0	260	37.4	277	67.7	166	85.9	81	94.7	32	98.2	11	99.5	4	99.9	1	100.0
			114	8.7	88.7	65	7.0	292	30.5	274	58.0	235	81.5	109	92.4	49	97.3	19	99.2	5	99.7	2	100.0
Teesside High School for	CLEVE	96	64	8.9	98.4	82	14.4	147	40.2	208	76.7	106	95.3	22	99.1	5	100.0						
Girls			62	8.7	89.1	54	11.2	217	42.5	150	70.4	116	92.0	33	98.1	8	99.6	2	100.0				
Tettenhall College	W MIDS	290	54	9.0	70.4	15	3.1	67	16.8	125	42.4	145	72.1	100	92.6	26	98.0	9	99.8	1	100.0		
			61	8.7	75.9	26	4.8	68	13.9	114	35.6	139	62.0	106	82.1	55	92.6	28	97.9	7	99.2	4	100.0
Thetford Grammar School	NORFOLK	217	37	9.0	94.6	31	9.3	112	42.9	120	79.0	49	93.7	15	98.2	4	99.4	2	100.0				
			39	8.9	94.9	18	5.1	94	28.2	105	58.4	89	84.1	35	94.1	16	98.7	4	99.9	0	99.9	1	100.0
Thornlow School	DORSET	112	29	8.2	65.5	8	3.4	28	15.1	63	41.6	61	67.2	46	86.6	11	97.9	1	98.3	4	100.0		
			31	7.8	58.3	10	5.2	26	11.5	47	30.9	61	56.0	44	74.1	32	87.2	23	96.7	6	99.2	2	100.0
Thorpe Hall School	ESSEX	121	30	8.1	56.7	5	2.1	25	12.4	55	35.1	69	63.6	54	86.0	28	97.5	6	100.0				
			30	7.7	69.0	4	1.7	22	9.8	54	33.0	75	65.1	49	86.0	21	95.0	10	99.3	1	99.7	0	100.0
Thorpe House School	NORFOLK	217	40	8.8	85.0	43	12.2	79	34.7	101	63.4	78	85.5	40	96.9	7	98.9	2	99.4	2	100.0		
			40	8.4	78.9	5	1.6	50	15.2	87	41.2	100	71.0	59	88.7	24	95.8	12	99.4	2	100.0		
Thornton College	BUCKS	84	25	8.4	80.0	11	5.2	41	24.8	65	53.3	65	84.3	19	93.3	13	99.5	1	100.0				
			41	8.7	77.4	13	4.9	65	19.1	91	44.7	96	71.7	58	88.0	25	95.1	14	99.0	3	99.8	0	100.0
Tonbridge School	KENT	164	128	9.5	100	205	16.9	527	60.3	355	89.6	120	99.5	6	100.0								
			128	10.4	100	172	13.9	604	47.7	445	80.9	205	96.2	40	99.2	9	99.9	1	100.0	0	100.0	0	100.0
Tormead School	SURREY	265	62	8.8	95.2	101	18.6	193	54.1	149	81.6	73	95.0	20	98.7	4	99.4	3	100.0				
			54	8.9	100	103	21.6	257	57.3	147	87.6	50	97.9	8	99.6	2	100.0						
Tower College	MERSEY	214	21	9.2	100	16	8.2	75	46.9	69	82.5	29	97.4	5	100.0								
			27	8.8	96.6	24	9.3	87	38.7	76	70.6	53	92.9	14	98.7	3	100.0						
Tower House	N WALES	310	11	8.0	72.7	6	6.8	22	31.8	12	45.5	32	81.8	11	94.3	4	98.9	1	100.0				
			12	9.5	85.7	2	2.9	23	20.1	23	40.3	30	66.5	19	83.2	11	92.8	7	98.9	1	99.8	0	100.0
Towers Convent School, The	W SUSSEX	279	32	9.7	84.4	10	3.2	81	29.2	105	62.8	68	84.6	34	95.5	10	98.7	4	100.0				
			31	8.7	82.6	7	3.2	67	25.2	74	52.6	73	79.6	35	92.6	14	97.8	5	99.6	1	100.0		
Trent College	DERBYS	102	110	8.7	97.3	100	14.2	255	33.2	335	64.5	263	89.1	75	96.2	39	99.7	4	100.0	0	99.6	4	100.0
			85	9.6	93.1	36	4.2	265	33.2	286	68.1	190	91.3	52	97.7	15	99.5	4	100.0				
Trinity School	DEVON	106	33	8.6	81.8	5	1.8	28	11.6	92	43.9	91	75.8	48	92.6	15	97.9	6	100.0				
			36	7.7	0.0	0	0.0	37	13.3	60	34.8	92	67.8	46	84.3	28	94.3	11	98.3	4	99.7	0	100.0
Trinity School	GR LON	206	125	10.7	100	96	7.2	348	33.3	578	76.6	255	95.7	50	99.5	7	100.0						
			116	9.6	97.3	109	9.1	431	40.7	366	73.6	216	93.0	61	98.5	14	99.8	2	100.0	0	100.0	0	100.0
Truro High School for Girls	CORNWALL	98	40	8.5	87.5	31	9.1	104	39.8	117	74.3	56	90.9	14	95.0	17	100.0						
			62	8.7	94.5	72	14.7	191	38.2	165	68.9	113	89.9	38	97.0	13	99.4	3	100.0	0	100.0	0	100.0
Truro School	CORNWALL	98	127	9.1	98.4	127	11.0	396	45.1	381	78.0	204	95.6	43	99.3	7	99.9	0	99.9	0	99.9	1	100.0
			113	9.0	89.5	75	7.4	323	33.0	271	59.5	253	84.3	109	94.9	34	98.2	14	99.6	2	99.8	2	100.0
Tudor Hall School	OXON	230	43	9.2	100	41	10.3	172	53.7	157	93.2	27	100.0										
			41	9.0	100	32	7.5	146	41.2	108	78.0	68	96.4	12	99.7	1	99.9	0	99.9	0	99.9		
University College School	GR LON	207	107	9.0	100	190	16.7	447	66.0	247	91.6	77	99.6	3	99.9	1	100.0						
			105	8.9	99.1	159	16.5	517	58.7	245	84.9	108	96.4	25	99.1	6	99.7	2	99.9	0	99.9	0	100.0
Uplands School	DORSET	112	22	10.0	86.4	3	1.4	26	13.2	69	44.5	76	79.1	27	91.4	9	95.5	4	97.3	6	100.0		
			29	8.2	84.0	1	0.5	26	11.1	52	33.3	80	67.4	45	86.6	21	95.6	6	98.1	3	99.4	1	100.0

389

GCSE ENGLAND & WALES RESULTS 1995

School	County	P	*A		A		B		C		D		E		F		G		U	
Uppingham School	LEICS	173	90	9.6	95.6	74	8.6	267	39.7	314	76.2	156	94.3	40	99.0	8	99.9	1 100.0		
			112	9.1	92.6	77	9.2	316	32.5	319	63.9	283	91.7	71	98.7	11	99.8	2 100.0		
Ursuline College	KENT	164	48	9.3	77.1	32	7.2	81	25.3	136	55.8	93	76.7	81	94.8	19	99.1	4 100.0		
			50	8.6	89.7	11	2.1	104	24.5	129	54.4	103	78.2	56	91.2	28	97.7	9 99.8	1 100.0	
Victoria College	C.I.	88	86	9.4	84.9	71	8.8	180	31.1	235	60.1	186	83.2	78	92.8	37	97.4	17 99.5	2 99.8	2 100.0
			88	8.8	93.4	41	4.6	211	28.2	255	61.0	190	85.5	74	95.0	24	98.1	12 99.6	2 99.9	0 100.0
Virgo Fidelis School	GR LON	207	34	8.5	97.1	13	4.5	63	26.4	89	57.3	99	91.7	17	97.6	6	99.7	1 100.0		
			27	8.6	74.1	10	4.5	52	24.7	54	48.1	68	77.5	34	92.2	11	97.0	7 100.0		
Wakefield Girls' High School	W YORKS	307	128	9.0	100	264	22.8	395	56.9	385	90.2	104	99.1	10 100.0							
			118	9.0	100	211	19.9	502	51.4	315	81.1	156	95.8	33	99.0	10	99.9	1 100.0		
Walthamstow Hall	KENT	164	72	9.0	94.4	77	11.9	202	43.2	206	75.1	109	92.0	37	97.7	11	99.4	4 100.0		
			62	9.0	93.7	98	14.2	223	43.6	180	75.9	98	93.5	28	98.6	6	99.6	2 100.0		
Warminster School	WILTS	294	64	8.1	85.9	37	7.1	111	28.6	162	59.8	126	84.2	60	95.8	17	99.0	5 100.0		
			66	8.2	82.6	25	4.4	78	15.4	133	40.1	166	71.0	95	88.6	43	96.6	14 99.2	3 99.8	1 100.0
Warwick School	W'WICKS	285	145	9.8	97.9	245	17.2	470	50.2	459	82.5	201	96.6	43	99.6	4	99.9	1 100.0		
			124	9.4	97.5	75	6.3	533	47.1	356	77.7	197	94.7	48	98.8	12	99.8	1 99.9	1 100.0	
Wellingborough School	N'HANTS	219	77	8.7	94.8	89	13.3	159	37.1	206	67.9	160	91.8	46	98.7	7	99.7	2 100.0		
			94	8.8	94.0	55	7.5	247	31.3	232	59.5	212	85.2	86	95.6	28	99.0	7 99.9	1 100.0	
Wellington College	BERKS	79	156	10.0	98.7	248	15.9	468	46.0	536	80.4	255	96.7	35	99.0	13	99.8	2 99.9	1 100.0	
			155	10.1	99.3	116	8.3	572	37.9	561	73.6	334	94.9	67	99.2	12	99.9	1 100.0		
Wellington School	MERSEY		26	8.8	80.8	10	4.4	21	13.5	60	39.7	83	76.0	27	87.8	19	96.1	8 99.6	1 100.0	
			40	8.5	64.5	15	5.7	31	10.1	61	28.3	104	59.2	70	80.0	42	92.5	18 97.9	5 99.3	2 100.0
Wellington School	SOMERSET	238	143	8.9	92.3	129	10.1	333	36.3	415	68.8	267	89.6	101	97.7	22	99.5	7 100.0		
			126	8.8	92.0	113	9.2	342	33.0	313	61.2	279	86.4	96	95.1	40	98.7	11 99.7	1 99.8	2 100.0
Wells Cathedral School	SOMERSET	238	87	8.5	94.3	135	18.2	180	42.4	212	70.9	163	92.9	42	98.5	9	99.7	2 100.0		.
			94	8.6	91.2	108	12.4	258	34.9	248	65.8	172	87.3	73	96.4	22	99.1	6 99.9	1 100.0	0 100.0
Wentworth Milton Mount School	DORSET	113	52	8.7	92.3	45	10.0	88	29.4	179	69.0	101	91.4	26	97.1	9	99.1	4 100.0		
			58	8.7	80.4	9	2.3	109	22.0	145	50.8	148	80.2	69	93.9	24	98.7	6 99.9	0 99.9	0 100.0
West Buckland School	DEVON	107	77	9.2	94.8	77	10.8	171	34.9	283	74.7	141	94.5	26	98.2	9	99.4	4 100.0		
			79	8.4	87.8	68	8.2	179	29.2	176	55.9	188	84.3	70	94.9	25	98.7	7 99.8	1 99.9	0 100.0
West Heath School	KENT	165	27	8.7	96.3	12	5.1	45	24.2	103	67.8	55	91.1	16	97.6	5 100.0				
			29	8.5	100	9	3.7	60	25.0	83	58.5	73	87.9	24	97.6	5	99.6	1 100.0		
Westbourne College	S WALES		11	10.6	100	29	24.8	35	54.7	38	87.2	15 100.0								
			17	9.6	80.0	13	8.6	48	30.9	49	60.6	41	85.5	19	97.0	3	98.8	1 99.4	0 99.4	1 100.0
Westfield School	TYNE	282	32	9.0	87.5	17	5.9	67	29.3	76	55.7	83	84.7	26	93.7	12	97.9	6 100.0		
			34	8.5	87.5	28	10.1	65	24.4	73	49.5	94	81.8	36	94.2	11	98.0	4 99.4	1 99.7	0 100.0
Westholme School	LANCS	170	102	9.0	97.0	193	21.0	290	52.6	297	85.0	122	98.3	12	99.6	4 100.0				
			99	9.0	97.0	170	18.7	376	46.1	268	76.2	159	94.1	38	98.4	12	99.6	2 100.0	0 100.0	0 100.0
Westminster School	GR LON	208	130	10.1	100	396	30.1	572	73.5	298	96.1	46	99.6	4	99.9	0	99.9	1 100.0		
			105	10.1	100	237	21.0	599	60.7	285	87.5	107	97.6	21	99.6	4 100.0	0 100.0	0 100.0		
Westonbirt School	GLOS	125	50	9.4	90.0	37	7.9	119	33.1	188	73.0	77	89.4	36	97.0	10	99.2	4 100.0		
			41	8.8	87.5	30	6.7	63	18.9	129	54.1	110	84.2	43	95.9	13	99.5	2 100.0		
Westwing School	AVON	67	9	7.8	55.6	0	0.0	6	8.6	20	37.1	22	68.6	9	81.4	10	95.7	1 97.1	2 100.0	
			17	7.5	52.4	5	3.2	10	8.6	29	31.4	37	60.4	23	78.5	18	92.6	6 97.3	3 99.7	0 100.0
Whitgift School	GR LON	208	150	10.1	100	218	14.4	483	46.4	517	80.6	249	97.1	37	99.5	6	99.9	1 100.0		
			131	9.7	99.2	171	13.0	523	44.0	408	76.2	212	92.9	62	97.8	18	99.3	5 99.7	1 99.7	3 100.0
William Hulme's Grammar School	GR MANCH	211	113	6.6	94.7	57	5.9	291	35.8	336	70.3	215	92.4	56	98.2	17	99.9	0 99.9	0 99.9	1 100.0
			115	8.5	96.3	101	10.8	343	37.2	322	70.1	196	90.2	68	97.2	21	99.3	5 99.8	1 99.9	0 100.0
Wimbledon High School GPDST	GR LON	208	80	10.1	100	211	26.1	335	67.7	202	92.7	49	98.8	3	99.1	0	99.1	0 99.1	0 99.1	7 100.0
			69	9.0	99.8	147	19.9	345	59.8	170	87.0	64	97.3	16	99.8	1 100.0				
Winchester College	HANTS	135	132	8.4	100	244	22.0	600	76.2	236	97.6	26	99.9	1 100.0							
			131	8.9	98.4	118	11.2	813	71.2	271	94.3	62	99.6	5 100.0							
Wisbech Grammar School	CAMBS	87	91	9.0	92.3	57	7.0	199	31.3	291	66.8	166	87.1	83	97.2	18	99.4	5 100.0		
			93	8.8	92.0	36	4.0	214	27.1	250	57.7	239	87.0	75	96.2	23	99.0	6 99.8	1 99.9	0 100.0
Wispers School	SURREY	266	18	7.9	72.2	1	0.7	26	18.9	45	50.3	47	83.2	15	93.7	6	97.9	2 99.3	1 100.0	
			30	7.5	62.5	1	0.5	25	11.0	56	35.7	75	68.7	41	86.7	22	96.4	6 99.0	1 99.5	1 100.0
Withington Girls School	GR MANCH	211	70	9.0	100	336	53.2	213	87.0	80	99.7	2 100.0									
			68	8.6	100	285	44.9	407	79.2	99	96.1	21	99.7	2 100.0							
Woldingham School	SURREY	266	68	9.4	97.1	74	11.6	193	41.7	255	81.6	95	96.4	17	99.1	6 100.0				
			67	9.2	100	34	5.3	215	36.0	212	70.3	145	93.8	33	99.2	5 100.0					

School	County	P				*A		A		B		C		D		E		F		G		U	
olverhampton Grammar School	W MIDS	291	91	9.9	98.9	139	15.4	329	51.8	313	86.4	102	97.7	17	99.6	3	99.9	1	100.0				
			90	9.2	100	73	7.9	391	48.9	284	83.0	109	96.1	27	99.4	4	99.9	1	100.0				
oodbridge School	SUFFOLK	246	83	9.5	94.0	66	8.4	242	39.0	263	72.3	157	92.2	56	99.2	5	99.9	0	99.9	0	99.9	1	100.0
			84	9.2	96.7	66	7.5	258	35.2	258	68.8	166	90.3	51	97.0	16	99.0	5	99.7	1	99.8	1	100.0
oodhouse Grove School	W YORKS	307	87	8.9	78.2	31	4.0	129	20.8	222	49.6	236	80.3	102	93.5	28	97.1	15	99.1	5	99.7	2	100.0
			85	9.3	93.5	26	3.5	155	20.3	221	48.3	251	80.1	109	94.0	38	98.8	7	99.7	2	99.9	0	100.0
orksop College	NOTTS	224	66	8.8	77.3	25	4.3	106	22.6	157	49.7	157	76.9	69	88.8	41	95.9	16	98.6	4	99.3	4	100.0
			85	8.6	85.7	18	2.5	146	20.7	203	48.6	212	77.8	103	92.0	42	97.8	13	99.6	2	99.8	1	100.0
orth School	W SUSSEX	279	75	9.4	100	47	6.7	239	40.6	279	80.3	107	95.5	28	99.4	3	99.9	1	100.0				
			65	10.4	89.4	32	4.4	130	20.1	207	50.6	210	81.7	83	93.9	32	98.6	6	99.5	1	99.7	2	100.0
rekin College	SALOP	234	59	8.7	89.8	22	4.3	91	21.9	194	59.6	152	89.1	46	98.1	9	99.8	1	100.0				
			71	9.3	82.8	10	1.7	119	18.3	183	46.1	224	80.0	93	94.1	31	98.8	6	99.8	1	99.9	0	100.0
roxall Abbey	W'WICKS	285	13	7.8	53.8	1	1.0	5	5.9	19	24.8	31	55.4	23	78.2	16	94.1	5	99.0	1	100.0		
			16	7.6	44.4	0	0.0	7	5.6	19	20.9	37	50.5	30	74.6	16	87.4	9	94.7	3	97.1	3	100.0
ychwood School	OXON	230	24	8.2	91.7	7	3.6	43	25.5	77	64.8	44	87.2	16	95.4	8	99.5	1	100.0				
			25	8.9	90.0	8	3.0	72	32.9	69	63.5	53	87.0	21	96.4	6	99.0	2	99.9	0	99.9	0	100.0
ycliffe College	GLOS	126	57	9.3	93.0	37	7.0	127	30.9	165	62.0	148	89.8	36	96.6	13	99.1	4	99.8	0	99.8	1	100.0
			54	10.0	90.4	25	4.9	131	25.4	147	52.8	158	82.3	61	93.7	24	98.2	7	99.5	2	99.9	0	100.0
ycombe Abbey School	BUCKS	84	79	9.3	100	251	34.1	340	80.3	133	98.4	12	100.0										
			80	9.5	100	170	22.2	507	71.7	170	94.3	34	98.8	7	99.7	2	100.0	0	100.0	0	100.0	0	100.0
keham House School	HANTS	135	36	8.5	91.7	15	4.9	95	36.1	122	76.1	53	93.4	16	98.7	4	100.0						
			34	8.6	89.1	51	12.4	81	31.5	83	60.2	79	87.5	27	96.9	8	99.7	1	100.0				
rm School	CLEVE	96	72	9.7	97.2	44	6.3	168	30.4	286	71.3	165	95.0	28	99.0	6	99.9	1	100.0				
			62	9.6	100	49	9.0	194	34.5	199	68.2	138	91.5	37	97.8	9	99.3	3	99.8	1	100.0		
hudi Menuhin School	SURREY	267	14	2.4	21.4	7	21.2	19	78.8	5	93.9	2	100.0										
			14	2.2	21.4	6	19.4	13	61.3	7	83.9	2	90.3	2	96.8	1	100.0						
rk College for Girls	N YORKS	301	25	8.9	92.0	26	11.7	38	28.8	79	64.4	59	91.0	17	98.6	3	100.0						
			29	9.1	92.9	45	18.1	95	39.4	71	66.3	63	90.2	17	96.6	7	99.2	2	100.0				

GCSE ENGLAND & WALES RESULTS 1995

SCOTTISH EXAMINATION RESULTS 1995

NAME OF SCHOOL		No PUPILS		No CANDIDATES		No PRESENTATIONS	GRADES ACHIEVED A B C D E N L
Albyn School for Girls	6th yr	32	Highers	24	Highers	50	7 14 18 10 0
			CSYS	20	CSYS	42	3 20 14 5 0
			A-level		A-level		
	5th yr	41	Highers	40	Highers	173	57 75 28 12 0
							1 2 3 4 5 6
	4th yr	38	Standard	38	Standard	287	126 128 25 8 0 0
							*A A B C D E F/G
			GCSE		GCSE		
Dollar Academy	6th yr	113	Highers	113	Highers	220	40 59 81 31 0
			CSYS	80	CSYS	139	20 30 54 26 9
			A-level	16	A-level	16	2 6 1 3 1 2
	5th yr	129	Highers	129	Highers	540	144 153 126 97 0
							1 2 3 4 5 6
	4th yr	138	Standard	138	Standard	1071	513 389 130 28 8 0
							*A A B C D E F/G
			GCSE		GCSE		
Dundee High School	6th yr	102	Highers	90	Highers	185	21 50 57 41 0 1
			CSYS	69	CSYS	124	39 36 40 3 6
			A-level		A-level		
	5th yr	137	Highers	137	Highers	602	224 159 140 58 0
							1 2 3 4 5 6
	4th yr	128	Standard	128	Standard	1063	659 297 83 20 4 0
							*A A B C D E F/G
			GCSE		GCSE		
Edinburgh Academy, The	6th yr	70	Highers	30	Highers	77	7 19 31 17 0
			CSYS		CSYS		
			A-level	61	A-level	153	44 31 34 20 10 11
	5th yr	76	Highers	60	Highers	205	34 58 68 33 0
	4th yr	78	Standard		Standard		1 2 3 4 5 6
							*A A B C D E F/G
			GCSE	78	GCSE	688	44 112 201 221 80 23 7
Fettes College	6th yr	79	Highers	47	Highers	185	37 51 59 25 0
			CSYS		CSYS		
			A-level	45	A-level	135	38 38 33 22 3 1
	5th yr	77	Highers	27	Highers	29	11 8 10 0 0
	4th yr	76	Standard		Standard		1 2 3 4 5 6
							*A A B C D E F/G
			GCSE	76	GCSE	658	134 211 162 91 43 12 5

NAME OF SCHOOL	No PUPILS		No CANDIDATES		No PRESENTATIONS		GRADES ACHIEVED						
							A	B	C	D	E	N	U
George Heriot's School	6th yr	138	Highers	113	Highers	249	20	48	99	63	0		19
			CSYS	102	CSYS	216	30	54	62	40	27		3
			A-level		A-level								
	5th yr	165	Highers	164	Highers	715	188	179	221	101	0		26
							1	2	3	4	5	6	
	4th yr	173	Standard	172	Standard	1125	475	438	161	39	4	4	4
							*A	A	B	C	D	E F/G	U
			GCSE		GCSE								
George Watson's College	6th yr	197	Highers	173	Highers	392	48	100	118	97	0		29
			CSYS	114	CSYS	230	56	68	59	33	11		3
			A-level		A-level								
	5th yr	217	Highers	213	Highers	875	315	280	172	93	0		15
							1	2	3	4	5	6	
	4th yr	216	Standard	216	Standard	1231	408	498	227	78	13	2	5
							*A	A	B	C	D	E F/G	U
			GCSE		GCSE								
Glasgow Academy,The	6th yr	103	Highers	83	Highers	207	15	56	71	45	0		20
			CSYS		CSYS								
			A-level	50	A-level	92	23	22	25	18	2	2	0
	5th yr	98	Highers	97	Highers	398	114	106	113	52	0		13
							1	2	3	4	5	6	
	4th yr	113	Standard	113	Standard	902	379	341	141	35	5	1	0
							*A	A	B	C	D	E F/G	U
			GCSE		GCSE								
Glasgow,The High School of	6th yr	89	Highers	68	Highers	113	34	33	23	15	0		8
			CSYS	73	CSYS	135	33	44	41	11	6		0
			A-level		A-level		-						
	5th yr	87	Highers	87	Highers	414	196	125	69	21	0		3
							1	2	3	4	5	6	
	4th yr	91	Standard	91	Standard	723	546	143	30	4	0	0	0
							*A	A	B	C	D	E F/G	U
			GCSE		GCSE								
Glenalmond College	6th yr	61	Highers	22	Highers	100	17	25	41	11	0		6
			CSYS		CSYS								
			A-level	48	A-level	136	46	39	31	14	4	2	0
	5th yr	40	Highers	18	Highers	18	3	6	9	0	0		0
							1	2	3	4	5	6	
	4th yr	40	Standard		Standard								
							*A	A	B	C	D	E F/G	U
			GCSE	40	GCSE	362	34	85	107	101	25	7 3	0
Gordonstoun School	6th yr		Highers										
			CSYS		CSYS								
			A-level	105	A-level	319	42	70	76	65	37	20	9
	5th yr		Highers		Highers								
							1	2	3	4	5	6	
	4th yr	74	Standard		Standard								
							*A	A	B	C	D	E F/G	U
			GCSE	74	GCSE	661	25	140	227	161	91	14 3	0
Hutchesons' Grammar School	6th yr	147	Highers	109	Highers	219	52	82	63	17	0		5
			CSYS	73	CSYS	94	25	26	23	15	4		1
			A-level	85	A-level	130	45	27	29	16	8	3	2
	5th yr	207	Highers	207	Highers	1006	607	206	149	35	0		9
							1	2	3	4	5	6	
	4th yr	193	Standard	193	Standard	1011	753	235	20	3	0	0	0
							*A	A	B	C	D	E F/G	U
			GCSE		GCSE								

SCOTTISH EXAMINATION RESULTS 1995

393

SCOTTISH EXAMINATION RESULTS 1995

NAME OF SCHOOL		No PUPILS		No CANDIDATES		No PRESENTATIONS		GRADES ACHIEVED						
								A	B	C	D	E	N	U
Keil School	6th yr	31	Highers	30	Highers	69		5	13	29	12	0		10
			CSYS	4	CSYS	5		0	3	1	1	0		0
			A-level	8	A-level	13		0	3	2	5	0	1	2
	5th yr	23	Highers	23	Highers	82		13	22	23	17	0		7
								1	2	3	4	5	6	
	4th yr	33	Standard	33	Standard	265		62	106	70	24	3	0	0
							*A	A	B	C	D	E	F/G	U
			GCSE		GCSE									
Kelvinside Academy	6th yr	51	Highers	48	Highers	137		10	29	47	28	0		23
			CSYS	5	CSYS	8		0	4	4	0	0		0
			A-level	14	A-level	30		4	3	6	8	5	2	2
	5th yr	66	Highers	61	Highers	243		58	55	65	51	0		14
								1	2	3	4	5	6	
	4th yr	85	Standard	85	Standard	593		185	209	135	43	20	1	0
							*A	A	B	C	D	E	F/G	U
			GCSE		GCSE									
Kilgraston School	6th yr	36	Highers	34	Highers	84		12	21	33	16	0		2
			CSYS		CSYS									
			A-level	20	A-level	25		8	2	5	5	3	2	0
	5th yr	44	Highers	41	Highers	148		22	41	52	30	0		3
								1	2	3	4	5	6	
	4th yr	41	Standard	41	Standard	296		102	115	57	18	2	2	0
							*A	A	B	C	D	E	F/G	U
			GCSE		GCSE									
Laurel Bank School	6th yr	32	Highers	30	Highers	60		22	17	14	7	0		0
			CSYS	18	CSYS	28		11	9	5	3	0		0
			A-level		A-level									
	5th yr	31	Highers	31	Highers	134		55	48	26	5	0		0
								1	2	3	4	5	6	
	4th yr	47	Standard	47	Standard	361		172	126	47	14	2	0	0
							*A	A	B	C	D	E	F/G	U
			GCSE		GCSE									
Lomond School	6th yr	46	Highers	23	Highers	90		14	16	25	20	0		15
			CSYS		CSYS									
			A-level	24	A-level	41		12	7	10	6	4	1	1
	5th yr	52	Highers	50	Highers	199		42	41	56	43	0		17
								1	2	3	4	5	6	
	4th yr	57	Standard	57	Standard	442		179	160	74	26	2	1	0
							*A	A	B	C	D	E	F/G	U
			GCSE		GCSE									
Loretto School	6th yr	74	Highers	39	Highers	56		11	13	16	13	0		3
			CSYS		CSYS									
			A-level	74	A-level	202		39	43	49	31	23	13	4
	5th yr	75	Highers	5	Highers	5		4	1	0	0	0		0
								1	2	3	4	5	6	
	4th yr	53	Standard		Standard									
							*A	A	B	C	D	E	F/G	U
			GCSE	53	GCSE	476	38	129	199	83	23	4	0	0
Mary Erskine School	6th yr	91	Highers	81	Highers	180		47	46	54	28	0		5
			CSYS	59	CSYS	106		18	31	39	14	3		1
			A-level	9	A-level	8		1	2	4	0	1	0	0
	5th yr	99	Highers	99	Highers	444		174	122	100	39	0		9
								1	2	3	4	5	6	
	4th yr	115	Standard	115	Standard	881		452	327	85	16	1	0	0
							*A	A	B	C	D	E	F/G	U
			GCSE	30	GCSE	30	1	11	10	8	0	0	0	0

NAME OF SCHOOL		No PUPILS		No CANDIDATES		No PRESENTATIONS	GRADES ACHIEVED						
							A	B	C	D	E	N	U
Merchiston Castle School	6th yr	74	Highers	38	Highers	166	16	36	87	23	0		4
			CSYS		CSYS								
			A-level	36	A-level	107	43	22	16	16	4	5	1
	5th yr		Highers		Highers								
	4th yr	66	Standard		Standard		1	2	3	4	5	6	
			GCSE	66	GCSE	636	A	A B	B	C	D	E F/G	U
							12	156	213	173	62	16 4	0
Morrison's Academy	6th yr	77	Highers	51	Highers	121	16	25	43	21	0		16
			CSYS	15	CSYS	23	7	5	6	4	1		0
			A-level	46	A-level	79	22	16	17	12	6	5	1
	5th yr	94	Highers	94	Highers	424	157	79	91	69	0		28
	4th yr	85	Standard	85	Standard	666	1	2	3	4	5	6	
							237	257	134	27	6	5	0
			GCSE		GCSE		A	A B	B	C	D	E F/G	U
Park School	6th yr	23	Highers	18	Highers	32	7	10	9	1	0		5
			CSYS	4	CSYS	4	0	0	3	1	0		0
			A-level	10	A-level	11	1	1	5	1	2	1	0
	5th yr	38	Highers	38	Highers	154	55	47	39	11	0		2
	4th yr	35	Standard	35	Standard	300	1	2	3	4	5	6	
							127	111	35	22	5	0	0
			GCSE		GCSE		A	A B	B	C	D	E F/G	U
Rannoch School	6th yr	44	Highers	42	Highers	161	24	54	43	25	0		15
			CSYS		CSYS								
			A-level		A-level		-						
	5th yr	36	Highers	1	Highers	1	1	0	0	0	0		0
	4th yr	49	Standard	49	Standard	365	1	2	3	4	5	6	
							71	129	100	50	14	1	0
			GCSE		GCSE		A	A B	B	C	D	E F/G	U
Robert Gordon's College	6th yr	115	Highers	98	Highers	223	32	68	54	51	0		18
			CSYS	65	CSYS	118	20	33	39	16	10		0
			A-level		A-level								
	5th yr	160	Highers	160	Highers	739	208	265	194	53	0		19
	4th yr	170	Standard	170	Standard	1187	1	2	3	4	5	6	
							653	409	102	20	2	1	0
			GCSE		GCSE		A	A B	B	C	D	E F/G	U
St Aloysius' College	6th yr	88	Highers	83	Highers	222	32	82	76	24	0		8
			CSYS	5	CSYS	5	0	2	2	1	0		0
			A-level	38	A-level	62	10	13	21	10	4	4	0
	5th yr	140	Highers	140	Highers	643	223	177	130	89	0		24
	4th yr	144	Standard	144	Standard	849	1	2	3	4	5	6	
							513	243	76	13	4	0	0
			GCSE		GCSE		A	A B	B	C	D	E F/G	U
St Columba's School	6th yr	36	Highers	32	Highers	48	13	14	15	4	0		2
			CSYS	29	CSYS	48	14	13	11	8	2		0
			A-level		A-level								
	5th yr	43	Highers	43	Highers	179	69	53	43	9	0		5
	4th yr	51	Standard	51	Standard	363	1	2	3	4	5	6	
							238	92	29	4	0	0	0
			GCSE		GCSE		A	A B	B	C	D	E F/G	U

NAME OF SCHOOL	No PUPILS		No CANDIDATES		No PRESENTATIONS		GRADES ACHIEVED						
							A	B	C	D	E	N	U
St Denis and Cranley School	6th yr	10	Highers	8	Highers	15	3	2	2	6	0		2
			CSYS	6	CSYS	11	2	2	3	4	0		0
			A-level		A-level								
	5th yr	31	Highers	29	Highers	86	15	27	23	16	0		5
							1	2	3	4	5	6	
	4th yr	20	Standard	20	Standard	143	46	34	23	27	9	3	1
							*A	A	B	C	D	E F/G	U
			GCSE		GCSE								
St George's School for Girls	6th yr	69	Highers	60	Highers	325	105	124	75	19	0		2
			CSYS	11	CSYS	13	3	6	4	0	0		0
			A-level	42	A-level	95	27	37	17	10	4	0	0
	5th yr	89	Highers	83	Highers	352	158	114	63	14	0		3
							1	2	3	4	5	6	
	4th yr	87	Standard	87	Standard	294	223	49	19	2	1	0	0
							*A	A	B	C	D	E F/G	U
			GCSE	87	GCSE	464	90	205	121	42	6	0	0
St Leonards School	6th yr	47	Highers	14	Highers	32	6	10	12	4	0		0
			CSYS		CSYS								
			A-level	42	A-level	126	37	35	27	12	7	6	2
	5th yr	47	Highers	13	Highers	16	11	4	1	0	0		0
	4th yr		Standard		Standard								
							1	2	3	4	5	6	
							*A	A	B	C	D	E F/G	U
			GCSE	52	GCSE	394	70	108	125	69	19	3	0
St Margaret's School for Girls	6th yr	29	Highers	26	Highers	49	15	14	16	3	0		1
			CSYS	21	CSYS	35	10	12	12	1	0		0
			A-level		A-level								
	5th yr	44	Highers	41	Highers	170	65	45	42	16	0		2
							1	2	3	4	5	6	
	4th yr	44	Standard	44	Standard	340	168	123	37	11	1	0	0
							*A	A	B	C	D	E F/G	U
			GCSE		GCSE								
St Margaret's School	6th yr	48	Highers	44	Highers	98	14	25	33	22	0		4
			CSYS	29	CSYS	37	4	14	15	4	0		0
			A-level	9	A-level	9	3	2	0	2	2	0	0
	5th yr	75	Highers	75	Highers	315	82	110	92	28	0		3
							1	2	3	4	5	6	
	4th yr	49	Standard	49	Standard	383	165	149	61	8	0	0	0
							*A	A	B	C	D	E F/G	U
			GCSE		GCSE								
Stewart's Melville College	6th yr	101	Highers	89	Highers	189	34	43	63	36	0		13
			CSYS	77	CSYS	171	34	45	59	28	4		1
			A-level		A-level								
	5th yr	124	Highers	122	Highers	540	159	148	129	66	0		38
							1	2	3	4	5	6	
	4th yr	141	Standard	141	Standard	1068	447	450	140	28	3	0	0
							*A	A	B	C	D	E F/G	U
			GCSE	51	GCSE	51	0	0	12	25	11	2	0	1
Strathallan School	6th yr	72	Highers	65	Highers	177	35	66	51	23	0		2
			CSYS		CSYS								
			A-level	48	A-level	131	41	33	36	12	9	0	0
	5th yr	83	Highers	1	Highers	1	0	0	1	0	0		0
							1	2	3	4	5	6	
	4th yr	96	Standard	92	Standard	92	44	38	10	0	0	0	0
							*A	A	B	C	D	E F/G	U
			GCSE	92	GCSE	738	96	198	217	151	57	16	3	0

SCOTTISH EXAMINATION RESULTS 1995

NAME OF SCHOOL	No PUPILS		No CANDIDATES		No PRESENTATIONS		GRADES ACHIEVED						
							A	B	C	D	E	N	U
Wellington School	6th yr	29	Highers	27	Highers	50	8	14	19	9	0		0
			CSYS	17	CSYS	29	6	14	8	1	0		0
			A-level		A-level								
	5th yr	39	Highers	39	Highers	146	41	51	36	18	0		0
							1	2	3	4	5	6	
	4th yr	39	Standard	39	Standard	288	151	94	33	7	2	1	0
							*A	A	B	C	D	E F/G	U
			GCSE		GCSE								

SCOTTISH EXAMINATION RESULTS 1995

**ALPHABETICAL
INDEX
TO SCHOOLS**

Abberley Hall *Hereford & worcester* Bg. 138
Abbey Gate College *Cheshire* C 90
Abbey Gate School *Cheshire* C 91
Abbey School *Glos* C 124
Abbey School Woodbridge,The *Suffolk* C 244
Abbey School,The *Berks* Gb 70
Abbot's Hill *Herts* G 144
Abbotsford School *Warks* C 284
Abbotsholme School *Staffs* C 240
Aberdour School *Surrey* C 249
Aberlour House *Scotland* C 315
Abingdon School *Oxon* B 226
Ackworth School *W yorks* C 304
Adcote School for Girls *Salop* G 233
Albyn School for Girls *Scotland* G 315
Aldenham School *Herts* Bg 144
Aldro School *Surrey* B 249
Aldwickbury School *Herts* Bg 144
Alice Ottley School,The *Hereford & worcester* G 138
All Hallows School *Somerset* C 236
Alleyn Court and Eton House *Essex* C 116
Alleyn's Junior School *London (greater)* C 177
Alleyn's School *London (greater)* C 177
Allhallows College *Dorset* C 109
Alpha Prep. School *London (greater)* C 177
Altrincham Prep. School *Cheshire* B 91
Amberfield School *Suffolk* Gb 244
Amberleigh Prep. School *Manchester (greater)* C 211
American Community School *London (greater)* C 178
American Community School *Surrey* C 249
Amesbury School *Surrey* C 249
Ampleforth College Junior School L*Yorkshire (north)* B 297
Ampleforth College *N yorks* B 296
Aravon Preparatory School *RofI* C 327
Ardingly College Junior School *Sussex (west)* C 275
Ardingly College *Sussex (west)* C 275
Ardvreck School *Scotland* C 316
Arnold House School *London (greater)* B 178
Arnold Junior School *Lancs* C 167
Arnold Lodge School *Warks* C 284
Arnold School *Lancs* C 168
Arts Educational London Schools,The *London (greater)* C 178
Arts Educational School *Herts* C 145
Arundale School *Sussex (west)* C 275
Ascham House School *Tyne* B 281
Ashbourne PNEU School *Derbys* C 102
Ashdell Preparatory School *Yorkshire (south)* G 303
Ashdown House *Sussex (east)* C 269
Ashfold *Bucks* C 81
Ashford Junior School *Kent* G 155
Ashford School *Kent* G 156
Ashton House School *London (greater)* C 178
Ashville College *Yorkshire (north)* C 297
Atherley School,The *Hants* Gb 128
Austin Friars School *Cumbria* C 100
Aymestrey School *Hereford & worcester* B 138
Aysgarth School Trust Ltd *Yorkshire (north)* B 297
Ayton School *Yorkshire (north)* C 297
Babington House School *Kent* Gb 156
Bablake Junior School *W Mid* C 287
Bablake School *W Mid* C 287
Badminton Junior School *Avon* G 63
Badminton School *Avon* G 63
Ballard College *Hants* G 128
Ballard Lake Prep School *Hants* G 128
Bancroft's School *Essex* C 117
Bangor Grammar School *N ire* B 325
Barfield School *Surrey* C 249
Barnard Castle School *Durham* C 115
Barnardiston Hall Preparatory School *Suffolk* C 244
Barrow Hills *Surrey* C 250
Baston School *Kent* G 156
Bath High School GPDST *Avon* G 63
Batley Grammar School *Yorkshire* L*(west)* Bg 305
Battle Abbey School *Sussex (east)* C 269
Beachborough School *Bucks* C 82
Beacon School & Winterbourn *Bucks* B 82
Beaconhurst Grange *Scotland* C 316
Bearwood College *Berks* Bg 71
Beaudesert Park *Glos* C 124
Bedales School *Hants* C 128
Bedford High School *Beds* G 69
Bedford Modern Junior School *Beds* B 69
Bedford Modern School *Beds* B 69
Bedford Preparatory School *Beds* B 69
Bedford School *Beds* B 70
Bedgebury School *Kent* Gb 156
Bedstone College *Salop* C 233
Beech Hall School *Cheshire* C 91
Beechwood Park *Herts* C 145
Beechwood School Sacred Heart *Kent* Gb 156
Beeston Hall *Norfolk* C 216
Belfast Royal Academy *NI* C 326
Belhaven Hill *Scotland* C 316
Belmont *London (greater)* B 178
Belmont School *Surrey* C 250
Belvedere School GPDST,The L*Merseyside* G 213
Bembridge School *IoW* C 155
Benenden School *Kent* G 157
Bentham School *Yorkshire (north)* C 297
Berkhamsted Junior School *Herts* B 145
Berkhamsted School for Girls *Herts* Gb 145
Berkhamsted School *Herts* Bg 145
Bethany School *Kent* C 157
Bickley Park School *London (greater)* Bg 179
Bilton Grange *Warks* C 285
Birchfield School *Salop* B 233
Birkdale School *Yorkshire (south)* B 303
Birkenhead High School GPDST L*Merseyside* G 213
Birkenhead School *Merseyside* B 214
Bishop Challoner School *London* L*(greater)* C 179
Bishop's Stortford College *Herts* C 146
Bishop's Stortford College Junior LSchool *Herts* C 146
Blackheath High School GPDST *London (greater)* G 179
Bloxham School *Oxon* Bg 226
Blue Coat School,The *W Mid* C 288
Blundell's School *Devon* C 104
Bodiam Manor *Sussex (east)* C 269
Bolitho School,The *Cornwall* Gb 98
Bolton School (Boys Div.) *Lancs* B 168
Bolton School (Girls Div.) *Lancs* Gb 168
Bootham School *Yorkshire (north)* C 298
Boundary Oak School *Hants* C 129
Bow School *Durham* Bg 115
Bowbrook House School *Hereford & worcester* C 138
Bowbrook School *Hereford & worcester* C 138
Box Hill School *Surrey* C 250
Brabyns School *Cheshire* C 91
Bradfield College *Berks* Bg 71
Bradford Girls' Grammar School L*Yorkshire (west)* Gb 305
Bradford Grammar School *Yorkshire (west)* C 305
Braeside School For Girls *Essex* G 117
Brambletye *Sussex (west)* B 275
Bramcote School *Notts* C 222
Bramcote School *Yorkshire (north)* Bg 298
Bramley School *Surrey* G 250
Brantwood Independent School for Girls *Yorkshire (south)* G 303
Bredon School *Glos* C 124
Brentwood Preparatory School *Essex* B 117
Brentwood School *Essex* C 117
Bretby House School *London (greater)* C 179
Bricklehurst Manor *Sussex (east)* Gb 270
Bridgewater School *Manchester* L*(greater)* C 211
Brigg Preparatory School *Humberside* C 153
Brighton & Hove High School GPDST *Sussex (east)* G 270
Brighton College Junior School *Sussex (east)* C 270
Brighton College *Sussex (east)* C 270
Brigidine School,The *Berks* Gb 71
Bristol Cathedral School *Avon* Bg 63
Bristol Grammar Lower School *Avon* C 63
Bristol Grammar School *Avon* C 64
Broadgate School *Notts* C 223
Broadwater Manor School *Sussex* L*(west)* C 275
Brockhurst *Berks* Bg 71
Bromley High School GPDST *Kent* G 157
Bromsgrove Lower School *Hereford & worcester* C 139
Bromsgrove School *Hereford &* L*worcester* C 139
Bronte House School *Yorkshire (west)* C 305
Bronte School *Kent* C 157
Brooklands School *Staffs* C 241
Bruton School for Girls *Somerset* G 236
Bryanston School *Dorset* C 109
Buchan School,The *IoM* C 154
Buckingham College *London (greater)* Bg 179
Burgess Hill School *Sussex (west)* G 276
Bury Grammar School (Girls) *Lancs* Gb 168
Bury Grammar School *Lancs* B 168
Bury Lawn School *Bucks* C 82
Burys Court *Surrey* C 250
Bute House Preparatory School for Girls *London (greater)* G 180
Butterstone School *Scotland* Gb 316
Cabin Hill *NI* B 326
Caius House School *Manchester* L*(greater)* C 211
Caldicott *Bucks* B 82
Cameron House *London (greater)* C 180
Canbury School *Surrey* C 251
Canford School *Dorset* C 110
Cargilfield *Scotland* C 316
Carleton House Preparatory School *Merseyside* C 214
Carmel College *Oxon* C 227
Carrdus School,The *Oxon* Gb 227
Casterton School *Cumbria* Gb 100
Castle Court *Dorset* C 110
Castle Park *RofI* C 327
Caterham Preparatory School *Surrey* C 251
Caterham School *Surrey* C 251
Cathedral School Llandaff,The *Wales (south)* C 312
Catteral Hall *Yorkshire (north)* C 298
Cavendish School *London (greater)* Gb 180
Cawston College *Norfolk* C 216
Central Newcastle High School GPDST *Tyne And Wear* G 282
Chafyn Grove School *Wilts* C 293
Channing School *London (greater)* G 180
Charterhouse *Surrey* Bg 251
Cheadle Hulme School *Cheshire* C 91
Cheam Hawtreys *Berks* B 71
Cheltenham College *Glos* Bg 125
Cheltenham College Junior School *Glos* C 124
Cheltenham Ladies' College,The *Glos* G 125
Cherry Trees School *Suffolk* C 244
Chesham Prep. School *Bucks* C 82
Chetham's School of Music *Manchester (greater)* C 211
Chigwell Junior School *Essex* B 117
Chigwell School *Essex* Bg 118
Chinthurst School *Surrey* B 251
Chorister School,The *Durham* Bg 115
Christ Church Cathedral School *Oxon* B 227
Christ College *Wales (south)* Bg 312
Christ's Hospital *Sussex (west)* C 276
Churcher's College *Hants* C 129
City of London Freemen's School *Surrey* C 252
City of London School For Girls *London (greater)* G 181
City of London School *London (greater)* B 180
Claires Court School *Berks* B 72
Claremont Fan Court School *Surrey* C 252
Clayesmore Prep. School *Dorset* C 110
Clayesmore School *Dorset* C 110
Clewborough House Prep. School L*Surrey* C 252
Cliff School *Yorkshire (west)* C 305
Clifton College *Avon* C 64
Clifton College Prep. School *Avon* C 64
Clifton Hall School *Scotland* C 317
Clifton High School *Avon* Gb 64
Cobham Hall School *Kent* G 157
Cokethorpe School *Oxon* C 227
Colchester Boys High School *Essex* Bg 118
Coleraine Academical Institution *NI* B 326
Colfe's Prep. School *London (greater)* B 181
Colfe's School *London (greater)* B 181
Collingwood School *London (greater)* C 181
Colston's Collegiate Lower School *Avon* C 65

Colston's Collegiate School *Avon* C......... 65
Colston's Girls' School *Avon* C................ 64
Combe Bank School *Kent* Gb.................. 158
Commonweal Lodge School *London (greater)* G.. 181
Copthorne School Trust Ltd. *Sussex (west)* C.. 276
Cothill House *Oxon* B.............................. 227
Cottesmore School *Sussex (west)* C....... 276
Coventry Prep. School *W Mid* C............. 288
Coworth Park School *Surrey* Gb............. 252
Craigclowan Prep. School *Scotland* C.... 317
Cranbrook College *London (greater)* B. 182
Cranford House School *Oxon* Gb........... 228
Cranleigh Preparatory School *Surrey* B 252
Cranleigh School *Surrey* Bg.................... 253
Cranmore School *Surrey* B...................... 253
Cransley School *Cheshire* Gb.................... 92
Crescent School *Warks* C.......................... 285
Croft House School *Dorset* G................... 110
Croft House School *Nthd* C...................... 222
Croft School,The *Warks* C......................... 285
Croftinloan School *Scotland* C................ 317
Croham Hurst School *London (greater)* G182
Crosfields School *Berks* B........................... 72
Crown House School *Bucks* C.................... 83
Crowstone Prep. School *Essex* C............ 118
Croydon High School GPDST *London (greater)* G.. 182
Culcheth Hall *Cheshire* Gb........................ 92
Culford School *Suffolk* C........................... 245
Cumnor House School *London (greater)* B.. 182
Cumnor House School *Sussex (east)* C. 270
Cundall Manor *Yorkshire (north)* C........ 298
Dagfa House School *Notts* C.................... 223
Daiglen School,The *Essex* B..................... 118
Dair House School *Bucks* C....................... 83
Dame Alice Harpur School *Beds* G.......... 70
Dame Allan's Boys' School *Tyne And Wear* B.. 282
Dame Allan's Girls' School *Tyne And Wear* G.. 282
Dame Johane Bradbury's School *Essex* C118
Danes Hill *Surrey* C................................... 253
Daneshill School *Hants* C......................... 129
Dauntsey's School *Wilts* C........................ 293
Davenies School *Bucks* B........................... 83
Davenport Lodge School *W Mid* C......... 288
Dean Close Junior School *Glos* C.......... 125
Dean Close School *Glos* C........................ 125
Denmead School *London (greater)* B.... 182
Denstone College Prep. School *Staffs* C 241
Denstone College *Staffs* C........................ 241
Derby High School *Derbys* Gb................ 102
Derwent Lodge Preparatory School for Girls *Kent* G.. 158
Devonshire House Preparatory School *London (greater)* C.............................. 183
Ditcham Park School *Hants* C.................. 129
Dixie Grammar & Wolstan Prep Schools *Leics* C... 172
Dodderhill School *Hereford & worcester* G.. 139
Dollar Academy *Scotland* C..................... 317
Dolphin School *Berks* C.............................. 72
Dorchester Preparatory School *Dorset* C111
Dorset House *Sussex (west)* B................ 276
Douai School *Berks* C.................................. 72
Dover College *Kent* C................................ 158
Downe House *Berks* G................................ 72
Downs School,The *Avon* C.......................... 65
Downs School,The *Hereford & worcester* C.. 139
Downsend Girls Preparatory School *Surrey* Gb.. 253
Downsend School *Surrey* B...................... 253
Downside School *Avon* Gb.......................... 65
Downside School *London (greater)* B.... 183
Dragon School *Oxon* C.............................. 228
Drumley House School *Scotland* C......... 317
Duchy Grammar School,The *Cornwall* C. 99
Duke of Kent School *Surrey* C................ 254
Duke of York's Royal Military School *Kent* C... 158
Dulwich College *London (greater)* B...... 183
Dulwich College Prep. School *Kent* C... 158
Dulwich College Prep. School *London (greater)* Bg.. 183
Dumpton School *Dorset* C........................ 111
Duncombe School *Herts* C....................... 146
Dundee High School *Scotland* C............. 318
Dunhurst (Bedales Junior School) *Hants* C... 129
Dunottar School *Surrey* G......................... 254
Durham High School for Girls *Durham* G115
Durham School *Durham* C....................... 116
Durlston Court *Hants* C............................. 130
Durston House *London (greater)* B......... 183
Eagle House *Surrey* B................................ 254
Ealing College Upper School *London (greater)* Bg.. 184
Eastbourne College *Sussex (east)* Bg..... 271
Eastbourne House School *W Mid* C....... 288
Eastcliffe Grammar School *Tyne And Wear* C.. 282
Edenhurst Preparatory School *Staffs* C. 241
Edgarley Hall *Somerset* C......................... 236
Edgbaston C of E College *W Mid* G....... 288
Edgbaston College *W Mid* C.................... 289
Edgbaston High School for Girls *W Mid* G289
Edge Grove *Herts* B.................................... 146
Edgeborough *Surrey* C.............................. 254
Edgehill College *Devon* C.......................... 104
Edinburgh Academy Prep. School,The *Scotland* Bg.. 318
Edinburgh Academy,The *Scotland* Bg... 318
Edington and Shapwick School L*Somerset* C.. 237
Egerton-Rothesay School Limited *Herts* C.. 146
Elizabeth College *Channel Is.* Bg............. 89
Ellesmere College *Salop* C....................... 233
Elm Green Prep.School *Essex* C............ 119
Elm Tree House School *Wales (south)* Gb312
Elmhurst Ballet School *Surrey* C............ 254
Elmhurst School *London (greater)* B..... 184
Elms,The *Hereford & worcester* Bg.......... 139
Elmslie Girls School *Lancs* G.................. 169
Elstree School *Berks* Bg.............................. 73
Eltham College *London (greater)* Bg..... 184
Emanuel School *London (greater)* Bg.... 184
Embley Park School *Hants* C.................. 130
Emscote Lawn *Warks* C............................ 285
Epsom College *Surrey* Bg......................... 255
Eton College *Berks* B.................................. 73
Eton End PNEU School *Berks* Gb............ 73
Eversfield Prep. School *W Mid* Bg......... 289
Ewell Castle Junior School *Surrey* C..... 255
Ewell Castle School *Surrey* Bg................ 255
Exeter Cathedral School *Devon* C.......... 104
Exeter Preparatory School *Devon* B...... 104
Exeter School *Devon* Bg............................ 105
Fairfield PNEU School *Avon* C.................. 65
Fairfield School *Leics* C............................ 172
Fairstead House School *Suffolk* C.......... 245
Falcon Manor School *N'hants* C............. 219
Falkiand St. Gabriel *Berks* Gb.................. 73
Falkner House *London (greater)* G........ 184
Farleigh School *Hants* C........................... 130
Farlington School *Sussex (west)* G......... 277
Farnborough Hill *Hants* G........................ 130
Farringtons and Stratford House *Kent* Gb159
Felsted Preparatory School *Essex* C...... 119
Felsted School *Essex* C............................. 119
Feltonfleet School *Surrey* C..................... 255
Fettes College *Scotland* C........................ 318
Finborough School *Suffolk* C................... 245
Finton House School *London (greater)* C185
Flexlands School Educational Trust Ltd *Surrey* Gb.. 255
Fonthill Lodge School *Sussex (west)* C. 277
Forest Girls' School *London (greater)* G185
Forest Park School *Cheshire* C.................. 92
Forest Preparatory School *London (greater)* C... 185
Forest School *Cheshire* C........................... 92
Forest School *London (greater)* B.......... 185
Forres Sandle Manor *Hants* C................. 130
Framlingham College Junior School *Suffolk* C.. 245
Framlingham College *Suffolk* C.............. 245
Francis Holland School Clarence Gate *London (greater)* G.............................. 185
Francis Holland School London L*(greater)* G... 186
Frensham Heights *Surrey* C..................... 256
Friars School *Kent* C.................................. 159
Friends School *Essex* C............................. 119
Froebelian School,The *Yorkshire (west)* C.. 306
Fulneck School *Yorkshire (west)* C........ 306
Fyling Hall School *Yorkshire (north)* C. 298
Garden House School *London (greater)* Gb.. 186
Gateway School *Bucks* C............................ 83
Gateways School *Yorkshire (west)* G..... 306
Gayhurst School *Bucks* B............................ 83
George Heriot's School *Scotland* C........ 318
George Watson's College *Scotland* C..... 319
Giggleswick School *Yorkshire (north)* C 299
Glaisdale School *London (greater)* C..... 186
Glasgow Academy,The *Scotland* C......... 319
Glasgow,The High School of *Scotland* C319
Glebe House *Norfolk* C............................. 217
Glenalmond College *Scotland* C............ 319
Glenarm College *London (greater)* Gb... 186
Glendower Prep. School London L*(greater)* G... 186
Glenesk School *Surrey* C.......................... 256
Godolphin & Latymer School,The L*London (greater)* G.............................. 187
Godolphin School,The *Wilts* G................ 293
Godstowe Prep. School *Bucks* Gb............ 84
Gordonstoun School *Scotland* C............ 319
Gosfield School *Essex* C........................... 119
Grace Dieu Manor Preparatory School *Leics* C... 172
Grange School,The *Cheshire* C.................. 92
Granville School,The *Kent* Gb................ 159
Great Ballard *Sussex (west)* C................. 277
Great Houghton Prep. School *Northants* C.. 220
Great Walstead *Sussex (west)* C............. 277
Greenacre School *Surrey* G..................... 256
Greenbank School *Cheshire* C.................. 93
Greenfields School *Sussex (east)* C........ 271
Greenhayes School for Boys *Kent* B..... 159
Greenholme School *Notts* C.................... 223
Gregg School,The *Hants* C....................... 131
Grenville College *Devon* C....................... 105
Gresham's Preparatory School *Norfolk* C217
Gresham's School *Norfolk* C.................... 217
Greycotes School *Oxon* Gb...................... 228
Grosvenor House School *Yorkshire (north)* Bg... 299
Grosvenor School *Notts* C........................ 223
Guildford High School for Girls *Surrey* G256
Haberdashers' Aske's Prep Sch,The *Herts* B... 147
Haberdashers' Aske's Sch. for Girls *Herts* G... 147
Haberdashers' Aske's School,The *Herts* B.. 147
Haberdashers' Monmouth School for Girls *Wales (south)* G......................... 313
Haden Hill School *W Mid* C..................... 289
Haileybury *Herts* Bg.................................. 147
Haileybury Junior School *Berks* B.......... 73
Hale Prep. School *Cheshire* C................... 93
Hall Grove *Surrey* B.................................. 256
Hall School *London (greater)* B............. 187
Hallfield School *W Mid* B........................ 289
Halliford School *London (greater)* B..... 187
Halstead Prep. School for Girls *Surrey* G257
Hammond School *Cheshire* Gb................ 93
Hampshire School,The London L*(greater)* C... 187
Hampton School *London (greater)* B..... 187
Handcross Park School *Sussex (west)* C277
Hanford School *Dorset* G......................... 111
Harecroft School *Cumbria* C................... 101
Harenc School *Kent* B............................... 159
Haresfoot Preparatory School *Herts* C.. 148
Haresfoot Senior School *Herts* C........... 147
Harrogate Ladies' College *Yorkshire (north)* G.. 299
Harrow School *London (greater)* B....... 188
Harvington School *London (greater)* Gb188
Haslemere Prep. School *Surrey* B.......... 257
Hatherop Castle Preparatory School *Glos* C... 125
Hawford Lodge *Hereford & worcester* C 140
Hawley Place School *Hants* C................. 131
Hawthorns,The *Surrey* C.......................... 257
Haylett Grange School *Wales (south)* C 313
Hazelhurst School *London (greater)* Gb 188
Hazelwood School *Surrey* C.................... 257
Headfort School *Rofl* C............................ 328

Headington School *Oxon* Gb 228
Heath Mount School *Herts* C 148
Heathcote School *Essex* C 120
Heatherton House School *Bucks* Gb 84
Heathfield School *Berks* G 74
Heathfield School GPDST *London* L*(greater)* G 188
Heathfield School *Hereford & worcester* C140
Hellenic College of London *London (greater)* C 188
Hemdean House School *Berks* Gb 74
Hendon Preparatory School *London (greater)* C 189
Hereford Cathedral Junior School L*Hereford & worcester* C 140
Hereford Cathedral School *Hereford & worcester* C 140
Hereward House School *London* L*(greater)* B 189
Herington House School *Essex* Gb 120
Herries School *Berks* C 74
Hethersett Old Hall School *Norfolk* G 217
Heywood Preparatory School *Wilts* C 294
High March School *Bucks* Gb 84
Highclare School *W Mid* Gb 290
Highfield Priory School *Lancs* C 169
Highfield School and Nursery *London (greater)* C 189
Highfield School *Berks* C 74
Highfield School *Hants* C 131
Highfield School *London (greater)* C 189
Highfields School *Notts* C 223
Highgate Junior School *London* L*(greater)* Bg 189
Highgate School *London (greater)* B 190
Highlands School *Berks* C 74
Hilden Grange School *Kent* C 160
Hilden Oaks *Kent* Gb 160
Hill House Prep School *Yorkshire (south)* C 304
Hill School *Kent* C 160
Hillcrest Grammar School *Cheshire* C 93
Hillcroft Preparatory School *Suffolk* C 246
Hillgrove School *Wales (north)* C 310
Hillstone School *Hereford & worcester* C140
Hipperholme Grammar School L*Yorkshire (west)* C 306
Hoe Bridge School *Surrey* C 257
Hollygirt School *Notts* G 224
Holme Grange *Berks* C 75
Holmewood House *Kent* C 160
Holmwood House *Essex* C 120
Holy Child School *W Mid* Gb 290
Holy Cross Preparatory School *Surrey* C258
Holy Trinity College *Kent* Gb 160
Holy Trinity School *Hereford &* L*worcester* Gb 141
Homefield School *Dorset* C 111
Homefield School *London (greater)* B 190
Homewood Independent School *Herts* C148
Hordle House Preparatory School L*Hants* C 131
Horler's Pre-Preparatory School *Cambs* C86
Horris Hill *Berks* B 75
Howe Green House School *Herts* C 148
Howell's Preparatory School *Wales (north)* G 310
Howell's School Llandaff GPDST *Wales (south)* G 313
Howell's School *Wales (north)* G 310
Howsham Hall *Yorkshire (north)* Bg 299
Hull Grammar School *Humberside* C 153
Hull High School *Humberside* Gb 153
Hulme Grammar School for Girls *Lancs* G169
Hulme Grammar School *Lancs* B 169
Hulme Hall Schools *Cheshire* C 93
Hurst Lodge School *Berks* Gb 75
Hurstpierpoint College Junior School *Sussex (west)* C 278
Hurstpierpoint College *Sussex (west)* C 278
Hutchesons' Grammar School *Scotland* C320
Hydesville Tower School *W Mid* C 290
Hymers College *Humberside* C 154
Ibstock Place - The Froebel School *London (greater)* C 190
Ilford Ursuline High School *London (greater)* G 190
Innellan House St. Andrew's School Group *London (greater)* C 190
Ipswich High School GPDST *Suffolk* Gb246
Ipswich Prep. School *Suffolk* B 246
Ipswich School *Suffolk* Bg 246
Italia Conti Academy Of Theatre Arts Ltd. *London (greater)* C 191
James Allen's Girls' School *London (greater)* Gb 191
James Allen's Preparatory School L*London (greater)* C 191
John Lyon School,The *London (greater)* B 191
Josca's Prep. *Oxon* Bg 228
Junior King's School *Kent* C 161
Keble Prep. School *London (greater)* B 191
Keil School *Scotland* C 320
Kelly College *Devon* C 105
Kelly College Junior School - St. Michael's *Devon* C 105
Kelvinside Academy *Scotland* B 320
Kensington Prep. School for Girls GPDST *London (greater)* G 192
Kent College Infant & Junior School *Kent* C 161
Kent College Junior School *Kent* G 161
Kent College *Kent* C 161
Kent College Pembury *Kent* G 161
Kilgraston School *Scotland* G 320
Kimbolton School *Cambs* C 86
King Alfred School,The *London* L*(greater)* C 192
King Edward VI High Sch. for Girls *W Mid* G 290
King Edward VI School *Hants* C 131
King Edward VII School *Lancs* B 169
King Edward's School *Avon* Bg 66
King Edward's School *Surrey* C 258
King Edward's School *W Mid* B 290
King Henry VIII Junior School *W Mid* C291
King Henry VIII *W Mid* C 291
King William's College *IoW* C 155
King's College Junior School *London (greater)* B 192
King's College School *Cambs* C 87
King's College School *London (greater)* B192
King's College *Somerset* C 237
King's Hall *Somerset* C 237
King's High School for Girls *Warks* G 285
King's Hospital *RofI* C 328
King's House *London (greater)* B 192
King's Junior School *Cambs* C 87
King's Junior School *Hereford &* L*worcester* C 141
King's Preparatory School *Kent* C 162
King's School Bruton Junior Sch. *Somerset* C 237
King's School Bruton Pre-Preparatory *Somerset* C 237
King's School *Cambs* C 87
King's School *Cheshire* B 94
King's School *Glos* C 126
King's School *Kent* C 162
King's School Rochester *Kent* C 162
King's School *Somerset* Bg 238
King's School,The *Cheshire* C 94
King's School,The *Hereford & worcester* C 141
King's School,The *Tyne And Wear* C 282
Kingham Hill School *Oxon* C 229
Kings Monkton School *Wales (south)* C 313
Kingshott School *Herts* C 148
Kingsland Grange *Salop* B 233
Kingsley School *Warks* Gb 286
Kingsmead School *Merseyside* C 214
Kingston Grammar School *London (greater)* C 193
Kingswood House *Surrey* B 258
Kingswood School *Avon* C 66
Kingswood Schools *Merseyside* C 214
Kirkham Grammar School *Lancs* C 170
Kirkstone House School *Lincs* C 175
Kitebrook House *Glos* Gb 126
Knighton House *Dorset* Gb 111
Knoll School,The *Hereford & worcester* C141
La Retraite School *Wilts* Gb 294
La Sagesse Convent High School *Tyne And Wear* G 283
La Sagesse Convent Junior School *Tyne And Wear* G 283
Ladies College *CI* Gb 90
Lady Barn House School *Cheshire* C 94
Lady Eden's School *London (greater)* G193
Lady Eleanor Holles School,The L*London (greater)* G 193
Lady Lane Park Preparatory School *Yorkshire (west)* C 306
Lambrook *Berks* Bg 75
Lancing College *Sussex (west)* Bg 278
Lanesborough School *Surrey* B 258
Langley Preparatory School and LNursery *Norfolk* C 217
Langley School *Norfolk* C 218
Lathallan School *Scotland* C 320
Latymer Upper School *London* L*(greater)* B 193
Laurel Bank School *Scotland* Gb 321
Lavant House - Rosemead *Sussex (west)* Gb 278
Laverock School *Surrey* G 258
Laxton Junior School *Northants* C 220
Lea House School *Hereford & worcester* C141
Leaden Hall School *Wilts* Gb 294
Leeds Girls' High School *Yorkshire (west)* Gb 307
Leeds Grammar School *Yorkshire* L*(west)* B 307
Leicester Grammar School *Leics* C 172
Leicester High School for Girls *Leics* G 173
Leighton Park School *Berks* C 75
Leys School,The *Cambs* C 87
Licensed Victuallers' School *Berks* C 76
Lichfield Cathedral Sch.(St.Chad's) L*Staffs* C 241
Lime House School *Cumbria* C 101
Lincoln Cathedral School *Lincs* C 175
Lisvane - Scarborough College Junior School *Yorkshire (north)* C 302
Littlegarth School *Essex* C 120
Liverpool College *Merseyside* C 214
Llandovery College *Wales (south)* C 313
Lochinver House School *Herts* B 149
Lockers Park School *Herts* B 149
Lomond School *Scotland* C 321
Long Close *Berks* C 76
Longacre Preparatory School *Surrey* C 259
Longridge Towers School *Nthd* C 222
Lord Mayor Treloar College *Hants* C 132
Lord Wandsworth College *Hants* C 132
Loreto Convent Preparatory School *Cheshire* Gb 94
Loretto Junior School *Scotland* C 321
Loretto School *Scotland* C 321
Lorne House *Notts* C 224
Loughborough Grammar School *Leics* B173
Loughborough High School *Leics* G 173
Loyola Prep. School *Essex* B 120
Luckley-Oakfield School *Berks* G 76
Ludgrove *Berks* B 76
Lyndhurst House Prep. School *London (greater)* B 193
Lyndhurst School *Surrey* C 259
Lyndon School *Wales (north)* C 310
Magdalen College School *Oxon* B 229
Maidwell Hall *Northants* C 220
Maldon Court Preparatory School *Essex* C 121
Mall School *London (greater)* B 194
Malsis School *Yorkshire (north)* B 299
Maltman's Green *Bucks* G 84
Malvern College *Hereford & worcester* C142
Malvern Girls' College *Hereford & worcester* G 142
Manchester Grammar School L*Manchester (greater)* B 212
Manchester High School for Girls *Manchester (greater)* G 212
Manor House Prep. School *Leics* C 173
Manor House School *Devon* C 105
Manor House School *Surrey* Gb 259
Manor Prep. School *Oxon* Gb 229
Maple Hayes Hall School for Dyslexics *Staffs* C 242
Margaret Allen Preparatory School *Hereford & worcester* G 142
Mark College *Somerset* B 238
Marlborough College *Wilts* C 294
Marlborough House School *Kent* C 162
Mary Erskine and Stewart's Melville Jnr School,The *Scotland* C 321
Mary Erskine School *Scotland* G 322
Marymount International School L*London (greater)* G 194

Mayfield College *Sussex (east)* B 271
Mayfield Prep. School *W Mid* C.............. 291
Mayfield Preparatory School *Hants* C ... 132
Maynard School *Devon* G 106
Mayville High School *Hants* Gb 132
Mead School *Kent* C.............................. 162
Merchant Taylors' School for Girls *Merseyside* Gb.. 215
Merchant Taylors' School *London* L*(greater)* B 194
Merchant Taylors' School *Merseyside* B215
Merchiston Castle School *Scotland* B.... 322
Methodist College *NI* C.......................... 326
Micklefield School *Surrey* Gb................. 259
Micklefield Wadhurst *Sussex (east)* Gb. 271
Milbourne Lodge Junior School *Surrey* Bg.. 259
Milbourne Lodge School *Surrey* Bg....... 260
Mill Hill School *London (greater)* Bg 194
Millfield School *Somerset* C.................. 238
Milton Abbey School *Dorset* B 112
Milton Keynes Preparatory School *Bucks* C... 84
Minster School York,The *Yorkshire (north)* C... 300
Moffats School *Hereford & worcester* C. 142
Moira House School *Sussex (east)* G..... 271
Monkton Combe Junior School *Avon* C.. 66
Monkton Combe School *Avon* C 66
Monmouth School *Wales (south)* B 314
Moor Allerton School *Manchester* L*(greater)* C 212
Moor Park *Salop* C 234
Moorfield School *Yorkshire (west)* G..... 307
Moorland School *Lancs* C 170
Moorlands School *Yorkshire (west)* C ... 307
More House School *London (greater)* G194
More House School *Surrey* B................. 260
Moreton Hall School *Salop* G 234
Moreton Hall *Suffolk* C 246
Morrison's Academy *Scotland* C............ 322
Mostyn House School *Cheshire* C 94
Moulsford Preparatory School *Oxon* B. 229
Mount Carmel Junior School *Cheshire* Gb95
Mount Carmel School *Cheshire* G 95
Mount House School *Devon* B 106
Mount School *Hereford & worcester* C... 142
Mount School *London (greater)* G 195
Mount School,The *Yorkshire (north)* Gb300
Mount St. Mary's College *Derbys* C 102
Mount St. Mary's Convent School *Devon* Gb 106
Mowden Hall School *Nthd* C.................. 222
Mowden School *Sussex (east)* B............ 272
Moyles Court School *Hants* C................ 132
Nethercliffe School *Hants* C................... 133
Netherwood School *Wales (south)* C..... 314
Nevill Holt *Leics* C.................................. 173
New Beacon,The *Kent* B......................... 163
New College School *Oxon* B 229
New Hall School *Essex* G 121
New Park School *Scotland* C.................. 322
Newbridge Preparatory School *W Mid* Gb.. 291
Newcastle Prep. School *Tyne And Wear* C283
Newcastle U Tyne Church High Sch *Tyne And Wear* G................................... 283
Newcastle-under-Lyme School *Staffs* C. 242
Newell House School *Dorset* C.............. 112
Newland House School *London* L*(greater)* C 195
Newlands Manor School *Sussex (east)* C272
Newlands Pre-Preparatory School L*Sussex (east)* C................................ 272
Newlands School *Sussex (east)* C 272
Newlands School *Tyne And Wear* B 283
Norland Place School *London (greater)* C195
Norman Court *Hants* C........................... 133
North Cestrian Grammar School L*Cheshire* B.. 95
North Foreland Lodge *Hants* G 133
North Leeds and St. Edmund's Hall *Yorkshire (west)* C................................ 307
North London Collegiate School,The *London (greater)* G 195
Northampton High School *Northants* G 220
Northbourne Park *Kent* C....................... 163
Northfield School *Herts* Gb.................... 149
Northgate School *Wales (north)* C 310
Northwood College *London (greater)* G 195
Northwood Preparatory School *Herts* B 149
Norwich High School for Girls GPDST *Norfolk* G... 218
Norwich School *Norfolk* B...................... 218
Notre Dame Prep. School *Surrey* C........ 260
Notre Dame School *Surrey* Gb................ 260
Notre Dame Senior School *Surrey* G 260
Notting Hill & Ealing High School GPDST *London (greater)* G................ 196
Nottingham High School for Girls GPDST *Notts* G 224
Nottingham High School *Notts* B 224
Nottingham High School Prep. School *Notts* B.. 224
Nower Lodge School *Surrey* C................ 261
Nunnykirk Hall School *Nthd* C 222
Oakfield Preparatory School *London (greater)* C... 196
Oakham School *Leics* C.......................... 174
Oakhyrst Grange School *Surrey* B.......... 261
Oaklands Preparatory School L*Manchester (greater)* C 212
Oakwood *Sussex (west)* C 278
Ockbrook School *Derbys* Gb.................. 102
Old Buckenham Hall School *Suffolk* Bg 247
Old Hall School *Salop* C......................... 234
Old Malthouse,The *Dorset* Bg 112
Old Palace School of John Whitgift *London (greater)* G 196
Old School,The *Suffolk* C....................... 247
Old Vicarage School *London (greater)* G196
Oratory Prep. School *Berks* C................... 76
Oratory School,The *Berks* B 77
Oriel Bank High School *Cheshire* G......... 95
Orley Farm School *London (greater)* C. 196
Orwell Park School *Suffolk* C 247
Oswestry Junior School *Salop* C 234
Oswestry School *Salop* C 234
Oundle School *Northants* C 220
Our Lady of Sion School *Sussex (west)* C279
Our Lady's Convent Senior School *Oxon* G.. 230
Oxford High School GPDST *Oxon* G...... 230
Oxford House *Essex* C............................ 121
Packwood Haugh *Salop* C 235
Palmers Green High School *London (greater)* G 197
Pangbourne College *Berks* Bg.................. 77
Papplewick *Berks* B................................... 77
Paragon School *Avon* C 66
Parayhouse School *London (greater)* C. 197
Park School *Avon* Bg 67
Park School for Girls *Essex* G................ 121
Park School *Scotland* G.......................... 322
Park School,The *Dorset* C 112
Park School,The *Somerset* C.................. 238
Parkside School *Surrey* Bg..................... 261
Parsons Mead School *Surrey* G 261
Pembridge Hall School *London* L*(greater)* G 197
Pennthorpe School *Sussex (west)* C 279
Perrott Hill School *Somerset* C.............. 238
Perse Prep. School *Cambs* B 87
Perse School for Girls *Cambs* G............... 88
Perse School,The *Cambs* Bg..................... 88
Peterborough & St. Margarets *London (greater)* G 197
Peterborough High School *Cambs* Gb..... 88
Pilgrims' School *Hants* B........................ 133
Pinewood School *Wilts* C........................ 294
Pipers Corner School *Bucks* G................. 85
Plumtree School *Notts* C........................ 225
Plymouth College *Devon* C 106
Plymouth College Prep. School *Devon* C106
PNEU School *Notts* C 225
Pocklington School *Humberside* C 154
Polam Hall Junior School *Durham* G 116
Polam Hall School *Durham* G................. 116
Polwhele House School *Cornwall* C......... 99
Port Regis *Dorset* C 112
Portora Royal School *NI* B..................... 326
Portsmouth Grammar Lower LSchool,The *Hants* C.......................... 133
Portsmouth Grammar School,The L*Hants* C... 134
Portsmouth High School GPDST *Hants* G134
Pownall Hall School *Cheshire* B 95
Prebendal School *Sussex (west)* C 279
Prenton Preparatory School *Merseyside* C.. 215
Presentation College *Berks* Bg 77
Prestfelde *Salop* Bg 235
Prince's Mead School *Hants* C 134
Princess Helena College,The *Herts* G.... 149
Princethorpe College *Warks* Bg 286
Prior Park College *Avon* C 67
Prior Park Preparatory School *Wilts* C.. 295
Prior's Court *Berks* C 77
Prior's Field *Surrey* G............................. 261
Priory School *Surrey* B 262
Prospect House School *London* L*(greater)* C 197
Purcell School of Music *London* L*(greater)* C 198
Putney High School GPDST *London (greater)* G 198
Putney Park School *London (greater)* Gb198
Quainton Hall School *London (greater)* B198
Quantock School *Somerset* C................. 239
Queen Anne's School *Berks* G.................. 78
Queen Elizabeth Grammar Jnr School *Yorkshire (west)* B................................ 308
Queen Elizabeth Grammar School L*Yorkshire (west)* B 308
Queen Elizabeth's Grammar School *Lancs* Bg 170
Queen Elizabeth's Hospital *Avon* B 67
Queen Ethelburga's College *Yorkshire (north)* Gb 300
Queen Margaret's School *Yorkshire (north)* G 300
Queen Mary School *Lancs* Gb 170
Queen Mary's School *Yorkshire (north)* G300
Queen's College Junior School L*Somerset* C... 239
Queen's College London *London* L*(greater)* G 198
Queen's College *Somerset* C................... 239
Queen's Gate School *London (greater)* G199
Queen's Park School *Salop* C 235
Queen's School,The *Cheshire* Gb 96
Queenswood School *Herts* G 150
Quinton House School *Northants* C 221
R.N.I.B. New College Worcester L*Hereford & worcester* C 143
Radley College *Oxon* B........................... 230
Ramillies Hall *Cheshire* C 96
Ranby House *Notts* C 225
Rannoch School *Scotland* C 323
Ratcliffe College *Leics* C 174
Read School *Yorkshire (north)* C........... 301
Reading Blue Coat School *Berks* Bg 78
Red House School Ltd *Cleveland* C 98
Red House School *Yorkshire (north)* C . 301
Red Maids' Junior School *Avon* G........... 67
Red Maids' School *Avon* G 67
Redcliffe School *London (greater)* C...... 199
Reddiford School *London (greater)* C ... 199
Redland High School *Avon* G................... 68
Reed's School *Surrey* Bg......................... 262
Reigate Grammar School *Surrey* C......... 262
Reigate St.Mary's Prep.& Choir Sch *Surrey* B.. 262
Rendcomb College *Glos* C...................... 126
Repton Prep. School *Derbys* C 102
Repton School *Derbys* C 103
Richard Pate School,The *Glos* C 126
Richmond House School *Yorkshire (west)* C 308
Rickmansworth Masonic School *Herts* G150
Rickmansworth P.N.E.U. School *Herts* Gb.. 150
Riddlesworth Hall *Norfolk* Gb 218
Ridgeway *Berks* B 78
Ripley Court School *Surrey* C 262
Ripon Cathedral Choir School L*Yorkshire (north)* C........................... 301
Rishworth School *Yorkshire (west)* C.... 308
Riverston School *London (greater)* C ... 199
Robert Gordon's College *Scotland* C..... 323
Rockport *NI* C... 327
Rodney School *Notts* C 225
Roedean School *Sussex (east)* G 272
Rokeby *London (greater)* B.................... 199
Rookesbury Park School *Hants* G.......... 134
Rookwood School *Hants* C 134
Rose Hill School *Glos* C.......................... 126
Rose Hill School *Kent* C 163
Rosecroft School Didsbury *Manchester (greater)* Gb 212

Roselyon School *Cornwall* C 99
Rosemead Preparatory School *London (greater)* C 200
Rossall Preparatory School *Lancs* C 170
Rossall School *Lancs* C 171
Rougemont School *Wales (south)* C 314
Rowan Prep. School *Surrey* Gb 263
Royal Belfast Academical Inst. *NI* B 327
Royal Grammar School *Hereford & worcester* B 143
Royal Grammar School *Surrey* B 263
Royal Grammar School *Tyne And Wear* B284
Royal Hospital School *Suffolk* C 247
Royal Russell Preparatory School L*London (greater)* C 200
Royal Russell School *London (greater)* C200
Royal School Hindhead *Surrey* G 263
Royal School,The *Avon* Gb 68
Royal School,The *NI* C 327
Royal Wolverhampton Junior School *W Mid* C 291
Royal Wolverhampton School *W Mid* C 292
Ruckleigh School *W Mid* C 292
Rudston Preparatory School *Yorkshire (south)* C 304
Rugby School *Warks* C 286
Rupert House School *Oxon* Gb 230
Rushmoor Independent School *Hants* C135
Rushmoor School *Beds* B 70
Russell House School *Kent* C 163
Ruthin School *Wales (north)* C 311
Rydal Penrhos Preparatory School *Wales (north)* C 311
Rydal Penrhos Snr Sch (Co-ed Div) *Wales (north)* C 311
Rydal Penrhos Snr Sch (Girls' Div) *Wales (north)* G 311
Ryde School (Junior School) *IoW* C 155
Ryde School with Upper Chine *IoW* C .. 155
Rydes Hill Preparatory *Surrey* C 263
Rye St.Antony School *Oxon* G 230
Ryleys,The *Cheshire* B 96
S. Anselm's School *Derbys* C 103
S. Gabriels School *Berks* G 79
Sackville School *Kent* C 163
Saint Felix School *Suffolk* G 247
Salcombe Preparatory School *London (greater)* C 204
Salisbury Cathedral School *Wilts* C 295
Salterford House School *Notts* C 226
Sanderstead Junior School *Surrey* C 267
Sandhurst School *Sussex (west)* C 279
Sandroyd School *Wilts* B 296
Sarum Hall *London (greater)* Gb 205
Scaitcliffe *Surrey* B 267
Scarborough College *Yorkshire (north)* C302
Scarisbrick Hall School *Lancs* C 171
School of S.Mary & S.Anne *Staffs* G 243
Seaford College *Sussex (west)* Bg 280
Sedbergh School *Cumbria* B 101
Selwyn School *Glos* Gb 127
Sevenoaks Prep. School *Kent* C 165
Sevenoaks School *Kent* C 165
Shaftesbury Independent School L*London (greater)* C 205
Shebbear College *Devon* C 108
Sheffield High School GPDST *Yorkshire (south)* G 304
Sherborne House School *Hants* C 136
Sherborne Preparatory School *Dorset* C113
Sherborne School *Dorset* B 114
Sherborne School For Girls *Dorset* G 113
Sherrardswood School *Herts* C 152
Shiplake College *Oxon* B 232
Shoreham College *Sussex (west)* C 280
Shrewsbury High School GPDST *Salop* G235
Shrewsbury House School *London* L*(greater)* B 205
Shrewsbury School *Salop* B 236
Sibford School *Oxon* C 232
Sibton Park Girls' Preparatory School *Kent* Gb 165
Sidcot School *Avon* C 68
Silcoates School *Yorkshire (west)* C 309
Sir William Perkins's School *Surrey* G 267
Skippers Hill Prep. School *Sussex (east)* C 274
Slindon College *Sussex (west)* B 280
Solefield School *Kent* B 166
Solihull School *W Mid* Bg 292
Sompting Abbotts *Sussex (west)* B 280
South Hampstead High School GPDST *London (greater)* G 205
South Lee *Suffolk* C 248
Southbank International School L*London (greater)* C 205
Spratton Hall School *Northants* C 221
St Ambrose College *Cheshire* B 96
St Anne's High School *Durham* C 116
St Catherine's Preparatory School L*Cambs* G 88
St Clotilde's School *Glos* Gb 127
St Edward's School *Oxon* Bg 231
St Helen & St Katharine,The School of *Oxon* G 231
St James Independent School Jnr Boys Dept *London (greater)* B 202
St James Independent School Jnr Girls Dept *London (greater)* G 203
St. Agnes PNEU School *Yorkshire (west)* C 308
St. Albans High School for Girls *Herts* G150
St. Albans School *Herts* Bg 150
St. Aloysius' College *Scotland* C 323
St. Andrew's School *Beds* Gb 70
St. Andrew's School *Berks* C 78
St. Andrew's School *Surrey* Bg 263
St. Andrews School *Sussex (east)* C 273
St. Anne's Preparatory School *Essex* C . 121
St. Anne's School *Cumbria* Gb 101
St. Anthony's *London (greater)* B 200
St. Antony's-Leweston School *Dorset* Gb113
St. Aubyn's School *Devon* C 107
St. Aubyn's School *Essex* Bg 122
St. Aubyns *Sussex (east)* B 273
St. Bede's College *Manchester (greater)* C213
St. Bede's School *Staffs* C 242
St. Bede's School *Sussex (east)* C 273
St. Bede's School *Sussex (east)* C 273
St. Bees School *Cumbria* C 101
St. Benedict's Convent School *Hants* Gb135
St. Benedict's School *London (greater)* Bg 200
St. Bernard's Prep. School *Berks* C 78
St. Catherine's Junior School *Surrey* G . 264
St. Catherine's Preparatory School *Cheshire* C 96
St. Catherine's School *London (greater)* G 201
St. Catherine's School *Surrey* G 264
St. Cedd's School *Essex* C 122
St. Christopher School *Herts* C 151
St. Christopher's School London L*(greater)* C 201
St. Christopher's School London L*(greater)* G 201
St. Christopher's School *Norfolk* C 218
St. Christopher's *Somerset* Gb 239
St. Christopher's *Surrey* C 264
St. Colette's Preparatory School *Cambs* C88
St. Columba's College *RofI* C 328
St. Columba's School *Scotland* C 323
St. Crispin's School *Leics* B 174
St. David's College *London (greater)* C . 201
St. David's College *Wales (north)* B 311
St. David's Junior School for Girls *Surrey* G 264
St. David's School *London (greater)* C .. 201
St. David's Senior School *Surrey* G 264
St. Denis and Cranley School *Scotland* Gb323
St. Dominic's Priory School *Staffs* Gb 242
St. Dominic's School *Staffs* Gb 242
St. Dunstan's Abbey School *Devon* Gb . 107
St. Dunstan's College *London (greater)* C202
St. Edmund's College *Herts* C 151
St. Edmund's Junior School *Kent* C 164
St. Edmund's School *Kent* C 164
St. Edmund's School *Surrey* B 265
St. Edward's College *Merseyside* C 215
St. Edward's School *Berks* B 79
St. Edward's School *Glos* C 127
St. Elphin's School *Derbys* Gb 103
St. Faith's *Cambs* C 89
St. Francis School *Wilts* C 295
St. Francis' College *Herts* Gb 151
St. George's College Junior School *Surrey* Bg 265
St. George's College *Surrey* C 265
St. George's School *Berks* B 79
St. George's School *Berks* G 79
St. George's School for Girls *Scotland* Gb324
St. George's School *Suffolk* C 248
St. Gerards School *Wales (north)* C 312
St. Helen's School *London (greater)* G .. 202
St. Hilary's School *Cheshire* G 97
St. Hilary's School *Surrey* Gb 265
St. Hilda's School *Essex* G 122
St. Hilda's School *Herts* G 151
St. Hilda's School *Herts* Gb 151
St. Hilda's School *Yorkshire (north)* C ... 301
St. Hugh's *Lincs* C 175
St. Hugh's School *Oxon* C 231
St. Ives School *Surrey* G 265
St. James Independent Sch.for Boys *London (greater)* B 202
St. James Independent Sch.for Girls *London (greater)* G 202
St. James School *Humberside* C 154
St. James's and The Abbey *Hereford & worcester* G 143
St. John's Beaumont *Berks* B 79
St. John's College *Hants* Bg 135
St. John's College School *Cambs* C 89
St. John's School *Devon* C 107
St. John's School *Essex* C 122
St. John's School *London (greater)* B 203
St. John's School *Surrey* Bg 266
St. John's School *Wales (south)* C 314
St. John's-on-the-Hill *Wales (south)* C .. 314
St. Joseph's College *Staffs* C 243
St. Joseph's College with the School of Jesus and Mary *Suffolk* Bg 248
St. Joseph's Convent School *Berks* G 80
St. Joseph's School *Cornwall* Gb 99
St. Joseph's School *Lincs* Gb 175
St. Joseph's School *Notts* C 225
St. Joseph's School *Warks* Gb 286
St. Katharines School *Scotland* G 324
St. Lawrence College Junior School *Kent* C 164
St. Lawrence College *Kent* C 164
St. Leonards School *Scotland* G 324
St. Leonards-Mayfield School *Sussex (east)* G 273
St. Margaret's Junior School *Sussex (west)* C 279
St. Margaret's Preparatory School *Essex* C 122
St. Margaret's School for Girls *Devon* G107
St. Margaret's School for Girls *Scotland* Gb 324
St. Margaret's School *Herts* G 152
St. Margaret's School *London (greater)* G203
St. Margaret's School *Scotland* Gb 324
St. Margaret's School *Wilts* C 295
St. Martin's Preparatory School L*Humberside* C 154
St. Martin's School *London (greater)* B . 203
St. Martin's School *Yorkshire (north)* C 301
St. Martin's *W Mid* G 292
St. Mary's College *Kent* C 164
St. Mary's College *Merseyside* C 215
St. Mary's Convent School *Hereford & worcester* Gb 143
St. Mary's Hall *Lancs* B 171
St. Mary's Hall *Sussex (east)* Gb 274
St. Mary's Preparatory School *Oxon* C .. 231
St. Mary's School *Berks* G 80
St. Mary's School *Bucks* G 85
St. Mary's School *Cambs* G 89
St. Mary's School *Dorset* G 113
St. Mary's School *Essex* G 123
St. Mary's School *Lincs* C 176
St. Mary's School *Oxon* G 231
St. Mary's School *Scotland* C 325
St. Mary's School *Wilts* G 295
St. Maur's School *Surrey* Gb 266
St. Michael's *Devon* C 107
St. Michael's *Kent* C 165
St. Michael's School *CI* C 90
St. Michael's School *Essex* C 123
St. Michael's School *Surrey* Gb 266
St. Michael's School *Wales (south)* C 315
St. Monica's *Dorset* C 113
St. Neots *Hants* C 135
St. Nicholas House Preparatory School *Herts* C 152
St. Nicholas School *Essex* C 123
St. Nicholas' School *Hants* Gb 135

St. Olave's Preparatory School *London (greater)* C 203
St. Olave's School *Yorkshire (north)* C 302
St. Paul's Cathedral Choir School *London (greater)* B 204
St. Paul's Girls' School *London (greater)* G 204
St. Paul's Prep.School *London (greater)* B 204
St. Paul's School *London (greater)* B 204
St. Peter's School *Devon* C 108
St. Peter's School *Northants* Gb 221
St. Peter's School *Yorkshire (north)* C 302
St. Petroc's School *Cornwall* C 99
St. Piran's School *Berks* C 80
St. Pius X Preparatory School *Lancs* C 171
St. Richard's *Hereford & worcester* C 143
St. Ronan's *Kent* B 165
St. Swithun's Junior School *Hants* C 136
St. Swithun's School *Hants* G 136
St. Teresa's Preparatory School *Surrey* G 266
St. Teresa's School *Bucks* C 85
St. Teresa's School *Surrey* G 266
St. Ursula's High School *Avon* Gb 68
St. Winefride's Convent Jnr. Sch. *Salop* C 235
St. Wystan's School *Derbys* C 103
Stafford Grammar School *Staffs* C 243
Stamford High Junior School *Lincs* Gb 176
Stamford High School for Girls *Lincs* G 176
Stamford School Junior School *Lincs* B 176
Stamford School *Lincs* B 176
Stanborough School *Herts* C 152
Stanbridge Earls School *Hants* C 136
Stancliffe Hall *Derbys* C 103
Stanway School *Surrey* Gb 267
Stella Maris (Grenville Coll Jnr Sch) *Devon* C 108
Stewart's Melville College *Scotland* B 325
Stockport Grammar Junior School L*Cheshire* C 97
Stockport Grammar School *Cheshire* C 97
Stoke Brunswick *Sussex (west)* C 280
Stoke College *Suffolk* C 248
Stonar School *Wilts* Gb 296
Stonefield House School *Lincs* C 177
Stoneygate College *Leics* C 174
Stoneygate Prep. School *Leics* C 174
Stonyhurst College *Lancs* Bg 171
Stormont *Herts* G 152
Stover School *Devon* G 108
Stowe School *Bucks* Bg 85
Stowford *London (greater)* C 206
Stratford Preparatory School *Warks* C 286
Strathallan School *Scotland* C 325
Streatham Hill & Clapham High School GPDST *London (greater)* G 206
Stroud School *Hants* C 136
Study Preparatory School,The *London (greater)* G 206
Study School,The *London (greater)* C 206
Summer Fields *Oxon* B 232
Sunderland High School *Tyne And Wear* C 284
Sunningdale School *Berks* B 80
Sunninghill Prep. School *Dorset* C 114
Sunny Hill House School *Yorkshire (west)* C 309
Sunnymede School *Merseyside* C 216
Surbiton High School *London (greater)* Gb 206
Sussex House *London (greater)* B 207
Sutton High School GPDST *London (greater)* G 207
Sutton Valence School *Kent* C 166
Swanbourne House *Bucks* C 85
Syddal Park School *Cheshire* C 97
Sydenham High School GPDST *London (greater)* G 207
Sylvia Young Theatre School *London (greater)* C 207
Talbot Heath School *Dorset* Gb 114
Taunton Preparatory School *Somerset* C 239
Taunton School *Somerset* C 240
Taverham Hall School *Norfolk* C 219
Teesside High School for Girls L*Cleveland* G 98
Temple Grove with St. Nicholas *Sussex (east)* C 274
Terra Nova *Cheshire* C 97
Terrington Hall *Yorkshire (north)* C 302
Tettenhall College *W Mid* C 292
The New Eccles Hall School *Norfolk* C 216
Thetford Grammar School *Norfolk* C 219
Thomas's Preparatory School *London (greater)* C 207
Thornlow School *Dorset* C 114
Thornton College *Bucks* Gb 86
Thorpe Hall School *Essex* C 123
Thorpe House School *Bucks* B 86
Thorpe House School *Norfolk* G 219
Tockington Manor *Avon* C 68
Tonbridge School *Kent* B 166
Tormead School *Surrey* G 267
Tower College *Merseyside* C 216
Tower House School *London (greater)* B 208
Tower House *Wales (north)* C 312
Towers Convent School,The *Sussex (west)* Gb 281
Town Close House Prep.School *Norfolk* C 219
Treliske Preparatory School *Cornwall* C 100
Trent College *Devon* C 104
Trinity School *Devon* C 108
Trinity School *London (greater)* B 208
Truro High School for Girls *Cornwall* Gb 100
Truro School *Cornwall* C 100
Tudor Hall School *Oxon* G 232
Twickenham Prep.School *London* L*(greater)* C 208
Twyford School *Hants* C 137
Unicorn School *London (greater)* C 208
University College School Jnr.Br L*London (greater)* B 208
University College School *London* L*(greater)* B 209
Uplands School *Dorset* C 114
Uppingham School *Leics* Bg 175
Upton House School *Berks* Gb 80
Ursuline College *Kent* G 166
Vernon Lodge Preparatory School L*Staffs* C 243
Victoria College *CI* B 90
Victoria College Prep.School *CI* B 90
Vinehall *Sussex (east)* C 274
Virginia Water Prep School *Surrey* C 268
Virgo Fidelis School *London (greater)* Gb 209
Wakefield Girls' High School Junior School *Yorkshire (west)* C 309
Wakefield Girls' High School *Yorkshire (west)* G 309
Walhampton School *Hants* C 137
Wallop School *Surrey* Bg 268
Walthamstow Hall *Kent* G 166
Warminster Junior School *Wilts* C 296
Warminster School *Wilts* C 296
Warwick Prep. School *Warks* Gb 287
Warwick School *Warks* B 287
Waverley School *Berks* C 81
Wellesley House *Kent* C 167
Wellingborough School *Northants* C 221
Wellington College *Berks* Bg 81
Wellington School *Scotland* C 325
Wellington School *Somerset* C 240
Wellow House School *Notts* C 226
Wells Cathedral Junior School *Somerset* C 240
Wells Cathedral School *Somerset* C 240
Wentworth Milton Mount School L*Durham* G 115
West Buckland School *Devon* C 109
West Dene School *London (greater)* C 209
West Heath School *Kent* G 167
West Hill Park *Hants* C 137
West House School *W Mid* B 293
Westbourne College *Wales (south)* C 315
Westbourne House *Sussex (west)* C 281
Westbourne House *Wales (south)* C 315
Westbourne Prep. School *Yorkshire (south)* B 304
Westbrook Hay Educational Trust Ltd *Herts* C 153
Westbrook House *Kent* C 167
Westerleigh *Sussex (east)* C 274
Westfield School *Tyne And Wear* G 284
Westholme School *Lancs* Gb 172
Westminster Abbey Choir School L*London (greater)* B 209
Westminster Cathedral Choir School *London (greater)* B 209
Westminster School *London (greater)* Bg 210
Westminster Under School *London (greater)* B 210
Westonbirt School *Glos* G 127
Westwing School *Beds* Gb 69
White House School *Berks* C 81
White House School,The *Devon* C 109
Whitford Hall School *Hereford &* L*worcester* C 144
Whitgift School *London (greater)* B 210
Widford Lodge *Essex* B 123
William Hulme's Grammar School L*Manchester (greater)* C 213
Willington School *London (greater)* B 210
Wilmslow Prep. School *Cheshire* G 98
Wimbledon High School GPDST L*London (greater)* G 210
Winbury School *Berks* C 81
Winchester College *Hants* B 137
Winchester House School *Northants* C 221
Windlesham House School *Sussex* L*(west)* C 281
Winterfold House *Hereford & worcester* C 144
Wisbech Grammar School *Cambs* C 89
Wispers School *Surrey* G 268
Witham Hall *Lincs* C 177
Withington Girls School *Manchester (greater)* G 213
Wolborough Hill School *Devon* C 109
Woldingham School *Surrey* G 268
Wolstanton Preparatory School *Staffs* C 243
Wolverhampton Grammar School L*W Mid* C 293
Woodbridge School *Suffolk* C 248
Woodcote House School *Surrey* B 268
Woodford Green Prep. School *Glos* C 124
Woodhouse Grove School *Yorkshire (west)* C 309
Woodleigh School *Yorkshire (north)* C 303
Woodside Park School *Manchester* L*(greater)* C 211
Worksop College *Notts* C 226
Worth School *Sussex (west)* B 281
Wrekin College *Salop* C 236
Wroxall Abbey *Warks* G 287
Wychwood School *Oxon* G 232
Wycliffe College *Hants* C 128
Wycliffe College Jnr School *Glos* C 127
Wycombe Abbey School *Bucks* G 86
Wykeham House School *Hants* G 137
Yardley Court Prep. School *Kent* Bg 167
Yarlet Schools,The *Staffs* C 244
Yarm School *Cleveland* Bg 98
Yateley Manor School *Surrey* C 269
Yehudi Menuhin School *Surrey* C 269
York College for Girls *Yorkshire (north)* Gb 303
York House School *Herts* B 153

ISIS
INDEPENDENT SCHOOLS
INFORMATION SERVICE

The ISIS **New Perspective**
range of School Fees Plans

■ Offer you a sophisticated financial planning strategy for the provision of school fees

■ Enable you to spread the cost of school fees

■ Cater for both current and future school fees

■ Give you peace of mind

Contact the Bowring School Fees Practice on 0171 357 3333

Bowring
Committed to Education

IF YOU HAVEN'T PLANNED YOUR CHILDRENS SCHOOL FEES, IT'S NOT TOO LATE TO LEARN YOUR LESSON.

I must talk to EIG
I must talk to EIG
I must talk to EIG
I must talk to EIG
I must talk to EIG
I must talk to EIG
I must talk to EIG
I must talk to EIG
I must talk to EIG
I must talk to EIG
I must talk to EIG
I must talk to EIG
I must talk to EIG
I must talk to EIG

Don't worry, we're not going to give you a ticking off, we realise that you've probably had a lot more than school fees to think about while your children have been growing up.

That's why our school fees funding plan is designed to cater for all your financial concerns when putting your children through private and further education.

With our 'loan plan' you can take advantage of a long term loan through Allchurches Mortgage Company Limited, which you can draw on as required, and repay in a variety of ways.

For more information write, 100 times, your full name and address. Or you could just fill in the coupon below. But no spelling mistakes.

ISIS
INDEPENDENT SCHOOLS
INFORMATION SERVICE

SEND NOW TO: EIG, CUSTOMER SERVICE DEPT, FREEPOST, BEAUFORT HOUSE, BRUNSWICK ROAD, GLOUCESTER GL1 1BR (NO STAMP NECESSARY), OR PHONE 01452 526265.

Name _____
Title _____
Address _____
_____
Postcode _____
Telephone _____
Date of birth _____

Your home is at risk if you do not keep up repayments on a mortgage or other loan secured on it.   IY/96

EIG
ECCLESIASTICAL
INSURANCE GROUP
INSURANCE YOU CAN BELIEVE IN

Schooling yourself now could cut the cost of your child's education later.

You don't have to be well-off to provide an independent education for your child – as long as you're well organised. By planning ahead and schooling yourself to start a school fee programme in advance, you could cut the cost to yourself quite dramatically.

At The Equitable Life, we have helped individuals set up school fee programmes for many years, and can therefore provide a great deal of assistance. Since there are several ways of providing for school fees, we can supply the services of an expert to guide you through the alternatives and find the method best suited to your particular circumstances.

The Equitable Life is listed as a school fee specialist by ISIS.

To receive further information, by post and by telephone, on how The Equitable Life can help you provide for your child's school fees, ring Aylesbury (01296) 26226 or return the coupon.

Regulated by the Personal Investment Authority

To: The Equitable Life, FREEPOST, Walton Street, Aylesbury, Bucks HP21 7BR

I would welcome further information on financing school fees by means of a lump sum ❏ spread over a period ❏ .

Name (Mr/Mrs/Miss) _____

Address _____

_____

_____

Postcode _____

Date of Birth _____

Tel: (Office) _____

Tel: (Home) _____

ISKD5A

Founded 1762
The Equitable Life
You profit from our principles

HOGG ROBINSON FINANCIAL SERVICES LIMITED

We can help provide the fees

We advise on forward planning, capital investment and special loan facilities

Hogg Robinson Independent Financial Advisers are at the forefront of personal financial planning and employee benefits consultancy. Through our regional network we provide a full range of specialist services, drawing on the expertise of our high-calibre professionals, to ensure that our clients receive truly first class advice.

For further information please contact:-

Nigel Stallworthy
Hogg Robinson Independent Financial Advisers
St Paul's House
Park Square South
Leeds
West Yorkshire
LS1 2ND
Telephone : 0113 246 8146

Approved by the Independent Schools Information Service
Hogg Robinson Financial Services Limited
Registered Office: Concorde House 165 Church Street East Woking Surrey GU21 1HF
Registered in England and Wales No. 1125618 Regulated by the Personal Investment Authority
Amember of SPC Consumer Credit Licence No 024702

HR
A Hogg Robinson plc Company

> Halls of Residence
> University College
> Borchester
>
> Dear Mum and Dad,
>
> When I went off to college and the last school bill had been paid, I didn't have the knowledge of the great foundation you'd laid.
>
> It wasn't till I found all my student friends in debt, that I realised just how sound were the financial plans you'd set.
>
> I've had the opportunity to study hard and learn and now that I have my degree I'm ready to return.
>
> See you at the weekend.
>
> P.S. Can I have my old room back 'till I start my job?

If you want to see a happy return like this

you can with Gan

Through Gan Financial Services we have years of experience in providing help to parents in meeting expenses of higher education as well as an independent education. Gan Insurance Company has also insured over 600,000 children against accident and extended its insurances to give assistance to parents when a child's education is interrupted by absence due to injury or sickness, and care is needed at home.

It's no wonder Gan Financial Services is an ISIS approved company.

If you want to find out more please complete and return the coupon to 'The School Fees Unit', Gan Financial Services Ltd, Freepost, Harlow, Essex CM20 2EW.

I would like to know how Gan can help me:-

gan

- plan for my children's independent education* ☐
- plan for my children's higher education* ☐
- if my children have an accident or become sick+ ☐

ISIS
INDEPENDENT SCHOOLS
INFORMATION SERVICE

Name _____

Address _____

Telephone no. (day) _____ (eve) _____

* through products of Gan Life and Pensions PLC and Gan Pep Managers
\+ through products of Gan Insurance

Gan Financial Services Limited is an appointed representative of the Gan marketing group, which provides specialist advice on educational expenses planning and life insurance, pensions, personal equity plans and unit trusts. Members of the marketing group are regulated by the Personal Investment Authority. Registered in England no. 1035097 Registered office: Gan House, Harlow, Essex CM20 2EW.

115OK6066

SCHOOL FEES FROM £25 A WEEK.

A SMALL SUM TO PAY FOR YOUR CHILD'S FUTURE

£25 a week does not buy much nowadays but, with Invest for School Fees, it could start to buy your children or grandchildren an independent education. That means an education of your choice suited to your child's personality.

By planning as early as possible the savings achieved are impressive.

Call us or complete the coupon below. It commits you to nothing but it may be the start of your commitment to the kind of education and future we'd all like our children to have.

INVEST FOR SCHOOL FEES
☎ 0171-290 2510

FAX: 0171-493 4313

Approved by
ISIS
INDEPENDENT SCHOOLS INFORMATION SERVICE

INVEST FOR SCHOOL FEES IS A DIVISION OF WILLIS CORROON FINANCIAL PLANNING LIMITED. WHICH IS REGULATED BY THE PERSONAL INVESTMENT AUTHORITY.

Post to: Invest for School Fees, 58 St. James's Street, London SW1A 1LD

Name _____

Address _____

_____

Home Tel. _____ Office Tel. _____

Child's / Children's Age (s) _____
Preferred method of payment   TT 14/6

From Income ☐   Income & Lump Sum ☐   Lump Sum ☐

AN EDUCATION IS FOR LIFE .... ENSURE THE BEST FOR YOUR CHILD

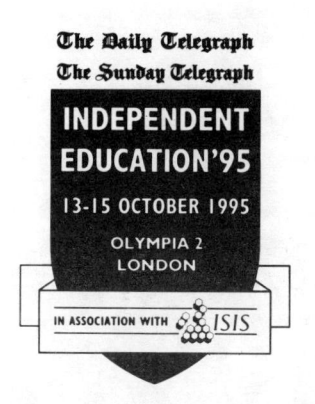

The Daily Telegraph
The Sunday Telegraph

INDEPENDENT EDUCATION'95
13-15 OCTOBER 1995
OLYMPIA 2
LONDON

IN ASSOCIATION WITH ISIS

Visit the annual National ISIS exhibition held each October at Olympia 2, London and gain an overview of all the independent sector has to offer:

* Over 300 of the UK's finest Day, Boarding, Prep and Senior Schools
* Comprehensive Free Seminars Daily
* Art Exhibition and Music Recitals
* Free Financial Advice and Creche

For further details, opening hours or dates for '96, please call 0171 571 6603

Schools
aren't all uniform...

...neither is the
planning

For further information
please contact
Lawrence Bernstein
0171 956 7955

Kleinwort Benson
PRIVATE BANK

ISIS

SCHOOL FEE PROTECTION AND SCHOOL FEES FUNDING PLANS

Lower your annual school fee expenditure by up to 50%

For forward planning and independent expert advice on meeting your school fee commitments, now or in the future, telephone our head office.

Individual and Group fee protection schemes are available for schools and parents to protect the school fees in the event of death, disability or unemployment.

We are also pleased to offer independent advice on meeting the shortfall in student grants for university or college.

MASON & MASON
L I M I T E D

18/20 Manchester Road
Wilmslow, Cheshire SK9 1BG
Tel: 01625 529536

INDEPENDENT FINANCIAL ADVISER

FIMBRA MEMBER

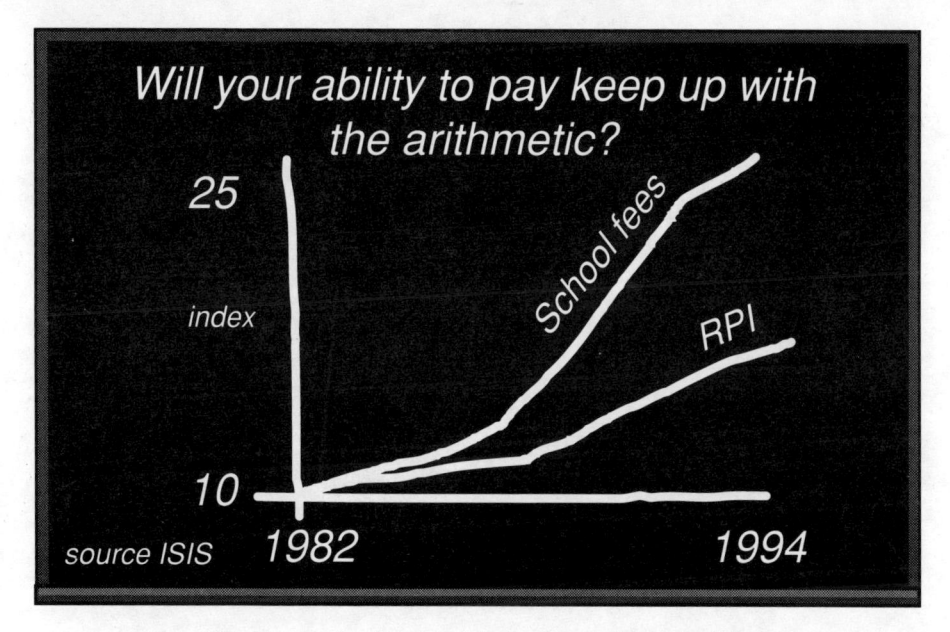

Will your ability to pay keep up with the arithmetic?

Chart showing index from 10 to 25, from 1982 to 1994, comparing School fees (rising steeply) and RPI (rising moderately). source ISIS

By planning ahead you could save thousands of pounds in independent and higher education costs, helping you to provide the schooling you want for your family.

Sedgwick Financial Services is one of the UK's leading providers of independent financial advice. Our size, security, expertise and independence have led more than 130,000 individuals from all walks of life to place their trust in us. To find out how you and your family can benefit from our specialist education funding service, please complete and return the slip below – no stamp required.

Sedgwick Financial Services
Sedgwick Financial Services Limited
PO Box 144, Norfolk House, Wellesley Road, Croydon CR9 3GB
Regulated by the Personal Investment Authority

ISIS
INDEPENDENT SCHOOLS INFORMATION SERVICE

Return to: Maureen Drinkwater, Education funding, Sedgwick Financial Services, FREEPOST CN87 Croydon CR9 3WZ

Name:

Address:

Postcode

Telephone (home):   Telephone (office):

SFIA
Investment Advisers

School Fees
and Further Education Costs

Planning for independence

With school fees rising and university grants frozen - there's never been a more important time to plan for the costs of education.

Whether you are planning in advance or require immediate help with fees, an SFIA tailor-made plan could help you manage more easily.

To find out more about how parents (and grandparents) can afford to provide for an independent education, clip and return the coupon today or telephone

Freephone 0800 282997

**School Fees
Insurance Agency Limited**
SFIA House, 15 Forlease Road,
Maidenhead,
Berkshire SL6 1JA

PIA ISIS
Regulated by the
Personal Investment Authority

Name ....

Address ....

....

Home telephone ....

Office telephone ....

ISIS 95/6

A simple lesson in financing children's education.

Planning for children's independent education is a simple lesson well worth learning. And the earlier plans are made, the easier it is to avoid financial hardship in the future. Standard Life now offer a range of plans which can be tailored to suit individual needs and circumstances. Our financial strength and past performance mean that there is no better company to plan early with. To find our more about our Educational Planning services, contact your financial adviser.

STANDARD LIFE

Past performance is not necessarily a guide to future performance.

The Standard Life Assurance Company* is a mutual company registered in Scotland (no SZ4)
Head Office 3 George Street Edinburgh Tel (0131) 225 2552

Regulated by the Personal Investment Authority for investment business

SCHOOL FEES...

Your Children depend on you to make the decisions that could affect the rest of their lives.

Independent advice from Whitehead & Partners will ensure that you find the school fee plan to suit you, your children and your budget.

Plan now and you could save up to two thirds on school fees.

Talk to one of our Independent Planning Specialists now for friendly, professional advice or return the coupon below. You owe it to yourself and your children.

To receive a copy of our FREE booklet, simply complete the enquiry form below or phone us FREE on 0800 413903.

Please cut out and post to: Whitehead & Partners Ltd, FREEPOST, Altrincham, Cheshire WA14 2BR

Name ....
Address ....
....
.... Post Code ....
Tel (day) .... Tel (evening) ....
Child/Children's ages ....

ISIS HB AUG 95

I am interested in (please tick)
☐ MONTHLY INVESTMENT ☐ LUMP SUM ☐ A COMBINATION ☐ FREE BOOKLET

Whitehead & Partners
INDEPENDENT FINANCIAL ADVISERS

INCORPORATING
FRASER MARR

HOWARD HOUSE LLOYD STREET ALTRINCHAM CHESHIRE WA14 2BR TEL: 0161 928 2209 FAX: 0161 927 7202

ISIS   FIMBRA MEMBER

Other offices at London and Bristol